THE
VISUAL FOOD
ENCYCLOPEDIA

Wiley Publishing, Inc.

Library of Congress Cataloging -in-Publication Data

Encyclopédie visuelle des aliments. English
    The visual food encyclopedia
    p.   cm.
    "Editorial director, François Fortin"--P. 2.
    "This book is adapted from 'Dictionnaire encyclopédique des aliments'"--P. 3.
    Include index.
    ISBN 0-02-861006-7 (alk. paper)
    1. Foods--Encyclopedias--Pictorial works.   2. Cookery--Encyclopedias--Pictorial works.
    I. Fortin, François.   II. Dictionnaire encyclopédique des aliments.   III.   Title.

    TX349.E48   1996
    641.3'03--dc20   96-7081
                                                                                                                  CIP

Published by Wiley Publishing, Inc., New York, NY

This book is adapted from "Dictionnaire encyclopédique des aliments", Solange Monette, Les Éditions Québec Amérique inc.

The visual food encyclopedia was created and produced by:

QA International
329, rue de la Commune Ouest, 3ᵉ étage, Montréal, Québec, H2Y 2E1
T (514) 499-3000 **F** (514) 499-3010
www.qa-international.com

For general information on our other products and services or to obtain technical support please contact our Customer Care Department within the U.S. at 800-762-2974, outside the U.S. at 317-572-3993 or fax 317-572-4002.

Wiley also publishes its books in a variety of electronic formats. Some content that appears in print may not be available in electronic books.

Manufactured in Slovakia

10 9 8 7 6 5 4   04

First Edition

THE
VISUAL FOOD
ENCYCLOPEDIA

Wiley Publishing, Inc.

EDITORIAL STAFF FOR THE ORIGINAL EDITION

Publisher
Jacques Fortin

Editorial Director
François Fortin

Executive Editor
Serge D'Amico

Nutrition Consultants
Marie Breton Dt. P.   Isabelle Emond Dt. P.

Graphic design
Anne Tremblay

Computer Graphics Artists
Jean-Yves Ahern   Marc Lalumière
Rielle Lévesque   Michel Rouleau
Pascal Bilodeau   Mamadou Togola
François Escalmel

Page Setup
Lucie Mc Brearty   Pascal Goyette
Georges Audet   Chantal Boyer

Computer Programming
Daniel Beaulieu

Research
Nathalie Daneau

Photo-retouching/coordination
Josée Gagnon

Recipes
Ariane Archambault

Photographs
Studio Focus-Pocus

Cook
Laurent Saget

Production and Technical Support
Tony O'Riley

Translators
Winifred Langeard   Peter Malden
Gordon Martin   Andrea Neuhofer

IV

Foreword

Modern life has profoundly changed our eating habits. As a result of the increasing availability of a greater variety of foods and a growing awareness of our nutritional requirements, as well as our interest in experimenting with new foods, we are now confronted by a vast array of products that we must learn how to distinguish between and use.

The Visual Food Encyclopedia is designed to help the reader (both the novice and the experienced cook) find clear and precise information about a particular food item as quickly as possible. Above all, it is a practical guide and reference tool that provides inquisitive readers with the opportunity to discover new products or new ways to use familiar products.

Although this encyclopedia includes some recipes, it is not a cook book, but rather a summary of everything that is known about food. It contains practical information about the origin, description, purchasing, preparation, uses, cooking methods, storage and nutritional value of foods. The information is arranged on dynamic, well-designed pages featuring clearly visible headings.

The Visual Food Encyclopedia provides the reader with complete information about foods as diverse as meat, spices, vegetables, and fish, in a single volume. It is an invaluable guide that will help readers make well-informed choices, and sort through the overwhelming amount of information now available about food and nutrition.

An integral part of the encyclopedia, the illustrations are instructive as well as attractive. They allow the reader to identify and distinguish between products at a glance. State-of-the-art, exceptionally precise photographs and/or illustrations reveal every detail of the item in question and help eliminate any lingering doubts. The images complement the descriptions, and help the reader distinguish between varieties and species.

This reference guide is the result of three years of effort by a large team of writers, researchers, editors, illustrators and designers. It contains entries on over 1,000 different foods, as well as more than 1,300 illustrations, photographs and recipes. Divided into topics and subtopics, the encyclopedia also includes a table of contents, a detailed index and a glossary of specialized terms to help the reader access information as quickly as possible.

Whether you want to improve your eating habits, enhance your knowledge of food, verify the nutritional value of a product or just delight in the amazing diversity of foods described in the book, *The Visual Food Encyclopedia* will be a pleasure to consult and a feast for your eyes.

The Editor

User's Guide

Each topic is divided into easy-to-spot sections. The headings lead you through the necessary steps, from shopping to preserving.

Full-color illustrations and an exceptional presentation make this food guide as attractive as it is useful.

Each entry begins with an insight into the origins of everyday foods.

Serving ideas: what to do with unusual food, and new ways of using familiar food.

You can select fresh produce with buying tips, and take advantage of seasonal bounty. We explain how to select each item at its peak, and how to choose from the large variety available in your local store.

The icons help you find the right heading at a glance.

Asparagus
Asparagus officinalis, Liliaceae

green asparagus

A perennial garden plant originating in the eastern Mediterranean region. Remnants of wild varieties of asparagus have been discovered in northern and southern Africa, and archeologists believe that it may also have been cultivated in ancient Egypt. Consumed for over 2,000 years, asparagus was originally valued for its medicinal properties. It fell into obscurity during the Middle Ages, although it continued to be cultivated by the Arabs. Under the influence of Louis XIV, asparagus was rediscovered in the 18th century, and since then several new varieties have been developed. Today the principal producers of asparagus are the United States, Europe, Mexico, and Taiwan.

Asparagus is actually a young edible shoot, commonly called a "spear"; the spear rises from an underground stem called a "crown," which is capable of producing spears for 15 to 20 years. Most asparagus is harvested in spring, when it is 6 to 8 inches high and has tender, fleshy spears and tight, compact heads. Once they reach maturity, the asparagus stalks become woody and fernlike foliage grows from the heads, making them inedible. Although grown on quite a large scale and in many countries, asparagus is available in abundance only from March to late June.

There are over 300 varieties of asparagus, only 20 of which are edible. They are divided into three main categories:

• Green asparagus. This is the most common type of asparagus. It is harvested at a height of about 8 inches.

• White asparagus. Grown in the dark (covered with soil to keep it from turning green), white asparagus is harvested as soon as it emerges from the ground. Although more tender than the green variety, it tends to be less flavorful and is also more expensive, since more work is required to grow it.

• Purple asparagus. This variety has a fruity flavor and is harvested when only 2 or 3 inches high.

Stalk Vegetables

106

Buying
Choose asparagus with firm, crisp stalks and compact, brightly colored heads with no traces of rust. Selecting similarly sized specimens will help ensure even cooking. Avoid yellowish asparagus with soft stalks and heads that are beginning to flower, which are signs of age.

Serving Ideas
Asparagus is always eaten cooked, either boiled or steamed. It can be served warm or hot, dressed in a generous helping of butter or hollandaise sauce. It is also good cold, topped with a dressing, mayonnaise, or mustard sauce. Puréed asparagus can be used to make soups, soufflés, or veloutés. Asparagus can also be used, cut or whole, to garnish omelets, poultry, quiches, salads, or pasta dishes. It also makes an interesting addition to a stir-fry

white asparagus

Helpful advice on the preparation and use of hundreds of ingredients.

Easy-to-follow steps clearly describe specific cooking techniques.

Focus on healthful eating as a key to fitness.

Asparagus

Preparing

Before cooking asparagus, cut off the base of the stalk (which can be cooked and puréed to make a soup). While it is not necessary to peel asparagus, it should be washed well in cold water to rid it of sand and soil.

Cut off the ends of the asparagus stalks with a sharp knife.

2 *Peel the asparagus from top to bottom.*

Tie the asparagus in bundles.

4 *Bundled asparagus is easier to remove from the pan after cooking.*

Polish-Style Asparagus

2 lb. (1 kg) fresh asparagus
2 hard-boiled eggs
3 tbsp. chopped fresh parsley
¼ lb. (125 g) butter
3 tbsp. fresh bread crumbs

1. Cut off the tough base of the asparagus stalks. Peel and wash the spears, and divide them evenly into four bunches. Tie the bundles with string.

2. Immerse the asparagus in a large skillet filled with salted boiling water, and blanch for about 10 minutes, or until a spear is easily pierced with the tip of a sharp knife. Drain well and remove the strings. Arrange the spears in a serving dish and keep warm.

3. While the asparagus is cooking, peel the eggs and discard the whites. Mash the yolks with a fork in a small bowl, and stir in the parsley.

4. Melt the butter in a small saucepan, and add the bread crumbs, stirring until they are golden brown. Remove from the heat.

5. Sprinkle the egg/parsley mixture over the asparagus spears, pour the butter sauce over them, and serve immediately.

Nutritional Information

	raw
water	92%
protein	2.6 g
fat	0.3 g
carbohydrates	4.2 g
calories	24
	per 100 g

Asparagus is an excellent source of folic acid and contains vitamin C, potassium, thiamine, riboflavine, vitamin B$_6$, copper, vitamin A, iron, phosphorus, and zinc. Asparagus contains a sulfurous substance that imparts an odor to urine. It also contains asparagine, an acid substance that gives the vegetable its characteristic flavor and is also diuretic. Asparagus is said to be laxative, remineralizing, and tonic.

Cooking

Avoid overcooking asparagus, as this causes it to lose flavor, color, and nutrients. When boiling asparagus spears, tie them in bundles to make it easier to remove them once they are cooked. Steaming is the best cooking method, and there are special tall, narrow asparagus steamers on the market in which the asparagus stands upright in an inner basket. This method cooks the asparagus to perfection, as the more fibrous bottoms are thoroughly cooked in the boiling water while the fragile tips are merely steamed. Asparagus is ready when the stalks are tender but still firm. If you are planning to eat the asparagus cold, plunge it immediately into cold water to halt the cooking process, but do not let it soak. Asparagus can also be cooked in a microwave oven. Avoid cooking it in iron pots, as this vegetable contains tannins which react on contact with iron, altering the color of the asparagus.

Storing

Asparagus is very perishable. Wrapped in a damp cloth and placed in a perforated plastic bag in the refrigerator, it will keep for a maximum of 3 days. Blanched asparagus will keep for up to 9 months in the freezer.

Asparagus is actually a young edible shoot, commonly called a "spear," that rises from an underground crown capable of producing spears for 15 to 20 years.

Stalk Vegetables

107

An illustration focuses on a specific historic or botanical aspect of each item.

Most suitable methods of cooking.

Easy-to-spot divisions help find the subject you're looking for.

Details on storing food.

VII

Although it is not a cookbook, The Visual Food Encyclopedia *highlights the main ways in which a food may be used, often giving popular recipes.*

Contents

Contents

The nutritional requirements of the body represent the quantities of food required for growth and maintenance of good health. In order to ensure that its nutritional needs are met, the body is equipped with a unique signal – the sensation of hunger. Although hunger may appear to prompt us to eat for pleasure, its primary role is to ensure that the body is provided with the substances that are essential for its survival. If the body does not receive enough food, it manifests this deficiency by means of various symptoms, including fatigue, concentration problems, shortness of breath, and certain recurring infections. Everything the human body does (sleeping, eating, moving, shivering) depends on the work of cells, and in order for the body to function well, cells require minimum amounts of various foods.

Nutritionists have identified three types of food with unique roles:

• **building blocks** allow cells to grow and/or multiply, thus maintaining the body and ensuring that it develops normally; they include protein and certain minerals (calcium, magnesium, and phosphorus);

• **energy sources** play a role in the formation of cells and in the digestive process, or simply maintain bodily functions such as the regulation of body temperature; they include carbohydrates and fats;

• **regulatory substances** ensure that building blocks and energy sources are used efficiently by the body, or more specifically by cells; they include water, vitamins, and minerals.

During the digestive process, the nutrients in food are made available to the body in order to ensure that it functions at peak capacity. Since the quantities of nutrients in food vary, it is important to ensure that you consume sufficient amounts of a variety of foods on a daily basis. All nutrients are essential because each of them plays a specific role.

Protein

Protein derives its name from the Greek word *protos,* meaning «first» or «of primary importance,» because it is the basic building block of living cells. Protein builds, repairs, and maintains the body, thus performing three functions that are essential to the survival of living matter. It also accelerates various biochemical reactions and acts as a hormonal messenger, neurotransmitter and component of the immune system. If the body is not supplied with sufficient quantities of carbohydrates and fat, protein can also be used as source of energy; 1 gram of protein contains 4 calories.

Depending on the relative proportions of the amino acids they contain, proteins are referred to as either «complete» or «incomplete.» Of the 20 amino acids that make up proteins, 8 are regarded as «essential» because they cannot be produced by the human body. Animal proteins are considered to be complete, while vegetable proteins are said to be incomplete. Strict vegetarians thus have to consume a broad range of vegetable proteins in order to ensure that they obtain ideal proportions of all the essential amino acids. A deficiency in even one of these amino acids constitutes a "limiting factor," meaning that the body can synthesize only corresponding amounts of the other essential amino acids. However, when a protein deficient in a certain amino acid is combined with a protein rich in this acid, they are said to be "complementary" because the nutritional value of the combination is relatively high (see *Complementary proteins*). Meat, poultry, protein, eggs, and dairy products are the main sources of animal proteins. Vegetable proteins are found in legumes, nuts, grains, and cereals. These are among the best sources of protein because they are low in fat and high in fiber.

Carbohydrates

As their name suggests, carbohydrates are organic compounds containing carbon, hydrogen, and water. They are the main source of metabolic energy, and provide the energy required for the operation of the brain and the nervous system. Carbohydrates are also one of the components of cell walls. Since they are digested relatively quickly, carbohydrates release energy faster than protein and fat. Carbohydrates contain 4 calories per gram. There are three main types of carbohydrates:

• **Simple carbohydrates** consist of one or two sugars – such as glucose, fructose, sucrose, and lactose – and are directly absorbed by the body, without being digested. They are found in fruits, vegetables, honey, and table sugar (brown sugar, corn syrup, molasses, maple syrup).

• **Complex carbohydrates** consist of three or more sugars, such as starch, glycogen, and cellulose; they have to be broken down into simple carbohydrates by means of the digestive process before they can be absorbed. They are found in cereals, legumes, nuts, and seeds, as well as in certain starchy vegetables such as potatoes, peas, corn, and sweet potatoes.

• **Fiber** consists of carbohydrates and those parts of plants that cannot be digested. It can be either hard and stringy (insoluble fiber) or gelatinous and mucilaginous (soluble fiber). Since it is not digested, fiber provides almost no food energy, but it does help to stimulate intestinal functions and is thus used to prevent and treat constipation. Fiber is found in varying proportions in cereals (especially whole-grain cereals), legumes, vegetables, fruits, nuts, and seeds.

A diet rich in complex carbohydrates (starch and fiber) is considered to be healthy because it may play a role in the prevention of certain illnesses such as colon cancer and conditions such as high blood pressure. Foods that contain large amounts of simple sugars should be eaten in moderation, not only because they can cause tooth decay but also because they contain so few nutrients that they are often referred to as "empty calories."

Fat

The word "fat" is derived from the past participle of an Old English verb meaning "to cram." Despite their bad reputation, fats play an essential role in the maintenance of good health. They are not only involved in the formation of cell walls and the production of hormones, they also enhance the flavor of food and create the sensation of fullness. It is also important to remember that they are a concentrated source of energy: a single gram of fat contains 9 calories – twice the amount in either carbohydrates or protein. Furthermore, fats also facilitate the circulation and absorption of the fat-soluble vitamins (A, D, E, and K). They are the only source of the two essential fatty acids, linoleic acid and alpha-linoleic acid, which are the only fats that must be included in the diet, because the body cannot produce them on its own. These acids ensure that all of the cells in the body remain intact by allowing them to absorb and expel substances without placing their contents at risk. The main sources of these essential fatty acids are whole-grain cereals, oils, nuts, and seeds.

Cholesterol is a type of fat normally found in the blood that is essential for the production of sex hormones, biliary acids, and vitamin A, as well as for the formation of cell walls. Only foods from animal sources contain cholesterol; vegetables are cholesterol-free. Unlike essential fatty acids, most cholesterol (70%) is produced inside the body; only about a third (30%) comes from food. Even a diet that does not include cholesterol will not lead to a deficiency in cholesterol, because the fatty acids in food have a much greater impact on blood-cholesterol levels than does the cholesterol in food.

Most of the fat in food is in the form of triglycerides, which are composed of fatty acids. These fatty acids can be either polyunsaturated, monounsaturated, or saturated, depending on the presence or absence of double links between the carbon atoms of which they are comprised. They are found in varying proportions in oils and other fats. Foods from animal sources generally contain more saturated fatty acids than foods from vegetable sources. The exceptions are palm and coconut oils, which contain mainly saturated fat, and fish and seafood, which contain significant amounts of polyunsaturated fatty acids. Polyunsaturated fatty acids are found mainly in vegetable oils, while monounsaturated fatty acids are found in olive oil, canola oil, hazelnut oil, avocados, and almonds.

Saturated fatty acids tend to raise blood-cholesterol levels, especially among people who consume excessive amounts of these acids and are particularly vulnerable to their effects. On the other hand, polyunsaturated and monounsaturated fatty acids tend to lower blood-cholesterol levels. It is common knowledge that there is a strong link between fatty foods and heart disease. However, clinical studies suggest that slightly reducing the amount of fat in the diet – or more specifically, reducing the amount of saturated fat and increasing the amount of mono- and polyunsaturated fats – can significantly lower the risk of heart disease.

13

Vitamins

The word "vitamin" is derived from the Latin word *vita,* meaning "life." Vitamins are organic substances that are indispensable for the maintenance of good health, despite the fact that they are present in minuscule quantities in food; 13 vitamins are considered to be essential. Although they are not a source of energy, vitamins play a crucial role in transforming fats and carbohydrates into a form of energy that can be used by the human body; they also facilitate growth and reproduction and help maintain bodily functions. Each vitamin plays a specific role, and they are not interchangeable because their structures are very different. A distinction is often made between water-soluble and fat-soluble vitamins.

Among the water-soluble vitamins are vitamin C and the B-complex vitamins, which include thiamin (B_1), riboflavin (B_2), niacin (B_3), pantothenic acid (B_5), pyridoxine (B_6), cyanocobalamin (B_{12}), biotin, and folic acid. Water-soluble vitamins are not stored in significant quantities in the body; since they are soluble in water, they are eliminated in urine and sweat and must be replaced on a daily basis. Vitamin C is found mainly in fruits and vegetables, while B vitamins are found mainly in whole-grain cereals, meat, and dairy products. Water-soluble vitamins play a role in a large number of biochemical reactions involved in the regeneration of skin, blood, and nerve cells. For example, vitamin C, which is also known as ascorbic acid, helps the body absorb the iron in food and is involved in the formation of collagen, a substance that enhances the resistance of skin, cartilage, bones, teeth, and blood vessels. B vitamins work together; if any one of them is lacking, the others cannot be used efficiently. They play a key role in the transformation of protein, carbohydrates, and fat into a form of energy that can be distributed throughout the body. They are also involved in the formation of antibodies and red blood cells, and ensure that the nervous and digestive systems function normally.

The fat-soluble vitamins include vitamins A, D, E, and K. Since they are soluble in fats, they can be stored in body fat and in the liver. They are eliminated very slowly in bile, and can thus be toxic if consumed in excessive quantities, especially in the form of supplements containing vitamin A or D.

Vitamin A, which is found mainly in dairy products, liver, and egg yolks, plays an important role in the enhancement of night vision and ensures that the immune system functions normally. This vitamin is also found in the form of precursors (such as carotene, a substance that promotes the formation of vitamins in the body) in yellow, green, and orange fruits and vegetables.

Vitamin D is often referred to as the "sun vitamin" because the skin contains a precursor that turns into vitamin D when exposed to the ultraviolet rays of the sun. This vitamin promotes the absorption of calcium and phosphorus, which are required for the formation of bone tissue. A deficiency in vitamin D during periods of growth can lead to rickets, or rachitis, a disease that has adverse effects on the development of bones. Although a few minutes of exposure to the sun provides all the vitamin D the body requires, it is commonly added to milk because many people are not exposed to sufficiently sunny conditions for long enough periods of time. Vitamin D is thus found in milk as well as in eggs, liver, and fatty fish.

Vitamin E is an antioxidant that prevents the formation of free radicals, substances that stimulate the growth of potentially cancerous cells. Vitamin E is found mainly in vegetable oils, wheat germ, and fish oils.

Vitamin K is essential for the normal clotting of blood; in fact, its name is derived from the German word *Koagulation*. Over half of the vitamin K required by the body is produced by the bacterial flora in the intestine; small amounts of vitamin K are also found in foods such as spinach, cabbage, milk, liver, and eggs.

Minerals

Minerals are inorganic substances that play a role in the formation of bones and in the metabolism of fat, protein, and carbohydrates; they also ensure that muscles and the nervous system function normally. Like vitamins, they are not a source of energy. The 22 essential minerals are divided into two groups, macrominerals and microminerals.

The body requires relatively large amounts of macrominerals (hence their name); this group includes calcium, phosphorus, magnesium, sodium, chlorine, and potassium. The microminerals, which are required in much smaller quantities, include iron, zinc, copper, iodine, fluorine, and selenium. Although many foods contain only small amounts of minerals, these quantities are generally sufficient to meet the body's needs. The exceptions to this rule are iron and calcium; the body requires relatively large amounts of these minerals, and many people do not consume them in sufficient quantities. The foods containing iron include meat and meat substitutes, especially liver and legumes, as well as cereals and dark-green vegetables. Calcium is found mainly in dairy products, as well as in mollusks, crustaceans, legumes, green vegetables, nuts, and seeds. It is thus important to eat a variety of foods to ensure that the body receives sufficient quantities of protein, fat, carbohydrates, vitamins, and minerals.

Water

In terms of volume, water is the most important component of the human body; approximately 55% of the adult body is made up of water. It is so essential for survival that the body must replenish lost water within 2 or 3 days. It plays a role in the regulation of body temperature, the lubrication of joints, and the transmission of sound in the ear; it also functions as a shock absorber in the nervous system. In fact, all bodily functions are dependent on water. It is essential for digestion, absorption, and circulation, as well as for the excretion of bodily waste, the distribution of nutrients, and the regeneration of tissue.

The supply of water in the body is regulated by thirst and must be replenished on a daily basis; people should thus drink at least six to eight 8-ounce glasses of liquid (1.5 to 2 liters) per day. The term "liquid" here refers to milk, juice, decaffeinated coffee, decaffeinated tea, herbal tea, and soft drinks, as well as to pure water; fruits and vegetables are also an important dietary source of liquid, since they contain 60% to 90% water.

Recommendations

Certain countries, including the United States, have established guidelines to ensure that the body's basic nutritional requirements are met – not to combat deficiency diseases but rather to guard against the development of chronic illnesses. In fact, in industrialized countries, overeating is a more serious problem than malnutrition. When combined with a sedentary lifestyle, the overconsumption of foods rich in saturated fat contributes to the development of diseases associated with opulence, which include diabetes, cancers of the digestive system, heart disease, cerebrovascular disease, breast cancer, certain liver problems, and tooth decay. Numerous studies have clearly demonstrated that there is a link between diet and the possible prevention of these diseases. However, these studies have not yet had a significant impact on behavior. In fact, most of the dietary recommendations made by Hippocrates in 500 B.C. remain valid today. Current nutritional guidelines had to be designed with two goals in mind: reducing the risks of chronic illnesses and ensuring that the body's nutritional needs are met. A balanced diet should thus:

• provide the recommended amounts of essential nutrients;

• provide no more than 30% of total calories in the form of fat and no more than 10% in form of saturated fat.

However, these guidelines have not led to permanent changes in eating habits of the population as a whole, because people are very reluctant to make changes in their diet. Although nutritional guidelines do not provide any guarantees, they can increase your chances of remaining healthy and thus enhance your quality of life.

Vegetables

contents

Introduction

The term applied to the many varieties of garden plants used for food. While the importance of vegetables as a food has varied across the ages and from one culture to another, vegetables, along with rice, have long served as a staple of the human diet. It is very difficult for scientists to trace the history of all the vegetables we consume, although a number of hypotheses have been proposed regarding the origins of vegetable cultivation.

Well before the beginning of agriculture (12,000 years ago), humans were nomads who lived on hunting, fishing, and gathering. This period lasted for over 2 million years. As these nomadic peoples gradually settled in certain regions, they began to keep animals and to gather wild plants for food. It is not known exactly how human beings learned to grow food, but it would appear that two techniques were used. The first method involved sowing seeds, while the second consisted of producing new plants from the shoots or roots. With subsequent migrations of peoples and their plants, new varieties of plants were created through hybridization. Over many generations, these plants adapted to environmental changes.

The most significant improvements in a number of vegetable varieties are actually quite recent and are largely attributable to the discovery of the principles of genetics as elaborated by Darwin and Mendel in the late 19th and early 20th centuries. These discoveries have made it possible to produce new varieties with specific crop yields and qualities such as flavor, color, and so on. Today vegetables are consumed mainly as an accompaniment to main courses in most of the Western Hemisphere, although they continue to play a central role in the diet in Asia and the Middle East. In North America, the consumption of vegetables has been on the rise since the mid-1970s, largely as a result of increased public awareness of their importance in a healthy diet. The recommendations of health professionals, as well as scientific research establishing a close link between a high consumption of fruits and vegetables and the prevention of certain diseases, have contributed to making the health benefits of vegetables more widely known. The greater diversity and availability of vegetables in the marketplace have also contributed to the increase in their consumption.

A simple way to classify vegetables is on the basis of the portion of the plant that is used for food. This gives us:

• *bulb vegetables,* which include garlic, scallion, chive, shallot, onion, and leek;

• *leaf vegetables,* including chicory, cabbage, watercress, spinach, various types of lettuce, nettle, sorrel, dandelion, and radicchio;

• *inflorescent vegetables* such as artichoke, broccoli, cauliflower, and broccoli rape;

• *fruit vegetables,* including eggplant, avocado, chayote, cucumber, squash, okra, olive, and peppers;

• *root vegetables* such as beets, burdock, carrots, celeriac, malanga, turnip, parsnip, radish, rutabaga, and salsify;

• *stalk vegetables,* including asparagus, bamboo, chard, cardoon, celery, kohlrabi, fiddlehead fern, and fennel; and

• *tuber vegetables,* which include crosne, yam, jicama, manioc, sweet potato, potato, taro, and Jerusalem artichoke.

Buying

The outer appearance of vegetables can provide an indication of their freshness. To preserve this freshness, producers often cover their vegetables with a wax coating, notably in the case of the eggplant, cucumber, squash, turnip, sweet potato, parsnip, sweet pepper, and tomato. This treatment minimizes moisture loss and the rate of deterioration. Look for firm, undamaged, and well-colored vegetables that show no sign of mold, bruising, frost damage, or softness. Avoid buying fragile vegetables that look as if they have been on the shelf for too long; peeled vegetables and vegetables with wilted leaves or shriveled skin should also be avoided.

Preparing

The manner in which vegetables are prepared, used, and preserved has an effect on their flavor, nutritional value, texture, and appearance. Like fruits, vegetables react to air and heat and continue to be living organisms even after harvesting. A single hour left out at room temperature will cause them to deteriorate twice as quickly as if they were refrigerated, since heat speeds up their rate of maturation.

When preparing vegetables, it is important to avoid lengthy exposure to air, heat, and water:

• Rinse the vegetables well under running water, but avoid soaking them, whether before or after cutting them, in order to minimize the loss of water-soluble vitamins (including B-complex vitamins and vitamin C). However, some vegetables (even if they have been treated with pesticides) may contain parasites, making it necessary to soak them in cold salted water for about 30 minutes before preparing them; this is often the case for cabbage, broccoli, and cauliflower, among others.

• Avoid leaving the vegetables out at room temperature once they are ripe.

• Vegetables to be eaten raw should be prepared at the last minute using stainless-steel utensils; to minimize the loss of vitamins (vitamin C in particular), sprinkle them with an acid ingredient such as vinegar or citrus juice and refrigerate them until ready to serve.

• Vegetables to be cooked should be cut in evenly sized pieces to ensure uniform cooking; the more finely chopped the vegetable, the greater the loss of vitamins (especially vitamins B and C), minerals, and flavor.

Serving Ideas

Most vegetables can be eaten raw. It is important to include raw vegetables in one's diet, since the quality of their nutrients has not been altered by cooking. However, fresh vegetables that have been stored too long or in unsuitable conditions are not necessarily more nutritious than frozen, canned, or properly cooked vegetables, although the nutritional value of cooked vegetables also depends on the cooking method used. Vegetables have an endless number of culinary uses; they work well in everything from appetizers to desserts, and are even used in wine making.

Vegetables

19

Cooking

Certain vegetables with a high starch content, such as the potato, are inedible raw and must be cooked in order to convert their starch into a form that can be assimilated by the body. Cooking converts the starch into sugar, as well as softening the cellulose, releasing the substances in the fiber, and dissolving the pectin contained in vegetables. Other vegetables, including the malanga and taro, contain irritating or harmful substances that are neutralized by cooking.

Vegetables should be cooked as briefly as possible, as overcooking makes them bland and soggy, while also depriving them of a portion of their vitamins and minerals. The loss of vitamins B and C can be minimized by cooking the vegetables at a high temperature for a short time (in a pressure cooker, for example).

The most suitable cooking method for vegetables often depends on whether one is preparing green, yellow, red, or white vegetables, which tend to react differently to cooking.

Green vegetables tend to lose their color quickly when cooked. This is because the heat releases the acids in the vegetables, which then react with the chlorophyll (the substance responsible for their green color), part of which is eliminated, causing the vegetables to lose their bright color and turning them a brownish green.

Yellow and orange vegetables are rich in carotene, a provitamin that the body converts into vitamin A. This substance is not very soluble in water, remains stable when heated, and is unaltered by the addition of an acid ingredient to the vegetables.

Red and purple vegetables obtain their color (which sometimes verges on blue) from the pigment anthocyanin. The addition of an acid ingredient during cooking enhances the color of red and purple vegetables, which tend to lose some of their color during cooking, especially if they are cut; this is because the acidity in the vegetables evaporates at the same time as the water.

White vegetables contain a pigment called anthoxanthine; adding an acid ingredient during cooking enhances their color. Overcooking or the addition of an alkaline substance causes these vegetables to turn yellow or brown; they also react to contact with iron and aluminum, which makes them turn brownish, greenish, or yellowish. It is therefore preferable to use stainless-steel or glass utensils.

Certain vegetables, including celeriac, parsnips, artichoke hearts, salsify, and Jerusalem artichokes, oxidize and turn brown as soon as they are peeled; to prevent discoloration, immediately soak the vegetables in an acid solution (lemon juice, vinegar water, vinaigrette) and refrigerate them until you are ready to use them. Cooking vegetables with their peel reduces the loss of vitamins and minerals.

The choice of a cooking method can influence the nutritional quality of vegetables as well as their color.

Boiling

This is a simple method that involves cooking the vegetables in boiling water. However, boiling results in a significant loss of flavor and nutritional value, particularly if the vegetables are boiled too long and if the cooking liquid is discarded. Although this is the most common method of cooking vegetables, it is also the one that is the most improperly used.

It is generally preferable to use a small quantity of water and to reserve the cooking water, which contains many of the vitamins and minerals lost by the vegetables during cooking; the liquid can be used to make soups and sauces. For uniform cooking, use a pan that is suitable for the quantity of vegetables and check the water level occasionally to prevent the vegetables from sticking to the bottom.

The vegetables should be added once the water reaches a full boil; lower the heat when the water resumes boiling and simmer the vegetables until they are cooked. This method allows for a slightly shorter cooking time and helps retain the color and flavor of the vegetables.

Use of a cover

With the exception of green vegetables, vegetables should be cooked in a covered pot; this shortens the cooking time as well as reducing the evaporation of volatile substances, thus preserving the flavor, color, and nutritional value of the vegetables. When cooking green vegetables, it is recommended to remove the cover in order to prevent concentration of their acids, which has the effect of destroying their chlorophyll and discoloring them.

Cooking temperature

Vegetables should not be added to the water until it reaches a full boil, as this quickly neutralizes the enzymes that destroy their vitamins. Once the vegetables have been immersed in the boiling water, maintain a high heat until the boiling resumes, and then reduce the heat. Vegetables do not cook more quickly at a full boil, since the temperature of the simmering water remains at 212°F.

Adding an alkaline ingredient

An alkaline ingredient, such as baking soda, is sometimes added to the cooking water to help retain the color of green vegetables. This practice is unnecessary for yellow vegetables and is not recommended for red vegetables, as it discolors them, making them turn a purple, blue, or greenish color; it also causes white vegetables to turn yellow if they are cooked too long. This practice also has disadvantages for green vegetables: the baking soda attacks the cells of the vegetable, causing it to soften; it also alters the vegetable's flavor, destroys its thiamine content, and hastens the loss of vitamin C. It is therefore preferable to shorten the cooking time or to choose another cooking method in order to prevent the discoloration of vegetables.

Adding an acid ingredient

Adding an acid ingredient such as vinegar, citrus juice, dry wine, or cider to the cooking liquid maintains the firmness and color of red and white vegetables; in the case of red vegetables (notably beets), these ingredients can sometimes even restore and enhance the color.

This practice is not recommended for green vegetables, however, as it acts on the chlorophyll molecules, imparting an unappetizing green color to the vegetables.

It is also unnecessary for yellow vegetables, whose color is stable. To cook vegetables that darken readily when cut or peeled (artichokes, salsify), mix 1 tablespoon of flour with 3 tablespoons of water and the juice of half a lemon and add this mixture to 1 quart of salted boiling water.

Adding salt

Salt has the effect of softening vegetables by extracting water from them, either by absorption or by osmosis. Thus, when added at the start of cooking, salt drains vegetables of some of their juices, leading to a loss of nutrients. Moreover, prolonged cooking leads to a concentration of the salt in the vegetables. It is unadvisable to add salt when cooking vegetables with a high water content (mushrooms, cucumbers, tomatoes), and it is preferable not to use it with several other vegetables (red cabbage, peppers), as it causes them to lose flavor and firmness.

Cooking time

Vegetables should be cooked as briefly as possible. Those that are still crunchy after cooking are more flavorful and more nutritious. Once they are cooked, drain the vegetables and reserve the liquid for cooking other foods. Shorten the cooking time if the vegetables are to be reheated or served cold, since they continue to cook as long as they are hot. You can halt the cooking process by running the vegetables under cold water, but this practice causes a slight loss of vitamins and minerals.

Steaming

The vegetables cook in the hot vapor released by a small quantity of boiling water. This method of cooking retains nutrients and flavor better than boiling and can be used for all types of vegetables, although it is particularly well suited to fragile vegetables such as cauliflower, broccoli, and asparagus. The vegetables are arranged in a single layer (for uniform cooking) in the bottom of a steamer basket about an inch above the boiling liquid. Normally, a vegetable steamer with a tight-fitting lid is used. The vegetables are not placed in the steamer until the water begins to boil. When the cover begins to vibrate or steam starts to escape, reduce the heat to a simmer; avoid opening the cover unnecessarily, as this lengthens the cooking time and causes the nutritional substances contained in the vegetables to evaporate. If the cover is not close-fitting enough or if the heat is too high, it may be necessary to add more water. Cooking times for steaming are slightly longer than for boiling.

Pressure cooking

This method of cooking also uses steam, but it differs from regular steaming in that the vapor accumulates in a hermetically sealed cooker, producing pressure and raising the temperature above the boiling point, with the result that the vegetables cook very rapidly. While this method saves time and energy, it is important to time the cooking very carefully.

Stewing

Stewing is similar to steaming, except that the vegetables are cooked, covered, in their own evaporating moisture after having been briefly browned in a little butter or oil. A small quantity of liquid (water, wine, tomato sauce) can be added at the start of cooking, but this is not essential. The vegetables are cooked over gentle heat until tender. Usually, very little liquid is left at the end of cooking. This is the perfect cooking method for squash, mushrooms, tomatoes, onions, and shallots.

Cooking fish fillets and potatoes *en papillote* (wrapped in parchment or foil) so that they steam in their own moisture is a cooking method that is similar to stewing.

Braising

Braising is a particularly effective method of cooking tougher vegetables such as fennel, cardoon, artichoke, cabbage, and celery. After having been gently browned in a bit of fat, the vegetables (whole or in pieces) are cooked slowly in a small quantity of liquid in a covered pan over gentle heat. They can be braised alone, but they also make a savory dish when combined with meat. Ratatouille is a delicious braised vegetable stew. As with other methods of cooking, the vegetables should be cut into similarly sized pieces to ensure even cooking.

Dry-heat cooking

This method uses the dry heat of an oven or barbecue grill to cook the food and produces tender, juicy, and tasty vegetables. It is not necessary to add an acid or alkaline ingredient. Vegetables cooked in the oven can be cooked whole in their skin or cut into pieces. Unpeeled vegetables lose fewer nutrients, since less surface is exposed to the air. When cooked whole, certain vegetables, including the potato and eggplant, may burst as a result of inner pressure; to prevent this and to ensure even cooking, pierce them or make a slit in the skin.

Cooking in a wok

A wok is a special round-bottomed pan, traditional in Asian cooking, in which vegetables are quickly fried (stir-fried) or steamed, or both. The vegetables are rapidly fried in hot oil over very high heat and then cooked briefly; this seals in the nutrients and retains the color, texture, flavor, and nutritional value of the vegetables. The vegetables are cut into evenly sized pieces to ensure uniform cooking. This method is well suited a number of vegetables, in particular cauliflower, broccoli, and carrots. It is important to prepare all the vegetables and to group them according to their cooking time before starting to cook so as not to interrupt the cooking process. Once the vegetables are ready, heat a sufficient amount of oil in the wok along with the desired seasoning ingredients (ginger, garlic, etc). When the oil is hot, add the vegetables, those requiring the longest cooking time first, stirring constantly.

Once all the vegetables are coated with the oil, lower the heat slightly and, if desired, add a little liquid (water, tamari sauce, stock) thickened with cornstarch to make a sauce. If necessary, continue cooking while stirring or cover the wok for a few more minutes until the vegetables reach the desired tenderness.

Deep-frying

This method involves cooking food by immersing it in boiling oil. The oil used must be able to withstand very high temperatures; peanut oil, safflower oil, and soybean oil are all suitable for this method of cooking (see *Oil*). A cooking thermometer can be used to monitor the cooking temperature, which should be between 350° and 420°F. The temperature should not be allowed to exceed 475° to 490°F, as the oil could ignite spontaneously.

If the vegetables are not dried well or coated before being immersed in the oil, the water will evaporate immediately on contact with the hot oil, causing it to splatter. Different coatings can be used depending on the food; it can be coated with flour, with a mixture of flour, beaten egg, and bread crumbs, or with a batter. Coating has the advantage of sealing in the moisture of the vegetables, thus preventing them from drying out. Vegetables that take long to cook (broccoli, cauliflower) can be blanched prior to being deep-fried.

While the cooking time varies from one vegetable to another, all vegetables will float to the surface of the oil when they are cooked. They are then removed with a slotted spoon and drained on paper towels. When frying several types of vegetables together, start with those requiring the longest cooking time. Frying significantly increases the fat content of vegetables without improving their nutritional value; for example, 100 grams of fried potatoes contain 3 times more calories than baked potatoes. A number of studies have also shown that an excessive consumption of fat in the diet can have adverse health effects, making it preferable to limit one's consumption of fried foods.

Microwave cooking

Cooking vegetables in the microwave oven produces excellent results, as it retains their color and flavor better than any other cooking method. The microwaves act on the fat, sugar, and water molecules in the food; since vegetables have a high moisture content, they cook very quickly in the microwave oven. As always, for best results it is important that the vegetables be very fresh.

Microwave cooking uses short waves that are similar in nature to radio waves and that have two basic characteristics: they are absorbed by food and reflected by metal.

Upon penetrating food, microwaves excite the molecules in the food; the heat caused by the friction of the molecules cooks the food. The heat is conducted from the surface of the food toward the center. As with all foods, the molecules continue to vibrate for a while even after the oven or heat source is turned off. This phenomenon is accentuated in microwave cooking; the heat, or degree of activation of the molecules, is measured in terms of the power level to which the oven is set (as opposed to temperature).

Microwave cooking requires the use of cooking containers that are specially designed for the microwave oven. Glass and china cookware can be used as long as it does not have metallic trim. Plastic bags and containers that are not designated as being microwave-safe are not recommended, since they tend to melt and part of the toxic substances they contain may be transferred to the food when activated by the microwaves. Glazed dishes are also unsuitable for this reason.

Cooking time

Cooking times are approximate and vary according to the wattage of the oven, its size, and the power level; for example, a powerful 800-watt oven will cook food faster than a 400-watt oven. It is important to read the manual provided by the manufacturer, since there are wide variations among microwave ovens in terms of wattage. Cooking times also vary depending on the amount and size of the food being cooked, its water, sugar, and fat content, the amount of liquid added, the initial temperature of the food, and the how the food is arranged in the oven. The size of the oven also has a bearing on cooking time; the smaller the oven, the shorter the cooking time.

If the quantity of food called for in a recipe is increased or reduced, the cooking time should be adjusted accordingly; a greater quantity of food will require a longer cooking time than that indicated.

• Vegetables with a high water, fat, or sugar content cook more rapidly, and sometimes more unevenly.

• The more liquid in the container, the longer the cooking time.

• Food at room temperature cooks more quickly than refrigerated or frozen food.

• Food cooks more quickly and evenly when placed in the center of the oven. Newer microwave ovens are usually equipped with a distributor, fan, or rotating antenna that distributes the microwaves evenly, avoiding the need to turn the food manually during cooking. Most microwave ovens have a revolving turntable allowing for more even cooking of foods.

• Arrange vegetables that take longer to cook (or thicker portions) on the outside edges of the cooking dish, placing those that cook more quickly in the center; smaller pieces will cook more rapidly and evenly if they are the same size. To calculate the cooking time when cooking several vegetables together, add up the cooking times required for each vegetable, and then shorten this total slightly. To avoid overcooking, check for doneness, and then continue cooking if necessary.

When cooking in the microwave, remember to take the standing time into account, since foods continue to cook by conduction even after they are removed from the oven. If the vegetables are not going to be consumed immediately, stop cooking when they are still firm. Although foods generally cook more quickly in the microwave than in a conventional oven, large portions may take as long to cook in the microwave.

Vegetables that are cooked whole and that have a firm or thick skin (eggplant, manioc, potato, squash, tomato) must be pierced several times with a fork or knife before cooking to allow the steam to escape and to prevent them from bursting. Vegetables should not be wrapped in aluminum foil; instead, arrange large pieces on a paper towel.

It is important to cover the dish when cooking peeled or sliced vegetables in order to keep them from drying out. Use the container lid or cover the dish with microwave-safe plastic wrap. Pierce the wrap in two or three places with a fork, or fold back a small section from the edge to allow steam to escape. Salt and seasoning should be added after cooking, since salt can cause blackish spots to appear on the vegetables, while seasonings may either lose flavor or intensify in flavor. Use only a small quantity of water when cooking fibrous vegetables; fresh vegetables do not usually require water. Using too much water lengthens the cooking time and results in a loss of nutrients. It is not necessary to add water to frozen vegetables when cooking them in the microwave.

Among its many other uses, the microwave oven is perfect for boiling, poaching, and steaming foods; it can also be used to blanch vegetables before freezing, providing that they are uniformly sized and that the quantity is not too large.

To blanch vegetables in the microwave, add ⅓ cup of water for every 2 cups of vegetables. Cover the dish and cook for the required time. Remove the vegetables from the oven, immerse them in ice water, and then drain and pat them dry. Wrap the vegetables, and label the bag or container before freezing them.

Nutritional Information

All vegetables supply certain nutritional elements in proportions that vary depending on the type of vegetable. However, they also share certain nutritional characteristics:

• They provide a range of vitamins and minerals, particularly vitamin A in the form of carotene, vitamin B_6, vitamin C, and folic acid, as well as potassium, iron, magnesium and calcium.

• They have a high water content (80% to 95% of their total composition).

• They provide soluble and insoluble fiber.

• They are low in fat, with the exception of avocados and olives.

• They are generally low in protein.

• Most vegetables have a low calorie content, and since they are of plant origin, they contain no cholesterol.

Various factors, including the season and the type of soil, influence the flavor and nutritional value of vegetables before, during, and after harvesting. While some of these factors are uncontrollable (the climate, for example), others are influenced by humans; the latter include cultivation methods and the use of pesticides. The increase in the use of pesticides throughout the 20th century coincided with the development of industrial methods of cultivation and consumer demands. The esthetic preferences of consumers have made the use of pesticides unavoidable, since most consumers will avoid vegetables that are less than perfect in color or shape, even if they are of equivalent nutritional value.

Most vegetables are exposed to chemicals at some point. Part of these products remain on the vegetables in the form of residues, a certain quantity of which penetrates the vegetable itself (systemic contamination), while others remain on the surface (topical contamination). The medium— and long-term health effects of many of these chemical products is uncertain. In the past years, farm producers have modified their use of pesticides in order to reduce the amount of residue that finds its way into food.

To reduce the amount of residual pesticides consumed, vegetables should be carefully scrubbed under cold running water or peeled (although peeling results in a loss of nutrients and fiber contained in the skin). Peeling vegetables removes almost all of the topical pesticides, while cooking vegetables in boiling water greatly reduces the amount of systemic pesticides. Another solution is to consume organically grown vegetables, but this remains a costly alternative, since these products are generally very expensive.

Storing

There are several methods of preserving vegetables, including refrigeration, cold storage, freezing, canning, drying, marinating, and so on. The healthier looking and firmer the vegetable, the longer it will keep. While vegetables such as winter squash, garlic, potato, and taro tend to keep well even when stored at room temperature, most vegetables need to be refrigerated upon purchase. The vegetable compartment of the refrigerator is the best place to keep perishable vegetables, as it is less cold and more humid than the upper shelves, where the drier air causes them to dry out. For this reason, vegetables stored on refrigerator shelves should always be wrapped.

For many vegetables, a distinction is usually made between summer storage and winter storage. For example, carrots, cabbage, turnips, parsnips, and beets can all be stored for quite a while in a cold room where they can be buried, unwashed, in sand, moss, or sawdust. In summer, however, it is better to consume these vegetables immediately and to keep any surplus in the refrigerator.

Vegetables are stored differently depending on their specific characteristics; these characteristics are addressed under "Storing" in the individual entries. In general, however, it is preferable not to store or soak vegetables in cold water, as this drains them of some of their nutrients. Instead, wilted vegetables can be refreshed, and their crispness restored, by adding a bit of moisture to the container (using a wet paper towel, for example) or by misting them with water or immersing them in ice water for a few minutes. Avoid sealing the container completely, however, as this may cause the vegetables to rot.

Irradiation

Irradiation is another technique used by producers to improve the shelf life and overall quality of vegetables. They are exposed to radiation in the form of cobalt 60 or cesium 137, which act directly on the molecules without making the vegetables radioactive. Radiation reduces germination, destroys bacteria and insects, and reduces the need to treat fruits and vegetables with pesticides following harvesting. Presently, the U.S. government approves irradiation of flour, spices, fruit, and vegetables; a regulation requires that irradiated foods be clearly identified with a symbol indicating that they have been treated with radiation. However, research has thus far not shown the consumption of irradiated food to present a danger to public health.

Freezing

Freezing is a method of preservation that is widely used for vegetables, most of which stand up to the process. The advantages of this method are that it makes it possible to consume seasonal vegetables throughout the year and, when properly done, it preserves the color, texture, flavor, and most of the nutritional value of vegetables. For best results, use vegetables that are fresh and in good condition, and that reach peak ripeness soon after harvesting or purchasing; before being frozen, unripe vegetables should be placed in the refrigerator until ripe. While freezing does not keep vegetables from deteriorating, it does slow down this process, as well as halting the development of microorganisms (without destroying them); it also slows down the activity of the enzymes responsible for unpleasant odors and for the loss of color and nutrients in vegetables. These enzymes can be neutralized if the vegetables are blanched before being frozen. The nutritional value of a vegetable that has been properly blanched and frozen will be comparable to that of a fresh vegetable. Only vegetables with a high acid content do not need to be blanched prior to freezing. Because even frozen vegetables can dry out when exposed to dry freezer air, it is important to use airtight containers and bags.

Blanching consists of immersing raw vegetables in boiling water for a given length of time (depending on the type and size of vegetable); the vegetables are then refreshed and drained. For successful blanching, it is important to time it carefully and to refresh the vegetables immediately; vegetables that are not adequately blanched deteriorate rapidly, while those that are blanched too long will be almost cooked, in addition to having been subjected to all the disadvantages of boiling vegetables.

To blanch vegetables in water:

• Boil a generous quantity of water (4 quarts per pound of vegetables or 8 quarts per pound of leaf vegetables).

• Place the vegetables in a metal basket or in a cheesecloth bag to make it easy to quickly remove them from the water.

• Immerse the vegetables in the boiling water, cover the pan, and begin timing (the water should return to a boil rapidly).

• Once the blanching time is up, refresh the vegetables immediately by immersing them in very cold water (50°F) just long enough for them to cool (do not let them soak).

• Drain the vegetables, then dry them before placing them in a freezer bag, taking care to expel any remaining air. Label each bag with the type and quantity of vegetable and the date of freezing.

Because of their high water content, it is important to freeze vegetables rapidly in order to prevent the formation of large ice crystals, which damage the vegetables' cells, causing them to turn soft and to lose juice and nutritional value. For this reason, it is best to avoid overloading the freezer with a large quantity of food to be frozen at one time; prepare only the quantity that will freeze within 24 hours (between 2 and 3 pounds per cubic foot of space), bearing in mind that small packages freeze more quickly. For maximum storage life and quality when freezing vegetables, it is important to maintain a constant temperature of 0°F or less. At this temperature, vegetables will keep for an average of 1 year.

Most vegetables do not need to be thawed before being cooked; in fact, it is often preferable to avoid thawing them completely prior to cooking in order to limit the loss of flavor and nutritional value. However, some vegetables must be totally or partially thawed before being cooked. Vegetables can be thawed in their sealed package or container, either at room temperature or in the refrigerator. In the latter case, allow a longer time for thawing.

To cook frozen vegetables, add them to boiling water, cover the pot, and wait until the boiling resumes before lowering the heat. Because they are already partially cooked during blanching, frozen vegetables require a shorter cooking time than fresh vegetables.

Canning

Canning is a much older method of preserving food preservation than freezing. The consumption of certain canned vegetables largely surpasses that of frozen vegetables. The nutritional value of canned vegetables is usually less than or comparable to that of fresh or frozen vegetables. The loss of vitamins and minerals is increased by the common practice of discarding the canning liquid.

During commercial canning, food additives (EDTA, calcium gluconate, various calcium salts, citric acid) may be added to improve the color, texture, flavor, and keeping qualities of the vegetables.

Never buy a can that has bulges or dents, as the contents may be spoiled and potentially dangerous. In addition, always discard cans whose contents leak or overflow when the can is opened; canned food that produces foam or bubbles, that is moldy, or that smells rotten or sulfurous should also be thrown away. When in doubt, it is better to discard the can without tasting the contents.

Vegetables canned at home must be sterilized by a process of steaming under pressure, since, like all low-acid foods (meat, seafood, etc.), they can become highly toxic if they are merely sterilized in a boiling-water bath. This is because the toxin that causes botulism thrives in low-acid environments. This toxin is destroyed by temperatures of around 280°F, which can be obtained only with a pressure canner. Only the tomato has a sufficient acid level to permit sterilization by boiling water only; all other vegetables must be sterilized by steam under pressure.

Chive

Allium schoenoprasum and *Allium tuberosum,* Liliaceae

chive

The chive is the smallest member of the onion family; when cut, the thin, pointed, hollow stems will grow back continuously.

Aromatic plants native to Asia, the chive and the Chinese chive belong to the same family as garlic, onion, and leek.

The **chive** *(Allium schoenoprasum)* is the smallest member of the onion family. A native of Europe and northern Asia, it was not until the Middle Ages that it was widely cultivated and appreciated. Chives are easy to cultivate and also grow abundantly wild; they can be found in North America as well as in Europe and Asia. The long green filiform leaves typically reach a height of 6 inches. Thin, hollow, and pointed, these grasslike stems grow from tiny, barely formed white bulbs found in clumps just above the soil level. Pink, white, or purplish flowers will blossom at the tip of unharvested stems. Chives should not be torn out of the soil, but rather cut just above the ground; they will grow back continuously. Chives have a very mild and delicate flavor.

The **Chinese chive** *(Allium tuberosum)* has been cultivated in China for over 2,000 years and is an important ingredient in Asian cooking. Its flavor is more pronounced than that of the chive grown in the West.

Chinese chives grow in clumps; the plants have rhizomes with barely developed shoots. Each bulb sprouts four or five narrow, flat leaves of a dark-green color. The Chinese chive is harvested when its leaves reach a height of 14 to 18 inches and are ⅕ inch thick. At the end of summer, Chinese chives are often blanched and covered to protect them from the light and conserve the yellowish color of the stems.

Bulb Vegetables

30

Buying

When buying chives, choose fresh, evenly green leaves that show no signs of yellowing, softness, or drying out.

Preparing

 Use scissors to cut chives finely.

Nutritional Information

	chive	*Chinese chive*
water	92%	92%
protein	0.1 g	2.8 g
fat		0.6 g
carbohydrate	0.1 g	0.1 g
fiber	0.1 g	3.8 g
	per 3 g (15 ml)	**per 100 g**

Chive juice is used as a vermifuge.

Serving Ideas

 The chive and Chinese chive are often included in the family of *fines herbes.* They are used to season a wide variety of dishes, both warm and cold. They serve to flavor and garnish everything from vinaigrettes to mayonnaise, salads, dips, vegetables, soups, sauces, cheeses, omelets, pasta, tofu, fish, seafood, meat, and poultry.

Add chives at the end of cooking in order to preserve their flavor; however, it is best not to cook them at all and to add them just before serving.

Storing

Chives and Chinese chives may be kept in the vegetable compartment of the refrigerator for a few days. They freeze very well without being blanched.

Chinese chive

Scallion

Allium fistulosum, **Liliaceae**

Also known as cibol, this aromatic plant originated in southwestern Siberia. Although it has been cultivated in China for over 2,000 years, it was not introduced into Europe until the 16th century.

Scallions do not form a bulb as such, although the base of the plant is slightly swollen. The white shaft of the plant, which extends from the roots to the leaves, is fleshier and longer than that of chives. The long green leaves are slender and hollow; they can grow as high as 5 feet but are usually between 1 and 2 feet in height. Scallions are often partially covered with soil during cultivation in order to obtain a longer white stem. The scallion has a slightly hot flavor that is milder than the common onion but stronger than chives. There are several varieties of this plant.

Scallions have long, slender, hollow green leaves; their slightly hot flavor is milder than that of the common onion but stronger than that of chives.

Buying

Choose scallions with fresh, evenly green leaves and a pleasant odor.

Preparing

Cut the stems of scallions into small pieces with scissors or chop them with a knife.

Serving Ideas

 The green part of this plant is often included in the family of *fines herbes* and is used to season a wide variety of dishes, both warm and cold. It is used as a flavoring and as a garnish in vinaigrettes, mayonnaise, salads, dips, vegetables, soups, sauces, cheeses, omelets, pastas, tofu, fish, seafood, meat, and poultry. For maximum flavor, it is best to add it at the end of cooking. The leaves can substitute for chives, but should be used in smaller quantities. The white shaft of scallions is used like the common onion.

Nutritional Information

water	90.5%
protein	1.9 g
fat	0.4 g
carbohydrates	6.5 g
fiber	1.7 g
calories	34
	per 100 g

Raw scallion is a good source of vitamin C and potassium; it also contains vitamin A, iron, folic acid, zinc, and phosphorus. Scallion juice is used to relieve intestinal ailments.

Storing

Scallions will keep for a few days in the vegetable drawer of the refrigerator. They freeze well and do not need to be blanched beforehand. Freezing is a better method of preserving this vegetable than drying.

Bulb Vegetables

Leek

Allium porrum, Liliaceae

A biennial garden vegetable thought to have originated in central Asia, leeks have been known since antiquity and are mentioned several times in the Bible. Already cultivated by the ancient Egyptians, this vegetable was probably introduced into Great Britain by the Romans, where it came to be held in high esteem by the Celts. The leek is regarded as the "national vegetable" of Wales.

Leeks have a subtle and delicate flavor that is milder and sweeter than that of onions. The white part grows underground and is formed of sheathed cylindrical leaves; it is the more tender part of this vegetable and that which is the most appreciated and most commonly used. The white adds a subtle touch to various dishes without masking other flavors. The green ends are usually cut off at the point where they separate from the bulb and are primarily used as a flavoring ingredient in broths, soups, and stews. This vegetable, which grows to between 1½ and 3 feet high, is harvested when the bulb is at least 1 inch in diameter.

Buying

Look for leeks that are straight, firm, and intact; they should have bright green tops and be free of brownish patches. Avoid limp leeks, as well as those with cracked or swollen bulbs or dried-out and discolored leaves.

Serving Ideas

Leeks are eaten raw as well as cooked. Finely chopped raw leek is often added to salads; it can also be used either in combination with or in place of onions. Sometimes dubbed "poor man's asparagus" in Europe, leeks can be cooked and prepared in much the same way as that vegetable. They are excellent with a vinaigrette or a cream sauce and are often combined with potatoes, as in the famous vichyssoise, a delicious soup made with puréed potatoes and leeks and traditionally served cold. Leeks can also replace chicory in dishes baked au gratin. The green part is often used to add flavor to broths, stews, and other similar dishes; it can substitute for shallots or chives. Leeks are a good accompaniment to veal, ham, and cheese, and blend well with lemon, basil, sage, thyme, and mustard. The white part of leeks can be finely shredded or cut into strips and used as a flavoring in stocks and court bouillons.

Preparing

It is important to wash leeks thoroughly to rid them of the earth and sand trapped between the leaves. To do so, trim off the rootlets and the green tops, leaving a little green if desired, and remove any wilted outer leaves. Make a few equally spaced lengthwise cuts in the bulb, stopping about ¾ inch from the base, and pry open the layers of leaves; wash thoroughly under running water and drain.

1 *Remove any wilted outer leaves and trim off the green tops.*

2 *Trim off the rootlets.*

3 *Make several lengthwise cuts in the leek, stopping about ¾ inch from the base.*

4 *Separate the layers of leaves and rinse under running water. Drain and slice or shred, according to the recipe.*

Cooking

This vegetable should be cooked briefly, as it tends to become soft and mealy when overcooked. To ensure uniform cooking, buy similarly sized leeks. When cooking whole or split leeks, allow 15 to 20 minutes if boiling them and 25 to 35 minutes if braising or baking them. Sliced leeks can be sautéed for 3 to 5 minutes, simmered for 10 to 15 minutes, or melted in butter for 20 to 25 minutes.

Vichyssoise

SERVES 8

5 leeks (white parts only)
4 medium potatoes
1 rib celery
¼ cup (60 ml) unsalted butter
4 cups (1 l) chicken stock

½ tsp. salt
3 cups (750 ml) milk
2 cups (500 ml) heavy cream
2 tbsp. minced chives

1. Wash and slice the leeks. Peel, rinse, and dice the potatoes. Cut the celery into thin slices.

2. Melt the butter in a saucepan and add the leeks. Cook, covered, for 5 minutes or until the leeks are just tender but not brown. Add the potatoes, celery, stock, and salt. Bring to a boil, and simmer over a moderate heat for 35 minutes.

3. Transfer the soup to a blender and purée it.

4. Return the mixture to the saucepan, and stir in the milk and 1 cup of the cream. Bring to a boil again, stirring frequently. Remove from the stove immediately and allow to cool.

5. Pour the soup into a soup tureen. Mix in the rest of the cream and chill for 1 hour in the refrigerator.

Serve the soup cold, garnished with the chives.

Nutritional Information

	raw
water	83%
protein	1.5 g
fat	0.3 g
carbohydrates	14 g
fiber	1.8 g
calories	61
	per 100 g

Raw leeks are an excellent source of folic acid and a good source of iron and potassium; they also supply vitamin C, vitamin B$_6$, magnesium, calcium, and copper. Leeks are said to be laxative, antiseptic, diuretic, tonic, and anti-arthritic. They are also known for their cleansing effect on the digestive system.

Storing

Leeks can be stored in the refrigerator for about 2 weeks. It is also possible to store them, unwashed, in a cool damp place (90% to 95% humidity), where they will keep between 1 and 3 months.

Once cooked, this vegetable will keep for only about 2 days in the refrigerator, after which it tends to spoil rapidly and become indigestible. Leeks can be frozen, but their texture and flavor are altered when thawed. Cut raw leeks into slices, or blanch them whole for 2 minutes, before freezing. Frozen leeks will keep for about 3 months. For maximum flavor, cook them without thawing.

Bulb Vegetables

33

Garlic

Allium sativum, Liliaceae

The Egyptians elevated garlic to the status of a divinity and it was frequently depicted in wall paintings in tombs; it was also used as a form of payment.

An annual bulbous herb native to central Asia, garlic has been known since ancient times and has been grown for over 5,000 years, making it one of the oldest cultivated plants. During the building of the pyramids, the Egyptians gave their slaves a daily ration of garlic, believing that it had the power to increase strength and endurance. They also raised garlic to the status of a divinity. Greek athletes consumed garlic as a stimulant before competitions and soldiers ate it before going into battle. The Crusades contributed to spreading the use of garlic across Europe. Over the ages, garlic has been recognized as having many therapeutic properties, including the power to protect against the plague. Today the principal garlic-producing countries are China, South Korea, India, Spain, and the United States. Garlic is known for its persistent flavor that tends to linger on the breath and permeate perspiration, an unpleasant quality that has earned it a somewhat bad reputation in some societies.

The bulb, or "head," of garlic is made up of a cluster of 12 to 16 cloves. Both the head and the individual cloves are covered with a paperlike whitish skin. Garlic is ready for harvesting when its long, flat green leaves, which can grow to a length of 1 foot, begin to wilt; it is then left to dry in the sun for several days. Although it is most often sold dried, garlic can also be eaten fresh.

There are over 30 varieties of garlic, the most popular being white garlic, pink garlic, and purple garlic (only the skin is colored). Giant, or elephant, garlic, also called Spanish garlic *(A. scorodoprasum),* is a similar but slightly milder-flavored variety.

Buying

Choose plump, firm heads that are free of sprouts and spots. The skin should be intact. Garlic can be found in flake, powder, chopped, and paste form. While these preparations are practical, it is best to use fresh garlic for maximum flavor.

Preparing

For easy peeling, crush the garlic lightly with the flat side of a knife, after which the peel should practically come off by itself. Remove the green sprout that is sometimes found at the center of each clove, as it is difficult to digest and causes the odor to linger on the breath.

Serving Ideas

Although it can be eaten as a vegetable, garlic is most commonly used as a flavoring agent in a wide variety of foods, including vinaigrettes, soups, vegetables, tofu, meats, stews, cold meats, and marinades. Raw chopped or crushed garlic is an important ingredient in aioli sauce, rouille, tapenade, pistou, pesto, and garlic butter. Meat dishes, such as leg of lamb, can be flavored by making incisions in the meat and inserting slices of garlic.

For a mild garlic flavor, rub the inside of salad bowls or fondue dishes with the peeled half of a raw clove. A few cloves of garlic can also be added to oil to give it extra flavor; the longer the cloves are macerated, the more pronounced the taste of the oil. The green stems of fresh garlic may be used in place of shallots or chives. To freshen the breath after consuming garlic, chew on some parsley, mint leaves, or coffee grains.

pink garlic

Cooking

The flavor of garlic is released only when it is cut, crushed, or chopped; rupturing the skin causes the release of substances that are activated on contact with air. The more finely the garlic is chopped or crushed, the stronger its flavor.

For maximum flavor, add the garlic at the end of cooking; cooking it too long will detract from its flavor. For a more discreet flavor that is reminiscent of hazelnuts and does not cause "garlic breath," cook the garlic whole without peeling or cutting it. Do not let garlic brown when you are sautéing it, as this destroys its flavor and makes it, as well as the food it accompanies, bitter.

Storing

It is not necessary to refrigerate garlic, whose odor spreads quickly to the other food in the refrigerator. It will keep for several months at room temperature when stored in a cool, dry, well-ventilated place. When stored in hot and humid conditions, the garlic will begin to sprout and turn moldy. For a lengthy storage life, the temperature should be in the 32°F range and the humidity should not surpass 60%. Garlic heads are sometimes braided together by their stems; a braid will keep for several months. Fresh white garlic will usually keep for about 6 months. Garlic can be frozen as is, after removing the outer skin, for about 2 months.

Aioli Sauce

SERVES 6

6 cloves garlic	1 cup (250 ml) olive oil
2 salmonella-free egg yolks	Salt and pepper
	2 tbsp. lemon juice

All ingredients should be at room temperature.

1. Peel the garlic cloves, cutting them in half and removing the sprout.

2. In a food processor, blend the garlic with the egg yolks, ¼ cup of the oil, and salt and pepper to taste. While continuing to blend, incorporate the rest of the oil in a thin stream until the mixture has the consistency of thick mayonnaise. Add the lemon juice last. Serve Aioli Sauce with eggs, steamed vegetables, poached fish, or cold meats. Aioli is traditionally made in a mortar, but the food processor is easy, efficient, and reliable!

Nutritional Information

water	59%
protein	0.6 g
fat	0.1 g
fiber	0.14 g
carbohydrates	3 g
calories	13
	per 3 cloves (9 g)

The bulb, or "head," of garlic is made up of a cluster of 12 to 16 cloves. Both the head and the individual cloves are covered with a paperlike whitish skin.

Consumed in large quantities, in the manner of a vegetable, garlic is an excellent source of selenium. Some people have difficulty digesting garlic or experience allergic reactions to it, usually in the form of a skin rash or irritation.

Garlic is well known for its numerous medicinal qualities and has long been considered a veritable panacea by many. It is credited notably with diuretic, stomachic, tonic, antispasmodic, antiarthritic, antiseptic, and cleansing properties. It is used to relieve a wide range of health problems, including colic, bronchitis, gout, hypertension, and digestive troubles.

Medical studies have confirmed some of garlic's medicinal properties. It was widely used as an antibiotic during World War I, and researchers have since discovered that it contains allyl sulfide, a powerful antibiotic.

Other studies have proven that garlic contains allicin, which in concentrated form has a beneficial effect on the cardiovascular system, notably on the blood cholesterol level. According to these studies, the quantities of allicin needed to be effective correspond to the consumption of 7 to 28 fresh garlic cloves per day. It is interesting to note, however, that the active property of allicin may be destroyed during its extraction for the manufacture of tablets. Moreover, its effect is short-lived, lasting no more than 24 hours. Thus it is too early to know whether garlic, in fresh or tablet form, significantly reduces the blood cholesterol level.

Bulb Vegetables

35

garlic cloves

Onion

Allium cepa, Liliaceae

The onion was held in high esteem by the Egyptians, who used it to pay tribute to their gods. Onion remains were discovered in the tomb of the Egyptian king Tutankhamen.

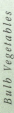

A garden plant native to central Asia and Palestine, the onion is widely appreciated both as a vegetable and as a condiment, in addition to having many medicinal properties. Cultivated for over 5,000 years, the onion was held in high esteem by the Egyptians, who used it to pay tribute to their gods and as a form of payment to the slaves during the building of the pyramids. Onions were also placed in tombs for use in the afterworld; remains of onions were discovered in the tomb of the Egyptian king Tutankhamen. The belief that onions can aid in the prediction of weather comes from the Gauls, who held that many layers of skin signaled the coming of a harsh winter. The onion has been an essential cooking ingredient and vegetable since the Middle Ages, particularly in the northern European countries. Christopher Columbus is responsible for introducing onions into the New World upon his second voyage in 1493. One of the most universal flavoring ingredients, onions are cultivated in many countries, including China, India, the United States, Russia, and Turkey.

The onion is a biennial vegetable cultivated as an annual; it is made up of numerous concentric layers of fleshy, juicy whitish leaves, which are covered by several outer layers of paper-thin skin. When the onion dries, pigments in the skin cause it to turn white, purple, yellow, brown, or red, depending on the variety. Onions are consumed fresh, semi-dry, or dry, and vary in shape, size, and flavor. Climate and variety determine how sharp or mild the onion will be. Spanish onions are among the mildest, while white onions are mild and sweet, and red onions are the sweetest. Certain varieties known as scallions, green onions, or spring onions *(Allium cepa)* are often sold fresh in bunches.

Onions can be harvested before the bulb has had a chance to mature, while it is still green and very small (as in the case of green onions), or once the bulb has reached maturity and dried, when the surface leaves begin to yellow and wilt.

Some people have difficulty digesting onions, particularly raw onions. Onions also tend to linger on the breath, which can be freshened by chewing on a few sprigs of parsley, a mint leaf, or a few coffee grains. The pungent taste that is characteristic of the onion is produced by its volatile oils, which are rich in allyl sulfide.

Spanish onion

red onion

white onion

Serving Ideas

Onions can be used in an endless variety of ways; they are indispensable in almost everything but desserts! They are used both raw (especially when mild) and cooked. To moderate the sharpness of raw cut onion, blanch it for a few minutes (rinsing it with cold water afterward to halt the cooking process), or soak it in cold water or vinegar; note, however, that this causes a very slight loss of nutrients. Yellow onions are an essential ingredient in numerous classic dishes, including onion quiche, pizza, onion soup, and dishes à la soubise and à la niçoise. Onions are also frequently baked au gratin, fried, stir-fried, creamed, or stuffed. They are a widely popular condiment in a multitude of both hot and cold dishes, where they are used raw or cooked, chopped, minced, or sliced. Studded with cloves, a whole onion can also be used to add flavor to stews and stocks.

Small onions are often glazed or pickled; they are also added to stews and simmered dishes, such as the classic bœuf bourguignon.

Onion Quiche

SERVES 4 TO 6

1 unbaked 9-inch short-crust pie crust
1½ lb. (750 g) onions
2 tbsp. butter
1 tbsp. oil
2 eggs
½ cup (125 ml) milk
½ cup (125 ml) whipping cream
2 tbsp. flour
Salt and white pepper to taste
Dash of nutmeg

1. Preheat the oven to 375°F (190°C).

2. Grease a 9-inch pie plate and dust it with flour. Line it with the pastry. Prick the bottom with a fork, and bake for 5 minutes. Set the crust aside.

3. Peel and thinly slice the onions. In a saucepan, heat the butter and oil. Add the onions and cook them over low heat for 5 to 7 minutes, or until tender, stirring constantly.

4. In a bowl, lightly beat the eggs. Add the milk, cream, and flour. Season with the salt, pepper, and nutmeg, and mix well.

5. Sprinkle the onions over the pastry shell, and pour the egg mixture on top.

6. Bake in the oven for 30 minutes, or until the mixture has risen and is golden on top.

Buying

When buying dry onions, look for firm specimens with a dry, smooth, crisp outer skin and a small neck. There should be no signs of sprouting or mold.

Onions are often treated by irradiation to prevent sprouting; this is rarely indicated on packaging, despite the fact that most countries have laws requiring producers to mention it. Onions bought in early fall are less likely to be treated, as they do not remain stocked in warehouses for long. Onion is also available in dried form, either as flakes or as plain or seasoned powder (such as onion salt). Although practical, seasoned onion powder is not always a good buy, as it often contains more salt than onion.

Nutritional Information

	raw
water	89.7%
protein	1.2 g
fat	0.2 g
carbohydrates	8.6 g
fiber	1.6 g
calories	38
	per 100 g

Onions contain potassium, vitamin C, folic acid, and vitamin B$_6$. Cooked onions have more or less the same vitamin and mineral content as raw onions. The onion has been credited with so many medicinal qualities that it can almost be called a panacea. It is notably said to prevent scurvy and to be diuretic, antibiotic, a stimulant, and an expectorant. It is also used in the treatment of colds, intestinal parasites, gallstones, diarrhea, and rheumatism.

Bulb Vegetables

37

green onion

Onion

Onions can be harvested before the bulb has had a chance to mature, while it is still green and very small (as in the case of green onions), or once the bulb has reached maturity and dried, when the surface leaves begin to yellow and wilt.

Preparing

Preparing onions can be a teary business; the tears are caused by the rupture of the onion's cells when it is cut; these cells release their sulfurous contents which, on contact with the air, create a new molecule, allyl sulfate, which is irritating to the eyes. The stronger the onion, the more it irritates. Here are a few hints to help reduce the tears:

• Use a very sharp knife and keep your face as far away from the onion as possible, by standing up while cutting it, for example.

• Cool the onion for 1 hour in the refrigerator or 15 minutes in the freezer before cutting it, to reduce the effect of the enzyme.

• Wear something over the eyes – such as goggles or eyeglasses – to avoid direct contact with the irritating substance.

• Cut the onion under a stream of cold water; this dissolves the irritating molecules.

To make it easier to separate the layers, completely remove the fibrous part of the base. While a finely chopped onion will cook more quickly, it will also tend to have less flavor. Avoid preparing onions too far in advance, since they tend to lose their juice when cut, and it is absorbed by countertops and wooden cutting surfaces. To remove the odor of onion from the hands, rub them with lemon juice or vinegar. Avoid chopping onions in a food processor, which tends to turn them into a purée.

Cooking

Onions become sweeter and lose their sulfurous enzymes during cooking, making them milder. Onion is more flavorful if it is sweated in a little fat until it is slightly soft but not colored.

Storing

Most dry onions enter a period of dormancy after harvesting, which explains why they can usually be stored for several weeks without sprouting. Their keeping qualities depend on the variety. It is a well-known fact that the sharper the onion, the longer it will keep; this is because the compound responsible for the onion's pungency also helps to preserve it. Strong onions that do not have a high water content, such as the yellow onion, have better keeping qualities than the white onion. Yellow onions will keep for 2 to 3 months in a cool, dry place, while red onions will keep for only 2 to 4 weeks. A good way to store dry onions is to hang them in a basket in a well-ventilated, cool, dry place. Do not store them in the refrigerator, as their odor tends to spread to other food. In addition, keep onions away from potatoes; they absorb their moisture, causing them to rot and sprout. Once cut, onions should be consumed in short order, as they tend to lose their vitamins and oxidize quickly. Green onions can be stored in the refrigerator for about 1 week.

Although it is possible to freeze onions, they tend to become soft and to lose some of their flavor, making it necessary to increase the quantity needed to flavor dishes. Before freezing, simply peel and chop the onion; blanching is not necessary.

Onions can be dried very easily: cut the onion into thin slices and place it on a cookie sheet in the sun for 2 to 3 days; then place it in a 185°F oven for about 10 minutes, or put it in a dehydrater for a few hours (180° to 190°F).

caption: gray shallot

Shallot

Allium ascalonicum, Alliaceae

A bulbous herb, probably of Near Eastern origin, since its scientific name is said to be derived from the name of an ancient Palestinian port. The shallot was widely consumed in ancient times by the Greeks and Romans. The Romans considered it as much an aphrodisiac as a food. Many historians and botanists believe that the shallot was introduced into Europe in the 17th and 18th centuries by crusaders returning from the Near East. Whatever its origin, this herb is particularly popular in France, a country recognized for the quality of its shallots.

The shallot is a hardy perennial that is cultivated as an annual. It is more aromatic and subtle in flavor than the onion and less pungent than garlic. Unlike both of these herbs, shallots do not cause "bad breath." The size of a garlic bulb, the shallot has two or three cloves. There are several varieties of the shallot, the most common of which include the **gray shallot** or common shallot, which is small and slender, with gray skin and a purple-colored head and flesh that is firm and piquant; the **Jersey shallot,** which has a short round bulb and pink skin, and veiny and milder-tasting flesh; and the ***cuisse de poulet*** shallot, which has an elongated bulb with copper-colored skin resembling that of the onion.

Buying

 Choose shallots that are firm and dry-skinned. Avoid sprouted, soft, or blemished shallots.

Serving Ideas

Shallots may be eaten raw or cooked. They are more commonly used as a condiment than as a vegetable, and lend a touch of refinement to numerous dishes. They are an important ingredient in béarnaise sauce and in white- and red-wine sauces in particular. They frequently accompany salads, fish, and grilled or fried meats. Shallots are also used as a seasoning in *beurre blanc*. Once cooked, they are more easily digested than onions. The green stems are very flavorful and can be chopped and used like chives in the spring. The cloves can be used to season vinegar or oil. Shallots also add flavor to soups, vinaigrettes, and vegetable dishes.

Storing

Shallots can be kept for about 1 month when stored in a dark, cool, dry place that is well ventilated. They will keep for only about 2 weeks in the refrigerator.

Once cut, store them in plastic wrap or place them in a container and cover with olive oil. The oil will become very aromatic and can be used for cooking.

Cooking

Shallots should not be browned or roasted in fat or butter, as this will make them bitter; it is better to cook them slowly over a low heat until softened.

Nutritional Information

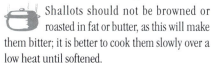

	raw
water	80%
protein	0.3 g
carbohydrates	1.7 g
calories	7
	per 10 g (15 ml)

The shallot is said to be rich in minerals, and is used as an appetite enhancer and a stimulant. It is also used to relieve burns and insect bites.

caption: ***cuisse de poulet*** shallot

caption: **Jersey shallot**

Water chestnut

Eleocharis dulcis and *Trapa* spp., **Cyperaceae**

The edible tuber of an aquatic plant believed to have originated in southern China, the water chestnut (also known as Chinese water chestnut) has been consumed since ancient times and continues to play an important role in Chinese, Japanese, and Vietnamese cooking. In China, where they were originally used for their medicinal qualities, water chestnuts have been cultivated for centuries. From that country, cultivation of the water chestnut spread first to India and then as far as Madagascar. China is the world's leading producer of water chestnuts, although they are also grown on a smaller scale in other areas of Europe. North Americans are most familiar with the variety *Eleocharis dulcis,* imported from China and usually sold canned in specialty shops.

The water caltrop *Trapa natans,* which is cultivated in parts of Asia and Europe, is often thought to be a relative of the water chestnut *Eleocharis dulcis,* but it actually belongs to a different family altogether, the Trapaceae family. The water chestnut grows in the shallow waters of lakes, rivers, and marshes. Like rice, it requires a lot of water to grow; in Asia it is often cultivated in rice fields, where it is planted in spring and harvested in fall when the fields have dried up. The water chestnut *Eleocharis dulcis* resembles the common chestnut; round in shape, it is about 1 to 1¾ inches in diameter and has a slightly flattened top that is capped by a small tuft out of which leaves would sprout if the chestnut were not harvested. The bulb is covered by a dark brown shell; the whitish flesh inside is crisp, juicy, sweet, and fragrant and is encased in a thin beige-colored skin. The flavor of cooked water chestnuts is reminiscent of corn.

There are two types of water caltrop: the *Trapa bicornis* variety has two recurved horns, while the *Trapa natans* consists of four slender horns. The shells of water caltrop were often used to make rosaries. While very popular in Europe at one time, the water caltrop has fallen into relative obscurity. The nuts of this plant cannot be eaten raw, as they contain toxic substances that are neutralized only during cooking.

Nutritional Information

	raw	canned
water	74%	86%
protein	1.5 g	1.1 g
fat	0.2 g	0.1 g
carbohydrates	24 g	12 g
calories	107	50
		par 100 g

Raw water chestnuts are an excellent source of potassium and contain riboflavin, magnesium, vitamin C, and phosphorus. Canned water chestnuts contain potassium and iron. Water chestnuts are held to be a good tonic.

Serving Ideas

Water chestnuts can be eaten raw (the variety *Eleocharis dulcis* only) or cooked. Raw water chestnuts are served as an appetizer or eaten out of hand, as a snack. Cooked, they are delicious on their own or simply topped with a little butter. They add an original and crispy touch to a large variety of dishes, including soups, mixed salads and fruit salads, pastas, quiches, meats, poultry, and seafood. They can also be sautéed with tofu or vegetables and are delicious cooked with rice and spinach and then gratinéed.

A delicious soup can be made by adding puréed water chestnuts to a chicken stock with onions, apples, and light cream. Water chestnuts are also good puréed together with potatoes, sweet potatoes, or winter squash.

Preparing

Water chestnuts should be washed thoroughly to rid them of any traces of dirt; remove soft or brown patches and discard any damaged or fermented water chestnuts. Water chestnuts can be peeled before or after cooking. While there is less waste if they are peeled after cooking, this causes the flesh to turn a beige color similar to that of the skin. Water chestnuts are easier to peel if a very sharp knife is used. To prevent peeled water chestnuts from discoloring, immerse them in water acidulated with a bit of lemon juice. To peel cooked water chestnuts, cut an "X" in the flat part of each chestnut and immerse them in boiling water for 4 to 5 minutes. Remove them from the water and peel them, removing their thin brownish membrane at the same time.

Cooking

While cooking makes water chestnuts slightly sweeter and causes them to discolor, it does not alter the crisp texture of their flesh. Add a little lemon juice to the cooking water to prevent discoloration. Water chestnuts can also be cooked in stock or in a mixture of equal parts of water and milk. Before adding them to a stir-fry, boil the chestnuts for 5 minutes or steam them for 7 to 8 minutes. Water chestnuts can be used whole, halved, sliced, diced, cut into julienne strips, or puréed.

Water Chestnuts Wrapped in Bacon

MAKES ABOUT 16

1 can water chestnuts	*1 tsp. ground ginger*
(8 oz.)	*8 slices bacon*
½ cup (125 ml) soy sauce	*½ cup (125 ml) sugar*

1. Drain and rinse the water chestnuts.

2. In a bowl, mix the soy sauce and ginger. Add the drained water chestnuts. Let soak 1 hour at room temperature, stirring frequently.

3. Preheat the oven to 400°F (200°C).

4. Cut the bacon slices in half. Drain the water chestnuts.

5. Pour the sugar into a bowl and roll each chestnut in the sugar; then roll it in a half slice of bacon. Attach the bacon with a toothpick. Arrange the chestnuts on a baking sheet.

6. Bake for about 15 minutes. Serve with an aperitif.

Buying

When choosing fresh water chestnuts, look for very hard specimens that are free of bruises and soft patches.

Storing

Because water chestnuts are quite perishable, it is better to store them unpeeled. Fresh water chestnuts can be covered with water and placed in a container in the refrigerator, where they will keep for up to 2 weeks. While this method of storage makes them slightly less flavorful, it keeps them fresh and crunchy. Fresh water chestnuts can also be stored unwashed in a paper bag and placed in the coldest part of the refrigerator, where they will also keep for 2 weeks, although it is a good idea to check on them periodically to make sure they haven't begun to dry out or ferment. Peeled water chestnuts will keep for 2 or 3 days in the refrigerator. Refrigerate unused portions covered in water, changing the water every day. Water chestnuts can also be frozen, either raw or cooked, peeled or unpeeled. Raw unpeeled water chestnuts will keep for about 6 months in the freezer, while if they are cooked and puréed, they will keep for about a year. Freezing may cause puréed water chestnuts to separate; simply mix them again after thawing to restore their consistency, or add a tablespoon of butter or honey to the purée before freezing to keep it from separating.

Bulb Vegetables

41

Beet

Beta vulgaris, Chenopodiaceae

The flesh of the beet is usually deep red, but it can also be white.

red beet

The beet is the fleshy root of a plant believed to have originated in North Africa. Red and white beets were well known to the Romans, who used them for their roots, while other peoples consumed only the leaves. In the 16th century, the English and Germans began to consume the so-called garden beet as a vegetable, while the white beetroot was used as livestock feed. The first sugar beet factory was built in the early 19th century in Poland, around the same time that beets began to be cultivated in the United States.

Beets can be more or less fleshy and have a thin, smooth skin. The flesh is usually deep red but can also be white. The edible leaves are quite colorful and curly, and often measure over 14 inches in length and 10 inches in width. There are several varieties of beet, including the fodder beet, used to feed livestock, and the sugar beet, which is processed to make sugar and alcohol.

Red beets owe their characteristic color to betacyanin, a pigment of the anthocyanin family that is extremely soluble in water. The slightest bruise causes the beet to "bleed" during cooking, releasing its purple juice upon contact with the cooking liquid. This characteristic is exploited in borscht, a colorful soup from Eastern Europe that is made of finely cut slices of beets and usually served with sour cream. Lemon juice can be used to remove the stains left on the hands by beets (wearing gloves avoids this problem). Beets may also discolor urine and stools, but this is not a cause for concern.

Buying

Choose firm, smooth-skinned beets with a deep red color and no signs of spots or bruises. To ensure even cooking, look for beets of a similar size, avoiding those that are very large or elongated, as they may be fibrous. The leaves do not give an indication of the quality of the root; however, if you are planning to use the leaves, they should be tender and a healthy green color.

Serving Ideas

Beets can be eaten raw, cooked, canned, or pickled. Raw, they can be peeled, sliced, or grated and seasoned as desired. Cooked beets can be eaten warm or cold; they are often served with a vinaigrette or added to salads. The leaves are delicious cooked and can be prepared much like spinach or Swiss chard.

Beets can also serve as a substitute for coffee; the finely cut slices are dried, roasted, and ground to a powder that can be used on its own or mixed with other ingredients such as chicory.

42

Storing

Fresh beets that still have their roots and their leaves (or 2 to 3 inches of stem) will keep for 2 to 4 weeks in the refrigerator or in a cool (32°F) and humid (90% to 95%) place. Stored in soil or in a cellar, they will keep longer, but they have a tendency to harden if left for too long. Unwashed leaves will stay fresh for 3 to 5 days in the refrigerator when stored in a perforated plastic bag.

While raw beets cannot be frozen because they become soft during thawing, cooked beets freeze without any problem.

Borscht

SERVES 8

4 raw beets	*2 tbsp. oil*
¼ lb. (100 g) green cabbage	*8 cups (2 l) water*
1 carrot	*Salt and ground pepper*
1 rib celery	*2 tbsp. tomato paste*
1 onion	*1 tbsp. lemon juice*
1 clove garlic	*½ cup (125 ml) sour cream*
2 tbsp. flat-leaf parsley	

1. Peel and wash the beets and cut them into small cubes; you should have 2 cups (500 ml). Cut the cabbage into thin strips; you should have 1 cup (250 ml). Peel and slice the carrot. Rinse the celery, remove the strings, and cut it into strips. Peel and chop the onion and the garlic. Chop the parsley.

2. Heat the oil in a flameproof casserole and cook the onion until it is soft and transparent. Add the beets, carrot, celery, water, and salt and pepper and bring to a boil. Cover and cook over medium heat for 45 minutes. Add the cabbage, garlic, and tomato paste, and cook for another 30 minutes.

3. Add the lemon juice and parsley. Adjust the seasoning.

4. Garnish each serving with a spoonful of sour cream, and serve.

Cooking

Wash beets under running water, taking care not to bruise them; scrub them delicately if necessary. Cook the beet whole, without peeling it or bruising it, leaving the roots and 1 to 2 inches of stem. The color of beets can be restored or revived by adding an acidic ingredient such as lemon juice or vinegar. Alkaline ingredients like baking soda make beets turn purple, while salt makes them paler; salt should be added only at the end of cooking.

Depending on their size, allow 30 to 60 minutes when boiling or steaming beets. Baking beets in the oven preserves their flavor and enhances their color. To verify whether the beet is cooked, hold the vegetable under a thin stream of cold water; the peel will detach itself easily if it is ready. Avoid piercing the beet with a fork or knife, as this will cause it to "bleed" and lose color during cooking.

Nutritional Information

	cooked	*cooked leaves*
water	89%	90.9%
protein	2.6 g	1.1 g
fat	0.2 g	0.1 g
carbohydrates	5.5 g	6.7 g
fiber	2.9 g	2.2 g
calories	27	31
		per 100 g

Beets are an excellent source of potassium and vitamin A, and a good source of vitamin C, magnesium, and riboflavin; they also contain iron, copper, calcium, thiamine, vitamin B_6, folic acid, zinc, and niacin.

Beet greens are an excellent source of potassium; they are also a good source of folic acid and magnesium, and contain vitamin C and iron.

Beets are said to stimulate the appetite and are easily digested. They are also used to relieve headaches and are believed to combat colds and anemia.

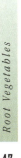

Root Vegetables

43

orange beet

Turnip

Brassica rapa, Cruciferae

A root vegetable of European origin, the turnip belongs to the large family that includes the cabbage, mustard, and radish. The roots and leaves of the wild turnip were apparently used long before the development of agriculture. Cultivated for the first time some 4,000 years ago in the Near East, it came to be much appreciated by the Greeks and the Romans, who developed several varieties of the turnip. The turnip remained very popular in Europe throughout the Middle Ages, until it was somewhat replaced by the potato in the 18th century.

The turnip's white fleshy root is covered with a thin layer of skin that is pale yellow or white, with a purple-tinged ring around the top of the vegetable. The leaves of the turnip (turnip greens) are slightly hairy but edible.
The turnip is often confused with the rutabaga (swede), a related yellow-fleshed species. They can be distinguished by the fact that the leaves of the turnip are attached directly to the top of the root, while the rutabaga's leaves issue from the neck of the root.

Buying

Turnips should be firm, heavy, smooth, and without cracks or blemishes. Avoid oversize roots, as they tend to be fibrous and bitter tasting. When leaves are present, they should be crisp and deep green in color.

Nutritional Information

	raw
water	92%
protein	0.9 g
fat	0.1 g
carbohydrates	6.2 g
fiber	1.8 g
calories	27
	per 100 g

The turnip is a good source of vitamin C and potassium and also contains folic acid. The sulfur in turnips may cause flatulence, especially in the case of larger turnips or those that are hollow or overcooked. Turnip greens are rich in vitamins A, B, and C, and in potassium and magnesium.

The turnip is said to act as a revitalizer, a diuretic, and an emollient. It combats scurvy and alleviates respiratory ailments.

Preparing

Small turnips do not need to be peeled if they are very fresh and do not have a waxy coating, in which case a simple scrubbing will do. Otherwise they should be peeled and washed, preferably shortly before cooking to prevent darkening of the flesh. It is a good idea to blanch turnips for 10 minutes before preparing them; this makes them easier to digest, conserves more of their nutritional value, and somewhat attenuates their pungent odor.

Serving Ideas

Turnips can be eaten raw or cooked, and are often prepared in much the same manner as carrots. They are delicious in soups and stews, and can be puréed, stuffed, or braised. Tender young turnips are often baked with grated cheese, or served with a cream or Mornay sauce; they can also be added to fresh or cooked salads. Turnip greens also make a savory dish and can be prepared much like spinach.

Cooking

Turnips take a little longer than carrots to cook; allow 10 to 15 minutes when boiling them, and slightly more when steaming them, depending on the size of the pieces. This vegetable absorbs fat easily, making it very high in calories when fried.

Storing

Turnips will keep, unwashed and in a perforated plastic bag, for 1 to 3 weeks in the refrigerator. The leaves should be removed and stored separately in a perforated plastic bag; they will keep for 4 or 5 days in the refrigerator. This vegetable freezes well after being blanched for a couple of minutes, or in cooked or puréed form.

Parsnip

Pastinaca sativa, **Umbelliferae**

A root vegetable native to the Mediterranean, the parsnip was widely used by the ancient Greeks and Romans, but it was not until the Middle Ages that the variety we know today was developed. During the Middle Ages and the Renaissance, the parsnip enjoyed the same popularity among Europeans as the potato does today. Although introduced into the United States by the first English settlers in the early 16th century, it did not gain much popularity among early Americans, who had little appreciation for its taste and found it too slow-growing to be profitable as a crop. It is still relatively unfamiliar here today.

The parsnip is a root measuring 7 to 12 inches in length and 2 to 3 inches in diameter. It is similar in texture to the turnip, and its foliage resembles that of celery; both these vegetables belong to the same family as parsnip. Its yellowish, fruity flesh has a flavor reminiscent of hazelnut. Parsnips are sweeter when they have been exposed to a light frost while still in the ground, as the cold converts their starch into sugar.

Preparing

Parsnips need to be peeled only if they are waxed, which is often the case. Scrub or peel them in the same way as carrots. It is very easy to remove the thin skin after cooking, particularly if the parsnip is cooked whole or if it is old. Because the flesh darkens on contact with the air, cut parsnips should either be cooked immediately or be placed in lemon or vinegar water in the meantime. The core of old or large parsnips may have to be removed, as it is often hard, fibrous, and tasteless.

Serving Ideas

The parsnip is prepared in much the same way as the carrot, salsify, or turnip, vegetables which it can also replace in most recipes. Parsnips are delicious puréed, fried like French fries, glazed like carrots, served cold dressed in a vinaigrette, or simply as a vegetable side dish. They are very good raw and make a pleasant addition to soups and stews. The flavor is best when parsnips are cooked whole and for a short time. They require approximately the same cooking time as carrots.

Storing

The parsnip has good keeping and freezing qualities. It can be stored for about 4 weeks in the refrigerator, but should be wrapped in a paper towel and placed it a perforated plastic bag, as it loses moisture rapidly when exposed to air.

Parsnips can be frozen whole or in chunks. Blanch whole parsnips for 5 minutes and cut parsnips for 3 minutes before freezing.

Buying

Choose parsnips that are firm and smooth and without bruises; smaller specimens will be more tender.

Nutritional Information

	cooked parsnip
water	77.7%
protein	1.3 g
fat	0.3 g
carbohydrates	19.5 g
fiber	4 g
	per 100 g

The parsnip is known for its carbohydrate content, which is much higher than that of carrots, making it sweet and fairly high in calories.

This vegetable is an excellent source of potassium and folic acid; it also contains vitamin C, magnesium, pantothenic acid, copper, phosphorus, and vitamin B_6. It is said to aid menstruation and to be purifying, antirheumatic, and diuretic.

Carrot

Daucus carota var. *sativa*, Umbelliferae

A root vegetable originating in the Middle East and central Asia, where it has been cultivated for thousands of years, the carrot is a biennial plant that is cultivated as an annual. The ancestor of the carrot we know today was purple in color, verging on black. The yellow variety is most likely the result of a mutation. Both the purple and yellow varieties were used by the Greeks and Romans for their medicinal qualities. Until the Renaissance, carrots were not a very popular vegetable; they were yellow and tough, with a woody core, making them rather unappetizing. The texture of the carrot was subsequently improved, and the orange-colored carrot was developed by French agronomists in the mid-19th century.

There are over 100 varieties of the carrot, some of which are very long while others are short. Indeed, they range from 2 inches to 3 feet in length and from ½ inch to 2½ inches in diameter. They can be orange, white, yellow, red, purple, or black. The largest producers of carrots are China, the United States, Poland, Japan, France, and England.

Carrots developed their orange color in the 19th century; the ancestor of the carrot was purple verging on black.

Root Vegetables

46

Nutritional Information

	raw	*cooked*
water	87.8%	87.4%
protein	0.9 g	1.2 g
fat	0.1 g	0.1 g
carbohydrates	3.2 g	10.5 g
fiber	1.9 g	3.2 g
calories	43	45
		per 100 g

Raw carrots are an excellent source of vitamin A and potassium; they contain vitamin C, vitamin B_6, thiamine, folic acid, and magnesium. Cooked carrots are an excellent source of vitamin A, a good source of potassium, and contain vitamin B_6, copper, folic acid, and magnesium.

In order to assimilate the greatest quantity of the nutrients present in carrots, it is important to chew them well. Carrots are credited with many medicinal properties; they are said to cleanse the intestines and to be diuretic, remineralizing, antidiarrheal, tonic, and antianemic. The carrot has a reputation as a vegetable that helps to maintain good eyesight. Raw grated carrot can be applied as a compress to burns for a soothing effect. Its highly energizing juice has a particularly beneficial effect on the liver. Consumed in excessive quantities, carrots cause the skin to turn yellow; this phenomenon, which is caused by the carotene contained in carrots, is frequently seen in young children but is not at all dangerous.

An infusion of carrot seeds (1 teaspoon per cup of boiling water) is believed to be diuretic, to stimulate the appetite, reduce colic, and help alleviate menstrual cramps.

Buying

Choose firm and brightly colored carrots. This vegetable is usually sold without its top (stems and leaves), which is removed during harvesting to reduce moisture loss. If the tops are present, they should be firm and well colored. Avoid soft and sprouting carrots, as well as those with moist patches.

Serving Ideas

Carrots can be used in an endless variety of ways; they feature in everything from appetizers to desserts and are even used to make wine. Raw carrots are eaten on their own or used in salads and appetizers. They are also used in baking to make cakes and cookies. Cooked carrots make an excellent vegetable side dish, either on their own or combined with other vegetables. They are often served with a cream sauce, glazed, or simply dressed with a little butter. They are also delicious puréed with potatoes, and are a common ingredient in a wide variety of dishes, including soups, stews, quiches, soufflés, and omelets. They can also be preserved in vinegar. Carrot tops, which are very rich in minerals, can be added to soups, salads, and sauces.

Storing

Carrots have good keeping qualities. Stored in the refrigerator, they will keep for 1 to 3 weeks (2 weeks in the case of new carrots), but it is best to wrap them first, as they lose moisture quickly when exposed to air. Place them in a perforated plastic bag or wrap them in a paper towel to prevent the formation of condensation, which causes them to spoil. Carrots can also be stored in a dark, cool (33°F), humid (93% to 98% humidity), and well-ventilated place; the cooler the temperature, the longer the carrots will preserve their flavor.

Do not store carrots near fruits or vegetables that produce a lot of ethylene gas, such as pears, apples, or potatoes, as this gas causes them to age more quickly and to become bitter. One of the best methods of storing carrots is to cover them, unwashed, with sand; they will keep for up to 6 months. Carrots will also hibernate in the garden, well buried and covered with mulch, ready to be harvested as they are needed, as long as the temperature does not fall too low. Carrots take well to freezing; blanch them for 3 minutes first if they are cut and 5 minutes if they are whole; they will keep for about 1 year at a temperature of 0°F.

Preparing

Carrots should be washed or gently scraped; only old carrots need to be peeled. A green stem end indicates that the carrot was exposed to sunlight; this part is bitter and should be removed. Carrots can be eaten raw or cooked, either whole or cut into sticks, slices, julienne strips, cubes, or chopped or grated.

Cooking

All methods of cooking are suitable for carrots, but to ensure maximum flavor and nutritional value, avoid overcooking them.

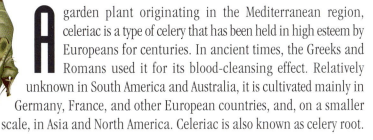

Celeriac

Apium graveolens var. *rapaceum,* **Umbelliferae**

A garden plant originating in the Mediterranean region, celeriac is a type of celery that has been held in high esteem by Europeans for centuries. In ancient times, the Greeks and Romans used it for its blood-cleansing effect. Relatively unknown in South America and Australia, it is cultivated mainly in Germany, France, and other European countries, and, on a smaller scale, in Asia and North America. Celeriac is also known as celery root.

Similar in size to the turnip, celeriac usually measures about 4 inches in diameter and weighs between 1 and 2 pounds. It is irregularly shaped and its surface is dotted with tufts of rootlets. The thick, rough brownish skin covers a creamy white, crisp flesh that is slightly hotter tasting than celery. Celeriac also grows more easily and keeps longer than celery, making it an excellent winter vegetable.

Buying

Look for a heavy, firm, undamaged celeriac; the more regular its shape, the easier it will be to peel it. Avoid celeriac that is bruised or that sounds hollow when tapped. Specimens measuring over 4½ inches in diameter and weighing more than 1 pound tend to be more fibrous.

Preparing

Celeriac is very easy to prepare: simply wash it, peel it (either before or after cooking), and cut it. Since it oxidizes quickly on contact with air, it should be sprinkled with vinegar or lemon juice or cooked as soon as it is cut to prevent discoloration.

Serving Ideas

Celeriac is most often eaten raw. A classic way of using it is to grate it or cut it into thin strips or cubes, and to serve it as a salad seasoned with a rémoulade dressing. Celeriac can also be cooked, either on its own or in combination with other vegetables. It makes a good purée mixed with potatoes and also adds a pleasant aroma to soups and stews. Celeriac lends itself particularly well to braising, and is delicious topped with a Mornay or béchamel sauce and gratinéed.

Nutritional Information

	raw	*cooked*
water	88%	92.3%
protein	1.5 g	1 g
fat	0.3 g	0.2 g
carbohydrates	9.2 g	5.9 g
calories	39	25
		per 100 g

Raw celeriac is an excellent source of potassium and a good source of vitamin C, phosphorus, vitamin B$_6$, magnesium, and iron. Cooked celeriac is a good source of potassium and contains vitamin C, phosphorus, vitamin B$_6$, and magnesium. Celeriac is said to be diuretic, stomachic, remineralizing, and tonic, and to stimulate the appetite and cleanse the system.

Root Vegetables

47

Cooking

A short cooking time is recommended for celeriac, since overcooking tends to transform it into a rather tasteless and sticky paste. Allow 10 to 15 minutes when boiling it and 12 to 18 minutes when steaming it. Adding a teaspoon of lemon juice or vinegar to the cooking liquid will prevent the celeriac from oxidizing.

Storing

Celeriac can be kept for several weeks in the refrigerator. If it is sold with its leaves, remove them and place the vegetable in a perforated plastic bag to prevent it from drying out. While it will keep at temperatures slightly above the freezing point, celeriac, like celery, does not freeze well.

Black radish

Raphanus sativus var. *niger,* **Cruciferae**

A root plant believed to have originated in the eastern Mediterranean region, the black radish is particularly popular in eastern Europe. It is almost as pungent as its close relative horseradish.

Black radishes usually measure between 2 and 3 inches in diameter and up to 6 inches in length; they can weigh over 1 pound. A rough blackish skin covers the firm white flesh, which is less juicy than that of the red radish.

Buying

Choose black radishes that are very firm, unblemished, and uncracked. The leaves, if present, should be bright green.

Preparing

Black radishes are usually scraped, scrubbed, and peeled.

Nutritional Information

The freshly extracted juice of black radish is said to have an antiscorbutic and antiallergenic effect when taken in doses of 1 or 2 ounces per day. It is also used as a sedative and a respiratory tonic and to treat liver problems, dyspepsia, cholelithiasis, urinary lithiasis, pulmonary problems (cough, chronic bronchitis, asthma, whooping cough), rheumatism, arthritis, gout, and eczema.

Cooking

Black radish is often used in a stir-fry. It requires a cooking time of 10 to 25 minutes, depending on its freshness.

Serving Ideas

Because of their pungency, black radishes are rarely consumed as they are; they are more commonly drained or cooked. To drain a black radish, grate it coarsely or cut it into thin slices or sticks and sprinkle with salt; mix well and cover the bowl tightly to keep in the strong odor; let stand for about 1 hour and then rinse and drain the radish; proceed with the chosen recipe.

Drained black radish is often seasoned with shallots and sour cream or added to salads; it is also good with a rémoulade sauce. Black radish is very decorative when unpeeled.

Cooked black radish tastes somewhat like rutabaga and can be added to soups, stews, omelets, and tofu.

Storing

Black radish has good keeping qualities; placed in a perforated plastic bag in the refrigerator, it will keep for several weeks, although it tends to lose some of its firmness as it ages. Wash it just before using it. If present, the tops should be removed before storing black radish, as they cause it to dry out more quickly.

Radish

Raphanus sativus, **Cruciferae**

The edible root of an annual vegetable plant, thought to be a native of the Near East. The radish was one of the first vegetables to be domesticated; ancient documents reveal that it was consumed some 4,000 years ago by the Egyptians and Babylonians, who valued it particularly for its medicinal properties. Radishes were introduced into China around 500 B.C.; the Chinese developed new varieties with larger and longer roots and a much milder taste than the small round radish known today. The Latin name of this root is derived from the Greek *raphanos,* meaning "that which rises easily," and refers to the fact that radishes grow swiftly and easily.

There are many varieties of radishes, including the red radish, the black radish, and the white radish (also known as daikon or Japanese radish). The red radish is round or elongated, about 1 inch in diameter, with a crisp and juicy flesh that can be white or cream colored, or sometimes reddish. It is less sharp than the black radish, and its rough greens are edible.

Radish greens are edible and can be prepared like spinach when they are still fresh and tender.

Buying

Choose firm, smooth-skinned radishes with no cracks or blemishes. Avoid larger specimens, which tend to be more fibrous and to have a sharper flavor. If the greens are present, they should be brightly colored.

Serving Ideas

Radishes are eaten raw as well as cooked. In Western countries, they are usually served raw in appetizers, salads, sandwiches, or with a dip, while in the East, cooked or marinated radishes are quite popular. Cooked radishes have a less pungent flavor that is comparable to that of small turnips. They can be added to soups, stews, omelets, or stir-fries.

When fresh and tender, the greens are prepared like spinach. They add a refreshing touch to soups or mashed potatoes. The leaves can also be dried and infused for a tea.

Radish seeds can be sprouted like alfalfa seeds; the sprouts have a piquant flavor that is reminiscent of watercress. They are used in soups, sandwiches, omelets, or as a flavoring with fish and tofu. To preserve crispness and flavor, add them near the end of cooking.

Storing

Radishes keep well, particularly without their greens, which tend to accelerate the loss of moisture. Place the radishes, unwashed, in a perforated plastic bag and store them in the refrigerator, where they will keep for about 1 week.

Cooking

To restore, and even enhance, the color of red radishes during cooking, add an acid ingredient such as lemon juice to the cooking liquid. An alkaline ingredient such as baking soda will have the opposite effect, discoloring the red radish and reducing its already low thiamine content.

Nutritional Information

	raw
water	95%
protein	0.6 g
fat	0.5 g
carbohydrates	3.6 g
fiber	2.2 g
calories	17
	per 100 g

The radish is a good source of vitamin C and potassium and supplies folic acid. It is said to be antiseptic, antiarthritic, antirheumatic, to stimulate the appetite, and to combat scurvy and rickets. It also aids in digestion and is used in the treatment of asthma, bronchitis, mineral deficiencies, and liver and gallbladder troubles. Many people find radishes difficult to digest.

Preparing

Radishes owe their peppery flavor to their essential oil, which is concentrated at the surface of the vegetable, just beneath the skin. They are not usually peeled unless a milder flavor is preferred. Trim off the roots and leaves, wash in plenty of water, and drain. Radishes can be served whole, sliced or diced, cut into sticks, minced, or grated.

Root Vegetables

49

Daikon

Raphanus sativus var. *longipinnatus,* Cruciferae

daikon

A root vegetable believed to have originated in the eastern Mediterranean, daikon is a variety of radish that was brought to China around 500 B.C. Also known as Oriental radish, it is held in high esteem in Asia, where it is prepared in a wide variety of ways. It is also used for its leaves and sprouted seeds.

Daikon is a white-fleshed winter radish; its thin, smooth skin is usually whitish but may also be black, pink, or green. It has a firm, crisp flesh with a relatively mild flavor that can be sweet in some varieties. The variety most commonly available in Western markets is shaped like a large carrot and is usually about 1 foot long, although it can measure anywhere from 4 inches to 2 feet in length and from 1 to 4 inches in diameter.

Buying

When choosing daikon, look for firm and slightly shiny roots without spots or bruises. Avoid very large specimens, which tend to be more fibrous and spongy in texture and less tasty. A clear skin is a sign of freshness. If sold with its tops, they should be a bright green color.

Nutritional Information

water	94.5%
protein	0.3 g
carbohydrates	1.8 g
calories	8
	per 45 g

Raw daikon contains vitamin C and potassium.

It is said to stimulate the appetite and to be antiseptic, diuretic, and tonic. In phytotherapy, it is used notably to bring down fever, to relieve coughs and hemorrhaging, to aid digestion, and to treat the liver and the gallbladder.

Preparing

Scrub the daikon or peel it, removing only a thin layer from the surface. It can then be grated, cut into sticks, cubes, julienne strips, or thin slices; it can also be puréed once it is cooked. Avoid overcooking it, which makes it softer and less flavorful.

Serving Ideas

Daikon can be eaten raw or cooked. Raw daikon makes a refreshing appetizer and is often served with a dip or added to salads and sandwiches. Grated and sprinkled with vinaigrette or simply with vinegar or lemon juice, it can accompany vegetables, poultry, seafood, or fish. In Japan, grated daikon is commonly served with sashimi and tempura.

In Asia, daikon is popular preserved in salt or cooked. Cooking gives it a milder flavor. Cooked daikon is used like the turnip; it is often added to soups and stews and is delicious in a stir-fry with other vegetables. Its tops can be prepared like spinach. Raw, they are added to salads, especially when young and tender, or to soups.

The seeds, which are sprouted, have a hot flavor that is slightly reminiscent of watercress. The sprouts are often added to soups, sandwiches, and omelets, or used to season tofu and fish. Add them at the last minute to ensure maximum crispness and flavor.

Storing

Despite its appearance, daikon is actually a perishable vegetable; it tends to wilt and dry out quickly and should be stored in a perforated plastic bag in the refrigerator, preferably without its tops, as they tend to accelerate the loss of moisture. When consumed raw, daikon should be used no later than 3 or 4 days after purchase. If it is intended for cooking, it can be kept for about 1 week.

red winter radish

green winter radish

Rutabaga

Brassica napus var. *napobrassica*, **Cruciferae**

The rutabaga is a cross between a member of the cabbage family (Savoy cabbage) and the turnip, developed by the Scandinavians in the Middle Ages. Rutabaga, which comes from the Swedish *rotabaggar*, is also known as "swede." It became a staple in Europe during World War II when food supplies were scarce, and since then it is often associated with privation. Some varieties of this vegetable are used as fodder for cattle.

Although often confused with the turnip, rutabagas are longer and rounder than the turnip, and their leaves larger and fleshier. Both the skin and the flesh of rutabagas are yellowish in color, although there is also a white-fleshed variety. The flavor of the rutabaga is more pungent than that of the turnip. The plant is also distinguished from the turnip by a projection at the top of the root, from which the leaves develop.

Buying

 Choose a rutabaga that is firm, heavy for its size, and without blemishes. Avoid very large roots, as they tend to be hard and fibrous. This vegetable is usually sold without its leaves, which are removed during harvesting to prevent the root from drying out. Rutabaga greens are not as palatable as turnip greens.

Preparing

Peel the rutabaga and cut it into pieces. Remove the core if it is brownish (this is caused by a lack of boron in the soil). The more pronounced the odor of the rutabaga, the more pungent its flavor. Its pungency can be reduced by blanching it for about 5 minutes before cooking.

Serving Ideas

The rutabaga can be eaten raw or cooked. It is incorporated into soups and stews, and is particularly delicious puréed on its own or mixed with mashed potatoes and carrots. It can replace turnips in most recipes. The rutabaga also makes a good soufflé and is often served with a sauce or with cream.

Cooking

The rutabaga takes longer to cook than the turnip; allow 15 minutes for boiling and slightly longer for steaming.

Nutritional Information

	cooked
water	90%
protein	1.1 g
fat	0.2 g
carbohydrates	7.7 g
fiber	2.1 g
calories	34
	per 100 g

The rutabaga is an excellent source of potassium and a good source of vitamin C. It contains magnesium, folic acid, and phosphorus. It is said to be a source of minerals and a good diuretic.

Storing

Store the vegetable, unwashed, in a perforated plastic bag in the refrigerator, where it will keep for about 3 weeks. Like carrots, rutabagas can be stored buried in sand (see *Carrot*). Rutabagas freeze well after being blanched for 2 minutes, or cooked and puréed.

Root Vegetables

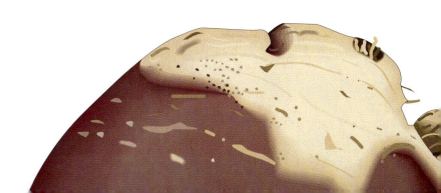

Malanga

Xanthosoma sagittifolium, **Araceae**

The tuber of a plant originating in South America and the West Indies, the malanga grows mainly in tropical and subtropical regions; it is a staple food in the West Indies and in all the tropical Spanish-speaking countries. The term *malanga* is used in Cuba, while in Puerto Rico it is known as *yautia.*

The malanga belongs to a family of ornamental plants that includes the philodendron and the dieffenbachia. Approximately 40 different species of malanga have been identified, some of which, like the yellow malanga, are often confused with the taro, a related variety. Although they can be distinguished by their flavor and by the appearance of their leaves, neither of these characteristics can be judged at the moment of purchase.

The malanga plant can reach over 6 feet high; its large luxuriant leaves are often more than 3 feet long, and although edible, they are rarely offered in Western markets. The irregularly shaped tubers are 7 to 10 inches long and usually weigh between 9 ounces and 2 pounds. Their thin layer of brownish skin may be smooth, downy, or studded with radicles, depending on the variety. The skin partially covers a firm, crisp, and slightly viscous pulp that can be whitish, yellow, orange, pink, or reddish. The malanga has a strong flavor reminiscent of hazelnuts, with a slightly earthy aftertaste. Some varieties resemble the sweet potato, while others resemble the taro. Like the potato, the malanga has a high starch content.

Buying

Choose very firm malangas, with no sign of mold or soft spots. Ideally, the tuber should be cut in half in order to judge the quality of the flesh, but when shopping, a slight incision with the fingernail will suffice to determine juiciness.

Preparing

Peel the malanga and soak it in cold water if it is not to be used right away.

Nutritional Information

	raw
water	66%
protein	1.7 g
fat	0.3 g
carbohydrates	31 g
calories	132
	per 100 g

The malanga contains thiamine, vitamin C, iron, and phosphorus. Some varieties contain bitter irritants which are neutralized by cooking.

Serving Ideas

The starch in malangas becomes digestible when they are cooked; cooking also neutralizes the calcium oxalate crystals they contain, a substance that irritates the digestive system. The malanga can be grated and used to make crêpes. In the West Indies, grated malanga is mixed with fish or vegetables seasoned with herbs to make a special kind of dumpling. The malanga also makes a tasty dish when deep-fried or served with a sauce. It should be used in moderation, however, since its strong flavor tends to mask that of other foods. Malanga is also made into a starch used in the manufacture of alcohol. Malanga leaves are prepared like spinach, and may be used to wrap other foods for baking. The leaves also contain calcium oxalates, whose bitter taste and irritating properties are neutralized by cooking.

Cooking

It is best to boil or steam the malanga before adding it to soups and stews, and it should be incorporated at the last minute to prevent it from overcooking and falling apart. Malangas can also be boiled for 20 minutes and served as an accompanying vegetable, either whole or puréed, like potatoes.

Storing

The malanga spoils rapidly, becoming soft and shriveled and losing its characteristic hazelnut flavor. It will keep for only a few days at room temperature or in the refrigerator. Malanga leaves will keep for several days in the refrigerator; wipe them with a damp cloth and place them in a perforated plastic bag.

Salsify

Tragopogon porrifolius and *Scorzonera hispanica,* **Compositae**

O riginally from the Mediterranean region, salsify and scorzonera (black salsify) are closely related root vegetables; they are similar in shape and share a subtle, sweet flavor that is often likened to the delicate flavor of oysters, which explains why they are also known as "oyster plant." The taste of salsify is also said to bear a slight resemblance to that of asparagus or artichoke, with what some people describe as a coconut aftertaste. The flesh of salsify and scorzonera becomes sweeter when the plants are exposed to a light frost while still in the ground, as the cold temperatures activate the conversion of the starch into sugar. Although known in southern Europe for more than 2,000 years, salsify was not cultivated until the 17th century. It was introduced into North America by the Pilgrims, but remains relatively unknown even today. Belgium is one of the main producers of scorzonera.

Salsify has an elongated shape resembling that of the parsnip, although the roots of salsify grow in bunches. The whitish flesh is covered with a thin, light brown skin that is studded with rootlets. The root can measure 1 foot in length and 2 inches in diameter. The long and narrow leaves of salsify are edible, particularly the young shoots, whose delicious taste is reminiscent of chicory.

Scorzonera, or **black salsify**, is long and tapering and looks like a long, thin carrot, except that it has blackish brown skin and cream-colored flesh. Easier to peel than salsify, scorzonera is also less fibrous and more savory.

Salsify and scorzonera are root vegetables resembling the carrot and parsnip; salsify is light brown in color, while scorzonera is black.

scorzonera

salsify

Buying

Choose roots that are firm (salsify is not as firm as the carrot, however) and free of wet patches. Medium-size specimens are less fibrous than the larger roots.

Preparing

Unlike carrots, salsify and scorzonera blacken on contact with the air when they are peeled and cut. This can be prevented by plunging the vegetables in vinegar or lemon water or by boiling them for 15 minutes before peeling and preparing them. Note that the skin of these vegetables can leave temporary stains on the hands during peeling.

Serving Ideas

Salsify and scorzonera are delicious in soups and stews, baked au gratin, or topped with a béchamel or cheese sauce. They can also be eaten cold, dressed in a vinaigrette. These vegetables blend particularly well with potatoes, leeks, celery, onion, and spinach. They are delicious braised with veal, poultry, or fish, and can also be glazed like carrots.

Cooking

Salsify and scorzonera should not be overcooked, as this tends to turn their flesh into an unappetizing mush. The best cooking method is to steam them for 10 to 15 minutes, but they can also be boiled for 8 to 12 minutes.

Nutritional Information

	cooked salsify
water	81%
protein	2.7 g
fat	0.2 g
carbohydrates	15.4 g
fiber	3.1 g
	per 100 g

Salsify is a good source of potassium; it also supplies vitamin B_6, vitamin C, folic acid, magnesium, and phosphorus. This vegetable contains inulin, a carbohydrate occurring in place of starch that can be consumed by diabetics since it does not seem to affect the level of blood sugar. Inulin may cause flatulence in certain people, however, and should therefore be used in moderation by those who are sensitive to this problem or who are eating it for the first time. Salsify is said to help cleanse the blood and to relieve congestion of the liver and kidneys.

Storing

Place the vegetables, unwashed, in a perforated plastic bag and store them in the refrigerator, where they will keep for several days. They are best, however, when consumed as fresh as possible.

Burdock

Arctium lappa, **Compositae**

The edible roots are dug up before the appearance of the floral stem; their flavor is reminiscent of that of salsify.

A large herbaceous biennial plant believed to have originated in Siberia and the Caucasus, the burdock is known for its burrs, the prickly fruits that cling to animal fur and clothes. It grows wild along roadsides and on vacant lots in temperate regions, particularly in Asia, Europe, and North America. The Japanese cultivate it as a vegetable. The edible parts of this plant include the young shoots, the large pale-green oval leaves, and the roots. The roots can grow to a length of 1 to 2 feet, and their whitish flesh is fibrous and spongy. They are covered with a thin brownish edible skin. The roots are dug up before the floral stem makes its appearance. The flavor of burdock is similar to that of salsify, and it can be prepared in the same way as salsify or asparagus.

Buying

Choose firm roots measuring ¾ inch in diameter and no more than 16 inches in length, as these are the tenderest and tastiest.

Nutritional Information

	boiled roots
water	76%
protein	2.1 g
fat	0.2 g
carbohydrates	21 g
calories	88
	per 100 g

Burdock roots are an excellent source of potassium and a good source of magnesium. They contain phosphorus, iron, and calcium. Burdock has been renowned for its medicinal properties since ancient times. It is said to be sudorific, diuretic, depurative, and choleretic. It also has a reputation as a blood purifier and makes a good poultice for skin problems. Chinese doctors use it to treat throat infections, colds, the flu, pneumonia, and poisoning. All parts of the plant are thought to have curative properties against cancer.

To make burdock tea, use 1 tablespoon of burdock flowers and leaves for 1 cup of water and steep for 10 minutes. To prepare a decoction from the roots, use 2 teaspoons for 1 cup of water and boil for 10 minutes.

Preparing

The burdock can be cooked with its skin, especially if it is thin. Wash it well to remove all traces of soil. Because the flesh of the burdock oxidizes quickly, it should be cooked as soon as it is cut. It can also be soaked for a few minutes in cold water to which a bit of vinegar or lemon juice has been added. To eliminate the slightly bitter aftertaste of this vegetable, soak it in salty water for 5 to 10 minutes before cooking.

The burdock is often grated, as its flesh remains slightly fibrous after cooking. It may also be finely sliced or diced.

Serving Ideas

The burdock is used both as a vegetable and as a seasoning, depending on one's appreciation of its slightly earthy flavor. It is often added to stews and marinades, and is also good stir-fried. The leaves of this plant are used to prepare soups, or they can be eaten braised. The leaves can also be prepared like leaf vegetables such as Chinese cabbage and spinach.

Storing

Wrapped in damp paper towels and placed in a perforated plastic bag, burdock will keep for several days in the refrigerator.

Okra

Hibiscus esculentus and *Abelmoschus esculentus,* **Malvaceae**

F ruit of a magnificent vegetable plant, the okra belongs to the same family as the mallow, hibiscus, and cotton plant. Most likely of African origin, it grows in tropical and warm temperate climates. It is common fare in Africa, India, the Middle East, the West Indies, South America, and Louisiana. Historians attribute its introduction into Spain from Africa to Moorish invasions of Europe in the 8th century. Okra was brought to the United States by African slaves and has long been considered a food for the poor, which explains why it has been ignored by many.

The thin edible skin of okra can be smooth or downy, depending on the variety; the inside is divided into sections containing numerous edible green or brownish seeds. When cut, the pod of this fruit vegetable releases a sticky substance whose thickening properties make it useful in soups and stews, as well as in the well-known gumbo. Its subtle flavor can be compared to that of eggplant, for which it is an appropriate substitute. However, okra has a rather unusual texture. The pods are picked before they are completely ripe, as they become tough and fibrous upon reaching maturity. The young pod is tender and measures 2 to 4 inches in length; its small seeds are not yet completely developed. The fruit is at its best at this point.

The inside of the okra is divided into sections filled with numerous edible seeds; this vegetable contains a sticky substance whose thickening properties make it useful in soups and stews.

Buying

Choose okra that is healthy in color, tender without being soft, free of marks and bruises, and no more than 4 inches long. If too ripe, okra will have a very sticky texture.

Preparing

Gently scrub the surface of the downy variety of okra with a vegetable brush or paper towel. Rinse and drain the okra, and slice off only the top and the tail if they are to be cooked whole. Once cooked, okra can be cut into slices and used to thicken preparations such as soups or ragouts.

Serving Ideas

Okra is eaten raw or cooked. It can be prepared in the same manner as asparagus or eggplant and may replace these vegetables in most recipes (cooking time should be reduced). Okra goes well with tomatoes, onions, peppers, and eggplant, as well as with such seasonings as curry, coriander, oregano, lemon, and vinegar.

A useful thickening agent in soups and stews, it should be added about 10 minutes before the end of cooking. It is also delicious cold, sprinkled with vinaigrette or added to a salad after being quickly blanched. Okra is a common ingredient in Creole dishes and is often served with chicken in the United States. It may also be dried and ground into flour, and an edible oil can be extracted from the seeds. The seeds were at one time dried and roasted to be used as a coffee substitute.

Cooking

Okra can be prepared in many different ways; it can be braised, boiled, steamed, dressed with bread crumbs and fried, sautéed, or marinated, but it does not purée well. It can be steamed alone or with other vegetables (8 to 15 minutes) or served as a side dish. Iron or copper pans should be avoided, as contact with these metals affects the color, although not the taste, of okra. Okra has a sticky texture when overcooked.

Nutritional Information

	cooked
water	90%
protein	22 g
fat	0.2 g
carbohydrates	7.2 g
fiber	3.2 g
calories	32
	per 100 g

Cooked okra is an excellent source of potassium; it is a good source of magnesium and folic acid; it also supplies vitamin C, thiamine, vitamin B_6, zinc, vitamin A, calcium, phosphorus, and niacin. Easy to digest, okra is mildly laxative and has emollient properties.

Storing

Okra is perishable and should be stored in the refrigerator in a paper bag, or wrapped in a paper towel inside a perforated plastic bag. Stored in this manner, it will keep for 2 to 3 days. Okra can be frozen after blanching it whole for 2 minutes.

Eggplant

Solanum melongena, Solanaceae

common eggplant

The fruit of a plant originating in India, the eggplant is a berry that is consumed like a vegetable. Also called "aubergine," it has been known in Asia for over 2,500 years, having been cultivated in China since around 500 B.C. The Arabs and Persians presumably brought it to Africa prior to the Middle Ages, and it was from there that it was introduced into Italy in the 14th century. Because the first varieties of eggplant were very bitter, Europeans initially valued it for its ornamental qualities. They also believed it could cause insanity. Years of cultivation and crossbreeding of the eggplant have greatly improved its flavor. Today eggplant is cultivated mainly in China, Turkey, Japan, Egypt, and Italy.

There are a number of different varieties of eggplant; most prefer warm climates, but some varieties have been adapted to temperate zones as well. The most common variety both in North America and in Europe is the deep purple, oval eggplant that resembles a large pear. It grows on a 3-foot-high plant that bears beautiful purple-blue flowers. Several other varieties, often classified as Asian varieties, are also now available. Some can be as small as an egg, others are long and slender, and some resemble a bunch of grapes. The color of the thin, smooth, shiny skin varies from deep purple to lavender, cream, white, green, or orange. The skin is edible, although in certain varieties it can be bitter. The yellowish white flesh is spongy and contains small brownish edible seeds. Small and young specimens of eggplant contain fewer seeds and their skin is more tender and less bitter.

Buying

When purchasing eggplant, look for firmness and heaviness; it should have a smooth and evenly colored skin. Avoid fruits with shriveled or mottled skin, as they are likely to be old and bitter-tasting. To check for ripeness, press lightly on the skin with your fingers; if the imprint remains visible, the eggplant is ripe; if the flesh springs back, it is not yet ready for consumption.

Preparing

Since the flesh of eggplant discolors quickly when cut, cook it soon after cutting or sprinkle it with lemon juice in the meantime. If the eggplant is large, sprinkle the slices or chunks with salt and let them "sweat" for 1 or 2 hours to reduce their water content and to rid them of some of their bitterness. (Not all eggplants are bitter enough to necessitate this operation.) Soaking eggplant in water for 15 minutes will also draw out some of its bitter juices. Since the bitterness is concentrated just under the skin, it can also be peeled. Less bitter varieties can simply be cooked as they are.

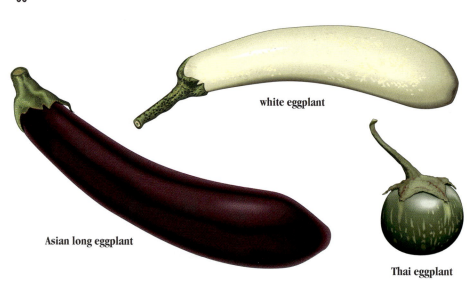

white eggplant

Asian long eggplant

Thai eggplant

Western eggplant

Serving Ideas

Eggplant is delicious hot or cold and can be prepared in a wide variety of ways. It is excellent stuffed, roasted, au gratin, puréed, as a casserole, or on brochettes. It is an essential ingredient in Asian and Mediterranean cuisine, where it is often prepared with tomatoes, garlic, and olive oil, as in ratatouille, eggplant spread, or moussaka. Certain Asian varieties can be eaten raw in a salad.

Ratatouille Niçoise

SERVES 6

2 lb. (1 kg) tomatoes
4 cloves garlic
3 onions
1 lb. (500 g) eggplant
2 lb. (1 kg) zucchini
1 lb. (500 g) sweet
   green peppers

2 tbsp. fresh basil leaves
1 tbsp. fresh parsley
   leaves
⅓ cup (80 ml) olive oil
1 bay leaf
1 bouquet garni
salt and pepper

1. Blanch and peel the tomatoes, remove the seeds, and cut into quarters. Peel and chop the garlic and the onions. Slice the unpeeled eggplant and zucchini. Remove the stems from the peppers and cut them in half, removing the seeds and white membranes. Cut them into strips. Chop the basil and parsley.

2. Heat 2 tbsp. of the oil in a casserole. Sauté the eggplant slices and set them aside. Heat the rest of the oil in the casserole. One ingredient at a time, sauté the zucchini, peppers, onions, tomatoes, and garlic. Stir occasionally, adjusting the seasoning, and set them aside as they are cooked.

3. Return all the ingredients to the casserole, adding the bay leaf, bouquet garni, and salt and pepper. Stir for a few minutes over high heat, then reduce the heat and simmer, covered, for about 1 hour, or until the vegetables are tender and their juices have evaporated.

4. Transfer to a shallow dish and garnish with the chopped basil and parsley.

Nutritional Information

	raw
water	92%
protein	1.2 g
carbohydrates	6.3 g
fiber	1.5 g
calories	27
	per 100 g

Eggplant is a good source of potassium and contains folic acid, copper, vitamin B_6, and magnesium. It is regarded as a diuretic, a laxative, and a sedative.

Cooking

Although eggplant absorbs oil like a sponge, the quantity of oil absorbed can be limited by coating the slices of eggplant with layers of flour, beaten egg, and bread crumbs before deep-frying or pan-frying. To bake eggplant in the oven, pierce the whole, unpeeled eggplant several times to let the steam escape; depending on the size, bake it for 15 to 25 minutes at 350°F (180°C). It can also be cut in half and baked; make incisions in the flesh to ensure uniform cooking, and depending on whether the halves are stuffed or not, allow 35 minutes to 1 hour at 350°F (180°C). The baking time for sliced or cubed eggplant is 15 to 20 minutes. For added flavor, brush the eggplant with olive oil and seasonings. Eggplant can also be boiled, steamed, microwaved, or broiled; blanch it for a few minutes before preparing it. It becomes very soft during cooking. Avoid salting eggplant, especially at the start of cooking.

Storing

Eggplant bruises easily and should be handled with care. It is also sensitive to temperature fluctuations. It is often sold wrapped in a plastic film that prevents it from breathing; remove the wrapping as soon as possible and store the eggplant in a perforated plastic bag in the refrigerator, where it will keep for about 1 week.

Eggplants that have been blanched or steamed will keep in the freezer for 6 to 8 months.

There are a number of varieties of eggplant, of varying sizes and colors; they can be as small as an egg or very large.

Fruit Vegetables

57

Avocado

Persea americana, Lauraceae

With the exception of the cocktail avocado, all varieties of avocado have a large pit at their center, which detaches easily from the flesh.

The avocado is the pear-shaped fruit of a tree that is native to Central or South America, where it has been known for centuries. The word "avocado" comes from the Aztec word *ahuacalt,* from which the Spanish derived *ahuacate* or *agucate* (still used today) and finally *avocado.* The avocado is sometimes also called "alligator pear." The popularity of the avocado in North America and Europe is quite recent. The early Spanish explorers observed that the cultivation of avocados extended from Mexico to Peru. Today the largest producers are Mexico, the United States, the Dominican Republic, Brazil, and Colombia.

The avocado tree grows in tropical and subtropical climates, reaching up to 65 feet in height. It has oval, waxy evergreen leaves. There are about a dozen varieties, most of which bear small whitish or greenish yellow flowers that are very fragrant. The tree flowers in two stages but produces only a small yield of fruits. Avocados come in varying shapes, colors, and sizes, depending on the variety. The most common variety, the Hass avocado, is oval and has a rugged black or dark brown shiny skin when the fruit is ripe. Over 75% of the American crop consists of Hass avocados. Ripe Fuerte, Zutano, and Bacon avocados, all of which are oval, have a green, glossy skin. There is also a miniature variety called the "cocktail" avocado. The skin of avocados is inedible. The different types vary in weight from 8 ounces to over 2 pounds. All varieties have a rich, buttery-textured flesh with a slightly nutty taste. The flesh is yellowish green in color.

All except the cocktail avocado have a large pit at their center, which detaches easily from the flesh; it is covered with a milky substance that turns reddish when exposed to air and can stain fabrics.

Buying

Choose avocados that are heavy for their size, not too hard, and free of black spots and bruises. Avocados that are too soft will be overly ripe; the color of the skin differs from one variety to another and is not a good indication of ripeness. The avocado is ready for consumption when it yields to the touch.

Preparing

The avocado is usually cut in half lengthwise with a stainless-steel knife. If the flesh clings to the pit, twist the two halves gently in opposite directions when separating them and remove the pit by spearing it with a knife or by scooping it out with a spoon. Avocado flesh darkens when exposed to air; to prevent discoloration, sprinkle it with lemon juice or vinegar.

Serving Ideas

The avocado is most commonly eaten raw. Indeed, it does not stand up well to cooking, and should therefore be added only at the end of cooking; it should not be boiled, as this will detract from its flavor. It is often served on its own, simply cut in half and topped with a bit of vinaigrette, mayonnaise, or lemon juice seasoned with salt and pepper.

Avocados also go well in sandwiches and salads, and can be added to hot or cold soups. They also appear in desserts such as ice cream, mousses, and fruit salads. They are excellent stuffed with seafood or chicken. Guacamole, one of the most popular dishes of Mexico, is made by puréeing avocados with chiles, onions, spices, and lime juice and is served with tortillas.

Guacamole

SERVES 4

2 very ripe avocados
juice of 2 limes
2 tbsp. extra-virgin
  olive oil
1 tomato
2 tbsp. cilantro leaves

1 small green sweet
  pepper
2 tbsp. finely chopped
  onion
Salt and ground pepper
4 drops Tabasco sauce

1. Halve the avocados and remove the pits. Scoop out and purée the flesh, adding the lime juice and the olive oil.

2. Peel and dice the tomato. Finely chop the cilantro. Chop the green pepper and remove the seeds.

3. Mix all the ingredients well, cover, and refrigerate until ready to serve. Serve as an appetizer with raw vegetables and tortillas.

Storing

Avocados can be left to ripen at room temperature; to accelerate the process, place them in a paper bag (this locks in the ethylene gas responsible for ripening). Avocados will not continue to ripen once they are refrigerated. Whole ripe avocados will keep for 2 or 3 days in the refrigerator; cut avocados will keep for a day or two (sprinkle the exposed flesh with lemon juice to prevent discoloration). Frozen puréed avocado (to which lemon juice has been added) will keep for about a year.

Nutritional Information

	raw
water	74.3%
protein	2 g
fat	15.3 g
carbohydrates	7.4 g
fiber	2.1 g
calories	161
	per 100 g

The avocado is an excellent source of potassium and folic acid, and a good source of vitamin B_6. It also contains magnesium, pantothenic acid, vitamin C, copper, niacin, iron, vitamin A, and zinc. The avocado is a very nutritious and energizing food. Despite its high fat content, it is easy to digest because it contains numerous enzymes that facilitate the breakdown of fats. The avocado is said to be good for the stomach and the intestines.

Fruit Vegetables

59

Bacon avocado

Sweet pepper

Capsicum annuum, Solanaceae

green pepper

Fruit of a plant originally from Latin America, the sweet pepper (also known as the bell pepper) is a member of the large family of plants that includes the eggplant, the potato, the tomato, the alkekengi, and the tamarillo. It was one of the first plants to be cultivated in South America. Pepper seeds dating back some 5,000 years B.C. are believed to belong to a wild variety of the sweet pepper we know today. The expansion of the cultivation of sweet peppers is mainly attributed to Spanish and Portuguese explorers, but it is also a result of the pepper's adaptability. The pepper plant is a perennial in tropical regions and an annual in temperate zones. The main producers of sweet peppers today are China, Turkey, Nigeria, Spain, Mexico, and Romania.

The sweet pepper is a fleshy-walled berry containing numerous whitish seeds in its inner cavity. The plant that produces it can grow to a height of 3 feet. There are dozens of varieties of the sweet pepper, varying in size, shape, color, and flavor. Sweet peppers are plump, with a soft, delicately sweet flesh. They are usually range from 2½ to 6 inches in length and from 2 to 4½ inches in diameter. The most popular variety in North America is the bell pepper, which has four lobes and is somewhat square in shape. Certain varieties have three lobes, while others are more tapered in shape and have no lobes at all.

Green peppers are harvested before they are fully ripe; left on the plant, the green pepper will turn yellow and then red as it matures. Inversely, purple, brown, and black peppers will become green if left to ripen on the plant. Peppers ripened on the plant are sweeter and more fragrant, with red and orange peppers being the sweetest.

Buying

Choose firm, glossy, plump peppers that have no blemishes or soft spots. The flesh should be brightly colored and should yield to gentle pressure.

Preparing

Peppers may be cut into slices, strips, or pieces. Remove the stem, the core, and the seeds before cutting. When stuffing a pepper, make a cut around the stem and remove it; carefully scratch out the seeds and core and cut out the whitish veins; fill with the stuffing and replace the top. To shorten the cooking time for stuffed sweet peppers, blanch the peppers before coring and stuffing them. To remove the pepper's skin, place the pepper under the oven broiler and grill it on all sides for 10 to 12 minutes, or until the skin blackens and swells. Cover it with a damp cloth, place it in a plastic bag, or wrap it in a large sheet of aluminum foil, and when it has cooled, peel it with a knife and rinse it under running water.

stem

core

seeds

vein

Serving Ideas

Sweet peppers can be eaten raw or cooked. Although they are a fruit, they are used like a vegetable. Raw, the sweet pepper is eaten on its own, served with a dip or as an appetizer, or in salads. It is also frequently added to soups, omelets, tofu, stews, brochettes, rice, pasta, and pizza. It is a good accompaniment to chicken, rabbit, ham, tuna, and eggs, as well as being indispensable in dishes such as gazpacho, piperade, and ratatouille. It is also used in marinades and is often served stuffed. Portuguese and Mexican cooking make wide use of the sweet pepper.

Sweet Peppers Marinated in Oil

SERVES 4

4 sweet peppers: 2 green, 1 red, 1 yellow
2 cloves garlic

1 tbsp. flat-leaf parsley
Salt
¾ cup (180 ml) olive oil

1. Preheat the broiler.

2. Place the peppers under the broiler and grill until their skin is slightly burned, 10 minutes on each side.

3. Peel and crush the garlic. Chop the parsley fine.

4. Remove the peppers from the broiler, wrap them in a large sheet of aluminum foil, and leave them for about 15 minutes, or until they are no longer hot.

5. Peel the skin with a knife (it should come off easily now), and cut the peppers in half; remove the seeds and the white veins. Wipe the inside well. Cut the peppers into strips and arrange them by color in a glass serving dish. Sprinkle with the garlic and parsley, and season with salt.

6. Cover with the olive oil, and let marinate in the refrigerator for at least 1 hour before serving.

Cooking

Sweet peppers become sweeter when cooked; they should not be overcooked, however, as this will cause them to lose flavor and nutrients. Cooking causes brown, black, and purple peppers to turn green.

Nutritional Information

water	92.2%
protein	0.9 g
fat	0.2 g
carbohydrates	6.4 g
fiber	2 g
calories	27
	per 100 g

Red and green peppers are an excellent source of vitamin C and vitamin A, and a good source of potassium. They also contain vitamin B_6 and folic acid. The nutritional value is almost the same for raw peppers as for cooked peppers. They contain more vitamin C than oranges of the same weight. The proportion of the different nutritional elements varies greatly from one variety to another. For example, red peppers contain much more vitamin A and vitamin C than green peppers.

Sweet peppers have a number of medicinal properties: they are held to be a good stomachic, diuretic, stimulant, digestive, and antiseptic. Some people may find it difficult to digest sweet peppers, but peeling them alleviates this problem.

Storing

Sweet peppers can be stored unwashed in a perforated plastic bag or in the vegetable compartment of the refrigerator, where they will keep for about a week. They freeze well without being blanched, but it is better to wash them first. For maximum flavor and nutritional value, store them whole, as fewer parts are exposed to the air. Sweet peppers lend themselves well to drying, and keep at least 1 year when dried. They are also good marinated.

yellow pepper   **red pepper**

Fruit Vegetables

61

Olive

Olea europaea, Oleaceae

green olives

ruit of the olive tree, which has an exceptionally long lifespan, the olive is one of the oldest cultivated fruits. Although it is not known for certain when the wild olive tree was first cultivated, information gathered from archeological sites has led some historians to believe that it might have been somewhere between 5000 and 3000 B.C. in Crete, from which cultivation then spread to Egypt, Greece, Palestine, and Asia Minor. The history of the olive tree is also the history of agriculture and of the Mediterranean basin. The olive branch is present in the story of the Flood, and oil mills existed as early as 3000 B.C. A symbol of peace and wisdom, the olive tree plays an important role in mythology, where it was venerated by the Egyptians, the Greeks, and the Romans. The olive tree was introduced into America during the Renaissance by the Spanish and Portuguese. Entire populations were able to live on olives and olive oil, which also provided lamp fuel and medicinal remedies. Today the cultivation of olives still constitutes an essential part of the economy of many Mediterranean countries. Italy and Spain account for approximately 50% of the global production of olives and olive oil. Greece, Turkey, Syria, Morocco, Tunisia, Portugal, and the United States are the main producers of table olives.

The olive tree usually grows to between 10 and 23 feet in height, but it can sometimes grow as high as 50 feet. It produces an abundance of fleshy fruits differing in size, flesh, and color according to the climate, the method of cultivation, and the variety of the tree. The flesh contains a ligneous pit.

Olives reach their maximum weight 6 to 8 months after the tree has bloomed. Olives directly off the branch are inedible, as they contain an extremely bitter glycoside that irritates the digestive tract. To make them suitable for consumption, they must first be macerated and then undergo various processes, which differ according to the variety of olive and the region of cultivation. Table olives must be medium- or large-sized, the ideal weight being between ⅛ and ¼ ounce. They must also be easy to pit, and their skin should be fine-grained and elastic, so that it is able to resist shocks and brine. For optimal preservation, they must contain a minimum of 4% carbohydrate and very little oil.

Green olives are harvested when they reach their normal size and just before they change color. They are processed according to two methods: the Spanish method, which uses fermentation, and the American method, which does not. The Greek method, which involves soaking the olives in brine, is only used for ripe olives (black). The aim of all of these methods is to make olives suitable for consumption by reducing their bitterness.

The Spanish method, which produces **green fermented olives**, involves soaking the still firm and unripe fruits (which are a light green at this point) in a caustic soda solution to reduce their natural bitterness; they are then washed and soaked in brine, which promotes fermentation and changes the color of the olives to their characteristic "olive green." The original brine is changed before marketing and the olives are packed in smaller containers. They are often sold pitted and stuffed.

The American method (canned ripe olives) differs from the Spanish method in that the olives are soaked in brine without fermentation. The olives are picked when half ripe, just as their color starts to turn from yellow to red. They are then soaked in an alkaline solution and exposed to air, which causes them to turn black. These "black" olives are then packed in brine, canned and sterilized. This method is widely used in California.

black olives

The Greek method uses fully ripe dark purple or **black olives**. Because the use of caustic soda solutions is not authorized in Greece, the olives are prepared according to a gradual process of fermentation in brine, lasting 6 months. Other methods can also be used which may or may not call for brine in addition to caustic soda. Another method involves preserving the olives in salt; this method causes their skin to wrinkle, but leaves the olives otherwise intact. Olives prepared in this way have a fruity and slightly bitter taste. Once ready for consumption, the olives are either left in their barrels or packed in containers to be sent to market. They are often pitted and stuffed with sweet pepper, onion, almonds or anchovies, or spiced. Olives may also be sold halved, quartered, sliced, chopped, or puréed.

Buying

 Olives are sold in bulk, in jars, or in cans. When buying bulk olives, make sure they have been stored and handled with care.

Serving Ideas

Though commonly known as an appetizer, the olive has a multitude of other uses. It may be added to salads, as well as to meat or poultry dishes. Olives feature in numerous dishes, including tapenade (a purée of black olives, capers, and anchovies), pizza, stuffed veal scallops, beef casserole, and duck. They are also a popular ingredient in Spanish tapas, as well as in dishes prepared *à la niçoise* or *à la provençale*.

To reduce the saltiness or the acridity of olives, boil them for about 15 minutes (this will make them lose some of their flavor, however). The original packing solution can also be substituted with water or with a solution of water and vinegar seasoned with garlic, thyme, oregano, etc.

Tapenade

4 TO 6 SERVINGS

¾ cup pitted black olives
3 tbsp. capers, drained
¼ cup anchovy fillets
2 garlic cloves, peeled and germ removed

½ cup (125 ml) olive oil
1 tbsp. lemon juice
Ground black pepper

Tapenade is an excellent dip for raw vegetables. It may also be served with hard-boiled eggs, fish or grilled meat, or as a spread on toast.

1. Place the olives, capers, anchovies, and garlic in a food processor and purée at high speed.

2. Add the oil slowly, processing until the tapenade is smooth and thick like mayonnaise.

3. Incorporate the lemon juice and pepper.

Nutritional Information

	marinated green olive	black olive
protein	28 g	16 g
fat	2.5 g	2.5 g
carbohydrates	0.3 g	1.5 g
fiber	0.8 g	0.5 g
calories	23	25
		per 100 g

Olives have a very high fat content, which may vary between 12% and 30%, depending on the variety and the season they were picked. A deliciously fragrant oil is extracted from them. Green olives contain more fat and calories than black olives. Olives also contain some vitamins and minerals, but mostly in trace quantities. Black olives contain iron. Olives are thought to have laxative qualities, and to stimulate the appetite and aid the liver.

Used externally, olive oil is thought to prevent hair loss and boils. The olive tree's leaves are thought to be astringent, and to reduce high blood pressure and high blood sugar.

Unprocessed olives contain a very bitter substance that makes them inedible. To be suitable for consumption, they must first be soaked and then undergo various processes.

Storing

Olives keep in a sealed container for about a year; once opened, the container must be refrigerated. Green olives and black olives dry-packed in salt tend to spoil faster. Refrigerate bulk olives in an airtight container.

Cucumber

Cucumis sativus, Cucurbitaceae

American cucumber

Fruit of an annual herbaceous plant originating in southern Asia, where cucumber seeds believed to date back some 10,000 years have been discovered. It is speculated that navigators introduced cucumbers into the Far East, central Asia, and India. This vegetable was extremely popular among the Egyptians, Greeks, and Romans, who used it both as a food and for its beneficial effect on the skin. Jean de La Quintinie, a French agronomist during the reign of Louis XIV, invented the sheltered cultivation of cucumbers as a way of obtaining earlier harvests so that the vegetable could be served more often to the king, who was very fond of them. The early colonists introduced the cucumber into North America. The *gherkin* variety was introduced into the New World with the arrival of African slaves and was also widely cultivated in western India. More recently, the British developed a seedless variety of cucumber, grown exclusively in hothouses without fertilization.

The cucumber belongs to the same family as squash and melons. It grows on a climbing plant that is 3 to 10 feet long; the plant's tendrils allow it to cling to other plants or objects. The fruit emerges after the plant's large yellow flowers have blossomed. Cucumbers are long and cylindrical in shape, and range in length from 3 inches to 2 feet. There are over 40 varieties of cucumber; the English varieties are the longest, while the American varieties are shorter and fatter. The color of the skin varies from green to white; the skin may be smooth, ridged, or rough, but it is always glossy. Certain varieties have spiny bumps. The whitish flesh is crisp and refreshing, with a slightly bitter taste. Most varieties contain a varying number of edible seeds. What are usually called "pickles" are in fact certain varieties of cucumbers that are harvested while still green and very immature and used to make pickles.

The *gherkin* is a variety of cucumber *(C. anguria)* that is grown specifically for this purpose; it is oblong and measures about 2 inches in length and 1 inch in diameter. Its thorny skin has also earned it the name "prickly gherkin." Cucumbers have a reputation for being difficult to digest, but the English variety, along with some of the new varieties, is more easily digested. Today China, Japan, Turkey, the United States, and Romania are the largest producers of cucumbers.

Cucumbers emerge after the plant's large yellow flowers have blossomed; they are long and cylindrical in shape.

Fruit Vegetables

64

English cucumber

Buying

Cucumbers should be green and firm, with no sign of bruising or yellowing. Medium-size cucumbers are preferable to overly large specimens, which tend to be bitter and bland tasting and contain numerous hard seeds.

Preparing

Although they are usually eaten raw, cucumbers may also be cooked, in which case they are prepared much like squash, which they can replace in most recipes. The seeds should be removed if they are hard. It is not necessary to peel cucumbers, especially those that are very fresh, not too large, and that do not have a wax coating.

Some recipes recommend sprinkling the cucumber with salt and letting it drain to remove excess moisture and bitterness. While draining causes the flesh to become softer and less tasty, it also makes it easier to digest. It is important to drain the cucumber well to prevent it from making the dish to which it is added too watery.

Serving Ideas

Raw cucumber can be grated or cut into strips, slices or cubes, and accompanied with a vinaigrette, yogurt, or sour cream. It is also good stuffed with seafood. Cucumbers are a popular ingredient in Greek salads and in salads seasoned with mint. Cucumbers may also be cooked, pickled, or marinated. They are great in stews and soups, an excellent example being the famous Spanish soup gazpacho. They may also accompany meats and fish, and are good served au gratin or with a béchamel sauce. They can also be sautéed or steamed. For a low-calorie salad dressing, use puréed cucumber to replace up to three-quarters of the oil in the dressing.

Nutritional Information

water	96%
protein	0.5 g
fat	0.1 g
carbohydrates	2.9 g
fiber	0.7 g
calories	13
	per 100 g

Cucumbers are very refreshing and constitute an excellent source of potassium, vitamin C, and folic acid. They are said to have the properties of a diuretic, a purifier, and a relaxant.

Cucumbers are reputed to be good for the skin and are often puréed and mixed with other ingredients to make facial masks.

Storing

Cucumbers are sensitive to extreme temperatures. Store them in the refrigerator, where they will keep for 3 to 5 days. Cut cucumber should be well wrapped in order to prevent its odor from spreading to surrounding foods. Cucumbers do not stand up well to freezing, which makes them become soft.

pickle

Fruit Vegetables

65

Tomato

Lycopersicon esculentum, Solanaceae

common tomato

Native to Mexico and Central America, the tomato was originally a small round fruit resembling what is known today as the cherry tomato. Spanish settlers were introduced to the tomato by the Indians who cultivated it. Long considered poisonous, it was used mainly as an ornamental plant until the 18th century. The belief that tomatoes can make people sick is not so far-fetched, considering that the unripe fruits as well as the leaves and stems of this plant contain a toxic alkaloid. Nevertheless, the tomato found its way into Italian cooking by the 16th century; the Italians named it *pomodoro,* meaning "golden apple." This fruit became popular in the United States in the 19th century. The word "tomato" is derived from *tomalt,* the name for this fruit in Nahuatl, the language of the Aztecs.

A short-lived perennial in tropical regions and an annual in temperate climates, the tomato grows on a bushy, sometimes creeping plant requiring long periods of sunshine and warm temperatures. It is produced mainly in the United States, Russia, Turkey, Egypt, China, Spain, and Italy. There are over 1,000 different varieties of tomatoes, including the cherry tomato and the plum tomato (also known as the Italian tomato); there is also a bioengineered variety that has been genetically altered for longer preservation, while another variety is cultivated in soilless conditions. Tomatoes can be round, globular, or oval. There is even a square variety that was created by American agronomists in 1984 to meet industry requirements for a tomato that is easy to pick and ideal for packing.

The size of the fruit varies according to the species; the small cherry tomato is about 1 inch in diameter. The plum tomato, which resembles a small pear, is 2 to 4 inches long and between 1 and 2 inches in diameter; this variety is less juicy and contains fewer seeds than the others. The common round type is 2 to 5 inches in diameter and varies in weight between 3 ounces and more than 2 pounds. Some varieties stay green even as they ripen, but most tomatoes turn red, pink, orange, or yellow. The flavor of tomatoes depends on a number of factors, including when they were harvested, their degree of acidity, their sugar and water content, as well as the texture of their skin and flesh (which can be relatively starchy). Most tomatoes on the market today are firm and thick-skinned.

plum tomato

cherry tomatoes

yellow tomato

pear tomato

Buying

 Choose firm, smooth tomatoes with good color and no wrinkles or cracks. They should be pleasant-smelling and yield to light pressure of the fingers. Avoid soft, mottled, or bruised fruits, as they are likely to be watery and quite flavorless, and will spoil rapidly. Fresh tomatoes are best bought at the end of summer, when local vine-ripened tomatoes are abundant.

Imported cans may contain more lead than U.S.-produced cans. In the case of high-acid foods like tomatoes, this could cause a problem since the acidity can lead to corrosion, causing some of the metal to be transferred from the can to its contents. If you are concerned about lead poisoning, look for U.S. brands of tomato products.

Preparing

To prepare tomatoes, wash them first, and then, depending on the use, peel, seed, and pare them.

To peel tomatoes

Immerse the tomatoes in boiling water for 15 to 30 seconds (without cooking or soaking them), and let cool or rinse under cold water before peeling them with a knife. A strainer or metal basket can be used to facilitate this operation. Overripe tomatoes can be peeled directly, by piercing the skin with a knife and grasping it between the thumb and the blade to peel it off.

To seed tomatoes

Simply cut the tomato in half and squeeze the halves to extract the seeds and the juice; remove any remaining seeds by hand.

To pare tomatoes

Cut a circle around the stem end and remove the hard part to which the peduncle was attached.

Serving Ideas

Tomatoes are eaten raw or cooked and can be prepared in a wide variety of ways. Raw, they may be consumed on their own, with or without dressing, or added to salads, appetizers, and sandwiches. Cherry tomatoes are often used raw as ornamental garnishes. The versatility of cooked tomatoes is endless: they can be stuffed, incorporated into soups, sauces, stews, omelets, and risottos, or made into jam or marinades. They are also the basic ingredient in gazpacho, ratatouille, pizza, and caponata. They blend deliciously with garlic, shallots, basil, tarragon, thyme, bay leaf, oregano, and cumin, and are often combined with olives, peppers, and eggplant. Tomatoes figure prominently in the cuisine of a number of countries and regions, including Italy, Provence, Greece, Mexico, and Spain. Tomato purée and crushed tomatoes are used to flavor or garnish numerous dishes. Tomatoes are perfect as an accompaniment to mullet, sardines, and tuna fish, or to beef, chicken, veal, and eggs, in addition to being a classic ingredient in various Italian sauces and dishes.

Green tomatoes can also be eaten when cooked beforehand. They are often sautéed, fried, or used to make marinades. Tomatoes can be processed to make juice, sauce, purée, or concentrate; these preparations are sometimes interchangeable in recipes. Dried tomatoes are wrinkled and reddish brown in appearance and have an exquisite flavor that goes particularly well with antipasto. Store them in a container, preferably covered with olive oil.

Tomato plants were long considered poisonous; the unripe fruits as well as the leaves and stems of this plant contain a toxic alkaloid.

Fruit Vegetables

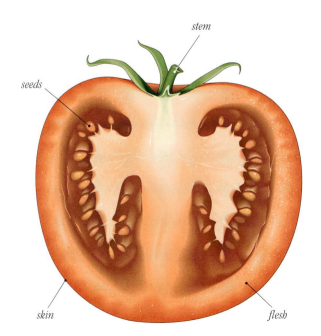

seeds

stem

skin

flesh

currant tomatoes

Storing

Tomatoes can be kept for a week at room temperature, as long as they are not exposed to direct sunlight. Overripe tomatoes should be stored in the refrigerator, where they will keep for 2 or 3 days. For the fullest flavor, take them out about 30 minutes before serving. Tomatoes should be washed just before use.

Green tomatoes can be ripened slowly at room temperature and will keep for several weeks away from direct sunlight. To hasten the ripening process, wrap them individually in paper or cover them with a cloth. Temperatures below 50°F (10°C) will halt the ripening process. Tomatoes can be frozen, but they tend to fall apart and lose their juice when thawed and are thus mainly used for cooking, preferably before they have completely thawed. Whole frozen tomatoes can be blanched for 30 to 60 seconds and rinsed briefly under cold water before being peeled. Tomatoes can also be cooked for 5 or 6 minutes, or until tender, with a teaspoon of salt and sugar before freezing.

Home preserving of tomatoes is very popular, but the success of this method requires that the appropriate jars be used and that they be properly sterilized. The tomatoes should also be sufficiently acidic to prevent the development of microorganisms. Since the acid content of tomatoes depends on the variety, climatic conditions, and the time of harvesting (unripe tomatoes are particularly acid), it is best to add a bit of citric acid or bottled lemon juice, which is more concentrated than fresh lemon juice. Use 1 tablespoon lemon juice or ⅓ teaspoon citric acid for every pound of tomatoes. A little added salt (less than half a teaspoon) will also ensure better conservation. Incorporate these ingredients once the tomatoes have been poured into the jars.

Cooking

Avoid cooking tomatoes in aluminum pots, as the corrosive effect of their acid makes them take on an unpleasant metal taste that can also be harmful. The acidity of cooked tomatoes can be diminished by adding a small amount of sugar or honey; the quantity required depends on the variety of tomato. Tomato sauce should be cooked slowly over low heat, as prolonged cooking over high heat can make the sauce difficult to digest.

Nutritional Information

	raw red tomato	*cooked red tomato*
water	93.8%	92.2%
protein	0.8 g	1.1 g
fat	0.3 g	0.4 g
carbohydrates	4.6 g	5.8 g
fiber	1.2 g	1.5 g
calories	21	27
		per 100 g

Tomatoes are a good source of vitamin C and potassium; they also supply folic acid and vitamin A. Green tomatoes are very acidic and contain solanine, a toxic substance that is neutralized during cooking. Tomatoes are said to be diuretic and mineralizing; they also stimulate the appetite, combat scurvy, and cleanse the system of toxins.

Tomato and Bocconcini Salad

SERVES 4

4 medium-size tomatoes
2 balls bocconcini
  cheese

2 tbsp. fresh basil leaves
Salt and ground pepper
2 tbsp. olive oil

This salad can be served as an entrée.

1. Slice the tomatoes and the bocconcini. Chop the basil.

2. On a flat plate, arrange the tomato and bocconcini slices in concentric circles, slightly overlapping each other.

3. Add salt and pepper generously. Sprinkle with the oil and chopped basil.

Tomatillo

Physalis ixocarpa, Solanaceae

The tomatillo, or Mexican husk tomato, is native to Mexico, where it has been cultivated since the time of the Aztecs. It is relatively unknown to Americans outside of Mexico and Southern California, where there is a large Mexican population. As a member of the nightshade family, the tomatillo is related to the tomato, eggplant, pepper, and potato.

The fruit is actually a berry that is about 1 inch in diameter and grows on a plant measuring from 3 to 4 feet in height. Firmer and glossier than the tomato, it is usually picked when it is still green; it becomes yellowish or purple when ripe. The tomatillo is covered with a thin membrane, or calyx, that is a brownish orange color with purple veins. The berry has a slightly gelatinous texture and a rather acidic flavor that is more pungent than that of other varieties of *Physalis,* such as the alkakengi.

Buying

Choose tomatillos that are firm and evenly colored. When sold with their calyx, it should be free of mold and crisp, a sign that the fruits are ripe.

Preparing

Peel off the husk and wash the fruit just before using it, taking particular care to wash off the sticky resin accumulated at the base of the stem. Remove the core.

Serving Ideas

The tomatillo is most often cooked, but it can also be eaten raw, either on its own or added to a salad. Firmer than the tomato, tomatillos are perfect for sauces and are widely used for this purpose in Mexico, where the famous tomatillo-based *mole verde* sauce is used to season numerous dishes, including tacos, burritos, enchiladas, and various meats. Raw tomatillos are also minced and added to gazpacho and guacamole. Because of its unusual appearance, the tomatillo is sometimes used as an ornamental fruit by turning it over on its stem or peeling back the husk.

Storing

Tomatillos can be kept for about 1 week in the vegetable drawer of the refrigerator. Like tomatoes, they freeze well when cooked. They will keep at room temperature if used within 2 days.

Nutritional Information

	raw
water	91.7%
protein	0.9 g
fat	1.2 g
carbohydrates	6 g
calories	32
	per 100 g

This fruit is a good source of potassium and also contains vitamin C, magnesium, niacin, and thiamine. It is said to reduce fever, alleviate rheumatism, and act as a diuretic and a cleansing agent.

Fruit Vegetables

69

Wax Gourd

Benincasa hispida, **Curcubitaceae**

Fruit of an annual garden plant originating in Malaysia, the wax gourd belongs to the same family as the cucumber, squash, and other melons, with which it also shares its growing characteristics. It is cultivated in the tropical and subtropical regions of Asia and is an important part of the diet in many countries, particularly in India and Southeast Asia, although it is relatively new on Western markets.

The wax gourd grows on a long trailing vine. It has a round or oblong shape similar to that of the watermelon and typically measures 6 to 10 inches in diameter and 8 to 14 inches in length. Some specimens can weigh as much as 30 pounds. As the gourd ripens, the pale green rind thickens and becomes covered with a thin white down that continues to develop even after harvesting. The firm, white flesh of the wax gourd is sweet and tasty. The cavity contains numerous seeds that are similar to cucumber seeds.

Nutritional Information

	cooked
water	96%
protein	0.5 g
fat	0.2 g
carbohydrates	2.9 g
fiber	0.8 g
	per 100 g

The wax gourd contains vitamin C.

Buying

Some of the larger varieties of wax gourds are often sold cut, although smaller varieties are also exported to Western markets. Choose a gourd that is firm and unbruised.

Preparing

Remove the rind and the fibrous part containing the seeds. Cut the flesh into uniformly sized pieces to ensure even cooking.

Serving Ideas

 The most common use of the wax gourd is in stir-fries and soups. It can be used like the squash or pumpkin, with which it is interchangeable in most recipes. This type of gourd is a good accompaniment to spicy dishes and is sometimes also candied. The young leaves and flower buds of the wax gourd are edible, as are the seeds, which are often eaten roasted or fried.

Storing

Whole wax gourds will keep for several weeks in a cool and dry place, away from direct sunlight. When stored at a temperature of 55 to 59 °F and at a humidity of 70 to 75%, they will keep for over 6 months. This type of gourd does not stand up well to freezing, which makes it turn soft.

Bitter melon

Momordica charantia, **Cucurbitaceae**

Fruit of an annual vegetable plant originating in tropical India, the bitter melon (also known as the balsam pear) is related to the gourd, the melon, and the cucumber and grows in the same way as those plants. Bitter melons are found growing in tropical and subtropical regions. They have been consumed for centuries in Asia, where they were first used for their medicinal properties. While the bitter melon is quite popular in India, Indonesia, and Southeast Asia, it is still a relative newcomer in Western markets.

The bitter melon grows on a climbing plant measuring between 22 and 32 feet in length; the vines have tendrils by which they attach themselves to plants or other objects. The fruit is 3 to 10 inches long and is shaped like a cucumber, with an inedible pale green skin that is wrinkled and warty. The thick, pearly flesh is rather dry and contains numerous whitish seeds; its high quinine content gives it a bitter taste, although it is less bitter before it reaches maturity. The ripeness of bitter melons is indicated by their color, which becomes yellow or orange as they mature.

Preparing

Peel the bitter melon and cut it in half lengthwise. Remove the seeds and the surrounding white substance. Cut the flesh into similarly sized pieces to ensure uniform cooking. The bitterness of the melon can be reduced by blanching it for a few minutes. It can also be sweated: Sprinkle the flesh with salt and let it macerate for about 30 minutes; then rinse it with cold water. Sweated bitter melons do not need to be peeled.

Serving Ideas

The uses of the bitter melon are rather limited because of its bitterness, which makes it unsuitable for eating raw. In Chinese cooking, this fruit is often steamed and is added to a dish consisting of pork, onions, ginger, and black bean sauce. The bitter melon is also a frequent ingredient in Chinese soups. In India the bitter melon is often served at the beginning of the meal, either alone or combined with lentils or potatoes and seasoned with cumin and turmeric. The bitter melon can also be marinated.

Buying

When choosing a bitter melon, look for one that is firm and without mold. Dark green specimens will be less bitter.

Storing

Bitter melons should be wrapped in a perforated plastic bag and placed in the vegetable drawer of the refrigerator, where they will keep for about a week. They do not freeze well.

Nutritional Information

water		94%
protein		1 g
fat		0.2 g
carbohydrates		3.7 g
fiber		1.4 g
calories		17
		per 100 g

Squash

Cucurbita spp., **Cucurbitaceae**

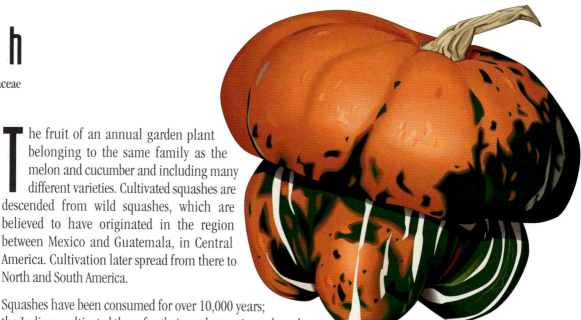

The squash family embraces an impressive number of different varieties; they are related to the cucumber and melon, and like those vegetables, they grow on trailing plants.

The fruit of an annual garden plant belonging to the same family as the melon and cucumber and including many different varieties. Cultivated squashes are descended from wild squashes, which are believed to have originated in the region between Mexico and Guatemala, in Central America. Cultivation later spread from there to North and South America.

Squashes have been consumed for over 10,000 years; the Indians cultivated them for their seeds at a time when they were not yet very fleshy. Over the centuries, improved varieties having more flesh and a fruitier taste were developed; these varieties were cultivated along with corn and bean crops by the Aztec, Incan, and Mayan peoples of Latin America. Christopher Columbus was the first westerner to discover these fruits, and cultivation began in Europe shortly after the discovery of America.

Most varieties of squash are classified as being either summer squash or winter squash, depending on their storage life. Summer squash cannot be stored for very long, whereas winter squash will keep for a good part of the winter under adequate storage conditions. Today, most squashes and pumpkins are produced in China, Romania, Egypt, Argentina, Turkey, Italy, and Japan.

SUMMER SQUASH

Summer squashes are picked when still very young, from 2 to 7 days after flowering. Both their skin and seeds are tender enough to be edible. These varieties are perishable and do not keep for very long. Although summer squashes that have reached maturity are still edible, they tend to be drier, with harder seeds and a thicker skin.

The list of the different types of summer squash, and of winter squash for that matter, is quite impressive, and it is getting longer all the time as new hybrid varieties are developed.

The **zucchini** *(C. pepo)* is probably the best-known member of the summer squash family. Originally from Italy, the zucchini is a variety of marrow squash that is harvested before it is fully ripe and that resembles a large cucumber. It is also known as "courgette." The thin, smooth skin can be yellow or green, and sometimes has grayish green or yellowish speckles or stripes. The cream-colored, watery flesh is rather bland tasting and contains a varying number of seeds. The most flavorful zucchinis usually measure between 6 and 8 inches, with flavor and quality declining as the fruit matures. French and Italian cooking make use of zucchini flowers, which can be stuffed or deep-fried in batter.

The **marrow squash**, or vegetable marrow, is green with white stripes and looks like a large zucchini.

The **crookneck squash** and the **straightneck squash** (var. *melopepo* f. *torticolis*) are usually yellow both inside and out, but they may also have a green-colored skin. This variety is covered with small bumps and has a swollen base. The crookneck squash has a slender, crooked, swan-like neck. This variety has been genetically improved to produce the straightneck squash. These squashes are most flavorful when they measure between 8 and 10 inches in length.

The **pattypan squash** (var. *melopepo* f. *clypeiformis*) has an unusual saucer-like shape that is often likened to a mushroom cap. The skin is usually a very pale green, bordering on white, but it can also be golden yellow. Less soft than the skin of zucchini, it turns white and becomes as hard as a winter squash when very ripe, making it necessary to remove the skin. The firm, whitish flesh is less watery than that of zucchini and has a slightly sweet taste that is reminiscent of the artichoke. Pattypan squashes are best when they measure between 3 and 4 inches in diameter. Very small specimens are sometimes preserved in vinegar.

WINTER SQUASH

Winter squashes are harvested when fully ripe. They vary in shape, size, color, and flavor, depending on the variety. The orange-colored flesh is drier, more fibrous, and much sweeter than that of summer squash, and it becomes creamy when cooked. Like melons, winter squashes have a hollow inner cavity containing hard, fully developed seeds; these seeds can be washed, dried, and roasted, either salted or plain, and make a delicious and nourishing snack. Pumpkin seeds are commonly used in this way. The thick, hard shell of winter squashes is inedible; difficult to pierce, it acts as effective protection for a storage period ranging between 30 and 180 days, depending on the variety.

The already large family of winter squashes is continually expanding and includes the following well-known varieties:

The **butternut squash** (*C. moschata)* is best when 8 to 12 inches long and about 4 to 5 inches in diameter around the base. Similar in shape to a large pear, the butternut squash has a finely textured, fairly sweet-tasting flesh with a high carotene content that gives it its deep orange color. The smooth, cream-colored skin is easy to remove. Greenish-colored skin is an indication that this squash is not yet ripe.

The **Hubbard squash** has a very hard, rough skin that can be moderately or sharply ribbed and varies in color from dark green to gray-blue or orange-red. This squash is quite large and can be oval or round in shape. The thick, dry flesh is less sweet and often less orange in color than most other varieties of winter squash. Green Hubbard squashes usually weigh around 11 pounds and can be stored for 6 months.

The **turban squash** (*Cucurbita maxima* var. *turbaniformis*) has an orange-yellow or golden-yellow flesh that is dry, thick but fine-textured, and very sweet, with a hazelnut-like flavor. The seed cavity is quite small. The rugged shell is hard and thin; it is green with variously colored stripes or speckles. When fully ripe, the turban squash measures between 6 and 8 inches in diameter and weighs about 3 pounds.

The **buttercup squash** (*Cucurbita maxima* var. *turbaniformis*) has a creamy, orange-colored flesh resembling that of the butternut squash. The orange or green shell is thick and smooth. This squash has a turban-like crown that is paler in color, with yellow flesh. The skin of certain varieties is so hard that a knife will pierce it only if hit with a blunt object such as a wooden mallet or rolling pin, or sometimes even a hammer. This squash, which usually weighs about 3 pounds, can be stored for approximately 1 month.

The **acorn squash** has wide ribs that make peeling difficult. Its smooth, hard skin is deep green, with orange patches when harvested at maturity. The pale orange-yellow flesh is tender and fine-textured, with a flavor reminiscent of hazelnuts and pepper. The most flavorful acorn squashes are about 5 inches long and from 6 to 8 inches in diameter. This variety will keep for 30 to 50 days.

Less common varieties of winter squash include the cylindrical **banana squash** *(C. maxima)*, which measures between 20 and 24 inches in length and about 6 inches in diameter. The skin can be ivory or pinkish in color, and the orange flesh is firm and fine-textured. Since this type of squash is often sold cut, it is easier to judge the quality of its flesh at the time of purchase.

The same holds true for the **mammoth** variety; although similar in shape to the pumpkin, it is often white but can also be dark green, grayish green, blue-green, or orange in color. Some specimens weigh over 140 pounds.

The **pumpkin** *(C. pepo)* is very similar to the **autumn squash** *(C. maxima),* with which it is often confused, even in dictionaries. Pumpkins are more commonly used in North America, while the autumn squash is more popular in Europe. Both of these varieties are quite large and can be distinguished only by their peduncle; the pumpkin's is hard and fibrous, with five angular ridges and no swelling at the stem end, while that of the autumn squash is soft, spongy, cylindrical, and flared at the point of attachment. The flesh of these squashes is slightly thicker, and they have a more pronounced flavor than the other varieties of winter squash. Rarely used on their own as a vegetable, they are more commonly used in soups, desserts, and jams. They can weigh up to 110 pounds and can have a circumference of as much as 5 feet. The smooth, hard skin of pumpkins is usually orange, while that of autumn squash is often yellow or green. The flesh is a deep orange-yellow color, and is quite thick, dry, and sweet. Pumpkin seeds are more popular than the seeds of other varieties of squash; the seeds of the "Tripletreat" variety have the advantage of having no shell. Although most commonly purchased for use as a Halloween decoration, pumpkins can also be substituted for or combined with other squashes in most recipes.

pumpkin

squash flower

autumn squash

turban squash

Buying

When choosing summer squash, look for firm, undamaged specimens with a glossy skin that is free of cracks and blemishes. Dull-colored squashes lack freshness, while those with spots have been damaged by exposure to cold. Overly large specimens tend to be fibrous and bitter, while too-small ones lack flavor.

It is important to verify the condition of winter squash. If it is not ripe, the skin will be shiny and it will be rather flavorless; if the squash is too old, it will be slightly woolly looking and the flesh will be fibrous. Look for a squash that is firm and intact, heavy for its size, and with a dull-colored skin, indicating that it was picked when fully ripe. It should still have a part of its stem, which slows down the loss of moisture. Avoid winter squashes that are cracked or that have brownish or soft spots.

Nutritional Information

	cooked summer squash	*cooked winter squash*
water	93.7%	89%
protein	0.9 g	0.9 g
fat	0.3 g	0.6 g
carbohydrates	4.3 g	8.8 g
fiber	1.6 g	2.8 g
calories	20	39
		per 100 g

Cooked winter squashes contain more carbohydrates than summer squash, making them higher in calories. They are an excellent source of potassium and vitamin A; they also contain vitamin C, folic acid, pantothenic acid, and copper.

Storing

Summer squashes are easily damaged and should be handled with care. Place them in a perforated plastic bag in the refrigerator, where they will keep for about 1 week. Wash them just before using them.

Summer squash can be frozen, but this results in a softer flesh. Cut it into slices and blanch it for 2 minutes before freezing. Once frozen, summer squash will keep for 3 to 4 months.

Depending on the variety, winter squash will keep for a period ranging from 1 week to 6 months; it should be stored away from the light and should not be exposed to cold, which damages it, or to heat, which converts its starch too rapidly. A temperature between 50° and 60°F and a humidity of 60%, along with good ventilation, are recommended. Leave on a portion of the stem, and remove all traces of soil. Refrigerate winter squash only if it has been cut or cooked. A cut piece of raw squash can be wrapped in plastic and stored for a day or two in the refrigerator. Winter squash freezes well, especially in puréed form. It is more practical to freeze it in individual portions for use in recipes.

Fruit Vegetables

75

acorn squash

pattypan squash

zucchini

Sweet Dumpling squash

mammoth squash

straightneck squash

Preparing

To prepare summer squash, wash it and cut off both ends. It can be used whole, grated, halved, or cut into cubes, strips, or slices. It can also be stuffed by cutting it in half lengthwise and scooping out some of the flesh. Because of its high water content, squash is often drained; although not essential, draining may be necessary if there is a possibility that the squash will make the dish to which it is being added too watery.

To drain the squash, cut it into slices and arrange them in a shallow dish; sprinkle uniformly with coarse salt and let drain for 20 to 30 minutes. Using a strainer, rinse the slices under cold running water. Pat them dry and proceed with the recipe.

Very ripe squash should be peeled and seeded, but because it is less watery, it does not need to be drained, although it does require a longer cooking time. The less subtle flavor of ripe squash makes it more useful in soups and stews, or in puréed form.

Wash and peel winter squash, and scoop out the seeds and filaments with a spoon. Keep the seeds, which are excellent when dried. It is sometimes easier to peel winter squash if it is first halved or quartered. Whenever possible, cook the squash in its skin (this may be necessary when stuffing squash or if its skin is very hard).

Serving Ideas

Summer squash can be eaten raw or cooked. Raw squash is good on its own or served with a dip; it can also be added to appetizers, salads, or sandwiches, and is good marinated. Great crêpes can be made by grating raw squash and mixing it with eggs, flour, and seasonings. Squash is delicious cooked in its juice with garlic, onions, and tomatoes. Squash is often stuffed and baked, gratinéed, braised, fried in batter or bread crumbs, or roasted. It is also added to soups, stews, quiches, and omelets. Zucchini is one of the basic ingredients in ratatouille.

To enhance the flavor of summer squashes, season them with spices or herbs: dill and mint are particularly well suited to squash. These varieties of squash can replace cucumbers in most recipes; since they are less flavorful, they produce a milder-tasting dish.

Squash flowers are edible and never fail to add an original touch to a menu. Their delicate flavor adds aroma and visual appeal to soups, fritters, crêpes, omelets, rice, seafood, and poultry. They are often quickly sautéed over high heat or stuffed and baked. The flowers should be picked when open to avoid finding a bee trapped inside.

Winter squashes are often added to soups, stews, couscous, curries, and other similar dishes. Cooked and puréed, they are delicious in combination with puréed potatoes or used in soups. They also make a number of excellent desserts, including pies, cakes, muffins, cookies, puddings, soufflés, and cream desserts. The rather bland flavor of winter squash can be enhanced through generous seasoning. Sweet potatoes can be replaced with winter squash in most recipes.

marrow squash

buttercup squash

Hubbard squash

banana squash

Zucchini with Mustard Sauce

SERVES 4

4 medium zucchini
3 tbsp. mayonnaise
1 tbsp. Dijon mustard
1 tbsp. plain yogurt

4 drops Tabasco Sauce
Salt and ground pepper
1 tbsp. chopped chives

1. If you like, peel the zucchini. Cut them into thin slices, and place them in a salad bowl.

2. In a small bowl, blend the mayonnaise and mustard well, and add the yogurt, Tabasco Sauce, salt and pepper, and the chives. Pour over the sliced zucchini. Let stand for 15 minutes before serving.

Serve as an appetizer.

Cooking

Squashes can be boiled, steamed, baked, microwaved, or cooked in the pressure-cooker.

• Boiling is not the best method of cooking squashes, as it tends to detract from their flavor and to make them very watery. Cut the squash into ½- to ¾-inch cubes, use very little water, and cook for 10 to 15 minutes or until tender.

• It is also possible to boil squash whole and unpeeled. Poke a few holes in the squash with a fork, cover with water, and boil for about 1 hour.

• Steaming is a highly recommended means of cooking squash. Simply cut the squash into halves, slices, or pieces, season with salt, and place on a steamer rack in a large saucepan. The cooking time can vary from 15 to 40 minutes, depending on the size of the pieces.

• To bake squash in the oven, cut the unpeeled squash in half (or in quarters if it is large), remove the seeds, put a little oil or butter in the cavity, add salt and pepper, and season with nutmeg and cinnamon or any other seasoning; pour a little water, orange juice, or lemon juice in the cavity; place the squash in an baking dish with ¾ to 2 inches of water, and bake for 30 to 60 minutes or until tender. Another method is to place a little brown sugar, honey, or maple syrup in the cavity, top it with cheese, and bake it au gratin. Squash can also be stuffed before being baked.

To cook squash in a microwave, cut it in half, remove the seeds, cover the squash with plastic wrap, leaving one corner open (or place it in a microwavable plastic bag), and cook on high power until tender, 10 to 15 minutes depending on the size.

1 Cut the squash in half and scoop out the seeds with a spoon.

2 Cut the squash into quarters and remove the skin with a sharp knife.

crookneck squash

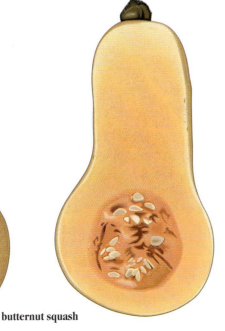

butternut squash

Fruit Vegetables

77

Dried squash seeds

Nutritional Information

	winter squash seeds
water	7%
protein	33 g
fat	42 g
carbohydrates	13.4 g
fiber	13.8 g
calories	522
	per 100 g

The seeds of winter squash are very nourishing and energizing. They are an excellent source of magnesium, iron, phosphorus, zinc, copper, potassium, niacin, and folic acid, in addition to being a good source of riboflavin and thiamin. They also contain pantothenic acid.

Seeds roasted in oil generally contain saturated acids, making them even more energizing than plain-roasted seeds. Squash seeds have been credited with a number of medicinal properties; they are said to be diuretic and to help in the treatment of urinary tract infections and prostate disorders. They also have a reputation for being an aphrodisiac.

Storing

Store winter squash seeds in a cool dry place, away from insects and rodents. They may also be frozen. Chopped or ground seeds should be stored in the refrigerator to prevent them from going rancid.

Preparing

To roast the seeds:

• gently remove all the seeds, along with the surrounding filaments, from the cavity of the squash; discard the filaments and pat the seeds dry with a paper towel. Do not rinse them.

• spread the seeds on a cookie sheet and leave them out to dry at room temperature for several days if possible; otherwise, leave them out at least overnight;

• place the seeds in the oven and roast them at 350°F until they are golden, shaking them occasionally. Coat them with a little oil and salt if desired;

• remove the seeds from the oven and take them off the cookie sheet to end roasting;

• to prevent the formation of mold during storage, ensure that the seeds are cool and dry before placing them in an airtight container.

Serving Ideas

The seeds of winter squash can be used as they are or roasted, either whole, chopped, or ground. They make a good snack, either on their own or mixed with walnuts, almonds, peanuts, and dried fruits. They also add a pleasant crunch to salads, pasta dishes, sauces, and vegetables.

whole pumpkin seeds

shelled pumpkin seeds

Spaghetti squash

Cucurbita pepo, Cucurbitaceae

The spaghetti squash is the edible fruit of a plant that is thought to have originated in North America or Central America, although little is known about its history. Unlike that of other squash, the flesh of the spaghetti squash can be separated into spaghetti-like strands after it is cooked. Whole spaghetti squash measure between 8 and 14 inches in length and weigh approximately 4½ pounds. Their off-white or yellowish skin is smooth and moderately tough. The flesh of the spaghetti squash is a very pale yellow color that can be slightly green; its taste is similar to that of summer squash.

Buying

Choose a spaghetti squash that is hard, intact and unbruised; patches of green indicate that the squash is not quite ripe.

Serving Ideas

Spaghetti squash can replace spaghetti in most recipes and can thus be topped with a variety of pasta sauces. It can also be used like other squash, especially in soups and stews.

Cooked and chilled spaghetti squash can be used in salads and dressed with a vinaigrette or mayonnaise. It can also be grated and eaten raw. It is usually necessary to remove excess moisture from the squash by spinning it in a salad spinner.

Cooking

When baking or boiling spaghetti squash, leave it whole or split it lengthwise (remove the seeds in the central cavity). Pierce whole squash in several places, and bake halved squash hollow side up. The riper the squash, the faster it will cook. Bake whole squash for about one hour at 350°F (180°C) and halved squash for 30 to 45 minutes. Boil whole squash for 30 to 45 minutes, and sliced squash for about 20 minutes. Check to see if a whole squash is ready by piercing it with a fork (it should be soft); the flesh of sliced squash should separate easily into strands when done. Spin the squash for several minutes if it contains too much moisture. Avoid overcooking squash because the flesh will become bland and mushy; the flesh is best when still slightly crunchy.

When cooking spaghetti squash in the microwave, cut it in two and remove the seeds, then place each half on a plate hollow side up and cover them with plastic wrap, leaving one corner open. Cook each half separately on high power for 6 to 8 minutes, or until the flesh separates easily. Remove the flesh and prepare it as directed.

Nutritional Information

	cooked
water	92.3%
protein	0.7g
fat	0.3 g
carbohydrates	6.5 g
fiber	1.4 g
	per 100 g

Spaghetti squash contains potassium, vitamin C and pantothenic acid.

Storing

Spaghetti squash should be protected from heat, cold and light. A spaghetti squash that it is in good condition can be stored for up to 3 months at temperatures between 50 and 60°F. Remove all traces of soil from the squash, but do not remove the part of the stem that attaches the squash to the plant. Sliced or cooked spaghetti squash should be stored in the refrigerator. Raw, grated or cooked spaghetti squash can be frozen. When freezing premeasured quantities of raw spaghetti squash, include ½ cup extra to compensate for the moisture and volume that will be lost when the squash is defrosted.

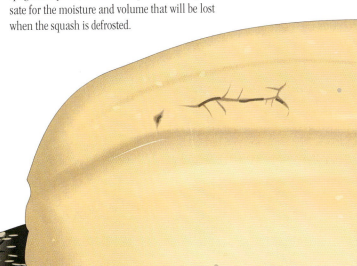

Chayote

Sechium edule, Cucurbitaceae

F ruit of an annual edible plant native to Mexico and Central America, the chayote (also known as the christophine) is a squash that prefers tropical and subtropical climates but can also be cultivated in moderate climates where the temperature remains warm throughout most of the fall. The chayote is cultivated in the Caribbean and several other areas, with most of the crop coming from Costa Rica. It was originally cultivated by the Mayans and the Aztecs; in fact, the word is derived from *chayot,* the word for this vegetable in Nahuatl, the language of the Aztecs.

The chayote resembles the pear, and can grow to between 3 and 8 inches in length. Its thin, rough skin is edible and varies in color from yellowish white to pale green to dark green. It has several deep longitudinal ribs. The firm, crisp whitish flesh has a high water content and a rather subtle flavor. It contains a single stone that is 1 to 2 inches long and that sprouts inside the ripe fruit. This stone can be eaten when cooked.

Buying

Choose an unblemished chayote that is firm but not too hard. Very hard-skinned chayote will have fibrous flesh.

Nutritional Information

water	93%
protein	0.6 g
fat	0.5 g
carbohydrates	5.1 g
fiber	0.7 g
calories	24
	per 100 g

Raw chayote is a good source of potassium and contains vitamin C, folic acid, vitamin B_6, copper, and magnesium.

Preparing

The skin of the chayote remains firm during cooking; for this reason, it is almost always peeled, either before or after cooking. It may be a good idea to wear gloves or to peel the fruit under running water, as it secretes a sticky substance during peeling.

Serving Ideas

The chayote can be eaten raw or cooked. In raw form, it is often added to salads or served on its own with a bit of vinaigrette. It can be prepared in a wide variety of ways.

When very ripe (the sprout beginning to emerge), the chayote can be peeled and cooked for use in Creole-style dishes; it goes into the making of acras and gratins. Cooked, it is delicious topped with a sauce, au gratin, or as a compote. The addition of sugar and seasoning (lime juice, cinnamon, and nutmeg, for example) turns this compote into an excellent dessert.

Chayotes can also be added to soups and stews, stir-fried, stuffed, or added to marinades and chutneys. They may replace summer squash in most recipes.

Cooking

The delicate flavor of the chayote is better if the fruit is still slightly crisp after cooking; allow 10 to 15 minutes for boiling and steaming.

Storing

Placed in a perforated plastic bag, chayotes will keep for a few weeks in the vegetable compartment of the refrigerator.

Spinach

Spinacia oleracea, **Chenopodiaceae**

Spinach is harvested when the leaves are still young and tender, before the floral stem appears.

T his annual vegetable plant is believed to be a native of Persia. Unknown to the Greek and Roman civilizations, spinach was introduced into Spain by the Moors, after which it spread across the rest of Europe. In the Middle Ages, cooked spinach leaves were sold molded in the shape of round balls called *espinoche*. When Catherine de Médicis left her native Florence to marry the king of France in 1533, she brought along Italian cooks capable of preparing her favorite vegetable in a variety of ways; since then, dishes served on a bed of spinach are usually referred to as "à la Florentine."

Spinach grows in most temperate regions, with the largest producers being the United States, the Netherlands, and Scandinavia. The plant is harvested when the leaves are still young and tender, before the floral stem appears.

Preparing

Spinach, when not sold prewashed, is very sandy and must be washed thoroughly, preferably just before using it to prevent the leaves from becoming soft. Wash the spinach rapidly in a large basin of water, immersing and shaking the leaves gently; change the water if necessary, but do not let the spinach soak. Trim or section any tough stems to ensure even cooking of the leaves and stems.

Serving Ideas

Spinach can be eaten raw as well as cooked. Raw spinach is delicious in salads and sandwiches. When cooked, it can be eaten plain, with a little butter and lemon juice, or with a sauce; Mornay, béchamel, and cream sauces are particularly well suited to spinach. It can also be baked au gratin or puréed, either on its own or with potatoes. Spinach blends well with milk (which offsets its acidity) and eggs and is frequently combined with these foods in such dishes as omelets and quiches. A classic accompaniment to veal, poultry, and fish, spinach is also used in stuffings and soufflés.

Cooking

Spinach can usually be cooked in the water remaining on its leaves after it has been washed and briefly drained. Cook it quickly (1 to 3 minutes) in a covered saucepan over high heat. Cooking reduces the volume of spinach significantly. When using spinach in simmered dishes, add it at the end of cooking. Spinach should not be cooked in a pressure cooker, as this tends to overcook it. Steaming tends to bring out the bitterness of spinach. To prevent oxidation, use glass or stainless-steel pans and utensils when preparing spinach; avoid untreated aluminum and cast-iron pans. When overcooked, spinach tends to become brownish.

Buying

Choose fresh-looking spinach with deep green leaves that are tender and supple to the touch. Avoid dull-looking vegetables with limp, sodden, or yellowing leaves.

Nutritional Information

	raw
water	91.6%
protein	2.9 g
fat	0.3 g
carbohydrates	3.5 g
fiber	2.6 g
calories	23
	per 100 g

Raw spinach is an excellent source of folic acid, vitamin A, potassium, and magnesium; it is a good source of vitamin C and iron, and also supplies riboflavin, niacin, vitamin B_6, calcium, phosphorus, zinc, and copper. Spinach is said to prevent scurvy and anemia, and to replenish minerals.

Storing

While fresh spinach will keep in the refrigerator for 4 or 5 days, cooked spinach does not keep well. Wash the leaves just before using them, as wet spinach tends to spoil rapidly. This vegetable freezes well as long as it is very fresh; blanch it for 2 minutes before freezing. Since freezing makes the leaves go quite soft, avoid thawing frozen spinach completely before using it.

Sorrel

Rumex spp., Polygonaceae

Sorrel has large, tender, bright green leaves. Its tart and acid flavor is similar to that of rhubarb.

82

Sorrel and patience dock, or dock sorrel, are two varieties of the same species, which originated in northern Asia and in Europe. These hardy perennials can be found growing wild or under cultivation in most temperate regions of the world. They are related to rhubarb, with which they share their tart and acid flavor; indeed, the name "sorrel" is derived from the ancient French *surel,* meaning sour. The Romans and Egyptians appreciated sorrel for its digestive properties. Quite popular in Europe since ancient times, sorrel is still held in high esteem today and is an important ingredient in both French and English culinary traditions. As early as the Middle Ages, herbalists discovered that sorrel helped to prevent scurvy. The plant was introduced into North America by the Pilgrims, who grew it in their New England gardens. From there, sorrel rapidly spread north to Canada.

Garden sorrel or large sorrel *(Rumex acetosa)* has large, tender, bright green leaves with more or less serrated edges depending on the variety. The arrow-shaped leaves are usually 6 to 8 inches long on average, but they can grow to 3 feet. The bell-shaped reddish flowers grow in clusters.

Patience dock *(Rumex patientia)* is larger than sorrel, with coarse rounded leaves and clustered green flowers. Often considered a weed, this plant grows up to 5 feet in height. The leaves are not as savory as those of sorrel.

Buying

Look for sorrel with firm and glossy green leaves and slender stems, which tend to be less fibrous.

Nutritional Information

	raw sorrel
water	92.9%
protein	1.9 g
fat	0.8 g
carbohydrates	3.1 g
	per 100 g

Sorrel is an excellent source of vitamins A and C, magnesium, and potassium; it is also a good source of iron and supplies phosphorus. The vitamin and mineral content of cooked sorrel is similar to that of raw sorrel. Like spinach and rhubarb, sorrel and patience dock contain a fair amount of oxalic acid, and should therefore be consumed in moderation. They are said to be reinvigorating, regenerative, diuretic, aperitive, digestive, antiscorbutic, and mildly laxative.

Preparing

Wash sorrel just before consuming it to preserve the freshness of the leaves. Immerse the leaves in a bowlful of water and shake them delicately, changing the water if necessary, but do not soak. Sorrel is usually cooked without its stems; to remove them, simply fold the leaves in half lengthwise and pull off the stem, which should come away easily.

Serving Ideas

Sorrel can be eaten raw or cooked. Its acid flavor is reminiscent of lemon and adds a refreshing note to salads, especially when the leaves are young and tender. It can also be cooked and prepared like spinach, and is particularly delicious in soups and sauces. In fact, sorrel soup is a classic in a number of European culinary traditions, particularly in central Europe and Russia. Sorrel sauce blends well with poultry, eggs, and quiches. This vegetable is also traditionally served as a vegetable side dish with fish (shad, pike) and veal. Puréed sorrel is often mixed with other puréed vegetables, such as potatoes or beans. The acid flavor of sorrel can be moderated by adding lettuce leaves to the preparation or by topping the vegetable with a cream sauce.

Cooking

Avoid cooking sorrel and patience dock in aluminum or iron pans, as they tend to blacken upon contact with these metals; also, when cutting them, use a stainless-steel knife. Note that steaming tends to bring out the bitterness of these vegetables.

Storing

Sorrel is quite perishable and should be consumed as soon as possible. The leaves can be stored for 1 or 2 days in a perforated plastic bag in the refrigerator. Wash just before using. Cooked sorrel can also be frozen.

Nettle

Urtica dioca, **Urticaceae**

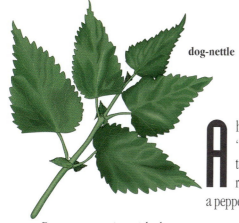

dog-nettle

A herbaceous plant originating in Eurasia, the nettle (also known as "bigstring") is covered with stinging hairs and can be found in most temperate climates growing alongside roads, on waterfronts, and on raw land. Despite its bad reputation, the nettle is an edible plant with a peppery flavor.

Pungency varies with the variety, great nettle and dog-nettle being the most common. **Great nettle** or **stinging nettle** *(U. dioca)* is a perennial plant. Sometimes called "common nettle," it can grow to a height of 5 feet. The plant's long, hairy stems are grooved and harden gradually as it matures. The dark-green oval leaves are long and wide, and are also covered with hairs. The tips of the plant's flowers feature a small reservoir containing an irritating liquid. Nettle leaves may be prepared on their own or with sorrel.

Dog-nettle *(U. urens)* is an annual. Sometimes called "burning nettle," it can grow up to 20 inches high. Its smooth dentated leaves are rounder and more irritating than the great nettle's. This variety is usually eaten in salads.

Nettle leaves may cause a rash, but they lose their irritating properties as soon as they are cooked or dried.

Buying

Nettle must be picked before its stems harden. You may want to wear gloves to cut it, but this is unnecessary if you avoid touching the top of the leaves.

Serving Ideas

Nettle leaves become non-irritating as soon as they are cooked or dried. Nettle may be used the same way as spinach. Nettle soup, made with potatoes, leeks, watercress, cabbage, or beans, is particularly delicious. This plant is often braised with onions and garlic, with a touch of nutmeg added. Very young nettle leaves or those of less irritating varieties can be eaten raw, finely chopped. Because of their high chlorophyll content, they stay a rich green when cooked for a short time.

Storing

Nettle is fragile. Refrigerate it unwashed in a perforated plastic bag.

Nutritional Information

protein	5.5 g
fat	0.7 g
carbohydrates	7 g
calories	57
	per 100 g

Nettle is an excellent source of iron, calcium, potassium, and magnesium, as well as of vitamins A and C. It is thought to have astringent, tonic, digestive, cleansing, and diuretic properties. It is believed to aid in lactation and to relieve rheumatism. It may be used in a gargling solution to prevent mouth infections, or in a decoction as a dandruff remedy.

To make nettle tea, use 2 ounces (60 g) of roots and leaves for every quart (liter) of water; boil for 2 to 3 minutes, and steep for 20 minutes.

Dandelion

Taraxacum officinale, **Compositae**

T he dandelion is a perennial plant thought to be native to Europe, North Africa, central and northern Asia, and North America. A common plant with yellow flowers, it is often looked upon as a weed, since it can be found growing just about anywhere. However, for centuries the dandelion was highly valued for its medicinal and culinary properties, particularly in Europe. It is still quite popular in France. The word "dandelion" actually comes from the French *dents-de-lion* (lion's teeth) and refers to its serrated leaves; the French word for dandelion, *pissenlit,* refers to the plant's diuretic qualities.

The wild dandelion has bright green leaves, whereas the cultivated dandelion, which is grown in the dark like Belgian endive and white asparagus, has whitish leaves that have a delicate and slightly acid taste. The leaves of the wild dandelion are smaller and more bitter-tasting than those of its cultivated counterpart. The leaves have long thin whitish stems that contain a milky sap, also found in the flower stalks. The long fleshy roots are whitish on the inside and brown on the outside.

The dandelion is a common plant with yellow flowers that can be found growing just about everywhere and that is usually considered a weed.

Preparing

Blanching dandelions in boiling water for 1 or 2 minutes before preparing them will reduce the bitterness.

Nutritional Information

	raw leaves
water	85.6%
protein	1.6 g
fat	0.4 g
carbohydrates	5.3 g
fiber	2 g
calories	26
	per 250 ml (60 g)

Raw dandelion leaves are an excellent source of vitamin A and a good source of vitamin C and potassium; they also contain iron, calcium, riboflavin, thiamine, magnesium, and vitamin B_6, as well as folic acid and copper.

The dandelion is known for its properties as a tonic and a decongestant; it aids the appetite, counteracts scurvy, and cleanses the system. It has been used since ancient times to treat ulcers and hepatitis, and to sooth itching. Substances contained in the root of the dandelion are responsible for its stimulating action on the liver and the gallbladder. The root is also used for its effect as a mild laxative. The leaves have a reputation for their powerful diuretic properties. Dandelions may cause an allergic reaction, most often in the form of a benign skin rash, in sensitive people.

Buying

When choosing dandelions, look for fresh leaves that still have their roots, as they will keep longer. Avoid plants with dried-out, dull, or limp leaves. Dandelions are most tender and least bitter when picked while the leaves are very young, before the flower stalks have formed.

Do not pick plants that have been exposed to pollution; those growing along roadsides, for example, usually have a high lead content from the exhaust fumes.

Serving Ideas

Dandelion leaves may be eaten raw or cooked. Raw, the fresh young leaves are frequently added to salads. Their bitter flavor blends particularly well with strong-tasting oils and vinegars, such as hazelnut oil, olive oil, raspberry vinegar, or wine vinegar. Dandelions are delicious in a warm vinaigrette; the heat takes away some of the bitterness and tenderizes the leaves. In France, the traditional dandelion salad is made with bacon, vinegar, and garlic croutons.

Dandelions are often braised with pork (either ham, *lardons,* or bacon). They can also be prepared as a vegetable, in the same way as spinach. As for the different parts of the plant, the flower buds are sometimes marinated, the flowers are used to make wine, and the roots can be used, like the chicory root, as a substitute for coffee.

Storing

Stored in a perforated plastic bag in the refrigerator, dandelions will keep for a maximum of 5 days. Since they are most flavorful when fresh, it is best to use them as soon as possible; wash them at the last minute.

Although dandelions freeze well after being blanched for 2 minutes, they tend to wilt during thawing. If possible, do not thaw them completely before preparing them.

Purslane

Portulaca oleracea, **Portulacaceae**

 perennial plant that is very common in the relatively warm regions of Central Europe and North and South America, where it is often found growing wild. There are over 40 different varieties of this decorative plant, which has been used for more than 3,500 years both as a vegetable and for its medicinal properties. Purslane was very popular in medieval Europe, particularly among the English. It grows to between 2 and 4 inches high. Its branched stalks have a rubbery texture and are saturated with water, as are its thick, tender, fleshy leaves. The leaves are tear-shaped and yellowish green in color. Purslane is harvested before flowering. It has a slightly acid and peppery taste.

The branched stalks have a rubbery texture; purslane is harvested before flowering and has a slightly acid and peppery taste.

Serving Ideas

Purslane can be eaten raw or cooked. The tender stalks can be prepared like spinach or cardoon, but use them in moderation if you are unaccustomed to the sharp flavor. The leaves are more tender toward the top of the stalk and can be prepared in the same manner as watercress.

Purslane is used to flavor and decorate soups, sauces, mayonnaise, omelets, and stews. Excellent served with grated carrots or puréed potatoes, it also accompanies lettuce and tomatoes. Its stalks and leaves can be marinated in vinegar like capers. In the Middle East, purslane is used in a type of salad called *fattouch.*

Buying

When choosing purslane, look for firm stalks and leaves.

Nutritional Information

water	93%
protein	1.6 g
fat	0.1 g
carbohydrates	3.6 g
calories	17
	per 100 g

Purslane is an excellent source of potassium and magnesium, and a good source of vitamin A; it also supplies vitamin C, calcium, and iron. It contains mucilages and antioxidants. Its high water content makes it quite thirst-quenching. Purslane is said to make a good diuretic, intestinal cleanser, and emollient.

Storing

Because purslane is very perishable, it should be used promptly.

Lamb's lettuce

Valerianella locusta and *Valerianella olitoria*, **Valerianaceae**

Lamb's lettuce is cultivated and consumed like lettuce. The leaves are very tender and delicately flavored.

Also known as corn salad and mâche, this annual plant is believed to have originated in the Mediterranean region. It is a frost-resistant vegetable that is cultivated and consumed like lettuce. The delicate flavor of its tender leaves has been appreciated by Europeans since the time of the Roman Empire. Relatively unknown in North America, it is mainly produced in France and the Netherlands.

Lamb's lettuce is a close relative of valerian, a plant which is also called "catnip" because its odor is attractive to cats. There are several varieties of lamb's lettuce, all of which produce clusters of leaves at soil level. The leaves measure 4 to 12 inches in length; depending on the variety, they may be wide or narrow, with rounded or pointed tips, and come in varying shades of green. Some varieties of lamb's lettuce have a hazelnut flavor. A very tender vegetable, fresh lamb's lettuce has a delicate flavor; if they are wilted, however, the leaves may have a bitter taste.

Buying

Lamb's lettuce is sold in small bunches still attached to the roots. Choose a bunch with crisp, glossy leaves of an even green color. Avoid wilted or discolored leaves.

Nutritional Information

	raw
water	93%
protein	2 g
fat	0.4 g
carbohydrates	3.6 g
calories	21
	per 100 g

Raw lamb's lettuce is an excellent source of potassium and vitamins A and C; it is a good source of iron and vitamin B_6. This vegetable also contains copper, zinc, folic acid, magnesium, and phosphorus. It is said to act as a stimulant, a diuretic, and a laxative.

Preparing

Wash lamb's lettuce just before serving. Remove the roots and rinse the leaves well, since this plant grows in sandy soil. Handle the leaves delicately and change the water if necessary, but avoid soaking the leaves; drain thoroughly. Add the dressing at the last minute to ensure maximum tenderness and flavor.

Serving Ideas

Lamb's lettuce is delicious on its own or combined with other tender-leaf lettuces such as Boston or Bibb. Avoid mixing it with strong-tasting vegetables or dressings, as they tend to overpower its subtle flavor. A dash of hazelnut oil, a few drops of lemon, and a pinch of salt will suffice to enhance the flavor of this delicate vegetable.

Lamb's lettuce can also be used as a garnish on soups; simply cut it into little pieces and add it before serving. It also adds a colorful touch to omelets and rice or potato salads; add it at the last minute for the best effect. This vegetable blends deliciously in a mixed salad with nuts, apples, or beets and also makes a pleasant addition to poultry stuffings.

Storing

Lamb's lettuce spoils very rapidly. It can be kept in the refrigerator for 2 days, wrapped in a paper towel and placed in a perforated plastic bag. The delicate flavor of the leaves will be at its best if they are consumed without delay.

Arugula

Eruca sativa, Cruciferae

Arugula is a herbaceous annual plant native to Europe and western Asia. Also known as rocket, this pungent-smelling vegetable was known to the Romans, who used its leaves and seeds. A member of the cabbage family, arugula is related to watercress, mustard, and radishes. It is particularly popular in the South of France, in Italy, and in Egypt.

The plant grows to a height of about 20 inches and has tender green leaves that are smooth, sharply indented, and irregularly shaped, like those of dandelion. The piquant flavor of arugula is reminiscent of watercress.

Buying

Choose tender and fresh-looking arugula with bright green leaves that are deeply indented. Avoid limp, yellowing, or spotted leaves. When harvesting this vegetable, it is best to choose young leaves and to pick them before the plant blooms, as more mature plants tend to be rather coarse and too pungent.

Preparing

Trim off the roots and any fibrous stems. The leaves should be washed thoroughly, as they tend to harbor a lot of sand and soil. Wash them without soaking and just before using, in order to preserve their fresh appearance.

Serving Ideas

Arugula can be eaten raw or cooked, but it should be used with discretion, as it has quite a sharp flavor. It makes an attractive and flavorful seasoning in broths, salads, mayonnaise, sandwiches, potato salads, and pasta. It is also delicious puréed and incorporated into soups and sauces. Arugula seeds are used to prepare a very strong mustard that is much appreciated in the Mediterranean region and in the Middle East.

Nutritional Information

	raw
water	92%
protein	0.3 g
carbohydrates	0.4 g
fat	0.1 g
	per 10 g (½ cup)

Arugula is said to have the properties of a stimulant, a diuretic, and a stomachic.

Storing

Arugula is highly perishable and does not keep well, even when refrigerated. Before storing it in the refrigerator, wrap a damp paper towel around the roots and place the vegetable in a perforated plastic bag; it will keep for 2 or 3 days but should be consumed as soon as possible.

Arugula can also be preserved standing up in a glass of water, like flowers; change the water daily.

Leaf Vegetables

87

Cress

Nasturtium officinale and *Lepidium sativum,* Cruciferae

Cress grows in streams. Its leaves have a slightly pungent and peppery flavor.

A herbaceous perennial plant believed to have its origins in the Middle East, cress has been known for its medicinal properties since ancient times. It is mentioned in Greek writings dating back to the 1st century A.D., although it was not yet cultivated extensively, as it requires very specific growing conditions. Cress was introduced into various parts of the world by European immigrants. The Latin (and Greek) name for this plant, *nasturtium,* is derived from *nasus tortus,* meaning "twisted nose," in reference to the grimaces provoked by its pronounced hot and peppery taste. There are several types of cress, the most common varieties being watercress *(Nasturtium officinale)* and garden cress or peppergrass *(Lepidium sativum).*

Cress is an aquatic plant; its roots grow in fresh cold-water streams. The thin stalks can grow to between 8 and 20 inches in height and bear glossy compound leaves of 3 to 11 dark green leaflets; they can be round or oval in shape. Tiny white cruciferous flowers appear on unharvested plants. The leaves of cress have a slightly pungent and peppery flavor.

Nutritional Information

	raw
water	95%
protein	2.3 g
fat	0.1 g
carbohydrates	1.3 g
fiber	1.8 g
calories	11
	per 100 g

Cress is an excellent source of vitamin C, vitamin A and potassium; it also contains calcium, magnesium, riboflavin, vitamin B$_6$, and phosphorus. It is said to be tonic, diuretic, remineralizing, and antianemic, and to stimulate the appetite, cleanse the intestines, and combat scurvy.

Buying

Cress is most often sold in containers. Look for fresh, tender leaves of a deep green color. Avoid cress with wilted, yellowing, or spotted leaves.

Preparing

Remove the roots and any yellowing leaves, and wash the cress thoroughly to rid it of clinging sand and soil. To do so, place the leaves in a large bowl with enough water to cover them and swirl them around gently, changing the water as many times as necessary. Do not let the cress soak. Wash it just before serving to keep the leaves crisp.

garden cress

Serving Ideas

Cress can be eaten raw or cooked. The tender, juicy leaves are particularly good raw, and their mustardy flavor is very pleasant in salads. The hot flavor of garden cress adds bite to salads, sauces, and sandwiches.

It is best to use cress with discretion in order to avoid overpowering the flavor of the other foods. Cress makes both an attractive garnish and a good seasoning in mayonnaise, dips, potato salad, pasta dishes, and tofu. It can be cooked and prepared like spinach and makes an excellent purée, which can be added to sauces and soups or combined with puréed potatoes.

Storing

Cress is extremely perishable and should be consumed as soon as possible. Wrap its roots in a damp paper towel and place the plant in a perforated plastic bag in the refrigerator, where it will keep no longer than 1 or 2 days. It is best kept standing with its stalks in a bowl of water, which should be changed every day.

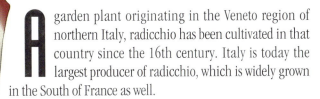

Radicchio

Cichorium intybus var. *foliosum*, **Compositae**

A garden plant originating in the Veneto region of northern Italy, radicchio has been cultivated in that country since the 16th century. Italy is today the largest producer of radicchio, which is widely grown in the South of France as well.

Radicchio is a variety of red chicory. Its leaves start out green but turn a reddish color when the temperature drops, although the leaves of certain varieties remain green or acquire only a slight pinkish or reddish coloring even when exposed to colder temperatures. Radicchio can be the size of a Boston lettuce or chicory. The most commonly known variety has round, glossy leaves that are deep red with white veins. The flavor of radicchio is slightly bitter and acid.

Buying

Look for a radicchio head with a firm and undamaged base and compact, well-colored leaves. Avoid those with brown-edged leaves.

Preparing

Remove the core and separate the leaves, removing any brown spots; rinse and dry the leaves.

Serving Ideas

Radicchio can be eaten raw or cooked. The decorative leaves of raw radicchio can be used as cups to contain crudités, olives, cheese, potato salad, rice salad, or fruit salad. They add a crispy note to salads, where their fairly bitter taste is best appreciated when combined with other types of lettuce. Cooked radicchio adds color to soups, rice, legumes, pasta, omelets, and tofu. It can also be cooked whole on a spit and is interchangeable with chicory and escarole in most recipes.

Nutritional Information

water	93%
protein	0.6 g
fat	0.2 g
carbohydrates	1.8 g
	per 40 g

Radicchio contains folic acid, potassium, copper, and vitamin C. It is said to stimulate the appetite, cleanse the blood, and to be diuretic, stomachic, remineralizing, and tonic.

Storing

Radicchio can be stored unwashed in a perforated plastic bag in the refrigerator, where it will keep for about 1 week, but it is at its tastiest and crispest when consumed as soon as possible.

Leaf Vegetables

89

Chicory

Cichorium intybus and *Cichorium endivia,* Compositae

Annual plants presumed to have originated in the Mediterranean area, chicory and escarole were originally used by the Greeks and Romans for their medicinal properties. In Europe, chicory and escarole have been consumed as a vegetable since the 14th century.

Wild chicory (*Cichorium intybus*) can be found growing naturally throughout North America, Europe, and the temperate regions of northern Africa. It is very bitter tasting and its short stems consist of green, tooth-edged leaves similar to those of the dandelion. Young and tender wild chicory is used in salads.

Wild chicory root can be forced into a savory vegetable that is less bitter, more crisp, and sweeter tasting. Known as *witloof,* meaning "white leaf" in Dutch, this vegetable is also commonly called endive.

Curly chicory (*Cichorium endivia* var. *crispa*) can grow to 18 inches in length, forming a voluminous plant that is mainly used in salads. Its green dentated leaves are slender and pointed and form a rosette; they have whitish or reddish ribs and are fairly bitter tasting. The heart and inner leaves are yellowish or whitish.

Escarole (*Cichorium endivia* var. *latifolia*) has broad leaves that are less curly and less bitter than those of chicory. The leaves have slightly dentated edges and form a plant that is smaller than curly chicory. The inner leaves are paler (white with yellow edges) and less bitter than the outer leaves. Escarole is frequently subject to an infection that causes the tips of its leaves to turn brown, particularly those at the heart of the plant; any such brown tips should be removed and discarded.

Buying

Look for chicory with a light-colored heart surrounded by firm, crisp, shiny leaves. The leaves should be curly and a healthy green color.

Storing

To keep chicory and escarole fresh, place them in a perforated plastic bag or wrap them loosely in a wet cloth; they will keep for up to 1 week. Do not store them airtight, as these vegetables will spoil if they are not allowed to breathe. They should be dried as much as possible before refrigerating them to prevent spoiling or wilting. Wilted chicory and escarole can be revived by immersing them in ice water. These vegetables do not stand up well to freezing, however.

Wild chicory is very bitter; its short stems consist of green tooth-edged leaves similar to those of the dandelion.

escarole

Serving Ideas

Chicory and escarole are most often eaten raw but may also be cooked. They are used like lettuce and spinach, which they can replace or accompany in most recipes. Raw chicory and escarole are most commonly added to salads dressed in a vinaigrette or mayonnaise. Combined with other greens, they add flavor and nutrients, as well as visual appeal. Chicory and escarole can also be braised or used to flavor soups (add them at the end of cooking).

They are good braised and gratinéed, added to flans and quiches, or served with béchamel sauce. These are all excellent ways to use leaves that are no longer fresh. When preparing chicory or escarole, remove the outer leaves unless the vegetable is organically grown.

Chicory and Bacon Salad

SERVES 4

1 head chicory	1 tbsp. butter
1 small onion	Salt and pepper
1 tbsp. parsley leaves	2 tbsp. red wine vinegar
1 tbsp. chopped chives	1 tsp. Dijon mustard
¼ lb. (125 g) smoked bacon	⅓ cup (80 ml) olive oil

1. Remove the damaged outermost leaves from the head of chicory. Wash and drain the chicory, and tear it into bite-size pieces. Place in a salad bowl.

2. Peel and chop the onion, and chop the parsley. Add the onion, parsley, and chives to the chicory.

3. Remove the rind from the bacon and cut the bacon into small pieces. Brown them in the butter in a pan.

4. To prepare the vinaigrette, combine the salt, pepper, and wine vinegar in a small bowl. Add the mustard and olive oil and whisk vigorously. Pour over the salad and toss.

5. Top with the warm bacon, taking care not to add the cooking grease. Toss again.

Preparing

Rinse a head of chicory or escarole quickly in water (avoid soaking) just before serving in order to preserve the attractive appearance of the leaves. Remove any wilted leaves and tough ribs. Cut and season these vegetables at the last minute to prevent them from softening and from losing vitamins.

Nutritional Information

	raw wild chicory	chicory and escarole
water	92 %	94 %
protein	1.7 g	1.2 g
carbohydrates	4.7 g	3.4 g
calories	23	17
fat	0.3 g	0.2 g
		per 100 g

Wild chicory is an excellent source of folic acid, vitamin A, and potassium; it is also a good source of vitamin C, pantothenic acid, and copper. It contains magnesium, calcium, iron, riboflavin, vitamin B_6, and zinc.

Chicory and escarole are an excellent source of folic acid and potassium, and a good source of vitamin A; they also contain pantothenic acid, vitamin C, zinc, iron, copper, and calcium.

These vegetables are held to be diuretic, stomachic, remineralizing, and tonic, to stimulate the appetite, cleanse the intestines, and aid digestion. Coffee made with chicory root is said to be slightly laxative and to act as a tonic on the intestines.

Leaf Vegetables

91

Endive

Cichorium intybus, Compositae

A garden vegetable that was discovered in around 1850 when a Belgian peasant accidentally dug up wild chicory roots that resembled long, yellowish shoots. Following this discovery, a Belgian botanist by the name of Brézier made a number of improvements to the endive, to finally obtain the vegetable with which we are familiar today. It is also known as Belgian endive and by its Flemish name, *witloof,* meaning "white leaf." Although the endive was slow to become known in North America, it is now cultivated there, particularly in Quebec. In Europe it is cultivated in France, Holland, Belgium, and Italy.

Cultivation of the endive involves a rather complex process. In spring, a shoot develops at soil level; it is harvested in fall when its roots have become well developed. The freshly gathered roots are stored outdoors for at least 1 month, during which time the cool temperatures stimulate the metabolism of the roots, making production of the endive possible. These roots are then "forced," meaning that they are transplanted in a dark, warm environment (to keep them from turning green and to preserve their mild flavor), where they develop into the endive, which is harvested 3 to 4 weeks later.

Endives usually measure between 4 and 8 inches in length and about 2 inches in diameter. The crisp leaves are a creamy white color, with a hint of yellow around the edge. They have a slightly bitter taste. A new variety called red endive has recently become available; a cross between white endive and red radicchio, it is milder tasting than the white endive. It cannot be cooked, however, as this causes it to discolor and to lose its distinctive flavor.

Buying

Choose firm heads with compact and creamy white leaves. The best specimens are 5 times longer than they are wide and have only two visible outer leaves. Avoid endives with brown-edged leaves, as well as limp endives with green leaves, which are an indication of bitterness.

Preparing

It is not necessary to wash endives; simply wipe the outer leaves with a damp cloth. Soaking is not recommended, as it tends to bring out the bitterness of this vegetable. Endives should be cut and seasoned at the last minute before serving to prevent them from darkening on contact with the air. Endive leaves can be left whole or chopped. To separate the leaves, cut out a small cone about an inch long at the base of the endive, where most of the bitterness is concentrated.

Baked Endive with Ham

SERVES 4

8 endives
4 tbsp. butter
Salt
Juice of ½ lemon
1 pinch of sugar
8 thin slices of ham

2 cups (500 ml)
    béchamel sauce
½ cup (125 ml)
    grated Gruyère
    cheese
Butter

1. Wipe the outside of the endives and remove the outer leaves. Remove the cone-shaped heart, using a small knife.

2. First stew the endives: melt the butter in a skillet and arrange the endives side by side, adding a pinch of salt and the lemon juice. Sprinkle with the sugar, and cook over very gentle heat for 45 minutes.

3. Preheat the oven to 400°F (200°C). Grease a baking dish.

4. Remove the endives from the skillet and drain them; roll each endive up in a slice of ham. Arrange the rolled endives in the baking dish, and top with the heated béchamel sauce. Sprinkle with the Gruyère and a few dabs of butter. Bake in the oven for about 20 minutes.

Serving Ideas

 Endives are somewhat of a delicacy and can be consumed raw or cooked. Raw endive is often served in salads, sprinkled with vinaigrette or mayonnaise. The leaves can also be stuffed with cheese. Combining endive with other greens makes for an attractive, tasty, and nutritious dish. Endives are also braised or steamed and served with a béchamel sauce or simply topped with a little butter and seasoned with a few herbs. A classic way of serving endives is to steam them and wrap them in a slice of ham, after which they are baked au gratin.

Cooking

Endive can be braised in the oven for 30 to 45 minutes or steamed for 25 to 35 minutes.

Storing

Placed in a perforated plastic bag or loosely wrapped in a damp cloth, endive will keep for 5 to 7 days in the refrigerator. It is best eaten as soon as possible, however. Endives do not freeze well.

Nutritional Information

	raw
water	95%
protein	1 g
fat	0.1 g
carbohydrates	3.2 g
calories	15
	per 100 g

Endives are an excellent source of folic acid and a good source of potassium, as well as containing vitamin C, pantothenic acid, riboflavin, and zinc.

They are said to be stimulate the appetite, cleanse the system, aid the liver, and function as a diuretic, digestive, remineralizer, and tonic.

shoot

Lettuce

Lactuca sativa, Compositae

Boston lettuce

This vegetable plant is a native of the eastern Mediterranean and western Asia. The cultivation of lettuce can be traced back as far as 4500 B.C., at which time it was most likely grown for the oil of its seeds. It has been well established that the Persians consumed lettuce leaves around the year 600 B.C. Firmly implanted in the Mediterranean basin, lettuce was held in high esteem by the Greeks and Romans, both as a vegetable and as a remedy. Columbus is said to have introduced lettuce into the Caribbean.

The word "lettuce" comes from the Latin *lactuca,* which is derived from *lactus,* meaning "milk"; it was so named for the milky sap secreted by the stems when they are cut. Lettuce is an annual plant that comes in about 100 varieties. The crisp, tender leaves are usually green but may also be red; they vary in shape and flavor, depending on the variety. The most common varieties on the market are head lettuce, butterhead lettuce, leaf lettuce, romaine (also known as cos) lettuce, and celtuce.

Head lettuce (var. *capitata*). In North America, the most common type of head lettuce is *iceberg lettuce,* so called because when it first began to be commercialized on a large scale, it had to be covered with ice to keep it fresh during shipping. The leaves of this lettuce are crisp and green on the outside, while the inner leaves, which are not exposed to light, are rather yellowish or whitish. This variety is less colorful and less nutritious than the other varieties.

Butterhead lettuce (var. *capitata*). *Bibb* and *Boston* are the two most popular types of butterhead lettuce in North America. There are some variations between these two groups in terms of color, size, and appearance. Both are known for the tenderness of their large leaves, which form a loose head and are easily separated from the stem. Boston lettuce has larger leaves and is a paler green than Bibb. Some varieties of Bibb have reddish leaves. All butterhead lettuces have yellowish leaves at the heart. This variety of lettuce is widely appreciated for its delicate flavor, particularly in Europe.

Leaf lettuce (var. *crispa*). A type of lettuce with loose, curly leaves that do not grow in a head. There are a number of varieties of leaf lettuce, all of which have long, broad leaves that are tender and flavorful; the leaves can be green or reddish, or simply tinged with red at the tips. Some varieties of leaf lettuce have a slight hazelnut-like flavor.

Romaine lettuce (var. *longifolia*). The long, deep green leaves of this lettuce are quite firm and crisp, with a stiff central rib that is particularly crisp and fibrous. The more tender inner leaves are a lighter green color and have a yellowish rib.

Celtuce (var. *angustana*). This lettuce is a cross between celery and lettuce, with a flavor that is reminiscent of both of these vegetables. Relatively rare in North America, celtuce is well known in Asia, where its stems are consumed raw or cooked like celery, while the leaves are usually served cooked.

Buying

Look for a lettuce with a dense heart (in varieties where this applies) and glossy, firm, crisp leaves. Avoid soft, dull-looking, rusting, sodden, or yellowing lettuces, as well as those with dried-out or brown edges.

Nutritional Information

	Boston	iceberg	leaf	romaine	celtuce
water	95.6%	95.9%	94%	94.9%	94.5%
protein	0.7 g	0.6 g	0.8 g	1 g	0.5 g
fat	0.1 g	0.1 g	0.2 g	0.1 g	0.2 g
carbohydrates	1.3 g	1.2 g	2.1 g	1.4 g	2.2 g
calories	8	8	11	9	13

per cup

Lettuce is rich in water and low in calories. Most varieties are rich in folic acid, although the vitamin and mineral content can differ from one variety to another.

As a general rule, the greener the lettuce, the more vitamins and minerals it contains. Lettuce is said to stimulate the appetite and to have analgesic, emollient, and sedative properties; it is recommended for insomnia, nervous or sexual excitement, and as a cough remedy. In the Middle Ages, monks were advised to eat lettuce to purge the body of lust.

Caesar Salad

SERVES 4

1 head romaine lettuce
2 eggs
4 anchovy fillets in oil
1 clove garlic
2 oz. (60 g) softened
    butter
3 slices sandwich bread

4 tbsp. olive oil
Juice of ½ lemon
Salt and ground
    pepper
1 tbsp. capers
⅓ cup (80 ml) grated
    Parmesan cheese

1. Preheat the oven to 350°F (175°C).

2. Shred, wash, and drain the lettuce. Place it in a salad bowl.

3. Boil the eggs for 10 minutes or until hard. Rinse the eggs under cold water, remove the shell, and cut them into quarters.

4. Drain and chop the anchovies.

5. Peel and chop the garlic. Mix garlic with the softened butter.

6. Remove the crusts from the bread and spread garlic butter on each slice. Cut the slices into small cubes. Place on a baking sheet and bake in the oven until the cubes are crisp and golden (2 minutes).

7. Mix together the oil, lemon juice, and salt and pepper.

8. Pour the dressing over the romaine lettuce and toss it well.

9. Add the eggs, anchovies, and capers. Top with the garlic croutons and sprinkle with the Parmesan cheese.

Serving Ideas

Lettuce is usually eaten raw, but it may also be cooked. Like parsley, it has many uses. Raw, it is most commonly topped with dressing or mayonnaise and served as a salad, or added to sandwiches. To enhance the appearance, flavor, and nutritional value of a salad, try combining several different types of lettuce.

Lettuce is often braised or used to flavor soups. Add the shredded leaves at the end of cooking; the heat of the broth will cook them sufficiently. This is an excellent way to use leftover lettuce or wilted leaves. Discard the outermost leaves of the lettuce, unless it it organic or hydroponic lettuce. Lettuce leaves can also be puréed and made into a delicious soup.

Lettuce leaves, peas, and baby onions are used to prepare a vegetable side dish called *petits pois à la française*. Caesar salad is a classic salad made with romaine lettuce.

Lettuce is an annual plant that comes in about 100 varieties. The crisp, tender leaves are usually green but may also be red; they vary in shape and flavor, depending on the variety.

romaine lettuce

Leaf Vegetables

95

leaf lettuce

iceberg lettuce

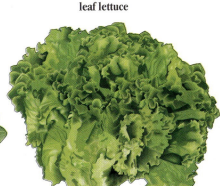

celtuce

Preparing

Remove the wilted outermost leaves and the tougher bottom part of the rib. Wash the leaves well to rid them of any soil, sand, and insects. Varieties such as leaf lettuce need to be washed thoroughly in plenty of water; change the water several times and shake the leaves gently if necessary, without soaking them. Drain the lettuce well, using a salad spinner for best results. Dressing will be more evenly distributed if the lettuce has been well dried. Shred the lettuce by hand rather than cutting it with a knife, which may cause it to rust. The leaves will come off easily if the heart is removed first. To prevent its leaves from wilting, lettuce should be taken out of the refrigerator and seasoned with dressing just before serving. The more bitter varieties of lettuce can be blanched for a few minutes before being used.

Storing

Lettuce must be properly stored to prevent it from spoiling or wilting. Leaf and romaine lettuce should be washed before being placed in the refrigerator in order to rid them of soil, insects, and, very frequently, excess moisture, which can cause them to deteriorate quickly.

Boston, Bibb, and iceberg lettuce are very fragile and should be washed only at the last minute. Tender varieties spoil more quickly and should be eaten without delay. Boston and leaf lettuce will keep for 2 to 3 days, iceberg lettuce can be kept for 1 to 2 weeks, and romaine lettuce for 3 to 5 days. All types of lettuce should be stored in the refrigerator, wrapped loosely in a damp cloth or placed in an airtight container. Limp or wilted lettuce can be revived by plunging it in cold water. Keep lettuce away from ethylene-producing fruits and vegetables such as pears, apples, bananas, tomatoes, and cantaloupes, as this gas can cause lettuce leaves to turn brown.

Lettuce is too fragile to be frozen.

Violet

Viola odorata, **Violaceae**

A hardy perennial, the violet is a decorative plant whose leaves and flowers are used in cooking as well as for medicinal purposes. The violet belongs to a large family of some 500 varieties which includes, notably, the pansy. Like the violet, wild pansies also have edible leaves.

Violets may grow to be approximately 6 inches in height. The plant's leaves and flowers have a subtle and delicate flavor. In the past, violets were used mainly as a cough suppressant; today they are frequently used in confectionery.

Buying

Violets purchased at plant and flower shops are not intended for human consumption and may be treated with harmful chemicals; buy edible violet leaves and flowers at fine grocers instead.

Storing

The leaves and flowers of the violet are fragile and should be eaten as fresh as possible. They will, however, keep for a few days in the refrigerator.

Serving Ideas

The leaves and flowers of the violet can be used fresh, dried, or candied. They add a decorative touch to salads, pastries, and drinks, as well as lending an aromatic note to desserts. Violets may also be added to stuffing for poultry or fish.

Garnish salads with the flowers after the dressing has been added in order to prevent them from absorbing the oil. The essential oil extracted from violets is used as a flavoring in pastries, ice cream, sweets, and liquor, as well as being widely used in the manufacture of cosmetics.

Nutritional Information

Violets have a number of medicinal properties; they are notably used as an expectorant, to soothe migraines, and to bring down fever. A poultice made from violet leaves is also used to relieve skin irritations.

Violets make a delicious tea: steep 1 teaspoon of the leaves or flowers in 1 cup of boiling water for 10 minutes.

Nasturtium

Tropaeolum majus, **Tropaeolaceae**

An ornamental plant native to South America and having edible leaves, flowers, and buds. In tropical climates, the nasturtium is a hardy perennial, while in temperate climates it grows as an annual. The nasturtium was originally called "Indian cress," due to its sharp flavor, reminiscent of cress, and to the confusion of America with the Indies.

There are a hundred different varieties of the nasturtium, some of which may reach a height of 10 to 13 feet. The common variety is low and compact, rarely growing more than 1 foot high. Its leaves are round and flat, and its delicate flowers are shades of bright yellow, orange, and red.

Buying

Nasturtium leaves and flowers should be bought at specialized grocers, as those sold at plant and flower shops are not intended for consumption and may be treated with harmful chemicals.

Serving Ideas

The young leaves and the flowers of the nasturtium are decorative and lend a spicy note to salads; add the flowers to the salad after the vinaigrette, in order to prevent them from absorbing the oil. The flowers may also be used to garnish soups, vegetable dishes, poultry, fish, red meats, pastries, and drinks. Nasturtium buds and the tender green fruits may be pickled in tarragon vinegar and used in place of capers.

Nutritional Information

The nasturtium has a number of medicinal properties: it is used as a stimulant, an expectorant, an antiscorbutic, a diuretic, and as a topical remedy. A lotion made from the nasturtium and applied to the scalp is said to prevent hair loss. Nasturtium seeds are also used as a purgative.

Storing

The leaves and flowers of the nasturtium are delicate and should be eaten as fresh as possible.

Leaf Vegetables

97

Cabbage

Brassica oleracea, Cruciferae

A garden plant believed to have been brought from Asia Minor to Europe around 600 B.C. Although a number of varieties of cabbage were developed by the Greeks and Romans in the Mediterranean region, these varieties did not yet form the closed head of cabbage that we know today. The ability of cabbage to withstand cold climates favored the spread of its cultivation across northern Europe, and it came to be held in high esteem in Germany, Poland, and Russia in particular. Today the largest producers of cabbage include Russia, China, South Korea, Japan, and Poland. Cabbage has long been valued for its many medicinal properties; it was considered a veritable panacea by the Greeks and Romans.

Cabbage belongs to the large Cruciferae family, which includes kale, broccoli, collards, Brussels sprouts, salad Savoy, Chinese cabbage, cauliflower, Savoy cabbage, sea kale, and kohlrabi. It consists of superposed layers of thick leaves that may or may not form a head, that may be smooth or curled, and that vary in color from green to white or red. Because they are sheltered from direct sunlight, the inner leaves are paler than those on the outside. A cabbage head usually ranges in weight from 2 to 7 pounds and has a diameter of between 4 and 8 inches. There are roughly 400 varieties of cabbage; although they all share certain structural characteristics and medicinal properties, they vary greatly in shape, type, and color. The different types include inflorescent cabbage (broccoli, cauliflower), stem cabbage (kohlrabi, kale, collards, Chinese cabbage), and smooth-leaf and curled-leaf cabbage (Savoy cabbage, green, white, and red cabbage).

Leaf Vegetables

98

green cabbage

Savoy cabbage

white cabbage

red cabbage

Buying

 Choose a cabbage that is heavy and compact; it should have shiny, crisp, well-colored leaves that are unblemished and free of cracks and bruises.

Preparing

Some cabbages may contain worms; for many people this is a welcome indication that no chemical pesticides were used during cultivation. To rid cabbage of any clinging insects, soak it in salt water or vinegar water for about 15 minutes. Cabbage containing no worms can simply be washed under running water after removal of the thicker and more fibrous outer leaves.

Stuffed Cabbage Leaves

SERVES 6

1 medium green cabbage	3 tbsp. chopped fresh
1 clove garlic	parsley
1 tbsp. butter	1 cup cooked rice
½ cup (125 ml) finely	2 tbsp. tomato purée
chopped onion	Juice of ½ lemon
1 lb. (500 g) ground meat	½ tsp. lemon zest
(beef, veal, or pork)	10 oz. (1¼ cups) beef stock
Salt and ground pepper	10 oz. (1¼ cups) tomato
1 pinch oregano	juice

1. Preheat the oven to 350°F (175°C).

2. Remove the core of the cabbage and plunge the cabbage into a large pot of salted boiling water. Boil the cabbage, uncovered, for about 10 minutes or until the outer leaves are tender. Drain and let cool.

3. Peel and finely chop the garlic.

4. Melt the butter in a pan and brown the onion, garlic, and meat over moderate heat. Season, and add the oregano and parsley. Add the cooked rice, the tomato purée, and the lemon juice and zest. Stir for 2 minutes. Then remove from the heat and let cool.

5. Gently separate the cabbage leaves, discarding those that are too big. Pat 12 leaves dry with paper towels and lay them out; place an equal amount of stuffing on each. Roll the cabbage leaves by folding the outer edges toward the inside.

6. Butter a baking dish and place the rolls in it.

7. In a bowl, combine the beef stock and the tomato juice. Pour this over the rolls and cover the dish with aluminum foil. Bake for at least 1 hour, or until the rolls are tender.

Serving Ideas

Cabbage can be eaten raw or cooked. It can also be salted to make sauerkraut. This process involves fermenting the finely shredded cabbage in salt to produce lactic acid. This fermentation makes the cabbage easier to digest and alters its texture and flavor while preserving most of its vitamins and mineral salts. Raw cabbage can be shredded or chopped to make a delicious salad known as coleslaw. Coleslaw is tastier if it is left to sit in the refrigerator for at least 30 minutes before serving. Cabbage is used in both rustic and refined dishes and may be cooked in any number of ways; it can be steamed, braised, sautéed, or stuffed. It is often added to soups, stews, and stir-fries, and it blends well with carrots, onions, and potatoes as well as bacon and sausages.

Cooking

When cooked too long or in too much water, cabbage tends to lose its color and become pasty; it also loses some of its nutrients and flavor and acquires a strong and unpleasant odor. Use very little water (about ¾ inch will do), and avoid adding acidic ingredients such as vinegar or lemon juice (except in the case of white cabbage) or alkaline ingredients such as baking soda. Add the cabbage only once the water is boiling, and cook it briefly (5 to 8 minutes for shredded cabbage and 10 to 15 minutes for cabbage cut into quarters). To prevent red cabbage from discoloring, use a stainless-steel knife to cut it, and when using it in a salad, sprinkle it with a bit of vinegar. Adding an acidic ingredient to the cooking water preserves its color, while too much water detracts from its color.

Leaf Vegetables

99

Storing

Cabbage will keep for about 2 weeks in the vegetable drawer or in a perforated plastic bag in the refrigerator. Because it takes on a more pronounced odor as it ages, especially once cut, it should be stored wrapped and placed away from other foods. Cabbage can also be kept in a cold room under suitable conditions; that is, at a humidity of 90% to 95% and at a maximum temperature of 38°F, but preferably closer to 32°F. Cabbage can be frozen after being blanched: 1 minute for shredded cabbage and 2 minutes for cabbage cut into wedges. The texture will be less crunchy once the cabbage is thawed, however. Cabbages can also be dried.

Nutritional Information

	raw	*cooked*
water	93%	93.6%
protein	1.2 g	1.0 g
fat	0.2 g	0.2 g
carbohydrate	5.4 g	4.8 g
fiber	1.8 g	1.7 g
calories	24	21
		per 100 g

Raw cabbage is an excellent source of vitamin C and folic acid, and a good source of potassium; it also contains vitamin B$_6$. Cooked cabbage is a good source of vitamin C and potassium and contains folic acid. Cabbage is said to have cancer-inhibiting properties, and its juice is held to be effective in the treatment of stomach ulcers. It is also credited with the properties of an antidiarrheal, an antibiotic, and a remineralizer; it stimulates the appetite and combats scurvy. In phytotherapy, cabbage is used to treat over 100 illnesses. Cabbage contains a flatulence-inducing substance as well as sulfurous substances that are responsible for its characteristic flavor and odor. These sulfurous substances are released when the cabbage is cut and become active on contact with air.

Sea kale

Crambe maritima, **Cruciferae**

Like the endive, the leaves of sea kale are often covered to delay their development and to obtain very meaty, almost yellow stems.

A vegetable native to western Europe, sea kale is more widely known in Europe than in North America. It is now a protected species in France, where it has practically disappeared from the coasts of Brittany. Sea kale is still cultivated in France and England, and also grows along the shores of the Atlantic Ocean, the Baltic Sea, and the Black Sea.

A hardy perennial measuring between 6 inches and 2 feet in height, sea kale has pale green leaves with wide, fleshy, edible leaf stalks. Like the endive, they are often covered to delay their development and to obtain very meaty, almost yellow stems. There are between 20 and 30 varieties of sea kale.

Nutritional Information

	cooked
water	95%
protein	1.4 g
carbohydrates	0.8 g
	per 100 g

Sea kale leaves are said to have diuretic properties and to combat scurvy.

Cooking

When steaming sea kale leaves, allow approximately 10 minutes.

Serving Ideas

 Boiled sea kale is especially delicious topped with a spicy sauce or simply sautéed with garlic. Its blanched stems are edible and may be served like asparagus, with butter or a light sauce. They are most flavorful when they are around 8 inches long. Sea kale can also be eaten raw, dressed in a vinaigrette.

Storing

 Sea kale will keep for 2 to 3 days in the refrigerator, or for 1 year in the freezer after being blanched.

Collards

Brassica oleracea var. *viridis,* **Cruciferae**

A garden plant originating in the eastern Mediterranean region or Asia, collards are one of the oldest and hardiest members of the large cabbage family. Like kale, they can withstand both high and low temperatures (as low as 5°F). Collards were introduced to North America by African slaves and for a long time were consumed almost exclusively in the southern States.

The leaves are smooth, thick, and veined, and may have flat or curled edges, depending on the variety. The whitish central ribs are tough and rather unpalatable. While the flavor of collards is quite pronounced, it is milder than that of borecole.

Buying

 Choose collards with firm, brightly colored, relatively small leaves that are unblemished and free of mold.

Preparing

Wash collards well under running water to rid the leaves of sand and soil. Separate each leaf from the central rib, which can be discarded unless the collards are young and tender.

Serving Ideas

Fresh collards add a spicy note to salads, but should be used in moderation because of their unusual texture and strong flavor. To moderate the flavor, blanch the collards for a few minutes before cooking them. They can be prepared in much the same manner as spinach.

Collards blend particularly well with barley, brown rice, kasha, potatoes, and beans, and they add spice to soups and stews. They are delicious topped with a sauce and gratinéed, or puréed, either on their own or combined with mashed potatoes, sweet potatoes, or legumes. They also make an interesting addition to omelets and quiches. They can be steamed to the desired degree of firmness and accompanied with smoked pork. Collard leaves can also be served with a little butter and lemon juice.

Storing

Store collards, unwashed, in the refrigerator, wrapped in a damp paper towel and a perforated plastic bag. They will keep for several days, but are tastier and less bitter when eaten without delay. Collards can be frozen after being blanched for 2 or 3 minutes, or until the leaves become slightly soft.

Cooking

 Collards can be steamed, braised, or stir-fried.

Nutritional Information

	raw	*cooked*
water	90.5%	92%
protein	1.6 g	1.4 g
fat	0.2 g	0.2 g
carbohydrates	7.1 g	6.1 g
calories	31	27
		per 100 g

Raw collards are an excellent source of vitamin A and a good source of vitamin C; they contain potassium and folic acid. Cooked, they are an excellent source of vitamin A and contain some vitamin C and potassium.

Kale

Brassica oleracea var. *acephala f. sabellica,* **Cruciferae**

A garden vegetable originally cultivated in the Mediterranean region, kale (also known as borecole and curly kale) was an important crop in Roman times and became a staple food among peasants during the Middle Ages. It was brought to the United States from England in the 17th century.

Kale is one of the hardiest members of the cabbage family; it is able to withstand temperatures as low as 5°F, although it is not quite as tolerant of warm temperatures. Because of its ability to withstand cold and the ease with which it grows, kale has long been a popular winter vegetable, particularly in Scotland, Germany, Holland, and Scandinavia. Today it is consumed in many countries throughout the world.

Kale has large, fibrous, finely curled leaves. They have a pungent flavor and vary in color from light to dark green, with some varieties having a bluish green hue. The leaves do not form a head – hence the Latin varietal name *acephala,* meaning "without a head." Rather, they are attached to thin whitish stems that are very fibrous and measure between 12 and 16 inches in length. Curly kale is a highly decorative plant, and some varieties have been developed specifically for ornamental purposes (see *Ornamental kale*).

Buying

Look for kale with firm, brightly colored, and relatively small leaves; it should be free of spots and mold.

Nutritional Information

	raw	*cooked*
water	84.5%	91%
protein	3.3 g	1.9 g
fat	0.7 g	0.4 g
carbohydrates	10 g	5.6 g
fiber	1.5 g	2.0 g
calories	50	32
		per 100 g

Kale is an excellent source of vitamins A and C and of potassium; it is also a good source of vitamin B_6 and copper, and provides folic acid, calcium, iron, thiamine, riboflavin, niacin, and zinc. Cooked kale is an excellent source of vitamins A and C and a good source of potassium; it also contains copper, vitamin B_6, calcium, iron, and folic acid.

Preparing

Separate and trim the leaves, and wash them thoroughly under running water or in vinegar water to rid them of any remaining soil or insects.

Serving Ideas

Because it is fairly tough and has a pronounced flavor, kale is rarely eaten raw; used in moderation, however, fresh kale can add a spicy note to salads. Its strong flavor also goes well in soups and stews. Blanch it for a few minutes in salted boiling water before cooking to moderate its bitterness. Kale is delicious dressed in a sauce and gratinéed, or puréed on its own or with potatoes.

Cooking

Kale can be boiled or steamed (allow 20 to 30 minutes), braised in a casserole, stuffed, or added to a stir-fry.

Storing

Store kale with its leaves close together in a perforated plastic bag in the refrigerator. It will keep for 5 to 10 days, but it is tastier and less bitter when consumed as soon as possible. Kale can also be frozen after being blanched for 2 to 3 minutes, or until the leaves become slightly soft.

Ornamental kale

Brassica oleracea var. *acephala*, **Cruciferae**

A leafy vegetable belonging to the large cabbage family, ornamental kale, a close relative of kale, is sometimes also called salad savoy. It is a newcomer on the market, having been commercialized by a California vegetable grower, John Moore, who discovered it growing in a garden in Sweden and was so impressed by its beauty that he decided to improve its flavor.

Ornamental kale is indeed a decorative plant, more closely resembling a flower than a vegetable; its loose, curly leaves are connected to short stems and vary in color from pinkish purple to cream, green, or white. While crunchy, it is tenderer than cabbage although firmer than lettuce. Its mellow flavor is reminiscent of that of broccoli and cauliflower.

Serving Ideas

Ornamental kale can be eaten raw or cooked. Raw, it adds crunch and color to salads. It also adds a colorful note to soups, rice, beans, pasta, omelets, and tofu. Its attractive appearance makes it useful as a decorative lining for serving dishes or as a natural bowl to hold dips, appetizers, cheeses, potato salad, and rice or fruit salads.

Cooking

Ornamental kale can be eaten steamed, braised, or stir-fried. Avoid overcooking to preserve its color, flavor, and nutritional value. To help it keep its color during cooking, add an acid ingredient such as vinegar or lemon juice.

Storing

Store ornamental kale unwashed in the refrigerator; wrap it in a damp paper towel and place it in a perforated plastic bag. Its flavor is best when consumed as soon as possible, but it will keep for up to 1 week in the refrigerator.

Buying

Choose ornamental kale with firm, brightly colored leaves that are free of spots and mold.

Preparing

Separate each leaf, and trim and discard the stem if it is tough. Wash the leaves under running water.

Nutritional Information

water	92%
protein	2.1 g
fat	0.4 g
carbohydrates	3 g
calories	12
	per 100 g

Ornamental kale is rich in vitamins A and C, as well as in potassium, phosphorus, calcium, and iron.

Brussels sprouts

Brassica oleracea var. *gemmifera*, **Cruciferae**

A garden plant whose exact origin is not known. Although it is related to the wild variety of cabbage, which was used for thousands of years, it would appear that the Brussels sprout as we know it today was developed only a few centuries ago in northern Europe, close to Brussels, the city after which it is named.

Brussels sprouts resemble small cabbages and are found growing densely in the leaf axils of upright stems that can grow as high as 3 feet. Each stem can bear as many as 20 to 40 heads. They are usually harvested when they reach a diameter of about 1 inch, when they are at their most tender.

Preparing

Remove the stems and any yellowish or loose leaves, and wash the sprouts well under running water or soak them for 15 minutes in lemon or vinegar water to rid them of any clinging insects.

Nutritional Information

	cooked
water	87%
protein	2.5 g
fat	0.5 g
carbohydrates	8.7 g
fiber	4.3 g
calories	39
	per 100 g

Brussels sprouts are an excellent source of vitamin C, folic acid, and potassium; they also contain vitamin B_6, iron, thiamine, magnesium, vitamin A, phosphorus, and niacin. Like all members of the cabbage family, they are thought to have cancer-inhibiting properties.

Buying

Choose firm and compact Brussels sprouts that are bright green in color and have no yellowing leaves. Select similarly sized specimens to ensure uniform cooking.

Serving Ideas

Unlike the other members of the cabbage family, Brussels sprouts are only eaten cooked. They are often served as a vegetable side dish, either on their own or with butter or a béchamel sauce. They may also be served au gratin, added to soups or stews, stir-fried, or puréed with potatoes. Once cooked, they are also good served cold in a salad.

Cooking

Brussels sprouts are usually cooked whole. To shorten the cooking time and to ensure even cooking, cut a shallow "X" in the stem end before cooking.

Brussels sprouts should be cooked rapidly to prevent them from becoming pasty. To boil them, use about ¾ inch of water and cook for 8 to 12 minutes. When steaming or braising Brussels sprouts, allow about 15 minutes. The cooking time depends on how tender one likes one's sprouts.

Storing

Brussels sprouts will keep for 3 or 4 days, unwashed, in a perforated plastic bag in the vegetable compartment of the refrigerator. They may also be frozen after being blanched for 3 minutes in the case of small Brussels sprouts and 5 minutes for larger specimens. Frozen Brussels sprouts will keep for about 1 year.

Chinese cabbage

Brassica rapa, **Cruciferae**

A plant believed to have originated in China and eastern Asia. As many as 33 varieties of Chinese cabbage have been identified in Asia, few of which are known in the West, although some varieties are gradually beginning to appear in Western markets. While this vegetable has been known for thousands of years in China, Europeans only discovered it in the early 18th century. The most common varieties in the West are celery cabbage or pe-tsai, pak-choi or bok choy, and gai-lohn. There is much confusion surrounding the scientific and common names for these vegetables.

pak-choi

Celery cabbage or **pe-tsai** (var. *pekinensis*) is native to China, where it has been consumed for thousands of years. In northern China, it is eaten on a daily basis, often marinated. Celery cabbage is similar in shape to romaine lettuce and was the first variety to gain recognition in the West. The most common varieties are the Michihili, which can reach 18 inches in length and 4 inches in width and has flattened leaves and ribs, and the Napa, which is broad and compact. The pale green outer leaves are darker than the inner leaves, which are greenish white in color. The water content of celery cabbage is higher than that of the other varieties of cabbage, making it crisper and more refreshing. It is also less fibrous and has a more subtle and pleasant flavor than head cabbage.

Pak-choi or **bok choy** (var. *chinensis*) is also a native of China and was introduced into the United States by Chinese prospectors during the gold rush of the late 19th century. Pak-choi resembles celery and Swiss chard; its whitish ribs are fleshy, crisp, and mild flavored, and its veined dark green leaves have a more subtle flavor than those of head cabbage. There are many varieties of pak-choi, some of which are short-ribbed while others have long ribs.

Gai-lohn (var. *alboglabra*) is also called *tsai shim* or "Chinese broccoli," and is indeed a type of broccoli. The leaves and thin floral stems are edible. It has been said that gai-lohn is the most delicate-tasting member of the cabbage family.

Serving Ideas

Celery cabbage can be eaten raw, cooked, or marinated. It should be washed at the last minute. Remove the desired number of leaves and trim the base of each. Wash, drain, and use them cooked or raw. Raw celery cabbage is delicious in salads, where its crisp ribs can even replace celery. Cooked, it adds delicate flavor to soups, stews, pasta dishes, and stir-fries. Marinated celery cabbage is particularly delicious as a salad side dish. To prepare it, chop the celery cabbage coarsely, sprinkle it with salt, and leave it to sweat for a few hours, stirring occasionally, until it is slightly soft. Drain thoroughly and add 2 or 3 crushed garlic cloves, a little grated ginger, some finely chopped scallions, rice vinegar, soy sauce, and a pinch each of sugar, salt, and cayenne pepper. Pak-choi can also be eaten raw, cooked, or marinated. Trim the base of as many ribs as needed, and cut the ribs into large chunks after removing the leafy part.

Pak-choi is delicious in a stir-fry mixed with other Asian vegetables; cook the ribs first, adding the leaves at the last minute since they require a very short cooking time. The ribs should be cooked for only a few minutes in order to keep them crisp.

Pak-choi can be added to soups, gratinéed, mixed with rice, or served as a vegetable side dish. The ribs and leaves of pak-choi are often used separately; the ribs can replace celery and the leaves can be used in place of spinach or chard. Gai-lohn is consumed raw or cooked and can be prepared and served like broccoli, although it requires a shorter cooking time. It too makes a delicious addition to a stir-fry.

Buying

When buying Chinese cabbage, look for compact, firm, fresh ribs with no brown spots. The leaves can be slightly wilted, particularly if they are going to be cooked.

Nutritional Information

	cooked celery cabbage	*cooked pak-choi*
water	95%	95.5%
fat	0.2 g	0.2 g
protein	1.5 g	1.6 g
carbohydrates	2.4 g	1.8 g
fiber	1.6 g	
calories	13	12
		per 100 g

Cooked celery cabbage is a good source of vitamin C, folic acid, and potassium, and contains some vitamin A. Cooked pak-choi is an excellent source of potassium and vitamin A, and a good source of vitamin C and folic acid, as well as containing vitamin B_6, calcium, and iron. Gai-lohn is rich in vitamins A and C, calcium, and iron.

Storing

The different varieties of Chinese cabbage can be stored in a perforated plastic bag in the vegetable compartment of the refrigerator. Celery cabbage will keep for about 2 weeks, but it is crisper and more flavorful when eaten as soon as possible. Pak-choi and gai-lohn are more perishable and will keep for only a few days; wash pak-choi at the last minute.

Leaf Vegetables

105

celery cabbage   **Gai-lohn**

Asparagus

Asparagus officinalis, Liliaceae

A perennial garden plant originating in the eastern Mediterranean region. Remnants of wild varieties of asparagus have been discovered in northern and southern Africa, and archeologists believe that it may also have been cultivated in ancient Egypt. Consumed for over 2,000 years, asparagus was originally valued for its medicinal properties. It fell into obscurity during the Middle Ages, although it continued to be cultivated by the Arabs. Under the influence of Louis XIV, asparagus was rediscovered in the 18th century, and since then several new varieties have been developed. Today the principal producers of asparagus are the United States, Europe, Mexico, and Taiwan.

Asparagus is actually a young edible shoot, commonly called a "spear"; the spear rises from an underground stem called a "crown," which is capable of producing spears for 15 to 20 years. Most asparagus is harvested in spring, when it is 6 to 8 inches high and has tender, fleshy spears and tight, compact heads. Once they reach maturity, the asparagus stalks become woody and fernlike foliage grows from the heads, making them inedible. Although grown on quite a large scale and in many countries, asparagus is available in abundance only from March to late June.

There are over 300 varieties of asparagus, only 20 of which are edible. They are divided into three main categories:

• Green asparagus. This is the most common type of asparagus. It is harvested at a height of about 8 inches.

• White asparagus. Grown in the dark (covered with soil to keep it from turning green), white asparagus is harvested as soon as it emerges from the ground. Although more tender than the green variety, it tends to be less flavorful and is also more expensive, since more work is required to grow it.

• Purple asparagus. This variety has a fruity flavor and is harvested when only 2 or 3 inches high.

Buying

Choose asparagus with firm, crisp stalks and compact, brightly colored heads with no traces of rust. Selecting similarly sized specimens will help ensure even cooking. Avoid yellowish asparagus with soft stalks and heads that are beginning to flower, which are signs of age.

Serving Ideas

Asparagus is always eaten cooked, either boiled or steamed. It can be served warm or hot, dressed in a generous helping of butter or hollandaise sauce. It is also good cold, topped with a dressing, mayonnaise, or mustard sauce. Puréed asparagus can be used to make soups, soufflés, or veloutés. Asparagus can also be used, cut or whole, to garnish omelets, poultry, quiches, salads, or pasta dishes. It also makes an interesting addition to a stir-fry.

white asparagus

Preparing

Before cooking asparagus, cut off the base of the stalk (which can be cooked and puréed to make a soup). While it is not necessary to peel asparagus, it should be washed well in cold water to rid it of sand and soil.

1 *Cut off the ends of the asparagus stalks with a sharp knife.*

2 *Peel the asparagus from top to bottom.*

3 *Tie the asparagus in bundles.*

4 *Bundled asparagus is easier to remove from the pan after cooking.*

Polish-Style Asparagus

2 lb. (1 kg) fresh
asparagus
2 hard-boiled eggs
3 tbsp. chopped fresh parsley

¼ lb. (125 g) butter
3 tbsp. fresh bread
crumbs

1. Cut off the tough base of the asparagus stalks. Peel and wash the spears, and divide them evenly into four bunches. Tie the bundles with string.

2. Immerse the asparagus in a large skillet filled with salted boiling water, and blanch for about 10 minutes, or until a spear is easily pierced with the tip of a sharp knife. Drain well and remove the strings. Arrange the spears in a serving dish and keep warm.

3. While the asparagus is cooking, peel the eggs and discard the whites. Mash the yolks with a fork in a small bowl, and stir in the parsley.

4. Melt the butter in a small saucepan, and add the bread crumbs, stirring until they are golden brown. Remove from the heat.

5. Sprinkle the egg/parsley mixture over the asparagus spears, pour the butter sauce over them, and serve immediately.

Nutritional Information

	raw
water	92%
protein	2.6 g
fat	0.3 g
carbohydrates	4.2 g
calories	24
	per 100 g

Asparagus is an excellent source of folic acid and contains vitamin C, potassium, thiamine, riboflavine, vitamin B$_6$, copper, vitamin A, iron, phosphorus, and zinc. Asparagus contains a sulfurous substance that imparts an odor to urine. It also contains asparagine, an acid substance that gives the vegetable its characteristic flavor and is also diuretic. Asparagus is said to be laxative, remineralizing, and tonic.

Cooking

Avoid overcooking asparagus, as this causes it to lose flavor, color, and nutrients. When boiling asparagus spears, tie them in bundles to make it easier to remove them once they are cooked. Steaming is the best cooking method, and there are special tall, narrow asparagus steamers on the market in which the asparagus stands upright in an inner basket. This method cooks the asparagus to perfection, as the more fibrous bottoms are thoroughly cooked in the boiling water while the fragile tips are merely steamed. Asparagus is ready when the stalks are tender but still firm. If you are planning to eat the asparagus cold, plunge it immediately into cold water to halt the cooking process, but do not let it soak. Asparagus can also be cooked in a microwave oven. Avoid cooking it in iron pots, as this vegetable contains tannins which react on contact with iron, altering the color of the asparagus.

Storing

Asparagus is very perishable. Wrapped in a damp cloth and placed in a perforated plastic bag in the refrigerator, it will keep for a maximum of 3 days. Blanched asparagus will keep for up to 9 months in the freezer.

Asparagus is actually a young edible shoot, commonly called a "spear," that rises from an underground crown capable of producing spears for 15 to 20 years.

Stalk Vegetables

107

Bamboo shoot

Phyllostachys spp., Gramineae

A perennial plant that grows in tropical regions, the bamboo shoot is native to Asia, where it has been consumed for thousands of years. The edible parts of the plant include not only the shoots but also the leaves, the heart, and the sweet liquid extracted from its cut stems. There are more than 200 varieties of this plant, all of which are edible. It has deciduous or evergreen leaves and woody stems that can grow to a height of 98 feet.

The cone-shaped shoots measure an average of 2¾ inches in diameter at the base and are 6 inches long. Certain varieties of bamboo can be processed to make paper pulp or fertilizer. Bamboo shoots are harvested as soon as they grow above the soil, generally when they are 6 inches long. Because they are cultivated in the dark, they are ivory in color; as they grow, they are covered with soil to prevent them from turning green. Fresh shoots are covered with slender but sharp hairs which must be removed before blanching. Bamboo shoots contain toxic substances that make them inedible in raw form, but that are destroyed during cooking.

Nutritional Information

	canned
water	94%
protein	1.8 g
fat	0.4 g
carbohydrates	3.2 g
calories	19
	per 100 g

Bamboo shoots contain potassium.

peeled bamboo shoot

Buying

In the West, bamboo shoots are available mainly dried or canned (on their own or in vinegar); they can be found in gourmet shops. Fresh bamboo shoots may occasionally be found in Asian markets.

Serving Ideas

Bamboo shoots are very popular in China and in Asia in general. Canned bamboo shoots can be eaten as they are, or sliced thinly and boiled, sautéed, or braised to serve as an accompaniment to meat or fish, or to use in Oriental dishes. They are often sold in thin strips or sticks that can be used in appetizers, soups, and stews. In Japan, bamboo shoots are an essential ingredient in sukiyaki.

Cooking

Cut raw bamboo shoots into sticks, cubes, or slices and cook them in lightly salted water for 30 minutes or until tender; then prepare them according to the recipe directions.

Storing

Unused portions of canned bamboo shoots should be covered with fresh water and placed in an airtight container in the refrigerator; the water should be changed every day or two. Fresh bamboo shoots will also keep in the refrigerator for several days.

Cardoon

Cynara cardunculus, Compositae

A perennial native to the Mediterranean region, the cardoon is closely related to the artichoke; both are edible members of the thistle family. The cardoon was cultivated on a wide scale in Europe during the Middle Ages and is still very popular in Italy, Spain, and France as well as Argentina and Australia, where it is cultivated. It also grows wild in a number of countries. This vegetable is not as popular in North America. The flavor of cardoon can be likened to a combination of artichoke, celery, and salsify.

Cardoon looks a little like celery because of its long, flexible ribs. The outer ribs of wild cardoon are woody, hard, and covered with soft spikes; they are usually discarded. The inner ribs are used after removal of their leaves and of the long tough strings from the ribs. Cultivated cardoon that is grown in the dark for a few weeks before harvesting tends to be more tender. Its large upper leaves are cut during harvesting, causing the top of the ribs to turn slightly brown.

Cardoon is a close relative of the artichoke; both are edible members of the thistle family.

Buying

When buying cardoon, look for firm, crisp ribs that are creamy white, rather broad, and fleshy.

Serving Ideas

Cardoon can be prepared in the same ways as celery or asparagus. It cannot be eaten raw. It is often cooked with a cream or cheese sauce, browned, or puréed with potatoes. It may be served as a vegetable side dish or added to soups and stews, and it is sometimes eaten cold with vinaigrette or mayonnaise.

Cooking

Cardoon is almost always blanched before being cooked in order to make it more tender and to rid it of some of its bitterness. Using a vegetable peeler, pull off the tough strings from the sides of the outer ribs. Cut the ribs into 3- or 4-inch-long pieces and add a tablespoon of vinegar to the cooking water to prevent the stalks from darkening. (The pieces of cardoon may discolor during preparation, but their color will be restored during cooking.) Immerse the ribs in this acidulated water and boil for 10 to 15 minutes to blanch them or 30 minutes to cook them; then drain and follow the recipe.

Nutritional Information

	cooked
water	93.5%
protein	0.8 g
fat	0.1 g
carbohydrates	5.3 g
calories	22
	per 100 g

Cardoon is an excellent source of potassium and a good source of magnesium; it also contains calcium and iron. It is said to have sedative properties.

Storing

Wrap the base of the cardoon in a paper towel and store it in a perforated plastic bag in the refrigerator, preferably in the vegetable drawer, where it will keep for 1 to 2 weeks at most. Cardoon can also be stored buried in sand in a cold room.

Chard

Beta vulgaris var. *cicla*, Chenopodiaceae

Swiss chard

This biennial plant, also known as Swiss chard, is related to the beet and is grown for its edible stalks and leaves. Greek writings dating from the 4th century A.D. contain descriptions of chard, which was held in high esteem by both the Greeks and the Romans for its medicinal properties. Cultivation of chard later spread throughout Europe.

Although often compared to spinach, chard leaves are actually larger and milder tasting. The leaves can measure up to 6 inches across and range in color from light to dark green; depending on the variety, they may be smooth or curly. They grow at the top of long, fleshy red or white stalks that are tender and crisp and that can grow up to 2 feet in height.

Buying

 Choose chard with firm, unblemished stalks and crisp, evenly colored leaves.

Nutritional Information

	raw	*cooked*
water	92.7%	92.7%
protein	1.8 g	1.9 g
fat	0.2 g	0.1 g
carbohydrates	3.7 g	4.1 g
fiber	1.6 g	2.1 g
calories	19	20
		per 100 g

Raw chard is an excellent source of vitamin C, vitamin A, magnesium, and potassium; it contains iron, copper, folic acid, riboflavin, vitamin B$_6$, and calcium. Cooked chard is an excellent source of potassium, magnesium, and vitamin A, a good source of vitamin C and iron, and contains copper, riboflavin, calcium, and vitamin B$_6$. Chard leaves are used as a laxative and a diuretic.

Preparing

Like spinach, chard should be washed carefully to rid it of the sand and soil concealed in its leaves. It the stalks are fibrous, cut them off near the base and peel off the fibers like threads. Depending on the intended use, separate the leaves from the stalks using a knife or scissors.

Serving Ideas

Chard can be eaten raw or cooked. When tender and fresh, the raw leaves are delicious in salads. Cooked chard is good warm or cold. It can be cooked whole, or the stalks and leaves can be cooked separately. The stalks are prepared like spinach or celery, and may be served with a Mornay or hollandaise sauce or with a vinaigrette. In addition to being a good substitute for Chinese cabbage in sautéed dishes, they can be added to soup or ragouts.

Chard leaves are prepared much like spinach, with which they are interchangeable in most recipes.

Cooking

The stalks may be blanched in salted water for 1 or 2 minutes or until tender, or they can be sprinkled with lemon juice or vinegar. To prevent them from darkening during cooking, cook them in acidulated water, avoiding aluminum or iron pots. When braised in the oven, the stalks take 20 to 30 minutes to cook, while steaming requires a cooking time of 8 to 15 minutes. Allow 5 to 8 minutes when steaming or boiling chard leaves. It is best to cook the leaves and stalks separately if the stalks are more than ½ inch wide.

Storing

Chard can be stored unwashed in a perforated plastic bag in the refrigerator for a maximum of 4 days. Like spinach, the leaves freeze well after being blanched for 2 minutes; the stalks do not take well to freezing.

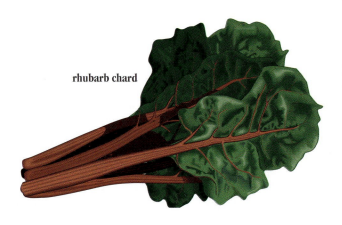

rhubarb chard

Fennel

Foeniculum vulgare, Umbelliferae

A vegetable originating from the Mediterranean region, fennel is a hardy perennial when grown in favorable climates and soils, and a biennial in less suitable conditions. The varieties of this vegetable include sweet fennel and Florence fennel. It has been used as a vegetable, a herb, and a medicinal plant since ancient times, and was particularly valued by the Greeks and Romans. In Latin, the word "fennel" means "little hay," while in Greek it was named "marathon," after the battle site of the Greek victory over the Persians. Indeed, the ancient Greeks regarded fennel as a symbol of victory and success. Fennel occupied an important place in the diet of the Romans, who used it mainly as a vegetable and who believed that it had the ability to sharpen eyesight. It is still widely enjoyed in Italy and Scandinavia, where it is cooked and served in the same way as asparagus.

Today we associate fennel with Italian cuisine in particular. Its mild, slightly sweet flavor is reminiscent of anise or licorice, which is why it is sometimes erroneously labeled anise or dill.

The base of the fennel plant is composed of overlapping leaves growing out of a pale-green or whitish fleshy bulb and surmounted by several robust, slightly striated pale-green stalks. The stalks of sweet fennel can grow up to 6 feet high. They have many long, thin, feathery leaves that are dark green in color and supported by tiny stems. The plant's small yellow umbellate flowers each produce two elongated ribbed seeds that are pale green in color.

The plant's small yellow umbellate flowers each produce two elongated ribbed seeds that are pale green in color.

Buying

 Choose fennel that is firm, rounded, fragrant, white, and unblemished, with healthy stalks. The stems, which are sometimes sold separately as an aromatic herb, should be fresh and of a healthy green color.

Serving Ideas

Fennel may be used raw or cooked once the tough outer leaves have been removed. Cook fennel as little as possible in order to preserve its flavor. Fennel is delicious with cream or yogurt. Raw, it may be cut in slices or long thin strips and added to salads. Fennel can also be blanched and then braised, or sautéed with other vegetables or on its own. It is good cooked in cream, au gratin, or grilled and served with lemon. Like celery, fennel is a versatile vegetable, and its anise-like flavor makes it even more delicious. Fennel also complements other vegetables and legumes, as well as rabbit, pork, lamb, beef, fish, and seafood. Sea bass accompanied by fennel is a regional specialty in Provence, France. Fennel seeds are used to flavor cheese, bread, soups, sauces, pastries, and wine. The leaves are traditionally associated with fish, but they may also be used as a herb in numerous other dishes. Fennel's essential oil is used in the making of wine and spirits and in perfume.

Storing

Fennel will keep in the refrigerator for about 1 week, but it has a tendency to become stringy and to lose flavor as it ages.

It may be frozen if blanched first, but this tends to diminish its flavor significantly.

The leaves dry best if placed in a microwave for 30 seconds to 2 minutes.

Nutritional Information

	raw	*seeds*
water	90.2%	8.8%
protein	1.3 g	0.3 g
fat	0.2 g	0.2 g
carbohydrates	7.2 g	1.1 g
	per 100 g	per 2 g

Raw fennel is an excellent source of potassium; it contains vitamin C, folic acid, magnesium, calcium, and phosphorus.

Fennel is thought to have the properties of a diuretic, an antispasmodic, and a stimulant. It is also said to soothe gastric pain, to aid the digestion of fatty or indigestible foods, to stimulate the appetite, to cleanse the system, and to prevent flatulence. The essential oil extracted from fennel contains anethole, a substance that is also present in anise; hence the similarity in flavor.

To make an infusion of fennel, boil 2 tablespoons of the root in 4 cups of water for 5 minutes and steep for 10 minutes, or boil 1 teaspoon of fennel seed in 1 cup of water and steep for 10 minutes.

Stalk Vegetables

111

sweet fennel

fennel seeds

Fiddlehead fern

Matteuccia struthiopteris and *Osmunda cinnamomea,* **Polypodiaceae**

*Fiddleheads
are young, edible,
fern shoots that are
gathered when
they are still curled.*

Fiddleheads are young fern shoots that are very similar in shape to the head of a violin, hence their name. These vegetables are gathered in the spring when they are still tightly curled and between 4 and 6 inches high. This period lasts for about 15 days between mid-April and early July, depending on the region. Fiddleheads must be collected just days after they emerge, as the plants become inedible once they uncoil. North American Indians appreciated fiddleheads long before the arrival of Europeans. The plant has also long been known to the Japanese and the aboriginal peoples of Australia and New Zealand.

There are thousands of varieties of ferns, only a few of which produce edible shoots. Edible varieties include the ostrich fern *(Matteuccia struthiopteris)* and the buckhorn, or cinnamon fern *(Osmunda cinnamomea).* The fiddleheads of the bracken fern, which are highly prized in Japan, contain a carcinogenic substance that can be neutralized by roasting the plants before using them. Brakes rise in single fronds, and the fiddleheads are more bitter tasting than those of the ostrich fern.

Nutritional Information

water	62%
protein	2.5 g
fat	0.3 g
carbohydrates	3.3 g
calories	20
	per 100 g

Fresh fiddleheads are a good source of potassium; they also supply vitamin C, niacin, and iron.

Preparing

To rid the fiddleheads of their scales, rub them between your hands or place them in a bag and shake it. Wash fiddleheads well, preferably at the last minute, and drain them before using them.

Cooking

Avoid overcooking fiddleheads and do not add baking soda to the cooking liquid, as this will affect their color. For the best-tasting fiddleheads, add a little salt to the water and boil them just the right amount of time, ideally 5 to 7 minutes. Do not be alarmed if the water turns brownish; this is normal. Fiddleheads are also very good steamed or braised; cook them for 5 to 10 minutes, or until they reach the desired tenderness.

Buying

Fiddleheads are sold fresh, frozen, or canned. Fresh fiddleheads are available only in the spring. They should be bright green, firm, and tightly curled, and they should still have their brown scales. The stems should be short and the heads between ¾ and 1½ inches in diameter. When picking your own fiddleheads, be sure to correctly identify the different types of ferns, as some inedible varieties cause food poisoning. It is very important not to cut the plant to the ground, as it will be unable to reproduce; in the case of the ostrich fern, collect three to five fiddleheads per plant.

Serving Ideas

Both the head and a small part of the fern's stem are edible. Uncoiled plants are inedible and should never be consumed. Fiddleheads are usually cooked and can be eaten either warm or cold. They are delicious served simply with a dab of butter or topped with vinaigrette or with a hollandaise, cheese, or béchamel sauce, or baked au gratin. Fiddleheads are often used as a vegetable side dish or incorporated into salads, pasta, omelets, and stews. They also make an excellent soup. Fiddleheads are sometimes also eaten raw.

Storing

Fiddleheads are very perishable and should be refrigerated as soon as possible to prevent them from ripening further. Wrap them in a paper towel and place them in a plastic bag in the refrigerator, where they will keep for 1 or 2 days. Fiddleheads stand up well to freezing when blanched for 1 or 2 minutes. Plunge them into cold water immediately after blanching and dry them thoroughly before placing them on a cookie sheet in the freezer; once frozen, they can be transferred to an airtight container. Cook without thawing.

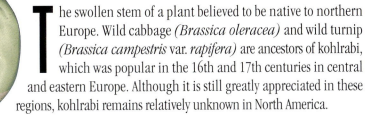

Kohlrabi

Brassica oleracea var. *gongylodes,* **Cruciferae**

The swollen stem of a plant believed to be native to northern Europe. Wild cabbage *(Brassica oleracea)* and wild turnip *(Brassica campestris* var. *rapifera)* are ancestors of kohlrabi, which was popular in the 16th and 17th centuries in central and eastern Europe. Although it is still greatly appreciated in these regions, kohlrabi remains relatively unknown in North America.

The size of an orange, kohlrabi has a peculiar shape; its bulbous base grows aboveground and produces thin stems that grow in all directions and end in large edible leaves. Kohlrabi may be a very pale green, white, or purple and is covered with a thin edible skin. The flesh is sweet and crisp, with a flavor slightly reminiscent of radish, while the stems and leaves taste like cabbage.

Preparing

Kohlrabi can be peeled before or after cooking, but the peel is easier to remove once the vegetable has been cooked. To eat kohlrabi raw, first remove the stems, then peel it, taking care to remove the fibrous layer just below the skin. Kohlrabi can be grated or cut into strips, cubes, slices, or wedges.

Serving Ideas

Kohlrabi can be eaten raw or cooked. Raw, it is delicious on its own, served with a dip or dressed in a vinaigrette; it also often appears in salads. Cooked kohlrabi is served as a vegetable side dish, added to soups and stews, puréed, or stuffed. It is also delicious steamed and sprinkled with lemon juice and melted butter. It can also be accompanied by a sauce or sour cream, gratinéed, or seasoned with ginger and garlic.

Most herbs and spices blend well with the delicate flavor of kohlrabi. When young and tender, it is prepared like turnips, for which it is a good substitute, or like celeriac. The flesh is prepared in the same manner as turnips, while the leaves can be used like spinach. The leaves require a very short cooking time and are delicious sprinkled with a bit of lemon juice and a dollop of butter. Purple kohlrabi changes color during cooking.

Cooking

When boiling or steaming kohlrabi, it is best to peel it after cooking. Depending on the size, cook it for 20 to 30 minutes, or until it is tender. To braise, sauté, roast, or bake it, it is best to peel it before cooking.

Buying

Choose kohlrabi that is smooth and unblemished; smaller specimens (under 3 inches in diameter) tend to be less fibrous. The leaves, if present, should be firm and bright green.

Nutritional Information

	raw
water	91%
protein	1.7 g
fat	0.1 g
carbohydrates	6.2 g
fiber	1 g
calories	27
	per 100 g

Kohlrabi is an excellent source of vitamin C and potassium; it also contains vitamin B_6, folic acid, magnesium, and copper, and its leaves are rich in vitamin A.

Storing

Stored in a perforated plastic bag, kohlrabi will keep for about 1 week in the refrigerator. The leaves remain fresh for only a day or two and should be stored separately.

Freezing is not the best method of preserving this vegetable, as it alters its texture and, in the case of puréed kohlrabi, its color.

Celery

Apium graveolens var. *dulce,* Umbelliferae

Celery is a garden plant used for its stalks, leaves, roots, and seeds.

A biennial garden vegetable native to the Mediterranean area and grown for its stalks (also called ribs), leaves, roots, and seeds. Celery leaves were originally used for their medicinal properties and were long regarded as a powerful aphrodisiac. In ancient times, the Greeks used celery leaves, like bay leaves, to crown victorious athletes, to whom celery wine was also served. Celery was used as a seasoning in Roman times, and during the Middle Ages, an elixir made from celery was consumed to soothe arthritic pain and to aid digestion. The first cultivated form of celery was developed from wild celery in the 16th century. Two varieties were obtained: celeriac, which has a fleshy root, and stalk celery, which was developed for its leafy stems. For a long time celery was only consumed cooked; it was not until the 18th century in Europe that people began to eat it raw. Celery was introduced into the United States in the 19th century.

Celery can grow to a height of 12 to 16 inches and has fleshy ribbed stalks that join at the base to form a head. The inner stalks, called the heart, are the tenderest. There are several varieties of celery, with stalks varying in color from different shades of green to whitish. Europeans prefer white celery, while Americans have adopted the green variety. When grown for its seeds, the celery is left in the ground unharvested; it flowers the following year, bearing white umbellate flowers that give way to strongly aromatic seeds, commonly used in cooking. (Celery salt is a seasoning derived from ground dried celeriac.) To obtain milder-tasting and lighter-colored celery, the plant is often blanched during cultivation; this consists of covering the growing celery with earth, paper, or boards to protect it from direct sunlight. Certain improved varieties of celery are self-blanching.

Buying

Choose celery with shiny, firm, crisp stalks; if it is sold with its leaves, they should be a healthy green color. Avoid soft or damaged stalks, as well as those with brown patches or yellowing leaves.

Preparing

Celery is easy to prepare: simply trim the base, wash the stalks under running water, and cut them to the desired length. The tougher surface fibers, or strings, of the outermost stalks can be removed by cutting a thin slice at the base or top of the stalk and peeling the fibers away with it.

Serving Ideas

Celery can be eaten raw or cooked. Raw celery is often served as an appetizer, either on its own or stuffed with cheese, a seafood mixture, poultry, or eggs. It is also frequently added to salads and sandwiches. Cooked celery is a popular flavoring ingredient in a wide variety of dishes, including soups, sauces, stews, pasta, tofu, quiches, omelets, and rice. It also makes a good accompanying vegetable, either braised, gratineed, topped with a béchamel sauce, or simply served with melted butter.

There is no need to throw away celery leaves, which can be used to add flavor to preparations such as salads, soups, sauces, or court bouillons. They can be chopped or used as they are, in fresh or dried form. The seeds are slightly bitter and have a concentrated celery flavor. They are used whole or crushed in stuffings, poached vegetables, crackers, marinades, and sauces.

Braised Celery

SERVES 6

6 medium heads of celery
2 tbsp. olive oil
1 tbsp. unsalted butter
1 bay leaf
1 onion, chopped
1 clove garlic, finely
  chopped

Salt and ground pepper
1 cup (250 ml) chicken
  stock
½ cup (125 ml) dry white
  wine
Chopped curly-leaf parsley

1. Preheat the oven to 350°F (175°C).

2. Detach the outer ribs of the celery, and set them aside for another use. Trim the celery hearts 6 inches from the base, and rinse them well in cold water.

3. Blanch the celery hearts in boiling salted water for 10 minutes. Drain.

4. In a flameproof casserole, heat the olive oil and butter. Add the bay leaf. Add the onion and garlic, and cook until just tender, without browning. Add the drained celery hearts and brown for a few minutes on all sides. Season to taste with salt and pepper.

5. Add the chicken stock and wine, and bring to the boil. Bake in the oven for approximately 45 minutes or until the celery is tender.

6. Remove the celery and cut it lengthwise in half or in quarters, depending on the size of the hearts. Place in a warm serving dish.

7. Place the casserole on the stove and reduce the cooking liquid. Taste for seasoning. Pour the sauce over the celery, and garnish with the parsley. Serve immediately.

celery seeds

Nutritional Information

	raw	cooked
water	95%	94%
protein	0.8 g	0.8 g
fat	3.8 g	4 g
carbohydrates	9.2 g	5.9 g
calories	15	17
fiber	0.7 g	0.6 g
		per 100 g

Celery is an excellent source of potassium; it also contains vitamin C, folic acid, and vitamin B$_6$.

Celery is credited with many curative properties: it is said to stimulate the appetite, cleanse the system, prevent scurvy, and to be diuretic, stomachic, remineralizing, antiseptic, antirheumatic, and tonic. When applied directly as a compress, celery juice is believed to promote the healing of ulcers and wounds. Celery seeds also have numerous medicinal properties: they are used to treat colds, flus, insomnia, indigestion, and arthritis. Celery is also said to contain an active ingredient that lowers high blood pressure by reducing the level of hormones associated with stress.

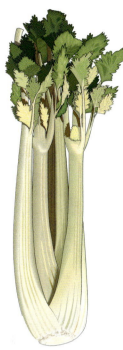

white celery

Storing

Celery will keep for a week in the refrigerator, wrapped in a perforated plastic bag or damp cloth or placed in a sealed container. Because it has a high water content and wilts quickly, it should not be left out at room temperature for too long. Celery will also keep for several days standing in a dish of cold salted water. Avoid storing peeled and cut celery in water, as this drains it of some of its nutrients. To revive wilted celery, sprinkle it with a little water and refrigerate it for a few hours or until it regains its crispness. Celery can also be stored, unwashed and with its roots still attached, in a cool (32°F) and very humid place, wrapped in a perforated plastic bag. Celery takes very poorly to freezing, which makes it wilt, although this is not important if it is to be used for cooking.

Stalk Vegetables

115

Cassava

Manihot esculenta and *Manihot dulcis,* Euphorbiaceae

The cassava is a tuber vegetable that grows in tropical and subtropical climates; it is a staple food in many countries of Africa, Asia, and South and Central America.

 sweet cassava

Tuber of a shrub that has large palmate leaves and can grow to a height of 3 to 10 feet, the cassava is native to northeastern Brazil and southwestern Mexico. It grows in tropical and subtropical climates, and is a staple food in many countries of Africa, Asia, and Central and South America. It is also known as manioc, and in some countries goes by the name *yuca* (not to be confused with the yucca, a decorative plant of the Liliaceae family). The main producers of cassava are Nigeria, Brazil, Thailand, Zaire, and Indonesia.

This tuber is conical or cylindrical in shape, and when small it resembles the sweet potato. Its skin is brown and the flesh can be whitish, yellowish, or reddish. Cassavas are harvested between 6 months and 1 year after planting, when they measure 8 to 16 inches in length and 2 to 4 inches in diameter. However, in Africa, where the tubers are sometimes left in the fields for up to 6 years to ensure supplies in the event of a famine, they can grow to over 3 feet in length and weigh 50 pounds or more; such large tubers tend to be hard and fibrous. Cassavas are extremely perishable and do not stand up well to shipping. There are many varieties of cassava, all of which contain hydrocyanic acid, a poisonous substance that is eliminated by cooking or dehydration. They are usually classified as bitter cassava or sweet cassava, according to the quantity of this acid present.

Bitter cassava *(M.esculenta)* owes its taste to its high hydrocyanic acid content; it must undergo several processes before it becomes edible. This variety is rich in starch and is used in the preparation of tapioca. The word "tapioca" is derived from *tipioca,* which is the name for this food in the language of the Tupi peoples of Brazil. Using modern extracting processes, 4 tons of cassava tubers are required to produce 1 ton of tapioca.

Buying

Look for tubers that show no signs of mold or sticky patches. While the skin of cassavas is rarely perfect, choose those that have as little damage as possible, since spoiled cassavas contain higher amounts of hydrocyanic acid. Avoid acrid or sour-smelling tubers as well as those with gray-blue mottling.

instant tapioca

Preparing

Even though the bitter cassava contains much higher amounts of hydrocyanic acid than the sweet cassava, both varieties should be soaked in water to rid them of as much of this poison as possible. Cut the tuber lengthwise into two or three pieces before peeling it with a knife; then dice or grate it and leave it to soak. Before cooking, rinse it well under running water. Boil the cassava in fresh water, keeping the lid on the saucepan to prevent evaporation of the hydrocyanic vapors. The process of boiling or baking the cassava, whether whole or cut into pieces, neutralizes the enzyme responsible for the production of hydrocyanic acid.

Manufacture of tapioca

• The tubers are washed, peeled, and grated, after which the pulp is left to macerate. It is then passed through a sieve, drained, and dried. During the dehydration process, the starch obtained (the tapioca) forms into whitish beads of varying sizes. This "pearl tapioca" must be soaked for 45 to 75 minutes before being cooked.

• Tapioca is also processed into flake, flour, or granular form to obtain what is called "instant tapioca," which takes only 10 minutes to prepare, since it is almost entirely precooked before being marketed. Tapioca can also be used to make flour.

Nutritional Information

	uncooked instant tapioca	*uncooked pearl tapioca*	*raw cassava*
calories	64	102	120
water			68.5%
protein	0.2 g	0.1 g	3.1 g
carbohydrates	15.6 g	26.6 g	26.9 g
fat			0.4 g
fiber			0.1 g
	per 30 g		**per 100 g**

The cassava contains more calories than the potato because of its higher carbohydrate content. It is an excellent source of vitamin C, potassium, iron, and magnesium, and a good source of thiamine and vitamin B_6; it also supplies folic acid, niacin, copper, calcium, phosphorus, riboflavin, and pantothenic acid.

Serving Ideas

Because tapioca is a bland food that tends to absorb the flavor of the dishes to which it is added, it is very useful as a thickening agent in soups, sauces, stews, pies, fruits, and puddings. Delicious desserts are made from tapioca cooked in milk. The pulp and paper industry uses tapioca in the production of embossed paper, and it is also used in the glue on the back of postage stamps.

The **sweet cassava** *(M. dulcis)* can be consumed on its own, in the same way as the potato or the sweet potato, with which it is interchangeable in most recipes. In Brazil, roasted cassava flour, seasoned and flavored with onions, raisins, and cashews, is served as a side dish to that country's national speciality, *feijoada,* which is made with black beans *feijao,* sausage, and onion. The flour derived from sweet cassavas is used in the preparation of sauces, stews, breads, cakes, and biscuits. Cassava also goes into the making of a brandy called *cavim,* which is very popular in Brazil.

Cooking

Tapioca is easy to make, but it should be stirred constantly to prevent the formation of lumps.

Storing

This tuber vegetable spoils easily and is damaged by exposure to high humidity or to temperatures above 68°F. It will keep for several days in the refrigerator, and can also be peeled and cut into pieces for freezing.

Potato

Solanum tuberosum, Solanaceae

Potatoes are harvested after flowering, when the plants begin to yellow. The only edible part of the plant is the tuber, the thickened end of the stem.

The edible tuber of a plant that has been cultivated for between 4,000 and 7,000 years in the Andean regions of Bolivia and Peru, the potato has been a staple in the diet of Andean societies since ancient times. It was originally a wild plant, and it is believed that the variety selected for cultivation was less bitter than its wild-growing relative.

At the beginning of the 16th century, Spanish explorers discovered that potatoes prevented scurvy and began to carry them on their ships. Shortly after the potato was introduced into Europe by the Spanish, the Italians and Germans began to grow and consume it.

Seventeenth-century attempts by an English scientific council and German leaders to promote the cultivation and use of the potato failed due to the belief that the potato transmitted leprosy. As a result, it wasn't until the 18th century that potato cultivation became more widely spread across northern Europe. This development followed the popularization of the potato by the French agronomist Antoine-Auguste Parmentier, who allowed peasants to steal potatoes from the royal gardens and served potatoes mashed with butter and seasoning, thus making them unrecognizable. In creating a potato dish that still bears his name, Parmentier won a contest sponsored by the French government to find a replacement food for bread, which had become a rare commodity.

Around the same period in Ireland, potatoes were cultivated as a solution to frequent food shortages. However, in 1845 and 1846, a parasite destroyed the potato crop, resulting in a terrible famine that led to a massive exodus of the population, with many people emigrating to the United States. It was only in the 19th century that the potato began to be cultivated on a large scale in the United States. Today the main potato-producing countries include the Commonwealth of Independent States countries, Poland, China, the United States, and India.

The potato is a perennial plant that is cultivated as an annual; the aerial portion of the plant consists of stems that can sometimes grow to a height of 3 feet and that bear oblong leaves. Potatoes are harvested after flowering, when the plants begin to yellow. Of the 3,000 existing varieties of potato, only about 100 are used for human consumption. These varieties differ widely not only in shape, color, and size, but also in flavor and starch content.

The only edible part of the plant is the tuber, the thickened end of the plant's stem, which grows underground and may be round, oval, or elongated in shape. The tubers can be smooth or rough and often have "eyes," out of which new buds eventually grow. The skin can be varying shades of red, brown, yellow, green, or purplish red, and covers a white or yellow flesh. Potatoes are perishable and bruise easily.

Preparing

Dispose of any potato more than half of which is green, as it will be bitter and inedible. Scrub the potato well if it is to be cooked with its skin, and remove the eyes and any traces of green. It is not necessary to peel early or new potatoes; simply cook them as they are or scrub them first, after having removed any green flesh.

To prevent the flesh of the potato from darkening on contact with air, cook it as soon as it is cut or place it in cold water until you are ready to use it. This brief soaking will also prevent the potato from falling apart during cooking (use fresh water for cooking).

Potatoes au Gratin

SERVES 4

2 lb. (1 kg) potatoes	*Salt and white pepper*
1 clove garlic	*Light cream*
1 tbsp. butter	*1 pinch of nutmeg*

1. Preheat the oven to 400°F (200°C).

2. Peel, rinse, and dry the potatoes, and cut them into very fine slices.

3. Rub a casserole with the garlic and coat it with the butter. Layer the potatoes in the dish, seasoning each layer with salt and pepper.

4. Pour in enough cream to cover all but the top layer. Season with the pinch of nutmeg.

5. Bake for about 25 minutes, or until the dish is golden brown on top.

Buying

Choose firm, undamaged potatoes that show no signs of sprouting or green patches. Although it can be difficult to judge the quality of tubers packaged in opaque paper bags, paper is preferable over plastic for storing potatoes because it allows the moisture to escape and protects them from the light. If plastic bags are used, they should be perforated so that the potatoes can breathe.

Ready-cleaned potatoes have a shorter storage life, since washing removes their protective coating, making them more susceptible to bacteria. They are also more expensive – an impractical expense considering that they are almost always rewashed before use. When buying ready-cleaned potatoes, avoid those with green patches; because they are often sold in bulk, they are not protected from the light (see Nutritional Information).

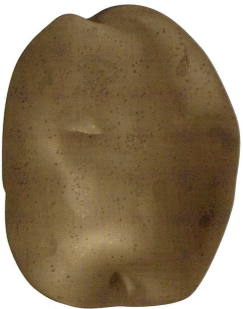

white Marfona potato

All Blue potato

Tuber Vegetables

119

Serving Ideas

Because 20% of the potato is comprised of an indigestible starch, potatoes must be eaten cooked; during cooking, this starch is converted to sugar. In addition to being the ideal accompaniment to almost all meats, poultry, and fish, potatoes are also the featured ingredient in a number of tasty dishes, including aligot, goulash, Swiss rösti, and Irish stew. The somewhat neutral flavor of the potato can be enhanced with cheese, onion, herbs, or seasoning. Potatoes are often added to soups, stews, soufflés, and omelets, and are the essential ingredient in croquettes, quenelles, and gnocchi. Although often considered poor man's fare, potatoes actually enter into the preparation of a number of elaborate and refined dishes, including *gratin dauphinois* and *pommes duchesse*. The potato is also the basic ingredient in vodka. It can be frozen, dehydrated, or canned.

Potato starch is used in the making of pastries, cold meats, and puddings, and as a thickening and setting agent.

To make good mashed potatoes, it is important to use cold water at the start of cooking and to add the salt after the peeled potatoes have been placed in the water. Once they have been boiled and drained, incorporate the butter and then the hot milk with a wooden spatula. For lighter mashed potatoes, increase the mixing time and the quantity of milk or cream added.

Cooking

 The potato can be cooked in many different ways, including boiling, steaming, baking, frying, browning, and mashing.

Boiled or steamed potatoes. Potatoes should be cooked whole with their skin in a small quantity of water (instead of throwing out the cooking water, use it for soups and sauces). It is best to bring the pot of salted water to the boil before immersing the potatoes; cover the pot, and make sure that the potatoes do not stick. Water with a high alkaline content will sometimes cause the potatoes to turn yellow during cooking; to help them stay white, add a bit of lemon juice to the cooking water. Whole potatoes should be boiled for 20 to 30 minutes (30 to 45 minutes if steamed), while cut potatoes require 10 to 15 minutes whether boiled or steamed.

Oven-baked potatoes. Before putting them in the oven, pierce the skin of the potatoes several times with a fork to allow the steam to escape and to prevent them from splitting. While it is not mandatory to bake the potatoes wrapped in aluminum foil, they do tend to become drier if not wrapped. The aluminum foil traps the heat, keeping the skin tender and the flesh moist; wrapped potatoes take longer to bake.

A medium-size potato will take 40 to 50 minutes when baked at 425°F. To save time and energy, it can also be baked for 70 minutes at 350°F at the same time as a meat dish.

French fries. The best potatoes for frying are those with the lowest moisture content, such as Russet and Idaho.

Potatoes can be fried with their skin.

Cut the potatoes into thin strips of equal thickness to ensure even cooking, but no thicker than ½ inch; otherwise they will become too greasy.

As soon as they are peeled, rinse the potatoes in water (do not soak them); pat them dry to avoid splattering when they are immersed in the boiling oil. These procedures help to reduce the amount of grease absorbed by the potato and to prevent them from sticking, while at the same time ensuring crispness.

Once peeled, the potatoes can also be merely patted dry, without being rinsed.

For frying, use an oil that can withstand a temperature of 340°F (see *Oil*) without decomposing.

Fill the pot with oil to one third of its capacity so the potatoes can float freely without sticking; there should be no risk of the oil overflowing once heated.

Preheat the cooking oil, and using a thermometer if possible, add the potatoes when the temperature reaches 340° to 350°F. (If it is overheated, the oil will start to smoke and will become toxic; this generally occurs between 410° and 425°F, depending on the type of oil.) The oil is hot enough if it sizzles when the potatoes are added.

Fry the potatoes in small batches in order to avoid reducing the temperature of the oil and preventing the fries from sealing; if they don't seal, they will absorb too much oil and turn soft. The heat can be increased to compensate for the drop in temperature when the potatoes are added, but it must be reduced again as soon as the maximum temperature is restored.

Potatoes can be single-fried or, to make them crisper, double-fried. To double-fry potatoes, fry them first for 5 to 6 minutes in moderately hot oil (300° to 320°F), and remove them before they turn golden. After they have drained and cooled, heat the cooking oil to 350°F and re-fry the potatoes for 2 to 3 minutes, until golden brown. Pat them dry with a paper towel, and add salt just before serving.

Used cooking oil that is not in good condition will quickly become toxic. Before storing it in the refrigerator or in a cool place, filter the oil to prevent the debris from previous frying from burning and spoiling the oil. If the oil becomes very dark, thick, or rancid, or if it smokes when heated below 300°F, discard it. Avoid mixing fresh and used oil to replenish the quantity, as the fresh oil will turn quickly on contact with the old oil.

For a less fatty alternative to deep-frying, potatoes can also be fried in the oven:

• Coat the potatoes with heated oil, using 1 tablespoon of oil for 1 cup of potatoes, and cook them at 450°F for about 8 minutes;

• reduce the heat to 375°F and cook them until tender, or broil them 3 inches from the grill for 15 to 20 minutes, turning them occasionally.

Frozen French fries can also be deep-fried or oven-fried, although oven-fried potatoes tend to be soft and greasy, undercooked, and rather tasteless. Commercial frozen French fries are rarely as good as fresh fries and often contain food additives, including sulfates, artificial flavoring, BHA, and monosodium glutamate. Check the list of ingredients on the package.

Chips are also fried potatoes, which have been cut into thin slices and soaked in water to rid them of the starch that prevents them from becoming crisp. To make potato chips, it is necessary to eliminate the moisture from the potatoes using a very high cooking temperature, but this method makes them turn very dark and causes the oil to decompose quickly. To prevent this, three methods are used for frying chips. The first calls for already partially fried chips to be completely fried in a microwave oven; the second method uses dry frying; and the third uses a vacuum method to complete the frying.

Microwave-baked potatoes.

• Pierce the whole unpeeled potato several times to allow the steam to escape during cooking, and place it on a paper towel;

• cook it on high power for 3 to 4 minutes (if microwaving more than one potato at a time, increase the cooking time);

• if the oven does not have a turntable, turn the potato once during cooking;

• let the potato cool for 2 minutes, wrapped in the paper towel, before serving it.

Storing

Once picked, potatoes are stored for a period of 4 to 15 weeks, depending on the variety. They then enter a period of dormancy, after which they begin to sprout. The storage conditions influence the length of time potatoes will keep; stored at a maximum temperature of 39°F, they will keep for up to 9 months.

Stored in a cool, dark, dry, well-ventilated place, at temperatures ranging between 44° and 50°F, potatoes will keep for about 2 months. The higher the temperature, the shorter the storage period; the common practice of storing them in the pantry at room temperature promotes sprouting and dehydration.

When possible, avoid storing potatoes in plastic bags, which favor the development of mold; if plastic bags are used, perforate them several times.

New potatoes or very old potatoes may be kept in the refrigerator, but should be placed away from pungent foods such as onions. New potatoes will keep for only about 1 week, as will cooked potatoes, which take on an unpleasant taste after this time, especially if they are boiled or mashed.

Nutritional Information

The water content of the potato is 79.4% of the total composition. It is an excellent source of potassium and a good source of vitamin C; it also contains vitamin B$_6$, copper, niacin, magnesium, folic acid, iron, and pantothenic acid.

The vitamin C contained in potatoes disappears gradually over time; after 3 months of dark storage at 53°F, only 68% of the vitamin C remains, and after 6 months, only 50% is left. Close to 40% of the vitamin C is lost during the first 2 months of storage, after which the loss of this nutrient slows down and starts to stabilize in the seventh month of storage.

The potato is credited with a number of medicinal properties; the raw juice is believed to have antispasmodic, diuretic, sedative, and healing qualities, and is used to relieve scurvy and ulcers. Raw and sliced or grated or converted into starch, the potato is also used to treat inflammations, sunstroke, burns, and chapped skin.

Exposure of the potato to light or sun will cause the formation of green or dark green patches, which impart a bitter taste to the potato and may contain significant quantities of a toxic alkaloid substance called solanine. Small doses of solanine may cause stomach cramps, headaches, or diarrhea, while strong doses may affect the nervous system. All traces of green should be removed from the potato, as the solanine is not neutralized by cooking. The sprouts and eyes should also be removed, since the solanine tends to accumulate in them.

red Desiree potato

early potato

	raw	*baked (whole)*	*boiled (whole)*	*boiled (peeled)*	*deep-fried*	*chips*
protein	2.1 g	2.3 g	1.9 g	1.7 g	4.0 g	6.6 g
carbohydrates	18 g	25.2 g	20.1 g	20 g	39.6 g	48.5 g
fat	0.1 g	0.1 g	0.1 g	0.1 g	10.6 g	35.4 g
calories	79	109	87	86	315	539
fiber	1.5 g	2.3 g	1.5 g	1.4 g	-	3.8 g
vitamin C	19 mg	13 mg	13 mg	7 mg	11 mg	58 mg

per 100 g

Taro

Colocasia esculenta, **Araceae**

The tuber of a plant presumed to be native to Southeast Asia, the taro (or dasheen) grows in tropical as well as warmer temperate regions, having as its natural habitat virgin forests. The cultivation of taro dates back some 4,000 to 7,000 years, but the plant was probably introduced into Japan and China at a later period. It is a staple food in several tropical countries of Asia, the Pacific Islands, and the West Indies.

The taro belongs to a family of ornamental plants and is related to the philodendron and the dieffenbachia. More than 100 different varieties have been identified; some are oblong, resembling the sweet potato, while others are more rounded and resemble celeriac. They tend to have smoother, less twisted shapes than other tubers. The plant can grow up to 6 feet in height and has very large leaves; the young shoots are edible after being blanched. The leaves and shoots are rarely available in Western markets, however. The tubers have a thick brownish, ringed skin that is rather rugged and hairy. The flesh can be white, cream-colored, or purple-gray, sometimes veined with pink or brown. It has a high starch content and a sweet flavor.

Buying

Look for firm taros, with no sign of mold or soft patches. A small incision can be made in the flesh to check for freshness and juiciness, although the best way to judge the quality of the flesh is to cut the taro in half.

Preparing

Peel the tuber and soak it in fresh water if it is not to be used immediately. It is best to peel taros under running water or to wear gloves, since they contain a sticky juice that may irritate the skin.

Serving Ideas

The taro must be consumed cooked, as it contains an indigestible starch as well as calcium oxalate crystals, a bitter and irritating substance that is neutralized during cooking. When cooked, the flesh of the taro becomes grayish or mauve. The taro is used in the same way as the potato. It is best served very hot, as the texture of the flesh is altered by cooling. Soups and stews can be thickened with this tuber, which tends to absorb the flavor of the food to which it is added.

Like potatoes, taros are delicious fried or served with a sauce and can be grated to make crêpes. Cut into pieces and cooked in syrup, they can also be served as a dessert. Taro flour is used in Asian cooking. The leaves can be cooked like spinach or used to wrap other food for baking. The calcium oxalates present in the leaves are also destroyed by cooking.

Storing

Keep taros in a dark, cool, dry place that is well ventilated. They should be consumed as soon as possible after purchase, as they tend to soften quickly. Taro leaves will keep for several days in the refrigerator; store them in a perforated plastic bag after wiping them with a damp cloth.

Nutritional Information

	cooked
water	64%
protein	0.4 g
fat	0.2 g
carbohydrates	34.5 g
calories	142
	per 100 g

The taro is rich in potassium; it also contains magnesium, phosphorus, and iron.

Cooking

Taro can be boiled (allow about 20 minutes), steamed, or cooked in the microwave. It can also be oven-baked (allow 25 minutes), but this tends to make the flesh very dry and the flavor more pungent. To make it less dry, baste it often with butter, margarine, or sauce and serve very hot.

Because the taro becomes very viscous when puréed, it is best to dry the purée by cooking it further, as croquettes or a soufflé, for example. To prevent the taro from overcooking and falling apart when it is incorporated into soups or stews, steam or boil it first and add it at the last minute.

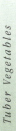

Yam

Dioscorea spp., Dioscoreaceae

The yam is oblong like the sweet potato, with which it is often confused. The Chinese yam is the only variety that grows in temperate climates.

The yam is the tuber of a climbing plant whose country of origin is not known, although archeological excavations show some evidence that it was cultivated over 10,000 years ago in Africa and eastern Asia. Yams were introduced into South America at a later date. The yam is one of the most widely consumed foods in the world, constituting a staple food in many countries, particularly in South America and the West Indies.

In North America, the yam is often confused with the sweet potato, although it actually belongs to a different family which includes some 600 species, about 200 of which are varieties of yam. This tuber grows mainly in the tropical and subtropical regions of Africa, Asia, and America; the Chinese yam *(D. batata)* is the only variety that grows in temperate zones. The yam can be round in shape or oblong like the sweet potato. Its flesh varies in color from white to yellow, ivory, pink, or brownish pink; it is very starchy and contains a mucilaginous substance that gives it a rather slippery texture. Depending on the variety, the yam's flesh will either become creamy or remain firm when cooked. The thick skin can be coarse or downy, and varies in color from white to pink or brownish black. This tuber can weigh up to 45 pounds and measure 20 inches in diameter. It is similar in taste to certain varieties of the sweet potato, although it is less sweet and more earthy.

Tuber Vegetables

124

Buying

 Choose yams that are firm and intact, with no soft patches or signs of mold.

Nutritional Information

	raw
water	70%
protein	1.5 g
fat	0.1 g
carbohydrates	28 g
fiber	3.9 g
calories	116
	per 100 g

Yams are an excellent source of potassium; they also supply vitamin C, vitamin B_6, thiamine, folic acid, magnesium, phosphorus, and copper. The yam contains more starch than the potato, making it more mealy. Certain wild varieties of yams contain steroids that are used by the pharmaceutical industry, notably to make contraceptives.

Serving Ideas

The yam can be used like the potato. It is often added to soups and stews, and can also be grated and made into breads and cakes. Because the yam is rather bland when boiled or puréed, it is rarely served this way in countries where it is a staple food. It is more commonly seasoned with spices, served with a sauce, or combined with other foods. In the West Indies, it is also used to moderate the flavor of hot and spicy dishes.

Fried yams make a savory treat. Oven-baked yams tend to become quite dry and are best served with a sauce. Yams can be used in place of potatoes and sweet potatoes in most recipes. Only the smallest tubers should be cooked in their skins. The starch obtained from the yam is known as "Guyanese arrowroot."

Cooking

Like potatoes, yams contain a large amount of indigestible starch that is converted into sugar during cooking; for this reason, they are only consumed cooked. To prepare yams, peel them, cut them into pieces, and blanch them for 10 to 20 minutes in salted boiling water.

Storing

Yams should be stored in a dark, cool, dry, and well-ventilated place. The warmer the temperature, the faster these tubers will spoil. Do not store yams in a plastic bag, as this favors the formation of mold.

Jicama

Pachyrhizus erosus and *Pachyrhizus tuberosus,* **Leguminosae**

The edible tuber of a plant native to Mexico and Central and South America, the jicama (also called yam bean) was known to the Aztecs, who used its seeds as medicine. The word is derived from *xicamalt,* the Aztec term for this vegetable. In the 17th century, Spanish explorers brought the jicama plant to the Philippines, and cultivation subsequently spread throughout Asia and the Pacific.

The jicama grows on a climbing plant that produces one or more tubers. There are two varieties of jicama, the largest of which, *Pachyrhizus tuberosus,* is native to the Amazon; it grows in the tropical and temperate zones of America, including the Andes region and Ecuador, as well as in China and the Caribbean. The jicama is harvested when it attains a length of 8 to 12 inches and a diameter of 1 inch; if left to mature, it can reach a diameter of as much as 12 inches, although it is no longer edible at this point because it contains a toxic substance called rotenone that is used mainly as an insecticide. This variety of jicama is very juicy and is almost always eaten raw.

The second variety, *Pachyrhizus erosus,* comes from Mexico and Central America and is smaller, measuring between 6 and 8 inches in length. It is widely cultivated in South America, where it is eaten raw or cooked. Depending on the variety, jicamas often look like a turnip with slightly flattened ends. Their thin brown skin is inedible and covers a juicy white flesh that is crisp and sweet; the delicate flavor of the jicama is reminiscent of that of the water chestnut.

Buying

 Choose a jicama that is firm, medium-size or small, with thin skin and no bruises. Large thick-skinned specimens tend to be fibrous and dry. To verify the thickness of the skin and the juiciness of the flesh, make a small incision in the skin with a fingernail.

Preparing

Jicamas are easier to peel with a knife. Once it is peeled, grate the jicama or cut it into cubes, julienne strips, or slices.

Serving Ideas

Jicamas can be eaten raw or cooked. Raw, they are used in salads, dips, and appetizers. For a typically Mexican snack, cut them into thin slices, sprinkle with lemon or lime juice, and season with chili powder and salt.

Jicamas remain crisp even when cooked. They add an original and crunchy touch to a wide array of dishes, including soups, vegetables, rice, tofu, quiches, meat, poultry, seafood, and even fruit salads. Since they absorb other flavors without losing their texture, they also make a delicious addition to stews and sweet-and-sour dishes. The jicama can be used in place of bamboo shoots and water chestnuts in most recipes.

Cooking

Jicamas are cooked in the same manner as potatoes; they are also good lightly fried.

Storing

Jicamas will keep, unwrapped, for about 3 weeks in the vegetable drawer of the refrigerator. Stored in the same way as potatoes, in a cool, dry place, they will also keep for several weeks.

Once cut, jicamas will keep for about a week in the refrigerator; store cut jicama in a perforated plastic bag.

Nutritional Information

water	85%
protein	1.4 g
carbohydrates	12.8 g
calories	55
	per 100 g

Sweet potato

Ipomoea batatas, Convolvulaceae

Tuber of a plant native to Central America. Despite its name, the sweet potato is not related to the potato. Rather, it belongs to the Convolvulaceae family of plants, which includes the morning glory and with which it shares its bell-shaped flowers.

The remains of sweet potatoes discovered in a cave in Peru and dating back 10,000 and 12,000 years provide evidence that the vegetable has been consumed since prehistoric times. The sweet potato we know is thought to be a hybrid of a wild-growing ancestor that originated somewhere in the region between Mexico and the northern part of South America. In the 16th century, the sweet potato migrated to the Philippines via Spanish explorers; it was introduced into Africa, India, southern Asia, and Indonesia by the Portuguese. Today the main producers of sweet potatoes are China, Indonesia, Vietnam, Uganda, Japan, and India.

This vegetable is a staple in many Asian and Latin American countries. It is also very popular in the southern United States, where cultivation was established in the 16th century. Although the sweet potato is often confused with the yam, the yam is actually starchier and less flavorful than the sweet potato.

The aerial part of the plant is composed of long creeping stems that can reach 16 feet and that bear leaves that are used in the same manner as spinach. The more than 400 varieties of sweet potato are grouped into two main categories. In the first group, the flesh is firm and dry, almost mealy, when cooked, while the flesh of the second variety becomes soft and moist when cooked. The thin edible skin of the sweet potato can be smooth or rough in texture, and ranges in color from white to yellow, orange, red, or purple; its flesh may be white, yellow, or orange.

Buying

When buying sweet potatoes, choose firm specimens without soft spots, cracks, or bruises. Avoid refrigerated sweet potatoes, as their taste is altered by the cold.

Preparing

Since the sweet potato is often dyed or given a waxy coating, some people may prefer to peel it before eating it. To prevent the flesh from darkening on contact with air, as soon as the potato is cut, put it in cold water until you are ready to use it or cook it as soon as possible (it should be completely covered with water).

Serving Ideas

Like the potato, the sweet potato is always eaten cooked, but because it is sweeter than the potato, it can be prepared in a greater variety of ways. Like winter squash, which is also sweet and which it can replace in most recipes, the sweet potato is often used to make cakes, pies, bread, pudding, marmalades, cookies, and muffins. It can be used to make croquettes or soufflés, or served au gratin or à la crème. The sweet potato is popular in Creole cooking. It blends well with cinnamon, honey, coconut, nutmeg, and lime, and constitutes an excellent accompaniment to pork, ham, and poultry. It is equally delicious baked in the oven or mashed, and can also be dried to make flakes or chips. Sweet potatoes also go into the making of alcohol, starch, and flour.

Tuber Vegetables

Cooking

The sweet potato may be prepared and cooked like the potato; the required cooking time is identical.

To cook a whole unpeeled sweet potato in a microwave oven, prick it several times with a fork, wrap it in a paper towel, and cook it on high for 5 to 7 minutes; halfway through cooking, turn the potato over. Let it cool for 2 minutes before serving.

When baking it whole in the oven, leave it unpeeled, prick it in several spots to prevent it from splitting, and bake it for 45 to 60 minutes, until tender. When boiling sweet potatoes, it is best not to peel them; after boiling for 20 to 30 minutes, the peel will come away easily.

Baked Sweet Potatoes

SERVES 4

2 large sweet potatoes
2 tbsp. olive oil

Salt and ground
pepper
1 tsp. chopped parsley

Serve with poultry.

1. Preheat the oven to 350°F (175°C).

2. Wash the potatoes well under running water and drain well. Without peeling them, cut the sweet potatoes in half lengthwise.

3. Place the potato halves in a baking dish (cut side up) and brush with the olive oil. Season with salt and pepper, and sprinkle with the parsley. Bake for about 45 minutes.

Nutritional Information

	baked or boiled (without the skin)
water	73%
protein	1.6 g
fat	0.3 g
carbohydrates	24.3 g
fiber	2.5 g
calories	105
	per 100 g

The sweet potato is an excellent source of vitamin A; it is also a good source of potassium and contains vitamin C, vitamin B_6, riboflavin, copper, pantothenic acid, and folic acid. The deeper its color, the higher its vitamin A content. Although the sweet potato contains more starch than the potato (up to 18%, depending on the variety), its carbohydrate content is roughly the same.

Storing

The sweet potato is more fragile than the potato and should be handled with care. Stored in a cool, dark, well-ventilated place, it will keep from 7 to 10 days. Avoid storing it at temperatures above 60°F, as this will cause it to sprout or ferment and in some varieties the flesh may become woody. Although the sweet potato should not be stored in the refrigerator when raw, once cooked, it will keep for about a week in the refrigerator; it can also be frozen after being cooked.

The aerial part of the sweet potato is composed of long creeping stems; its thin edible skin can be smooth or rough and varies in color from white to yellow, orange, red, or purple.

Tuber Vegetables

127

Jerusalem artichoke

Helianthus tuberosus, **Compositae**

Because of its height and ornamental features, this plant is used in certain regions to mark property boundaries.

Tuber Vegetables

128

The tuber of a perennial plant native to North America, this vegetable (also known as sunchoke) was originally cultivated by Indians settled in the region now known as New England. At one time much appreciated, the popularity of the Jerusalem artichoke was eventually overshadowed by the potato. During World War II, Jerusalem artichokes were one of the few vegetables available, and they thus came to be considered a poor man's vegetable.

The plant can grow to a height of 6 to 12 feet. Because of its height and ornamental features, it is sometimes used to mark property boundaries in certain regions, such as in the southern United States and in the Middle East. The Jerusalem artichoke plant is easy to grow and very resistant; in fact, it can be difficult to get rid of it. Jerusalem artichokes are 3 to 4 inches long and 1 to 2 inches in diameter. Their knobby roots resemble ginger. The yellowish white flesh is crisp and juicy, with a sweet, delicate flavor. The thin beige skin is edible and can have tinges of red or purple, depending on the type of soil in which the vegetable is grown. The flavor of Jerusalem artichokes tends to improve with time, and they are particularly tasty when dug up following a light frost.

Nutritional Information

	raw
water	78%
protein	2 g
fat	2 g
carbohydrates	17.4 g
fiber	1.6 g
calories	76
	per 100 g

Raw Jerusalem artichoke is an excellent source of potassium, as well as a good source of iron and thiamine; it also supplies niacin, phosphorus, copper and magnesium, folic acid and pantothenic acid.

This vegetable contains inulin, a sugar that, like starch, changes into fructose. Since inulin can cause flatulence in some people, it is recommended that it be consumed in small quantities the first time, especially by those prone to this problem. The Jerusalem artichoke is said to be energizing, disinfectant, and lactogenic.

Buying

Choose Jerusalem artichokes that are small and firm, with unblemished skin. Do not buy them if they are greenish in color or if they have begun to sprout.

Preparing

Jerusalem artichokes tend to oxidize rapidly when cut. To prevent this, soak them in water to which a little lemon juice or vinegar has been added.

Since they are not easy to peel, Jerusalem artichokes are often cooked in their skin after being brushed well; if necessary, the skin can be removed once they are cooked, but this should be done right away, before it cools and hardens again.

Serving Ideas

The Jerusalem artichoke can be consumed raw, cooked, or marinated. It is prepared in various ways, including puréed, au gratin, and *à la crème*. Raw, it can be served as an appetizer (sprinkled with citrus juice or vinegar to prevent darkening) or used to add a refreshing touch to salads. Cooked, it is a pleasant substitute for water chestnuts and potatoes. It is often added to soups, stews, crêpes, and fritters, and marries well with poultry and leeks.

Jerusalem artichokes can also be made into alcohol, or dried to make a very nutritive flour.

Cooking

It is better to shorten the cooking time for this vegetable, as 1 or 2 minutes too long could turn the flesh into an unappetizing mush.

For best results, the Jerusalem artichoke should be baked, steamed, or sautéed in a wok. Depending on its size, allow 30 to 45 minutes to bake it whole in the oven (about the same amount of time as for potatoes), 10 to 15 minutes for steaming, and 5 to 7 minutes for sautéing, adding it to the wok at the last minute. Avoid aluminum or iron pans, as contact with these metals will cause oxidation.

Storing

Jerusalem artichokes should be handled with care, as they bruise easily. Wrap them unwashed in a paper towel to absorb the humidity, and place them in a plastic bag in the refrigerator, where they will keep for up to 2 weeks. Like carrots, they can also be buried in sand, and will keep for 1 to 2 months stored in this way. This vegetable should not be frozen or canned, as it causes the flesh to darken and spoils its texture. It can be marinated instead.

Crosne

Stachys spp., **Labiatae**

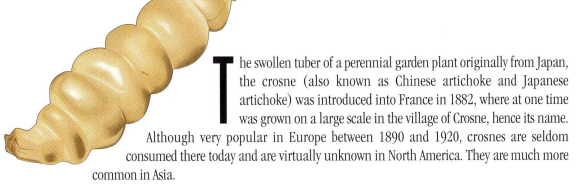

The swollen tuber of a perennial garden plant originally from Japan, the crosne (also known as Chinese artichoke and Japanese artichoke) was introduced into France in 1882, where at one time was grown on a large scale in the village of Crosne, hence its name. Although very popular in Europe between 1890 and 1920, crosnes are seldom consumed there today and are virtually unknown in North America. They are much more common in Asia.

The crosne (pronounced crone) grows on a plant with stems measuring 12 to 16 inches in height and bearing large oval dull-green leaves that are rough and puffy. The tubers are covered with a thin edible skin and measure 2 to 3 inches in length and ½ to ¾ inch in diameter. Their delicate, slightly sweet taste is reminiscent of salsify or artichoke.

Tuber Vegetables

129

Preparing

This vegetable does not need to be peeled, which is fortunate considering its twisted shape. The easiest way to clean it is to place it in a bag with coarse salt and to shake it vigorously, after which it can be rinsed under running water to remove any remaining dirt.

Serving Ideas

Crosnes are used and prepared like the potato, Jerusalem artichoke, and salsify. They can be boiled, braised, fried, pickled in vinegar, or puréed. They are sometimes added to salads or cooked in combination with other vegetables. They are often blanched for 2 minutes before being cooked. Crosnes are excellent sautéed in butter or topped with a bit of cream.

Storing

Crosnes are perishable and dry out quickly. Avoid leaving them out at room temperature for long periods. Store them in the refrigerator.

Buying

It is best to consume crosnes soon after harvesting, as they tend to dry out and lose their flavor quickly. Look for firm, unwrinkled specimens with evenly colored ends.

Nutritional Information

protein	2.7 g
carbohydrates	17.3 g
calories	80
	per 100 g

Cauliflower

Brassica oleracea var. *botrytis,* **Cruciferae**

A garden plant whose primitive ancestor is believed to have originated in Asia Minor, cauliflower was later introduced into Italy, where it underwent several transformations. France discovered cauliflower in the mid-16th century; it was subsequently brought to northern Europe and the British Isles, where it is still greatly appreciated. Today the most important producers of cauliflower are China, India, France, Italy, and the United States. Historical evidence suggests that this vegetable was known more than 2,500 years ago. Cauliflower was cultivated in Egypt as early as the 4th century B.C.

white cauliflower

Cauliflower consists of a compact head (or curd) comprised of numerous undeveloped flower buds attached to a short central stalk. If left to develop, these buds become small yellow flowers that are relatively unsavory. Cauliflower is usually white, but certain varieties have a purplish hue (they turn green during cooking). Purple cauliflower is very similar to broccoli; it cooks faster than white cauliflower and is milder tasting.

Cauliflower is covered with several layers of green leaves attached to the stalk. These leaves form a screen that protects the head from direct sunlight. They are sometimes hand-tied around the curd in order to preserve its white color. The outer leaves are long, coarse, and dark green in color. The edible inner leaves are smaller, more tender, and yellowish green.

Buying

Choose a cauliflower with a firm and compact head; it should be creamy white and still have its leaves, which should be bright green. The freshness of the outer leaves is the best indication of the freshness of the head. Avoid dull-colored or spotted cauliflower, as well as cauliflower that has started to flower.

Preparing

Remove the outer leaves and the stalk (reserve them for soups), keeping the small green leaves. Separate the florets from the main stalk, leaving a part of the stem. The florets can be cut if they are too big; this will shorten the cooking time and ensure uniform cooking. Wash the cauliflower under running water or soak it in vinegar water or salted water to rid it of any insects.

Serving Ideas

Cauliflower is just as good raw as it is cooked. Raw cauliflower can be eaten on its own or served with a dip; it is also used in appetizers and salads. Cooked, it can be eaten warm or cold, but it is better if still slightly firm. Good as a vegetable side dish, cauliflower can also be added to soups, stews, pasta, omelets, or quiches. It is excellent topped with a Mornay or hollandaise sauce, or covered with a béchamel sauce and gratinéed. Cooked cauliflower can be puréed and added to soufflés and soups. It is also an ingredient in pickles, relishes, and chutneys. Cauliflower is prepared in much the same way as broccoli, with which it is interchangeable in most recipes.

Cauliflower au Gratin

SERVES 4

2 lb. cauliflower

Mornay sauce:
2 tbsp. butter
1 heaping tbsp. flour
2 cups (500 ml) milk

1 pinch nutmeg
Salt and white pepper
¼ cup (60 ml) grated
Gruyère cheese
Few pats of butter

1. Break the cauliflower into florets and soak them for 10 minutes in cold water with a bit of vinegar. Drain.

2. Cook the cauliflower florets in boiling salted water, or steam them, until tender but still firm.

3. Drain them well if they were boiled, and arrange them in a gratin dish. Cover and place to the side.

4. To make the Mornay sauce, melt the butter over low heat. Add the flour and stir for a few seconds until the mixture begins to foam. Add the milk all at once. Add the nutmeg, salt, and white pepper. Mix and cook, stirring constantly, until thick. Remove from the heat and add half of the grated Gruyère.

5. Pour the Mornay sauce over the cauliflower florets and sprinkle with the remaining Gruyère and a few pats of butter.

6. Place under a preheated broiler and cook for a few minutes, or until the top is golden brown.

Cooking

Cauliflower cooks very quickly and should not be overcooked, as it tends to fall apart and become pasty, in addition to losing some of its flavor and nutritional value. It requires the same treatment given to other white vegetables (see *Introduction*). It can be boiled, steamed, stir-fried, or microwaved. When boiling it in water, you can add a piece of bread to the cooking liquid to absorb some of the odor.

Nutritional Information

	raw	*cooked*
water	92%	92.5%
protein	2 g	1.9 g
fat	0.2 g	0.2 g
carbohydrates	5 g	4.6 g
fiber	1.8 g	1.8 g
calories	24	24
		per 100 g

Cauliflower is an excellent source of vitamin C, folic acid, and potassium; it also contains vitamin B_6 and niacin. Cooked cauliflower is an excellent source of vitamin C and potassium; it is also a good source of folic acid and contains vitamin B_6 and copper. Cauliflower contains citric acid and malic acid and is the most easily digestible member of the cabbage family. Like the other members of this family, it is believed to have cancer-inhibiting properties.

Storing

Cauliflower can be kept unwashed in a perforated plastic bag in the refrigerator for about 10 days. Cooked cauliflower spoils more quickly and will keep for only 2 or 3 days. The odor and taste of cauliflower become more pronounced as it ages. Cauliflower can be frozen after being blanched for 3 minutes in boiling water. However, this will make it more watery once it is thawed.

purple cauliflower

Inflorescent Vegetables

131

Broccoli

Brassica oleracea var. *italica,* Cruciferae

A vegetable believed to have originated in southern Italy, broccoli has a long history of cultivation, having been developed by the Romans from wild cabbage. The Romans had high esteem for this vegetable, which to this day is often associated with Italian cuisine. It is held that broccoli was grown for its floral shoots in Asia Minor, and that it was later brought by navigators to Italy, where it was subsequently developed and much improved. Catherine de Médicis introduced it into France.

The word "broccoli" comes from the Latin *bracchium,* meaning "branch" or "arm," and refers to the treelike shape of the vegetable. Usually green, broccoli can also be white or purple; it is harvested before its yellow flowers blossom. The different varieties of broccoli include the cauliflower broccoli (var. *botrytis*), which is similar to cauliflower, and the broccoflower, a cross between broccoli and cauliflower.

Nutritional Information

	cooked
water	90.6%
protein	2.9 g
carbohydrates	5.1 g
fiber	2.6 g
fat	0.4 g
calories	28
	per 100 g

Cooked broccoli is an excellent source of vitamin C and potassium; it is a good source of folic acid and contains vitamin A, magnesium, pantothenic acid, iron, and phosphorus. Like the other members of the large cabbage family, broccoli contains beta-carotenes, which are believed to be anticarcinogenic.

Preparing

Remove any wilted or fibrous leaves (use them in soups and stews for flavor), keeping the tender small leaves. The heads can be cooked whole, or if they are too large, they can be separated into florets to ensure rapid and uniform cooking. Wash the broccoli under running water or soak it for 15 minutes in salted water or vinegar water to dislodge any insects.

Buying

Choose broccoli that is firm and evenly colored, with compact bud clusters. Broccoli with open flowers, or yellow, wilted, or bruised broccoli that is losing its buds, should be avoided, as it is neither fresh nor tender. The outer leaves should be a deep green and the stems should be firm.

Serving Ideas

Broccoli can be eaten raw or cooked. Raw, it is often served on its own, with a dip, in an appetizer, or added to salad. Cooked broccoli is good warm or cold and is best when still slightly firm. It is delicious served with a dressing, with béchamel, Mornay, or hollandaise sauce, au gratin, or simply with butter or puréed. It makes a good vegetable side dish and is also frequently added to soups, stews, omelets, soufflés, quiches, and pasta. Broccoli can be prepared in the same manner as cauliflower.

Cooking

Since the stems take longer to cook than the florets, they can be cooked separately for a few minutes, or peeled if they are very fibrous, or cut into pieces (necessary if they are very thick). Lengthwise incisions can also be made in the stems for quicker cooking. Broccoli can be boiled, steamed, stir-fried, or cooked in the microwave. Allow 10 to 15 minutes when boiling or steaming whole broccoli. Adding a bit of sugar during cooking will help it stay greener.

Storing

This vegetable is very perishable; signs of spoiling include wilted leaves, open buds that are yellow or falling, and a hardened stem. Store broccoli in the vegetable drawer of the refrigerator, where it will keep for 5 days. Blanched and frozen, broccoli will keep for up to 1 year at 1°F.

Italian broccoli

Brassica rapa var. *ruvo* or *italica,* **Cruciferae**

Native to the Mediterranean region, Italian broccoli (also called broccoli raab, rabe, and di rape) is related to broccoli, cabbage, and the other members of the crucifer family. Consumed in Italy for centuries, it was carried across the Atlantic by Italian immigrants who settled in the United States at the beginning of the century; however, this vegetable is still relatively unknown in North America.

The thin green stalks of Italian broccoli are topped by serrated leaves. Unlike broccoli, it does not have green heads, although some stems produce clusters of small floral buds which open into yellow florets. The stems, leaves, buds, and flowers of Italian broccoli are all edible.

Italian broccoli has a slightly bitter flavor, and its stalks are usually preferred to the more bitter leaves.

Buying

Choose Italian broccoli with thin, firm stems bearing relatively few bud clusters. Avoid specimens with soft stems, wilted or yellow leaves, or open florets.

Preparing

Wash the stalks well under running water and trim them near the bottom. They can be prepared whole or cut into pieces. The stalks take longer to cook and may be prepared separately from the leaves.

Serving Ideas

Italian broccoli can be eaten raw, but the pungent flavor of this vegetable may not suit everyone's taste. Broccoli and Italian broccoli are prepared in the same way and are interchangeable in most recipes, although Italian broccoli cooks faster.

Once cooked, it is consumed hot or cold and makes a savory dish when served with an oil and vinegar dressing. Steaming is not the best method of cooking this vegetable because it tends to retain a lot of its bitterness. Italian broccoli adds a lively note to bland foods such as tofu, potatoes, and pasta. It is delicious with béchamel sauce, grated with cheese, or simply topped with a dash of lemon and a pat of butter.

Cooking

Cook the stalks for 1 minute in a small quantity of water, then add the leaves and buds and cook for 2 to 4 minutes longer. This way, the stalks will be tender and the leaves will remain an attractive green. Italian broccoli can also be blanched for 1 minute before cooking to make it less pungent.

Storing

Unwashed and stored in a perforated plastic bag, Italian broccoli will keep for a week in the refrigerator. Since it is most flavorful when fresh, it should be consumed as soon as possible after purchase.

Nutritional Information

	raw
water	89%
protein	3.6 g
carbohydrates	5.9 g
fiber	1.5 g
calories	32
	per 100 g

Inflorescent Vegetables

133

Artichoke

Cynara scolymus, Compositae

The artichoke is the flower bud of a plant that developed from the cardoon; it is edible prior to blossoming.

The flower bud of a garden plant that developed from the cardoon. A native of the Mediterranean area, the artichoke was held in high esteem by the Greeks and Romans. During the Middle Ages it acquired the reputation for being an aphrodisiac, and it became quite rare during this period. Catherine de Médicis was very fond of artichokes and brought them to France from her native Italy when she married the king of France. The artichoke was introduced into America by French and Spanish explorers.

The artichoke is widely cultivated in Italy, Spain, and France, which together represent over 80% of world production of this vegetable. It is also cultivated on a large scale in the western United States, particularly in Castroville, California.

The artichoke grows on a plant that stands 3 to 5 feet high and has indented leaves. It can be eaten prior to flowering; the edible parts of the plant include the heart of the bud and the bases of the leaves, which are actually bracts. The fuzzy choke at the center, which would develop into a flower if the plant were allowed to mature, is inedible.

There are over a dozen varieties of artichoke, differing in shape (although usually round and slightly pointed) and color (dark green bordering on blue or violet). The only variety that can be eaten raw is the small purple Provençal artichoke, since it has an undeveloped choke. The artichoke grows best in warm climates, where it is a perennial; elsewhere, it is often grown as an annual.

Buying

Choose an artichoke that is compact and heavy for its size, with crisp, tightly packed, bright green leaves. The size of the artichoke varies according to variety and is no indication of the vegetable's quality. Avoid artichokes with discolored or brown-tipped leaves, as they lack freshness and tend to have a pungent flavor. Loosely spread leaves are a sign of overripeness; overripe artichokes have a large choke and tend to be tough. Artichoke bottoms are often available ready to eat preserved in salted or unsalted water or in vinegar. Artichoke hearts are sold frozen or in vinaigrette.

Serving Ideas

With the exception of the purple Provençal artichoke, artichokes are always eaten cooked. Once cooked, they may be served hot, warm, or cold. They are often boiled or steamed whole and served warm or cold. The usual method of eating artichokes consists of removing the leaves one at a time and scraping off their flesh with the teeth. Once all the leaves have been removed, the central pink- or purple-colored cone and the choke covering the bottom are cut out so that the tender bottom can be savored. Artichokes prepared this way are often served with a dressing or mayonnaise in which the leaves and heart can be dipped.

Artichoke hearts are frequently added to salads and appetizers or used as a garnish.

Whole artichokes are good stuffed and baked in the oven; they can also be served with a béchamel, butter, or hollandaise sauce.

Preparing

To clean an artichoke, wash it under running water and soak it in acidulated water to rid it of any dirt and insects. Avoid touching the prickly leaf ends. Break off the stem with your hands rather than with a knife, removing some of the tough outer leaves around the base at the same time. Then use a knife to cut the stem off flush with the base so that the artichoke can be stood up. Rub the base with lemon to avoid oxidation. Trim off the spiky tips of the leaves with scissors, and slice off the top one third of the artichoke with a knife.

PREPARING ARTICHOKE BOTTOMS

1 *Break off the stem of the artichoke along with the tough fibers from the heart.*

2 *Cut off the outer leaves surrounding the heart, leaving the more tender inner leaves.*

3 *Trim off the top two thirds of each artichoke.*

4 *Remove the rest of the leaves from the base of the artichoke, and trim it so that it is flat.*

5 *Rub the base of the artichoke with a slice of lemon to prevent discoloration, and keep the artichokes in lemon water until ready to be used.*

Cooking

Among the many different ways in which artichokes can be cooked, baking, boiling, and steaming are the most common. Although boiling has its disadvantages (see *Introduction*), this is the most frequent method used; allow 35 to 45 minutes depending on the size. Whole artichokes will darken during cooking if they are not completely covered with salted water. To keep them from floating to the surface, cover them with a heatproof dish or a cloth. Do not add baking soda to the water, as the alkalinity causes the artichokes to turn an unappetizing green color and reduces their vitamin content slightly. Avoid cooking them in aluminum or iron pots, which tend to make them turn grayish. Whole artichokes are cooked when the outer leaves can be easily detached. Before serving, drain the artichokes for a few minutes by turning them upside down to let all the water run off the leaves. Artichoke hearts should be cooked in water acidulated with lemon juice or vinegar to keep them from discoloring. Simmer them for 15 to 20 minutes, or until they are easily pierced with a knife.

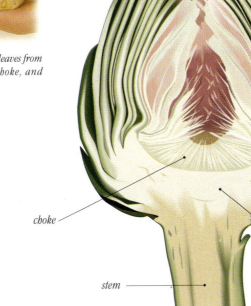

leaves

choke

bottom

stem

Nutritional Information

	cooked
water	84%
protein	3.5 g
fat	0.2 g
carbohydrates	11.2 g
calories	50
	per 100 g

The artichoke is an excellent source of potassium and magnesium and a good source of folic acid; it also supplies vitamin C, copper, iron, phosphorus, niacin, vitamin B$_6$, zinc, pantothenic acid, and calcium. Artichokes contain substances that are said to stimulate the secretion of bile. They are also credited with a number of medicinal properties: they are said to be a good appetite stimulant, blood cleanser, antitoxin, and diuretic, in addition to being excellent for the liver. The therapeutic effects of the artichoke are maximized by infusing the plant's large indented leaves (not the bracts that are eaten).

Storing

Store artichokes unwashed and well wrapped in a perforated plastic bag in the refrigerator, where they will keep for 4 to 5 days. If they still have their stems, you can stand them in a bowl of water, like cut flowers, and store them in the refrigerator. Cooked artichokes should not be left out at room temperature for too long, as they deteriorate quickly. Once cooked, artichokes will keep for 24 hours in the refrigerator. Cooked artichoke hearts will keep for 6 to 8 months in the freezer.

Artichoke Hearts in Lemon Sauce

SERVES 4

4 large artichokes
1 slice lemon
1 cup (250 ml) heavy cream
1 tbsp. flour
5 tbsp. (75 ml) butter, in pieces

1 pinch of sugar
6 tbsp. (90 ml) lemon juice
Salt
Nutmeg

To prepare the artichokes:

1. Break off the artichoke stems at the base. Slice off the top third of each artichoke, and trim the tips of the outer leaves with scissors. Wash and drain the artichokes, and rub the base of each with the slice of lemon.

2. Plunge the artichokes into boiling salted water and simmer for 30 to 40 minutes. The artichokes are ready when the outer leaves pull away easily.

3. Remove the artichokes from the water and place them upside down in a strainer to drain.

4. When ready to serve, discard the leaves and remove the choke.

To prepare the sauce:

While the artichokes are cooking, make the sauce:

1. In a pot, combine the cream and flour.

2. Cook over a low heat, stirring constantly, for 3 or 4 minutes or until the sauce is smooth and creamy. During this time, stir in the butter, sugar, and lemon juice, and season with salt and nutmeg to taste.

3. Pour a bit of sauce over each artichoke, and pour the rest into a warm sauceboat.

Provençal artichoke

Legumes

Introduction

The term "legume" is used to refer to plants that produce edible seeds in pods, to the seeds themselves, as well as to the family of these plants. The family of legumes is extremely vast, encompassing more than 600 genuses and 13,000 species. Lentils *(Lens)*, beans *(Phaseolus)*, broad beans *(Vicia)*, soybeans *(Glycine)*, and peanuts *(Arachis)* all belong to the family of legumes. The dried seeds of leguminous plants are also known as "pulses."

An important part of the human diet since ancient times, legumes were also among the first plants to be cultivated. Several varieties of legumes were grown as early as prehistoric times. Recent archeological discoveries of remains of beans and other legumes dating back over 11,000 years suggest that the first legume crops were planted in southeastern Asia, rather than in the Middle East, as was originally believed. Lentils and chickpeas are also natives of this region of Asia.

While legumes were held in high esteem by some civilizations, others had only contempt for them. The ancient Greeks and Romans regarded legumes as poor man's fare and the Greek philosopher Pythagoras was their declared enemy. Throughout the Middle Ages, legumes were a dietary staple in Northern Europe where the climate was unsuitable for the cultivation of good cereal crops. In the 15th and 16th centuries, the explorations and the expansion of trade contributed to the spread of the different varieties of legumes to other regions of the world. To this day, legumes play a major role in the diet of many societies, particularly in North Africa, Latin America, and Asia.

Most legumes grow on annual plants that can be of the bushy, dwarf or giant variety (some of which attain over 6 feet in height). Many of these plants have tendrils which permit them to cling to their immediate surroundings. While peas and beans grow best in cool temperatures and can even be planted in early spring, most varieties of legumes require warmer weather. The pods emerge once the flowers have blossomed; the flowers vary in color from one variety to another. Averaging between 3 and 8 inches in length, the pods contain 4 to 12 seeds, often kidney-shaped, that vary in size and range in color from green to brown, black, red, yellow or white. Whether they are consumed fresh or dried, the seeds of leguminous plants are always cooked beforehand. The immature pods are also edible (dolichos bean, adzuki bean, lima bean, soybean, etc.).

Buying

When choosing dried legumes, look for specimens that are intact, brightly colored, uniform in size, and smooth (except for bumpy varieties like the chickpea). Avoid any that are dull looking or wrinkled, as well as those with insect holes, as they are likely either too old or they were improperly stored, making it difficult to rehydrate them.

Preparing

 Dried legumes are easy to prepare for cooking; simply soak them and add the seasoning ingredients.

Soaking

The purpose of the soaking process is to restore the moisture that has been lost by the dried legumes; it also shortens the cooking time and preserves vitamins and minerals, as well as reducing the flatulence caused by legumes. Certain legumes, including lentils, split peas, mung beans, and adzuki beans, do not need to be soaked before being cooked. Soaking generally takes 6 to 8 hours, which is why it is often done overnight, although a quick-soaking method can also be used. Legumes cooked in a pressure cooker do not need to be presoaked. It is a good idea to soak a large quantity of legumes at once and to freeze part of them for future use.

Overnight soaking

Before soaking, wash and sort the dried legumes. Remove any debris, as well as any stained or cracked beans. It is important to wash the legumes several times in cold water, letting them soak between rinses and skimming off any impurities or any beans that float to the surface (they often harbor parasites); a sieve can be used to facilitate this process. Transfer the washed legumes to a large bowl and cover them with 3 parts water to 1 part legumes. Let the legumes soak overnight in a cool place or in the refrigerator.

Quick soaking

Wash and sort the dried legumes. In a large pot, add 3 to 4 parts water to 1 part legumes and slowly bring to a boil. Simmer for 2 minutes and remove from the heat. Let the legumes stand in the covered pot for 1 or 2 hours, or until they swell. Drain and cook according to the chosen recipe.

When using a microwave oven, make sure the pot is large enough to hold the legumes once they expand; add enough cold water to cover the legumes and cook on high for 8 to 10 minutes or until they start boiling. Boil for 2 minutes more and let stand for 1 hour.

Certain precautions can be taken to reduce the flatulence caused by legumes when their sugars, starch, and fiber are fermented by the action of bacteria in the intestine:

• change the soaking water several times and do not use it to cook the legumes; alternatively, change the cooking water after 30 minutes, simmering the legumes until they are very tender. Some of the water-soluble nutrients will be discarded with the soaking and cooking water, but this loss can be compensated for by adding a little yeast just before serving;

• cook legumes slowly and thoroughly;

• masticate legumes well;

• do not add sugar or any other sweet ingredients when cooking legumes and avoid sweet desserts at the end of the meal.

Serving Ideas

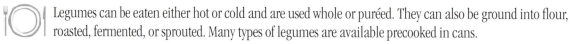 Legumes can be eaten either hot or cold and are used whole or puréed. They can also be ground into flour, roasted, fermented, or sprouted. Many types of legumes are available precooked in cans.

The uses of dried legumes or pulses are many and varied: they can be served as an appetizer or a snack (roasted like peanuts), in salads or soups, as a main dish or as a dessert. The Middle Eastern specialty known as hummus is prepared from a purée of chickpeas, while Indian dahl is made from puréed and spiced lentils. Many varieties of legumes are ground into flour that is used to make crêpes, flat breads, cakes, quiches, and sweets. Asians use adzuki beans and mung beans to make various sweet, jelly-like desserts that are very popular. Legumes are often used to prepare side dishes or as the essential ingredient in main dishes; Mexican tacos and burritos, the Lebanese specialty falafel, the famous French cassoulet, and Brazil's national dish feijoada are all made from legumes.

Cooking

 Many people regard the cooking of legumes as a chore; indeed, most legumes must be rehydrated (soaked) before being cooked and the cooking time is relatively long (unless they are pressure cooked).

Legumes can be cooked on the stove top, in the oven, or in a pressure cooker. In America, legumes were traditionally simmered for up to 2 days in clay pots, giving them a unique flavor. With modern cooking methods, most legumes require only 2 hours of cooking; place the dry legumes in a large pot, cover them with cold water and bring to a boil; reduce the heat and simmer gently until the legumes are tender. Never use hot water at the start of cooking, as it may cause the legumes to ferment.

Legumes cook much more quickly in a pressure cooker; the end result is not as flavorful, however, since once they are cooked, the legumes have little time to absorb the flavor of other foods. A pressure cooker is most useful when cooking legumes on their own or in the case of recipes which do not require the addition of many ingredients or seasonings at the beginning of cooking of the legumes. When cooking legumes with other ingredients, it is better to use slower cooking methods which give the legumes time to absorb the other flavors.

There are certain risks involved in pressure cooking, particularly with dry legumes such as soybeans, lima beans, and peas, all of which tend to produce a lot of foam. Pressure cooking is not recommended for lentils and split peas.

For best results:

• Add a little oil to the cooking water to prevent the formation of foam that could block the pressure control valve and the safety valve; bring the legumes to a boil without the cover and skim off the foam; reduce the heat and simmer for a while before covering the pot and starting to cook under pressure; once the desired pressure is reached, set the timer according to the size and variety of legume.

• Avoid overfilling; the volume of water and legumes should not exceed ⅓ of the capacity of the pot.

• Do not cook on high.

• Rinse the pot under cold water as soon as the legumes are cooked and make sure that the control valve and safety valve are cleaned thoroughly after each use to prevent clogging.

• If the control valve and safety valve become blocked, rinse the pot immediately under cold water and clean the valves thoroughly.

Dried legumes expand when cooked; 1 cup of most types of dried legumes will produce 2 to 3 cups of cooked legumes.

Baking soda is sometimes added to the soaking or cooking water to soften the legumes and shorten the cooking time. However, this practice tends to destroy part of the thiamine content of legumes and to make their amino acids less assimilable; it may also alter the flavor. Adding a little algae will soften the legumes more quickly while at the same time increasing their nutritional value.

Salt and acidic ingredients (lemon juice, vinegar, tomatoes) should only be added near the end of cooking, as they cause the legumes to remain hard longer. Some legumes should not be stirred once they start boiling, as this could cause them to stick to the bottom of the pot. If more water is required during cooking, add boiling water. Lard or oil are often included in recipes for legumes; whenever possible, reduce the quantity of these ingredients or eliminate them altogether; it is best to add a little oil just before serving.

Although the majority of legumes are interchangeable in most recipes, it is not a good idea to cook different varieties simultaneously; a number of factors may affect their moisture content, making it difficult to obtain uniformly cooked legumes. For best results, cook them separately. It is also important to cook legumes thoroughly in order to neutralize the substances that interfere with the absorption of their nutrients. A number of condiments and seasonings blend particularly well with legumes, including mustard, tamari, vinegar, thyme, laurel, summer savory, sage, garlic, fennel, onion, tomato, and celery. They are frequently associated with savory, which makes them more easily digestible and reduces flatulence.

Nutritional Information

Legumes are highly nutritious. Cooked, they supply 6 to 9 g protein, 0.1 to 0.7 g fat, 18 to 28 g carbohydrates, 5 to 8 g fiber, and 105 to 140 calories per 100 g.

The proteins in legumes are different from those found in meat. They are said to be "incomplete" because they are lacking in certain essential amino acids, notably methionine, cystine, and tryptophan (called the "limiting" amino acids, to the extent that they are present in lower quantities than the other amino acids). To make up for these deficiencies, legumes should be combined with other sources of protein, such as cereals. Most legumes are an excellent source of folic acid and potassium and a good source of iron and magnesium, as well as supplying thiamine, zinc, and copper. Legumes are also a very rich source of dietary fiber. Fresh legumes and legume sprouts contain small amounts of vitamin C as well.

To increase the body's absorption of the iron present in legumes, they should be consumed in combination with foods that are rich in vitamin C, such as citrus fruits, sweet peppers, or any member of the cabbage family. Avoid drinking tea, which contains tannins that interfere with the absorption of iron.

Legumes

141

Storing

Legumes will keep for a full year without significant loss of nutritional value if they are placed in an airtight container and stored in a cool, dry place. Avoid mixing legumes bought at different times or in different stores in the same container. Cooked beans can be refrigerated for about 5 days and frozen for up to 3 months; it may be a good idea to drain the legumes before freezing them. Canned legumes should be stored in a cool, dry place and used within a year.

Bean

Phaseolus spp., Leguminosae

Seed of a plant native to Central and South America. The term "bean" is used to refer to both the pod, which is consumed as a vegetable, and its edible seeds. Beans were cultivated over 7,000 years ago by Indian tribes in Mexico and Peru. Indian migrations contributed to the gradual spread of bean plant cultivation right across America. By the time Spanish explorers arrived on the continent in the 15th and 16th centuries, beans could be found growing all over Latin America. Seventeenth-century English settlers also encountered them on the east coast of the United States. Spanish and Portuguese explorers are credited with having introduced beans and the culture of beans into Africa, Asia, and Europe in the early 17th century. In Europe, this plant was originally cultivated for its seeds, and it wasn't until the end of the 19th century in Italy that fresh green beans began to be eaten as a vegetable. Today the major producers of dried beans are India, Brazil, China, the United States, Mexico, and Indonesia.

There are over 100 varieties of beans, varying in shape, color, flavor, and nutritional value. The pods of most varieties can be eaten fresh before they reach maturity, like the common green bean and the wax bean of the variety *Phaseolus vulgaris*. Once the pods mature they are no longer edible; they are shelled and their seeds are used fresh or dried (but always cooked). The bean seeds are known as "legumes." Fresh beans usually come from dwarf species that are cultivated in many regions of the world, including China, Turkey, Spain, Italy, France, Egypt, the United States, Romania, and Japan. The pods can be green (sometimes with purple or red mottling), yellow, or purple; purple varieties turn green during cooking. Long and slender, the pods can be straight or slightly curved. Some varieties, such as the snap bean, are stringless. The pods usually measure 3 to 8 inches in length and contain 4 to 12 seeds that vary in color from one variety to another and that can be uniformly colored, mottled, or striped. The bean seeds are either kidney-shaped or round and usually measure less than ⅜ of an inch in length.

White beans include a wide array of varieties, including:

• the **white kidney bean**, which is kidney-shaped, fairly large, and slightly squared at the ends, and the smaller **small white bean**;

• the **Great Northern bean**, which is medium-size, less kidney-shaped and rounder than the white kidney bean, with rounded ends;

• the **cannellini bean**, a variety that is highly prized in Italy, with somewhat of a kidney shape and squared ends;

• the oval-shaped **navy bean or white pea bean**, which is the size of a pea;

• the **cranberry bean**, which is large, round, and creamy white with splashes of pink or brown; very popular in Europe, it has a low starch content and is used mainly in stews and cassoulet.

All of these types of beans are interchangeable in most recipes. They have a less pronounced taste than red kidney beans and readily absorb the flavor of the foods with which they are cooked.

The **pinto bean** is medium-size, fairly flat, and kidney-shaped; it is beige with light brown spots resembling splashes of paint (in fact, the word *pinto* means "painted" in Spanish). The mottling disappears during cooking, however, and the bean takes on a pinkish hue. This flavorful bean acquires a creamy texture when cooked and is a good replacement for red kidney beans; it also adds a colorful touch to dishes and is delicious puréed.

The **Roman bean** is kidney-shaped, brownish in color (certain varieties are beige) with mottling, and resembles the pinto bean, although it is often larger and darker. It is very popular in Italy, where it is called *fagiolo romano*. This excellent bean loses its mottling during cooking; it has a smooth texture and readily absorbs the flavor of dishes to which it is added. It can be used in place of the pinto bean or the red kidney bean.

The **red kidney bean** is one of the most widely known beans; as its name suggests, it is dark red and kidney-shaped, with a delicate texture and flavor. It is commonly used in simmered dishes, where it readily absorbs flavors. It is a key ingredient in the nourishing dish known as *chili con carne*. Its ability to retain its shape and texture make it particularly suitable for canning. Red kidney beans can be substituted for Roman beans and pinto beans in most recipes.

The **flageolet** is a pale green, thin, flat bean; less starchy than most other legumes, it is often called "fayot" in Europe. It is particularly prized in France, where it is the traditional accompaniment to roast leg of lamb *(gigot d'agneau)*. This bean is mainly available in dried or canned form.

The **black bean** is slightly kidney-shaped and completely black. It is rarely available outside of its native United States, Central America, and Mexico, where it has long been a staple food. Mexican cooking makes particularly abundant use of this bean, notably in *frijoles refritos* (refried beans). Black beans are also traditionally served with Mexican burritos and enchiladas or added to soups and salads.

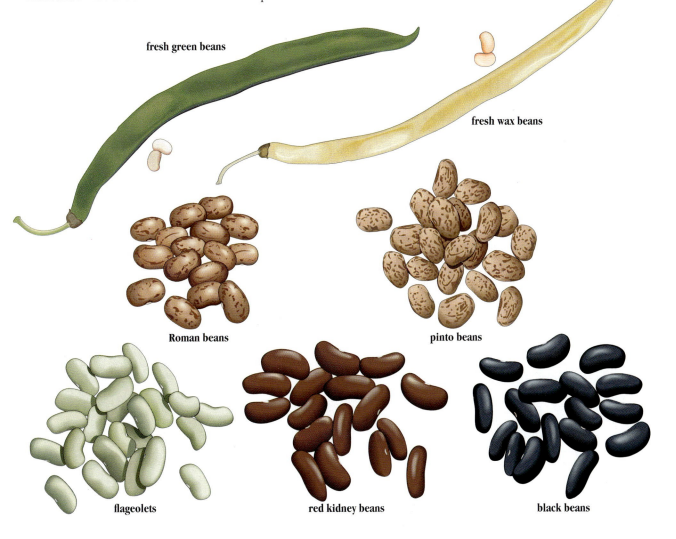

fresh green beans

fresh wax beans

Roman beans

pinto beans

flageolets

red kidney beans

black beans

The pods of most varieties of beans can be eaten fresh before they reach maturity, like the yellow and green beans with which most of us are familiar. Once mature, however, these pods are inedible; then they are seeded and their bean seeds used fresh or dried.

Legumes

144

Buying

When buying fresh beans, look for firm, crisp pods with a healthy green or yellow color and a regular shape; they should be free of bruises and brown spots. The beans are fresh if beads of moisture form around the break when they are snapped in two. Overripe or old beans tend to be tough and starchy.

Preparing

Fresh bean pods should be washed just before using them; remove the top and tail and any strings (some varieties are stringless).

Storing

Place fresh bean pods, unwashed, in a perforated plastic bag in the refrigerator, where they will keep for 2 to 3 days.

Fresh beans may also be frozen after being blanched, although prolonged freezing (more than 12 months) detracts from their flavor. Before freezing, blanch cut beans for 3 minutes and whole beans for 4 minutes.

Nutritional Information

Raw fresh beans are a good source of potassium and folic acid; they also contain vitamin C, magnesium, thiamine, iron, vitamin A, and niacin, as well as traces of copper, phosphorus, and calcium. Cooked fresh beans are an excellent source of potassium, a good source of folic acid, and contain vitamin C, magnesium, iron, vitamin A, and copper.

Most varieties of dried beans are an excellent source of potassium and folic acid, a good source of magnesium and iron, and contain copper, phosphorus, zinc, thiamine, niacin, and vitamin B$_6$.

Fresh beans are said to be diuretic and tonic, and to cleanse the blood and protect against infection.

Serving Ideas

Fresh beans are most commonly eaten cooked, either warm or cold. In addition to their frequent use as a vegetable side dish, they are added to salads, soups, stews, and stir-fries. They are delicious marinated, baked au gratin, or topped with a sauce or vinaigrette. Their flavor blends particularly well with tomato, thyme, oregano, rosemary, mint, marjoram, mustard, aniseed, nutmeg, and cardamom.

Dried beans can also be eaten warm or cold, in whole or puréed form. They are a popular addition to soups, salads, sandwich spreads, and main dishes, and sometimes even serve to make desserts. Puréed dried beans can be used as a side dish or as the basis of main dishes, in croquettes and fritters, for example.

Cooking

Green and purple beans should be cooked with care in order to preserve their flavor, color, and nutritional value. They tend to lose their color during cooking (see *Cooking vegetables*). Cook them as briefly as possible; allow 5 to 15 minutes for boiling or steaming, depending on the size of the beans and whether they are whole or cut.

Dried beans are cooked after being soaked (see *Cooking legumes*). The cooking time differs from one variety to another but is generally between 1½ and 2 hours.

Greek-Style Beans

SERVES 4

2 large onions
3 tbsp. flat-leaf parsley
3 cloves garlic
2 large fresh tomatoes
¼ cup (60 ml) olive oil

1 lb. (500 g) fresh green beans
Salt and ground pepper
Oregano and basil to taste
1 bay leaf

Serve hot or warm to accompany meat or broiled fish.

1. Chop the onions and parsley. Finely chop the garlic. Blanch and peel the tomatoes, and cut into chunks.

2. Pour the oil into a casserole (preferably cast iron) and add the beans, onions, tomatoes, and garlic. Season with salt and pepper. Add the oregano, the parsley, and basil, and place the bay leaf on top. Cover and simmer over low heat for about 1 hour.

	raw fresh bean	cooked fresh bean	boiled white bean	boiled pinto beanred	boiled kidney bean
water	90.3%	89.2%	63.0%	64.0%	66.9%
protein	1.8 g	1.9 g	9.7 g	8.2 g	8.7 g
fat	0.1 g	0.3 g	0.3 g	0.5 g	0.5 g
carbohydrates	7.1 g	7.9 g	25.0 g	25.6 g	22.8 g
fiber	1.8 g	2.4 g	6.3 g	8.6 g	7.4 g

per 100 g

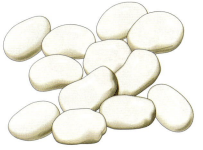

Lima beans

Phaseolus lunatus, Leguminosae

Thaceous plant originating in South America and also known as the "butter bean." Remains of the lima bean dating back over 7,000 years have been discovered in Peru, and it is known to have been cultivated throughout the Caribbean and Central and South America around the time of Columbus's discovery of America. Spanish explorers are credited with having introduced the lima bean into Europe.

There are numerous varieties of lima beans, which are often named after their place of cultivation, particularly the European varieties.

Lima beans grow on a bushy or climbing plant ranging in height from 1½ to 13 feet. The flat oblong pods measure 2 to 4 inches in length and contain two to four smooth kidney-shaped seeds that are flat with rounded ends. The seeds vary in size from one variety to another; some are quite tiny, while others are very large, measuring over ¼ inch thick. Lima beans are usually cream-colored or green but may also be white, red, purple, brownish, or blackish; some are uniformly colored, while others are spotted. They are very tasty and have a rather starchy texture.

Certain varieties of lima beans from the Caribbean contain a high level of toxic compounds called cyanogenetic glycosides; these are neutralized by soaking and cooking. Varieties cultivated in the United States contain negligible quantities of these substances.

Buying

Fresh lima beans should be glossy and clean. Avoid those that are wrinkled, yellowed, or blemished, as they tend to be rather hard and bland. Shelled lima beans should be plump, with tender pale or whitish green skin.

Serving Ideas

Young lima beans can be eaten fresh with or without their pods and are often served as a vegetable or added to salads, soups, and stews. Their delicate flavor makes them suitable for use in a wide variety of recipes, particularly in finer dishes where stronger-tasting beans would mask the flavor of the other ingredients. Lima beans can also be puréed and served as a pleasant substitute for potatoes. Like other beans, they can also be sprouted.

Cooking

It is important not to overcook lima beans, as they tend to turn mushy quickly once they have softened. Lima beans also produce a lot of foam during cooking, which can be dangerous in a pressure cooker, where the foam could block the safety valve (see *Introduction*).

Varieties of dried lima beans with large seeds cook in 15 minutes in the pressure cooker, while small-seeded varieties require only 10 minutes. When cooking them in water, allow 15 to 25 minutes for fresh lima beans and about 1½ hours for dried beans, depending on their size.

Nutritional Information

	boiled lima beans
water	69.8%
protein	7.8 g
fat	0.4 g
carbohydrates	20.9 g
fiber	7.2 g
calories	115
	per 100 g

Lima beans are an excellent source of folic acid and potassium and a good source of iron and magnesium; they also contain thiamine, niacin, pantothenic acid, zinc, phosphorus, and copper. Lima beans are also a very good source of dietary fiber. The proteins they contain are said to be incomplete because they are lacking in certain essential amino acids (see *Complementary proteins*).

Storing

Lima beans are as perishable as garden peas and will keep for only a short time once they are shelled. Avoid leaving them out at room temperature, as they lose their flavor and become viscous quite quickly.

Mung bean

Phaseolus aureus or *Vigna radiata,* **Leguminosae**

The fruits of a herbaceous annual plant originating in India, mung beans, or green gram beans, have been widely cultivated since ancient times and continue to play an important role in the culinary traditions of several Asian countries, particularly India. The world's leading producers of mung beans are India and Pakistan. In the Western Hemisphere, the mung bean is most frequently used sprouted; mung bean sprouts are one of the key ingredients in chop suey.

The plant on which mung beans grow is 1 to 4 feet high and has long, thin, slightly downy pods that are 1 to 4 inches in length and contain 10 to 20 tiny seeds. The most common variety is green, but among the over 200 different varieties of mung beans one also finds golden yellow, brown, olive, and brownish purple varieties, some of which are speckled while others are evenly colored.

Buying

Mung bean sprouts are usually sold fresh in plastic bags or cooked and canned.

Serving Ideas

 Mung beans can be used like any other legume, either as a substitute or in combination. In Asia they are often served in puréed form or converted into a flour, which is used by the Chinese to make noodles. The sprouts are added to chop suey, salads, and various other Asian-style dishes. The young pods are edible and can be cooked and served like green beans.

Cooking

Mung beans can be cooked whole or cracked; it is not really necessary to soak them. Allow 45 to 60 minutes when boiling them, or 10 minutes in the pressure cooker for unsoaked beans and 5 to 7 minutes for soaked beans.

Nutritional Information

	raw mung bean sprouts	*boiled mung beans*
water	90.4%	72.7%
protein	3.1 g	7.0 g
fat	0.2 g	0.4 g
carbohydrates	5.9 g	19.2 g
fiber	1.5 g	2.5 g
calories	30.8	105.4
		per 100 g

Mung beans are an excellent source of folic acid and a good source of potassium and magnesium; they contain thiamine, pantothenic acid, iron, phosphorus, zinc, and copper. Mung beans are also a source of dietary fiber.

The proteins supplied by mung beans are said to be incomplete, meaning that they lack certain essential amino acids (see *Complementary proteins*).

Black gram

Phaseolus mungo or *Vigna mungo,* **Leguminosae**

The fruit of an annual plant of Asian origin, the black gram, or urd bean, is a widely popular bean in India, Burma, and Pakistan. It grows in dry tropical climates on a plant that can attain a height of 8 inches to 3 feet. The straight pods are very downy and measure between 1¼ and 3 inches in length; they contain four to ten fairly small, slightly kidney-shaped seeds. Usually black or grayish, the seeds can also be dark green or brownish; they have a white hilum, or eye, and are a creamy white color inside.

Serving Ideas

Young black gram pods are edible and are often used as a vegetable. Upon maturing, however, they become too hairy to be edible. Black gram beans can be prepared like other beans; they have quite a strong flavor and a fine texture. In Asia they are the key ingredient in a popular black sauce. Indians shell and split black gram beans and mix them with rice to prepare a type of flat bread called *dhosai;* they also use them to make a spicy lentil and bean pure called *dahl.* Black gram beans can also be ground into a flour that is used to make sweets, flat cakes, and bread.

Cooking

Black gram beans require a cooking time of about 1½ hours when boiled (don't be surprised if the cooking water turns black). In the pressure cooker, allow 20 to 25 minutes for unsoaked beans and 15 minutes for soaked beans.

Nutritional Information

	boiled
water	72.5%
protein	7.6 g
fat	0.6 g
carbohydrates	18 g
fiber	1 g
calories	105
	per 100 g

Boiled black gram beans are an excellent source of folic acid and magnesium; they are a good source of potassium and also provide thiamine, niacin, pantothenic acid, riboflavin, iron, calcium, zinc, phosphorus, and copper. The proteins they contain are said to be incomplete, as they are lacking in certain essential amino acids (see *Complementary proteins*).

Adzuki bean

Phaseolus angularis or *Vigna angularis,* Leguminosae

The fruit of an annual herbaceous plant originating in Asia, most likely in Japan or China, where adzuki beans have been cultivated and greatly appreciated for centuries. Today the adzuki bean (also called aduki bean) ranks second in commercial importance behind the soybean. The Chinese believe this bean brings good luck, and it is a popular food on festival menus. The increasing popularity of adzuki beans in the United States since the 1960s may be related to the promotion of macrobiotic diets.

This legume is the seed of a bushy plant measuring between 10 inches and 3 feet high. The cylindrical pods are 2½ to 5 inches long and contain 4 to 12 tiny rectangular seeds with rounded edges. Usually brownish red in color, the seeds can also be pale yellow, green, gray, or black; they may be uniformly colored or speckled, and have a creamy white scar, or hilum, at the point of attachment.

Serving Ideas

Young adzuki bean pods are edible and can be prepared like green beans. The beans, which have a delicate flavor, are more commonly available dried, in which case they are prepared in the same way as other legumes.

Adzuki beans are frequently served with rice. In Asia they are often made into a paste that is used in numerous dishes, both savory and sweet, and that can replace tomato paste. Adzuki beans can also be finely ground into a flour that is added to cakes, soups, and milk substitutes. They are also puffed like corn, sprouted, or roasted to make a coffee substitute.

Cooking

Adzuki beans should be soaked in cold water for 2 or 3 hours and then simmered for 1½ to 2 hours. When using a pressure cooker, allow about 20 minutes for soaked beans and 25 minutes for unsoaked beans.

Nutritional Information

	boiled adzuki beans
water	66%
protein	7.5 g
fat	0.1 g
carbohydrates	25 g
fiber	8 g
	per 100 g

Adzuki beans are an excellent source of potassium and a good source of magnesium, phosphorus, zinc, and copper; they also supply iron and thiamine and are an extremely rich source of dietary fiber. The proteins in adzuki beans are said to be incomplete, as they are lacking in certain essential amino acids (see *Complementary proteins*).

Scarlet runner bean

Phaseolus coccineus or *Phaseolus multiflorus,* Leguminosae

Fruit of a herbaceous plant that is thought to be native to Mexico or Central America, or possibly both of these places. Historical remains provide evidence that runner beans were used as food by Mexican Indians some 9,000 years ago, at a time when only wild varieties existed. Cultivation of these beans is believed to have begun about 4,000 years ago. In Europe, the first cultivated runner beans date back to the 18th century. Today this bean is grown principally in cooler regions, particularly in England, where it is mainly eaten fresh, and in Central America, where it is consumed as a legume.

There are numerous varieties of the runner bean plant, including a widely popular North American variety with bright red ornamental flowers, and a variety much appreciated by Europeans that produces seeds similar in appearance to lima beans.

Runner beans are the seeds of a plant that can attain a height of more than 13 feet. The pinkish pods measure 4 to 16 inches in length and contain from six to ten seeds each. The seeds can be convex, flattened, or oblong and are white with red spots or red with black spots.

Nutritional Information

	cooked scarlet runner beans
water	12%
protein	23 g
fat	2 g
carbohydrates	70 g
fiber	5 g
calories	385
	per 100 g

The proteins in scarlet runner beans are said to be incomplete, as they are lacking in certain essential amino acids (see *Complementary proteins*).

Serving Ideas

Fully mature seeds can be consumed fresh or dried. They are cooked and prepared in the same manner as red kidney beans or like the seeds of other legumes. Scarlet runner beans blend particularly well with onions, tomatoes, and tuna fish.

The edible young pods are prepared and served like green beans.

Cooking

Soak dried scarlet runner beans for several hours before cooking them for 1 to 1½ hours. The cooking time can be reduced by using a pressure cooker; soaked beans will cook in 10 to 15 minutes, while unsoaked beans require 15 to 20 minutes.

Lupine

Lupinus spp., Leguminosae

yellow lupine

The seed of a herbaceous plant, the lupine has been grown in Europe for over 2,000 years. While certain varieties of lupines originated in the Mediterranean region, others are native to North and South America. The lupine was farmed intensively by both the Greeks and the Romans, but it was considered to be a food for the poor by the Romans, who cooked enormous cauldrons of lupines to distribute free during festivals and religious feasts. Uncommon in North America, the lupine grows in countries with hot climates and is eaten primarily in Italy, the Middle East, North Africa, and South America.

There are approximately 100 species of lupines, some of which contain bitter-tasting toxic alkaloids and can thus be eaten only after a great deal of preparation. The white lupine *(L. albus)* is probably the most commonly consumed of these legumes, largely because several nontoxic varieties have been developed since 1930. It grows on an annual plant that can be up to 4 feet high.

The straight pods of the lupine plant are 2 to 4 inches long and 1 to 2 inches wide; they contain three to six dull pale-yellow seeds that are between ¼ and ½ inch in diameter. Smooth and slightly rectangular, these seeds are usually somewhat compressed.

The smooth, compressed seeds of the white lupine are probably the most frequently consumed of these legumes, because they do not contain any toxic substances and are thus relatively easy to prepare.

Preparing

Most lupines have to be treated in order to neutralize the alkaloids that make them taste bitter:

• cover 2 cups (500 ml) of lupines with 6 cups (1.5 l) of cold water and allow them to soak for 12 hours; strain and rinse the lupines, then cover them with cold water again;

• gently cook the lupines until they are tender (about 2 hours). Since they remain firm on the outside, pierce them with the point of a knife to determine whether or not they are ready;

• strain the lupines again and cover them with cold water one more time; then add 2 tablespoons salt and store them in a cool place (not in the refrigerator); allow them to soak for 6 or 7 days, changing the salted water twice daily;

• once the bitter taste has been completely eliminated, cover the lupines with salted water and refrigerate them in a tightly sealed container;

• when you are ready to use the lupines, strain the desired quantity and serve them plain or with a little lemon juice.

Serving Ideas

Lupines are often served plain or with a little lemon juice, either skinned or unskinned. Like olives, they are sometimes eaten plain as an appetizer or snack, especially in Italy and the Middle East. Lupines are made into a flour that is added to soups, sauces, pasta, baked goods, and breads; they can also be roasted and ground to make a coffee substitute.

Nutritional Information

water	71%
protein	15.5 g
fat	2.9 g
carbohydrates	9.9 g
fiber	0.7 g
calories	119
	per 100 g

White lupines are very nourishing. When boiled, they are a good source of magnesium, potassium, and zinc. They also contain phosphorus, copper, thiamine, iron, and calcium. Their proteins are considered to be incomplete because they are lacking in certain amino acids (see *Complementary proteins*).

Lentil

Lens ensculenta or *Lens culinarus,* **Leguminosae**

green lentils

The seed of an annual herbaceous plant thought to have originated in central Asia, the lentil has been eaten since prehistoric times and was one of the first foods ever grown by man; it is mentioned in the book of Genesis. Archeologists have found lentil seeds in Middle Eastern agricultural sites dating back 8,000 years; these lentils were eaten with barley and wheat, which originated in the same region. All three of these foods spread throughout Europe and Africa during various migrations. The lentil was introduced into India prior to the first century A.D., and spiced lentil dishes known as *dal* have long been a staple of the Indian diet. Today the leading producers of lentils are Turkey, India, Canada, Bangladesh, China, and Syria.

The lentil grows on a small bushy plant that has very thin, angular stems and is between 14 and 18 inches high. The short, flat, oblong pods, which are rarely more than half an inch long, contain one or two seeds.

Lentils are divided into two groups according to their size: *macrospermae* (large lentils) and *microspermae* (small lentils). There are dozens of varieties of each type of lentil. One of the most common varieties in Western countries is a round, unhusked, green or brownish lentil shaped like a biconvex disk. However, lentils can also be black, yellow, red, or orange and somewhat less round, as well as oval, flat, or heart-shaped. Lentils are sold whole or husked and are sometimes separated into halves like split peas. Their texture and flavor vary from one species to another.

Preparing

Lentils do not have to be soaked, but they should be washed carefully because they often contain small stones. Lentils that have been plunged into boiling water are easier to digest.

Serving Ideas

Lentil pods are not picked until they are fully grown. Dried lentils are not only used to make nourishing soups, they are also added to salads and main-course dishes. Puréed lentils are often used to make croquettes. In India, lentils are frequently eaten with rice, which enhances the nutritional value of both foods because their amino acids are complementary. Lentil curries are highly flavored, thick and stew-like.

Lentils can also be sprouted or made into flour, which is to used to make flat breads and is added to cereal flours as a protein supplement.

Cooking

Lentils will turn to mush if they are cooked for too long. Brown lentils take about 60 minutes to cook, while orange lentils take only about 20 to 30 minutes. When cooking lentils in a pressure cooker, add a little oil to prevent the scum that forms on top of the lentils from blocking the safety valve. Brown lentils can be cooked in 15 to 20 minutes in a pressure cooker, and orange lentils take as little as 5 minutes.

Nutritional Information

	boiled dry lentils
water	69.6%
protein	9 g
fat	0.4 g
carbohydrates	20 g
fiber	3.9 g
calories	116
	per 100 g

Lentils are an excellent source of folic acid and potassium, and a good source of iron and phosphorus; they also contain magnesium, zinc, thiamine, copper, niacin, vitamin B$_6$, and pantothenic acid.

Lentil Soup

SERVES 4

1 cup (250 ml) brown lentils
1 medium onion
2 cloves garlic
1 carrot
1 rib celery
2 tomatoes
4 tbsp. (60 ml) olive oil
1 tbsp. tomato paste
6 cups (1.5 l) water
1 bay leaf
Salt and ground pepper
2 tbsp. white wine vinegar
1 tsp. chopped parsley

1. Sort and wash the lentils. Soak them for 1 or 2 hours in cold water, then strain them.

2. Thinly slice the onion and finely chop the garlic. Dice the carrot and the celery. Blanch, peel, and seed the tomatoes, then cut them into small pieces.

3. Heat the oil in a soup pot and rapidly brown all the vegetables along with the tomato paste.

4. Add the lentils to the vegetable mixture along with the water, the bay leaf, and salt and pepper. Bring the soup to a boil, then cover it and allow it to simmer over low heat for 45 minutes.

5. Add the vinegar and the parsley, and allow the soup to simmer for another 10 minutes or until the lentils are tender.

red lentils

Dolichos bean

Vigna spp. or *Dolichos lablab*, **Leguminosae**

black-eyed peas

U sed to describe legumes of the genus *Vigna,* the term "dolichos" comes from the Greek word *dolikhos,* meaning "long" or "elongated." However, dolichos beans should not be confused with broad beans, which belong to the *Vicia* genus.

There are several different kinds of dolichos beans, including the black-eyed pea, the yard-long bean, and the lablab bean.

The **black-eyed pea** (*Vigna unguiculata* or *Vigna sinensis*) is also known as the "cowpea," especially in Britain. Thought to have originated in North Africa, where it has been eaten for centuries, it may have been introduced into India as long as 3,000 years ago; it was also a staple of the Greek and Roman diets. However, it was not brought to the New World until much later, probably by Spanish explorers and African slaves. It is named the "black-eyed pea" because its dark, spot-like hilum (the point where the seed is attached to the pod) makes it look like an eye; the hilum, which disappears when the legume is cooked, is usually black, but it can also be brown, red, or dark crimson, depending on the species. There are over 7,000 different varieties of black-eyed peas; they can be solid-colored, spotted, or marbled, and white, red, brown, black, yellowish green, or cream-colored. The pea grows on a tropical or subtropical annual plant that can be almost 3 feet tall. The straight, spiral, or curved pods of this plant are 1 to 3 inches long and contain 2 to 12 seeds, which can be smooth, wrinkled, kidney-shaped, globular, or slightly rectangular.

The **yard-long bean** *(Vigna sesquipedalis)* grows on a climbing plant that reaches from 6 to 13 feet; its beautiful flowers are a mauvish shade of azure blue. The yard-long bean was once thought to have originated in the Asian tropics, but it is now widely believed that the wild ancestors of domestic yard-long species came from central Africa. The latest evidence suggests that these original African species spread eastward to India and China, northward to the Mediterranean and Europe, and westward to the Caribbean and North America. Cultivated in tropical and subtropical regions, the yard-long bean is particularly popular in the Far East, Africa, and the Caribbean, but it is also grown in Hawaii and California. The Latin name of the yard-long bean, *sesquipedalis,* means "foot and a half long" and refers to the extraordinary length of its straight or hooked pods, which can be anywhere from 1 to 3 feet long. These pods contain between 15 and 20 elongated, kidney-shaped seeds, which are usually black or brown. Between ½ and ¾ inch long, the seeds taste like a cross between navy beans and asparagus.

The **lablab** or **hyacinth bean** (*Lablab purpureus, Lablab niger, Lablab vulgaris,* or *Dolichos lablab*) probably originated in India, where it has been eaten for centuries; it is also popular in Africa, Central and South America, and Asia. Lablab beans grow on a tropical and subtropical plant that can withstand severe droughts. The lablab plant is usually between 6 and 10 feet long but can grow to be as long as 20 feet. It has oblong, flat, swollen, and occasionally curved pods that measure between 2 and 8 inches. They contain flat, elongated seeds that can be white, brown, black, or red and either solid-colored or spotted, depending on the species. Approximately 50 such seeds are attached to each pod by means of long, white protruding hila. Often used as a decorative plant, the lablab has crimson flowers and beautiful crimson-red pods.

Legumes

Nutritional Information

	cooked black-eyed peas	boiled yard-long beans	boiled fresh lablab beans
water	70%	68.8%	86.9%
protein	7.7 g	8.3 g	2.9 g
fat	0.5 g	0.5 g	0.2 g
carbohydrates	20.8 g	21.1 g	9.2 g
fiber	9.6 g	2 g	1.8 g
calories	116	118	49
			per 100 g

Black-eyed peas are an excellent source of folic acid and a good source of potassium, magnesium, iron, and thiamine; they also contain phosphorus, zinc, copper, niacin, pantothenic acid, and vitamin B_6.

Yard-long beans are an excellent source of folic acid, magnesium, and potassium, and a good source of iron, phosphorus, and thiamine; they also contain zinc, copper, pantothenic acid, and vitamin B_6.

Lablab beans are an excellent source of copper and a good source of potassium and magnesium; they also contain riboflavin, iron, and phosphorus.

Dolichos beans are a source of fiber, but their proteins are considered to be incomplete because they are deficient in certain amino acids (see *Complementary proteins*).

Cooking

Black-eyed peas should be cooked for about 1 hour. If they are even slightly overcooked, they can become mushy. When cooked in a pressure cooker (at 15 pounds pressure), presoaked beans can be ready in as little as 10 minutes, while unsoaked beans will take 10 to 20 minutes.

Serving Ideas

Immature black-eyed-pea pods can be eaten whole and are often served as a green vegetable, like string beans. The leaves and roots of the plant are also edible.

Black-eyed peas are very flavorful and are used to make soups, salads, fritters, and casseroles; they can also be puréed or sprouted. Black-eyed peas cooked with pork is a traditional dish in the southern United States, where this legume is a particularly common food.

Yard-long beans are usually eaten fresh, like string beans, but they are not quite as juicy and sweet, and their relatively strong flavor is more like that of dried beans. They are particularly good in Asian dishes, and their dried seeds can be prepared like those of other legumes.

Dried lablab beans can be used like other legumes and can replace them in most recipes. Ground dried lablabs are used as a flour combined with other flours to make a bread dough or made into small balls and cooked like oatmeal. The seeds are also sprouted, and the pods are eaten fresh, like green beans. In India, lablab beans are dried and split, then cooked quickly, like split peas.

Dolichos beans resemble navy beans and can be used in the same ways, either fresh or dried.

lablab beans

yard-long beans

Broad Bean

Vicia faba, Leguminosae

The hardy pods are 6 to 12 inches long; inside, a whitish, downy lining encloses 5 to 10 flat seeds

Fruit of an annual herbaceous plant believed by botanists to originate in North Africa and the Mediterranean region. Ancient writings make reference to the use of this bean as food by the Chinese more than 5000 years ago. The broad bean was also cultivated in biblical times by the Hebrews and later by the Egyptians, Greeks and Romans. The Greeks used broad beans as ballots in voting and believed that souls could be reincarnated in this food. During Saturnalia celebrations in ancient Rome, the broad bean was used to designate the king of the banquet, a custom which may be at the origin of the use of a broad bean in the traditional cake of Twelfth Night celebrations.

Introduced onto the America continent shortly after the arrival of Columbus, the broad bean is now cultivated in several Latin American countries. The broad bean was the only variety of legume known to Europeans until the Spanish brought back the green bean *(Phaseolus vulgaris)* from South America in the 16th century.

The broad bean plant can attain a height of between 1 and 6 feet and prefers the cooler climates of temperate regions or the higher altitudes of tropical regions. The largest producers of broad beans are China, Egypt, Ethiopia, Morocco, Germany, and Italy.

The hardy pods are 6 to 12 inches long and have a pointed tip at one end. Inside, a whitish, downy lining encloses 5 to 10 flat, round-ended seeds that are usually ¾ to 2 inches in length. There are many varieties of the broad bean, with seeds varying in color from green to reddish, brownish, or purple.

Nutritional Information

	boiled broad beans
water	71.5%
protein	7.6 g
fat	0.4 g
carbohydrates	19.6 g
fiber	5.1 g
	per 100 g

Broad beans are an excellent source of folic acid and a good source of potassium and magnesium; they also supply thiamine, riboflavin, iron, zinc, phosphorus, copper, and they are rich in dietary fiber. Because they lack certain essential amino acids, the proteins of broad beans are said to be incomplete (see *Complementary proteins*).

Serving Ideas

Broad beans are starchy and have a rather strong flavor. Fresh young beans can be eaten raw without their thick outer skin, whose high tannin content gives them a bitter taste. Fresh or dried broad beans are delicious in soups and simmered dishes, either whole or in their traditional puréed form. The Spanish specialty *fabada,* is a type of bean cassoulet that also includes blood pudding, pork, chorizo sausages, and cabbage. Italians prepare broad beans *alla pancetta,* meaning with onions and lard. In Middle Eastern cooking, they are often served puréed, as fritters, and in salads.

Sautéed broad beans make a great snack. Once cooked, broad beans can be used cold, either whole or puréed, in salads, appetizers, and as a sandwich spread. The edible young pods are prepared like green beans.

Cooking

Fresh or dried broad beans can be cooked with or without their skin, depending on one's appreciation of their bitter taste. To remove the skin, plunge the beans in boiling water for a few minutes, drain and rinse under cold water. The skin also comes off easily if the beans are soaked for 12 to 24 hours (change the water frequently).

Whole dried beans require a cooking time of about 2½ hours, while fresh beans are ready in about 20 minutes. Skinned dried beans only need to be soaked for 8 to 12 hours and cook in about 1½ hour. In the Mediterranean and the Middle East, particularly in Egypt and Italy, broad beans are soaked for 48 hours in water that is changed frequently, making it very easy to remove their skin before cooking. Falafel is made using uncooked broad beans that have been soaked.

When using a pressure cooker (103 kPa), allow 25 minutes for unsoaked beans and 20 minutes for previously soaked beans.

Broad Bean Salad

SERVES 4

½ lb. dried broad beans
2 cloves garlic
4 tbsp. olive oil

Juice of 1 lemon
1 tbsp. fresh coriander
Salt and ground pepper

1. Peel and crush the garlic. Chop the coriander.

2. Cook the beans in salted water for 1 hour or until tender. They are done when they can be crushed between the fingers. Drain and let cool.

3. Add the lemon juice, garlic, and then the oil and toss well. Adjust the seasoning to taste.

Garnish with the fresh minced coriander and serve cold as an appetizer.

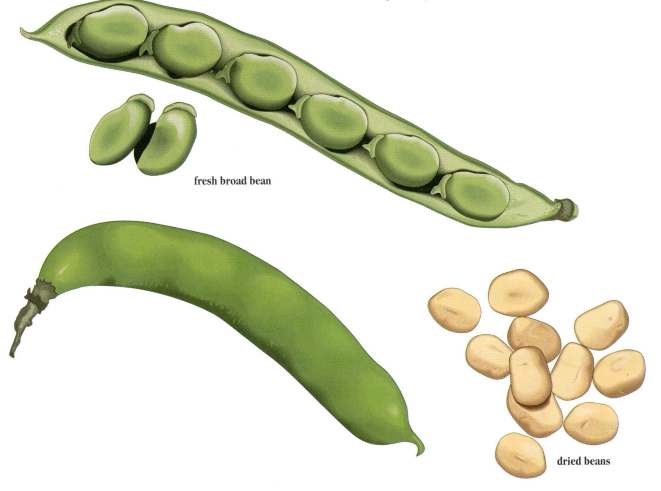

fresh broad bean

dried beans

Pea

Pisum sativum, Leguminosae

The seed of a herbaceous annual plant, the pea (also known as the green pea or garden pea) is believed to have descended from the field pea and is the product of centuries of cultivation and selection. Peas are indigenous to central Asia and Europe and have been known to the Chinese for over 4,000 years. They were very popular among the ancient Greeks, Romans, and Egyptians. Peas were introduced into America in the 19th century.

For a long time, peas were consumed dried and made into a purée that constituted a staple food for many peoples. The Chinese were apparently the first to consume the pod and seeds as a vegetable. Green peas did not appear on European tables until the 16th century, having been popularized by the French royalty. The first vegetable to be hybridized, by the end of the 19th century, garden peas had undergone numerous improvements, thanks notably to the experiments of the Austrian monk and botanist Gregor Mendel, one of the forefathers of modern-day genetics, the scientific study of the transmission of genetic characteristics.

Peas grow on a bushy or climbing plant that can grow to a height of 1 to 5 feet. They grow better in cool climates, where they can be sown in early spring. The smooth green pods can be straight or slightly curved, and are either swollen or flat. They usually measure from 1¾ to 6 inches in length and contain between two and ten seeds of varying sizes. The seeds are generally round but may also have a slightly square form. While most peas are green, certain varieties may be grayish, whitish, or brownish in color. Dried peas are yellow or green and are sold whole or split.

There are over 1,000 varieties of the pea, including smooth peas, wrinkled peas, and snow peas (also known as mange-tout peas). Smooth peas are the variety most commonly sold in frozen form; they grow better in cold climates and are starchier than the wrinkled varieties, which are sweeter and used mainly for canning. Snow peas (var. *saccharatum* and *macrocarpon*) are distinguished by their edible pods, which are sweet and crisp. Snow peas should have flat pods with barely developed seeds; those with swollen pods have tough strings and are inedible. The opposite is true of sugar snap peas, a fairly recent variety whose pods are tasty even when the seeds are fully developed.

The leading producers of dried peas are Russia, France, China, and Denmark, while fresh peas are produced mainly by the United States, Great Britain, China, Hungary, and India.

wrinkled peas

Legumes

156

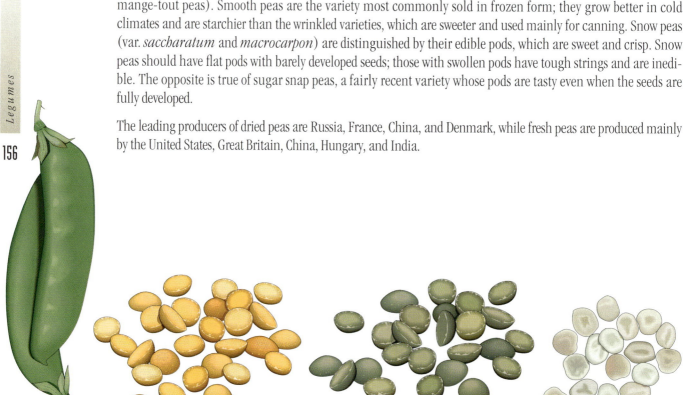

snow peas

yellow split peas

green split peas

dried peas

Buying

It is important to pick fresh peas at just the right time, when they are neither too large nor too small; if harvested too late, their sugar converts into starch rapidly, making them drier and less sweet. Dried peas are obtained by leaving the peas in the field until they are fully mature, at which point they are harvested and dried. Peas are rarely available on the market in their fresh state, and when they are, they tend to be quite expensive. Choose shiny, bright green, smooth-looking pods that seem to contain a good number of small seeds. The majority of the pea crop is used for freezing and canning.

Snow peas are usually sold fresh; choose medium-size peas with a firm, crisp, unblemished pod that is bright green in color. Avoid pods that appear to be soft, wrinkled, yellowed, or spotted.

Preparing

Some people believe that fresh peas should not be left in their pods for more than 12 hours after purchase and suggest shelling the peas and keeping them in the refrigerator until ready for use. Before shelling the peas, give them a quick rinse under running water and snap off the top of the pod, pulling off the thread along the seam (some varieties have no thread). Do the same at the other end and pry open the pod to remove the seeds. It is not necessary to wash the peas.

Home-Style Peas

SERVES 4

12 small pearl onions	1 cup (250 ml) chicken
¼ lb. (125 g) lean slab	stock
bacon	1 bouquet garni
1 tbsp. butter	1½ lb. (750 g) frozen
1 tbsp. flour	peas
Salt and ground pepper	1 tsp. sugar

1. Peel the onions. Remove the rind from the bacon and discard it. Cut the bacon into cubes and blanch it for 1 minute in a pot of boiling water.

2. In a casserole, melt the butter, add the onions and bacon cubes, and cook for 5 to 10 minutes or until golden brown. Remove the bacon and onions and set aside.

3. Add the flour to the cooking butter, stirring with a wooden spoon until it forms a smooth paste. Add salt and pepper to taste. Pour in the chicken stock. Add the bouquet garni, onions, and bacon. Bring to a boil, stirring constantly. Add the peas and sugar, and mix. Cover and simmer for about 10 minutes.

Serve warm as an accompaniment to veal or lamb.

fresh peas

Serving Ideas

Snow peas and very young and fresh garden peas can be eaten raw, although they are slightly sweeter when cooked.

Fresh green peas can be cooked in boiling water or in a little butter and are good combined with carrots or asparagus spears, as well as being an excellent accompaniment to meat and poultry. They are also used in soups and stews. Cold peas are often added to mixed salads; they are usually included in diced vegetable mixtures called *macédoines* and in *jardinières*. Frozen green peas have the same uses as fresh peas.

Snow peas are excellent raw or cooked and are used in the same way as green beans, with which they are interchangeable in most recipes. Raw snow peas are good in salads and appetizers, while cooked snow peas can be used like fresh peas. The most delicious way of serving them is in a stir-fry, however.

Whole dried peas are mainly cooked and used in soups, traditionally accompanied with a ham bone or ham cubes. Split peas are usually puréed and can be used in soups, stews, or as a side dish.

Cooking

To preserve their color and flavor, peas should be cooked very briefly. Ten to 15 minutes (depending on the size) is sufficient when boiling fresh peas. They may also be steamed or braised. A good way to braise peas is between two layers of undrained rinsed lettuce leaves.

Snow peas can be prepared like green beans and require a cooking time of 6 to 15 minutes for boiling and steaming. They tend to become mushy when overcooked.

Dried peas are available whole, halved, or split. Only whole dried peas need to be soaked before being cooked; they should be cooked gently for 1 to 2 hours.

Yellow or green split peas are less starchy and take less time to cook (1 to 1½ hours). They should be cooked until tender, but avoid overcooking them, which makes them turn mushy and fall apart.

It is not a good idea to cook split peas in a pressure cooker, as they tend to produce a lot of foam which can block the safety valve (see *Cooking legumes*).

Legumes

157

Nutritional Information

Cooked green peas are a good source of folic acid, potassium, thiamine, and magnesium; they also contain vitamin C, zinc, vitamin B$_6$, niacin, iron, and phosphorus.

Dried peas have certain amino acid deficiencies (see *Complementary proteins*). However, they are an excellent source of potassium and folacin, a good source of thiamine, and contain magnesium, zinc, iron, copper, phosphorus, and pantothenic acid.

Cooked snow peas are an excellent source of vitamin C, a good source of potassium, and contain iron, folic acid, magnesium, thiamine, pantothenic acid, vitamin B$_6$, and phosphorus.

	cooked green peas	*cooked dried peas*	*cooked snow peas*
water	77.9%	69.5%	88.9%
protein	5.4 g	8.4 g	3.3 g
fat	0.2 g	0.4 g	0.2 g
carbohydrates	15.6 g	21.1 g	7.0 g
fiber	6.7 g	4.0 g	2.8 g
			per 100 g

Storing

Fresh green peas should be refrigerated as soon as possible to delay the conversion of their sugar into starch. Stored in a non-airtight container or a perforated bag, they will keep for 4 to 5 days.

Green peas and snow peas stand up very well to freezing; blanch them for 1 or 2 minutes beforehand.

Chickpea

Cicer arietinum, Leguminosae

Chickpeas are the seeds of a bushy leguminous plant that grows best in warm, dry climates. The short swollen pods contain between one and four roundish bumpy seeds.

The fruit of an annual herbaceous plant believed to have originated in the Middle East, the chickpea, or garbanzo bean, has played an important role in the culinary traditions of many countries since ancient times, particularly in North Africa, India, Spain, and southern France. Historical evidence indicates that this legume was used as food some 7,000 years ago, while the cultivation of chickpeas is thought to date back 5,000 years in the Mediterranean region and 4,000 years in India. Chickpeas were very popular among the ancient Greeks, Romans, and Egyptians. The cultivation of chickpeas subsequently spread throughout the world via Spanish and Portuguese explorers and Indian immigrants, who introduced them into the subtropical regions.

The Latin word for chickpea, *arietinum,* means "small ram," an allusion to the irregular shape of the chickpea, held to resemble a ram's head.

Chickpeas are the seeds of a bushy leguminous plant measuring 8 inches to 3 feet in height that grows best in warm dry climates. The leading producers of chickpeas are India and Turkey, which supply three fourths of the world crop, followed by Pakistan, China, Mexico, and Ethiopia.

The short, swollen pods of chickpeas are usually about an inch long and contain between one and four roundish, bumpy seeds measuring roughly ½ inch in diameter. Depending on the variety, the seeds range in color from creamy beige to blackish, green, yellow, reddish, or brownish. They also differ in terms of texture, with some being pastier than others, and in flavor, with some varieties having a nutty taste.

Preparing

Dried chickpeas should be soaked for 12 to 16 hours before being cooked. To reduce the cooking time by 1 hour, they can be soaked overnight, frozen in the same water, and then thawed just before cooking.

Serving Ideas

Chickpeas that are gathered before their pods reach maturity can be prepared and served like green beans, while fresh or dried fully mature chickpeas are used in the same way as other legumes, although they are harder and do not fall apart as easily as most other legumes during cooking.

Along with green beans, chickpeas are one of the most versatile legumes. They are used in appetizers, soups, and main dishes and are delicious cold in mixed salads or puréed. Middle Eastern specialties such as *hummus,* a cold purée, and *falafel,* fried balls or patties, have chickpeas as their main ingredient. Many traditional dishes from the South of France, including *estouffade, cocido, puchero,* and other stewed dishes, make use of chickpeas. They are also traditionally added to couscous dishes.

Chickpeas can be roasted, sprouted, or ground into a flour that is used mainly for unleavened breads, flat cakes, and frying batter. Ground chickpea flour is also an important ingredient in Indian cooking.

Roasted chickpeas, plain or salted, make a good snack.

Hummus

SERVES 10

1 can (19 ounces)
  chickpeas
1 clove garlic
3 tbsp. tahini
¼ cup (60 ml) lemon juice

Salt
1 tbsp. olive oil
Paprika
Black olives

Note: Tahini is a paste made from crushed sesame seeds; it is sold in health-food stores and gourmet shops.

1. Drain the chickpeas and rinse under running water.

2. Peel and press the garlic, removing the germ.

3. Mash the chickpeas with a fork.

4. In a blender, process the chickpeas with the tahini, garlic, lemon juice, salt, and olive oil to form a thick, smooth purée.

5. Transfer the purée to a deep serving dish, and smooth the surface with the back of a spoon. Sprinkle generously with paprika, drizzle with a little olive oil, and garnish with a few black olives.

Hummus is often served as an appetizer or as a dip for raw vegetables.

Cooking

To cook dried chickpeas, boil them for 2 to 2½ hours after soaking them. When cooking them in a pressure cooker, allow 20 to 25 minutes for soaked beans and 35 to 40 minutes for unsoaked beans.

Nutritional Information

	boiled dried chickpeas
water	60%
protein	8.9 g
fat	2.6 g
carbohydrates	27.4 g
fiber	3.5 g
calories	164
	per 100 g

Chickpeas are an excellent source of folic acid and potassium and a good source of magnesium, phosphorus, zinc, and copper; they also contain thiamine, niacin, vitamin B_6, and calcium, in addition to being a source of dietary fiber. The proteins in chickpeas are said to be incomplete, as they lack certain essential amino acids (see *Complementary proteins*).

Chickpeas are said to have the properties of a diuretic, a stomachic, and an intestinal cleanser.

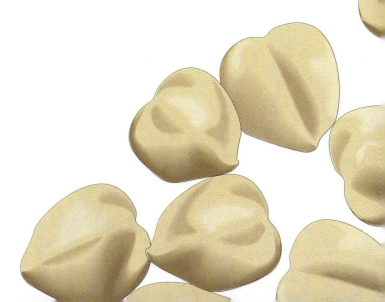

Peanut

Arachis hypogaea, Leguminosae

Peanuts grow in a very unusual way. The stems of the flowers lengthen and bend until they reach the ground, which they penetrate before developing into peanuts.

The peanut is the seed of an annual plant that is thought to have originated in South America (Brazil or Bolivia) or China. It has been a staple of the South American diet for centuries, and was grown by the Aztecs and eaten throughout South America long before the arrival of the Spanish and the Portuguese colonists in the 15th century. Introduced by these colonists into Africa and the Philippines, it was first brought to United States at the time of the slave trade. Toward the end of the 19th and the beginning of the 20th century, vast numbers of peanut plants were grown in North America, and in 1890 peanut butter was invented, quickly becoming just as popular as it is today. Over 90% of the world's peanuts are grown in Asia and Africa, and along with the United States, the leading peanut-producing countries are India, China, Nigeria, and Indonesia.

Although it is commonly referred to as a nut, the peanut is in fact a legume that belongs to the same family as peas and beans, and can be used in the same ways. It is also referred to as the "goober" or "goober pea" – a name derived from the word *nguba,* which means "peanut" in Kongo, a Bantu language spoken in Zaire, the Congo Republic, and Angola.

The peanut plant thrives in tropical and subtropical climates, but it can also be grown in temperate regions. A climbing or bushlike plant that reach 30 inches in height, it is covered with small yellow flowers for 2 or 3 months of the year. The buds of these flowers open at sunrise, are fertilized during the early morning hours, and wither and die before noon. Over the next few days, the stems of the flowers grow longer and bend toward the ground, which they penetrate to a depth of 1 to 3 inches; the ends of the stems then expand and ripen underground, becoming seed-bearing pods. Usually 1 to 1½ inches long, these veined pods contain two or three seeds and become brittle when dried. Each of the oval seeds is covered with a reddish brown membrane and is made up of two thick, fleshy off-white cotyledons and a visible embryo. These cotyledons and the embryo they enclose comprise what is commonly known as the "nut," which can be eaten either plain or roasted.

Peanuts are harvested by uprooting the whole plant and removing the pods after the plant has been allowed to dry for a few days in the fields or in a drying shed. There are approximately ten different species of peanuts and a large number of varieties.

Cooking

Peanuts expand slightly when cooked and remain somewhat firm, but they can become soft if they are reheated or overcooked. To preserve their crunchiness, add them, whenever possible, to only those portions of food that are going to be eaten right away. Peanuts take about 30 minutes to cook.

Buying

The peanut can be contaminated by aflatoxin, a mold caused by the fungus *Aspergillus flavus.* Invisible to the naked eye, this mold has been associated with cancer in laboratory animals but has yet to be linked to cancer in humans. Most foods can be contaminated by aflatoxin, but peanuts are particularly vulnerable because of their exposure to heat and humidity; temperatures between 86°F (30°C) and 95°F (35°C) combined with a relative-humidity rate of 80% are the ideal conditions for growing peanuts. Manufacturers and health-protection agencies are responsible for detecting peanuts that are not fit for human consumption by strictly monitoring storage conditions, as well as the quality of all nuts and nut products (including peanut butter). To avoid eating contaminated peanuts, discard those that are old, discolored, blackened, rancid, or moldy.

Serving Ideas

Peanuts are left whole, crushed, ground, or made into a paste. They are available salted or unsalted, peeled or unpeeled, dry- or honey-roasted, and coated in chocolate or oil. Often eaten as appetizers or snacks, they are also substituted for almonds and pistachios in pastries.

Peanut butter (an excellent source of protein) is not really an American invention, as its popularity in North America might suggest. Africans, Indians, South Americans, and Indonesians have been making a similar paste for centuries. The peanut is a key ingredient in their national cuisines: served with meat, fish, and poultry, peanuts are also used to flavor soups, sauces, salads, simmered dishes, and desserts. In Indonesia, for example, the peanut is the basic ingredient in a spicy sauce known as satay sauce, as well as in gado gado, a vegetable dish served with a sauce containing peanuts, coconut milk, peppers, and garlic. The seed of the peanut plant yields an excellent multipurpose, mild-tasting oil that can withstand high temperatures and can be refried again and again (see *Oil*). Approximately two thirds of the world's output of peanuts is made into oil.

Shrimp with Peanut Sauce

SERVES 4

⅓ cup (80 ml) shelled roasted peanuts
1 small onion
1 clove garlic
5 tbsp. (75 ml) peanut oil
1 tsp. chopped cilantro
1 tsp. ground cumin
1 tsp. freshly grated ginger

⅓ cup (80 ml) coconut milk
1 pinch cayenne pepper
1 pinch salt
1 lb. (500 g) shelled fresh shrimp
1 tbsp. lime or lemon juice

1. Crush the peanuts in a blender or food processor until they form a smooth paste, then set the paste aside.

2. Chop the onion and garlic.

3. Heat 2 tablespoons of the peanut oil in a saucepan, and gently brown the onions. Add the garlic, cilantro, cumin, and grated ginger, as well as the peanut paste, and cook for 1 minute over low heat, mixing all the ingredients thoroughly.

4. Gradually add the coconut milk to this mixture and season it with the cayenne pepper and salt. Allow the mixture to cook until it forms a smooth, thick sauce, then just keep it warm.

5. Heat the remaining peanut oil in a frying pan and quickly sauté the shrimp until they are pink on both sides.

6. Add the lime or lemon juice to the peanut sauce, and allow it simmer for a moment before adjusting the seasoning. Top the shrimp with this sauce and serve them with plain rice.

Nutritional Information

	raw	*dry-roasted*
water	5.6%	1.4%
protein	13 g	11.8 g
fat	23.8 g	24.8 g
carbohydrates	9.3 g	10.7 g
fibre	1.2 g	3.9 g
calories	282	293
		per 50 g

A nutritious food, the peanut is rich in protein, fat, and calories. Raw peanuts are an excellent source of thiamine, niacin, magnesium, and potassium, and a good source of pantothenic acid, copper, zinc, and phosphorus; they also contain iron.

Dry-roasted peanuts are an excellent source of magnesium, niacin, and potassium, and a good source of zinc, copper, thiamine, and phosphorus; high in fiber, they also contain pantothenic acid, iron, and vitamin B_6. Peanuts that are roasted in oil contain comparable amounts of these nutrients. The proteins in peanuts are said to be incomplete because they contain relatively small amounts of certain amino acids (see *Complementary proteins*).

The fat in peanuts consists of 85.5% unsaturated fatty acids – 57% monounsaturates and 28.5% polyunsaturates (see *Fats*). Peanuts can be difficult to digest, especially if they are roasted in oil. You can of course buy dry-roasted peanuts, but they are just as fatty and often contain food additives.

Storing

Raw peanuts deteriorate more quickly than roasted peanuts, and are thus more difficult to store and much less commonly available. Store them in the refrigerator in a sealed container. Roasted peanuts should be kept in a cool, dry place that is inaccessible to insects and rodents. Peanuts can be stored in the freezer for up to 6 months. Unshelled peanuts can be refrigerated for 9 months, but shelled peanuts should not be refrigerated for any longer than 3 months.

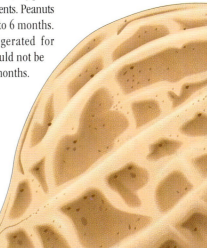

Alfalfa

Medicago sativa, Leguminosae

The seeds found inside the pods of the alfalfa plant are sprouted for human consumption; the plant itself is used as forage.

Alfalfa seeds grow on a herbaceous perennial plant that almost certainly originated in southwestern Asia. The alfalfa plant is cultivated for use as forage much more commonly than as a food for human consumption; in fact, it has been fed to animals for centuries, dating back to prehistoric times. Thought to have been grown in Greece and Italy during the first century A.D., it was subsequently introduced into other parts of Europe, then brought to South America by Spanish explorers.

Alfalfa is usually eaten by humans in the form of sprouted seeds. Germination enhances its value as a food by making the seeds easier to digest and increasing their nutritional content. Immature leaves from the alfalfa plant are sometimes eaten as a vegetable or used to make tea. The alfalfa plant has numerous branches and can grow to be 1 to 3 feet high. It thrives in the hottest parts of temperate regions and in the coolest parts of subtropical regions. Its spiral pods contain six to eight tiny brownish or yellowish seeds, which can be oval or kidney-shaped.

Buying

Buy dry seeds that are meant to be sprouted, not planted, to ensure that they have not been treated with chemicals. There is no need to buy a large amount at any one time, because the small, light seeds produce a high volume of sprouts. When buying sprouted seeds, ensure that the sprouts are firm and that their small leaves are very green. Avoid sprouts that are soggy or colorless, as well as those that smell moldy.

Nutritional Information

	raw sprouted alfalfa seed
water	91%
protein	1.4 g
fat	0.2 g
carbohydrates	1.3 g
fiber	1 g
calories	10
	per 35 g (250 ml)

Raw sprouted alfalfa seeds contain folic acid and zinc. They are also reputed to be diuretic and a stimulant, and are said to alleviate scurvy, peptic ulcers, and urinary and intestinal problems.

Serving Ideas

Unlike mung-bean sprouts, alfalfa sprouts are thin and tasty enough to be eaten raw. Used in salads, sandwiches, and hors d'oeuvres, they are also added to cooked dishes such as soups, stews, omelets, vegetables, and tacos immediately before they are served. Small amounts of the flour made from alfalfa leaves can be added to various cereal products.

Preparing

Sprouting alfalfa seeds in a glass jar

• Measure approximately 1 tablespoon of dry alfalfa seeds;

• soak the seeds in water overnight; strain the seeds and rinse them thoroughly, then put them in a large sterilized glass jar with a wide mouth;

• cover the opening of the jar with cheesecloth or muslin, and secure it with a metal ring or an elastic band; turn the jar over and put it in a warm, dark place;

• rinse the seeds with lukewarm water twice daily for 3 or 4 days, straining the seeds and returning the jar to the same location, where it should be able to drain completely (it is important that the seeds not be allowed to dry out);

• when the sprouts are between 1½ and 2 inches long, expose them to sunlight for a day to allow the leaves to turn green;

• serve or refrigerate the sprouts.

Storing

Alfalfa sprouts can be kept in the refrigerator for about a week. Dried alfalfa seeds can be stored for about a year in a cool, dry place, if they are kept in tightly sealed container.

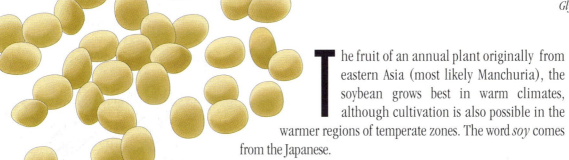

Soybean

Glycine max, Leguminosae

The fruit of an annual plant originally from eastern Asia (most likely Manchuria), the soybean grows best in warm climates, although cultivation is also possible in the warmer regions of temperate zones. The word *soy* comes from the Japanese.

The soybean, also known as soya bean, has been cultivated in Asia since the earliest times, particularly in Korea, Manchuria, Japan, and China. Cultivated for over 13,000 years in China, it was one of the first foods to be domesticated by humans. To the Chinese, soybeans represented one of the five essential grains of life, along with rice, barley, wheat, and millet. It was not until the 17th century that a German botanist introduced the cultivation of soybeans into Europe. Although introduced into America in the early 19th century, soybeans only began to be cultivated on a large scale there in the 1930s.

Today the United States is the largest producer of soybeans, supplying 50% of the world crop, followed by Brazil, China, Argentina, India, and Italy. In Asia, China is still the largest soybean-producing country, while Japan imports more soybeans than any other country. The United States has built a thriving and powerful industry around soybeans; they are used in particular to make soybean oil (for the manufacture of margarine, which was invented as an outlet for the abundance of oil produced the beans), while the residue from the pressing stage (oil meal) is used as livestock feed.

Soybeans grow on a branching plant that can reach a height of 1 to 6 feet. The oblong down-covered pods can be pale yellow, gray, brown, or black. They usually measure from 1 to 2 inches in length and contain one to four hard seeds that vary in color from one variety to another. The fresh beans are harvested young, before they become oily and starchy. Soybeans can be eaten alone or with the pod and are often served as a vegetable or prepared in the same manner as dried beans. The beans can also be cooked with or without their pod; to make shelling easier, blanch the beans for about 5 minutes in boiling water.

Soybeans are excellent in stews; they remain firm during cooking and impart a pleasant hazelnut-like flavor to the stew. Dried soybeans are prepared and used like other legumes. It is important to cook them thoroughly in order to deactivate their antinutrients, which are neutralized by cooking.

Ground soybean has had the outer shell removed before being ground into fine granules. It cooks much more quickly than whole soybeans; allow about 30 minutes, using 4 cups of water per cup of ground soybean.

Ground soybean is added to a wide variety of dishes, enriching everything from soups and stews to spaghetti sauces, cookies, and breads. Depending on the intended use, pour boiling water over ground soybeans or boil them for a few minutes beforehand to make them more digestible and to neutralize their antinutrients. This step is not necessary if the soybeans are used in dishes that cook for a long time, such as soups.

Soybean sprouts are ready to be eaten after germinating for a few days, when they are about 4 inches tall. They are more nourishing and tastier than mung bean sprouts, and can be used in the same way, either slightly cooked or raw. The Vietnamese use soybean sprouts in spring rolls.

Since **soybean flour** does not contain any gluten, it does not rise during cooking. This flour contains 2 to 3 times more protein than wheat flour and, in the case of non-defatted soybean flour, 10 times more fat.

Defatted soybean flour can be stored at room temperature, while non-defatted soybean flour must be refrigerated to prevent it from turning rancid.

Soybean flour is used mainly to thicken sauces and to enrich cakes, muffins, and cookies. It must be combined with wheat flour in order to produce leavening. Soybean flour is best used in small doses, as it has a quite pronounced flavor.

A **coffee substitute** is obtained by roasting and grinding soybeans; it is brewed like regular coffee, which it somewhat resembles in taste.

Preparing

Soybeans must be soaked before being cooked in order to restore their moisture; this shortens the cooking time slightly and helps preserve the vitamins and minerals, as well as reducing the risk of flatulence.

Serving Ideas

Fresh soybeans contain antinutrients such as trypsin and phytic acid inhibitors. Since these substances are neutralized during cooking and fermentation, it is essential that soybeans be properly cooked. Asians usually consume soybeans in a transformed state (as miso, tamari, soy milk, and tofu, for example), using processes that neutralize the antinutrients in the beans. Well-cooked soybeans are also more easily digested and assimilated.

Soybeans are the only legume from which a liquid, called soy milk or soya milk, is extracted; among its other uses, soy milk enters into the making of tofu (see *Soy milk, Tofu*). Soybeans can be consumed fresh or dried in various forms, including cracked, sprouted, roasted, ground (flour), pressed (see *Oil*), or fermented (see *Miso, Soy sauce, Tempeh*). They are also used to make a coffee substitute, and processed to make texturized proteins which are used as a substitute for meat and to prepare various other products (see *Texturized vegetable protein*).

Soybean Sprout Salad

SERVES 4

2 cups (500 ml) soybean sprouts
2 cups (500 ml) spinach leaves
½ rib celery
½ zucchini
4 large fresh mushrooms
1 red sweet pepper
1 tbsp. fresh coriander (cilantro) leaves

⅓ cup (80 ml) cashews
⅓ cup (80 ml) raisins

Vinaigrette
1 clove garlic, minced
1 tbsp. minced fresh ginger
⅓ cup (80 ml) vegetable oil
2 tbsp. soy sauce
A few drops of sesame oil

1. Rinse and drain the soybean sprouts and the spinach. Tear the spinach into pieces. Finely slice the celery, zucchini, mushrooms, and sweet pepper. Chop the coriander.

2. Place all the salad vegetables in a large bowl, and add the cashews and raisins.

3. Mix the ingredients for the vinaigrette, and pour over the salad.

Cooking

Dried soybeans must be cooked for at least 3 hours, and sometimes up to 7 or even 9 hours, depending on the variety. Soybeans are cooked when they can be easily mashed with a fork. Use slightly more water than for other legumes, and check the level of the water regularly, as soybeans tend to absorb a lot of liquid.

To cook soybeans in a pressure cooker, first bring them to a boil in the pressure cooker without its cover and skim the foam from the surface; reduce the heat and let the beans simmer. Then attach the lid and pressure-cook the soybeans; when the required pressure is attained, set the timer for 30 minutes for soybeans that have been presoaked. The soybeans and cooking water should not fill more than one third of the pressure cooker.

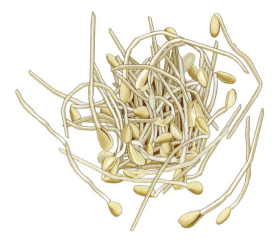

soybean sprouts

Nutritional Information

	boiled soybeans	non-defatted soybean flour	defatted soybean flour
water	62.5%	5.2%	7.2%
protein	16.6 g	34.5 g	47 g
fat	9 g	20.6 g	1.2 g
carbohydrates	9.9 g	35.2 g	38.4 g
fiber	2 g		
calories	173	436	329
			per 100 g

Soybeans are more nourishing and contain more protein and calories than any other legume. In fact, 1 cup of cooked soybeans contains as much protein as ¼ pound of cooked meat, poultry, or fish. In addition, the protein in soybeans is of excellent quality, since it has a balanced supply of amino acids, although it is lacking in methionine. It is high in lysine, however, making soybean an ideal complement to cereals, in which lysine is often deficient (see *Complementary proteins*). The fat in soybeans is 78% unsaturated, non-cholesterol, and contains lecithin. Soybeans are said to be good for the liver, in addition to being remineralizing and energizing. Studies show that the fiber contained in soybeans may lower the cholesterol level in people with high blood cholesterol, although it seems to have little effect on people with a normal blood cholesterol level. Experimental studies also indicate that soybeans contain several compounds that are potentially anticarcinogenic and that consuming soybeans reduces the risks of contracting colon cancer.

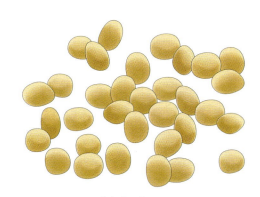

dried soybeans

Soybeans are an excellent source of potassium, magnesium, iron, and folic acid and a good source of phosphorus, copper, niacin, and riboflavin; they also contain vitamin B_6, zinc, thiamine, and calcium.

Soybean flour (defatted or non-defatted) is an excellent source of potassium, magnesium, folic acid, copper, niacin, iron, phosphorus, thiamine, zinc, and vitamin B_6, as well as being a good source of calcium.

In addition, non-defatted soybean flour is an excellent source of riboflavin and a good source of pantothenic acid, while defatted soybean flour is an excellent source of pantothenic acid and a good source of riboflavin.

soybean flour

Soy milk

As its name suggests, soy milk is a milklike liquid that is made from crushed soybeans. In fact, the soybean is the only legume from which such a liquid can be made. Used like milk from animals, soy milk has been consumed in Asia for several centuries, and it has long been used as a milk substitute for nursing infants in the West. Innumerable other uses for soy milk have recently been discovered.

Soy milk has a strong flavor associated with an enzyme that is released when soybeans are crushed. The intensity of this flavor is directly affected by the way the milk is produced and can be greatly reduced if the soybeans are crushed in boiling water.

In order to produce soy milk, the beans are washed and soaked, then crushed. The resultant liquid is then filtered and heated (the order in which this is done depends on the method of production). In most cases, the milk is also pasteurized or sterilized. Soy milk can also be made from soy flour from which the fat has not been removed. It is sold as a liquid (often artificially flavored and heavily sweetened) or a powder. The production of soy milk results in the creation of an edible residue known as "okara" (see *Okara*).

Nutritional Information

water	93.3%
protein	7 g
carbohydrates	4.6 g
fat	4.8 g
calories	84
	per 250 ml

Soy milk is an excellent source of thiamine and potassium, and a good source of magnesium and copper; it also contains phosphorus, riboflavin, iron, niacin, and vitamin B_6. The proteins in soy milk are of a very high quality, but they are lacking in methionine, an essential amino acid (see *Complementary proteins*). The fat in soy milk is mainly comprised of unsaturated acids; like all vegetable fat, it contains lecithin and is cholesterol-free. Unlike milk from animals, soy milk does not contain lactose, a substance that some people cannot digest (see *Milk*). Soy milk has numerous medicinal properties. It is reputed to be alkalizing and beneficial for the digestive system. Since it contains iron, it may also prevent anemia and stimulate the production of hemo-globin. The lecithin contained in soy milk may reduce triglyceride levels and blood cholesterol. Exclusive or extensive use of soy milk as part of a strict vegetarian diet can lead to a deficiency in calcium and vitamin B_{12}. This can be avoided by drinking soy milk that has been fortified with calcium, by eating other foods that are rich in calcium and vitamin B_{12}, or by taking a vitamin supplement containing these nutrients.

Preparing

Making soy milk

• Wash 1 cup (8 oz., 250 g) of soybeans and combine them with enough water to cover by 2 inches to allow them to expand; let them soak overnight or for at least 10 hours;

• heat 1 cup (250 ml) of water in a large saucepan;

• meanwhile, purée the beans, adding 3 or 4 cups (700 ml to 1 l) of water;

• add the purée to the saucepan and bring it to a boil, then reduce the heat and allow the mixture to simmer for 12 to 25 minutes (30 minutes for milk with a milder flavor);

• pour the mixture into a container through a sieve lined with several layers of cheesecloth; squeeze or twist the cheesecloth to remove any remaining liquid;

• spread the cheesecloth in the sieve again and pour 1 cup of water (hot or cold) through it, then roll it up and wring it out again.

Serving Ideas

Soy milk can be used in countless ways; like milk from animals, it can be used to make soups, sauces, yogurt, sherbet, ice cream, puddings, drinks, and pastries. Curdled soy milk is known as tofu, a nourishing food that is often compared to cheese (see *Tofu*).

Storing

Liquid soy milk can be kept in the refrigerator for several days. It can also be frozen, but it separates when defrosted. Powdered soy milk, which is very low in fat, can be stored at room temperature in a tightly sealed container.

The Japanese name for the curd obtained from the milky liquid extracted from soybeans. Called *doufu* (dow-foo) in its native China, tofu was invented over 2,000 years ago by a Chinese scholar and is a very important food in Asian cooking. The Japanese discovered this product in the 8th century and are credited with having introduced it into the Western Hemisphere at a much later date.

Although the dictionary defines it as a soft vegetable cheese, tofu is actually not a dairy product, and it is neither fermented nor aged nor matured like cheese. Usually sold in the form of a rectangular block, tofu has a somewhat gelatinous but firm texture that can be likened to a firm custard. Although somewhat bland tasting on its own, the flavor of tofu can be modified at will, since it readily absorbs the flavors of the foods with which it is combined.

Buying

Tofu is available in bulk (covered in water), individually wrapped (usually vacuum sealed), as well as in dried or frozen form.

When buying tofu sold in bulk, make sure that it is fresh and that the basic rules of hygiene are respected; in particular, the water should be fresh and the tofu should be handled with clean utensils only.

Sealed packaging eliminates the risk of contamination and prolongs the storage life of tofu. Packaged tofu can be kept for a maximum of 90 days unopened. Manufacturers must indicate the expiration date on the package; this date is valid as long as the package has not been opened.

firm tofu

Preparing

Preparation of tofu:

The first step in the preparation of tofu is the same as that for soy milk (see *Soy milk*), except that tofu requires a thicker soy milk than that consumed as a beverage. The formation of curds is then induced using a salt or acidic ingredient. The salt usually used is nigari, a sea salt extract available in its natural form, a beige or whitish crystal powder. Other possible coagulating agents include magnesium chloride (nigari extract), calcium chloride (derived from a mineral ore), calcium sulfate (gypsum), and magnesium sulfate (Epsom salt). Vinegar, lemon or lime juice, or lactone can also be used.

Fifteen to 20 minutes after the coagulant has been added to the hot milk, whitish curds form. The curds are drained in cheesecloth to remove the whey, after which the tofu is usually pressed to give it shape and consistency. It can be marketed plain or flavored.

The type of coagulant used has an effect on the texture and flavor of plain tofu. For example, magnesium chloride, nigari, and seawater produce a lighter and more delicately flavored tofu, while tofu made using gypsum is blander and softer. Epsom salts produce a firmer tofu with a subtle flavor. The length of draining also influences the tofu's consistency; the longer it is drained, the firmer and denser it will be.

Tofu

1 *Rinse the soybeans (½ lb.) in cold water. Place them in a bowl, cover them with water, and soak for 8 hours.*

2 *Rinse again, drain, and purée the beans in a food processor with 3 cups of water.*

3 *Bring 8 cups of water to a boil and add the soybean purée. Cook for 10 minutes over medium heat, stirring constantly.*

4 *Pour the soybean paste into a strainer covered with cheesecloth (stand the strainer over a bowl). Wring the cheesecloth to extract the soybean milk from the paste.*

5 *Heat the soybean milk until it begins to simmer; add one third of the coagulant that has been previously dissolved in a little cold water. Stir, pour in the rest of the coagulant, and stir again. Let stand for 5 minutes.*

6 *When the curd forms, scoop out the remaining liquid (the whey) with a ladle.*

7 *Transfer the soybean curd to a strainer covered with a cloth and wrap it in the cloth.*

8 *Place a heavy object on the wrapped curd and let stand for 15 to 30 minutes, depending on the desired firmness.*

Tofu with Ginger

SERVES 4

8 slices of tofu
2 tbsp. soybean oil

Marinade:
¾ inch fresh ginger root
1 clove garlic

1 tbsp. cilantro leaves
2 tbsp. soy sauce
2 tbsp. water or sake
1 tbsp. lemon juice
2 tbsp. honey

1. Cut each slice of tofu into two triangles. Finely chop the ginger root, the garlic, and the cilantro.

2. Combine the marinade ingredients and marinate the tofu in this sauce for 1 hour. Drain the tofu, reserving the marinade.

3. In a skillet, sauté the tofu in the soybean oil until lightly browned. Remove and place to the side.

4. Deglaze the pan with the marinade and reduce to the desired consistency. Pour the sauce over the tofu slices and serve.

Serving Ideas

Tofu can be used in an endless number of ways. Its bland taste makes it suitable for use in everything from main courses to desserts, and even in beverages. The type of dish one is preparing determines whether soft or firm tofu should be used. It can be served hot or cold and is often added to soups, pastas, pizzas, meat loaves, cakes, tarts, cookies, and muffins. Raw tofu can be ground and seasoned for use in sandwiches, salads, and appetizers. Soft tofu, which is easily liquified in the blender, can be used in place of sour cream, yogurt, and soft cheeses such as cottage cheese, ricotta, or cream cheese. It can also be prepared in the same way as scrambled eggs or used as a sandwich spread.

Firm tofu cooks in a matter of minutes and can be sautéed, braised, simmered, fried, or grilled. It can also be transformed to make a vinaigrette, dip, or spread. Tofu is the basic ingredient in a product resembling ice cream that is often marketed under the name Tofutti. A number of ready-made food products are also made from tofu, including croquettes, burgers, and hot dogs. While these products are often more expensive than their meat-based equivalents, their nutritional value is usually much higher, as they contain more protein, much less fat and salt, and very few additives.

The flavor of tofu is enhanced by using Worcestershire sauce, chili sauce, or soy sauce; garlic, fresh ginger, curry powder, chili powder, or hot mustard can also be used.

Cooking

Tofu is a food product of amazing versatility; not only does it absorb the flavor of the food with which it is mixed, but its texture can also be adapted to that of the dish to which it is added. It can be drained, pressed, crumbled, ground, and braised; the more it is drained, the more it absorbs other flavors.

The moisture content and texture of tofu depend on the method of preparation. Firm tofu keeps its shape better and is easier to slice and cut into cubes than soft tofu, which is more easily crumbled and mashed.

Freezing makes tofu thicker, spongier, and more rubbery; it also makes it absorb sauces and flavors more readily. Boiling has a similar effect, with the consistency of the tofu depending on the length of time it is boiled. Boil tofu whole or cubed for 4 to 20 minutes, depending on the size of the pieces and the desired texture. For maximum flavor, tofu should be consumed as soon as possible after the date of purchase. Older tofu is firmer and has a stronger taste, and is best seasoned generously.

Nutritional Information

	firm tofu
water	69.8%
protein	15.7 g
fat	8.6 g
carbohydrates	4.3 g
fiber	0.1 g
calories	146
	per 100 g

Tofu is a highly nutritious food. It is an excellent source of iron and magnesium, a good source of potassium, niacin, copper, calcium, zinc, and phosphorus, and contains folic acid, thiamine, riboflavin, and vitamin B$_6$.

The proteins in tofu are high in lysine, making it an ideal complement to cereals (see *Soybean*). Its fats are 78% unsaturated and contain no cholesterol, since they are of vegetable origin. It has a low carbohydrate content, since most of the carbohydrates are concentrated in the whey, which is drained after curdling. Although a normal portion of tofu (3½ ounces) contains only half as much protein as a 2-ounce portion of cooked meat, additional protein needs can be derived from other sources in the course of a day. Moreover, combining tofu with cereal products or a food of animal origin during a meal will make the quality of the proteins in tofu comparable to that of the proteins in meat, cheese, and eggs.

During the process of making tofu, most of the fiber contained in the soybeans is lost. Tofu contains two to three times more iron than a portion of cooked meat; the absorption of this iron can be facilitated by combining the tofu with a good source of vitamin C.

Storing

Fresh tofu can be kept in the refrigerator or the freezer. Bulk tofu and tofu from vacuum-sealed packages that have been opened must be stored, covered in water, in an airtight container in the refrigerator. The tofu will keep for about 1 week if the water is changed every 2 days. Vacuum-packed tofu that has passed its expiration date can also be stored in this way, but make sure upon opening the package that the tofu does not give off an unpleasant odor and that it is not viscous.

Tofu can be frozen in its original vacuum pack or in an airtight container without water (let the air escape when closing it). Freezing makes tofu more rubbery and gives it a yellowish white color. Thaw it in the refrigerator in order to minimize the alteration of its texture and the spread of bacteria.

Okara

The drained pulp of soybeans, okara is a by-product of the fabrication of soy milk. It has a fine crumbly texture similar to that of freshly grated coconut and is beige in color.

Nutritional Information

water	82%
protein	3.3 g
fat	1.8 g
carbohydrates	12.6 g
fiber	4.1 g
calories	77
	per 100 g

Okara is a good source of potassium and contains magnesium, iron, calcium, and phosphorus. It is also rich in dietary fiber. Its high cellulose content helps prevent constipation.

Serving Ideas

Okara is used to enrich various foods and to enhance their consistency; it also serves as a thickening agent. It makes breads and pastries lighter and improves their keeping qualities by making them dry out less quickly. Because it readily absorbs the flavor of other foods, okara is useful in a wide variety of foods, including cereals, frying batter, crêpes, muffins, biscuits, hamburgers, croquettes, and stews. It is also used as a meat substitute, to make bread crumbs, and to thicken soups (although not consommés, which become cloudy) and sauces. Okara can be used moist or dried. Its moisture content, which has a bearing on how it is used, depends on the proportion of milk extracted. Okara can be dried in the sun, in a dehydrator, or in the oven at 250° to 450°F. Stir it occasionally; for a more finely textured product, mix the okara in a blender.

Storing

Dried okara keeps almost indefinitely when stored in a cool dry place away from insects and rodents. Moist okara will keep for about 1 week in the refrigerator.

Tempeh

A fermented product with a slightly rubbery texture and a pronounced flavor, tempeh is a highly nutritious food believed to have originated in Indonesia, where it has been a staple for over 2,000 years. Although traditionally made from soybeans, tempeh can also be prepared using other legumes (peanuts or red or white kidney beans), cereals (wheat, oats, barley), or coconut.

The beans are first split in half and their skin is removed; they are then briefly cooked before being inoculated with the fermenting agent *Rhizopus oligosporus,* a filamentous fungus that grows at a temperature of 85° to 95°F. Fermentation usually takes place over a period of 24 hours. White mold spreads throughout the product, which acquires a nougatlike texture and an outer appearance resembling the downy rind of certain cheeses, such as Camembert and Brie.

Buying

Tempeh can be purchased in Asian markets and in health-food stores. Fresh tempeh is covered with a thin whitish outer layer and has a mushroom-like smell. It may contain black or grayish spots where the product has fermented more; while these spots are no cause for concern, it is best not to let the tempeh ferment to that stage. If the tempeh has pink, yellow, or blue spots, or if it smells of ammonia or rot, it has not fermented properly and is not fit for consumption.

Serving Ideas

Tempeh has a strong flavor and a surprising texture that not everyone will appreciate. It can be used as a replacement for or in combination with tofu in numerous recipes. It is more commonly used as a main ingredient than as a seasoning. Like tofu, it is tastier when marinated (allow at least 20 minutes) or when flavored with garlic and fresh ginger or hot mustard. Tempeh is good in soups, sauces, stuffings, dips, sandwiches, mixed salads, stews, lasagna, and pizzas.

Cooking

Tempeh must always be eaten cooked. It is often sautéed or fried until it becomes golden brown and crisp (5 to 10 minutes); drain it on a paper towel before serving.

Storing

Tempeh should be stored in the refrigerator. It can be frozen after being blanched to deactivate the enzymes.

Nutritional Information

	soy tempeh
water	55%
protein	18.9 g
fat	7.7 g
carbohydrates	17 g
fiber	3.0 g
calories	199
	per 100 g

Soy tempeh is an excellent source of vitamin B$_{12}$, niacin, copper, potassium, and magnesium and a good source of folic acid, zinc, phosphorus, vitamin B$_6$, and iron; it also contains thiamine, calcium, vitamin A, riboflavin, and pantothenic acid. It is a source of dietary fiber.

Tempeh is one of the rare foods of vegetable origin to contain significant quantities of vitamin B$_{12}$; this is a result of the fermenting process.

Like all fermented foods, tempeh is rich in nutrients. Fermenting transforms the nutrients in several ways; for example, the proteins are partially hydrolyzed, making them easier to digest and increasing their rate of assimilation. Fermentation also increases tempeh's methionine content, which is the limiting amino acid in legumes. Tempeh is also rich in vitamins and minerals.

Textured vegetable proteins

roteins extracted (isolated) from certain vegetable plants by a chemical process, textured vegetable proteins are added to a wide array of food products and serve primarily as a substitute for meat. The chemical process enabling the isolation of vegetable proteins was developed in the latter half of the 20th century; because of the low production cost involved and the high protein content of the resulting product, the process was hailed as an effective solution for replacing meat in the diet.

Textured vegetable proteins (TVP's) often come from soybeans, which are ideal for this type of transformation because they are abundant and relatively inexpensive, they provide a rich and balanced source of amino acids, and their proteins can be easily isolated. Wheat, sunflower, and alfalfa have similar qualities and are therefore also suitable for this procedure. Depending on the manufacturing method used, the isolated proteins can be more or less gelatinous, viscous, and soluble. The nutritional value of the proteins also varies.

For a homemade product resembling textured vegetable proteins but without the additives, thaw frozen tofu in a strainer and extract as much water as possible; mash the drained tofu with a fork or pestle and season it as desired (with stock, tomato juice, tamari, spices, herbs). Mix well, and use it as is or dry the mixture in the oven (275° to 300°F) for later use.

Buying

Since the number of additives in textured vegetable proteins varies from one product to the next, it is important to read the label carefully before purchasing.

Preparing

To rehydrate dried proteins, add ¾ cup of boiling water per cup of granules and let stand for 10 to 15 minutes. Wet your hands to prevent the rehydrated proteins from sticking to them when you are shaping the product.

Storing

Dried textured soybean proteins can be stored at room temperature, but once rehydrated they should be placed in the refrigerator, where they will keep for about 1 week.

Serving Ideas

Textured vegetable proteins are available plain or seasoned, in the form of granules, powder, cubes, or slices. They readily absorb flavors and can be seasoned with just about anything, including various meat, vegetable, nut, fish, and seafood flavors. They are also used in sauces, stews, lasagna, hamburgers, frozen desserts, and breakfast cereals.

We often consume textured vegetable proteins without realizing it; indeed, these proteins are used as an ingredient or as an additive in numerous products. They can either replace meat or be combined with meat (the law requires producers to mention this on the label). Powdered vegetable proteins are well suited for use in deli meats. Among their multiple other uses, textured vegetable proteins enter into the fabrication of cereal products as well as of commercial pastries and breads.

Nutritional Information

The composition of textured soybean proteins is extremely variable, since it depends on the manufacturing process as well as on the ingredients used. In cooked commercial preparations, there is so much variety that it is often very difficult to know the nutritional value of the product unless it is indicated on the label. The advantage of textured protein vegetables from a nutritional point of view is that they are extremely low in fat and rich in proteins.

Fruits

contents

Introduction

Botanically speaking, the fruit is the part of the plant that develops from the fertilized ovary of the flower and that house the ovules once they develop into seeds. In common usage, the term fruit is applied to a range of usually sweet foods that are consumed in desserts, at breakfast, or as a snack. However, certain foods that many people take to be vegetables are considered by botanists to be fruits, including the eggplant, tomato, squash, olive, avocado, and nuts. Until the 18th century, vegetables were included in the category of fruits, as they were considered to belong to what were called the "fruits of the earth."

Fruits have been consumed by both humans and animals since prehistoric times, while their cultivation dates back over 6000 years. Seasonal fruits played an important role in the diets of primitive peoples. With the discovery of the process of drying, it became possible to consume them out of season as well. Over thousands of years, natural crossbreeding and the repeated selection of resistant species made it possible to introduce crop plants into the different continents. Considering the crudeness of the methods used by early fruit cultivators, their techniques of plant propagation were surprisingly effective. Knowledge of the basic principles of plant propagation only came much later, when scientific "proof" of the sexuality of flowers was developed in the 17th century. Once the cultivation of a certain variety of fruit was well established in one place, it became possible to disperse it intentionally or accidentally. The expeditions of the Spanish, Portuguese, English, French and Dutch played a major role in the exchange of fruits and vegetables between the Old and New World and the creation of botanical gardens contributed to the distribution of fruits throughout the world.

Never before in history has such a wide variety of fruit been available on markets as today. This evolution can be attributed to a number of factors:

• The improvement of preservation methods has made it possible to offer a greater variety of fresher fruit all year round.

• With the development of international trade, many exotic fruits have been successfully marketed worldwide.

• The diversity of supply sources assures constant availability. Fruit is now produced by numerous countries in both hemispheres, and when North America and Europe lie covered in snow and fruit production is low, South America and Australia are in the middle of their summer and at the height of the fruit-growing season. The production of fruit has been rising constantly throughout the 20th century. The fruits produced in greatest quantity internationally include grapes, oranges, bananas, apples, watermelon, and plantains.

Buying

Choose undamaged, brightly colored, and pleasant-smelling fruit that is neither too firm nor too soft; it should be free of mold and bruises. The fine powdery coating or "bloom" that forms naturally on the surface of plums and grapes is a sign of freshness and not a chemical residue.

Preparing

With the exception of some of the more delicate fruits, like raspberries and blackberries, fruit should be washed prior to consumption.

The flesh of many fruits (including apricots, bananas, apples, pears, peaches, and nectarines) oxidizes and turns brown readily when exposed to air, particularly if the fruit is not eaten or cooked immediately once cut. To avoid darkening of the fruit, prepare it at the last minute and sprinkle it with an acid ingredient such as citrus juice, vinegar, vinaigrette, or alcohol (depending on the intended use) or poach it in a sweet syrup. It is also a good idea to use stainless steel utensils when cutting these fruits. The higher the acid content, the longer the fruit will resist darkening. Refrigeration also delays oxidation, while cooking halts it completely. Fruit should be cooked as briefly as possible in order to preserve its flavor and nutritional value.

Serving Ideas

The culinary uses of fruits are endless. They are eaten raw, cooked, dried, candied, flambéed, poached, fried in batter, canned, or macerated in alcohol. They are also used to make compote, coulis, jelly, jam, marmalade, butter, vinegar, alcoholic beverages (liqueurs, spirits, wine, cider), as well as non-alcoholic beverages (fruit juice).

Fruits can be used in desserts as well as in savory dishes. They are added to sauces, soups, fruit salads, mixed salads, cakes, muffins, mousses, charlottes, Bavarian cream, tarts, ice cream, sorbets, crêpes, flans, strudels, clafoutis and puddings. An excellent way to make use of overripe or damaged fruits is to cook them to make a compote.

Fruit that is at peak ripeness, juicy, and firm can be poached in a sugar syrup.

Some fruits, including apples, pears, bananas, and pineapple can also be used to make fritters; the fruits are cut into pieces, covered with batter and deep fried until golden brown.

Fruits blend particularly well with cheese, ham, shellfish, smoked fish, wild game, pork, and poultry; the lemon is the fruit that is most commonly used in cooking.

Fruits

Nutritional Information

While each type of fruit has its own specific concentration of nutritional elements, as a food group, fruits have certain nutritional characteristics in common:

• Most fruits have a high water content (80 to 95%), and are therefore thirst-quenching.

• They usually contain 13 to 23 g of carbohydrates.

• They are generally low in calories, with ½ cup of unsweetened fruit containing between 30 and 100 calories.

• They have a low protein and fat content (ranging from minute traces to about 1 g of fat per 100 g of fruit). Exceptions to this are nuts (almonds, cashews, coconut, etc.), avocados, and olives, which contain between 8 and 35 g of fat per 50 g.

• Most fruits are rich in vitamin A, vitamin B_6, vitamin C, potassium, calcium, iron, and magnesium. Citrus fruits (lemons, oranges, lime, etc.) are particularly high in vitamin C. Generally speaking, the more brightly colored and the darker the fruit, the higher its vitamin and mineral content.

• Fruits contain several organic acids (including citric acid, tartaric, malic, acetic and oxalic acid) which produce alkaline salts that stimulate the secretion of gastric juices. The tannin content is higher before the fruit reaches full ripeness, giving unripe fruit a bitter taste.

• Fruits are rich in soluble and insoluble fiber, which, among other effects, increases intestinal motility.

Fresh fruit should be eaten with its peel whenever possible, since most of the vitamins, fiber and minerals in fruit are concentrated near the surface. Some people have problems digesting raw fruit however.

Several factors influence the flavor and nutritional value of fruits before, during, and after harvesting. While some of these factors, such as the weather, are uncontrollable, most can be controlled by humans, particularly since the development of industrial methods of cultivation at the beginning of the 20th century.

Most fruits come into contact with chemical products at some point during growth and after harvesting; these chemicals are contained in fertilizers, herbicides and insecticides, wax, dyes, etc. Some fruits acquire a natural protective coating of wax, much like that added by fruit producers to delay the loss of moisture in fruits. Although this waxy coating is edible, it is best to scrub fruits thoroughly under running water before eating them. Some of these substances remain in the fruit in the form of residues which can be found inside the fruit (systemic contamination) or only on the surface (topical contamination). Numerous studies are under way to develop safer phytosanitary products and natural techniques to replace these chemical substances. It should be pointed out, however, that the pesticide content of fruits can be reduced considerably if they are blanched (prior to freezing, for example), cooked, or canned. Fruit juices contain very few traces of pesticides, since 90% of these substances are eliminated with the peel, while the rest are eliminated by sterilization. Among the pesticides used, none are considered to cause cancer in humans, according to the International Cancer Research Agency.

Most fruits are gathered before they are fully ripe in order to withstand the rigors of shipping and storage. They are placed in cold rooms or in cold atmosphere storage for periods varying from several days to a few months. Cold atmosphere storage of fruits helps to control their breathing; the quicker they breath, the quicker the fruits «age.» By storing them in a sealed, refrigerated chamber with carefully controlled levels of oxygen and carbon dioxide, the rate of respiration is reduced. Lower temperatures also reduce the development of micro-organisms and enzymes, thus delaying the maturing process. Cold atmosphere (CA) storage makes it possible to offer seasonal products over a longer period of time. The sugar content of most fruits does not increase after harvesting, although their texture and acidity continue to evolve.

Storing

Most fruits are perishable. They continue to live or "breath" after harvesting, and the ambient temperature has a major effect on their rate of respiration. The higher the temperature, the more fruits breath, resulting in a loss of moisture and accelerating the ripening process. All fruits are not equally perishable, however; for example, oranges keep much longer than strawberries.

Stored at a suitable temperature and humidity level, fruits will stay fresh longer; the higher the humidity, the longer it takes for them to dry out.

Unripe fruits can be left out at room temperature away from direct sunlight until they are ripe. However, because many fruits ripen very quickly, check them frequently to make sure they do not become overripe. Fruits are ripe when they yield under gentle pressure of the fingers and when they have a pleasant odor. Once ripe, fruit should be kept in the refrigerator and used as soon as possible.

Fruit emits a large amount of ethylene, a gas that hastens the ripening process. Unripe fruit will thus ripen more quickly if it is placed in a paper bag; the bag seals in the ethylene gas and maximizes its effect. Remove the fruit from the bag as soon as it is ripe, however, to prevent it from becoming overripe. Fruit should not be stored in an airtight plastic bag or container, as the plastic holds in the moisture, causing the fruit to rot more quickly. As for fruit juices, it is best to keep them in an opaque and sealed container in order to minimize the loss of nutrients.

Because the ethylene gas given off by fruit causes vegetables to spoil, it is best to store fruits and vegetables separately. On the other hand, the ethylene in fruits can help to accelerate the flowering of plants if the plant is placed in a bag with an ethylene-producing fruit such as an apple or banana. Fruits should be handled with care, as once they are bruised, they tend to deteriorate very quickly. Also, keep them away from strong-smelling foods, as most fruits have a tendency to absorb odors.

Almost all fruits are suitable for freezing; two exceptions are pears and sweet cherries, which become too soft when thawed. During freezing, certain enzymes cause the fruit to turn brown; the addition of sugar or acid ingredients such as lemon juice or ascorbic acid will delay this process.

To make good-quality fruit preserves, the fruits, even those that are very acid, must be sterilized in order to destroy any bacteria, mold, and enzymes that could cause the fruit to spoil. It is also important to use only ripe fruit that is firm and in good condition. Home-made preserves that are properly prepared will keep for up to one year; it is best to store them in a dark and cool place.

Drying is one of the most ancient methods of preserving food and was used over 5000 years ago in the Middle East. The most frequently dried fruits are apricots, dates, figs, and grapes. The basic principle behind the drying of fruits and other foods is that it drains them of their moisture, making it difficult for micro-organisms to grow. However, because the enzymes present in fruits can cause alterations in color and flavor during the drying process, the fruits are either blanched or sulfated beforehand to minimize the effects of these enzymes. They are then dried until there is no more water at their core. Dried fruits have a supple texture that is similar to that of leather. The amount of time required for the drying process varies between 5 to 15 hours, depending on the type of fruit and the size of the pieces.

Dried fruits

dried apples

Dried fruits are fruits from which a major part of the water content has been removed. Drying is one of the oldest means of preserving food. Humans discovered this process by observing that fruits that had been left on the branches of trees were still edible. For centuries after this discovery, fruits were deliberately left to dry in the sun. Today commercial dehydration is highly mechanized and is carried out under precisely controlled temperatures.

Buying

Dried fruits are sold in bulk or pre-packaged. It is often difficult for the consumer to know whether these fruits contain additives, but their appearance may provide an indication. For example, fruits that appear drier and darker, or that are more brownish in color, are more likely not to contain sulfites. Dried pineapple, papayas, and apricots are often treated with sulfites in order to conserve their bright color.

When buying dried fruits, the best way to be assured of their quality and freshness is to purchase them in stores with a rapid turnover. Avoid sulfite-treated fruits that have hardened, as they may be old.

Preparing

Dried fruits can be rehydrated by soaking them in water, juice, or alcohol until they swell and soften. Let them soak for 6 to 8 hours in cold liquid and for at least 30 minutes in hot liquid.

Serving Ideas

Dried fruits can be eaten as they are or rehydrated, cooked or uncooked. They make a pleasant snack or dessert, and are also good puréed. Dried fruits are often added to cereals, fruit salads or mixed salads, sauces, stuffings, rice, cakes, cookies, puddings, and pastries. Since they are very sweet, it is a good idea to reduce the quantity of sugar in dishes to which they are added.

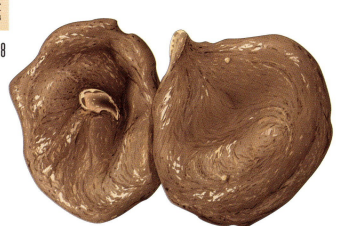

dried figs

dried papayas

dried apricots

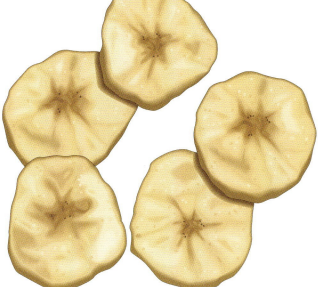

dried bananas

Nutritional Information

Because dried fruits contain one third the water of their fresh counterparts, their nutritional elements are much more concentrated. In fact, they contain four to five times more nutrients than fresh fruits of equal weight, making them a very energizing food. The energy they provide is immediately available, since the sugars they contain are rapidly metabolized. Given their high sugar content and the fact that they tend to get stuck in the teeth, dried fruits may cause tooth decay.

They often contain food preservatives to prevent them from discoloring and hardening, and to suppress the growth of mold and fungi. Some of the additives found in dried fruits include sorbic acid, potassium sorbate, potassium bisulfite, and sodium bisulfite. Their use is not absolutely necessary, however, and some dried fruits contain no sulfites. Although they have been shown to be harmless, some consumers object to the use of additives in dried fruits. They can provoke an allergic reaction in hypersensitive people.

Storing

Store dried fruits in airtight containers and place them in a cool, dry place away from insects. Depending on the variety, they will keep for 6 to 12 months. Dried fruits also freeze very well.

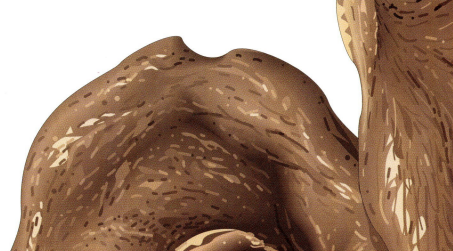

Candied fruits

Fruits preserved in sugar. This method of preserving fruits, by replacing their moisture content with sugar, dates back to ancient times. There are historical records which show that candied fruits were consumed in Egypt 4,000 years ago, although the art of candying fruits only really developed in Europe in the 15th century, when white sugar became more readily available. By the end of the 14th century, the town of Apt, France, was already renowned for the quality of its candied fruits; this reputation still holds today.

The fruits are picked just before they are fully ripe to ensure maximum flavor. The traditional process of candying consists of blanching the fruits to soften them (with the exception of strawberries and apricots); they are then macerated in increasingly concentrated syrups which penetrate the fruit without damaging it. The amount of sugar in the syrups depends on the fruit being candied. The syrups are heated to precise temperatures to prevent them from crystallizing or caramelizing. The traditional method takes up to 2 months and is used mainly for perishable or fragile fruits, while the more rapid, continuous method is used for hardier fruit and takes 1 week on average. After being drained, the fruits are dried. They are then sold as they are or iced with sugar to make them less sticky and easier to keep.

Almost all fruits can be candied, whether whole or in pieces; the rinds of citrus fruits are also commonly preserved in this way, as are violet petals and the stems of angelica.

Nutritional Information

	candied apricot
water	12%
protein	0.6 g
fat	0.2 g
carbohydrates	86.5 g
calories	351
	per 100 g

Because they are extremely rich in sugar, candied fruits have a high calorie content.

Serving Ideas

Candied fruits are used for decoration, in pastry making, and simply to be eaten as sweets. They are indispensable in plum pudding and in fruitcakes, and in Italy are often added to ice cream.

Storing

Candied fruits should be kept in an airtight container in a cool dry place, away from insects. If protected from the heat, they will keep for as long as 6 months.

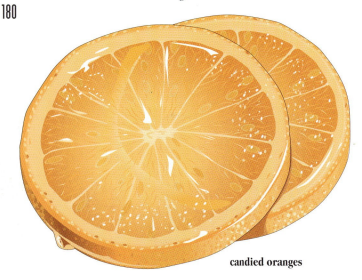

candied oranges

candied apricots

Rhubarb

Rheum rhaponticum, **Polygonaceae**

A plant originating in northern Asia (Tibet or Mongolia), rhubarb is frequently regarded as a fruit but is technically a vegetable, belonging to the same family as sorrel and buckwheat. The word "rhubarb" comes from the Latin *reubarbarum,* meaning "root of the barbarians," a term used at one time to designate anything unfamiliar or foreign. Although widely consumed by the "barbarians," this plant was unknown in the Western world. Used initially for its medicinal properties or as an ornamental plant, it did not enter into the culinary preparations of Europeans until the 18th century. North Americans discovered it a century later.

Rhubarb is a perennial plant reaching more than 3 feet high. Some 20 varieties have been identified. The edible part of the plant is the crisp fleshy stalk, which is between 1 and 3 inches thick. The red, pinkish, or green stems end in wide veined leaves whose high oxalic acid content makes them toxic; this substance also makes them an effective laxative. Rhubarb is at its most flavorful in the spring.

Preparing

To prepare rhubarb, first trim off the leaf ends and the lower ends of the stalks; wash the stalks and cut them into ¾-inch pieces. Stems that are too fibrous may need to be pared; pull off the strings as for celery.

Serving Ideas

Rhubarb is sometimes eaten raw, coated with a little sugar or salt. However, it is more commonly cooked and made into compote, marmalade, or marinades. It is also baked in pies, cakes, and muffins, and incorporated into sorbets, ice cream, and punches. Rhubarb blends deliciously with other fruits, and especially with strawberries and apples. It is also pleasant seasoned with lemon, cinnamon, and ginger. Rhubarb can be used in savory dishes or as an accompaniment to meats and fish. It is interchangeable with cranberries in most recipes.

Cooking

Rhubarb should be cooked in a small quantity of water over moderate heat for about 20 minutes or until the fibers become soft; it is not necessary to cook it to a purée.

Storing

Rhubarb tends to wilt rapidly and will stay fresh in the refrigerator for only a few days. It freezes well in stewed form or simply cut into pieces (they do not need to be blanched or sweetened with sugar beforehand). Rhubarb can be preserved either by cooking it first and placing it in warm sterilized jars, or by filling jars with alternating layers of raw rhubarb pieces and sugar and sealing the jars, then sterilizing them in boiling water.

Buying

Choose stalks that are firm and crisp, without blemishes.

Nutritional Information

water	94%
protein	0.9 g
fat	0.2 g
carbohydrates	4.5 g
calories	21
	per 100 g

Rhubarb is rich in potassium and also contains vitamin C and calcium. It is rarely consumed on its own because of its high acidity. Because of this, generous quantities of sugar are often added, increasing its calorie content significantly. Rhubarb is known for its tonic and purgative properties. It is also said to be aid the appetite and digestion, and promote the flow of bile.

Red currant

Ribes spp., Saxifragaceae

Fruit of the red-currant bush, a dense and thorny shrub that can grow up to 3 feet high. During the 19th century, red-currant bushes growing in North America were host to a fungus that destroyed millions of pine trees. As a consequence, the cultivation of these berries practically disappeared from this region, and they are still rarely available fresh there.

There are close to 150 varieties of these berries, divided into two main categories: currants and gooseberries. The major producers are Germany, Poland, and Russia.

The **red currant** (*Ribes rubrum, sativum, vulgare,* etc.) is thought to have originated in northern Europe and Asia. It is a round red or white berry less than a quarter of an inch in diameter.

The **black currant** *(Ribes nigrum)* is a black berry resembling the bilberry. It grows on the black-currant bush, which is native to northern Europe. Produced in Europe since the mid-18th century, it is not cultivated in North America. The skin of this berry is thin and translucent, similar to that of grapes. The pulp is fragrant, tart, and juicy, and contains tiny seeds.

The **gooseberry** *(Ribes grossularioides)* is believed to come from Europe, where it is held in high esteem. It is particularly popular in English cooking – for instance in a sweet-and-sour sauce to accompany mackerel. The gooseberry differs from the currant in that it grows on a thorny shrub, it is larger, and the fruits form singly instead of in clusters. Depending on the variety, it may be yellowish, green, whitish, or reddish in color, with a downy or smooth skin. The flesh, which contains numerous small edible seeds, is tart and often has a bitter aftertaste.

Buying

 Look for fruits that are undamaged and uniformly colored.

Preparing

 To strip red currants off the stalk, use your fingers, a fork, or a wide-toothed comb.

Serving Ideas

Red currants may be eaten raw, either on their own or in salads. However, because of their rather tart flavor, they are more frequently consumed cooked than raw. They may be added to puddings, cakes, and pies, and they blend well with pears, plums, pineapple, and raspberries. Currants are used mainly to make compote, jelly, jam, syrup, and wine. Red-currant juice makes an excellent substitute for vinegar in vinaigrettes.

Gooseberries can be enjoyed in a wide variety of ways. They are delicious eaten fresh with sugar or added to fruit salads. They are also used to make pies, jellies, sorbets, and syrup, and often appear in puddings and chutneys. Gooseberries are also an excellent garnish for meat and fish dishes.

The black currant is chiefly used in the fabrication of liquors, wines, jellies, and *coulis* but can also be prepared in the same way as the red currant. However, it is rarely sold fresh as a table fruit.

Nutritional Information

	red currant	*black currant*	*gooseberry*
water	84%	82%	88%
protein	1.4 g	1.4 g	0.9 g
fat	0.2 g	0.4 g	0.6 g
carbohydrates	14 g	15 g	10 g
fiber	4.3 g	5.4 g	4.3 g
calories	55	64	45
			per 100 g

The red currant is rich in vitamin C and potassium, and contains iron, magnesium, and traces of phosphorus, calcium, and sodium. The black currant is an excellent source of vitamin C and potassium, as well as supplying iron, magnesium, pantothenic acid, phosphorus, calcium, and traces of vitamin A.

One cup (250 ml) of fresh black currants contains three times more vitamin C than a small orange.

The gooseberry is a good source of vitamin C and potassium and contains traces of pantothenic acid, phosphorus, and vitamin A.

All of these fruits are rich in citric acid (which gives them their tartness) and pectin. When used to make jams and jellies, it is best to choose them not completely ripe, when their pectin content is the highest. If they are to be consumed fresh, however, choose ripe berries for the best flavor. These berries are said to have aperitive, digestive, diuretic, and depurator properties. They are an excellent natural laxative, particularly the black currant.

Gooseberry Sauce

SERVES 4

½ lb. (250 g) gooseberries
1 cup (250 ml) water

2 tbsp. sugar
2 tbsp. unsalted butter
½ tsp. grated lemon zest

1. Wash the gooseberries and remove the stems. Place them in a saucepan with the water and bring to a boil. Simmer the berries over moderate heat for 3 to 5 minutes until very tender or until the skins begin to separate.

2. Remove the pan from the heat, and pass the mixture through a fine sieve without pressing too hard on the fruits (to prevent the sauce from clouding). Discard the skins and the pulp remaining in the sieve.

3. Add the sugar, butter, and grated lemon zest to the purée and mix well. Serve hot as an accompaniment to fish, duck, or goose.

Cooking

The berries should be cooked slowly for 3 to 5 minutes in a small quantity of water or juice (just enough to keep them from sticking). Sugar can be added after cooking.

Storing

Fresh, these fruits will keep in the refrigerator for no more than 2 to 3 days. They should be washed just before use. They freeze well whole, with or without sugar. The berries will be more flavorful if used before they are fully thawed.

gooseberries

red currants

black currants

Berry Fruits

183

Blueberry/Bilberry

Vaccinium spp., Ericaceae

bilberries

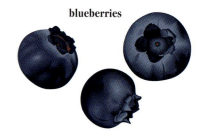
blueberries

Blueberry shrubs, less than 1 foot high, produce tiny fruits the size of small peas.

Blueberries and bilberries belong to the heath family, which includes close to 150 varieties, not all of which are edible.

The **blueberry** is native to North America and is cultivated mainly in Canada and the United States. It is rare in Europe and was only recently introduced into Australia. The fruit of a wild plant, the blueberry grows best in woods, mountainous regions, and peaty soils. North American Indians used blueberries to season pemmican, a mixture of dried meat and fat.

There are about 30 varieties of blueberry plants. Most of them are shrubs less than 1 foot high that produce tiny fruits the size of small peas. Some giant varieties of blueberry shrubs can grow to a height of 7 feet and produce fruits the size of marbles. The pinkish white flowers are bell-shaped and the fruits grow in clusters. The sweet flesh harbors tiny seeds.

The lowbush blueberry *(Vaccinium angustifolium)* is often sweeter and tastier than its relative the highbush blueberry *(Vaccinium corymbosum)*. Blueberries are often naturally covered with a thin waxy coating called the bloom, which tends to dull their color.

The **bilberry** *(Vaccinium myrtillus)* comes from Europe and Asia and grows on wild shrubs that stand 1 to 2 feet high. Their green foliage turns a deep red color in the fall. The tiny white flowers of the shrub give way to clusters of small fruits measuring about ⅓ inch in diameter. Although it resembles the blueberry, the bilberry belongs to a different species.

Buying

Choose fruits that are uniformly blue, firm, and free of mold.

Preparing

As blueberries and bilberries are highly perishable fruits, wash them briefly, and only if necessary, just before consuming them.

Nutritional Information

water	85%
protein	0.7 g
fat	0.4 g
carbohydrates	14 g
fiber	2.3 g
calories	56
	per 100 g

Blueberries and bilberries are a source of vitamin C, potassium, sodium, and fiber. They contain several acids, including oxalic, malic, and citric acid. They also contain anthocyanides, which may explain the effectiveness of blueberries in the treatment of urinary-tract infections. They are said to be astringent, antibacterial, and antidiarrheal.

Serving Ideas

These fruits are delicious fresh, whether eaten on their own, mixed in fruit salads or cereals, or used as a topping for crêpes and waffles. They are also served topped with fresh cream, orange juice, vodka, or Grand Marnier. Like all berries, they appear in numerous desserts, including pies, cakes, muffins, ice cream, yogurt, and sorbets. They make succulent jams and jellies, and are also used in the making of juice and alcoholic beverages. They can also be dried. North American Indians used to cook blueberries to make a concentrated paste, which they then left to dry in the sun, thus ensuring a supply of these fruits during the off-season.

Storing

Blueberries and bilberries are extremely fragile. They can be stored unwashed in the refrigerator, where they will keep for a few days. Remove any damaged berries in order to prevent the spread of mold. They can also be canned or frozen. Prior to freezing, they should be sorted, washed, and drained; it is not necessary to add sugar. Freezing may alter the flavor and texture of these berries, but this is of little consequence if they are used in cooking. To retain maximum flavor, cook the berries while they are still frozen.

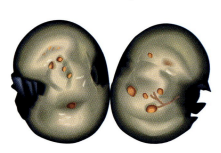

Blackberry

Rubus spp., **Rosaceae**

The fruit of a bramble belonging to the same family as the raspberry and the strawberry, blackberries grow in gardens, fields, and woods, climbing over walls and any other obstacles in their path. Blackberries are not to be confused with mulberries, which grow on the mulberry bush (*Morus* spp.) of the Urticaceae family, and which is host to the silkworm. A native of temperate climates, the blackberry is grown in North America, Europe, the British Isles, and Australia. They are usually thorny shrubs that produce clusters of delicate whitish or pinkish flowers. More than a thousand varieties of blackberries have been identified, most of which grow wild.

The blackberry is a compound of small juicy fruits called drupelets, each of which contains a tiny seed. The berry can be black, burgundy red, or even yellowish white in color. It is difficult to know when to harvest the black-colored blackberry, since it tends to turn black before it is ripe. At peak ripeness, when they are sweetest and least acidic, the berries are soft and come off the stem easily. As with raspberries, the best moment to pick them is in the morning. Unlike the raspberry, however, the central receptacle of the blackberry remains in the fruit after it is detached from the plant. Hybridizations of blackberries with raspberries have produced new fruits, such as loganberries and boysenberries, which are often named after their inventors.

The blackberry can be black, burgundy red, or even yellowish white in color. There are more than 1,000 varieties.

Buying

Blackberries are delicate fruits that do not stand up well to heat, handling, or shipping. They tend to spoil rapidly, contaminating surrounding berries as well. When buying blackberries, choose fruits that are firm and glossy, avoiding soft, dull-colored, or closely packed blackberries, which are probably lacking in freshness and may be overripe or moldy. Whenever possible, pick blackberries fresh from the bush; they will keep longer and be sweeter if picked in the morning.

Preparing

Blackberries should be washed only if absolutely necessary, as they tend to absorb water and turn soft. Rinse them delicately and briefly just before using them. Shake freshly picked berries lightly in their container to rid them of any insects.

Storing

Blackberries are highly perishable fruits. Avoid exposing them to the sun or leaving them out at room temperature for any length of time. Stored in the refrigerator, they will keep for several days. They tend to keep longer if stored unwashed and loosely packed, after the removal of any damaged berries. Adding a little sugar will also help them keep longer and will prevent discoloration. The berries can be frozen whole or in a coulis, with or without sugar. They will retain more of their nutritional value if frozen whole, as this reduces the fruit surface that is exposed to air. To limit the loss of nutrients, add a little lemon juice to puréed blackberries. When sugar has been added to the berries, the amount of sugar called for in recipes should be modified accordingly.

To freeze blackberries, spread them in a single layer on a cookie sheet; once they are frozen solid, they can be stored in an airtight container. Blackberries taste better if they are thawed completely before being used.

Serving Ideas

Blackberries may be used in the same manner as raspberries. They are delicious fresh, served with ice cream, yogurt, or fresh cream. They can be added to fruit salads, crêpes, and tarts, and make a tasty topping on breakfast cereals. Blackberries are also made into jam, jelly, syrup, juice, wine, and brandy (ratafia).

Blackberry coulis can be used as a garnish or as a topping on cakes, puddings, ice cream, sorbets, custards, and Bavarian cream. Coulis is prepared by puréeing the berries in a food processor and then passing the mixture through a sieve in order to remove the numerous tiny seeds. Blackberries can also be dried, as was once a common practice among American Indians. In addition to drying them whole, they made a paste from crushed berries that was left to dry in the sun or over a fire.

Nutritional Information

water	86%
protein	0.7 g
fat	0.4 g
carbohydrates	13 g
fiber	4.6 g
calories	51
	per 100 g

The blackberry is a good source of vitamin C and potassium, and contains magnesium and copper. It has also been credited with astringent, cleansing, and laxative properties.

Raisin

Raisins are grapes that have been dried. The practice of drying grapes dates back to ancient times and has always ensured a supply of grapes in the off-season. Damascus was renowned for its raisins as early as the 13th century. The largest producers of raisins today are the United States, Turkey, and Greece; other raisin-producing countries include Australia, South Africa, Spain, and Chile, as well as some countries in the eastern Mediterranean basin and in the Middle East.

The grapes most commonly used for drying are table grapes (wine grapes are rarely used for this purpose); they usually have a tender skin, a rich flavor, and a high sugar content. The Muscat, Malaga, Sultana, and Thompson Seedless varieties (the latter accounts for over 95% of American grape production) are among the most commonly marketed. Over 30% of the American grape crop is dried to produce raisins. Raisins may or may not contain seeds, depending on the variety. The seeds of the Muscat variety, which is larger than the Sultana and Thompson, are removed after drying.

Corinth grapes, also known as **Zante currants**, are tiny black seedless grapes that are particularly popular in the making of pastries. They are named after the places in Greece where they were produced on a large scale over 2,000 years ago. Most raisins are produced by sun-drying grapes directly in the vineyard between the rows of vines. Depending on the temperature, this takes from 2 to 4 weeks, during which the fruit's color changes from green to purplish brown and the moisture content drops from 75% to less than 16% of the fruit's total composition. Golden raisins are obtained by treating Thompson grapes with sulfites before they are dried in order to conserve their light color, which varies from golden yellow to amber.

Nutritional Information

water	15 to 19%
protein	3 to 4 g
fat	0.3 to 0.5 g
carbohydrates	74 to 80 g
fiber	3.7 to 6.8 g
calories	283 to 302
	per 100 g

Like all dried fruit, raisins are very nourishing and supply energy rapidly, since the drying processes concentrates their nutritional elements. They are an excellent source of potassium and a good source of iron, magnesium, and copper; they also contain calcium, phosphorus, zinc, and vitamin C. Golden raisins are treated with sulfites to prevent them from darkening.

Buying

Raisins are usually sold in sealed packages, which makes it difficult to determine their quality before purchasing them. If the package is transparent, ensure that the raisins are undamaged and not overly dry.

Serving Ideas

Raisins are often eaten out of hand as a snack food. They are used both as a condiment and as an ingredient in a wide range of foods, including cereals, salads, sauces (port sauce), fricassees, poultry stuffing, meat loaf, pâtés, tarts, breads, muffins, biscuits, brioches, and puddings. They are also used in stuffed grape leaves, couscous, tajines, and pilafs.

Northern and eastern European cooking mixes raisins with other dried fruits. They can be used dried or rehydrated in water, juice, or alcohol.

Storing

Raisins will keep for about 1 year if stored in an airtight container in a cool dry place.

Grape

Vitis spp., Vitaceae

Fruit of the climbing woody vine. While the exact place of origin of the grape is not known, it is believed to be either Asia Minor, the Caspian Sea region, or Armenia. The grape is one of the oldest and most widely distributed fruits in the world, dating back thousands of years to the earliest civilizations. Some studies suggest that grapes were cultivated in western Asia over 7,000 years ago, while drawings found in Egyptian burial sites indicate that they may have been grown as early as 2375 B.C.; grape cultivation in China may have begun even earlier. Grapes are the basic ingredient in wine and various other alcoholic beverages, including Armagnac, cognac, port, champagne, and so on. Winemaking is nearly as old as civilization itself. Wine was highly valued by the Greeks and Romans, who consumed it in abundance and venerated the wine gods Dionysus and Bacchus. At the time of the fall of the Roman Empire, viticulture was promoted by the Gauls; the monasteries followed suit, greatly improving winemaking methods.

The species native to Europe, Vitis vinifera, produces the best grapes for winemaking.

The family of grapes includes three principal species. The species native to Europe, *Vitis vinifera,* produces the best grapes for winemaking and is the most widely cultivated (95% of grapes are produced by this species). There are thousands of varieties of *vinifera* grapes. The second species is native to North America and includes two main varieties of grapes: *Vitis labrusca* and *Vitis rotundifolia.* The Concord (black), the Niagara (green), and the Catawba (red) are varieties of the *labrusca.* The Delaware (red) is a cross between the *vinifera* and the *labrusca.* The skin of *labrusca* grapes peels away easily from the pulp. The third species includes the hybrids, also called "French hybrids," which were developed from the European species *Vitis vinifera.*

In 1863 the *vinifera* species was almost totally destroyed in France, the world's largest wine-producing country, following the unintentional importation into Europe from North America of a tiny louse, *Phylloxera vastatrix,* that lives and feeds on vine roots, destroying them. Unlike the *vinifera* species, American vines are resistant to this insect. In 1865 the Rhone valley and the Bordeaux region were totally infested by it, and it is estimated that 2,500,000 acres of grapevines were decimated in Europe. The only thing that saved the vineyards was the decision to graft *vinifera* vines to the resistant American rootstock of the *Vitis labrusca* species. Chile, Cyprus, southern Australia, some regions of Hungary, Austria, and the northwestern United States were miraculously spared and are the only areas where the *Vitis vinifera* is still found today. The largest grape-producing countries are Italy, France, and Spain.

The vines can grow to a length of 55 feet or more, but they are usually trained in order to facilitate harvesting. In fact, vines of wine grapes are pruned to limit the production to a few bunches of grapes, thus concentrating the flavors. The vine develops tendrils by which the plant is able to attach itself solidly just about anywhere, and which help to support the weight of the clusters of fruit. As many as 50 bunches can grow on one vine; when they first appear, they are concealed by the large five-lobed palmate leaves, which measure between 4 and 8 inches in length. The vine flowers in spring and the fruit is ripe and ready for harvesting just 3 months later. The fruit of the grapevine is a berry that is round or elongated in shape, and more or less fleshy depending on the variety. The grapes grow in bunches, each of which contains from 6 to 300 grapes. They vary in color from green (known as white in Europe) to greenish yellow, reddish, and blue-black or purple. The sweet, juicy pulp is covered with a skin that has a thin powdery coating called the "bloom." While some varieties of grapes are seedless, others contain between 1 and 4 seeds.

Grapes are often classified according to their use: certain varieties are grown as table fruit or to be used in baking and cooking, others for winemaking or for the production of raisins. Most varieties grow better in hot climates, although some do tolerate temperate climates. Some of the most common European varieties include the Cardinal, the Muscat of Hamburg, the Lival, and the Ribier in the category of blue or black grapes. The green or white grapes include the Chasselas, the White Muscat, the Gros-vert, and the Servant. Common North American varieties include the Concord (a blue seeded grape), the Flame, Delaware, and Ruby (red seedless), and the Thompson and Niagara (green seedless). Unlike the European varieties, the skin of American grapes does not cling to the pulp. Black Corinth grapes are distinguished from other varieties by their tiny size; they are also called Zante currants or champagne grapes. Corinth is the name of a Greek city and Zante is the name of a Greek island where these grapes were cultivated intensively over 2,000 years ago. The term "champagne grapes" originated in California, where champagne is often served in glasses garnished with small clusters of these grapes. These decorative grapes are seedless and very sweet and flavorful.

bunch of grapes

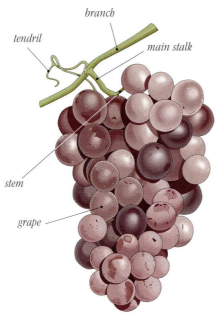

branch

tendril

main stalk

stem

grape

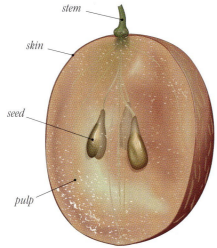

stem

skin

seed

pulp

Buying

Choose grapes that are firm, undamaged, and evenly colored; they should still have their bloom and be firmly attached to the stem. Green grapes are sweeter if they have a yellow tint. Avoid grapes that are soft, wrinkled, blemished, or whitened at the stem end, as they are probably not fresh.

Preparing

Because they are almost always treated with chemical substances (copper sulfate and calcium hydrate), grapes must be washed carefully before being consumed. The residue from spraying (which is stopped well before harvesting) is not to be confused with the grape's bloom, which is a natural coating. It is better to remove small clusters of grapes from the main stem with scissors rather than pulling off individual grapes, as this causes the stem to dry out and the other grapes to soften and shrivel.

Nutritional Information

	American grape	*European grape*
water	81%	81%
protein	0.7 g	0.7 g
fat	0.3 g	0.6 g
carbohydrates	17 g	18 g
fiber	0.9 g	1.2 g
calories	63	71
		per 100 g

The grape is a good source of potassium and contains vitamin C, thiamine, and vitamin B_6. It is credited with numerous medicinal properties and is notably used as a diuretic, an energy food, a digestive, a laxative, a tonic, and a remineralizer. The natural coloring matter of black grapes, oenocyanin, makes them an excellent tonic. Grapes help to purify the system thanks to their invigorating and cleansing qualities.

Serving Ideas

 Grapes are delicious fresh, cooked, dried, and in juice form. They can be eaten out of hand or added to fruit salads, tarts, and custards. In pastry making they can be used in place of cherries or apples. They are often used to make jam and jelly, and are frequently added to sauces, stuffings, curries, stews, and mixed salads. Grapes blend well with poultry, wild game, rabbit, fish, and seafood, and make a particularly pleasant accompaniment to calf's liver, duck, and quail.

The juice of grapes is very popular, whether fresh or fermented. A table oil is extracted from the seeds of the grape (see *Oil*). The edible leaves are used mainly in North America, Greece, Israel, and Iran, often stuffed with rice or meat.

Grape Jam

Ripe but firm grapes   *Sugar*

1. Pick the grapes off the stems, discarding those that are too soft or damaged. After washing the grapes well, cut them in half and remove the seeds, if any.

2. Weigh the grapes. If you will be storing the jam, use an equal amount of sugar. If you will be using it soon, use half the amount of sugar.

3. Pour the sugar into a saucepan and add 1/5 cup (50 ml) of water for every 2 pounds (1 kg) of sugar. Cook gently until the sugar dissolves. Bring to a boil and cook for 4 minutes.

4. Add the grapes, return the mixture to a boil, and cook for 15 minutes.

5. Skim the foam off the liquid, and remove the grapes from the liquid; set them aside.

6. Boil the syrup until it thickens, and then return the grapes to the pan. As soon as the mixture resumes boiling, remove the pan from the heat and pour the jam into hot sterilized jars and seal.

Storing

Grapes tend to shrivel and ferment if stored at room temperature. Wrapped in a paper towel and placed in a perforated plastic bag, they will keep for several days in the refrigerator. For the best flavor, take them out of the refrigerator 15 minutes before serving. Although they do not take well to freezing, grapes are very good macerated in alcohol.

Muscat grapes

Corinth grapes

Chasselas grapes

Thompson grapes

Cardinal grapes

Strawberry

Fragaria, Rosaceae

Wild strawberries are the ancestors of cultivated strawberries.

Fruit of the strawberry plant, a perennial that grows in temperate zones all over the world. Some varieties of the strawberry come from the temperate zones of Europe, while others are native to North and South America.

Wild strawberries are the ancestors of today's cultivated strawberries. They are small and juicy, and tend to be more flavorful and fragrant than the cultivated variety. In 1714 a Frenchman, François Amédée Frézier, created large fleshy strawberries by crossing two varieties of wild strawberries. These plants became widely cultivated in Europe and, many crossings later, are thought to be the source of the large-fruit strawberry plants that are popular today. The more than 600 varieties of strawberries differ in size, texture, color, and flavor.

The strawberry is a low-growing plant with horizontal runners (stolons) that spread out from the base and take root to produce new plants. Strawberries are not really fruits in the botanical sense of the term. The flesh we eat is in fact the result of the swelling of the strawberry plant's stalks, which occurs after its flowers have been pollinated. Officially, the "fruit" part of the strawberry is the small yellowish seeds (achene) that dot the berry's surface. Picking season and use differ according to the variety of strawberry, some of which, such as everbearing strawberry plants, produce berries more than once a year.

Buying

Some varieties of strawberries are better suited for freezing, while others are best eaten fresh and others yet are more suitable for cooking. These qualities are difficult to identify, however, since they are rarely indicated in the marketplace.

When buying strawberries, choose firm, shiny berries with a healthy color. Most strawberries on the market are a bright red; dull-colored strawberries are usually overripe. Strawberries stand up poorly to heat, handling, and shipping. The smallest bump will bruise them, causing them to rot and contaminate the other berries in the container. Avoid soft, dull, or moldy strawberries, and check at the bottom of the container to make sure all the berries are in good condition.

Preparing

Wash strawberries before hulling them to prevent losing their juice, and not until they are to be used, for they are very fragile and will rot quickly. Rinse the berries in cold water and avoid soaking them, as they tend to absorb water and thus lose their flavor.

Serving Ideas

Strawberries can be used in many different ways. They may be eaten plain, whole, sliced, or crushed. When they are ripe and very sweet, they can be eaten raw with yogurt or ice cream, with fresh cream, or sprinkled with a liqueur. They are also delicious dipped in chocolate fondue. To restore the color of strawberries that have been cooked, puréed, or strained to make a *coulis,* add a bit of citrus juice to the mixture. Strawberries may also be added to fruit salads, omelettes, ice cream, or sorbets. Strawberries that are past their prime can be used in pies, cookies, mousses, soufflés, flans, puddings, and cakes. Strawberries are also used to decorate appetizers and cheese platters.

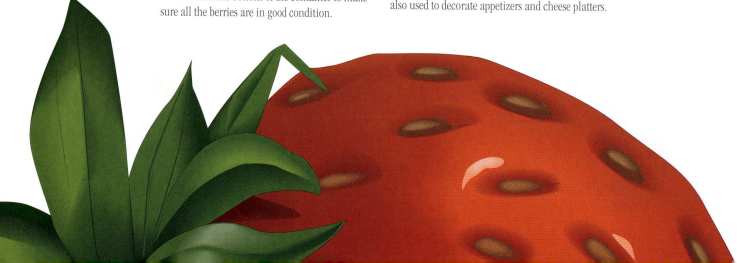

Storing

Strawberries are highly perishable. Avoid leaving them in the sun or at room temperature for any length of time. To ensure optimal freshness, sort strawberries before storing them, discarding the damaged berries. Without washing or hulling them, pack the strawberries loosely in a covered container (to prevent their odor from spreading to other foods) and store them in the refrigerator, where they will keep for 2 to 3 days. Strawberries that have already been washed or that are slightly overripe will keep a while longer if you add a bit of sugar. Strawberries freeze well, but take care to discard unripe or overripe berries first. They may be frozen whole, sliced, quartered, or crushed, with or without sugar. Whole strawberries maintain a higher nutritional value (and particularly vitamin C) than cut or sliced berries, since less of their surface is exposed to air. Vitamin C loss can by reduced by adding lemon or apple juice to the berries. Though sugar is not indispensable, adding it will help preserve the color of the berries, just as citrus juice would. When using pre-sweetened strawberries, reduce the amount of sugar that is called for in a recipe. Frozen strawberries keep their shape better when they are not completely thawed before being used.

Strawberries with Lemon

SERVES 4

1 lb. (500 g) strawberries	3 tbsp. sugar
	Juice of 1 lemon

1. Rince, drain, and hull the strawberries.

2. Place them in a serving dish and add the sugar and lemon juice.

3. Allow the fruit to macerate for 2 hours before serving.

Nutritional Information

water	92%
protein	0.6 g
fat	0.4 g
carbohydrates	7 g
fiber	2.6 g
calories	30
	per 100 g

Strawberries are an excellent source of vitamin C, a good source of potassium, and a source of folic acid, vitamin B_5 and magnesium. They are thought to have tonic, depurator, diuretic, remineralizing, and astringent properties. Strawberry essence is used in beauty products to combat wrinkles and freckles, and is also a good skin tonic. Strawberry leaves are brewed to produce a mild astringent tea used to relieve diarrhea. On the other hand, when eaten in large quantities, strawberries will act as a laxative. Brewed strawberry plant root is used to make a diuretic tea. In some people, eating strawberries may produce an allergic reaction. This type of allergy usually flares up as a benign skin rash, which disappears relatively quickly.

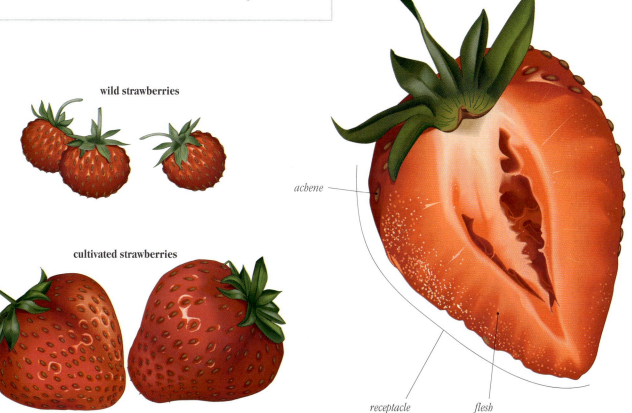

wild strawberries

cultivated strawberries

achene

receptacle

flesh

Raspberry

Rubus spp., **Rosaceae**

ruit of the raspberry bush, the raspberry is believed to be of East Asian origin. Traces of the wild raspberry have been found at prehistoric sites. The first variety to be cultivated in Europe was the *rubus idaeus,* or red raspberry; it was brought there by Crusaders who had discovered it growing in the region of Mount Ida in Turkey (hence its name *rubus idaeus*). While the culture of raspberries improved during the 18th century, it was not until the 19th century that they became more widely cultivated in Europe and North America.

The raspberry bush has thorny woody branches; they produce delicate white flowers that ripen into berries. These aggregate fruits consist of numerous smaller fruits called "drupelets," each of which contains a small seed, and which are clustered on a central receptacle. Separating the berry from the stem creates a hollow cavity at the base.

The raspberry bush has thorny woody branches bearing delicate white flowers that ripen into raspberries.

Raspberries vary in size, with wild raspberries being smaller than the cultivated varieties. Although most often red in color, raspberries can also be black (not to be confused with blackberries), yellow, orange, amber, or white. Fragrant and sweet, they have a slightly tart taste and are more delicate than strawberries. Loganberries and boysenberries are hybrids of the raspberry and the blackberry, and are named after their creators.

Preparing

Raspberries should not be washed, as they tend to absorb the water and become soft. When it is absolutely necessary to wash them, it is best to do so rapidly and gently just before consuming them. Containers of freshly picked raspberries can be shaken gently to dislodge any insects, such as the raspberry aphid, that may be hiding among them.

Serving Ideas

Raspberries can be used in the same manner as strawberries, with which they are interchangeable in most recipes. To make a finely textured coulis, toss the berries in the blender and pass the pulp through a sieve to remove the tiny seeds. Raspberry coulis goes well in a number of desserts, including cakes, puddings, ice creams, sorbets, custards, and Bavarian cream. It also makes an exquisite topping. As with strawberries, a touch of lemon or orange juice will liven the color of raspberry coulis and cooked raspberries. Delicious fresh, raspberries are also an excellent accompaniment to ice cream, yogurt, or fresh cream, and can be used to garnish fruit salads, cereals, cakes, and crêpes. They are fermented to make beverages, liqueurs, and spirits. These fruits are equally popular in tarts, syrups, jams, jellies, compotes, wine, and beer. Raspberries can be preserved in syrup, brandy, or as they are. The juice is used as a flavoring in ice creams and sorbets. Raspberry vinegar is also very popular.

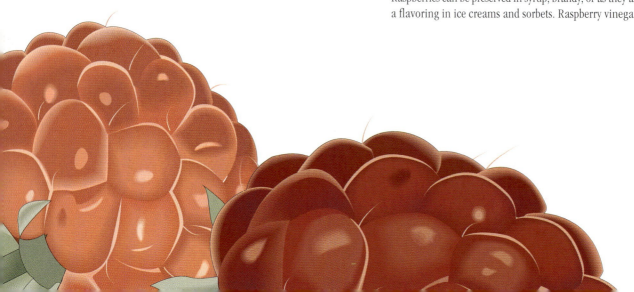

Buying

Raspberries are highly perishable fruits; they do not stand up well to heat, handling, or shipping. Because they spoil rapidly, they can be bought fresh for a reasonable price at farm stands when in season. When buying raspberries, choose plump and lustrous fruits, avoiding those that are soft and dull-colored, or that are too closely packed, as they will be either too ripe or moldy. Picking your own raspberries is the best option; make sure to choose ripe berries, as they do not ripen once they have been picked. Raspberries picked in the morning are sweeter and tend to keep longer.

peduncle

seed

receptacle

drupelet

Nutritional Information

water	87%
protein	0.9 g
fat	0.6 g
carbohydrates	11.5 g
fiber	4.7 g
calories	50
	per 100 g

Raspberries are a good source of vitamin C; they contain potassium and magnesium, as well as traces of calcium and vitamin A, and are high in fiber. Raspberries are said to have diuretic, tonic, depurator, sudorific, aperitive, stomachic, and laxative properties. They can also help relieve heartburn and constipation. A tea made from raspberry leaves is used as a diuretic, a laxative, an emmenagogue, and for its astringent properties. In the spring, the tender young shoots of the raspberry bush can be peeled and eaten raw.

Storing

Raspberries are highly perishable fruits; they should not be exposed to the sun or left at room temperature for long periods of time. For a longer storage life, store them unwashed and pack them loosely after removing any spoiled berries. They will keep for a day or two in the refrigerator. Adding a little sugar will also help preserve them longer. Raspberries freeze well whole or as a coulis, with or without sugar.

To reduce the loss of vitamin C, freeze raspberries whole or with a little lemon juice added to purées and coulis. While the addition of sugar or lemon juice is not indispensable, it may help to preserve the color of the berries. If you do add sugar, reduce the quantity of sugar called for in a recipe using those raspberries.

The berries will keep their shape better if they are used while still partially frozen – to decorate a cake, for example.

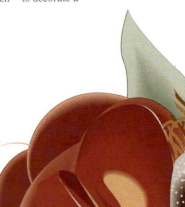

Berry Fruits

193

Cranberry

Vaccinium macrocarpon and *Vaccinium oxycoccos,* **Ericacae**

This berry grows in North America and Europe, and belongs to a large family that includes the blueberry, the bilberry, the arbutus berry, and heather. The Amerindian name *atoca* is often used in Canada. Cranberries are widely cultivated in the United States, especially in Massachussets; in Canada, cultivation of this fruit for commercial purposes is more recent and rather modest. This fruit is relatively unknown in Europe, apart from the smaller wild variety (*Vaccinium oxycoccos*) that grows there.

Cranberries grow on bushes that require sandy, damp, peaty soil to develop. Very sensitive to cold temperatures, these bushes consist of ligneous branches growing vertically from the roots, in a way similar to the raspberry bush. After 3 years, they yield berries resembling small cherries and measuring about ½ to ¾ inch in diameter. In the fall, the berries are harvested by flooding the fields; this causes the mechanically detached berries to float to the surface. Cranberries are juicy and have a tart taste. They contain numerous small edible seeds.

Buying

Choose cranberries that are firm, plump, and lustrous. Avoid those that are discolored and dull-looking, that have whitish spots on the skin, or that appear to be soft, wrinkled, or damaged.

Nutritional Information

water	87%
protein	0.4 g
fat	0.7 g
fiber	1.4 g
calories	46
	per 100 g

Cranberries are a source of vitamin C and potassium. Their characteristic tart flavor is attributable to the presence of several acids, including oxalic and citric acid. Known for their astringent properties, cranberries are said to be good for blood circulation, the complexion, and the digestive system. They are also used in the treatment of urinary-tract infections.

Preparing

Cranberries should be washed just before use. Remove the stalks and sort the berries, discarding those that are soft, wrinkled, or moldy.

Serving Ideas

Because of their high acidity, cranberries are rarely eaten raw. They are either incorporated unmodified into baked goods such as muffins, breads, and cakes, or cooked briefly (just enough to make them split open) for use in pies, crêpes, mousses, and sorbets. They are also made into jam, jelly, chutney, and cranberry sauce, all of which go well with poultry. In both Canada and the United States, the combination of turkey and cranberries is an integral part of the traditional Thanksgiving and Christmas meals.

In addition to blending well with citrus fruits, apples, and pears, cranberries make excellent juice. They are also used to season pâtés, sausages, and terrines, as a dressing on baked potatoes, and as a stuffing for squash.

Cooking

Cook cranberries in a small quantity of water. The pot should be left uncovered; otherwise the steam will cause them to swell and explode like popcorn.

Storing

Cranberries should be kept in the refrigerator, as they will spoil rapidly when left at room temperature. They freeze well as they are, without the addition of sugar, and do not need to be thawed before cooking, although they should be washed first. To dry cranberries, simply place them in a warm oven, leaving the door ajar, until they dry. To rehydrate them, soak them for a few hours in water, juice, or alcohol.

Alkekengi

Physalis alkekengi, **Solanaceae**

otanists do not agree on the origin of this fruit-bearing annual plant; some trace it back to South America, while others believe it came from Europe, China, or Japan. The alkekengi grows easily and can be found on all five continents. Along with the tomato, eggplant, sweet pepper, and potato, it belongs to the large family of Solanaceae. Cultivated as an ornamental garden plant, it is also used in dried flower arrangements.

This fruit is known under different names, including "Cape gooseberry," which refers to the fact that the alkekengi has been widely cultivated on the Cape of Good Hope for more than a century. It has also been called "Chinese lantern" because of the resemblance of its parchment-like membrane to a Chinese lampshade. The Latin name *physalis* comes from the Greek *phusan,* which means "to puff out" and is a reference to the shape of the alkekengi flower.

The alkekengi is a red, orange, or greenish yellow berry the size of a cherry. It is covered with an inedible paper-thin membrane, or calyx, which is the color of sand. There are about 100 varieties of this sweet-tasting berry, which is not very juicy and leaves a slightly acid and astringent aftertaste. The alkekengi produces a large quantity of edible seeds.

The Latin name physalis *refers to the shape of the alkekengi flower and comes from the Greek* phusan, *which means "to puff out."*

Buying

Choose firm, uniformly colored fruits that show no sign of mold. A crisp calyx is an indication that the berry is ripe.

Preparing

Remove the calyx and wash both the fruit and around the stem in order to remove the resinous substance that lodges there.

Serving Ideas

The alkekengi is usually cooked but may also be eaten fresh, whether on its own, in fruit salads, or in mixed salads. It is used to make pies, sorbets, and ice cream. Because of its high pectin content, it is easily made into jams, jellies, or marinades. It may also be pressed to make juice.

Storing

Alkekengis will ripen at room temperature. Wrapped in a cloth, they can be stored in the refrigerator; they should be used within 2 days. The berries may be frozen once the calyx is removed.

Nutritional Information

water	85%
protein	2 g
fat	0.7 g
carbohydrate	11 g
calories	53
	per 100 g

The alkekengi is a source of iron, niacin, and vitamin A. It is said to be a good febrifuge, diuretic, and antirheumatic.

Berry Fruits

195

Plum

Prunus spp., **Rosaceae**

Some varieties of plums are as small as a cherry, while others can be as large as a nectarine.

Stone Fleshy Fruits

196

The plum is the fruit of a tree that is thought to be native to China, although the exact origin is not known because it has been cultivated in many regions of the world since prehistoric times. What is known, however, is that the first varieties of plums were rather sour. The Romans were already familiar with over 300 varieties and consumed dried Damson plums, a variety cultivated since ancient times in the region of Damascus. This variety was introduced into Europe by the Crusaders in the 12th century. Later, in the 17th century, the European, or common, plum was introduced into America by the first European settlers. Today there are more than 2,000 varieties of plums.

The plum tree grows in warm and temperate climates. Although usually between 13 and 20 feet high, there also exist dwarf varieties that are only about half as tall, making it easier to harvest their fruit. The plum tree has oval leaves that are preceded in the spring by its white flowers. The flesh of plums can vary in color from red or orange to yellow or greenish yellow. Some are clingstone varieties, while others are freestone. Depending on the variety, the flesh may be more or less fragrant and juicy, sweet or sour, and crisp or mealy. When exposed to cold temperatures, plum flesh turns brownish and deteriorates in flavor. Plums are generally classified according to six main varieties:

The **European plum** *(Prunus domestica),* also known as the common plum, is of medium size, oval-shaped, and dark blue or red in color. It has a thick skin and firm yellow or greenish yellow flesh. It is sold fresh or canned, although most of the crop is dried to make prunes.

The **Japanese plum** *(Prunus salicina)* varies in color from crimson or purple to greenish or yellow; it comes in various sizes and is usually round, although it can also have a more prominent apex, making it slightly heart-shaped. The sweet and juicy flesh is pale green or golden yellow. This variety is available fresh or canned.

The **American plum** comprises a number of different varieties, including the *Prunus americana.* They are resistant to cold and have amber-colored skin and flesh. American plums are grown particularly on the east and west coasts of the United States.

The **Damson plum** *(Prunus insititia)* is a blue-skinned variety with a rather acid, tart flavor. Ideal for preserves and jellies, this group includes the mirabelle plum.

The **ornamental plum** *(Prunus cerasifera)* is a red fruit which is also used in the making of jams and jellies.

The **wild plum** *(Prunus spinoza, Prunus nigra)* is a small, round, blue-black plum that is also very tart.

The main producers of plums include Russia, China, the United States, Romania, and Yugoslavia. Most of the plums in North America come from California, which produces 89% of the American crop, including over 140 varieties, the most widely cultivated being the Japanese plum. The Santa Rosa is one of the best-known varieties. In France, popular varieties include the greengage (also known as the *reine claude,* named after Queen Claude of France, the wife of François I), the mirabelle, the quetsche (mainly cultivated in Alsace, hence its Germanic name), and the French plum or Agen plum, which comes from the southwest of France and is usually dried to make prunes.

Storing

Plums are fairly perishable. They can be left out at room temperature if underripe, but check on them frequently, as they tend to ripen very quickly. Ripe plums will keep in the refrigerator for a few days. Plums freeze well; remove the stones, however, as they impart a bitter taste to the flesh.

Buying

Look for healthy colored fruits that have a pleasant scent and that yield to a slight pressure of the fingers. Ideally, the skin should still have its powdery "bloom," a sign that the plum has not been handled too much. Avoid plums that are hard and dull-colored, an indication of underripeness, as well as those that are too soft, bruised, or stained.

Preparing

Plums can usually be used with their skin, but if peeling is required, the fruits can first be blanched in boiling water for 30 seconds; rinse them immediately afterward in cold water to halt the cooking process. Do not let them soak, however. Avoid overcooking plums, as it turns the flesh into a purée.

Plum Tart

SERVES 4 TO 6

1 9-in. (23 cm) pie crust, unbaked
1½ lb. (750 g) fresh plums
¾ cup (185 ml) sugar
Apricot jelly
½ cup (125 ml) slivered almonds

1. Preheat the oven to 350°F (175°C).

2. Butter and flour a 9-in. pie plate. Line it with the pie crust. Prick the crust with a fork, and bake in the oven for 5 minutes.

3. Wash the plums, cut them in half, and remove the stones.

4. Sprinkle 3 tablespoons of the sugar over the bottom of the pastry shell. Arrange the plum halves on the pastry, cut side up. Sprinkle with the rest of the sugar. Bake in a 400°F oven for 30 minutes or until the crust is golden and the plums are soft and caramelized.

5. Once the pie is cooled, spread a layer of apricot jelly over the fruit, and garnish with the almonds.

Nutritional Information

water	85%
protein	0.8 g
fat	0.6 g
carbohydrates	13 g
fiber	1.6 g
calories	55
	per 100 g

Plums are a good source of potassium; they also supply vitamin C and riboflavin. These fruits are known for their laxative properties, which are more potent in the case of unripe fruits. Plums are said to be diuretic and energizing, and to cleanse the blood of toxins.

Serving Ideas

Plums are excellent eaten fresh, whether on their own or added to a fruit salad. Cooked plums be can used in a wide variety of ways; they are often stewed or made into jams and jellies. They are used to make sweet-and-sour sauce and are a good accompaniment to pork, game, and poultry in addition to being delicious in pies, cakes, puddings, muffins, and ice cream. They can also replace fresh cherries in most desserts. These fruits are available canned, candied, dried (in which case they are known as prunes), or preserved in vinegar (particularly the quetsche). They also go into the making of juice, brandy (prunelle, mirabelle), and wine.

Stone Fleshy Fruits

197

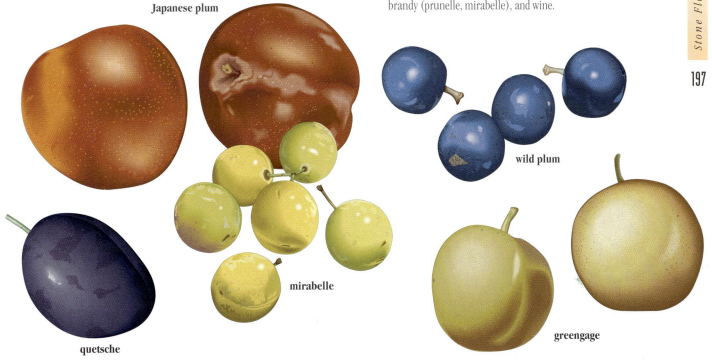

Japanese plum

wild plum

mirabelle

greengage

quetsche

Prune

Prunus domestica, Rosaceae

Name given to a dried plum and to the varieties of plums that dry well without requiring removal of their stone. Only a few varieties of plums are suitable for drying, including the Agen prune, grown in southwestern France. Those that have a firm flesh and a high sugar content are generally the best plums for drying.

For a long time, plums were dried in the sun. Today they are usually dried industrially in ovens where the temperature, humidity, and air circulation are strictly controlled. Effective oven-drying takes 3 or 4 days, after which the fruits retain only 18% to 19% of their original moisture content. High-performance desiccators give the same results in 12 to 24 hours. Approximately 5 pounds of fresh plums are required to yield 2 pounds of prunes. Prunes are also processed to make juice.

Nutritional Information

water	32%
protein	2.6 g
fat	0.5 g
carbohydrates	63 g
fiber	7 g
calories	239
	per 100 g

Prunes are an excellent source of potassium and a good source of vitamin A, vitamin B_6, magnesium, iron, and copper; they also supply niacin, pantothenic acid, vitamin C, phosphorus, zinc, and calcium. These fruits have a laxative effect, particularly when they are soaked or eaten before bedtime. Prune juice has similar laxative properties.

Buying

Prunes are sold with or without their stone. They vary in size as well as in quality. Choose prunes that are black and shiny, plump, and fairly soft without being sticky or moldy. Overly dry-looking prunes are either too old or have not been treated with food preservatives.

Serving Ideas

Prunes can be eaten out of hand or stewed. They are cut up or left whole and incorporated into sauces, cakes, muffins, biscuits, and puddings. Prunes are a classic and delicious accompaniment to rabbit and also work well with pork, poultry, and game. In the culinary traditions of Iran and the Near East, lamb is often served with prunes. When soaked beforehand in water, juice, or alcohol, prunes do not take long to cook. Overly dry prunes can be soaked in boiling water, drained, and patted dry before being used.

When making stewed prunes, add the sugar only at the end of cooking; otherwise it will prevent the prunes from absorbing enough water. The almond-like kernel lodged inside the stone of the prune contains hydrocyanic acid, a toxic substance; it is therefore recommended to consume the kernels in small quantities only.

Storing

Prunes should be stored in an airtight container in a place that is neither too dry nor too damp. They keep longer in the refrigerator.

Nectarine

Prunus persica var. *nectarina*, **Rosaceae**

A fruit native to China, the nectarine belongs to the same family as the peach, of which it is a smooth-skinned variety. A distinction is made between the freestone nectarine *(scleronucipersica)*, which is more common in North America, and the clingstone nectarine *(aganonucipersica)*. Although it is often believed that the nectarine is a cross between the peach and the plum, it is actually the result of relatively recent mutations of the downy-skinned peach. Recent discoveries provide evidence that it was consumed in China over 2,000 years ago.

There are numerous varieties of the nectarine, 85 of which have been created in the United States alone since the early 1950s. Their harvesting season extends from spring to fall. They are distinguished from the peach by their smooth, more colorful skin, and by the fact that their flesh is somewhat tastier. The flesh of the nectarine is firm and juicy and may be white or yellow in color, with tinges of red close to the stone and a sweet but slightly tart taste.

The nectarine is distinguished from the peach by its smooth, more colorful skin, and by the fact that its flesh is somewhat tastier.

Buying

Since nectarines are extremely perishable, they are often harvested when mature but still firm. Look for fragrant fruits that are not too hard, and that are free of spots, cracks, and bruises. Avoid greenish-colored nectarines, an indication that they were picked prematurely and may not ripen properly, particularly since the sugar content of unripe nectarines does not increase once they have been picked.

Preparing

Because the flesh of the nectarine tends to oxidize quickly, it should be consumed immediately or sprinkled with lime or lemon juice, wine, vinegar, or vinaigrette, depending on the intended use. While it is not necessary to peel the skin, this can be done easily by first immersing the nectarine in boiling water for a minute and cooling it immediately under cold water (without letting it soak).

Storing

These fruits spoil easily and should therefore be handled with care. Wash nectarines just before using them, and store them loosely packed to prevent the spread of mold. They may be left to ripen at room temperature; place them in a paper bag to hasten the ripening process. Once ripe, they will keep for a few days at room temperature, and slightly longer if refrigerated, but they will be more flavorful if taken out of the refrigerator shortly before being served.

Nectarines lend themselves well to canning and freezing. Blanch and peel the fruit first, and be sure to remove the pit, as it imparts a bitter taste. Overripe fruits can be made into a compote or purée and frozen; add a bit of lemon juice to prevent discoloration.

Serving Ideas

Delicious eaten out of hand, nectarines may also be cooked, dried, canned, candied, or frozen. They are prepared like peaches, which they can replace in most recipes, and often turn up in fruit salads, crêpes, cakes and pies, yogurt, ice cream, and sorbets. Nectarines are also made into jams and jellies, marinated, pressed to make juice, and used in the making of liqueurs and brandies.

Nutritional Information

water	86%
protein	0.9 g
fat	0.4 g
carbohydrates	12 g
fiber	1.6 g
calories	49
	per 100 g

The nectarine is a good source of potassium and contains vitamins A and C.

Peach

Prunus persica, **Rosaceae**

Fruit of the peach tree, which is native to China. Westerners are said to have discovered the peach in Persia during the conquest of Alexander the Great. Believing it to be native to that region, where it grew in abundance, they named it *persica*. The Chinese have cultivated the peach since earliest antiquity. Their fascination for the sweetness and exquisite flavor of this fruit led them to create many legends and superstitions about it, one of which attributes it with the power to confer immortality. The peach is a close relative of the apricot, almond, cherry, and plum.

Peach trees can grow to a height of 16 to 26 feet; they have deciduous leaves and bear magnificent pink flowers which emerge even before the leaves have opened in spring. Although they prefer warm climates, certain hybrids can tolerate cooler conditions. The largest producers of peaches are Italy, the United States, China, and Greece.

The edible skin of the peach is fairly thin, downy, and yellowish in color. The skin of certain varieties has a crimson hue even before the peach is ripe, but this is more a genetic characteristic than an indication of the fruit's quality. The flesh of the peach is yellow or greenish white. The latter variety is more perishable but also sweeter and juicier, and while it accounts for 30% of the market in France, it is rarely sold commercially in North America. The flesh of the peach is juicy, sweet, fragrant, and fairly firm. It encloses an oval woody stone that is usually about an inch long. Peaches are often classified according to whether the stone adheres to the flesh (clingstone) or falls out easily when the fruit is cut in half (freestone and semi-freestone). The kernel inside the pit is edible but should be eaten only in small quantities, as it contains a toxic substance called hydrocyanic acid. Certain varieties of peaches are available early in the season, while others mature later.

Buying

Peaches spoil very easily, even when unripe. It is therefore best to buy only the quantity needed and to consume them as soon as possible. Choose fragrant peaches that are unblemished and not too hard. Avoid peaches with green coloring, as they were probably picked too early and will not ripen properly. They will also be less sweet than peaches harvested when ripe, since the sugar content no longer increases after picking.

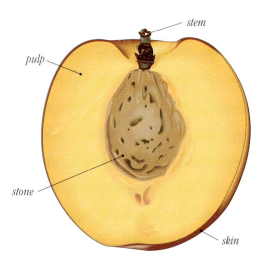

stem

pulp

stone

skin

Peach Melba

SERVES 4

4 fresh peaches	1 tbsp. Kirsch or raspberry
2 cups (500 ml) water	brandy (optional)
⅔ cup (170 g) sugar	1 tbsp. sugar
1 cup (250 ml)	2 cups (500 ml) vanilla
raspberries	ice cream
Juice of ½ lime	2 tbsp. slivered almonds

This recipe can also be made using peaches canned in syrup.

1. Blanch the peaches for 1 minute in boiling water, and peel them. Cut them in half and remove the stones.

2. Combine the water and ⅔ cup sugar in a saucepan. Bring to a boil and cook for 1 minute; then add the peaches and poach them for 8 minutes. Cool them in the syrup and then drain them. Place them in the refrigerator.

3. To make the raspberry coulis, purée the raspberries in a food processor and then pass them through a fine sieve. Add the lime juice, the optional Kirsch, and the tablespoon of sugar.

4. Divide the ice cream among four dessert bowls. Add the peach halves, and drizzle with the raspberry coulis. Sprinkle with the slivered almonds.

Preparing

Peaches will peel more easily if blanched for a minute (a strainer can be used to do this); cool them immediately in cold water to stop the effect of the heat, but do not let them soak.

The flesh of the peach tends to oxidize and turn brown on contact with air. To prevent this, eat or cook the peach immediately, or sprinkle it with lemon, orange, or lime juice, or alcohol.

Serving Ideas

Peaches are excellent fresh but can also be cooked, dried, canned, candied, or frozen. They are often added to tarts, crêpes, fruit salads, yogurts, ice creams, sorbets, and soufflés. Peach Melba is a dessert that was created in 1892 by the famous French chef Escoffier, in honor of the Australian opera singer Nellie Melba. The classic recipe for Peach Melba consists of a half peach poached in syrup, served with a scoop of vanilla ice cream and topped with raspberry purée. Peaches can also be used to make jelly, jam, marinade, juice, compote, liqueurs, and brandy. They constitute a good accompaniment to savory dishes such as seafood, poultry, and pork, and are delicious drizzled with vinaigrette. Puréed peaches can be dried.

Storing

Handle peaches with care, as they spoil rapidly once they are bruised. Do not pack peaches too closely, to prevent them from spoiling and causing the other peaches to rot. Unripe peaches can be left to ripen at room temperature. This process can be hastened by placing them in a paper bag, although they should be checked occasionally for rotting. Peaches will keep for only 3 or 4 days at room temperature and slightly longer in the refrigerator. They are tastier if taken out of the refrigerator shortly before consuming them. Wash the fruit just before eating it. Peaches lend themselves well to canning and freezing. Remove the stone first, however, as it imparts a bitter taste.

When the fruits are very ripe, freeze them as a compote or purée. Adding a bit of lemon juice will prevent discoloration.

Nutritional Information

	fresh	*dried*
water	88%	31%
protein	0.7 g	3.6 g
fat	0.1 g	0.8 g
carbohydrates	11 g	61 g
fiber	1.6 g	8.2 g
calories	43	240
		per 100 g

The peach is a good source of potassium and contains vitamin C, vitamin A, and niacin. Since peach producers often coat the fruit with a thin layer of wax to prolong its shelf life, it is important to wash it well before eating it. Peaches are easily digested when ripe. They are said to be diuretic, stomachic, and mildly laxative.

Drying tends to concentrate the nutritional elements of peaches; dried peaches are rich in potassium and iron and are a good source of vitamin A, niacin, copper, magnesium, and riboflavin, as well as containing phosphorus, vitamin C, and zinc. Dried peaches often contain an additive (sulfur dioxide, potassium sorbate, sorbic acid, or sodium bisulfite) that acts to enhance their color and prolong their storage life.

The skin of the peach is fairly thin, downy, and yellowish in color. In certain varieties, the skin has a crimson hue even before the peach is ripe.

Cherry

Prunus spp., Rosaceae

Fruit of the cherry tree, believed to have originated in northeastern Asia. It is difficult to establish the exact country of origin of this fruit, however, since cherries have been cultivated in many regions of the world ever since prehistoric times. Birds are very fond of cherries and through their migrations most likely contributed to the spread of cherry trees all over the world.

This tree belongs to the large family that includes the apricot, apple, plum, and peach. The cherry tree can grow to a height of 65 feet but is usually pruned to more modest proportions in order to facilitate harvesting. Cherry trees blossom in early spring, producing magnificent white flowers.

Cherries are round, smooth-skinned drupes with a pulpy and juicy flesh. They hang from long, thin stems attached in clusters to the bark of the branch. There are three main categories of cherries: sweet cherries, sour cherries, and wild cherries.

Sweet cherries *(P. avium)* are sweet and fleshy. They are usually light or dark red, and sometimes yellow. Round, oblong, or heart-shaped, sweet cherries have a thin skin and come in some 500 different varieties. The **Bing,** which is very juicy, is the most common variety in North America. In France, the most popular varieties of sweet cherry are the heart-shaped **bigaroon,** a crisp, firm-fleshed fruit that is red or yellow with a scarlet hue, and the **gean,** a red or black soft-fleshed fruit that is very sweet and tasty. Certain varieties of gean cherries are used in the making of kirsch.

Sour cherries *(P. cerasus)* are usually dark red and grow easily under harsh climatic conditions. There are over 250 varieties of this cherry, including the **Montmorency,** which is medium-size, deep red, soft, and quite tart, and the **Morello,** a smaller variety. These varieties are more often cooked than eaten raw. Their delicate aroma adds a pleasant note to preserves, jams, pies, clafoutis, and various liqueurs.

Wild cherries *(Prunus avium)* are small, almost black in color, and not as fleshy as the other varieties. Their high astringency makes the mouth pucker. They are produced by the Pennsylvanian and the Virginian cherry trees.

Buying

Cherries must be picked ripe, as they do not ripen after harvesting. Choose brightly colored glossy fruits that are plump and firm; the stems should not be dried out. Avoid unripe cherries, which are usually small, pale in color, and hard, as well as overripe cherries, which are soft, with brownish spots or bruised or wrinkled skin.

Serving Ideas

Cherries are delicious eaten raw, but they may also be cooked, candied, dried, preserved in syrup, macerated in alcohol, or distilled. Fresh cherries are often used in fruit salads, custards, sorbets, ice cream and yogurt, pies, and clafoutis, while candied cherries are an essential ingredient in fruitcake and Black Forest cake. This fruit also makes a delicious compote and jam. Cherries are often converted into wine or spirits; they are notably used to make Alsatian kirsch, Italian maraschino, and Provençal ratafia. Cherries can also be used to accompany game and poultry.

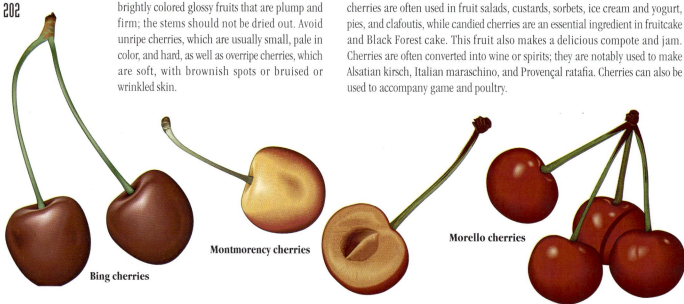

Montmorency cherries

Morello cherries

Bing cherries

Clafoutis

SERVES 4

1 lb. (500 g) black cherries	*3 eggs*
¼ cup (60 ml) sugar	*1 cup (250 ml) cold milk*
⅓ cup (80 ml) flour	*½ tsp. vanilla extract*
1 pinch salt	*Sugar*

1. Preheat the oven to 375°F (190°C).

2. Wash and drain the fruits, and remove their stems and stones. Place the cherries in a buttered baking dish and sprinkle with half of the sugar.

3. In a bowl, combine the flour, salt, and remaining sugar. Beat in the eggs, one at a time, followed by the cold milk and the vanilla extract, and continue mixing until the batter is smooth.

4. Pour the batter evenly over the cherries. Bake in the oven for 45 minutes or until the top is puffed and golden. Sprinkle the clafoutis with a little sugar. Serve lukewarm or cold.

Storing

Cherries can be left at room temperature but they tend to spoil rapidly; they should be placed in the refrigerator, where they will keep for a few days or longer if they are still firm. They should be stored away from strong-smelling foods, as they tend to absorb odors and deteriorate in flavor. Store cherries in a perforated plastic bag to prevent them from drying out. Cherries can be frozen whole or pitted, and may be coated with sugar or syrup before freezing; frozen cherries are best used for cooking. Dried cherries will keep for about a year when stored in an airtight container in a cool, dry place.

Nutritional Information

	sweet cherry	sour cherry
water	81%	86%
protein	1.2 g	1 g
fat	1 g	0.3 g
carbohydrates	17 g	12 g
fiber	1.6 g	1.2 g
calories	72	50
		per 100 g

Sweet cherries are a good source of potassium, while sour cherries have a high potassium content in addition to providing fiber and vitamin A. Wild cherries are said to be a good diuretic, anti-rheumatic, antiarthritic, remineralizer, and a mild laxative. They are also known for their blood-cleansing properties. An infusion can be made from cherry stems and is sometimes used as a diuretic.

Preparing

Cherries should be washed, but avoid soaking them. They can be pitted by cutting them in half or making an incision with the tip of a knife and removing the stone. A cherry pitter may also be used.

Cherries are round, smooth-skinned drupes with pulpy, juicy flesh. They hang from long, thin stems.

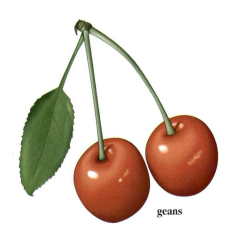

Using a pitter, make a hole in the flesh to remove the stone.

wild cherries

bigaroons

geans

Date

Phoenix dactylifera, **Palmaceae**

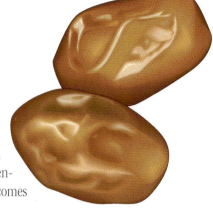

Dates are the fruit of the date palm, which, like all palm trees, grows in warm and humid climates. A native of the Middle East, the date palm has held great significance for Mediterranean peoples since ancient times. Known as the "tree of life," it is mentioned in the Bible. The word "date" refers to the shape of the fruit and comes from the Greek *daktulos,* meaning "finger."

In addition to its fruits, the buds and sap of the date palm can also be consumed. The date's fibers are used in the making of fabrics, while the stones are used for fuel or as oil meal to feed sheep and camels. Egypt, Iran, and Saudi Arabia are among the major producers of this fruit. The date palm can reach 100 feet in height and yields over 1,000 dates each year. The fruits grow in hanging bunches of more than 200 dates, with each bunch weighing close to 40 pounds. The dates themselves are between 1 and 2½ inches long and about ¾ inch in diameter. The flesh of unripe dates is green, becoming a golden or brownish color as the fruit matures. The small stone at the date's center is in fact a corneous albumin. Dates vary in texture, flavor, and sugar content. The three main types of dates are soft, semi-dry, and dry dates. While there are close to 100 different varieties of this fruit, only a few of them have been widely commercialized. The most common varieties in the United States include the Deglet Noor, the Medjool, the Zahidi, the Halawy, and the Bardhi. The Arab name *Deglet Noor* means "date of the light;" this variety is one of the most highly prized in the world and represents about 85% of date production in the United States.

Buying

Choose dates that are plump, soft, and well colored. Avoid dull-looking fruits, or those that appear to be dried out, moldy, or fermented. Dates are sold with or without their stone.

Preparing

Dates can be rehydrated by soaking them in water for a few hours.

Serving Ideas

Dates are good eaten out of hand, but they also enter into the preparation of many dishes. In North America they are usually associated with sweet foods such as cakes, cookies, date squares, muffins, and cereals. Elsewhere their use is more diversified; for example, in Arab countries they are stuffed, candied, incorporated into salads and couscous, and used to make spirits. In India dates are often used in chutneys and added to curries. Because dates are very sweet, the amount of sugar called for in recipes that use them can be significantly reduced or omitted altogether. Dates themselves can be converted into sugar, to be used like any other sugar.

To make sugar from dates, arrange some sliced pitted dates on an ungreased baking sheet. Bake in a 460°F (240°C) oven for 12 to 15 hours, opening the door occasionally to check on the dates and to allow the moisture to escape. The dates are ready once they are as hard as stone. Set them aside to cool. Grind the dates in a blender or food processor at low or moderate speed.

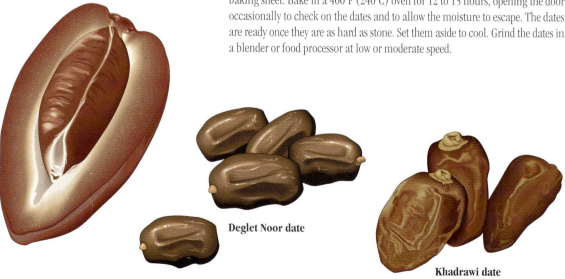

Deglet Noor date

Khadrawi date

Nutritional Information

water	24%
protein	1.9 g
fat	0.5 g
carbohydrates	72 g
fiber	2.3 g
calories	271
	per 100 g

The high sugar content of dates makes them a very nourishing fruit. Dried dates are very high in potassium; they are also a source of iron, magnesium, copper, pantothenic acid, vitamin B_6, and niacin. Dates are said to be tonic and remineralizing. They are often treated with sulfites and sometimes coated with syrup (corn syrup or other) to keep them soft, a practice that increases their already high sugar content.

The date palm can reach 100 feet in height and yields over 1,000 dates each year.

Dates Stuffed with Almond Paste

24 DATES

24 dates
⅓ cup (80 ml) ground almonds
⅓ cup (80 ml) sugar
1 egg white, lightly beaten
1 tsp. almond extract

1. Split open the dates lengthwise and remove the stones.

2. To make the almond paste, combine the ground almonds and the sugar in a small bowl, mixing them well. Stir in the egg white and the almond extract. Make sure all the ingredients are well blended.

3. Divide the paste into 24 mounds similar in shape to date stones but twice their size. Stuff the dates generously with the almond paste. Place each date in a small paper baking cup.

Storing

To prevent dates from drying out further, store them in an airtight container in a dark, cool, dry place; they will keep for 6 to 12 months, depending on the variety. Fresh dates can be stored in the refrigerator, where they will keep for at least 2 weeks. Dates should be well wrapped to prevent them from absorbing the odor of other foods. It may not be a good idea to freeze dates, as they are often frozen during shipping.

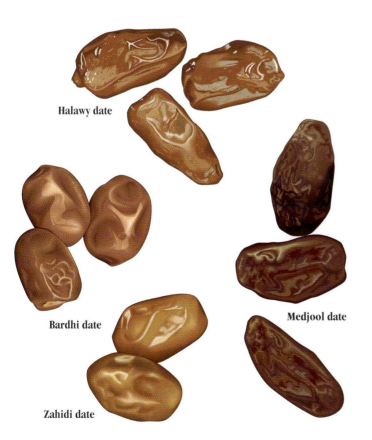

Halawy date

Bardhi date

Zahidi date

Medjool date

Apricot

Prunus armeniaca, Rosaceae

This delicate fruit is often harvested unripe to help it withstand the delays and rigors of shipping.

Fruit of the apricot tree, a native of China. Westerners initially believed that the apricot tree originated in Armenia, which is why they gave it the name *Prunus armeniaca.* For a long time they believed that the fruit of this tree was cursed and caused the onset of fever. Alexander the Great is said to have introduced the apricot into the Western world; the Arabs brought it to the Mediterranean. The apricot derives its name from the Spanish Arabic word *al barquq,* meaning "precocious," and was so named because the tree blossoms very early in the spring.

The apricot tree has deciduous leaves and can stand over 30 feet high. It produces magnificent fragrant flowers that have the unusual characteristic of developing directly from the trunk and branches. There are more than 40 varieties of the apricot tree, most of which are grown in warm climates, although certain hybrids have been adapted to temperate regions. Turkey, Italy, and the CIS (Commonwealth of Independent States), formerly parts of the Soviet Union, are the world's largest producers of apricots.

The apricot has an edible downy skin that becomes smooth when the fruit is fully ripe. The tender orange flesh is sweet and aromatic. Unfortunately, this delicate fruit is often harvested unripe to help it withstand the delays and rigors of shipping, a practice that can make the flesh mealy and rather bland.

Nutritional Information

	fresh	*dried*
water	86%	31%
protein	1.4 g	3.7 g
fat	0.4 g	0.5 g
carbohydrates	11 g	62 g
fiber	7.7 g	2.9 g
calories	48	237
		per 100 g

The apricot is known for its very high vitamin A content; it is also rich in potassium and is a source of vitamin C. Apricots are said to be astringent, to stimulate the appetite, and to help fight anemia. Dried apricots have a higher concentration of nutrients, making them rich in vitamin A, potassium, iron, and riboflavin. They are also a good source of copper and magnesium. Most dried apricots are treated with sulfites to prevent discoloration and the growth of bacteria, thus preserving their freshness and color. When dried, apricots are mildly laxative and should be consumed in moderation.

Buying

Choose undamaged apricots that are neither too firm nor too soft. Avoid fruits with whitish spots, cracks, or blemishes.

Preparing

The flesh of the apricot tends to darken rapidly when exposed to air. To prevent discoloration, sprinkle cut apricots with citrus juice or alcohol if they are not eaten or cooked immediately.

Serving Ideas

Fresh apricots are delicious eaten raw, either on their own or added to a fruit salad. They can be cooked in the same manner as peaches and nectarines, with which they are interchangeable in most recipes. They are good in pies, cakes, sorbets, ice cream, yogurt, and crêpes, and make savory jams and chutneys. They can also be stewed or pressed to make juice. Apricots are often enjoyed macerated in alcohol, candied, canned, or dried.

Dried apricots can be eaten as they are, or soaked in water, juice, or alcohol. *Kamraddin* is a paste made from apricots that is popular in Arab countries. The almond-like kernel lodged inside the apricot pit is edible but should be consumed only in small quantities, as it contains a toxic substance called hydrocyanic acid.

Storing

Handle apricots with care, since they tend to spoil rapidly when bruised. Wash them just before use and pack them loosely to avoid the spread of mold. Apricots ripen at room temperature, and ripe apricots will keep for up to 1 week in the refrigerator.

Apricots freeze well; blanching them for 30 seconds will make it easier to peel the skin. Remove the pit, as it imparts a bitter taste to the fruit. Very ripe apricots may be frozen in stewed or puréed form. Lemon juice or citric acid can be added to prevent discoloration.

McIntosh

The fruit of the apple tree, one of the oldest and most widely cultivated fruit trees, believed to be native to southwestern Asia. Archeological remains provide evidence that apples have been cultivated since ancient times and could already be found growing wild in prehistoric Europe. A highly symbolic fruit, the apple is known as the forbidden fruit and the fruit of knowledge. In the 6th century B.C., the Romans knew of 37 different varieties of apples. In the meantime, there has been an incalculable number of mutations and crossbreedings. The Romans contributed to the spread of the apple to England and across Europe. Around 1620, the early settlers brought the apple with them to North America. Today over 7,500 varieties of apple are known to exist.

The word "apple" comes from the Latin *pomum,* meaning "fruit." The apple tree grows best in temperate zones; it cannot be cultivated in tropical climates because it requires a period of cold and dormancy in order to thrive. Some varieties are able to withstand temperatures as low as -40°F. The largest producers of apples are Russia, China, the United States, Germany, and France.

The height of the apple tree can vary widely, particularly since the creation of dwarf hybrids. It is generally as tall as it is wide and produces pretty clusters of highly fragrant and decorative pink or white flowers. An apple tree in blossom is quite a beautiful sight. There are a great many varieties of apples, differing in shape, color, flavor, texture, nutritional value, harvesting period, use, and keeping qualities. The flesh of the different varieties comes in varying degrees of firmness, crispness, acidity, juiciness, and sweetness.

Varieties of apples that ripen in late summer do not keep long and are best eaten quickly, as opposed to fall apples, which have good storing qualities. When deciding which apples to use for a particular purpose, it is important to consider a number of factors, including firmness, cellulose, sugar and pectin content, the degree of acidity, and the rate of discoloration of the flesh when cut. Some varieties do not stand up well to cooking, while others become bitter when baked in the oven. Generally, the qualities to look for include:

for eating out of hand	a firm, juicy, tasty, crisp apple
for pies	a drier, slightly acid apple;
for oven baking	a sweet apple that does not disintegrate easily
for jellies	a barely ripe apple that is acid, juicy, and high in pectin
for applesauce	an apple that does not discolor easily

Because market demand dictates which varieties of apples are offered, several varieties are slowly disappearing, not considered profitable enough to grow on a large scale. In Canada, McIntosh has long been the most widely grown, but it is now losing ground to competing varieties like the Granny Smith, Delicious, and Cortland. In the United States, the market is dominated by eight major varieties: Red and Golden Delicious, McIntosh, Rome Beauty, Jonathan, Winesap, York, and Stayman. In Europe, the Golden Delicious is very popular.

The Romans recognized 37 varieties of apples, which is quite considerable for the time period. Today over 7,500 varieties are known to exist.

Pome Fleshy Fruits

207

Variety	Origin and Description	Use
CORTLAND	Developed from the McIntosh, large, round with flat ends, bright red skin with streaks, very white and aromatic flesh, does not discolor; superior in quality to the Spartan, it remains firm when baked whole	All-purpose, good for eating out of hand, perfect for pies, oven-baking, and applesauce
MELBA	Medium-size, round and irregular shape, red skin with yellow streaks, juicy, tender flesh, turns mealy quickly	Good for eating out of hand, makes excellent applesauce
GOLDEN DELICIOUS	Created in the United States at the end of the 19th century, slightly elongated, narrowing at the base and ending in 5 distinguishing bumps, yellow skin, semi-firm flesh, juicy, sweet, fine, only slightly acid	Good for eating out of hand, pies, applesauce
RED DELICIOUS	Same characteristics as the golden variety except the flesh is crisper and the skin is bright red with streaks	Eating out of hand
EMPIRE	Originally from the United States, a cross between the McIntosh and Red Delicious, almost the same flavor as the McIntosh, but more resistant to bruising, keeps longer, medium-size and round, its skin is streaked with dark red and has spots	All-purpose
GALA	Created in New Zealand, a cross between the Cox's Orange Pippin and the Red and Golden Delicious, thin pale yellow skin with pink streaks, juicy, crisp, sweet, and very aromatic	Excellent for eating out of hand, cooks well
GOLDEN RUSSETT	Medium or small, round, reddish-brown skin the thickness of a potato peel, corky yellow flesh, very tasty, poor keeping qualities	Good for eating out of hand
GRANNY SMITH	Originally from Australia, introduced into North America about 30 years ago; cultivated for the first time in 1868 by a grandmother named Smith, medium-size, green skin, juicy and acid	Good for eating out of hand and pies
IDARED	Large, dark red with greenish-yellow spots, firm, juicy, and aromatic flesh that remains firm when cooked	All-purpose, excellent baked or for applesauce
MCINTOSH	Created in Ontario, Canada, around 1870, medium size, round, firm, juicy, crisp flesh, dark red skin with green streaks	Excellent for eating out of hand, good for baking and applesauce
ROME BEAUTY	Large, round, red stripes with little spots, shiny, firm, juicy, acid, and aromatic	All-purpose, oven baking
SPARTAN	Cross between a McIntosh and Yellow Newton, crisper, more colorful and sweeter than the McIntosh, medium to large, round, dark red skin with small white spots	All-purpose

Buying

The diversification of sources as well as technological advances have made it possible to offer fresh apples all year round. The three main methods of storing apples are in refrigerated storage, in nonrefrigerated storage, and in controlled-atmosphere (CA) storage, all of which aim to slow down the apples' rate of "breathing" and to prevent them from shriveling and rotting. Nonrefrigerated storage makes use of air currents, replacing the warm air inside the warehouse with the colder air from outside; it is effective provided that the air outside the warehouse is sufficiently cool. In refrigerated warehouses, the apples are stored at temperatures slightly above freezing with a humidity of 85% to 90%. They continue to ripen slowly, consuming oxygen and producing carbon dioxide, and remain pleasant for eating out of hand for 3 or 4 months, after which they lose their lustre and become mealy. Some varieties can be successfully stored in this manner for up to 6 months.

In controlled-atmosphere storage, the apples "hibernate" in a hermetically sealed room where the amount of oxygen is reduced to slow down the breathing rate, thus delaying the ripening process and allowing storage for up to 1 year. This type of controlled atmosphere can be effectively reproduced on a smaller scale using a hermetically sealed apple bag, a technique that is often combined with refrigeration. Apples stored in this way are usually marketed later in the year than those that have been refrigerated.

Apples are almost always harvested before they ripen in order to help them withstand shipping and marketing delays. When harvested at maturity, their flesh tends to become starchy quickly and the area around the core turns brown. Immature or overripe apples tend to be dull-colored, although it is difficult to judge this quality accurately, since most apples are shiny only because they have either been covered with wax (beeswax, paraffin wax, and shellac all give fruit a shiny lustre) or polished. To test the degree of ripeness, give the apple a flick close to the stalk; a dull sound indicates ripeness, while a hollow sound is a sign of overripeness. Choose apples that are firm, brightly colored, and free of bruises (these cause the apple as well as surrounding fruit to rot). If the flesh yields under pressure of the fingers, the apple will be mealy. Unless the date of harvesting is indicated, apples are best bought from a refrigerated display, since they tend to ripen very quickly at room temperature. Apples are graded according to their shape, size, and qualities. Those without any defects are the most expensive, but the extra expense is unnecessary if you are planning to use the apples for cooking, in which case less perfect apples are fine. Before eating or cooking apples, it is best to scrub them under cold water.

Preparing

The flesh of apples oxidizes and darkens when exposed to air. To prevent oxidation, eat or cook the apples immediately, or sprinkle them with citrus juice (lemon, lime, orange), vinegar, or vinaigrette, depending on the intended use.

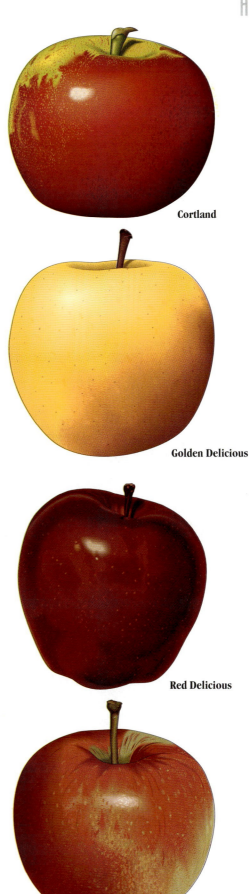

Cortland

Golden Delicious

Red Delicious

Melba

Serving Ideas

There is practically no limit to the uses of the apple. It is eaten raw, cooked, dried, or candied, and can be made into applesauce, jelly, jam, marmalade, syrup, butter, chutney, or vinegar. Apples are used in a wide variety of desserts, including cakes, muffins, crêpes, flans, strudels, clafoutis, charlottes, pies, and puddings, and are delicious flavored with cinnamon and vanilla.

Apples also accompany savory foods such as cheese, meat, poultry, wild game, blood pudding, and salads (as in the famous Waldorf Salad). Apples are also used in distilling to make Calvados and in the manufacture of cider and apple juice.

Cooking

For cooked apples with a firmer texture, use less watery varieties, like the Rome Beauty or the Cortland; cook them gently in just enough liquid to prevent the apples from sticking to the pot. When baking apples in the oven, make a cavity in the center to hold the filling (raisins, coconut, nuts, honey, tahini, etc.).

To make a quick applesauce, cut a few apples into cubes and cook them, covered with plastic wrap, for 2 minutes in the microwave. Depending on the variety of apple used, some applesauces are just as good with no or very little sugar added. For a more exciting sauce, try cooking new varieties of apples or combining different varieties, or add strawberries, cranberries, or rhubarb.

Storing

Apples can be stored in a perforated plastic bag or in the fruit drawer of the refrigerator, where they will keep for a few weeks. For longer-term storage, place them in a dark, cool (32° to 40°F), and very humid (85% to 90%) place. To maintain the necessary degree of humidity to prevent the apples from drying out, cover them with thin plastic film. Discard or isolate overripe or damaged apples. Insufficiently ripe apples can be left out at room temperature, but check them regularly, as they ripen 10 times more quickly than when refrigerated. Apples freeze very well when puréed, with or without added sugar. Uncooked apples do not stand up as well to freezing. Peel, core, and slice the apples and sprinkle them with lemon juice or ascorbic acid prior to freezing to prevent discoloration.

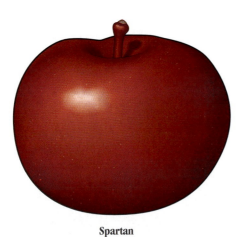

Spartan

Granny Smith

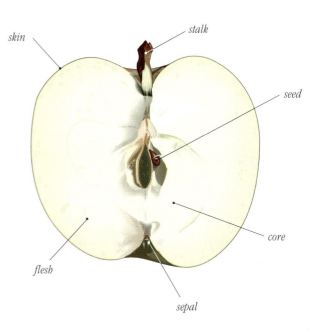

skin · *stalk* · *seed* · *core* · *sepal* · *flesh*

Apple Tart

SERVES 4 TO 6

*1 unbaked 9-in. short-
crust pie crust
1½ lb. (750 g) Cortland
or Idared apples
¼ cup (60 ml) sugar*

*3 pinches of ground
cinnamon
Apricot jelly, melted
(optional)*

1. Preheat the oven to 350°F.

2. Grease and flour a 9-in. tart pan, and line it with the pastry.

3. Peel and core the apples. Quarter them and cut the quarters lengthwise into thin sections. Arrange the slices on the pastry in tightly overlapping circles. Sprinkle with the sugar and cinnamon. Bake in the oven for about 30 minutes, until golden brown.

4. Remove from the oven and brush melted apricot jelly over the apples.

Nutritional Information

water	84%
protein	0.2 g
fat	0.4 g
carbohydrates	15 g
fiber	2.2 g
calories	59
	per 100 g

A medium-size apple weighs about 5 ounces. Apples are a source of potassium and vitamin C. They contain pectin, which helps to control cholesterol, blood sugar, and cellulose levels, as well as improving intestinal functioning. Because most of the apple's nutrients are concentrated just under the skin, it is best to eat it unpeeled. While they are not a miracle cure, apples do have a number of medicinal properties – hence the popular saying "An apple a day keeps the doctor away." They are said to be diuretic, laxative, antidiarrheal, a muscle tonic, antirheumatic, stomachic, and beneficial for the digestive system and the liver. Eating raw apples cleans the teeth and massages the gums.

1 *Using an apple corer, pierce the center of the fruit down to the work surface. Rotate and remove the corer.*

2 *Or cut the apple in half and remove the core with a vegetable peeler.*

3 *Depending on the recipe, the cored apple can then be cut into slices.*

Russet

Empire

Pome Fleshy Fruits

211

Pear

Pyrus communis, **Rosaceae**

There are hundreds of varieties of pears; most of those known today are the result of crosses carried out in the 17th and 18th centuries in order to improve the fruit's characteristics.

Fruit of the pear tree, a native of the northern regions of central Asia, where it could be found growing wild as far back as prehistoric times. Held in high esteem by the ancient Egyptians, Greeks, Romans, and Chinese, the pear has been under cultivation for 3,000 years and the different varieties number in the hundreds. Most of the varieties known today are the product of crosses performed in the 17th and 18th centuries in order to improve the fruit's characteristics.

A member of the large rose family, the pear is related to the apple, the almond, and the apricot. Like the apple tree, it grows well in most temperate zones, although it is slightly more sensitive to temperature variations. The largest pear-producing countries today are China, Italy, the United States, and Russia. While some varieties are almost completely round, most pears are oblong with a swollen end that gives them a teardrop shape. Their edible skin may be yellow, brown, red, or green and is usually quite soft and thin. The white or cream-colored flesh is finely textured, although in some varieties it may be slightly gritty near the center. The core is similar to the apple core and houses up to ten seeds. Pear flesh can be more or less juicy, soft, and fragrant according to the variety. While some varieties are harvested in summer, others are gathered in fall or even in winter in warmer regions.

Like the banana and the avocado, pears do not ripen well on the tree and are usually picked before they are fully ripe in order to prevent their flesh from becoming gritty and granular. The ripening process is continued in refrigerated warehouses or in cold-atmosphere storage. As the starch is gradually converted into sugar, the fruit remains firm, with a smooth, tender, pleasant texture.

The **Anjou** pear originated in France. It is medium-size with a very short neck and light green or yellowish green skin. The flesh is very juicy and has a fine, buttery texture.

The **Bartlett** is an English variety that was introduced into the United States by Enoch Bartlett of Dorchester, Massachusetts; it is known in Europe as the Williams pear. The skin of the Bartlett changes from light green to golden yellow during ripening. Its smooth white flesh is highly aromatic. The Red Bartlett, or Red Williams, has the same fine flavor; both are good cooking pears.

The **Bosc** pear, originally from Belgium, has a thicker and rougher skin than that of other varieties; the skin is brown verging on yellow. The Bosc is elongated, with a long thin neck and a juicy white flesh that is granular and strongly perfumed. It stands up quite well to cooking and poaching.

The **Comice** pear was developed in France and has been cultivated in North America for over a century. Large and round with a short neck, it has tender greenish yellow skin with pink or brown tinges when ripe. Its fragrant yellowish white flesh is exceptionally juicy and sweet. It is considered to be one of the finest pears in the world. The Comice is often served with good-quality cheeses.

The **Conference** pear owes its name to the fact that it won first prize at the International Pear Conference held in London in 1885. It creamy white flesh is juicy, sweet, and refreshing. This variety closely resembles the Bosc.

The **Packham** pear is an Australian variety that was created in 1896 by Charles Henry Packham when he crossed a Bartlett with an Yvedale Saint-Germain pear. The Packham pear is similar in color and flavor to the Bartlett, but less symmetrical in shape. It is a large pear with a small neck and green skin that turns slightly yellowish as the fruit matures. The white flesh of this variety is juicy and sweet.

The **Passe-Crassane** originated in Normandy, France, where it was created in 1855 by an orchard cultivator named Louis Boisbunel when he crossed a pear with a quince. It is an excellent winter pear, as it has very good keeping qualities. The Passe-Crassane is large and round with a thick skin. Its white flesh, which is slightly granular, is very sweet and tasty and melts in the mouth.

The **Rocha**, a native of Portugal, is medium-size and round with a short brownish neck. Its yellow skin is dotted with green. Initially firm and crisp, its flesh becomes soft and buttery when ripe.

Anjou   **Bartlett**

Buying

Choose pears that are smooth and firm but not overly hard; they should be free of bruises and mold. When it is ripe, a pear has a pleasant odor and its flesh yields when pressed near the stem.

Storing

Pears are quite perishable. Unripe pears should be left to ripen at room temperature; at peak ripeness, they will keep for a few days in the refrigerator. Some varieties do not change color, but remain green upon ripening; they are ready to eat when the skin yields slightly under gentle pressure. Once ripe, they should be eaten as soon as possible as they tend to spoil rapidly.

Do not stack pears too closely together, and avoid storing them in an airtight bag or container, as they produce ethylene gas, which accelerates spoiling. Also, to prevent the absorption of odors, store pears away from strong-smelling foods such as apples, onions, potatoes, and cabbage. Pears do not stand up well to freezing unless they are cooked.

Chocolate-Covered Pears

4 large pears
½ lemon
2 cups (500 ml) water
½ cup (125 ml) sugar
¼ tsp. vanilla extract

4 oz. (125 g) dark
   chocolate
2 tbsp. whipping cream
2 tbsp. unsalted butter

This recipe can be made using pears canned in syrup.

1. Peel the pears, leaving them whole with their stems attached. Sprinkle them with the juice of the half lemon to prevent oxidation. Cut a thin slice from the bottom of each pear so it will stand up.

2. In a saucepan, heat the water with the sugar. As soon as the sugar has dissolved, add the vanilla extract and the pears, and poach them over low heat for 15 to 20 minutes, or until they are translucent. Leave them to cool in the syrup. Then drain them and set them aside.

3. To make the chocolate sauce, break the chocolate into small pieces and melt it in a double boiler. When it has melted, mix in the cream and the butter. Serve the pears covered with the chocolate sauce.

Conference

Packham

Comice

Preparing

The flesh of pears oxidizes and turns brown when exposed to air. To prevent discoloration, eat or cook the pear as soon as it is cut or sprinkle it with lemon, lime, or orange juice or with alcohol.

Serving Ideas

There are almost as many uses for the pear as for the apple. It can be eaten fresh, cooked, dried, or candied. It is also used to make compote, coulis, jelly, jam, juice, vinegar, spirits, and liqueurs; Poire Williams is made from Williams (Bartlett) pears. When cooking pears to make compote or when poaching them in wine or syrup, choose fruit that is not yet totally ripe. The flavor of pears blends very well with apples, quinces, chocolate, and ginger.

Pears are added to fruit salads, sorbets, yogurt, souffls, pies, and charlottes; they can be served dressed in a sauce or with various garnishes. Chutneys and marinades often contain pears. In addition to lending an original touch to mixed salads, pears are delicious with sweet onions and slightly bitter vegetables such as watercress, raddichio, dandelion, and chicory. They are the perfect accompaniment to cheeses such as Brie, Camembert, Cheddar, goat's cheese, and Roquefort. Pears are also delicious in an appetizer with prosciutto or Parma ham.

Nutritional Information

	fresh	*dried*
water	84%	27%
protein	0.4 g	1.9 g
fat	0.4 g	0.6 g
carbohydrates	15 g	70 g
fiber	1.4 g	6.4 g
calories	59	262
		per 100 g

Pears are rich in fiber and contain potassium and copper. The nutrients in dried pears are much more concentrated; dried pears are rich in potassium and constitute a good source of copper and iron, in addition to containing magnesium, vitamin C, phosphorus, and sodium. Unripe pears are difficult to digest and have a laxative effect, while ripe pears are said to be diuretic, remineralizing, stomachic, and sedative.

Passe-Crassane

Bosc

Rocha

Pome Flesby Fruits

215

Quince

Cydonia oblonga, **Rosaceae**

Fruit of the quince tree, a small tree believed to be native to Iran and that grows only in warm climates.

Fruit of the quince tree, believed to be native to Iran. The quince grows only in warm climates and typically reaches a height of 13 to 20 feet. It was popular among the Greeks and Romans. The Greeks believed that it warded off bad luck and valued it as a symbol of love and fertility. They also used it in wedding rites. The Romans used its essential oil to make perfume.

Since ancient times, the traditional use of the quince has been in jams and jellies. This is attributable to its large amount of pectin, a mucilaginous substance that acts as a thickening agent. The word "marmalade" comes from the Portuguese *marmelada,* which means "quince jam" (marmelo). The seeds of the quince contain a high concentration of a mucilage that was once used in the preparation of hair spray.

The thin skin of the quince turns from green to yellow as the fruit ripens. Like the pear, the quince does not ripen well on the tree, and it is therefore picked just before it reaches full maturity and allowed to ripen at temperatures varying from 57° to 67°F and at a humidity of roughly 85%. The flesh of the quince has a pronounced aroma that fills a room with a pleasant scent. It is firm, dry, and rich in pectin. It cannot be eaten raw, however, because its high tannin content gives it a bitter taste; the bitterness disappears during cooking. The quince oxidizes rapidly once cut, and should be sprinkled with lemon juice or cooked immediately to prevent discoloration. The flesh turns a pink or red color when cooked.

Nutritional Information

water	84%
protein	0.4 g
fat	0.1 g
carbohydrates	15 g
fiber	1.7 g
calories	57
	per 100 g

The quince is a good source of potassium and contains vitamin C and copper. It is sometimes used as an astringent and as an aperitive. It is also believed to be good for the gastrointestinal system.

Buying

Choose quinces that are plump, firm, and undamaged, and look for partially yellow skin. Fresh quinces often have spots, but this does not matter if they are cooked immediately. Avoid fruits that are hard and green, a sign that they are not ripe.

Serving Ideas

The quince maintains its shape and texture during cooking. It is cooked like the apple, after being cored and, if desired, peeled. It is used to make jam, jelly, compote, syrup, and wine, and blends well with apples, pears, strawberries, and raspberries. A paste made from the quince, *cotignac,* is particularly popular in Europe, especially among Spanish-speaking peoples, who call it *dulce de membrillo.* In eastern Europe, the Near East, and northern Africa, the quince is often served with meat and poultry dishes. It can be added to simmered dishes or served as a compote.

Storing

Buy quinces slightly green and leave them to ripen at room temperature. Ripe quinces can be wrapped individually and refrigerated; they will keep for a few weeks if in good condition. Puréed quince freezes very well, with or without the addition of sugar. It does not freeze as well raw (peel it, cut it, and sprinkle it with lemon juice or ascorbic acid to prevent browning).

Loquat

Eriobotrya japonica, **Rosaceae**

Fruit of a tree native to China and Japan, the loquat was popularized by the Japanese, who have been growing it for a long time and have considerably improved it. Also called the "Japanese medlar," the loquat is grown in the subtropical climates of many countries, including Israel, India, the United States, Italy, Spain, Chile, and Brazil. The loquat tree, an evergreen that can grow to a height of approximately 23 feet, was introduced into Europe at the end of the 18th century. Initially it was grown for ornamental purposes. Its superb wood is much sought after by stringed-instrument makers.

The loquat belongs to the Rosaceae family, which also includes the pear, the peach, and the apple. A tree of a similar variety, known as the medlar tree *(Mespilus germanica),* also grows in temperate climates, particularly in Europe. It produces a small fruit, the medlar, which is edible only when it is extremely ripe; however, it is rarely found on the market today.

Loquats grow in clusters that appear in early spring. They are pear-shaped, approximately 3 inches long, and have a diameter of 1½ inches at their widest point. Their thin yellowish skin is edible and is sometimes covered with a fine down. The flesh of the loquat is rather scarce, cream- or orange-colored, and may be firm or soft, depending on the variety. It is juicy, sourish but sweet at the same time, and quite refreshing, with a taste similar to the cherry or plum. However, it can be very acid when the fruit isn't sufficiently ripe. The loquat usually contains from 4 to 10 hard, smooth, black inedible seeds. Loquats are highly perishable and stand up poorly to shipping, which has a direct impact on their commercial success.

Buying

Choose tender, smooth-skinned loquats. Usually those covered with brown spots are surprisingly tastier.

Serving Ideas

Loquats are delicious eaten on their own, with or without their skin, raw or cooked. Poaching brings out their flavor. They are used in fruit salads, pies, jellies, and jams. They are also made into an alcohol and can be candied or canned. Whole or ground, loquat seeds are used as a spice.

Nutritional Information

water	87%
protein	0.4 g
fat	0.2 g
carbohydrates	12 g
calories	47
	per 100 g

Loquats are a good source of potassium and vitamin A. They are thought to have diuretic and tonic properties.

Storing

Since loquats are picked ripe, they are best eaten without delay.

Pomelo

Citrus maxima, Rutaceae

F ruit of a tree that can grow to a height of 20 feet, the pomelo, or pummelo, has been grown in Asia for over 4,000 years. Greatly appreciated in many Asian countries, particularly in China, Thailand, and Indonesia, it has only recently been marketed in North America.

The pomelo is sometimes also called "shaddock," after the English sea captain who brought it to the Caribbean during the 17th century. In Guadeloupe and Martinique, it is known as *chadèque.* During the 18th century, it seems that a cross between the shaddock tree *(Citrus grandis)* and the sweet orange tree *(Citrus sinensis)* occurred naturally, resulting in the grapefruit tree *(Citrus paradisi),* which produces the fruit that is widely consumed in the Western Hemisphere.

The pomelo may be spherical or pear-shaped, and varies in diameter from 4 to 12 inches (which explains why it is called *maxima*). It can weigh over 13 pounds. Its thick, fragrant skin peels easily and may be green, yellow, or pink, and smooth or rough in texture. The pomelo is less juicy than the grapefruit. Depending on the variety, its flesh may be flavorless or tasty, very sweet or very acidic, and may contain seeds or not. Pomelos are often candied or cooked.

Nutritional Information

water	89%
protein	0.7 g
carbohydrates	9.6 g
calories	37
	per 100 g

Pomelo is an excellent source of vitamin C and a good source of potassium. A stomachic, it is also known to stimulate the appetite and to facilitate digestion.

Buying

When buying pomelos, choose relatively firm fruits that seem heavy for their size. Blemishes on the skin, such as scarring or hard spots, do not necessarily affect the quality of the fruit. Avoid very soft, dull-skinned fruits that yield too easily to slight pressure and those that appear dried-out on the stem end.

Serving Ideas

Unlike grapefruit, the pomelo is rarely eaten with a spoon; it is more commonly cooked or candied. It can also be peeled, de-membraned, and added to fruit or vegetable salads served with a dressing.

Storing

Pomelos keep for a week when refrigerated and for a few days when left at room temperature. Their juice and zest freeze well.

white grapefruit

Grapefruit

Citrus paradisi, Rutaceae

A fruit believed to be native to Jamaica, the grapefruit is sometimes confused with the pomelo *(Citrus maxima),* which is a close relation but is larger and pear-shaped. Many botanists maintain that the grapefruit is a natural hybrid of the pomelo with either the sweet orange or the bitter orange. The term "grapefruit," first used in Jamaica in 1814, probably refers to the fact that grapefruits grow in clusters like grapes.

The grapefruit tree can grow to a height of 26 to 30 feet. Grapefruits are round, with a diameter of between 4 and 6 inches. Their thin skin may be either completely yellow or yellow with a pinkish hue. The yellow, pinkish, or reddish pulp of the grapefruit can be more or less sharp-tasting, acidic, sweet, and fragrant (less so in the case of yellow grapefruits). While some grapefruits are seedless, most do contain seeds. Because it tends to fall from the tree and begins to lose its acidic flavor when ripe, the grapefruit is harvested before it reaches full maturity. The color of citrus fruits is not a good indication of their ripeness and cannot be relied upon to determine the best moment for picking. In fact, grapefruits do not lose their green color until they are exposed to cool nights, with temperatures of 39 to 50°F. Once picked, they can also be ripened by exposure to ethylene gas in a heated room.

The grapefruit was first marketed toward the late 19th century. The United States is the largest producer of this citrus fruit, accounting for over 40% of global production. Approximately 60% of the grapefruit crop is used for the manufacture of juice and canned grapefruit, while the rest is sold fresh.

Buying

Choose grapefruits that are heavy for their size, quite firm, with tight and shiny skin. While the quality of the fruit is not affected by the presence of marks or hard spots on the skin, avoid overly soft fruits with dull-colored skin.

Serving Ideas

The grapefruit is most often cut in half and scooped out with a spoon, with or without a sprinkling of sugar. It is easier to eat if the segments are first loosened with a curved grapefruit knife or a special serrated spoon. It is a good idea to wash the grapefruit before cutting it.

The grapefruit can be used in a variety of ways. Grilled, it can accompany main dishes of duck, chicken, pork, or shrimp. It also goes well in mixed salads and in a number of desserts, including cheesecakes, flans, fruit salads, and sorbets. It can be used as a substitute for the orange or the pineapple in most recipes. The grapefruit provides a most refreshing juice, and the skin can be candied.

Storing

Grapefruits will keep at room temperature for 8 to 15 days. If they are to be kept longer, they should be placed in the refrigerator. Both the juice and the zest of grapefruits can be frozen.

Nutritional Information

water	91%
protein	0.6 g
fat	0.1 g
carbohydrates	8 g
fiber	0.6 g
calories	30 to 33
	per 100 g

The nutritional value of the grapefruit varies with the color (white, pink, or red). Red and pink grapefruits have a higher amount of vitamin A. Grapefruit is slightly less nutritious than the orange. It is rich in vitamin C and contains potassium and folic acid. It stimulates the appetite and is used for its digestive, stomachic, antiseptic, tonic, and diuretic qualities.

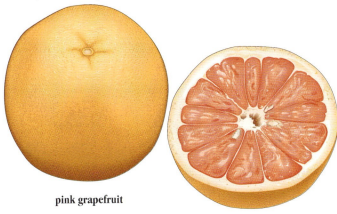
pink grapefruit

Orange

Citrus spp., **Rutaceae**

T he fruit of the orange tree, which is native to China. The orange tree has been cultivated in Asia for over 4,000 years and was introduced into Persia, Egypt, Spain, and northern Africa by the Arabs. In fact, the word "orange" is derived from the Arab *narandj,* which is in turn derived from the Sanskrit word *nagarunga.*

While still considered an exotic fruit at the beginning of this century, oranges today constitute one of the most important commercial fruit crops in the world. They are usually classified as being either bitter oranges or sweet oranges. Each of these categories embraces many different varieties.

The **bitter orange** *(Citrus aurantium)* is believed to be the ancestor of the sweet orange. It is also called the "Seville orange" because it was once cultivated on a large scale by the Moors near Seville, Spain.

The bitter orange tree is a spiny shrub with shiny oval evergreen leaves and strongly scented white or pink flowers. The skin of the bitter orange is thick and rough, with green or yellow coloring. It is smaller than the sweet orange, and its pulp is rather dry and extremely bitter.

The **sweet orange** *(Citrus sinensis)* is that which is most popular for its juiciness, sweetness, and tartness. Native to China or Indochina, it is believed to have been introduced into Europe by the Arabs in the 15th century. Christopher Columbus apparently brought orange seeds with him to Hispaniola on his second voyage in 1493. The orange tree was later brought to Florida by the Spanish in the 16th century.

The orange tree can grow a height of 26 to 43 feet and bears strongly scented flowers, considered in many Mediterranean countries to symbolize virginity and marriage. There are many different varieties of sweet oranges.

The **Valencia orange** is named after the Spanish city where it was once cultivated on a large scale. Introduced into the United States around 1870, it now represents close to 50% of the American orange crop. Valencia oranges are also cultivated in many other parts of the world, including South America, Australia, and South Africa. Its flesh is very juicy and acid and contains few or no seeds. This variety is considered to be the best juice orange.

The **navel orange** is thought to be native to Brazil. It was introduced into the United States around 1600 and is also cultivated in Spain, Israel, Australia, South America, and South Africa. Its orange-colored rind is thick, coarse, and easy to peel. Its pulp is juicy and sweet and almost always seedless.

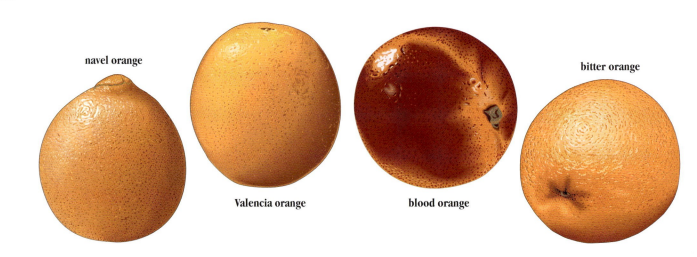

navel orange

Valencia orange

blood orange

bitter orange

The **blood orange** is a hybrid that first appeared in Europe around 1850. The flesh of blood oranges is red or orange with bright red streaks and is sweet, juicy, and very aromatic. Certain varieties are slightly oval in shape. Blood oranges are usually seedless and are cultivated mainly in Spain, Italy, and North Africa.

Oranges are often identified by a brand name, such as "Sunkist," "Jaffa," or "Outspan." Sunkist is the name of a marketing cooperative of American citrus growers that includes 8,000 members from California and Arizona. The name Jaffa was chosen by the Israeli government, while Outspan is a South African brand. Each brand name actually embraces several different varieties of oranges that correspond to certain standards of quality, size, and so on established by these organizations. The largest producers of oranges are Brazil, the United States, China, Spain, and Mexico. Close to 14% of the world production is supplied by the United States, particularly Florida.

The orange tree has been cultivated in Asia for over 4,000 years and bears strongly scented flowers.

Buying

Choose oranges that are firm and heavy for their size; the skin should be smooth and show no traces of soft or black spots or mold.

Serving Ideas

Oranges can be used in a wide variety of ways. They are eaten out of hand, used in cooking, made into marmalade, or pressed to make juice. Their zest and pulp can be candied. The essential oil and essence of the orange are used in pastry making, confectionery, cosmetics, pharmacy, and even in chemistry, while the fragrant flowers of the orange tree are distilled to manufacture orange-flower water. Oranges are a frequent addition to fruit salads, soufflés, flans, crêpes, ice cream, sorbets, and punch.

Oranges also add an original touch to savory dishes and are much used in sauces, salad dressings, vegetables, rice salads, chicken salads, and seafood. They blend very well with fish, duck, beef, and pork. Blood oranges are often used for decorative purposes, while orange-flower water adds a pleasant aroma to crêpes, flans, syrups, pastries, and infusions.

Bitter oranges are usually canned or cooked to make marmalade, jam, jelly, syrup, or sauce. An infusion of orange leaves is said to stimulate digestion and to be antispasmodic. The flowers of the bitter orange tree are used to make "oil of neroli" and orange-flower water. Bitter-orange essence is also extracted from the rind of bitter oranges. Cointreau, Curaçao, and Grand Marnier owe their orange flavor to the zest of the bitter orange.

Storing

Oranges can be stored at room temperature for about 1 week. For a longer storage life, keep them in the refrigerator. The juice and zest of oranges can be frozen.

Oranges are often treated with chemical preservatives and should be washed first if used for their zest. Candied or dried orange peel should be stored in an airtight container in a cool dry place away from insects.

Nutritional Information

water	87%
protein	0.9 g
fat -	0.1 g
carbohydrates	12 g
fiber	1.8 g
calories	47
	per 100 g

Oranges are known for their high vitamin C content; they are also a good source of potassium.

Oranges are diuretic, tonic, digestive, combat scurvy, and have a mild laxative effect. Their flowers have antispasmodic properties, and the water contained in the flowers is said to have a soporific effect.

segment

zest

skin

flesh

Mandarin

Citrus reticula or *Citrus nobilis,* **Rutaceae**

Fruit of the mandarin tree, a native of China or Indochina, for a long time the mandarin was known only in Asia. It owes its name to the fact that its rind is the same color as the robes worn by the mandarins, the public officials of the Chinese empire. Despite having been cultivated for some 3,000 years in China, mandarins were not introduced into Europe and America until the 19th century. While cultivation of the fruit was limited to the Mediterranean basin for some time, a number of hybrids have since been produced, and today the main producers include Japan, Spain, and Brazil.

The **mandarin** *(Citrus reticula)* resembles a small, slightly flattened orange. Its skin is easy to peel and the delicate flesh is fragrant and sweet; it is less acidic than most citrus fruits. Among the numerous varieties, some have many seeds while others are seedless. The mandarin's flesh is divided into small segments that come apart easily.

The **tangerine** is the result of a cross between the mandarin orange and the bitter orange *(Citrus reticula* X *Citrus aurantium)* ; it is named after Tangier, the Moroccan port which for many years was the main point of departure for shipments of mandarins destined for export. Most tangerines are grown in the southeastern United States. Like the mandarin, tangerines are easy to peel, but their skin is usually darker in color, with an almost reddish hue.

Like the tangerine, the **clementine** is a hybrid between the mandarin and the bitter orange. It derives its name from Father Clément Dozier, a French missionary living in Algeria, who created this hybrid at the beginning of the 20th century. Its thin easy-to-peel skin is reddish orange and often has a rough texture. The clementine's flesh is juicy, slightly acid, and not quite as fragrant as that of the mandarin orange. This fruit is widely grown in Europe (Corsica, Spain, Italy), North Africa (Algeria, Morocco), and Israel. Certain varieties have no or very few seeds, while others contain up to 20.

The **satsuma** mandarin is a Japanese variety that is very small and virtually seedless. In North America, it is most commonly available in canned form.

The **tangor** *(Citrus nobilis)* is a cross between the tangerine and the sweet orange. The name comes from the word "tangy" and refers to its tartly sweet taste. The tangor is also loose-skinned.

222

tangelo

ugli fruit

tangerine

The **tangelo** *(Citrus paradisi* x *Citrus reticula)* is a hybrid between the mandarin orange and the grapefruit. Like the tangor, it was named for its tartness. The tangelo is often identified according to its different varieties, which include the Minneola, the Seminole, and the Orlando. Some of these varieties are distinguished by a bump at one end. The fragrant, juicy flesh of the tangelo is sweeter and less acidic than that of the grapefruit. Depending on the variety, the brightly colored skin can be either tight or loose, and the flesh may contain only a few or many seeds. The tangelo is larger and more acidic than the orange.

The **ugli fruit** *(Citrus paradisi* x *Citrus reticula)* is a surprising variety that was discovered in Jamaica at the beginning of this century. There are some doubts about the origin of this fruit, which some claim is a hybrid of the tangerine with the grapefruit or the pomelo, while others point to the bitter orange. It is a delicious fruit in spite of its rather unattractive appearance (hence the name "ugli"). The thick, wrinkled skin is easy to peel; depending on the variety, ugli fruits are either green, yellowish red, or orange-yellow. The juicy flesh is sweeter than that of the grapefruit, orange or pink in color, slightly acid, and seedless.

Buying

Choose fruits that are undamaged and heavy for their size, with no signs of mold, dark spots, or soft areas. While dark spots on the peel of ugli fruits do not alter the flavor of this variety, avoid those with a dried-out stem end.

Serving Ideas

The mandarin and its hybrids are most frequently eaten on their own. Indeed, they make practical and refreshing snacks or desserts. They are often used like oranges and added to fruit salads, sauces, or sweet-and-sour dishes. They are also used to decorate cakes, puddings, pies, or Bavarian creams, and add an original touch to rice salads, chicken, and seafood. Mandarin oranges make a special treat served with ice cream (a bit of Grand Marnier can be poured on top) or with chocolate fondue. Mandarin peel has a superb exotic flavor. Because it is thinner than orange peel, less pressure is required when grating it for its zest or when squeezing the fruit to make juice. Tangerine juice is particularly delicious and refreshing.

Nutritional Information

water	88%
protein	0.6 g
fat	0.2 g
carbohydrates	11 g
fiber	1 g
calories	44
	per 100 g

Mandarins are an excellent source of vitamin C. They also supply potassium, vitamin A, and folic acid.

Storing

Mandarins are best when consumed as fresh as possible but will keep in the refrigerator for 1 to 2 weeks.

Citrus Fruits

223

mandarin

tangor

Lemon

Citrus limon, **Rutaceae**

Fruit of the lemon tree, believed to have originated in China or India, lemons have been cultivated in Asia for at least 2,500 years. The Arabs introduced the lemon into Spain in the 11th century, while the Crusaders returning from Palestine were largely responsible for spreading it across the rest of Europe. It was not until the 15th century that western Europeans began to use lemons in cooking instead of verjuice, the sour juice extracted from unripe grapes. Columbus apparently brought the lemon to Hispaniola on his second voyage to the Americas in 1493.

The size and acidity of lemons differ according to the variety, as does the coarseness and thickness of the yellow peel. The number of seeds contained in the juicy flesh also varies, with some lemons being seedless. When lemons are picked ripe, they are sweet and only slightly acid. For this reason, commercially sold lemons are usually harvested when still green and left to ripen artificially in warehouses for 1 to 4 months.

Buying

Choose lemons that are firm and heavy for their size, with a close-grained, slightly glossy yellow peel. Green-tinged lemons tend to be more acid, while coarse-skinned specimens are likely to have a very thick skin and relatively little flesh. Avoid wrinkled fruits, as well as those with hard or soft patches, or with dull or excessively yellow peel, all indications that the fruit is no longer fresh.

Serving Ideas

Lemons can serve both decorative and culinary purposes, and their uses are many. They are a popular flavor enhancer and a good substitute for salt. They also prevent certain fruits and vegetables from discoloring. Lemons add zest to soups and sauces, vegetables, cakes, custards, ice creams, and sorbets, and enter into the making of marmalade and jelly.

Lemon juice may replace vinegar in dressings and is also used to marinate and tenderize meat, poultry, fish, and game. It is the thirst-quenching ingredient in lemonade and is often added to teas. The zest of lemons can be grated or sliced and is available candied or dried. It is used as a flavoring in meats, sauces, and desserts.

1 *Pare off the zest with a lemon zester.*

2 *Cut strips of zest using a vegetable peeler.*

3 *Chop the zest strips with a knife.*

Lemon Sorbet

SERVES 4

4 large thick-skinned lemons	2 cups (500 ml) water
2 cups (1 lb., 500 g) sugar	4 fresh mint leaves

1. Cut a cap off the stem end of each lemon and set them aside.

2. Using a grapefruit spoon, scoop out the flesh, taking care not to pierce the peel. Place the lemon shells and the caps in the freezer.

3. In a blender, purée the lemon pulp.

4. In a saucepan, dissolve the sugar in the water over low heat. Remove the syrup from the heat and set it aside to cool.

5. Mix the puréed pulp with the syrup, and freeze the mixture for about 3 hours or until it forms a sorbet.

6. Fill the frozen hollowed-out lemon shells with the sorbet and cover with the caps. Garnish with a leaf of fresh mint and keep in the freezer until serving time.

Nutritional Information

water	89%	
protein	1 g	
fat	0.3 g	
carbohydrates	9.3 g	
fiber	2.1 g	
calories	29	
	per 100 g	

Like all citrus fruits, lemons are very rich in vitamin C. They also provide potassium and folic acid.

Lemons contain 6% to 10% citric acid; their high acidity makes their juice too sour to be consumed undiluted. The essential oils of the lemon are made up of 95% terpene and have expectorant properties. This fruit is also an excellent natural antiseptic; it relieves insect bites and combats scurvy. Among their numerous other medicinal properties, lemons are said to be diuretic and tonic, and to alleviate rheumatism and intestinal problems.

The size and acidity of lemons differs according to the variety. The number of seeds contained in the juicy flesh also varies, with some lemons being seedless.

Storing

Lemons will keep at room temperature for about 1 week. For longer keeping, they should be stored in the refrigerator. Both the juice and the zest of lemons can be frozen. The candied or dried zest should be placed in an airtight container and stored in a dry and cool place, away from insects.

Citrus Fruits

Kumquat

Fortunella spp., **Rutaceae**

Fruit of a tree originating in China. The kumquat tree stands 16 to 20 feet high and is commonly grown for ornamental purposes. It owes its botanical name to the British botanist Robert Fortune, who introduced it into Europe in 1846. The word "kumquat" comes from the Cantonese *kin kü,* meaning "golden orange." This fruit is grown in many parts of the world, including California, Florida, the Mediterranean countries, Japan, China, Indochina, Indonesia, Israel, Peru, and Brazil. The kumquat is often crossed with other citrus fruits, such as the lime (limequat), the lemon (lemonquat), the orange (orangequat), and the mandarin orange (calamondin).

The kumquat measures between 1 and 2 inches in length and is covered with a thin, tender edible rind. The rind is fragrant and sweet, and varies in color from dark orange to golden yellow. The flesh, which is divided into five or six sections containing rather large seeds, is pleasantly acidic.

Nutritional Information

water	82%
protein	1.1 g
carbohydrates	16 g
fiber	3.7 g
calories	63
	per 100 g

The kumquat is rich in vitamin C; it is also a good source of potassium and contains some copper. People who are allergic to the rind of citrus fruits may also experience an allergic reaction to the skin of the kumquat.

Buying

Choose firm, glossy fruits that are free of cracks and blemishes. Avoid soft kumquats, as they tend to spoil rapidly. Kumquats are sometimes sold still attached to their branch, with a few remaining decorative green leaves.

Preparing

Kumquats should be washed thoroughly before being eaten. They can be blanched for about 20 seconds and then rinsed under cold water to soften the skin.

Serving Ideas

The kumquat tastes best if it is gently rolled between the fingers before being eaten, as this releases the essential oils in the rind. This fruit is delicious eaten on its own, unpeeled. It can be added to fruit salads or mixed salads, or used as an ornamental garnish. Kumquats are also cooked in stuffings, baked in cakes and muffins, and used to enhance the flavor of sweet-and-sour sauces. The kumquat can be candied, marinated, made into jam or marmalade, poached in syrup, or preserved in alcohol. It blends well with fish and is particularly good as an accompaniment to poultry, duck, or lamb.

Storing

Because of their thin skin, kumquats are more perishable than oranges. They will keep at room temperature if consumed within 5 or 6 days of purchase; they will keep for about 3 weeks in the refrigerator.

Lime

Citrus aurantifolia, **Rutaceae**

Fruit of the lime tree, a thorny tree believed to be native to a region somewhere between India and Malaysia. The lime tree was brought to France and Italy by the Crusaders in the 13th century. There is also historical evidence that Christopher Columbus took lime seeds to Hispaniola on his second trip to the New World in 1493. The lime tree is an evergreen that can grow from 10 to 16 feet high. It flowers continually, bearing fruit all year long. Its small, fragrant flowers are white with tinges of red. Lime trees are cultivated in Mexico, the West Indies, the United States, India, Spain, and Italy.

The lime typically has a diameter of between 1 and 2 inches; its thin tight skin covers a fragrant and juicy pulp that is very acid in taste. Both the flesh and the skin are a green color, eventually becoming more yellow as the fruit ripens. Some varieties of lime have seeds, while others are seedless. The variety usually seen on display in the supermarket is the sour lime. The sweet lime variety is not commercialized in North America.

Buying

Choose limes that are firm, plump, and heavy for their size; the skin should be a deep green, smooth, and slightly glossy. Avoid dull-colored, soft, or dried-out fruits. Brownish spots on the skin of limes do not affect their flavor.

Serving Ideas

Limes and lemons have basically the same uses and are interchangeable in most recipes. The lime goes just as well in main dishes as in soups, sauces, vinaigrettes, cakes, Bavarian cream, ice cream, and sorbets. It adds zest to punches and tropical cocktails, and enhances the flavor of poultry, fish, beans, and vegetable soups.

The lime is a basic cooking ingredient in several regions, including Latin America, the West Indies, Africa, India, Southeast Asia, and the Pacific Islands. The classic Peruvian dish *seviche* is made of raw fish marinated in lime juice.

Storing

Limes are more perishable than lemons and should be handled with care. Left at room temperature, they will keep for about a week. They may be stored for a longer time in the refrigerator. When exposed to bright light, limes tend to yellow and to lose their characteristic acid taste. The juice and the zest of limes can be frozen. Candied or dried lime zest should be kept in an airtight container in a cool and dry place, away from insects.

Nutritional Information

water	88%
protein	0.8 g
fat	0.2 g
carbohydrates	10.6 g
fiber	2.1 g
calories	30
	per 100 g

The lime is an excellent source of vitamin C, although it contains less than the lemon. It also supplies potassium and traces of iron, folic acid, and calcium. The medicinal properties of the lime are similar to the lemon. Like the lemon, it combats scurvy.

Citrus Fruits

227

Citron

Citrus medica, Rutaceae

Cultivated in Asia since ancient times, the citron tree, a member of the large rue family of citrus fruits, is thought to have originated in China. Various man-uscripts and archeological sites in Egypt provide evidence that citrons were cultivated as early as 300 B.C. In Judaism, the citron is believed to be the fruit of knowledge eaten by Adam. The citron tree has thorny branches and white flowers with shades of purple. Corsica is one of the main producers of the citron, along with other Mediterranean countries such as Greece, Italy, and Israel, where it is grown on a smaller scale. The fruit is 6 to 10 inches long and can weigh from 8 to 10 pounds. Its thick greenish yellow skin is strongly scented and often verrucose. The green or yellowish flesh is divided into several sections enclosed in a thick white membrane; rather dry and tart, the flesh contains numerous pits.

Buying

 Rarely available fresh, citrons are most commonly sold as candied fruits.

Storing

Candied citron should be kept in an airtight container in a cool place where insects cannot get at it.

Serving Ideas

Citrons are commonly used in baking and confectionery; they are often candied and used for decorative purposes. A frequent ingredient in cakes, biscuits, cookies, and puddings, the citron can also be added to salty dishes or made into jam or marmalade. Corsicans use citrons to prepare the liquor "cedratine," as well as consuming them as sweets. Fresh citron can add a pleasant scent to a room or to furniture.

Nutritional Information

Because of its high vitamin C content, the citron is a good antiscorbutic. It is also said to be a good sudorific, febrifuge, and digestive. The seeds can be ground and used as an intestinal cleanser.

Bergamot

Citrus bergamia, Rutaceae

The fruit of the bergamot tree, which has evergreen leaves and highly fragrant flowers, the bergamot resembles a small orange and is thought to be a cross between the lime and the bitter orange *(Citrus aurantium).*

This fruit, which has been used for several centuries, is today mainly cultivated in southern Europe, notably in Sicily and Calabria. Its greenish pulp is divided into sections, and although very juicy, it is too acid and bitter tasting to be edible. The yellowish rind is rich in an essential oil that exudes a refined fragrance.

Serving Ideas

The bergamot cannot be eaten as a fruit. It is used mainly for its zest and its essential oil. The zest serves as a flavoring ingredient in pastries and confections, while the essential oil goes into the making of confections and is used in perfumery (eau de cologne) and distilling. Bergamot is also a flavoring in Earl Grey tea. In France, the city of Nancy has specialized in the production of bergamot-flavored barley sugar *(sucre d'orge)* since 1850.

Plantain

Musa paradisiaca, **Musaceae**

Fruit of the banana tree, a giant herbaceous plant native to Malaysia, the plantain is related to the sweet banana. It is also referred to as the "cooking banana." This food, a staple in many regions, is grown mainly in Africa but is also common in India, Malaysia, the West Indies, and South America.

The plantain is 10 to 15 inches long; its green skin is thicker than that of the banana, and its flesh is firmer and not as sweet. As the fruit ripens, the skin tends to turn yellow and then black. The fruit of this plant should not be eaten raw, even when ripe, because although its starch (different from that of the banana) is converted into sugar as it ripens, it is not enough to make it pleasant tasting. Plantains may, however, be cooked as a fruit.

Buying

Choose plantains that are firm and intact. Brownish or blackish skin does not affect the quality of the flesh.

Serving Ideas

The plantain is most commonly used as a vegetable; its texture and flavor are somewhat reminiscent of the sweet potato or, when very ripe, the banana. It can be cooked in soups or stews, and blends well with apples, sweet potatoes, and squash. In East African countries such as Tanzania and Uganda, the plantain is fermented to make banana beer.

Cooking

The plantain may be prepared sliced or whole, and will retain its shape and consistency when cooked. To cook it in water, allow about 25 minutes; on the grill, place it 4 inches from the heat for about 45 minutes. The plantain is often eaten fried. It can also be baked in its skin (after cleaning it) at an oven temperature of 350°F (180°C) for an hour. To bake it without the skin, simply make a cut at both ends and peel off the skin. The skin can also be sliced open lengthwise before placing the plantain in the oven.

Nutritional Information

water	65%
protein	1.3 g
fat	0.4 g
carbohydrates	32 g
fiber	2.3 g
	per 100 g

The plantain is rich in potassium and is a good source of vitamin C, vitamin B_6, and magnesium. It also supplies vitamin A and folic acid. It contains tannins that are neutralized during cooking.

Storing

Plantains should be kept at room temperature. Refrigerate them only if they are very ripe. Ripe plantains freeze very easily; simply peel the fruits and wrap them individually before placing them in the freezer.

Tropical Fruits

229

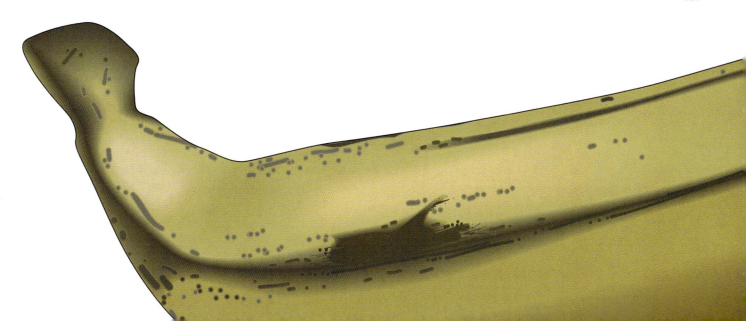

Banana

Musa spp., **Musaceae**

Fruit of the banana tree, a gigantic herbaceous plant belonging to the same family as the lily and the orchid. The banana is believed to have originated in Malaysia. The first record of its existence dates back to the 6th or 5th century B.C. in India, but it is thought to be close to a million years old. According to an Indian legend, the banana was the fruit offered to Adam, which explains why it is called the "fruit of paradise" in that country. The same legend is also the origin of the Latin name *paradisiaca* given to the plantain banana. For a long time, the difficulty of transporting this fragile fruit greatly limited its availability on the market. It was not until the beginning of the 20th century that it became more widely available, with the development of methods of preservation and more rapid means of transportation. Today bananas are stored in giant warehouses under closely controlled temperatures. They are often exposed to ethylene gas in order to artificially accelerate the ripening process.

Bananas grow in tropical and subtropical climates. The main producers of this fruit are India, Brazil, the Philippines, Ecuador, and Indonesia. Bananas develop on a large flower spike after its clusters of purplish flowers have blossomed. The banana plant can grow to a height of 10 to 26 feet and has enormous leaves that can attain a length of as much as 10 feet. The leaves join at the base to form a false trunk. Each plant produces only one bunch of fruit, after which it dries out and is replaced by new shoots. It takes almost a year before the bananas are ready to be picked. Bananas grow in bunches of 10 to 25 fruits, called "hands."

There are three distinct species of bananas: the sweet banana *(M. sapienta, M. nana)*, the plantain banana *(M. paradisiaca)*, also called the cooking banana (see *Plantain*), and the inedible variety *(M. textilis, M. ensete)*. There are a number of different kinds of sweet banana; most have a thick inedible skin that is usually yellow but can also range from red to pink or purple. Certain varieties are very small; these dwarf bananas are more fragile and for many years were available only in the countries where they were grown. The flavor and texture of bananas also depends on the variety, with some being starchier or sweeter than others. Bananas are usually harvested while still green, as they are more flavorful when allowed to ripen off the plant.

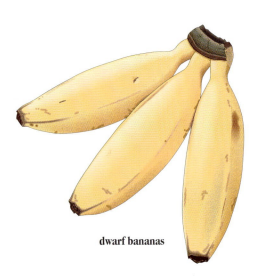

dwarf bananas

Buying

An indication of the degree of ripeness of bananas is given by the color of their peel; when fully ripe, yellow bananas have a slightly lustrous peel with some black or brown spots; there should be no remaining green coloring. The peel of reddish bananas darkens as the fruit ripens. Choose bananas that are undamaged, avoiding those that are too hard, as they are probably unripe. Fruits that are overly green, or that are split or very soft, should also be avoided unless they are intended for cooking.

Bananas are also sold in the form of flour or cut into thin slices and fried to make banana chips, a snack that is particularly high in calories.

Preparing

Because bananas discolor rapidly on contact with air, it is best to peel them at the last minute; if this is not possible, sprinkle them with a little citrus juice to prevent them from oxidizing.

Serving Ideas

The banana is most commonly eaten on its own, but it can also be baked, steamed, boiled, sautéed, or fried. It is used both as a fruit and as a vegetable. Green bananas maintain their consistency better and are less sweet than ripe bananas, which is why they are often used as a vegetable. Bananas are delicious sprinkled with ginger or cinnamon, mixed with brown sugar and lemon or lime juice, and flambéed in rum or orange liqueur. This dish can also be baked in the oven for about 20 minutes.

The banana blends very well with dairy products, including yogurt, ice cream, sorbet, milkshakes, tapioca, and custards. The banana split is a classic dessert. Bananas can also be made into a purée, which can be eaten on its own or used in pies, cakes, muffins, puddings, and donuts. It is not necessary to add sugar to the purée, particularly if it is not consumed right away, as its starch turns to sugar.

An essence derived from bananas is used as a flavoring in numerous dishes and is particularly popular in Asian cooking. The banana can be dried or distilled. In central Africa, a beer is made from bananas.

Bananas Flamed in Rum

4 ripe bananas
3 tbsp. unsalted butter

⅓ cup (80 ml) confectioners' sugar
1 oz. (30 ml) dark rum

1. Peel the bananas and cut them in half lengthwise.

2. Melt the butter in a frying pan. Add the bananas and fry over low heat for 3 minutes on each side until golden. Sprinkle in the sugar. Lower the heat and let the sugar melt and caramelize slightly.

3. Add the rum and carefully set it alight. Cover the pan for 2 minutes.

4. Pour the caramel mixture over the bananas, and serve.

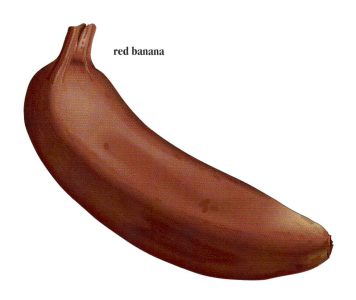

red banana

Nutritional Information

water	74%
protein	1 g
fat	0.5 g
carbohydrates	23 g
calories	92
	per 100 g

As the banana ripens, the sugars in it are transformed. Initially present in the form of starch, which is difficult to digest, they gradually convert into sugars such as fructose, glucose, and sucrose, which are easily assimilated. This explains why the green banana is difficult to digest, while the overripe banana is so sweet-tasting and nourishing.

Bananas are an excellent source of vitamin B_6 and potassium; they are also a source of vitamin C, riboflavin, folic acid, and magnesium. They are a mild laxative when overripe.

Bananas develop on a large flower spike after its clusters of purplish flowers have blossomed.

Storing

Despite their hardy appearance, bananas are actually very fragile fruits. They do not stand up well to sudden changes in temperature or to temperatures below 28°F; this is especially true of unripe bananas, as the cold halts the ripening process. Store bananas at room temperature. To accelerate the ripening process, place them in a paper bag or wrap them in newspaper. Very ripe bananas will keep for a few days in the refrigerator, during which time their peel will darken in color, although this will not affect the pulp. For maximum flavor, take them out of the refrigerator just prior to consuming them.

Bananas will keep in the freezer for about 2 months. Purée them first, adding a touch of lemon juice to prevent discoloration and to preserve their flavor. Thawed bananas are often used in baked goods, such as cakes, muffins, or other desserts. When whipped, partially thawed bananas have a curious tendency to froth, producing a dessert resembling ice cream.

Pineapple

Ananas comosus, **Bromeliaceae**

Fruit of a herbaceous plant originating in the tropical and subtropical countries of America, most likely in Brazil. The pineapple belongs to the large Bromeliaceae family; unlike most plants in this family, pineapples do not grow on trees, and they are the only plant in this family to bear edible fruit.

The pineapple has been cultivated in South America and the West Indies since ancient times. Christopher Columbus discovered it during his voyage to Guadeloupe in 1493 and brought it to Europe, where attempts to cultivate it met with little success. The Portuguese and the Spanish introduced it into their Asian colonies. In the early 1800s, the Azores, Australia, Hawaii, and South Africa began to grow pineapples for commercial purposes. The main producers today are Thailand and the Philippines. For a long time, the commercialization of pineapples was limited by the fact that this fragile fruit does not stand up well to shipping, particularly when ripe. The market for pineapples expanded greatly with the advent of modern refrigeration methods and rapid means of transportation. Pineapples are now produced in most tropical regions, including South and Central America, the Caribbean, Australia, the Pacific Islands, and in several countries in Asia and Africa.

The Spanish named this fruit *piña* because of its likeness to a pine cone; this resemblance also inspired the English word "pineapple." The pineapple grows on a herbaceous perennial plant that is about 3 feet high. Its fruits are harvested for only the first 2 or 3 years, after which they become too small. The long slender leaves are stiff and have spiny edges. The plant bears a hundred or more purple flowers that grow in a spiral pattern around a central axis; these unfertilized flowers join together to form a single fruit, the pineapple, which is ready for harvesting some 18 to 20 months after planting. The pineapple is thus actually a compound of small individual fruits, called "eyes," merged into one large fruit. Pineapples are seedless and have a thick, scale-like skin that is various shades of yellow, green, greenish brown, or reddish brown. The yellowish flesh is fibrous, sweet, and juicy. The flesh near the base of the fruit is even sweeter and more tender, and has a darker color. Pineapples usually weigh between 4 and 9 pounds.

There are numerous varieties of pineapples, four of which are of particular commercial importance:

• **Cayenne** pineapples are large and have golden-yellow flesh. The firm and fibrous flesh is juicy, tart, and very sweet; this is the most common variety of pineapple.

• **Queen** pineapples are rather small. Their yellow flesh is firmer, less acidic, and slightly drier than the cayenne variety, and not quite as sweet.

• **Red Spanish** pineapples are a medium-size variety with purplish skin and pale-colored flesh that is very fragrant, acidic, and slightly fibrous.

• **Pernambuco** pineapples are medium-size, with whitish or yellowish flesh that is moderately acidic, tender, and sweet.

A significant proportion of commercially grown pineapples is used for canning. Certain varieties, such as the firm-fleshed cayenne pineapple, are more suitable for canning than others. Pineapple trimmings, including the skin, the core, and the ends, are also used to make compote, vinegar, alcohol, and food for livestock.

Preparing

Different techniques can be used to peel the pineapple:

• Cut off the top and bottom of the pineapple and slice off the skin with vertical strokes of a knife; remove any remaining "eyes" with the tip of a knife. Cut the flesh into slices and, as desired, into chunks or small cubes. Ripe pineapples do not have to be cored.

• Trim both ends and cut the pineapple in half lengthwise. Separate the flesh from the skin with a knife, remove the core if desired, and cut the flesh into pieces.

• Slice off only the top of the pineapple, and separate the flesh from the skin with a knife. After the flesh has been cut in pieces, it can be replaced in the hollowed-out skin.

• Another alternative is to use a commercial pineapple peeler and corer. These instruments do not adjust to the size of the pineapple, however, and tend to waste a lot of flesh. To recover the juice that is lost during peeling and cutting, prepare the pineapple in a deep plate.

1 *Trim off the top and bottom of the pineapple.*

2 *Slice off the skin just below the surface in vertical strips.*

3 *Remove the remaining eyes with a knife.*

4 *Cut the pineapple into slices.*

5 *Remove the core, using a peeler-corer.*

Buying

Choose a pineapple that is heavy for its size and pleasantly aromatic; it should have deep green leaves and yield to a slight pressure of the fingers. Avoid pineapples with spots, mold, or sodden skin. Tap the pineapple lightly with the palm of the hand; a muffled sound is a sign of ripeness, while a hollow sound is an indication that the fruit may be dried out. An overly strong odor may indicate that the fruit has begun to ferment. Darkened "eyes," soft spots, and yellowing leaves denote a lack of freshness. The quality of this fruit is largely dependent on the moment of harvest; pineapples should be picked at peak ripeness, as their sugar content does not increase once they are harvested.

Nutritional Information

water	87%
protein	0.4 g
fat	0.5 g
carbohydrates	12 g
fiber	0.5 g
calories	50
	per 100 g

Pineapple supplies vitamin C, potassium, magnesium, and folic acid. It is said to make a good diuretic, stomachic, and detoxicant. Like the kiwi, the pineapple contains bromelin, an enzyme whose properties include that of a meat tenderizer; it also keeps gelatin from setting, turns milk sour (although it has no effect on yogurt or ice cream), and softens the other fruits in a fruit salad (unless added at the last minute). Since these properties are neutralized by cooking, canned pineapple may be used freely with gelatin or in fruit salads.

Tropical Fruits

233

Pineapple

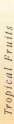

Serving Ideas

🍽 Pineapple is excellent fresh, whether on its own or dressed with rum or kirsch. It can be prepared in a number of ways, and is equally good raw, cooked, dried, candied, or made into juice. It is often incorporated into sauces, pies, cakes, fruit salads, sweets, yogurt, ice cream, sorbets, and punches. Upside-down pineapple cake is a dessert classic in North America.

The flesh of this fruit also blends well with savory foods and is a popular ingredient in sweet-and-sour dishes; it often accompanies seafood, chicken, duck, and pork. Ham with pineapple is a traditional dish in Canada and the United States. Pineapple also combines pleasantly with cottage cheese, rice, coleslaw, and with chicken or shrimp salad. Dried pineapple can be eaten as is or soaked in water, juice, or alcohol.

The pineapple is actually a compound of small, individual fruits called "eyes," merged into one large fruit.

Sliced Ham with Pineapple

SERVES 4

4 tbsp. butter
4 slices precooked ham
   (¼ in. thick)
4 slices pineapple
½ tsp. cornstarch

1 tbsp. lemon juice
½ cup (125 ml)
   pineapple juice
sherry (optional)

1. Preheat the oven to 200°F (93°C).

2. In a large pan, melt half the butter and brown the ham slices on both sides over low heat. Set aside on a warm serving dish.

3. Add the rest of the butter to the pan and heat the pineapple slices until golden. Place with the ham.

4. Mix the cornstarch with the lemon juice. Pour the pineapple juice in the pan, add the cornstarch mixture, and bring to a boil. Lower the heat and simmer the sauce until it is smooth. Flavor with a few drops of sherry at the end of cooking.

5. Coat the pineapple and ham with the sauce and serve immediately.

queen pineapple

cayenne pineapple

Storing

Pineapples are very perishable and bruise easily. This fruit tends to ferment when kept too long at room temperature and deteriorates if exposed to temperatures below 44°F. It should be consumed as soon as possible. Pineapple will keep for 1 or 2 days at room temperature but it will not become any sweeter, only slightly less acid. Keep a close eye on it to make sure it does not spoil before you get a chance to eat it. Pineapple can be stored wrapped in a perforated plastic bag in the refrigerator, where it will keep for 3 to 5 days. It is tastier when taken out of the refrigerator a few minutes before serving. Cut pineapple will also keep in the refrigerator for several days if it is immersed in liquid and stored in an airtight container. Pineapple can be cut and frozen in its juice or in syrup, but it tends to lose some of its flavor when frozen.

red Spanish pineapple

Jaboticaba

Myrciaria cauliflora, **Myrtaceae**

The jaboticaba tree is a native of Brazil. Standing close to 40 feet high, this evergreen grows in warm subtropical and cool tropical regions. Its spear-shaped leaves are 1 to 4 inches long, and it has small white flowers. Jaboticabas are harvested five or six times a year. Very popular in Brazil, this fruit is still relatively unknown elsewhere, although it has been introduced into South America, the United States, and more recently into Australia.

Jaboticabas develop on the trunk and larger branches of the tree and measure between ½ and 1½ inches in diameter. They are thick-skinned fruits and can be black or purple in color. The translucent whitish or pinkish flesh is juicy and sweet. It contains up to four small seeds.

Serving Ideas

Fresh jaboticabas can be eaten on their own, like grapes. They can also be added to fruit salads or used to garnish cheese plates or appetizers. They make succulent jams, jellies, juice, and wine.

Buying

Choose brightly colored jaboticabas that are undamaged, firm, and glossy.

Nutritional Information

water	87%
carbohydrates	13 g
calories	46
	per 100 g

Because of its high sugar content, the jaboticaba is a nourishing fruit. It is a source of vitamin C.

Storing

Jaboticabas can be wrapped in a perforated plastic bag and kept for 2 weeks in the refrigerator.

Carambola

Averrhoa carambola, Oxalidaceae

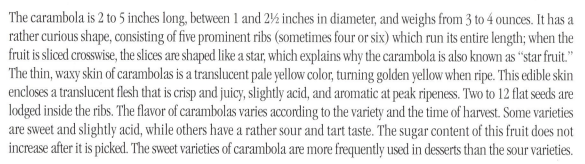

A native of Ceylon and the Moluccas, the carambola has been cultivated in Asia since ancient times. The carambola tree is between 20 and 33 feet high and bears clusters of sweet-smelling pink or purplish flowers. It grows in tropical and subtropical climates, and is cultivated in many countries around the world, including Brazil, Malaysia, China, Australia, Israel, the West Indies, and the United States. The arrival of carambolas in Western markets is relatively recent.

The carambola is 2 to 5 inches long, between 1 and 2½ inches in diameter, and weighs from 3 to 4 ounces. It has a rather curious shape, consisting of five prominent ribs (sometimes four or six) which run its entire length; when the fruit is sliced crosswise, the slices are shaped like a star, which explains why the carambola is also known as "star fruit." The thin, waxy skin of carambolas is a translucent pale yellow color, turning golden yellow when ripe. This edible skin encloses a translucent flesh that is crisp and juicy, slightly acid, and aromatic at peak ripeness. Two to 12 flat seeds are lodged inside the ribs. The flavor of carambolas varies according to the variety and the time of harvest. Some varieties are sweet and slightly acid, while others have a rather sour and tart taste. The sugar content of this fruit does not increase after it is picked. The sweet varieties of carambola are more frequently used in desserts than the sour varieties.

The **bilimbi** *(Averrhoa bilimbe),* a related species originating in Malaysia, is available mainly in Asian markets. The main producers are Asia, Australia, South and Central America, and the United States. The ribs of the bilimbi, which is smaller than the carambola, are barely visible. Its juicy flesh contains six or seven flat seeds and is a greenish yellow color; it is firmer and much more acidic than the flesh of carambola. This fruit is rarely eaten raw.

Buying

Choose a well-colored, firm fruit that is unbruised and has a pleasant fruity aroma.

Nutritional Information

water	91%
protein	0.6 g
fat	0.3 g
carbohydrates	7.8 g
calories	33
	per 100 g

Carambola is rich in vitamin C and is a source of vitamin A and potassium. It also contains several acids, including oxalic, tartaric, and malic acid.

Preparing

The carambola should be washed before it is consumed. If the edges of the ribs are blackened, remove them with a peeler or a knife. The seeds should also be removed. The carambola is often sliced crosswise to emphasize its decorative star shape.

Serving Ideas

Carambola can be eaten raw or cooked, and blends just as well with vegetables as with fruits. It makes a savory treat sprinkled with a vinaigrette and can be used as a vegetable side dish or cooked in a stir-fry with seafood and vegetables. To preserve its flavor, cook carambola for a very short time. Thin carambola slices make a decorative substitute for lemon slices to accompany fish or seafood dishes and are also used to garnish cocktails, appetizers, cakes and pies, and cheese platters. Carambola can also be used to make marinades and jellies, incorporated into sorbets and puddings, and made into a refreshing juice. The bilimbi is usually consumed cooked. It is used in marinades, jams, and jellies, and can also be added to soups, sauces, and sweet-and-sour dishes. It makes a good juice and often replaces mango in Indian chutneys.

Storing

Despite its fragile appearance, carambola keeps well. It can be left out at room temperature if eaten within a few days or if it is not yet quite ripe. When stored in the refrigerator, a carambola that is in good condition will keep for as long as 15 days.

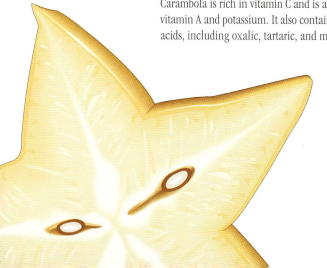

Cherimoya

Annona cherimola, **Annonaceae**

Some varieties of cherimoya are covered with large scales. The skin, whose color ranges from bronze to green, is fragile and inedible.

This fruit, native to the Andes, can be found growing in tropical and subtropical regions, and is borne by a thorny-branched tree that can reach up to 24 feet high. Because the scent of cherimoya flowers is too strong to attract insects, the trees are often pollinated manually to produce more fruits. The cherimoya is cultivated in a number of countries, including the United States (California), Chile, Mexico, Peru, Ecuador, Spain, Israel, and Australia.

The name "cherimoya" is derived from *chirimoya,* a word meaning "cold seed" in Quechua (the Inca language still spoken by the Indian peoples of Peru and Bolivia). There are over 50 varieties of this fruit.

The cherimoya belongs to the custard-apple family, which includes the soursop and the sweetsop. Depending on the variety, the fruit may be cone-shaped, oval, spherical, or heart-shaped, and can weigh anywhere between ½ and 4½ pounds. Some varieties are covered with large scales. The skin color varies from bronze to green, turning to yellow and eventually almost black as the fruit ripens. This fragile layer of skin is too bitter to be eaten. The fragrant whitish pulp of the cherimoya is sweet and juicy, with a slightly acid taste and granular texture (although less so than the pear). It has the consistency of custard and contains numerous hard and inedible seeds.

The pleasing fragrance of the ripe cherimoya can turn into an unpleasant odor and spoil the fruit's flavor when it becomes overripe. Because it spoils so easily and does not stand up well to transportation, the cherimoya is usually picked before it is fully ripe. However fragile, the cherimoya is considered by many to be one of the finest and most flavorful of fruits.

Preparing

The cherimoya should be washed briefly before peeling it and cutting it into two or more sections. The fibrous center is discarded only if it is still hard. The seeds can be removed immediately, while eating the fruit, or before dicing or puréeing it.

Serving Ideas

The cherimoya is usually consumed raw, as cooking greatly alters its flavor. It is usually eaten chilled and scooped out with a spoon. Once cut, this fruit tends to oxidize quickly, and is therefore frequently sprinkled with orange juice to prevent discoloration. In Chile this is a classic way to enjoy the cherimoya. The cherimoya blends well in fruit salads; it is used in sorbets, ice cream, yogurt, pastry, and cookies. The fruit can also be cooked to make jam, jelly, or compote, or pressed to make juice.

Storing

The cherimoya ripens best at room temperature. It should therefore be refrigerated only once ripe; it will keep for 1 or 2 days in the refrigerator. Since it tends to ferment when overripe, the cherimoya should not be left out for too long.

This fruit is difficult to freeze, even when puréed, as it must be frozen at a specific stage in its maturation that is difficult to determine with accuracy. When frozen under suitable conditions, puréed cherimoya will keep for up to 4 months.

Buying

Choose a fragrant fruit that is intact and not too firm. Avoid bruised or blackish skin, and handle the cherimoya with care, as it is extremely fragile.

Nutritional Information

water	74%
protein	1.3 g
fat	0.4 g
carbohydrate	24 g
fiber	3.4 g
calories	94
	per 100 g

Because of its high carbohydrate content, the cherimoya is a very nutritious fruit. It is also a source of vitamin C and niacin.

Durian

Durio zibethinus, Bombaceae

F ruit of a tree native to the Malay Archipelago, which can grow as high as 65 to 130 feet. It is closely related to the baobab, the cacao tree, the cotton plant, and the mallow. The durian is rarely cultivated outside of Asia, as it does not adapt well to different climates. It is a large, oddly shaped fruit that resembles the jackfruit but does not belong to the same family. Although it gives off a foul odor when ripe, this fruit is extremely popular in the countries where it is grown. Because of its large size, its spines, and its strong odor, the durian is difficult to ship.

Durians can weigh up to 11 pounds and typically measure between 8 and 12 inches in diameter and 16 inches in length. The durian's rind has several grooves which crack when the fruit is ripe, providing a handy means to open the fruit. The inside is divided into five or six sections separated by an inedible white membrane. Each section contains up to six shiny edible seeds embedded in the pulp, which is whitish or light brown in color and is mild, creamy, and compact. The durian has a peculiar flavor that is difficult to describe and that is not to everyone's liking.

Buying

Choose durians with undamaged skin in order to reduce the risk of spoiling. A yellowish rind is a good indication of the fruit's ripeness.

Nutritional Information

water	81.1%
fat	0.8 g
carbohydrates	15 g
fiber	1.6 g
calories	81
	per 100 g

The durian is rich in potassium and is a good source of vitamin C. It is said to be an aphrodisiac. It is best not to soak this fruit in alcohol and not to drink alcohol when eating it, as an unpleasant fermentation is caused by the mixing of alcohol and durians.

Preparing

Open the durian by running a sharpened knife along its grooves. Scoop out the flesh with a spoon and remove the seeds.

Serving Ideas

Once accustomed to the foul smell of the durian, many people find this fruit very pleasant tasting. The durian is often eaten fresh using a spoon. It can also be added to yogurt and ice cream, and is sometimes cooked to make jam. In Asia, a popular way to eat it is with sticky rice or, as in China, in pastries.

Roasted or baked, the seeds of the durian can be eaten like nuts. The powder obtained from crushed seeds is used to make confections.

Storing

The durian will ripen at room temperature. Because its skin cracks at maturity, avoid spoilage by consuming it immediately or refrigerating it. Wrap it well and store it away from the other food in the refrigerator. In Malaysia durians are preserved in brine to ensure their availability throughout the year.

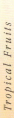

Jackfruit

Artocarpus heterophyllus, **Moraceae**

Jackfruit is entirely covered with short, sharp spines.

Fruit of the jackfruit, a tree believed to be native to the region between India and Malaysia. Jackfruit is currently grown in most tropical countries. While it is a staple food in many Asian countries, its commercial value is limited by its relative fragility and by its large size, which complicates handling. This fruit is particularly popular in Sri Lanka and India.

Jackfruit is a close relative of breadfruit, but while the former is used only as a vegetable, the latter is also eaten as a fruit. The jackfruit is also an ornamental tree which can grow as high as 33 to 50 feet. Like all trees of its family, it secretes a white viscous liquid.

The trunk of the tree produces a number of flowers which ripen into fruits that are attached to the trunk and branches by a long woody stem. Jackfruit is very large; its length varies between 1 and 3 feet and its diameter between 10 and 20 inches, depending on the variety. It usually weighs between 15 and 33 pounds, but some varieties can weigh up to 65 pounds. The fruit's pale green or yellowish green skin turns a deeper shade of yellow as it ripens and is entirely covered with short, sharp spines.

The many varieties of jackfruit are divided into two main categories: soft-flesh varieties, which have a sweet, juicy pulp, and crisp-flesh varieties, whose pulp is less sweet and juicy. Jackfruit's whitish or yellowish pulp becomes golden yellow when it is perfectly ripe. It contains numerous large seeds (depending on the variety, fruits may contain between 50 and 500 seeds) of a whitish color. These seeds are edible and vary in length from ¾ to 1½ inches and in thickness from ½ to ¾ inch. Approximately 30% of a jackfruit's weight is composed of pulp and 11% of seeds. While fertilized jackfruit flowers can be eaten, the fruit's skin and core, as well as the skin of the seeds, are inedible. These parts are commonly used for livestock feed. Like the banana, jackfruit continues to ripen after picking. Its flavor is not altered significantly, even when it is picked slightly unripe.

Buying

When buying jackfruits, choose fruit without bruises or soft spots. When ripe, jackfruit should have a strong aroma. Because it is so large, this fruit is often sold precut.

Preparing

When cutting a jackfruit, oil your fingers and the knife in order to keep them from brecoming sticky with the fruit's viscous juice. Cut the fruit, discarding its seeds and the surrounding flesh.

Serving Ideas

Jackfruit is eaten as a vegetable when unripe and as a fruit when ripe. It can be eaten raw or cooked, on its own, shredded, or cut into pieces. It can also be used in fruit salads or added to ice cream. Cooked, it may be puréed or made into jam. Jackfruit can also be processed to make juice or flour, and it can be frozen or dried. Boiled or fried jackfruit is served as a dish, either on its own or with other vegetables. It is also made into chutney and added to curries.

In producing countries, jackfruit is often canned in brine or syrup. Its rind is candied or made into jelly, and is also used for its pectin. Boiled, the seeds are used as a vegetable; they can also be roasted and eaten like peanuts. The seeds may be canned on their own or with other vegetables, in brine or tomato sauce. They are also dried and ground to make a flour, which is used in India to make chapatis and *papadums*.

Nutritional Information

	jackfruit	*seeds*
water	72%	
protein	1.5 g	19 g
fat	0.3 g	1 g
carbohydrates	24 g	74 g
fiber	1 g	4 g
calories	98	383
		per 100 g

Jackfruit is rich in potassium. Dried jackfruit seeds contain B-complex vitamins, calcium, potassium, magnesium, phosphorus, iron, and sulfur.

Storing

Jackfruit will keep at room temperature for 3 to 10 days. Cut or ripe jackfruit should be refrigerated. It will freeze better if covered with a syrup containing equal quantities of sugar and water, to which a bit of citric acid has been added.

Tree tomato

Cyphomandra betacea, **Solanaceae**

O riginally from the Andean region of South America, the tree tomato belongs to the large nightshade family, which also includes the tomato, pepper, potato, and eggplant. The tree on which it grows is from 6 to 10 feet in height and begins to yield fruits after 18 months, reaching its peak production after 3 or 4 years. It also goes by the more exotic name of "tamarillo," given to it in 1967 by New Zealand producers for marketing purposes. New Zealand is one of the largest producers of this fruit, which is also cultivated in Central and South America, the West Indies, India, Australia, Southeast Asia, and certain countries of Africa, Kenya in particular.

Two varieties of tree tomatoes are widely commercialized, one being golden orange with yellowish flesh, and the other burgundy or purple with orange-colored flesh.

The tree tomato is oval and about the size of an egg, measuring 2 to 4 inches in length. Its smooth, satiny skin is bitter and inedible, and its firm flesh has a slightly tart flavor. The golden variety is milder and sweeter. Both varieties contain numerous edible blackish seeds similar to those of the tomato. The sweet-and-sour flavor of the tree tomato can be compared to the tomato, gooseberry, and alkakengi.

Buying

Choose tree tomatoes that are firm and intact with smooth, bright red, unblemished skin. When ripe, they should yield to light pressure of the fingers. Avoid unripe tree tomatoes, as they tend to be bitter.

Nutritional Information

water	86%
protein	2 g
fat	0.9 g
carbohydrates	10 g
fiber	1.6 g
calories	50
	per 100 g

The tree tomato is rich in vitamins A and C as well as calcium, potassium, phosphorus, sodium, and magnesium.

Preparing

Peel tree tomatoes with a knife, or blanch them first for easy removal of the skin. The juice of the red tree tomato leaves indelible stains.

Serving Ideas

The tree tomato can be eaten raw when it is very ripe; simply cut it in half and sprinkle it with a little sugar or salt, or with lime or lemon juice. It can also be puréed and used to flavor yogurt, ice cream, sorbets, and cocktails. Unripe, it is often cooked like a vegetable. When cooked with other fruits, it should be used in moderation, as its flavor can be overpowering.

The tree tomato and the tomato are interchangeable in most recipes. It is good as an accompaniment to meat, poultry, and fish, and makes delicious sauces as well as marinades, jams, and jellies. For a refreshingly different salad, add tree tomatoes that have been marinated in oil and vinegar for 1 or 2 hours.

Storing

Leave tree tomatoes to ripen at room temperature. Once ripe, they can be stored in the refrigerator in a perforated plastic bag, where they will stay fresh for about 2 weeks. Tree tomatoes freeze well, either whole after being peeled, or cut into pieces and sprinkled with sugar. They are also cooked and frozen as a purée.

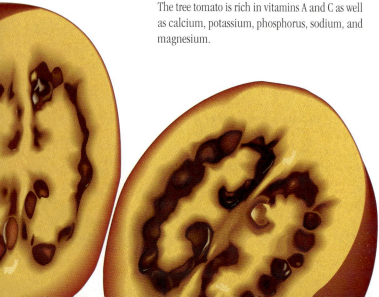
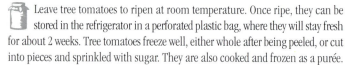

Rambutan

Nephelium lappaceum, Sapindaceae

Originally from Malaysia, the rambutan grows in clusters on a small evergreen tree. Related to the lychee and the longan, it is widely grown in Southeast Asia, particularly in Indonesia. There are over 50 varieties of this fruit. Covered on the outside with soft spikes, it looks rather like a small hedgehog. Its appearance accounts for its Malayan name, *rambout,* which means "hair"; it is also known as the "hairy lychee."

Rambutans have a diameter of about 2 inches and are covered with a fragile shell that is easily split open and varies in color from red to yellowish brown. The whitish pulp is juicy and translucent, and is similar in texture to the lychee. Like the lychee, the flesh surrounds a single inedible seed that is flat and almond-shaped. The flavor of the rambutan varies from sweet, mild, and fragrant to slightly sour or acid, depending on the variety. Its scent is less pronounced than that of the lychee.

Buying

Choose rambutans with a light reddish hue and greenish spikes; the skin should show no signs of moisture. Avoid dark-skinned and dry fruits or those leaking a sour-smelling juice, as they are likely to be old.

Preparing

Rambutans can be peeled easily by slicing open and gently removing the shell with the fingers or a knife, taking care not to cut the flesh. An original way of serving a rambutan consists of removing only the top half of the shell and serving it like an egg in the bottom half.

Serving Ideas

This fruit is often used like the lychee, for which it can substitute in all recipes. It is delicious on its own, added to a fruit salad, or served with ice cream. Cooked rambutan may accompany vegetables and meat, or it can be used as a stuffing. Rambutans are also canned in syrup.

Storing

Rambutans are perishable fruits and are most flavorful when fresh. They will keep for only a few days in the refrigerator. Conserved in a light syrup or made into jam, they will keep for 3 to 4 months.

Nutritional Information

water	82%
protein	1.0 g
fat	0.1 g
carbohydrates	16.5 g
fiber	1.1 g
calories	64
	per 100 g

The rambutan is rich in vitamin C and contains iron and potassium.

Tropical Fruits

241

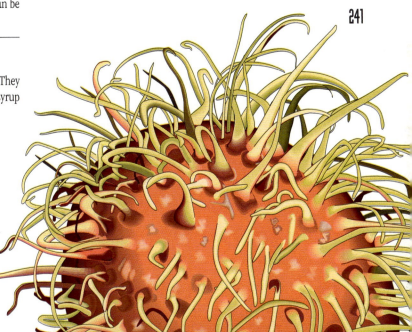

Persimmon

Diospyros spp., **Ebenaceae**

The persimmon tree, thought to be of Chinese origin, belongs to the large family of hardwoods that includes ebony; however, it is the only tree in this family to bear edible fruits. The persimmon is a winter fruit that remains on the tree even after the leaves have fallen. In Japan, where it is called "kaki," it is the national fruit. Other producers include China, Korea, Israel, and the United States. The hundreds of varieties of persimmons are classified into two main groups: the Asian persimmon *(Diospyros Kaki)*, known and cultivated for over a thousand years, and the American persimmon *(Diospyros virginiana)*, which grows wild in the southeastern United States. American Indians dried persimmons to ensure their availability year-round.

Among the Asian varieties, the *hachiya* and the *fuyu*, rather like tomatoes in size and appearance, are the most common. The *hachiya* is heart-shaped, with bright orange flesh and skin. It should be consumed when it is soft, a sign that it is fully ripe. Unripe, the *hachiya* is astringent and inedible. This fruit turns from green or yellow to bright red as it ripens. At peak ripeness, the tender flesh of these varieties is sweet and very fragrant, slightly viscous, with an almost liquid texture. The other well-known variety, the *fuyu*, contains no tannins and can thus be eaten either firm or ripe. Israel is a major producer of a type of *fuyu* called *Sharon*. The flesh contains up to eight large brown inedible seeds.

Nutritional Information

water	80%
protein	0.6 g
fat	0.2 g
carbohydrates	19 g
fiber	1.6 g
calories	70
	per 100 g

The persimmon is a good source of vitamin A and contains potassium, vitamin C, and copper. It is said to have a mild laxative effect.

Buying

When shopping for persimmons, ask which variety is on display. Since the persimmon is a very colorful fruit, its color cannot be relied upon as a sign of ripeness. In general, however, look for undamaged specimens and avoid those that are greenish or yellow.

Serving Ideas

The persimmon is delicious raw; simply remove the top or cut the fruit in half, and scoop out the flesh with a spoon. The *fuyu* variety can be eaten like an apple. Persimmons are also made into purée, with a few drops of lemon juice added to prevent discoloration. They make a good topping on ice cream, cakes, Bavarian cream, and crêpes, and they enliven fruit salads, rice, seafood, and poultry. The persimmon also adds a pleasant flavor to yogurts, custards, and other desserts, and is a good accompaniment to cheese. It can be dried, canned, or made into jam.

Storing

Persimmons will ripen at room temperature. To hasten this process, place the fruits in a paper bag, either alone or with another fruit that produces ethylene gas, such as an apple or banana. Keep ripe persimmons in the refrigerator. They may be frozen whole or puréed; add 1½ tablespoons of lemon juice to the purée (1 cup) to prevent discoloration.

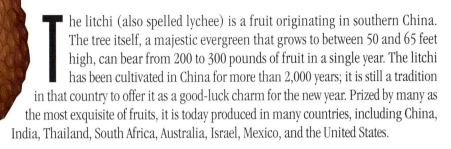

Litchi

Litchi chinensis, Sapindaceae

he litchi (also spelled lychee) is a fruit originating in southern China. The tree itself, a majestic evergreen that grows to between 50 and 65 feet high, can bear from 200 to 300 pounds of fruit in a single year. The litchi has been cultivated in China for more than 2,000 years; it is still a tradition in that country to offer it as a good-luck charm for the new year. Prized by many as the most exquisite of fruits, it is today produced in many countries, including China, India, Thailand, South Africa, Australia, Israel, Mexico, and the United States.

When ripe, the shell of the litchi is pinkish or reddish in color, turning brownish as the fruit ages. The flesh encloses an inedible brownish stone.

The litchi is 1 to 2 inches in diameter and is covered with a thin shell that is rough on the outside and smooth inside. This shell hardens after the fruit is picked and is very easy to remove. It is pinkish or reddish in color, and turns brownish as the fruit ages. Litchis are very vulnerable to cold temperatures. The translucent, pearly white flesh is crisp, refreshingly juicy, and very fragrant and sweet. It encloses a smooth, nonclinging brown stone that is hard and inedible. Although the flavor of the litchi varies with its degree of maturity, it generally resembles a combination of the strawberry, the rose, and the muscat grape.

Litchis should be eaten at peak ripeness, since unripe litchis are gelatinous and rather bland, while overripe fruits have lost much of their flavor. Once picked, the litchi does not continue to ripen. The fact that it does not stand up well to the rigors of shipping may explain why it is sometimes brownish and rather tasteless by the time it reaches Western markets.

Buying

 Litchis are sold fresh or canned in syrup; they can also be found dried or candied. When buying fresh litchis, look for fruits with a healthy blush and no cracks.

Preparing

Peeling litchis is easy: Simply split the shell open with your fingers or a knife, taking care not to cut the flesh, and peel the skin off. Depending on the use, the stones may also be removed.

Serving Ideas

The litchi is delicious fresh; it makes a tasty dessert on its own, or as an exotic addition to fruit salads. It can also be used to flavor or accompany rice, vegetables, stuffings, and sauces. In Chinese cooking, litchis are often blended with meat and fish.

Cooking

Cook litchis as briefly as possible to preserve their delicate flavor. When prepared with other food, they should be added at the end.

Storing

Litchis will keep for several weeks wrapped in a paper towel and placed in a perforated plastic bag in the refrigerator. However, they are at their best when eaten as fresh as possible. If left too long, they will ferment and become acid. Litchis may be frozen in their shell.

Nutritional Information

water	82%
protein	0.8 g
fat	0.4 g
carbohydrates	16.5 g
fiber	0.5 g
calories	66
	per 100 g

Fresh litchis are rich in vitamin C and are a good source of potassium; they also contain copper and magnesium.

Longan

Dimocarpus longan, Sapindaceae

The fruit of a majestic tree that can grow as high as 130 feet, the longan, a native of India, is closely related to the litchi and rambutan. Consumed in Asia for thousands of years, this tropical fruit is now cultivated mainly in Asian countries, the United States, and Australia. In China, shampoo is made from the seeds of longan, which have a high saponin content.

Longans grow in clusters and are covered with a smooth, thin orange shell that changes to brown and hardens when the fruit is ripe. Inside, the transparent white flesh is juicy and sweet, although slightly less flavorful than that of the litchi. The flesh encloses a large, smooth brown seed that is inedible. The Chinese call this fruit "eye of the dragon" because of the white eye-shaped spot on the seed.

Buying

 When choosing longans, look for uncracked, brightly colored specimens.

Nutritional Information

	fresh longan
water	83%
protein	1.3 g
fat	0.1 g
carbohydrates	15 g
fiber	0.4 g
	per 100 g

Longans are an excellent source of vitamin C and potassium, and contain magnesium and copper.

Cooking

To preserve their flavor, add longans at the end of cooking and avoid overcooking them.

Preparing

The longan's shell can be removed by splitting it open at the stem end and peeling it off. Depending on the intended use, longans can be pitted in advance or at the moment of consumption.

Serving Ideas

Longans are delicious eaten out of hand. They also add an exotic touch to fruit salads, rice, vegetables, salads, and sauces. They are good poached or added to a stir-fry. Longans are also available canned in syrup or in dried form; dried longans look like large raisins.

Storing

To store longans, wrap them in a paper towel to absorb excess moisture and place them in a perforated plastic bag in the refrigerator. They will keep for 2 to 3 weeks, although they tend to lose some of their flavor as they age. For maximum flavor, they should be eaten as soon as possible. Longans can be frozen in their shell.

Papaya

Carica papaya, Caricaceae

papaya

Fruit of the papaya tree, which is believed to be native to Central America. The papaya tree usually measures between 6 and 33 feet in height. According to botanical criteria, it is not truly a tree, since its long trunk is not sufficiently woody and its leaves grow only at the top. A papaya tree may produce from 30 to 150 fruits per year. The papaya is ready to be picked as soon as its skin is streaked with yellow; 4 to 5 days later, it is usually ripe. Papaya has long been appreciated by Latin American Indians. The Spanish and Portuguese had a hand in spreading its culture throughout the world, and papayas are now cultivated in most tropical and subtropical climates, particularly in Brazil, Mexico, Thailand, Indonesia, and India.

The papaya tree propagates easily, grows quickly, and blooms continuously, producing fruits all year long. However, it has a limited lifespan. Unripe papayas contain an odorless, whitish liquid; it is from this latex that papain, an enzyme with properties similar to the bromelin in pineapples or to the actidin in kiwis, is extracted. This enzyme tenderizes meat and prevents gelatin from gelling. This "solvent" sap is present in the tree's trunk, limbs, leaves, and fruit, particularly when it is still unripe. It is used for medicinal purposes and in various fields, including the food, leather, silk, wool, and brewing industries. Green papaya latex is also used in chewing gum.

There are about 50 types of papayas of the *Carica* variety, most of which are inedible. The mountain papaya *(Carica pubescens)* and the babaco *(Carica pentagonia)* are less common.

Papayas are usually pear- or cylinder-shaped and measure from 4 to 20 inches; they can weigh anywhere from a few ounces to over 20 pounds. Commercial varieties are generally small, the Hawaiian "Solo" being one of the most common. The papaya's thin, smooth skin is inedible; it ranges in color from orange to reddish yellow or yellowish green. The color of its juicy pulp is usually a yellowish orange of varying intensity, but it may also be yellow or red. Its texture is similar to that of the cantaloupe, yet softer. The fruit's central cavity contains numerous seeds embedded in a mucilaginous substance. They resemble large peppercorns and have a peppery taste. The papaya's mellow flavor resembles that of the melon; its sweetness and fragrance may vary.

Papayas grow in clusters at the top of the tree. They are picked as soon as they are streaked with yellow.

Buying

When buying papayas, choose fruits with an almost completely reddish orange skin that yields slightly to the touch. A few black or moldy spots will not affect the flavor. Avoid hard, completely green papayas, as they have been picked too early and will be flavorless. They will never ripen. Also avoid very soft or bruised fruit.

Serving Ideas

Papaya is delicious scooped out with a spoon and eaten just like melon, with or without sugar; sprinkle it with lime or lemon juice, Port, or rum. It is added to yogurt, pudding, sorbet, and ice cream. To avoid softening the other fruits, add papaya to fruit salads just before serving them. Papaya may be puréed or pressed to make juice. It is also cooked to make jam, chutney, and ketchup. Like melon, papaya goes well with baked ham, prosciutto, and smoked salmon. It is delicious stuffed with fruit, chicken, or seafood salads.

Green papaya can be used like winter squash and may even serve as a substitute for it in most recipes. Before using it, it is sometimes necessary to drain it of its white, acidic sap. Green papaya can also be stuffed, fried, added to fricassees or ratatouille, marinated, or served with dressing.

Papaya seeds may be ground and used like pepper. Some people like to crunch on a few of them when they eat the fruit. The babaco papaya is made into jam or canned. In South America, it is often used as an ingredient in cake recipes. The babaco is rarely made into juice because it is too acidic.

Nutritional Information

water	89%
protein	0.6 g
fat	0.1 g
carbohydrates	10 g
fiber	0.9 g
calories	39
	per 100 g

Papaya is an excellent source of vitamin C, as well as a good source of potassium and vitamin A. It is thought to have stomachic and diuretic properties. Its seeds cleanse the intestines. Brazilians make a sedative syrup from papaya juice.

Tropical Fruits

245

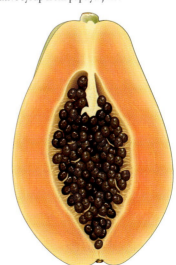

babaco

Storing

Papaya is a relatively fragile fruit. Leave it out at room temperature if it needs to ripen, placing it in a paper bag to accelerate the process. Papayas must be eaten as soon as they are ripe. Do not store unripe papayas at temperatures below 45°F, as this will halt the ripening process. Ripe papaya keeps for a few days in the refrigerator but does not freeze well.

Pepino

Solanum muricatum, Solanaceae

Fruit of a plant native to Peru. While cultivation of the pepino in the Andean region goes back many years, this fruit is a relative newcomer to Western markets. *Pepino* is a Spanish word meaning "cucumber," a misleading name considering that this fruit differs greatly from the cucumber. Like the eggplant, pepper, tomato, and potato, the pepino belongs to the Solanaceae family.

The pepino grows on a shrub that can reach a height of 3 feet; it has evergreen leaves and bears magnificent purple flowers. The fruit resembles a small melon; it has a slightly elongated shape and measures between 4 and 6 inches in length. Its thin satiny skin turns from pale green to golden yellow as the fruit ripens, and is always streaked with purple. Its flesh can be orange or yellowish in color and contains soft edible seeds at its core. The flesh is somewhat floury and slightly sweeter than a melon's.

Buying

 Choose pepinos that are firm and undamaged, with a delicate fragrance.

Nutritional Information

water	93%
protein	0.6 g
fat	0.1 g
carbohydrates	5 g
fiber	1 g
calories	22
	per 100 g

In addition to being rich in vitamin C, pepinos are said to relieve rheumatism and are used to treat bronchitis and various skin problems.

Storing

The pepino will ripen at room temperature. Once ripe, it will keep for a day or two in the vegetable compartment of the refrigerator.

Preparing

Washed and cut in half, the pepino can be served as is, or the flesh can be scooped out with a spoon. It can also be peeled and cut into slices.

Serving Ideas

 Unripe pepinos are often served cooked, and can be prepared like squash. When ripe, they are often simply cut in half and served like a melon. Some people prefer to eat them chilled. Pepinos are delicious flavored with ginger, or sprinkled with lemon or lime juice, Grand Marnier, or Cointreau. The pepino may be added to appetizers, fruits salads, and mixed salads. Puréed, it is used to make ice cream, sorbets, and beverages. It can also be macerated in alcohol.

Feijoa

Feijoa sellowiana, **Myrtaceae**

Fruit of a shrub native to South America, the feijoa has evergreen leaves and magnificent bright red flowers. Certain varieties are cultivated for decorative use. The feijoa (also known as pineapple guava) belongs to the same family as the guava, the clove, and the eucalyptus. It was named after a Spaniard, Don J. da Silva Feijó, who was director of a museum of history in Brazil in the 19th century. Today New Zealand is one of the world's largest producers of this fruit.

The feijoa is 2 to 3 inches long and measures roughly 1 inch in diameter. Although its smooth but tough green skin is too bitter to be consumed, its cream-colored flesh is sweet and fragrant, with a slightly granular texture resembling that of a pear. The fruit's center is slightly gelatinous and contains tiny black seeds which are tender and edible. Depending on its stage of maturity, this fruit can have a sourish taste.

Buying

Choose a feijoa that is fragrant, tender to the touch, and unblemished. If the fruit is too firm, it will not be ripe and may have an acidy and sometimes even bitter taste.

Preparing

The flesh of the feijoa darkens when it is not consumed immediately. To prevent oxidation, sprinkle it with a bit of citrus juice.

Storing

Leave the feijoa out at room temperature until it ripens. This fruit should be eaten when exactly ripe. Store it in the refrigerator, where it will keep for a few days. Feijoa can be frozen fresh or cooked.

Serving Ideas

Peeled feijoa can be eaten fresh or cooked. It is delicious as is or added to fruit salads, yogurt, and other desserts. It should be used in moderate doses, however, as it has a rather strong fragrance. Feijoa can be cooked and made into jam or jelly. It is also good puréed and used as a flavoring for ice cream, sherbet, flans, or puddings. Feijoa goes well with apples and bananas, with which it is interchangeable in most recipes.

Nutritional Information

water	87%
protein	1.2 g
fat	0.8 g
carbohydrate	10.6 g
fiber	4.3 g
calories	50
	per 100 g

Feijoa is a good source of folic acid and contains vitamin C and potassium.

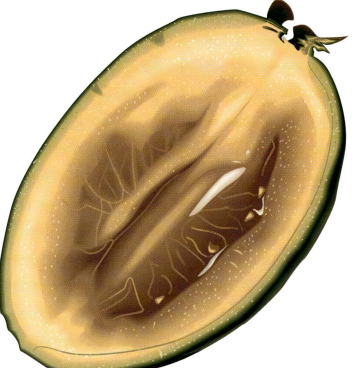

Jujube

Ziziphus jujuba, **Rhamnaceae**

Fruit of the jujube tree, a Chinese tree that grows in tropical and subtropical climates to heights varying between 26 and 33 feet. Also known as Chinese dates, these fruits have been used for their curative properties since ancient times. They are relatively rare in Europe and little known in North America, where they were introduced during the 19th century. Chinese dates are produced in small quantities in China, India, and Africa, as well as in the United States and in Mediterranean countries. North Americans are more familiar with the candy called the "jujube," which is made from jujube paste.

Depending on the variety, jujubes may be the size of an olive or of a date and may be round or oblong in shape. They contain an extremely hard and long two-part stone, one part of which contains an oily seed. Their smooth, firm, and shiny skin turns from green to maroon as they ripen. The greenish or whitish flesh of jujubes is not particularly juicy. It has a slightly floury texture but is crunchy at the same time. It is also mucilaginous and has a sweet-and-sour taste. Dried jujubes are slightly spongy and sweeter still.

Depending on the variety, jujubes are the size of an olive or a date and are round or oblong.

Nutritional Information

	fresh	dried
water	78%	
protein	1.2 g	
fat	0.2 g	
carbohydrates	20 g	74 g
fiber	1.4 g	
calories	70	287
		per 100 g

Fresh jujubes are an excellent source of vitamin C and a good source of potassium. They contain small quantities of magnesium, niacin, copper, and iron.

Dried jujubes provide a richer supply of energy. They are an excellent source of potassium, a good source of magnesium, and a source of vitamin C, copper, iron, phosphorus, and calcium. They are thought to have expectorant, emollient, calming, and diuretic properties.

Buying

When buying jujubes, choose firm, unblemished fruits. Dried jujubes should be heavy and wrinkled. Canned jujubes may be found in gourmet shops.

Serving Ideas

Fresh or dried, jujubes may be eaten plain or cooked. They are used like dates (which they can also replace) in desserts, soups, stuffing, and stews. Cooked jujubes are used in compotes and jams or made into a paste. This fruit may also be marinated, pressed to make juice, or fermented to make an alcoholic beverage.

Storing

Fresh jujubes should be refrigerated. Dried jujubes will keep indefinitely when stored away from heat and light in an airtight container.

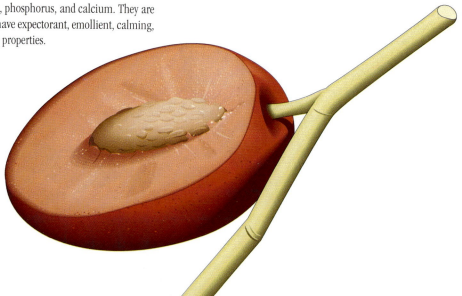

Kiwi fruit

Actinidia chinensis, **Actinidiaceae**

The kiwi fruit, native to China, was originally called "Chinese gooseberry" by westerners. Introduced into New Zealand in 1906, the variety was much improved, and for many years that country monopolized commercial production of the fruit. It wasn't until 1953 that it was renamed "kiwi" after a flightless bird (also known as the apteryx) native to New Zealand, which it resembles by virtue of its fuzzy brown skin.

The kiwi is the fruit of a long, flexible, climbing creeper resembling a vine; the plant is generally pruned when it reaches a length of 7 to 10 feet. Today about ten varieties of kiwi fruit are cultivated worldwide, including in the United States, France, Italy, Spain, Israel, Chile, Australia, South Africa, and Russia. In North America, the Hayward variety is the most common.

The kiwi fruit is an egg-shaped berry some 3 inches long and weighing between 2 and 4 ounces. The emerald-green flesh is sweet and juicy, and slightly acid. Small edible black seeds form a decorative circle around the yellowish core of the fruit. Although the thin and downy brownish skin is edible, most people prefer to peel it.

Buying

Kiwis are picked when they are ripe but still firm. Unlike most other fruits, they become sweeter if left to ripen at room temperature. Choose kiwis that are intact and unblemished. When ripe, the flesh should be soft, yielding to light pressure of the fingers. Those that are very soft or damaged will lack flavor. The size of the fruits is no indication of their quality.

Serving Ideas

This fruit is very good fresh; it can be peeled and eaten as it is, or cut in half and scooped out with a spoon. It may be sliced into cereals, yogurt, ice cream, sorbets, and fruit salads, but it should be added at the last minute to prevent it from softening the other fruits. It makes a colorful garnish on appetizers, cheese plates, cakes, pies, and Bavarian creams, and blends well with meat, poultry, and fish. It is also used to make a sweet-and-sour sauce to accompany meat, and can be incorporated into other sauces and soups. Kiwis are also an excellent addition to mixed salads. When pressing kiwis to make juice, avoid grinding the seeds, as they tend to impart a bitter taste to the juice.

Cooking

Kiwis should be cooked as little as possible, to preserve their color and delicate flavor.

Storing

Leave kiwis to ripen at room temperature until they yield to a light pressure of the fingers. To speed the ripening process, place the fruits in a paper bag, either alone or, to accelerate things even further, with an apple or a banana. Ripe kiwis can be kept in the refrigerator for several days, while unripe kiwis will keep for 2 to 3 weeks.

Nutritional Information

water	83%
protein	1 g
fat	0.4 g
carbohydrates	15 g
fiber	3.4 g
calories	61
	per 100 g

The kiwi is an excellent source of vitamin C and potassium. It contains magnesium as well as traces of phosphorus, iron, and vitamin A. Kiwis supply twice as much vitamin C as do oranges and lemons; so they are used to combat scurvy. They are also diuretic and laxative.

The kiwi contains actinic and bromic acids, enzymes that are activated on contact with air and that give it certain properties, the most notable being that of a food tenderizer. Unripe kiwis that are peeled and left out will even tenderize themselves. This trait becomes undesirable in a fruit salad, however, as it causes the other fruits to soften. It also stops gelatin from solidifying and causes milk to turn sour (although it does not affect yogurt or ice cream).

Pomegranate

Punica granatum, Punicaceae

The pomegranate tree is thought to be a native of Persia, where the pomegranate was cultivated as early as 4,000 years ago. Highly prized in Mesopotamia and ancient Egypt, this fruit still plays a important role in Iranian cooking today. In Western countries the pomegranate was fairly popular until the 19th century, but it has since lost some of its appeal, particularly as a fresh fruit. The pomegranate is mentioned in the Bible and is often represented as a symbol of fertility in mythology. The prophet Mohammed advocated that believers eat pomegranates to purge the body of longing. This fruit also appears in ancient Chinese paintings. Ancient Egyptians buried pomegranates with their dead.

The pomegranate grows in most tropical and subtropical climates. Although the tree can adapt to different climatic conditions and soil types, it grows best in regions with cold winters and very hot summers. The main producers of pomegranates are Iran, India, and the United States.

The pomegranate tree can reach 20 to 23 feet in height, but domestic varieties are usually pruned to a height of 6 to 12 feet. The tree bears large trumpet-shaped flowers, and its fruits are generally harvested 5 to 7 months after flowering. Pomegranates are picked when they are fully mature, as they do not continue to ripen after harvesting. The name of this fruit is derived from the Latin *granatum,* meaning "fruit of many seeds."

Measuring around 3 inches in diameter, the pomegranate has a thick, leathery skin, which is inedible. The skin of pomegranates is usually bright red, although some varieties may be yellowish. Inside, thick white membranes divide the fruit into six sections enclosing a large number of small edible seeds. The membranes are bitter and inedible. Depending on the variety, the small pulpy seeds are crimson red, dark pink, or pinkish; they contain a small pip at their center. The flesh of pomegranate seeds is very juicy and pleasantly refreshing, with a tangy-sweet flavor. Many people prefer to eat only the pulp and to discard the more bitter-tasting inner pips.

Buying

Choose a large and unblemished pomegranate that is heavy for its size; it should be brightly colored with tinges of brown. Avoid wrinkled fruits, as well as those with dull or pale skin.

Storing

Pomegranates can be left out at room temperature for a few days or stored in the refrigerator, where they will keep for about 3 weeks. Pomegranates freeze well; simply remove the seeds and freeze them, wrapped in plastic wrap.

Serving Ideas

Pomegranate seeds are often eaten fresh. In many tropical countries, they are popular both as an ingredient and as a condiment. They enhance both the appearance and the taste of fruit salads, mixed salads, soups and sauces, cheeses, vegetables, poultry, fish, and seafood. Pomegranates play a major role in Iranian cuisine; in Europe the fruit is best known for its juice, which is sold as grenadine syrup. Grenadine is used to prepare beverages and cocktails, ice cream, sorbets, and other desserts.

Preparing

Slice the skin of the pomegranate into four equal parts and pry it open carefully. The seeds and surrounding pulp can be eaten directly or placed in a bowl and scooped up with a spoon. Discard the bitter-tasting membranes.

The juice of the pomegranate can be sipped by inserting a straw through a hole in the skin. Roll the fruit first, pressing it lightly to release the juice from the seeds. This juice is relatively bitter because it contains some of the tannins from the membranes and skin. The fruit should be handled with care, as pomegranate juice stains readily.

1 *Slice the skin of the pomegranate into four equal parts with a knife.*

2 *Divide the fruit into halves, and then into quarters.*

3 *Detach the seeds and place them in a bowl to enjoy when desired.*

Nutritional Information

water	81%
protein	1 g
fat	0.3 g
carbohydrates	17 g
fiber	0.2 g
calories	68
	per 100 g

The pomegranate is a good source of potassium. It also supplies vitamin C and pantothenic acid, as well as traces of sodium and niacin. The characteristic tart flavor of pomegranates is accounted for by the presence of numerous organic acids, including a high citric acid content.

The pomegranate is produced by large flowers that blossom amidst a shiny and luxuriant foliage.

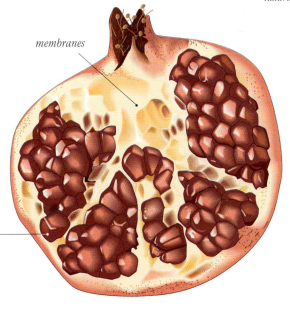

membranes

seeds

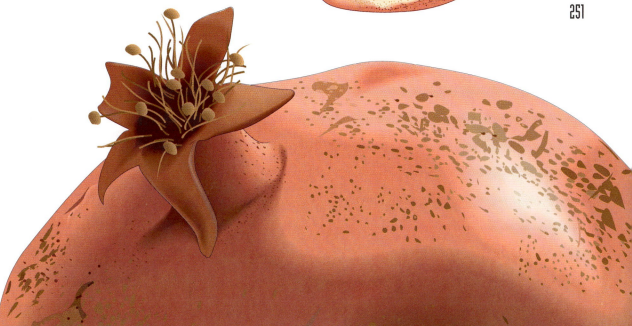

Tropical Fruits

251

Passion fruit

Passiflora spp., **Passifloraceae**

The shape of the beautiful flowers is said resemble instruments of Christ's Passion (crown of thorns, hammers, and nails).

Fruit of a climbing vine native to Brazil, also known as the granadilla. The name "passion fruit" comes from Spanish missionaries who, upon discovering the plant in South America, found that parts of the flowers resembled instruments of the Passion and crucifixion of Christ (crown of thorns, hammers, and nails).

Passion fruit is cultivated in most tropical regions, including New Zealand, Africa, Malaysia, and the West Indies. There are some 400 different varieties of this plant, of which only about 30 produce edible fruits; few of these are sold commercially. The most common varieties found on the market are the size of an egg, but passion fruit can grow to be the size of a small melon.

Passion fruit has a thick, smooth, lustrous skin that is inedible. In commercially sold varieties, the skin is yellow, orange, or purple in color. As the fruit ripens, the skin becomes thinner and wrinkles. The pulp of passion fruit has a gelatinous texture and ranges in color from pinkish green to shades of orange or yellow; it may also be white or colorless. The pulp is sweet and juicy, slightly tart, very fragrant, and refreshing. Unripe passion fruits are very tart. The pulp contains small blackish seeds that are crisp and edible.

Nutritional Information

water	73%
protein	2.2 g
fat	0.7 g
carbohydrates	23 g
calories	100
	per 100 g

Passion fruit is an excellent source of vitamin C, potassium, and sodium; it is also a source of iron, magnesium, phosphorus, niacin, and vitamin A.

The leaves and flowers of passion fruit are said to have an antispasmodic and narcotic effect; the seeds are used as a vermifuge.

Storing

Ripe passion fruit can be stored in the refrigerator, with or without its skin; it will keep for about a week.

The pulp can be frozen in an ice-cube tray, and will keep for several months if well wrapped.

Buying

Choose fruits that are wrinkled, unbruised, and heavy. Smooth skin is a sign that the fruit is unripe.

Serving Ideas

Passion fruit is tastiest when it is quite ripe; dimpled skin indicates that the fruit is ready for consumption. It is delicious fresh, scooped out with a spoon. Extremely fragrant, passion fruit makes an excellent flavoring in a number of dishes, even when used in small quantities; it is added to punches and cocktails, as well as to fruit salads, custards, crêpes, yogurt, ice creams and sorbets, cakes, puddings, and beverages. The pulp should be strained to remove the seeds. Passion fruit is also cooked to make jams and jellies, and can be fermented to make alcoholic beverages.

Guava

Psidium spp., **Myrtaceae**

ruit of the guava tree, which is native to tropical America and a member of the large myrtle family, along with cinnamon, nutmeg, clove, the eucalyptus, and the feijoa. The guava tree was widely cultivated by the Incas and is still very common in South America. It grows in a number of tropical and subtropical countries, chiefly in Africa, Australia, India, the southern United States, Brazil, and Taiwan.

The guava tree can grow up to 30 feet high and has aromatic flowers. The more than 150 species of guava bear fruits that vary in shape, size, color, and taste. The guava typically has a diameter of 2 to 3 inches. Its thin edible skin ranges in color from white to yellow, red, or green and sometimes has black or pink spots. The color of its flesh may be white, yellow, or salmon. It is extremely fragrant and has a slightly acid taste, which makes it a very refreshing fruit. It contains numerous small, hard edible seeds. The assertive flavor of the guava can be surprising.

The flesh of the guava is very fragrant and slightly acid, giving it a refreshing taste. It contains many small, hard edible seeds.

Buying

 When buying guavas, look for smooth, unblemished fruits that are neither too soft nor too hard. The overripe guava has a rather unappealing odor, while the unripe guava is inedible because it is too astringent.

Preparing

When ripe, the guava will yield to gentle pressure. It can be eaten before or after peeling it; simply cut the fruit in half and, if desired, remove the seeds.

Serving Ideas

The guava can be eaten fresh or cooked, and is used in both savory and sweet dishes. Cooked, it is made into jams, jellies, and chutneys. It can also be a delicious addition to sauces, fruit salads, pies, puddings, tapioca, ice cream, yogurt, and beverages. In Mexico, guava and sweet potato is a favorite combination.

Storing

The guava can be left to ripen at room temperature. Placing it in a paper bag will hasten the ripening process, while placing it in the refrigerator will have the opposite effect. A ripe guava will keep for a few days in the refrigerator.

Nutritional Information

water	86%
protein	0.8 g
fat	0.6 g
carbohydrates	12 g
fiber	5.6 g
calories	50
	per 100 g

Guavas are an excellent source of vitamin C and potassium; they contain vitamin A and niacin, as well as traces of phosphorus and calcium. They are known for their astringent and laxative properties.

Fig

Ficus carica, **Moraceae**

T he fruit of the fig tree, a majestic tree that is believed to have originated in the Mediterranean. The fig is not a fruit in the botanical sense of the word, but rather a fleshy receptacle containing a large number of small brittle seeds, or achenes, that are the actual fruits.

The history of the fig is a very ancient one; it has been valued for its nutritional and medicinal properties since the earliest times. As food, figs were consumed fresh, dried, or roasted; they were also used as a remedy and as a sweetening agent. In fact, figs were used as a sweetener well before sugar was even known. Figs were highly prized by the Greeks and the Romans, who introduced them into Europe. They were brought to America by Spanish conquistadors and missionaries, after whom "Mission" figs were named.

The fig is cultivated in many countries. The main producers today, in order of importance, are Turkey, Greece, the United States, Portugal, and Spain. The fig tree can live as long as 100 years. While they can grow to 100 feet, domestic fig trees are usually pruned to a height of about 16 feet. The trunk and branches contain a latex that has coagulating properties; in ancient Greece, shepherds used fig tree branches to stir cheese, thus accelerating the process of coagulation.

There are over 150 varieties of figs; colors vary from white to green, brown, red or purple, and sometimes almost black. The most common commercial varieties include:

- the **black fig,** which is sweet and rather dry, and is not as perishable as the others;

- the **green fig,** a thin-skinned, juicy variety;

- the **purple fig,** the juiciest and sweetest of the three, it is also the most perishable and is relatively rare.

Because they are highly perishable fruits, fresh figs are most frequently dried or preserved. They can be dried artificially or through exposure to the sun. Figs are sometimes coated with sugar or soaked in water to increase their weight and moisture content. It takes over 6 pounds of fresh figs to produce 2 pounds of dried figs.

Tropical Fruits

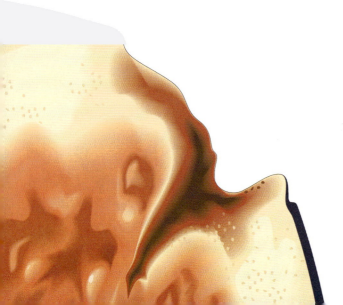

black fig

Buying

 When buying fresh figs, choose soft, plump specimens with firm stems. Avoid sodden, bruised, moldy, or sour-smelling fruits, as they are probably overripe. Dried figs should have a pleasant smell and be reasonably soft.

Preparing

Wash fresh figs gently and briefly before consuming them. Dried figs can be eaten as they are or soaked in water, juice, or alcohol.

Serving Ideas

Fresh and dried figs are often eaten out of hand. They are also incorporated into fruit salads and appetizers or served with cheese and ham. They can also be cooked to make compote or jam. Dried figs can be prepared in a variety of ways; they are excellent stuffed with almonds or other nuts, or with sections of orange. They are a popular dessert fruit.

Figs also play a role in savory cooking, blending well with rabbit, poultry, and game. They can be used in place of prunes in most recipes. Like barley and chicory, roasted figs are used as a coffee substitute. North Africans use figs to make *boukha,* a popular spirit. Figs are succulent poached or soaked in whisky, port, or semi-dry sherry.

Figs with Red Wine

SERVES 4

2 lb. (1 kg) fresh figs   *1 bottle strong red wine*
Sugar to taste

1. Peel the figs and cut them in half.

2. In a deep dish, arrange a first layer of figs; sprinkle with sugar and then with wine. Fill the dish with successive layers, sprinkling a little sugar and wine over each. The level of wine should rise to the surface of the last layer.

3. Leave to cool in the refrigerator for at least 2 hours before serving.

Nutritional Information

	fresh	*dried*
water	79%	28%
protein	0.8 g	3 g
fat	0.4 g	1.2 g
carbohydrates	19 g	65 g
fiber	3.3 g	9.3 g
calories	74	255
		per 100 g

Fresh figs are very nutritious. They are a good source of potassium and fiber. The nutritional elements of dried figs are more concentrated, making them even more nourishing. They are an excellent source of potassium and a good source of magnesium, iron, and copper; they also supply calcium, sodium, phosphorus, vitamin B_6, pantothenic acid, riboflavin, thiamine, and zinc.

Figs are held to be a good diuretic and laxative. The milky latex contained in the branches and leaves is said to rid the skin of calluses and corns.

The fig is not a fruit in the botanical sense of the word, but rather a fleshy receptacle containing a large number of small brittle seeds, or achenes, that are the actual fruits.

Storing

Fresh figs are highly perishable. They can be kept in the refrigerator for 1 or 2 days, but should be wrapped well to prevent them from absorbing odors. Dried figs should be kept in a cool, dry place, away from insects.

green fig

purple fig

Prickly pear

Opuntia ficus-indica, Cactaceae

The leaves of the prickly pear are covered with spines or prickly hairs. In season, the plant bears beautiful flowers that ripen into tasty pear-shaped fruits.

Also known as the Indian fig, the prickly pear is a member of the cactus family and is native to the tropical regions of the Americas, where it has been consumed by Indians since ancient times. It was introduced into Spain by Spanish explorers, who originally called it "tuna," as it was named in South America. The Moors, who called it the "Christian fig," brought it to North Africa.

The long flat leaves of the prickly pear are covered with spines or prickly hairs. In season they bear beautiful flowers that ripen into tasty pear-shaped fruits. Today prickly pears are grown all over the world, including in Mediterranean countries, South America, Mexico, the United States, Africa, and Asia. In Israel, where it is known as "Sharon's fruit," the prickly pear is the official national fruit. The berry is 2 to 4 inches long and has a thick, coarse skin that varies in color from green to yellow, orange, pink, or red depending on the variety. The skin has tubercles studded with thin, often invisible spines that prick the skin when the fruit is handled. The juicy pulp, which can be green, orange-yellow, or dark red in color, is tart, fairly sweet and fragrant, and contains numerous crisp edible seeds.

Buying

Most prickly pears sold commercially have had their spines removed. If not, they should be handled with care. When buying prickly pears, choose smooth fruits with unblemished skin.

Nutritional Information

water	81%
protein	0.8 g
fat	0.5 g
carbohydrates	17 g
fiber	1.1 g
calories	67
	per 100 g

The prickly pear is a very good source of magnesium and a good source of potassium. It also contains calcium, vitamin C, and sodium. It has astringent properties.

Preparing

The prickly pear should yield to gentle pressure of the fingers when ripe. To remove the skin, first cut off a slice at one end of the fruit and then make lengthwise incisions (not too deep) to make it easy to peel off. If the spines have not already been removed, do so before cutting by rubbing the skin with a cloth or thick paper or by brushing it under water; use gloves to protect your hands.

Serving Ideas

This fruit can be enjoyed eaten on its own or sprinkled with lemon or lime juice. If it is to be cooked, it should be passed through a sieve first in order to remove the seeds, which are not to everyone's taste and which tend to harden when heated. Prickly pears may be used to flavor sorbets, yogurts, and fruit salads, along with various other desserts. They add a surprising touch to green salads, and can also be puréed or made into jam or juice.

The long blade-shaped leaves of the prickly pear plant are edible, either raw or cooked. Remove the needles; then peel and cut the leaves into pieces before steaming, sautéeing, or stewing them. Mexicans like to add them to salads, omelets, and mashed beans. They can also be added to soup about 10 minutes before the end of cooking.

Storing

Prickly pears ripen at room temperature. When ripe, they should be consumed immediately or placed in the refrigerator, where they will keep for a few days.

Mangosteen

Garcinia mangostana, **Guttifereae**

F ruit of the mangosteen tree, native to Malaysia, the Philippines, and Indonesia. The cultivation of the mangosteen (also known as the mangostan) dates back several thousand years. The tree bears magnificent large pink flowers and is often grown for decorative purposes. Introduced into the West Indies toward the mid-19th century, this tropical tree is difficult to grow outside of its natural habitat and takes 10 to 15 years to bear fruit. More than 100 varieties are produced today.

The mangosteen is a round and peculiar-looking fruit that measures about 3 inches in diameter. Its thick hard rind is inedible and contains tannins, which are used for dyeing in the leather industry. As the fruit ages, the rind takes on a deep purple color. Under this shell is a thick reddish membrane which encloses the flesh and is also inedible. The exquisite pearly white flesh inside is sweet and juicy; it is divided into five or six segments, some of which contain an edible pinkish stone. The fleshy part represents only a quarter of the fruit's total weight. The mangosteen is prized as one of the most succulent fruits of Asia.

The mangosteen tree bears magnificent large pink flowers and is often grown for decorative purposes. The mangosteen is prized as one of the most succulent fruits of Asia.

Buying

Choose mangosteens at their peak of ripeness; at their most flavorful, they have purple skin and should yield to gentle pressure. Avoid fruits with very hard skin, an indication that they are overripe.

Preparing

The best way to peel a mangosteen is to make an incision around the center of the fruit with a knife (taking care not to cut into the flesh) and remove the skin with a slight twisting movement.

Serving Ideas

The best way to enjoy a mangosteen is to eat it raw, as cooking detracts from its delicate flavor. Once peeled, it is divided into sections and eaten like an orange. Mangosteens are delicious served with strawberry or raspberry coulis, made into jam, or added to fruit salads. Puréed, they are used to flavor yogurt, ice cream, sorbets, cakes, and puddings. In Asia a vinegar is made from the mangosteen and oil is extracted from the seeds.

Storing

Mangosteens tend to spoil rapidly, so they should be consumed as soon as possible. While they will keep for 2 to 3 days at room temperature, and for a week or so in the refrigerator, they do not stand up well to freezing.

Nutritional Information

water	84%
protein	0.5 g
fat	0.3 g
carbohydrates	14.7 g
fiber	5.0 g
calories	57
	per 100 g

The mangosteen contains potassium and vitamin C, as well as traces of iron and niacin.

Mango

Mangifera indica, **Anacardiaceae**

The mango can be round, oval, or kidney-shaped; its smooth perfumed flesh clings to a large flattened stone.

Fruit of the mango tree, thought to be a native of India. Cultivated for over 6,000 years, mangoes were long unknown outside of Asia. They were introduced into Brazil by Portuguese explorers in the 18th century, after which they gradually became known throughout the world. The Portuguese named this fruit *manga,* an adaptation of *man-gay,* as the fruit is called in the Tamil language of southeastern India. Thailand, India, Pakistan, and Mexico are among the largest producers of mangoes today.

A relative of the pistachio and cashew, the mango tree grows in tropical climates and measures an average of 50 feet in height, although it can sometimes reach 100 feet. It produces an annual yield of about 100 fruits. There are over 1,000 different varieties of the mango, some of which are round, while others are oval or kidney-shaped. The fruit averages about 4 inches in length and weighs between 9 ounces and 3 pounds. Mangoes have a thin smooth skin that can be greenish, yellowish, or reddish in color, often tinged with purple, pink, orange-yellow, or red. The flesh is orange or orange-yellow, like that of the peach. While mangoes are sometimes fibrous, the flesh of most varieties is smooth, buttery, sweet, and fragrant. The flesh clings to the stone, which is quite large and flat. The slightly tart and spicy flavor of mangoes is surprisingly pleasant. Certain varieties, especially wild mangoes, have very little flesh and often leave an aftertaste of turpentine.

Buying

When ripe, mangoes have a wonderful, sweetly fragrant aroma and yield slightly to the touch. The skin may have a few black spots, an indication that the fruit is very ripe. Mangoes that are picked too early will have shriveled skin and a fibrous flesh that is very acid and unpleasant tasting, in addition to being of inferior nutritional value. Choose mangoes that are neither too hard nor too soft.

Preparing

Mangoes should be eaten peeled, as their skin may be irritating to the mouth. Mango juice leaves indelible stains on clothing.

1 Cut the mango in half by sliding the knife along each side of the stone, from top to bottom.

2 With the tip of a knife, cut a crisscross pattern in the flesh, without cutting the skin.

3 Turn the skin inside out so that the cubes of flesh pop up.

4 Detach the mango cubes from the skin with a knife.

Serving Ideas

The mango is delicious whether eaten on its own, in a fruit salad, or atop cereals or crêpes. It is a popular flavoring in yogurt, ice cream, and sorbets. Mangoes are also made into jams, jellies, marmalades, coulis, compote, and juice.

In Asia and the West Indies, it is not uncommon to eat unripe mangoes. They are used both raw and cooked in a variety of dishes, including appetizers, soups, and sauces; they are also cooked like a vegetable to accompany meat or fish. In India, green mangoes are a basic ingredient of traditional chutneys, as well as being used to flavor a yogurt-based beverage. In Thailand, puréed mangoes are dried in the sun to produce a nutritive paste that is very popular. At peak ripeness, mangoes blend deliciously with ham, duck, poultry, pork, fish, and legumes.

Chicken with Mangoes

SERVES 4

1 chicken (about 3 lb./1.5 kg)
Salt and pepper to taste
1 onion
2 mangoes
2 tbsp. butter
3 tbsp. peanut oil
1 cup (250 ml) chicken stock
1 tsp. grated lemon zest
Pinch of ground cinnamon
Pinch of ground coriander

1. Cut the chicken into pieces. Season with salt and pepper and set aside. Finely chop the onion. Peel the mangoes, cut them in half, and remove the stone. Cut the flesh into slices.

2. In a frying pan, melt the butter with 1 tablespoon of the oil. Brown the chicken pieces on all sides for 10 minutes. Remove the chicken from the pan and set it aside, keeping it warm.

3. Heat the rest of the oil in a flameproof casserole and sauté the onion for a few minutes, until it is soft and transparent. Add the mango slices and cook them briefly on each side.

4. Add the chicken, stock, lemon zest, cinnamon, and coriander to the casserole. Adjust the seasoning. Cover and simmer for 45 minutes.

Nutritional Information

water	82%
protein	0.5 g
fat	0.3 g
carbohydrates	17 g
calories	65
	per 100 g

The mango is an excellent source of vitamins A and C; it is also a good source of potassium, and it supplies copper. When unripe, this fruit may have a laxative effect. The skin of mangoes can cause an allergic reaction, irritating the mouth and skin.

Storing

Mangoes keep relatively well. Unripe fruit can be left to ripen at room temperature; a fruit that is still green will ripen in a week, or faster if it is placed in a paper bag. Mangoes taste best when eaten at peak ripeness. Ripe mangoes can be kept in the refrigerator for 1 or 2 weeks. Unripe fruits will not ripen at temperatures below 55°F. Mangoes can be frozen, cooked in syrup or puréed; sugar and lime or lemon juice may be added if desired.

Tropical Fruits

259

Horned melon

Cucumis metuliferus, Cucurbitaceae

The horned melon is native to southwestern Africa and belongs to the large family of Cucurbitaceae, along with the cucumber, the zucchini, and the melon. Introduced into New Zealand in 1930, it was initially cultivated for decorative purposes. New Zealanders called it "kiwano" because its flesh bears a slight resemblance to that of the kiwi fruit, which is named after the country's national bird and which New Zealand has marketed with great success for over 80 years. It was only recently made available in North American and European markets.

The horned melon is roughly 4 inches long, 2 inches wide, and weighs between ½ and 1 pound. Its firm inedible skin is bright orange mottled with yellow and is covered with spikes resembling small horns. The brighter the orange color, the riper the fruit. The juicy flesh of the horned melon is emerald green and contains numerous soft edible seeds. Its flavor is reminiscent of a cross between the melon and the cucumber, with a hint of lime and banana.

The firm inedible skin is covered with spikes resembling small horns. The brighter the orange color, the riper the fruit.

Buying

When buying a horned melon, look for a yellow- or orange-colored fruit with firm spikes and firm undamaged skin. Avoid dull-colored or blemished fruits.

Nutritional Information

water	90.4%
protein	0.9 g
carbohydrates	3.1 g
calories	24
	per 100 g

The horned melon is rich in vitamin C and contains iron and potassium.

Preparing

After being rinsed and peeled, the horned melon can be served cut into thin slices or cubes, or made into juice. The fruit can also be cut in half and the pulp scooped out with a spoon.

Serving Ideas

The unusual shape of the horned melon makes it an interesting fruit. The scooped-out halves are sometimes used for decorative purposes. Since it contains numerous seeds, it is a good fruit from which to make juice; after blending the flesh and seeds in a food processor, strain the liquid through a sieve to remove the seeds. This juice is excellent in salad dressings, where it can be substituted for vinegar. For a particularly thirst-quenching beverage, add a few drops of lime or lemon juice and a bit of sugar to horned melon juice, and if desired, flavor it with orange liqueur. The pulp of horned melons can be added to sauces, soups, salads, sorbets, and yogurts.

Storing

Handled with care, the horned melon will keep for several weeks. However, it is best if consumed within 10 days of purchase. It can be stored at room temperature, or in the refrigerator if it is to be eaten promptly (it is more flavorful when chilled).

Asian pear

Pyrus ussuriensis and *Pyrus pyrifolia*, **Rosaceae**

Also known as the sand pear, the Asian pear is the fruit of a tree originating in Asia. It is thought to be the ancestor of the common pear and belongs to the same family of fruits. The Asian pear has been widely consumed in Asia for centuries, where it is a favorite fruit, but it is still relatively unknown in most Western markets. It was introduced into the United States only at the end of the 19th century. The largest producers of the Asian pear are Japan, China, Taiwan, and Korea; the United States, New Zealand, and Brazil began cultivating this fruit a few years ago.

There are more than 1,000 varieties of the Asian pear, most of which are round in shape and about the size of an apple (some are quite small, while others can weigh up to 1 pound). Only a few of these varieties are actually pear-shaped. The thin, smooth edible skin may be yellow, green, or golden-brown in color. The juicy flesh is slightly sweet and mildly flavored, like the pear, but has the crispness of an apple. Some varieties have a granular texture. Unlike the pear, the Asian pear is picked when ripe and ready for consumption.

Most Asian pears are round and about the size of an apple. Only a few varieties are actually pear-shaped.

Buying

Choose a fragrant, unblemished fruit that is heavy for its weight, a sign of juiciness. Surface bruises will not affect the quality of the flesh. Although the Asian pear is very firm even when ripe, it is nonetheless fragile because of the thinness of its skin.

Preparing

The Asian pear is often served sliced horizontally to show off its star-shaped seed center. It is frequently peeled to allow full enjoyment of the subtly flavored flesh.

Serving Ideas

The Asian pear is best eaten fresh on its own, as other foods tend to mask its delicate flavor. It can be added to fruit salads or mixed salads, and imparts an interesting texture to sauted and Chinese-style dishes. It blends particularly well with cream cheese and yogurt. Its juice is excellent and quite refreshing.

Cooking

The Asian pear keeps its shape and remains quite firm during cooking. It requires a slightly longer cooking time than the common pear. Because of its high moisture content, poaching or baking it in the oven tends to bring out its flavor.

Storing

Asian pears will keep for a few days at room temperature and for up to 2 months in the refrigerator if they are in good condition. To protect them, wrap them individually in paper towels and place them in a perforated plastic bag in the refrigerator. Browned-skinned fruits tend to keep longer than those with green skin, while the yellow variety is the most perishable. Asian pears do not freeze well.

Nutritional Information

water	88%
protein	0.5 g
fat	0.3 g
carbohydrates	11 g
calories	42
	per 100 g

The Asian pear contains potassium.

Sapodilla

Manilkara zapota, Sapotaceae

The fruit of a tree native to Central America and Mexico. Sapodilla, sometimes also called naseberry, secretes a white latex called chicle which is used in the manufacture of chewing gum. The sapodilla tree was much prized by the Aztecs, who named its fruit *tzapotl,* from which the Spanish derived the name *sapodilla*. The term "sapota" refers to a different fruit and should not be confused with the sapodilla. The sapodilla was introduced into the Philippines by the Spanish. Because it is very perishable and does not stand up well to shipping, this fruit is relatively unknown outside the countries where it is cultivated.

The sapodilla tree is a stately evergreen standing up to 100 feet high and yielding from 2,000 to 3,000 fruits in a single year. When burned, the wood gives off an odor of incense. It is produced mainly in Central America, India, Indonesia, California, and Australia. The fruit is the size and shape of an egg, about 2 to 3 inches in diameter, with a rugged grayish or brown skin that peels off easily. The flesh of the sapodilla is a translucent brownish yellow or reddish yellow, with a slightly granular texture similar to the pear. Juicy and very fragrant, it melts in the mouth. Its sweet flavor is often compared to honey or apricots. The core of the fruit contains two to ten flat, rectangular seeds; their bitter white inner kernels are used to make tea. The sapodilla should be eaten when very ripe; otherwise its high tannin content makes it rather unpalatable.

Buying

 Choose sapodillas that are firm and intact.

Preparing

The sapodilla can be eaten whole after being washed and peeled, or its flesh can be cut into pieces and the seeds removed. The fruit can also be cut in half and scooped out with a spoon.

Serving Ideas

 This fruit is consumed raw or cooked. It can be incorporated into fruit salads or eaten on its own. Sapodillas are often puréed or pressed to make juice. They are delicious in sauces, sorbets, and ice cream, and make an excellent wine. They can also be poached or cooked to make jam.

Storing

Sapodillas should be left to ripen at room temperature, after which they can be stored in the refrigerator.

Nutritional Information

water	78%
protein	0.4 g
fat	1.1 g
carbohydrates	20 g
fiber	5.3 g
calories	82
	per 100 g

The sapodilla is very high in fiber and is a good source of potassium; it contains vitamin C, sodium, and iron.

Watermelon

Citrullus lanatus, Cucurbitaceae

A variety of melon believed to be of African origin, the watermelon is so named because of its high water content (between 92% and 95%), which gives it its reputation as a very refreshing fruit. Watermelon has been widely consumed since ancient times, particularly in Mediterranean countries and in Egypt, where it frequently plays an important role when water is polluted or in short supply. Over 5,000 years ago in Egypt, it was customary for peasants to offer watermelon to thirsty voyagers.

Like all melons, watermelons are the fruit of an annual plant that prefers warm climates; in the case of the watermelon, the warmer the climate the better. However, among the more than 50 varieties of watermelon, certain hybrids do grow in temperate zones. China, Russia, and Turkey are among the main producers of this fruit today.

Watermelons can be round, oblong, or spherical, and range in weight from a few pounds to close to 90 pounds, depending on the variety. The rind of the watermelon is thick but fragile; it ranges in color from pale to dark green and is often striped or spotted. The pulp is usually red, but it can also be white, yellow, or pinkish. It contains numerous smooth seeds ranging in color from black to brown, white, green, yellow, or red. Only a few varieties of watermelon have no seeds at all. Compared to other melons, the flesh of the watermelon is more crumbly (because more aqueous), crisper, and more thirst-quenching.

Watermelons can be round, oblong, or spherical and range in weight from a few pounds to close to 90 pounds, depending on the variety.

Buying

It is difficult to know whether a watermelon will be flavorful, short of cutting it open and actually tasting it, which is rarely an option. However, there are certain things one can look for: Choose a firm, heavy melon that is slightly waxy (but not dull) in appearance. There should be a paler, almost yellow area on the skin where the melon lay on the ground during ripening. If it doesn't have one, it means that the watermelon was picked prematurely. Tap the watermelon lightly with the palm of your hand; a thudding sound is an indication that the fruit is full of water and ready to eat. Avoid melons that are cracked or have soft spots. It is possible to tell the freshness of precut watermelon by observing whether the flesh looks firm and juicy, is a healthy red color, and is free of white streaks.

Nutritional Information

water	92%
protein	0.6 g
fat	0.4 g
carbohydrates	7 g
calories	31
	per 100 g

Watermelon contains vitamin C and potassium. It is said to be a good cleansing agent, diuretic, and detoxifier.

Storing

Watermelons are sensitive to the cold, particularly to temperatures below 50°F. On the other hand, once picked they should be refrigerated, as the flesh ripens more quickly in the heat, becoming dry and fibrous. In addition to keeping longer when refrigerated, watermelons are also more refreshing when eaten chilled. Once cut, watermelon should be kept in the refrigerator, covered with plastic wrap in order to prevent it from drying out and from absorbing the odors of the other food. Eat it as soon as possible.

Serving Ideas

Watermelon is usually eaten on its own, either sliced or quartered; it can also be cut into cubes or scooped out to form balls. Once the seeds have been removed, it can be added to fruit salads or cooked to make jam. Puréed, it makes a tasty sorbet and a delicious juice. The Russians make a popular wine from watermelon juice. Unripe watermelon is used in the same way as summer squash.

Watermelon seeds are edible, and in certain regions of Asia they are eaten roasted or salted and are sometimes even ground (as a form of cereal) to make bread. The rind of the watermelon may be marinated or candied.

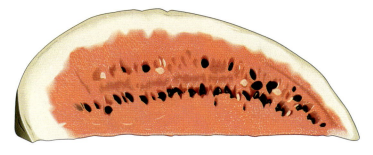

Melon

Cucumis melo, Cucurbitaceae

Charentais

A fruit believed to have originated in India or Africa, the melon has been cultivated in India since ancient times and was probably introduced into Europe at the beginning of the Christian era. Today it is cultivated in many countries, including Israel and Japan, which have created a number of hybrid varieties. Melons belong to the same family as the cucumber, pumpkin, squash, watermelon, and gourd. Like these fruits, they grow on a trailing vine, but melons require warmer temperatures and more sunlight. There are many varieties of melon, some of which can grow in temperate regions. Like squashes, the different varieties are classified as being either summer melons or winter melons. Cantaloupe and muskmelon (or netted melon) are summer melons. Winter melons, which are more oblong in shape and have a longer storage life, include the honeydew melon, prince melon, casaba melon, Persian melon, canary melon, Ogen melon, Galia melon, and Santa Claus melon.

SUMMER MELONS

The true **cantaloupe** (*C. melo* var. *cantalupensis*) derives its name from the papal villa of Cantalupo, near Rome, where it was cultivated around 1700. This orange-fleshed melon is rough-skinned with deep grooves. The most widely cultivated variety is the Charentais, which is lightly ribbed and has a pale green skin; this variety accounts for almost the entire French crop. True cantaloupes are rarely found in America; what North Americans call cantaloupe is actually a variety of muskmelon.

The **muskmelon** or **netted melon** (*C. melo* var. *reticulatus*) is round and often ribless with a distinctly netted skin. A number of hybrid varieties combine the characteristics of the cantaloupe and the muskmelon (oval, netted, ribbed or ribless), which causes some confusion when it comes to classifying them. All of these tasty melons have salmon-colored or orange-yellow flesh; they are often named after the place where they are cultivated (notably Cavaillon, Charente, and Touraine in France).

WINTER MELONS

The **honeydew melon** is a smooth-skinned variety which changes from pale green to creamy yellow color as it ripens. Its green-colored pulp is very sweet. Honeydews usually weigh between 3 and 7 pounds and are more ovoid than round in shape.

The **prince melon** is round in shape and closely resembles the honeydew, except that the flesh of this hybrid is orange.

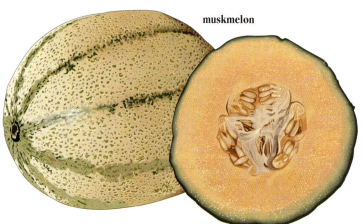

muskmelon

honeydew melon

The **casaba melon** can be round or ovoid and usually weighs between 4 and 7 pounds. It has a wrinkled yellow or orange skin with a greenish tinge at the stem end. Its whitish flesh is creamy but often less fragrant than that of other melons.

The **Persian melon** is round and usually weighs about 6½ pounds. Its dark green skin acquires a fine brownish netting at maturity, and it has firm orange flesh. This variety resembles a large muskmelon.

The **canary melon** is oblong with smooth canary-yellow skin. It has deliciously sweet whitish flesh with a hint of pink near the cavity and is very fragrant when ripe.

The **Ogen melon** is a hybrid variety that was created on an Israeli kibbutz in the 1960s. It is a small round melon with hard, smooth, ribbed skin with greenish yellow coloring. The flesh is very juicy and can be either deep pink or pale green.

The **Galia melon** is another Israeli hybrid and bears the name of the family that created it. Its brownish skin is ribbed and netted, and it has a very aromatic pale green flesh.

The **Santa Claus melon** is oblong and looks like a small watermelon, except that its skin is golden yellow with black and green stripes; its pale green flesh more closely resembles that of the honeydew.

The melon belongs to the same family as the cucumber and squash. Like these fruits, it grows on a trailing vine, but it requires more warmth and sunlight.

Buying

Obtaining a truly tasty melon is no easy task, mainly because they are almost always harvested before they are fully ripe in order to help them withstand the rigors of shipping. Have a look at the stalk end of the melon, especially in the case of muskmelons and cantaloupes; if it is very hard or unevenly colored, or if part of the greenish stalk is still attached, the fruit may not be sufficiently mature. In ripe melons, this part softens – although this is not always an indication of ripeness, as it can also be caused by excessive handling. The end opposite the stalk should have a delicate aroma if the melon is ripe.

A ripe melon will give off a hollow sound when it is tapped lightly with the palm of the hand. Choose a melon that is heavy and free of bruises or soft or damp spots. Avoid overly soft melons, as well as those with a strong odor or unusual color; chances are that they are overripe and have begun to ferment.

Preparing

Cut the melon into quarters or halves. Scoop the seeds out of the cavity, but leave the seeds in any unused portions to keep them from drying out. The melon can be served cut into slices or cubes, or the flesh can be scooped out with a melon baller.

Ogen melon

Santa Claus melon

Persian melon

Serving Ideas

Melon is usually eaten fresh. It can be cut in half and its cavity filled with port wine to be served as an appetizer; this ancient custom was practised by the popes, who used a sweeter wine. Melon is also delicious flavored with ginger, lemon or lime juice, or sherry. It can be added to cereals and fruit salads, or made into juice or puréed and used to flavor sorbets and ice cream. It can also be cooked and made into jam, marmalade, or chutney. Melon blends well with ham, deli meats, prosciutto or other dried meats, smoked fish, and cheese. It can also accompany meat, poultry, and seafood as well as adding an original touch to vegetable salads, rice salads, and chicken salads. Melon can also be dried, marinated, or distilled.

Nutritional Information

water	90%
protein	0.5 to 1 g
carbohydrates	8 to 9 g
calories	35
	per 100 g

White or pale-colored melons are an excellent source of potassium and a good source of vitamin C and folic acid. Some people find it hard to digest melons. Melons are reinvigorating, diuretic, laxative, and stimulate the appetite.

Melon with Port Wine

SERVES 4

4 small melons (one per person) *¾ cup (185 ml) port wine*

1. Cut a cap off the stem end of each melon. Place the caps to the side.

2. Scoop out the seeds with a spoon, and extract the flesh, taking care not to pierce the skin. Cut the flesh into cubes and place them in a bowl. Add the port and place in the refrigerator, along with the melon shells and caps. Macerate for 2 hours.

3. Just before serving, fill the hollowed-out shells with the macerated melon cubes and top with the caps.

Storing

Despite their appearance, melons are very perishable; their skin offers only minimal protection and they tend to spoil rapidly. Leave the melon to ripen at room temperature until it has a delicate aroma. Do not keep it near other fruits and vegetables, as it produces a lot of ethylene gas, which hastens ripening and alters the flavor of other foods. Ripe melons should be kept in the refrigerator, but wrap them in plastic to prevent surrounding food from absorbing their odor. For maximum flavor, take the melon out of the refrigerator shortly before serving it.

Melons can be frozen, but their flesh tends to soften when thawed. Remove the skin and seeds, cut the flesh into slices, balls, or cubes, add sugar (½ cup per 4 cups of fruit) and lemon juice, then seal the fruit in an airtight container or freezer bag.

casaba melon

canary melon

Galia melon

Nuts
and Seeds

Introduction

The term "nut" is applied to various fruits having a hard outer shell enclosing a kernel (also called a nut), while "seeds" are contained in the fruits of plants and are capable of producing a new plant when released from the fleshy part of the fruit. Nuts and seeds have been used as food by humans for thousands of years; they were an essential part of the diet for primitive hunter-gatherer cultures and are also a source of nourishment for many animal species. Pistachios, walnuts, and almonds were already under cultivation in biblical times in Southeast Asia and were held in high esteem by the ancient Greeks and Romans.

The most commercially important varieties of nuts produced in the world today are the coconut, almond, walnut, hazelnut, chestnut, cashew, and pistachio. Nuts and seeds continue to be a popular food, for they are highly nutritious and require little preparation.

Buying

The market offers nuts and seeds in many different forms: they are available with or without their shell, whole, halved, cut in fine slices or slivers, chopped, ground, plain, roasted, with or without their brown skin, salted, smoked, sweetened, or coated in candy or chocolate. They are also processed to make butter, oil, and sweetened or unsweetened spreads. The shells of nuts provide a protective coating that prevents the nuts from turning rancid as quickly. When purchasing unshelled nuts, choose those with undamaged shells.

When buying shelled nuts, it is best to buy those sold in vacuum-sealed glass jars, in cans, or in sealed bags, all of which ensure maximum freshness. It is also a good idea to buy nuts in stores with a rapid turnover.

Serving Ideas

Nuts and seeds have a wide array of culinary and decorative uses. They go just as well with savory dishes as with sweet dishes, and they make an ideal snack or appetizer. They are also a good complement to or replacement for meat. Nuts sold with their skin have a stronger flavor than skinned nuts. A number of savory oils are extracted from nuts and seeds, which are also processed to make butter and flour.

Storing

Nuts sold in the shell tend to keep better than shelled, cut, chopped, or ground nuts. They should be stored in an airtight container away from direct light, heat, and moisture. Depending on the variety, nuts will keep for 2 to 9 months in the refrigerator.

Unshelled nuts freeze well and will keep for about a year in the freezer. Shelled, cut, chopped, or ground nuts and seeds should be stored at room temperature in an airtight container or package. Once the package has been opened, transfer the nuts to a sealed container and keep them in a cool, dry, dark place for short-term storage or in the refrigerator or freezer for longer storage.

Nutritional Information

Nuts and seeds are high in fat and calories. While their nutritional value varies widely, in general nuts contain from 3 to 10 grams of protein, 17 to 37 grams of fat, and 8 to 16 grams of carbohydrates. Two exceptions are the ginkgo, which contains only 1.1 grams of fat while containing 37 grams of carbohydrates, and 175 to 355 calories per 50 grams; and the chestnut, with 0.6 gram of fat, 22 grams of carbohydrates, and 98 calories per 50 grams.

The fat in nuts is mainly in the form of monounsaturated and polyunsaturated fatty acids, with the exception of the coconut, which contains mainly saturated fatty acids (see *Fats*). Since they are of plant origin, nuts and seeds do not contain cholesterol. While all nuts are a source of dietary fiber, Brazil nuts and sunflower seeds are particularly high in fiber. Because of their high fat and calorie content, and because they are often salted, it is best to consume nuts and seeds in moderate quantities. They are also easier to digest when chewed thoroughly or when finely ground.

Most nuts and seeds are excellent sources of magnesium, copper, and potassium; they are also a good source of thiamine and folic acid, and usually contain iron, pantothenic acid, and riboflavin.

Walnut

Juglans spp., **Juglandaceae**

The walnut tree has been cultivated for thousands of years; it originated on the shores of the Caspian Sea and in northern India. In many languages, including French, the equivalent of the word "nut" refers primarily to the fruit of the walnut tree, its generic meaning being secondary. By contrast, the English word "walnut" is derived from an Old English word meaning "foreign nut," which may be a reference to the fact that the walnut was associated with the Gauls.

The walnut tree was introduced into Europe by the Romans and has been grown there since the 4th century. The Greeks cultivated the tree intensively, mainly for walnut oil, and the Romans regarded it as a sacred tree. In fact, the walnut tree has always been held in high esteem because it outlives several generations of humans.

The walnut tree has long been regarded as an important plant, especially in rural areas. The nourishing nuts of the tree were invaluable during the winter, when only a very limited number of foods were available. The edible oil extracted from the nuts was used to provide light, and the leaves were prized for their medicinal properties; the husk was used, as it still is, to make liqueurs, ratafias, and flavored wines, and the shell was used to make a dye for furniture craftsmen and dyers.

There are numerous species of walnut trees. The species *Juglans regia,* which originated in southeastern Europe and western Asia, can live for 300 to 400 years and usually grows to be between 30 and 80 feet high. Also referred to as "English walnuts" or "royal walnuts," the nuts of this variety were produced in large numbers by the British, who introduced the tree into numerous countries around the world. Today the leading producers of walnuts are the United States, Turkey, China, Romania, Iran, France, and the Balkan countries.

The black walnut *(Juglans nigra)* and the white walnut or butternut *(Juglans cinerea)* are two of the most common walnut species in North America, their place of origin. The black walnut is a magnificent tree that generally measures between 100 and 130 feet in height. Its deeply cracked bark is very dark in color. The nut of this tree has a very strong flavor and is enclosed in a very hard shell that is difficult to break open. The most sought-after varieties of French walnuts are known as *noix de Grenoble* because they are grown in the Grenoble region, which is renowned worldwide for the quality of its walnuts.

The walnut contains a very bumpy kernel in two pieces; approximately one third of each piece is joined to the other piece or lobe, but the remaining portions are separated by a membrane. Off-white in color, the kernel has a strong flavor and is covered with a thin layer of skin whose color ranges from light to dark yellow. It is enclosed in a hard convex shell that can be either round or oblong; some varieties have woodier shells than others. The shell is covered with a smooth, sticky green husk known as the "shuck."

Walnuts are harvested either manually (fallen nuts are gathered by hand) or mechanically (a machine shakes the trees, then gathers the fallen nuts). The nuts are then processed, which involves removing the husk and drying them. The shells are often whitened with chlorine or sulfur dioxide.

Buying

Walnuts deteriorate quickly when exposed to humidity, heat, air, or light. When buying unshelled walnuts, look for nuts that seem relatively heavy and full, with intact shells that are not cracked or pierced. Shelled walnuts should be crunchy; avoid those that are soft, shriveled, or rancid. Walnuts sold in vacuum-packed jars or in cans are usually the freshest.

Serving Ideas

Walnuts can be eaten whole, chopped, or ground, either plain or roasted. Often eaten as snacks, they are also added to desserts (cakes, brioches, muffins, pies, cookies, ice cream) as well as to sauces, sandwiches, cheese, and main-course dishes (omelets, legumes, Asian foods). Walnuts can also be used as a condiment in stuffings, pâtés, and pasta sauces.

Pickled in vinegar, unripe walnuts can also be added to jams and marinades. An expensive oil is extracted from walnuts; stronger-tasting than olive oil, it is used primarily in salads.

The shucks of walnuts contain an aromatic substance that is used to make liqueurs (ratafia, *brou de noix*).

Storing

Store walnuts in a tightly sealed container, away from heat and humidity; unshelled walnuts will keep for 2 to 3 months. Shelled walnuts should be refrigerated to prevent them from going rancid; they will keep for 6 months. Walnuts can also be frozen; shelled walnuts can be stored in the freezer for up to 1 year.

Nutritional Information

water	3.6%
protein	7.2 g
fat	31 g
carbohydrates	9.2 g
fiber	2.4 g
	per 50 g

The fat in walnuts consists of 86% unsaturated acids (see *Fats*).

Walnuts are an excellent source of copper and magnesium, and a good source of potassium, vitamin B$_6$, folic acid, and thiamine; a source of fiber, they also contain phosphorus, niacin, iron, riboflavin, and pantothenic acid. Walnuts have long been said to have various medicinal properties. Dried walnuts are reputed to be mildly laxative and cleansing. It was once thought that walnuts could ward off headaches because their shape was said to be comparable to that of the human brain. Since the leaves of the walnut tree contain an antibiotic substance, they can be used to destroy bacteria.

The British produced "royal walnuts" in large numbers and introduced the royal walnut tree into numerous countries around the world.

whole walnut

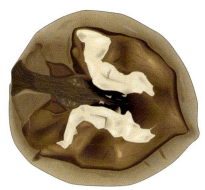
shelled walnuts

whole unshucked walnut

Nuts and Seeds

271

Pecan

Carya spp., Juglandaceae

The edible fruit of a giant tree originating in the Mississippi river valley in the United States. An important part of the diet of American Indians before the arrival of European settlers, pecans are still very popular in the United States today, especially in the South. They are widely cultivated in Texas (the pecan tree is the official state tree), New Mexico, Louisiana, Mississippi, Georgia, and Florida. There are over 300 varieties of pecan, one of which is adapted to the colder climate of Canada.

The pecan tree was successfully grafted for the first time in 1846 by a slave named Antoine, a gardener on a Louisiana plantation who grafted a total of 126 trees. While the cultivation of the pecan tree subsequently increased steadily, the technique of grafting only resurfaced in 1877 to the detriment of sowing. However, the technique of sowing pecan trees was to remain the most effective, being easier to carry out and having a higher success rate. In Australia, the pecan tree began to be a productive crop in 1960, while in Israel the cultivation of pecans increased markedly in the 1970s.

The pecan tree can live to be very old; in fact, it is not uncommon to find specimens that are 100 years old, and some even live as long as 1,000 years. The tree can have a circumference of over 6 feet and can grow up to 180 feet in height, although the average height is between 80 and 100 feet. It is a very decorative tree, with catkin flowers similar to those of the hazel, a member of the same family. The pecan tree only begins to produce a profitable crop of nuts after 10 years, but in a good year it can yield over 400 pounds of pecans. On large plantations, the pecans are harvested mechanically by machines that shake the trees to cause the nuts to fall to the ground, where they are sucked up by another machine.

The pecan consists of an elongated seed, or kernel, that has two lobes, like the walnut. The seeds are whitish in color and are covered by a thin brown skin. They are encased in a smooth, oval, brownish shell that is easy to break; the seed separates from the shell easily. The shell is contained in a fleshy green outer covering that splits into four parts when the fruit is ripe. Producers often alter the appearance of pecans in order to increase sales; the shells are washed and sanded, dyed brown or red, and waxed and polished to give them a more uniform and attractive appearance.

Most varieties of pecans are 1 to 1½ inches in length, although size varies and is not an indication of quality. The flavor of fresh pecans improves in the 3 weeks following harvesting, after which their extremely high fat content causes them to slowly begin to turn rancid. Pecans have a slightly more delicate flavor than walnuts.

whole pecans

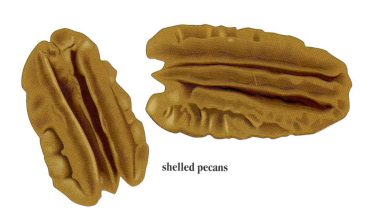

shelled pecans

Buying

When choosing pecans in their shell, look for nuts that are heavy for their size, that do not rattle when shaken, and that are unstained; there should be no cracks or holes in the shell. The shelled pecans one buys in the store are often rancid or lacking in flavor. It is better to buy them either in their shell or in vacuum-sealed glass jars or cans, as these containers ensure maximum flavor.

Serving Ideas

Pecans are eaten whole, ground, or chopped and are good plain, salted, sweetened, or spiced. They are used in both savory and sweet dishes. Pecan pie is a traditional dessert in North America. They are also commonly added to cookies, ice cream, cakes, and candies, or coated with chocolate. Pecans are also used in stuffings for wild game and poultry.

A transparent and mildly flavored oil is extracted from pecans; of the same quality as olive oil, it is very expensive to produce and is used mainly in salads.

Pecan Pie

SERVES 4 TO 6

1 unbaked 9-in. short-crust pie crust	½ tsp. vanilla extract
¾ cup (185 ml) pecan halves	¼ cup (60 ml) butter
3 eggs	¾ cup (185 ml) packed dark brown sugar
1 cup (250 ml) corn syrup	1 pinch of salt

1. Preheat the oven to 350°F (175°C).

2. Grease and flour a 9-inch pie plate, and line it with the pie crust. Prick the crust with a fork in several places, and bake it for 5 minutes.

3. Arrange the nuts in concentric circles on the bottom of the crust.

4. Beat the eggs until light and fluffy. Mix in the syrup and vanilla.

5. Cream the butter and gradually add the brown sugar and salt. Beat until the brown sugar is completely dissolved. Incorporate into the egg mixture.

6. Gently pour this mixture into the pie crust, taking care not to disturb the nuts, which will rise to the surface. Bake for 40 to 45 minutes.

Nutritional Information

	dried pecans	oil-roasted pecans
water	4.8%	4%
protein	3.9 g	3.5 g
fat	33.8 g	35.6 g
carbohydrates	9.1 g	8.1 g
fiber	3.3 g	3.6 g
		per 50 g

The fats in pecans are composed of 87% unsaturated fatty acids (62% monounsaturated and 25% polyunsaturated; see *Fats and Oils*). Pecans are an excellent source of thiamine, zinc, copper, and magnesium; they are also a good source of potassium and contain phosphorus, pantothenic acid, niacin, folic acid, iron, and vitamin B$_6$. They are a source of fiber.

Oil-roasted pecans are an excellent source of zinc, copper, and magnesium and a good source of potassium, in addition to containing phosphorus, pantothenic acid, thiamine, folic acid, niacin, iron, and vitamin B$_6$. They are a high source of fiber. Oil-roasted pecans and dried pecans have about the same nutritional value.

Storing

Unshelled pecans will keep for about 3 months at room temperature. Once they are shelled, store them in the refrigerator, where they will keep for 6 months, or in the freezer, where they will keep for a year.

Shelled pecans absorb odors readily and tend to turn rancid quickly. They should be kept in an airtight container in the refrigerator. Pecans can be frozen with or without their shell.

Nuts and Seeds

273

Cashew

Anacardium occidentale, Anacardiaceae

Cashew apples are gathered by hand once they ripen and fall to the ground. The nuts are removed from the apples, then left to dry in the sun.

cashew nut

The cashew tree originated in Brazil and is related to the pistachio and the mango. It now grows mainly in Africa and India, where it was introduced by the Portuguese during the 16th century. The nut of the cashew tree did not become commercially valuable until the beginning of the 20th century. The leading producers of cashews are India, Brazil, Mozambique, Nigeria, and Tanzania. India, which produces 90% of the world's cashews, exports more than any other country.

The cashew tree usually grows to be 32 to 40 feet high and can produce nuts for 3 to 20 years, and occasionally for as long as 45 years. Cashew nuts hang from fleshy fruitlike peduncles that are sometimes referred to as "apples" but actually look more like pears. Cashew apples, each of which produces a single nut, are soft and contain an abundance of milky juice, which can stain clothing. Either yellow or bright red in color, they are 2 to 4 inches long and 1½ to 2 inches wide. Their fine yellow flesh is refreshing and very rich in vitamin C; in fact, it contains much more vitamin C than oranges.

Cashew nuts measure just over 1 inch in diameter and are enclosed in two shells. The smooth, thin exterior shell is initially olive green but becomes brownish red as the fruit develops. The interior shell is very hard and can be difficult to break open. There is a very caustic resinous oil known as "cashew balm" between the two shells; it can burn and blister your fingers or lips if you try to remove the nuts manually or by biting into them. This corrosive liquid is used primarily to make varnishes and resins that protect wood against termites, as well as waterproofing products, ink, and insecticides. The wood of the cashew tree is very hard and precious, and its bark contains a yellowish gum that is used like gum arabic.

Cashew "apples" are gathered by hand after they ripen and fall to ground. The nuts are removed from the apples and then dried for 2 days in the sun. They are always shelled and treated before being sold. Treating cashew nuts is quite an elaborate process. After being removed from the fleshy portion of the fruit, the nuts are cleaned, then stored in a humid environment for 12 hours, until they become fragile. These fragile nuts are then roasted in a rotating cylinder, which removes and recovers the corrosive cashew balm. After this initial roasting, the nuts are sprayed with water, then chilled and dried. At this point, they are ready to be shelled (which is often done mechanically) and peeled. Finally, they are roasted again, in two stages: halfway through this final roasting, they are sprayed with a mixture of gum arabic, salt, and water.

Buying

Cashew nuts spoil very quickly. Those sold in vacuum-packed glass jars or in cans tend to be freshest. Avoid nuts that are very shriveled as well those that smell rancid.

Storing

Cashew nuts spoil quickly at room temperature, but they can be refrigerated for up to 6 months and frozen for up to a year. Store them in a tightly sealed container to prevent them from absorbing food odors. Cashew apples are difficult to store because they begin to ferment soon after they are gathered.

Serving Ideas

Cashew nuts can be used whole, in pieces, chopped, roasted, dry-roasted, salted or unsalted. When ground, they turn into a creamy butter that can be used like peanut butter, although its flavor is much milder. Cashew nuts are often eaten as snacks, either alone or with dried fruit, seeds, and other nuts. They are added to various foods, including salads, rice, pasta, cakes, cookies, puddings, and Asian dishes. A particularly common ingredient in Indian cuisine, they are added to lamb curry as well as to various stews and rice dishes. However, they are cooked less frequently than other nuts because they become soft relatively quickly; it is thus important that they not be added to hot food until just before it is served.

Cashew apples can be eaten raw or cooked and have a bittersweet flavor. They are usually made into juice, which is used primarily to make alcoholic beverages like wines and liqueurs. They are also canned or used to make jams. In some of the regions where cashew trees are grown, especially in Brazil and the Caribbean, they are regarded as a delicacy and are much more highly prized than cashew nuts, which are sometimes even discarded.

Nutritional Information

	dry-roasted cashew nuts
water	1.7%
protein	7.7 g
fat	23.2 g
carbohydrates	16.4 g
fiber	0.9 g
	per 50 g

Dry-roasted cashews contain less fat than any other kind of nut. The fat in cashew nuts consists of 76% unsaturated fatty acids (60% monounsaturated acids and 16% polyunsaturated acids; see *Fats*).

Cashew nuts are an excellent source of copper, magnesium, and zinc, and a good source of potassium, phosphorus, iron, and folic acid; they also contain niacin, pantothenic acid, thiamine, vitamin B_6, and riboflavin.

cashew apple

Cola nut

Cola spp., Sterculiaceae

The cola nut is the fruit of a tree that is thought to have originated in tropical western Africa. Closely related to the cacao tree, the cola tree grows mainly in Africa and South America. African cola trees are usually between 50 and 65 feet high, but South American varieties never grow to be any larger than a small bush. There are approximately 50 different species of cola trees, two of which are of great commercial importance because they are used to make cola drinks – the *Cola nitida* and the *Cola acuminata*.

Cola trees start to produce fruit after about 15 years, and adult trees can produce 90 to 110 pounds of nuts per year. The capsular fruit contains three to ten irregularly shaped, fleshy seeds, each of which is 1 to 1½ inches long. Pink, red, or white when fresh, the seeds turn brown and harden when dried. Their taste is quite bitter and harsh, which is why they have come to be referred to as nuts.

Serving Ideas

Cola nuts are chewed by the indigenous populations of several countries, particularly in Africa. They have numerous effects, including diminishing thirst, hunger, and fatigue, as well as increasing energy levels by stimulating muscles and nerves.

In other parts of the world, cola nuts are used to make refreshing drinks known as "colas." One of the most famous of these drinks, Coca-Cola, was created in the United States in 1886; it is a carbonated drink containing cola extract.

Nutritional Information

Cola nuts contain several stimulants, including caffeine (up to 2%) and theobromine, that affect the body in various ways. Reputed to have diuretic and aphrodisiac properties, cola nuts are a milder stimulant than coffee, which has harsher and more prolonged effects.

Coconut

Cocos nucifera, **Palmaceae**

The coconut is the fruit of the coconut palm, a tree belonging to the large *Palmaceae* family, that is thought to have originated in Southeast Asia and the Melanesian islands in the Pacific Ocean. The coconut palm grows in almost all tropical countries, including Indonesia, the Philippines, India, Sri Lanka, Thailand, and Mexico – the world's leading producers of coconuts. It is cultivated but also grows wild. Indonesians say that there are as many uses for coconuts as there are days in the year. The wood of the coconut palm is used by cabinetmakers and carpenters; the leaves are comprised of large fibers that are used to make rope, baskets, brushes, carpets, and fabric; the shell is used as a container; the sap is made into an alcoholic drink; and the milk and the pulp are very popular foods.

The coconut palm can grow to be 100 feet high and is topped by a crown of enormous leaves. Its fruit, or "drupes," usually grow in five or six bunches, each of which contains about a dozen coconuts. While on the tree, coconuts are protected by a fibrous husk (the pericarp) 2 to 6 inches thick. Beneath this fibrous husk is a very hard, thin brownish shell that has to be broken open to reach the pulp (nut) that adheres to its interior walls. The cavity at the center of the fruit is filled with a sweet, refreshing opalescent white liquid known as "coconut water" (not to be confused with coconut milk, which is produced by crushing the pulp). An albuminous liquid, coconut water turns into ivory-white pulp as the coconut matures. The edible portions of the coconut are the pulp (known simply as "coconut") and the very refreshing liquid in the hollow center of the fruit.

Buying

Choose an uncracked coconut that still contains water (this can be easily verified by shaking the fruit) and has intact, firm "eyes" that are free of mold.

Coconut is sold whole, dried, grated, flaked, or roasted and as canned milk, or sweetened or unsweetened cream. It is often coated with sugar, which increases the number of calories it contains. Dried grated unsweetened coconut is available in natural-food stores.

coconut

Nutritional Information

	raw	*sweetened dried and grated pulp*	*unsweetened dried and grated pulp*	*coconut milk*	*coconut water*
protein	1.7 g	1.7 g	3.5 g	4.6 g	1.8 g
fat	16.8 g	16.1 g	32.3 g	48.2 g	0.5 g
carbohydrates	7.6 g	23.8 g	12.2 g	6.3 g	9.4 g
fiber	4.5 g	2.7 g	2.6 g		2.8 g
	per 50 g			**(250 ml)**	

As shown above, the nutritional value of coconut depends on whether it is fresh or dried pulp, or coconut milk or water.

Fresh coconut is a good source of potassium and is high in fiber; it also contains copper, iron, magnesium, folic acid, zinc, and phosphorus.

Unsweetened dried coconut is good source of potassium, copper, and magnesium. A source of fiber, it also contains iron, zinc, phosphorus, vitamin B_6, and pantothenic acid.

Coconut is said to be a laxative and a diuretic, and coconut water is used to alleviate intestinal problems.

Storing

An unopened coconut can be stored at room temperature for 2 to 4 months. Once opened, it can be refrigerated for 1 week or frozen for up to 9 months.

Fresh coconut and coconut milk should be refrigerated; cover the pulp with water to prevent it from drying out. The pulp also freezes readily and thaws quickly. Dried coconut should be stored in a cool, dry place and protected from air and insects.

Preparing

To open a coconut, start by piercing holes in the soft areas at the top of the shell (the "eyes") with a pointed instrument. Pour the water inside the shell into a container, then break the outside of the shell in half by turning the coconut slowly and hitting it about one third of the way down (just below the eyes) with a hammer or a heavy knife. Remove the white pulp, which will be more or less difficult depending on the ripeness of the coconut.

The coconut can also be placed in a hot oven (350°F or 180°C), once the eyes have been pierced and the liquid has been poured out; after 30 minutes in the oven, the shell will crack open and the pulp will be easier to remove.

It is impossible to tell whether or not the pulp is rancid without opening the shell.

Shrimp in Coconut Milk

SERVES 4

1 lb. (500 g) large raw shrimp	1 tsp. turmeric powder
1 onion	1 tsp. curry powder
2 cloves garlic	1 cup (250 ml) coconut milk
2 red or green bell peppers	½ tsp. salt
2 tbsp. peanut oil	1 lemon, sliced
1 tsp. grated fresh ginger	

1. Wash the shrimp. Either shell them or leave them in their shells.

2. Peel and chop the onion, and mince the garlic. Halve and seed the peppers, then chop them coarsely.

3. Heat the oil in a large frying pan, and cook the onions, garlic, and ginger, without letting the onions brown. Add the peppers, turmeric, and curry powder, and fry the mixture for another minute. Add the shrimp and sauté them until they change color, about 3 minutes. Pour in the coconut milk, then add the salt. Allow the mixture to simmer uncovered, stirring it constantly, until the liquid thickens, 3 to 5 minutes.

4. Place the shrimp and the sauce in a serving dish, garnishing it with lemon slices. Serve the shrimp with plain rice.

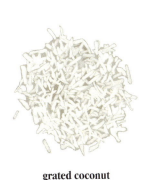

grated coconut

coconut milk

Serving Ideas

Coconut is a common ingredient in Asian, African, Indian, Indonesian, and South American cuisines. Fresh or dried coconut pulp, as well as coconut milk and cream, are widely used ingredients. The pulp of unripe coconuts can also be eaten fresh, by cutting through the shell with a knife and eating the pulp right off the shell with a spoon.

Dried coconut is mainly used as an ingredient in recipes, for decorative purposes, and to prepare condiments. It is added to a vast number of dishes, both sweet and savory (appetizers, soups, main-course dishes, desserts).

Like cow's milk, coconut milk is used in many different ways. A common ingredient in Indian cuisine, it is used to make curries, sauces, and rice. It is also added to soups, marinades, stews, flans, puddings, and drinks, and used to cook meat, poultry, and seafood.

To make coconut milk, mix 4 ounces of grated unsweetened coconut (add more coconut for more concentrated milk) and 1 cup of hot water, milk, or coconut water in a small saucepan. Cover the saucepan and let the mixture simmer over low heat for 30 minutes. Strain the mixture through muslin, pressing on the coconut to extract as much liquid as possible. If the milk is set aside for a moment, a layer of "cream" will form on the surface; it can be mixed back into the milk or skimmed off with a spoon and put to some other use. Meat and poultry can be simmered in coconut cream.

A vegetable oil known as coconut oil or copra oil is extracted from the pulp of the coconut (see *Oil*). It can be used as is or made into coconut butter. Since coconut oil contains a large percentage (91%) of saturated fatty acids, it remains solid at room temperature. It is widely used in the food industry, especially for baking, frying, and candy-making. It is also used to make soaps, shampoos, and detergents, and is often added to milk substitutes, lotions, and creams.

Coconuts are protected by a fibrous green exterior husk and a very hard brown interior shell that must be broken open to reach the pulp (coconut) inside the fruit. The hollow center of the fruit is filled with coconut water.

Macadamia nut

Macadamia integrifolia, **Proteaceae**

The macadamia nut is the fruit of a tree that is thought to have originated in Australia, probably in the state of Queensland in the northeastern part of the country. The nut of the macadamia tree has been eaten by Australian aborigines since ancient times. Ferdinand van Mueller, a European who first discovered this nut around 1850, named it the macadamia in honor of the Australian naturalist John Macadam. The Europeans who settled in Australia were quick to develop a taste for the macadamia nut, but it did not become a commercially important food until the early 20th century in Hawaii, where it was successfully introduced at the end of the 19th century. The Australians began to cultivate the macadamia nut intensively several decades later, and like Hawaii, Australia is now a leading producer of macadamia nuts.

There are half a dozen different species of macadamia trees, which grow in very humid environments and are sensitive to the cold as well as to changes in temperature. The macadamia tree can be up to 65 feet high, and its tough evergreen leaves are dark green in color. The small nuts, which grow in bunches of about 20, are approximately 1 inch in diameter and fall to the ground when fully grown.

The macadamia nut consists of an off-white kernel enclosed in a brownish shell that is smooth, thick, and very hard. Varieties with softer shells have recently been developed. The shell itself is enclosed in a thin, fleshy green membrane that cracks open when the nut is fully grown and has to be completely removed before the shell can be broken. Ripe macadamia nuts are crunchy, flavorful, and hold up better than underripe nuts when cooked.

Macadamia nuts are generally fatty, smooth, sweet, and flavorful, but these characteristics vary from one species to another. Their flavor, which is similar to that of coconuts, is largely dependent on how much oil they contain. The lower the amount of oil, the heavier, darker, and less flavorful the nut. Fattier nuts are generally plump, smooth, and relatively pale. The nuts are sorted by floating them in water and then are dried naturally in the open air; they are shelled and cooked in one of two ways, depending on their fat content. The oiliest nuts are dry-roasted, and the others are plunged into hot oil, which improves their appearance but increases their already considerable fat content.

Nutritional Information

water	2.9%
protein	4.3 g
fat	37.3 g
carbohydrates	6.9 g
fiber	2.5 g
calories	355
	per 50 g

Macadamia nuts are high in calories because they are very high in fat, 81% of which consists of unsaturated fatty acids (see *Fats*). A good source of magnesium and potassium, they also contain thiamine, zinc, iron, copper, phosphorus, and niacin.

Preparing

Since macadamia nuts are very hard to break open, a special macadamia nutcracker has been developed. A hammer can also be used.

Buying

Macadamia nuts are often sold shelled, raw or roasted, plain or salted, or covered in chocolate, honey, or carob. They are also available whole, split, chopped, powdered, or ground. The freshness of macadamia nuts can be gauged by their color and texture. Choose plump, crunchy nuts that are relatively light in color. Nuts sold in vacuum-packed glass jars or in cans remain fresh the longest.

Serving Ideas

Macadamia nuts make foods unusually crunchy. They are added to curries, salads, stews, vegetables, rice, cookies, cakes, candies, chocolates, and ice cream, as well as to other sweet and savory dishes. They can be used as a substitute for Brazil nuts. Macadamia nuts are also ground into a creamy butter that can be used like peanut butter.

Storing

Macadamia nuts spoil less quickly than other fatty nuts, but they should be refrigerated once shelled to prevent them from going rancid. If stored in a tightly sealed container, they will not absorb food odors and can be refrigerated for up to 2 months. Unshelled macadamia nuts can be stored at room temperature for about 1 year.

Brazil nut

Bertholletia excelsa, Lecythidaceae

The Brazil nut is the fruit of a tree that originated in Brazil and Paraguay. The Brazil-nut tree can grow to be 250 feet high with a trunk 3 to 7 feet in diameter. It grows wild in the tropical forests of the Amazon region, Guyana, Venezuela, Bolivia, Peru, and Ecuador; attempts to cultivate it elsewhere have generally been unsuccessful. It does not begin to produce nuts in significant quantities until after 12 to 15 years.

The oblong Brazil nut has a crunchy yellowish kernel that tastes like coconut and is covered with a thin layer of brownish skin. The kernel is enclosed in a rough, hard, fibrous shell that is reddish brown in color and measures ¼ to 1 inch in diameter; the shell has three irregularly shaped sides, resembling an orange segment. From 12 to 20 Brazil nuts are crammed inside a coconut-like capsule that measures 3 to 8 inches in diameter and weighs 2 to 4½ pounds. Like orange segments, the nuts are held in place by a fibrous substance; this becomes increasingly dry as the fruit ripens and breaks open, revealing the nuts inside the capsule when it falls to the ground.

Brazil nuts are harvested only in good weather. Workers comb through the forest, gathering nuts that have fallen to the ground. Brazil-nut trees are too tall to climb, and they cannot be shaken because the nut-bearing capsules are too heavy. On windy or rainy days, the workers do not venture into the forest because the capsules can cause fatal injuries when they fall from the trees; in fact, they fall with such force that they dig into the ground. The workers spend the days after the harvest opening the fruit with machetes or axes.

Brazil nuts are difficult to shell; producers soak them for 24 hours in huge vats of water, then boil them for 3 to 5 minutes before straining them. The nuts can then be opened using manually operated machines; this is a delicate operation because the irregularly shaped nuts can be easily damaged.

Preparing

To make Brazil nuts easier to shell, steam them for a few minutes; or freeze them, let them defrost slightly, and then break them open. However, it is best to do as little as possible to them before they are shelled.

Serving Ideas

Brazil nuts can be eaten whole, sliced, chopped, or ground. They are often served as snacks or added to foods such as fruitcakes, cookies, salads, stuffings, and ice cream. When sold as candy, they are usually chocolate-covered.

Brazil nuts can replace coconut and macadamia nuts in most recipes because they have a similar taste and texture. A light yellow oil is extracted from Brazil nuts; very expensive to manufacture, it is used primarily to make soap and other industrial products.

Storing

Shelled Brazil nuts should be refrigerated because they spoil quickly. Store them in a tightly sealed container to prevent them from absorbing food odors. Unshelled nuts will last for up to 2 months if stored in a dry, cool place that is inaccessible to insects.

Buying

When buying shelled Brazil nuts, look for nuts in vacuum-packed jars or in cans because they tend to be freshest.

Nutritional Information

	dried
water	3.3%
protein	7.2 g
fat	33.1 g
carbohydrates	6.4 g
fiber	5.7 g
	per 50 g

Brazil nuts are second only to macadamia nuts in terms of their fat content, which consists of 71% unsaturated acids (see *Fats*).

Brazil nuts are an excellent source of magnesium, copper, thiamine, phosphorus, potassium, and zinc; very high in fiber, they also contain niacin, iron, calcium, and vitamin B_6.

Pine nut

Pinus spp, **Coniferae**

The seed produced by several varieties of pine tree, including the umbrella pine or stone pine *(P. pinea)*. Pine nuts (also called pine seeds) are borne on the scales of pine cones. The trees which produce them grow mainly in Southern Europe, notably in Italy and the south of France, as well as in the Southern United States; some varieties are also found in Spain, Portugal, Siberia, and Australia.

The pine nuts available on markets outside of producing countries are usually quite expensive, since their conditions of cultivation make fertilization and harvesting difficult. In fact, the seeds are often harvested by hand. Moreover, pine trees only start producing nuts after 25 years and only become commercially viable after 75 years.

The Bible contains mention of pine nuts. They were also cultivated and widely appreciated by the Romans; remains of pine seeds were found among the ruins of Pompeii. Modern-day Italian cuisine still makes use of pine nuts in several dishes. For a long time, pine nuts were an important food for many Indian tribes of Mexico and the Southern United States.

Pine nuts are covered in a hard shell; the kernels are small, elongated, and cream-colored, with an average length of about ½ inch. They have a soft texture and a delicate, sweet flavor, although some varieties have a resinous taste. A large cone can bear close to 100 seeds, some of which are so small that an average of 1500 seeds are required to obtain a pound. When the mature pine cones open up in the fall, the seeds are harvested by hand or by machine. The araucaria *(Araucaria araucana)* is a variety of pine tree that produces larger nuts, averaging about 1½ inch in length and ¾ inch in width and enclosed in a thin, red-tinged, slightly woody shell. Araucaria nuts are more commonly eaten cooked (they are frequently boiled for 30 minutes). The word "araucaria" is derived from *Arauco*, the name of the tree's native region in Chile.

Pine nuts, or pignoli or pine seeds, are borne on the scales of the pinecone and are often harvested by hand. They are quite expensive.

Nutritional Information

	dried pine nut
water	6.7%
protein	18 g
fat	38 g
carbohydrates	10.7 g
fiber	10.7 g
calories	390
	per 75 g

The fat in pine nuts is composed of 80% unsaturated fatty acids (38% monounsaturated and 42% polyunsaturated) (see *Fats*).

Pine nuts are an excellent source of magnesium, potassium, phosphorus, iron, zinc, copper, and niacin; they are a good source of folic acid and provide riboflavin as well as vitamin B_6. Pine nuts are also a very rich source of dietary fiber.

Buying

Pine nuts are almost always sold shelled. It is best to buy them from stores with a rapid turnover, as they go rancid quickly. Avoid purchasing nuts with a rancid odor.

Serving Ideas

Pine nuts can be eaten whole, ground, or crushed. While most varieties are not eaten raw, the variety *P. pinea* is delicious whether raw or roasted.

The resinous flavor of pine nuts is largely neutralized during roasting. Roast the nuts for 10 minutes in the oven (350 °F) or in a pan on the stove. Pine nuts are used as both an ingredient and as a garnish. They are good in salads, stuffings, and sauces, as well as adding flavor and a decorative touch to puddings, flans, cakes, pastries, and biscuits. They can also be served with meat or fish. Pine nuts are an essential ingredient in Italian pesto sauce. They are also ground into a flour that is used in confectionery.

Pine nuts play an important role in the culinary traditions of many parts of the world, including India, the Middle East, Southern France and the Southern United States.

Storing

Shelled pine seeds turn rancid within 3 to 6 months of harvesting. Store them in an airtight container, preferably in the refrigerator, where they will keep for a month at the most. Frozen, they can be kept for 2 to 3 months, with or without their shell.

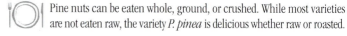

Ginkgo nut

Ginkgo biloba, Ginkgoaceae

The ginkgo nut is the fruit of a very decorative Asian tree that can grow to be 165 feet tall; the last surviving member of a group of species dating back several hundred million years, the ginkgo tree is said to have been called a "living fossil" by Darwin because it has remained relatively unchanged down through the ages. China is the only country where it still grows wild; regarded as a sacred tree in both China and Japan, it is often planted in parks and near Buddhist temples. Its remarkable longevity can be partially attributed to the length of its reproductive period, which lasts for over 1,000 years, as well as to the fact that the tree is extraordinarily resistant to insects, bacteria, and viruses. When the ginkgo tree was introduced into Europe during the 18th century, its very unusual appearance aroused considerable curiosity. It is now also grown in the United States and Australia. Since ginkgo nuts are rarely commercially available in the West, very few people are familiar with them.

Ginkgo nuts are enclosed in a fleshy membrane that is an orange shade of yellow; this membrane is removed before the nuts are sold because it starts to smell rancid shortly after the fruit is harvested and because the juice it contains can provoke itching in some people. Beneath this membrane is a very hard and smooth cream-colored oval shell that encloses a yellow-green kernel about the size of a small plum or olive. This kernel, which is covered with a layer of thin brown skin, has a mild resinous flavor.

Ginkgo nuts are covered with an orangey-yellow membrane that is removed before they are sold because it starts to smell rancid shortly after the nuts are gathered.

Buying

 Choose ginkgo nuts that are relatively heavy for their size. They are usually sold canned in water.

Preparing

 To make ginkgo nuts easier to peel, plunge them into simmering water for a few seconds.

Serving Ideas

Ginkgo nuts are usually roasted before being eaten plain or cooked further. They are added to soups, as well as to Asian vegetable, fish, seafood, pork, and poultry dishes. The Japanese, who use ginkgo nuts in many different ways, also eat them as a dessert fruit.

Storing

 Store ginkgo nuts in a tightly sealed container, away from heat and humidity.

Nutritional Information

	dried ginkgo nuts
water	12.5%
protein	5.2 g
fat	1.1 g
carbohydrates	37 g
fiber	0.3 g
	per 50 g

Ginkgo nuts are an excellent source of potassium and niacin, and a good source of thiamin; they also contain vitamin C, copper, phosphorus, magnesium, pantothenic acid, iron, riboflavin, and vitamin A.

Nuts and seeds

281

Chestnut

Castanea spp., **Fagaceae**

The fruit of the majestic chestnut tree, which is thought to have originated in the Mediterranean basin and Asia Minor, the chestnut has been eaten since prehistoric times in both of these regions, as well as in China. A very nourishing nut, it has long been a staple food in several parts of world, including the South of France, Italy, Corsica, and North Africa. Chestnuts are usually roasted, boiled, or ground into a flour that is used to make bread, cakes, and cookies. Most of the world's chestnuts are now grown in China, South Korea, Italy, Japan, and Spain.

The chestnut tree is related to the oak and can live for up to 500 years; it usually measures about 50 feet but can grow to be 100 feet tall with a trunk over 3 feet in diameter. Its long, veined deciduous leaves have jagged edges and are a very dark shade of green. Used to make parquet floors and furniture, the hard, finely grained wood of the chestnut tree is much sought after. It also contains numerous tannins that are used to cure leather.

There are over 100 different species of chestnut trees, several of which produce clusters of two or three separate nuts at the base of their leaves. Single chestnut trees start to produce nuts after 25 or 30 years, but it is usually 40 to 60 years before nuts begin to grow on trees planted close together.

Chestnuts are enclosed in spiky husks or burrs, most of which hold three separate small, flat triangular nuts. Each chestnut contains a very wrinkled cream-colored kernel that is covered with a layer of thin brown skin. The nut is protected by a hard, inedible reddish brown membrane known as the pericarp. Improved cultivated varieties of the chestnut tree produce a single large nut, which is fleshier and more flavorful. The French refer to these larger chestnuts, which are better for cooking, as *marrons* and to ordinary chestnuts as *châtaignes*. The inedible nuts of horse chestnut trees, which belong to the *Aesculus* genus of the Hippocastanaceae family, were once used to treat respiratory disease in horses; they are known as "conkers" in Britain because they are used to play a child's game in which they are struck against each other.

The husk is the spiky membrane surrounding the nuts; it holds three chestnuts, each of which contains a cream-colored kernel covered with a thin layer of beige or brown skin. It is enclosed in a hard, inedible brown membrane.

282

Buying

 Choose chestnuts that are heavy and firm, with shiny, taut shells.

Soft, light chestnuts with dull, wrinkled shells are no longer fresh and should be discarded.

Preparing

Peeling chestnuts requires patience; it involves removing both the shell and the bitter-tasting layer of thin brown skin. It is easier, but just as time-consuming, to peel chestnuts if they have been cooked and are still hot. To prevent chestnuts from bursting when cooked, use the point of a knife to make a cross-shaped incision on the rounded side of the shell.

Chestnuts can be peeled in one of three ways. (If they are not completely cooked before they are peeled, be sure to finish cooking them afterward or they will be difficult to digest.)

The first method is to simply remove the shell and the skin of raw chestnuts with a small, very sharp knife.

The second method involves piercing a hole in each of the chestnuts, then roasting them until they burst open. Allow them to cool before peeling them.

The third option is to boil the chestnuts after making an incision in the shell. In this case, they should be peeled while still hot.

Serving Ideas

Chestnuts can be boiled, steamed, braised, or roasted. They are added to soups, stuffings, and salads. Peeled whole chestnuts are canned in water or syrup, candied or crystallized with sugar *(marrons glacés),* preserved in alcohol, and used to make sweetened or unsweetened jams and purées.

Chestnuts are ground into a flour that is added to cakes or made into flat cakes (polenta), pancakes, waffles, porridge, or bread.

Chestnut purée is used to flavor ices, puddings, pastry creams, Bavarian cream, pies, and the like. Mont blanc, a famous dessert, consists of a meringue base covered with a dome of chestnut purée topped with Chantilly cream.

In Europe, chestnuts are traditionally served with game and poultry, especially during the Christmas and New Year season; in France and Italy, they are served as an alternative to other vegetable side dishes like potatoes. In Sardinia and Corsica, chestnuts are the main ingredient in several special dishes.

Storing

Store chestnuts in a cool, dry place that is inaccessible to rodents and insects. Peeled cooked chestnuts can be stored in the refrigerator for a few days. Both fresh and cooked chestnuts can be frozen, either peeled or in their shells. Fresh unpeeled chestnuts can be stored at room temperature for a week or refrigerated in a perforated plastic bag for 1 month; they can be frozen for up to 6 months. Dried chestnuts can be stored in a cool, dry place for 2 months or frozen for up to 6 months.

Nutritional Information

	fresh chestnuts	*boiled chestnuts*
water	52%	68.2%
protein	3.0 g	2.0 g
fat	1.2 g	1.4 g
carbohydrates	44.2 g	28.0 g
fiber	20.0 g	0.7 g
		per 100 g

Starch makes up 40% of the carbohydrates in chestnuts; in fact, chestnuts contain twice as much starch as do potatoes. Fresh chestnuts are a good source of vitamin C and potassium; they also contain folic acid, copper, vitamin B_6, magnesium, and thiamine.

Cooked chestnuts are an excellent source of potassium; they also contain vitamin C, copper, magnesium, folic acid, vitamin B_6, iron, thiamine, and phosphorus. Chestnuts are reputed to have antiseptic properties, and are said to prevent anemia and alleviate stomach problems. They can cause bloating and flatulence, especially when eaten raw, but these effects can be minimized by chewing the chestnuts thoroughly.

1 *Slice open the shell of the chestnut with the point of a sharp knife or paring knife.*

2 *Remove the shell, along with the thin layer of brown skin covering the chestnut.*

3 *Prepare the raw chestnuts as directed.*

dried chestnuts

peeled chestnut

Beechnut

Fagus spp., **Fagaceae**

The beechnut is the fruit of the common beech tree, an immense, sturdy tree that grows in the temperate forests of the Northern Hemisphere. There are over ten different species of beech trees, each of which produces a large quantity of nuts approximately every 3 years. Used mainly as feed for animals, beechnuts were initially eaten by humans only during food shortages, when they were ground into flour to make bread or used as a coffee substitute.

Beechnuts resemble small off-white chestnuts and taste somewhat like hazelnuts, a related species. Fleshy and spiky, each pyramid-shaped, brownish beechnut capsule contains two or three seeds. When fully grown, the capsule splits into four segments, revealing the beechnuts.

Beechnuts resemble small off-white chestnuts and taste somewhat like hazelnuts.

Nutritional Information

water	7%
protein	6 g
fat	50 g
carbohydrates	34 g
fiber	4 g
	per 100 g

Seventy-five percent of the fat in beechnuts consists of unsaturated acids (see *Fats*).

Serving Ideas

 Beechnuts can be eaten raw, but their flavor is less harsh when they are roasted like chestnuts. Very fatty, they yield an excellent edible oil, which is renowned for its flavor; beechnut oil can be stored for a very long time and is a versatile cooking oil, not unlike olive oil.

Storing

Store beechnuts in a tightly sealed container, away from heat and humidity.

Hazelnut

Corylus spp., **Corylaceae**

The hazelnut is the fruit of the hazel tree, a small, very decorative tree that thrives in humid and temperate climates. The hazel tree is thought to have originated in Asia Minor and to have spread to Italy, Spain, France, and Germany by way of ancient Greece.

The hazelnut is mentioned in Chinese manuscripts dating back 5,000 years, to very beginning of the history of agriculture. The Greeks and Romans ate hazelnuts as food but valued them most highly for their medicinal properties. The name of the hazelnut genus, *Corylus,* is derived from the Greek word *korys* and refers to the helmet- or hoodlike shape of the exterior membrane of the nut.

There are over 100 different varieties of hazel trees. Certain varieties are known as "filberts" because their nuts ripen around the feast day of St. Philbert, a 7th-century Frankish abbot. Slightly larger than other hazelnuts, filberts are referred to as *avelines* in France, because for many centuries they were cultivated intensively around the Italian city of Avellino.

Hazelnuts are round or oblong dry fruits that grow in pairs or in groups of three. Each nut is at least partially covered with a foliated membrane; as long as or longer than the nut itself, this membrane has to be removed before the nut can be broken open. The nut is enclosed in a shell whose hardness varies from one variety to another; yellowish in color, it is covered with a layer of thin brown skin.

Hazelnuts are gathered when completely ripe, usually after they have fallen to the ground; they are then washed, dried, and, quite frequently, shelled. When roasted, they are rubbed vigorously in a cloth while they are still hot to remove their thin brown skin.

Hazelnuts are covered with a green husk that has to be removed before they can be broken open. They are gathered when fully ripe, usually after they have fallen to the ground.

Buying

Hazelnuts are sold shelled or unshelled, peeled or unpeeled, whole or ground, and plain, roasted, or salted. Choose hazelnuts with no cracks or holes in their shells. The freshest shelled hazelnuts available are those sold in vacuum-packed glass jars or in cans.

Preparing

To roast hazelnuts, arrange them on a cookie sheet and bake them in the oven at 200° to 285°F until they turn golden brown, stirring them from time to time.

To peel hazelnuts (to remove their thin brown skin), roast them until the skin can be removed by rubbing it with a thick cloth. Roasting, grinding, and chopping hazelnuts enhances their flavor.

Serving Ideas

Hazelnuts can be used whole, ground, or chopped. Delicious both fresh and dried, they are often eaten as snacks or appetizers. Hazelnuts are added to cereals, salads, sauces, muffins, puddings, and ice cream. Ground hazelnuts are added cakes and cookies. Finely chopped hazelnuts can be used to make a flavored butter that is served with fish and shellfish. Hazelnuts go particularly well with poultry and game.

Hazelnuts can be made into pastes or butters that are used in same way as almond paste and almond butter, which they resemble. Hazelnuts are often added to nougat and are frequently combined with chocolate. A very fine oil is extracted from hazelnuts; it cannot be heated but is excellent in salads.

Nutritional Information

water	5%
protein	6.6 g
fat	32 g
carbohydrates	8 g
fiber	3 g
	per 50 g

Hazelnuts are an excellent source of magnesium and copper, and a good source of thiamine, potassium, vitamin B_6, and folic acid; they also contain phosphorus, zinc, iron, calcium, and pantothenic acid. They are a source of fiber, and the fat they contain is 88% unsaturated (see *Fats*).

Storing

Fresh hazelnuts are very perishable, especially if they have been shelled. They should be eaten as soon as possible. Hazelnuts are less fatty and less perishable than pecans, Brazil nuts, and macadamia nuts, but they tend to turn bitter and dry out relatively quickly. Store them at room temperature, away from heat and insects. Unshelled hazelnuts can be stored in a cool, dry place for up to 1 month. Shelled hazelnuts can be refrigerated for 3 to 4 months and frozen for up to 1 year.

Nuts and seeds

285

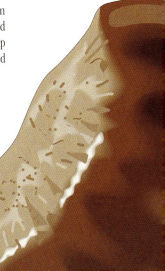

Sesame

Sesamum indicum, **Pedaliaceae**

The edible seeds of the sesame plant are highly valued for their precious oil, which represents more than half their total weight.

A n annual oil-producing plant native to Indonesia and East Africa, from where it later spread throughout Asia and North Africa. Cultivated in Mesopotamia more than 3,500 years ago, sesame is believed to have been one of the first condiments as well as one of the first plants to be used for its edible oil. Archeological remains show that sesame was grown in Palestine and in Syria some 3,000 years before the Christian era. An Egyptian tomb dating back 4,000 years depicts a baker adding sesame seeds to his dough.

The edible seeds of this plant are highly valued for their oil, which represents more than half of their total weight and which is extremely resistant to rancidity. In addition to its use as a food, sesame is used in the fabrication of cosmetics and as livestock feed (the residue from the extraction of the oil). At the end of the 17th century, sesame was introduced into the southern United States by African slaves. It is cultivated on a modest scale in America today, where it is used mainly as a condiment. The largest producers of sesame are India, China, and Mexico.

Sesame is a thick, bushy plant averaging about 2 feet in height; it bears pretty white or pink flowers from which the pods develop. Each pod contains numerous flat seeds that are creamy white, yellow, reddish, or blackish in color, depending on the variety. The tiny oval seeds are covered with a thin edible hull and have a nutty flavor. The famous magic formula "Open sesame!" from Arabian tales is thought to have been inspired by the fact that the pods of the sesame plant burst open when the enclosed seeds reach maturity.

Sesame seeds are harvested by hand; the plant is principally cultivated in countries where labor is cheap and readily available.

Buying

Sesame seeds are marketed raw or roasted, with or without their hulls.

Storing

Hulled sesame seeds should be kept in the refrigerator as they tend to turn rancid quickly. Whole seeds can be stored in an airtight container, away from heat and humidity. Sesame seeds can also be frozen.

Serving Ideas

Sesame seeds can be used as they are, plain or roasted. They often serve to garnish breads and cakes and are the basic ingredient, along with honey and almonds, in halvah, a Middle Eastern sweet. Sesame seeds can be ground into flour, but the flour will not rise since it does not contain gluten; sesame flour can be used alone or in combination with other flours.

Plain or roasted sesame seeds can be ground into a paste. When thick, this paste is called **sesame butter** and is used like peanut butter. The runnier version of sesame paste is called **tahini**; it is a very popular condiment, particularly in Asia and the Middle East, where it is used to flavor sauces, main dishes, and desserts. It is often combined with lemon juice, salt, pepper, and seasonings and used as a vinaigrette on vegetables, salads, or appetizers.

The oil extracted from sesame seeds is amber or yellow in color, with a thick consistency and a pronounced flavor. It is excellent for frying and does not turn rancid easily. Chinese, Japanese, Indian, and Arab cuisines use sesame oil as a condiment and as a seasoning, as well as for cooking. The Lebanese combine chickpeas and sesame oil to make hummus.

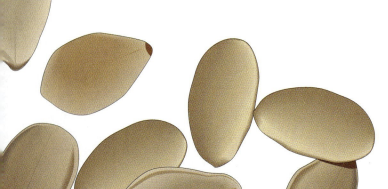

Baba Ghanoush

SERVES 4 TO 6

2 lb. (1 kg) eggplant	1 tbsp. olive oil
2 cloves garlic	A few drops of sesame oil
1 tbsp. fresh coriander (cilantro) leaves	¼ cup (60 ml) lemon juice
2 tbsp. sesame butter	Salt and ground pepper

Sesame butter is available in health-food stores and in grocery stores specializing in imported products.

1. Preheat the oven to 350°F (175°C).

2. Wash the eggplants and prick them in several places with a fork; place them on a cookie sheet and bake in the oven for 30 minutes.

3. Let the eggplants cool, and then peel them and cut the pulp into small cubes.

4. Chop the garlic and coriander.

5. In a blender, combine the eggplant with the garlic, coriander, sesame butter, olive oil, sesame oil, and lemon juice. Add salt and pepper to taste.

Blend the ingredients to obtain a smooth and homogenous purée.

Serve garnished with a few coriander leaves.

Nutritional Information

	dried whole sesame seed
water	4.7%
protein	13.3 g
fat	37.3 g
carbohydrates	17.6 g
fiber	7.6 g
	per 75 g

Dried sesame seeds are an excellent source of magnesium, potassium, iron, calcium, phosphorus, zinc, copper, thiamine, niacin, folic acid, and vitamin B_6; they are a very rich source of dietary fiber and contain riboflavin.

Sesame fat is composed of 82% unsaturated fatty acids (38% monounsaturates and 44% polyunsaturates). (See *Fats and Oils*.)

Sesame is said to have laxative, antiarthritic, and emollient properties. It is also beneficial for the nervous system, and is used to aid in digestion and to activate blood circulation. Sesame oil makes an excellent massage oil.

Because their tiny size makes it difficult to chew them well, sesame seeds are easier to digest when ground. The nutrients in sesame seeds are better assimilated by the body when they are consumed in the form of an oil, paste, or butter.

Almond

Prunus amygdalus or *Prunus dulcis,* Rosaceae

The almond is the sede almond tree, which is thought to have originated in Asia and North Africa; the almond has been appreciated since the earliest days of human history and is mentioned in ancient texts such as the Bible. Archeologists have found traces of the cultivation of almonds dating back to the time of the Assyrians and the ancient Persians, but evidence suggests that the Greeks were the first to cultivate the seed; in fact, the Romans referred to the almond as the "Greek nut." The ancients used the almond as both a food and a medicine.

The almond tree usually grows to a height of 20 to 30 feet. It resembles the peach tree and belongs to same family, but unlike the peach, the dry fruit of the almond tree is not fleshy. Very sensitive to the cold, the almond tree thrives in regions with Mediterranean climates, and it is grown in South America, California, and Australia as well as in Europe.

The fruit of the almond tree contains an off-white oval seed (the almond) that is covered with thin brownish "skin" and surrounded by a shell whose firmness depends on the particular variety of almond (over 100 varieties are grown in California). The shell itself is covered with a tough, fibrous green husk that breaks open when the almond is fully grown. Although the shell usually houses only one almond, it can contain twin seeds, known as Philippine almonds. The word "almond" can refer to anything that is almond-shaped, including the seeds of other fruits (especially in France). Almonds are classified as either bitter or sweet:

The **bitter almond** (*P. amygdalus* var. *amara*) contains several rather toxic substances, including the hydrocyanic acid that makes it taste bitter; these toxins are removed from bitter-almond oil before it is used in the preparation of food. A clear liquid, the essential oil of the bitter almond is used as a flavoring (almond essence) and to make liqueurs such as amaretto.

The **sweet almond** (*P. amygdalus* var. *dulcis*) is the widely available edible seed commonly known as the "almond"; although it is usually eaten dried, it can be eaten fresh if its shell is green, firm, and still somewhat tender.

The almond is composed of an off-white seed that is covered with thin brownish "skin" and surrounded by a shell, itself is covered with a tough, fibrous green husk that breaks open when the almond is fully grown.

Nutritional Information

	dried unbleached almonds
water	4.4%
protein	9.9 g
fat	26 g
carbohydrates	10.2 g
fiber	3.4 g
	per 50 g

The fat in almonds is comprised of 86% unsaturated acids (65% monounsaturated and 21% polyunsaturated, see *Fats*). A nutritious food, the sweet almond is an excellent source of magnesium and potassium, and a good source of phosphorous, riboflavin, copper, niacin, and zinc; it also contains folic acid, iron, calcium, and thiamin.

The sweet almond is said to have remineralizing properties, while almond milk is reputed to alleviate inflammations of the intestine and stomach. Almond oil may promote the elimination of gallstones, and it is sometimes applied externally to speed the healing of burns and cracks, as well as to relieve dry skin.

Buying

Almonds are sold in many different forms: shelled or unshelled, whole or split, cut into slivers or small sticks, minced or ground, plain or roasted, peeled or unpeeled, salted, smoked or sweetened, covered in sugar or chocolate, and as almond butter, almond oil, or sweetened or unsweetened almond paste.

Almonds that are still inside their shells do not spoil as quickly as shelled almonds; choose almonds with undamaged shells. When buying shelled almonds, look for almonds that are packed in hermetically sealed jars, cans, or bags; these types of packaging ensure maximum freshness. Buy almonds in stores where the merchandise is restocked on a regular basis.

Preparing

It is easy to peel almonds (to remove the thin layer of brown "skin") once they have been blanched. This involves plunging the almonds into boiling water for 2 to 3 minutes. Once their "skin" starts to swell, drain the almonds and rinse them under cold water to cool them down. Remove the "skin" by pinching the almonds between your thumb and index finger; then dry or roast them.

Storing

Almonds should be stored in a tightly sealed container, away from sunlight and humidity.

Both shelled and unshelled almonds can be frozen for up to 1 year. Unshelled almonds can also be stored for up to 1 year in a cool, dry place, but shelled almonds must be refrigerated and should not be kept for any longer than 6 months.

Cooking

Almonds can be roasted dry or in oil, either in the oven or in a frying pan on the stovetop. They can be roasted whole, in pieces or in slices, either peeled or unpeeled.

Dry-roasting almonds in the oven

Heat the oven to 350°F (175°C). Arrange a single layer of almonds on a baking sheet. Cook them until they turn golden brown, stirring them from time to time to ensure that they are evenly roasted. The cooking time will vary depending on the intensity of the heat and the size of the almonds. Remove the almonds from the oven and place them in a container to cool.

Oven-roasting almonds in oil

Follow the instructions for dry-roasting, but reduce the temperature to between 200° and 275°F (100° and 140°C), and coat the almonds with a little oil.

Roasting almonds in a frying pan

Roast the almonds in a dry nonstick pan or in a little oil. Cook them over medium heat, stirring constantly.

Trout with Almonds

SERVES 4

4 gutted trout, each
  weighing approximately
  ½ lb. (250 g)
½ cup (125 ml) milk
¼ cup (60 ml) flour
Salt and ground pepper

2 tbsp. oil
¼ cup (60 ml) butter
¼ cup (60 ml) split
  almonds
1 lemon

1. Wash the trout and pat them dry, then dip them first in the milk and then in the seasoned flour.

2. In a large frying pan, heat the oil and half the butter. Brown the trout over medium heat, for approximately 7 minutes per side or until the skin can be easily removed with a fork.

3. While the trout are cooking, melt the rest of the butter in a small saucepan, and lightly brown the almonds in the butter. Pour this mixture over the trout and decorate the fish with slices or wedges of lemon.

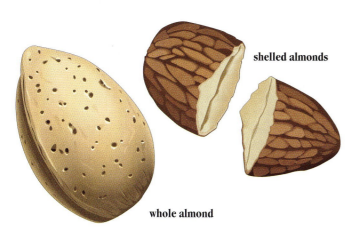

shelled almonds

whole almond

Serving Ideas

Almonds can be used in many different ways because their mild flavor complements practically every kind of food. They are added to a wide variety of both sweet and savory dishes, including cereals, salads, cakes, cookies, pastries, ice cream, and other sweet snacks.

Whole, split, or ground almonds are particularly good with fish (such as trout) and chicken, especially in dishes like chicken *à l'indienne* with Royale sauce. Split almonds browned in butter *(amandine)* are used to garnish fillets of fish, chicken pieces, and vegetables. Ground sweetened almonds can also be made into a paste. Sometimes referred to as "marzipan," almond paste is used to decorate cakes as well as to make candies and chocolates. Almonds are often eaten as appetizers or snacks, either alone or with dried fruit, seeds, and other nuts. They are particularly good with dates, coffee, and chocolate.

When ground, almonds turn into a creamy butter, which, like peanut butter, can be used as a sandwich spread or to flavor sauces, soups, and stews. Almond butter has a much milder flavor than peanut butter.

To make almond milk, add milk or hot water to ground almonds, then cover the mixture and allow it to cook over low heat for 30 minutes. Once the mixture has cooled, strain it through muslin, applying pressure to squeeze out the liquid. Almond milk is used to flavor various dishes and is the main ingredient in *orgeat,* a syrup flavored with orange-flower water that is diluted with water and served as a refreshment.

Dry ground almonds are used to make stuffings and are added to a variety of desserts. In some recipes, almond powder is substituted for some or all of the flour. Cakes made with almond powder have a rich texture and are very flavorful.

The many sweet snacks made with almonds include sugar-coated almonds and pralines (almonds coated with carmelized sugar), nougat, and chocolates.

Sweet almonds yield an edible oil that cannot be heated but is often used in salads. Not merely a foodstuff, almond oil is also used by drug and cosmetic manufacturers, as well as by massage therapists. Almond essence is used to flavor numerous foods, including cakes, cookies, flans, pies, puddings, and drinks. It is also a key ingredient in amaretto, a delicious Italian liqueur.

Sunflower seed

Helianthus annuus, **Compositae**

An annual plant that originated in Mexico and Peru, the sunflower is believed to be one of the first plants ever grown as a crop in the United States. Native Americans have used various parts of the sunflower for over 5,000 years – the oil-producing seeds, the stems, the flowers, and the roots. The sunflower was first grown in Europe by the Spanish during the 15th century and was then introduced into numerous other countries. The plant has great commercial importance because the edible oil extracted from its seeds is rich in polyunsaturated fatty acids, its flowers are the source of a substance used to treat malaria, and its petals are used by the dyeing industry. The countries that make up the former Soviet Union are the world's leading producers of sunflowers, followed by Argentina, France, China, Spain, and the United States.

The Latin name of the sunflower, *Helianthus annuus,* also refers to the sun – *Helianthus* is a conflation of the Greek words for "sun" *(helios)* and "flower" *(anthos)* ; it was once believed that the flower followed the movements of the sun, which does not in fact appear to be the case. This magnificent plant is adorned with a large yellow flower that sits atop a long, thick, hairy stem. The flowers, or capitula, can grow to be 20 inches in diameter, and the plants can be anywhere from 3 to 20 feet tall. The capitula consist of thousands of individual flowers (as many as 20,000) arranged side by side, forming a flat disk that is surrounded by yellow petals. These flowers produce grayish green or black seeds (depending on the species) that are enclosed in thin gray or black shells, some of which are adorned with black and white stripes. Bees feed on the nectar covering the shells. Sunflower seeds have a mild flavor not unlike that of the Jerusalem artichoke, a related species.

The *Helianthus* genus includes over 100 different species, but only two varieties are generally considered to be sunflowers – the oil-producing Russian variety, whose small seeds are over 40% oil, and the non-oil-producing North American variety, whose large seeds are used mainly for human consumption and as birdseed.

Buying

Sunflower seeds are sold shelled or unshelled, raw or roasted, and salted or unsalted. For maximum freshness, buy sunflower seeds in stores where the stock turns over rapidly. When buying raw shelled seeds, avoid yellowish seeds, which are no longer fresh and may be rancid.

Preparing

Shelling sunflower seeds by hand requires time and patience. They can be shelled in a seed mill or an electric mixer, but this is delicate operation. When using a seed mill, put the seeds through the largest opening; most of the shells should open without doing too much damage to the seeds. To separate the seeds from the shells, plunge the entire mixture into cold water; the relatively light shells will float to the surface and can be skimmed off. Strain the seeds as quickly as possible, then dry them.

When using a mixer, pour a small amount of seeds into the bowl and turn the mixer on for a few seconds, then separate the seeds from the shells in water. This method is less efficient because more of the seeds are crushed, especially if they are mixed for any longer than is absolutely necessary.

Nutritional Information

	dried sunflower seeds	*oil-roasted sunflower seeds*
water	5.4%	2.6%
protein	17.1 g	16.1 g
fat	37.2 g	43.1 g
carbohydrates	14.1 g	11.0 g
fiber	9.9 g	5.1 g
		per 75 g

The fat in sunflowers is made up of 85% unsaturated acids – 19% monoun-saturated acids and 66% polyunsaturated acids (see *Fats*). Very rich in nutrients, dried sunflower seeds are an excellent source of thiamine, magnesium, folic acid, pantothenic acid, copper, phosphorus, potassium, zinc, iron, niacin, and vitamin B_6; very high in fiber, they also contain riboflavin and calcium.

Oil-roasted sunflower seeds are an excellent source of folic acid, phosphorus, pantothenic acid, copper, zinc, magnesium, iron, vitamin B_6, niacin, and potassium, and a good source of thiamine; they also contain riboflavin and are high in fiber.

Sunflower seeds are an excellent source of potassium; foods rich in potassium are often recommended for people with high blood pressure because they promote the elimination of sodium by means of urination. Sunflower seeds are also said to promote expectoration and to alleviate the symptoms of colds, coughs, and asthma. They are sometimes used to treat anemia, gastroduodenal ulcers, and poor vision.

Serving Ideas

Sunflower seeds can be used plain or roasted, either whole or chopped; they can also be ground or sprouted. A versatile food, they can be added to virtually any dish. Since they are rich in protein, they enhance the nutritional value of foods to which they are added; however, they are also high in fat and calories. Whole sunflower seeds can add a unique crunchiness to salads, stuffings, sauces, vegetable dishes, cakes, and yogurt. Ground sunflower seeds can be combined with flour to make pancakes, cookies, and cakes. The seeds often turn green when cooked – the result of a reaction between the chlorogenic acid and the amino acids. The floral buds of sunflowers can be eaten like artichokes.

Cooking

Usually roasted in saturated oil, commercially available sunflower seeds are often fatty, overcooked, salty, and laden with additives (gum arabic, monosodium glutamate, etc.). However, it is easy to roast fresh sunflower seeds at home. Cook them in a frying pan over medium heat (no oil is required), stirring constantly, or bake them for 10 minutes in the oven (200°F), stirring them from time to time. Once they have been baked, the seeds can be coated with a small amount of oil so salt will stick to them.

Storing

Store sunflower seeds in a cool, dry place that is inaccessible to rodents and insects. If they are shelled, ground, chopped, or in the form of a butter, store them in the refrigerator to prevent them from going rancid. Sunflower seeds can be frozen.

The thousands of flowers that constitute the flat disk of the sunflower produce seeds that are enclosed in gray or black shells, which are sometimes adorned with black and white stripes.

Nuts and Seeds

291

Pistachio Nut

Pistacia vera, Anacardiaceae

The seed of the pistachio tree, a deciduous tree native to Asia Minor that yields fruits twice a year. Pistachio nuts were introduced into the Mediterranean region in the 1st century B.C.

A relative of the cashew, the pistachio tree can attain 16 to 32 feet in height and grows best in hot, dry climates, particularly at high altitudes. More drought-resistant than any other fruit tree, the pistachio is also extremely frost-resistant. In its natural habitat, the pistachio tree has a life span of over 150 years.

The pistachio tree grows wild in the mountainous regions of Russia and Turkistan (central Asia) and is cultivated in most countries of central Asia and the Near East, in the Mediterranean region of Europe, and in the United States, especially in California, where it was introduced in the 1890s. Turkey, Iran, Palestine, and Syria are important producers of pistachio nuts today.

Pistachios grow in clusters and are harvested by hand or by machines that shake the nuts from the trees, allowing for them to be gathered from the ground. After harvesting, the nuts are soaked in order to rid them of their fleshy reddish or yellow shell. The pistachio nuts are then dried in the sun.

The greenish kernel of the pistachio nut is small and round and has a delicately sweet taste. It is covered with a fine brownish skin and encased in a thin, fairly hard shell that splits open along its lengthwise seam when the fruit is ripe. Initially cream-colored, the shell takes on a pinkish hue as it dries; the food industry often treats the shells of pistachios with a red dye to make them even pinker.

Pistachios grow in clusters and are harvested by hand or by machines that shake the nuts from the trees, allowing for them to be gathered from the ground.

Nutritional Information

	dried pistachio nut	*dry-roasted pistachio nut*
water	4%	2.1%
protein	10.3 g	7.5 g
fat	24.2 g	26.4 g
carbohydrates	12.4 g	13.8 g
fiber	5.4 g	2.9 g
calories	288	303
		per 50 g

The fat content of pistachio nuts is composed of 83% unsaturated fatty acids, including 68% monounsaturated fats and 15% polyunsaturated fats (see *Fats*). Dried pistachio nuts are an excellent source of potassium, magnesium, copper, and thiamine; they are also a good source of iron and phosphorus, as well as supplying folic acid, pantothenic acid, niacin, riboflavin, vitamin C, vitamin B_6, calcium, and zinc. Dried pistachio nuts are rich in dietary fiber.

Dry-roasted pistachio nuts are an excellent source of potassium, magnesium, and copper; they are a good source of thiamine and phosphorus and provide folic acid, pantothenic acid, niacin, riboflavin, vitamin C, vitamin B_6, iron, and zinc. Dry-roasted pistachio nuts are also a source of dietary fiber.

Buying

Pistachio nuts are often sold roasted and salted in their shells. When buying shelled nuts, it is best to buy them vacuum-packed in glass jars or in cans for maximum freshness.

Preparing

For easy removal of the brownish layer of skin, blanch the pistachio nuts in boiling water for 2 to 3 minutes; drain and cool, and rub the skins off while the nuts are still lukewarm.

Serving Ideas

Pistachio nuts are eaten whole, ground, or chopped, with or without salt. For cooking, it is best to use nuts that have not been dyed red. Pistachio nuts are added to salads, sauces, stuffings, pâtés, and cereals, as well as to dessert foods like puddings, cakes, pastries, and ice cream. They are often used in confectionery (as in nougat) and in delicatessen meats.

Mediterranean and Asian cuisines make wide use of pistachio nuts, particularly in pastries and in meat and poultry dishes. In Indian cooking, these nuts are often purÇed and served as a condiment with rice and vegetables.

Storing

Store pistachio nuts in an airtight container in a dry place, preferably in the refrigerator; unshelled, they can be refrigerated for 3 months or frozen for 1 year. Shelled pistachio nuts will keep for 3 months in the refrigerator but are not suitable for freezing.

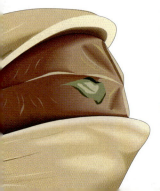

Seaweed

Introduction

Plants that grow in, or near, salt water or fresh water, seaweed has been eaten since ancient times in certain parts of the world, mainly by the inhabitants of coastal regions in northwestern Europe (Scotland, Ireland, Norway, Iceland), Hawaii, South America, the Pacific islands, New Zealand, and Asia (especially in Japan, China, and Korea). Archeological evidence found in Japan suggests that seaweed has been part of the human diet for at least 10,000 years. The Japanese eat more seaweed per capita than people of any other nationality, and Japan is the world's leading producer and exporter of seaweed; this explains why individual varieties of seaweed are often referred to by their Japanese names (kombu, wakame, hijiki, arame, etc.).

Seaweed has no leaves, stems, or roots; the plant body of seaweed, which consists of nonvascular tissue, is referred to as the "thallus," a term derived from the Greek word *thallos,* meaning "green shoot." These perennial or annual plants grow in warm, temperate, or cold water. Their size and shape are determined by their habitat. The plants found in warm seas are grasses or bushes that rarely grow to heights of more than 12 inches, while seaweed that grows in colder waters is quite lush and can measure anywhere from 3 to 33 feet in length.

Like plants that grow on land, seaweed photosynthesizes organic compounds by means of pigments such as chlorophyl. The texture and flavor of seaweed vary greatly from one species to another; for example, it can be rubbery, tender, or crisp. There are almost 25,000 different species of seaweed, only a very small number of which have a pleasant taste (between 40 and 50 species). These edible varieties belong to one of four groups – brown algae (Pheophyceae), green algae (Chlorophyceae), red algae (Rhodophyceae), and blue-green algae (Cyanophyceae).

Several species of seaweed are cultivated by placing spore-bearing shoots, plastic tubes, or ropes in temperature-controlled reservoirs of seawater, or in the sea itself. Each class of seaweed has particular characteristics.

Brown algae is the most abundant and most commonly used variety. It is brown in color because yellow and brown pigments known as xanthophyls mask the green chlorophyl. The species of brown seaweed harvested in Japan include arame, hijiki, kombu, and wakame. Kelp is the most common variety of brown seaweed in North America. Brown seaweed grows at moderate depths.

The chlorophyl in **green algae** is not masked by other pigments. Among the plants classified as green algae are those comprising the *Ulva* and *Caulerpa* genuses. Certain species belonging to the *Ulva* genus are referred to as "sea lettuce," and *Caulerpa* algae are known as "sea grapes" due to their grapelike shape (they too taste like lettuce). Green seaweed grows to be 2 to 4 inches long and generally has a delicate taste and texture.

Red algae is colored by a red pigment known as phycoerythrin, which masks the green chlorophyl. The numerous plants classified as red algae include the 30 species comprising the *Porphyra* genus, dulse *(Palmaria palmata),* and carrageen *(Chondrus crispus).* Galactose, a simple sugar found in red algae, combines with other monosaccharides to form various viscous polysaccharides. These are extracted from several different species of seaweed to produce agar-agar and carrageen, substances used in the food industry as gelling, emulsifying, and stabilizing agents.

Blue-green algae are primitive microscopic plants that are sometimes classified as bacteria. These include spirulina, which is often consumed as a nutritional supplement.

Buying

 Fresh seaweed should be dark and richly colored, not pale or discolored. Dried or fresh seaweed is available in health-food stores.

Preparing

Seaweed should be washed before it is used because it often contains sand and small shells. Dried seaweed is almost always soaked before it is eaten or cooked (for 5 to 60 minutes or longer). The water in which it is soaked can be used to make broths or sauces and to cook pasta or grains.

Serving Ideas

Seaweed can be eaten either hot or cold and is used as a seasoning, garnish, or nutritional supplement (as a powder or flakes, or in capsules or tablets). Prepared in a variety of ways, it can be boiled, roasted, steamed, fried, sautéed, or marinated in vinegar or tamari. It can be served as an appetizer, a vegetable side dish, or a dessert, and can also be used to make tea. It is often added to hors d'oeuvres, soups, salads, and pasta dishes. Sea lettuce is a common ingredient in salads and soups.

Dried seaweed can be rehydrated or eaten as is as a snack.

Seaweed can be used in a variety of ways. It is used as a food additive, fertilizer, and fodder, as well as to develop photographs and to make glue, paper, rubber, cement, paint, fabric, gunpowder, glass, toothpaste, and cosmetics.

Nutritional Information

The nutritional value of seaweed depends on the species, as well as on where it is grown and when it is harvested. Spirulina is exceptionally rich in protein; 100 grams of dried spirulina contains 54 to 65 grams of protein.

The proteins in seaweed are comprised of a better balance of amino acids than those found in plants that grow on land but are not as well balanced as animal proteins. Most varieties of seaweed are deficient only in sulfuric amino acids (see *Complementary proteins*).

Carbohydrates are a major component of seaweed, usually comprising from 40% to 60% of their total weight. Most of these carbohydrates are complex organic compounds; in fact, only 5% to 10% of them are simple sugars. Relatively little research has been done on the digestibility of the carbohydrates found in seaweed, but they are known to be quite difficult to digest, which means that seaweed is not very fattening. However, it appears that when people eat seaweed on a regular basis, their digestive systems develop enzymes that are better able to assimilate the polysaccharides.

Seaweed is low in fat and calories. It is an excellent source of minerals (which comprise approximately 5% to 10% of the total weight of dried seaweed), especially calcium and iodine. It also contains significant quantities of several vitamins, including vitamin A (in the form of betacarotene), certain B-complex vitamins (especially thiamine, riboflavin, and niacin), and vitamin C.

Seaweed is thought to have numerous medicinal properties. The ailments seaweed is reputed to alleviate or cure include arteriosclerosis, hypertension, obesity, constipation, hyperthyroidism, tumors, bacterial infections, and intestinal worms. Unfortunately, much research remains to be done concerning the actual impact of seaweed on some of these conditions. Therapies involving seawater and seaweed baths make use of the medicinal properties of seaweed, as do certain pharmacological preparations. The medications containing seaweed include anticoagulants, vermifuges, and drugs used to treat high blood pressure.

Storing

Most varieties of fresh seaweed can be refrigerated for a few days. Store dehydrated seaweed in a tightly sealed container (such as a glass jar) in a cool, dry, dark place. Cooked seaweed should be refrigerated.

Most varieties of seaweed can be frozen, with the notable exception of kelp.

Arame

Eisenia bicyclis, Pheophyceae

A plant with large serrated fronds that are approximately 12 inches long and 1½ inches wide, arame is thicker than other kinds of seaweed. Like hijiki, it is cooked for several hours to soften its tough fibers before being dried. Sold in thin strips, it resembles hijiki but is composed of flat rather than round strands. Arame is yellowish brown when fresh and becomes blackish when cooked. More tender if picked before it is fully grown, it is slightly crisper than hijiki and has a milder, sweeter taste. Most arame is gathered near the Ise Peninsula in Japan. It grows on rocks beneath the surface of the sea.

Nutritional Information

	raw
protein	8 g
fat	0.1 g
carbohydrates	56 g
	per 100 g

Preparing

Wash arame twice in cold water, stirring it thoroughly to eliminate sand and other impurities. Soak it for 5 minutes before eating it raw, boil it for 5 to 10 minutes, or sauté it for a few minutes. Arame doubles in volume when soaked.

Serving Ideas

Arame is particularly good with tofu and vegetables. It is added to soups, especially miso soup, and salads (it is delicious when marinated in vinegar, soy sauce, and sugar). Frequently served as a vegetable side dish, it is often fried.

Wakame

Undaria pinnatifida, Pheophyceae

Wakame is a seaweed that grows at depths of 20 to 40 feet and resembles a large, deeply serrated leaf. There is a thick mucilaginous rib in the center of the upper portion of the leaf. The Japanese are especially fond of wakame, whether it is salted, seasoned with vinegar, or prepared in some other way. Wakame is usually 2 to 4 feet long and 12 to 16 inches wide. It has a delicate texture and flavor.

Nutritional Information

	dried wakame
protein	13 g
fat	2.7g
carbohydrates	46 g
	per 100 g

Wakame is particularly rich in calcium.

Serving Ideas

Wakame can be eaten raw after it has been soaked for 3 to 5 minutes. It is also frequently cooked (for no more than a few minutes). Since it has a mild flavor, it can be used in a variety of ways. It goes well with rice, pasta, vegetables, tofu, meat, poultry, fish, and shellfish. It can also be added to soups, salads, and marinades. Like kombu, wakame softens the hard fibers of foods with which it is cooked, shortening the time required to cook them. It is especially good with legumes.

Kombu

Laminaria spp., Pheophyceae

K ombu is a large seaweed with flat, smooth fronds that can be quite broad and thick, like the leafy fronds of the most popular variety, ma-kombu *(Laminaria japonica),* which grows to be 3 to 10 feet high. The extract of kombu roots is a traditional remedy for high blood pressure, and kombu itself has been eaten since ancient times, both in Asia and along the coasts of the Atlantic and the Pacific. In Japan, there are special boutiques that sell nothing but kombu and kombu products; many of the over 300 kombu products that are available, which include teas and condiments, have specific uses.

Kombu is rich in glutamic acid, an amino acid that enhances the flavor of foods when combined with water. Monosodium glutamate, the sodium salt of glutamic acid, is commonly used as a flavoring in Asian cuisine (the monosodium glutamate used today is an industrial product made by fermenting cane sugar, beets, pineapple, or tapioca). Glutamic acid also tenderizes fiber and makes food easier to digest. Kombu is particularly good when prepared with vegetables, which cook faster when the seaweed is added.

Preparing

To make kombu broth, begin by washing the kombu thoroughly to eliminate sand and other impurities. Use between 1 and 2 ounces of dried kombu per quart of broth. First, soak the kombu for 30 minutes in 10% to 20% more water than is required to make the broth. Then drain it, add fresh water, and heat it gently. Remove the kombu before the water comes to a boil.

Serving Ideas

Kombu is used primarily to make broths. In Japan, kombu broth is known as *dashi* and is the basic ingredient in many dishes.

If kombu is boiled for any longer than 10 to 15 minutes, inorganic magnesium, sulfuric acid, and calcium will be released into the water, giving the broth an unpleasant flavor and dissolving carbohydrates that can make it sticky. Do not discard the boiled kombu, which can be used to make other dishes. It is infused to make kombu tea, a popular drink, and is also added to numerous marinated, boiled, roasted, and fried dishes.

Nutritional Information

	dried
protein	6.0 g
fat	1.0 g
carbohydrates	56 g
	per 100 g

Kombu is particularly rich in calcium, iron, and potassium. Like arame, it contains a large amount of iodine, which is why the Chinese have used it to treat gout for centuries.

Seaweed

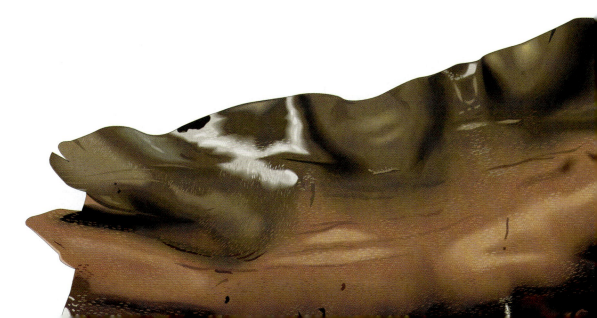

Hijiki

Hizikia fusiforme, Pheophyceae

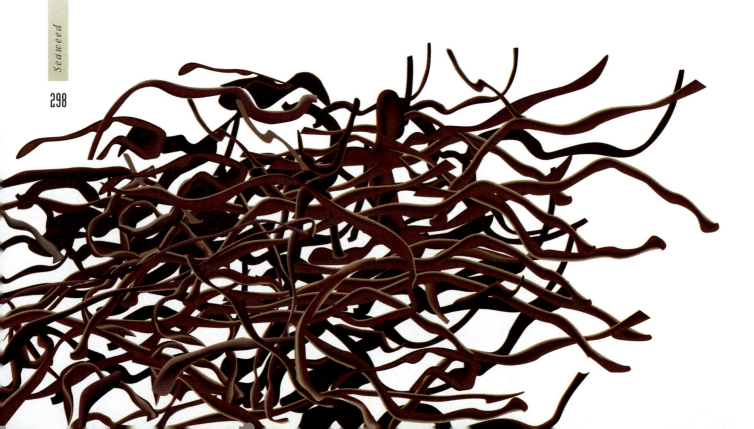

A plant that grows on rocks beneath the surface of the sea, hijiki consists of numerous cylindrical twigs that are attached to stems. It is shaped like a bush and can be anywhere from 16 to 40 inches high.

Hijiki is first dried, then boiled or steamed for a few hours. Once it becomes tender, it is dried again and soaked in arame juice, then dried one last time in the sun. A blackish brown color, dehydrated hijiki twigs are minuscule but swell to at least five times their size when soaked. At this stage, they resemble black noodles. Stronger-tasting than arame, hijiki has a somewhat crunchy texture.

Preparing

Hijiki should be soaked for 20 to 30 minutes in lukewarm water before being eaten raw, steamed, or cooked in water or oil.

Cooking

Hijiki is often steamed for about 20 minutes, then sautéed or simmered. The Japanese like to sauté hijiki, then simmer it in a liquid flavored with soy sauce and sugar.

Nutritional Information

	dried
protein	8 g
fat	0.1 g
carbohydrates	56 g
	per 100 g

Serving Ideas

Hijiki is particularly good when served with root vegetables, grains (rice, millet, etc.), fish, and shellfish. It is often added to soups, sandwiches, salads, and pancakes. It can be served as a vegetable or as an infusion.

Kelp

Macrocystis pyrifera, Pheophyceae

A rapidly growing plant, giant kelp *(Macrocystis pyrifera)* is the largest variety of seaweed, sometimes attaining heights of almost 200 feet. Kelp is common on the Pacific and Atlantic coasts of North America.

Serving Ideas

The large fronds of the kelp plant are rich in alginic acid; also found in other varieties of brown seaweed, alginic acid becomes extremely viscous when mixed with water. Alginate, the salt in alginic acid, is used as an additive by the food industry, especially as a thickening, stabilizing, and emulsifying agent. Alginate is also used to make products such as medicines, paper, fabrics, paint, and cosmetics.

Dried kelp is ground, then compressed into capsules for use as a nutritional supplement. Ground kelp can also be used as a condiment.

Nutritional Information

	raw
proteins	1.7 g
fat	0.6 g
carbohydrates	10 g
	per 100 g

Kelp is particularly rich in iodine.

Sea lettuce

Ulva lactuca and *Ulva fasciata*, Chlorophyceae

Some kinds of green seaweed are known as "sea lettuce" because they resemble lettuce leaves. Sea lettuce can be anywhere from 4 to 20 inches long, but all varieties are tender and have a very similar taste.

Preparing

Rehydrate sea lettuce by soaking it in water for 3 to 4 minutes; then cook it for 5 minutes or eat it raw. It can be added to salads and soups.

Nutritional Information

	raw
protein	17 g
fat	0.9 g
carbohydrates	37 g
calories	223
	per 100 g

Agar-agar

A transparent mucilaginous substance, agar-agar is used like gelatin, which it can replace in most recipes. Foods thickened with agar-agar are firmer and melt less readily than those containing gelatin. Agar-agar is also known by its Japanese name, *kanten; agar* is the Malay word for "seaweed."

Agar-agar is derived from several species of red seaweed (usually those belonging to the genus Gelidium). It consists of two polysaccharides (or carbohydrates) agarose (70%) and agaropectin (30%). Traditionally, agar-agar is made by chopping dried seaweed, then boiling it in water along with an acid ingredient (diluted acetic or sulfuric acid). The hot liquid is filtered to remove any remaining pieces of seaweed, then neutralized with an alkaline ingredient such as sodium bicarbonate (baking soda). A jelly forms when the temperature of the liquid falls below 104°F (40°C). To eliminate the aftertaste of seaweed and any remaining traces of color, the jelly is frozen, defrosted, and dehydrated, either two or three times.

Nutritional Information

	dry
protein	6 g
fat	0.3 g
carbohydrates	81 g
calories	306
	per 100 g

Agar-agar is particularly rich in iron. Since it is eight to ten times more efficient than gelatin, it adds far fewer calories to foods. Agar-agar is a mild laxative and can provoke allergic reactions in some people.

Buying

Agar-agar is available as a powder, flakes, bars, or strands.

Preparing

Although agar-agar will not dissolve in cold water, it does absorb moisture, becoming soft and swollen. It melts when heated and forms a jelly as it cools. To use agar-agar, bring the liquid containing the substance to the boiling point and melt it over low heat. The amount of agar-agar required depends on the desired consistency of the final product, as well as on the nature of the substance to which the agar-agar is added: the thicker or more acidic the liquid, the greater the amount of agar-agar required. Generally, ¼ to ½ ounce (usually ⅓ ounce) of agar-agar is required per quart of liquid (water, juice, stock). When using bars of agar-agar, break them into small pieces before attempting to melt them in liquid.

Serving Ideas

Agar-agar is used to thicken jellies containing fruit juices or puréed fruit. Vegetarians often use it as substitute for gelatin, which is an animal protein. Among the ways in which agar-agar is used in the food industry is as a stabilizing agent; it is added to fruit jellies, cream, flavored milk, ice cream, and sherbets.

Dulse

Palmaria palmata, Rhodophyceae

A seaweed that grows in the cold, turbulent waters of rocky coasts, dulse is particularly abundant in the Atlantic and has been eaten in the coastal regions of western Europe for thousands of years.

Usually between 6 and 12 inches long, it grows below the low-tide line. Its crimson-red fronds have a mild texture and a strong flavor.

Serving Ideas

Once it has been soaked, dulse can be used raw or cooked like other kinds of seaweed, which it can replace in most recipes. It is delicious in soups and salads.

Nutritional Information

protein	20 g
fat	3.2 g
carbohydrates	44 g
	per 100 g

Dulse is especially rich in iron.

Carrageen

Chondrus crispus, Rhodophyceae

A seaweed measuring between 2 and 5 inches wide, carrageen is abundant in the North Atlantic, especially along the Irish coast, as well as in France, Britain, Spain, and Canada. It can be yellowish green, brown, or crimson in color and cannot be eaten raw. Carrageen is used to make a viscous polysaccharide that shares its name (this substance is also made from other types of red seaweed). Also known as Irish moss, carrageen has been used in Ireland for centuries and is named for an Irish coastal village, Carragheen, where it is gathered and distributed.

The food additive known as carrageen is a powerful gelling agent. The Irish use it to stiffen blancmange and other foods made with dairy products. The United States is the leading producer of carrageen. It is used extensively in the food industry as a stabilizing, thickening, and gelling agent in products such as ice creams, sherbets, condensed milks, instant soups, cakes, cookies, and candies.

Serving Ideas

Fresh carrageen can be added to soups and simmered dishes or used as a vegetable.

Nutritional Information

	raw
protein	1.5 g
fat	0.2 g
carbohydrates	12 g
	per 100 g

Nori

Porphyra spp., Rhodophyceae

Several species belonging to the genus *Porphyra* are generally referred to by their Japanese name, *nori,* because they are produced almost exclusively in Japan, though they grow in most of the world's seas. The production of this kind of seaweed, all which is cultivated, is a major industry employing over 300,000 people. Nori has been cultivated since ancient times because the quantity that grows naturally is insufficient to satisfy the great demand for this food. Red or crimson in colr, nori becomes dark or blackish when dried, and green when cooked. It is usually sold in the form of dry, thin, paper-like sheets. Asakusa-nori *(Porphyra tenera)* is especially popular in Japan.

Buying

Nori is sold in various forms, including in packages of dried, folded sheets, as roasted sheets and in pieces. Shiny, brittle and green, good-quality dried nori should be transparent when held up to the light.

Nutritional Information

	dried nori
protein	17 g
fat	0.8 g
carbohydrates	36 g
	per 100 g

Nori is particularly rich in vitamin A.

Sushi

32 PIECES OF SUSHI

4 sheets dried seaweed (nori)
1 avocado
1 European-style cucumber, seeded
4 ounces smoked salmon or crab
1 teaspoon Japanese horseradish (wasabi) paste
1 tablespoon roasted sesame seeds

1 cup short-grained Japanese rice, uncooked

Rice seasonings:
⅓ cup rice vinegar
4 teaspoons sugar
2 teaspoons salt

Accompanying sauce:
½ teaspoon oil
¼ cup rice vinegar
¼ cup tamari soy sauce
1 bamboo sushi mat (maki-su)

Serve the sushi with the accompanying sauce.

1. Before cooking the rice, wash it in a large quantity of water several times. Cook it in 1 cup of cold water. Bring the rice and water to a boil over high heat, then lower the heat and allow the rice to cook for another 15 minutes before straining it.

2. While the rice is cooking, prepare the seasonings. Mix the rice vinegar, sugar and salt in a saucepan. Bring the mixture to a boil, uncovered. Pour the seasonings over the cooked rice, then mix everything together with a wooden spatula. Allow the mixture to cool.

3. Cut the sheets of seaweed (nori) in two. Spread some of the horseradish paste (wasabi) on each of the pieces.

4. Put a strip (about 4 tablespoons) of cooked rice on each of the half-sheets of seaweed, leaving a ¾-inch border. Sprinkle on some roasted sesame seeds.

5. Cut the smoked salmon into narrow strips, the seeded cumber into thin sticks and the avocado into thin slices. Arrange these ingredients on top of the rice in successive strips.

6. Roll the half-sheets of seaweed around the assembled ingredients in the bamboo mat, forming a tight cylinder. Allow the sushi to take shape for five minutes, then remove the mat and cut each roll into four pieces.

Serving Ideas

Nori can be eaten fresh, dried or rehydrated. Before being used, it is usually roasted over a small flame to make it crispy and more flavorful, then crumbled or reduced to a powder. Roasted nori has a delicious sardine-like taste.

Nori is used to make sushi and added to soups, salads, appetizers and breads. Cooked with fish, tofu, vegetables, pasta and rice, it is also used as a condiment and drunk as an infusion.

1 *Place a sheet of nori on the bamboo mat, then add a row of the chilled cooked rice.*

2 *Arrange the strips of smoked salmon and the sticks of cucumber on top of the rice in successive layers.*

3 *Roll the garnished sheets of seaweed into tight cylinders in the bamboo mat, allowing them to take shape for 5 minutes.*

4 *Remove the mat and cut each roll into pieces about ¾ of an inch thick.*

Glasswort

Salicornia spp., Chenopodiaceae

An annual or perennial plant that is seaweed in only the broadest sense of the word, glasswort (also called salicornia or marsh samphire) grows wild in the salty marshes of both hemispheres, as well as on the coasts of the Atlantic, the Pacific, and the English Channel; it is generally found on beaches, below the high-tide line. Consisting of leafless stems arranged in a pattern resembling a bird's foot, the plant measures between 8 and 24 inches across. Glasswort is usually harvested from the beginning of spring to the middle of summer.

Serving Ideas

Glasswort can be eaten raw in salads, or cooked like asparagus or green beans and served with a little butter. It goes well with fish, seafood, and poultry. It can also be pickled in vinegar and served as an hors d'oeuvre. Glasswort is salty enough to replace the salt in stews.

Cooking

Glasswort is often steamed or boiled for a few minutes in unsalted water. Cooking it for too long alters its flavor.

Buying

Look for firm, evenly colored glasswort without any soft or spoiled patches; the center and base should not be fibrous or hard.

Preparing

Remove any remaining roots, as well as any hard pieces at the base of the plant.

Spirulina

Spirulina spp., Cyanophyceae

O ne of the best-known varieties of blue-green seaweed, spirulina grows in the fresh and alkaline waters of lakes in various parts of the world, including Mexico, Peru, and Africa. Spirulina is also grown on a large scale in shallow ponds in Hawaii, California, and Thailand. It is estimated that this microscopic seaweed (or microalga), which is shaped like spiraling thread, has existed for over 3 billion years. Its blue-green color is the product of two main pigments, phycocyanine and chlorophyll. Spirulina reproduces very rapidly, splitting into two plants three times every 24 hours.

Spirulina was eaten by the Aztecs and has also been consumed for centuries by people living along the shores of Lake Chad in central Africa. Formed into a seaweed pancake known as a *dihé,* it is served on millet or vegetables with a thick, spicy tomato sauce, not unlike the *chilimolli* sauce eaten by the Aztecs.

Since the 1960s, spirulina has become increasingly popular because it is rich in certain nutrients; it is now regarded as a very valuable food extract.

Buying

Spirulina is available as a powder or flakes, and in tablets or capsules. Buy spirulina that is sold in glass bottles or laminated polyester packages rather than in plastic containers, which provide little protection against oxidization.

Serving Ideas

Spirulina is often dissolved in juice or water, or mixed with yogurt or cereal. It is also added to broths, soups, sauces, rice, and pasta just before they are eaten. People who do not like the taste or color of spirulina, which turns food green, often consume it in the form of tablets.

Since spirulina is a highly concentrated food, it should be incorporated into your diet gradually. Start by consuming 1 gram per day for a week; then increase your daily intake by 1 gram each week until you are consuming 5 to 10 grams per day.

Nutritional Information

	dried spirulina
protein	60 g
fat	6 g
carbohydrates	18 g
	per 100 g

The nutritional value of spirulina depends on when and where it is grown, as well as on how it is harvested and dried. It is rich in chlorophyll and various other nutrients, including beta-carotene and other carotenoids (which are converted into vitamin A), iron (10 mg per 10 g), thiamin, riboflavin, and magnesium. It is also rich in protein, but it contains relatively little methionine, an essential amino acid.

Although the nutrients in spirulina are inferior to those found in animal products (eggs, dairy products, meat), they are of a higher quality than those contained in grains and legumes, including soy products. Spirulina also contains gamma-linoleic acid, a fatty acid for which the only other source is mother's milk. It is low in sodium (1 to 9 mg/g) and contains no iodine. The value of the vitamin B_{12} in spirulina is questionable because studies suggest that only 5% of the total amount can be absorbed by the human body.

Spirulina is said to be revitalizing and is reputed to be an appetite suppressant.

Mushrooms

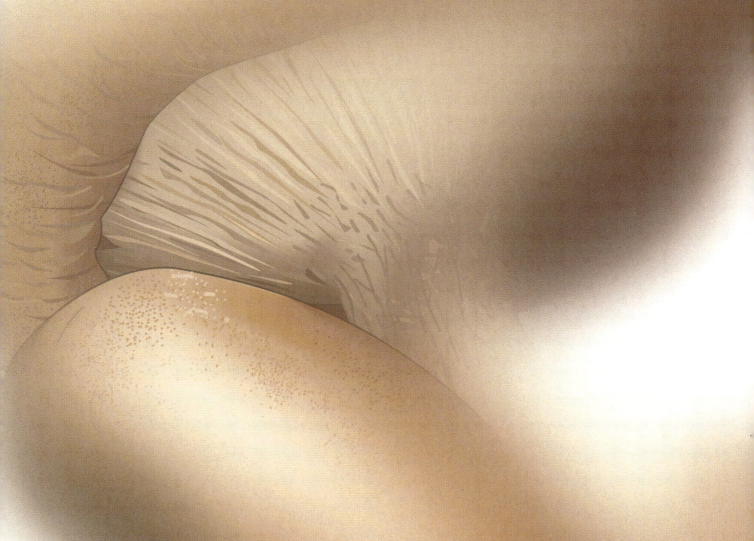

Introduction

Mushrooms, like other fungi (over 50,000 species, including truffles, molds, and yeasts), stand apart from other plants by their lack of leaves, chlorophyll, flowers, and roots. Without chlorophyll, they are obliged to draw nutrition from existing organic materials, and thus they attach themselves to a wide variety of objects such as wood, humus, and even decayed rags, dirty glass, and rusted metal.

Consumed since time immemorial, mushrooms have a reputation – perfectly warranted, moreover – for causing death. Nevertheless, very few of the thousands of species that have been indexed are actually poisonous. On the other hand, numerous varieties cause problems such as diarrhea, stomachaches, and vomiting. Amateurs should strictly avoid eating mushrooms with which they are unfamiliar.

The Egyptian pharaohs considered mushrooms to be a food of the gods and prohibited their consumption by the population. The Romans believed that the fleshy fungi gave people strength and included them in their soldiers' diet. Throughout history, mushrooms have been one of the poisoner's preferred tools, as the cause of the victim's death is often hard to identify. In A.D. 54 the emperor Claudius died after eating mushrooms fed to him by his wife Agrippina; Pope Clement VII met a similar fate in 1534; and Holy Roman Emperor Charles VI died after being fed poisonous mushrooms in 1740. Mushrooms have also been associated with witchcraft, which adds to the aura of fear and distrust that surrounds them.

Various types of mushrooms and other fungi are hallucinogenic, 1% to 2% of species are poisonous, and certain others are used for their medicinal properties. Although most mushrooms are edible, few species are actually consumed, as most species can be tough, woody, or gelatinous, give off an unpleasant smell, or taste bad. Only about 20 varieties are truly flavorful. A number of species can be cultivated, including boletes, pleurotus mushrooms, shiitakes, wood ears, and common ("button") mushrooms. Truffles, highly prized fungi often mistakenly classified with mushrooms, are also grown commercially.

Unlike plants that grow from seeds, mushrooms reproduce by single-cell spores. As they develop, the tiny spores sprout minute filaments called mycelia, which commercial growers normally use for propagation purposes. Some mushrooms, including common mushrooms, are cultivated on natural manure (mainly that of horses) that has been fermented and pasteurized, or on synthetic manure made from hay, straw, bark, gypsum, and potassium or corncobs.

Buying

Mushrooms are sold fresh, dried, frozen, canned, and blanched and sliced. When buying fresh mushrooms, be sure to choose specimens that are firm and intact. Avoid those that are wrinkled, spotted, or slimy, as well as discolored mushrooms with a split cap and dry stem, as they are not fresh.

Preparing

Clean and prepare mushrooms just before using them to avoid discoloration and rotting. Do not soak them, as they will become saturated with water. Rinse them quickly under the tap or in water to which you have added a bit of vinegar (to slow down blackening), using a soft brush if desired (special brushes are available for just this purpose). Then drain them and pat them dry with a cloth or paper towel. If you prefer, you can simply wipe the unwashed mushrooms with a damp cloth or paper towel.

Dried mushrooms should be soaked for 10 minutes in warm water. Drain them, change the water, and leave them to soak for a further 10 to 15 minutes.

You can use mushrooms whole, remove the stems, cut them into pieces, slice them, or chop them. Although some recipes advise cooks to peel mushrooms (especially common white mushrooms), this reduces their flavor and nutritional value. You may, however, wish to peel or scrape old mushrooms.

Mushroom stems, or stalks, are generally edible. Those of certain species are tough and stringy and should be removed; otherwise, merely slice off the base of the stem if it is dirty or dry. Various recipes advise you to remove the stems for esthetic reasons or suggest that you use them to prepare delicately flavored bouillons.

Serving Ideas

Often used in condiments, mushrooms add flavor to a wide range of dishes, including appetizers, salads, dips, soups, sauces, omelets, stews, and pizzas. They go well with meat, poultry, fish, and shellfish.

Several types of mushrooms can be eaten raw (common mushroom, king bolete, wood ear, puffball, etc.). They are excellent as is or marinated. Almost all wild mushrooms need to be cooked longer than commercially grown varieties.

Cooking

Mushrooms can be sautéed, broiled, fried, and so on. To prevent blackening, avoid cooking them in aluminum pans. Add salt only at the end of the cooking process; otherwise, the mushrooms will lose their water. For optimum flavor in simmered dishes, add mushrooms about 15 minutes before the end of cooking or brown them separately in oil and add them to the dish just before serving.

As far as possible, leave mushrooms out of dishes you intend to freeze, adding them just before serving, as freezing alters their texture and reduces their flavor.

Storing

Raw or cooked, mushrooms are fragile and deteriorate quickly. Handle them with care and refrigerate them as soon as possible. Store fresh mushrooms unwashed in a non-airtight container, preferably a paper bag, to allow them to breathe. At the very least, poke holes in the plastic packaging, as poor air circulation promotes rotting and the growth of *Clostridium botulinum,* a bacterium naturally found in soil, which proliferates in damp oxygen-poor environments and can cause serious food poisoning (botulism).

Mushrooms keep for about a week in the refrigerator. They freeze well; simply slice them and place them carefully in a freezer bag. Blanching makes them tough and is unnecessary if you intend to freeze them for less than 3 months. If you plan to freeze mushrooms for a longer period, sprinkle them with lemon juice diluted with water and then blanch them for 2½ minutes. Use them unthawed. You can also dry mushrooms; they lose up to 90% of their initial volume and keep for up to a year.

Nutritional Information

	most varieties, raw
water	89%
protein	3 g
fat	0.4 g
carbohydrates	6 g
calories	30
	per 100 g

Mushrooms are high in potassium and riboflavin, and are believed to have a number of medicinal properties. They are said to be laxative, antibiotic, cholesterol-lowering, and even aphrodisiac.

Common mushroom

Agaricus bisporus, **Agaricaceae**

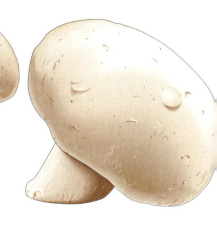

The most widely cultivated and consumed mushroom, the common (or cultivated) mushroom is found in various world regions, including North and South America, Europe, Australia, and New Zealand. Easily grown, it owes its French name, *champignon de Paris,* to the fact that it has been cultivated intensively in abandoned quarries around the French capital for close to 200 years.

Mushrooms are grown in a carefully controlled environment. Producers spread mycelia (very fine filaments from the single-celled spores that constitute the mushroom's reproductive body) over either natural manure (generally horse manure) that has been pasteurized following fermentation or synthetic manure made from hay, straw, bark, corncobs, gypsum, and potassium.

The fleshy white cap of the common mushroom can measure up to 4 inches across. The stem, which is also white, is ¾ inch to 2 inches long.

A less widely sold variety, the cremini mushroom, is coffee-colored. Some people avoid these darker mushrooms in the mistaken belief that they are old, whereas they are in fact more flavorful than their pale cousins.

In the United States, one of the most popular types of common mushroom is the portobello mushroom. Larger, darker-colored, and stronger tasting, it has an exceptional flavor reminiscent of wild mushrooms. Portobello mushrooms, which are sold riper than other common mushrooms, are delicious fried and can be added to dishes cooked in sauce.

Buying

Common mushrooms are available fresh, canned, and dried. Choose fresh mushrooms that are intact, firm, and fleshy. Avoid those that are wrinkled, slimy, spotted, or whose caps are split, all signs of age. Supermarkets often sell presliced fresh mushrooms, which keep up to 90 days as they have been quickly blanched and placed in a salt or ascorbic-acid solution. Their flavor and nutritional value are somewhere between those of fresh and canned mushrooms.

Preparing

Just before using fresh mushrooms, rinse them under the tap or dip them in water acidulated with a bit of vinegar; this slows down browning. Then clean them, if desired, with a soft brush (you can buy brushes specially designed for this purpose). Don't leave them to soak, as they will absorb too much water. If you prefer, you can simply brush them carefully or wipe them with a damp paper towel.

Remove the base of the stem. You can use mushrooms whole, in pieces, sliced, diced, chopped, or puréed. If you intend to serve cut mushrooms raw, sprinkle them with lemon juice, vinegar, salad dressing, or another acidic liquid to prevent them from turning brown.

Fresh Mushroom and Cream Salad

SERVES 4

½ lb. (250 g) fresh mushrooms
Juice of ½ lemon
3 shallots

3 tbsp. chopped parsley leaves
Salt and ground pepper
¼ cup (60 ml) heavy cream

1. Slice the mushrooms thinly. Place them in a salad bowl and sprinkle them with the lemon juice; make sure they soak up the juice.

2. Finely chop the shallots and add them with the parsley to the mushrooms. Add a generous amount of salt and pepper. Stir.

3. Add the cream and stir again. Adjust seasoning to taste.

Serve the salad as a first course.

Add more cream if desired.

Serving Ideas

Common mushrooms can be eaten raw or cooked. They are delicious in appetizers, salads, and with dips. Traditionally linked with meat, they go particularly well with onions and rice. Mushrooms are included in a wide variety of dishes, including soups, sauces, stuffings, stews, omelets, and quiches. They can also be served like snails *à la bourguignonne*.

Nutritional Information

	raw
water	91%
protein	3 g
fat	0.2 g
carbohydrates	0.3 g
calories	14
	per 100 g

The common mushroom is rich in potassium and a good source of riboflavin.

Cooking

Common mushrooms shrink and lose their water content when cooked for a long time at low heat. Brown them for a few minutes at high heat, stirring them continually. Take them off the burner if they start to ooze water. Rather than throwing out this water, which is rich in taste and nutrients, use it to flavor sauces, soups, and simmered dishes.

Storing

Keep common mushrooms in the refrigerator, in a paper bag or wrapped in a damp cloth. They will last for about a week. You can also freeze them, can them, or dry them.

Enoki mushroom

Flammulina velutipes, Collybia

The delicate-tasting enoki mushroom – also called the velvet shank – has a long stem (up to 4 inches tall) topped with a tiny white cap. It grows in clusters on live or dead tree trunks, as well as on tree roots and branches covered with soil. The mushrooms are cultivated on stumps or in a sawdust medium, and are picked about 2 months after inoculation. Cultivated enoki mushrooms are paler than those that grow wild.

The enoki mushroom is highly esteemed in Asia and figures prominently in various Asian dishes. About 80% of world production comes from Japan, where it is called *enokitake*. The mushroom's white flesh is soft but resistant. It has a mild flavor and a slightly fruity odor.

Preparing

 Remove the lower 1 to 2 inches of the stem, as it is tough.

Nutritional Information

	raw
water	90%
protein	2 g
carbohydrates	0.3 g
calories	9 g
	per 100 g

Buying

Fresh enoki mushrooms, bundled in plastic bags, are available mainly in Asian specialty food stores. Choose mushrooms with firm, white, shiny caps. Avoid buying enoki mushrooms with slimy or brownish stalks. The mushrooms are also sold canned and in jars.

Serving Ideas

 Enoki mushrooms are delicious raw. Use them to decorate and add flavor to salads and sandwiches. They are also good in soups and Asian dishes, and with pasta and vegetables. Add them at the end of the cooking process to retain their delicate flavor.

Storing

You can store enoki mushrooms in the refrigerator for about a week. Leave them in their plastic packaging.

Morel

Morchella spp., **Discomycetes**

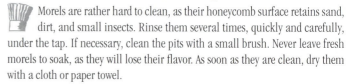

E dible, relatively rare spring mushrooms, morels are highly prized for their pleasant taste. They grow in temperate regions. Easily identifiable, they are among the simplest wild mushrooms to pick. Although morels can be cultivated, the practice is not widespread.

The morel's globular or conical cap is honeycombed, which makes it look porous. Yellowish ochre, brown, or whitish, the cap is from 1 to 5 inches high. It grows atop a fairly thick stalk of the same color and height. There are said to be over 20 different species of morels. Their thin, fragile flesh is highly aromatic. The most sought-after morels are those with darker caps.

Buying

 Morels are generally sold dried or canned.

Storing

 Fresh morels can be kept for 2 to 3 days in the refrigerator.

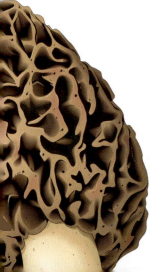

Preparing

Morels are rather hard to clean, as their honeycomb surface retains sand, dirt, and small insects. Rinse them several times, quickly and carefully, under the tap. If necessary, clean the pits with a small brush. Never leave fresh morels to soak, as they will lose their flavor. As soon as they are clean, dry them with a cloth or paper towel.

Cover dried morels with warm water and leave them to soak for 10 minutes. Drain them, change the water, and let them soak for another 10 to 15 minutes.

Cooking

 Brown morels for 5 to 7 minutes at low heat in butter or oil, or simmer them for 15 to 20 minutes in a sauce, soup, or stew.

Serving Ideas

Morels should always be eaten well cooked, as they irritate the stomach when raw. Delicious stuffed and in sauces, they are often associated with cream, which brings out their flavor. They go well with meat, poultry, game, and fish. You can use them in soups and stews, or with rice, pasta, and eggs.

Nutritional Information

water	90%
protein	2 g
carbohydrates	0.3 g
calories	9
	per 100 g

Morels are rich in potassium.

Pleurotus mushrooms

Pleurotus spp., **Agaricaceae**

Mushrooms belonging to the genus *Pleurotus* often have a cap 6 inches or more in diameter, reminiscent of an oversized ear or an ear trumpet. They grow on trees and dead wood. Some varieties have a short lateral stalk or "stipe." Unlike the common mushroom, which is cultivated on a bed of manure, pleurotus mushrooms are grown on wood (trunks, stumps, logs) or non-fermented organic waste (straw, corncobs, sawdust, bark) and are thus always clean.

There are 35 to 40 different species of pleurotus mushrooms, most of which are edible. None of the varieties are toxic, and many of them are grown commercially. The mushrooms can be white, cream, light yellow, or reddish brown, with a short whitish stalk. Pleurotus mushrooms are highly esteemed, particularly the oyster mushroom *(Pleurotus ostreatus),* with its tender white flesh, subtle taste, and sometimes strong fragrance.

Buying

Avoid pleurotus mushrooms that are slimy or black-spotted. Choose specimens that are uniform in color with smooth caps.

Serving Ideas

 Pleurotus mushrooms are delicious and make a pleasant substitute for common mushrooms. Avoid combining them with highly flavorful foods or cooking them in large quantities of fat, which would overpower their flavor. Their normally firm, crisp flesh has more taste when the mushrooms are young. They are used in soups and sauces and go very well with rice, pasta, eggs, tofu, poultry, and seafood.

Storing

Pleurotus mushrooms are highly perishable and tend to take on the flavors of other foods. Eat them without delay. They can nevertheless be kept in the refrigerator, in a paper bag or a dish covered with a cloth, for a few days. Remove the cloth if the mushrooms become wet, or dampen it a bit if they begin to dry out.

Preparing

There is usually no need to wash cultivated pleurotus mushrooms.

Cooking

 Sauté or fry pleurotus mushrooms for 3 to 5 minutes; or cook them with very little liquid in a tightly closed pan, either on the stove for 10 to 15 minutes or in a 375°F (180°C) oven for 10 to 15 minutes. The stems, which tend to be tough, should be cooked longer; it is a good idea to chop them beforehand.

Mushrooms

311

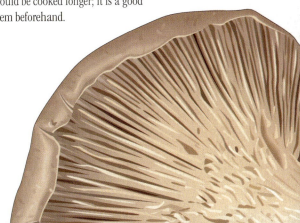

Shiitake

Lentinus edodes, **Polyporaceae**

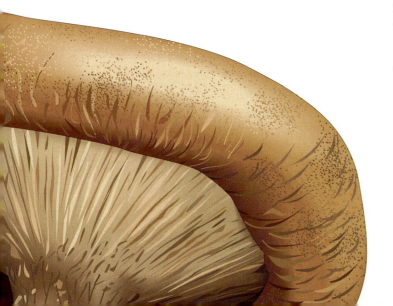

An edible mushroom that grows on wood, the shiitake is indigenous to Asia, where it has been known for at least 2,000 years. Today it is cultivated intensively in countries such as China, Korea, and Japan (a major exporter). Indeed, it is second in importance only to the cultivated, or common, mushroom used widely in Western cuisine and may be considered the equivalent of the latter species in Japanese cooking. Shiitake mushrooms are grown on logs, dead tree trunks, and sawdust. They are convex or almost flat, occasionally with a small raised central area. Their fleshy brownish caps are generally from 2 to 4 inches across, and their stems are woodier than those of most other mushrooms. The time of picking is crucial, as the caps of shiitake mushrooms that are harvested too late tend to be split and sporeless, which makes the mushrooms thin, flat, and relatively tasteless.

Shiitakes are used in cooking and for various therapeutic purposes. When dried, their tasty white flesh is slightly acidic and has a stronger aroma. In Western countries, the mushrooms are most often sold in this form.

Nutritional Information

	dried
protein	9 g
fat	1 g
calories	293
	per 100 g

Shiitake mushrooms are a good source of potassium. In Asian cultures, they are thought to have numerous medicinal properties and are used to treat problems such as high blood pressure, flu, tumors, stomach ulcers, diabetes, anemia, obesity, and gallstones.

Preparing

Clean shiitake mushrooms with a damp cloth or paper towel, or use a soft brush. They can also be rinsed briefly under the tap; don't allow them to soak, as they will swell with water.

Dried shiitakes, which have a stronger flavor than the fresh mushrooms, should be covered with warm water and left to sit for about an hour. Add the used water to stocks, soups, and sauces. Chop or finely slice the stems and cook them separately, as they are firm and stringy.

Serving Ideas

Shiitakes can easily replace other mushrooms in recipes. They have a pleasant flavor and absorb the taste of other ingredients. They are delicious in soups, sauces, stews, and Asian dishes, as well as with pasta and rice.

Cooking

Cooking brings out the flavor of shiitakes. Sauté or fry them (dabbed with oil) for 5 to 7 minutes; or cook them with very little liquid in a tightly closed pan, either on the stove for 15 minutes or in a 375°F (180°C) oven for 15 to 20 minutes.

Storing

Shiitakes are a bit less fragile than other mushrooms. If you store them unwashed in a paper bag in the refrigerator, they will keep for at least a week.

Boletus mushrooms

Boletus spp., Polyporaceae

Boletes are fleshy edible mushrooms native to temperate regions including Europe, North America, and Australia. They generally grow in evergreen forests (pine, fir, spruce) or deciduous woods (oak, beech, chestnut). Boletes are relatively hard to find unless you know exactly where to look. Unfortunately, most specimens are infested with insect larvae.

Also known as *cèpes* or *porcini,* boletes have a long, fleshy stalk up to 10 inches high. Thick and firm, it is topped by a fleshy cap. Depending on the type of bolete, the generally round, convex cap can be either smooth or velvety. Anywhere from 2½ to 12 inches across, it can be a number of different colors: yellow, red, brown, pink, whitish, grayish. The underside of the cap is covered with vertical tubelike pores; this aids identification, as most other mushrooms have gills. Young boletes are more tender and flavorful. Certain species are cultivated *in situ,* i.e., in their natural environment. There are several dozen varieties of boletes (king bolete, bragger's bolete, painted slippery cap, etc.).

Buying

 Boletes are usually sold dried. When buying fresh boletes, choose young specimens, as they have more flavor.

Preparing

Boletes sold in stores are generally clean, except for the base of the stem, which should often be removed (if it is overripe or worm-eaten) or brushed. Remove the vertical tubes under the cap if they are slimy; they detach easily.

Dried boletes must be rehydrated by soaking them in hot water for 20 minutes; the soaking liquid can be strained and used for its flavor.

Serving Ideas

Boletes can be eaten raw but are better cooked. Use them like other mushrooms, which they can replace in recipes. Avoid combining them with strong-tasting ingredients, which would mask their flavor. They are delicious braised or cooked in oil; add shallots, garlic, parsley, and white wine. They are also good in soups and casseroles, and are often used in Italian cooking (pasta sauces, risottos, stuffed pasta).

Cooking

Sauté or fry boletes for 5 to 7 minutes; or cook them with very little liquid in a tightly closed pan, either on the stove for 15 minutes or in a 375°F (180°C) oven for 15 to 20 minutes.

Nutritional Information

water	89%
protein	3 g
fat	0.4 g
calories	14
	per 100 g

Boletes are rich in potassium and a good source of riboflavin.

Storing

 Boletes are fragile and should be eaten as soon as possible. You can keep them in the refrigerator for a few days.

Avoid storing them in a plastic bag: keep them in a paper bag or in a dish covered with a clean cloth.

Certain species change color quickly when cut or broken.

Truffle

Tuber spp., Tuberales

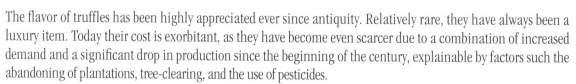

Truffles are hard-to-find edible fungi that grow on the roots of trees, particularly oaks. For a long time, experts had trouble deciding how they grew and how to classify them. People used to believe that truffles sprang up after lightning struck the ground during electrical storms; this myth can be explained by the fact that heavy rains can wash away soil, exposing the highly prized fungi.

The flavor of truffles has been highly appreciated ever since antiquity. Relatively rare, they have always been a luxury item. Today their cost is exorbitant, as they have become even scarcer due to a combination of increased demand and a significant drop in production since the beginning of the century, explainable by factors such the abandoning of plantations, tree-clearing, and the use of pesticides.

Modern-day truffle growers sometimes inoculate the roots of young trees (oak, hazel, pine, lime) with truffle mycelia (very fine filaments). Most of the mycelia develop into truffles, which can be gathered about 5 years later.

Truffles are often hunted by animals specially trained to recognize their odor. For many years, pigs were used for this purpose. As they love the fungi and aren't satisfied with merely sniffing them out, the swine are fitted with muzzles, which also prevent them from fighting over truffles. The trend today is to use trained dogs for this purpose. Truffles can sometimes be located by the presence of a species of fly that lays its eggs over the fungi.

There are several types of truffles. The most sought after is the **black truffle** *(Tuber melanosporum),* a globular fungus covered with small blackish warts, which grows abundantly but not exclusively in the French region of Périgord. Its dark, white-veined flesh is highly odoriferous.

The **white truffle** *(Tuber magnatum)* is also highly esteemed, particularly specimens gathered around Alba, Italy. Somewhat rough textured, it is whitish, yellowish, or greenish yellow in color and resembles an irregularly shaped tuber. The largest of all edible truffles, it grows to a diameter of over 4 inches and can weigh up to a pound. Its white or ochre flesh, streaked with white veins, has a garlicky or cheeselike taste.

Another variety, known by its Latin name *Tuber aestivum,* is less flavorful. Its flesh is pale or beige.

Mushrooms

314

Buying

Fresh truffles are generally available only in regions where they are gathered; their peak growing season is January to March. Choose specimens that are firm, fleshy, and bruise-free. Some stores carry truffles preserved in water.

Preparing

Don't wash truffles. Clean them gently with a soft brush. They can be sliced, cut into thin strips, shaved, or diced.

Serving Ideas

Truffles are eaten raw or cooked, and are also used in the form of juice, concentrate, essence, and the like. They are included in a number of products, including foie gras and pâté. They can also be added to salads, stuffings, sauces, pasta, rice, and eggs, and are delicious raw or cooked alone. They are traditionally associated with game and poultry, particularly Christmas turkey in France. A few thin slices are enough to flavor an entire dish.

Cooking

Truffles can be sautéed for 2 to 3 minutes, cooked in a sealed vessel in very little water for 10 to 15 minutes, or braised for 45 to 60 minutes.

Storing

 Fresh truffles can be kept in a sealed container in the refrigerator for about a week.

You can also cut them into pieces, place them in a sealed container, and cover them with Madeira or white wine before refrigerating. Canned truffles should be stored in the refrigerator once they have been opened. If covered with oil or Madeira, truffles keep for about a month.

Nutritional Information

	raw
water	76%
protein	6 g
fat	0.5 g
calories	25
	per 100 g

Truffles are rich in potassium and are a good source of iron.

Wood ear

Auricularia auricula-judae, Auriculariales

T he wood ear (also known as the tree ear or Jew's ear) is an edible mushroom that grows on the trunks of beech, elder, and walnut trees. Originally known as Judas's ear (later corrupted to Jew's ear), it owes that name to its flat earlike shape and to the legend that Judas hanged himself from an elder tree. The mushroom has a very short stalk. Its translucent brownish beige flesh is gelatinous but firm, and relatively tasteless. Wood ears are particularly popular in Asia.

Buying

 Wood ears are often sold fresh in Asian specialty food stores. They are also available dried.

Preparing

Wash the fresh mushrooms quickly in cold water and remove the sticky parts. Soak dried wood ears in warm water for 10 minutes. Drain them, change the water, and let them soak for a further 10 to 15 minutes. They will expand to up to five times their initial dry size.

Serving Ideas

Wood ears can be eaten raw, blanched (for 1 minute), or cooked (e.g., fried or boiled). They add an unusual texture to foods, particularly soups, salads, vegetables, stews, and pasta dishes. They absorb the liquid in which they are cooked and take on the taste of the other ingredients.

Cooking

 Sauté or fry wood ears for 3 to 5 minutes, or steam them or cook them in a tightly closed pan with little liquid for 10 to 15 minutes.

Nutritional Information

water	93%
protein	0.5 g
carbohydrates	7 g
calories	25
	per 100 g

Wood ears are rich in iron, potassium, and magnesium. They are a good source of riboflavin.

Storing

Store fresh wood ears unwashed in the refrigerator. Although they keep for up to a month, it is best to use them within a week. They can be frozen as is.

Mushrooms

315

Chanterelle

Cantharellus spp., Agaricaceae

Cantharellus cibarius

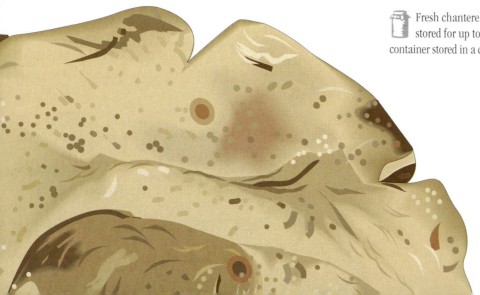

Chanterelles are delicious edible mushrooms that grow in coniferous and deciduous forests in temperate regions. Highly prized by European connoisseurs, they are less well known in North America and Australia.

Chanterelles have a cup-shaped cap ranging from ¾ inch to 4 inches across. Depending on the variety, it can be yellowish, orangey, whitish, brownish gray, or blackish. The cap's wrinkled underside distinguishes chanterelles from most other mushrooms, which are gilled. The lower surface of some species tapers downward to the narrow stem, which may be ⅓ inch to 4 inches long. All types of chanterelles are edible. The flesh of some varieties is soft. That of the best types, such as *Cantharellus cibarius,* is firm, fruity, and yellowish white. Often peppery tasting, the flesh loses this characteristic with cooking.

Buying

Chanterelles are sold fresh, dried, and canned. When buying fresh specimens, make sure the cap is spongy, firm, and fleshy. Beware: chanterelles that have turned translucent are poisonous!

Nutritional Information

water		92%
protein		2 g
fat		0.5 g
calories		10
		per 100 g

Chanterelles are rich in potassium and iron.

Preparing

Wash chanterelles quickly under the tap to keep them from soaking up too much water. Drain them immediately, and dry them with a clean cloth or paper towel. You can also brush them carefully if they are young and relatively dirt-free.

Cover dried chanterelles with warm water and allow them to soak for about an hour.

Serving Ideas

Chanterelles are a traditional favorite with meat and omelets. They are delicious in soups and sauces, and with pasta, rice, buckwheat, and millet.

Cooking

Sauté or fry chanterelles for 3 to 5 minutes; or cook them with very little liquid in a tightly closed pan, either on the stove for 15 to 20 minutes or in a 375°F (180°C) oven for 10 to 15 minutes.

Storing

Fresh chanterelles keep for about a week in the refrigerator and can be stored for up to a year in the freezer. Keep dried chanterelles in a sealed container stored in a cool, dry place.

Cereals and Grains

Introduction

The edible seeds of various plants belonging to the grass family, cereals have been an essential part of the human diet since the beginnings of agriculture in the first millennium B.C. Inhabitants of Syria, Palestine, and the eastern shores of the Mediterranean were already cultivating primitive varieties of barley and wheat over 8,000 years ago. By 3000 B.C., the Egyptians had mastered the techniques of irrigation, allowing for further development of cereal cultivation. Cereals have played an essential role in world history; in fact, the evolution of certain civilizations actually coincided with the cultivation of cereal grains. Each continent has its dominant cereal culture: rice is the most important grain in the Far East, while the predominance of wheat and barley extends from India to the Atlantic, rye and oats dominate in northeastern Europe, corn in America, and millet and sorghum in Africa.

While cereal consumption has declined in industrial countries over the last century, cereals remain the most important crop in the Third World, where they represent the major source of food energy and up to 90% of protein intake, compared to a mere 25% in industrialized countries.

All cereals belong to the family of grasses. Buckwheat, although often considered a grain, is actually a member of the Polygonaceae family. While most grains share a common structure, the proportions constituted by the different parts vary from one cereal to another. The cereal grain (caryopsis) consists of three main parts: an outer layer (the bran), the endosperm (or kernel), and the germ.

The seed is enclosed in an **outer shell**, or hull, that cannot be assimilated by the human digestive system. For this reason, the grains must be hulled to make them edible.

The **endosperm** (kernel) is the largest part of the grain and is composed mainly of starch, a complex carbohydrate that is absorbed slowly by the body, producing a long-lasting feeling of satiety.

The kernel is enclosed in the **bran** (pericarp), which is made up of several fibrous layers. Rich in vitamins and minerals, it also plays an important role in the functioning of the gastrointestinal system by helping to prevent constipation.

The **germ** (embryo) is located in the lower end of the grain and contains the seed of a new plant. Despite its small size, the germ has the highest concentration of nutritional elements, including various vitamins, minerals, and proteins. It also contains a high level of fat, which makes it perishable.

Serving Ideas

Cereal grains play a central role in the human diet and are used in a wide variety of ways. While the word «cereal» is most commonly associated with the ready-to-eat breakfast food, cereal grains are also available in many other forms; for example, they can be ground or crushed to make pasta, flour, semolina, and starch, as well as being sold in the form of puffs or flakes. Wheat, triticale, barley, and rye grains can be added to soups and legume dishes, to which they lend an original note while at the same time improving their nutritional quality.

Cereals are also used to make croquettes or as an accompaniment to main courses or vegetable dishes, in addition to being served with fruits and spices. They are often sprouted and added to salads, soups, and stews. Sprouted cereal grains can also be ground and incorporated into bread dough or baked into flat cakes. (For easier digestion of raw sprouted cereal grains, it is recommended to chew them well.) Cereals are also an important ingredient in the production of a number of alcoholic beverages, including beer, whiskey, bourbon, sake (Japan), and chicha (Latin America).

Cooking

Cereals are cooked in water, milk, or stock, either on the stovetop, in a double boiler, or, more rarely, in the oven. Cooking transforms the grain in several ways, notably by gelatinizing the starch, softening the hull, and altering the flavor. In order for the starch to be converted, it is important to use a sufficient quantity of cooking water, with most cereals requiring 2 to 3 times their volume in liquid. A larger quantity of liquid produces a mushy grain, while less liquid leaves the grain drier and harder. The final texture also depends on whether the cereals are initially immersed in boiling liquid, which produces a lighter, less mushy grain, or in liquid that is still cold. Small grains cook more rapidly and tend to form a sticky mass; to reduce the degree of stickiness, mix the cereals in a small amount of cold liquid before immersing them in the boiling liquid. Roasting the grains for 4 to 5 minutes before cooking also minimizes stickiness, while at the same time facilitating digestion and imparting a slightly nutty flavor to the grains. Avoid roasting them too long, however, as this can give the grains a bitter taste. Cooking times vary according to the type of cereal, its freshness, and the degree of refining to which it has been subjected. Cereals must be sufficiently cooked in order to facilitate digestion of their starch. Most whole-grain cereals remain slightly crunchy even when cooked. Prior to cooking, wash whole-grain cereals in cold water and soak them for 12 to 24 hours; this will shorten the cooking time and reduce the effect of the phytic acid (a component of bran). The soaking water can be used to cook the grains.

Cereals should be cooked in a heavy saucepan; slowly pour the grains into lightly salted boiling water, stirring constantly. Boil for 1 to 2 minutes, then lower the heat and simmer, covered, until the liquid is absorbed, stirring occasionally. Cooking can be completed in a double boiler as soon as the preparation begins to thicken, avoiding the need for stirring. Any remaining cooking liquid will be rich in nutrients from the cereals and can be used to cook other foods. Cereals expand to 3 or 4 times their original volume during cooking. The following table provides cooking times for whole and processed cereals.

1 cup	Liquid (cups)	Cooking time
OATS (GRAINS)	2-3	1 hr
CRACKED WHEAT	2-3	30-40 min
WHEAT (GRAINS)	2	60-90 min
BULGUR	2	cover and simmer 25-35 min
COUSCOUS	1	add boiling water, let stand 5 min
ROLLED OATS	1	5 min
WHEAT FLAKES	2	1 hr
RYE FLAKES	2	1 hr
SOYA FLAKES	2	1 hr
MILLET	2	30-40 min
BARLEY (GRAINS)	2	45 min
HULLED BARLEY	3-4	1 hr
BROWN RICE	2	45-60 min
WILD RICE	3	45-60 min
BUCKWHEAT (KASHA)	2	10-15 min
CORNMEAL	4	25-30 min

Nutritional Information

Cereals generally consist of 8% to 15% protein. While cereal proteins contain the eight essential amino acids, some of them, the so-called limiting amino acids, are present in limited quantity; lysine is especially deficient in cereals. Because of these deficiencies, cereals are said to be an «incomplete» food (see *Complementary proteins*). Cereals are relatively low in fat (1% to 7%), an element that is concentrated in the germ and that mainly takes the form of polyunsaturated fatty acids (see *Fats*). Being of plant origin, cereals do not contain cholesterol. On the other hand, they are very rich in carbohydrates (usually 60% to 80%), principally in the form of starch. On average, cereals contain between 330 and 390 calories per 100 grams. Cereals also contain minerals, the most important of which are iron, phosphorus, magnesium, and zinc; they are also rich in the B-complex vitamins (niacin, thiamine, and riboflavin) and in folic acid. Because most of the B-complex vitamins are contained in the outer layers of the grain, they are practically absent from refined products such as white flour and polished rice (unless these products are enriched), since hulling and polishing strips away these layers. The refining process also deprives cereals of much of their vitamin E content, which is concentrated in the germ.

The amount of phytic acid present in cereals varies from one variety to the next. It is often said that this acid interferes with the absorption of calcium by binding with it and making it difficult for the body to assimilate it. Indeed, the consumption of dietary fiber can reduce the absorption of zinc, calcium, and iron, since these minerals bind with the fiber itself or with the phytate or phytic acid it contains. However, it is unclear whether these effects are significant from a nutritional point of view in a diet that includes a balanced intake of protein, vitamin C, and minerals. Moreover, the metabolism of minerals should not be adversely affected by a normal intake of dietary fiber. In addition, many cereals have high levels of phytase, an enzyme that hydrolyzes phytic acid, neutralizing some of its negative effects.

Gluten is another substance present in varying proportions in cereal protein. Mainly comprised of gliadin and glutenin, gluten becomes viscous and elastic when flour is mixed with a liquid (the word «gluten» is derived from the Latin *glu,* meaning glue). Gluten is the substance that causes dough to rise; it is stretched by the expansion of the gas produced by the fermentation of bread dough and is activated by kneading. Only flours made from wheat, rye, and triticale contain a sufficient quantity of gluten to be suitable for bread making, with wheat flour producing the most successful results.

Storing

Cereals are best kept in an airtight container away from heat and moisture. Storing them in the refrigerator or at a temperature of about 40°F delays rancidity and the development of mold, while also preventing insect infestation.

Complementary proteins

A vegetarian diet must include foods that contain complementary amino acids. Amino acids are the main constituents of protein, a nutrient of utmost importance in maintaining good health. Protein is made up of 20 amino acids, 8 of which are said to be essential because they cannot be synthesized (produced) by the human body; these essential amino acids must therefore come from the food we eat. Protein of animal origin is different from that provided by plants in that it contains all the essential amino acids, both in adequate proportions and in sufficient amounts to fulfill human needs. On the other hand, protein of plant origin is deficient in certain essential amino acids and is only partially used by the human body. When a plant protein is short of a particular amino acid, this amino acid is referred to as the limiting factor, because its limited quantity reduces the overall efficiency of the protein by 30%.

Since the early 20th century, proteins of animal origin have been referred to as "complete," while proteins of plant origin are said to be "incomplete." With better knowledge of the composition of foods, scientists have come to understand how the shortage of certain amino acids in one type of food can be compensated by their abundance in another. For example, most legumes are rich in lysine while being deficient in methionine, cystine, and tryptophan; on the other hand, cereals, nuts, and seeds contain plenty of methionine and tryptophan but very little lysine. Thus, when these food groups are combined, they complement and enrich each other. This example shows that the perfect combination of plant proteins provides the complete protein that is required by the human body. Cereals complement legumes (bread + peanut butter), as do nuts and seeds; in the same way, dairy products complement cereals. All foods belonging to the same family can be interchanged in such combinations.

This theory of compensating for a plant food's deficiency in amino acids by combining it with another (becoming its complement) has been put to practice instinctively by numerous peoples for thousands of years. For example, Mexicans have always combined legumes and corn in their diet, while Arabs associate chickpeas and bulgur, Indians eat lentils with rice, and Italians combine pasta with legumes (as in minestrone). The complementarity of proteins is effective when the complementing foods are consumed during the course of a meal or within the same day. However, growing children as well as pregnant or breast-feeding women should complement their proteins at every meal; this rule also applies to vegans, people who eliminate all foods of animal origin from their diet, including dairy products and eggs (unlike vegetarians, whose diet usually includes dairy products and eggs), and who are thus more prone to nutritional deficiencies.

Being a vegetarian and having a balanced diet is not as difficult as is generally thought; variety is the key word in a healthy diet and it is particularly important to consume complementary sources of protein.

By lowering the consumption of fat and increasing the intake of fiber, a balanced vegetarian diet can lead to a lower incidence of heart disease, high blood pressure, and colon cancer. These benefits are also attainable by non-vegetarians who follow the recommendations of dieticians.

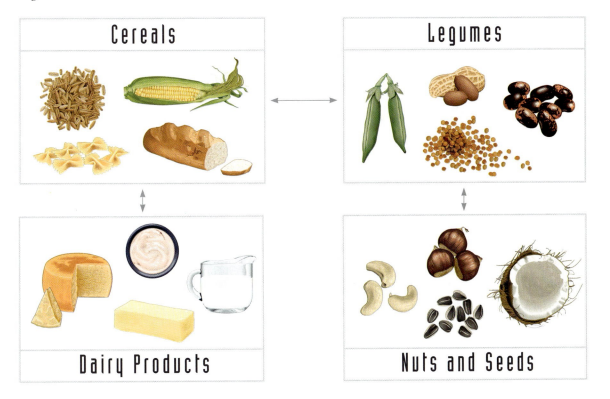

Cereals

Legumes

Dairy Products

Nuts and Seeds

Wheat

Triticum spp., Gramineae

A cereal believed to be native to southwestern Asia, although its exact origins are uncertain. What is certain, however, is that the history and evolution of human civilization are closely related to the history of wheat. The common ancestor of all varieties of wheat is thought to be wild einkorn wheat *(Triticum monococcum),* remains of which have been discovered in ruins in Mesopotamia and southwestern Asia. It would appear that humans used wheat for food more than 12,000 years ago. Tombs located in the Nile valley and dating from 5000 B.C. contain wall paintings depicting wheat, and it is well known that the ancient Egyptians produced the first leavened bread. Wheat has long been of religious significance and was a part of numerous primitive rituals. Both the Greeks and the Romans worshipped gods of wheat and of bread. To this day, wheat is still considered a sacred crop in some regions of China.

Before the Spanish first landed in America, wheat was cultivated exclusively in the Old World; Columbus introduced it into the New World upon his second expedition, in 1493. Some four centuries later, in the late 19th century, Russian immigrants settling in Kansas brought with them a red wheat variety called *Turkey red* wheat, which was superior to the varieties cultivated until then. The commercial importance of the American cereal industry is largely attributable to red wheat.

Wheat, along with rice, has been a primary source of nourishment for the human race since prehistoric times. While rice constitutes a staple food in Asia, wheat is the principal food in Europe, Africa, America, Australia, and large parts of Asia. Close to one third of the world's population depends on wheat for sustenance.

Wheat is an extremely adaptable plant that grows in most parts of the world. Although frost-resistant, most wheat requires long summers in order for its flowers to produce grains. However, varieties have recently been developed that can grow in northern regions where summers are very short. The world's largest producers of wheat are Russia, China, the United States, India, France, and Canada.

Wheat is an annual plant that grows to between 2 and 4 feet high, depending on the variety, the degree of humidity, the fertility of the soil, and the amount of sunlight. The wheat grass develops spikes, or ears, of wheat consisting of groups of three to five flowers called spikelets, which are arranged on the rachis, or central axis. Each spikelet has two sterile bracts (glumes) at its base and two fertile bracts (glumellas). After fertilization, the flower, which remains closed at maturity, develops into a more or less plump oval-shaped grain, or kernel (called the caryopsis), which has a deep crease extending its entire length. The apex of the kernel has a tuft of fine hairs, while the lower end encloses a tiny germ, or embryo, out of which a new plant will eventually grow; each plant produces an average of 50 wheat grains per year. There are a great many varieties of wheat, varying in size, shape, and color. The grains can be white, yellow, red, or purple.

The two main types of wheat are winter wheat and spring wheat. Winter wheat is cultivated in temperate regions and is planted in the fall, while spring wheat grows in countries with colder winters and is sown in the spring when there is no more risk of frost. Each group produces both hard and soft varieties of wheat (depending on the texture of the grains); grains are usually red or white, with tinges of yellow or amber.

The protein content of wheat is determined by the hardness of the grain; thus, hard wheat is richer in protein and its principal use is in the making of bread and pasta. Soft wheat has a lower protein content and is used mainly in the production of cake and pastry flours.

The most common type of wheat is *Triticum vulgare,* commonly referred to as bread wheat; it is the most widely cultivated species in the world, representing 90% of all wheat production. Durum wheat *(Triticum durum)* is also of considerable commercial importance and is used mainly in the manufacture of pasta.

Spelt wheat *(Triticum speltum)* is a variety that was cultivated on a large scale in Germany, Switzerland, and France until the beginning of the century. The grains of spelt are small and brown, and unlike other wheat grains, they are very difficult to separate from the hull (the outer coating of the grain). Hulled spelt wheat is a good replacement for rice and can be prepared in the same manner as rice; it requires a cooking time of 1 hour. Spelt wheat is also mixed with durum wheat to be used for flour in bread making. Its nutrient content is similar to that of soft wheat.

The outermost layer, or hull, of the wheat kernel, or berry, cannot be digested by humans and must be removed. The three main parts of the hulled wheat kernel are the endosperm, the germ, and the bran.

The **endosperm** represents about 83% of the total weight of the kernel, most of which is starch (70% to 72%).

The proteins in wheat, in particular its glutamic acid (a mixture of gliadin and glutelin), form a sticky mass called gluten when they come into contact with water (the word "gluten" is derived from the Latin *glu,* meaning "glue"). It is gluten that is responsible for the appearance, texture, and volume of dough. By allowing the dough to retain the gas released by the leavening agent, such as yeast or baking powder, the gluten gives the dough the ability to rise. Without it, the gas would simply escape into the air.

The elasticity of gluten differs from one type of flour to another. Mixing and kneading activate the gluten; the more the dough is kneaded, the more the gluten develops, reinforcing the structure of the dough. Wheat gluten is also used in the fabrication of monosodium glutamate, a flavor enhancer.

Bran is the multilayer fibrous coating of the endosperm; it is made up of three main types of fiber: 32.7% non-cellulosic fiber, 8% cellulose, and 3% lignin. Most of the fibers in wheat are water-insoluble. Bran represents 14.5% of the weight of the wheat grain, and in addition to being rich in fiber, it has a high protein, vitamin, and mineral content. It also supplies 80% of the wheat grain's niacin, as well as a fair amount of other B-complex vitamins. Bran is able to absorb up to three times its weight in water.

wheat grains

whole wheat flour

spelt wheat

Serving Ideas

Wheat bran and wheat germ are often added to breakfast cereals or incorporated into stuffings, pâtés, crêpes, pastries, muffins, and breads. The nutritive value of refined white flour can be increased by mixing it with wheat germ or bran (replace ¼ cup of each cup of white flour with ¼ cup of wheat germ). A sprinkling of wheat germ enriches the nutritional value of vegetables, omelets, beans, and yogurt; it can also replace nuts in cakes and cookies.

Wheat is not only used as flour or for its bran or germ, but can also be consumed in whole, cracked, or puffed form, or as flakes, semolina (couscous), or bulgur. Wheat germ is also pressed to make oil.

Whole wheat is simply wheat from which the outer coating has been removed. Whole wheat grains (or berries) can be cooked on their own or added to soups, stews, or beans. For best results, soak the grains for 12 hours in warm water before simmering them for 60 to 90 minutes (the soaking liquid can be used for cooking). Use 3 to 4 cups of liquid for each cup of hard wheat, and 3 cups of liquid per cup of soft wheat. Wheat berries can also be eaten raw after being soaked for 12 hours and coarsely ground; they are a good addition to mueslis, salads, pilafs, and baked goods. Whole wheat grains are also used in the fabrication of starch and alcohol (whiskey), and may be germinated to produce wheat sprouts.

Cracked wheat is obtained by crushing whole wheat grains into small pieces. Its uses are similar to those of whole wheat and it must also be soaked, although it requires less liquid (2 cups per cup of grains) and a shorter cooking time (30 to 40 minutes). Cracked wheat is sometimes added to bread dough. It can also be prepared like rice, eaten as a breakfast cereal, or cooked to make a cream dessert.

Puffed wheat is made by heating and applying extremely high pressure to hulled wheat grains; the pressure is then sharply reduced and the steam expands, causing the grains to burst. Puffed wheat is usually eaten as a breakfast cereal and is also used in confectionery.

Wheat flakes in cooked or raw form are also available on the market. The nutritive value of precooked flakes can vary greatly from one product to another and depends on the degree of refining and on the processing to which the wheat has been subjected. Raw flakes are obtained in the same way as rolled oats, by flattening the berries under massive rollers. Raw wheat flakes must be soaked for several hours before being cooked for about 1 hour (use about 2 cups of liquid for every cup of flakes).

The term **semolina** can be confusing, as it has a number of different uses. Generally speaking, it refers to the product obtained by grinding wheat, rice, corn, or other cereal grains.

More specifically, semolina is the flour obtained by milling hard durum wheat; it is often used as a basis for pastas. The word "semolina" comes from the Latin *simila,* meaning "finest wheat flour."

Semolina is usually made from the endosperm of the grain, which is humidified before being finely ground; it does not include the germ and bran.

The hot cereal known as Cream of Wheat is made from very fine semolina, which is also an ingredient in puddings, custards, soufflés, and soups.

Semolina is also used to make **couscous**, a word referring both to the grain itself and to the national dish of the North African countries of Algeria, Morocco, and Tunisia. Couscous is traditionally made by hand; the semolina is mixed with flour and sprinkled with cold salted water before being pressed or rolled to obtain tiny beads.

Cooked on its own, couscous can be consumed like rice or other cereal grains. It often accompanies meat and vegetable dishes or is added to soups and salads. It can also be cooked and made into a dessert or eaten as a hot cereal. Instant couscous is precooked and requires a very short cooking time.

The traditional way of cooking couscous is by steaming it in a special double pot called a *couscoussière;* the semolina is placed in the upper part or sieve, while a seasoned broth of meat, vegetables, and spices simmers in the pot below. During cooking, the couscous is turned out onto a plate and separated with a fork to eliminate any lumps that may have formed; each time, the couscous is sprinkled with a little cold salted water and olive oil.

Bulgur is made from whole wheat grains without the bran that are prepared according to an Near Eastern tradition dating back thousands of years. The wheat is partially steamed and then dried before being more or less finely ground to produce a readily made cereal having a golden color and a slight hazelnut flavor.

Bulgur can be prepared in one of two ways, either by cooking it or by simply rehydrating it. When using it in cold dishes or salads, soak the cereal for an hour in boiling water, using 2 cups of water per cup of cereal, and then drain. If the grain is still not soft enough, add a little more liquid and wait until it is absorbed by the cereal. When serving bulgur hot, either on its own or in a pilaf or stew, cook it over low heat for about 30 minutes, using 2 cups of liquid per cup of bulgur. The leftover liquid can be saved and used for soups, sauces, or stir-fries.

In addition to being consumed as a cereal, bulgur is used in a large variety of dishes. One of its better-known uses is in tabbouleh, a salad of Lebanese origin made of a mixture of bulgur, parsley, tomatoes, fresh mint, oil, and lemon juice. In Turkey, bulgur is used to make stuffed vine leaves. It can also be added to soups, salads, and stuffings, or served as a main dish combined with beans or meat. Bulgur also works well as a substitute for rice.

Wheat germ oil is obtained by cold pressing or with the help of solvents. It is added to other foods as a vitamin supplement and is an excellent source of vitamin E in particular, although it is rather expensive to produce.

couscous

semolina

bulgur

Cereals

325

Storing

Wheat berries should be stored in a cool dry place, away from insects and rodents. Wheat by-products such as bulgur, bran, and semolina should be stored in the refrigerator to prevent them from turning rancid and to preserve their nutritional value.

Wheat germ that is not vacuum packed should also be kept in the refrigerator, as it tends to turn rancid quite quickly. It is best to keep it frozen and to use it unthawed.

wheat berry

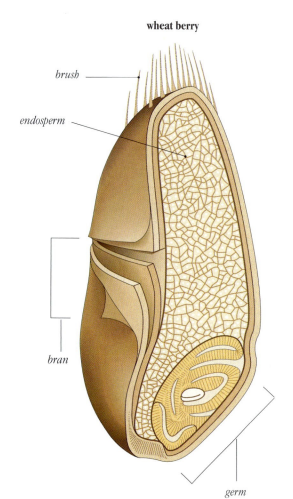

brush

endosperm

bran

germ

Nutritional Information

	raw wheat bran	*raw wheat germ*	*hard durum wheat*	*cooked couscous*	*bulgur*
water	9.9%	11.1%	10.9%	72.6%	10 %
protein	4.7 g	6.9 g	10.2 g	3.8 g	11.2 g
fat	1.3 g	2.9 g	1.9 g	0.2 g	1.5 g
carbohydrates	19.4 g	15.5 g	53.3 g	23.2 g	75.7 g
fiber	12.7 g	4.5 g	1.8 g	1.4 g	1.7 g
	per 30 g (½ cup)	**per 30 g (¼ cup)**	**per 75 g**	**100 g**	**100 g**

Raw wheat bran is an excellent source of magnesium, potassium, and phosphorus; it is also a good source of niacin, vitamin B_6, iron, zinc, and copper, and supplies some thiamine, riboflavin, folic acid, and pantothenic acid; it is very rich in dietary fiber.

Couscous contains niacin, folic acid, pantothenic acid, thiamine, and potassium.

Bulgur supplies magnesium, potassium, iron, zinc, folic acid, niacin, pantothenic acid, vitamin B_6, and thiamine.

The **wheat germ**, which is located at the base of the kernel, is the embryo that develops to form a new plant. Although it represents a mere 2.5% of the total weight of the kernel, the germ contains the most nutrients. It is also rich in fatty acids (about 10%), making it quite perishable. Most of its fatty acid is in the form of linoleic acid (see *Fats and Oils*).

Wheat germ also contains a considerable amount of lysine, an essential amino acid and one of the main constituents of protein; surprisingly, lysine is a deficient amino acid in the rest of the kernel.

Raw wheat germ is an excellent source of thiamine, folic acid, niacin, magnesium, and zinc; it is a good source of vitamin B_6, phosphorus, and potassium, and contains pantothenic acid, riboflavin, iron, and copper. Wheat germ is also rich in dietary fiber.

Durum wheat is an excellent source of niacin, magnesium, potassium, phosphorus, and zinc; it is a good source of thiamine, vitamin B_6, folic acid, iron, and copper, and contains pantothenic acid as well as riboflavin.

Wheat, like most cereal grains, lacks sufficient quantities of certain essential amino acids, notably lysine, tryptophan, and methionine. However, it is possible to compensate for this deficiency by varying the types of foods one eats (see *Introduction*). Although the crossbreeding of different varieties of wheat has produced hybrids that are richer in lysine and protein, farmers are reluctant to grow these new crops, as their yield is 10% to 15% lower than the common varieties.

Some people may experience an allergy to the gluten in wheat. Major symptoms can affect the gastrointestinal system (stomach pain, colic, diarrhea), the skin (hives, eczema), the respiratory system (cough, asthma), circulation, and the central nervous system (fatigue, migraine, irritability).

Seitan

A spongy food made from the proteins (gluten) extracted from durum wheat flour.

The wheat flour is stripped of its starch and bran by kneading it in a bowl of water until only the gluten is left; the starch dissolves in the water, while the bran separates and sinks to the bottom of the bowl. This dough is then cooked for 1 to 2 hours in a stock seasoned with tamari and kombu (seaweed). To become seitan, the gluten must be cooked in soy or tamari sauce. It is important that the protein concentrate absorb the minerals contained in the stock, as this makes the seitan easily digestible and highly nutritious (a protein concentrate that is low in minerals is more difficult to digest). The longer the gluten cooks, the firmer it becomes.

Buying

 Seitan is available ready made at natural health food stores.

Preparing

Since the process of making seitan is rather long, it is a good idea to prepare a large quantity and to freeze a portion of it. It is recommended that durum wheat flour be used.

Kneading

• Pour 4 cups of water into a large bowl and add enough flour to obtain the consistency of a thick soup;

• Stir vigorously with a wooden spoon and add the rest of the flour, for a total of 8 cups of durum whole wheat flour;

• Form the dough into a ball (at this point, there should be roughly 2½ cups of raw seitan, which expands during cooking);

• Knead the dough for 10 to 20 minutes, adding flour or water as needed to work the dough (this operation is important, since the kneading binds the gluten molecules and allows the starch to dilute in the water);

• Let the dough stand, covered with cold water, for 30 minutes to 8 hours; although this step is not essential, it shortens the rinsing time, thus facilitating the separation of the starch and the gluten.

Rinsing

• Fill a large bowl with cold water; place the dough in a strainer in the water;

• Gently knead the dough in the water until it thickens and takes on a whitish color;

• The rinsing process is finished when the dough becomes rubbery and has been rid of its starch; change the water as many times as necessary until it is clear. Do not worry about overkneading the dough – it regains its elasticity quickly;

• The rinse water containing the starch and bran can be used to thicken soups, sauces, braised dishes, and desserts. Another alternative is to slowly pour out the water and to keep the starch that has settled at the bottom of the bowl, which can be dried and used like cornstarch.

Cooking

• Prepare a stock with 8 cups of water, ½ cup or more of tamari sauce, a 3-inch piece of kombu, and a pinch of salt.

• If desired, flavor the stock by adding vegetables, spices, and fines herbes (garlic, onion, ginger, thyme, bay leaf, etc.);

• Cut the gluten into pieces the size of a potato; since it expands during cooking, it is better to separate it this way, especially when making a large quantity;

• Bring the stock to a boil; add the gluten to the stock, cover the casserole, lower the heat, and let simmer;

• Stir occasionally, adding water if necessary.

Cooking time varies depending on the size of the pieces and their intended use; allow about 30 minutes if planning to recook the seitan in another dish, and 1 hour if planning to eat the seitan in strips.

Nutritional Information

protein	18 g
calories	118
	per 100 g

Fresh seitan is low in fat and carbohydrates.

Since it is of plant origin, seitan contains no cholesterol. However, because it is made using only the wheat gluten, it lacks certain essential amino acids and does not have the same nutritive value as meat. It should therefore be served with legumes or dairy products in order to constitute a protein-rich meal containing sufficient quantities of the essential amino acids.

Serving Ideas

 Seitan can be used like meat; in fact, its taste, texture, and versatility make seitan a good substitute for meat in most recipes. It can be cooked in the same way one would prepare a cutlet, roast, meat loaf, hamburger, or brochette. Seitan is also good added to soups, sauces, stuffings, savory tarts, stews, sandwiches, lasagna, and tacos. It can also be stir-fried.

Storing

Seitan will keep for 1 to 2 weeks in the refrigerator or 2 to 6 months in the freezer.

Buckwheat

Fagopyrum esculentum and *Fagopyrum tataricum*, Polygonaceae

buckwheat flour

This bushy plant produces clusters of very fragrant white or pink flowers that bloom for over a month; bees are particularly fond of these flowers, from which they produce a dark, strongly flavored honey.

Although commonly regarded as a cereal, buckwheat is in fact the fruit of a plant belonging to a different family altogether; this family includes sorrel and rhubarb. A native of northern Europe and Asia, buckwheat was widely cultivated in China from the 10th through the 13th century. It found its way into Europe via Turkey and Russia in the 14th and 15th centuries, and was introduced into Great Britain and the United States in the 17th century. Today the largest producers of buckwheat are Russia and Poland, where it is a staple food, consumed mainly in soup and porridge. The Brittany region of France also produces a lot of buckwheat and is famous for its buckwheat crêpes. In North America, buckwheat is mainly used to make pancakes.

This bushy annual plant can grow as high as 3 feet and produces clusters of highly fragrant white or pink flowers that bloom for over a month; bees are particularly fond of these flowers, from which they produce a strongly flavored dark honey. The blackish seeds are triangular in shape and are about the size of a grain of wheat. Buckwheat can grow in poor soil and drought conditions, although the yield will be smaller; its short vegetative cycle makes it suitable for cultivation in temperate regions.

Buckwheat grains must be hulled in order to be edible; their triangular shape requires special hulling equipment. The grains are first washed and sorted according to size, after which they are crushed between two millstones to remove the hard outer shell without altering the grain. They are then sold, either roasted or plain, and graded according to size. Roasted cracked or whole buckwheat is called "kasha," used to make a dish that is popular in eastern Europe; kasha has a distinctive flavor and color. Flour is also made from buckwheat; the darker the flour, the higher its nutritional value.

Nutritional Information

	whole buckwheat flour	cooked and roasted buckwheat grains
water	11.2%	75.7%
protein	15.1 g	3.4 g
fat	3.7 g	0.6 g
carbohydrates	84.7 g	19.9 g
	per 120 g (250 ml)	per 100 g

Buckwheat flour is an excellent source of magnesium, potassium, zinc, vitamin B$_6$, thiamine, phosphorus, iron, niacin, copper, and folic acid; it also contains riboflavin, pantothenic acid, and calcium.

Cooked and roasted buckwheat grains are a good source of magnesium; they also contain potassium, copper, zinc, phosphorus, folic acid, iron, and pantothenic acid. The profile of essential amino acids in buckwheat reveals a high level of lysine, with methionine being the limiting factor (see *Introduction*). Buckwheat contains rutin (1% to 6%), which is used in the treatment of certain forms of hemorrhaging and frostbite. In addition to being easily digested, buckwheat is energizing and nutritious.

Cooking

Whole-grain buckwheat takes about 30 minutes to cook, while cracked buckwheat requires a cooking time of 15 to 30 minutes. Add the buckwheat to a boiling liquid, using 2 cups of liquid per cup of buckwheat; reduce the amount of liquid if the buckwheat is sautéed in a little fat prior to cooking. Improper cooking of buckwheat results in a rather tasteless mush, but this can be avoided by mixing the cereal with a beaten egg and cooking it briefly in a pan before adding it to the boiling water. The albumin in the egg seals the grains, making them less mushy. Buckwheat can also be cooked together with white rice.

Serving Ideas

Roasted cracked or whole buckwheat, or kasha, can be used in the same way as rice or potatoes. It is usually served as an accompanying dish or added to soups, stews, or muffins. Unroasted buckwheat has a more subtle flavor and is better suited to fine-flavored foods such as fish and desserts; it also makes a good breakfast cereal. It can be cooked on its own as hot cereal or combined with other cereals for variety.

Because buckwheat flour contains no gluten, it does not rise during baking and must be mixed with wheat flour to make bread or other leavened foods. Buckwheat flour is used in noodles, pancakes, polenta, cakes, cookies, and the traditional buckwheat cakes. Buckwheat flour is also used to make blinis (small Russian crêpes served with caviar) and is combined with wheat flour to make a type of Japanese noodle called *soba*.

Storing

Refrigerate unrefined buckwheat flour in an airtight container to prolong its storage life. Kasha can be kept in an airtight container in a cool dry place.

Stored under cool and dry conditions, whole-grain buckwheat will keep for up to 1 year, while buckwheat flour will keep for several months.

roasted buckwheat

Oats

Avena sativa, **Gramineae**

Oats grow easily in conditions where it would be impossible to cultivate other cereals. Their spikelets, which yellow at maturity, are similar to those of millet. There are several hundred varieties of oats.

oats

A cereal grain believed to be native to Asia. Several archeological finds have provided firm evidence that all varieties of oats are derived from the wild red oat. The first documents to make reference to the cultivation of this cereal date from the beginning of the Christian era. Oats were used primarily for medicinal purposes before serving as a food. They were long regarded as a weed, particularly by the ancient Greeks and Romans.

The cultivation of oats was an extremely important economic activity in Europe long before the discovery of America; in fact, until the 19th century, oats constituted a dietary staple in Scotland, Scandinavia, Germany, and Great Britain. They were introduced into North America by the first Scottish settlers in the early 17th century. Russia is presently the largest oat-producing country, followed by the United States, Canada, Germany, Poland, and Finland.

Oats are best suited to cool, moist climates, but they adapt easily to a range of climatic conditions and can be grown easily in poor soils where it would be impossible to cultivate most other cereals. An annual plant ranging from 2 to 5 feet in height, the oat produces panicles, or heads, consisting of 10 to 75 spikelets each; the spikelets, which yellow upon maturing, resemble those of millet. The several hundred varieties of oats are divided into two classes: winter oats and summer oats. The grains of most varieties are covered in hairs and vary in color from white and yellow to gray, red, and black.

After harvesting, oats are washed to rid them of sand, twigs, and other impurities. The grains are then dried and roasted. In addition to giving them their distinctive flavor, roasting improves their keeping qualities and facilitates the separation of the hull (the inedible outer surface coating) from the kernel. Once roasted, the grains are cooled and sorted; the largest and best-shaped kernels are reserved for human consumption, while broken grains are used for animal feed. The hulled grains are then cut to obtain uniformly sized granules, which are rolled into flakes.

The hulled seed, or groat, can be sold as it is, rolled, or ground. Unlike wheat, oats retain their bran and germ during processing, as they are not refined. The different stages and methods of processing produce steel-cut oats, old-fashioned rolled oats, quick-cooking oats, instant oats, oat bran, and oat flour.

Steel-cut oats are made from hulled roasted oats that are passed between steel blades which cut them into slices of varying thickness. The more finely the oats are cut, the faster they cook. Use 2 to 3 cups of water per cup of oats for cooking.

For **old-fashioned rolled oats**, the hulled grains are steamed and rolled to produce flat flakes. To cook them, use 2 to 3 cups of water per cup of oats and allow 10 to 25 minutes.

Quick-cooking oats are simply old-fashioned rolled oats that have been cut more finely in order to shorten their cooking time. While their nutritional value is equivalent to that of old-fashioned rolled oats, they are not as flavorful. Quick-cooking oats can be cooked for 3 to 5 minutes in 2½ cups of liquid per cup of oats.

To obtain **instant oats**, the grain is partially cooked and then dried and rolled very thin; it is ready to eat simply by adding boiling water. The nutritional value is equal to that of quick-cooking oats. Oats are often seasoned or flavored and marketed as a breakfast cereal known as oatmeal. The different types of oatmeal on the market almost always contain sugar and salt and often contain food additives.

The **oat bran** is located in the outer layers of the grain under the inedible hull and is longer and narrower than wheat bran. It is available as a separate product but may also be present in rolled oats and steel-cut oats. It can be cooked on its own, like oatmeal, or used in combination with other foods, in the same way as wheat germ.

Oat flour does not contain gluten and therefore does not rise during baking. It must be combined with wheat flour to make breads and other leavened foods, and tends to produce denser products.

Nutritional Information

	uncooked oat bran	*dry oats*
water		8.9%
protein	5.4 g	4.3 g
fat	2.2 g	1.7 g
carbohydrates	20.5 g	18.1 g
fiber	4.9 g	2.8 g
calories	76	104
		per 30 g

Unlike most cereals, oats retain almost all of their nutritional elements even after hulling, since the bran and germ do not separate from the kernel. This makes them a very nourishing cereal. Although the quality of their protein is also good, like all cereals, oats are lacking in sufficient quantities of certain essential amino acids (see *Introduction*).

Oatmeal is a good source of magnesium and thiamine; it also contains phosphorus, potassium, iron, pantothenic acid, and copper, and is a source of dietary fiber.

Uncooked oat bran is an excellent source of magnesium, thiamine, and phosphorus, a good source of potassium, and contains iron, zinc, folic acid, pantothenic acid, and copper.

Oats contain a natural antioxydant that makes them extremely resistant to rancidity. They also contain phytic acid and lipase, an enzyme that produces a soapy taste upon contact with substances such as baking soda, palm oil, and coconut oil. Heat treatment of the oats neutralizes the effect of the lipase.

The main advantage of oats from a nutritional point of view is that they are rich in soluble fiber, which helps to reduce blood cholesterol levels. Their auxin content (a plant hormone that promotes the growth of plants) makes them beneficial for children, and their high silica content gives them a diuretic effect.

Serving Ideas

 Although most commonly known for their use as a hot breakfast cereal, oats actually have a wide variety of other possible uses; they are notably added to granola and muesli mixtures, muffins, cookies, cakes, crêpes, and bread (in bread, use approximately 4 cups of wheat flour for 2 cups of oats).

Oats are also added to soups (as a thickener), meat loaves, pâtés, and puddings, as well as being used to make date squares, fruit crisps, cakes, jellies, beers, and beverages. Scottish and Austrian cooking use oats in stews and stuffings.

rolled oats

Barley

Hordeum vulgare, Gramineae

One of the oldest cultivated cereals, barley is mentioned in historical documents dating from the very beginning of agriculture and has been an important cereal crop throughout history. It was initially believed that barley originated more than 10,000 years ago in the deserts of southwestern Asia, where it was apparently used as food for humans and animals. However, recent studies point to the mountain regions of Ethiopia and southeastern Asia as other possible points of origin.

During the Middle Ages, when wheat was not widely available, people ate a bread made from barley and rye. The Spanish introduced barley into America in the mid-15th century.

An annual plant with a short growing period, barley is sown in the spring and harvested before summer. It is the most adaptable cereal crop, being able to resist cold, drought, and poor soil conditions. The plant varies in height from 1 to 4 feet, depending on the variety and growing conditions. The head of barley consists of two or six rows of grains arranged on a central axis, or rachis. The United States and Canada grow as many as 150 varieties of barley. The leading barley-producing countries are Russia, Germany, Canada, France, Spain, and the United States.

In many countries of Asia, North Africa, and the Middle East, barley flour and grains are used to make types of porridge. In the Western Hemisphere, barley is not as important as a food crop and is principally used for animal feed, in bread making, brewing (beer), and distilling (whiskey).

The drier growing conditions of the northern plains produce a harder and more protein-rich barley grain than the softer grains grown in the midwestern United States and on the Pacific coast. Distillers prefer the protein-rich variety for the manufacture of whiskey, while brewers use the softer, starchier variety to make beer.

Barley grains are oval and are usually milky white in color, although they may also be black or purple. For the grains to be edible, the outer coating, or hull, must be removed. The nutritional value of barley is largely determined by the way in which the grains are hulled, since most of the nutrients are concentrated near the outer coating. The various stages of processing produce hulled barley, pot (or scotch) barley, and pearled (or pearl) barley.

Hulled barley is barley from which the outer husk has been removed and which still has almost all of its bran. The seed is most nutritious in this form, as only a small portion of the nutrients are lost.

Pot or scotch barley has been subjected to a triple polishing process. This abrasion causes the grain to lose various nutrients (for the most part vitamins and minerals) and almost all of its bran.

Pearled barley undergoes five or six polishing operations, after which it is further processed to create grains of the same size and shape. In the process, the grain is stripped of its germ, in addition to a certain quantity of its vitamins, minerals, fiber, fat, and protein.

Barley flakes are processed and used like rolled oats, while **barley flour** is available in varying degrees of refinement. Whole-grain barley flour has a nutty flavor and is darker than whole-grain wheat flour.

Certain varieties of barley constitute the raw material used to make **malt**; this cereal withstands germination, or malting, better than others. Malt is produced by germinating, drying, roasting, and then grinding the barley grains. The flour obtained is left to ferment, during which time the grain's starch is converted into various sugars and then into alcohol. Germination of the barley seeds results in an increase in their vitamin B complex, as well as a reduction of the starch content. The main use of malt is in the production of beer and whiskey. The longer the malt is roasted, the darker the beer.

The hard, protein-rich variety of barley is used by the distilling industry to make whiskey, while the softer, starchier variety is more sought after by brewers.

Serving Ideas

The many uses of barley are similar to those of most other cereals. Frequently added to soups and stews, it is also cooked on its own or, in the case of pearled barley, mixed with rice. It can be used in pâtés, croquettes, puddings, and desserts, and its somewhat rubbery texture adds an original touch to mixed salads.

Barley also goes into the making of miso (see *Miso*). Ground roasted barley produces a malt that serves as a substitute for coffee, while barley flour is used to thicken soups and sauces and to add a slightly sweet taste to various foods. Barley flour is also used to make cookies, bread, crêpes, and cakes, but because it has a low gluten content, it must be combined with wheat flour to produce leavening.

Barley is a staple food of Tibetans, who use roasted barley flour to make a thick porridge called *tsampa* and an alcoholic beverage called *chang*. The malt is used to make beer and whiskey, and as a coffee substitute; it also serves to enhance the flavor and texture of certain foods. Malted syrups are used to flavor milk beverages and commercial cakes. The market also offers malted barley breakfast cereals.

Pearled Barley Consommé

SERVES 4 TO 6

½ cup (125 ml)
  pearled barley
8 cups (2 l) beef stock
1 carrot
1 onion

1 rib celery
Salt and ground
  pepper
1 tsp. chopped curly
  parsley leaves

1. Wash the barley in warm water.

2. Pour the beef stock into a large soup pot, and add the barley and vegetables (uncut). Bring to a boil and simmer for 2 hours.

3. Remove the vegetables and season the consommé with salt and pepper to taste. Garnish with the chopped parsley, and serve.

Nutritional Information

	cooked pearled barley
water	68.8%
protein	2.3 g
fat	0.4 g
carbohydrates	28.2 g
fiber	6.5 g
	per 100 g

Like all cereals, barley is not a complete food, as it lacks sufficient quantities of certain proteins; the limiting amino acids in barley are tryptophan and lysine (see *Introduction*). Cooked pearled barley contains niacin, iron, zinc, magnesium, potassium, folic acid, vitamin B_6, thiamine, copper, and phosphorus. Barley is an excellent source of water-soluble fiber and a good source of dietary fiber in general.

Barley is said to be fortifying, emollient, regenerative, antidiarrheal, and good for the respiratory system. Barley tea has long been used to soothe coughs.

Cooking

Hulled barley takes about 1 hour to cook over low heat, using 3 to 4 cups of cooking liquid for 1 cup of grains. Hulled and pot barley should be soaked for several hours before cooking (the soaking liquid can be used to cook the barley). If desired, drain and roast the barley before cooking it.

Pearled barley takes about 30 minutes to cook and does not need to be soaked beforehand.

Cereals

333

Millet

Panicum miliaceum and *Setaria italica,* Grameneae

The term "millet" is used to refer to several cereal grains that do not necessarily belong to the same genus. While it is known that millet has been cultivated in Asia and North Africa since prehistoric times, the exact origin of this cereal is unclear. Some believe millet to be a native of eastern or central Asia, while others point to Ethiopia as its place of origin. Millet is a very important food grain in Africa. During the Middle Ages, when corn and potatoes were still unknown in Europe, this cereal was common fare, and it remains a popular grain to this day, particularly in eastern Europe. In North America and western Europe, however, millet is cultivated almost exclusively for use as forage. Asia and Africa produce 87% of the world's millet crop, with the major producing countries being India (with 40%), followed by China and Nigeria.

Millet is a drought-resistant plant that can withstand poor soils but that is less tolerant of cold temperatures. Unlike the majority of other cereals, which form ears, most varieties of millet form panicles, or heads. Millet berries are small and round and vary in color from white, gray, or yellow to red or reddish brown. The seeds of most varieties remain enclosed in their hull even after threshing. Once hulled, the berries are sold as they are, in the form of flakes, or ground.

Botanically speaking, there are significant differences among the main varieties of millet cultivated around the world. **Common millet** *(Panicum miliaceum),* a variety dating from prehistoric times, is cultivated in Russia, China, Japan, India, southern Europe, and in some regions of North America; it is used mainly for human consumption and animal feed. **Foxtail millet** *(Setaria italica)* is an Asian variety that was held to be sacred by the Chinese. Introduced into the United States in the 19th century, this is the best-known variety and is grown mainly for forage. In Russia foxtail millet is used mainly to make beer, while in England it is used primarily for birdseed. **Pearl millet** *(Panicum miliare)* is cultivated principally in India; this variety can grow in impoverished soils and is much more resistant to droughts and floods than other millets.

Sorghum *(Sorghum vulgare),* also known as "milo," has been cultivated in Africa and Asia for 4,000 years. It is one of the most widely consumed food grains in the world (after wheat, rice, corn, and barley), and it is particularly important in Africa, India, and China. Some 70 varieties of this grain have been identified, most of which are annual, while some are perennial. Sorghum is a tropical or subtropical plant that grows easily in regions that are too dry for rice, wheat, and corn; it adapts just as well to wet climates as to semi-arid climates.

Teff *(Eragrostis abyssinica)* is another variety classified among the millets; it originated in Africa, most likely in Ethiopia, where it has been consumed for thousands of years. Cultivated as a cereal crop exclusively in Ethiopia until 1988, the availability of teff in Western markets is quite recent, although India, Kenya, and South Africa also produce this grain for forage. Today teff is grown both for forage and for human consumption.

Serving Ideas

 Millet can be used in place of most other cereals, although its strong flavor might not be appreciated by everyone. It can be added to soups, omelets, croquettes, meat pies, puddings, and muesli.

Since millet flour does not contain gluten, it is unsuitable for making leavened breads, although it is commonly made into flat breads that are widely consumed in Africa and Asia. Millet is also cooked to make porridge, fermented to make alcohol or beer (particularly in Africa), or sprouted like alfalfa sprouts and used to enrich other foods. Millet meal or ground millet can be incorporated into breads, cakes, pies, and biscuits.

Sorghum flour is also devoid of gluten and must be mixed with wheat flour to make leavened breads; it is also used to make flat breads. Sorghum is prepared like rice or millet and can be used in whole grain or semolina form. It is cooked into porridge and incorporated into cakes. Africans make beer from sorghum, while the Chinese use it to make alcoholic beverages such as the aperitif known as *mao-tai,* which has an alcohol content of 53%. In North America, only 1.4% of the sorghum crop is used for human consumption; the rest is used for forage.

Teff is eaten whole or ground into a slightly granular flour; although this flour does not rise, it is baked into delicious flat breads and sweet breads, such as *injera,* the national bread of Ethiopia. *Faffa* is a dietary supplement that is prepared from a finely ground mixture of teff flour, chickpeas, skim milk, sugar, and salt.

Cooking

To cook millet, use 2 cups of liquid per cup of grains and simmer it for 30 to 40 minutes. Before cooking, soak the berries or roast them dry or in a little oil. Roasting gives them a delicious nutlike flavor: roast the berries in a skillet over medium-low heat, stirring them constantly to keep them from burning; when the millet is golden, add the cooking liquid.

To make porridge from teff, use 3 cups of water or milk per cup of grains and simmer it for about 15 minutes.

Storing

Whole grain millet and sorghum will keep for several months in an airtight container stored in a cool, dry, and preferably dark place.

Nutritional Information

	cooked millet
water	71.4%
protein	3.5 g
fat	1 g
carbohydrates	23.7 g
calories	119
	per 100 g

Millet is a good source of magnesium; it also supplies niacin, thiamine, riboflavin, folic acid, vitamin B_6, potassium, phosphorus, iron, zinc, and copper. Millet protein is superior to that of wheat, rice, or corn, although it is deficient in the two essential amino acids lysine and tryptophan. Millet is one of the few cereals that is alkaline; it is also easy to digest and nonallergenic. The characteristic flavor of millet may be explained by its high silica content, a mineral that has a beneficial effect on the blood cholesterol level and on bones.

Millet is said to have a mild laxative effect and to combat gallstones, stomach ulcers, and colitis; it also contains a mucilaginous substance that may have a positive effect on the bladder and kidneys, and on the gastrointestinal system in general.

The nutritive value of sorghum is similar to that of corn, although sorghum has more protein and starch and less fat. Sorghum also contains niacin, thiamine, iron, potassium, and phosphorus.

Rice

Oryza sativa, Grameneae

One of the most important cereal grains, rice is known to have been cultivated in China over 6,000 years ago. A descendant of wild species of rice native to Southeast Asia, where they can still be found growing today, rice was introduced into Greece by Arab travelers and was brought to India by Alexander the Great around 326 B.C. (The scientific name, *Oryza,* comes from the Greek word for rice.) In A.D. 700, the Moors introduced it into Spain during their conquest of that country. The Spanish in turn brought rice with them to South America at the beginning of the 17th century. The Crusaders are credited with having introduced this grain into France.

Next to wheat, rice is the largest food crop in the world, representing as much as half the caloric intake for at least half the world's population. It is the most important crop in Asia, where 94% of the world production is concentrated. The importance of rice in this part of the world is reflected in the language; for example, the Chinese word for rice is the same word used for agriculture, and in several official languages and local dialects the word "to eat" translates into "to eat rice." In a number of other Asian languages, the same word designates both "rice" and "food." Although other countries have also emerged as important producers, the China, India, Indonesia, Bangladesh, and Thailand remain the largest rice producers.

Rice is an annual grass that grows best in tropical climates. Although originally a dry plant, over the course of repeated mutations, rice developed into a semiaquatic plant. While it can withstand a wide range of climatic conditions, it grows more rapidly and vigorously in hot, humid areas. Depending on the climate, rice plants produce one or several crops per year.

The plant can measure from 2 to 6 feet in height and has branching stems ending in panicles 8 to 12 inches long; each panicle is made up of 50 to 300 flowers, or "spikelets," which form the rice grain when fertilized.

While it is possible to grow rice in unflooded conditions, most varieties (90%) are grown in flooded fields where the water level rises to between 4 and 6 inches.

Traditional methods of rice farming involve several stages requiring many hours of hard labor. In Asian countries, field workers often carry out this work under extremely harsh conditions. The rice is sown by hand and transplanted when it reaches a certain height, at which point the field is flooded. Once blooming has taken place, the field is drained and the rice is harvested manually. The crop is usually ready for harvesting 4 to 6 months after sowing.

In many areas, particularly in the United States, these century old practices have been largely replaced by highly mechanized means of production. Almost all of those crops are seeded by airplanes that spread sprouted rice seeds, and combines are used for harvesting. These automated means of rice production are, of course, more common in the wealthier countries.

There are two main species of cultivated rice. The most common is the *sativa* or white rice, which is a native of Asia. The species *glaberrima,* or "African rice," is grown mainly in Africa; the latter is more recent and less widespread, as it does not adapt as well to different climatic conditions.

The over 8,000 varieties of rice are generally divided into short grain (or round grain), medium grain, and long grain types. What is known as "wild rice" belongs to a different species altogether (see *Wild Rice*).

Short grain rice or **round grain rice** measures 4 to 5 millimeters (less than ⅕ inch) in length and 2.5 millimeters in width; its higher starch content makes it stickier when cooked.

Medium grain rice (5 to 6 millimeters, or ⅕ to ¼ inch, long) is slightly shorter and plumper than long grain rice; these varieties remain firm and light when cooked but tend to stick when cooled.

Long grain rice (6 millimeters/¼ inch and over) is light, and the grains remain separate when cooked; however, this rice can become sticky if it is overcooked or stirred too frequently during cooking.

The grain of rice is covered by a hard inedible hull, which is always removed during milling. The milling process influences the flavor, nutritional value, and keeping qualities of rice, since rice is composed of several layers containing varying proportions of nutrients. For example, more than 80% of the thiamine, 56% of the riboflavin, 65% of the niacin, 60% of the pantothenic acid, and 85% of the fat in rice are concentrated near the surface. Therefore the quantity of nutrients lost during milling depends on the number of layers removed from the grain. There are many different hulling methods, from the traditional practices of hand threshing and pounding to the more modern industrial methods using mechanical brushes. The market offers several kinds of rice which vary according to the degree of milling.

Brown rice (or whole rice) is the whole grain with the fibrous inedible outer hull removed. This type of rice is also called "cargo rice." Brown rice almost always contains some green grains that were not fully ripe at the time of harvesting. (This is inevitable because the grains do not mature at the same rate and it is difficult and costly to sort them before or after harvesting.) While these immature grains are also found in white rice, they are less noticeable because white rice is milled to a greater degree. Brown rice is the most nutritious form of rice; its nutty flavor is stronger than that of white rice.

Instant brown rice has been treated in the same way as instant white rice (see below) in order to reduce the cooking time to 5 minutes, with a 5-minute rest period, as opposed to the normal cooking time of 45 minutes required for brown rice.

Parboiled brown rice (ready in 25 minutes) is processed in the same way as parboiled white rice (see below) in order to shorten its cooking time. Parboiling has the added advantage of improving the keeping qualities of brown rice by neutralizing the substances that cause the oils in the germ to turn rancid. Unlike parboiled white rice, parboiled brown rice always retains the bran and germ.

Parboiled white rice or **converted white rice** is soaked and then steamed before being milled. The parboiling process transfers the water soluble vitamins and minerals contained in the germ and outer layers to the interior, so that they are not eliminated during polishing. Parboiled rice is slightly translucent and yellowish, but turns white when cooked. It does not usually stick and is lighter and more delicately flavored than brown rice. Next to brown rice, this is the most nourishing rice, although it is not as high in fiber because the bran has been removed. Equal quantities of uncooked white and brown rice will yield about the same volume of rice when cooked. Parboiling improves the keeping qualities of rice by delaying rancidity.

White rice has been hulled and polished, stripping it of a significant proportion of its nutrients. Compared to brown rice, it is much lower in niacin, thiamine, magnesium, zinc, iron, and fiber. In some countries, including the United States, white rice is commonly enriched with iron, niacin, and thiamine in order to restore some of its nutritional value. It is also sometimes given a coating of magnesium silicate or of a mixture of glucose and talc (polished rice) to make it whiter and shiny. Polished rice is preferred in many countries, particularly in Puerto Rico, for its more attractive appearance.

Instant rice is white rice that is precooked and then dried to shorten its cooking time. Once cooked, this rice is dry and fluffy in appearance. It is fairly bland-tasting and even less nutritious than white rice, although it is more expensive than the latter because it requires more processing. It is often referred to as Minute Rice, a familiar brand name.

Arborio rice is a classic round white rice that is the essential element in Italian dish. It is considered to be one of the finest types of rice because of its ability to absorb large quantities of liquid without becoming too mushy.

Most varieties of rice are cultivated in flooded fields; next to wheat, rice is the most important cereal crop in the world.

brown rice

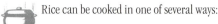

Perfumed rices have a much more distinct flavor than other varieties. **Basmati rice** is one of the best known and most popular of the perfumed varieties; a standard in Indian cooking, it has a light, dry texture and a perfumed flavor. **Jasmine rice** is also a popular variety.

Seasoned rices are almost always made from precooked or parboiled rice to which salt and various seasoning ingredients have been added. They also often contain food additives.

Preparing

Parboiled, white, and instant rice do not need to be soaked prior to cooking. Medium-grain and round rice should be washed before being cooked to keep them from sticking; rinse the rice under running water until the water is clear.

Basmati rice (and, optionally, jasmine rice and other perfumed rices) should be soaked in cold water before being cooked. Stir the rice in water and replace the water when it turns milky; repeat the operation four or five times or until the water is clear. Rinsing rice prior to cooking gives it a lighter, less creamy texture.

arborio rice

white rice

Cooking

Rice can be cooked in one of several ways:

Boiling

Rice can be boiled in water, stock, juice, or milk (rice cooked in milk is usually used to make desserts) according to different methods:

• Use 1 part rice with 2 parts cooking liquid. Place the liquid and the rice in a pot and bring to a boil; lower the heat, cover, and simmer gently until all the liquid is absorbed. Alternatively, bring the liquid to a boil before adding the rice and then simmer until the liquid is absorbed.

• Place the rice in a saucepan and cover it with a generous quantity of water. Bring to a boil, lower the heat, and cook the rice uncovered; drain it when it is ready. To remove excess moisture after cooking, dry the rice in the oven at 300°F for 7 to 15 minutes.

• For brown rice that does not stick, soak it in water for 1 hour and then cook it in its soaking water for 45 minutes; or cook it for 35 minutes, then turn off the heat and let the rice stand in the covered pot for another 10 minutes.

• The absorption method is a very popular way of cooking rice, as it produces a light and nonsticky final product. First, wash the rice according to the method described above for basmati rice. Then place the rice in a saucepan and just cover it with cold water. Cover the pan and bring to a boil over high heat; cook over medium heat, without stirring, until small craters form on the surface; at this point, most of the water has evaporated and the rice is moist. Lower the heat and simmer, covered, for 15 minutes. Avoid overcooking the rice, as this will make it stick to the bottom of the pot. For rice that doesn't stick, it is also important not to stir the rice (or to stir it one time only) once the craters have formed.

• Basmati rice is delicate and aromatic and requires less cooking liquid (about 1¼ cup for 1 cup of presoaked rice, or slightly more liquid for unsoaked rice). It should be cooked over low heat. Soak 1 cup of rice for 30 minutes in 2 cups of water, drain, and let stand for 10 minutes. Pour the rice into the saucepan, add the water (or 1¼ cup milk per cup of presoaked rice), and cook, covered, over very low heat for 20 minutes. Turn off the heat and let the rice stand for 10 minutes.

The cooking time varies depending on the type of rice and on individual preference. The following cooking times are therefore approximate:

brown rice, 40 to 45 minutes; parboiled rice, 25 minutes; white rice, 15 minutes; instant rice, 5 minutes.

When boiling rice:

• For firm rice, reduce the quantity of water and do not overcook it. For softer rice, use slightly more water.

• If the rice is not to be served immediately, shorten the cooking time slightly to allow for reheating. The greater the quantity of rice, the longer the heat is retained, and the shorter the cooking time. To halt the cooking process, remove the cover from the pot when the rice is done.

• If there is a little liquid remaining once the rice is cooked, remove the cover and raise the heat to evaporate the liquid quickly (make sure that the rice does not stick to the pan).

• If there is a lot of cooking liquid remaining, drain the rice (the leftover cooking liquid can be used to make soups, sauces, or stews). Place the drained rice in the oven or on the stove briefly to dry it.

• To prevent it from becoming sticky, avoid stirring the rice during cooking.

Steaming

Pour the rice into the top of a double boiler and place it over boiling water; cover and simmer over moderate to high heat. The rice can be blanched for a few minutes beforehand, but this deprives it of some of its vitamins and minerals.

Cooking in fat

First, cook the rice in a little fat or butter for a few minutes, stirring constantly. Then add twice its volume in liquid, cover the pan, and simmer until the liquid is absorbed. Rice cooked in this manner remains firm and does not stick (this is the traditional method of preparing risotto, paella, Greek-style rice, rice pilaf, and Creole rice).

Serving Ideas

Rice is an extremely important element in cooking and is used in a variety of ways. It is added to soups, croquettes, meat and vegetable stuffings, salads, puddings, pies, and cakes, as well as constituting the key ingredient in risotto, pilaf, paella, and curry dishes. It is also used to make rice noodles, cereals, syrup, wine, vinegar, and miso. As a replacement for potatoes, rice is commonly served with meat, poultry, fish, and seafood dishes, and it traditionally accompanies grilled fish and brochettes. It can be served plain or in a stir-fry. A delicately sweet and slightly granular flour can be made by grinding rice in a food processor or coffee grinder; rice flour gives cakes and pastries a slightly crunchy texture. It can also be used to thicken sauces, although it is not suitable for bread making, as it does not contain gluten.

Rice is used in the fabrication of a number of alcoholic beverages that are popular in Asia, including Japanese sake and mirin and a Chinese yellow wine called *chao xing*. Sake is a sweet alcoholic drink that is served hot, warm, or cold, usually in tiny cups; it has an alcohol content of 14% to 16%. Mirin is a sweet or savory wine with a lower alcohol content (some varieties contain about 8% alcohol); it is used mainly as a cooking wine in sauces or various preparations.

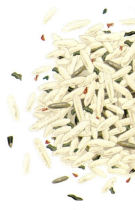

seasoned rice

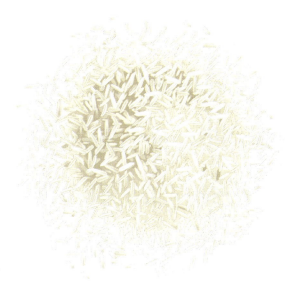

jasmine rice

parboiled rice

rice flour

Nutritional Information

Rice is a good source of magnesium and contains niacin, vitamin B_6, thiamine, phosphorus, zinc, and copper, as well as traces of pantothenic acid and potassium.

Long-grain parboiled white rice contains niacin, magnesium, copper, and pantothenic acid, as well as traces of phosphorus, zinc, and potassium. Cooked long-grain white rice contains pantothenic acid, vitamin B_6, magnesium, and zinc, as well as traces of phosphorus, niacin, and potassium. Rice has the lowest protein content of all the cereal grains (although certain improved varieties may contain up to 14%). As with all cereals, its proteins are incomplete, with lysine being the limiting amino acid (see *Introduction*). The starch in rice is composed of amylose and amylopectin; it expands during cooking and is highly digestible.

With the exception of brown rice, rice contains only traces of thiamine (vitamin B_1). Consequently, in countries where unenriched white rice is the main source of nourishment, thiamine deficiency causes a serious disease known as beriberi. The main symptoms of this disease are edema, heart failure, and a form of paralysis. A lack of thiamine can lead to muscular weakness and improper functioning of the digestive system.

Rice is known to be an effective remedy for diarrhea (its cooking water is particularly effective). It is also said to be effective against hypertension and it is used as an astringent.

Storing

Brown rice still contains the oil rich germ and should therefore be stored in the refrigerator to keep it from going rancid; place it in an airtight container to prevent the absorption of odors.

White rice should be stored in a cool, dry place where insects cannot get at it. An unopened box of white rice will keep for a year.

Cooked rice is perishable and will keep for only a few days in the refrigerator; store it in a covered container. It can also be frozen for 6 to 8 months. A practical idea when cooking rice is to make a large batch and to freeze the excess for future use.

Rice Pudding

SERVES 4 TO 6

2½ (625 ml) cups milk
½ cup (125 ml) long-grain rice
Sugar
Salt
1 tsp. cornstarch

1 tbsp. cold milk
1 egg yolk
⅓ cup (80 ml) raisins
Vanilla extract
Nutmeg
Grated orange zest

1. Heat the milk in a saucepan over low heat.

2. Rinse the rice under cold water.

3. Add the rice, 2 tablespoons of sugar, and a pinch of salt to the hot milk. Cook, covered, over very gentle heat for 25 minutes, stirring occasionally.

4. In a small bowl, mix 1 teaspoon of sugar with the cornstarch. Add the 1 tablespoon of cold milk and the egg yolk, and mix with a fork.

5. Add this mixture to the cooked rice, and heat while stirring. Remove from the heat and add the raisins and a few drops of vanilla.

6. Pour the rice pudding into individual dessert bowls and sprinkle with nutmeg. Garnish with a little orange zest.

Serve warm or cold.

---

	cooked long-grain brown rice	cooked parboiled long-grain white rice	cooked long-grain white rice	instant long-grain white rice
water	73%	72.5%	68.7%	76.4%
protein	2.6 g	2.3 g	2.7 g	2.1 g
fat	0.9 g	0.3 g	0.3 g	0.2 g
carbohydrates	23 g	24.7 g	27 g	21.3 g
fiber	1.7 g	0.5 g	0.4 g	0.8 g

per 100 g

Wild rice

Zizania aquatica, Grameae

The seed of an aquatic plant that is native to the Great Lakes area of North America, wild rice grows in marshes and along the muddy banks of calm freshwater lakes. It is found growing mainly in Canada and the United States, where the Indians have harvested and valued it for centuries; in the past, certain tribes even waged long wars over wild rice territories.

American Indians have harvested and appreciated wild rice for centuries. The traditional method of gathering wild rice consists of bending the stalks over the side of the boat and striking the ripe heads to dislodge the grains.

Wild rice comes from an annual grass that can grow as high as 10 feet. It is much sought after, and commercial production has expanded rapidly in recent years. It is an expensive crop to grow, however, since it is sensitive to climatic variations, shifts in water levels, and parasites, resulting in fairly limited crop yields. In addition, wild rice is difficult to harvest. The traditional method of gathering consists of bending the stalks over the side of the boat and striking the ripe heads to dislodge the grains. Today mechanical harvesters of the kind used for wheat are increasingly used in place of traditional methods.

Wild rice grains acquire their blackish color once they are washed, dried, and hulled. They are longer than ordinary rice grains, often measuring close to ½ inch in length. The hulls are easily removed once the grains are dried. Wild rice has a crisp texture and a pronounced hazelnut-like flavor.

Preparing

Wash wild rice thoroughly to remove any debris.

If the grains have not already been hulled, spread them on a cookie sheet and dry them in a warm oven (200°F) for 2 to 3 hours, stirring them occasionally, or store them in a warm place for 2 or 3 days. Another possibility is to heat the rice in a warm frying pan, stirring constantly.

Once dried, the hulls can be easily loosened by threshing the grains or rubbing them together. Allow the hulled rice to dry for an additional hour in the oven (250°F).

Serving Ideas

Wild rice is often served as an accompaniment to poultry, wild game, and seafood; the dark color and distinctive flavor of the rice contrast pleasantly with these foods. It can be served on its own or mixed with other kinds of rice and blends well with mushrooms, vegetables, fruits, and nuts. Cooked wild rice is also a popular ingredient in stuffings and crêpes. Wild rice can be popped like corn and is also ground to make flour.

Nutritional Information

	cooked
water	73.9%
protein	4 g
fat	0.3 g
carbohydrates	21.3 g
	per 100 g

Not only is wild rice richer in protein than ordinary rice, but its proteins are more complete, as they contain more lysine (see *Complementary proteins*).

Wild rice is a highly nutritious grain. It is a good source of zinc and supplies folic acid, niacin, vitamin B_6, riboflavin, magnesium, potassium, phosphorus, and copper.

Cereals

341

Cooking

Wild rice is prepared by boiling it in water or stock after it has been soaked for several hours or overnight. For a more rapid soaking method, boil the rice for 5 minutes in four times its volume of water; remove from the heat and allow the rice to soak for 1 hour in the covered saucepan. Drain the rice. Return the pan to the heat, adding fresh water or broth (using three times the volume of rice, or slightly less for a drier rice) and ½ teaspoon of salt. Bring to a boil and add the rice; reduce the heat and simmer for about 20 minutes or until tender.

Avoid overcooking wild rice as this causes it to lose flavor and firmness and to become sticky.

Unsoaked rice should be cooked for about 40 minutes in three times its volume of water. The rice grains expand to four times their initial volume during cooking.

Wild Rice au Gratin

SERVES 4 TO 6

¾ cup (185 ml) wild rice	1 rib celery
1⅓ cups (330 ml)	3 tbsp. butter
chicken stock, soaked	½ cup (125 ml) grated
Salt and ground pepper	aged Cheddar cheese
1 small onion	
¾ cup (185 ml) chopped	
fresh mushrooms	

1. Preheat the oven at 375°F (190°C). Rinse the wild rice in hot water. Pour the stock and rice into a saucepan, add salt and pepper to taste, and bring to a boil. Reduce the heat and simmer, covered, for 45 minutes. Drain the rice and separate the grains with a fork. Set aside in the covered pan.

2. Chop the onion. Slice the mushrooms. Dice the celery.

3. Cook the celery briefly (3 minutes) in boiling water to soften it. In a frying pan, sauté the onion in the butter 5 minutes until golden and tender. Add the mushrooms and sauté for 2 minutes. Add the cooked celery. Season to taste.

4. Mix the cooked wild rice with the vegetables, and transfer to a baking dish. Top with the grated cheese and bake in the oven for 20 to 25 minutes or until a golden crust forms.

Serve as an accompaniment to chicken, quail, or duck.

Quinoa

Chenopodium quinoa, **Chenopodiaceae**

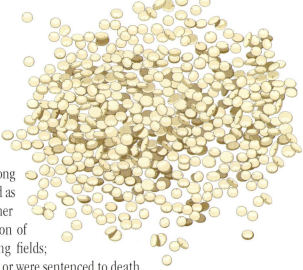

An annual plant native to South America, where it has been cultivated for over 5,000 years in the Andes of Bolivia, Chile, and Peru. Quinoa was once a staple food of the Andean peoples, along with the potato, tomato, bean, and corn. It was regarded as a sacred food by the Incas, who called it "the mother seed." Spanish conquerors prohibited the cultivation of quinoa by the Indians and destroyed their growing fields; those who disobeyed the ban had their hands cut off or were sentenced to death.

These harsh measures were ultimately effective in eliminating cultivation of this cereal. Quinoa disappeared for centuries, only to be restored by Americans, who recognized the potential of this nourishing plant, with its edible seeds and leaves. In 1982, Americans Stephan Gorad and Don McKinley played a major role in rehabilitating quinoa when they decided to begin cultivating it in Colorado. Quinoa has been gaining in popularity ever since, thanks also to more effective methods of cultivation and commercialization.

The quinoa plant can attain a height of 3 to 10 feet and produces numerous tiny seeds that resemble a cross between millet and sesame seeds. Depending on the variety, the outer layer of the seed can be transparent or pink, orange, red, purple, or black. Quinoa is more resistant to harsh conditions than most other cereals, being able to withstand dry and sandy soils, cold, drought, and high altitudes. Although commonly regarded as a cereal, in botanical terms, quinoa is actually the fruit of a plant that belongs to the same family as the beet, chard, and spinach. There are thousands of varieties of this plant.

Most of the quinoa sold on the market is available in health-food stores. The quinoa seed, which is usually yellow, contains a large germ, or embryo, that eventually grows to produce a new plant. Most of the nutrients are concentrated in this part of the seed, and it is also the germ that allows the quinoa to withstand adverse growing conditions. Quinoa seeds are covered with a layer of saponin, a bitter, soapy resin that forms a lather on contact with water and that must be washed off before the seeds can be eaten. During commercial processing, the seeds are washed in an alkaline solution or by dry friction.

Preparing

Rinse the quinoa thoroughly under running water while rubbing the seeds together, and then let it drain. If the raw seeds still have a bitter taste after washing, saponin is still present and they should be washed again; when all traces of the substance have been eliminated, the water no longer appears soapy.

Serving Ideas

Quinoa can be substituted for most cereals and is a good replacement for rice in particular. It can be eaten cooked like a porridge or added to various dishes, including soups, savory pies, and croquettes. Ground quinoa is incorporated into breads, cookies, puddings, crêpes, muffins, and pasta.

Quinoa seeds have a low gluten content. They can be sprouted and used like alfalfa sprouts.

In South America, quinoa is often used to prepare an alcoholic beverage called *chicha* that has been widely appreciated for thousands of years.

Quinoa leaves can be cooked like spinach.

Cooking

Quinoa cooks quickly, requiring only about 15 minutes; use 2 cups of liquid per cup of seed. The seeds remain slightly crunchy and do not stick after cooking. The texture of quinoa resembles that of caviar, while its flavor is reminiscent of hazelnut.

Storing

Store quinoa in an airtight container in a cool dry place. To prevent ground quinoa from turning rancid, store it in the refrigerator, where it will keep for 3 to 6 months.

Nutritional Information

	raw quinoa
water	9%
protein	5.2 g
fat	2.3 g
carbohydrates	27.6 g
	per 100 g

Quinoa is an excellent source of magnesium, iron, and potassium; it is also a good source of copper, zinc, and phosphorus and contains riboflavin, thiamin, and niacin.

Not only does quinoa contain more protein than most cereals, but its proteins are of a higher quality, since its amino acids are more evenly balanced; in particular, it contains a high level of lysine, as well as of methionine and cystine. This food is a good complement to other cereals, legumes, nuts, and grains (see *Complementary proteins*).

Cereals

343

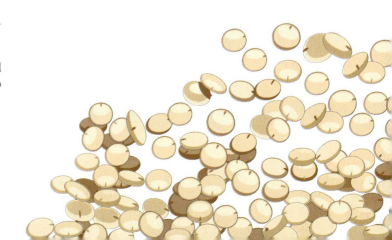

Corn

Zea mays, **Gramineae**

Upon arriving in the New World, the first explorers discovered that the cultivation of corn extended all the way from Canada to Chile; it was a staple food of pre-Columbian civilizations as far back as primitive times.

The only native American cereal grain, corn is believed to have originated in Mexico or Central America and constituted the staple food of pre-Columbian civilizations as far back as primitive times. Archeological remains discovered in southern Mexico and dating back over 7,000 years provide the earliest traces of a meal made from small ears of corn. Mayan, Aztec, and Incan mythology contain abundant references to corn; it was also used by these civilizations in religious ceremonies, as a form of currency, fuel, construction material, and to make jewelry and tobacco (from the silky threads). Upon arriving in the New World, the first explorers found corn growing all the way from Canada to Chile. Native Indians from Mexico northward to lower Canada consumed a type of cornmeal sweetened with honey or spiced with peppers and accompanied by vegetables, meat, or fish.

Early colonists were attracted by the presence of this cereal grain, which the natives had adapted to various climatic and soil conditions; the cultivation techniques developed by the Indians encouraged rapid settlement. In the Old World, the first reports of corn's existence were provided by Christopher Columbus, who discovered it growing in Hispaniola in 1492. It was introduced into Europe in the early 16th century by the Spanish explorer Hernán Cortés, and the Portuguese introduced it into Africa at the beginning of the 16th century. Corn remains a very important commodity in present-day America.

Corn grows on a robust annual plant that can attain a height of 6 to 10 feet; the plant has drooping leaves and bears both male and female flowers. The kernels are borne on ears of corn measuring 6 to 12 inches in length. Each ear has numerous long slender threads called "styles," or "silks," which protrude from the top of the husk and through which pollination occurs; each style is connected to a flower, which when pollinated develops into an ovary, or kernel. An ear of corn can contain between 750 and 1,000 kernels, which grow in an even number of rows (usually between 8 and 24). The kernels can be yellow, white, orange, red, purple, blue, black, or brown, according to the variety.

The kernel of corn is composed of three main parts: the pericarp (the outer layers), the endosperm (which is approximately 90% starch), and the embryo, or germ (rich in nutrients). The many different varieties of corn can be divided into six general categories. The most commercially important type of corn is *dent corn,* which is used mainly as livestock feed; the kernels are firm, low in sugar, and high in starch and may be deep yellow, white, or red. *Sweet corn* ranks second in economic importance and is grown principally for human consumption; the pale yellow or white kernels are tender, juicy, and sweet. Sweet corn should be refrigerated, as heat converts the sugar present in the kernels into starch, causing it to lose its sweetness quite quickly. Other important types of corn include popcorn, which is a small-grained variety, and various decorative types of corn that are inedible. Within each general category, there are wide variations in characteristics such as sweetness, firmness, fat content, and flavor. The United States is the largest corn-producing country, followed by China, Brazil, Russia, Mexico, and India.

Nutritional Information

The primary fats present in corn are polyunsaturated fatty acids (46%), monounsaturated acids (28%), and saturated fatty acids (15%) (see *Fats*).

Carbohydrate content varies from one type of corn to another; starchy varieties contain less sugar, while sweet varieties contain a gene that delays the conversion of sugar into starch; however, once the sweet corn is harvested, this conversion process begins immediately, resulting in a loss of flavor in a matter of a few hours.

Cooked fresh corn is a good source of folic acid, potassium, and thiamine; it also contains magnesium, pantothenic acid, vitamin C, phosphorus, niacin, zinc, and riboflavin and is rich in dietary fiber.

Cream-style corn is a good source of folic acid and contains potassium, vitamin C, magnesium, zinc, niacin, and phosphorus.

Whole yellow cornmeal is an excellent source of magnesium, thiamine, iron, and potassium, a good source of phosphorus, zinc, niacin, and vitamin B_6, and contains riboflavin, folic acid, copper, pantothenic acid, and vitamin A. It is extremely high in fiber.

Degermed yellow cornmeal is a good source of folic acid and magnesium; it also contains vitamin B_6, potassium, niacin, thiamine, zinc, iron, and phosphorus.

Whole yellow corn flour is an excellent source of magnesium, potassium, and phosphorus, a good source of vitamin B_6, thiamine, zinc, and iron, and contains niacin, copper, folic acid, pantothenic acid, riboflavin, and vitamin A; it is also very rich in fiber.

Corn bran contains magnesium and iron and has a very high fiber content.

Corn germ is an excellent source of magnesium, phosphorus, thiamine, potassium, and zinc and a good source of vitamin B_6 and iron, in addition to containing riboflavin, folic acid, and copper.

Whether it is fresh, boiled, or dried, corn is lacking in the essential amino acids lysine and tryptophan. To compensate for this deficiency, it is important to include a wide variety of foods in one's diet (see *Complementary proteins*).

The yellow variety of corn is the only cereal grain to contain vitamin A.

Fifty to 80% of the niacin in corn cannot be assimilated by the human body; consequently, people whose diet is comprised almost solely of corn often suffer from pellagra, a disease caused by a niacin-deficient diet, which affects the central nervous system, the digestive system, the skin, and the mucous lining of the mouth. The ancestral practice of adding lime, caustic soda, or ashes to corn was an instinctive way of compensating for the nutritional deficiencies of this cereal, as the addition of these substances makes the niacin in corn assimilable.

Buying

To ensure maximum flavor when buying fresh sweet corn, examine the kernels carefully. To test their juiciness, press on a kernel with your fingernail; if it is fresh, a milky juice will squirt out. Discolored or shriveled kernels are a sign that the corn is not fresh. Dark and dried corn silks and dull or yellowed husks also indicate a lack of freshness.

Avoid corn that is sold on displays exposed to direct sunlight or high temperatures, as heat accelerates the process that makes corn starchy. In a single day, corn stored at a temperature of 86°F will lose up to 50% of its sugar; at 68°F, 26% of the corn's sugar is lost.

Cooking

Corn can be cooked with or without its husk. Suitable cooking methods include boiling, steaming, dry heat (oven or barbecue), and microwaving. Husked corn is sometimes wrapped in aluminum foil before being cooked in the oven or on the barbecue.

When boiling corn, avoid adding salt to the water and do not overcook it, as this will cause it to harden and to lose flavor. It is recommended to cook it in slightly sweetened water, leaving a bit of the husk and adding a little milk or beer to the cooking water. Immerse the ears of corn in the boiling water and cook for 3 to 4 minutes for small ears and 5 to 7 minutes for larger ears.

When cooking corn in a pressure cooker, use 1 cup of water and cook it for 3 to 5 minutes. In the oven, cook it for about 35 minutes at 425°F; in the microwave, cook corn on the cob for about 3 minutes on high power and let the corn sit for 5 minutes before serving it.

Corn grows on a hardy annual plant that can attain 6 to 10 feet in height; the kernels develop on ears measuring 6 to 12 inches in length; corn is the only cereal grain that is native to the Americas.

	cooked fresh corn	cream-style corn	cornmeal (whole kernels)	cornmeal (degermed kernels)	flour (whole kernels)	corn bran
water	69.6%	78.7%	10.3%	11.6%	10.9%	4.8%
protein	3.3 g	1.7 g	8.1 g	8.5 g	6.9 g	2.5 g
fat	1.3 g	0.4 g	3.6 g	1.6 g	3.9 g	0.2 g
carbohydrates	25.1 g	18.1 g	76.9 g	77.7 g	76.8 g	25.7 g
fiber	3.7 g	1.3 g	11 g	5.2 g	13.4 g	25.4 g
calories	108	72	362	366	361	67,2
	per 100 g	**per 100 g**	**per 100 g**	**per 100 g**	**per 100 g**	**per 30 g**

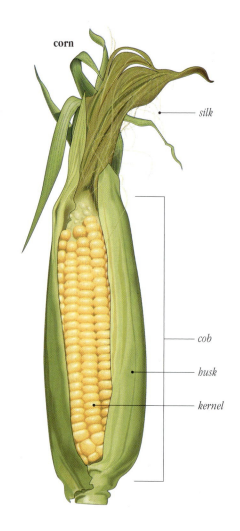

corn

silk

cob

husk

kernel

corn flour

cornmeal

Serving Ideas

Corn has a wide array of uses as a vegetable. It can be eaten cooked, either on the cob or shelled, or processed to make hominy. Corn flour and cornmeal are made from the ground endosperm of the corn kernel, while corn oil is extracted from the germ.

Corn on the cob is traditionally eaten flavored with butter and salt.

Corn kernels can be removed from the cob before or after cooking. The raw kernels are often added to soups, mixed vegetables, stews, and relishes, while cooked kernels are served as a vegetable side dish or in salads. Allow 20 minutes when steaming corn kernels.

Hominy is made from flint or dent corn, varieties with hard kernels that are dried on the cob before being removed and soaked in a solution of baking soda, lime, or wood ash, causing the hulls to soften and swell. The kernels are hulled and the germ is removed by friction. The hulled and degermed kernels are dried; they resemble popcorn but are softer in texture. Although commonly available canned, hominy can also be found in dried or cooked form. It is often used in simmered dishes such as soups and stews.

The dried kernels are ground to make *masa harina,* the flour from which tortillas are made, as well as *hominy grits,* coarse whitish grains that are used mainly to make a hot cereal, but that are sometimes also added to convenience foods. In the United States, hominy grits are traditionally served with bacon and eggs.

Cornstarch is obtained by extracting the starch from the endosperm of the corn kernel. This fine white powder is used as a gelling agent and as a thickener (like wheat or other flours), producing a more opaque result than cassava starch (tapioca). To prevent the formation of lumps when adding cornstach to a hot mixture, dissolve it first in a cold liquid. It should be cooked for at least 1 minute to rid it of its bitterness. The food industry makes wide use of cornstarch as a thickener in everything from sauces and desserts to pastries, vinaigrettes, sour cream, peanut butter, confectionery, baby foods, and cold meats. Cornstarch that has been treated by hydrolysis or other processes to alter its properties and control its action is known as "modified cornstarch."

Cornmeal is obtained by grinding dried corn kernels to varying degrees of coarseness. In order to improve the keeping qualities of cornmeal, the germ is almost always removed from the kernels before grinding. Cornmeal lends a slightly crunchy texture to foods such as cookies, muffins, cakes, and bread. It is also cooked to make a porridge-like dish known as polenta, as well as serving to thicken soups and sauces. Cornmeal is used to make tortillas and corn chips, as well as the dough for tamales. It is difficult to handle and often results in a crumbly product.

Corn flour is finely ground cornmeal obtained from kernels from which the germ has been removed in order to improve the storage life of the flour. Corn flour is used in crêpes, cakes, muffins, and breads, but it has a low gluten content and must be combined with wheat flour to produce leavening.

Corn germ is the embryo that eventually develops into a new plant; rich in nutrients, it also has a high fat content, supplying 46% of the calories in the kernel. Because these fats cause the kernel to turn rancid more quickly, the germ is almost always removed and products like cornmeal and corn flour are usually sold degermed. Larger than wheat germ, corn germ has a crunchy texture and a hazelnut-like flavor; it can be eaten as a cold cereal with milk or used to enrich foods such as salads, legume dishes, and stews. Since it is highly perishable, corn germ is commonly sold in hermetically sealed packages that must be stored in the refrigerator or freezer once they are opened.

Corn oil is a dark yellow color when unrefined and pale yellow when refined. It contains 58.7% polyunsaturated fatty acids, 24.2% monounsaturated fats, and 12.7% saturated fats (see *Oil*).

Corn flakes are a popular ready-to-eat breakfast cereal that was invented by the Kellogg brothers in 1894; they discovered the process of corn flake fabrication by accident when they passed corn kernels that had been left too long in their cooking water through rollers, resulting in flakes with a surprisingly good taste.

Among its other uses, corn also enters into the fabrication of beer, whiskey, gin, and chicha (a fermented beverage popular among South American Indians).

Corn Bread

*1 cup (250 ml) corn
  flour (masa harina)*
*½ cup (125 ml) all-
  purpose flour*
1 tsp. sugar
2 tsp. baking powder

1 tsp. salt
*¼ cup (60 ml) butter,
  softened*
2 eggs
1 cup (250 ml) milk

1. Preheat the oven to 400°F (200°C).

2. Grease the bottom and sides of an 8-inch baking pan.

3. In a bowl, mix the corn flour, all-purpose flour, sugar, baking powder, salt, and butter with a spatula.

4. In a separate bowl, beat the eggs with the milk, using a fork.

5. Using a wooden spoon, incorporate the milk and egg mixture into the flour mixture. Mix until all the ingredients are well blended.

6. Pour this batter into the greased pan, and bake in the oven for 25 minutes or until a knife inserted into the center of the bread comes out clean. Let the corn bread cool in the pan; then remove it.

Storing

Corn on the cob loses its flavor rapidly and is best when eaten as soon as possible, preferably on the day of purchase. If it is not eaten immediately, it should be stored in its husk in the refrigerator. Husked corn can be stored in a plastic bag in the refrigerator.

Fresh corn stands up well to canning and freezing. Corn can be frozen on the cob after blanching (7 to 11 minutes, depending on the size), or the kernels can be frozen on their own (blanch the cob for 4 minutes before removing the kernels). Blanched and frozen corn on the cob will keep for 1 year, while frozen corn kernels will keep for up to 3 months.

Corn flour and cornstarch should be stored in airtight containers in a cool, dry place. Whole cornmeal and corn flour spoil rapidly because they still contain the oil-rich germ; they should be stored in an airtight container in the refrigerator. They can also be kept for 1 to 2 years in the freezer.

corn oil

dried kernels

corn flakes

Popcorn

Zea mays var. *everta,* Gramineae

popcorn kernels

Corn kernels that burst open when heated. Known since ancient times, popcorn is made from a primitive variety of corn that has small hard ears and kernels. Remains of these kernels dating back some 5,000 years have been found in archeological sites in Mexico. The endosperm of this type of corn is much larger in proportion to its weight than that of other varieties, with the result that it has a higher starch content. It is also characterized by its firm and glossy hull. When exposed to extreme heat, the moisture in the endosperm is converted into steam and the resulting pressure causes the hull of the kernel to burst, exposing the inner part, which forms a crisp and puffy mass. The different varieties of popcorn are identified according to the shape of the kernels; they also vary in color, which ranges from the usual white or yellow to the occasional red or brown. Once popped, however, popcorn is always white or yellow, regardless of the color of the raw kernels. Corn kernels can expand to between 25 and 30 times their initial volume when popped.

Buying

To ensure freshness, buy popcorn from stores that have a rapid turnover, as fresh kernels will be puffier and better tasting.

Preparing

Popcorn is cooked in an airtight container that retains the steam. It is not really necessary to add oil, particularly if the corn is fairly fresh. A little oil can be dribbled over the popcorn once it is cooked to make the salt cling better.

Serving Ideas

Popcorn is eaten plain or flavored with butter and, if desired, salt or spices. It can also be eaten with a caramel coating.

Cooking

Cook popcorn over medium heat, shaking the pot often to ensure uniform popping of the kernels and to prevent them from burning. When all the kernels have popped, remove the pot from the heat and transfer the popcorn to a serving dish right away so that it does not burn.

Popcorn is now sold in ready-made packets that can be microwaved in minutes, but they are far more expensive than plain popcorn kernels. Popcorn can also be made in a special hot-air popper that uses dry heat and does not require any fat.

Storing

Popcorn kernels should be stored in an airtight container to prevent them from becoming too dry; once they lose their moisture, they do not pop as well.

Nutritional Information

	popcorn (with oil and salt)	sweetened popcorn	plain popcorn
water	3.1%	4.0%	4.0%
protein	1.8 g	4.6 g	2.8 g
fat	4.2 g	2.6 g	1.0 g
carbohydrates	11.2 g	63.2 g	16.8 g
fiber	1.6 g	4.4 g	1.8 g
	per 20 g (500 ml)	**per 74 g (500 ml)**	**per 22 g**

Plain popcorn contains thiamin, magnesium, potassium, phosphorus, zinc, and copper; it is also a source of dietary fiber. Popcorn contains the same nutrients as sweet corn, but in lower quantities. Sweetened and buttered popcorn have a much higher calorie count than plain popcorn.

popcorn

Amaranth

Amaranthus spp., **Amaranthaceae**

A herbaceous annual plant with long clusters of red flowers, the amaranth is now used mainly for ornamental purposes. However, the large leaves and tiny seeds of the amaranth plant are edible, and they were once a staple of the human diet. Before the Spanish conquest of Mexico, the Aztecs farmed amaranth intensively on over 10,000 acres of land. Amaranth also played a part in religious rituals; since it was a staple food, farmers were expected to offer a portion of their harvests as a tribute to the gods. The conquistador Hernando Cortés ordered that the fields of amaranth be destroyed and made growing the plant a punishable offense, cutting off the hands of recalcitrant farmers and even imposing the death penalty. These extreme measures put an end to the cultivation of amaranth for centuries, but the plant has recently made something of a comeback because it is rich in nutrients and can be grown in a wide variety of environments; it is particularly resistant to drought.

The amaranth is thought to have originated in Mexico. It has flaming-red leaves and can grow to a height of 12 to 36 inches. Its small red flowers form dense tassels; the tiny seeds are enclosed in individual capsules, which are arranged in tight, spike-shaped formations. A single amaranth plant can produce up to 500,000 seeds. There are several different varieties of amaranth, but only those with white seeds are grown as food. Like buckwheat and quinoa, amaranth is not really a cereal, but it is used as one and can be ground into a flour.

Serving Ideas

Amaranth leaves are used like spinach, and they are often an appropriate substitute for spinach. Amaranth seeds can be cooked alone (for about 30 minutes in 2 to 3 parts water) and eaten as a cereal. They do not stick together or burst when cooked, and they taste somewhat spicy. They can also be popped, sprouted, or ground into flour.

Pastry made with amaranth flour is unusually moist and sweet; however, amaranth flour does not contain gluten and does not rise when baked. Plain amaranth flour can be used to make things like cookies, pancakes, or waffles, but it has to be combined with wheat flour in order to make baked goods like breads and cakes. The delicate flavor of wheat flour does not obscure the unique taste of amaranth flour, and the protein in amaranth flour heightens the nutritional value of wheat flour.

Storing

Amaranth flour will keep for longer than wheat flour. Store it in an opaque container in a cool, dry place. Amaranth seeds can be stored in the same way. Amaranth leaves can be refrigerated for a few days or frozen like spinach.

Nutritional Information

	seeds
water	9.8%
protein	10.8 g
fat	4.9 g
carbohydrates	49.6 g
fiber	11.4 g
calories	280
	per 75 g

Amaranth contains more protein than most cereals and is richer in nutrients, because its amino acids are remarkably well balanced. It is unusually rich in lysine, as well as in methionine and tryptophan. These proteins complement those found in cereals, legumes, nuts, and seeds (see *Complementary proteins*). Amaranth is an excellent source of magnesium, iron, phosphorus, copper, and zinc, and a good source of potassium and folic acid; it also contains pantothenic acid, calcium, riboflavin, vitamin B_6, vitamin C, thiamin, and niacin. It contains twice as much iron and four times as much calcium as durum wheat.

Rye

Secale cereale, Gramineae

Rye grains are used to make alcoholic beverages such as whiskey, beer, bourbon, and certain types of vodka.

A cereal grain believed to be native to Anatolia or Asia Minor, rye would appear to be one of the more recently domesticated cereal crops to be used for human food. Cultivation is thought to have begun around 400 B.C. The ancient Greeks were not very fond of rye, and the Romans regarded it as a food for the poor. As standards of living rose, rye gradually disappeared from the daily diet of most westerners, although it remained an important food crop in many parts of the world, notably in Scandinavia and eastern Europe. Rye is still widely cultivated in modern-day Europe, which supplies 90% of the world crop, more than half of which comes from Russia. Other producers include Poland, Germany, China, Canada, the former Czechoslovakia, Denmark, Austria, Sweden, and Spain. Worldwide consumption of rye by humans is on the decline, however, and this cereal is used mainly as livestock feed.

There are about a dozen species and many varieties of rye, which are usually classified as being either winter rye or spring rye. While some varieties grow as perennials, others are annuals. Rye is slightly bushy at the base and usually stands 5 feet high, although it occasionally attains a height of as much as 8 feet. Unlike most other cereals, it is tolerant of poor soil conditions and cold temperatures. The rye grain is similar in appearance to the wheat grain, although it is longer and less plump. It has a shallow lateral crease and is crowned by a tuft of short hairs called the "brush." It varies in color from yellowish brown to greenish gray. Rye grains are subject to attack by a fungus called ergot, which contains a toxic alkaloid; the grains must be hulled after being cleaned and sorted to remove any ergot that may be present. Once the outer layer, or hull, has been removed, the grains are used whole or cracked or are ground to make flakes or flour.

Rye flour is used extensively in bread making, but the fact that its gluten is less elastic and retains less gas than wheat flour makes it rise less; rye bread is therefore denser and more compact than wheat bread. It also keeps longer since it does not dry out as quickly. The greater the proportion of the grain's germ and bran remaining in flour, the greater the flour's nutritional value. This proportion is particularly high in rye (it is difficult to separate the endosperm from the bran of rye grains), with the result that rye flour retains a large quanitity of nutritional elements.

The more refined a flour is, the whiter it is, and the more it has been stripped of its nutrients (see *Flour*). Slightly refined and unrefined rye flours are used to make the strong-tasting, almost black bread called "pumpernickel." Because this bread is less popular than lighter bread, wheat flour is often combined with refined rye flour to lighten it. Rye and wheat are sometimes also ground together to make flour. At one time, it was common practice to sow these two cereals in the same field; the cereal mixture obtained was called "maslin."

rye grains

Buying

 When purchasing rye bread, check the list of ingredients, because this bread is sometimes made with wheat flour colored with caramel.

Serving Ideas

Whole rye grains are highly nutritious and can be cooked and consumed in the same way as other cereal grains, in particular rice. Soak whole rye grains overnight in 2 to 3 cups of liquid per cup of rye, and then boil them until tender. Rye flakes can be used like rolled oats; they are cooked to make hot breakfast cereal or added to muesli or granola mixtures.

The most common use of rye is as flour, however; coarsely ground and with all of its nutrients intact, rye flour is used to make the famous German pumpernickel bread, which has a slightly sour taste and dense texture. Rye flour also goes into the making of rusks, gingerbread, crêpes, pâtés, and muffins.

Rye grains are used to make alcoholic beverages such as whiskey, beer, bourbon, and certain types of vodka. When sprouted, they may be used like wheat germ.

Storing

Store rye flour and grains in an airtight container in a cool dry place.

Nutritional Information

	dark rye flour	light rye flour
water	11%	8.8%
protein	14 g	8.4 g
fat	2.6 g	1.4 g
carbohydrates	68.8 g	80.2 g
fiber	2.4 g	0.4 g
		per 100 g

Dark rye flour is an excellent source of magnesium, potassium, zinc, phosphorus, iron, copper, folic acid, and vitamin B_6; it is also a good source of thiamine, pantothenic acid, niacin, and riboflavin; and it contains calcium.

Light rye flour is an excellent source of magnesium and thiamine, a good source of potassium, zinc, and phosphorus, and also contains iron, vitamin B_6, copper, folic acid, pantothenic acid, riboflavin, and niacin. Like all cereals, rye has essential amino acid deficiencies, the limiting amino acids being tryptophan and methionine (see *Introduction*).

Ergot, the parasite that infects rye, is used to help relieve migraines and headaches, to control bleeding, and to aid in the birthing process. Rye is said to have properties that help to control high blood pressure, arteriosclerosis, and vascular disease.

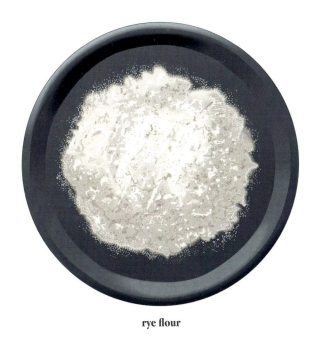

rye flour

Triticale

Triticum X Secale, **Gramineae**

A cereal created in the 20th century by hybridization, triticale is a cross between wheat and rye. Its name is derived from the Latin names for these cereals: *triti*cum (wheat) and se*cale* (rye).

Triticale is the result of many years of research. The first hybrid was created by a Scottish scientist in 1875. Later, in 1937, a Frenchman produced the first fertile cultivar. Triticale combines the nutritional assets of both its parents, including the high protein content of wheat and the high lysine content of rye. This makes it a very nutritional cereal. There are a number of cultivated varieties of triticale with differing characteristics, and more research is needed to improve the yield and adaptability of this crop.

Triticale inherited the hardiness of rye without the fragility of wheat; it can adapt to a wide range of soil and climatic conditions, growing in tropical as well as in temperate regions.

Serving Ideas

Triticale is used like wheat or rye. The triticale berry is consumed whole, cracked, in flake form, or ground into flour. It can also be sprouted. Triticale flour has a flavor that is reminiscent of hazelnut and it can be added to various foods to improve their fiber and nutrient content. Because the gluten in triticale flour is very delicate, bread dough made with 100% triticale flour should be handled very gently; it requires little kneading and only one rising and usually produces a flatter bread than other flours. In most recipes, wheat flour can be replaced by triticale flour providing that less liquid is used, as wheat flour is finer and absorbs more water than triticale flour.

Among its other uses, triticale is found in pasta, tortillas, pancakes, muffins, cakes, and pies. This cereal is also fermented and distilled to make spirits and beer.

Cooking

Cook whole triticale berries in two to three times their volume of water for 45 to 60 minutes.

Nutritional Information

	triticale flour
water	13%
protein	17 g
fat	2.4 g
carbohydrates	95. 1 g
fiber	19 g
	per 130 g (1 cup)

Triticale supplies slightly more protein than wheat; its proteins are also better balanced in terms of the essential amino acids, notably containing more lysine (see *Introduction*). The gluten content of triticale is average, about halfway between that of rye (low) and wheat (high). However, the quality of triticale's gluten is lower than that of wheat, making it less suitable for bread making.

Triticale flour is an excellent source of magnesium, potassium, folic acid, pantothenic acid, vitamin B_6, thiamin, iron, zinc, phosphorus, and copper; it is a good source of niacin and supplies calcium as well as riboflavin. Certain nutrients are present in greater concentrations in triticale flour than in wheat flour, particularly folic acid, pantothenic acid, vitamin B_6, and copper; other nutrients, such as niacin, are not as abundant in triticale flour as in wheat flour.

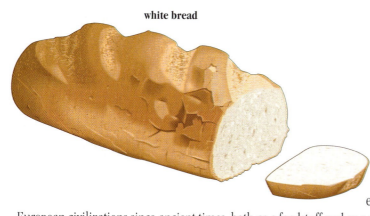

white bread

A food typically made from flour mixed with water and salt, and then kneaded, allowed to rise, formed into loaves or shapes, and baked in the oven. Bread has played an essential role in Middle Eastern and European civilizations since ancient times, both as a foodstuff and as a symbol. For Christians, bread represents the body of Christ, and numerous expressions in the English language reflect the importance accorded to bread — "to earn one's daily bread," "breadwinner," "to take the bread out of somebody's mouth," and "to break bread." Legend has it that leavened bread was discovered accidentally by an Egyptian baker who had left out a mixture of cereals and water for several hours; the mixture was contaminated by a wild yeast or by bacteria, causing it to ferment and rise due to the multiplication of microorganisms in the flour.

Bread can be "leavened," in which case it contains a fermenting agent (yeast or sourdough), or "unleavened," such as the Middle Eastern pita or the Indian chapatti. The first type of leavening agent used by the Egyptians was sourdough, or dough that had been fermented the previous day by wild yeast spores and bacteria present in the air. Later, yeast spores were cultivated in order to obtain a more uniform final product. The Egyptians thus became the first professional bakers, in addition to inventing the first bread oven equipped with separate compartments for combustion and baking. The ancient Hebrews learned how to make leavened bread from the Egyptians in 1300 B.C. However, at the time of the Exodus, the Jews brought only unleavened dough with them as they fled, from which they created the matzoh. Later, the Romans also adopted the baking methods of the Egyptians and spread them throughout their empire. They were apparently the first to use mechanical means of mixing bread dough. It is also said that by 300 B.C., the Greeks had mastered the art of bread making, becoming the best bakers in the ancient world; at least 70 different types of bread were known at this time. Nobles consumed bread made from finely sifted flour, while the commoners had to be content with whole wheat bread, which was much cheaper and easier to prepare. The Middle Ages brought with them a notable increase in the diversity of breads. During that period the bakers' guilds, which had disappeared with the Roman Empire, reemerged and laws were enacted forbidding the milling of grains by anyone other than professional millers. Bakers were required to obtain a license in order to run a bakery and sell bread.

The use of a crude form of baking soda dates back to the late 18th century in the United States. This discovery made it possible to significantly shorten the time required to prepare bread, as this powder acted much more rapidly than yeast (it was activated by the heat of the oven). Consequently, as of 1850, bakers worldwide began to adopt this chemical leavening agent. Subsequent improvements in the milling process led to increased supplies of white flour. Today the baking industry is highly automated, allowing for the mass production of bread.

In the course of the 20th century, bread acquired a reputation for causing corpulence, with the result that bread consumption dropped significantly in the Western Hemisphere. In recent years, however, bread is again being promoted for its high nutritional value and moderate calorie content, although consumers are advised to pay more attention when selecting the foods they eat with bread.

Because the spontaneous fermentation of bread dough (when the flour and water mixture are left out at room temperature) is a long and unpredictable process, people learned very early on how to use sourdough, a portion of unbaked fermented dough saved from a previous batch. Sourdough contains yeast and bacteria. It is prepared by dissolving 7 grams of dried yeast in 2½ cups of warm water with 1 tablespoon of sugar; 2 cups of hot water and about ½ pound of white flour are then added to create a dough; the dough is covered with a cloth and left to ferment for

3 to 5 days away from drafts. The acid in the sourdough prevents the development of pathogenic bacteria. If it is not used within 1 week, the composition of the sourdough changes and it becomes necessary to add flour and warm water in order to keep it longer. In recipes, ½ cup of sourdough can be used in place of 7 grams of dried yeast. The use of sourdough has declined over the last century because the sourdough must be reactivated by adding water and flour before it can be panned and baked. To avoid this long and painstaking process, baker's yeast (or brewer's yeast) is now widely used in place of sourdough; it is easier to use and acts more quickly and uniformly. Yeast is composed of microscopic fungi *(Saccharomyces cerevisiae)* and, like sourdough, it is a live culture. It is produced industrially by inoculating cereal worts or a solution of molasses, phosphoric acid, and ammoniac. Once the fungi have stopped growing, they are centrifuged, washed, and then compressed or dried. Yeast interacts with sugar (either that added to the dough or that present in the flour starch), fermenting it to produce carbon dioxide and alcohol which become trapped in the gluten, a protein substance in flour that becomes sticky and elastic when water is added and that causes the dough to rise by retaining the gas produced by the fermentation of the dough. During baking, the alcohol evaporates and the gas trapped in the dough forms bubbles; the gas is released into the surrounding air when the bread cools.

As its name suggests, sourdough bread has a slightly sour taste; it is more strongly flavored and more easily digested than yeast bread, in addition to having better keeping qualities. However, it does not rise as high as yeast bread and its crumb has irregularly shaped and smaller cells.

Buying

There are a number of factors to consider when deciding what type of bread to purchase, including the flavor, the use, and the nutritional value desired. "Good" bread should have a firm, golden, fairly thick crust and a soft crumb.

Preparing

To prevent bread from drying out and for maximum flavor, cut bread at the last minute before serving it. To refreshen slightly stale bread, place it in the oven (175°F) for about 10 minutes.

rye bread

multigrain bread

1 Dissolve the yeast in the luke-warm water with 1 teaspoon of the sugar.

2 Pour the yeast and water into the mixture of flour, sugar, and salt. Add the oil.

3 Blend until the dough forms a homogeneous mass. If the dough is too dry, add a little more water.

4 Turn the dough out onto the work surface, and knead it with regular movements until it no longer sticks.

5 Place the dough in a bowl, cover with plastic wrap, and let it rise in a warm place until it doubles in volume (1½ to 2½ hours).

6 Punch the dough with your hand to release the gas bubbles, and turn it back out on the work surface.

7 Divide the dough into two portions.

8 Form each portion into a ball and place them on a cookie sheet. Cover with a cloth, let rise again for 30 to 50 minutes, and bake in the oven.

Serving Ideas

🍽 Bread is used in an endless variety of ways, in everything from appetizers to desserts. In many households, bread accompanies every meal of the day. It is indispensable for sandwiches, canapés, toast, and bread crumbs; it is also added to certain soups (French onion soup, gazpacho, garlic soup) and is an integral part of cheese fondue. For most people, bread is an essential breakfast food, whether toasted or untoasted. It also goes into the making of charlottes and bread pudding, as well as French toast. Stale bread is often dried to make rusks and bread crumbs, in addition to being useful in stuffings and bread soup. Bread fresh from the oven tends to be indigestible; in the case of a traditional leavened loaf, it is best to wait until the next day before eating the bread, and rye bread is best when eaten slightly stale. Toasting detracts from the nutritional value of bread by reducing its thiamine, riboflavin, and niacin content by 15% to 20%. The more toasted the bread, the greater the loss of nutrients.

Bread

2 MEDIUM LOAVES

2 tsp. sugar	3½ cups (875 ml) all-purpose flour
2 cups (500 ml) lukewarm water	1 tsp. salt
1 envelope of dry yeast (¼ ounce/8 g)	2 tbsp. vegetable oil

1. Dissolve 1 teaspoon of the sugar in ½ cup of the lukewarm water, and sprinkle with the yeast. Let stand for 10 minutes. The yeast should become frothy.

2. In a large bowl, sift the flour with the remaining 1 teaspoon sugar and the salt. Make a well in the center and add the dissolved yeast, the rest of the water, and the oil to the well. Mix with a wooden spoon, adding a little extra water if necessary to form a smooth dough. Once the ingredients are mixed, shape the dough into a ball.

3. Place the dough on a generously floured working surface and knead it until it is firm and elastic.

4. Rub a little oil on the outside of the dough and place it in a lightly greased bowl. Cover with plastic wrap and let stand in a warm place until it rises to double its initial volume (about 1½ to 2½ hours).

5. Punch the dough with your fist to release the bubbles of carbon dioxide. Turn the dough out on the work surface and knead it again.

6. Grease a cookie sheet. Divide the dough into two portions, form them into balls, and place them on the cookie sheet. Let rise again for about 30-50 minutes. Meanwhile, preheat the oven to 350°F (175°C).

7. Bake the loaves for 30 minutes, or until the crust is golden brown.

pita

chapatti

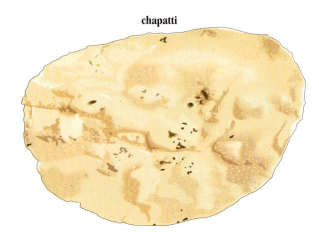

tortilla

Storing

Bread should be stored wrapped to keep it from drying out. An uncut loaf of traditional bread will keep for a few days in a cool place; once cut, place it face down on a wood or marble surface. Sliced bread can be stored in a plastic bag for no more than 5 to 7 days at room temperature. Bread stands up very well to freezing and will keep for about 2 months in the freezer.

Nutritional Information

As the nutritional table shows, the protein, carbohydrate, fat, and calorie content of the different varieties of bread is relatively similar. On the other hand, the vitamin, mineral, and fiber content varies significantly from one type of bread to another.

White bread (enriched) is a good source of thiamine, niacin, iron, and folic acid; it also contains riboflavin, phosphorus, potassium, calcium, and pantothenic acid.

Whole wheat bread contains folic acid, phosphorus, thiamine, iron, potassium, and niacin.

Dark rye bread contains potassium, phosphorus, magnesium, iron, thiamine, copper, and zinc.

Whole wheat bread, cracked wheat bread, and dark rye bread are all highly nutritious.

In addition to whole wheat and rye breads, the market also offers breads made from rice, corn, and oat flour. Some breads are flavored with cumin or poppy seeds or with salt (as in the pretzels available in German bakeries). Daily consumption of bread also supplies complex carbohydrates, fiber, B-complex vitamins, and minerals such as iron and zinc, which are rarely found in other foods.

whole wheat bread

	enriched white bread (28 g/slice)	cracked wheat bread (25 g/slice)	wholewheat bread (28 g/slice)	dark rye bread (32 g/slice)	light rye bread (25 g/slice)
water	35.8%	34.9%	36.4%	34.0%	35.5%
protein	2.4 g	2.2 g	2.5 g	2.9 g	2.3 g
carbohydrates	14.1 g	13.0 g	13.8 g	17.0 g	13.0 g
fat	0.9 g	0.6 g	0.7 g	0.4 g	0.3 g
fiber	0.5 g	1 g	1.6 g	1.7 g	0.7 g
calories	75	66	67	79	61

Cereals

357

Flour

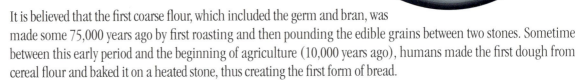

Flour is the product of milling or grinding wheat, other cereal grains, or certain vegetables (chestnuts, chickpeas, lentils, potatoes, peanuts, manioc). While all cereals can be ground into flour, the term generally refers to flour produced from wheat, and flour made from other cereal grains is usually qualified as such (oat flour, rye flour, buckwheat flour, etc.).

It is believed that the first coarse flour, which included the germ and bran, was made some 75,000 years ago by first roasting and then pounding the edible grains between two stones. Sometime between this early period and the beginning of agriculture (10,000 years ago), humans made the first dough from cereal flour and baked it on a heated stone, thus creating the first form of bread.

In the early days, the grains were separated from the harvested ears of wheat using stones, after which they were ground by hand. Later, the grains were crushed by cows. The invention of the millstone and the water wheel greatly improved production, clearing the way for the development of the art of bread making.

The Romans produced several grades of flour, including one that was whiter than previous flours, although not as white as that commonly used today. However, only the rich could afford this white flour (the whiter it was, the higher its price), and white flour became a symbol of social standing and wealth.

The first windmill was built in England in the 11th century, with Belgium, Luxembourg, and Holland following suit in the 12th century. Water and wind were used as energy sources by the early inhabitants of America to grind the corn used to make corn bread.

In the meantime, major developments in the production of flour were occurring on both sides of the Atlantic. In the late 18th century, the steam engine was invented by the Scotsman James Watt and began to be used in milling operations. Around the same time, the American Oliver Evans invented a highly automated mill that permitted the continuous milling of flour.

The advent of the Industrial Revolution gave rise to gigantic industrial mills. Over the course of 50 years during the 19th century, the invention of increasingly sophisticated machines led to the gradual replacement of millstones by steel rollers, which improved the grinding and pulverization operations as well as allowing for better separation of the germ and bran.

In present-day milling, the wheat is subjected to several processes in order to produce flour. The grains are first cleaned, finely ground, and pulverized, after which they are sifted, or bolted, to rid them of their bran (comprising the outer layers) in order to obtain a finer flour. The germ is also removed to improve the flour's keeping qualities. The germ can be sold separately or transformed into oil. The part of the grain that is converted into flour is called the endosperm.

The quality of the finished flour depends on the characteristics of the wheat used. For example, soft wheat contains little gluten and is very well suited to cake making, while hard wheat has a higher gluten content, making it more suitable for bread making.

The baking qualities of all types of flour are improved if the flour is stored for several weeks after milling; during this aging stage, a natural process of oxidation causes the flour to become whiter.

To hasten the maturing process and to control the end results, the flour industry now adds bleaching agents such as chlorine dioxide and maturing agents such as potassium bromate, depending on the type of flour.

In order to compensate for the loss of nutrients caused by the removal of the bran and germ during milling, various vitamins (thiamine, riboflavin, niacin) and minerals (iron) are added to the flour to fortify it. This practice is mandatory for white flour in Canada and the United States.

The bran and germ are sold separately and are used primarily as livestock feed. Refined flour and refined flour products have better keeping qualities, since without the oily germ they turn rancid less quickly.

A wide array of flours is available on the market, including whole wheat flour, all-purpose flour, cake flour, self-rising flour, unrefined flour, high-gluten flour, and bread flour.

Whole wheat flour is obtained by milling the entire grain (endosperm, germ, and bran); it is darker in color and has a slight hazelnut-like taste. Some brands of whole wheat flour are still stone-ground in the traditional way. In many countries, whole wheat flour is available mainly in health-food stores.

When purchasing whole wheat flour, read the label carefully: enriched flour to which bran has been added is not necessarily whole wheat flour, even if it is darker in color. Whole wheat flour can be used in place of white flour in most recipes, although in some cases it may be necessary to increase the quantity slightly. While products made with whole wheat flour are more nutritious, their color, flavor, and often their volume are somewhat altered; they tend to be darker, with a more pronounced flavor and less volume.

The loss of volume is caused by the higher concentration of bran, which contains an enzyme called glutinase that reduces the elasticity of the gluten in flour. For a lighter product, sift the flour several times before using it, taking care to return any bran particles caught in the sieve back into the flour.

Graham flour is named for the 19th-century American nutritionist Sylvester Graham, who was an ardent advocate of the health benefits of bran in the diet and who believed that bread should be made using only whole-grain flour.

Although it is not always properly distinguished from whole wheat flour, graham flour usually contains flakes of bran ground to varying degrees of coarseness, and the germ is commonly removed to improve the flour's shelf life. Graham flour can be used alone or combined with other flours.

All-purpose flour is a blend of different varieties of hard and soft wheat flours. It is suitable for a wide variety of baked goods, including breads and pastries, although best results are obtained by using hard wheat flour for bread and soft wheat flour for pastries and cakes.

Cake flour is made exclusively from very finely ground soft wheat and is extremely soft to the touch. Since it is almost always the product of the last stages of the milling process, cake flour is usually highly refined. With its high starch content and low protein (and therefore gluten) content, it produces very light cakes but is not suitable for making leavened breads. When using it in place of all-purpose flour, replace 1 cup of all-purpose flour with 1⅓ cups of cake flour.

Pastry flour is usually made from soft wheat varieties, although hard wheat is also sometimes used. Low in gluten, it is finely ground, but not as finely as cake flour, and it is used in the making of pastries, biscuits, and cakes, among other things. Pastry flour is not suitable for leavened bread.

Self-rising flour is all-purpose flour to which salt and a leavening agent are added, usually baking soda with either sodium acid pyrophosphate or monocalcium phosphate. These food additives increase the sodium content of the flour. Self-rising flour can save time, depending on the recipe, by eliminating the need to add baking soda and salt to the flour; 1 cup of self-rising flour contains 1½ teaspoons of chemical leavener and ½ teaspoon of salt. Self-rising flour is not recommended for leavened bread.

Unbleached flour is white flour that is bleached naturally. For aesthetic and economic reasons, flour is usually bleached artificially, using food additives. At one time, flour had to be aged by storing it or by manipulating it in order to expose it to oxidation by air. Today the same effect can be obtained by the use of bleaching agents that do not require a long storage period. Oxidation of the flour makes the gluten stronger or more elastic, thus improving the flour's baking characteristics. Moreover, certain bleaching agents contain calcium or phosphorus, which increase the nutritional value of the flour slightly. Unbleached flour has a more natural flavor since it does not contain any additives. The presence of bleaching agents results in a lighter, higher, finer-grained, and lighter-colored product.

Gluten flour is a starch-free, high-gluten whole wheat flour. To obtain gluten flour, high-protein hard wheat flour is cleaned to rid it of its starch; it is then dried and reground. Gluten flour normally contains 45% gluten and 55% white flour. It can be used in combination with whole wheat flour or low-gluten flours like rye, barley, or oat flour.

Bread flour is a blend of hard wheat flours; slightly granular, its gluten content is too high for domestic use, and it is used mainly in the baking industry.

Buying

For maximum freshness, flour should be purchased in a store with a rapid turnover. Real whole wheat flour is generally available in health-food stores, but it is a good idea to read the label, as not all whole wheat flours have the same nutritional value.

Serving Ideas

Flour is widely used in bread and pastry making as well as in cooking to prepare a large variety of foods (crêpes, waffles, rolls, donuts, tarts, puddings, muffins, biscuits, tempura). The thickening properties of flour are used to give consistency to numerous preparations, including cheese fondues, sauces, soups, syrups, and pastry creams. The non-culinary uses of flour include plasticine and homemade glue.

Flour

Nutritional Information

	whole wheat flour	*enriched all-purpose flour*
water	10.3%	11.9%
protein	13.7 g	10.3 g
fat	1.9 g	1 g
carbohydrates	72.6 g	76.3 g
fiber	12.6 g	3.1 g
calories	339	364
		per 100 g

The nutritional value of flour depends on a number of factors, including the type of cereal, the degree of aging, and, especially, the degree of milling or the extraction rate of the flour. The extraction rate indicates the proportion of the germ and bran that remain after milling; an extraction rate of 100% designates a whole-grain flour. The nutritional value of flour is thus directly related to its percentage of extraction; the lower the figure, the less nutritious the flour. The common rate of extraction of white flour in industrialized countries is 60% to 72%.

Since the mid-20th century, flour mills have been fortifying white flour to compensate for the loss of nutrients resulting from the removal of the bran and germ. The law requires the addition of specific quantities of niacin, riboflavin, thiamine, and iron. Prescribed quantities of calcium and vitamin D may also be added to flour and bread, but this is optional. The added nutrients only partially make up for those lost during extraction, since the mineral content (notably magnesium, zinc, and copper) and the fiber content are also affected by removal of the bran and germ. On the other hand, the added vitamin content (niacin, riboflavin, and thiamine) is usually higher for enriched flour than for unenriched flour, whether whole or refined.

Certain countries, including Canada, the United States, and Great Britain, routinely enrich their flour, while in other countries, such as France, this practice is forbidden.

Whole wheat flour is an excellent source of magnesium, niacin, thiamine, potassium, zinc, phosphorus, and iron and a good source of folic acid, vitamin B$_6$, and copper; it also contains pantothenic acid and riboflavin.

All-purpose flour is an excellent source of thiamine, niacin, and iron, as well as a good source riboflavin; it contains folic acid, phosphorus, potassium, magnesium, zinc, copper, and pantothenic acid.

Gluten flour is an excellent source of niacin; it also contains phosphorus, folic acid, and potassium.

Storing

Whole wheat flour, whether stone-ground or not, must be stored in the refrigerator or freezer in order to preserve its vitamin E and to keep the oil in the germ from going rancid. Once it has thawed, store the flour in a paper bag, since an airtight container or a plastic bag will retain moisture, favoring the development of mold.

Refined flours should be stored in cool, dry, dark conditions, away from insects and rodents.

unbleached flour

cake flour

gluten flour

whole wheat flour

bran flour

361

Cereals

361

Pasta

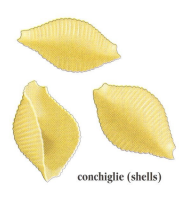

A food product made of cereal flour mixed with water. Several countries claim credit for the invention of pasta, including China, Japan, France, and Italy. According to some sources, pasta was introduced into Italy by Marco Polo upon his return from China at the end of the 13th century. There is also evidence that buckwheat, rice, wheat, and soybean noodles were consumed by the Chinese long before Marco Polo's travels. While the exact origins of pasta remain obscure, industrial fabrication is known to have begun in Naples at the beginning of the 15th century, although it did not become popular until the 19th century, with the discovery of the process of drying pasta, which greatly improved its keeping qualities. According to 16th-century Italian historians, stuffed pasta was invented by an Italian peasant woman.

In the Western Hemisphere, good-quality pasta is made from durum wheat, a variety of hard wheat that is rich in protein, with a high gluten content and a relatively low starch content. The wheat grains are ground into fine particles (semolina) or into flour. Durum wheat tends to remain slightly granular when ground, giving good results when cooked and producing firm pasta that does not stick. Pasta can also be made using soft wheat flour, a blend of hard and soft wheat, buckwheat flour, rice flour, or corn flour (rarely). A wide array of other ingredients can also be found in the different types of pasta, including soybean and mung bean flour, vegetables (spinach, tomatoes, beets, carrots), gluten, whey, eggs, herbs, spices, and flavorings. The color of some pastas may be provided by food coloring agents instead of vegetable purées. Egg noodles are made from soft wheat flour. In Asia, noodles are more commonly made from rice, buckwheat, or soft wheat flour. In several countries, pasta is enriched with B vitamins (thiamine, riboflavin, and niacin) and sometimes with iron. Also available on the market are high-protein pastas in which eggs and whey powder are added to the water and semolina mixture, thus greatly enhancing the natural protein content of the pasta. The fiber supplement in fiber-enriched pasta is provided by ground pea pods.

The industrial production of pasta takes place in large automated factories. In the fabrication process, the semolina is mixed with water and kneaded into a dough. The dough is rolled out into thin sheets that will be further cut into strands or passed through extruding machines to be pressed into various shapes. After being shaped, the pasta is ready to be marketed as either fresh or dried pasta. Dehydration is performed by exposing the pasta to hot, humid airstreams, which gradually reduce the water content of the pasta to about 12%. The drying process is delicate, because if it is done too slowly the pasta may develop mold, while if it is too rapid, the final product will be cracked and brittle. The choice of a shape of pasta is, of course, a matter of taste, but also depends on how the pasta will be served. For example, thinner pastas are primarily used in soups and broths, while curved, twisted, or tubular shapes are excellent for soaking up sauces; ridged pasta is best served with a meat sauce, while smooth-surfaced pasta is perfect with cream or cheese sauces.

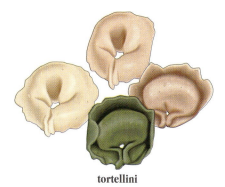

tortellini

gnocchi

conchiglie (shells)

Buying

Choose intact, smooth-textured, and uniformly colored pasta (ivory tending toward yellow). Fresh pasta should have a pleasant smell.

Spaghetti alla Bolognese

SERVES 4

Salt
2 tbsp. olive oil
¾ lb. (375 g) spaghetti or spaghettini
Butter
4 servings Bolognese Sauce (see below)
Freshly grated Parmesan cheese

Sauce ingredients

1 onion
1 rib celery
½ green sweet pepper
2 28-oz. (840 g) cans tomatoes
1 5½-oz. (165 g) can tomato paste
1 7½-oz. (225 g) can tomato sauce
2 bay leaves
2 pinches of Italian seasoning
2 pinches of dried tarragon
2 pinches of dried basil
2 pinches of dried thyme
2 pinches of celery salt
Salt and ground pepper
2 cloves garlic, finely chopped
3 tbsp. olive oil
1 lb. (500 g) lean ground beef

For a spicy sauce, add 2 pinches of ground red chile pepper.

To make the sauce:

1. Finely chop the onion, celery, and green pepper. Set aside.

2. In a blender or large bowl, purée the tomatoes. Stir in the tomato paste and tomato sauce. Set aside.

3. Combine the spices and seasonings, along with the garlic, in a small bowl. Set aside.

4. In a large pot, heat the oil and sauté the vegetables until soft.

5. Add the meat and brown it until it is thoroughly cooked.

6. Add the tomato and spice mixtures to the meat and mix well.

7. Simmer the sauce for 1½ to 2 hours, stirring frequently, until much of the liquid has been reduced. Adjust the seasoning.

8. Cool the sauce and divide it into separate portions for freezing, if desired.

To cook the pasta:

1. Fill a large pot three-fourths full of water. Add salt and the oil.

2. Bring the water to a full boil, add the pasta, and reduce the heat slightly; boil for 7 or 8 minutes or until al dente. When the pasta is cooked, drain it and add a pat of butter.

3. Serve the spaghetti topped with the sauce. Offer the Parmesan separately.

Serving Ideas

Pasta is one of the most versatile, easy-to-prepare, and inexpensive foods. Just as good cold as warm, it can be used to make both simple dishes and elaborate preparations like lasagna or cannelloni. Pasta finds multiple uses in everything from appetizers to soups, mixed salads, main dishes, and even desserts; it can be served as an accompaniment to meat, poultry, and seafood. In Asia, pasta is frequently used in spring rolls and wonton. The mild flavor of pasta makes it possible to combine it with a wide variety of foods. It is commonly served with a tomato-based sauce to which minced meat, seafood, poultry, ham, cheese, or vegetables are added. Pasta can also be stuffed with ground meat, cheese, spinach, mushrooms, or various seasonings.

ravioli

In order to reduce the calorie content of pasta dishes,

• choose vegetable and herb sauces instead of rich, high-fat sauces made with cream;

• use skim milk instead of cream;

• use low-fat cheeses such as cottage cheese and ricotta whenever possible, and reduce the amount of high-fat cheeses used as a topping on dishes baked au gratin;

• reduce the quantity of meat in sauces and use poultry whenever possible;

• cut down on saturated fats by replacing butter with olive oil (see Oil).

Cereals

363

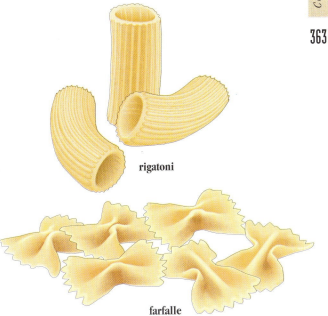

rigatoni

farfalle

1 *Place ¾ cup flour in a pile on a work surface and make a well in the middle of it; place 2 eggs, 1 tbsp. oil, and 1tsp. salt in the middle of the well.*

2 *Gradually fold the flour into the middle from the edges, mixing the ingredients to form a dough; add a little water if necessary;*

3 *Form the dough into a ball and let it stand for 30 minutes to 1 hour.*

4 *Sprinkle flour on the work surface and flatten the dough slightly with a rolling pin; divide it into two portions.*

5 *Roll out the dough into the shape of a circle.*

6 *Continue rolling to obtain as thin a sheet of dough as possible.*

7 *Sprinkle the sheets of dough with flour and roll them up so they form a roll.*

8 *Cut to make strips about ⅓ inch wide.*

9 *Unroll the fresh pasta strips and spread them out on a cloth to dry before cooking them.*

penne (quills)   **ziti**   **ditali**   **rotini**

Cooking

Pasta should be cooked in rapidly boiling water. Add long pasta, like spaghetti, in a bunch, gradually pushing it down as it softens; add other types of pasta to the rapidly boiling water in a stream. A brisk boil seals the pasta and is the best way to cook pasta *al dente,* meaning slightly firm to the bite. Use 1 tablespoon of salt in the water for each pound of fresh or dried pasta. A little oil can also be added to the water to keep the pasta from clumping. As it begins to soften, stir the pasta gently. For pasta to cook evenly without sticking together, it is important to use plenty of water and a pot that is large enough to allow for swelling (good-quality pasta will expand to 4 times its initial size). Use 12 cups of water per pound of pasta, adding 4 cups of water for each additional ½ pound of fresh or dried pasta. Too much water is better than too little when cooking pasta.

The required cooking time for pasta is partly a matter of taste and partly a matter of the size and quantity of pasta and of the hardness of the water. Some experts recommend adding a little oil to the water to prevent it from overflowing when the starch is released from the pasta (pasta that produces a large quantity of foam is usually of inferior quality). The best way to know when the pasta is *al dente* is to test it regularly during cooking. The initial moisture content of the pasta will also influence its cooking time:

• Pasta made from hard wheat flour must be cooked longer than pasta made from soft wheat flour.

• Fresh pasta cooks much faster than dried pasta.

• Pasta that is to be cooked a second time or frozen should be cooked for a shorter time.

• Drain pasta as soon as it is cooked or it will continue to cook and become too soft.

• Rinse cooked pasta in cold water only if it is very starchy (in the case of soft wheat pasta, for example) to prevent it from sticking, if it is to be used cold (as in a salad), or to halt the cooking process immediately (for example, in the case of pasta to be cooked a second time with other ingredients).

Some types of dried pasta intended for use in baked dishes (lasagna, manicotti, cannelloni) do not have to be precooked. However, these dishes usually require a greater quantity of liquid or sauce, as much of it is absorbed by the pasta as it cooks.

whole wheat spaghetti   **fettucine**

cannelloni

macaroni

fusilli

Nutritional Information

	hard wheat pasta (cooked)	cooked whole wheat spaghetti	cooked egg noodle
water	63.6%	67.2%	68.7%
protein	4.8 g	5.3 g	4.8 g
fat	0.7 g	0.5 g	1.5 g
carbohydrates	28.3 g	26.5 g	24.8 g
fiber	0.1 g	0.1 g	2.2 g
calories	141	124	133
			per 100 g

Pasta has the reputation of being an energy-giving but calorie-rich food. In fact, it is not the pasta itself that is the major source of calories (unless, of course, it is eaten in enormous quantities), but rather what is added to it: butter, cream, and cheese are the main culprits. The nutritional value of pasta varies slightly depending on the ingredients used in its fabrication (unrefined flour, eggs, milk powder, vegetables) and on how long it is cooked. For example, pasta that is cooked for a long time loses slightly more of its water-soluble B vitamins into the water than pasta cooked *al dente*.

Pasta is a good source of energy and protein, in addition to being practically fat-free. It is rich in carbohydrates, mainly in the form of starch that is easily digested. Because its starch is absorbed slowly by the body, pasta provides a long-lasting feeling of satiety, which is why it is recommended for athletes needing long-term muscle fuel, particularly for endurance competitions.

Whole wheat pasta provides thiamine, niacin, pantothenic acid, magnesium, phosphorus, iron, zinc, and copper.

Cooked egg noodles contain magnesium, zinc, phosphorus, niacin, and vitamin B_{12}.

Storing

Fresh pasta will keep for 1 to 2 days in the refrigerator and can also be frozen. Stuffed pasta or fresh pasta made with eggs will keep for 1 day in the refrigerator or 2 months in the freezer. Cooked pasta will also keep in the refrigerator (3 to 5 days) or the freezer. Cover it well to prevent the absorption of odors. Dried pasta will keep indefinitely in a container stored in a dry place, away from rodents and insects.

spaghetti

spaghettini

spinach lasagna

spinach tagliatelle

Asian noodles

The use of noodles in Asia is believed to date back over 2,000 years; they are known to have been consumed by the Chinese as early as 200 B.C. In the northern regions of China, where the cultivation of wheat is widespread, most noodles are made from this cereal, whereas rice noodles are more commonly consumed in southern China. To this day, noodles play an essential role in Asian cuisine.

Most Asian noodles are made in the shape of long strands (symbolizing a long life) of varying widths and thicknesses. They are distinguished by the ingredients used; one can buy wheat noodles, rice noodles, mung bean noodles, and buckwheat noodles.

Chinese **wheat noodles** are yellow or white in color and are usually made from a mixture of wheat, water, and salt. Eggs are also sometimes added; **egg wheat noodles** are available fresh or dried. Fresh egg noodles are cooked by plunging them into boiling water for 2 to 4 minutes after separating them with a fork; frozen egg noodles should be thawed before they are cooked. Dried egg noodles are used in the preparation of chow mein; after being cooked in boiling water, they are fried to give them their characteristic crispness.

In Japan, wheat noodles (and sometimes corn noodles) are classified according to size; thin noodles are called *somen* while thick noodles are called *udon*.

Rice noodles are made from rice flour and water and come in different sizes and textures, from the fine and brittle rice vermicelli to broader noodles. Rice noodles are often fried or added to soups. They should be soaked in cold or lukewarm water before being boiled or stir-fried. **Rice vermicelli** are delicious fried in peanut oil (at 375° to 400°F), which makes them turn golden and expand, forming a nest; this is used to garnish several dishes, including the succulent Thai dish called *mee krob*.

Mung bean noodles are transparent and are usually sold in 3½-ounce packages. They should be soaked in lukewarm or hot water for 10 minutes before being added to a dish (other than soups). Mung bean noodles absorb a fair amount of liquid during cooking.

Buckwheat noodles, which also contain wheat, are very popular among the Japanese, who call them *soba*. These yellowish brown or gray noodles are available fresh or dried; green tea (chasoba) or beets are sometimes added as coloring agents. Buckwheat noodles should be cooked in rapidly boiling water until they reach the desired tenderness (they do not need to be presoaked). They are often served cold with soy sauce in the summertime and are also added to soups.

Wonton wrappers are very fine sheets of dough made from wheat, water, eggs, and salt that can be stuffed with meat, fish, seafood, or vegetables. This Asian version of Italian ravioli noodles can be purchased fresh or frozen.

Asian noodles

Buying

When purchasing fresh Asian noodles, make sure they really are fresh; they should be soft without being limp, sticky, or brittle.

Storing

Fresh egg noodles will keep for 3 or 4 days in the refrigerator and for 1 month in the freezer.

Dried noodles can be kept almost indefinitely in a cool, dry, dark place.

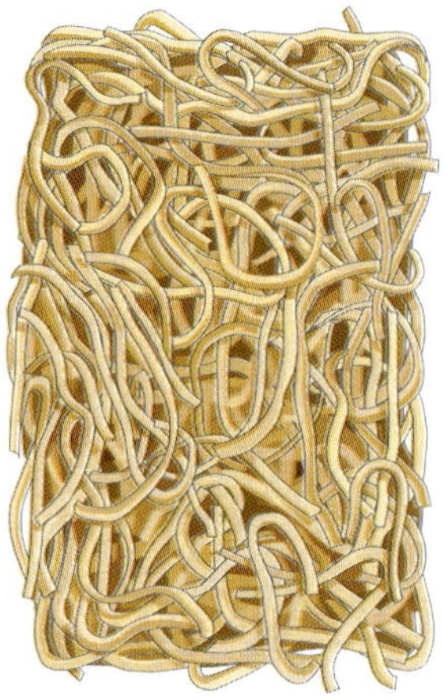

dried egg noodles

mung bean noodles

somen

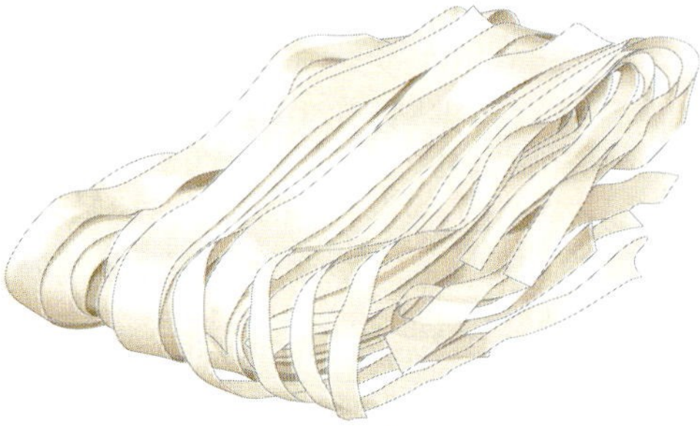

rice noodles

fresh egg noodles

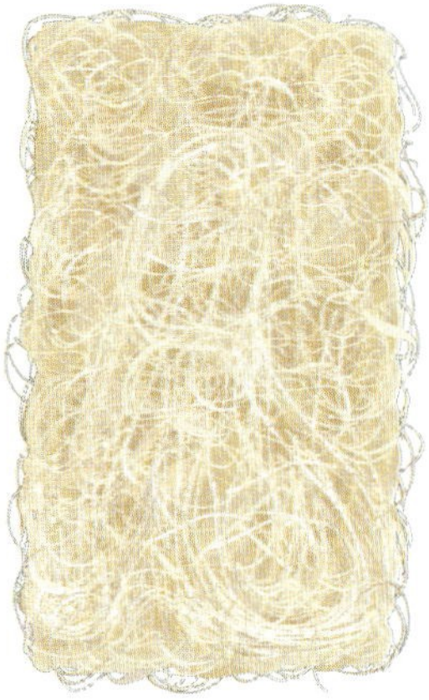

rice vermicelli

wonton wrappers

soba

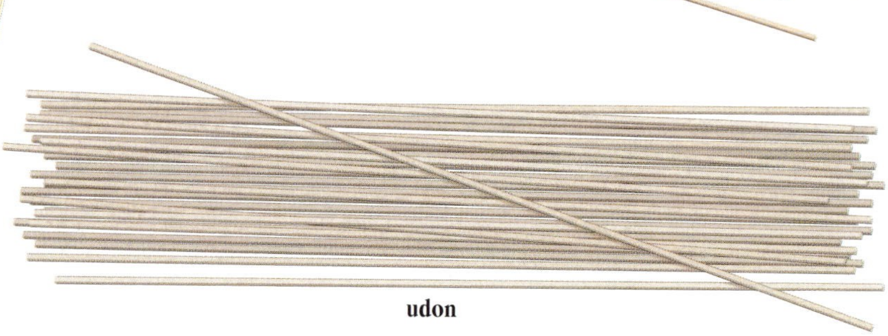

udon

Fish

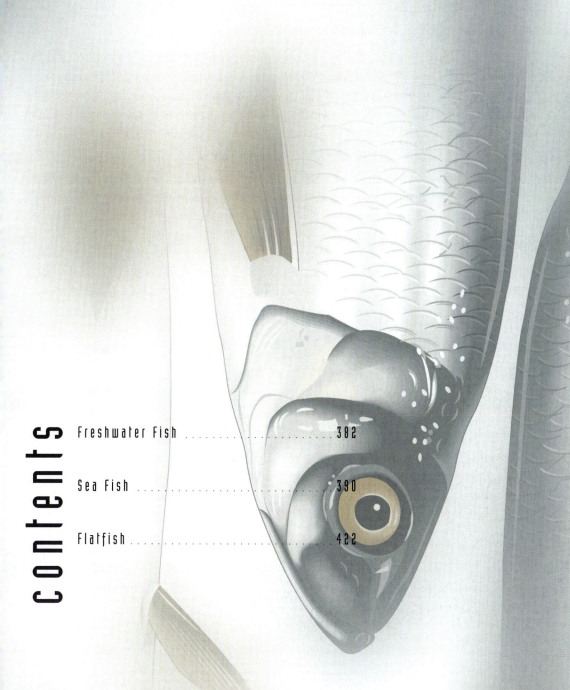

contents

Introduction

Fish has always been a staple part of the diets of coastal populations.

Vertebrate animals that live in water, fish have always been a staple of the human diet, especially among coastal populations. Although fish once constituted an abundant resource, the stocks of numerous species have declined alarmingly during the 20th century. This dramatic change is the result of numerous factors, including overfishing, pollution, and the development of industrial fishing techniques.

Fish farming (or pisciculture), which is a rapidly expanding industry, has begun to compensate for declining fish stocks. Although fish farming has existed for over 4,000 years, it initially involved nothing more than keeping fish in captivity; fish were not bred in captivity until 1733, when a German succeeded in breeding trout. The numerous species now bred in captivity include salmon, carp, redfish, and sturgeon.

There are over 20,000 different species of fish. The vast majority of these species live in the sea, but some are found in fresh water (rivers, lakes, streams). Certain so-called anadromous species, such as salmon, leave the sea to spawn in fresh water, while catadromous species, such as eels, leave fresh water to spawn in the sea.

Flatfish are the same shape as other fish at birth, but at a certain point in their development they tilt to one side, gradually becoming flatter and less oval; eventually the eye on the underside shifts to the exposed side, and the fish swim on one side for the rest of their lives. The underside or blind side of flatfish loses pigment and becomes white, while the exposed side changes color, allowing the fish to blend in with its environment by burrowing into the sand on the ocean floor. The entire length of the body of a flatfish is covered with fins. Depending on the species, the dorsal fins consist of 60 to 155 rays and the anal fins of 35 to 63.

The dorsal fins of some fish are spiny, providing a measure of protection, while the anal fins serve as rudders and the lateral fins as stabilizers; fish use their tails to propel themselves forward. These appendages vary greatly from one species to another, as do the shape, size, and color of the fish, and the texture and taste of the flesh.

There are several significant differences between fish and meat:

• The proportion of muscle is greater because the connective tissue that links the muscles together comprises only 3% of the flesh (as compared to 13% of meat), which is why fish can be cooked quickly and is always tender.

• The muscle fibers are shorter, which makes the flesh more tender.

• The flesh can be cooked very quickly and contains very little fat; it is thus easy to digest, which explains why people often feel hungry after eating fish, especially leaner varieties.

• Since the flesh contains far fewer blood vessels than meat and little or no pigment, it is almost invariably white in color.

• The fat in fish consists mainly of omega-3 polyunsaturated fatty acids, which are found in few other foods (meat contains mainly saturated fatty acids). Numerous studies have demonstrated that omega-3 polyunsaturated fatty acids have a beneficial impact on health. For example, they slow the rate at which blood coagulates, lower blood pressure, and reduce the levels of triglycerides and lipoproteins in the blood, all of which help prevent heart disease. The fattier the fish, the more polyunsaturated omega-3 fat it contains.

• Since polyunsaturated fat oxidizes faster than saturated fat, fish is more perishable than meat. The fattier the fish, the faster it spoils.

• Since the juices in fish are less dense than those in meat, the liquid that is released as fish cooks can be used to make relatively clear, delicately flavored sauces.

Buying

 The criteria for buying fish vary slightly depending on whether it is whole fresh fish or fresh fish in pieces, or frozen, salted, or smoked fish.

WHOLE FRESH FISH

• The gills should be moist and bright red.

• The eyes should be full, shiny, and slightly protruding.

• The skin should be shiny, iridescent, tight, and firmly attached to the flesh.

• The elastic, unmarked flesh should spring back when pressed and should not fall away easily from the bones.

• The shiny, intact scales should adhere firmly to the skin.

• The belly should not be swollen or faded, and the fish should have a mild, pleasant smell (a strong, fishy odor indicates that it is less than fresh).

• A muddy odor does not indicate that the fish is no longer fresh, but rather that the fish was caught in muddy waters.

FRESH FISH in fillets (pieces of flesh cut along the backbone), in steaks, (thick cross-sections), or in pieces

• Firm, shiny, elastic flesh that has a pleasant odor and is firmly attached to the bones. It should not be brownish, yellowish, or dry.

U.S. regulations require that defrosted fish be clearly labeled as such, because it can often be difficult, if not impossible, to distinguish between fresh and defrosted fish. This information is important because freezing slightly alters the taste and texture of fish; furthermore, fish should be eaten as soon as possible after it is defrosted and should never be refrozen until after it has been cooked.

FROZEN FISH

The fresh, firm, and shiny flesh should not show any traces of dryness or freezer burn; it should also be thoroughly frozen and wrapped in airtight, intact packaging that contains no frost or ice crystals.

SALTED FISH

• The flesh should be an attractive color and have a pleasant odor, and should not be dried out.

SMOKED FISH

• The flesh should have a pleasant odor and should retain its juices.

Fish is also canned (whole, in fillets, in pieces, flaked) in various substances (water, oil, vinegar, white wine, tomatoes, sauces). It is also frozen in sauces and in the form of croquettes, sticks, and breaded portions.

Fish

371

Preparing

The amount of preparation involved in cooking fish varies, depending on whether it is fresh or frozen.

FRESH FISH

Your fish merchant can make your job easier by scaling, trimming (removing the fins), and gutting the fish, or even cutting it into fillets. The head does not have to be removed because the eyes and cheeks are edible, and less of the juices are lost if the fish is cooked with the head on.

If the fish has a muddy odor, soak it for 1 or 2 hours in a mixture of vinegar and water (1 to 2 tablespoons of vinegar per cup of water), changing the mixture several times, or pour a tablespoon of vinegar into the mouth of the fish, closing the gills to prevent it from leaking out; another option is to add a little white wine or vinegar when the fish is cooking.

Scaling fish

Fish are easier to scale before they are gutted, when the ventral walls are still rounded. They are usually scaled with a scaler, a fork, the blunt edge of a knife or a knife that has been dulled (to reduce the risk of cutting yourself). With one hand hold the fish firmly by the tail, and use the other hand to scale the fish by placing the scaler at a 45° angle and scraping toward the head. This can be done under running water to prevent the scales from scattering. If the fish is going to be cooked with the skin on, be careful not to damage it. Fish can be skinned without removing the scales.

Flatfish do not have to be skinned before they are cooked, but they do have to be scaled.

Trimming fish

To trim the fish (remove the fins), cut across the rays comprising the fins. Trimming is not absolutely essential; in fact, the dorsal fins will help hold the fish together as it cooks.

Gutting fish

There are several ways to gut a fish – that is, to remove its entrails. The easiest way is to open the belly, but this method involves cutting into the sides of the fish, which distorts the shape of the fish and makes it more difficult to stuff.

Fish can also be gutted by making a small incision (½ to ¾ inch long) behind the gills and pulling the entrails out with your index finger or a spoon. The head can be cut at the base of the gills, then pushed gently toward the rear. Live large fish (halibut, turbot, brill) have to bled completely before they are gutted. This can be done by severing the fish near the tail. The liver, the hard roe (egg-filled ovaries), and the soft roe (testes) of certain species of fish are edible.

GUTTING A FISH THROUGH THE BELLY

1 *Make an incision from the anus to the gills with a pair of scissors.*

2 *Detach and remove the intestines.*

3 *Remove the gills*

4 *Rinse the inside of the fish under cold water. The surface of the cavity can then be scraped with a spoon.*

Filleting fish

Fish is usually filleted after it has been gutted to avoid soiling the flesh. First attempts at filleting can be frustrating, but it becomes much easier with practice.

Before preparing the fish, rinse it quickly but thoroughly under running water. If the ventral cavity has not been opened, clean it by forcing some water inside the fish.

FILLETING A ROUNDED FISH

1 *Turn the fish on its side and make an incision in the middle of the back (as deep as the backbone), from the tail to the back of the head.*

2 *Separate the flesh from the backbone, from the tail to the head.*

3 *Detach the fillet from the head by cutting it behind the gills.*

4 *Hold the end of the tail firmly; make an incision about ¾ inch from the tail, then slide the knife in and gently separate the fillet from the skin. Turn the fish over and repeat the process to remove the second fillet.*

FILLETING A FLATFISH

1 Start skinning the fish by cutting into the skin near the tail.

2 Using a cloth, pull the skin back as far as the head.

3 Make a lengthwise incision in the center of the fish to divide it into two fillets.

4 Insert the blade of the knife between the flesh and the backbone, gradually detaching the fillet.

5 Detach the fillet from the lateral bones by running the blade along its entire length.

6 Remove the other fillet in the same way. Then turn the fish over and repeat the process, thus producing a total of four fillets.

FROZEN FISH

Frozen fish requires a minimum of preparation because it has already been scaled, gutted, and trimmed; furthermore, fish is almost always skinned and is often filleted before it is frozen. In fact, the only thing you have to do is to plan your menu and defrost the fish if necessary. If the fish is thin, cook it frozen or defrost it only slightly (just enough to separate the fillets or pieces). If it is relatively thick, defrost it partially or completely; otherwise, it will cook too much on the outside and remain raw on the inside. Fish should be defrosted completely before it is grilled or fried.

The best way to defrost fish is to put it in the refrigerator, in its original packaging, for 18 to 24 hours (for 1 pound). Never defrost fish at room temperature; if you are short of time, put it in cold water (1 or 2 hours per pound); never use hot water because it will cook the fish.

Serving Ideas

Fish is eaten raw in dishes like Japanese sushi and sashimi and South American ceviche. Raw fish can be eaten plain or marinated in lemon or lime juice. However, some species of fish cannot be prepared in this way because they are too fatty, or because they have been contaminated by pollution or bacteria that cannot be eliminated without cooking the fish.

Fish can be prepared in any number of ways: marinated, smoked, stuffed, and cooked in sauces, mousses, quenelles, pâtés, terrines, rillettes, and *paupiettes* (rolled thin slices cooked in stock).

The size of the portions of fish served depends on various factors, including the species, the recipe, and the accompanying dishes. Cook about 1 pound per person if the fish is whole, 9 ounces if the fish has been dressed (gutted, with the fins, head, gills, tail, and scales removed), and 7 ounces if it has been cut into fillets or steaks.

Cooking

Fish is usually cooked before it is eaten. It can be cooked whole (gutted), in pieces, in steaks, or in fillets. Unless fish is cooked quickly, it can be dry and bland. However, it can be difficult to determine just how long fish should be cooked because several factors come into play, including the shape, the size, and the fat content. To get a rough idea, measure the thickest part of the fish and cook it for 6 to 8 minutes per ½ inch in a 425°F (220°C) oven; if the fish is partially frozen, increase the temperature to 450°F (230°C), and if it is frozen solid cook it for 13 to 15 minutes per ½ inch.

The flesh is cooked when it becomes opaque, falls apart easily, and is uniform in color (milky white if the flesh is white) but is still moist. Fish will continue to cook in a warm oven because it is very sensitive to heat. Shorten the cooking time if the fish will not be served immediately.

To ensure that fish does not shrivel up as it cooks, make small incisions in the skin or in the thin layer of nerve tissue beneath the skin.

Flatfish can be cooked in any way, but should be prepared as simply as possible to avoid masking its delicate flavor. The skin can be left on or removed, depending on how the flatfish is cooked; for example, pan-fried fillets will hold together better if the skin is left on.

Fish can be cooked in numerous ways. The most common methods involve dry heat, moist heat, and frying.

DRY HEAT

Baking fish

• Make several cuts in a whole fish to ensure that the heat penetrates it thoroughly; the stomach cavity can be filled with seasonings such as sliced onions, garlic, thyme, pepper, ginger, or other herbs and spices.

• Place the fish in a dish and either dot it with butter or margarine or brush on a little oil; cover it with a selection of thinly sliced vegetables and slices of lemon (or place it on a bed of vegetables); moisten the fish and vegetables with a white-wine or cream sauce.

• Preheat the oven to 450°F (230°C). If the fish is covered with a sauce containing milk, eggs, and cheese, cook it at a lower temperature (350°F or 180°C) to ensure that the proteins do not separate or harden.

• Cook the fish for the appropriate length of time.

Grilling fish

The fish is placed on a grill or spit and exposed to direct heat.

• Dredge small fish with flour to prevent them from drying out.

• Make incisions in larger fish to speed up the cooking process.

• Brush the fish with oil, melted butter or margarine, or with a sauce, and season it before and during the cooking process.

• Place fragile fish (skinned, sliced, in fillets) on a very hot, lightly oiled grill to prevent them from sticking.

- Cook the skinless side of fillets first to prevent them from shriveling.

- Place the fish 6 to 8 inches away from the heat source (3 to 4 inches for large fish).

- Turn the fish over when it is half done (unless it is too thin to be turned without breaking).

- When broiling fish in the oven, leave the door slightly open.

MOIST HEAT

Poaching fish

Poaching fish involves cooking it gently in a simmering liquid (court bouillon, milk, salted water, etc.). This method of cooking is particularly appropriate for firm fillets and small whole fish.

- The liquid should contain an acidic ingredient (vinegar, dry wine, beer, or lemon juice), which produces a chemical reaction that moderates the strong odor that is released as fish cooks. It also improves the flavor and congeals the flesh, which remains firm. The liquid (court bouillon) can contain milk, vinegar, or wine, vegetables, and seasonings (garlic, salt, pepper, celery, onions, carrots, thyme, fennel, bay leaf, curry). Court bouillon made with milk is particularly appropriate for smoked fish, turbot, and skate, as well as for fish cooked *au gratin*.

- When poaching salted fish, do not add any additional salt to the cooking liquid. If the fish has to be poached for a relatively long time, reduce the amount of salt to prevent it from becoming too salty.

- To enhance the flavor of the court bouillon, let it simmer for about 20 minutes before adding the fish.

- Poach the fish in just enough liquid to cover it; then use this stock, which is rich in nutrients as well as flavor, to make a sauce.

- Place the fish in the cold liquid, then bring the liquid to a simmer; the flesh will cook evenly if the temperature is increased gradually.

- Do not allow the fish to boil, because the flesh will crumble and lose more of its flavor. The outside of the fish will also cook faster than the inside.

- Skinless fish (fillets, steaks) can be cooked in court bouillon. The heat congeals the surface of the fish, creating a layer that seals in the juices, preserves the taste, and prevents the flesh from crumbling.

- Cook the fish for a few minutes less if it is to be served cold; allow it to cool in the cooking liquid.

- It is easier to remove the fish from the pan if it is first placed on a grill or in a piece of muslin.

Steaming fish

The fish is cooked by the steam produced by boiling liquid in the bottom of a saucepan. It should not come into contact with this liquid. Steaming is one of the easiest ways to cook fish because it does not have to be stuffed or wrapped; however, the final product can be quite bland. To enhance the flavor, season the inside of the fish with herbs, spices, ginger, shallots, tamari sauce, or seaweed. Like court bouillons used for poaching, the cooking liquid should contain an acid ingredient.

- Place the fish on a rack or in a basket, or suspend it in a piece of muslin, to prevent it from coming into contact with the liquid.

- Bring the water (2 inches) to a boil before placing the fish in position.

- Cover the saucepan and cook the fish for the appropriate length of time.

Au bleu

This method of cooking involves poaching small fish (carp, trout, perch, pike) in liquid containing vinegar, salt, and other seasonings when they are still alive or have been dead for less than 2 hours. It is important that the fish still be covered with their sticky coating; they should thus be gutted but not scaled. They become blue when cooked as the result of a chemical reaction involving the sticky coating and the vinegar.

• Sprinkle both sides of the fish with approximately ⅓ cup of vinegar; then cook them in a very vinegary court bouillon.

• The fish can also be sprinkled with vinegar in the dish in which they are cooked. The vinegar then becomes part of the vinegary court bouillon, which becomes that much more acidic.

• Cook the fish for 8 to 10 minutes.

Cooking fish in aluminum foil

This method of cooking involves sealing the fish in an airtight package so that it is cooked by the steam produced by its natural juices and any vegetables or liquids that are added. The package usually consists of a piece of aluminum foil.

• Set out a piece of foil for each serving of fish.

• Place the fish on a mixture of sliced vegetables and seasonings, or spread the vegetables and seasonings on top of the fish.

• Add a little liquid (wine, soy sauce, court bouillon, sauce, cream, or water).

• Add lemon slices to taste, and dot the fish with butter or margarine.

• Fold the foil into a tightly sealed package. Place the foil package in an ovenproof dish.

• Cook it at 450°F (230°C) for the appropriate length of time.

• Open the foil package when serving the fish at the table.

Braising fish

Braising involves cooking food slowly at low temperatures in a closed dish containing a very small amount of liquid. It is a particularly appropriate cooking method for fish with firm flesh.

• Place the fish in a dish or fish kettle containing a layer of vegetables and herbs (if the fish is large, slice it open to ensure that the heat penetrates it thoroughly). Add only enough liquid (concentrated stock, white wine, or court bouillon) to cover the fish halfway, to prevent it from boiling.

• Cover the dish and cook the fish over low heat on top of the stove or in a relatively cool oven.

• Serve the fish as is or thicken the sauce by removing the fish, straining the liquid, and reducing it slightly over low heat, or by adding a mixture of butter and flour (1 tablespoon of each), 1 or 2 egg yolks, or even a little cream.

FRYING FISH

Although this is the most popular method of cooking fish, it is the worst choice from a nutritional point of view because it increases the fat content.

Fish can be deep-fried or pan-fried. In both cases, the fish is first dredged in flour, rolled in bread crumbs, or dipped in batter. This creates a layer that protects the fish from the intense heat, limits the amount of fat that is absorbed, and prevents the moisture in the fish from escaping (when water leaks out, the temperature drops, and the fish becomes soggy and greasy).

Deep-frying fish

Deep-frying involves submerging the fish in boiling fat.

• When cooking small fish, or a small quantity of fish, use only a very small amount of oil.

• Preheat the oil to 375°F (190°C).

• Soak the fish for 5 minutes in salted water, or dip it in an egg that has been beaten with a tablespoon (15 ml) of water; for an extra-special flavor, soak it in citrus juice for 30 minutes.

• Drain the fish slightly, then coat it thoroughly with flour, bread crumbs or batter; the coating can be flavored with seasonings or cheese.

• Butter and margarine are not suitable for deep-frying because they contain water and burn easily. Use fat or oil that has a high critical point (see *Oil*). A thermometer can help you avoid overheating the fat and determine how long the fish should be cooked. The fat should be heated to between 325° and 375°F (160° and 190°C). If cooked at lower temperatures, the fish will be soggy and greasy rather than crispy; and at higher temperatures, the fat will begin to break down and the fish may burn. For the best results, add the fish gradually to avoid a sudden drop in temperature. After the fish has finished cooking, drain it and place it on paper towels until it is served.

Pan-frying fish

• Use only a small amount of fat. You can use butter or margarine, especially if it is has been clarified (melted and filtered); clarified butter and margarine burn less easily because their impurities have been removed (see *Butter*).

• Roll the fish in bread crumbs or dredge it in flour (it does not have to be dipped in liquid).

• The fat should be very hot but not smoking. If pan is not hot enough, the protective layer that prevents the fish from sticking will not form.

• Cook the fish for the appropriate length of time.

• Turn the fish only once, when it is half done.

• Drain the fish when it has finished cooking, by placing it on a piece of paper towel.

Fish can be baked rather than fried. Baked fish can be cooked in even less fat than fried fish, does not have be turned halfway through the cooking process, and cooks more quickly and evenly. Preheat the oven to 500°F (260°C).

MICROWAVING FISH

Fish cooks well in the microwave, because unlike meat it is best when cooked rapidly at high temperatures. Microwaving enhances the delicate flavor of fish and gives it a moist, light texture without significantly reducing its nutritional value.

For the best results, cook one layer of fish at a time, placing the thickest portions toward the outside. If a whole fish is too large to fit inside the microwave, either bend it or remove the head and tail. Unless the recipe specifies otherwise, cover the fish with a layer of plastic wrap, leaving one corner open to allow excess steam to escape.

• Place the fish in a microwavable dish, dot it with butter or sprinkle on a little oil, and cover it with a selection of minced vegetables, spices, herbs and lemon slices (or place it on a bed of seasonings), or pour on a white wine or cream sauce.

- Make several cuts in the skin of larger fish to prevent them from splitting as they cook.

- Make several cuts in the skin of large fillets to ensure that they retain their shape as they cook.

- Cook whole fish (1½ lb.) on high power (in a 700-watt oven) for 8 to 10 minutes, and fillets or steaks (1 lb.) for 4 to 5 minutes, turning them halfway.

- Allow the fish to sit in the oven for 2 or 3 minutes before it is served.

Storing

Saltwater fish are less perishable than freshwater fish. Wipe the fresh fish thoroughly with a damp cloth, then wrap it in waxed paper, put it in a tightly sealed container, and place it in the coldest part of the refrigerator as soon as possible; it can be stored for 2 or 3 days.

During fishing trips, store the fish in a cooler, or place them in the shade and cover them with moss, or wrap them in a cloth moistened with vinegar and keep them cool. Gut and eat the fish as soon as possible.

Fish is sometimes preserved by means of smoking and salting. The fish is exposed to smoke from slow-burning, nonresinous wood and other woodlike products such as peat. This process partially dehydrates the fish and gives it a smoky flavor. Fish can be either hot- or cold-smoked. Hot-smoked fish is exposed to temperatures of up to 250°F (120°C). Since this congeals the proteins in the fish, it does not have to cooked any further.

Cold-smoked fish is not cooked; it is simply placed in a smoky location, far enough away from the heat source to ensure that the smoke cools before it comes into contact with the fish. It is less delicate and flavorful than hot-smoked fish.

Before being smoked, fish is dry-salted or pickled in brine.

Dry-salted fish is sliced into fillets, then arranged between layers of salt in a manner that allows the resultant brine to circulate freely. Pickled fish is soaked in salted water. Since there are several methods of salting fish, the amount of salt in the fish varies. Hot-smoked fish and fish that is dry-salted before it is cold-smoked can be eaten as is, but cold-smoked pickled fish has to be cooked. Smoked and salted fish can be refrigerated for several days or frozen for 3 to 4 weeks.

FREEZING FISH

Fish can be frozen quite easily. Wrap it well and keep it at a constant temperature no warmer than 0°F (-18°C). Lean fish can be frozen for longer (2 to 3 months) than fattier fish (1 or 2 months), because it spoils less quickly.

Avoid freezing fish you did not catch yourself. Do not attempt to freeze fresh store-bought fish because it cannot be frozen quickly enough (industrial methods are much faster). Fish should always be gutted before it is frozen and should be as fresh as possible. It can be frozen in one of four ways: in a block of ice, in layers of ice, after being soaked in lemon juice, or in a hermetically sealed package.

FREEZING FISH IN A BLOCK OF ICE

Wash the fish in salted water (1 tablespoon of salt per quart of water); then place the fish in a container and fill it with fresh water to within ¾ inch of the top. Cover the container and put it in the freezer.

When freezing steaks or fillets, remove the skin, rinse the fish under cold water, then place the pieces in a container, separating them with sheets of aluminum foil or plastic wrap. Cover them with water and freeze them as indicated above.

Fish

379

FREEZING FISH IN LAYERS OF ICE

Wash the fish, then freeze it unwrapped. Once it is frozen, plunge it into ice water and put it back in the freezer. Repeat this operation several times until the fish is covered with a layer of ice about ¼ inch thick. Wrap the fish well before returning it to the freezer for the last time.

FISH SOAKED IN LEMON JUICE

Place the fish in a bowl filled with lemon juice. Moisten one side of the fish, then turn it over and moisten the other side; repeat this process, then wrap and freeze the fish.

FREEZING FISH IN HERMETICALLY SEALED PACKAGES

Wash the fish and wrap it carefully in a layer of plastic wrap; then put it in a freezer bag, squeezing out all the air. Freeze the fish rapidly at a temperature no higher than 0°F (-18°C).

Nutritional Information

Fish can be lean, moderately fatty, or fatty. Lean fish such as plaice, haddock, and cod contain less than 5% fat (from 75 to 125 calories per 100 grams); moderately fatty fish such as halibut contain between 5% and 10% fat (125 to 150 calories per 100 grams); and fatty fish such as salmon, herring, and mackerel contain over 10% fat (over 150 calories per 100 grams). Fish contain between 15% and 20% so-called complete proteins (see *Complementary proteins).* They are also rich in certain minerals and vitamins, including phosphorus, iodine, fluorine, copper, vitamin A, magnesium, iron, zinc, selenium, and B-complex vitamins. Fatty fish are a very good source of vitamin D (which is not found in the flesh of land animals). However, fish is not a source of calcium, unless you consume the bones in canned fish such as salmon or sardines.

The flesh of spawning fish is less appetizing because its texture is not quite as good. The spawning season varies from one species to another, but generally lasts from January to June in the Northern Hemisphere.

Fish are susceptible to pollution. As waterways become increasingly polluted, many species of fish are being contaminated by various toxic substances such as DDT (dichlorodiphenyltrichloroethane). PCBs (polychlorinated biphenyls) and mercury can cause serious illness when present in high concentrations and when large amounts of contaminated foods are consumed. The level of contamination depends on the age of the fish and on its habitat. The older and larger the fish, the greater the impact of the pollution in its environment. An older fish can thus contain high levels of contamination if it comes from polluted waters. As a rule, predatory fish and freshwater fish are more contaminated than saltwater fish. Fatty fish and fish that eat other fish are particularly vulnerable to pollution. Bass, pike, dory, swordfish, halibut, shark, muskellunge, and tuna are thus often heavily contaminated. It is advisable to limit your consumption of fish caught in polluted waters.

Kamaboko

Kamaboko is the Japanese name for a seafood substitute made from surimi, a fish paste. First produced in Japan almost 900 years ago as the result of efforts to preserve fish, surimi is now the key ingredient in over 2,000 Japanese products, including imitation seafood (crab, shrimp, lobster, scallops, etc.) and fish sausages, balls, loaves, and noodles.

Surimi is made by processing fish in a variety of ways in order to destroy the enzymes and eliminate the blood, fat, and proteins that cause fish to spoil. After being skinned, thinly sliced, and washed in a series of stainless-steel tanks, the fish (usually pollock, but sometimes shark or cod) is put through a sieve, and the purified flesh is placed in a vat of salt water. Once it has been drained and slightly dehydrated, it is sieved again to separate the pinkish flesh (which makes up approximately 5% of the fish) from the white flesh, which is then completely dehydrated and dipped in a tank filled with sugar, sorbitol, and phosphates – preservatives that allow fish to be frozen for a longer period of time.

At this stage, surimi is a completely tasteless and unappetizing concentrate of fish proteins.

Buying

 It is often difficult to distinguish seafood substitutes from real seafood, but there are certain clues that can be helpful:

• the shape of imitation seafood is usually too perfect, and the individual pieces are identical;

• the flesh is comprised of long, uniform strands;

• the surface of the extremely white flesh is colored with pinkish or red dye.

Preparing

Kamaboko is imitation seafood that is made by combining minced surimi with ingredients that enhance its taste and texture, including water, starch, egg white, monosodium glutamate, and real or artificial flavoring. These ingredients are mixed together until they form a paste, which is partially cooked before being molded into various shapes (short sticks, shredded "crab meat," "shrimp," etc.). This molded seafood is then cooked further, pasteurized, and sterilized. A small amount of real seafood is sometimes added to the surimi, and the final product often tastes so much like the seafood being imitated that it is difficult to tell them apart. Kamaboko is much less expensive than real seafood and is often used as a seafood substitute, especially in restaurants.

Serving Ideas

Kamaboko can be eaten hot or cold and can be used as a substitute for real seafood in most recipes. Since it is precooked, it can be used "as is" in salads, sandwiches, canapés, and the like.

Nutritional Information

	steamed
protein	12 g
fat	1 g
calories	52
	per 100 g

Kamaboko is rich in protein and low in fat and calories, just like real seafood. It also contains very little cholesterol, unless shellfish have been added to the surimi. It does, however, contain several additives and up to three or four times as much sodium as the seafood it replaces. Since it often contains monosodium glutamate, it can cause allergic reactions in some people.

Storing

Kamaboko can be kept in the refrigerator for several days, and can be stored in the freezer if it has not been previously frozen.

Eel

Anguilla spp., Anguillidae

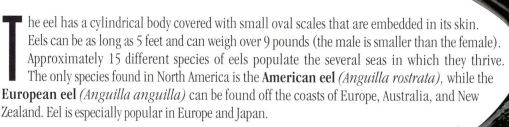

European eel

T he eel has a cylindrical body covered with small oval scales that are embedded in its skin. Eels can be as long as 5 feet and can weigh over 9 pounds (the male is smaller than the female). Approximately 15 different species of eels populate the several seas in which they thrive. The only species found in North America is the **American eel** *(Anguilla rostrata),* while the **European eel** *(Anguilla anguilla)* can be found off the coasts of Europe, Australia, and New Zealand. Eel is especially popular in Europe and Japan.

The eel has a small head, strong jaws, and small pointed teeth – characteristics that distinguish it from the lamprey, a species with which it is often confused. Its color depends on its age and habitat, and its dorsal, caudal, and anal fins form one large fin that covers fully one half of its body. The life cycle of the eel is quite unusual; unlike other fish, eels are born in the sea, spend most of their lives in fresh water, and return to the sea to reproduce.

Eels spawn in the Sargasso Sea, off the coast of Bermuda, and in the tropical waters of the Atlantic. Each female lays as many as 10 million eggs, which develop into larvae before being carried by ascending currents to waters where they are fertilized by sires that live just long enough to spawn. It takes eels a year to reach the fresh waters of North America, and 2 to 3 years to penetrate the rivers and lakes of Europe. Female eels spend 10 to 15 years in fresh water, while males return to the sea after 8 to 10 years. All eels are female at birth, but a certain number of them become male shortly thereafter. When eels reach the coast of Europe at approximately 3 years of age, they are transparent and measure between 2 and 4 inches long. These small, flavorful "glass-eels" or "elvers" are much sought after; there are approximately 1,000 individual fish in a single pound.

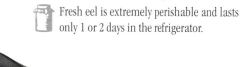

Nutritional Information

	raw
protein	18 g
fat	12 g
calories	184
	per 100 g

Raw eel is high in fat and rich in vitamins A and D. The firm flesh is fine and fatty. Eels are easy to debone, and much of the fat can be easily removed from larger eels because it is stored between the flesh and the skin.

Storing

Fresh eel is extremely perishable and lasts only 1 or 2 days in the refrigerator.

Buying

Eel is cut into fillets, slices, or pieces and sold fresh, smoked, marinated, or in cans. In some countries, eels are kept alive in water tanks until they are sold, because their flesh deteriorates rapidly and their blood can be poisonous if it enters a cut.

Preparing

Before cooking an eel, remove the thick skin. This can be done by cutting the eel into three sections and poaching it for 1 or 2 minutes in boiling water to soften the skin, or by grilling it briefly (the skin is easy to remove once it blisters). This method also removes excess fat from the eel.

Serving Ideas

Avoid cooking eel in ways that increase the fat content. If it is fried, it should first be poached for 8 to 12 minutes in salted water containing 1 or 2 teaspoons of lemon juice.

Cooking

Eel is often grilled, baked, poached, sautéed, or added to stews and soups (matelote, bouillabaisse). Smoked eel is also excellent.

Since the flesh of eels is firm, heat penetrates it quite slowly. This is another reason to avoid frying eel, because it tends to burn before it is cooked, especially if it weighs over a pound.

Freshwater bass

Micropterus spp., **Centrachidae**

A very difficult fish to catch, the freshwater bass thrives in the rivers and lakes of North America. *Achigan,* the Algonquin (and French) name for the freshwater bass, means "the fighter" and refers to the legendary aggressiveness of the fish. Capable of growing to a length of over 2 feet, the freshwater bass is a hunchbacked fish with spiny dorsal fins, rough scales, and a tapered head that comprises fully one third of its body. The characteristics of the various freshwater bass species vary from one habitat to another.

The **smallmouth bass** *(Micropterus dolomieni)* usually measures between 8 and 15 inches and rarely weighs more than 3 pounds. Its mouth contains numerous small teeth and sits atop a protruding lower jaw. Its dorsal skin can be green, brown, or golden brown, and its golden or bronze sides are adorned with dark stripes.

The **largemouth bass** *(Micropterus salmoides)* has a somewhat sturdier body than the smallmouth bass, and its mouth extends back to the middle of the eye, whereas that of the smallmouth barely reaches the front of the eye. Its dark green back and greenish sides are speckled with silver, and a lateral stripe often adorns each of its sides, especially among younger fish. While the smallmouth bass frequents the rocky waters of cold rivers and lakes, the largemouth bass prefers the relatively warm waters of slow-moving rivers and muddy lakes. Known as the speckled perch in Europe, the largemouth bass can be slightly longer and heavier than the smallmouth bass.

Preparing

The scales of the freshwater bass are very difficult to remove. Before attempting to scale the fish, plunge it briefly into boiling water that contains a little lemon juice. It is also possible to remove the skin.

Serving Ideas

Medium-size freshwater bass can be prepared like trout, and larger ones can be prepared like carp or shad; bass can be cooked whole, but it is usually filleted. Freshwater bass are often found in polluted waters, and the degree of contamination to which they have been exposed depends on their age and habitat; older, larger fish are likely to be more contaminated. It is best to limit your consumption of freshwater bass unless the fish comes from an area that is known to be free of pollution.

Buying

A favorite of sport fishermen, the freshwater bass is rarely sold commercially.

Cooking

Freshwater bass can be cooked in virtually any way.

Nutritional Information

	raw
protein	19 g
fat	4 g
calories	114
	per 100 g

The flesh of the freshwater bass is lean, white, flaky, and very flavorful.

largemouth bass

Pike

Esox spp., Esocidae

northern pike

The pike is a voracious eater with a particular fondness for frogs, ducks, and small mammals, and it is also in fierce competition with fishermen. Found in the rivers, lakes, and ponds of North America and Europe, the pike has a very large mouth that contains nearly 700 long pointed teeth. It also has a forked dorsal fin just in front of its tail. The following species are among the most common:

The **northern pike** *(Esox lucius),* which is the most common of all, has a very elongated body that varies in color and is decorated with yellowish spots. Northern pike usually weigh between 2 and 5 pounds and measure between 14 and 28 inches, but they can weigh in at 40 pounds and grow to be over 3 feet long.

The **grass pickerel** *(Esox americanus vermiculatus)* is often too small (6 to 8 inches) to eat. Its body is shorter and its head longer than those of other pikes. It has a rust-brown stripe on its back, as well as large vertical markings separated by the dense grasslike multitude of undulating and sinuous striae for which it is named.

The **chain pickerel** *(Esox niger)* is a rather small fish (16 to 20 inches), but its flesh is very tender. Its sides are green or brown with yellow-green patches and are decorated with markings that resemble the links of a chain.

The **muskellunge** *(Esox masquinongy)* was named by native Americans and is the largest member of the pike family. Although it can grow to be almost 7 feet long and can weigh as much as 100 pounds, most of the fish now caught are between 2 and 4 feet long and weigh between 5 and 35 pounds. Its color varies depending on its habitat, but the muskellunge is always decorated with dark stripes.

Buying

 This fish is usually sold fresh or frozen, either whole or in fillets.

Cooking

Pike can be cooked in virtually any way.

Nutritional Information

protein	19 g
fat	0.7 g
calories	88
	per 100 g

Lean, firm, and flaky, the white flesh of the pike contains many small bones. The eggs and soft roe of spawning pike are slightly toxic.

Preparing

 The flesh of pikes can be dry and can sometimes taste a little muddy. To get rid of this taste, soak the fish for 1 or 2 hours in fresh water or a mixture of water and vinegar (1 part vinegar to 10 parts water). Pike does not have to be scaled and can be cooked whole, in fillets, or in steaks (remove the skin before serving).

It is best not to wash pike too much before cooking it, because its viscous coating helps make it more tender.

Serving Ideas

Small pike are better than large ones, which tend to be less tender. Since pike contains a large number of small bones, it is often used in pâtés, quenelles, and fish loaves.

Carp

Cyprinus carpio, **Cyprinidae**

Found in the rivers, lakes, ponds, and canals of Europe and North America, the carp prefers warm shallow water. It is thought to have originated somewhere in Asia – probably in China – and has been raised in captivity for thousands of years. The Chinese are said to have established the first carp farms over 3,000 years ago. During the Middle Ages, the central European region of Bohemia was renowned for the quality of the carp it produced, and the fish is still a key ingredient in the cuisine of the area, especially during Easter and Christmas festivities.

The carp has a sturdy, laterally compressed body covered with large thick scales (certain hybrid species have few or no scales). It has a triangular head, a slightly prominent upper jaw, and two pairs of barbels around a toothless mouth. There is a hard spine in front of both its anal and dorsal fins. Carp are usually between 14 and 18 inches long and often weigh over 15 pounds, but can measure up to 30 inches and weigh as much as 55 pounds. The most common species of carp is brownish green, olive green, or bluish green with golden yellow sides and relatively pale ventral skin. Its flesh is firm.

Preparing

The flavor of carp varies, and wild carp often tastes slightly muddy. To get rid of this taste, scale and gut the carp (be sure to remove the gallbladder at the base of the throat); then soak it for 1 or 2 hours in water that contains a small amount of vinegar, changing the water from time to time. Carp is difficult to scale, but plunging the fish into boiling water for a few seconds makes scaling easier.

Serving Ideas

Carp can be cooked whole, in fillets, or in sections. The eggs, cheeks, tongue, and lips of the carp are considered to be delicacies.

Cooking

Carp can be cooked in any number of ways and is often steamed, roasted, poached, grilled, or fried.

Buying

Carp is sometimes smoked before being sold.

Nutritional Information

protein	18 g
fat	4.6 g
calories	127
	per 100 g

Moderately fatty, raw carp is an excellent source of niacin, phosphorus, and vitamin B_{12}.

Pike perch

Stizostedion spp., **Percidae**

Known as pike perch in Europe, the various fishes comprising the *Stizostedion* genuses are found in freshwater lakes and large rivers. Their long bodies are slightly flat, and they have large mouths, prominent jaws, and numerous teeth. What distinguishes pike perch from perch, with which they are often confused, is the fact that they have two dorsal fins rather than one. Pike perch are found in mainland Europe, Scandinavia, and England, as well as in North America, where the most common species are the walleye and the sauger.

The **European pike perch** *(Stizostedion lucioperca)* has an elongated body, powerful teeth, and grayish skin; it usually measures between 24 and 40 inches and can weigh up to 22 pounds. It is bred intensively in Europe.

The **sauger** *(Stizostedion canadense)* has a rather sturdy cylindrical body with the long pointed snout that is characteristic of pike perch. It is usually between 10 and 16 inches long and weighs about 1 pound. Its cheeks are covered with rough scales, its dorsal skin can be brown or gray, and its sides are yellow with dark brown marbling. The flesh of the sauger is often considered to be superior to that of the walleye.

The **walleye** *(Stizostedion vitreum)* has a more elevated head and a thicker body than the sauger; it also has larger, darker eyes and comparatively smooth cheeks. The largest member of the perch family, it is usually 13 to 20 inches long and weighs between 2 and 4 pounds. Its olive-brown or yellowish skin is adorned with small yellow or gold spots and dark, somewhat blurred, diagonal lines.

Buying

 Pike perch are sold whole, trimmed, or in fillets, either fresh or frozen.

Nutritional Information

	raw sauger
protein	17 g
fat	1 g
calories	83
	per 100 g

The lean white flesh of the pike perch is delicate and flavorful.

Serving Ideas

 Pike perch can be prepared like pike or perch, or like any other fish with firm flesh, either whole or in fillets.

Cooking

 Pike perch are very flavorful fish that can be cooked in any number of ways.

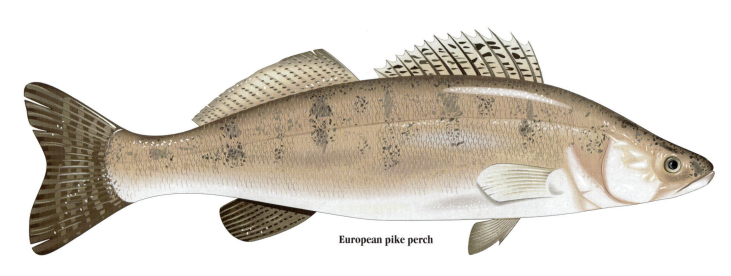

European pike perch

Perch

Perca spp., **Percidae**

O ne of the few fish that thrive in both briny and fresh water, the perch is found almost all over the world and is bred on fish farms in the United States and several other countries. The perch family is made up of 9 genuses and approximately 120 species, including the walleye, the sauger, and the yellow perch.

The perch has a slightly elongated, laterally compressed body. Its tapered head comprises a full third of its body, and its large mouth is equipped with numerous thin teeth. The two adjacent dorsal fins of the perch are brownish green, while its other fins are red or orangey. Its front dorsal fin is composed of slender spines, its second dorsal fin has one spine, and its anal fin has two. Perch are between 10 and 20 inches long, and though they can weigh as much as 8 pounds, their average weight is closer to l pound. Their skin is covered with small rough scales and is usually an olive color on the top and white on the bottom; their yellowish sides are striped with six to eight vertical bands.

Preparing

 It is best to scale perch as soon as they are caught; otherwise the scales can be very difficult to remove without skinning the fish. Another option is to poach it or plunge it into boiling water for a few moments before attempting to remove the scales. Beware of the spines on the fins.

Serving Ideas

A very bony fish, the perch has lean, firm white flesh with a delicate flavor, and recipes that overpower its taste should be avoided. Recipes for carp and trout are particularly appropriate for perch.

Cooking

Perch can be cooked whole or in fillets. It is often poached, steamed, or prepared *à la meunière* (lightly floured and fried in butter).

Buying

 Perch is rarely sold to consumers.

Nutritional Information

	raw
protein	19 g
fat	0.9 g
calories	91
	per 100 g

Perch is rich in niacin, vitamin B_{12}, phosphorus, and potassium.

Trout

Salmo spp., Salmonidae

The trout is found in the cold waters of lakes and rivers, as well as in the sea; trout that live in the sea return to fresh water to spawn. A member of the large Salmonidae family, the trout is closely related to the char and the grayling. The common characteristics of these fish include their somewhat elongated, slightly laterally compressed bodies and their pointed teeth. Highly prized by sports fishermen, they have very fine, much-sought-after flesh. The trout was the first fish ever raised in captivity, and the rainbow trout is a particular favorite of trout farmers.

The most common species of trout, char, and grayling include the brown trout, the rainbow trout, the lake trout, the brook trout, the arctic char, and the common grayling.

The **brown trout** *(Salmo trutta)* originated in Europe and was introduced into North American waters in 1883. The species of brown trout found exclusively in fresh water is usually about 16 inches long, while the variety that migrates between fresh water and the sea can grow to be almost 5 feet long. The brown trout usually weighs between 2 and 13 pounds but can be heavier. It has a large mouth equipped with several well-developed teeth. Its dorsal skin is brownish, its sides are silvery, and its ventral skin is off-white or cream-colored. Large black spots, many of which are encircled by relatively pale rings, adorn its head and dorsal fins as well as its sides, which are also speckled with irregularly shaped, rust-colored spots; there are very few spots on its square tail. The pinkish flesh of the brown trout is delicious.

The **rainbow trout** *(Salmo gairdneri)* originated on the west coast of North America and was introduced into European waters at the end of the 19th century. It resembles the brown trout and is approximately the same weight. Its dorsal skin is metallic blue, and its sides are adorned with a horizontal stripe whose color ranges from dark pink to bright red to crimson, which explains why the fish is known as the rainbow trout. Its back and sides, as well as its dorsal and adipose fins, are covered with black spots. The rainbow trout thrives in cold, clear water, but it can also live in warm water. It is the most common trout in North America and the trout most commonly bred on fish farms throughout the world.

The **lake trout** *(Salvelinus namaycush)* is distinguished from other trout by its forked tail and its remarkably elongated body, which is usually speckled with pale, sometimes yellowish blotches. The color of its skin ranges from gray or light green to brown or dark green verging on black. One the largest freshwater fish, it usually measures between 15 and 20 inches. Although it generally weighs between 4 and 7 pounds, it can tip the scales at over 75 pounds. It has very powerful teeth.

The **brook trout** *(Salvelinus fontinalis)* is a relatively small fish, usually weighing between ½ pound and 3 pounds and measuring between 10 and 12 inches. Its dorsal skin is often dark olive or black and is marbled with dark lines, while its silvery sides are speckled with small red spots encircled by bluish halos. One variety of brook trout lives mainly in the sea. The **arctic char** *(Salvelinus alpinus)* is distinguished by the beauty of its coloring, which is often dark blue or blue-green on the back, silvery blue on the sides, and white on the underside; its sides are speckled with large red, pink, or cream-colored blotches. Its size varies depending on its habitat; it usually weighs between 2 and 11 pounds, but it can be larger.

The **common grayling** *(Thymallus thymallus)* is a European species which, as its Latin name suggests, smells somewhat like thyme when freshly caught. It has an elongated, slightly compressed body with a small head and mouth, extremely long dorsal fins, and a forked tail. Its skin is covered with scales larger than those found on the trout, and its slightly rounded back can be dark blue, blue-gray, or crimson. Its entire body is speckled with an inconsistent number of diamond- or V-shaped marks. A very beautiful fish, it can be anywhere from 16 to 20 inches long.

Buying

 Available either fresh or frozen, trout are sold whole, trimmed, or in fillets, and are sometimes cut into steaks. Trout is also smoked, and a very small quantity is canned.

Trout Cooked in Aluminum Foil

SERVES 4

2 shallots
1 tbsp. fresh tarragon
  leaves
1 tbsp. fresh dill leaves
2 tbsp. fresh parsley leaves

1 lemon
4 trout, each weighing
  about ½ lb. (250 g)
Salt and ground pepper
Olive oil

1. Preheat the oven to 400°F (200°C).

2. Thinly slice the shallots. Chop the tarragon, dill, and parsley. Peel and slice the lemon.

3. Ensure that the trout have been gutted and are ready to cook, then pat them dry. Salt and pepper the insides of the fish, then stuff them with the shallots and herbs.

4. Cut four rectangular pieces of aluminum foil and brush each of them on one side with olive oil. Place the trout on the pieces of foil and cover them with the lemon slices. Bring the edges of the foil together, tightly sealing each of the rectangles. Arrange the packages in an ovenproof dish and cook the fish for 15 minutes.

Preparing

Trout does not have to be scaled and is very easy to fillet.

Serving Ideas

Trout should be prepared as simply as possible so as not to overpower its delicate flavor. Smoked trout is especially delicious, and trout is also particularly good when used in salmon recipes.

Nutritional Information

protein	21 g
fat	7 g
calories	148
	per 100 g

The flesh of the various species of trout is very fine and fragrant. Its remarkably delicate flavor varies slightly from one species to another, as does its color, which can be white, ivory, pink, or reddish. Trout is moderately fatty.

brook trout

rainbow trout

Freshwater Fish

389

Bluefish

Pomatomus saltatrix, Pomatomidae

The bluefish is a voracious and aggressive fish that moves through the water in enormous schools in the wake of other schools of fish, including mackerel and herring, on which it feeds. It is found primarily in the North and South American waters of the Atlantic, as well as in the Pacific. It is closely related to the horse mackerel and its flesh is much sought after, especially in North America and Australia.

The bluefish has an elongated body, a forked tail, and a large head and mouth. Covered with small scales, its skin is bluish green on the back and silvery on the underside. The bluefish can grow to a length of approximately 43 inches and can weigh as much as 50 pounds, but usually it is between 16 and 24 inches long and weighs from 10 to 15 pounds. It has lean, flavorful flesh.

Preparing

The bluefish should be bled as soon as it is caught to ensure that its flesh remains firm and flavorful. Fish that are only 4 to 6 inches long need not be scaled.

Nutritional Information

	raw
protein	20 g
fat	4 g
calories	124
	per 100 g

Serving Ideas

Bluefish is often grilled, braised, or poached. It can be prepared like mackerel and can replace it in most recipes. Only very small bluefish should be fried because larger ones tend to absorb too much fat.

Storing

Bluefish should be refrigerated immediately and eaten as soon as possible, because the flesh is extremely perishable. It should not be frozen for longer than 3 months.

*Saltwater Fish*

390

Shad

Prized for its eggs as well as its flesh, the shad is one of the most commercially important fish in North America and is also fished in western Europe and the Mediterranean. It spends most of its life in the ocean but swims back upriver in the spring to spawn.

The following are among the most common species of shad: The **American shad** *(Alosa sapidissima)* thrives in the Atlantic from Labrador to Florida, and it has also been found on the west coast of North America since its introduction into Pacific waters at the end of the 19th century. Usually 16 to 30 inches long, it can weigh anywhere from 2 to 7 pounds. Its dorsal skin is a dark shade of blue-green, its sides are silvery, and there are at least four dark spots behind each of its gills.

The **twaite shad** *(Alosa fallax)* usually measures between 8 and 16 inches but can grow to be 20 inches long. Although it is most common in the Atlantic, it is also found in the Baltic, the North Sea, and the Mediterranean. Its dorsal skin is blue-black, its sides and belly are silvery white, and the sides of its head are golden. It is distinguished from other shad by the six or seven dark spots that adorn the upper part of its back.

The **allis shad** *(Alosa alosa)* can grow to a length of 28 inches. Its dorsal skin is dark blue, its sides are silvery white, and there can be a dark spot behind each of its gills. It is most common off the Atlantic coasts of Europe as well as in the Mediterranean.

The **alewife** *(Alosa pseudoharengus)* usually measures between 10 and 14 inches but can grow to be 16 inches long. Known as the gaspareau in Canada, it has grayish green dorsal skin, silvery sides, and a single dark spot on the upper part of its back near the gills.

Buying

Shad is usually sold fresh or frozen, either whole or in fillets. Its white flesh is fatty, tender, and flaky. While certain species have very flavorful, much-sought-after flesh, others are less popular because their flesh contains a large number of bones that are very difficult to remove (the American shad contains 360 bones). There is a row of parallel bones on either side of the large bone, at a depth of about 1 inch; shad is easier to fillet if you locate these rows with your fingers. Female shad are more sought after than males because their relatively large bones are easier to remove and because their roe is delicious.

Serving Ideas

Shad is often prepared with highly acidic ingredients like sorrel, rhubarb, and gooseberries, which make the fish easier to digest and soften the bones. It can replace herring and mackerel in most recipes.

Cooking

If you are not used to filleting shad, cook it whole. If it is cooked quickly, the small bones will remain attached to the backbone.

Storing

Shad should be cooked as soon as possible after it is purchased because it spoils quickly.

Nutritional Information

	raw
protein	17 g
fat	14 g
calories	197
	per 100 g

Mullet

Mugil spp., **Mugilidae**

The mullet prefers the warm coastal waters of the Atlantic, the Mediterranean, and the Pacific, but schools of mullet also venture into briny and fresh water. An unusual feeder, the mullet sticks its mouth into mud and filters out the particles it can consume – a practice that accounts for the muddy taste of some freshwater mullet. There are 13 genuses and 95 species in the mullet family, and it can be difficult to tell them apart. The most common species is the gray mullet *(Mugil cephalus)*.

The gray mullet has a slender body that is covered with scales. It has blue-green dorsal skin and silvery sides. It is usually between 12 and 16 inches long but can grow to a maximum length of 40 inches. It has a short, flat head and a small mouth filled with short, tightly spaced teeth.

Nutritional Information

	raw
protein	19 g
fat	4 g
calories	116
	per 100 g

Serving Ideas

Mullet can be eaten hot or cold and is particularly flavorful when smoked. Its eggs are delicious; dried, pressed, salted mullet roe is used to make *boutargue,* one of the most popular dishes in the Provence region of France. Mullet roe is also the key ingredient in the Greek dish *taramasalata,* a creamy, flavorful pink paste.

Cooking

Mullet can be cooked in any number of ways. Small mullet do not have to be gutted before they are cooked.

Monkfish

Lophius spp., **Lophiidae**

A strange-looking fish that lives in the muddy waters at the bottom of the Atlantic, the Mediterranean, and other salt-water seas, the monkfish hides from its predators by burrowing into the seabed until it is indistinguishable from its surroundings. It attracts the large number of small fish required to satisfy its huge appetite by waving the two appendages that protrude from its upper jaw. Since this activity is similar to fishing, the monkfish is also known as the angler.

The monkfish has an enormous flat head that is wider than the rest of its body. Its equally enormous mouth contains several large pointed teeth, and its slimy, limp, scaleless skin is covered with spines and appendages. Its dorsal skin is an olive-green color, and its ventral skin is grayish. More popular in Europe than in North America, monkfish are between 20 inches and 7 feet long, and can weigh as much as 90 pounds.

Buying

 Monkfish is sold fresh, frozen, or smoked. The skin and the head are usually removed before the fish is sold.

Serving Ideas

The only edible part of the monkfish is its tail, which consists of lean, flavorful white flesh that is often compared to lobster meat. Other than its thick backbone, which is very easy to remove, the monkfish contains no bones. Monkfish is often prepared like lobster and can be substituted for lobster in most recipes. It is best when served with a sauce, because it has to be cooked a little longer than most fish and the flesh tends to dry out. It is also excellent when served cold with a vinaigrette. Its head can be used to flavor soups.

Cooking

Monkfish is often braised (30 minutes), poached, or grilled (20 minutes). When grilling, baste it frequently to prevent it from drying out.

Nutritional Information

protein	14 g
fat	1.5 g
calories	75
	per 100 g

Sea bass

Disentrarchus labrax, Serranidae

sea bass

Also known as the sea perch (because it resembles the perch), the sea bass is a voracious predator that ferociously pursues shrimp, mollusks, and small fish and often damages fishermen's nets. The sea bass is found in the North Atlantic, from Norway to Morocco, and is very common in the Mediterranean. Although the sea bass is not found off the coast of America, several related species, including the white perch or **American white bass** *(Morone americana),* do frequent American waters. The bass is not restricted to the sea but also thrives in the briny waters of estuaries and bays, as well as in rivers.

The rather elongated, laterally compressed body of the sea bass can grow to be over 3 feet long. It has a long spiny dorsal fin, a large triangular head, prominent eyes, strong teeth, and silvery bluish or greenish dorsal skin.

Preparing

Since the skin of the bass is fragile, the scales must be removed with care. If the bass is to be grilled or poached whole, it should not be scaled. The flesh will retain more moisture and flavor if the skin is left on, and the scales can be easily removed along with the skin once the fish is cooked.

Cooking

Bass can be poached, flambéed, grilled, braised, fried, or stuffed. Bass should be cooked as simply as possible to avoid overpowering its delicate flavor. It is particularly delicious when served cold.

Nutritional Information

	raw
protein	18 g
fat	2 g
calories	96
	per 100 g

The white flesh of the sea bass is delicate and flavorful. It is much sought after because it is lean and firm, contains few bones, and retains its flavor when cooked.

Sturgeon

Acipenser spp., **Acipenseridae**

A long and very slender migratory fish, the sturgeon can weigh more than a ton and grows to a length of over 13 feet. It first came into existence over 100 million years ago, and there are now 4 separate genesus and 25 individual species, including the white sturgeon, the shortnose sturgeon, the sevruga, the beluga, and the sterlet. Certain species are found only in fresh water, while others live in the sea but swim back upriver to spawn. The sturgeon is not only the largest freshwater fish, it also has the longest life span, sometimes living over 150 years. Exclusive to the Northern Hemisphere, it is found, among other places, in the North Atlantic, the North Pacific, the Arctic Ocean, the Caspian Sea, and the Black Sea, as well as in numerous rivers and lakes, including the Delaware River, the Rhine, the Garonne, the Elbe, the Volga, the Danube, and Lake Ladoga. Since the great demand for sturgeon itself is outstripped by the demand for its roe – the essential ingredient in genuine caviar – it has been the object of intensive fishing for many years, which has led to a dangerous reduction in the sturgeon population. To compensate for this overfishing, certain species are now bred on fish farms.

Like the ray and the shark, the sturgeon has a cartilaginous skeleton (other fish have bony skeletons). Its almost perfectly cylindrical body is covered with five rows of bony spines, and its hard skin is scaleless and rough. Its coloring varies in accordance with its species, age, and habitat. The sturgeon has a forked tail, no teeth, and a long pointed snout with four barbels.

Buying

Sturgeon is usually sold frozen or canned, rather than fresh; it can be smoked, salted, or marinated. The flesh contains very few bones and, depending on the species, can be quite moist, firm, and flavorful. Veined with blue when fresh, the white flesh becomes pink and the veins turn brown or yellow when it begins to lose its freshness.

Nutritional Information

	raw
protein	16 g
fat	4 g
calories	106
	per 100 g

Sturgeon is low in fat and rich in niacin, phosphorus, potassium, and vitamin B$_{12}$.

Preparing

Since the flesh is quite firm, it is better to let freshly caught sturgeon sit for 48 hours before it is cooked. Marinating also helps to make it more tender. To skin sturgeon or to make it easier to digest, poach it for few minutes.

Serving Ideas

Often compared to the flesh of land animals, sturgeon can be prepared like meat. Swordfish and tuna recipes are also ideal. Sturgeon is delicious when smoked and served cold. In Russia, the dried spinal marrow (*vesiga*) is used in the filling of fish pies (*koulibiaca*).

white sturgeon

Caviar

beluga caviar

Genuine caviar consists solely of salted sturgeon roe. Although the roe of several other species of fish (salmon, carp, cod, whitefish, herring, pike, tuna) can also be eaten, it cannot be sold as caviar. Salmon roe is sometimes incorrectly referred to as "red caviar." The United States was a major producer of caviar at the end of the 19th century, but overfishing has endangered sturgeon stocks and practically destroyed the caviar industry. Almost all the caviar sold throughout the world now comes from the Black and Caspian seas; Russia and, to a lesser extent, Iran now have a monopoly on the market.

Like champagne, caviar has great prestige and carries great symbolic weight; and like saffron and truffles, it has the "distinction" of being one of the most expensive foods on the market. It will always be rare because it comes from a specific species of fish and can be harvested only during a particular stage of the reproductive cycle.

Sturgeon roe is removed from live female fish before they begin to spawn. Its size, taste, and color depend on the particular variety of sturgeon (beluga, osetra, sevruga). The eggs can be golden, black, brown, dark green, or gray. After being washed in cold water, sifted, and sorted according to size, color, texture, and flavor, they are salted, left to mature, drained, placed in containers, and refrigerated. The salting process determines the quality of the caviar, and the quantity of salt added is strictly monitored.

Buying

Packed in glass or metal containers, caviar is sold in whole grains or, if made from more mature eggs, pressed. Caviar of the highest quality contains less than 5% salt and is referred to as *malassol,* a Russian word meaning "lightly salted." Pressed, or *payusnaya,* caviar contains 10% salt.

Serving Ideas

Caviar should never be cooked and should be kept cold, not frozen. Place it in the warmest part of your refrigerator and remove it about 15 minutes before serving (put the container on ice). Caviar can be eaten plain or with toast, butter, and 1 or 2 drops of lemon juice. Russians like to eat it with blini (small buckwheat pancakes), sour cream, and vodka.

Nutritional Information

protein	2.5 g
fat	1.8 g
calories	25
	per 10 g

Caviar is low in fat and rich in vitamins A and B_{12}, as well as in magnesium, iron, and sodium.

Storing

Unpressed caviar can be kept for several weeks at a temperature of 32° to 45°F (0° to 7°C), and pressed caviar can be stored in the refrigerator for several days.

Sardine

Sardina pilchardus, Clupeidae

A small fish with a slender body, the sardine is found in schools in the temperate waters of seas such as the Atlantic, the Mediterranean, and the Pacific. It was named the sardine because it was particularly abundant off the coast of Sardinia, an island in the Mediterranean. Sardines once traveled in enormous schools. At the end of the 19th century, an English author reported that a single boat had caught 80,000 fish in just one night. However, intensive fishing has led to a considerable decline in sardine stocks.

There are six different species of sardines in the large Clupeidae family, which also includes fish like the herring, the sprat, and the shad. The fish sold as sardines in North America are actually small herring. In several countries, including the United States, Canada, England, Australia, and New Zealand, adult sardines are known as "pilchards." In France, this term refers to herring or sardines canned in oil or tomato sauce. First canned at the beginning of the 19th century, the sardine was the first fish to be preserved in this way. Portugal, France, Spain, and Norway are now among the leading producers of canned sardines.

Usually between 6 and 8 inches long, the sardine is covered with thin scales. Its back can be green or olive green, it sides are golden, and its belly is a silvery color. It has a forked tail and a prominent lower jaw.

Preparing

Before cooking fresh sardines, scale, gut, and clean them, and remove their heads; small, very fresh sardines need only be cleaned.

Cooking

Fresh sardines are often grilled. Avoid cooking methods that increase the fat content of sardines.

Nutritional Information

protein	19 g
fat	5 g
calories	85
	per 100 g

Sardines are rich in phosphorus, vitamin B$_6$, and niacin; the bones are rich in calcium, and the delicious flesh is moderately fatty.

Buying

Sardines are rarely sold fresh because they are extremely perishable. They are sometimes sold smoked or salted, but more often than not their heads are removed and they are gutted, cooked (usually steamed), and canned in oil, tomato sauce, or white wine. Sardines packed an oil have the unique advantage of improving with age.

Serving Ideas

Fresh sardines are often grilled. Avoid cooking them in ways that increase their fat content. Canned sardines are generally eaten "as is," with or without a little lemon juice, often with buttered bread. They can also be marinated or made into a pâté containing lemon juice, a little butter or cream cheese, and spices.

Storing

Turn unopened cans over from time to time to ensure that all parts of the sardines remain moist. Store sardines in the refrigerator once the can has been opened.

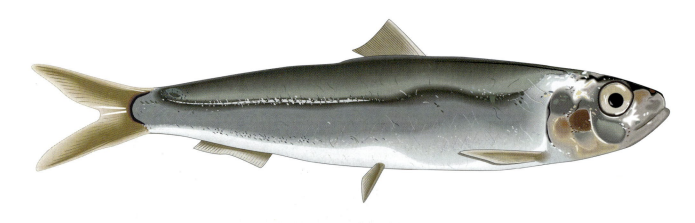

Anchovy

Engraulis encrasicolus, Engraulidae

The anchovy is a small fish with a laterally compressed head and body, protruding eyes, a deeply slit mouth, and a very prominent upper jaw enclosed in a rounded snout. Its dorsal skin can be either light green or blue-green, and the sides of some varieties are decorated with a silver band. Anchovies are between 5 and 8 inches long, and a pound of anchovies consists of 10 fish on average. Normally found in relatively warm seas, the anchovy is very abundant in the Mediterranean but is not uncommon in colder waters, including those of the Atlantic and the Black Sea.

In ancient times, the anchovy was a main ingredient in garum, a liquid condiment not unlike the fish sauces used in Asian cooking, especially the Vietnamese "fish water" known as *nuoc-mam.* Garum was made in processing plants by heavily salting anchovies and various other fish such as sprats and mackerel, along with the entrails of larger fish like tuna. Shrimp, oysters, and sea urchins were sometimes added to the garum, which was left to ferment in the sun for 2 or 3 months in order to produce a dark liquid that was strained and poured into small bottles.

Buying

Since anchovies are extremely perishable, they are rarely sold fresh. Usually bottled or canned in brine, oil, or salt, anchovies are also sold in the form of pastes, creams, butters, and essences.

Serving Ideas

Anchovies have been popular in Mediterranean countries for a very long time and are a key ingredient in several regional dishes *(pissaladière, tapenade, anchoïade,* salads). Anchovy essence is used to flavor soups and sauces, while anchovy butter and paste are used primarily to coat meat and fish in preparation for cooking, and as a spread on brown bread.

Preparing

To remove the salt from anchovies, rinse them gently under cold running water. The flavor of anchovies can be enhanced by soaking them in milk, dry wine, or wine vinegar for 30 to 90 minutes.

Nutritional Information

	canned in oil
protein	29 g
fat	10 g
calories	210
	per 100 g

Anchovies are high in fat and calories.

Herring

Clupea harengus, Clupeidae

One of most common saltwater fish, the herring is also among the most frequently caught fish in the world. Prehistoric engravings depicting its capture confirm that it has been eaten since the earliest days of human history.

Herring swim in dense schools near the surface of the ocean and were once so plentiful that these schools covered large parts of the Atlantic and the Pacific. Although overfishing has greatly reduced herring stocks, the herring fishery remains one of most important components of the fishing industry in many countries.

The herring usually measures between 6 and 12 inches but can grow to be almost 17 inches long, and it can weigh anywhere from 9 to 27 ounces. The shape of the herring varies slightly depending on its species and habitat. Covered with large, soft, easily removable scales, its body ends in a forked tail. The dorsal skin of the herring is blue-green or blue-black, and its sides are a silvery color. Its eggs are unusual in that they are denser than water, and thus sink to the bottom of the sea and become attached to seaweed and rocks.

Buying

Herring is usually sold fresh or frozen, either whole or in fillets, but is also canned, marinated, salted, and smoked.

Preparing

Herring can usually be scaled by merely washing them, and they can be gutted through the gills or by severing the spine just behind the head.

Cooking

Fresh herring is delicious grilled, baked, or fried but is too fragile to be steamed or poached. It should not be overcooked.

Serving Ideas

Herring can be substituted for mackerel in most recipes. Frequently marinated, smoked, or canned, herring is usually sold as one of following products: marinated herring, smoked herring, saur herring, bloaters, bucklings, or kippers. **Marinated herring** is completely deboned and fried, then marinated in oil, wine, tomato sauce, or vinegar. The canned sardines sold in North America are actually marinated herring.

Smoked herring is either hot-smoked (slightly cooked over direct heat) or cold-smoked (smoked for a longer period of time, away from the heat).

Saur herring is named for the reddish brown color the fish takes on when it is cold-smoked for a long period of time. It is salted for 2 to 6 days before it is smoked and may or may not be gutted. Whole saur herring are stored in barrels or wooden crates and are sold individually; saur herring fillets are sold either in packages or in cans. It is also possible to buy marinated saur herring and canned saur herring eggs. This kind of herring will keep for 12 to 15 days.

Bloaters are ungutted, usually whole herring that have been lightly salted (for 1 day at most) and then moderately hot- or cold-smoked. They will keep for about 5 days.

Bucklings are herring that have been pickled in brine for a few hours and then smoked. Particularly popular in Holland and Germany, they are partially cooked during the smoking process and can be eaten without being cooked any further. This kind of herring will keep for about 4 days.

Kippers are large herring that have been beheaded, slit open, deboned, flattened, and lightly cold-smoked. Sold fresh, frozen, canned, or in ready-to-cook bags, they can be eaten «as is» or cooked for a few minutes. They will keep for 4 days.

Saur herring fillets marinated in oil

SERVES 4

¾ lb. (375 g) saur
  herring fillets
Milk
1 onion
1 carrot

1 sprig of thyme
2 bay leaves
12 black peppercorns
1 lemon
Peanut oil

1. Desalt the saur herring for 6 hours in milk diluted with water. Wash them once they have been thoroughly desalted, then pat them dry.

2. Cut the onion into thin slices and separate the slices into rings. Peel the carrot and the lemon; then cut them into thin round slices.

3. Arrange the herring fillets in a glass dish, interspersing them with the onion rings, the carrot and lemon slices, the thyme, the bay leaves, and the peppercorns. Cover them with oil, and allow them to marinate for 2 days before eating them. Serve them with a potato salad.

Nutritional Information

	raw
protein	18 g
fat	9 g
calories	158
	per 100 g

Herring is high in fat and rich in B-complex vitamins, phosphorus, and potassium. Its white flesh is fatty and flavorful, and the many bones it contains are easy to remove.

fresh herring

Saltwater Fish

399

smoked herring

Mackerel

Scomber spp., Scombridae

A very beautiful fish with a slender body, the mackerel is found in most seas, including the Pacific, the Atlantic, and the Mediterranean. It is part of the Scombridae family, whose name is derived from the Greek word for mackerel, *skombros*. During the summer, mackerel can be found off the coasts of Canada and the United States, but they migrate to warmer waters in the fall. Certain species of mackerel (such as the common mackerel) have no swim bladder and have to swim constantly to avoid sinking. Capable of moving through the water with great speed, mackerel sometimes travel in immense schools several miles wide, and they often swim alongside schools of herring.

The mackerel is in the same family as the tuna and the kingfish. The most prevalent species of mackerel include the common mackerel and the Spanish mackerel.

The **common mackerel** *(Scomber scombrus)* usually measures between 12 and 20 inches and weighs between 1 and 2 pounds, but it can grow to be almost 2 feet long and weigh over 4 pounds. Its spindle-shaped body is covered with steel-blue dorsal skin, pearly ventral skin, and very thin scales (longer on the trunk and shorter toward the ends) that make the surface of the fish rather smooth. The top of its back is adorned with 23 to 33 dark wavy bands similar to the stripes of a tiger. Its two dorsal fins are farther apart than those of other members of the mackerel family, and it has a thin forked tail. The common mackerel is the species most frequently found in North America; a closely related species, the *Scomber australasicus,* inhabits the warm waters of the Pacific between Japan and Australia.

Capable of growing to a maximum length of 20 inches, the **Spanish mackerel** *(Scomber japonicus)* resembles the blue mackerel but has larger eyes and less visible stripes, as well as dark blotches on its ventral skin. It is found in the eastern Atlantic, the Mediterranean, the Black Sea, and the Pacific.

The off-white flesh of the mackerel is flavorful and rather fatty. Like tuna, it is enclosed in a relatively dark outer layer that enhances the flavor but makes the fish more difficult to digest. Removing this layer and marinating the remaining flesh, or brushing it with a marinade, makes mackerel easier to digest.

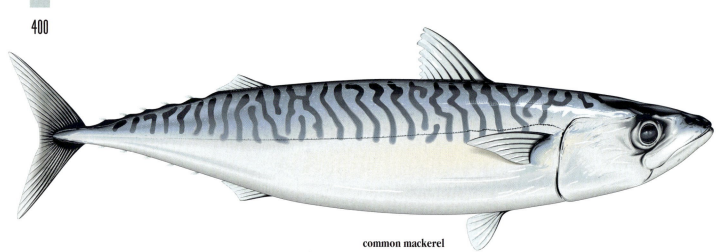

common mackerel

Buying

 Mackerel is sold whole or in fillets, either fresh or frozen. It is also canned in water, sauce, white wine, or oil. Like herring, mackerel is sometimes salted or smoked, then sold as bucklings or bloaters.

When buying fresh mackerel, look for fish that are firm and stiff (since they start to become limp as little as 24 hours after being caught, stiffness is sign of freshness); they should also have a metallic sheen, bright eyes, and very white rounded bellies (fish whose bellies have burst open are inedible).

Preparing

When filleting mackerel, locate the bones between the two sides of the fish and carefully separate the flesh from the bones with a knife.

Mackerel with Gooseberries

4 mackerel, each weighing ½ lb. (250 g)
2 cloves garlic
1 onion
⅓ cup (80 ml) fresh parsley leaves

½ lb. (250 g) gooseberries
Salt
2 tsp. ground pepper
2 tsp. ground nutmeg
1 lemon sliced

1. Wash the gutted mackerel and pat them dry.

2. Mince the garlic, onion, and parsley very finely. Stuff each of the fish with this mixture.

3. Butter the inside of a saucepan or ovenproof dish large enough to hold the fish in a single layer. Place the mackerel in the saucepan, arranging them head to tail.

4. Using a spoon, crush the gooseberries without completely mashing them. Add a glass of water (¾ cup) to the berries, and pour this mixture over the fish. Sprinkle on the salt, pepper, and nutmeg. Place a slice of lemon on top of each of the fish. Cover the saucepan with oiled aluminum foil, and cook on top of the stove over low heat for 30 minutes, or bake in the oven for 25 minutes at 375°F (190°C), until the mackerel are completely done.

Serving Ideas

 Mackerel should be eaten shortly after it is purchased because its flesh spoils very quickly; slight exposure to heat is enough to make the flesh turn bitter and begin to spoil. When fishing for mackerel, refrigerate them as soon as possible after they are caught.

Mackerel can be cooked in any number of ways, but it is preferable to avoid methods that increase its fat content. Traditionally served with gooseberry sauce, mackerel can be eaten hot or cold and is delicious when smoked or marinated. It is often added to ceviche, but it is important to ensure that it contains no parasites if it is to be eaten raw. Mackerel can replace canned tuna, herring, or shad in most recipes.

Cooking

It is best when baked, grilled, cooked in aluminum foil, or poached in court bouillon.

Storing

 Mackerel loses much of its flavor when frozen.

Nutritional Information

	raw
protein	19 g
fat	14 g
calories	205
	per 100 g

Sea bream

Chrysophrys aurata, Sparidae

Particularly abundant in Europe, Australia, and New Zealand, the sea bream is a coastal fish that is commonly found in the tropical waters of the Atlantic and the Mediterranean.

The sea bream has an oval body with flat sides that appears to be elongated although it is actually quite thickset. It is usually between 8 and 14 inches long, and weighs between 10 ounces and 7 pounds. The spines on its fins are very hard, and its pinkish or reddish skin is covered with small blue spots and numerous large scales. The sea bream has a large head, big eyes, a hooked forehead, a small mouth, and strong teeth that it uses to crush shellfish.

Buying

 The sea bream is usually sold fresh and gutted, or as frozen fillets.

Nutritional Information

protein	16 g
fat	0.5 g
calories	73
	per 100 g

The lean white flesh of the sea bream is very fine and flavorful.

Preparing

The scales of the sea bream are difficult to remove because they are large, numerous, and sticky (fish merchants often leave much of the work to the consumer). Ideally, the sea bream should be scaled shortly after it is caught. To avoid scaling fillets, simply lift them up and pull off the easily removable thick skin. The flesh contains many bones, but these can be removed once the fish has been skinned and cut into fillets. Just locate the bones with your fingers and try to remove them without damaging the flesh.

Serving Ideas

This fish can be prepared in any number of ways, but the simplest methods are best. It is delicious in sashimi and ceviche, and when smoked. Its eggs are excellent.

Conger

Conger spp., Congridae

The conger is shaped like a large snake and has very powerful teeth. It is often confused with eels belonging to the Anguillidae family, but unlike those fish the conger has a deeply slit mouth, relatively large oval (rather than round) eyes, a protruding upper jaw, and smooth scaleless skin. Its color varies in accordance with its habitat but is always quite even.

The conger can grow to be 10 feet long and can weigh over 100 pounds. The females are generally larger than the males. Found in most oceans, including the Atlantic, the Pacific, and the Mediterranean, the conger is particularly common in Chilean and European coastal waters. There are nine species of congers in North America, eight of which are found in the Atlantic. The black conger, which lives among rocks, often in the company of lobsters, is the most sought-after species.

Buying

 Conger is sold whole (after it has been gutted and the head has been removed), in sections, or in slices. The firm white flesh contains few bones, except near the tail. The flavor varies according to the species and the size of the fish; the smaller the fish, the blander its taste.

Serving Ideas

Conger is a common ingredient in bouillabaisse and matelote. It can be prepared in any number of ways-especially the flesh between the middle of the body and the head, which contains fewer bones than the flesh near the tail.

Nutritional Information

protein	20 g
fat	3 g
calories	100
	per 100 g

Low in fat, conger is rich in potassium and magnesium.

Swordfish

Xiphias gladius, Xiphiidae

The swordfish is named for its unusually shaped upper jaw, which is very long and slender. Found in most oceans, it is particularly common on both sides of the Atlantic, as well as in the North Sea, the Baltic Sea, and the Mediterranean. Since it likes to frolic in the sunshine, its tail and fins can often be seen above the surface of the water. Capable of moving through the water at 60 miles an hour, the adult swordfish is renowned for the speed and power of its muscular, scaleless body.

The swordfish has a large toothless mouth, and its main dorsal fin is very long and quite pointed. Its dorsal skin can be blue, blue-gray, or brown, and its ventral skin can be black, white, or silver. The swordfish usually measures between 6 and 10 feet and weighs between 200 and 500 pounds, but it can be as long as 15 feet and weigh over 1,100 pounds.

Buying

Swordfish is cut into steaks and sold fresh, but it can also be smoked, frozen, or canned. The tail and fins are edible.

Serving Ideas

Fresh swordfish is easier to digest if it is poached for 10 to 15 minutes before being cooked. It is prepared like other fish with firm flesh, such as halibut, sturgeon, and tuna.

Cooking

Swordfish is delicious grilled, braised, or fried, whether it has been marinated or not. Grill steaks or fillets for 5 to 7 minutes per side, braise them for 20 to 30 minutes, or sauté them for 4 to 6 minutes per side. Swordfish will dry out if it is overcooked.

Nutritional Information

	raw
protein	20 g
fat	4 g
calories	121
	per 100 g

Swordfish is rich in vitamin B_{12}, niacin, potassium, and phosphorus. The streaked white flesh is much sought after because it is very firm and flavorful.

Saltwater Fish

403

Gurnard

Trigla spp., **Triglidae**

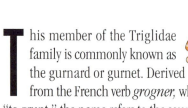

red gurnard

This member of the Triglidae family is commonly known as the gurnard or gurnet. Derived from the French verb *grogner,* which means "to grunt," the name refers to the sound produced by the swim bladder when the fish is removed from the water. The gurnard is most common in the Atlantic, the Mediterranean, and the Pacific, especially off the coasts of Australia, New Zealand, Japan, and South Africa.

A singularly unattractive fish, the gurnard has large oblique eyes and a large head covered with bony plates. Its elongated body, which is often red or pink, is covered with small rough scales and numerous spiny fins that resemble the wings of a bird. The gurnard uses its pectoral fin to move along the seabed, disturbing the sand and thus simultaneously rooting out food and providing itself with cover. Fishermen often throw the gurnard back, probably because of its unusual shape or because it contains very little flesh for a fish of its size. Its somewhat flaky pinkish flesh is delicious, however. There are several different species, including the gray gurnard, the red gurnard, and the sea robin.

The **gray gurnard** *(Eutrigla gurnardus)* can be up to 20 inches long. Its grayish dorsal skin is tinged with red and covered with numerous little white spots. Its habitat extends from the coasts of Iceland and Norway to the Mediterranean. It has firm, flavorful flesh.

The **red gurnard** *(Aspitrigla cuculus)* is usually about 12 inches long and, as its name suggests, is red in color. It is most common in the Mediterranean, the Atlantic, and the Pacific. Since it contains very little flesh, it is often used to make soup.

The **sea robin** *(Prionotus carolinus)* can grow to be 15 inches long and can weigh as much 14 ounces. Found off the Atlantic coast of North America, it has firm, flavorful, lean flesh.

Preparing

Remove the spiny fins to prevent injuries. Leave the fish whole, or cut it into fillets or sections. The skin is easy to remove.

Nutritional Information

	raw
protein	17 g
fat	3 g
calories	100
	per 100 g

Gurnard is rich in potassium and calcium.

Serving Ideas

The gurnard is often added to bouillabaisse and matelote. It is delicious when baked, poached, fried, or smoked.

Cooking

Gurnard tends to dry out if it is cooked at extremely high temperatures. When grilling or baking gurnard with the skin on, brush it generously with oil or a marinade to protect the fragile skin.

Lamprey

Petromyzon spp., Petromyzontidae

Like the eel, the conger, and the moray, the lamprey resembles a snake. It is one of the few surviving cyclostome vertebrates – animals with no lower jaw, round sucker-like mouths, and tongues covered with corneous pointed teeth. Most lampreys are parasites that live by attaching themselves to other fish (including salmon, cod, and carp) and feeding on their flesh and blood. They live in the sea but return to fresh water to reproduce. Lamprey is particularly popular in Europe and among the Native Americans on the Pacific Coast.

The lamprey has scaleless, smooth, viscous skin, the color of which changes from one stage of sexual development to another. Covered with spots, it is often bluish gray, brownish gray, or olive green. The lamprey is between 6 and 40 inches long, and has seven pairs of hole-shaped bronchi just behind its head.

There are 8 different lamprey genuses and approximately 30 individual species.

One of the species commonly found on both sides of the Atlantic is known as the **sea lamprey** *(P. marinus),* which measures between 20 and 36 inches.

The **river lamprey** *(Lampetra fluviatilis)* is found along European coasts, as far north as the cold waters of Siberia. A relatively small species, it is only 12 to 18 inches long.

The **Pacific lamprey** *(Entosphenus tridentatus)* is common in American coastal waters.

Serving Ideas

Fatty and boneless, the flesh of the lamprey is more delicate than that of the eel, but it is prepared in the same way. The sea lamprey has finer flesh than the river lamprey, and the flesh of male fish is more flavorful than that of females.

Lamprey *à la bordelaise,* which is cooked in red wine, is a famous French gourmet recipe.

Cooking

Lamprey is often grilled or cooked in fish stews (matelote) or pies.

Nutritional Information

	raw
protein	21 g
fat	18 g
calories	252
	per 100 g

Redfish

Sebastes spp., Scorpaenidae

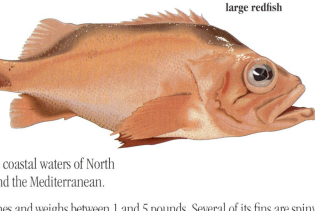

A member of the Scorpaenidae family, which includes approximately 60 genuses and 310 species, the redfish (or ocean perch) thrives in the depths of northern seas and in the shallow waters of southern seas. Over 100 species of redfish are found in the Pacific coastal waters of North America, and several species inhabit the Atlantic and the Mediterranean.

The redfish usually measures between 8 and 22 inches and weighs between 1 and 5 pounds. Several of its fins are spiny, and its skin is covered with irregularly shaped scales that are often a red, pink, or orange color. The redfish has a large mouth and a prominent lower jaw. A bony growth and large bulging eyes protrude from its decidedly unattractive head. Its firm flaky flesh is sometimes pinkish and always very flavorful. The large redfish, the large-scaled scorpion fish, and the small-scaled scorpion fish are among the most common members of the Scorpaenidae family.

The **large redfish** *(Sebastes marinus)* usually measures between 14 and 22 inches but can grow to be over 3 feet long. Its body is bright red with a dark spot on each of the operculums (the bony flaps covering its gill slits). Also known as the Norway haddock, it is found on both sides of the North Atlantic.

The **large-scaled scorpion fish** *(Scorpaena scrofa)* can grow to be as long as 20 inches but rarely measures more than 12 inches. Its dorsal skin is usually orangey red or light pink with dark marbling. Found in the deep waters of the Mediterranean and the eastern Atlantic, it known as the scorpion because its dorsal fin is studded with venomous spines. It is added to fish stews such as bouillabaisse and matelote, unless it contains enough flesh to be cooked in more elaborate ways.

The **small-scaled scorpion fish** *(Scorpaena porcus)* is a small fish that can grow to be 10 inches long but usually measures closer to 6 inches. Found in the shallow waters of the Mediterranean, it is also known as the brown scorpion fish because it has brown spots on its fins and brownish dorsal skin. It is cooked in bouillabaisse.

Buying

Redfish is sold fresh or frozen, either whole or in fillets.

Preparing

Remove its spiny fins as soon as it is possible do so.

Nutritional Information

	raw
protein	19 g
fat	2 g
calories	94
	per 100 g

Redfish and scorpion fish are low in fat.

Serving Ideas

These fish are equally good when eaten raw, cooked, smoked, or cold. In the South of France, the scorpion fish is considered to be an essential ingredient in bouillabaisse.

Cooking

These fish can be cooked in any number of ways, either whole or in fillets. The flesh tends to fall apart if the skin is removed before they are poached in court bouillon or grilled.

Goatfish

Mullus spp., **Mullidae**

The goatfish, or red mullet, thrives in the warm shallow waters of the Pacific, the Mediterranean, the Atlantic, and the Indian Ocean. It has big eyes on top of its large head, a spiny front dorsal fin, and a forked tail. It was named for the two long goatlike barbels that hang from its lower jaw, which enhance its senses of touch and taste. Covered with large scales, the skin of the goatfish varies in color but is often reddish or pinkish. Since the skin loses its sheen very quickly, it is invaluable when it comes to assessing the freshness of the fish.

An infrequent visitor to colder seas, this perchlike fish is rarely found in northern coastal waters. The most common species found in the Mediterranean include the surmullet, the red goatfish, and the striped goatfish.

The **surmullet** *(Mullus surmuletus)* usually measures between 8 and 10 inches. It has several rays on its front dorsal fin and two scales under its eyes. Its reddish skin is adorned with several yellow stripes and one brown stripe that extends from its eyes to its tail.

The **red goatfish** resembles the surmullet, but its dorsal stripe is yellow, and its front dorsal fin has an orange stripe at its base and a yellow stripe a little higher up.

The **striped goatfish** *(Mullus barbatus)* is usually between 4 and 8 inches long. It has three scales under its eyes, and its skin is golden.

Serving Ideas

 Although goatfish contains many bones, it has an extremely delicate flavor and is much sought after, especially in the South of France. Prepare it simply so as not to mask its flavor. Small goatfish can be cooked whole or gutted, but the very flavorful liver should never be discarded.

Preparing

Goatfish should be scaled very carefully because their skin is fragile.

Nutritional Information

	raw
protein	20 g
fat	2 g
calories	88
	per 100 g

Lean and firm, the flesh of the goatfish contains many small bones.

Saltwater Fish

407

surmullet

Salmon

Oncorhynchus spp. and *Salmo salar,* Salmonidae

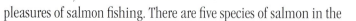

The salmon is a magnificent fish that has been greatly appreciated since ancient times, both for its flesh and for the pleasures of salmon fishing. There are five species of salmon in the Pacific (*Oncorhynchus* spp.) and one in the Atlantic *(Salmo salar).* A sixth variety is found only in fresh water (the ouananiche or landlocked salmon *Salmo salar ouananiche).*

Although once very plentiful, salmon is now much rarer due to overfishing, pollution, and the construction of dams. The Atlantic salmon was the first species to be threatened with extinction; it has survived thanks to salmon farms and the strict management of remaining stocks.

The salmon is born in fresh water, spends 1 to 4 years in the sea, depending on the rate at which it matures, and returns to its place of birth to spawn. Many salmon travel over 900 miles to get back to their spawning ground. The appearance of Pacific salmon changes considerably during the spawning season, especially among males; their snouts become misshapen, their jaws lengthen, and their teeth protrude. The females of certain species lay as many as 13,000 eggs, and the sires die after fulfilling their reproductive role. The salmon is distinguished from the trout, a closely related species, by its anal fin, which has 12 to 19 rays. The shape of its elongated, somewhat compressed body varies slightly from one species to another. Its skin is covered with smooth scales and is often dotted with markings that vary from species to species. The color of the skin depends on the species and on the time of year.

The Pacific salmon species include the Chinook salmon, the sockeye salmon, the coho salmon, the pink salmon, and the chum salmon.

The **Chinook salmon** or **king salmon** (*Oncorhynchus tshawytscha*) usually measures between 34 to 36 inches and weighs between 30 and 40 pounds. Its dorsal skin is olive green, its sides and belly are silvery, and its lower gums are black. Its back, the top of its head, and its sides are adorned with black spots. The color of its flesh ranges from light pink to dark orange. Sold fresh, frozen, or smoked, it is rarely canned. Smoked Chinook salmon is very much sought after.

The **sockeye salmon** or **red salmon** (*Oncorhynchus nerka*) is the second most prized species, after the Chinook salmon. It usually measures between 24 and 28 inches and weighs between 6 and 10 pounds. Its dorsal skin is bluish green, and its sides and belly are silvery. Its firm, very flavorful flesh is flat red in color and remains quite red even when canned. Rather thin, slender fish of uniform length, sockeye salmon are particularly well suited for canning. In fact, sockeye salmon is almost always canned, but it is also available smoked or salted.

The **coho salmon** or **silver salmon** (*Oncorhynchus kisutch*) usually measures between 18 and 24 inches and weighs between 4½ and 10 pounds. Its metallic-blue dorsal skin is adorned with small black spots, and its sides and belly are silvery. The coho salmon is the third most commercially important species. Its orange-red flesh is slightly inferior to that of the Chinook and the sockeye, but it too breaks into large pieces. It is lighter in color than the flesh of sockeye salmon. Frequently canned, coho salmon is also sold fresh, frozen, smoked, or lightly pickled.

The **pink salmon** (*Oncorhynchus gorbuscha)* is the smallest of the Pacific salmon. It matures very quickly (in 2 years). It usually measures between 17 and 19 inches and weighs between 3 and 5 pounds. Its bluish green dorsal skin is adorned with large black spots, and its sides are silvery. The pink salmon has long been regarded as an inferior species (like the chum) because its pinkish flesh is rather soft and breaks into small pieces. It is usually canned, but it is also sold fresh, smoked, or frozen.

salmon steak

Salmon

The **chum salmon** *(Oncorhynchus keta)* usually measures about 25 inches and weighs between 11 and 13 pounds. Its dorsal skin is metallic blue, and its sides and belly are silvery. Light crimson stripes adorn its sides. The chum has the least attractive and least flavorful flesh of any salmon. Only slightly pink, it is spongy, soft, and breaks into small pieces; however, it is less fatty than other kinds of salmon. Although best when fresh, it is also canned, frozen, dry-salted, and smoked. It is the least expensive kind of salmon.

The **Atlantic salmon** *(Salmo salar)* is the only salmon found in the Atlantic. It is quite different from the Pacific salmon and does not die after it spawns; in fact, it can reproduce two, three, or four times. The Atlantic salmon is renowned for its fighting spirit and for its pink, deliciously fragrant flesh. Its body is similar to that of other salmonid fish, and the color of its skin changes over time. Its dorsal skin can be brown, green, or blue, and its sides and belly are silvery. When caught, Atlantic salmon measure between 32 and 34 inches and weigh an average of 10 pounds. They are sold fresh, frozen, or smoked. Atlantic salmon should be prepared as simply as possible so as not to mask its flavor.

The **ouananiche** or **landlocked salmon** *(Salmo salar ouananiche)* is a delicious small freshwater salmon. It was trapped inland after the Ice Age because it was unable to make it back to the sea after the waters retreated. Even though the sea is readily accessible from many of the rivers the ouananiche now frequents, it has chosen to remain in fresh water. It is found on the east coast of North America, as well as in Scandinavia. *Ouananiche* means "little lost one" in Montagnais, the language of a Quebec native tribe. This fish is a species in its own right, not only because of its habitat but also because of certain physical modifications that set it apart from other salmon. It is shorter than most salmon (between 8 and 24 inches) and rarely weighs more than 13 pounds. Its comparatively long, powerful fins and its large, strong tail developed in response to the swift-running waters of its environment. It also has relatively large teeth and eyes. Its black dorsal skin is adorned with tightly spaced, well-defined spots, its sides are bluish gray, and its belly is silvery. Ouananiche can be prepared like salmon or trout.

Pacific salmon

Atlantic salmon

Saltwater Fish

409

smoked salmon

Buying

Salmon is sold fresh, frozen, smoked, salted, dried, and canned. Salmon roe is often packaged in glass jars. Fresh and frozen salmon can be purchased whole or as steaks, pieces, segments, or fillets. Smoked salmon is often sealed in plastic or frozen. It is best to buy salmon in a fish store where the stock turns over quickly to ensure that it is as fresh as possible. Avoid smoked salmon that has dry or brown edges or that is shiny or leaking moisture, because it is probably less than fresh. Dark salmon tends to be very salty.

Preparing

Salmon should be scaled and gutted before it is cooked. It does not have to washed, just wiped.

Cooking

Salmon can be cooked in any number of ways. It is often cut into steaks before being cooked. It is equally good when served hot or cold.

Storing

Salmon spoils quickly because the flesh is fatty. It should not be refrigerated for any longer than 2 or 3 days.

Nutritional Information

The Chinook is the fattiest salmon. The sockeye salmon, the Atlantic salmon, and the coho salmon are moderately fatty. Raw pink salmon and chum salmon are lean.

Serving Ideas

The flesh behind the head has a more delicate flavor than the flesh near the tail. Smoked salmon (also called lox) is often served with capers and thinly sliced sweet onions. It is added as a special finishing touch to foods such as sandwiches, salads, omelets, pasta dishes, mousses, and quiches. Avoid recipes that mask its unique flavor.

Canned salmon is cooked, then canned in its own juices. The bones and vertebrae are often included, but they are perfectly edible because they crumble easily; they are a good source of calcium. Canned salmon can be used in a wide variety of ways. It is added to sandwiches, salads, sauces, omelets, quiches, mousses, soufflés, pâtés, and crêpes. It is also sold in the form of a paste, which is used primarily to make sandwiches and canapés.

Salmon roe is delicious. It is sometimes referred to as "red caviar," but genuine caviar contains only sturgeon roe.

Cold Salmon in Aspic

SERVES 4

One 2-lb. (1-kg) piece of fresh salmon
8 cups (2 l) court bouillon

1 package Madeira aspic jelly
2 tablespoons Madeira
2 sprigs fresh parsley, chopped

1. Poach the salmon in the court bouillon for about 10 minutes; then let it cool in the liquid.

2. Drain the salmon and carefully remove the skin. Refrigerate the salmon on a serving plate.

3. Prepare the aspic and add the Madeira. Allow it to cool before using it.

4. Pour a thin layer of aspic over the cold salmon, sprinkle on some chopped parsley, and allow the aspic to set. Repeat. Then dress the salmon with a final layer of aspic and put it back in the refrigerator.

5. Pour the remaining aspic into a large dish and allow it to set.

6. Once the aspic has set, cut it into small cubes and place them around the salmon as a garnish.

Serve the salmon with mayonnaise or *gribiche* (a mayonnaise-like sauce containing hard-boiled eggs, capers, and herbs).

	Chinook salmon	*sockeye salmon*	*coho salmon*	*pink salmon*	*chum*	*Atlantic salmon*
protein	20 g	21 g	22 g	20 g	20 g	20 g
fat	10 g	9 g	6 g	3 g	4 g	6 g
calories	180	168	146	116	120	142

per 100 g

John Dory

Zeus faber, **Zeidae**

The John Dory is a strange-looking fish with a very compressed oval body. Found in the temperate seas of both hemispheres, it is especially common in the Atlantic between Norway and South Africa, and in the Pacific off the coasts of Japan, Australia, and New Zealand, as well as in the Mediterranean and the Indian Ocean. The French are said to have named this fish the *Saint-Pierre* because it has a rounded spot on each side of its body. Legend has it that these marks were left by the thumb and index finger of St. Peter, who was on the verge of strangling the fish but let it go when it started to moan loudly (it does in fact moan when removed from the water).

Although the John Dory can grow to be over 2 feet long, it usually measures between 8 and 20 inches and weighs between 28 and 32 ounces. Its eyes are positioned near the top of its enormous head, and its prominent jaw supports a large mouth. The name "dory" is derived from the French word *doré,* meaning "gilded" or "golden," and refers to the glints of gold that adorn the sides of the fish. The white flesh of the John Dory is firm and flavorful.

Serving Ideas

After gutting and trimming a John Dory, prepare it simply so as not to mask the delicate flavor of its flesh. It is particularly good when used in sole and turbot recipes. Its gelatinous bones create an appetizing aroma.

Storing

John Dory should not be frozen for longer than 3 months.

Nutritional Information

	raw
protein	18 g
fat	1 g
calories	80
	per 100 g

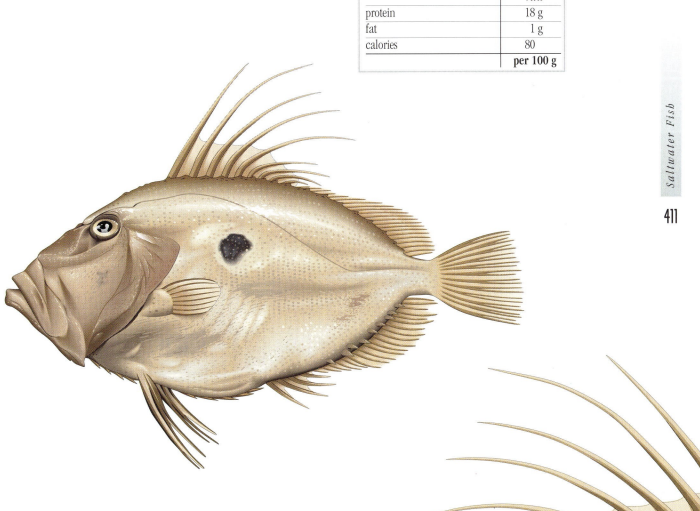

Saltwater Fish

411

Cod

Gadus spp., Gadidae

The cod lives in the cold, deep waters of the North Atlantic *(Gadus morhua)* and the North Pacific *(Gadus macrocephalus)*. Cod swim in large schools, especially during the reproductive season. The female cod is very prolific, laying approximately 5 million floating eggs at a time. The cod has always been among the most intensively fished species in the world. During the Middle Ages, it was one of the most commercially important fish in Europe. Since it could be smoked, dried, or salted, it was easy to transport and store, and could thus be made available to a great many people. The cod was once very abundant in the coastal waters of the United States and Canada – a fact reflected in place names such as Cape Cod, Massachusetts. It has been estimated that approximately 400 million Atlantic cod were fished on an annual basis at the height of the cod fishery. Intensive fishing in the North Atlantic over the past 20 years has greatly reduced cod stocks.

The cod has a large head and a deeply slit mouth; a thin, elongated barbel hangs from its lower jaw. It usually weighs between 4 and 9 pounds and measures between 16 and 32 inches. Its heavy, fleshy body is covered with small scales, and its skin color varies greatly from one habitat to another. A relatively pale lateral line runs the length of its body from head to tail. The French make a clear distinction between salted or dried cod *(morue)* and fresh or frozen cod *(cabillaud)*.

The large Gadidae family comprises approximately 60 different species. In addition to the cod, these include the haddock, the yellow pollock, the black pollock, the ling, the monkfish, the whiting, the hake, the silver hake, the three-bearded rockling, the forkbeard, the tomcod, and the pout. Most of these fish have similar flesh. The most common species include the haddock, the silver hake, the whiting, the black pollock, and the tomcod.

The **haddock** *(Melanogrammus aeglefinus)* resembles a small cod. It measures between 15 and 25 inches and weighs between 2 and 5 pounds. It has a slightly prominent upper jaw and a small mouth; a very short barbel hangs from its lower jaw. Its back and sides are purplish gray; each of its sides is adorned with a black lateral line, and there is a large black spot between this line and the pectoral fin. The haddock is found on both sides of the North Atlantic; in France, the English word "haddock" refers specifically to smoked haddock. Milder than cod, the white flesh of the haddock is lean and flavorful.

haddock

black pollock

The **hake** (*Merluccius* spp.) is a voracious fish that is found at various depths, from the shallowest of waters to those over 3,250 feet deep. The term "hake" refers to several different species, including the common hake *(Merluccius merluccius),* which is found in Atlantic coastal waters from Norway to Portugal and is particularly abundant off the Iberian coast. Its elongated body is a slate-gray color, its prominent lower jaw is free of barbels, and the inside of its mouth is blackish gray. The hake usually measures between 12 and 28 inches, but it can grow to almost 4 feet. It has flavorful flesh.

The **silver hake** *(Merluccius bilinearis)* inhabits the Atlantic coastal waters of North America from Newfoundland to South Carolina. When fully grown, the silver hake usually measures between 9 and 14 inches and weighs about 28 ounces. Its skin is flecked with silver, and its tender, flaky flesh is very flavorful.

The **whiting** *(Merlangius merlangus)* usually measures between 12 and 16 inches but can grow to be 28 inches long. Its dorsal skin can be yellowish brown, dark blue, or green. The whiting is found in the Mediterranean, the Black Sea, and the Baltic. Its very flavorful flesh crumbles easily.

The **black pollock** *(Pollachius virens),* which is commonly referred to as the "saithe" in Britain, usually measures from 20 to 35 inches and weighs from 2 to 15 pounds, but it can grow to be almost 5 feet long. Its olive-green dorsal skin can be almost black, which accounts for its name. Found on both sides of the Atlantic, it is particularly popular in Europe – especially in England, where it is known by over 50 different names, many of which are used to distinguish between fish of different sizes. Its firm white flesh can be rather coarse.

The **tomcod** *(Microgadus tomcod)* is a very small fish, usually measuring between 8 and 12 inches and rarely exceeding 14 inches. Found in both salt water and briny water, it inhabits the western Atlantic coasts from Labrador to Virginia and returns to rivers to spawn. A frequent visitor to the St. Lawrence River, it is sometimes referred to as the "frostfish" in Canada. Its long, filament-like pelvic fins and its rounded tail make it very easy to identify. The front of its body is cylindrical, but the rear portion is laterally compressed; it has three fins on its back and two on its belly. Its lean white flesh is much sought after.

whiting

Atlantic cod

Cod

Preparing

To remove the salt from salt cod, place the fish in a colander skin-side up (if the fish has not been skinned) to prevent the salt from accumulating between the flesh and the skin. Submerge the colander in a large container of water, and allow the salt to settle on the bottom of the container.

Another option is to put the container in the sink under a thin stream of water, and allow the salt to be flushed out as the water overflows. Dried salt cod has to be soaked for 8 to 12 hours before it can be cooked.

Serving Ideas

Cod is also canned, dried in the open air (stockfish), or salted (kippers). The roe of the cod is eaten fresh, smoked, or salted. Its tongue and liver are also edible. More fragile than the cod, the haddock is usually smoked or salted. The tomcod is often fried.

Cooking

Cod can be cooked in any number of ways. When poaching cod, do not to allow it to boil; simmer it for 8 minutes in court bouillon, or add it to liquid that has already come to a boil and immediately remove the pan from the heat, cover it, and set it aside for 15 minutes. Cod is particularly delicious in sauces.

Cod tongues are frequently poached before being prepared (in a sauce, floured, etc.). Place them in cold liquid and remove them as soon as it begins to boil.

414

Saltwater Fish

Nutritional Information

	cod	haddock	hake	whiting	black pollock	tomcod
protein	18 g	19 g	17 g	19 g	17 g	17 g
fat	0.7 g	0.7 g	0.9 g	1.3 g	1 g	0.4 g
calories	82	87	76	91	92	77

per 100 g

The oil extracted from cod livers is an important source of vitamin D. The flaky, milky-white flesh is lean, delicate, and firm, although its firmness depends on the freshness and size of the cod (the smaller the cod, the more tender the flesh).

Cod à la Portugaise

SERVES 4

1½ lb. (750 g) salt-cod fillets
2 onions
½ lb. (250 g) fresh tomatoes
2 tbsp. fresh parsley
2 cloves garlic
½ cup (125 ml) olive oil
2 tbsp. tomato paste
Salt and ground pepper
12 black olives
2 hard-boiled eggs

1. Preheat the oven to 375°F (190°C).

2. Desalt the fillets in cold water overnight. The next day, strain and rinse the cod to remove the remaining salt. Bring a pan of water to a boil, add the cod, and let it simmer for 15 minutes.

3. Peel and chop the onions. Peel and halve the tomatoes. Chop the parsley and the garlic.

4. Heat ¼ cup of the olive oil in a skillet. Cook the onions for about 5 minutes without letting them brown. Add the tomatoes, the tomato paste, the garlic, and the salt and pepper. Stir the mixture carefully for a few minutes. Remove it from the heat.

5. Pour the onion and tomato mixture into an ovenproof dish. Dry the cod fillets thoroughly, cut them into large pieces, and arrange them on top of the onions and tomatoes. Add the rest of the oil, and place the dish in the middle of the oven. Cook the cod for 30 minutes or until all the ingredients are very hot, turning it after 15 minutes to ensure that it is thoroughly coated with the sauce and remains tender. Garnish the dish with the black olives and slices of the hard-boiled eggs. Sprinkle on the chopped parsley.

Smelt

Osmerus spp., Osmeridae

A small thin fish with an elongated silvery body, the smelt inhabits the temperate or cold waters of seas and lakes. It is 6 to 14 inches long, and its slightly prominent lower jaw frames a large mouth filled with small or well-developed teeth. Its thin translucent skin, which is covered with thin scales, varies in color and is decorated with a lateral silver stripe.

Like trout and salmon, smelt return to fresh water to spawn, and some species live exclusively in fresh water. During the spawning season, smelt travel in such dense schools that they can be fished by the basketful; they prefer to spawn on beaches, which they invade in huge numbers at night. The smelt family consists of six genuses and ten species.

The **American smelt** *(Osmerus mordax)* is found off the Atlantic coasts of the United States and Canada from Labrador to Virginia, as well as in several lakes. It usually measures between 7 and 8 inches, but it can grow to be over a foot long. Its green dorsal skin is translucent, and a silvery stripe decorates its relatively pale sides.

The **European smelt** *(Osmerus eperlanus),* which is found in the Atlantic, the North Sea, and the Baltic Sea, is particularly popular in northern France. It can grow to be 14 inches long but usually measures about 8 inches. Its dorsal skin is a pale olive-green color, and each of its sides is adorned with a silvery stripe.

The **capelin** *(Mallotus villosus),* which is part of the smelt family, can grow to be over 9 inches long and is different from the Mediterranean capelin or the poor cod *(Trisopterus minutus capelanus),* which belongs to the Gadidae family. Its dorsal skin is an olive- or bottle-green color, its ventral skin is white, and its sides are silvery.

Buying

Smelt is sold fresh, frozen, lightly smoked, salted, or dried. Capelin is less common because it is fed to cod and other commercially available fish.

Preparing

Smelt is frequently just gutted and fried, but it is often marinated for about 10 minutes in a mixture of lemon juice, salt, and pepper, or dipped in milk and flour, before it is cooked.

Cooking

Smelt can be grilled or fried, and the largest of them can be cooked in more elaborate ways.

Serving Ideas

All parts of the smelt can be eaten, including the head, the flesh, the bones, the tail, the eggs, and the gonads.

Nutritional Information

	raw
protein	18 g
fat	2 g
calories	98
	per 100 g

Fine, flavorful, and quite fatty, the white flesh of the smelt smells like cucumber.

European smelt

Tuna

Thunnus spp., Scombridae

A migratory fish with a long, sturdy body, the tuna is found in the warm waters of the Mediterranean, the Pacific, the Atlantic, and the Indian Ocean. In the Atlantic, it is found as far north as Newfoundland during the summer months. A lively, powerful fish that travels in schools near the surface of the water, the tuna is a very agile and fast swimmer. It is a favorite of sport fishermen because the largest specimens will resist capture for hours on end, sometimes dragging boats several miles out to sea. The tuna has been fished since time immemorial, with rods and harpoons or with a *madraga* – an enclosure of compartmentalized nets set up permanently along the shore. In ancient times, smoked and pickled tuna were particularly popular.

Tuna are grouped into several species whose names highlight their distinguishing characteristics. The common characteristics of these fish include two dorsal fins (one of which is spiny), an anal fin, and a row of small fins located between the second dorsal fin and the anal fin. The most common species include the bluefin tuna, or tunny, the albacore, or white tuna, the bonito, and the yellowfin tuna.

The **bluefin tuna** or **tunny** *(Thunnus thynnus)* is by far the largest member of the tuna family. It usually measures between 3 and 7 feet and weighs from 220 to 400 pounds, but it can grow to be 13 feet long and weigh almost 2,000 pounds. It has a cone-shaped head, a large mouth, and a thin, crescent-shaped tail. Its dorsal skin is dark blue, and its underside is grayish with silvery spots. Its reddish brown flesh has a strong flavor.

The **albacore** or **white tuna** *(Thunnus alalunga)* has long saber-shaped pectoral fins, and its tail is adorned with a thin white stripe. It usually measures between 22 and 40 inches and weighs from 100 to 130 pounds. Its back and sides are a steel-blue color, and its underside is silvery. Its slightly pinkish skin is much sought after, as are its eggs. The French refer to the yellowfin tuna as the albacore, which leads to certain amount of confusion.

The **bonito** *(Sarda sarda)* has a rather small elongated body that is rarely more than 20 inches long and usually weighs under 5 pounds. The dark blue oblique stripes that adorn its sides make it very easy to identify. The lower half of its body is a silvery color. It is the most frequently caught species of tuna, and like the bluefin, the yellowfin, and the albacore, it is usually canned. In Japan it is often consumed in the form of dried flakes, which can be stored indefinitely. Its flesh is a dark red color.

bluefin tuna

The **yellowfin tuna** *(Thunnus albacares)* is a slender fish that usually measures between 2 and 5 feet. Its dorsal skin is a dark shade of metallic blue, and its sides and belly are silvery white. As its name suggests, the end of its tail, as well as its second dorsal fin and anal fin, is yellow. Its pale, delicious flesh is usually canned. The flesh of the tuna is fatty, firm, and dense. Its color varies from one species to another, as does its flavor, which can be very strong. The flesh located between the two flanks is the finest and most sought-after portion, as well as the most expensive.

Buying

Fresh tuna is sold as steaks, fillets, or pieces. Several varieties of tuna are almost always canned. Tuna is canned solid and in chunks. It can be packed in vegetable oil, broth, or water. Tuna packed in oil is the least dry, but it is also relatively high in fat. About ten different species of tuna are canned, but labels usually distinguish only between "white tuna" and "light tuna." Bluefin and yellowfin tuna should thus be marked "light tuna," while albacore should be labeled "white tuna." The bonito is usually marketed as "skipjack," the common name for the striped bonito. Solid tuna is always more expensive, but cheaper products such as crumbled tuna contain more fragments of bone and skin. When buying tuna, it may be helpful to consider how it is going to be used. If the appearance of the fish is important, buy solid tuna, but the other formats are fine for sauces or tuna salad (with mayonnaise).

Preparing

Freshly caught tuna should be bled as quickly as possible, which can be done by making an incision 1 or 2 inches above the tail. The tuna has a row of bones that juts into the middle of each of its sides. These can be removed by sliding the blade of a knife between them and the flesh. The choice light flesh of the tuna is enclosed in a layer of dark, fatty, strongly flavored flesh. Removing this layer makes the fish taste milder.

Cooking

Fresh tuna is poached, braised, grilled, roasted, and baked in aluminum foil. Tuna is particularly good when steamed or cooked in court bouillon.

albacore

Serving Ideas

Before tuna with strong-tasting flesh is cooked, it should be soaked for several hours in lightly salted water, then marinated in a mixture of lemon juice and herbs. Tuna is easier to digest if it is poached for about 10 minutes before being cooked. Avoid recipes that increase its fat content. Tuna is one of the main ingredients in *vitello tonnato,* an Italian dish that also contains cold veal, anchovies, capers, and mayonnaise. The Japanese are particularly fond of raw tuna, which is used in sashimi and sushi. Prepared in a variety of ways, canned tuna is used in salads, sandwiches, sauces, omelets, and quiches and is also cooked au gratin.

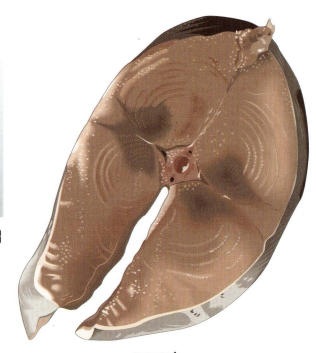

tuna steak

Tuna à la Basquaise

SERVES 4

8 tomatoes
2 green bell peppers
2 red bell peppers
1 onion
4 cloves garlic
¼ lb. (125 g) fresh mushrooms
4 tuna steaks, each weighing ½ lb. (250 g)

Salt and freshly ground pepper
⅓ cup (80 ml) olive oil
1 bouquet garni
½ cup (125 ml) dry white wine

1. Peel, seed, and dice the tomatoes. Core and seed the peppers, then cut them into strips. Chop the onion and 2 of the garlic cloves. Crush the other 2 cloves. Cut large mushrooms into 4 pieces; leave small ones whole.

2. Season the tuna steaks with salt and pepper. Heat 2 tablespoons of the oil in a flameproof casserole and brown the tuna steaks for 2 minutes on each side; then set them aside.

3. Add more oil to the casserole and brown the chopped onion, the crushed garlic cloves, and the peppers, stirring, for 3 minutes. Then add the mushrooms and the chopped garlic. Cook for 1 minute, adding more oil if necessary. Stir the mixture again so that all the ingredients are thoroughly mixed together.

4. Place the tuna steaks on top of the vegetables. Add the bouquet garni and pour in the white wine. Cover the casserole and cook over low heat for 15 minutes.

5. Add the tomatoes and mix the vegetables together, leaving the tuna steaks on top. Cover the casserole again, and cook over low heat for another 15 minutes.

6. Place the tuna steaks on a heated plate. Discard the bouquet garni and pour the vegetable mixture over the steaks. Serve with plain rice.

Nutritional Information

	fresh	*light tuna in oil*	*light tuna in water*
protein	23 g	29 g	30 g
fat	1 to 5 g	8 g	0.5 g
calories	105 to 145	198	131
			per 100 g

Fresh tuna can be lean or moderately fatty, depending on the species. Drained light tuna packed in oil is moderately fatty. Drained light tuna packed in water is lean.

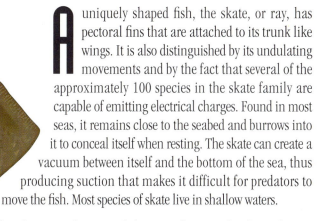

Skate

Raja spp., **Rajidae**

A uniquely shaped fish, the skate, or ray, has pectoral fins that are attached to its trunk like wings. It is also distinguished by its undulating movements and by the fact that several of the approximately 100 species in the skate family are capable of emitting electrical charges. Found in most seas, it remains close to the seabed and burrows into it to conceal itself when resting. The skate can create a vacuum between itself and the bottom of the sea, thus producing suction that makes it difficult for predators to move the fish. Most species of skate live in shallow waters.

The skate has a cartilaginous skeleton, and its mouth is located on its off-white underside beneath the head, like that of the shark. Its dorsal skin can be gray or brown and is often covered with blotches. Its flat diamond-shaped body can be rounded or relatively square, and its tail is long and narrow. Scales resembling small or large spines may cover its body and tail; certain species, such as the spinytail skate and the white skate, have more of these scales than others, and some even have venomous spines on their tails. Skates can measure anywhere from 1 foot to over 20 feet, depending on the species (the largest skate is the manta, which can weigh over a ton).

Buying

Small skates are sold whole and gutted, while larger ones are sold in pieces. The edible portions of the skate are the wings, the "cheeks," and the liver. Its boneless flesh can be pinkish or off-white and, depending on the species, may resemble that of scallops. Certain unscrupulous fish merchants have been known to cut skates into the shape of scallops and sell them as the higher-priced mollusk.

Preparing

The skate contains urea to prevent its bodily fluids, which are less salty than seawater, from being lost through osmosis; when the skate dies, this urea turns into ammonia. Although the ammonia disappears when the fish is cooked, skate tastes better if eaten 1 or 2 days after it is caught, when the smell of ammonia is less pronounced. To enhance the flavor of skate, rinse it before it is cooked, and let it soak for 2 hours in a mixture of water and lemon juice, vinegar, or milk.

To skin skate, cover it with boiling water and poach it for 1 or 2 minutes (it will start to cook if poached any longer); then lay the fish flat and use a knife to scrape the skin off, one side at a time. This should be done with care because there may be spines on the wings.

Serving Ideas

Skate can be prepared like scallops. It can be sticky if it is not cooked thoroughly and gelatinous if served less than piping hot.

Cooking

The thick skin of the skate should be removed before the fish is cooked. Skate is often poached (for about 15 minutes), baked (for 15 to 25 minutes), or served with black butter (fried for 4 to 6 minutes per side).

Nutritional Information

protein	22 g
fat	1 g
calories	98
	per 100 g

Shark

Selachians

Sharks are cartilaginous boneless fish that are found in most of the world's seas. There are approximately 225 different species of shark, comprising almost 80 individual genuses, 14 families, and between 3 and 7 suborders. Some sharks, such as the picked dogfish, are often simply referred to as "dogfish."

Although certain species have anal fins, others, including the picked dogfish, do not. Some sharks, like the spotted dogfish, are unique in that the female of the species is oviparous. Sharks have very poor vision but a very highly developed sense of smell. They can detect blood that has been diluted in a million parts water.

Most people have strong feelings about sharks, and any mention of them is usually enough to remind us of their reputation as "man-eaters." But not all sharks are voracious enough, or large enough, to inspire fear. Certain species can be as long as 50 feet, but some are only about 3 to 5 feet long and the smallest measure less than 2 feet. Although some sharks have as many as 3,000 teeth arranged in 6 to 20 separate rows, others have much smaller, relatively weak teeth. For example, species like the smooth hound, which eats mollusks and shellfish, have small blunt teeth. The most common species include the hammerhead shark, the picked dogfish, the smooth hound, the larger spotted dogfish, and the school shark.

The **hammerhead shark** (*Sphyrna zygaena*) can grow to a maximum length of approximately 13 feet. Named for its uniquely shaped head, it can have either brownish gray or greenish brown dorsal skin. The hammerhead thrives in the warm waters of temperate seas and can be found, among other places, on both sides of the Atlantic, in the Pacific, and in the Mediterranean. Its white flesh is extremely appetizing.

The **picked dogfish** (*Squalus acanthias*) usually measures between 24 and 40 inches but can be over 4 feet long. Its slate-gray dorsal skin, which can be somewhat brown, is speckled with off-white spots. It is referred to as "picked" because it has a hard spine at the front of each of its dorsal fins. The picked dogfish can be found in most cold-water seas. Its pinkish flesh has a very mild flavor.

The **smooth hound** (*Mustelus* spp.) usually measures between 20 and 40 inches and weighs between 7 and 9 pounds, but it can grow to be 5 feet long. The color of its dorsal skin varies from one species to another. The smooth hound is commonly found in the Mediterranean, the Atlantic, and the Pacific. Its white flesh smells of ammonia.

The **larger spotted dogfish** (*Scyliorhinus stellaris*) can grow to be over 5 feet long but usually measures just over 4 feet. Its dorsal skin, which is usually a gray or sandy color, is dotted with large black spots. The larger spotted dogfish is found, among other places, in the Mediterranean and the Atlantic. Its white flesh is best when very fresh and when served with a flavorful sauce.

The **school shark** (*Galeorhinus galeus*) usually grows to a length of between 4 and 6 feet and weighs between 10 and 35 pounds. It is commonly found in temperate and subtropical waters on both sides the Atlantic, as well as in the Pacific and the Mediterranean. It has brownish gray dorsal skin and firm white flesh.

Buying

Sharks are usually skinned before being sold because their very rough skin is difficult to remove. Their flesh is filleted or cut into steaks or pieces, and sold either fresh or frozen.

Preparing

Sharks are easiest to skin immediately after they are caught. To make skinning a shark less difficult, freeze it rapidly, then plunge it into boiling water.

The flesh of sharks contains urea to prevent the liquid in their bodies, which is less salty than seawater, from being lost through osmosis. In the hours after a shark is killed, this urea turns into ammonia. Shark meat should thus be eaten 1 or 2 days after the fish is caught, although no trace of ammonia remains once it is cooked.

To enhance the flavor of shark, rinse it under cold running water and marinate it for 4 hours in milk, or in water containing lemon or vinegar.

Serving Ideas

Shark is particularly delicious when served with a very flavorful sauce. In Asia, salted and dried shark fins are added to broths to give them a jelly-like consistency. Sharkfin soup is a particular favorite in China.

Cooking

Since shark meat is boneless, it does not fall apart when cooked and nothing is wasted. It is firm and, depending on the variety, can be quite flavorful and moist – even slightly gelatinous (picked dogfish is often said to have the best flavor). As a rule, the bigger the shark the stronger its flavor.

Shark can be cooked in a wide variety of ways. It can, for example, be grilled, braised, fried, baked, or poached in court bouillon.

Nutritional Information

	raw
protein	21 g
fat	4 g
calories	131
	per 100 g

larger spotted dogfish

smooth hound

Plaice

Pleuronectidae

common plaice

Abundant in the Atlantic and the Pacific, the plaice is often confused with the sole, but genuine sole are found only off the coast of Europe. (Since the flesh of the sole is finer than that of any other fish, an attempt was made in recent years to acclimatize the fish to the cold waters of the western Atlantic, but it was unsuccessful.) The fish sold as fillets of sole in North America is usually plaice, flounder, or dab. In several countries, including the United States and Australia, a wide variety of fish are sold under the name "plaice." Most of these fish are less than 2 feet long and weigh between 1 and 4 pounds.

The **American plaice** *(Hippoglossoides platessoides)* is abundant in New England and Canada, and is very common on both sides of the Atlantic. It can grow to a maximum length of 2 feet and has an almost perfectly straight lateral stripe, a large mouth, a rounded tail, and white-tipped fins. Covered with small rough scales, its skin is grayish, reddish, or brown on the right-hand or exposed side, on which both of its eyes are located.

The **common plaice** *(Pleuronectes platessa)* rarely measures more than 16 inches but can grow to be 3 feet long. The most abundant flatfish in European coastal waters, it has brownish skin with large orangey or red blotches on its exposed side and pearly white skin on its underside.

The **winter flounder** *(Pseudopleuronectes americanus)* is usually about 18 inches long but can grow to a maximum length of almost 2 feet. It is particularly abundant in New England and the Gulf of St. Lawrence, but its natural habitat extends all the way from Labrador to Georgia. Usually brownish red, its skin color varies depending on where the fish is found, and the lateral stripe that runs down the middle of its back is almost perfectly straight. The winter flounder is fleshier than any other member of the plaice family.

The **witch flounder** *(Glyptocephalus cynoglossus)* usually measures between 12 and 18 inches but can be over 30 inches long. Found on both sides of the Atlantic, it is similar to the winter flounder but is brownish gray and has more rays on its dorsal and anal fins.

The **common dab** *(Limanda limanda)* is usually between 8 and 10 inches long but can grow to a maximum length of 18 inches. Found off the Atlantic coasts of Europe, it is particularly common in French coastal waters. Its black dorsal skin is often covered with reddish brown spots, and its flesh is less flavorful than that of the common plaice.

The **yellowtail flounder** *(Limanda ferruginea)* usually measures between 10 and 16 inches but can be over 2 feet long. It has an almost perfectly oval, thin body and a small mouth. Its exposed side is olive green or reddish brown with large reddish brown blotches, and its lateral stripe is curved. Named for its yellow tail, it is commonly found in the Atlantic from Labrador to southern New England.

The **lemon sole** *(Microstomus kitt)* can grow to be over 2 feet long, but its head and mouth are relatively small. Its exposed side is usually brown and is covered with numerous irregularly shaped spots of various sizes and colors. Found in Atlantic coastal waters from France to Iceland, it is particularly abundant off the coast of France. Its flesh is bland and stringy.

The **flounder** *(Platichthys flesus)* is rarely more than 12 inches long but can grow to to a maximum length of 20 inches. Brownish, grayish brown, or greenish, the skin on its exposed side is dotted with blotches that are paler and less orange than those found on the skin of the common plaice. The lateral stripe that adorns its back curves slightly near the pectoral fin, and its blind side is usually white. Particularly abundant in the Baltic Sea, the flounder is fished in the Mediterranean. Its flesh is slightly less flavorful than that of the common plaice.

The **summer flounder** *(Paralichthys dentatus),* a member the Bothidae family, can grow to be 3 feet long. The largest species of plaice, it has a big mouth, pointed teeth, and small, closely set eyes. Its exposed side is covered with 10 to 14 dark spots and is usually brown or gray, but it can also be blackish or green. The summer flounder is abundant in American coastal waters from Maine to South Carolina.

Buying

Plaice, flounders, and dabs are very bony fish and are usually sold as fillets (fresh or frozen).

Cooking

Usually grilled or fried, plaice should be scaled but need not be skinned before being cooked. It is important not to mask its delicate flavor.

Nutritional Information

	raw
protein	19 g
fat	1.2 g
calories	92
	per 100 g

Plaice is low in fat.

Turbot

Psetta maxima, Scophthalmidae

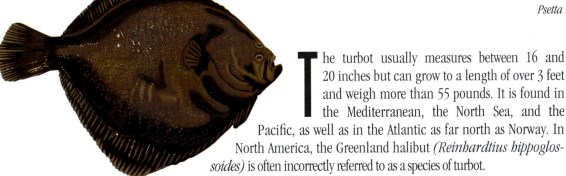

The turbot usually measures between 16 and 20 inches but can grow to a length of over 3 feet and weigh more than 55 pounds. It is found in the Mediterranean, the North Sea, and the Pacific, as well as in the Atlantic as far north as Norway. In North America, the Greenland halibut *(Reinhardtius hippoglossoides)* is often incorrectly referred to as a species of turbot.

The oval body of the turbot led to the creation of a special lozenge-shaped turbot kettle *(turbotière)* in which the flatfish can be cooked whole. Virtually scaleless, its skin is covered with bony tubercles and small black and white spots; it is usually brownish or yellowish gray on the exposed side and dark gray on the underside. The turbot has strong teeth, and its firm white flesh is very flavorful.

Buying

Turbot is sold whole or as skinned fillets. The size of the fish determines whether it is sold whole, gutted, or in pieces. One of the finest saltwater fish, it is also one of the most expensive.

Cooking

Turbot is usually just poached or grilled.

Nutritional Information

	raw
protein	16 g
fat	3 g
calories	95
	per 100 g

Turbot is low in fat.

Halibut

Hippoglossus spp., **Pleuronectidae**

The largest flatfish, and one of the largest saltwater fish of all, the halibut thrives in the cold waters of northern seas and is very common off the Atlantic coasts of Newfoundland and Greenland, as well as in the Pacific.

Covered with round scales, the smooth skin of the halibut is white or gray on the blind side and brownish on the sighted side, which becomes increasingly black with age. The halibut has a large mouth, a forked tail, and a lateral stripe. It usually measures between 20 and 55 inches and weighs between 10 and 155 pounds, but it can be over 8 feet long and weigh over 660 pounds. Commercial overfishing has made large halibut quite rare.

Nutritional Information

	raw
protein	21 g
fat	2.4 g
calories	109
	per 100 g

Lean, fine, firm, and flaky, the flesh of the halibut contains very few bones.

Serving Ideas

Halibut can be grilled or poached in red or white wine, but it is important not to overpower its delicate favor. It is particularly delicious with anchovy butter.

common sole

Sole

Solea spp., **Soleidae**

The sole thrives at the sandy bottom of seas such as the English Channel, the eastern Atlantic, the Mediterranean, the North Sea, and the Pacific. Genuine sole is not found off the coasts of the United States and Canada, and much of the fish called "sole" is actually plaice, which is very common in North American waters.

The sole usually measures between 8 and 18 inches but can grow to be about 28 inches long. The coloring of its exposed (right) side varies.

Sole is always very flavorful, but its quality depends on the species and on the location in which the fish is caught.

The most soughtafter species is the common sole *(Solea solea),* which is often identified with its place of origin and is thus also referred to as the Dover sole because it is fished intensively in the Straits of Dover. However, it is not exclusive to the English coast and is also found in the Mediterranean and as far north as Norway. Often gray or grayish brown and always marked with one or more dark spots, the common sole has a lobed snout that resembles the beak of a parrot.

Nutritional Information

	raw
protein	18 g
fat	1.4 g
calories	77
	per 100 g

Sole is low in fat.

Serving Ideas

Sole is prepared in an almost infinite variety of ways and fares well no matter how it is cooked.

Crustaceans

Introduction

Crustaceans are aquatic invertebrates whose bodies are protected by hard shells. They are generally found in the ocean (crab, shrimp, lobster, spiny lobster, scampi), but certain crustaceans, such as the crayfish and several species of shrimp and crabs, inhabit fresh water. The hardness of their shells varies from one species to another. Crustaceans shed and replace their shells several times over the course of their lives to allow their bodies to grow.

Decapod crustaceans have five pairs of limbs. In most of these species (lobster, crab, crayfish, scampi), the front pair of limbs is much more highly developed than the others; either the right or the left front limb ends in a powerful vise-like claw, while the other is equipped with a saw-toothed claw for crushing food. The limbs of shrimp, crayfish, and spiny lobsters are usually of uniform size and end in pincers (or hooklike appendages in the case of the spiny lobster). The thorax of crustaceans is directly attached to the head, forming the cephalothorax from which the limbs protrude.

Crustaceans move by walking, usually along the sea floor. Crabs can move very quickly, even from side to side, and certain species venture onto beaches. Crayfish can walk backward; in fact, the French equivalent of the expression "take one step forward and two steps back" is *"marcher comme une écrevisse,"* or "walk like a crayfish." Female crustaceans are distinguished from males by a sort of flipper, or fin, on the underside of the thorax, which is used to hold the eggs. In males, this appendage is thinner and harder and is not shaped like a fin. The red roe ("coral") of crustaceans is edible.

Buying

 Live crustaceans should be heavy and quite vigorous (lobsters and crabs should move their limbs); they should also have a pleasant odor and intact shells. Once crustaceans are cooked, their shells should be pink or bright red, with no greenish or blackish spots, and their flesh should be firm and have an appetizing smell; a folded tail indicates that the crustacean was still alive when cooked. There should be no frost inside packages of frozen crustaceans (raw or cooked); the presence of freezer burn indicates that the flesh has begun to dry out. It is important to determine whether or not fresh or cooked crustaceans have been defrosted, because the flesh should not be frozen more than once and should be used as quickly possible once defrosted.

Serving Ideas

 Crustaceans can eaten hot or cold but must always be cooked. They can be prepared in a wide variety of ways.

Cooking

For maximum freshness, crustaceans should be kept alive until they are cooked.

Almost all crustaceans turn pink when plunged into boiling water. Heat intensifies the color of the red pigment (carotene), which is just one of many pigments present in the shell.

Boiling crustaceans is a very easy way to cook them and requires little preparation; just fill any holes in the shell with compressed pieces of crustless bread. Opinion is divided with regard to the most appropriate method of boiling live crustaceans.

They are usually plunged headfirst into boiling water, which kills them instantly (watch out for the splashing caused by the folding tail); some people claim that the flesh is more flavorful when crustaceans are cooked in this way. However, others maintain that this method is cruel and makes the flesh tough. They suggest that crustaceans be placed in the freezer for an hour (this makes them sluggish and kills them gently), or that they be cooked in cold water that is brought slowly to a boil (seawater, salted fresh water [1 or 2 tablespoons of salt per quart], or court bouillon). The cooking time depends on the species and size of the animal; overcooking crustaceans makes the flesh tough and less flavorful.

The Japanese have developed a process of manufacturing substitute crustaceans, such as imitation shrimp, crab, and lobster, as well as various foods made with these products (see *Kamaboko*).

Nutritional Information

Crustaceans are low in fat and are an excellent source of protein, vitamins (including niacin and vitamin B_{12}), and minerals (especially zinc and copper). The flesh of many species of crustaceans contains cholesterol (between 50 to 150 milligrams per 100 grams).

Crustaceans can provoke allergic reactions such as migraine headaches in some people (see *Mollusks*).

Storing

Crustaceans can be refrigerated or frozen. Certain species, such as live lobsters and crabs, are stored in tanks in fish stores and some restaurants.

Shrimp

Pandalus spp., **Crustacea**

Crustaceans

S mall crustaceans that live in fresh, briny, and salt water of various temperatures, shrimp are found almost all over the world. There are nine different families of shrimp, comprising almost 160 individual species; however, some species are less flavorful than others and certain species are inedible. Shrimp are bred on farms in several countries, including the United States, Japan, Thailand, and Taiwan. Americans eat more shrimp than do the people of any other country, consuming almost 5 million pounds per year.

Shrimp have two long antennas and five pairs of legs; in certain species, all ten limbs are the same size and all but the middle pair are equipped with pincers, while in others the middle pair of limbs is relatively large. Usually between 1 and 12 inches long, shrimp tend to be smaller and more flavorful if they are found in cold water, where they grow more slowly. Some species of shrimp are born male and subsequently become female, usually between the ages of 18 and 30 months – after 1 or 2 years of life as sexually active males. However, this transformation can take up to 5 years in the particularly cold waters of countries such as Greenland. The firm, translucent flesh of the shrimp can be pink, yellow, gray, brownish, reddish, or dark red, depending on the species; it becomes opaque and pinkish when cooked.

The most commonly available shrimp are extremely flavorful. These include the **deep-water shrimp** *(Pandalus borealis),* which is one of the most commercially important species. Also known as the "pink shrimp," it is reddish pink in color and is usually between 3 and 4 inches long.

The **giant tiger prawn** *(Penaeus monodon)* is another commercially important species. It is the most common and the most frequently consumed shrimp in the Far East. Often referred to as the "black tiger shrimp," it is usually between 6 and 12 inches long.

In 1983, a machine capable of producing "reassembled" shrimp was developed in the United States. The flesh of the shrimp is first crushed and ground, then injected by means of high pressure into a device that heats it for a few seconds, causing the proteins to expand and combine. This substance is then molded into the shape of large shrimp, which are breaded and frozen. The shrimp machine can produce tens of thousands of relatively cheap shrimp in a single hour of operation.

Nutritional Information

water	76%
protein	20 g
fat	2 g
carbohydrates	0.9 g
cholesterol	153 mg
calories	106
	per 100 g

Shrimp are rich in vitamin B_{12} and niacin. Since they are extremely perishable, they are sometimes treated with sodium bisulphite so they can be stored for a longer period of time.

Buying

Since shrimp are extremely fragile, they are usually frozen, covered with ice, or cooked on board the boats on which they are fished. They are sold whole or with their heads removed, fresh or frozen, cooked or smoked, and shelled or unshelled; they can also be dried or canned. Shrimp are classified by size, the largest being the most expensive.

When buying fresh shrimp, ensure that their bodies are firm and that they smell only slightly fishy; avoid shrimp that are soft and sticky, as well as those whose bodies have become detached from their shells, that smell of ammonia, or that are covered with black spots, especially around the area where the head was removed from the body.

When buying frozen shrimp, ensure that they are not covered in frost and have not dried out. Since their flavor is affected by how and when they are defrosted, avoid shrimp that have already been defrosted. They are best when still slightly frozen or when defrosted slowly in the refrigerator.

Preparing

Shelling shrimp involves extracting the flesh from the shell in one piece. A whole shrimp can be shelled by holding the head in one hand and the body in the other, and pulling on the head so as to remove both the head and the shell. Any remaining pieces of the shell can then be removed. If the head has already been removed, it may be useful to slit the shell with scissors before attempting to remove it from the shrimp. Since shrimp are particularly difficult to shell once they have been defrosted, they should be shelled when still slightly frozen.

One pound of shrimp yields only about 8 ounces of cooked flesh because whole unshelled raw shrimp lose about 50% of their body weight – 25% when shelled and another 25% when cooked.

The shells can be used to make excellent stock for cooking the shrimp: cover the shells with boiling water and allow them to simmer for about 10 minutes, then strain the liquid and add the shrimp. Uncooked shells can also be ground and used to make flavorful butter.

The intestine (the dark vein that runs along the back) does not have to be removed before shrimp are eaten, but since many people prefer to eat shrimp that have been deveined, this intestine is sometimes removed before shrimp are sold. This involves cutting into the shrimp along the vein and pulling out the intestine.

Serving Ideas

Shrimp are delicious cold or hot and can be prepared in many different ways. They are used to make soups, mousses, sauces, salads, and stuffing, and are served as hors d'oeuvres, appetizers, or entrées, either alone or with meat, poultry, vegetables, or pasta.

Shrimp can replace other shellfish in most recipes, and they are a key ingredient in Southeast Asian cuisine, where they are often preserved in brine, or made into a paste or powder and used as a condiment.

Storing

Shrimp can be refrigerated for about 2 days and frozen for 1 month.

1 *Remove the shell of the shrimp.*

2 *Make a small incision in the flesh with the point of a knife.*

3 *Carefully remove the intestine which runs down the back.*

Crustaceans

429

Cooking

 The body of the shrimp curls up when it is cooked. Avoid overcooking shrimp because they can become hard and dry. Both shelled and unshelled shrimp are often cooked in water or court bouillon.

• The water can be either seawater or salted fresh water (2 tablespoons of salt per quart).

• The court bouillon can consist of nothing more than salted water, a slice of lemon, and a little thyme, but it can also be very elaborate, depending on your preference and level of inspiration.

• Bring the liquid in which the shrimp are to be cooked to a boil, add the shrimp and bring it to a boil again, then reduce the heat to a simmer. Small fresh shrimp should be ready within 3 to 5 minutes, but larger or frozen shrimp will take a little longer. To determine whether or not the shrimp are ready, rinse one under cold water, then taste it. Strain the shrimp as soon as they are ready, then rinse them under cold water to prevent them from cooking any further and losing their flavor.

Sautéed Shrimp with Garlic

SERVES 4

1 lb. (500 g) fresh shrimp	3 tbsp. olive oil
4 cloves garlic	2 pinches sea salt

1. Wash the shrimp and pat them dry.

2. Peel and finely chop the garlic.

3. Heat the oil in large frying pan.

4. Cook the shrimp rapidly in the hot oil, turning them only once to ensure that they are equally pink on both sides.

5. After removing the pan from the heat, add the garlic and sea salt, coating the shrimp thoroughly. Serve immediately with herbed rice.

deep-water shrimp

giant tiger prawn

Lobster

Homarus americanus (America) and *Homarus vulgaris* (Europe), **Crustacea**

European lobster

American lobster

A crustacean with an elongated body, the lobster thrives in the depths of the sea. Since lobsters generally crawl around at night among the rocks on the seabed, they can be easily caught in sunken cagelike traps.

Found mainly in the Atlantic, the lobster has all but disappeared from European coasts and is sold in Europe at exorbitant prices. It was so abundant in North America during the colonial period that it was regarded with disdain, but as its popularity increased it became the target of an overly aggressive fishery – so aggressive that many countries have been forced to regulate their lobster fisheries in order to protect the species. The North American lobster is a slightly different shape and color from the species found off European coasts.

The lobster has five pairs of claws, the front pair of which is much more highly developed than the others and is equipped with extremely powerful pincers. The largest of these two pincers – either the right or the left – is used to crush food, while the smaller one is used to cut food into pieces. The lobster has a rather well-developed abdomen (or tail) that is comprised of seven sections, the last of which is a powerful fan-shaped tail. The pointed head of the lobster is equipped with bulging eyes and is surmounted by a protruding spiny appendage known as the rostrum. Two of the six antennae attached to the rostrum are much longer than the others.

The female lobster is distinguished from the male by the appearance of the small fins located at the point where the thorax joins the abdomen: the female's fins, which are used to hold eggs, are thin and webbed, while the male's are long, stiff, and prickly. The flesh of female lobsters is often considered to be superior, especially during the egg-laying season, and is thus more sought after than that of males. Fortunately the overconsumption of female lobsters no longer constitutes as much of a threat to the species, since many of the lobsters now consumed are bred on vast lobster farms.

The lobster sheds its shell as it grows, replacing it 12 times over a 5-year period. Mature lobsters weigh approximately 1 pound and are usually about 1 foot long. The edible portions of the lobster are the flesh inside its abdomen (or tail) and claws (including the small ones, which are chewable), as well as the coral and the greenish liver inside the thorax. Lean, firm, delicate, and very flavorful, the white and pinkish flesh of the lobster comprises only about 30% of its total weight.

Buying

When buying a live lobster, ensure that the animal is in fact alive by picking it up by its sides; it should respond by abruptly tucking its tail under its body. The pincers are almost always restrained by an elastic band or a wooden peg, but if they are not, be extremely careful because they can grip very tightly.

A cooked lobster should have shiny black eyes, firm flesh, and a pleasant odor. Before cooking a lobster, pull on its tail to ensure that it still folds up on its own. Lobster is also sold frozen and canned (either in pieces or in the form of a spreadable paste).

Serving Ideas

Lobster can be eaten hot or cold but must always be cooked. It is often served with garlic butter, lemon, or mayonnaise, and is sometimes even eaten plain. A tool of some sort is required to remove the flesh from the claws: lobster pincers, a nutcracker, the handle of a heavy knife, or even a hammer will do the trick.

Prepared in many different ways, lobster is often cooked in bisques, soufflés, sauces, and au gratin. The classic recipes include lobster Thermidor, lobster Newburg, and lobster *à l'américaine* (or *à l'armoricaine*). Cold lobster is used in salads, sandwiches, and aspics. Lobster is also eaten in the form of a pâté. The shell can be used to flavor bisques, stews, and sauces. It can also be crushed or minced and added to flavor melted butter (which must then be strained). Lobster butter is used to cook fish, to make sauces and bisques, and as a sandwich spread.

Preparing

Before boiling a lobster, plug the holes in the shell with compressed pieces of crustless bread; the flesh will retain more of its flavor. To cut a lobster in two, press firmly on its belly and stick a knife through its shell at the intersection of the thorax and the tail; then split it lengthwise. Remove the intestines under the tail and the pockets at the back of the head.

1 *Place the lobster on a cutting board. Stick the point of a knife right through the head, until it hits the board.*

2 *Turn the lobster around and cut it lengthwise from head to tail.*

3 *Split the lobster in half, cutting the head lengthwise.*

4 *Reserve the coral (black when uncooked) and the liver (green) to make a sauce if desired.*

5 *Remove the sand sac, located near the head.*

6 *Carefully remove the intestine, which runs down the back.*

sand sac *liver* *coral* *intestine*

Cooking

Lobster can be cooked in water (seawater, salted fresh water, or court bouillon), steamed, or grilled. Opinions about how a lobster should be cooked vary. It is generally suggested that a lobster be cooked while it is still alive to ensure maximum freshness. When boiling a live lobster, plunge it headfirst into boiling water so that it dies instantly (beware of splashing, which is usually caused by the folding tail). However, some people maintain that this method not only is cruel but also makes the flesh tough. They suggest that a lobster can be killed more gradually and humanely by putting it in the freezer for an hour.

A lobster can also be cooked in cold water that is brought slowly to a boil. No matter which method is used, allow 12 minutes cooking time per pound and an extra minute for each additional quarter pound. When cooking a lobster in water that is already boiling, start timing as soon as it is plunged into the water; when cooking it in cold water, do not start timing until the water begins to boil. Always ensure that the lobster is completely submerged. Before serving the lobster, pierce the head to drain the water trapped inside the shell.

To grill a lobster, split it lengthwise and brush the flesh with oil, lemon juice, and, if desired, freshly ground pepper; then grill it gently for about 10 minutes. Do not defrost frozen lobster; it will retain more of its flavor if it is simply reheated for 2 minutes in boiling water.

Grilled Lobster

SERVES 2

*2 live lobsters,
1 to 1½ lb.
(500 to 750 g) each
½ cup (125 ml)
unsalted butter
Freshly ground pepper
or paprika*

*1 tablespoon finely
chopped parsley
1 tablespoon dry white
wine (optional)
Lemon wedges*

1. Split the lobsters in half and break open the claws.

2. Open each of the lobsters, and remove the sand sac and the intestine. Take out the liver (green) and the coral (black), reserving them to make a sauce if desired.

3. Melt the butter and preheat the broiler.

4. Arrange the lobsters on a broiling pan shell-side down. Brush them with the butter, and sprinkle with the pepper (or paprika) and the chopped parsley. (They can also be brushed with white wine if desired.)

5. Place the lobsters under the broiler and cook them for 15 to 20 minutes. (Large lobsters will take a little longer.) The lobsters are ready when their flesh is no longer translucent.

6. Remove the lobsters from the oven and serve them with the lemon wedges.

Nutritional Information

water	77%
protein	19 g
fat	1 g
cholesterol	95 mg
calories	91
	per 100 g

Lobster is rich in potassium, zinc, and niacin. The composition of the flesh varies from season to season and from one part of the body to another; the tail contains more nutrients than the claws.

Storing

A lobster can live for 3 to 5 days outside its natural habitat if stored in a tank filled with salt water. After buying a lobster, do not let it remain at room temperature for any length of time. Either cook it immediately or cover it with a damp cloth and put it in the refrigerator, where it will keep for 12 to 18 hours. Cooked lobster will keep for 1 or 2 days in the refrigerator.

Before being frozen, lobster should be cooked and strained; it can be frozen whole, but it is preferable to remove the flesh from the shell. Chill the flesh in the refrigerator, place it in freezer containers, and cover it with brine (1 tablespoon salt per cup of water); then seal the containers and put them in the freezer. A whole lobster can also be frozen in a freezer bag: chill the lobster and put it in the bag; then squeeze out the air, seal the bag, and put it in the freezer. Do not freeze lobster for longer than a month.

Crustaceans

433

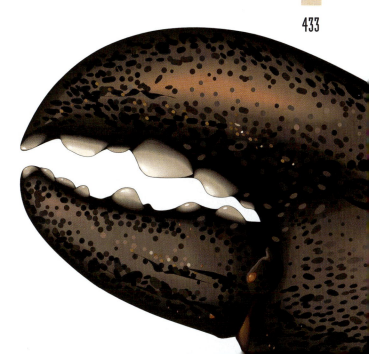

Crab

Cancer spp., Canceridae

Found in salt, fresh, and briny water, the crab hides under rocks, amid seaweed, and in crevices. Crabs are usually very aggressive and are skillful, combative predators that charge at their prey. If the leg of a crab becomes stuck or is restrained by an enemy, the crab simply detaches itself from the limb; any limbs lost in this way will grow back completely over the course of three moltings.

The crab has a rounded shell that is heart-shaped in certain species. Its underdeveloped tail and abdomen are tucked under its shell, which can be either hard or soft, depending on how recently it has molted. The crab has protruding eyes and five pairs of limbs, the front pair of which develops into powerful pincers. The ventral fin of female crabs is much more highly developed than that of male crabs because it is used to hold the eggs.

Although the crab is not a very fleshy animal, one quarter of its body is edible, including the flesh inside its body, legs, and pincers, as well as the liver and the creamy substance underneath the shell. The lean white flesh is stringy and flavorful. Of the approximately 4,000 different species that make up the crab family, the following are among the most common:

The **common shore crab** or **green crab** *(Carcinus maenus),* which is the single most common species, is frequently found on beaches. It is relentless in its pursuit of other crustaceans and mollusks, and moves in a very peculiar fashion – a trait highlighted by its Latin name *maenus,* which means "frenzied." The common shore crab weighs about 7 ounces and contains very little flesh; its rather small green shell is usually about 3 inches wide. Rarely sold commercially, it is sometimes used as bait by sports fishermen.

The **Atlantic common crab** *(Cancer pagurus)* inhabits rocky and sandy coasts and can dive to depths of over 300 feet. Its smooth, oval reddish-brown shell is usually 4 to 8 inches wide but can grow to almost 16 inches. Also known as the "edible crab," it has very flavorful flesh.

The **velvet swimming crab** *(Portunus puber)* measures from 3 to 6 inches in diameter, and as its name suggests, its shell and legs are covered with velvety hair. It has powerful pincers and flat rear legs that resemble fins. Its reddish brown shell is adorned with blue spots. The flesh of the velvet swimming crab is much sought after.

The **spider crab** *(Maïa squinado)* lives on sandy seabeds at depths of up to 165 feet. It can be pink, pinkish yellow, or reddish brown and is between 4 and 8 inches wide. Also known as the "spiny crab," it has a rounded triangular spiny shell that is somewhat heart-shaped, and long, slender legs that are arranged like those of a spider. Its flesh is considered to be excellent, but the flesh of the female is more flavorful than that of the male.

The **snow crab** *(Chionoecetes opilio)* is a member of the spider-crab family. Its shell is almost perfectly round but is slightly broader at the rear end; its legs are long and somewhat flat. Often orangey brown, its coloring varies depending on how recently the crab has molted. Only the male of the species is fished because it is much larger than the female. It can be over 5 inches wide and can weigh almost 3 pounds. The snow crab lives in cold water at depths ranging from 65 to 2,300 feet, which enhances the quality of its uniquely flavored, much-sought-after flesh.

The snow crab was long regarded as a nuisance by North American fishermen because it became entangled in their nets and had little commercial value. Initially marketed as "queen crab," with very little success, it is now sold under the more attractive name "snow crab," which originated in Asia. Now much sought after, the snow crab has even come to be regarded as a delicacy.

The **Pacific common crab** (*Cancer magister*) lives in cold waters and belongs to the same family of rock crabs as the Atlantic common crab. It can grow to be 9 inches wide and usually weighs between 2 and 4 pounds. Its shell is a brownish color. Whole Pacific common crabs are sold live, cooked, canned, or frozen. The delicious flesh is also available fresh or frozen.

The **blue crab** (*Callinectes sapidus*) is very popular in the United States. Usually between 6 and 8 inches wide, it thrives in Atlantic coastal waters from Delaware to Florida and is also known as the "Atlantic blue crab." It represents approximately one half of the output of the American crab fishery and has been introduced into European waters. Its sweet flesh is excellent.

Soft-shell crabs are blue crabs that have shed shells they have outgrown and have yet to replace them. These crabs are usually caught between 6 and 48 hours after they begin to molt, which generally occurs between mid-May and mid-September. This extremely short fishing season accounts for the rarity of soft-shell crabs, which many people regard as a delicacy. Soft-shell crabs are usually sold live but are generally in such a weakened state that they appear to be dead. Practically transparent, they are usually just cleaned (the gills and the tail are removed, and the crab is then rinsed in cold water) and sautéed in butter, or fried and served with tartar sauce. Other species of crabs are also eaten as soft-shell crab.

Buying

It is sometimes possible to buy live crabs, but the flesh is usually sold cooked, frozen, or canned. Imitation crab is also widely available (see *Kamaboko*). Never buy (or cook) a live crab unless its limbs are still moving. Hold the crab by the rear end to avoid the pincers, especially if it is large. When buying frozen crab, avoid those that have dried out or are covered with frost – signs that the crab is less than fresh.

Nutritional Information

	snow crab
protein	18 g
fat	1 g
cholesterol	60 mg
calories	89
	per 100 g

Crabmeat is rich in vitamin B_{12}, niacin, copper, and zinc.

Crustaceans

Preparing

To prepare a crab for cooking, make an incision between the underside and the shell, and pull the shell off from above. Be careful not to damage the shell if you intend to serve the crab in it. Remove the legs and pincers, then open them with a nutcracker or some other heavy utensil to remove the flesh.

Serving Ideas

Crab is delicious cold or hot. Prepared in any number of ways, it can replace shrimp, lobster, and other shellfish in most recipes. It is used to make hors d'oeuvres, salads, sandwiches, soups, and omelets, and is particularly tasty in sauces and pasta dishes. It is often fried in its shell.

1 *Remove the legs and pincers from the crab.*

2 *Break open the legs and pincers with lobster pincers or a nutcracker, then remove the flesh.*

3 *Unfold the tail from underneath the crab and twist it until it breaks off; throw it away.*

4 *Remove the plastron (the underside) and set it aside.*

5 *Remove the flesh from inside the shell. Discard the entrails and appendix, located behind the mouth of the animal.*

6 *Cut the plastron in half with a kitchen knife.*

7 *Remove the flesh from the alveoli (cavities) in the plastron.*

Crustaceans

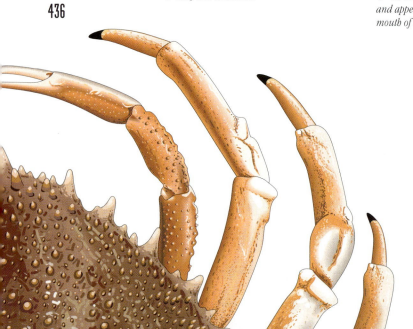

Avocados Stuffed with Crab

SERVES 4

2 ripe avocados   *¼ cup mayonnaise*
Juice of 1 lemon   *1 teaspoon ketchup*
1 rib celery   *1 teaspoon cognac*
1 can crabmeat   *Paprika*

1. Cut the avocados in half and remove the pits. Remove the flesh with a melon baller, being careful not to pierce the skin. Sprinkle the flesh with lemon juice to prevent it from becoming discolored.

2. Cut the celery into thin strips.

3. Drain the crab, then crumble it and remove any remaining pieces of cartilage.

4. Combine the mayonnaise, ketchup, and cognac, then add the crabmeat.

5. Mix the balls of avocado and the celery with the other ingredients, and fill the avocado halves with this stuffing. Sprinkle them with paprika and serve them cold.

Cooking

Like lobster (see *Lobster*), live crabs are cooked by plunging them into salted boiling water. The cooking time varies according to the size of the crab (from 10 to 20 minutes for a 6-inch crab and up to 30 minutes for a very large crab).

Storing

Crabs die soon after they are caught. Avoid storing them at room temperature for any significant length of time. Either cook them immediately or wrap them in a damp cloth and store them in the refrigerator (for no longer than 12 hours). Cooked crab can be refrigerated for 1 or 2 days, and whole crabs (preferably cooked and shelled) can be frozen for about 1 month.

spider crab

Atlantic common crab

Pacific common crab

Crustaceans

437

Scampi

Nephrops norvegicus, Nephropsidae

Scampi are large shellfish that live in the depths of the sea. Similar to small lobsters or large shrimp, they are also known as Norway lobsters or Dublin Bay prawns. The term "scampi" is the plural form of *scampo,* the Italian word for shrimp. Although several related species are found in the Pacific, scampi are most common in the coastal waters of the Atlantic from North Africa to Scandinavia.

Scampi are between 3 and 10 inches long and have large protruding eyes, a pair of very long antennae, thin bodies, and long tails. Like those of crabs, lobsters, and crayfish, the front limbs of scampi are much larger than the others, but they are equipped with long, thin pincers that contain very little flesh. The remaining limbs have white tips and are thinner than the rear limbs of lobsters.

Depending on the species, the shell can be pinkish white, salmon red, brick red, or grayish pink, and it is sometimes covered with reddish or brownish spots. Unlike other shellfish, scampi change color only slightly when cooked. Their flesh is more delicate than lobster and is considered to be excellent.

Nutritional Information

	raw
protein	21 g
fat	2 g
carbohydrates	2.4 g
cholesterol	70 mg
calories	112
	per 100 g

Scampi are rich in calcium, phosphorus, and iron.

Storing

Raw or cooked scampi will keep for 1 or 2 days in the refrigerator and for about 1 month in the freezer.

Buying

Scampi are rarely sold alive because they deteriorate very quickly when removed from water. They can be purchased raw (beheaded and frozen or preserved in crushed ice) or cooked. Look for firm scampi that do not smell of ammonia.

Serving Ideas

Frequently served with garlic butter, scampi can be used in most shellfish recipes and are one of the many ingredients in paella. They are often substituted for jumbo shrimp, and raw scampi can be shelled like shrimp (see *Shrimp*). Avoid overpowering their delicate flavor.

Cooking

Scampi should be cooked like shrimp, lobster, or spiny lobster. They will become tough and lose their flavor if overcooked. Boil them for 3 to 5 minutes, steam them for 6 to 7 minutes, or grill them for 3 minutes per side.

Crayfish

Astacus and *Cambarus* spp., **Crustacea**

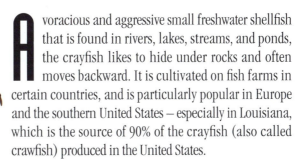

A voracious and aggressive small freshwater shellfish that is found in rivers, lakes, streams, and ponds, the crayfish likes to hide under rocks and often moves backward. It is cultivated on fish farms in certain countries, and is particularly popular in Europe and the southern United States – especially in Louisiana, which is the source of 90% of the crayfish (also called crawfish) produced in the United States.

There over 300 different species of crayfish, but only a few of them are large enough to eat. Some species are distinguished by the color of their claws ("white-clawed crayfish," "red-clawed crayfish").

Crayfish usually measure between 2 and 6 inches, but certain Australian species can grow to be over a foot long. The crayfish sold to consumers are usually about 4 inches long.

The crayfish has one pair of long antennae and five pairs of claws, the largest of which is equipped with pincers. Its shell can be red, brown, or purple, depending on the species. The density of its lean and delicate pinkish white flesh also varies from one species to another.

Buying

Crayfish are sold alive, cooked, frozen, or canned. When buying cooked crayfish, choose fish that have a pleasant odor, a firm shell, and intact claws.

Preparing

Before cooking crayfish, it is important to remove the gut, which can make the flesh taste bitter (the gut is usually removed before crayfish are frozen). The gut should come out if you pull gently on the small fin underneath the tail; if this technique fails, make a lengthwise cut with the point of a knife. This should be done just before crayfish are cooked, because they lose their flavor if the gut is removed too soon.

Serving Ideas

Since the claws contain very little flesh, the tail is the only part of the crayfish that is eaten. The shell can be crushed and used to flavor court bouillon, bisque, or butter. Crayfish is prepared like lobster, crab, and shrimp and can replace them in most recipes. Often served au gratin, it is also used to make bisque, mousse, soufflés, salads, and French onion soup.

Cooking

Allow whole crayfish to cook for 5 to 8 minutes in court bouillon. Steam crayfish tails for 10 to 12 minutes, or grill them for 3 to 5 minutes.

Nutritional Information

	raw
protein	19 g
fat	1 g
cholesterol	139 mg
calories	89
	per 100 g

Crayfish is rich in niacin, vitamin B$_{12}$, potassium, phosphorus, and copper.

Storing

Live crayfish can be covered with a damp cloth and stored in the refrigerator for up to 12 hours. Cooked crayfish can be refrigerated for 1 or 2 days and frozen for 1 or 2 months.

Spiny lobster

Palinurus spp. and *Jasus* spp., **Palinuridae**

As its name suggests, the spiny lobster is a crustacean that resembles the lobster but whose shell is covered with spines. Less aggressive than the lobster, it is also known as the rock lobster because it lives among rocks at the bottom of the sea. It prefers temperate or tropical waters and likes to hide in seaweed. Found in the Atlantic, the Adriatic, the Mediterranean, and the Pacific, the spiny lobster is particularly common off the coasts of California, Chile, Australia, New Zealand, and South Africa.

There are several different species of spiny lobster, and their color depends on their habitat. Those found in the Atlantic are usually reddish brown, while those in Pacific are slightly greener. Commercially available spiny lobsters are between 12 and 20 inches long and weigh between 1 and 5 pounds. Equipped with a pair of long antennae, the spiny lobster has hooks rather than large pincers on the ends of its limbs, and its tail is much longer than its chest, or thorax. Its white flesh is slightly less flavorful than lobster.

Buying

The spiny lobster is rarely sold alive or whole. In most cases only the tail is sold, either raw or cooked and usually frozen.

Nutritional Information

protein	17 g
fat	2 g
carbohydrates	0.5 g
calories	91
	per 100 g

Spiny lobster is rich in niacin, vitamin B$_{12}$, and zinc.

Serving Ideas

It is best to cook spiny lobster simply, so as not to mask its delicate flavor. Although it is less flavorful than lobster, it can be used as a substitute in most lobster recipes. Delicious in salads, it is often eaten with just a touch of garlic butter.

Cooking

It is important not to overcook spiny lobster because its flesh will quickly become tough and rubbery. It takes about 15 minutes to cook when boiled and only about 5 minutes when grilled.

Storing

Raw or cooked spiny lobster will keep for 1 or 2 days in the refrigerator and for about 1 month in the freezer.

Mollusks

Introduction

Invertebrates with soft bodies that are often protected by hard shells, mollusks are part of a large family that is divided into three main branches: gastropods, bivalves (or lamellibranchia), and cephalopods. Gastropods and bivalves are often referred to as shellfish.

Gastropods (periwinkle, whelk, abalone) are contained inside a single shell (univalve). The shells of the periwinkle and the whelk are spiral shaped. Gastropods are equipped with a flat ventral "foot" that allows them to move around.

Bivalves (oyster, clam, great scallop, scallop, mussel, quahog, queen scallop, carpet shell, soft-shell clam) have a shell that consists of two valves united by a hinge in the form of a ligament. Their gills resemble plates; hence the name "lamellibranchia," which means "plate-gilled" in New Latin. Most bivalves are sedentary; they remain stationary on the sea bed, nestling among rocks or other objects or burrowing into the sand. The scallop, the great scallop, and the queen scallop move through the water by closing their shells abruptly, thus expelling water and propelling themselves forward.

Cephalopods (squid, octopus, cuttlefish, little cuttle) have no external shell, but rather an internal cartilage or, in the case of the cuttlefish, a bone. They are equipped with numerous suckered "arms" or tentacles (eight to ten) that they use to capture prey and to move around.

Shellfish can be inedible if caught in polluted waters or if they have ingested a toxin-producing microscopic alga such as *Gonyaulax tamarensis* or *Alexandrium spp.* Carpet shells, clams, and soft-shell clams contaminated with this alga have caused several cases of paralyzing food poisoning in the past. The main symptoms of this kind of food poisoning are swelling and stinging (first affecting the lips, then the neck and face), a tingling sensation in the fingers and toes that can spread to the arms and legs, as well headaches, dizziness, overall weakness, muscular paralysis, and breathing difficulties. In fact, people who consume contaminated mollusks can die within 72 hours. Toxic algae are found primarily in the digestive system and gills of mollusks. Never eat mollusks that come from polluted waters or areas where toxic algae are present.

Buying

Mollusks should be kept very cool until they are eaten or cooked. When buying unshelled mollusks, ensure that they are still alive. The shells of live mollusks are either closed or will close when tapped. You can also try sliding the two halves of the shells against each other; if they do not move, the mollusk is still alive. When tapped, unshelled mollusks should emit a muffled sound, which indicates that they are full of water. Fresh octopus, squid, and cuttlefish should be firm and moist and should have a mild fishy smell.

The shells of mollusks should be brushed under running water. If they are full of sand, soak the mollusks for an hour or two in salted water (4 to 5 tablespoons of salt per quart of water). Scallops and abalones should be washed after their shells are opened.

To open live mollusks, slip a knife between the shells, then twist it (you may have to cut the adductor muscle that holds the shells together), or separate the shells when they are slightly open. Another option is to heat the mollusks in a dry saucepan or a medium oven for a few seconds; they can also be briefly steamed or microwaved (on high power).

Serving Ideas

 Several species of mollusks can be eaten either raw or cooked (oyster, scallop, clam, quahog, carpet shell), while others must always be cooked (periwinkle, whelk).

Mollusks become shriveled and tough when overcooked, and soft and pasty when cooked in liquid.

Mollusks from some regions can be inedible, especially if gathered during the hot months of summer, because they may have been contaminated by pathogenic bacteria or toxic algae in the water. Never gather mollusks in areas that have been closed to fishermen due to the possibility of contamination.

Nutritional Information

 Mollusks are rich in protein and minerals, and low in fat, cholesterol, and calories.

Storing

Fresh or cooked mollusks can be refrigerated for 1 or 2 days. Shelled mollusks can be frozen for about 3 months.

Mollusks

443

Abalone

Haliotis spp., Haliotidae

A gastropod mollusk with an ear-shaped shell, the abalone is also known as the ear shell, sea-ear, or ormer (a shortened form of the French name, *oreille de mer*). It has numerous small holes for eliminating water and waste around the edge of its shell. The edible portion of the abalone is the gray-brown muscle or "foot" with which it attaches itself to rocks. While the outside of its shell is often a reddish or pinkish color, the inside has a nacreous surface that is frequently used to make jewelry. Mature abalones are usually 4 to 10 inches in diameter. There are over 100 species of abalone around the world.

Most common in the Pacific and Indian oceans, the abalone is fished in California, Australia, New Zealand, Chile, Japan, and South Africa. The Japanese, who are particularly fond of abalones, buy most of the world's output of the mollusk.

Fished individually, abalones are easy to gather when caught by surprise, but they adhere firmly to their rocks if they know they are under attack. A task frequently performed by divers (poles are sometimes used), fishing for abalones can be very dangerous because sharks share many of the mollusk's habitats. The abalone fishery is regulated in many countries because the mollusk is threatened with extinction.

Usually white, the flesh of the abalone is firm, dense, and very flavorful. It is shaped like the scallop but is considerably larger. The abalone tenses up when it is caught, and its muscle remains contracted even after it has been removed from the shell. Although the flesh is often beaten before it is sold, it is important to ensure that it has been tenderized before it is cooked.

Buying

Rare and expensive, abalones are usually sold canned, dehydrated, or frozen.

When buying fresh unshelled abalones, touch the feet to ensure that they still move.

Serving Ideas

 Abalones can be eaten raw or cooked, and are excellent in appetizers, salads, soups, and steamed dishes. *Loco,* a classic Chilean dish, is comprised of abalones and mayonnaise.

Preparing

To shell fresh abalones, insert the blade of a knife into the thinnest part of the shell, behind the muscle. Move the blade around until the flesh is separated from the shell; then remove the entire foot. Wash raw abalones thoroughly, using a small brush if necessary, in order to remove the intestines and dislodge the sand that gets caught in the folds of their flesh. Abalones can be left whole or cut into slices.

To tenderize abalones, place them between two clean cloths or two sheets of plastic and flatten them with a rolling pin, a mallet, a rock, or any other heavy object. They can also placed in a strong bag and beaten against a hard surface for a few minutes.

Abalones can also be tenderized in a pressure cooker: Cook the abalone in 1 pint (500 ml) of water for 20 minutes; then allow it cool in the liquid or let it simmer for up to 4 hours. Prepare the tenderized abalone as desired.

Cooking

Abalones can be boiled, grilled, sautéed, braised, or fried. Thin slices should be cooked over high heat for about 30 seconds per side. Do not add abalones to cooked dishes until the last minute, and salt them just before they are served.

Storing

 Fresh unshelled abalones can be refrigerated for up to 3 days if covered with a damp cloth; fresh shelled abalones will keep for 1 or 2 days in the refrigerator. Freshly caught abalones should be soaked in salt water for 2 days to allow the contents of the stomach to be expelled (change the water from time to time). Shelled abalones can be frozen for about 3 months.

Nutritional Information

calories	105
carbohydrates	6 g
protein	17 g
fat	1 g
	per 100 g

Abalones are rich in vitamin B$_{12}$, niacin, and pantothenic acid.

Cockle

Cardium spp., **Cardiidae**

Bivalve mollusks that inhabit the sandy and muddy bottoms of marine coastal waters, cockles are readily accessible when the tide is low. The term "cockle" usually refers to the European cockle *(Cardium edule)*, which is found primarily in the Mediterranean, the Atlantic, and the Baltic; but there are in fact several species of cockles. Firmer and stronger-tasting than oysters and mussels, cockles are also less popular.

The number of radiating ridges on the thick, rounded shell of the cockle varies from one species to another. The shell can be an off-white, gray, or reddish brown color, and is adorned with brown, reddish, crimson, pink, or yellow stripes or marbling. Capable of growing to a length of about 3 inches, the cockle has a large external ligament and pale, lean flesh.

Buying

Live cockles are usually tightly sealed; if slightly open, they will close when tapped.

Preparing

Thoroughly wash and scrub the cockles, and discard any dead ones. If their shells are full of sand (as is often the case), allow them to soak for an hour or more in salted fresh water (1 or 2 tablespoons of salt per quart of water) or for 12 hours in seawater. Cockles can be opened with an oyster knife, or by heating them for a few minutes in a steamer or for a few seconds in a microwave oven (30 seconds at high power for 6 cockles).

Storing

Fresh cockles can be refrigerated for up to 3 days if covered with a damp cloth. Shelled cockles can be kept in the refrigerator for 1 or 2 days if stored in their own liquid in a tightly sealed container.

Shelled cockles can be frozen for about 3 months when covered with their own juices and stored in a freezer container.

Serving Ideas

Cockles can be eaten raw or cooked, either hot or cold, and can replace mussels and clams in most recipes. They are particularly delicious in fish soups.

Nutritional Information

	raw
protein	17 g
fat	1 g
calories	81
	per 100 g

Scallop

Pecten spp., Pectinidae

The scallop is a bivalve marine mollusk with rounded, almost identical shells that are joined by a small hinge. Unlike most other mollusks, the scallop can be quite mobile, propelling itself forward by means of the impetus created when it closes its shells abruptly. Sedentary unless it comes under attack, the scallop lives at the bottom of the sea, sometimes making itself practically invisible by attaching itself to objects on the ocean floor. The scallop grows relatively slowly, and its rate of growth is influenced by the temperature of the water in which it lives. The colder the water, the longer it takes for scallops to mature (from 4 to 7 years). The age of a scallop can be calculated by counting the number of rings on its upper shell. The Japanese were the first to breed scallops successfully.

The large Pectinidae family includes over 300 species, all of which are edible. The most popular species in Europe are the great scallop or *coquille Saint-Jacques* (the name of a popular scallop dish in North America) and the queen scallop, or quin. The most common species in North America are known simply as scallops. The flesh of all of these species is quite similar; what usually distinguishes one species from another is their size and the exterior of their shells.

The **great scallop** (*Pecten maximus* or *Pecten Jacobeus*) is found in the eastern Atlantic and the Mediterranean. It is particularly abundant in French and Spanish coastal waters. This variety of scallop was christened the *coquille Saint-Jacques* when medieval pilgrims visiting the shrine of St. James at Santiago de Compostella in Spain began to use the empty shells to eat from and to beg with. The shells became the symbol of the popular shrine, and all those who visited the site earned the right to use them. The poorest pilgrims hung the shells in full view above their doors, while the rich added them to their coats of arms. The great scallop is comprised of two large shells adorned with radiating ribs; one of the shells is rounded and the other is quite flat. A lug protrudes from either side of the hinge, which is joined by a ligament. The color of the shells, which can be pinkish, reddish, brownish, or yellowish, varies according to the habitat. The great scallop measures from 4 to 6 inches in diameter and weighs an average of 4 ounces.

The **queen scallop** or **quin** (*Chlamys opercularis*) is often confused with other very similar species known simply as scallops. Relatively small (2 to 3 inches), it has off-white shells with brown spots, several rather large radiating ribs, and two lugs of different sizes. The species referred to simply as **scallops** have two valves adorned with radiating ribs, and some have lugs of different sizes. Their flesh resembles that of the great scallop. Three of these species are particularly abundant in the Atlantic coastal waters of North America: the Atlantic deep-sea scallop, the Iceland scallop, and the bay scallop.

The **Atlantic deep-sea scallop** *(Placopecten magellanicus)* is the largest member of the scallop family. It can grow to be 6 to 12 inches in diameter. Its slightly rounded upper shell is usually reddish brown and is covered with numerous small protruding ribs. Its white or cream-colored lower shell is relatively flat and smooth, and its lugs are of equal size. The Atlantic deep-sea scallop is one of the most commercially important species in North America.

The **bay scallop** *(Aequipecten irradians)* is rather small (2 to 3 inches). Its grayish brown, crimson-gray, or blackish shells are adorned with approximately 18 rounded ribs and have identical lugs.

The **Iceland scallop** *(Chlamys islandicus)* has convex shells adorned with about 50 large, irregular ribs. Usually gray or crimson, these shells can be tinged with yellow, red, or crimson. One of the two lugs adjoining the shells is twice as long as the other. The edible portions of these mollusks are the "nut" – the delicate, flavorful flesh of the large white muscle that opens and closes the shells – and the coral, the relatively flaky flesh of the reproductive glands. When these glands mature at the end of spring, the female glands turn a beautiful shade of red and the male glands become cream-colored. The coral is rarely eaten in North America.

Buying

Since scallops are extremely perishable, they are often shelled and washed as soon as they are caught, then immediately covered with ice or frozen. The shells of live fresh scallops will close when tapped. When buying shelled fresh scallops, ensure that the flesh is white, firm, and odorless.

If scallops are not clearly marked "fresh" or "defrosted," be sure to ask if they have been frozen, because defrosted scallops have to be cooked before they can be refrozen. Frozen scallops should be firm, shiny, and moist, and the inside of their packaging should be free of frost.

Preparing

Scallops can be opened like oysters, once the closed shells have been rinsed under cold water. Detach the muscle by sliding the blade of a knife under the beards (the gray external edge); then remove the small black pocket and the beards, which can be used to make a fish fumet (a strongly flavored reduced stock that is added to sauces). Cut the small tough muscle on the side of the nut; remove the nut and the coral, then wash them carefully.

Serving Ideas

Scallops can be eaten raw or cooked, and are delicious with a little lemon juice, as well as in sashimi or ceviche. Prepared in a wide variety of ways, they can be grilled, poached, breaded, sautéed, steamed, fried, marinated, or cooked au gratin. The ovenproof shells of these mollusks are often used as cooking or serving dishes.

Storing

Fresh or cooked scallops can be refrigerated for 1 or 2 days in a sealed container. Frozen scallops will keep for up to 3 months. To defrost them, plunge them into boiling milk that has been removed from the heat or put them in the refrigerator. However, they will retain more of their flavor if they are cooked while still frozen.

Mollusks

447

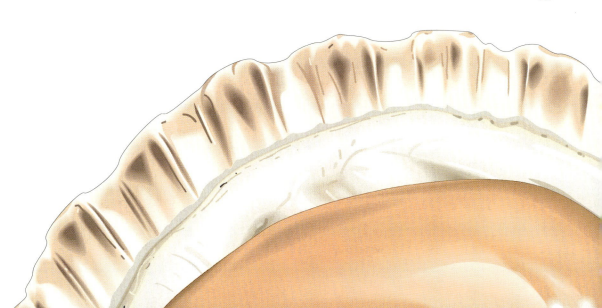

Cooking

 Small scallops can be cooked whole, but larger ones should be cut into pieces or slices. Scallops should not be cooked for very long (3 or 4 minutes is usually enough) because they quickly start to become tough, dry, and flavorless.

Nutritional Information

	raw
protein	17 g
fat	1 g
carbohydrates	2.4 g
calories	88
	per 100 g

Scallops are rich in vitamin B_{12} and potassium.

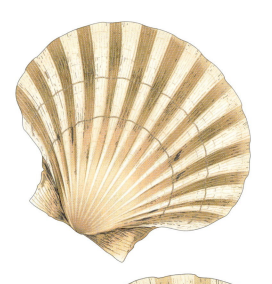

Scallops au Gratin

SERVES 4

1 lb. (500 g) fresh scallops	Bouquet garni
¼ lb. (125 g) fresh mushrooms	2 tbsp. butter
	1 tbsp. lemon juice
1 onion	4 tbsp. dried bread
1 rib celery	crumbs
½ cup (125 ml) cold water	**For the sauce:**
1 ½ cups (375 ml) dry white wine	3 tbsp. butter
	3 level tbsp. flour
Salt and ground pepper	¼ cup (60 ml) heavy cream

1. Rinse the scallops. Wash and dice the mushrooms. Finely chop the onion, and cut the celery rib into sections.

2. Bring the court bouillon (the cold water, white wine, celery, salt, pepper, and bouquet garni) to a boil. Add the scallops, then cover the saucepan and allow the scallops to poach for 10 minutes. After removing the pan from the heat, set the scallops aside (cut large ones into slices). Strain the liquid through a very fine sieve, then set it aside too.

3. Melt the 2 tablespoons butter in a saucepan, and gently brown the onions and the mushrooms. Add the lemon juice and allow the mixture to simmer over low heat for 5 minutes. Add the scallops, and cook for another 5 minutes.

4. Prepare the sauce: Mix the butter and flour in a saucepan over low heat. When this mixture starts to bubble, add ¾ cup (180 ml) of the reserved bouillon and the ¼ cup cream. Do this slowly to ensure that the sauce remains smooth. Stir the sauce constantly until it reaches the desired consistency (it should be quite thick).

5. Fill the buttered shells with equal portions of the scallop mixture, then pour on the sauce and sprinkle on the bread crumbs. Brown the topping under the broiler, and serve the shells immediately.

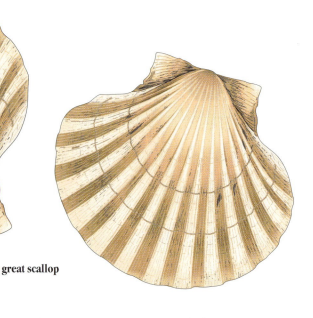

great scallop

Clam

Venus spp., Veneridae

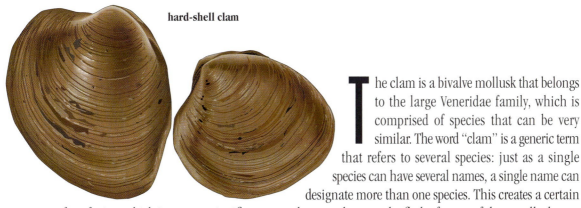

hard-shell clam

The clam is a bivalve mollusk that belongs to the large Veneridae family, which is comprised of species that can be very similar. The word "clam" is a generic term that refers to several species: just as a single species can have several names, a single name can designate more than one species. This creates a certain amount of confusion, which is not very significant to us, however, because the flesh of many of these mollusks can be quite similar.

Clams prefer to live in shallow water; they burrow into sandy or muddy seabeds by means of an extendable siphon, which they also use to feed and to expel waste once they have taken up their position in the sand. Found in seas throughout the world, they thrive in the Atlantic between Labrador and Mexico. Anthropologists have discovered evidence of the consumption of clams at prehistoric sites.

Most clams have very hard shells. In fact, "quahog," a name common to several species, is derived from an Algonquin word meaning "hard shell." The Latin name of the **surf clam,** *Spisula solidissima,* also refers to the hardness of the shell. Several species have smooth shells (the surf clam, the razor clam), while others, such as the **quahog** *(Venus mercenaria),* have ridged shells. The color, shape, and size of the shells vary from one species to another. They are often brown, brownish black, light gray, or chalk-white.

The **razor-shells** or **jackknife clams** (*Ensis* spp.) are long and thin. Sharp enough to cut through skin, their shell is six times as long as it is wide. However, most other clams have elliptical shells. One of the largest, the **surf clam** or **bar clam,** can be up to 7 inches wide but usually measures about 6 inches. The **ocean quahog** can be over 5 inches wide, and the **hard-shell clam** or **littleneck** (*Mercenaria mercenaria*) can be almost 6 inches wide. The **soft-shell clam** or **long-neck** (*Mya arenaria*) can also be over 5 inches wide but usually measures between 2 and 3 inches.

The flesh of these mollusks varies in color according to the species, ranging from creamy white to gray to dark orange.

Buying

Clams are sold fresh (either shelled or unshelled), cooked, frozen, or canned. When buying unshelled clams, ensure that they are still alive. The shells of live mollusks are tightly sealed, or will close slowly when tapped. Choose clams that have a mild, fresh smell and avoid those that smell of ammonia.

Mollusks

449

Clam

Nutritional Information

protein	13 g
fat	1 g
carbohydrates	3 g
cholesterol	34 mg
calories	74
	per 100 g

Clams are rich in vitamin B$_{12}$, potassium, and iron. Their flesh is lean.

Cooking

Avoid overcooking clams because they become tough very quickly. Poach, steam, or microwave them until their shells open.

Preparing

Fresh clams should be eaten as soon as possible because they will not live for long. Since their shells almost always contain sand, it is best to soak them before they are cooked; use seawater or salted water (5 or 6 tablespoons of salt per quart of water). Allow them to soak for 1 to 6 hours, changing the water from time to time (mollusks will run out of oxygen and die if they are soaked in the same water for a long period of time).

Clams are less difficult to open after they have been refrigerated for a while. This relaxes the adductor muscle and makes it easier to slip the blade of a knife between the shells. Be careful not to damage the shells, and be sure to reserve the liquid they contain for storing and cooking the mollusks. They can also be opened by exposing them to dry heat (oven, barbecue) for a few minutes, by microwaving them on high power for a few seconds, or by steaming them. Before opening or cooking clams, wash and scrub the shells to remove all traces of sand and lichen.

quahog

Serving Ideas

The smallest of these mollusks can be eaten raw or cooked; they are excellent plain or with a little lemon juice. The larger ones are tougher and usually have to be cooked. They are frequently chopped and added to sauces and fish soups. Clam chowder is very popular in the United States, especially in New England. Spaghetti *alle vongole* (with clams, tomatoes, and garlic) is a common Italian pasta dish.

Clams are particularly good when prepared with shallots, tomatoes, white wine, and thyme. They are used to make dips, sauces, salads, croquettes, vinaigrettes, paellas, soufflés, quiches, and stews. They can also be stuffed or marinated. Clams can replace other mollusks (oysters, mussels, scallops) in most recipes.

Storing

Fresh unshelled clams can be kept for up to 3 days in the refrigerator if stored in a container that is covered with a damp cloth. Fresh or cooked shelled clams will keep for 1 or 2 days. They can also be frozen for up to 3 months when shelled and stored in a freezer container filled with their own liquid. They will retain more of their flavor if they are cooked while still frozen.

Clam Chowder

SERVES 4 TO 6

2 oz. (60 g) salt pork	1 cup (250 ml) milk
2 potatoes	Salt and ground pepper
2 medium onions	Paprika
1 tablespoon fresh parsley leaves	1 bay leaf
1 lb. (500 g) canned clams	1 cup (250 ml) heavy cream
⅔ cup (160 ml) boiling water	4 tablespoons dry sherry

1. Trim and dice the salt pork. Peel and dice the potatoes. Peel and finely chop the onions. Chop the parsley.

2. Strain and chop the clams, reserving their liquid (there should be 1 cup/250 ml).

3. Cook the diced salt pork in a heavy saucepan over medium heat until most of the fat has melted. Add the onions and cook them in the lardons until they are transparent and the lardons are crisp and golden.

4. Gradually pour the boiling water and the milk into the saucepan; then add the potatoes, salt and pepper, paprika, and bay leaf. Bring the mixture to a boil. Reduce the heat and allow it to simmer for about 10 minutes, until the potatoes are tender.

5. Add the clams and their liquid, and bring the chowder to a boil again. Remove it from the heat and add the cream. Cook it over low heat just long enough to warm the cream, then remove it from the heat and stir in the sherry.

6. Serve the chowder, sprinkling each portion with chopped parsley.

Mussel

Muscullus spp. and *Mytilus* spp., **Mytilidae**

blue mussels

Bivalve mollusks that thrive in marine coastal waters, mussels attach themselves in clusters to sandbanks, rocks, and other objects by secreting a mass of strong silky threads known as a "byssus" or "beard." Although they are found all over the world, mussels prefer colder waters. Particularly vulnerable to pollution (because they filter up to 18 gallons of water per day), they are often bred in controlled environments. Cultivated mussels are pollution-free and contain no sand or parasites (the source of the small gray pearls often found inside mussel shells). Their flesh is more tender, more abundant, and paler than the flesh of natural mussels, which are rarely sold to consumers. Mussels are reared in a variety of ways. The *bouchot* method is named for the wooden hurdles on which the mussels cluster. An Irishman named Patrick Walton is thought to have stumbled upon this method after being shipwrecked off the coast of France at the end of the 13th century. In an attempt to catch birds for food, he strung nets from posts he set up in the water; after a while, he noticed that the posts were covered with mussels.

The mussel is comprised of two thin oblong valves of equal size. The shell of the most common species, the blue mussel *(Mytilus edulis),* is usually smooth but is sometimes covered with concentric ridges; blackish blue in color, it is frequently dotted with eroded crimson patches. The valves of the shell can be concave, convex, or straight, and the shiny, polished, iridescent interior is white or pale gray with darker, sometimes crimson edges. The blue mussel is between 1 and 4 inches in diameter, and the elastic ligament that connects its twin valves protrudes from the shell. The flesh of female mussels is orange, while that of males is a whitish color. There are a great many species of mussels, and the amount and firmness of their flesh varies from one species to another.

Buying

Mussels are sold fresh (either shelled or unshelled) or canned. Never buy unshelled mussels unless they are still alive. The shells of live mussels are usually closed, and those that are open should close slowly when tapped. Canned mussels are packed in a variety of substances, including water, oil, tomatoes, and white wine, and are sometimes smoked.

Preparing

Wash and scrub the mussels. It is not necessary to remove all the filaments attached to the outside of the shells if you like the flavor they add to the stock. Mussels that are open and will not close when tapped, as well as those with damaged shells, are inedible and should be discarded.

Mussels that are unusually heavy may be filled with mud or sand. Either throw them out or soak them for an hour or more in salted fresh water (4 or 5 tablespoons of salt per quart of water).

After mussels are soaked or scraped, the adductor sometimes protrudes from their shells, which suggests that they may no longer be alive. To determine if a mussel is dead or alive, try sliding the two valves of the shell back and forth; if you succeed in moving them, the mussel is in fact dead and should be discarded.

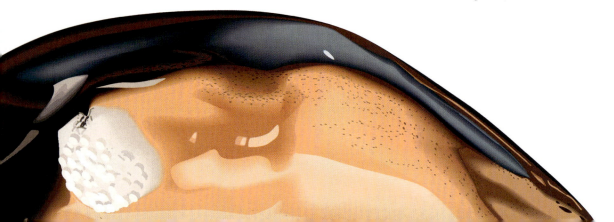

Serving Ideas

Mussels are rarely eaten raw, except when they have been freshly caught on the open sea and are thus unlikely to have been exposed to pollution. Cultivated mussels containing domoic acid, a toxic substance found in seaweed, have been known to cause food poisoning. As a result of such incidents, strict controls have been put in place to ensure that mussels are free of contaminants.

Of the many ways in which mussels can be prepared, the most famous is perhaps mussels *à la marinière:* cooked in their shells with white wine, butter, onions or shallots, parsley, and pepper. Use approximately 2 pounds of mussels per person when serving this dish as a main course.

Mussels can also be grilled, sautéed, fried, marinated, stuffed, or cooked au gratin or on brochettes. They are also a common ingredient in soups, sauces, hors d'oeuvres, salads, paellas, stews, and omelets.

Canned mussels can be eaten "as is," either hot or cold.

Cooking

Poach or steam mussels until their shells open (2 to 5 minutes). If the recipe calls for unshelled mussels, remove them from their shells as soon as this can be done with ease, then continue to cook them as directed. Discard mussels that do not open when cooked.

Mussels à la Marinière

SERVES 4

6 lb. (3 kg) mussels
2 shallots
2 tbsp. butter
1 bay leaf
2 tbsp. chopped parsley
Salt and freshly ground
   pepper

¾ cup (180 ml) dry
   white wine
3 tbsp. light cream or
   half-and-half

1. Scrape and wash the mussels.

2. Chop the shallots and divide the butter into several pieces.

3. Put the mussels in a large saucepan with the shallots, the bay leaf, the parsley, and the butter. Add the salt and pepper, then the wine.

4. Cover the saucepan and cook the mussels over high heat for 3 to 5 minutes until they open up, shaking the saucepan from time to time. When all of the mussels are open, put them in a bowl and reserve the liquid.

5. Strain the liquid and bring it to a boil in another saucepan. Add the cream and pour this mixture over the mussels. Serve very hot.

Nutritional Information

	raw
protein	12 g
fat	2 g
calories	86
	per 100 g

Blue mussels are rich in B-complex vitamins such as riboflavin, niacin, folic acid, and vitamin B_{12}. They are also rich in phosphorus, iron, and zinc.

Storing

Fresh unshelled mussels will keep for up to 3 days in the refrigerator when stored in a container and covered with a damp cloth. Shelled mussels stored in liquid in a tightly sealed container can be refrigerated for 24 to 48 hours. Mussels should always be eaten as soon as possible after they are purchased.

Raw shelled mussels can be frozen in their own juices in a freezer container for up to 3 months.

Oyster

Ostrea spp. and *Crassostrea* spp., Ostreidae

The oyster is a bivalve mollusk with thick, rough, irregular grayish or brownish shells. The top shell is larger and flatter than the lower one, which is concave and houses the body of the oyster. Oysters are classified as either flat or cupped, the flat varieties being more common in Europe.

Eaten since prehistoric times, the oyster was a particular favorite of the Romans, the Celts, and the Greeks. In ancient Greece, oysters were used as ballots as well as food: electors voted by scratching their choices onto the surface of the shells.

Relatively easy to breed, oysters have been grown in oyster beds for over 2,000 years and were first cultivated on a large scale by the Romans and the Gauls. Today the leading oyster-producing countries are the United States, Japan, Korea, and France, but the oyster is also farmed in numerous other countries, including South Africa, Australia, New Zealand, and Canada.

Oysters are also prized for their magnificent pearls, which, unlike those of other mollusks, are large enough to be fashioned into jewelry. These pearls are formed when a grain of sand or a piece of the shell becomes lodged inside the oyster, which then secretes a nacreous liquid in order to protect itself from this foreign body. Cultured pearls are produced by inserting a tiny pearl inside the shell, thus prompting the oyster to secrete layers of calcium carbonate. The most beautiful pearls are produced by the *Pinctada* genus, which lives in warm-water seas.

Oysters are either male or female, but it is not unusual for their gender to change at least once over the course of their lifetimes. Unlike mussels, oysters do not affix themselves to rocks or other objects by secreting a mass of silky threads, but rather by attaching themselves to other oysters or to a host. Capable of forming colonies, oysters feed on plankton, plants, and microscopic aquatic animals. Like all mollusks, they are particularly vulnerable to pollution (see *Mollusks*).

Oysters thrive in both tropical and temperate seas, but those found in temperate waters mature less quickly, often taking as long as 4 to 7 years to grow to a length of 3 inches – a size sometimes attained by tropical oysters in only 2 years. The slow-growing oysters found in temperate waters are renowned for their flavor.

The ample, shiny flesh of oysters can be grayish brown, pearl-gray, or beige, and may be even slightly green if the oyster has fed on seaweed. Its consistency changes during the reproductive season (from May to August in the Northern Hemisphere), becoming milky and soft. For this reason, it is often said that oysters are edible only during months that contain the letter "r" (from September to April); however, they are not actually inedible during the summer months, just less appetizing and more perishable. At any rate, this restriction is no longer always applicable – at least for cultivated oysters – because American researchers have invented a new genetic procedure that makes oysters sterile, effectively ending the reproductive cycle and eliminating the period during which they are less flavorful.

In North America, oysters are often named for the areas they inhabit. Blue Point and Cape Cod oysters are among the most popular varieties in the United States, while Caraquet (named for Caraquet Bay in New Brunswick) and Malpèque (cultivated in Prince Edward Island) oysters are renowned in eastern Canada. Likewise, the most sought-after Australian variety is known as the Sydney Rock oyster.

Preparing

Opening oysters requires a certain amount of skill. Oyster knives have solid handles and thick blades specially designed for opening the shells. (If you use an ordinary kitchen knife, the odds of cutting yourself are greater and the knife can break.) Use a knife with a stainless-steel blade to avoid transferring the taste of metal to the oysters.

Hold the oyster firmly in one hand, with the rounded side down so that less liquid is lost. Insert the blade of the knife between the shells, near the hinge. Twist the blade to separate the shells, then cut the muscle that joins them together. Next slip the blade of the knife underneath the oyster to detach it from the shell. All that remains to be done is to remove any fragments of shell that may be stuck to the oyster. You may want to protect your hand with a glove, a cloth, or thick paper, in case the knife slips.

Oysters are easier to open if the adductor muscle is softened by heating them in a medium oven for 30 to 60 seconds, steaming them for a few seconds, or microwaving them on high power for 1 minute. Before opening oysters, scrub them with a brush under cold running water. Never soak oysters in water, because they can die if they open and their liquid drains out.

It is impossible to assess the freshness of oysters without opening them. Never eat oysters unless they are firm and plump, and are stored in clear liquid that has a pleasant odor.

1 Hold the shell with a cloth. Insert the knife between the two valves of the shell.

2 Twist the knife to separate the shells.

3 Sever the muscle, then remove any fragments of shell that may be stuck to the oyster.

4 Slide the blade underneath the oyster to detach it from the shell.

Buying

Do not buy fresh unshelled oysters unless they are still alive and full of water. Live oysters are usually closed, and if they are slightly open, will close when tapped. Oysters that are filled with water are quite heavy. Unshelled oysters are usually sold by the dozen or the crate. Oysters are also shelled and sold either fresh or frozen, by the pound. Shelled fresh oysters should be firm, fleshy, and shiny, and the liquid in which they are stored should be clear, not milky. Shelled oysters are more expensive, but none of the flesh is wasted. Oysters are usually classified according to their size and shape, not their flavor.

Nutritional Information

	raw
water	80%
protein	7 g
fat	3 g
carbohydrates	4 g
cholesterol	55 mg
calories	65
	per 100 g

Oysters are rich in vitamin B_{12}, iron, zinc, and copper. They are said to be especially nourishing and are reputed to have regenerative and invigorating properties. Some people even consider them an aphrodisiac.

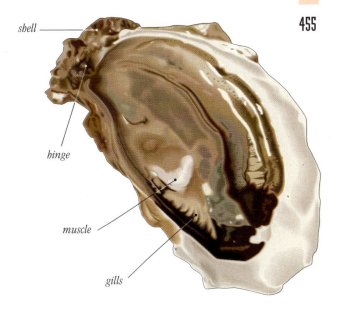

shell

hinge

muscle

gills

Serving Ideas

Oysters are usually eaten raw, either plain or with a little lemon juice or pepper. Cooked oysters are delicious hot or cold. Prepared in many different ways, oysters are often used in soups, pâtés, and sauces or cooked au gratin.

Preshelled oysters can be eaten raw if they are very fresh, but they are often less flavorful than unshelled oysters and are more suitable for use in cooked dishes. Although canned smoked oysters are sold "ready to eat," they can also be rinsed and marinated.

Storing

Shelled oysters stored in their own liquid will keep for about 10 days in the refrigerator and for about 3 months in the freezer, depending on how fresh they are when purchased. However, they should be eaten as soon as possible.

Unshelled oysters can be kept for up to 6 weeks in a container covered with a damp cloth. Never store them in a bag or a tightly sealed container because they will be unable to breathe.

Oysters cannot survive at temperatures lower than 33°F (1°C) or higher than 57°F (14°C). Never freeze unshelled oysters.

Cooking

Oysters can be cooked, but they become rubbery and pasty if even slightly overcooked.

To cook them, plunge them into boiling liquid and immediately remove the saucepan from the heat, leaving the oysters in the liquid for just a few minutes. If you decide to cook them a little more, allow them to simmer for a few minutes, but do not bring the liquid to a boil or the oysters will become hard and shriveled. They should never be cooked for longer than 5 minutes. As soon as the edges of the oysters start to curl up, remove them from the liquid.

Oyster Soup

SERVES 4 TO 6

1 onion
1 rib celery
Chives
1½ cups (375 ml) milk
1½ cups (375 ml) heavy cream
Salt and ground pepper

½ cup (125 ml) dry white wine
1 cup (250 ml) canned oysters in their juice
2 tbsp. butter
1 pinch cayenne pepper

1. Quarter the onion, cut the celery into sections, and chop the chives.

2. Put the milk, cream, vegetables, and salt and pepper in a saucepan and heat this mixture slowly for 20 minutes without allowing it to come to a boil. Once the vegetables are cooked, strain them and return the liquid to the saucepan, keeping it warm.

3. Heat the wine until it reaches the boiling point, then add the oysters and their juice. Cover the saucepan and poach the oysters for a few minutes.

4. Add the oysters to the mixture of hot milk and cream, then add the butter and the cayenne pepper. Sprinkle on the chives.

flat oyster

cupped Pacific oyster

Squid

Loligo spp., Loliginidae

The squid is a cephalopod mollusk with a soft body that is supported by an internal shell. Many of the 350 species of squid inhabit shallow coastal waters or live near the surface on the open sea, while others thrive in the depths of the ocean. The torpedo-shaped bodies of squid vary in color in accordance with their habitats. They are often white with flecks of red, brown, pink, or purple. Their eyes are very large and their mouths have several teeth. The ten suckered arms or tentacles that protrude from their heads allow them to feed and move around. Their bodies contain a feather-shaped transparent cartilage known as a "pen." Most of the back half of their bodies is comprised of two triangular fins that distinguish them from cuttlefish, a closely related species. The length of these fins, which vary greatly in size, depends on the particular species of squid. The squid moves through the water with astonishing speed.

Commercially sold squid are usually between 12 and 16 inches long. Their very flavorful flesh has been enjoyed since ancient times. Particularly popular in Europe and Japan, squid represents an important part of the North American commercial fishery.

The edible parts of the squid are its tentacles and its pocket-shaped body, which comprise 80% of the animal. The squid is equipped with a gland that produces sepia, a blackish liquid also known as "ink." This liquid is secreted when the squid comes under attack, creating a dark underwater cloud that shields it from its enemies. Often used in painting, this edible "ink" accounts for the fact that the squid is also known as "calamary" – a name derived from the Latin word *calamarius,* which means "writing." The white flesh of the squid is lean, firm, and slightly rubbery. Unlike the flesh of the octopus and the cuttlefish, it does not have to be pounded before it is cooked.

Buying

Squid is sold fresh, frozen, canned, or dried. Fresh or defrosted squid is not always prepared for cooking before being sold, and squid that is ready to cook can be relatively expensive (the ink sack has usually been removed). When buying fresh squid, look for moist, firm flesh that smells only faintly of the sea.

Preparing

When preparing fresh squid, remove the transparent cartilage (the pen) from the body and throw it away. Separate the head from the body by pulling firmly but gently. Spread the tentacles out flat, sever them just below the eyes, and remove the hard beaklike mouth from the center of the body. Wash the tentacles and the body, and then remove the membrane that covers them by scraping at it with your fingernails under running water. Leave the body whole (for stuffing) or cut it into sections.

Serving Ideas

Squid can be eaten hot or cold. Very small squid can be eaten raw and are used in Japanese dishes like sashimi and sushi. Prepared in many different ways, squid can be marinated, smoked, or stuffed, or added to soups, sauces, and salads. It is especially delicious with pasta, and some recipes even make use of the ink.

Storing

Fresh or cooked squid can be refrigerated for 1 or 2 days, and can last for up to 3 months in the freezer. Freshly caught squid should be refrigerated for 1 or 2 days to allow it to become more tender.

Nutritional Information

	raw
protein	16 g
fat	1 g
carbohydrates	3 g
calories	92
	per 100 g

Squid is rich in riboflavin and in vitamin B$_{12}$.

Cooking

Squid is often grilled or fried and can also be braised, sautéed, poached, or steamed. If squid is overcooked, it becomes hard and loses its flavor. Sauté or fry it for 1 or 2 minutes over medium heat, cook it in sauces for 10 minutes, or bake it in a 375°F (190°C) oven for 15 to 20 minutes.

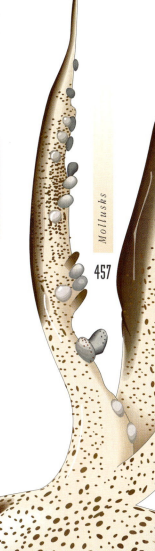

Mollusks

457

Octopus

Octopus spp., Octopoda

The octopus is a shell-less cephalopod mollusk that is found in most of the world's seas. It hides in holes and cracks in the sea floor when it comes under attack. Related to the squid and the cuttlefish, it is the largest member of the family and can grow to be almost 30 feet long.

The curved and pointed parrot-like mouth of the octopus is located at the center of its body and is surrounded by eight tentacles, each of which is usually equipped with two rows of suckers. The head contains all of its organs, including a gland that secretes a liquid known as "ink." The octopus ejects this liquid to provide cover when it is attacked. Fishermen usually kill octopuses before removing them from the water to prevent this indelible ink from staining their clothing.

Since octopuses adopt the color of their environment as camouflage, they can be found in a wide range of colors, including gray, black, pink, and brown. Octopus flesh is firm and flavorful, especially if it comes from a small animal. The tough flesh of large octopuses has to be pounded with a mallet before it is cooked, but flesh from octopuses under 4 inches is more than tender enough to eat. Fishermen often tenderize octopus flesh by beating the animals against rocks on the shore.

The flesh of certain species, including one commonly found along the coast of Australia, is poisonous. Octopus was a particular favorite of the Greeks and the Romans. In fact, the Romans considered it to be an aphrodisiac, and it continues to figure prominently in Greek and Italian cuisine. The Japanese have gone as far as to establish octopus farms. However, in many countries, including the United States and Australia, octopus is much less popular and usually serves only as bait.

Buying

Look for octopuses with firm flesh that smells only slightly fishy.

Preparing

Octopus is usually cleaned and tenderized before it is sold. If it has not been prepared for cooking, start by removing the tentacles from the body and then turn the stomach cavity inside out to remove the intestines. After locating and removing the eyes and mouth at the center of the head, begin skinning the octopus.

The skin is much easier to remove if the octopus has been pounded and then blanched for a couple of minutes.

Nutritional Information

protein	15 g
fat	1 g
calories	73
	per 100 g

Serving Ideas

Octopus is delicious when marinated or steamed, or when used in Asian dishes. It goes particularly well with garlic, tomatoes, onions, lemon, ginger, olive oil, cream, wine, and soy sauce.

Cooking

Octopus can be grilled, poached, sautéed, fried, or steamed. Cooking it slowly over low heat makes the flesh more tender. Although many recipes suggest that an octopus weighing over 4 pounds be left to simmer for 2 hours, 45 minutes is usually sufficient if it has been blanched prior to cooking. If it has not, let it simmer for 60 to 90 minutes. There is no need to skin small octopuses before grilling or frying them.

To evaporate the water that is produced when octopus is cooked, sauté it over low heat in a dry saucepan; then prepare it in the desired fashion.

Storing

Fresh or cooked octopus will last for 1 or 2 days in the refrigerator and for about 3 months in the freezer. It should always be washed before being refrigerated or frozen.

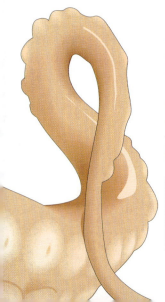

Cuttlefish

Sepia officinalis, Sepiidae

Very common in Europe and Asia, the cuttlefish is a cephalopod mollusk whose body is more oval and flatter than that of the squid, a closely related species. It contains an extremely light, chalky bone that is approximately 6 inches long. Rounded on one end and pointed on the other, the cuttlebone is often given to birds as a beak sharpener. In Roman times, it was ground and used by women to clean their teeth, powder their faces, and polish their jewels.

Yellow or beige and usually striped with black, the cuttlefish adopts the color of its environment as camouflage. It has ten tentacles, two of which are very long and are equipped with five or six rows of suckers. Like the octopus, it has small eyes not unlike those of vertebrates, as well as a sac full of ink that it ejects to provide cover when attacked. Known as sepia, cuttlefish ink is a dark brown liquid that is used as an artist's pigment.

The cuttlefish measures between 6 and 10 inches, and is thus much larger than the little cuttle or lesser cuttlefish, a closely related species that is only 1 to 2 inches long. Found in both the shallow and deep waters of most seas, the cuttlefish propels itself quickly forward by ejecting a jet of water. Cuttlefish is particularly popular in Italy, Greece, Spain, and Japan.

Buying

Look for fresh cuttlefish with moist, firm flesh that smells faintly of the sea. Cuttlefish is also sold frozen or canned.

Preparing

The white flesh of the cuttlefish is very firm, and its slippery skin is difficult to remove. Prepared like octopus, cuttlefish also has to beaten before it is cooked (see *Octopus*).

Serving Ideas

Cuttlefish is very flavorful and is used in much the same way as octopus and squid, which it can replace in most recipes. Stuffed cuttlefish is especially delicious. The sepia or "ink" is sometimes reserved and used in certain recipes.

Cooking

Unless cuttlefish is cooked rapidly, it tends to become tough. It can be poached or fried for 3 minutes per side, sautéed for 1 or 2 minutes per side, or steamed for 30 to 60 minutes.

Storing

Fresh or cooked cuttlefish will keep in the refrigerator for 1 or 2 days and can be frozen for about 3 months. It should be washed before being refrigerated or frozen.

Nutritional Information

protein	16 g
fat	1 g
calories	81
	per 100 g

Whelk

Buccinum spp., **Buccinidae**

Large and carnivorous, the whelk is a univalve gastropod mollusk that is especially common along the coasts of the Atlantic, the Pacific, and the Arctic oceans. More popular in Europe than in North America, it is a particular favorite of the British and the Italians. The most common species of whelk is the *Buccinum undatum,* which, like the crab, is caught in nets along the shore. Most of the several other species of whelks that exist are fished in deeper waters (at depths of up to 200 feet) or are gathered on the shore after storms.

The whelk resembles a large periwinkle (usually 1 to 4 inches, but it can be up to 6 inches in diameter). The color of its cone-shaped spiral shell ranges from dull gray to off-white, and the shell of certain species has a pearl-like interior.

Preparing

Before whelks are washed, they should be shaken to make them retreat back into their shells.

Nutritional Information

	raw
protein	24 g
fat	0.4 g
calories	138
	per 100 g

Serving Ideas

Prepared like periwinkles, whelks are often marinated or eaten plain with a little lemon juice. They are delicious in salads and when cooked in white-wine sauces.

Storing

Fresh whelks can last for up to 3 days in the refrigerator in a container that is covered with a damp cloth. Shelled whelks can be frozen for up to 3 months.

Cooking

Cook only live whelks whose shells are intact. They have to be cooked very carefully because the flesh becomes tough if it is even slightly overcooked. Ordinary whelks should be poached for 8 to 10 minutes in salted fresh water (1 tablespoon of salt per quart of water), seawater, or court bouillon. Place the whelks in a pot and cover them with liquid; then cover the pot and bring the liquid to a boil. Strain the whelks; then extract them from their shells with a pin after removing the operculum (the bony plate that covers the opening of the shell). Larger species of whelks (6 inches) have to be cooked for a longer period of time: poach them long enough make them protrude from their shells, extract them, then discard the soft tissue connecting the body to the shell and continue to cook the remaining firm flesh.

Periwinkle

Littorina spp., **Littorinidae**

A small gastropod mollusk that is very common in the Atlantic and the Pacific, the periwinkle resembles the snail and moves in a similar fashion. Since periwinkles do not move around during the day, it is best to fish for them at night. They live in colonies among coastal rocks and crevices, and attach themselves to the pillars of wharves just below the surface of the sea.

The small spiral shell of the periwinkle is thick and smooth. Closed by a bony protective plate called an operculum, it can be brown, grayish, or blackish with black or reddish spirals, depending on the species. Periwinkles are mature enough to be eaten when they measure approximately 1 inch across.

Serving Ideas

Periwinkles can be eaten hot or cold. Their lean flesh is similar to that of snails, and they can be substituted for snails in most recipes. Although they are often marinated, they can be eaten plain, with a touch of lemon or vinegar. Prepared in various ways, they are cooked in white-wine sauces and used in salads and appetizers. They are particularly delicious when grilled over wood (be careful not to overcook them).

Storing

Fresh periwinkles can last for up to 3 days in the refrigerator when stored in a container covered by a damp cloth. Shelled periwinkles can be frozen for approximately 3 months.

Cooking

Cook only live periwinkles whose shells are intact.

Cook periwinkles in salted fresh water (1 tablespoon of salt per quart of water), seawater, or court bouillon. Place the periwinkles in a pot and cover them with liquid; then cover the pot and bring the liquid to a boil. Cook the periwinkles for only 5 minutes (if they are cooked any longer, they become tough and are very difficult to remove from their increasingly fragile shells); then drain them. Extract them from their shells with a pin after removing the operculum.

Preparing

Before periwinkles are washed, they should be shaken to make them retreat back into their shells.

Nutritional Information

protein	20 g
fat	2 g
calories	100
	per 100 g

Snail

Helix spp., Helicidae

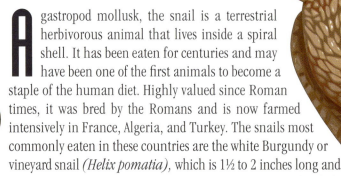

white Burgundy snail

A gastropod mollusk, the snail is a terrestrial herbivorous animal that lives inside a spiral shell. It has been eaten for centuries and may have been one of the first animals to become a staple of the human diet. Highly valued since Roman times, it was bred by the Romans and is now farmed intensively in France, Algeria, and Turkey. The snails most commonly eaten in these countries are the white Burgundy or vineyard snail *(Helix pomatia),* which is 1½ to 2 inches long and coiled inside a yellowish brown shell that is usually adorned with three to five brown spiral stripes, and the petit-gris or garden snail *(Helix aspersa),* which measures between 1 and 1¼ inches and lives inside a yellowish gray shell that is often decorated with one to five broken purplish brown stripes.

shelled snail

The firmness and delicacy of snail flesh vary from one species to another. To enhance their taste, snails are often starved for about 10 days before they are eaten, and in Provence they are fed a special thyme-based diet for added flavor.

Buying

Snails are sold frozen, canned, or cooked. In France and certain other countries, it is also possible to buy live snails.

Storing

Fresh or cooked snails can be refrigerated for up to 3 days, and shelled snails can be frozen for up to 3 months.

Nutritional Information

	raw
protein	16 g
fat	1.5 g
carbohydrates	2 g
calories	90
	per 100 g

Preparing

Preparing live snails

• Wash the snails in cold water; if necessary, remove the hard partition covering the opening of the shell;

• sweat the snails (3 or 4 dozen) for 3 hours in a mixture of coarse salt (a handful), vinegar (½ cup), and flour (1 tablespoon); cover the container and put a weight on top of it to prevent the snails from escaping; stir the mixture from time to time (some people omit this step because they feel it diminishes the quality of the flesh);

• remove the snails from the container and wash them thoroughly in cold water to remove all the mucous from their shells;

• put the snails in a saucepan and cover them with cold water; bring the water to a boil and allow it to boil gently for 5 minutes; strain the snails and rinse them under cold water;

• shell the snails and remove the black part (cloaca) at end of their tails; do not remove the glands and the liver, which are among the most flavorful and nourishing parts of the snail;

• cook the snails as desired.

Serving Ideas

Snails are often served in a special dish *(escargotière)* divided into 6 or 12 sections. They can be prepared in many different ways: grilled, sautéed, or cooked on brochettes or in sauces, court bouillon, or puff pastry. Snails served piping hot in garlic butter is a classic appetizer.

Sea urchin

Strongylocentrotus spp., Strongylocentrotidae

A small invertebrate marine animal that lives in coastal waters, the sea urchin has a spherical shell made of chalky platelets that is usually about 3 inches in diameter. Some species have flatter shells than others, and the shells of the most common species are covered with spines. Usually just under 1 inch long, these spines can measure 4 to 6 inches (it is no coincidence that "urchin" is the Old English word for "hedgehog"). Several of the spines are stationary, but those equipped with suckers are mobile and allow the sea urchin to move through the water; others are equipped with pincers that are used for feeding. Certain species also have venomous spines.

The underside of the sea urchin is completely covered with spines and contains no organs other the anus at its center. The lantern-shaped mouth is located under the shell; it contains five teeth and is surrounded by an area that is free of spines. For obscure reasons, the mouth is sometimes referred to as "Aristotle's lantern." The edible portion of the sea urchin is located under the mouth and consists of the five sexual organs (the ovaries and testicles of the unisexual animal) known as the "coral," as well as the liquid that surrounds them. The coral is an orange color, like that of the mussel and the scallop. The sea urchin is found in most seas, but many of the almost 500 species are inedible. Its consistency and smell are strongly iodized.

Buying

Sea urchins are sold whole (often packaged in small wooden boxes) or ready to serve (corals only), and are extremely perishable. When buying them whole, look for urchins with firm spines and tightly closed mouth holes.

Preparing

When opening sea urchins, protect your hands with sturdy gloves or a thick cloth. Hold the sea urchin in way that allows you to make an opening near the mouth with a small pair of scissors; then cut all the way around the soft spineless portion. Discard the black entrails. Remove the coral with a spoon and pour the liquid into a bowl; then remove any remaining pieces of the shell.

Serving Ideas

Sea urchins can be prepared in only a limited number of ways. They are often eaten raw, with or without their liquid, and with a little lemon or lime juice, shallots, and salt; they are served with buttered bread or on canapés. Sea-urchin coulis and purées are used to flavor sauces, mayonnaises, and dips. Sea urchins are also added to omelets, scrambled eggs, and crêpes. They are the main ingredient in a fish soup known as *oursinade,* and can also be cooked for a few minutes in salted boiling water, like poached eggs.

Storing

Sea urchins can be refrigerated for 1 or 2 days in a tightly sealed container. Before storing whole sea urchins, remove the crunchy parts of the mouth area (such as the eye) from beneath the shell.

Nutritional Information

protein	12 g
fat	4 g
calories	126
	per 100 g

Frog

Rana spp., **Batrachians**

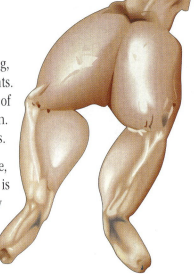

A web-footed amphibious animal that moves by swimming and hopping, the frog lives in fresh water and in damp terrestrial environments. The only edible parts of the frog are its legs, which are comprised of delicately flavored, tender white flesh that is often compared to chicken. Commercially available frogs' legs usually come from frogs bred on farms.

There are over 20 species of edible frogs of various sizes and colors. In Europe, the most frequently consumed species are the green or common frog, which is the most flavorful, and the rusty or mute frog, which is the most commonly available. The species of frogs eaten in North America tend to be larger.

Buying

Frogs' legs are sold skinned, fresh, frozen, or canned. When buying them fresh, look for legs that are plump, moist, and slightly pink.

Serving Ideas

Frogs' legs are often fried or sautéed and prepared with garlic, or with a mixture of chopped parsley and garlic known as *persillade*. Other popular recipes include frogs' legs *à la provençale* (with olive oil, tomatoes, and garlic) or *à la lyonnaise* (with butter and onions). They are also cooked in soups, omelets, and pies.

Storing

Fresh or cooked frogs' legs can be refrigerated for 2 or 3 days and frozen for 2 or 3 months. Be sure to wrap them well because they tend to dry out.

Nutritional Information

	raw
protein	16 g
fat	0.3 g
cholesterol	50 mg
calories	73
	per 100 g

Cooking

Frogs' legs should be grilled or fried for 2 to 3 minutes, sautéed for 1 to 2 minutes, poached for 3 to 5 minutes, or baked for 5 to 8 minutes.

Sautéed Frogs' Legs

4 PORTIONS

48 pairs of frogs legs	2 tbsp. chopped Italian
Salt and ground pepper	parsley
Flour	4 tbsp. (60 ml) butter
2 cloves garlic	Cayenne pepper
1 shallot	Lemon wedges

1. Wipe the frogs' legs dry, then sprinkle them with salt, pepper and flour.

2. Finely chop the garlic and the shallot, then combine these ingredients with the parsley.

3. Sauté the frogs' legs in two batches. In a large frying pan, melt 2 tablespoons of the butter. As soon as the butter heats up, sauté half of the frogs' legs over high heat for approximately 2 minutes. Once they have browned on one side, turn them over and lower the heat. Add a pinch of cayenne pepper and cook them for another 2 minutes. Keep them warm.

4. Repeat this operation with the remaining ingredients.

5. Return all of the frogs' legs to the pan. Add the chopped parsley, garlic, and shallots, then gently mix all of the ingredients together.

Serve with lemon wedges and boiled (in salted water) or steamed potatoes.

Herbs, Spices, and Condiments

Introduction

The generic term "seasoning" is often applied indiscriminately to herbs and spices. Spices are aromatic substances derived from plants native to tropical regions and are generally characterized by their pungent flavor. (Indeed, the term "spice" was formerly used to describe a much wider variety of hot tasting or aromatic foods and substances of exotic origin.) Herbs, on the other hand, are green-leafed plants indigenous to temperate zones and are often grown in vegetable gardens.

Soon after discovering spices in the early Middle Ages, Europeans became fervent consumers. At the time, spices were used to disguise the unpleasant taste of often tainted foods, the only preservative at the time being salt. People also appreciated the flavor, and in some cases the color, that spices added to dishes, and believed in their medicinal properties. Certain spices were used to make perfumes. A number of naval expeditions were launched to satisfy Europeans' lust for spices, and the spice trade sparked wars and led to the exploitation of aboriginal peoples.

Spices are obtained from fruits (allspice, chile, juniper, pepper), seeds (cardamom, poppy seed, cumin, nutmeg), roots (turmeric, ginger, horseradish), flower buds (cloves, capers), and bark (cinnamon).

Herbs are divided into two broad families: Labiatae (basil, marjoram, balm, mint, oregano, rosemary, summer savory, sage, thyme), which owe their Latin name to the fact that their petals form two liplike lobes; and Umbelliferae (dill, aniseed, caraway, chervil, coriander, cumin, fennel, parsley), whose flowers grow in «umbels,» that is, flat or rounded clusters.

The Latin names for herbs often highlight a particular aspect of the individual species. The terms *fragrans* and *odorata* are applied to aromatic herbs; *tinctoria* is part of the compound name of herbs used for their coloring agents; and *sativus* is assigned to herbs that are cultivated, as opposed to those that grow wild.

Buying

Spices are sold whole or ground. Buy them whole or in their original state (seeds, stems, roots) to obtain much longer-lasting flavor. Grind them in a spice grinder just before using them. Herbs are available fresh or dried. When fresh, they should be mold-free and their stems and leaves should not be dry or discolored. Dried herbs are sold whole, flaked, and ground (powdered). When possible, buy them in whole or flaked form, as ground herbs lose their taste quickly and have sometimes been adulterated.

For maximum flavor, buy herbs and spices in a shop that has a rapid inventory turnover. Avoid mixtures of salt and herbs, as they are costly and for the most part contain considerably more salt than herbs.

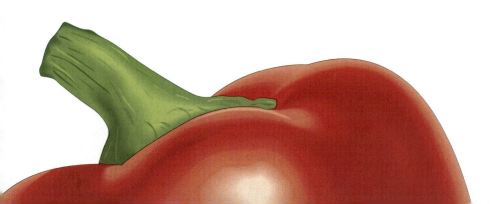

Preparing

Finely chopped fresh herbs impart more flavor to foods. Use a pair of scissors or a well-sharpened knife to avoid crushing them. Do, however, crush dried herbs briefly between your fingers or palms before using them, as the warmth brings out their flavor. You can also soak dried herbs (and spices) for about half an hour in water, milk, oil, or stock. In India, cooks roast spices before using them, as this enhances their aroma and is thought to make them easier to digest. Crushing (simplified by the use of a mortar and pestle) releases the essential oils contained in herbs and spices, thus producing a stronger taste.

Serving Ideas

There are virtually no limits, other than personal tastes and preferences, to the uses for herbs and spices. Don't be afraid to innovate. Although certain herbs are traditionally associated with particular foods – for example, basil with tomatoes, tarragon with vinegar or chicken, mint with lamb and peas – these combinations are far from exclusive.

Fresh herbs have a less concentrated flavor than dried herbs. A useful tip to remember is that 1 tablespoon of fresh herbs can be replaced by 1 teaspoon of dried herbs or ⅓ to ⅔ teaspoon of ground herbs. Food temperature also has a significant impact on the amount of flavor released by herbs. Although heat frees essential oils, the resulting taste and aroma quickly fade. Prolonged cooking, particularly vigorous boiling and lidless cooking, is thus inappropriate for most herbs. Generally speaking, you should add herbs at the end of cooking, particularly in the case of more fragile herbs. Rosemary, thyme, sage, bay leaf, and savory are nevertheless ideal seasonings in simmered dishes. When preparing cold dishes, add herbs well before serving to give them time to impart their flavor, as the cold temperature slows down the development of aromas and lessens their intensity; for the same reasons, you often need to increase the amount of seasoning in cold foods. Unlike herbs, most spices should be added early in the cooking process. In all cases, avoid over-seasoning, as it's easier to add more than to remove what you have already added!

Herbs and spices can also be used as substitutes for salt, both during and after cooking. Why not try filling your salt shaker with a herb or herbal blend?

Nutritional Information

Herbs and spices contain varying amounts of nutrients. Some of them are a significant source of calcium, potassium, and phosphorus (notably fennel, ground tarragon, dried parsley, ground cinnamon, ground basil, cloves, oregano, paprika, and savory, as well as all herbs and spices sold in seed form, for example, aniseed, caraway seed, cumin, dill seed, fennel, fenugreek, mustard, poppy seed, celery seed, coriander). Spices contain slighter more fat and carbohydrates than herbs.

Herbs and spices are thought to have a wide range of medicinal properties – some of them confirmed and others less certain. Over the centuries, a growing store of folk wisdom has been passed down from one generation to the next. Although these popular beliefs are not generally recognized by the world of science, some of them have been confirmed by observation. Phytotherapists draw from them in treating patients with plant products, particularly herbal teas and decoctions. In cooking, given the generally small amounts of herbs and spices used, the medicinal effects and nutritional value are minimal.

Storing

Dry herbs away from direct sun and artificial light. Spread them in a single layer on a piece of screen or nylon net to ensure sufficient air circulation. Keep only leaves that are completely dry, to avoid the growth of mold. If necessary, finish drying the herbs in the oven at 140°F for 15 minutes. Thyme, oregano, rosemary, bay leaf, and savory withstand drying particularly well.

Microwave drying also produces good results, particularly in the case of harder-to-dry herbs such as basil, parsley, fennel, coriander (cilantro), bay leaf, and juniper. Spread about ½ cup of herbs evenly between two sheets of paper towel and microwave them at high heat for 1½ to 2½ minutes or until they crumble. Repeat the process for any leaves that are not completely dry, checking them every 30 seconds.

Dried herbs and spices should be kept in sealed containers (ideally made of opaque glass) in a dry place away from light and heat.

Keep fresh herbs in the refrigerator. If they are dirty or sandy, rinse them gently just before using them. Wrapped in a paper towel and placed in a plastic bag, herbs stay fresh for several days. Those that still have their roots can be kept longer; place them in fresh water at room temperature, like cut flowers. You can also wrap the roots in a damp cloth and store the herbs in a plastic bag in the warmest part of your refrigerator.

Pick herbs just before they flower, ideally in the morning after any dew has evaporated and before the sun gets too hot. You can then freeze them whole or chopped, without blanching; if you wash them, be sure to dry them thoroughly.

Harder-to-dry herbs such as chives, chervil, fennel, coriander (cilantro), and parsley can easily be frozen. Put them in an ice cube tray and cover them with water or stock. You can then add the cubes (preferably unfrozen to maximize flavor) to soups, sauces, and stews. Formerly, people often preserved whole or chopped herbs by covering them with salt (alternate layers of herbs and salt in a glass or stoneware container) and stored the mixture in a cool place. If you try this method, avoid salting dishes seasoned with the herbs. Another simple solution is to preserve fresh herbs in vinegar, oil, or alcohol. The liquid absorbs the flavor and can be used as a convenient substitute for unavailable or overly expensive fresh herbs.

Dill

Anethum graveolens, **Umbelliferae**

fresh dill

An aromatic plant native to the Mediterranean basin and western Asia, dill is related to and resembles fennel, with which it is often confused. The yellow flowers of both plants are similar in appearance. Dill is particularly popular in Scandinavia, Russia, Central Europe, and North Africa.

Dill has been used as a seasoning for centuries. It is mentioned in ancient Egyptian texts and is referred to in the Bible. For the Romans, dill symbolized joy and pleasure. In medieval Europe, dill oil was known for its medicinal properties, notably in relieving colic and flatulence, as well as for its antiseptic, antispasmodic, and carminative effects. In England it was also used to counteract evil spells.

Unlike the roots of the fennel plant, dill roots are seldom topped by more than one stem.

The plant can grow to 2 feet in height. Its small flat seeds (dillseed) have thin winglike ridges. Their warm, sharp smell is reminiscent of fennel, caraway, and mint. When ripe, the seeds are toxic to birds.

Serving Ideas

Dillseed is perfect for seasoning vinegar, soups, pickles, marinades, cold sauces, and salads. It is excellent for pickling fish, particularly salmon and herring.

Dill goes very well with tomatoes, celeriac, beets, cucumbers, cabbage, fresh and sour cream, cream cheese, white sauces, melted butter, salad dressings, eggs, stews, and seafood. Its more subtle-tasting leaves (dillweed) should not be boiled, even when dried, as they will lose their flavor. Add them at the end of the cooking process.

Storing

Given its fragility, fresh dill can be kept for only about 2 days. Place the stems in a bowl of water, or wrap the leaves in a piece of damp paper towel and store them in the refrigerator. To optimize flavor, freeze fresh dill rather than drying it.

Dill can dried in the microwave.

Store dried dillseed in a sealed container kept in a cool, dry, dark place.

Buying

When buying fresh dill, don't worry if the leaves are wilted, as they droop very quickly after picking.

Nutritional Information

	Dried dillseed
potassium	25 mg
calcium	32 mg
magnesium	5 mg
fiber	0.4 g
zinc	0.1 mg
	per tsp. (2 g)

Dill has medicinal properties. It is said to be diuretic, carminative, antispasmodic, and slightly stimulating. To ease digestion, pour a quart of boiling water over 1 to 1½ tablespoons of dillseed and let steep.

Herbs, Spices, and Condiments

469

dillseed

Anise

Pimpinella anisum, Umbelliferae

The flowers, arranged in umbels, produce hard seeds with a spicy, slightly sweet flavor.

This aromatic herb is native to the western Mediterranean region and Egypt, where it still grows wild. Mentioned in the Bible, anise is one of the world's oldest seasonings. The Romans served desserts sprinkled with anise to ease digestion. In the Middle Ages, anise was used as a drug and an aphrodisiac. It was introduced to Europe only in the 14th century, originally to flavor bread.

Anise is particularly popular in Europe, North Africa, and Turkey. It is cultivated intensively in the South of France and is also grown in Italy, Spain, Russia, Bulgaria, and Mexico.

The hollow many-branched stalks can reach 20 to 30 inches in height. The upper leaves are feathery and the basal leaves are lobated. The small whitish flowers form a large number of umbels. The fruits, known as aniseed, are hard downy seeds about ¼ inch in length. Oval, they are grayish green and have a spicy, slightly sweet flavor. The seeds detach easily when ripe.

The fruit of the species *Pimpinella anisum,* aniseed is sometimes confused with the somewhat similar-tasting seeds of plants such as fennel, dill, caraway, and cumin. All of these plants belong to the Umbelliferae family.

Star anise, on the other hand, is the fruit of the *Illicium verum,* an evergreen tree of the Magnoliaceae family that grows to about 25 feet in height. Native to southeastern China, it is very common in central Asia. Also known as **badian**, star anise has much the same flavor and properties as aniseed.

The Chinese have been using star anise for thousands of years. It was introduced to Europe in the late 16th century by an English navigator, and was widely used as bait in mousetraps (whence its Latin name, *Illicium,* meaning "lure" or "bait"). The lance-shaped leaves resemble bay or magnolia leaves. Its large, highly aromatic flowers are light yellow and the woody fruits are reddish brown. Each point of the star-shaped fruit contains a green oval seed with longitudinal ridges. The flavor of these seeds is stronger and sharper than that of aniseed; indeed, a few star anise seeds are enough to flavor an entire dish. Star anise keeps its flavor longer than aniseed.

Buying

Unless you plan to use a large quantity of anise, buy only a small amount at a time to make sure the seeds keep their flavor.

Serving Ideas

Anise leaves, which are more delicate than the seeds, are delicious cooked or raw. Use them to season salads, soups, cream cheese, fish, vegetables, and tea. The more widely used fruits (both aniseed and star anise) heighten the taste of sweet and salty dishes alike. Use them to flavor or decorate compotes, cakes, cookies, breads (olive bread, pretzels, gingerbread), salads, soups, vegetables, fish, and fowl. The roots are sometimes utilized to make wine.

Anise can be used as a substitute for or be mixed with spices such as cinnamon and nutmeg in compotes, cakes, pies, breads, and so on.

Anise is a widely used to make licorice, cough drops, and candies, as well as alcoholic beverages such as pastis (France), anisette (North Africa), ouzo (Greece), raki (Turkey), arak (Egypt), and sambuca (Italy).

Anise is a common ingredient in Arab and Indian cuisine. In India it is sometimes used in hot spicy mixtures such as garam masala and curries. People chew it to freshen their breath. In Asia star anise is used to season pork, chicken, rice, coffee, and tea.

Nutritional Information

	seeds
potassium	30 mg
calcium	14 mg
phosphorus	9 mg
iron	0.7 mg
	per tsp. (2 g)

Anise is said to be diuretic, carminative, stomachic, antispasmodic, digestive, an expectorant, and a stimulant. It is used to tone up the heart, stimulate digestion, combat flatulence, and soothe coughs and asthma. Its essential oil contains anethole, a substance also found in fennel.

To make a herbal tea with a tonic effect on the nervous and digestive systems, add about 1 tablespoon crushed aniseed, 4 or 5 stars, or a few leaves to a cup of hot water. Boil the mixture for 2 minutes and let it steep for 10 minutes.

Herbs, Spices, and Condiments

471

aniseed

star anise seeds

star anise

Bay leaf

Laurus nobilis, **Lauraceae**

The sweet bay's clusters of small greenish yellow flowers produce shiny blue-black berries.

T he dark-green lanceolate leaves of the sweet bay tree (also known as the bay laurel or sweet laurel) are widely used as a seasoning. In ancient Greece, the laurel was dedicated to Apollo, god of light, and victorious athletes and renowned artists were crowned with laurel wreaths.

Although a number of trees and shrubs bear the name "laurel" (e.g., mountain laurel, dwarf laurel), many of them do not in fact belong to the laurel family.

An evergreen indigenous to the Mediterranean basin, the "true" laurel, or sweet bay, grows to a height of 10 to 20 feet. Its oval leaves, which are smooth, firm, and shiny, are about 2 to 4 inches long. The tree's clusters of tiny greenish yellow flowers produce shiny blue-black berries. Bay leaf has been used as a seasoning ever since the 1st century A.D.

Buying

Dried bay leaf should be light green.

Nutritional Information

vitamin A	4 ER
calcium	5 mg
potassium	3 mg
iron	0.3 mg
	per tsp. (1 g)

Bay leaves and berries are known for their numerous medicinal properties. They are believed to be antiseptic, digestive, expectorant, and antirheumatic.

The essential oil, which contains bitter elements and tannins that can be toxic in high doses, is used to produce an ointment that is said to be effective for soothing sprains and bruises.

To make herbal tea, boil a few dried leaves in a cup of water for 2 to 3 minutes and let the mixture steep for 10 minutes.

Serving Ideas

 Bay leaf can be used whole or in flakes, fresh or dried. For cooking purposes, it is normally used dried, as the fresh leaves are bitter. Even dried bay leaf is highly aromatic. Use it sparingly; often a single leaf is enough. The longer the leaves or flakes are cooked in liquid, the more taste they impart to the dish.

Bay leaf is used to flavor sauces, soups, stews, meat, poultry, fish, vegetables, legumes, pâtés, marinades – in short, almost anything, but especially simmered dishes. The ground seasoning is used in stuffings and marinades.

Along with parsley and thyme, bay leaf is an essential ingredient of *bouquet garni.*

Storing

Freshly picked leaves are dried in the dark so they keep their flavor. Dried bay leaf can be kept for a year in a sealed container stored in a dark place.

Marjoram/Oregano

Origanum spp., **Labiatae**

sweet marjoram

oregano (wild marjoram)

Marjoram and oregano, the generic names of which are frequently interchanged, are small aromatic shrubs that grow to a height of approximately 2 feet. There are about 30 different species. One of them, *Origanum vulgare,* commonly called wild marjoram or oregano, is native to northern Europe. A closely related species, *Origanum majorana,* or sweet marjoram, is believed to have originated in North Africa. It has been cultivated in France since the Middle Ages and is thought to have been imported from Palestine.

Oregano and sweet marjoram are perennials in Mediterranean climates (particularly in Italy). In North America they are generally annuals, as they cannot survive the harsh winters.

Sweet marjoram has been used since ancient times. It was long thought to prevent milk from souring. The Greeks and Romans looked on it as a symbol of happiness (the Latin *origanum* is derived from the Greek words for "mountain" and "joy"). Lovers were crowned with marjoram wreaths, and the Greeks planted the herb in cemeteries to ensure the dead of eternal peace. Oregano was known by the ancient Egyptians and prized by the Greeks.

The multibranched stems of these small shrubs are covered with small grayish green oval leaves. Small white or pink flowers (those of oregano are red) shaped like oval spikes grow at the tips of the branches; they produce tiny pale brown seeds that look like miniature nuts. Sweet marjoram's fragrance and taste are reminiscent of mint and basil.

Wild marjoram (Origanum vulgare) is often called oregano.

Buying

When buying fresh marjoram or oregano, look for firm stems.

Nutritional Information

	dried sweet marjoram	*ground oregano*
calcium	12 mg	24 mg
potassium	9 mg	25 mg
vitamin A	5 ER	10 ER
magnesium	2 mg	4 mg
phosphorus	1.8 mg	3 mg
iron	0.5 mg	0.6 mg
		per tsp. (1 g)

Sweet marjoram and oregano are said to be antispasmodic, antiseptic, bactericidal, stomachic, expectorant, and sedative. They alleviate colic, stimulate the appetite, facilitate digestion, and are thought to have a beneficial effect on the respiratory system. They are also believed to ease migraines, car sickness, insomnia, and bronchitis.

To make a herbal tea, use 1 teaspoon of dried leaves per cup of boiling water and let the mixture steep for 10 minutes.

Serving Ideas

Oregano and sweet marjoram are used fresh, dried, and ground. Sweet marjoram has a slightly more mellow flavor than oregano. Both herbs are essential ingredients of Mediterranean cuisine, particularly Italian and Provençal cooking.

They are used to season tomato-based dishes, salad dressings, sauces, stuffings, vegetables (onion, spinach, zucchini, eggplant), fish, seafood, legumes, eggs, meat, poultry, delicatessen meats – in a word, almost anything.

A branch of sweet marjoram or oregano placed in a bottle of oil or vinegar imparts an interesting taste. One or both of the herbs are included in the mixture known as *herbes de Provence.*

Tarragon

Artemisia dracunculus, **Compositae**

An aromatic herbaceous plant, tarragon is native to Central Asia or Siberia. This perennial is sometimes called the "dragon herb," probably because its roots resemble a tangle of small coiled-up snakes or because of its reputation as a cure for animal bites. Apparently introduced into Europe by Crusaders after they discovered it in the Near East, tarragon was at that time used both as a spice and as a remedy. Tarragon is a highly prized herb in French cuisine.

The plant can grow to a height of 3 feet, and its narrow, smooth-edged leaves are spear-shaped and pungent. For maximum flavor, tarragon is harvested before its tiny whitish or yellowish flowers blossom. Since the seeds are rarely fertile, this plant is more often grown by root division. The variety of tarragon said to be of Russian origin *(Artemisia dracunculoides)* is more pungent than the finer-flavored common or French tarragon.

Nutritional Information

potassium	48 mg
calcium	8 mg
magnesium	6 mg
phosphorus	5 mg
iron	0.5 mg
per 5 ml (1 teaspoon)	

Tarragon is said to be a stimulant, diuretic, antiseptic, carminative, vermifuge, and antispasmodic. It is also believed to regulate menstruation and to stimulate the appetite and digestion. The essential oil derived from tarragon has an anise fragrance and a turpentine-like flavor. For herb tea, use 1 teaspoon per cup of boiling water; brew 5 to 10 minutes.

Buying

For the best aroma and finest flavor, tarragon should be used fresh rather than dried.

Serving Ideas

Tarragon is used to flavor eggs, fish, seafood, turkey, salads, sauces, stuffing, mustard, vinegar, and pickles. Its appealing, slightly anise-like flavor, somewhat bitter and peppery, makes it useful as a seasoning for bland food. Tarragon stands up well to cooking and is frequently married with chicken. It is an essential ingredient in *sauce béarnaise* and is also used to season a number of other sauces *(gribiche, ravigote, tartar)*. Dried tarragon tends to mask the flavor of other food or herbs if used too generously.

green basil

Basil

Ocimum basilicum, Labiatae

An aromatic annual plant native to India, this highly fragrant herb has long been greatly appreciated. It was particularly esteemed by the ancient Greeks, who called it *basilikon,* meaning "royal." Basil is used abundantly in Mediterranean, Thai, Vietnamese, and Laotian cooking.

There are about 60 varieties of this stocky plant, which grows to a height of 8 inches to 2 feet. Its round or lance-shaped leaves are found in various shades of green, reddish, and purple. As the fragile leaves are most pungent just before the white flowers open at the tips of the stems, following which they lose their flavor, they should be picked before the plant blossoms. Their taste varies according to the variety: it can be reminiscent of lemon, camphor, jasmine, clove, anise, or thyme.

Basil's flavor reaches its peak just before the white flowers blossom at the tips of the stems.

Serving Ideas

Basil is the quintessential herb for seasoning tomatoes. It goes very well with garlic, onions, and olives, and is used to liven up pasta, salads, eggs, cheeses, vegetables, fish, seafood, fowl, and pork. Certain varieties are used in desserts and beverages.

Basil is the basic seasoning for *soupe au pistou,* a Mediterranean specialty; combined with garlic and olive oil, it is ground into a paste and added at the end of cooking. *Pistou* is a Provençal word derived from the Latin *pestare,* which means "to mash" or "to crush." In Italy the paste is combined with pine nuts and grated Parmesan to make *pesto,* which is served with pasta and soups.

The stems and leaves of the basil plant impart a subtle taste to cooking oil. Although basil does not go well with vinegar or other herbs, it blends perfectly with olive oil and lemon. Never simmer it, as its essence is highly volatile. Add it at the end of the cooking process.

Use basil to make herbal tea by pouring a cup of boiling water over a tablespoon of dried leaves. Allow the drink to steep for 10 minutes.

Storing

Keep fresh basil in the refrigerator. Wrap it in a slightly damp paper towel to help it stay fresh longer. Wash it just before using it. Fresh basil leaves can also be preserved in olive oil, or you can make them into a smooth paste by mixing them with oil in a blender or food processor. Store dried basil in a sealed container kept in a cool, dry, dark place.

Freezing is particularly suitable for basil, which loses much of its taste when dried. Freeze it whole or chopped; blanching is unnecessary. You can also cover it with stock or water and freeze it into cubes, which can be used in soups, sauces, and stews. Use it unthawed to maximize its flavor.

Nutritional Information

	dried	*fresh*
potassium	48 mg	24 mg
calcium	30 mg	8 mg
vitamin C		1 mg
iron	0.5 mg	0.1 mg
phosphorus	7 mg	4 mg
magnesium	6 mg	4 mg
vitamin A	13 ER	10 ER
		per tsp. (2 g)

Basil is believed to be antispasmodic, antiseptic, tonic, and stomachic. It is also said to help fight migraines, digestive problems, and insomnia.

purple basil

Sage

Salvia officinalis, **Labiatae**

Sage leaves are thick and downy, lance-shaped and veined. Purplish flowers grow in clusters at the tips of the stems.

An aromatic perennial plant indigenous to the Mediterranean region, sage is known for its medicinal properties. Indeed, its generic name, *Salvia,* is derived from the Latin *salvus,* which means "healthy." Sage has been consumed for thousands of years. The Greeks and Romans spoke highly of its healing properties and believed it helped to prolong life. According to an 18th-century author, the Chinese preferred sage tea to their traditional brew, and would willingly trade two cases of Chinese tea leaves for a single sage leaf.

There are various types of sage, some of them herbs and others shrubs. The most widespread variety is common or garden sage *(Salvia officinalis),* a bush that grows to a height of 1 to 3 feet. Its lance-shaped grayish green leaves are thick and have prominent veins. Clusters of purplish bell-shaped flowers bloom at the tips of the stems. The leaves and stems are covered with a silvery down, known in Arabic as "camel's tongue."

common sage

Buying

 Dried sage leaves are sold whole, in flakes, and ground.

Nutritional Information

	ground
calcium	12 mg
potassium	7 mg
vitamin A	4 ER
magnesium	3 mg
iron	0.2 mg
	per tsp. (1 g)

Sage is often considered a virtual panacea, combining the medicinal properties of 20-odd plants. According to a Medieval proverb from the school of medicine at Salerno, "He who has sage in his garden shall never die." Sage is said to have tonic, antispasmodic, antiseptic, diuretic, and cleansing properties. It is believed to be effective against sore throats and mouth cankers, to stimulate menstruation and the appetite, and to relieve flatulence.

To make sage tea, add a teaspoon of dried leaves to a cup of water, bring the mixture to a boil, and let it steep for 10 minutes.

Storing

 Dried sage can be kept for up to a year with little loss of flavor.

Serving Ideas

Sage's strong, sharp, slightly camphorated flavor adds a pleasant taste to a variety of foods (ham and other meats, poultry, delicatessen dishes, marinades, stuffings, vegetables, omelets, soups, stews, cheese). It goes well with dairy products and fatty fish. Sage is sometimes added to wines, beers, teas, and vinegars.

Sage is used widely in French cuisine to season white meat, soups, and vegetables; in Provence it is added to roast pork. The Germans use it to flavor ham, sausages, and beer. In England sage is used to flavor and color a type of cheese, and accompanies onion in stuffings and sauces. In Italian cooking, it is an essential ingredient of *saltimbocca, osso bucco,* and *rollatini.* The Chinese add it to roast mutton and tea.

Sage has a very strong taste; use it sparingly to avoid overpowering other ingredients. As it stands up poorly to boiling and heat, add it at the end of the cooking process. Sage eases the digestion of fatty foods and is often added to pork, goose, and duck.

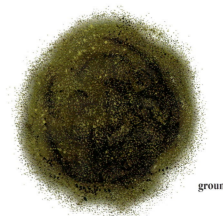

ground sage

Thyme

Thymus spp., Labiatae

An aromatic plant native to the Mediterranean region, thyme is a perennial shrub in hot climates and an annual herb in temperate zones. It grows to a height of 4 to 12 inches.

Thyme has been used for its aromatic and medicinal properties since ancient times. The Egyptians utilized it to embalm their dead. In Greek temples it was burned as incense, and the Romans dedicated it to Venus. In the Middle Ages, people believed that thyme gave them courage. Its name is derived from the Greek *thumos,* meaning "odor"; indeed, the plant is highly fragrant.

The long narrow leaves of **common** or **French thyme** *(Thymus vulgaris),* which are dark green on the upper side and whitish beneath, give off a penetrating aroma. They produce an essential oil with a warm, sharp taste. The plant's pink or purplish flowers grow in clusters at the base of the leaves. Thyme is most fragrant when it blossoms. There are about 60 different varieties, including wild thyme and lemon-scented thyme.

As indicated by its name, **wild** or **creeping thyme** *(Thymus serpyllum)* is an undomesticated creeper. Its oval leaves are smaller than those of common thyme and have darker undersides. Extremely fragrant, wild thyme has a spicy, slightly bitter taste.

Lemon-scented thyme *(Thymus citriodorus)* is a particularly interesting species, as it adds a lemony touch to poultry, veal, and seafood dishes. It loses its flavor, however, when cooked.

There are about 60 species of thyme, including wild thyme and lemon-scented thyme. It is most fragrant when it blooms.

common thyme

Serving Ideas

Fresh thyme goes particularly well with dried beans, sauces, eggs, tomato purée, vegetables, and stuffings, as well as on broiled meat and fish. Whether fresh or dried, common thyme stands up well to long cooking and is ideal in soups, stews, cassoulet, tomato sauces, and stocks. If you use it whole, remove the stems before serving.

Along with parsley and bay leaf, thyme is one of the components of bouquet garni. It adds an interesting flavor to vinegar, and its antiseptic properties make it a popular ingredient in delicatessen meats and marinades. Its essential oil is used to perfume soaps, bath oils, and other cosmetic products.

Buying

Whole thyme leaves have more flavor than ground leaves.

Nutritional Information

	ground
calcium	26 mg
potassium	11 mg
vitamin A	5 ER
magnesium	3 mg
phosphorus	3 mg
iron	1.7 mg
	per 5 ml (1 g)

Thyme is said to be diuretic, antispasmodic, aphrodisiac, a stimulant, and an expectorant; it stimulates perspiration and menstruation, relieves flatulence, and cleanses the intestines. Its essential oil contains thymol and carvacrol, which have excellent antiseptic and vermifuge properties (certain cough syrups contain thymol).

To make thyme tea, add a tablespoon of dried leaves to a cup of water, boil the mixture for 2 to 3 minutes, and let it steep for 10 minutes.

lemon-scented thyme

Mint

Mentha spp., **Labiatae**

Mint leaves have more flavor when picked before flowering.

A perennial aromatic herb native to the Mediterranean region, mint has been utilized ever since antiquity for a wide variety of purposes; it is mentioned in the Bible. In addition to its medicinal and culinary applications, it was once used to perfume temples and homes.

Mint grows so profusely in temperate regions that it can become a nuisance. There are about 25 different species. Some types have a flavor reminiscent of apple while others others taste lemony. The flavor varies in intensity from one species to another. Peppermint and spearmint are among the most popular species, as they are highly aromatic.

Peppermint *(Mentha piperata)* has purplish green stems and lance-shaped leaves veined with the same color. Small violet flowers grow at the tips of the branches. The plant's fragrance is pronounced and penetrating; indeed, peppermint is the strongest tasting of all mint species. A small amount is enough to season foods.

Spearmint *(Mentha spicata),* sometimes called garden mint, has shiny grayish green leaves with a strong odor. Almost round, they have very little down. The flowers are purplish.

Buying

Dried mint leaves are generally blackish green (except for those that have been dehydrated in a microwave oven). For maximum flavor, buy them in a shop with a quick inventory turnover.

Storing

Fresh mint can be kept for several days in the refrigerator. If stored in a sealed container kept in dry, dark place, dried mint remains flavorful for up to 2 years.

Serving Ideas

Mint can be used fresh or dried. It can be added to cold and hot soups, sauces, certain vegetables (zucchini, cabbage, cucumbers, peas, tomatoes), potato salad, meat, game, fish, and ice cream. Although mint is delicious with lemon, it is best to avoid mixing it with other aromatics. It imparts an interesting flavor to salad dressings and mayonnaise.

In the English-speaking world, lamb is traditionally served with mint sauce or jelly. Vietnamese spring rolls are wrapped in fresh spearmint, which is also an ingredient of Lebanese tabbouleh. Mint is a common component of North African, Middle Eastern, Indian, and Southeast Asian cuisines. It is used in curries, chutneys, shish kebabs, yogurt, salads, sauces, and tea.

Mint's essential oil is used to flavor chewing gum, chocolate, liqueurs, toothpaste, medicines, and cigarettes, and adds fragrance to certain cosmetics.

Nutritional Information

Peppermint owes its distinctive flavor and therapeutic properties to menthol, which leaves a fresh taste in the mouth. The compound is absent from spearmint, which is used only for its taste and has no effect on digestion. (The two species, however, are often confused.)

Peppermint essence can contain up to 92% menthol, which is believed to have a number of medicinal properties. It is said to alleviate colic, gallbladder problems, and spasms and to be antiseptic, tonic, expectorant, stomachic, and digestive.

Consumed in large quantities, mint can cause insomnia; in small doses, however, it promotes sleep.

To make mint tea, use a pinch of dried leaves per cup of boiling water and allow the mixture to steep for 10 minutes.

Various ointments used to treat headaches and muscular pain contain menthol.

spearmint   **peppermint**

Parsley

Petroselinum spp., Umbelliferae

curly parsley

Parsley is an aromatic biennial herb native to southern Europe. Over the centuries, people have ascribed to it various curative, and in some cases sinister, properties. In ancient Greece, parsley symbolized joy and festivity. It began to be used as seasoning only in the Middle Ages, thanks to Charlemagne, who ordered that it be grown on his estates. There are three main species of parsley.

Curly parsley has bright green leaves and long stems up to a foot in height.

Italian parsley has flat leaves and grows to a height of 1½ feet. Its highly fragrant taste, less bitter than that of curly parsley, is reminiscent of celery.

Turnip-rooted parsley (also known as Hamburg parsley) is grown mainly for its white roots; resembling salsify, they are generally about 6 inches long and 2 inches wide.

The taste of flat-leaf Italian parsley is reminiscent of celery.

Preparing

Wash parsley carefully: like spinach, it tends to retain sand and dirt. Swish it gently in cold water until it is clean, changing the water if necessary. Do not leave it to soak.

Serving Ideas

Parsley has an almost limitless number of uses. It can be consumed fresh, dried, frozen, or marinated. Its taste and nutritive value are greatest when it is fresh. Add it at the last minute to cooked foods; it will be crisper, greener, tastier, and more nutritious. Both the leaves and the stems are edible. Along with thyme and bay leaf, parsley is an essential ingredient of bouquet garni.

In addition to its more traditional uses, it can be added to sandwich fillings, omelets, and salads. In Lebanese cooking, parsley is the one of the main ingredients in tabbouleh, a cold dish also featuring cracked bulgur wheat, olive oil, onion, garlic, lemon juice, and mint. Parsley roots are prepared like turnips or carrots and are used mainly in soups, stews, and sauces. The roots can be cooked and eaten like asparagus or celeriac.

Storing

Keep parsley in the refrigerator in a perforated plastic bag. Wash it first if it is earthy, sandy, or very damp. If it is wilted, sprinkle it lightly with water before refrigerating it; or if you have just washed it, avoid drying it completely. Although parsley freezes well (without blanching), it loses its crispness; use it unthawed. Store dried parsley in an airtight container kept in a cool, dry, dark place.

Buying

Choose parsley that is crisp and green. Avoid sprigs that are yellow, brown, or wilted, as they lack flavor.

Nutritional Information

	fresh	*dried*
vitamin A	52 ER	30 ER
potassium	55 mg	49 mg
calcium	14 mg	19 mg
vitamin C	13 mg	2 mg
phosphorus	6 mg	5 mg
iron	0.6 mg	1.2 mg
per 10 sprigs (10 g)		

Parsley is said to be diuretic and a stimulant; it combats scurvy and intestinal problems, stimulates the appetite, and aids digestion. It also freshens breath.

Herbs, Spices, and Condiments

479

Italian parsley

Chervil

Anthriscus cerefolium, Umbelliferae

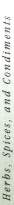

An aromatic annual herb, believed to be native to Russia. The word "chervil" comes from the Greek *kairephullon* from *khairein,* meaning "to rejoice," and *phullon,* meaning "leaf," and means literally "the leaf that rejoices." Chervil is a particularly important herb in French cuisine; its use in France dates back to the return of the Crusaders during the Middle Ages.

Chervil bears a slight resemblance to its close relative, parsley. In fact, it was known as "rich-man's parsley" in medieval Europe. It is, however, more delicately flavored than parsley, and of a more subdued shade of green.

Chervil has indented green leaves and small white umbellate flowers that produce long, thin dark-colored seeds; the seeds are not used in cooking. The plant, which grows to a height of 8 to 28 inches, is most flavorful just before it flowers. Chervil is a particularly refined aromatic plant whose delicate flavor is reminiscent of anise.

Chervil bears a slight resemblance to its close relative, parsley. In fact, it was called "rich-man's parsley" in medieval Europe.

Herbs, Spices, and Condiments

480

Buying

When buying fresh chervil, choose a plant that is firm and free of dark patches. Avoid yellow, brown, or wilted leaves.

Nutritional Information

	dried
potassium	28 mg
calcium	8 mg
iron	0.1 mg
	per 5 ml (1 g)

Chervil has been used as an aperitive, a stomachic, a depurator, and a diuretic. Chervil tea may be made by steeping 1 tablespoon of dried chervil leaves in 1 cup of boiling water for 10 minutes.

Serving Ideas

Chervil is used like parsley, for which it makes a delicious substitute. Along with parsley, tarragon, and chives, chervil belongs to the group of herbs known in French cuisine as *fines herbes.* It is commonly used to season soups, vinaigrettes, sauces (béarnaise, gribiche), raw vegetables, omelets, stews, cold dishes, and fish.

Because the essential oil of chervil is extremely volatile, it loses its flavor rapidly when it is boiled or dried. It should therefore be used as fresh as possible; it is best to cut it (preferably with scissors) and add it to dishes just before serving. Chervil should not be mixed with too much oil.

Storing

Fresh chervil is delicate. Place the stems directly in water, or wrap the chervil in slightly dampened paper and store it in the refrigerator. Chervil conserves its flavor better when frozen than when dried.

Rosemary

Rosmarinus officinalis, **Labiatae**

Rosemary is a small perennial shrub native to the Mediterranean area. Its highly aromatic leaves are used as a seasoning. The plant's Latin name, which means "dew of the sea," refers to the fact that rosemary grows best close to the seashore. It has been used since antiquity for its medicinal properties. People once believed that it reinforced memory. In certain cultures, including those of ancient Rome and Egypt, the plant was considered to be a cure-all. An excellent natural preservative, it can replace synthetic additives such as the antioxidants BHA (butylated hydroxyanisole) and BHT (butylated hydroxytoluene).

The plant generally grows to a height of 2 to 5 feet. Its leaves, which resemble fine needles, are dark green on top with a whitish underside. Clusters of tiny lavender, pale-blue, or in some cases white flowers attract bees, which produce an exquisite honey. Unlike other fresh herbs, rosemary is harvested during and after flowering, when the leaves are at their aromatic peak.

The evergreen leaves of the rosemary plant resemble fine needles. The upper side is dark green and the underside is whitish in color.

Serving Ideas

Rosemary has a pungent, heady flavor and a slightly camphorated aroma. Use it sparingly to avoid masking the taste of other ingredients. It is highly popular in the South of France and in Italy, where it is added in generous quantities to dishes such as soups, stuffings, sauces, and marinades. It is also used to flavor pasta, stews, fish, and meats such as lamb, poultry, and game (broiled, roasted, or in kebabs). Rosemary flowers add flavor to wines and salads. A few leaves add a delicate flavor to milk, which can then be used to make various desserts, including custards. Rosemary is an ingredient of the herb blend known as *herbes de Provence*. It is used to make perfumes and is a basic element of various ointments, soaps, and shampoos.

Nutritional Information

	dried
calcium	15 mg
potassium	11 mg
vitamin A	4 ER
magnesium	3 mg
vitamin C	1 mg
iron	0.3 mg
	per tsp. (2 g)

Rosemary is said to be antispasmodic, antiseptic, diuretic, stomachic, and a stimulant; it relieves rheumatism and flatulence, stimulates perspiration and menstruation, and aids the liver. Some people believe that it prevents wrinkles. Phytotherapists use it extensively. Strong doses of rosemary can irritate the stomach and intestines.

To make rosemary tea, add a teaspoon of dried leaves to a cup of water, boil the mixture for 2 to 3 minutes, and let it steep for 10 minutes.

Herbs, Spices, and Condiments

481

Juniper berry

Juniperus communis, Cupressaceae

The small berries of the juniper tree are initially green but eventually turn blue-black; they have a resinous odor and a pungent, slightly bitter flavor.

482

The juniper berry is the fruitlike cone of the juniper tree, which is native to the coniferous forests of the Northern Hemisphere. The juniper tree has stiff, prickly, evergreen needles that can be either gray-green or blue-green. Juniper trees grow wild in dry, sandy, or rocky soil in North America, Asia, and throughout Europe. Mentioned in Egyptian scrolls dating back to 2800 B.C., juniper berries have been renowned for their medicinal properties since ancient times.

The dimensions of the juniper tree vary; it can be tall (up to 40 feet) and dense, or of medium height, or a very compact and sturdy bush. The flowers of the tree produce fleshy green berries that turn blue-black or purple and develop a plum- or grapelike layer of skin after 1 or 2 years. All parts of the tree have a strong aroma. The berries have a resinous smell and a pungent, slightly bitter flavor.

Buying

Look for whole juniper berries, which are more flavorful than crushed berries. Choose blackish berries that are free of mold, avoiding those that are brown or greenish. Juniper berries are sometimes slightly shriveled.

Serving Ideas

Used whole and crushed, juniper berries are particularly popular in northern Europe. They are used as a flavoring for game, poultry, pork, rabbit, coleslaw, pâtés, marinades, stuffing, cold cuts, cabbage dishes, and court bouillon. Juniper berries are also one of the basic ingredients in dishes that are prepared *à la liégeoise* (with juniper berries and alcohol) and *à l'ardennaise* (game cooked with juniper berries or juniper-flavored alcohol).

Juniper berries are an indispensable component of gin, and they are also used to flavor a number of beers, Scandinavian aquavits, and German schnapps.

Nutritional Information

Juniper berries are used as an antiseptic, a diuretic, a tonic, a cleansing agent, and a digestive. They alleviate rheumatism and arthritis, as well gallbladder and urinary-tract problems. However, the essential oil of the juniper tree should not be used during pregnancy or for kidney problems without consulting a professional. The berries, bark, and needles of the juniper tree can be used to make tea: Add 1 teaspoon per cup of water, boil the mixture for 2 or 3 minutes, then let it brew for 10 minutes.

Clove

Syzygium aromaticum, **Myrtaceae**

Cloves are the dried flower buds of an evergreen tree indigenous to the Moluccas (formerly known as the Spice Islands), part of the Indonesian archipelago. They are characterized by their pungent, long-lasting taste, as well as by their resemblance to small nails (about ½ inch long with a ¼-inch-diameter head). The term "clove" is derived from *clavus,* the Latin word for "nail." Cloves have been used in Asia for more than 2,000 years. During the Han dynasty, Chinese courtiers placed cloves in their mouths to sweeten their breath when addressing the emperor. Although the use of cloves in Europe dates back to about the 4th century, it has been widespread only since the Middle Ages. Cloves were once as highly prized as pepper because of their ability to mask the often dubious flavor of poorly preserved food. For many years they were cultivated almost exclusively in Indonesia, under Dutch control. Today the Indonesian island of Zanzibar is the world's main clove-production center.

Clove trees can stretch upward to a height of 40 to 50 feet. Given their fragility, they grow best in tropical marine climates. Although the trees can live for over a century, their peak production period is between 10 and 20 years after planting. They start bearing fruit only in their seventh or eighth year. Their leaves, flower buds, and flowers are highly aromatic, filling the air with their heady scent. Clove trees rarely flower, however, as the buds are picked as soon as they begin to change from green to pink, before the petals appear. The buds are immediately dried until they turn brown. Given their exceptional hardness, cloves are difficult to grind.

Clove trees rarely flower, as the buds are picked and dried before they open.

Serving Ideas

Whole cloves are traditionally associated with roast ham. They are also added to onions in boiled dinners and pot roasts. They are good for seasoning fruit compotes, marinades, and vinegar pickles, and impart an interesting taste to coffee. Ground cloves are added to stuffings, blood sausage, delicatessen meats, beef, lamb, stews, meat loaf, head cheese, pickles, marinades, soups, vegetables, cakes, cookies, pies, puddings, pastries containing honey and dried fruits, fruit in brandy, juices, and mulled wine. They are one of the ingredients of gingerbread.

Cloves are often linked with cinnamon and nutmeg, and are included in spice mixtures such as *garam masala* and curries (India), *ras-el-hanout* (North Africa), and Chinese five-spices. Although they go well with garlic, onion, and pepper, they should not normally be combined with herbs. An essential oil, the main component of which is eugenol, is extracted from the flower buds, leaves, and stems. It is used to manufacture vanillin (synthetic vanilla), perfumes, soaps, medications (dental anesthetics), mouthwashes, and chewing gum.

Buying

It is best to buy whole cloves, as ground cloves lose their flavor quickly and cannot be kept for as long. To check the quality of a clove, put it in water: it should float vertically. If it sinks or floats horizontally, it is stale.

Nutritional Information

	ground
potassium	23 mg
calcium	14 mg
magnesium	6 mg
vitamin C	2 mg
iron	0.2 mg
	per tsp. (2 g)

Cloves are said to be tonic; they reduce neuralgia, spasms, and flatulence, and aid digestion. The essential oil, which contains 70% to 85% eugenol, is used to soothe toothaches and earaches. It contains stimulants that, if used in excessive quantities, can irritate the digestive system.

Herbs, Spices, and Condiments

483

ground cloves

Allspice

Pimenta dioica, **Myrtaceae**

allspice berries

A llspice is the highly aromatic berry of the allspice tree, native to the West Indies and Mexico. While Jamaica is the largest producer today, the spice is also cultivated in Honduras, Guatemala, and Brazil. Although allspice was used by the Aztecs in pre-Columbian times to flavor chocolate, it was introduced to Europe only in the 17th century. Its name refers to the fact that its flavor resembles a blend of cloves, cinnamon, and nutmeg.

The allspice tree is a tropical evergreen related to the clove tree. Its slender green trunk stretches upward to a height of about 40 feet. Tiny white flowers produce clusters of round pea-sized berries, which are picked before they ripen, while their flavor is at its peak. The green berries are then sun- or oven-dried, which changes their color to a dark reddish brown.

Buying

Allspice is sold whole or ground. It is best to buy it whole and grind it as needed, as it will keep its flavor longer. The berries are easy to crush. You can also use the leaves like bay leaf.

Nutritional Information

	ground
potassium	20 mg
calcium	13 mg
magnesium	3 mg
iron	0.1 mg
	per tsp. (2 g)

Allspice has medicinal properties similar to those of cloves: it stimulates the appetite and digestion, and alleviates flatulence and rheumatism. Its essential oil contains eugenol, used to manufacture vanillin (see *Cloves*).

Serving Ideas

Add allspice sparingly to avoid overpowering the flavor of other ingredients. It can be used to season both sweet and salty dishes. Use it like cloves, which it can replace in most recipes. Allspice goes well with roast meat and game, and can be added to marinades. It is used to flavor sauces (including applesauce), fruitcakes, custard tarts, rice, onions, cabbage, and poultry, and is an ingredient of certain delicatessen meats as well as liqueurs such as Chartreuse and Benedictine.

ground allspice

Herbs, Spices, and Condiments

Nutmeg

Myristica fragrans, **Myristicaceae**

utmeg is the seed of the nutmeg tree, an evergreen believed to be native to the Moluccas, or Spice Islands, which are part of Indonesia. Although nutmeg and mace have been traded ever since the 6th century, they have been known in Europe only since the 1300s. As in the case of cloves, the nutmeg trade was for many years a Dutch monopoly. The thin, ligneous covering of the nutmeg seed, known as the "aril," is commonly called mace. During the period of Dutch colonization, mace was a more profitable trade item than nutmeg.

Nutmeg trees, which grow in tropical climates, are cultivated mainly in Indonesia, India, Sri Lanka, and the West Indies. They grow to a height of about 30 feet, and their dark-green oblong leaves are about 4 inches long. The fruits, which resemble apricots, are golden yellow with red spots. When ripe, they split open to reveal a brown kernel (the nutmeg) about an inch long, which is covered by a bright red membrane (mace). Dark orange when dried, mace has a more subdued flavor than nutmeg, which is warm and spicy. Mace gives off an aroma reminiscent of cinnamon and pepper, and is sold in strips or powder form.

When the fruit is ripe, its flesh splits open to reveal a brown kernel (the nutmeg) covered in a red membrane (mace).

Buying

Nutmeg soon loses its flavor when ground. It is best to buy it whole and grate it as needed. It is often bleached with lime to protect it from insects. Be sure to choose kernels that are hard and heavy, with no insect holes. To check whether a kernel is fresh, nick it or poke it lightly with a needle: an oily film or droplet should rise to the surface. To ensure freshness, buy ground nutmeg or mace in a shop with a rapid inventory turnover.

Serving Ideas

Nutmeg is used to season both sweet and salty foods. It adds flavor to dishes containing potatoes, eggs, and cheese, as well as to cakes, puddings, pies, compotes, cabbage, spinach, sauces, onion soup, snails, meat, and marinades. It is an ingredient in liqueurs, punches, mulled wine, and various other beverages. Nutmeg goes particularly well with milk products. Avoid combining it with other fragrant spices.

Mace is used to flavor pastries, delicatessen meats, and spice blends. It is used much like nutmeg, which it can replace in omelets, béchamel sauce, and mashed potatoes. Add it at the beginning of the cooking process.

Nutritional Information

	ground nutmeg	*ground mace*
calories	12	8
fat	0.8 g	0.6 g
potassium	8 mg	8 mg
phosphorus	5 mg	2 mg
calcium	4 mg	4 mg
magnesium	4 mg	3 mg
iron	0.1 mg	0.2 mg
		per tsp. (2 g)

Nutmeg is said to be a stimulant, to aid digestion, and to reduce flatulence. It contains myristin, a narcotic substance with euphoric properties. Overconsumption leads to headaches and stomachaches.

mace

nutmeg

Cardamom

Elettaria cardamomum and *Amomun kravanh,* **Zingiberaceae**

Cardamom is the highly aromatic fruit of a ginger-family perennial native to India. The warm-flavored seeds are slightly peppery. Cardamom was known to the Greeks and Romans, who used it in cooking. Alexander the Great's soldiers introduced it to Europe upon returning from India. In the Middle Ages, people believed the spice had a wide variety of medicinal properties.

Cardamom is more commonly used in Eastern and Arab countries than in the West, with the exception of Scandinavia, where it is highly popular. The main producers are India, Sri Lanka, Cambodia, and Guatemala. Along with saffron and vanilla, cardamom is one of the most expensive spices. There are several varieties, the most commercially important of which are Malabar cardamom, Sri Lankan cardamom, and Cambodian cardamom.

Malabar cardamom *(Elettaria cardamomum,* var. *minuscula)* is produced by a large, bushy perennial found mainly near the Malabar coast. This rhizomatous plant grows wild in southern India's Cardamom Hills. Its long dark-green leaves are lance shaped, and its yellowish or bluish flowers blossom near the ground. The plant's greenish yellow or brown fruits are oval capsules about ½ inch long. They contain about a dozen small, black, highly aromatic seeds, which fetch a particularly high price.

Sri Lankan cardamom *(Elettaria cardamomum,* var. *major)* is not always considered a distinct species, as it closely resembles Malabar cardamom. Its pods are larger and longer, and its seeds are of lower quality.

Cambodian cardamom *(Amomun kravanh)* is a closely related plant common to Cambodia and Vietnam. It grows to a height of about 10 feet. Its small cylindrical flowers grow close together in dense clusters. The seeds are contained in round capsules similar in shape and flavor to Malabar cardamom.

The color of the capsules varies depending on how they are processed: green cardamom (preferred in India) is sun-dried; brown cardamom (most popular elsewhere in Asia and in Europe) is oven-dried; and white cardamom (United States) is bleached.

Nutritional Information

potassium	22 mg
calcium	8 mg
iron	0.3 mg
zinc	0.2 mg
	per tsp. (2 g)

Cardamom is said to be digestive, aperitive, carminative, and a stimulant. People chew the seeds to freshen their breath. You can make cardamom tea by adding a few seeds to water. Boil lightly for 2 to 3 minutes and allow the mixture to steep for 10 minutes.

brown cardamom

green cardamom

Serving Ideas

In the West, cardamom is used mainly to flavor cakes, cookies, fruit compotes, marinades, delicatessen meats, wines, and liqueurs. In Asia it is added to meats, fish, rice, omelets, and desserts. Cardamom is one of the main ingredients of Indian curry and is one of the basic spices in garam masala. In Arabia it is used to flavor coffee. Scandinavians use it for mulled wine, compotes, pies, and certain delicatessen meats (sausages, ground meat). It can replace ginger and cinnamon in most recipes.

Buying

Cardamom is sold as pods, as seed, and ground. It is best to buy it in the pod and grind it as needed, as it will keep its flavor longer and you will be able to use it for a greater variety of purposes (it can also be used whole). You will also be able to ensure that you are getting your money's worth, as cardamom is sometimes sold mixed with less expensive spices.

Caper

Capparis spinosa, **Capparidaceae**

The caper bush is a prickly perennial native to the Mediterranean region. The flower buds of this creeping shrub, known as capers, have been eaten since antiquity. The Romans used them to flavor fish sauces, and they are mentioned in the Old Testament.

Caper bushes are cultivated in southern Europe and North Africa. Highly decorative, they have magnificent white-petaled flowers with pink highlights and long stamens tipped with purple pollen. Their woody stems cling to walls and rocks. The bushes can reach about 3 feet in height. Their small green oval leaves are shiny, thick, and dense. The olive-green flower buds are picked before they open.

The olive-green flower buds are picked before they open.

Buying

Capers are sold pickled in vinegar, brine, or wine. Smaller capers, which are more expensive, have a more delicate flavor and are more aromatic. Nasturtium, broom, and marigold buds are often sold fraudulently as capers. They are less expensive and up to six times as large.

Serving Ideas

The sourish, somewhat bitter flavor of capers adds an interesting touch to mayonnaise, salads, and cold sauces such as remoulade. Capers are an essential ingredient of steak tartare. They can be used for sauces, hors d'oeuvres, mustard, sandwiches, pizza, rice, pasta, meat and poultry (roasted or braised), and, in particular, fish and seafood. To obtain optimum flavor, add capers at the end of the cooking process. The combination of capers, olives, and onion is characteristic of southern European cuisine: for example *tapenade,* an olive purée seasoned with capers and anchovies.

Nutritional Information

Capers contain a bitter glucoside that is an irritant, tonic, and diuretic. They are said to improve the appetite and digestion.

Storing

Pickled capers can be kept indefinitely. Once opened, the jar should be refrigerated.

Caraway

Carum carvi, Umbelliferae

Caraway is a biennial herb native to Europe and western Asia. Archeological digs at sites dating back to the third millennium B.C. have shown it to be the oldest of all European spices.

The plant, which grows to a height of 1 to 2 feet, is closely related to and is often mistaken for fennel and dill. Caraway is particularly popular in the Arabic countries and in India, Germany, Denmark, and Russia. It is unfamiliar in most other countries.

The caraway plant's lance-shaped leaves fan out into narrow strips resembling carrot tops. Its tiny white, pink, or purple flowers are grouped together in umbels. The fruits (seeds), which are about ⅕ inch long, are yellowish brown and have lateral ridges like cumin. Highly aromatic, caraway seeds have a warm, sharp taste, milder than cumin but stronger than dill.

The lance-shaped leaves split into narrow strips resembling carrot tops.

Herbs, Spices, and Condiments

488

Buying

It is best to buy whole seeds, as they have more flavor and keep longer than ground caraway.

Preparing

Crush and roast the seeds to bring out their full flavor. For a more subtle flavor, sauté them in fat or oil before crushing them.

Nutritional Information

potassium	28 mg
calcium	14 mg
phosphorus	12 mg
iron	0.3 mg
zinc	0.1 mg
	per tsp. (2 g)

Caraway is thought to be carminative, vermifuge, antispasmodic, stomachic, and a stimulant. Its inclusion in rich dishes facilitates digestion.

To make a herbal tea, add 1 tablespoon caraway seeds to a cup of water, boil for 2 minutes, and let steep for 10 minutes.

Serving Ideas

In India, caraway is added to a variety of foods including curries, lentil dishes, and rice. In Germany and eastern Europe, it is used to season delicatessen meats, sauerkraut, stews, fish, potato salad, pastries, and applesauce. Its full aroma is released by slow simmering. Caraway can be candied, used to decorate and season various cheeses (Gouda, Livarot, Munster), and used to flavor alcoholic drinks such as kummel, schnaps, aquavit, and vespetro.

Along with anise, fennel, and coriander, caraway is one of the "four hot seeds" included in the ancient pharmacopeia and favored by people from Arab cultures, who use them for salads, *méchouis,* and kebabs. The plant's roots, which are edible, can be boiled and served like carrots or parsnips. The leaves and young shoots add a pleasant flavor to soups and salads.

caraway seeds

Saffron

Crocus sativus, Iridaceae

A variety of crocus, saffron is believed to have originated in Asia Minor. Its stigmas and flowers are used as a seasoning and as a coloring agent. Saffron is said to be the most ancient of all spices. It is mentioned in a papyrus dating back to about 1500 B.C., and was thus known to the Egyptians, Greeks, and Romans. The Moors introduced it to Spain in the 8th century, and it eventually spread to France. Thanks to contacts with Arabic cultures, the Crusaders reintroduced saffron to Europe in the 11th century.

Saffron is a variety of crocus. Its flowers feature three orange-brown stigmas, which are hand-picked and dried.

Of the various types of saffron, *sativus* is the most highly prized variety. It is currently grown in various parts of the world, including Greece, Italy, the United States, and South America.

Saffron crocuses grow to a height of about 6 inches. Each purplish, red-veined flower has three orange-brown stigmas (upper extremities of the pistils), which are hand-picked and dried. They have a pungent aroma and a hot, bitter flavor. It takes an average of 100,000 flowers to produce just under a pound of saffron — the world's most expensive spice. Given its value, saffron is often mixed with safflower blossoms, arnica petals, or marigold flowers and sold fraudulently as "pure," or its weight is increased by the addition of water or oil.

Buying

Buy saffron stigmas rather than powder, which is often adulterated. The best saffron is orange-colored and has a warm, spicy flavor. As it ages, saffron gives off a moldy smell.

Preparing

To obtain a more even color, soak saffron in a hot liquid (use part of the liquid called for in your recipe) for about 15 minutes before adding it to the other ingredients.

Serving Ideas

Use saffron sparingly. A small pinch added at the beginning of the cooking process is enough to flavor an entire dish and give it a golden color. To preserve its aroma, avoid browning it at high temperatures in butter or oil. Saffron is a major seasoning in Arabic and Indian cooking. It is used to flavor and color soups, stews, rice, curries, couscous, pastries, liqueurs, and cheeses. It is an essential ingredient of bouillabaisse, paella, and *risotto alla milanese*. Saffron is also added to certain milk desserts and brioches, and is used to color and flavor poultry, seafood, and fish.

Nutritional Information

water	11.9%
calories	3.1
carbohydrates	0.7 g
potassium	7.2 mg
phosphorus	2.5 mg
	per tsp. (2 g)

Saffron is said to be antispasmodic, digestive, stomachic, and a stimulant; it relieves flatulence and stimulates menstruation.

It contains a bitter substance called picrocrocin and an aromatic essential oil. Although its yellow coloring matter, crocin, is extremely powerful, it cannot be used as a fabric dye because it is soluble in water.

Storing

Store saffron in an airtight container kept in a cool, dry, dark place.

Herbs, Spices, and Condiments

489

Coriander

Coriandrum sativum, Umbelliferae

Coriander is an annual or a biennial aromatic herb native to the Mediterranean basin. Its seeds are among the world's oldest known spices. The plant was cultivated in Egypt over 3,500 years ago, and there is evidence from around 1400 B.C. that the ancient Greeks used it as a remedy. The Romans used it to preserve meat.

The word "coriander" is derived from the Greek word *koris,* meaning "bug." Also known as cilantro or Chinese parsley, it is highly esteemed in Latin America and Asia, particularly in China, India, and Thailand. The Thais use the whole plant.

Coriander is closely related to caraway, fennel, dill, and anise. Its flat lobed leaves (which give off a strong smell when fresh) resemble those of flat-leaf parsley. Its thin, fragile stem can grow to a height of 3 feet. The plant's fruits look rather like lead shot with tiny longitudinal ridges. Each fruit contains a globular brownish mass can be broken into two separate spheres, or seeds. When dried, the seeds are yellowish brown and have a musky, lemon-like fragrance.

Serving Ideas

Fresh coriander is used like parsley and chervil, which it can sometimes replace as a seasoning or garnish. Asian cooks add it to salads, soups, and sauces. Use it with discretion, as people who are unaccustomed to coriander may find its flavor surprising or even unpleasant. In certain Middle Eastern countries, ground coriander is used as a table spice.

Whole or ground coriander seeds add flavor to a wide range of foods, including seafood, fish, rice, delicatessen meats, omelets, potatoes, cheeses, curries, marinades, chutneys, cookies, cakes, and gingerbread. They go well with parsley, lemon, and ginger, and are included in curry powder and garam masala, essential spice mixtures in Indian cuisine. Coriander is used to make balm water and liqueurs such as Chartreuse and Izarra, and is an ingredient of inferior-quality cocoa. Its delicious root can be crushed and used as a condiment or to replace garlic.

Nutritional Information

	fresh	*seeds*
vitamin A	11 ER	
potassium	22 mg	23 mg
calcium	4 mg	7 mg
phosphorus	1.4 mg	7 mg
magnesium	1 mg	6 mg
	per 50 ml (4 g)	**per tsp. (2 g)**

Coriander is known for its medicinal properties. It is said to be aid digestion and is used to ease rheumatism, joint pains, colds, and diarrhea. Some people chew the seeds to neutralize the smell of garlic.

Coriander makes a pleasant after-meal herbal tea. Use 1 teaspoon of seeds per cup of water. Boil the mixture for 2 to 3 minutes and let it steep for 10 minutes.

Storing

Fresh coriander is highly perishable. It lasts longer with its roots attached. You can keep it for up to a week in the refrigerator if you place the roots in water like flower stems and cover the leaves with a plastic bag. If the roots have been removed, cover the leaves with a damp cloth and store them in the refrigerator in a perforated plastic bag. They will last for 2 to 3 days.

Although fresh coriander freezes well and does not need to be blanched first, it loses some of its crispness and should be used unthawed. Dried coriander leaves have considerably less flavor. Keep them away from light and insects. If stored in an airtight container placed in a cool, dry, dark place, the dried seeds keep for about a year.

coriander seeds

Buying

Choose fresh coriander (usually labeled "cilantro") that is firm, crisp, and green. Avoid specimens with yellow, brown, or wilted leaves, as they are not fresh. When buying dried coriander seeds, opt for whole rather than ground seeds to obtain the maximum flavor.

Preparing

Wash fresh coriander at the last moment, as it is highly fragile and quickly loses its flavor. Swish it gently in cool water. To revive the aroma of dried coriander seeds, soak them for about 10 minutes in cold water and then drain them.

cumin seeds

Cumin

Cuminum cyminum, Umbelliferae

An aromatic herb native to the Mediterranean region, cumin has been used as a spice for thousands of years, particularly in the Middle East. The Bible mentions it as an ingredient of soup and bread. In addition to using cumin rather than pepper, the ancient Egyptians used the spice to mummify their deceased pharaohs. The Romans used it to flavor sauces, preserve meat, and season broiled fish. In medieval Europe, people believed that cumin reinforced fidelity between lovers and prevented chickens from straying.

The plant's fragile branched stem grows to a height of 12 to 20 inches. Split into a number of narrow leaflets, its foliage resembles that of fennel, to which cumin is related. Each white or pinkish flower produces two bristly oblong seeds about ¼ inch in length. Yellowish brown with longitudinal ridges, they are often confused with caraway seeds, which are produced by a plant belonging to the same family.

Cumin seeds' strong, penetrating, slightly bitter taste and aroma are not to everyone's liking. People often develop a taste for cumin by using it sparingly at first.

The white or pinkish flowers produce two small brown, bristly seeds. Oblong with longitudinal ridges, they have a strong aroma and a warm flavor.

Preparing

Roast and crush the seeds to bring out their full flavor. For a more subtle taste, sauté them briefly in oil or fat before crushing them.

Serving Ideas

Cumin is a common ingredient in Arabic, Indian, and Mexican dishes. It is used to flavor soups, vegetables, cheese, eggs, rice, legumes, sausages, stews, pâtés, beef, marinades, pastries, and bread. It is one of the basic components of chili powder, curry, and the North African spice blend known as *ras-el hanout.* Indeed, it is one of the leading spices in North Africa, where, under the name of *kamoun,* it is used to flavor *tajines* and couscous. In eastern Europe people use cumin in breads, delicatessen meats, and certain cheeses. A liquid paste made of ground cumin, pepper, and honey is considered in certain Arabic cultures to be an aphrodisiac.

Buying

It is best to buy whole seeds, as they have more flavor than ground cumin and can be kept longer.

Nutritional Information

potassium	38 mg
calcium	20 mg
phosphorus	10 mg
magnesium	8 mg
iron	1.3 mg
	per tsp. (2 g)

Cumin is said to be a diuretic and a sedative; it reduces flatulence and aids digestion.

To make cumin tea, add a teaspoon of seeds to a cup of water, bring the mixture to a boil, and let it steep for 10 minutes.

Lemon Balm

Melissa officinalis, **Labiatae**

An aromatic perennial herb native to southern Europe, lemon balm is a member of the mint family. It was cultivated by the Romans more than 2,000 years ago and is currently grown in a number of regions, including all of southern Europe, Germany, and Asia. It is sometimes referred to as "bee balm," as the plant attracts bees. Indeed, since ancient times, beekeepers have rubbed their hives with lemon balm to prevent the insects from swarming.

Lemon balm grows to a height of 1 to 3 feet. Its dark-green oval leaves have prominent veins. Their upper side is covered with down. Small whitish or pinkish flowers produce elongated oval seeds. Lemon balm is picked before it flowers, when its lemony flavor is at its peak.

Lemon balm (also known as bee balm) has dark-green oval leaves with prominent veins. Covered with down, they are picked before the plant flowers, when their lemony flavor is at its peak.

Herbs, Spices, and Condiments

492

Buying

When buying fresh lemon balm, make sure the stems and leaves are firm and free of dark spots.

Serving Ideas

Lemon balm can be used fresh or dried. It goes particularly well with pungent foods. Highly regarded in Asian cultures, it is used to flavor Indian curries, soups, and sauces. Add lemon balm just before serving, as its flavor is volatile. It can be used to season mixed salads, omelets, rice, fish, stuffings, orange- and lemon-based pastries, fruit salads, compotes, and fruit juices. Lemon balm is an ingredient in a number of liqueurs, including Benedictine and Chartreuse. In Holland it is used to season and tone down the taste of pickled herring and eel. The Spanish use it to perfume milk, sauces, and soups.

Nutritional Information

The essential oil contained in lemon balm is said to be tonic; it aids digestion, increases perspiration, reduces spasms, and combats bacteria and intestinal disorders. According to popular belief, lemon balm prolongs life.

Lemon balm tea is thought to relieve headaches, minor gastric problems, nervousness, and dizziness; boil a teaspoon of dried leaves in a cup of water for 1 to 2 minutes and let the mixture steep for 10 minutes. A cup of lemon balm tea after a meal helps reduce flatulence and colic. For maximum results, make the tea with fresh leaves, as the essential oil containing the active ingredients dissipates when the herb is dried.

Citral, one of the components of the essential oil, is used to perfume deodorants, ointments, and insecticides.

Lemon grass

Cymbopogon citratus, **Gramineae**

A perennial herb probably native to Malaysia, lemon grass is named for its subtle lemony flavor. It has been cultivated since antiquity for its essential oil, used in perfumes and cosmetics. About 60 herbaceous plants have a lemon-like aroma, including balm, which belongs to a different family. Lemon grass grows in most tropical and subtropical countries. Its tenacious roots help prevent soil erosion. In western Africa and Southeast Asia, where it is used to treat malaria, it is also known as "fever grass."

Lemon grass grows to a height of about 2 feet. Its bulbous stems are yellowish green with a cream-colored base; this is the tenderest part. The plant is cultivated today in Africa, the United States, South America, the Caribbean, and Australia.

Buying

Lemon grass is sold fresh, dried, and pickled. It is often used in herbal teas. When buying fresh lemon grass, choose specimens with a firm bulb.

Preparing

Peel the fresh stems and remove all but the lower 2½ inches, which is the tenderest part. The outer layer and upper portion of the stems are too stringy to be eaten but can be used to flavor stocks, sauces, soups, stews, fish, poultry, and herbal tea. Discard them after use.

Storing

Keep the bunch of lemon grass in the refrigerator, wrapped in plastic. It can be frozen without blanching (freeze the lower and upper stems separately).

Serving Ideas

Lemon grass is more flavorful fresh than dried. Use it sparingly, particularly if you are unfamiliar with its taste.

Lemon grass goes well with ginger, chile, coconut, garlic, shallots, and green pepper. It is particularly popular in Southeast Asia, where cooks use it to season a wide variety of foods, including soups, vegetables, curries, poultry, shellfish, fish, and marinades. It is often used to make herbal tea.

Nutritional Information

Lemon-grass oil contains geraniol and citral, which give the plant its lemony fragrance.

summer savory

Savory

Satureia hortensis, Labiatae

An aromatic herb native to the Mediterranean region, savory has been popular for over 2,000 years. The Romans used it to flavor sauces and vinegar and as an aphrodisiac – whence its Latin name, *Satureia,* which means "satyr's plant." Savory was introduced to New England in early colonial times.

There are two species of savory: an annual herb known as "summer savory" *(Satureia hortensis),* and a perennial plant called "winter savory" *(Satureia montana).* The former, which is the more common, grows to a height of about 10 inches. Its highly fragrant green leaves resemble thick needles. Before blossoming, the plant's pale purplish or white flowers, located in the leaf axils, give off a sweet aroma reminiscent of mint and thyme.

Savory's highly fragrant green leaves resemble thick needles.

Nutritional Information

	ground
calcium	30 mg
potassium	15 mg
vitamin A	7 ER
magnesium	5 mg
phosphorus	2 mg
iron	0.5 mg
	per tsp. (1 g)

Savory is said to be antispasmodic, antiseptic, an expectorant, and a stimulant. It is often used to season legumes, as it counteracts flatulence. To make savory tea, add a teaspoon of dried savory to a cup of boiling water and let the mixture steep for 10 minutes.

Serving Ideas

Savory leaves are used fresh or dried in cooking. Dried savory is available in flake and powder form. Add savory at the end of the cooking process to retain its full flavor. Avoid using too much, as it can make food taste bitter; a pinch of dried savory is enough. Savory is used to season goat cheese and vinegar. It is particularly appropriate with legumes, sauces, salads, soups, stews, marinades, meat and game, stuffings, pâtés, vegetables, and salad dressings. It goes perfectly with chervil and tarragon.

Curry

494

The term "curry" refers to a blend of spices as well as to fish, meat, lentil, and vegetable dishes that feature this seasoning. Native to India, curry is a basic element of the subcontinent's cuisine (both as a spice and as a main dish). In the Tamil language, *kari* means "sauce." As the spices included in the blend vary according to the region, caste, and customs, there is a virtually infinite range of curries. Curry can contain from as few as 5 to over 50 ingredients; most often, blends feature from 15 to 20 spices. Almost all curries include cinnamon, coriander, cumin, turmeric, pepper, cardamom, ginger, nutmeg, and cloves.

Depending on local traditions – and the cook's personal touch – curry may also feature mace, aniseed, caraway, fennel, fenugreek, bay leaf, poppy seeds, saffron, cayenne pepper, or mustard seeds. Cooks in Sri Lanka add coconut milk; in Thailand, curry sometimes contains shrimp paste. Indian curries come in a variety of colors, including white, golden brown, red, and green. They are available in liquid, dry, and powdered form. The sharpness of curry varies with the amount of pepper in the blend, which can be mild, semi-mild, hot, or very hot.

Buying

Curry is available commercially in powder and paste forms. A number of blends come from England, which adopted curry during colonial times.

Nutritional Information

Curry's nutritional value varies according to the type and quantity of ingredients.

Serving Ideas

Curry is used for a number of purposes. It is added to pork, lamb, and chicken entrées, vegetarian dishes (featuring chickpeas, lentils, or fish), appetizers, soups, vegetables, pasta, rice, sauces, mayonnaise, and butter. Before adding curry powder to a dish or sauce, heat it in oil or fat to bring out its aroma.

Storing

Keep curry powder in an airtight container stored in a cool, dry place. Curry paste should be refrigerated once the container has been opened.

Turmeric

Curcuma longa, Zingiberaceae

turmeric rhizome

Turmeric, a perennial plant belonging to the same family as ginger, is believed to have originated in Indonesia and Malaysia. It is grown for its rhizomes (underground stems) in tropical countries such as China, India, Indonesia, the Philippines, Taiwan, Haiti, Jamaica, and Peru.

The coloring matter contained in turmeric (curcumin) is virtually identical to the glycoside that gives saffron, a basic Indian spice, its yellow hue. Indeed, turmeric was formerly referred to as "Indian saffron" and is sometimes sold fraudulently as saffron.

Turmeric has been used for thousands of years. It was introduced to Europe by Arab merchants. The reedlike plant grows to a height of about 3 feet. Depending on the variety, its knotty rhizomes range from mustard yellow to lemon yellow. Seldom sold as is, the rhizomes are generally cooked, dehydrated, polished, and ground to a powder. A highly aromatic, pungent spice reminiscent of ginger, turmeric is quite different from saffron: its taste is more bitter, and this difference increases with cooking, which also darkens the spice. Turmeric is also used as a dye.

The rhizomes range from mustard yellow to lemon yellow. Similar in appearance to ginger, they are normally cooked, dehydrated, polished, and ground to a powder.

Buying

Turmeric's color is not a criterion of quality, as it differs from one variety to another.

Serving Ideas

Given its strong taste, use turmeric sparingly to avoid overwhelming the flavor of other ingredients. Turmeric is particularly popular in Southeast Asia, where it is used to color and flavor a wide variety of dishes, including soups, sauces, salads, lentils, rice, eggs, fish, and crustaceans.

In India it is one of the main ingredients of curry and *garam masala* spice blends, as well as chutneys. The English, who colonized India, also use turmeric in various dishes. It is an ingredient in Worcestershire sauce. Turmeric is used to color sauces, syrups, certain liqueurs, American mustard, marinades, candy, butter, margarine, cheese, and edible fats.

Nutritional Information

potassium	56 mg
phosphorus	6 mg
calcium	4 mg
magnesium	4 mg
iron	0.9 mg
	per tsp. (2 g)

In Chinese medicine, turmeric is used to treat shoulder pain, menstrual cramps, and colic. It is also said to be useful against coughs, indigestion, and conjunctivitis.

ground turmeric

Storing

Store turmeric in a dark place.

fresh turmeric

Borage

Borago officinalis, **Boraginaceae**

An aromatic and medicinal annual plant with blue flowers, borage is believed to have originated in Syria. It borrows its name from the Arab *sabu radj,* which means "father of sweat," and was so named because of the sweat-inducing properties of borage tea.

Borage is frequently found growing on vacant lots and along roadsides, particularly in America and Europe. Its leaves are most commonly used as a condiment but are also consumed as a vegetable, especially when they are still young and tender. Upon maturing, they become covered with a coarse down.

The plant has long stems which usually grow to a height of 1 to 1½ feet, but which can grow as high as 3 feet in the proper soil. Its long, broad leaves are wrinkled and coarsely textured, and are covered with long white hairs. The leaves become very stiff when the plant reaches maturity, and their flavor is similar to that of cucumber.

Borage leaves are consumed as a vegetable when they are young and tender, before they become covered with their hairy down.

Herbs, Spices, and Condiments

496

Nutritional Information

	cooked
water	92 %
protein	2.1 g
fat	0.8 g
carbohydrates	3.6 g
calories	25
	per 100 g

Borage is an excellent source of vitamin C, vitamin A, potassium, and iron; it is also a good source of magnesium and contains riboflavin, calcium, and phosphorus.

The relatively high mucilage content of borage flowers make them an effective remedy against colds and bronchitis when infused. Borage is said to be a good diuretic, laxative, depurator, and sudorific.

Serving Ideas

Borage can be eaten raw or cooked. The leaves can be added to salads, but it is best to marinate the older leaves in a vinaigrette for 30 minutes first, as they are much less tender than the young leaves. Borage is also used as a flavoring in yogurt, cream cheese, and vinaigrettes. It is best to use the leaves and flowers of borage when fresh, as they lose their flavor quite rapidly when dried.

The flowers are sometimes candied and used to decorate pastries. The fresh flowers can also be infused like mint (which they can replace), or they can be soaked in wine or iced tea, to which they add a refreshing flavor.

Cooking

Borage is cooked and prepared much like spinach, with which it is interchangeable in most recipes. However, it loses much of its flavor when boiled in water.

Storing

Borage can be kept in the refrigerator in a perforated plastic bag. It should be washed just before use.

cinnamon sticks

Cinnamon

Cinnamomum spp., **Lauraceae**

T he dried bark of the cinnamon tree (which belongs to the same family as the bay and the avocado) is one of the world's oldest known spices. It is mentioned in the earliest Chinese botanical treatise, which dates back to about 2800 B.C., as well as in Egyptian papyruses and the Bible.

Cultivators harvest cinnamon by cutting the 3-year-old shoots and slicing them open lengthwise in two or three places. The outer bark is removed. As it dries, the inner bark curls to form flaky tubular quills about 3 inches long and ½ inch in diameter.

There are about 100 different species of cinnamon trees with similar aromatic properties. The two leading commercial varieties are Ceylon cinnamon and Chinese cinnamon.

Ceylon cinnamon *(Cinnamomum zeylanicum)* is an evergreen that grows to a height of 30 to 40 feet. On plantations it is pruned back to about 8 feet. It is grown in various tropical regions, including Sri Lanka, India, the Seychelles, Madagascar, Brazil, and the Caribbean. Its large, tough aromatic leaves are shiny green on top and grayish blue underneath. The smooth thin bark, light brown and matte, is extremely aromatic. The paler the bark's color, the better the quality.

Chinese cinnamon *(Cinnamomum aromaticum)* can reach 40 feet in height. The tree grows wild in Southeast Asia and is cultivated in Indonesia and other Asian countries. Its bark, called "cassia," is a substitute for "true" cinnamon. Its flavor is sharper and less subtle, and the bark is thicker than that of the Ceylon cinnamon tree. Less expensive, it dominates the North American market.

For over 4,500 years, cultivators have harvested cinnamon by slicing the branches and drying the bark.

Buying

Cinnamon is sold in the form of sticks, powder, and essential oil. Ground cinnamon has a stronger flavor than cinnamon sticks, but it cannot be kept as long.

Serving Ideas

Cinnamon is used to flavor various foods, including cakes, cookies, apple pie, donuts, buns, puddings, pancakes, compotes, yogurt, and candies.

In regions such as Central Europe, Italy, Spain, and Canada, cinnamon is also used to season soups, meats, tomato sauces, vegetables, stews, couscous, pasta, and marinades. People in English-speaking countries often add it to baked zucchini. In France and northern nations, it is used in mulled wine. Asian cooks also use cinnamon flower buds, leaves, and dried berries. Cinnamon is used by the pharmaceutical industry to flavor various products, including toothpaste.

Storing

Keep cinnamon in a sealed container stored in a dry, dark place.

Nutritional Information

calcium	28 mg
potassium	11 mg
iron	0.8 mg
	per tsp. (2 g)

Cinnamon is said to be antispasmodic, antiseptic, vermifuge, and a stimulant. Added to tea or any other drink, ground cinnamon soothes digestive problems and diarrhea.

Make cinnamon tea by pouring boiling water over 1 to 1½ in. bark (2 g). Let the mixture steep for 10 minutes.

ground cinnamon

Herbs, Spices, and Condiments

497

Angelica

Angelica spp., Umbelliferae

A giant aromatic plant that grows abundantly in its native northern Europe, angelica is said to have been introduced into Europe by the Vikings. A related species, differing slightly in shape but with similar properties, grows in the northern part of the American continent. Angelica is much more widely used in Europe than in North America. It is cultivated in Belgium, Holland, and Germany.

This plant bears a slight resemblance to the celery plant. It varies in height from 1 foot to more than 6 feet. The more developed the plant, the more flavorful it will be. Its large emerald-green leaves are serrated, and its purplish ribbed, hollow stems appear in the second year. The small whitish or greenish yellow flowers form wide umbels with 30 to 40 rays. The plant is a biennial or a perennial. It has a warm and musky aroma, reminiscent of juniper berries.

The stems and roots of angelica are macerated in alcohol to make various alcoholic beverages.

Nutritional Information

Angelica is regarded as a good tonic, digestive, and expectorant. It improves the appetite and alleviates spasms. It is used as a remedy for asthma, chronic bronchitis, smoker's cough, colic, and migraines, and it also makes an excellent mouthwash.

Serving Ideas

Angelica is very popular in pastry making, where its candied stems are used to aromatize or decorate cakes, gingerbread, puddings, and soufflés. It is also used as a seasoning for fish and as a flavoring in vinegar. Raw, the chopped leaves add an original touch to salads. When cooked with acidic fruits, it makes them taste sweeter. The essential oil of angelica stems and roots is used in the manufacture of various alcoholic beverages, including Chartreuse, Benedictine, angelica liqueur, and gin.

To make angelica tea, boil 1 tablespoon of the root in 1 cup of water for 5 minutes; or boil 1 tablespoon leaves and seeds for 5 minutes and then steep for 10 minutes.

angelica stems

Fenugreek

Trigonella foenum-graecum, **Papitionaceae**

fenugreek seeds

Fruit of a herbaceous annual plant native to southeastern Europe and India. "Fenugreek" comes from the Latin *foenum graecum,* which literally means "Greek hay," while the Latin word *trigonella* refers to the shape of its seeds. Fenugreek has been used since ancient times, when it was more popular for its medicinal and condimentary properties than as a vegetable. In India, fenugreek has always been an ingredient of curries. The Egyptians consumed it as a vegetable and used it to embalm their dead. In ancient times, harem women sated themselves with roasted fenugreek seeds, mixed with olive oil and superfine sugar, in order to gain weight.

Fenugreek belongs to the same family as the pea and clover. The plant can grow to a height of 1 to 2 feet, and its yellow flowers, often slightly purple in color, grow in the axil of the leaves. The long, thin pods of the fruit contain 10 to 20 tiny, slightly flattened seeds that are quadrangular in shape and brownish yellow in color. Both the plant and the seeds give off a strong scent.

The seeds have a bittersweet flavor and leave a distinctive aftertaste of caramel or maple syrup when roasted. The food industry uses fenugreek in the preparation of an artificial flavor imitating maple syrup.

The long, thin pods of the fruit contain tiny seeds that are brownish yellow in color. Both the plant and the seeds give off a pungent aroma.

Serving Ideas

 Fenugreek seeds can be used dried, whole, ground, crushed, or sprouted. They are more flavorful when roasted and ground. They can be cooked in the same way as oatmeal, used as a condiment, or used to add flavor to soups, vegetables, cheeses, chutneys, pickles, and simmered dishes. Sprouted fenugreek seeds make a good salad. The seeds, leaves, and young sprouts are also used to make herbal tea, and the leaves and young sprouts are consumed as a vegetable in certain African countries and in India.

Storing

Store fenugreek in an airtight container and keep it in a cool, dry place away from the light.

Buying

Fenugreek is usually sold in specialized grocery stores.

Nutritional Information

water	7.5%
protein	0.9 g
fat	0.2 g
carbohydrates	2.2 g
calories	12
	per 5 ml (4 g)

Fenugreek seeds have a high mucilage content (up to 40%), and are said to be lactogenic, aphrodisiac, emollient, stomachic, and tonic. They also stimulate the appetite and are used in the treatment of abscesses and stomach pain, and as an emollient poultice. Fenugreek leaves are used as an expectorant, emollient, astringent, and diuretic.

ground seeds

Mustard

Brassica and *Sinapis* spp., Cruciferae

There are about 40 species of mustard, which can be distinguished mainly by their seeds.

An annual herb indigenous to the Mediterranean basin, mustard has been consumed from time immemorial and has been cultivated ever since antiquity. Known mainly for the condiment prepared from its seeds, the plant also has edible leaves (mustard greens). Indeed, like cabbage, it belongs to the crucifer family.

There are about 40 species of mustard, the most common being black mustard *(Brassica nigra),* white mustard *(Sinapsis alba),* Indian mustard *(Brassica juncea),* and wild mustard or charlock *(Sinapsis arvensis).*

Black mustard grows to a height of about 40 inches. Its lobed leaves are rough and hairy. The plant's small yellow flowers produce smooth, rounded red seeds, which turn black when ripe. Their flavor is extremely heady and pungent, more so than that of yellow mustard, as the seeds contain a high percentage of essential oil; this oil is used by the food industry.

White mustard reaches a height of 12 to 30 inches. Its flowers are larger than those of black mustard, and its seeds are easily distinguishable from those of other species as they are yellow and very large, with a bitter but less pungent taste.

The green leaves of the **Indian mustard** plant, known as mustard greens, are very popular in hot climates. Highly flavorful, they are sold fresh and used like spinach. The plant is said to be a cross between a member of the cabbage family *(Brassica rapa)* and black mustard.

Buying

Choose mustard greens that are fresh, pliant, and brightly colored. Avoid leaves that are dry, yellow, or wilted; also avoid those with hard, thick stems, as they tend to be stringy.

Preparing

Prepared mustard is made from mustard seeds, which are macerated in a liquid such as wine, must, vinegar, or water. The mixture is then ground to a fine paste. The color, flavor, and pungency of the resulting condiment depends on the seeds used and the seasonings that are added: e.g., garlic, tarragon, paprika, fines herbes, lemon, black pepper.

Dijon mustard is prepared with verjuice (the juice of unripened vine grapes), white wine, or wine vinegar, or a combination thereof; Bordeaux mustard is made with grape must; and Meaux mustard, which contains roughly crushed, multicolored seeds, is prepared with vinegar.

American mustard, which is milder than French mustard, is made with black and white mustard seeds and turmeric.

black mustard

Serving Ideas

Mustard greens can be eaten raw or cooked. They are prepared like spinach, which they can replace in most recipes. (Their flavor, however, is stronger.)

The greens go well in soups and make an excellent purée – particularly delicious when combined with mashed potatoes or puréed legumes, which cut the leaves' "bite." Avoid cooking the greens in aluminum or iron pots, as they turn black on contact with these metals.

Mustard seeds can be consumed whole, ground, or in condiment form. Whole, the seeds can be eaten as is or roasted. In India, cooks brown them in very hot oil until they burst open like popcorn. (Avoid cooking them too long, as they burn and turn bitter.)

Whole seeds are used to flavor a wide variety of foods, including marinades, legumes, sauces, and curries. Their highly aromatic oil is also extracted for commercial use. Powdered mustard can be added to salad dressings and mayonnaise and is used to season cooking ham. It can also be mixed with water to form a paste, which is used in much the same way as prepared mustard. Prepared mustard is used to add flavor to a wide range of foods, including rabbit, pork, chicken, and certain fatty fish (before cooking). It is a basic ingredient in numerous hot and cold sauces, including salad dressings, mayonnaise, and rémoulade.

Prepared mustard has been used for thousands of years. The Romans knew how to make it, and the Byzantines used it to flavor salad dressing. It was extremely popular in medieval times, as it made meats, commonly salted to prevent them from spoiling, palatable.

Indian mustard

Nutritional Information

	greens
water	91%
protein	2.7 g
fat	0.2 g
carbohydrates	5 g
fiber	1.1 g
calories	26
	per 100 g

Mustard greens are an excellent source of vitamin C, vitamin A, iron, and potassium.

Mustard is said to be a stimulant, a disinfectant, digestive, antiseptic, laxative, and vomitive. It promotes the secretion of gastric juices and saliva, stimulates the appetite, and if used in moderation, eases digestion (when overconsumed, however, it is an irritant).

Mustard oil is thought to have a strong antibacterial and antifungal effect. Mustard is used in foot baths and in mustard plasters, which are applied to the chest to clear the sinuses and decongest the lungs (to fight pneumonia, bronchitis, etc.).

Mustard's hot taste comes from the presence of myrosin and myronate. Myronate is found in black and Indian mustard seeds but not in white mustard, which explains why the latter variety is less hot.

Mustard greens contain substances that can cause the thyroid to increase in size. To avoid this problem, limit your consumption of this vegetable and eat foods with a high iodine content, such as seafood and kelp.

Storing

Prepared mustard should be kept in the refrigerator in a sealed container, as it loses its flavor at room temperature. Mustard powder and seeds should be stored in a cool, dry place.

Mustard greens are fragile. You can store them unwashed in the refrigerator, in a perforated plastic bag, for several days. They can also be frozen like spinach.

Mustard oil should be kept in the refrigerator or a cool place.

Ginger

Zingiber officinale, **Zingiberaceae**

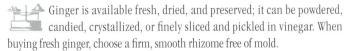

fresh ginger

The tuberous rhizome (underground stem) of a perennial plant native to Southeast Asia, ginger is cultivated in most tropical countries and can also be grown in hot and temperate regions. Long renowned for its aromatic and medicinal properties, ginger is mentioned in ancient Chinese and Indian writings and was known to the Greeks. The Romans imported it over 2,000 years ago. Only toward the end of the 13th century, however, did ginger begin to make inroads elsewhere in Europe, where it became highly prized as an aphrodisiac. In France it eventually faded in popularity.

The aboveground stems can reach 4½ feet in height. Ginger propagates by means of rhizome division. The fleshy rhizomes vary in size and color (sandy, yellow, white, or red), depending on the variety (of which there are many). Highly aromatic and pungent, the pulp can be extremely hot. Young rhizomes are covered with a thin edible skin.

Ginger is cultivated for the highly aromatic, pungent flesh of its underground stem (rhizome).

sliced fresh ginger

Buying

Ginger is available fresh, dried, and preserved; it can be powdered, candied, crystallized, or finely sliced and pickled in vinegar. When buying fresh ginger, choose a firm, smooth rhizome free of mold.

Serving Ideas

Fresh ginger is a basic ingredient in Asian cuisine. Used to season both sweet and salty dishes, it is added to sauces, meat, poultry, fish, seafood, vegetables, rice, tofu, marinades, stock, soups, fruits, cakes, and beverages. It is used to make jam and candy. In Japan, pickled ginger is traditionally served with sushi and sashimi. Powdered ginger is used widely in Western countries to flavor cakes, cookies, gingerbread, and compotes, and is also added to certain curries. The essential oil is an ingredient in certain beers and soft drinks (ginger ale). Ginger goes particularly well with apples and bananas. Fresh ginger has a much stronger taste than the dried and powdered varieties, which are poor substitutes.

Preparing

Fresh ginger can be peeled, sliced, grated, minced, or julienned.

Cooking

Like garlic, its flavor varies in strength depending on when it is added during the cooking process. Add ginger at the end of cooking for maximum taste, or at the beginning for a more subdued flavor.

Storing

Fresh ginger can be kept in the refrigerator for 2 to 3 weeks. Peel it just before using it. It can be frozen as is, and can be peeled and cut without thawing. Candied ginger keeps indefinitely. Preserved ginger should be refrigerated once the jar has been opened. Keep powdered ginger in an airtight container stored in a cool, dry, dark place.

Nutritional Information

potassium	24 mg
magnesium	3 mg
phosphorus	3 mg
	per tsp. (2 g)

Ginger has various medicinal properties. It is said to be tonic, antiseptic, diuretic, and an aphrodisiac; it reduces fever and aids the appetite. It is believed to stimulate digestion, combat flatulence, and be effective against colds, coughs, car sickness, and rheumatic pain. As it can irritate the digestive system, it should be used in moderation.

To make ginger tea, add about a teaspoon of chopped ginger root to a cup of water and boil for approximately 3 minutes.

1 Peel the fresh ginger.

2 Shave it into fine slices.

3 Mince it.

ground ginger

Pepper

Piper nigrum, Piperaceae

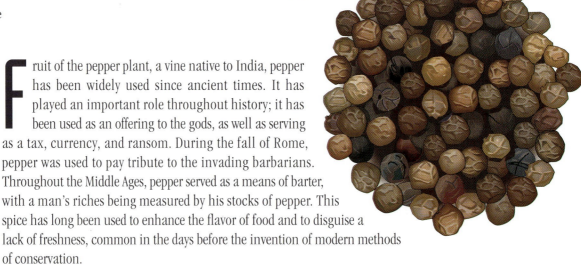

black peppercorns

Fruit of the pepper plant, a vine native to India, pepper has been widely used since ancient times. It has played an important role throughout history; it has been used as an offering to the gods, as well as serving as a tax, currency, and ransom. During the fall of Rome, pepper was used to pay tribute to the invading barbarians. Throughout the Middle Ages, pepper served as a means of barter, with a man's riches being measured by his stocks of pepper. This spice has long been used to enhance the flavor of food and to disguise a lack of freshness, common in the days before the invention of modern methods of conservation.

In days past, the search for pepper inspired explorers to take to the seas, leading to the discovery of new continents. The major merchant cities of Europe and Arabia grew rich on the thriving pepper trade. Today, Indonesia and India are the largest producers of pepper. There are several hundred varieties of the pepper plant, which grows only in very hot and humid tropical climates. The smooth woody vines can grow to a height of 33 feet and are supported by stakes. The trunk and vines have aerial roots that can cling to trees. The oval palm-shaped leaves are dark green. After 3 or 4 years, small white flowers, arranged in the form of spikes, develop into clusters of small round berries that turn from green to red and then to brown as they ripen. Green, black, and white pepper are all derived from the same plant and correspond to the different stages of maturity of the peppercorn.

Green pepper is derived from berries that are harvested while still green. It is not very spicy and has a slightly fruity flavor. Green peppercorns can be dried or preserved in brine or vinegar.

Black pepper comes from berries that are picked half-ripe, on the verge of turning red. When left to dry, they shrivel and take on a dark color. Black pepper is the most pungent and flavorful of peppers.

White pepper is derived from berries picked when very ripe and completely red. The berries are soaked in salt water for a few days in order to dissolve the dark outer shell covering the white inner seed, after which the corns are dried. White pepper tends to be milder than black pepper.

Gray pepper is black pepper that has been only slightly washed and still has its shell. It is quite rare on the market and is always sold ground. It can also be a mixture of black and white pepper. Gray pepper is fairly mild. All of these different peppers contain piperine, an alkaloid that gives them their distinctive flavor.

Pink pepper (or **red pepper**) comes from a different species altogether *(Schinus molle),* a small South American shrub of the same family as ragweed (Anacardiaceae). Like ragweed, pink pepper can also cause allergies. The dried berry has a delicate, fragrant, and slightly pungent flavor, which it loses rapidly.

Buying

Pepper is sold whole, crushed, or ground, in purée or seasoned form (onion pepper, garlic pepper, celery pepper, lemon pepper, etc.). Green peppercorns are sold dried or pickled in brine or vinegar. To obtain the best flavor, buy whole peppercorns and grind them just before adding them to a dish or preparation. Choose peppercorns that are heavy, compact, and unblemished, and that do not crumble easily. Ground pepper may contain impurities or mold, and it may sometimes be adulterated (an inferior spice may be added). To ensure maximum flavor and aroma, buy pepper in a store with a rapid turnover.

Serving Ideas

Pepper is one of the most popular spices in the world. It is found in almost all savory dishes, whether hot or cold, including sauces, vegetables, meat, cold cuts, vinaigrettes, and even certain desserts. White pepper is often used to season pale-colored dishes such as white sauces, poultry, and fish. Whole peppercorns are used to add flavor to marinades, pâtés, meat, cheeses and soups, court bouillons and ragouts. Freezing makes the flavor of the pepper in food become more pronounced.

Nutritional Information

	ground black pepper	ground white pepper
potassium	26 mg	2 mg
calcium	9 mg	6 mg
phosphorus	4 mg	4 mg
magnesium	4 mg	2 mg
iron	0.6 mg	0.3 mg
		per 5 ml (2 g)

Pepper is said to have fortifying, stimulating, carminative, and antibacterial properties. It contains piperine, an alkaloid that irritates the mucous lining of the stomach but also activates salivation and the production of gastric juices, thus aiding digestion. In strong doses, pepper becomes irritating and can burn the mouth.

Cooking

Ground pepper loses it flavor and aroma if it is cooked for over 2 hours. Add ground pepper at the end of cooking to prevent it from becoming bitter.

Storing

Whole peppercorns can be kept indefinitely at room temperature. Ground pepper can be conserved for 3 months. Green pepper will remain fresh for 1 week once the container has been opened; otherwise it lasts 1 year.

Green, black, and white pepper are derived from the same plant and correspond to the different stages of maturity of the peppercorn.

ground pepper

505

green peppercorns

white peppercorns

pink peppercorns

Chile pepper

Capsicum spp., Solanaceae

Hot peppers vary in size, shape, color, and flavor. Their flavor ranges from very hot to volcanic. They are smaller and more pointed than sweet peppers.

The fruit of a plant originally from South and Central America, the chile pepper, or hot pepper, is a member of the large nightshade family, which includes the eggplant, alkekengi, potato, tamarillo, and tomato. One of the first plants to be cultivated in South America (over 7,000 years ago), the chile pepper has been used throughout history for its therapeutic qualities, as a condiment, and as a vegetable. It was unknown in Europe before Columbus's voyages to the New World in the late 15th century.

Chile peppers were originally grown for decorative purposes; their usefulness as a culinary ingredient was discovered only later. Highly adaptable plants, they migrated quickly, thanks notably to the Portuguese navigator Ferdinand Magellan, who introduced them into Africa and Asia. Today chile peppers are cultivated on all continents, growing as a perennial in tropical regions and as an annual in temperate zones. Mexico and the West Indies produce the greatest number of varieties.

The chile pepper is a fleshy berry containing numerous seeds in its inner cavity. The plant on which it grows can attain a height of close to 5 feet.

There are about ten different species of hot peppers (*Capsicum frutescens, C. pubescens, C. baccatum, C. annuum,* etc.), varying considerably in size, shape, color, and flavor. Of these species, *annuum* and *frutescens* peppers are of particular culinary importance. Both have a very sharp, almost fiery, flavor.

Chile peppers are smaller and more pointed than sweet peppers. They are usually between ¾ and 6 inches long and ½ to 2 inches in diameter. They grow more abundantly in warm countries such as Mexico, where at least 15 different varieties have been identified. While some chile peppers are green (jalapeño, serrano, poblano), others are yellow-brown, purple, or red (ancho, Cascabel or cherry pepper, cayenne pepper, japone, Hontaka, pasilla), or yellow (carribe, guero). Certain varieties are so exceptionally hot that merely cutting them is enough to make the eyes water (guero, habanero, japone).

506

bird peppers

crushed chile

chili powder

Cayenne pepper is a powder made from ground dried red chile peppers; it is used as a spice. Cayenne pepper may contain one or several varieties of red chile pepper. The cayenne pepper itself *(Capsicum frutescens),* named after Cayenne in French Guiana, grows on a perennial plant that can reach 5 feet in height; the fruits are elongated and slender, about 1½ inches in length, and remain red when dried. Cayenne pepper is a very popular spice in Latin America and India and is used in the making of Tabasco Sauce, chili sauce, and curry powder.

Paprika is a powder made from sweet red peppers that have been dried and finely ground. These peppers, *Capsicum annuum,* grow on a shrub that is native to South America and was introduced into Hungary at the end of the 16th century. Paprika has since come to be closely associated with Hungarian cooking, which makes abundant use of it. In fact, *paprika* is the Hungarian word for sweet pepper; the term has been adopted by many languages. The color and flavor of paprika vary depending both on the type of pepper used (some mixtures include chile peppers) and on whether only the flesh is used, or the flesh, stem, core, and seeds. The more seeds present when the peppers are ground, the sharper the paprika. Check the label to avoid surprises. Hungarian paprika is labeled "sweet" or "hot."

Harissa is a hot pepper-based condiment that is extremely popular in the cuisines of the Middle East and North Africa; in fact, it is the Tunisian national condiment. Harissa is a purée of small red chile peppers and cayenne pepper mixed with oil, garlic, ground coriander, mint leaves, caraway seeds, and sometimes as many as 20 other spices.

Chili powder is a combination of various spices and dried hot peppers. It may contain black pepper, cumin, oregano, paprika, cloves, and garlic. The sharpness of the peppers used determines the pungency of the chili powder. The seasoning is of Mexican origin; *chilli* is the Aztec word for chile peppers.

The **tabasco pepper** *(Capsicum frutescens),* named after a state in Mexico, is a variety of hot pepper whose name has come to be associated with a popular hot sauce. Tabasco Sauce was invented and patented in Louisiana in 1870 by Edmund McIlhenny. To make it, red tabasco peppers are crushed and placed in oak barrels, where they macerate in salt for 3 years. They are then stored in distilled vinegar for up to 4 weeks, after which the liquid is filtered and bottled.

Herbs, Spices, and Condiments

507

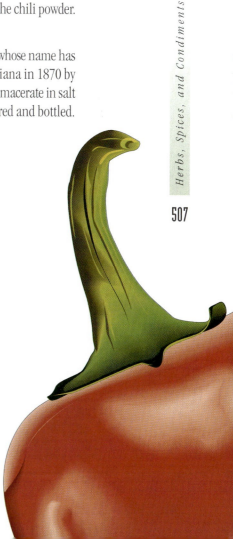

paprika pepper

paprika

Buying

It is normal for whole dry chile peppers to have wrinkled skin. Choose fresh or dried peppers that are brightly colored, glossy, and free of spots and soft patches. Ground peppers should be evenly colored and have a pleasant scent.

Cooking

Exercise caution when adding hot peppers to a dish; start with small doses, as cooking intensifies the hotness of the peppers. One safe way to flavor a dish with chile peppers is to sauté a hot pepper in oil and to then use the oil for cooking.

Avoid cooking paprika for too long, as this detracts from its flavor and color.

jalapeño pepper

Preparing

It is important to avoid touching your face – especially the lips and eyes – when cutting fresh or dried hot peppers, as they contain a powerful irritant called capsaicin; merely touching your face after handling hot peppers is enough to make the skin burn. Be sure to wash your hands, the knife, and the cutting board with soap and hot water to eliminate all traces of the irritant. In the case of very sensitive skin, wear rubber gloves when preparing hot peppers.

To moderate the sharpness of hot peppers, avoid consuming the seeds and the whitish inner ribs, or soak the peppers in cold water with a little vinegar for about 1 hour before eating them.

Harissa Sauce

½ lb. (250 g) dried red chile peppers	5 tsp. coriander seeds (optional)
15 cloves garlic	4 tsp. salt
5 tsp. caraway seeds	⅓ cup extra-virgin olive oil
5 tsp. ground cumin seeds	Olive oil

Store this sauce in the refrigerator.

1. Soak the peppers in warm water to cover for about 1 hour or until they soften. Drain and dry. Remove the stems and seeds and cut the peppers into cubes.

2. Peel the garlic and chop it fine.

3. In a mortar or spice grinder, crush the peppers with the garlic, caraway seeds, cumin seeds, coriander, and salt until the mixture has the consistency of a paste.

4. Add the ⅓ cup of oil, mixing constantly until it is completely absorbed by the sauce.

5. Pour the mixture into a glass jar, cover with olive oil, and seal tightly.

---

tabasco pepper

Tabasco Sauce

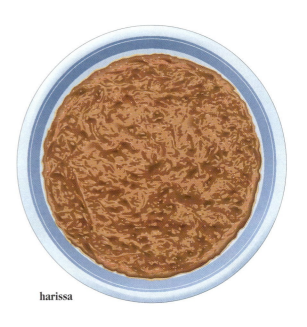

harissa

Serving Ideas

Hot peppers are much more popular as a condiment than as a vegetable. They are available dried, marinated, or cooked and puréed. Puréed preparations blend more evenly with other foods. A wide variety of dishes are seasoned with hot peppers, which also serve as a flavoring ingredient in numerous condiments. The Chinese make a red hot pepper purée with salt and oil called *öt*, which accompanies numerous dishes. Ground chile peppers are also used to make curry powders and ketchups.

Cayenne pepper is extremely hot and should be used with discretion. A mere pinch is usually enough to season an entire dish. Cayenne pepper is used to impart aroma to numerous dishes, particularly appetizers, soups, white and cream sauces, and main courses of shellfish or egg-based dishes.

Paprika and chili powder also add flavor and color to many foods; they are especially well suited to dull-colored or bland-tasting foods such as rice, pasta, béchamel sauces, and potato salads. Paprika, which is also used with eggs, poultry, seafood, mayonnaise, and cheese dips or unripened cheeses, is an essential ingredient in goulash, a Hungarian beef stew.

No Tunisian couscous is served without harissa, which also serves as a flavor enhancer in many other foods, including soups, salads, fish, stews, rice, sauces, mayonnaise, and eggs. Harissa can be used on its own, added to a stock, or combined with olive oil and lemon juice. Those unaccustomed to its hot taste are advised to use harissa in moderation.

Tabasco Sauce is added to soups, vinaigrettes, sauces, dips, mixed salads, beans, lentils, stews, meat, poultry, and seafood. Very little (1 to 3 drops) is often enough to season an entire dish.

Storing

Store fresh hot peppers in the refrigerator without washing them beforehand. Wrapped in a paper bag and placed in the vegetable compartment, they will keep for about 1 week.

Hot peppers freeze well, but it is best to broil or blanch them for 3 minutes and then peel them prior to freezing. They can also be marinated or dried. They dry very easily and will keep for 6 to 8 months in a plastic bag in the refrigerator. The powder obtained by grinding hot peppers should be stored in an airtight container in a dark, dry, cool place.

Because paprika tends to lose its flavor, color, and nutritional value quite rapidly, it is one of the few spices that keep better in the refrigerator. Store it in an airtight container.

Harissa should be kept in the refrigerator once the container has been opened.

Tabasco Sauce will keep indefinitely at room temperature.

Nutritional Information

	fresh whole chile pepper
water	88%
protein	2 g
fat	0.2 g
carbohydrates	9.6 g
fiber	1.8 g
calories	40
	per 100 g

Although chile peppers have a higher vitamin C content than oranges, the amount of vitamin C they actually provide is minimal considering that they are most often used in small quantities and in cooked form. Removing the seeds from chile peppers cuts their fiber content in half.

The proportion of nutrients present in chile peppers varies greatly from one variety to another, with red chile peppers usually containing more vitamins A and C than green chile peppers.

The hot taste of the chile pepper comes from its capsaicin, an alkaloid that is so powerful that it is possible to detect as little as 1 gram diluted in 2,500 gallons of water. This substance stimulates salivation and causes the gastric juices to flow, thus aiding digestion. The best way to soothe the burning sensation in the mouth is to eat a little yogurt, bread, cooked rice, sugar, or sweets; these foods are more effective than water, since capsaicin is soluble in oil but not in water. The *frutescens* varieties of chiles contain up to 20 times more capsaicin than sweet peppers.

The Scoville scale measures human tolerance to the sharpness of chiles, with a range up to 300,000 units. The jalapeño pepper is evaluated to be between 1,500 and 3,000 on this scale, the cayenne pepper between 20,000 and 60,000, and Tabasco Sauce between 80,000 and 120,000.

serrano pepper

Herbs, Spices, and Condiments

509

fresh green chile pepper

fresh red chile peppers

dried chile peppers

Horseradish

Armoracia rusticana, Cruciferae

horseradish root

Agarden vegetable native to eastern Europe, horseradish has been used in Europe since antiquity. It is mentioned in the Book of Exodus as one of the bitter herbs of the Jewish Passover. Initially popular in central Europe and Germany, it later spread to Scandinavia and England. In France it is often referred to as "German mustard." During the Middle Ages horseradish was known for its curative properties; it has been used in cooking only since the end of the 16th century. With a higher vitamin C content than oranges, horseradish was used by English and German sailors to prevent scurvy.

A member of the Cruciferae family, which includes cabbage, mustard, turnip, and radish, horseradish is a perennial plant that can grow to a height of about 3 feet. Its thick, hotly pungent root is topped by stems with wavy, jagged leaves. Horseradish roots are harvested in the second or third year. They are left underground until the fall, when their pungent taste reaches its peak. The fleshy roots resemble parsnips, although they are larger and have protuberances at one end. They can measure up to 20 inches in length and 1 to 3 inches in diameter. Their brownish peel is rough and wrinkled; underneath, the flesh is firm and creamy white. Horseradish contains an essential oil similar to that of mustard, which gives it its sharp, biting taste.

Buying

 Look for a firm, mold-free horseradish with no soft areas.

Nutritional Information

	Prepared horseradish
protein	0.2 g
carbohydrates	1.4 g
calories	6
calcium	9 mg
phosphorus	5 mg
	per tbsp. (15 g)

Horseradish is said to be antiseptic, diuretic, a stimulant, an expectorant, and a remedy for gout and scurvy. It relieves rheumatism and spasms, and aids the stomach and liver. When eaten in large amounts, it is purgative.

Cooking

It is best to avoid cooking horseradish.

Preparing

Wash and peel the horseradish. If you find any green areas under the peel, cut them out and discard them, as this flesh is excessively bitter. The heart of a large horseradish may be very hard and woody, and should also be discarded. To prevent peeled horseradish from turning brown, sprinkle it with lemon juice, vinegar, or vinaigrette as soon as you cut or grate it. Use a stainless-steel grater. If you use a food processor or a blender, grind the horseradish fine just before using it (fresh or in cooking) to obtain optimum flavor.

Serving Ideas

Horseradish can be eaten fresh or pickled. Although the leaves can be used in salads, the plant is more widely known for its root, most often added as a condiment to sauces. It can easily replace mustard. Usually grated, it can also be diced, julienned, or sliced. Finely minced horseradish can be added to sauces, salad dressings, soups, and sandwich fillings. Use horseradish sauce to liven up stews, boiled meat, smoked fish, and seafood. Horseradish also goes well with potatoes, beets, celery, parsnips, tuna, legumes, applesauce (served with a roast), delicatessen meats, and eggs. Add it to cream, yogurt, or mayonnaise to make a delicious, subtly flavored sauce.

Like those of other crucifers, horseradish leaves can be eaten raw or cooked.

Storing

Fresh horseradish can be kept for several weeks in the refrigerator. Wrap it in a damp paper towel and store it in a plastic bag in the vegetable crisper. If the root begins to soften, remove the soft parts and prepare the horseradish immediately. Horseradish can be frozen; when grated, it forms small, easy-to-use flakes. It can also be dried. Prepared horseradish sauce, which should be stored in the refrigerator, keeps for a long time; like frozen horseradish, however, it gradually loses its flavor. Horseradish in vinegar can be kept for about 6 months.

grated horseradish

Poppy

Papaver somniferum, **Papaveraceae**

An annual herb native to Asia Minor, *Papaver somniferum* is a member of the broad family of poppies, which includes a number of ornamental species. Known above all as a source of opium, it was already widely cultivated during antiquity by the Chinese, Egyptians, Greeks, and Romans.

The use of poppy seeds to flavor bread dates back to the second century A.D. *Papaver somniferum* grows to a height of 1 to 4 feet. Its large purplish white flowers produce capsules containing tiny dark grayish blue seeds. When gathered before they ripen, the seeds have powerful narcotic properties – as do the unripe capsules, from which opium is extracted in the form of a milky sap (which is also used for medical purposes, including the production of morphine and codeine). Opium poppies are grown widely in temperate regions. In Europe they are particularly common in Denmark, Holland, and France. They are also grown in India, China, and Iran. Their cultivation is prohibited in the United States.

When gathered before they ripen, poppy seeds have powerful narcotic properties, as do the unripe capsules, from which opium is extracted.

Buying

You can find poppy seeds in most grocery stores. To ensure maximum freshness and flavor, buy them in a shop where stocks are renewed regularly.

Serving Ideas

The grayish blue seeds have a subtle hazelnut-like flavor, which is enhanced with cooking. They are used to flavor breads, cakes, and pastries (particularly in Turkey, Egypt, and central Europe), as well as vegetables, pasta, potato salad, cheese, and marinades.

They are also used to produce a pleasant-tasting edible oil (poppy-seed oil), which can be added to salads instead of olive oil. The leaves can be served like spinach. Ground poppy seeds are a thickener.

Nutritional Information

calcium	41 mg
phosphorus	24 mg
potassium	20 mg
magnesium	9 mg
zinc	0.3 mg
iron	0.3 mg
	per tsp. (3 g)

Ripe poppy seeds have no narcotic effects. The seeds and latex (milky sap) extracted from green capsules, however, have sedative, tranquilizing, antispasmodic, and hypnotic properties.

poppy seeds

Tamarind

Tamarindus indica, **Leguminosae**

tamarind pod

Indigeneous to India, the tamarind tree towers up to 80 feet in height. Related to the carob tree, it grows in tropical and subtropical climates, particularly in Africa, Southeast Asia, the West Indies, and certain Middle Eastern countries. The word "tamarind" is derived from the Arabic *tamar hindi,* which means "date of India" — a reference to the fact that the tree has been cultivated for its fruits, or pods, ever since prehistoric times. Cooks in various Asian and Arabic cultures make wide use of tamarind products. Each cylindrical reddish brown tamarind pod, which can measure 4 to 6 inches in length, contains 1 to 12 hard, shiny, dark-cinnamon-colored seeds. They are surrounded by a dense pulp containing fibrous filaments. The pulp is bittersweet and highly acidic.

Each cylindrical reddish brown tamarind pod contains 1 to 12 hard, shiny seeds. The pulp has a strong acidic taste.

Buying

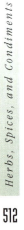 Tamarind products, including instant paste (merely add a bit of water) and compact cubes, are available mainly in specialty food stores.

Nutritional Information

	uncooked
water	31.4%
protein	2.8 g
fat	0.6 g
carbohydrates	62.5 g
fiber	3 g
calories	239
	per 100 g

Tamarind is an excellent source of potassium, magnesium, and thiamine and a good source of iron. It contains phosphorus, riboflavin, niacin, calcium, and vitamin C, as well as fiber. It is said to be laxative, to stimulate biliation, and to aid the liver.

Storing

Tamarind can be kept at room temperature.

Preparing

Soak pressed tamarind in hot water for about 15 minutes, until it softens and you can crumble the cubes with your fingers. Run it through a sieve to remove the fibers. The seeds, like other legumes, should be left overnight to soak and then be thoroughly cooked.

Serving Ideas

Tamarind pulp is used fresh, dried, candied, and pickled, as well as in liquid, paste, and syrup form. It can be consumed as a food or condiment. Cooks add it to soups, sauces, marinades, stews, cakes, and candies. It goes well with meat, game, and fish.

Tamarind's strong acidic flavor adds taste to fruits. The pulp is used in jams, sherbets, chutneys, beverages, and condiments, as well as to make a thirst-quenching beverage. The flowers and leaves are eaten like vegetables (for example, in salads) in producer countries. Although tamarind pulp can be replaced by lemon juice in most recipes, the result is not the same. The juice of 1 lemon is equivalent to 1 tablespoon of tamarind paste dissolved in ⅓ cup of water.

tamarind seeds

Vanilla

Vanilla planifolia, **Orchidaceae**

anilla beans are produced by climbing orchids indigenous to Mexico or Central America. The seeds enclosed in the beans have been used ever since ancient times. Vanilla was introduced to Europe by the Spanish, who were particularly impressed by a vanilla-flavored cocoa drunk by the Aztecs. By the end of the 16th century, Spanish producers had begun making chocolate flavored with vanilla. The word "vanilla" comes from the Spanish term *vainilla,* meaning "small sheath" (a reference to the pods).

Vanilla is cultivated in a number of tropical countries, including Mexico, Guatemala, Uganda, Brazil, Paraguay, Indonesia, and Madagascar (the number-one producer), and on certain Indian Ocean islands. The most prized variety comes from Mexico.

There are about 50 different types of vanilla orchids. "Real" vanilla comes from the species *Vanilla planifolia.* The plant's stems, which attach themselves to trees and other surfaces, can climb up to 200 feet toward the forest canopy. First harvested 3 years after the orchids are planted, the 8-inch beans, which resemble green beans, are picked when they turn golden yellow. They contain an aromatic pulp and a number of small seeds.

Freshly picked vanilla beans are odorless; the distinctive aroma develops during the complicated drying and fermentation process, which makes vanilla second only to saffron in price. The beans are dried until they turn soft and dark brown and are covered with a crystalline coating of vanillin, the substance that gives vanilla its characteristic taste. Vanillin can also be synthesized from eugenol, the chief component of clove oil. Although the artificial variety is often used to replace natural vanillin, its taste is less subtle.

The long, bean-like pods are picked when ripe, when their color changes from green to golden yellow.

Buying

Vanilla is available in bean, powder, liquid, and sugar form. Sold in glass tubes, jars, or pouches, the beans and seeds are less likely to be fake. Be sure to read the label on liquid or powdered vanilla, as they may also contain other ingredients. Pure vanilla tastes better than synthetic vanilla – and is much more expensive.

Serving Ideas

Vanilla is used to flavor tapioca, compotes, ice cream, yogurt, and puddings. It is virtually essential in baking and is also used in making candy and chocolate. In very small quantities, it can be added to certain savory foods, including fish soup, oysters, and poultry. It is also used in beverages (punches, wines, sangria, hot chocolate, and certain distilled alcohols). Liquid vanilla extract is often a pale imitation of real vanilla. As it loses much of its flavor during cooking, it should be added afterward if possible.

Vanilla beans can be used as is, finely chopped, or reduced to powder in a blender. You can use them to flavor milk, syrups, and fruits (split the beans in half lengthwise, let them steep in the cold liquid, and heat to the desired temperature). The beans can be used up to four times: remove them at the end of the process, rinse them, and store them.

Nutritional Information

Vanilla is said to be tonic, a stimulant, digestive, and antiseptic.

Storing

Vanilla should be kept at room temperature in a dry place. Store beans in an airtight container. To make vanilla sugar, bury a whole bean or part of a bean in a container of sugar.

Herbs, Spices, and Condiments

513

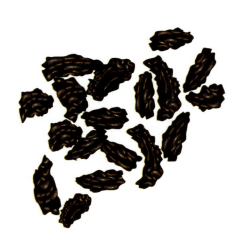

Miso

A very salty, occasionally sweetened fermented paste made from soybeans, miso is used primarily as a condiment. Developed in Asia, miso has been consumed in China for over 2,500 years and has been made in Japan since the 7th century. The fabrication of miso is a complex art comparable to Western practices like cheese- and wine-making.

Miso is a Japanese word; the Chinese refer to this paste as *chiang* and the Vietnamese call it *chao do*. Since miso is made with diverse ingredients and in many different ways, its color, taste, and texture vary greatly. In Japan alone, there almost 50 different kinds of miso. The most common Japanese variety, rice miso, is so popular that the word "miso" refers to rice miso unless otherwise specified. The current popularity of this variety is partially due to the fact that rice was once reserved exclusively for the aristocracy.

Traditionally, the soybeans are combined with salt, a fermenting agent *(Aspergillus oryzae),* and, depending on the desired result, rice or barley. This mixture is then slowly fermented in several stages for anywhere from a few months to 3 years; since they are made entirely from natural ingredients (unless ethyl alcohol is added as a preservative) and are not pasteurized, natural misos are very smooth and flavorful.

"Rapid" miso is fermented for only a very short period – a maximum of 3 weeks and a minumum of 3 days – and is relatively flavorless, colorless, and pale. It also spoils more quickly than other varieties of miso and contains various additives, including bleaching agents, colorings, and monosodium glutamate. It is fermented in a strictly controlled environment, then pasteurized in order to destroy the microorganisms, thus diminishing its nutritional value. It has a finer texture and a sweeter taste than traditional miso.

Each kind of miso has a unique color, texture, taste, and aroma; their nutritional content also varies. As a general rule, the darker the miso, the longer it has been fermented and the saltier it tastes. Conversely, the lighter the miso, the shorter the period of fermentation and the sweeter the taste. Miso made with barley is darker than rice miso and lighter than soy miso. Most varieties of miso are quite moist and smooth.

There is also a wide variety of miso containing a broad range of additional ingredients (honey, sugar, water, sake, nuts, seeds, vegetables, seafood, spices, seaweed, etc.).

Buying

Miso is usually sold in tightly sealed bags or in bulk, in plastic tubes or glass containers. When buying miso, read the list of ingredients carefully to determine whether or not it has been pasteurized and if it contains any additives.

Storing

Store miso in a tightly sealed container. Salted miso can be stored at room temperature, unless the weather is very hot; sweetened miso should be refrigerated.

Refrigeration prevents molds from forming on unpasteurized miso that contains no preservatives; however, these harmless molds can simply be removed from unrefrigerated miso.

Nutritional Information

The nutritional value of miso varies greatly; it depends on the ingredients and on the way the miso is made. Soy miso is an excellent source of zinc and a good source of iron, riboflavin, and folic acid; it also contains vitamin B_6, thiamine, calcium, and fiber.

Unpasteurized miso is a very nutritious food. Like yogurt and other fermented products, it contains living organisms, including lactic-acid bacteria (0.5% to 1%), enzymes, yeasts, and various other microorganisms, which can improve your health in a variety of ways. The proteins in miso are of a very high quality, not only because soy proteins are so nutritious but also because the proteins in beans and grains are complementary. Furthermore, fermentation increases the quantity of two essential amino acids – the methionine in soybeans and the lysine in grains (see *Complementary proteins*). Most of the fat in miso is unsaturated. The traditional fermentation process makes the various nutrients in miso easier to digest and assimilate.

The Japanese ascribe innumerable virtues to miso. Following the example of Westerners who say "an apple a day keeps the doctor away," they make a similar claim about their daily bowl of miso soup. Numerous medicinal properties are attributed to miso: it is said to be good for the digestive system (miso soup and drinks made with miso are reputed to help repair damage done to the intestinal flora by antibiotics) and to promote the elimination of toxic substances like heavy metals from the body; it also contains an alkaloid that is thought to prevent illness and to provide protection against the effects of pollution.

water	41%
protein	11.8 g
fat	6.1 g
carbohydrates	28 g
fiber	2.5 g
calories	206
	per 100 g

Cooking

Avoid cooking miso because heat destroys the microorganisms it contains. Add miso just before food is served, after it has stopped boiling. It best to dilute the miso in a small amount of broth or hot water.

Serving Ideas

Miso enhances the flavor and the nutritional value of foods. It can replace salt and tamari in most recipes. It is added to almost every kind of dish imaginable (soups, sauces, broths, vinaigrettes, pizzas, cereals, pasta, mixed salads, vegetables, tofu, seafood, meat, poultry, eggs, pancakes, marinades).

Sweetened misos are used mainly in vegetable dishes, sauces, spreadable pastes, pancakes, and desserts.

Miso can replace your morning coffee; most people in Japan eat miso soup as part of their morning meal. A nourishing food, miso soup is also an excellent stimulant that has none of the side effects of coffee.

Soy sauce

A condiment that originated in China, where it has been used for over 2,500 years, soy sauce is a key ingredient in Asian cuisine. *Shoyu* (its Japanese name) is thought to have been brought to Japan during the 7th century by Buddhist monks; *shoyu* and *tamari* (also a Japanese word) are now used in many countries because Japan is a leading exporter as well as consumer of these products.

Traditionally, the terms "soy sauce," "shoyu," and "tamari" refer to the liquid that is produced when miso is fermented for several months (see *Miso*). In fact, the word *tamari* is derived from the verb *tamaru,* which means "to accumulate."

Traditional Chinese **soy sauce** (or *chiang-yu*) is made with whole soybeans and ground wheat. In China a higher proportion of soybeans than grain is used, while in Japan the proportions are equal.

Tamari is made entirely from soybeans or from soy oil cake (the residue produced when soy oil is extracted from the beans) and thus contains no grain.

In order to make traditional Chinese soy sauce, the soybeans are cooked and the grain is roasted, then crushed. A fermenting agent *(Aspergillus oryzae)* is then added, and the mixture is allowed to ferment for 2 to 3 days; at this point, yeast and brine are added to the fermented mixture, which is referred to as *koji*. It is then aged for 18 to 24 months in cedar barrels. The soy sauce is obtained by filtering and pasteurizing this aged mixture; darker soy sauces are aged longer and contain caramel or molasses.

Tamari and *shoyu* (Japanese soy sauce) are aged in huge metal vats for only 4 to 6 months. Tamari sometimes contains additives such as monosodium glutamate and caramel. Shoyu is slightly sweet and is lighter in color than Chinese soy sauce. Tamari, which is also Japanese in origin, is thick and dark.

Soy sauce (both the Chinese and Japanese varieties) contains alcohol that is produced when the grain ferments, while tamari, which is usually made without grain, contains little or no alcohol. The only alcohol it may contain is 2% ethyl alcohol that is added after the tamari has been aged to prevent molds and fungi from developing.

The soy sauce available in supermarkets is usually a synthetic product that is a pale imitation of the original. It has neither the nutritional value nor the flavor of genuine soy sauce. Rather than being fermented, the soy oil cake is hydrolyzed with boiling hydrochloric acid. The resultant mixture is neutralized with sodium carbonate, then caramel and corn syrup are added for color and flavor. Synthetic soy sauce may also contain other additives.

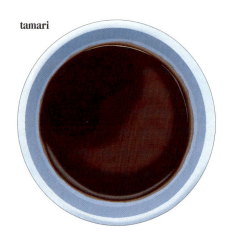

tamari

Serving Ideas

Shoyu, tamari, and soy sauce are used in a variety of ways; they can substituted for salt to give dishes a unique flavor. Shoyu should not be added until just before food is served, because it loses flavor if the alcohol evaporates. These sauces can be used as marinades or dips, as well as to season and color foods. They are all used to flavor tofu, for which they are the basic condiment, and can be used in combination with a variety of ingredients, including garlic, onions, fresh ginger, vinegar, and oil. Shoyu, tamari, and soy sauce are the basic ingredients in numerous other sauces, including teriyaki sauce and Worcestershire sauce.

Nutritional Information

	shoyu	*tamari*
water	71%	66%
protein	0.8 g	1.5 g
carbohydrates	1.2 g	0.9 g
calories	7.5	8.8
		per 15 ml

Storing

Shoyu and tamari should be refrigerated once the bottle has been opened. Synthetic soy sauce can be stored at room temperature indefinitely.

Most of these condiments are very salty, because they are 6% sodium (1 tablespoon of tamari contains 810 mg of sodium and 1 tablespoon of soy sauce contains 829 mg).

Over the past few years, low-sodium versions of these sauces have been introduced in response to the demands of consumers concerned about the amount of salt in their diets. Some of these sauces contain only 479 mg of sodium per tablespoon. People often become thirsty after eating foods seasoned with these condiments, because the human body requires extra liquid to metabolize excess sodium. Tamari and shoyu made in accordance with traditional methods have the same medicinal properties as miso, all of which are the result of fermentation (see *Miso*).

Vinegar

white wine vinegar

Vinegar is a liquid condiment that is produced by using bacteria to transform an alcoholic solution into a solution containing from 4% to 12% acetic acid. It can be made from an extremely broad range of raw materials: wine, ethyl alcohol (white vinegar), cider, cane sugar, malt, palm wine, dates, oranges, bananas, rice, and coconut milk. In fact, any food that can be fermented to produce alcohol can also be used to make vinegar. However, the best vinegars are made with wine or cider.

The production of vinegar probably dates back to the invention of wine, which starts to become acidic when left in the open air for any length of time. The word "vinegar," which is a conflation of the French words for "wine" *(vin)* and "sour" *(aigre),* is a reference to this transformation. Vinegar is mentioned in the Bible, and the Greeks and Romans are known to have ascribed numerous medicinal properties to it; soldiers of the Roman legions drank vinegar diluted with water. During the 14th century, Orléans, which was a major wine distribution center, became one of the first cities where vinegar was produced on a large scale. Until the 17th century, vinegar was strictly a by-product of the wine-and-beer-making process; it was not manufactured independently until a relatively late date. The first vinegar makers' guild was formed in 1394 in Orléans, which is still a major vinegar-producing center.

Vinegar is very easy to make because alcohol ferments spontaneously when exposed to air and microorganisms. The vinegar starts to develop when a velvety gray film forms on top of the liquid. This film gradually sinks to the bottom of the liquid, becoming a jelly-like mass known as the "mother of vinegar." Although vinegar can be produced naturally, it is usually manufactured using a bacterial culture. Some vinegars are still made by craftsmen in the traditional way, but most are produced industrially.

Traditional Orléans method

The vinegar is produced by adding wine to oak barrels containing a "mother" that has been left in the barrel for one or two generations. The wine is allowed to ferment for several weeks, sometimes for as long as 6 months, and the resultant vinegar is then drawn off, filtered, and bottled. This is an ongoing process; as vinegar is drawn off from the bottom, more wine is added at the top. Since vinegar made in this way is not pasteurized, it does not lose any of its natural flavor and color. After a certain amount of time, a "mother" may start to form in bottled unpasteurized vinegar; it can be left in the bottle, filtered out, or even used to make more vinegar.

Herbs, Spices, and Condiments

517

Industrial process

The liquid is poured into huge heated metallic vats equipped with boilers and pumps. It is brewed with vinegar-soaked beech-wood shavings. This rapid, so-called German method produces unperfumed vinegar in 24 hours. An alternative method speeds up the rate at which alcohol is transformed into acetic acid: the wine or alcohol is stirred continuously as air is pumped into it, producing vinegar within 3 to 5 days.

The liquid is then pasteurized and, occasionally, distilled; the resultant vinegar is a clear, relatively flavorless liquid containing no mother of vinegar.

Balsamic vinegar is a very famous vinegar produced in accordance with ancient methods that have been handed down from generation to generation; the quality of its most famous variety, traditional Modena balsamic vinegar, is strictly monitored.

Top-quality balsamic vinegar is made by harvesting very ripe sweet white grapes *(Trebbiano)* and preparing a must (freshly pressed juice ready to be fermented). At the first signs of fermentation, the liquid is filtered and gently boiled; it is then filtered again and allowed to cool before it is poured into the barrels in which it ferments, evaporates, and thickens. The concentrated liquid is decanted into smaller barrels made of various kinds of wood (oak, cherry, mulberry, ash, chestnut, etc.). Balsamic vinegar is usually aged for 4 to 5 years before it is sold. However, some balsamic vinegars are aged for 10 to 40 years; they are of an exceptional quality and have an indescribable flavor.

Balsamic vinegar is dark brown in color and has a fluid, somewhat syrupy consistency; it is only slightly acidic and has a unique taste.

Serving Ideas

Vinegar is used in various ways in cooking. As a condiment, it is used to make vinaigrettes, mayonnaises, and mustards. Since it is acidic, it can be used to prevent fruits and vegetables (apples, bananas, eggplants, etc.) from oxidizing, to slow down the rate at which enzymes destroy vitamin C, to lengthen the shelf life of soaked, pickled, or canned foods by preventing the development of harmful bacteria, and to give foods a bittersweet flavor. Vinegar is also added to marinades for meat, poultry, and game, as well as to dried beans; when used to flavor dried beans, vinegar should not be added until the last minute because acid ingredients can make the skin of legumes tough. Vinegar can be used to deglaze the bottom of pans. It can also be added to the water in which eggs are poached to make the egg whites congeal.

Since most vinegars are interchangeable, they can be used to adjust the flavor of foods. However, some vinegars have very specific uses. For example, white vinegar, which has relatively little flavor, is an ideal ingredient for pickling marinades and other liquids used to preserve food; cider and malt vinegars have too much color and flavor to be used in this way, but they are ideal for dark, spicy marinades and chutneys. Cider vinegar adds a hint of the flavor of apples to foods.

Cider and white wine vinegars are excellent with fish and shellfish, as well as with fruit and in delicate sauces such as hollandaise and Béarnaise. Red wine vinegar has a pungent flavor that can enhance the taste of bland foods; it goes very well calf's liver and other red meats.

Most Chinese or Japanese rice vinegars have a mild taste and can be used to flavor crudités, as well as soups and sweet-and-sour dishes.

Balsamic vinegar is much more of a seasoning than a vinegar. It is considered to be fragile and should never be boiled. It is not added to cooked dishes until they are almost ready. It can be added to hot foods (grilled meats, sauces) just before they are served.

red wine vinegar

balsamic vinegar

flavored vinegar

Balsamic vinegar is used in salads (as a replacement for, or in combination with, red wine vinegar), as well as to season a wide variety of foods: steaks, foie gras, fish, lobster, and mussels. You can even create an astonishing blend of flavors by spraying a touch of balsamic vinegar on sliced strawberries a few minutes before they are served.

Preparing

Homemade vinegar

To make your own vinegar, pour the liquid of your choice into a wooden, glass, or stoneware container and leave it at room temperature. You can use a mixture of unpasteurized vinegar and alcohol (6 oz. of vinegar to 3 cups of white or red wine, cider, etc.), but it will be 3 to 4 months before the vinegar is ready. You can shorten the process to 1 or 2 months by adding a piece of mother of vinegar to the mixture. Cover the container with two layers of muslin to allow air to get in, and store it in a warm place; it is important not to move the container. Once the wine has turned into vinegar, it can be filtered and bottled.

If you want to save the "mother" for future use, store it in a small amount of vinegar. When the "mother" becomes too large, cut off a piece and use it to make more vinegar.

You can make flavored vinegars by putting a selection of fresh herbs in a sterilized jar and adding preheated vinegar. Leave the herbs in the vinegar for 2 weeks, stirring the mixture from time to time; then filter it into a second sterilized jar and store it in cool, dark place.

1 Place the sprigs of herbs in a saucepan containing white wine vinegar. Then gently heat the vinegar, remove it from the heat, and allow the herbs to steep for 30 minutes.

2 Pour the flavored vinegar into a pitcher, leaving the herbs in the saucepan.

3 Fill a sterilized jar with the flavored vinegar; then add a sprig of fresh herbs.

4 This method can be used to make vinegars flavored with thyme, tarragon, and the like.

Nutritional Information

Vinegar consists mainly of water (approximately 95%). It contains no protein, fat, or vitamins, and only a small quantity of carbohydrates comprising very few calories (2 calories per tablespoon).

Unpasteurized vinegar contains trace amounts of various minerals and larger quantities of potassium and phosphorus. Pasteurized vinegar contains virtually no minerals.

The higher the percentage of acetic acid, the more acidic the vinegar; most vinegars contain between 4% and 12% acetic acid.

Vinegar is reputed to have numerous medicinal properties, especially if it is unpasteurized. It is used to treat wounds, insect bites, burns, headaches, and chronic fatigue. It is believed to be beneficial for the digestive system, improving your appetite, promoting digestion, and preventing or alleviating gastroenteritis. When taken internally, it should be diluted in water (2 teaspoons of vinegar per glass), with a touch of honey if desired, and drunk before each meal or whenever necessary. Consuming too much vinegar can irritate mucous membranes. If digestive problems arise, substitute lemon juice.

Storing

Vinegar can be stored indefinitely at room temperature; homemade vinegar should be refrigerated. It is still edible even if it becomes cloudy and a mother of vinegar starts to form, although you may want to filter it.

Salt

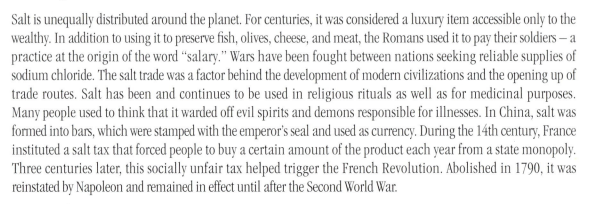

Odorless and sharp tasting, salt crystals are brittle and soluble in water. They are made up of sodium (40%) and chloride (60%), whence the scientific name for salt, sodium chloride.

Like water, salt is essential for the functioning of the human body. It has long been a precious condiment and food preservative. Given its critical importance for humanity, it has been referred to historically as "white gold."

Salt is unequally distributed around the planet. For centuries, it was considered a luxury item accessible only to the wealthy. In addition to using it to preserve fish, olives, cheese, and meat, the Romans used it to pay their soldiers – a practice at the origin of the word "salary." Wars have been fought between nations seeking reliable supplies of sodium chloride. The salt trade was a factor behind the development of modern civilizations and the opening up of trade routes. Salt has been and continues to be used in religious rituals as well as for medicinal purposes. Many people used to think that it warded off evil spirits and demons responsible for illnesses. In China, salt was formed into bars, which were stamped with the emperor's seal and used as currency. During the 14th century, France instituted a salt tax that forced people to buy a certain amount of the product each year from a state monopoly. Three centuries later, this socially unfair tax helped trigger the French Revolution. Abolished in 1790, it was reinstated by Napoleon and remained in effect until after the Second World War.

Today salt is plentiful and cheap. In many countries, along with bread, it remains a symbol of friendship and hospitality. Its cultural significance is underlined by common expressions such as "salt of the earth" and "take (a story) with a grain of salt." *Sal,* the Latin word for salt, has spawned a number of derivatives, including

- salary, from *salarium,* meaning payments made to purchase salt as well as salt rations allotted to Roman soldiers;

- sausage, from *salsus,* meaning salted;

- salami, from the Italian word *salame,* derived from the Latin *salare,* meaning to salt.

There are two types of sodium chloride: rock salt and sea salt.

Rock salt, or halite, is mined from natural deposits formed by the shrinking of seas during geological periods. Often, water is pumped into specially drilled wells to dissolve the rock-salt deposits. The brine is then pumped to the surface and heated until the water evaporates. The resulting product is white, as it has lost virtually all minerals other than sodium and chloride. Another technique consists in hauling the salt to the surface for refining. Table salt is halite that has been purified by a chemical process that prevents the mineral from absorbing moisture.

Ninety percent of the earth's water is salty, with each quart of seawater containing about an ounce of sodium chloride.

Sea salt generally comes from salt marshes, basins where seawater has been trapped and is allowed to evaporate under the combined effects of sun and wind. It is also produced from inland seas such as the Red Sea, Dead Sea, and Great Salt Lake, which have a higher than normal salt content.

Sea salt is grayish, as it contains traces of minerals such as calcium, magnesium, potassium, bromides, and other elements. Some chefs feel that these substances give sea salt a stronger, "purer" taste. They are often removed, however, as they fetch a higher price when sold separately.

Serving Ideas

Salt is used for a number of purposes in food preparation. Its effectiveness in inhibiting bacterial action and mold makes it an excellent preservative (in delicatessen meats, marinades, cheese, fish, etc.). It stabilizes the color, taste, and texture of foods, particularly vegetables. It slows down yeast growth in breads, cakes, cookies, and other baked goods. It masks bitter tastes and heightens flavor. It stimulates the appetite. Indeed, far from being merely a seasoning, salt has an estimated 10,000 different uses.

Processed food, restaurant food, and certain medications (laxatives, analgesics, and some antacids) are high in salt and should be consumed with moderation.

People wishing to cut back their sodium consumption should also avoid highly salted foods such as commercial soups and stocks; smoked, salted, and canned meats and fish (anchovies, sardines); marinades; sauerkraut; kelp; commercial sauces (soy sauce, chili sauce, ketchup, prepared mustard); foods sprinkled with salt (chips, crackers, pretzels); celery, garlic, and onion salt; and monosodium glutamate. (Some product labels indicate low or reduced salt or sodium content.) They should be careful not to use too much salt in cooking, avoid adding extra salt after serving, rinse canned vegetables before using them, and be sure to read the labels on commercial food products, which can contain various salt substitutes such as sodium bicarbonate, monosodium glutamate, sodium alginate, and sodium benzoate.

You are generally best advised to reduce your salt consumption gradually, to allow your taste buds to adapt. A sharp drop in salt intake can create a sodium deficiency, particularly for people who are used to eating highly salted dishes; this can lead to various symptoms, including a feeling of overall weakness.

Buying

Sodium chloride is generally marketed as coarse salt, fine-grain salt, crystal salt, or table salt. Table salt can comprise both halite and sea salt, and is often iodized. The addition of 0.01% of potassium iodide, which has no effect on taste, began in 1924 in the United States following the discovery that insufficient iodine causes goiter, an illness that had been endemic in America since the beginning of the century.

Salt is almost always treated with additives (magnesium carbonate, magnesium oxide, calcium silicate) to prevent it from absorbing moisture and ensure that it remains free flowing and granular.

Coarse salt, which may be less refined, is used by the food industry and in certain dishes and marinades. Various specialty salts for specific uses are available in stores: for example, tenderizer (salt fortified with enzymes such as papain, used to tenderize meat), salt enriched with sodium nitrate or a combination of sodium nitrate and potassium nitrate (used to cure meats and as a preservative), and flavored salt (garlic salt, onion salt, celery salt, etc.).

Various salt substitutes with little or no sodium chloride are available also. They often contain potassium chloride, a substance that leaves a bitter aftertaste and, particularly if consumed in large quantities by people who suffer from kidney disorders, can cause imbalances.

Herbs, Spices, and Condiments

521

coarse salt

table salt

sea salt

Nutritional Information

Sodium plays a number of vital roles in the human body, contributing to the metabolizing of protein and carbohydrates, the transmission of nerve impulses, muscle contraction, hormone regulation, consumption of oxygen by cells, control of urine production, thirst, and the production of liquids (blood, saliva, tears, perspiration, gastric juices, bile). Salt is also essential for the production of hydrochloric acid in the stomach.

Eating salty foods makes us feel thirsty, as the body reacts to excess salt by requiring extra liquid. Salt consumption is very high in industrialized countries: most Americans consume ten times more salt than the daily intake recommended by health specialists. Unfortunately, overconsumption frequently has a negative impact on health, contributing to hypertension and cardiovascular diseases among people at risk.

Excessive salt consumption can also lead to water retention, which boosts the heart rate and can increase blood pressure above recommended levels. You are therefore best advised to limit your salt intake, particularly as enough salt is naturally present in most foods to meet the body's normal needs. People with strictly vegetarian salt-free diets and individuals who suffer from diarrhea, vomiting, or heavy, prolonged sweating, however, could be suffering from salt deficiency.

Most of our salt intake (77%) comes from food products. Salt is said to be invisible, because we are often unaware of just how much salt is added to foods and our ability to detect saltiness decreases as we become accustomed to the seasoning. Less than one fourth or even one third of our total sodium intake comes from the salt we voluntarily sprinkle on our food.

Storing

Keep salt in an airtight container in a dry place. Add a few grains of uncooked rice to a salt shaker to prevent the salt from caking (the rice absorbs moisture).

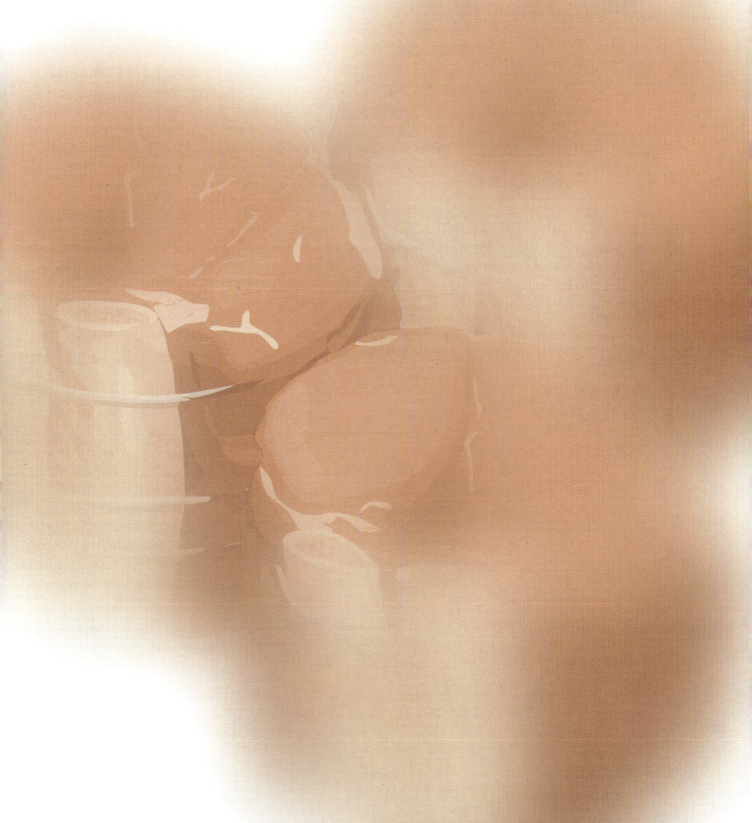

Meat

Introduction

The term "meat" refers to the flesh of animals, mainly of mammals and birds, that is eaten by humans. There is a distinction between red meat (mutton, lamb, beef, horse), white meat (veal, pork, rabbit, poultry), and dark meat (game), as well as between butcher's meat (beef, veal, mutton, horse, pork, and offal), poultry and game. The word "meat" is derived from the Old High German word *maz,* meaning "food," and can thus refer to anything edible, or to food in general as opposed to drink.

Humans have been consuming meat for thousands of years. It is thought that humans once fought with animals for the prey the animals had killed. For a long time, humans ate meat sporadically, depending on the season and the success of the hunt. Meat acquired a special status because it was less accessible and less abundant than other foods. The fact that meat was associated with hunting, an exclusively male activity from which men derived power, also increased its status. Meat eventually came to symbolize wealth and was regarded as an indication of social status, because only the rich could afford to eat it on a regular basis. It also acquired a reputation for being an essential part of a healthy diet. Meat continues to occupy a privileged position in the human diet.

For most of human history, our diet has consisted mainly of vegetables. Although meat has been plentiful at certain times, in particular places and within restricted milieus – for example, in the royal and noble households of Europe from the Middle Ages until the 17th century – it did not become widely available until relatively recently. With the advent of industrialization, standards of living improved and certain countries developed the capacity to produce meat on a massive scale, to transport it over long distances by rail and plane, and to preserve it in refrigerators and freezers.

In industrialized countries, meat is now consumed much more frequently than it was in the past. In fact, it is not unusual for people to consume meat several times a day – at breakfast, lunch, and dinner.

Buying

In general, between 35% and 65% of the carcass of an animal consists of muscle – the flesh – unless the animal is very fat. This muscle tissue is mainly comprised of long, tender muscular fibers held in place by tough fibers known as connective tissue. The tenderness of a cut of meat depends on how much connective tissue it contains, because this tissue is composed of two substances that react differently to heat: collagen (white), which turns into gelatin when heated in the presence of moisture, and elastin (yellow), which is hard and remains intact. The harder and longer a muscle works, the more highly developed, voluminous, and hard the connective tissue, and the tougher the meat. Since all the muscles in an animal's body do not work equally hard, the tenderness of a cut of meat depends on what part of the animal it comes from. The median part of butchered animals, which includes the ribs and the loin (back), is the source of the tenderest cuts of meat, while most of the moderately tender cuts come from the rear (rump) of the animal and most of the tougher cuts come from the front (flank, shank, brisket, shoulder, collar, and tip of the rib).

The older the animal, the more highly developed the connective tissue and the tougher the meat. When buying meat, consider how it is going to be prepared; there is no point in paying for a tender cut if is going to be simmered for a long period of time.

Choose fine-grained meat that is firm and smooth to the touch. Beef should be bright red and shiny, pork should be pinkish, mutton should be a dark shade of pink, and lamb a slightly paler shade of pink. The color of veal depends on the amount of iron in the calf's diet; grain-fed veal is thus pinker than milk-fed veal. Avoid limp and discolored meat, because it is probably less than fresh.

Meat is graded in accordance with government regulations that vary from one country to another. In Canada, meat is classified on the basis of precise criteria relating to the maturity, the quality (determined by the color, the texture, and the firmness of the lean and fatty portions of the carcass), and the amount of meat. The various grades of meat are identified by letters of different colors and by numbers corresponding to subsidiary grades (A1, A2, etc.). In the United States, meat is also graded in accordance with the quality of the meat and the yield from particular animals; the words "Prime," "Choice," "Standard" and "Commercial" are normally used to distinguish between the various grades. In Europe, a distinction is made between the condition or quality of the meat and the category to which it belongs; cuts belong to one of three categories, depending on how they are intended to be used (1st category, cuts for grilling or roasting; 2nd category, less tender cuts suitable for braising; 3rd category, cuts that should be slowly boiled or braised).

Making the best buy involves more than merely comparing the prices of various cuts. You should also consider the price per portion, which depends on the amount of bone, gristle, and fat the meat contains. As a rule, boneless meat yields more portions than meat that has not been removed from the bone.

The carcasses of animals are cut into numerous pieces that vary from one species to another. In North America, there are 25 different cuts of beef alone. Cuts also vary from one country to another. In certain countries, merchants cut meat up hastily with electric saws, rather than cutting carefully along the muscles and the bones to produce numerous cuts of various degrees of tenderness. The machine method is cheaper as well as faster.

Preparing

 Certain cuts of meat have to be prepared more elaborately in order to make them more tender and flavorful, or to ensure that they do not dry out as they cook.

Marinating meat

Marinating meat involves soaking it for several hours in liquid that is generally somewhat acidic (wine, lemon juice, etc.) and flavorful (oil, herbs, garlic, spices, etc.), in order to make the meat more tender or to enhance its flavor. The container in which the meat is marinated should be tightly sealed and placed in the refrigerator. Veal should not be marinated.

Larding meat

Larding involves sewing thin strips of fat into a piece of meat with a larding needle, in order to prevent lean cuts from drying out as they cook.

Barding meat

Barding serves the same purpose as larding and involves covering a piece of meat with a bard of fat prior to roasting. The fat drips onto the meat as it cooks and prevents it from drying out.

1 *Surround the piece of meat with a bard of fat and tie a piece of string around it, securing one end with a knot.*

2 *Starting at one end, wrap the string around your hand and slip this loop around the roast; pull the string tight with your other hand. Make a series of loops along the entire length of the roast.*

3 *Turn the roast over and wrap the string around it lengthwise.*

4 *Tie the loose end of the string tightly.*

Serving Ideas

Meat can be prepared in any number of ways. Depending on the cut and the manner in which it is cooked, it can be prepared very quickly or very slowly. It can also be prepared very simply or quite elaborately. Meat is usually cooked before it is consumed, but it is occasionally eaten raw (steak tartare and the Italian hors d'oeuvre *carpaccio*). Never eat meat raw unless it is very fresh and comes from a reputable supplier.

Cooking

Cooking meat can make it either more tender or more tough, depending on the intensity of the heat and the duration of the cooking process. The secret to cooking meat successfully is striking the right balance between the tenderness that results from the transformation of collagen into gelatin and the toughness that results from the solidification of the muscle fibers. Heat causes the proteins in meat to coagulate, turns the collagen into gelatin, and prompts the release of fat and water, which involves the loss of various nutrients and a certain amount of flavor. Too much heat can thus make meat tough and dry, shrink it considerably, and diminish its nutritional value and flavor.

The least tender cuts of meat – those that contain the most connective tissue – are best when cooked slowly in a relatively cool oven. This transforms the collagen in the connective tissue into gelatin (especially in the presence of liquid), thus tenderizing the meat, without causing too much of the protein to coagulate and harden. However, meat should not be cooked at extremely low temperatures (below 300°F or 150°C); it must be rapidly heated to a temperature high enough to destroy any microbes that may be present.

Meat is cooked when its internal temperature reaches a certain temperature, which varies depending on the kind of meat. The degree to which beef and lamb are cooked depends on individual taste, but this is generally not the case for other meats.

It is difficult to predict exactly how long a piece of meat will have to be cooked. The cooking time depends on a number of factors, including the cut of meat, its size, its initial temperature, and the efficiency of the heat source. Tender cuts do not have to be cooked for as long as tough cuts. A meat thermometer is very useful for determining precisely how long meat should be cooked, no matter how many variables come into play; insert the thermometer into the center of the piece of meat, ensuring that it does not touch fat or bone, which would result in a false reading. Position the thermometer so that you can read it without opening the oven door.

It is best to cook meat in heavy dishes or pans that conduct heat well. Meat should not be salted until the end of the cooking process, or after rather than before it is cooked, because salt draws the juices out of meat, making it drier and less flavorful. It should be salted prior to cooking only when used in dishes such as stew, which require a flavorful sauce or stock. Brown less tender roasts, cubes, and steaks before cooking them with moist heat (braising or poaching) to seal in the juices, and turn meat with tongs rather than a fork to prevent it from losing moisture as it cooks.

To reduce the fat content of meat, remove all visible fat before it is cooked and use only a small amount of fat for cooking. Meat sauces can be defatted by refrigerating them (an easily removable layer of fat forms on the surface) or by gently placing a piece of absorbent paper towel on the surface of the sauce (you may have to do this several times).

Meat can be tenderized before it is cooked, either by hand with a tool that breaks the fibers or with natural enzymes or acid ingredients. Certain fruits contain tenderizing enzymes (papayas, kiwis, figs, and pineapples) and can be used as is, in slices or pieces, or in the form of juice; the leaves are used whenever possible. Most commercial tenderizing agents are made from papaya. Among the acid ingredients that can be used are vinegar, yogurt, cider, wine, citrus juice, tomatoes, or beer; these ingredients are often used to make marinades in which the meat can be soaked for several hours in the refrigerator.

Meat can be cooked in various ways, with either dry or moist heat or a combination of both. It can be roasted, grilled, fried, braised, or poached.

Roasting

This method involves cooking meat with dry heat, either in the oven or on the barbecue, and is particularly appropriate for tender roasts or poultry. To reduce the fat content of meat as much as possible, remove all visible fat and brush the meat with a small amount of oil, butter, or margarine to prevent it from drying out. Place the meat on the rack of a roasting pan or directly on the barbecue grill (putting a pan underneath it to catch the juices). To prepare the base of a sauce, place the meat on top of bones or meat trimmings in a roasting pan. Season the meat, then insert a thermometer into the center. Place it in an oven that has been preheated to approximately 325°F (160°C); moderately tender or tough roasts are best when cooked slowly at 275° F (140°C).

The temperature at which meat is cooked depends on the desired result: higher temperatures (over 400°F or 200°C) seal the juices in the meat and make it crispy on the outside; however, meat also shrinks more when cooked in this way.

Meat cooks faster if it is already at room temperature and is only slightly marbled, relatively thin, and contains long, thin bones. The times specified in recipes are thus approximations, and a meat thermometer is always the best guide. Once the meat has finished cooking, let it sit for 5 to 15 minutes in an oven set at the desired internal temperature, or wrap it in aluminum foil (placing the shiny side toward the meat). This will allow the juices to spread evenly throughout the meat, making it more moist and tender. A roast or a bird that has finished cooking can be left at this temperature for a considerable length of time.

Grilling meat

This method involves cooking meat under the oven broiler or on a barbecue and is particularly appropriate for tender steaks and poultry. If the meat is too tough, marinate it for a few hours in the refridgerator or tenderize it with a mallet or a meat tenderizer. Cut into the fat on the outside of the meat to prevent it from curling up as it cooks; season the meat if desired, but do not salt it until near the end of the cooking process. Allow the broiler or the barbecue to become very hot. Place the meat about 4 or 5 inches away from the heat source and cook it for a few minutes on each side, turning it when drops of moisture appear on the surface (no more than once or twice). Leave the oven door slightly open and do not cover the barbecue. Do not pierce the meat, and wait several minutes before serving it to allow the juices to spread evenly throughout the meat.

Pan-frying meat

This method is much like grilling, but the meat is cooked in a pan in a small amount of fat. It is particularly appropriate for tender or tenderized steaks, as well as for ground meat and poultry. Make several cuts in the fat on the outside of the meat, and heat a little fat in the pan (no fat is required if a nonstick pan is used). Season the meat, then brown it uncovered over moderately high heat for a few minutes per side; avoid boiling the meat (too little heat) or allowing it to stick to pan (too much heat). Turn the meat when drops form on the surface (no more than once or twice). If melted fat accumulates in the bottom of the pan, it should be poured off to prevent the meat from being deep-fried. Do not add salt until the end of the cooking process.

Braising meat

This method involves cooking meat at a low temperature with moist heat (steam produced by liquid added to a closed pan in the oven or on the stovetop) and is particularly appropriate for tough or moderately tender steaks or roasts. The pan should be heavy and should have a tight-fitting cover. The meat will cook faster if it is cut into small pieces, but more moisture will be lost; before being braised, the pieces can be coated with flour and browned to seal in the juices.

Start by trimming the fat from the meat, then season it or coat it with flour. Brown it on all sides in a very small amount of hot fat. You can then remove the meat, drain off the fat, and briefly cook a selection of finely chopped vegetables. Place the meat on the vegetables, adjust the seasoning (do not add any salt at this point unless the meat has been coated with bread crumbs or flour), insert a thermometer in the meat (if cooking a roast), and add a small amount of liquid (stock, water, wine). Cover the pan and cook the meat over low heat or in a relatively cool oven (325°F or 160°C). If the meat is overcooked, it will become stringy and less flavorful. Defat the stock before serving the meat. If it is too runny, bring it to a boil (after removing the meat) and allow it reduce.

Poaching meat

This method is similar to braising, but more liquid is added to the meat; the resultant dish is referred to as *pot-au-feu* in France and "stew" in North America. Poaching is particularly appropriate for tough roasts or pieces. The meat is submerged in flavorful stock that is either hot or cold and cooked until it achieves the desired degree of tenderness.

The meat can be coated with flour and sautéed over moderately high heat on all sides before it is plunged into the cold or simmering liquid (this seals the juices inside the pieces); do not salt the stew until it is almost ready. For a richer stew, salt the meat before it is cooked and put it directly into cold liquid instead of browning it in fat. Skim the surface of the liquid if you prefer relatively clear stew. Add the desired seasonings and bring the stew to a gentle simmer; do not add vegetables until half an hour before the stew is ready. Defat the stew before it is served.

Microwaving meat

Most meats can be cooked in the microwave, especially less tender cuts that have to be cooked slowly with moist heat. However, it is best to roast, grill, or fry tender cuts in a conventional oven or on the stovetop. Meat can also be partially cooked in the microwave, then transferred to the stovetop or a conventional oven. Choose pieces of equal size and arrange them in a circle on a microwave-safe dish, placing the thickest portions toward the outside. Cover the meat before cooking it. Reduce the amount of liquid when making stew in the microwave, because very little of the moisture evaporates. Most cuts of meat can be cooked on high power, but tougher cuts will be more flavorful and tender if cooked slowly. Large pieces of meat will brown in the microwave because they have to be cooked for so long, but small pieces cook too quickly to brown. Brush thin cuts of meat with a marinade, soy sauce, melted butter, barbecue sauce, or Worcestershire sauce to improve their appearance and flavor. Since food cooks unevenly in the microwave, it is important to check the internal temperature of the meat in several places.

Nutritional Information

The composition of meat depends on several factors, including the species, the breed, the age, the sex, and the diet of the animal. Some of these factors influence the amount of myoglobin (pigment) in the flesh, which determines how red the meat is. Certain nutrients are present in more consistent quantities than others:

• the lean portion of meat (the muscle) contains approximately 75% water when raw; the fatty portion contains less water;

• meat contains 19% protein; fatty meat contains less protein than lean meat;

• meat generally contains 2.5% fat, but the fat content varies greatly (from 2 to 10 grams per 100 grams), which has a direct impact on the number of calories;

• 100 grams of raw lean meat can thus contain anywhere from 110 to 200 calories.

Meat contains no fiber and rarely contains any carbohydrates, with the notable exception of certain types of offal such as heart, kidney, and especially liver. The carbohydrates are in the form of glycogen, which gives meat a mild flavor. Glycogen turns into lactic acid after an animal is slaughtered, which stiffens the flesh.

Meat is an excellent source of certain B-complex vitamins such vitamin B_{12} (particularly beef, veal, and lamb) and niacin (especially pork). It is also an excellent source of zinc and potassium, and a good source of phosphorus and iron; the best sources of zinc and iron are beef, veal, and lamb. Offal contains vitamin A and is high in iron. Most of the vitamins and minerals in meat are not destroyed by cooking.

The proteins in meat are regarded as complete, whereas vegetable proteins are said to be incomplete. The difference is that meat contains more essential amino acids – substances the human body requires but cannot produce, which must therefore be included in the diet. Eight of the 20 amino acids have been deemed essential for adults, and all eight not only are found in meat, they are present in what are considered to be ideal proportions; vegetable sources contain insufficient amounts of one or more of these acids (see *Complementary proteins*).

Meat

530

It is generally agreed that in Western countries, people generally consume too much protein. A serving of cooked meat should weigh between 2 and 4 ounces (50 and 100 grams). The fat content of meat depends on the species, the cut, and the manner in which the animal was raised. Lean meat (white chicken and turkey, guinea fowl, pork tenderloin, bottom round steak, etc.) contains less than 3 grams of fat per 100 grams of raw meat, moderately fatty meat (most poultry and certain cuts of lamb, beef, veal, and pork) contains between 3 and 10 grams, and fatty meat over 10 grams. The amount of fat in meat affects its flavor.

Animal fat largely consists of saturated fatty acids and contains cholesterol (approximately 45 to 75 milligrams of cholesterol per 100 grams of raw meat; 100 grams of liver, heart, and tongue contain approximately 300 milligrams, 150 milligrams, and 100 milligrams respectively). Choosing lean cuts of meat and removing all of the visible fat can help reduce your consumption of these substances, which have been linked to various health problems.

Meat is generally ready for human consumption after it has been allowed to mature for at least 48 hours. Beef has to be matured for a longer period of time. In North America, beef is stored for at least 8 to 14 days, the minimum amount of time required for it to become sufficiently tender and flavorful.

Storing

Meat is very perishable. When left at room temperature, it can be contaminated by pathogenic bacteria very quickly, which can make it unfit for human consumption. Whether raw or cooked, meat should never be left at room temperature for any longer than 2 hours, and it should not be refrigerated for any longer than a few days (2 or 3 days for steaks, chops, cooked and raw poultry; 3 or 4 days for raw roasts and cooked roast; and only 1 or 2 days for ground meat). Wrap raw or cooked meat to prevent it from drying out and to prevent the juices in raw meat from contaminating other foods in the refrigerator.

Meat can be preserved by means of various processes, including smoking, salting, drying, canning, freeze-drying, irradiation, and freezing. No matter what the process, the results are largely dependent on the quality and condition of the meat that is used.

Smoking

Smoking traditionally involves impregnating the meat with smoke produced by burning resinous or aromatic wood (birch, pine, fir, beech, chestnut, walnut, oak), seeds, or various aromatic plants such as rosemary and sage. This process dries the meat and coats its surface with substances that prevent the development of bacteria. It also makes the meat darker in color and gives it a smoky flavor. Meat can be either cold-smoked (for 3 to 4 weeks) or hot-smoked (for just a few minutes or a few hours), after being salted or pickled. Most meat is now smoked by means of artificial rather than natural processes; more often than not, a smoke-flavored concentrate extracted from maple, oak, or other wood is used. Smoked meat can be refrigerated for 6 to 7 days or frozen for 1 to 2 months.

Salting is a process used to preserve raw meat (mainly pork). Some salted meat is also smoked and dried. Meat can be salted in a variety of ways: dry-salting involves placing layers of salt between flat, thin pieces of meat; salting in brine involves soaking meat in a saline solution; and salting by means of injection involves introducing brine containing controversial additives (nitrites or nitrates) directly into the joint. The presence of the salt means that less water is available for the development of microbes, and the chlorine in the salt also hinders their growth. Ideally, meat should be desalted before it is cooked.

Drying

Meat was originally dried in the sun in countries with hot, dry climates, but it can also be dehydrated by means of cryodessication – a relatively expensive, and thus little used, industrial process. Enough of the moisture is removed from dried meat to hinder the development of most bacteria. Some dried meat is also smoked or salted.

Freeze-drying (or cryodessication) is a recently developed process that involves freezing the meat, then dehydrating it by means of sublimation – that is, by transforming the water in the meat into gas by heating it in a vacuum. Freeze-dried meat contains less than 2% water.

Irradiation, a process that was invented around 1950, involves exposing food to gamma rays (usually rays emitted by cobalt 60 or cesium 137). The radiation breaks certain chemical bonds in the organisms that contaminate meat, thus reducing the number of pathogenic bacteria such as salmonella and trichina. This process is rarely used due to concerns about health risks.

Freezing preserves meat by retarding the action of enzymes and preventing the development of bacteria that cause deterioration. Meat should be frozen rapidly to prevent the formation of large ice crystals that can alter its taste and texture. Wrap the meat well to ensure that it does not dry out and to prevent the fatty portions from spoiling as a result of being exposed to air. Package the meat or put it in freezer bags, separating steaks, chops, and similar cuts with a double layer of waxed paper or freezer wrap so they can be used individually.

Defrost meat slowly – in the refrigerator, if possible – to prevent moisture loss, which reduces its flavor and nutritional value. Never refreeze meat that has been completely defrosted without cooking it thoroughly first.

The fat content of meat determines how long it can be frozen. Since fat deteriorates relatively quickly, fatty meat spoils faster than lean meat.

Meat

Beef

Bos, **Bovidae**

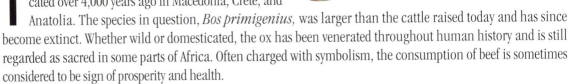

The word "ox" refers to the castrated male of any species of cattle. This mammal was first domesticated over 4,000 years ago in Macedonia, Crete, and Anatolia. The species in question, *Bos primigenius,* was larger than the cattle raised today and has since become extinct. Whether wild or domesticated, the ox has been venerated throughout human history and is still regarded as sacred in some parts of Africa. Often charged with symbolism, the consumption of beef is sometimes considered to be sign of prosperity and health.

There are several hundred different species of cattle and an incalculable number of crossbreeds. Only about 30 species are bred for human consumption because they yield unusually large amounts of particularly good meat. The word "beef" refers to meat from heifers, cows, bulls, bull-calves, oxen, and steers, although some of these meats are much more tender and flavorful than others. The quality of the meat is largely dependent on the age of the animal and the manner in which it was raised. For example, the older the animal and the harder it has worked, the tougher the meat.

Buying

Since cuts of beef vary not only from one country to another but also from region to region within individual countries, it can be difficult to sort out the names of the various cuts. No matter where the carcass is from, however, certain portions are referred to as "noble" cuts because they are particularly tender. These cuts comprise only about 30% of the animal and are thus rarer, more sought after, and more expensive than the less tender portions. However, the so-called inferior cuts can also be quite tender when prepared in the right way – that is, if they are tenderized with a marinade, a mallet, or a tenderizer, or if they are cooked slowly in liquid.

Always consider the cooking method when buying beef because there is no reason to pay for one of the more expensive, tender cuts if the meat is going to be simmered for long time. Conversely, never buy tougher cuts for grilling or roasting.

The composition and fat content of the ground beef sold in stores vary greatly. The best way to control these characteristics, and to ensure that the meat is as fresh as possible, is to grind it yourself. Although fattier beef is less expensive, more of its total weight is lost as it cooks because some of the fat melts. Regular ground beef, which contains the most fat, can be a good buy as long as the fat can be drained off as the dish cooks (a tomato meat sauce, for example), but it is best to use leaner beef when making dishes from which the fat cannot be removed (a meat loaf, for example).

Cooking

Like lamb, beef can be cooked for various lengths of time. It can be eaten very rare (raw on the inside and slightly cooked on the outside), rare, medium-rare, medium, or well-done. Since the amount of time separating one degree of doneness from another is often very short, beef has to be cooked quite carefully (a meat thermometer can be very useful).

Beef can also be cooked at a broad range of temperatures. The ideal temperature depends mainly on the type of cut. Tough or moderately tender cuts that contain a lot of connective tissue should be cooked at low temperatures for a long period of time, which transforms the collagen in this hard tissue into gelatin. Tender cuts can be cooked rapidly at high temperatures because they do have not be tenderized.

TENDER CUTS		
Degree of Doneness (325°F oven)	Minutes per Pound	Internal Temperature
VERY RARE	13 – 15	125° – 130°F
RARE	15 – 18	130° – 140°F
MEDIUM	18 – 20	140° – 150°F
WELL DONE	20 – 25	150° – 165°F

Serving Ideas

Beef can be eaten cold or hot and can be prepared in numerous ways. It is an ingredient in the simplest as well as the most elaborate dishes. Although beef is sometimes eaten raw (steak tartare), ground beef must always be cooked thoroughly (until no pink remains) because it may contain *E. coli*, a toxic bacterium that can cause food poisoning and other serious health problems; it can even be fatal if consumed by particularly vulnerable people such as children or seniors. Beef is especially delicious when salted or smoked. According to food guidelines issued by the U.S. government, the recommended daily allowance of meat (or meat substitutes) is two to three "servings"— 12% to 13% of the total diet.

Cooking Asian dishes, in which moderate amounts of meat are combined with vegetables and cereals (rice, noodles, millet, etc.), is an excellent way to ensure that you consume healthy portions of beef. Leftover beef and less tender cuts can be ground, either before or after they are cooked.

Oven-Baked Beef Tenderloin

SERVES 4

1½ lb. (750 g) beef tenderloin	1 tbsp. herbes de Provence (mixture of thyme, rosemary, bay, basil, savory)
3 tbsp. butter	
1 small carrot	
1 small onion	¼ cup (60 ml) dry sherry
Dijon mustard	1 bay leaf
¼ cup (60 ml) beef stock	Ground pepper

1. Remove the beef tenderloin from the refrigerator 30 minutes before it is to be cooked. Preheat the oven to 350°F (180°C).

2. Cut the carrot into thin rounds and slice the onion thinly. Coat the tenderloin with mustard.

3. Dot the bottom of an ovenproof dish with a portion of the butter, then add the sliced carrots and onions. Place the beef tenderloin on top of the vegetables, and sprinkle it with the *herbes de Provence*. Top it with the bay leaf and the remaining butter, then grind on pepper to taste. For rare meat, cook it for 40 minutes, then turn the oven off and leave the tenderloin in the cooling oven for another 10 minutes.

4. Remove the meat from the dish, pour in the sherry, and deglaze the pan. Add the beef stock and bring the mixture to a boil. Allow the sauce to reduce until it thickens.

The vegetables can be served as part of the sauce. Serve the fillet with potatoes *au gratin*.

Nutritional Information

The nutritional value of beef varies slightly depending on the breed and the breeding methods. The cut, the cooking method, and the amount of fat that is removed can also have a considerable impact on the nutritional value.

Beef is an excellent source of protein, potassium, zinc, and certain B-complex vitamins such as niacin and vitamin B_{12}. It is also a good source of iron and phosphorus. However, it may also contain large amounts of saturated fatty acids and cholesterol.

The marbling (the streaks of fat in the muscular portion of the meat) helps make the meat more tender, flavorful, and juicy. It does not significantly increase the fat content of cooked beef because most of it melts as the meat cooks.

You can reduce the amount of fat in the beef you consume by:

• choosing lean cuts (top round, bottom round, sirloin) and cooking them in a minimum amount of fat (roasting, grilling, braising, etc.);

• serving smaller portions, removing any visible fat before the meat is cooked, and eating only the lean meat;

• placing the meat on the grill of a roasting pan to allow the juices to drain off as it cooks;

• defatting the sauce.

Storing

Beef can be refrigerated or frozen. Ground beef can be refrigerated for 1 or 2 days, steaks for 2 to 3 days, and roasts and cooked beef for 3 to 4 days.

Ground or cooked beef can be frozen for 2 to 3 months, and steaks and roasts for 10 to 12 months.

sirloin *short loin* *rib* *chuck*

round

flank *short plate* *brisket* *fore shank*

Flank & Short plate

skirt steak

flank steak

Fore Shank and Brisket

shank (cross cut)   brisket (whole)

Rib

rib eye roast   rib roast (large end)

back ribs

Short Loin

T-bone steak   boneless top loin steak

tenderloin roast   porterhouse steak

Sirloin

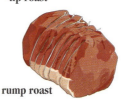

sirloin steak (flat bone)   top sirloin steak

Round

tip roast   eye round roast

rump roast   top round roast

Chuck

   short ribs

flanken-style ribs

   chuck eye roast

boneless top blade steak   under blade pot roast   chuck eye roast

boneless shoulder pot roast   arm pot roast   blade roast

Veal is meat from a calf less than 1 year old. Castrated males over 1 year old are referred to as steers, and females over 1 year old that have yet to give birth are known as heifers. Veal calves are generally killed when they are 4 to 6 months old; most of these animals are males because the majority of the females become dairy cows.

Veal has been enjoyed since Roman times and is still popular in Italy; in fact, it now serves as the basis for a wide variety of dishes.

Eating veal was once a symbol of wealth, because only the rich could afford to kill animals that provided so little meat. It was reserved for festive occasions; hence the association between the return of the prodigal child and the slaughter of a fatted calf.

In certain regions of France, including Normandy, calves were once fed up to 10 eggs per day just before they were killed. The yolks of the eggs colored the mouth of the animal, creating what was referred to as a *palais royal* (royal palate). Some calves were also fed milk-soaked biscuits to make the meat as white as possible.

Until about 20 years ago, veal came from very young animals (slaughtered at the age of 2 or 3 weeks) or from larger calves that spent the summer grazing and were killed in fall. The first kind of veal was limp, almost gelatinous, and relatively flavorless, while the second (known as grass-fed veal) was much darker (very red) and quite tough. Since producers began specializing in breeding calves, these varieties of veal have practically disappeared from the market. Most of the veal now available is either "milk-fed" or "grain-fed."

Milk-fed veal comes from animals that are raised indoors in individual stalls and feed almost exclusively on milk. Since milk contains very little iron, the flesh of the animals remains a very light, whitish shade of pink. The calves are killed at the age of 4 to 5 months, when they weigh approximately 300 pounds. Milk-fed veal is firmer than veal from very young calves, but it is still very tender and delicate.

Grain-fed veal comes from animals that feed on milk until the age of 6 to 8 weeks. At this point, the calves are removed from their individual interior stalls and placed in a fattening pen where they feed on grain. They are slaughtered at the age of 5 to 5½ months, when they weigh approximately 340 pounds. Since grain-fed animals consume relatively large amounts of iron, their flesh is pinker than that of milk-fed animals; it also has a somewhat stronger flavor and is slightly less tender.

Rather than slaughtering extremely young animals, producers now breed more milk- and grain-fed calves, thus providing consumers with a broad range of cheaper, meatier cuts of veal.

Meat

Serving Ideas

Veal can be prepared in numerous ways, including as fried scallops or *grenadins* (small, thick boneless slices) and as sautés, roasts, "birds" *(paupiettes),* and blanquettes (stewed in white stock). Veal Marengo is cooked in white wine, tomatoes, and garlic. Veal goes particularly well with cream, cheese, herbs (thyme, tarragon, rosemary, sage, basil, etc.), mushrooms, eggplant, spinach, onions, garlic, tomatoes, apples, citrus fruit, and alcohol (wine, Calvados, Madeira, cognac, etc.). Veal offal is renowned for its delicate flavor.

Nutritional Information

	raw loin	*roasted loin*
protein	20 g	26 g
fat	3 g	7 g
cholesterol	80 mg	106 mg
calories	116	175
		per 100 g

The nutritional value of veal depends on the age of the calf as well as on its diet and living conditions. Veal generally contains less fat and fewer calories than beef, pork, or lamb, but it is slightly higher in cholesterol.

Grain-fed veal contains more iron than milk-fed veal, which explains why it is pinker in color.

Cooking

Cuts of veal from the rib, loin (back), and sirloin are excellent roasted, grilled, or fried. Moderately tender cuts from the leg and hind shank can also be cooked with dry heat, especially if they have been marinated, or tenderized with a mallet or the handle of a knife. Cuts from the neck, shoulder, flank, shank, and breast, which are less tender, are best when braised or simmered.

Veal has to be cooked quite carefully because its lean flesh tends to dry out and become tough. It should thus be barded or coated with fat, cooked at moderate temperatures (275° to 300°F, or 140° to 150°C), and basted from time to time. Veal should never be overcooked and is best when still slightly pink.

Veal Birds (Paupiettes)

SERVES 4

4 very thin veal scallops	2 tablespoons olive oil
4 very thin slices of cooked ham	1 bay leaf
4 slices Swiss cheese	1 tablespoon capers (optional)
Ground pepper	½ cup (125 ml) Marsala wine
4 fresh tomatoes	
4 medium onions	

1. Cover each scallop with a matching slice of ham, then a slice of Swiss cheese. After grinding on some pepper, roll the scallops up to form "birds," or roulades, tying them crosswise.

2. Scald, peel, and seed the tomatoes, then cut them into large pieces. Peel and quarter the onions.

3. Heat the oil with the bay leaf in a pressure cooker. Brown the "birds" gently, being careful not let the oil burn. Add the onions, tomatoes, and capers, then pour in the Marsala. Cover the pressure cooker and simmer the veal for 30 minutes.

4. Adjust the seasoning. Untie the "birds" before serving them.

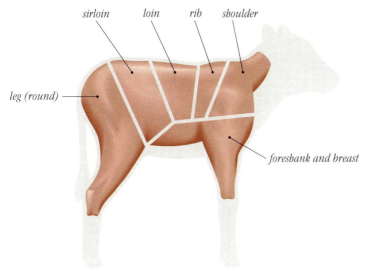

sirloin *loin* *rib* *shoulder*

leg (round)

foreshank and breast

Rib

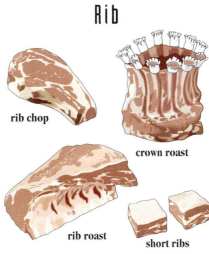

rib chop

crown roast

rib roast

short ribs

Leg (Round)

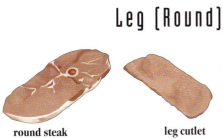

round steak

leg cutlet

boneless rump roast

Sirloin

sirloin roast

top sirloin steak

Shoulder

boneless shoulder arm roast

arm roast

blade steak

blade roast

boneless shoulder eye roast

arm steak

Loin

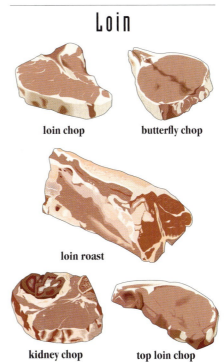

loin chop

butterfly chop

loin roast

kidney chop

top loin chop

Foreshank and Breast

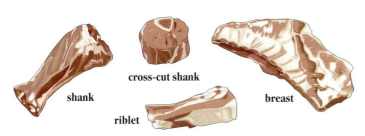

shank

cross-cut shank

riblet

breast

Pork

Sus, Suidae

The pig is an omnivorous mammal with a movable snout; it is raised for its flesh and its hide. Natural historians once thought that the pig was directly descended from the wild boar *(Sus scrofa),* which had more prominent tusks than the boars of today, but these animals are now considered to be no more than cousins. Male pigs are referred to as "boars," females as "sows," and young pigs as "piglets" or "porkers." Three- to 4-week-old pigs are known as "suckling pigs." The word "pork" refers to the flesh of pigs used as food. Pork has long been a staple of the human diet. Until the Second World War, the killing of a pig was the occasion for a major feast day in rural France, and families and neighbors still gather for ritual celebrations when pigs are slaughtered.

Pigs are prolific and easier to breed than other farm animals because they are docile and will feed on almost anything. On pig farms in times past, they traditionally shared the same space as their breeders, either occupying the lower floor of dwellings or living in close proximity – breeding conditions that persist in certain parts of the world today. Pigs are valued not only for their abundant flesh but also for almost every other part of their bodies, including their abdominal fat (lard), ears, hair (bristles), legs, feet, entrails, and tails, most of which are sold as fresh or prepared meat. The pig was once regarded as a scavenger because of its feeding habits. The Jewish and Muslim dietary restrictions regarding pork are thought to have been adopted because the consumption of pork was linked to illness. For example, the ancient Egyptians believed that pork was responsible for the spread of leprosy and banned pig-keepers from temples. It was not yet known that the real cause of the illness (trichinosis) was the presence in the pork of a parasitic worm *(Trichinella spiralis).* Invisible to the naked eye, trichinae can be destroyed by cooking pork thoroughly (to an internal temperature of 140°F, or 60°C) or by exposing it to radiation. The main symptoms of trichinosis are gastroenteritis, fever, vomiting, muscular pain, swollen eyelids, and headaches.

There are various breeds of pigs – including the Duroc, the Landrace, and the Yorkshire – as well as numerous crossbreeds. Over the past three decades, the demand for leaner meat has led to the development of breeds that are 30% to 50% less fatty (verified by measuring the thickness of the dorsal fat), by means of genetic manipulation and new diets. The stress related to transportation and slaughtering conditions can affect the quality of pork, which sometimes exudes moisture. Intensive research is currently being conducted in an effort to solve this problem, which leads to significant losses for slaughterhouses.

Serving Ideas

Pork can be eaten hot or cold but must always be cooked (until only slightly pink) in order to destroy any trichinae that may be present in the flesh. Pork is delicious when prepared with fresh or dried fruit (chestnuts, pineapples, apples, oranges, prunes, grapes, apricots).

Nutritional Information

Pork is higher in B-complex vitamins (riboflavin, niacin, and especially thiamine) than other meats. It is also rich in zinc and potassium, and is a good source of phosphorus.

The nutritional value of pork varies, depending on the cut and on whether or not the visible fat has been removed. Contrary to popular belief, cooked lean pork is no fattier or higher in calories than other lean meat. Pork fat is visible and can be easily removed.

Buying

European and North American cuts of pork differ more than those of any other kind of meat. Traditional European cuts date back to a time when economic efficiency was not the primary concern of butchers.

The most tender cuts of pork come from the loin (back) and include fillets (tenderloin), roasts, and chops. Cuts from the leg and shoulder are less tender; these also include roasts as well as various other pieces: feet, hocks, tail, etc.

Pork can be eaten fresh, salted, or smoked. Smoked picnic shoulder roasts are often referred to as "picnic hams," but genuine hams come only from the leg of the animal. Bacon comes from the loin (Canadian or back bacon) or the flank (sliced bacon). Both salt pork and pork fat (bards and lardons), which consist of dorsal fat located between the flesh and the skin, come from the shoulder. Lard is rendered pork fat.

Storing

Pork can be stored in the refrigerator or the freezer. Ground pork can be refrigerated for 1 to 2 days, pork chops and fresh sausages for 2 to 3 days, and roasts, cooked pork, and opened packages of prepared meat for 3 to 4 days. Chops and roasts can be frozen for 8 to 10 months, sausages for 2 to 3 months, bacon and ham for 1 to 2 months, and prepared meats for 1 month.

Pork Tenderloin with Prunes

SERVES 4

2 pieces of pork tenderloin
8 pitted prunes
Salt and ground pepper
2 tsp. ground ginger
¼ cup (60 ml) butter
1 cup (250 ml) beef consommé (soup made from stock)

1. Preheat the oven to 350°F (180°C).

2. Slit the pieces of tenderloin lengthwise, insert the prunes in the openings, and sew them closed.

3. Season the meat with the salt, pepper, and ginger. Then brown it on all sides in the butter in a heavy skillet.

4. Place the meat in an ovenproof dish, add the consommé, and cover the dish. Cook the meat in the oven for 1 hour, basting it frequently. Add more consommé as required.

Cooking

Pork must always be cooked, because this is the only way (other than irradiation) to kill any parasites that may be present in the flesh; these parasites are destroyed when the internal temperature reaches 140°F, or 60°C. To be extra-safe, wait until the internal temperature reaches 150°F, or 70°C (when the flesh is only slightly pink).

If the pork lacks flavor, it can be seasoned or marinated before it is cooked. Green peppers, mustard, onions, garlic, citrus juice, soy sauce, and herbs complement its flavor perfectly.

Since pork tends to dry out and harden as it cooks, it should not be overcooked, and if the visible fat is removed, a little fat should be added to protect the meat. Pork should also be cooked at low temperatures (250°F, or 120°C, in the oven, or over medium heat on the stove top or barbecue, for example) to allow the flesh to cook thoroughly without losing its flavor, juices, or tenderness.

Avoid cooking pork in the microwave because it may cook unevenly. Checking the internal temperature of various parts of the meat with a thermometer is a good way to ensure that it is evenly cooked.

Tender cuts of pork, most which come from the loin, are best when cooked with dry heat, in the absence of liquid (roasted, grilled, fried). Tougher cuts from the shoulder, leg, or flank are more tender when cooked with moist heat or in liquid (braised, simmered).

Meat

539

loin   *blade shoulder*

leg

arm shoulder

side

Shoulder

smoked hock

smoked picnic

blade roast

boneless arm picnic roast

Loin

top loin chop

loin chop

sirloin chop

butterfly chop

rib chop

Canadian-style bacon

center loin roast

sirloin roast

blade roast (loin)

Side

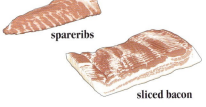
spareribs

sliced bacon

Leg

smoked ham, center slice

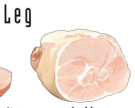
smoked ham
(shank portion)

country-style ribs

crown roast

center rib roast

smoked ham

smoked ham (rump portion)

top loin roast

tenderloin

back ribs

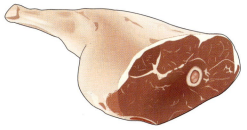

Lamb

Ovis, **Ovidae**

Lamb is a young sheep, a relatively docile ruminating mammal; meat from older sheep – castrated adult males, noncastrated adult males (rams), and adult females (ewes) — is known as "mutton."

The sheep was first domesticated in Iran about 13,000 years ago and has long played an important economic role in rural societies, providing families with fur, wool, leather, meat, and milk (which was used to make cheese, butter, and yogurt). Like goat's meat, kid's meat, and beef, roasted mutton and lamb were among the first foods prepared in honor of deities. In fact, the lamb remains a common religious symbol: Jews sacrifice the Paschal Lamb every year to commemorate their departure from Egypt, and Christians refer to Jesus Christ as the "Lamb of God."

Lamb usually comes from animals that are less then 12 months old, although norms vary from one country to another.

Baby lamb is slaughtered when it is 6 to 8 weeks old; spring lamb (slaughtered between March and October) is 3 to 5 months old. Regular lamb is up to 12 months old.

Mutton comes from adult sheep; the older the animal, the redder, tougher, fattier, and stronger-tasting the meat.

Unlike meat from other animals, lamb and mutton contain "hard fat," which rapidly solidifies once the meat is served. For this reason, lamb and mutton should be served on very hot plates.

Buying

The color, texture, and flavor of the meat depend on the breed and age of the animal as well as on how it was fed and reared. The condition of the bones, and the color of the fat and flesh, make it possible to distinguish between lamb and mutton. The joints of the forelegs of lambs are cartilaginous, while those of sheep are bony; furthermore, the fat on mutton is darker than the fat on lamb, and the meat itself is reddish rather than pinkish. The bone makes up about 25% of the total weight of a leg of lamb; take this into account when buying lamb to ensure that the leg is large enough to provide the appropriate number of servings. A leg of lamb weighing approximately 6 pounds will serve between 6 and 8 people.

Serving Ideas

The various seasonings that complement lamb and mutton include garlic, mustard, basil, mint, rosemary, and sage, as well as the zest of lemon, lime, and orange. Lamb and mutton are best when marinated, especially less tender cuts (shoulder, breast, shank) that are going to be cooked with dry heat. Leg of lamb is traditionally served at Eastertime in many countries. *Méchoui,* a whole eviscerated lamb or sheep roasted on a spit over a wood fire, is a traditional dish in North Africa and other parts of the Arab world. Lamb and sheep are also common ingredients in Arab couscous dishes.

Meat

541

Nutritional Information

	roasted leg of lamb
protein	28 g
fat	7 g
cholesterol	100 mg
calories	181
	per 100 g

The older the animal, the fattier the flesh and the greater the number of calories it contains; however, much of the fat is visible and can be easily removed. The leg, the rib, and the loin (back) are leaner than the shoulder.

Lamb is rich in protein, zinc, and B-complex vitamins, especially niacin, riboflavin, and vitamin B_{12}. It is also a good source of iron, potassium, and phosphorus.

Cooking

Lamb is usually roasted or grilled and is most flavorful when slightly pink. Like beef, it can be eaten rare (171°F or 63°C), medium (180°F or 68°C) or well done (approximately 189°F or 73°C). Since it tends to dry out and become tough, it should be cooked at moderate temperatures (275° to 325°F, or 140° to 160°C) and should not be overcooked. When roasting a leg, loin, or shoulder of deboned lamb, allow it to cook for 30 minutes per pound at 325°F (160°C) if it is to be eaten rare. Lamb is often braised or poached to make it more tender, but a leg or loin, of lamb can be roasted and lamb chops (cutlets) can be grilled, especially if they have been marinated.

Storing

Very fresh lamb can be refrigerated for about 3 days (1 or 2 days if ground). Pieces of lamb can be frozen for 8 to 10 months, and ground lamb for 2 to 3 months.

Loin of Lamb

SERVES 4

½ cup (125 ml) red wine
1 tbsp. rosemary
1 tbsp. thyme
1 tbsp. oregano
1 onion, chopped
2 cloves garlic, chopped

1 loin of lamb with
  8 ribs
3 tbsp. Italian parsley
Dijon mustard
⅔ cup (160 ml) beef
  stock
2 tbsp. butter

1. Pour the wine into a dish large enough to hold the loin of lamb, then add a third of the rosemary, thyme, and oregano, as well as all the chopped onion and garlic. Marinate the lamb in this mixture for 2 hours at room temperature, basting it regularly. Cover the dish with a layer of plastic wrap to seal in the flavors.

2. Preheat the oven to 350°F (180°C).

3. Chop the parsley.

4. Remove the lamb from the marinade and wipe it dry. Coat it with a thick layer of mustard, especially the ends. Sprinkle on the parsley and the remaining herbs, then place the loin in an ovenproof dish. Reserve the marinade.

5. Roast the lamb for 35 minutes (if it is to be served rare).

6. Remove the dish from the oven, then place the lamb on a hot serving platter and return it to the cooling oven to keep it warm.

7. Pour the stock and the marinade into a saucepan, and reduce this mixture over high heat. Remove it from the heat, then thicken the mixture with the butter. Pour it around the loin of lamb and serve the meat hot.

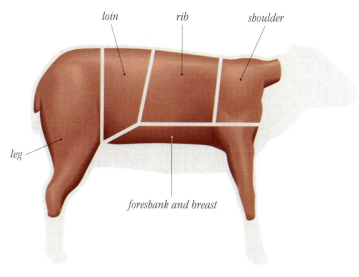

loin   rib   shoulder

leg

foreshank and breast

Loin

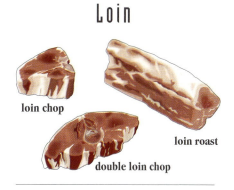

loin chop

loin roast

double loin chop

Foreshank and Breast

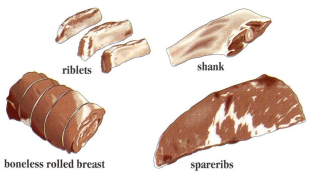

riblets

shank

boneless rolled breast

spareribs

Shoulder

boneless shoulder roast

arm chop

blade chop

square-cut shoulder (whole)

neck slice

Leg

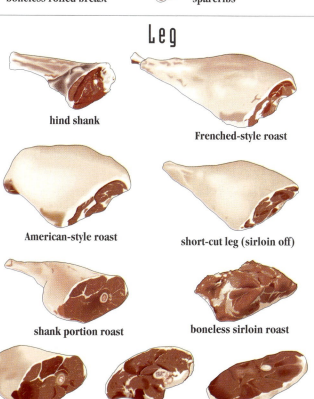

hind shank

Frenched-style roast

American-style roast

short-cut leg (sirloin off)

shank portion roast

boneless sirloin roast

center leg roast

sirloin chop

center slice

Rib

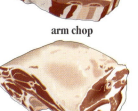

rib roast

rib chop

Frenched rib chop

crown roast

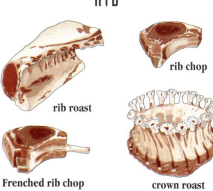

Venison

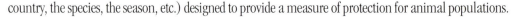

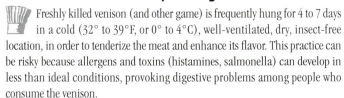

T he English word "venison" refers to the flesh of any kind of deer (reindeer, elk, caribou, moose, etc.) used as food; however, it once referred to the flesh of any large game animal, including the wild boar – a meaning that the French word *venaison* retains. The Greeks published the first treatises on hunting, but the Romans and the Gauls also extolled its pleasures. French kings and noblemen reserved hunting privileges for themselves. Hunting is now subject to various sets of regulations (depending on the country, the species, the season, etc.) designed to provide a measure of protection for animal populations.

It is important to note that much of the meat now marketed as "wild game" is wild in name only, because it comes from animals that are bred on farms. Although this meat is more tender than truly wild game, it is often less flavorful because the animals are fed a different diet.

The flavor of venison depends on the animal's diet, which can consist of wild berries, young shoots, grains, bark, or other foods. Since countries such as the United States and New Zealand began specializing in the production of farm-bred venison, it has been available year-round.

The roe deer *(Capreolus capreolus)* and red deer *(Cervus* spp.) are the most sought-after species.

Buying

 Meat from young deer is by far the most flavorful kind of venison; roe deer should be less than 2 years old, and red deer under 3.

Determining the age of the animal should be left to experts such as butchers or suppliers. As a rule, the younger the animal, the whiter the fat; the flesh is dark and very finely grained.

Venison is usually available fresh, vacuum-packed, or frozen.

Preparing

Freshly killed venison (and other game) is frequently hung for 4 to 7 days in a cold (32° to 39°F, or 0° to 4°C), well-ventilated, dry, insect-free location, in order to tenderize the meat and enhance its flavor. This practice can be risky because allergens and toxins (histamines, salmonella) can develop in less than ideal conditions, provoking digestive problems among people who consume the venison.

Venison does not have to be hung, especially if its strong flavor does not appeal to you or if the animal is young. Most of the venison sold in stores has already been aged and can be used immediately.

Traditional recipes suggest that venison be marinated before it is cooked, often for as long as a few days. However, marinades are now used only for meat from older animals; expert cooks would never consider marinating meat from a young animal because this could profoundly alter its flavor.

The only thing that absolutely has to be done when preparing venison is to bard pieces that are cooked in the oven; since venison is very lean, it tends to become tough when not cooked correctly. Remove the visible fat, which is strong-tasting and rancid, and replace it with a bard of lard, bacon, or caul.

Serving Ideas

Cuts from the shoulder can braised or stewed, and loin chops can be pan-fried or grilled. The choicest cuts (tenderloin) come from the saddle of the animal, and cuts suitable for roasting come from the haunch. Among the various seasonings and ingredients that complement venison are capers, mushrooms, pepper, Madeira, wine, lemon juice, and small fruits such as cranberries and cherries. It is often served with mashed potatoes or chestnuts. Venison can also be used to make pâtés and terrines.

Cooking

Since venison is very lean, it tends to become tough and dry if even slightly overcooked. The consensus among connoisseurs is that venison should be pink and juicy when served. Seal the meat in a frying pan, then transfer it to an ovenproof dish and roast it at 350° to 400°F (175° to 200°C), basting it every 15 minutes. Noisettes (small round boneless slices), chops, and cuts from the loin can be pan-fried, while cuts from the shoulder and other less tender pieces are best when braised. Roast pieces that weigh over 3 pounds for 10 to 15 minutes per pound, and pieces that weigh less than 3 pounds for 15 to 20 minutes per pound.

Nutritional Information

	raw
protein	23 g
fat	2.5 g
calories	120
	per 100 g

Venison is exceptionally lean; in fact, it is approximately 5 times less fatty than beef.

Storing

Venison can be refrigerated for 1 or 2 days. Individually wrapped pieces can be frozen for 3 to 6 months. They should be defrosted in the refrigerator; allow 2 to 3 hours per pound.

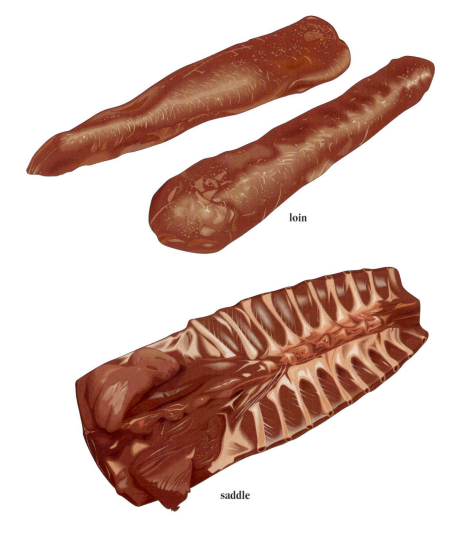

loin

saddle

Rabbit

Oryctolagus, Leporidae

The rabbit is a furry mammal thought to have originated in southern Europe and North Africa. It is so prolific that it has become a symbol of fertility; the female rabbit starts reproducing at the age of 4 or 5 months and gives birth to an average of 8 or 9 offspring at a time (litters of 18 are not uncommon); in a year and a half of reproductive activity (the maximum length of time for which they are used as breeders), domestic doe rabbits can give birth to over 100 offspring.

Wild rabbits can do a great deal of damage to crops, and when present in large numbers, they can make farming virtually impossible. In Australia, where the rabbit was introduced as a domestic animal during the 19th century, there are now approximately 300 million wild rabbits; since the rabbit has no natural predators in Australia, all efforts to reduce this population have failed.

The rabbit is related to the hare, a wild species regarded as game, which has darker, stronger-tasting flesh. The wild rabbit, which is probably the ancestor of the domestic rabbit, has lean, dark flesh with a gamy flavor. Meat from domestic rabbits resembles chicken.

Since rabbits are relatively easy to domesticate, they have been bred in captivity since ancient times. The rabbit was originally known as the "cony" or "coney," a name derived from the Old French word *conis* and, ultimately, from the Latin word for rabbit, *cuniculus.* In fact, the French still refer to the practice of breeding rabbits as *cuniculture.* It can be relatively expensive to raise rabbits because their feed alone accounts for as much as 40% to 50% of the cost of production. This is one of the reasons that they were raised on farms in limited numbers until the beginning of the 20th century, when the first industrial rabbit-breeding facilities were established. Commercially bred rabbits reach their optimal weight of 5 to 6 pounds in about 3 months, rather than the usual 4 to 6 months. Their flesh is somewhat fattier and blander than that of rabbits raised in more traditional ways. One commercially bred rabbit contains enough meat to feed 4 to 5 people, because there is very little waste or shrinkage. Rabbits are also bred for their fur, which is available in a variety shades and colors, as well as for the fertilizer they provide.

Buying

Rabbit meat is sold fresh or frozen, either whole or in four to six pieces, depending on the size of the animal. Rabbits are almost always skinned and gutted before being sold. When buying a fresh whole rabbit, ensure that the legs are still flexible. Choose a rabbit with shiny, slightly pink skin, an unmarked red liver, clearly visible red kidneys, and very white fat.

Preparing

When cutting a whole rabbit into pieces, first remove the four legs, then divide the saddle (the fleshy lower portion of the sides and the tail, which is often regarded as the best cut) into two or three pieces. If the animal is large enough, you may want to cut the relatively fleshy rear legs into two pieces.

Before cooking the rabbit, wash it, then soak it for a few hours in lightly salted cold water; this will bleach the meat and give it a more delicate flavor.

Rabbits and hares are not left to hang like pheasants, because they spoil too quickly.

However, they can be marinated, which not only tenderizes and whitens the meat but also makes it more moist and flavorful. In order to tenderize the meat, the marinade must contain an acid ingredient (red or white wine, lemon juice, vinegar) and oil; a wide variety of vegetables and seasonings can also be added. Farm-bred rabbits, which are naturally tender, do not have to be tenderized before they are cooked.

Rabbit with Cream

SERVES 4

½ lb. (250 g) firm salt
    pork
2 onions
4 shallots
2 tbsp. fresh parsley
    leaves
¼ cup (60 ml) sunflower
    oil
1 rabbit, cut into 8 pieces
1 cup (250 ml) white wine
1 cup (250 ml) chicken

stock
Salt and ground pepper
2 cups (500 ml) heavy
    cream
½ lb. (250 g) fresh
    mushrooms
1 tbsp. cornstarch
2 tbsp. cold water

1. Remove the rind from the pork fat, then cut it into lardons (strips). Desalt the lardons by boiling them in water for 10 minutes. Meanwhile, cut the onions and the shallots into thin slices; then chop the parsley. Drain the lardons.

2. Heat 1 tablespoon of the oil in a large frying pan, and brown the lardons; then put them in a casserole.

3. Brown the pieces of rabbit in the same frying pan, adding more oil when necessary. Place the browned rabbit in the casserole.

4. Brown the onions and shallots in the remaining oil; then add the wine and the chicken stock. Season this mixture with salt and pepper, and add the parsley. Bring the liquid to a boil, thoroughly deglazing the bottom of the pan. Pour the entire contents of the frying pan over the rabbit pieces in the casserole. If the liquid does not cover the bottom half of the rabbit pieces, add more chicken stock or a mixture of chicken stock and wine.

5. Bring the liquid to a boil, then cover and allow to simmer for about 2 hours, or until the rabbit is tender. Add the cream in small amounts while the rabbit is cooking.

6. Thirty minutes before the rabbit is ready, add the mushrooms (chop them coarsely if they are too large to be added whole).

7. Strain the cooking liquid. Arrange the rabbit, vegetables, and lardons on a serving plate, and put the plate in a warm oven. Stir the cornstarch into the water until dissolved. Add this to the cooking liquid, and simmer for 15 minutes or until thickened.

8. Pour the sauce over the rabbit, and serve the dish with small steamed potatoes or noodles.

Serving Ideas

Rabbit is often compared to chicken; like chicken, it can be cooked in a wide variety of ways and can be accompanied by a broad range of ingredients and seasonings. Since the meat of older rabbits is relatively tough, it should be cooked with liquid (braised, simmered); it is also frequently used to make pâtés or terrines. Hare can be prepared like rabbit; it is often served with acidic fruit or with a sweet-and-sour or spicy sauce, in order to reduce the intensity of its flavor.

Cooking

Rabbit has to be cooked somewhat more carefully than chicken because its lean flesh is not protected by a layer of skin or fat and tends to dry out. For this reason, it is often cooked in liquid or barded or brushed with fat before it is cooked. It takes between 1 and 1½ hours to cook, and is best when cooked at a moderate temperature, usually around 325°F (160°C).

Roasted or grilled rabbit should be basted as it cooks.

Nutritional Information

	roasted
protein	29 g
fat	8 g
cholesterol	821 mg
calories	197
	per 100 g

Rabbit is rich in protein, B-complex vitamins, calcium, and potassium. It is also a good source of iron and phosphorus.

Storing

Freshly killed hares and rabbits can be refrigerated for up to 1 week. Whether fresh or cooked, they can be frozen, but they will be somewhat less flavorful as a result.

Ground Meat

G round meat comes from various parts of the animal (shoulder, loin, haunch, brisket). Rather than buying prepackaged ground meat, which can be less than fresh, you can ask your butcher to grind it fresh or you can grind it yourself in a meat grinder or food processor.

Buying

In most countries, the fat content of ground meat sold in stores is regulated. In the United States, for example, "extra-lean" ground beef can contain no more than 5% fat, "lean" ground beef no more than 10%, and so on. The greater the number of visible white pieces, the fattier the meat.

The color of ground meat can be an indication of its freshness, because it tends to turn brown with age. In some countries, it is illegal to add food dyes and other additives to fresh meat. It is normal for the meat at the center of a package to be darker than the meat on the surface, because the pigment in meat changes color in the absence of oxygen.

Preparing

Good ground meat should be very fresh and should not contain any cartilage, bones, or nerves.

Fat affects the taste of ground meat, and some people claim that lean ground meat has less flavor than fattier meat. Regular ground beef is cheaper than lean ground beef, but more of its weight is lost when the fat melts as it cooks.

The best way to control the quality, freshness, and fat content of ground meat is to grind it yourself.

Cooking

Ground meat should always be cooked thoroughly – that is, until it is no longer pink in the center and the juice it secretes is clear.

Serving Ideas

Ground meat can be cooked in a variety of ways, in both simple and elaborate dishes. A staple food in numerous countries, it is served in countless ways. The most common dishes made with ground meat include the American hamburger, Greek moussaka, meat loaf, and bolognese sauce for pasta.

Hamburgers on the Grill

SERVES 4

1½ lb. (750 g) lean ground beef	Lettuce leaves
Salt and ground pepper	Dried oregano
8 hamburger buns	Mustard
2 tomatoes	Relish
2 onions	Ketchup

1. Shape the ground beef into flat patties that are the same diameter as the hamburger buns; then sprinkle them with salt and pepper. Refrigerate them until ready to cook.

2. Slice the tomatoes and cut the onions into thin rounds; then arrange them on a serving plate.

3. Rinse and spin-dry the lettuce leaves; then put them in a bowl.

4. Cook the hamburger patties on a grill, seasoning them with dried oregano.

5. Flip the burgers when they are half done. (The degree of doneness is a matter of personal taste.) Start toasting the hamburger buns.

6. When the patties are ready, invite your guests to assemble their own hamburgers, with their favorite garnish and condiments.

Potato chips are the perfect accompaniment for hamburgers.

Nutritional Information

The nutritional value of ground meat is largely dependent on its fat content; the more fat it contains, the greater the number of calories.

Storing

Ground meat is very perishable because it is an ideal medium for the development of bacteria. It should be kept in the refrigerator for no longer than 1 or 2 days, and frozen for no longer than 2 or 3 months. Ensure that it is well wrapped.

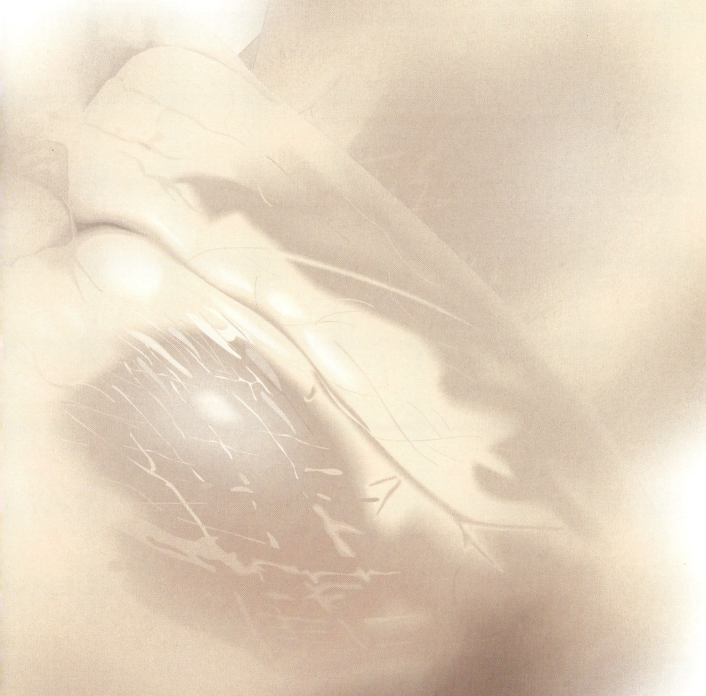

Variety
Meats

Introduction

Variety meats, also called "offal," consist of the edible nonmuscular parts of slaughter animals. Variety meats are generally broken down into organ meats (red offal, which includes heart, tongue, lungs or "lights," spleen, and kidneys) and white offal (brains, teats, marrow, testicles or "mountain oysters," feet, thymus or "sweetbreads," head, and tripe). Although certain variety meats are more highly appreciated (kidneys, veal liver and sweetbreads, brains, tongue, lamb testicles or "fries," etc.) and are thus more costly, most offal is little appreciated and is relatively inexpensive.

Pork provides the greatest variety of common variety meats. The main types of beef offal are tongue, liver, tripe, feet, and tail (oxtail). Sheep and lamb offal consist of brains, kidneys, fries, and feet. Veal offal (brains, marrow, kidneys, liver, and sweetbreads) is particularly prized, given its delicate flavor. Lungs and spleen are used mainly as animal feed and historically have been eaten in times of famine.

Buying

Always make sure that variety meats are very fresh, as they are much more perishable than other meats. They should have the characteristic offal color and should not be swimming in liquid. Buy about 5 ounces of raw offal for each 3½ ounces of cooked meat required.

Serving Ideas

Certain variety meats, such as heart and tongue, have to be cooked for a long time in moist heat (braised or poached) until they are tender. Others, including liver, kidneys, and brains, should be cooked quickly in dry heat. Marrow, particularly beef marrow, can be poached alone or in the bone. It can also be melted like butter and used to cook meats and vegetables.

Nutritional Information

Most variety meats are rich in iron and, especially in the case of kidneys and liver, vitamin A and folic acid. They also contain the same nutrients as other meats. Some health specialists thus recommend that we eat offal more frequently. The cholesterol content of variety meats such as brains, liver, and kidneys, however, is much higher than that of other meats.

Because the liver and kidneys filter undesirable substances found in the live animal's body, they can contain traces of heavy metals, medicines, and pesticides. Given government control of meat products and the fact that most people consume only moderate quantities of variety meats, the risk is probably negligible.

Variety meats such as brains, heart, liver, sweetbreads, and kidneys are rich in purines, precursors of uric acid. People who suffer from gout have trouble metabolizing uric acid and should thus limit their consumption of these foods.

Storing

Variety meats are highly perishable and can be kept for only a day or two, in the refrigerator. Prepare them as soon as possible, that is, within 24 hours of purchase. Although they can be frozen for 3 to 4 months, freezing alters the flavor, texture, and appearance of most types of offal.

ox (beef) heart

Heart

The heart is a muscle that is classified as a type of red offal. Eating the heart of an animal has often been considered to be a very symbolic gesture; in primitive societies, it was thought to bolster courage. But heart has very little importance in contemporary cuisine.

Although heart is quite a stringy meat, it can be excellent. The hearts of calves, lambs, and chickens are the most sought after, because they are small and tender. Pig's heart is moderately tender, while ox (beef) heart is the largest, firmest, and strongest-tasting.

Buying

Choose a plump heart that appears to be fresh and is reddish brown (lamb and beef), bright red (pig and chicken), or light red (calf). Avoid heart that has begun to turn gray. Buy 4½ ounces of raw heart for each 3-ounce portion of cooked heart required.

Preparing

Remove the fat around the heart, as well as the membranes and veins; then wash it. You may also want to tenderize the heart (especially beef heart) by soaking it for at least 1 hour, refrigerated, in a mixture of cold water and vinegar (1 tablespoon per quart). Rinse the heart thoroughly, then pat it dry. Leave the heart whole, slice it, or cut it into pieces.

Nutritional Information

Heart is rich in protein, iron, zinc, copper, and B-complex vitamins, especially niacin and vitamin B_{12}. It is also a good source of phosphorus and potassium. Heart contains more cholesterol than fresh meat but less than other types of variety meat like liver, kidney, and brain.

Serving Ideas

Heart is often cooked in stews and casseroles. Peruvians are particularly fond of *anticuchos,* grilled marinated ox hearts often cooked by street vendors.

Cooking

Heart can be sautéed, grilled, roasted, braised, or simmered. It becomes tough and dry when overcooked.

Pig and ox hearts, which are the least tender, are particularly flavorful when braised or simmered. Braising a whole ox heart takes about 3 to 4 hours; be sure to add liquid when necessary. The hearts of younger animals will cook in 2 to 3 hours. Sliced heart should be sautéed for 5 to 7 minutes. Heart should still be slightly pink when served.

Storing

Heart can be refrigerated for 1 or 2 days and frozen for 3 to 4 months.

Variety Meats

551

	simmered ox heart	*braised lamb heart*	*braised pig heart*	*braised calf heart*	*simmered chicken heart*
protein	29 g	25 g	24 g	29 g	26 g
fat	6 g	8 g	5 g	7 g	8 g
cholesterol	193 mg	249 mg	221 mg	176 mg	242 mg
calories	175	185	148	186	185

per 100 g

Liver

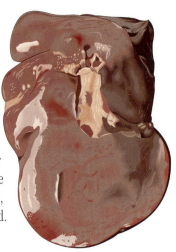

Liver is a type of edible red offal that comes from domesticated animals, poultry, and game, as well as from certain fish (cod, monkfish, skate). Liver from young animals is more tender and flavorful, and calf's (baby beef) liver is the most sought after. The livers of lambs, heifers, rabbits, and poultry are also renowned for their tenderness and their delicate flavor. Liver from oxen (beef), sheep, and pigs has a stronger flavor and becomes relatively pasty when cooked.

Buying

The color of liver ranges from pinkish brown to reddish brown, depending on the species and age of the animal. Look for shiny liver with a pleasant smell; it should not be soaking in a large amount of liquid. Buy approximately 6 ounces of raw liver for each 4-ounce portion of cooked liver required.

Nutritional Information

	braised calf's liver
protein	22 g
fat	7 g
cholesterol	561 mg
calories	165
	per 100 g

Many nutritionists recommend that liver be eaten on a regular basis because it is rich in protein as well as in various vitamins and minerals, including vitamin A, vitamin B_{12}, folic acid, vitamin C, phosphorus, zinc, and copper. Since it is also an excellent source of iron, it is often prescribed to prevent anemia.

Cod-liver oil is rich in vitamin D, which can prevent rickets.

It is important to note, however, that the liver filters impurities from the blood of the animal and can thus contain traces of heavy metals, medicines, or pesticides to which the animal has been exposed. That being said, some countries have implemented strict controls designed to ensure that liver is safe for human consumption. Furthermore, most people eat such small quantities of variety meats that there is very little cause for concern.

Preparing

Remove the thin membrane covering the liver to prevent the flesh from becoming misshapen when cooked, as well as any remaining veins.

Soak beef and pork liver in milk for 1 or 2 hours, refrigerated, to reduce the intensity of its flavor; then dry it thoroughly. Cut the liver into slices of equal size to ensure that it cooks evenly.

Serving Ideas

Liver is often sautéed, grilled, fried, or marinated; it is usually served with mushrooms, wine, cream, or onions. Pork liver is used mainly to make prepared meats like pâtés and terrines. Cod livers are often smoked.

Calf's Liver with Bacon

Salt and ground pepper
4 slices calf's liver, each
   weighing ¼ lb. (125 g)
Flour
2 tbsp. butter
2 tbsp. sunflower oil

4 slices bacon
½ cup (125 ml)
   chicken stock
½ lemon
1 tsp. fresh parsley

1. Preheat the oven to 200°F (100°C).

2. Salt and pepper the liver slices, then lightly flour them.

3. Heat 1 tbsp. butter and the sunflower oil over medium heat in a large frying pan. Cook the liver quickly on both sides, ensuring that it remains slightly pink in the center (5 to 8 minutes). Put it on a serving plate and keep it warm.

4. Brown the slices of bacon in the frying pan until they become slightly crispy; then set them aside with the liver.

5. Remove almost all of the bacon fat from the frying pan. Pour in the chicken stock and reduce it by half over high heat. Remove the pan from the heat, and add the rest of the butter and a few drops of lemon juice. Pour this mixture over the liver, and garnish the dish with the chopped parsley.

Serve with mashed potatoes.

Cooking

Liver should not be eaten rare, but it will become tough if overcooked. It is most flavorful when slightly pink in the center. Tender liver is usually grilled or sautéed (5 to 8 minutes).

Cook liver in as little fat as possible to avoid increasing its fat content. Liver that is somewhat tough should be cooked slowly in a small amount of liquid.

Storing

Since liver is extremely perishable, it should be cooked as soon as possible. It can be refrigerated for 1 or 2 days and frozen for 3 to 4 months.

Tongue

beef tongue

The tongue is a fleshy muscular organ that can be pinkish or grayish in color. It is covered with a rough, thick mucous membrane that can be easily removed once the tongue is cooked. Beef (ox) tongue, which is the thickest and largest variety, can weigh almost 5 pounds and is covered with numerous large taste buds, most of which are on the top surface. Calf's tongue is the most tender and flavorful variety, and also requires the least amount of cooking. Pork (pig's) tongue feels relatively soft.

Bird tongues are also edible, as are those of certain fish, such as cod. The skin on the tongues of land animals cannot be eaten.

Preparing

Brush the tongue under cold running water; then soak it in cold water for at least 4 hours, or preferably for 12 hours (or overnight), changing the water two or three times.

Cooking

Tongue is often poached, then braised. Beef tongue is poached for 2 hours, then braised for 4 hours; calves', lambs', and pigs' tongues are poached for 45 minutes, then braised for 2 hours or until tender. Remove the skin from cooked tongue after it has cooled down.

Buying

Choose tongue that is free of spots. Buy 6 to 7 ounces of raw whole tongue for each 4-ounce portion of cooked tongue required.

Serving Ideas

Tongue can also be breaded and fried (once it is cooked), smoked, or marinated. Sometimes eaten cold, it is delicious when served with mustard, a vinaigrette, or in brine. It can be used to make salads and sandwiches.

Storing

Tongue can be refrigerated for 1 or 2 days, but it should be cooked as soon as possible because it deteriorates rapidly, especially if left at room temperature for a long period of time in the liquid in which it was cooked. Tongue can be frozen for 3 to 4 months.

Nutritional Information

	simmered beef tongue	*braised pork tongue*	*braised calf's tongue*
protein	22 g	24 g	26 g
fat	21 g	19 g	10 g
cholesterol	107 mg	146 mg	238 mg
calories	283	271	202
			per 100 g

Tongue is rich in vitamin B$_{12}$ and in zinc. Pork and beef tongue are rich in iron.

Sweetbread

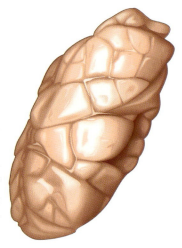

Sweetbreads is the name for the thymus gland of the calf and the lamb, a whitish gland found only in young animals because it atrophies with age. Located at the entrance to the chest, below the windpipe, the thymus gland consists of two parts – a central lobe known as the "heart sweetbread" or "kernel" and two lateral lobes known as the "throat sweetbread." Together, these lobes form a whole sweetbread; they have a very delicate flavor and are very tender. Calf's sweetbreads are the most sought-after variety.

Buying

Choose plump, shiny sweetbreads that have a pleasant odor and are a creamy white pinkish color.

Nutritional Information

protein	32 g
fat	4 g
cholesterol	469 mg
calories	174
	per 100 g

Braised sweetbreads are rich in protein, niacin, vitamin C, phosphorus, and zinc. Sweetbreads are one of the few foods from animal sources that contain vitamin C.

Since sweetbreads are low in fat, they are easy to digest (as long as they are cooked in small amount of fat).

Preparing

Wash the sweetbreads and soak them for 2 to 3 hours in lightly salted water, changing the water from time to time. Blanch them before they are cooked to make them firmer and easier to handle (2 to 3 minutes for lamb's sweetbreads and 7 to 10 minutes for calf's sweetbreads). Once they cool down, remove the membrane, the veins as well as the surrounding fat, and then dry the sweetbreads thoroughly.

Cooking

Sweetbreads can be grilled (6 to 8 minutes), sautéed (3 to 5 minutes), braised (30 to 40 minutes), poached (20 to 30 minutes), or fried (3 to 4 minutes). They are cooked in vol-au-vents, on brochettes, in puff pastry, and au gratin. They are also added to stuffings. Avoid overcooking them because they tend to dry out.

Storing

Since sweetbreads are very perishable, they should be cooked as soon as possible after they are purchased. They can be refrigerated for 1 or 2 days. Blanched sweetbreads can be frozen.

Brains

calf brains

The brains of certain slaughter animals are commonly cooked and eaten. The most delicate and sought after are those of sheep and lambs, which are very pale. The taste of calf brains, which are more highly colored, is comparable. Cow brains are firmer and red veined, and pork brains are seldom eaten.

Buying

Choose brains that are grayish pink, plump, pleasant smelling, and free of spots and blood clots. Buy about 4 ounces of fresh brains per serving.

Preparing

Soak the brains for 30 minutes in cold salted water (¼ teaspoon of salt per cup of water), changing the water several times. Carefully remove the thin outer membrane, and blanch the brains for 15 to 18 minutes in salted water (½ teaspoon of salt per quart of water) to which you have added a tablespoon of vinegar or lemon juice. Cool the brains in cold water and dry them well.

Nutritional Information

	braised veal brains	braised lamb brains
protein	12 g	13 g
fat	10 g	10 g
cholesterol	3,100 mg	2,040 mg
calories	136	145
		per 100 g

Brains are rich in vitamin B_{12} and phosphorus. Their cholesterol content is very high; as they are not eaten on a frequent basis, however, they do not pose a problem for most healthy people.

Serving Ideas

Brains are often cooked whole in stock (about 10 minutes for sheep and lamb brains and 15 minutes for calf brains), and are then sliced and sautéed (3 to 4 minutes) or fried (2 to 3 minutes).

The tenderest brains are served as is or in salads; the remainder are used in casseroles, croquettes, sauces, stuffings, and sometimes soups.

Storing

Brains are highly perishable; they can be kept for a day or two in the refrigerator. If not used immediately, they should be blanched in salted water with a bit of vinegar or lemon juice.

Kidney

calf kidneys

Kidney is a type of red offal that comes from various domesticated animals. Pork and sheep kidneys are comprised of a single lobe, while those of the calf and the ox (beef) have several. The kidneys of young animals like calves, heifers, and lambs are tender and flavorful. Pork, sheep, and beef kidneys have a strong, bitter taste and are relatively tough. Beef and lamb kidneys are dark brown, calves' kidneys are a lighter shade of brown, and pork kidneys are a light shade of reddish brown.

Nutritional Information

	braised lamb kidneys	simmered beef kidneys	braised pork kidneys	braised calf kidneys
protein	24 g	26 g	25 g	26 g
fat	4 g	3 g	5 g	6 g
cholesterol	565 mg	387 mg	480 mg	791 mg
calories	137	144	151	163
				per 100 g

Kidneys are rich in protein, vitamin A (beef kidneys), vitamin B (including vitamin B_{12}, riboflavin, niacin, and, in the case of lamb and beef kidneys, folic acid), iron, phosphorus, and zinc. Although they contain relatively little fat, they are high in cholesterol.

Buying

Choose plump, firm, shiny kidneys of the appropriate color; they should not smell of ammonia.

Preparing

Remove the thin membrane surrounding the kidneys, then cut them in two and remove the internal fat and blood vessels. To eliminate the odor of urine that can emanate from beef, sheep, or pork kidneys, boil them briefly and strain them before they are cooked; or alternatively, soak them for 1 or 2 hours, refrigerated, in salted water (1 tablespoon of salt per quart of water), then rinse them under cold water and dry them.

Cooking

The tenderest kidneys can be grilled, sautéed, or roasted; other kinds should be braised. Cook kidneys only until they are no longer red in the center; they will become rubbery if overcooked.

Serving Ideas

Kidneys are particularly good with tomatoes, mushrooms, mustard, lemon juice, cream, red wine, Madeira, and sherry.

Storing

Since kidneys are extremely perishable, they should not be refrigerated for longer than 1 day. They can be frozen but must be used as soon as they are defrosted.

Tripe

paunch

Tripe is a food made from the stomachs of cud-chewing animals (beef, mutton, and veal prepared in various ways), but the word "tripe" also refers to the intestines of butchered animals.

The stomachs of cud-chewing animals (ruminants) consist of four interconnected compartments: the paunch, the reticulum, the rumen, and the psalterium.

Buying

Tripe is usually blanched before it is sold. Choose white or cream-colored tripe (the color depends on the sex of the animal) that has a pleasant odor.

Nutritional Information

	raw beef tripe
protein	15 g
fat	4 g
cholesterol	95 mg
calories	98
	per 100 g

Tripe is rich in vitamin B_{12} and in zinc.

Storing

Tripe can be refrigerated for 1 or 2 days and frozen for 3 to 4 months.

Preparing

Before cooking tripe, soak it for about 10 minutes in cold water, then rinse it, brush it to remove the fat, and slice it.

Serving Ideas

Often served with potatoes, tripe is cooked with a broad range of ingredients, including ox, calf's, or pig's feet as well as lard, vegetables, wine, cream, and a variety of seasonings. The most famous tripe dish is *tripes à la mode de Caen,* which originated in the French city for which it was named.

Gras-double (scalded pieces of beef paunch cooked in water) is often marinated before being grilled or fried; it is also braised, served in stews, and cooked au gratin. It can be braised for as long 20 hours, which makes it very tender.

Cooking

Tripe can be poached for 1 or 2 hours, then sautéed or fried for about 10 minutes. It can also be blanched for about 15 minutes, then braised for 3 to 4 hours; it can be tough if not thoroughly cooked.

Delicatessen

Introduction

Prepared meats were once made mainly from pork meat or offal, but the flesh and internal organs of a variety of animals are now used to make products such as cold cuts, sausages, and pâtés. These products are also referred to as deli meats because many of them were originally available only in imported food stores known as delicatessens (derived from the German word *Delikatessen,* meaning "delicacies").

Most prepared meats were originally designed as a means of using animal parts that would otherwise go to waste, especially the least desirable parts such as the intestines, the head, the throat, the esophagus, and the blood. Such meats have been prepared in accordance with specific standards since Roman times; in fact, the Roman *porcella* law contained stipulations regarding the rearing and slaughtering of pigs as well as the preparation of pork.

For many centuries, pork was the main type of meat consumed by rural populations. In countries where long, severe winters limited the amount of pasture, pigs were killed at the end of autumn, and the meats prepared with this pork (chitterlings (or chitlins), bacon, blood sausage, galantine, foie gras, drippings, ham, pâtés, sausages, potted meat, headcheese, terrines, meat pies, etc.) constituted a major portion the food eaten during the winter months. Regarded for centuries as rather humble foods, prepared meats began to gain more respect at the end of the 19th century, thanks to the efforts of the famous Parisian butcher Louis-Franois Drone, who was known as the "Carème de la charcuterie." He was partly responsible for the inclusion of prepared meats on gala menus.

Prepared meats are made in wide variety of ways. In Europe, numerous regions have developed their own special recipes. Classifying prepared meats is no easy task, given the broad range of raw materials and methods of preparation. The meat is generally preserved in some way; it is either raw or cooked, and may be salted, smoked, or dried. Certain products can be consumed "as is" (foie gras, large cured sausages, cooked ham, potted meat, terrines), while others have to be cooked (fresh and smoked sausages, bacon).

Serving Ideas

 Prepared meats are very popular because they often require no further preparation; they are often eaten on bread or in sandwiches.

Storing

 Prepared meats should be refrigerated; wrap them well to ensure that they do not dry out or absorb food odors. They can be stored in the meat compartment of the refrigerator for 3 or 4 days.

To enhance the flavor of prepared meats, remove them from the refrigerator about 15 minutes before they are to be served.

Nutritional Information

Prepared meats are less nutritious than the meats from which they are made. They are also higher in fat, cholesterol, calories, and sodium, and they often contain additives. They should thus be consumed in moderation.

Salted pork (or boar or bear meat) that is often smoked and dried, ham was once reserved for royalty or for special occasions. It was very highly regarded during the Roman Empire, but was served only in the imperial dining room. During the Middle Ages, when pork was a very common food, the consumption of ham became associated with Holy Week, a custom that has persisted to this day.

Genuine ham comes from the leg of the animal. Similar products are prepared with pork shoulder (cottage roll, smoked picnic ham. etc.), but they are less tender and flavorful. Though prepared in the same way as ham, these products cannot be labeled "ham." Ham shank comes from the front or rear knees of the animal, just below the area from which ham is cut.

Ham is sold ready to serve (cooked or cured) or fresh.

Ready-to-serve cooked hams are steeped in brine or, more commonly, injected with brine, then steamed, smoked or cooked in water; ham must be heated until its internal temperature reaches at least 158°F (70°C), in order to destroy any trichinae or pathogenic bacteria that may be present. It is sometimes cured further in specially designed smokehouses. Cooked hams can be prepared and seasoned in various ways to make them even more tender and flavorful. Some ready-to-serve cooked hams are canned.

Fresh ham is precooked until its internal temperature reaches at least 140°F (60°C) in order to destroy any trichinae that may be present, but it must be cooked further before it can be eaten.

Cured hams (or dried hams) are salted, usually by rubbing salt into the meat repeatedly, then dried. The most famous varieties of cured ham include Bayonne, Savoy, Westphalian, Ardennes, Corsican and Parma ham (cured Italian prosciutto). Products referred to as "Corsican," "Parma" or "Westphalian" ham have to meet certain standards to ensure that their quality is consistent.

Modern industrial methods of salting and smoking ham make it possible to turn out a finished product is as little as 3 to 4 days. For example, rather than salting pork by steeping it in brine for several weeks and then smoking it naturally, manufacturers inject it with a mixture containing water, sugar (dextrose, sucrose, maple syrup, etc.), salt, sodium phosphate, spices, sodium erythrobate and sodium nitrate. The salt acts as a preservative and enhances the flavor of the meat; the sugar makes it taste sweeter and allows the surfaces of the meat to be caramelized. The phosphate promotes the absorption and retention of the brine, thus making the ham more tender. The sodium nitrate gives the ham the pinkish color that is characteristic of salted meats, inhibits the growth of bacteria such as *Clostridium botulinum* (which causes botulism) and enhances the flavor of the meat. However, the use of sodium nitrate is somewhat controversial, because under certain conditions it can be transformed into nitrosamines, which may be carcinogenic. The erythrobate stabilizes the color of the product. The ham is then cooked and smoked either naturally or by means of liquid smoke that is vaporized in the smokehouse. Lastly, it is chilled and refrigerated.

Preparing

If you wish, you can desalt ham by soaking it. It can be soaked overnight, but smaller or less salty hams need only be soaked for several hours.

Nutritional Information

	lean oven-roasted ham
protein	25 g
fat	6 g
cholesterol	55 mg
calories	157
	per 100 g

Since ham is usually quite salty (between 1,000 and 1,500 milligrams of sodium per 100 grams), it is best to consume only moderate amounts, especially if you have been advised to restrict the amount of sodium in your diet. Cured (or dried) ham is higher in fat and calories than precooked ham (which is known as *jambon blanc* in France). Eating only lean cuts of ham can help reduce your consumption of fat and calories.

Storing

Ham can be refrigerated for about 1 week. It can also be frozen for 1 to 2 months, but freezing can diminish its flavor and make it more difficult to slice.

Serving Ideas

Ham can be cooked simply or in more elaborate ways. Two of the classic recipes are braised ham with pineapple and ham cooked in pastry. Ham can be eaten either hot or cold. It can be served as a main course or added to a variety of other foods (quiches, omelets, croquettes, "au gratin" dishes, pâtés, mixed salads, canapés, terrines, aspics, mousses, stuffing, toasted cheese sandwiches, etc.). Ham bones can be used to make soup.

Cooking

Ham can be roasted, grilled, braised or boiled. If the ham has a rind, make a few incisions in it. When roasting ham, cook it uncovered on a rotating grill in an oven preheated to 325°F (160°C). A precooked ham can be removed from the oven when its internal temperature reaches 131°F (55°C), but a fresh ham has to be cooked until its internal temperature is about 153°F (67°C) (167°F or 75°C for a picnic ham). The bone can be easily removed from the flesh. Let the ham sit for about 10 minutes before it is served to allow the juices to spread throughout the meat.

UNCOOKED HAM ROASTING TIME		
Cut	Weight (lb.)	Roasting time (325°F)
Bone-in		
Whole	8 to 10	3 h 30
Butt End, Shank	5 to 8	3 h 15 - 3 h 30
Boneless		
Whole	10 to 12	3 h 30 - 4 h
Half	5 to 8	2 h 30 - 3 h 30
Shoulder	4 to 6	2 h 30 - 3 h
	6 to 8	3 h - 4 h
	8 to 10	4 h - 4 h 30

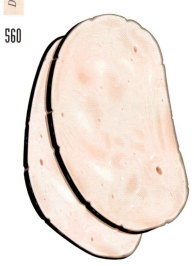

"Forêt Noire" ham

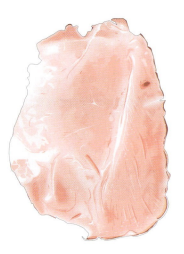

smoked ham

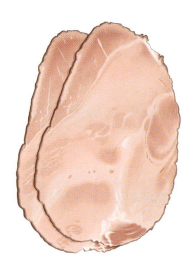

"jambon de Paris"

prosciutto

Bacon

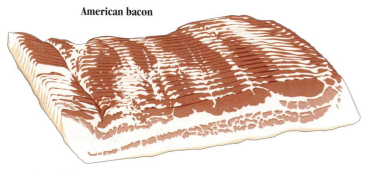

American bacon

B acon is pork that has been cured and, most often, smoked. Generally sold thinly sliced, it is usually produced from pork bellies (sliced bacon) or loins (back bacon). The word "bacon" comes from an Old French word, *bakko,* which means "ham." Eggs and fried bacon is a traditional breakfast in North America.

Serving Ideas

Bacon goes well with eggs: it is frequently included in quiches and omelets. It is often served with pancakes and adds flavor to salads and salad dressings.

"Bacon bits" are imitation bacon pieces made from hydrolyzed protein soya. Various additives give the product color and taste. The bits are used to season soups, salads, salad dressings, dips, and various prepared foods.

Cooking

Bacon is good fried or sautéed. Cook it at low heat for about 10 minutes, periodically draining the grease, as high heat speeds up the formation of nitrosamines, chemical compounds generated by the combination of fat and heat. Before serving it, pat the cooked bacon with paper towels to absorb any excess grease.

Storing

Vacuum-packed bacon can be kept in the refrigerator until the "Sell by" date. Once the package is opened, the bacon can be kept for about a week in the refrigerator. It can be frozen for 1 or 2 months, with a slight loss in flavor.

Nutritional Information

protein	4 g
fat	6 g
cholesterol	10 mg
calories	72
2 cooked slices (1 ounce)	

Bacon is high in sodium (approximately 1,600 mg per ¼ pound when cooked). It also contains an additive called sodium nitrate, which gives cured meats flavor and enhances their pinkish color while inhibiting the development of bacteria such as *Clostridium botulinum,* which can cause severe food poisoning. The use of the additive is controversial, however, as it can produce nitrosamines, substances that are reportedly carcinogenic.

Delicatessen

561

pancetta

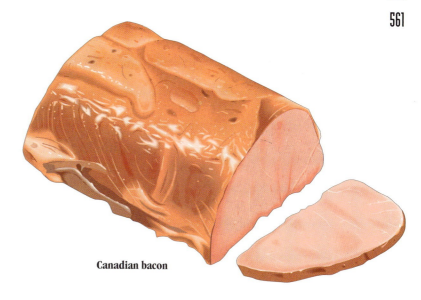

Canadian bacon

Sausage

Usually prepared by butchers, sausages consist of a piece of animal intestine stuffed with seasoned chopped meat. The French distinguish between small sausages *(saucisses),* which are usually fresh, and large sausages *(saucissons),* which are often precooked or cured. The word "sausage" is derived from these French terms, which are themselves derived from the Latin word *salsus,* meaning "salted."

Although Germany lays claim to the sausage, it now appears that the first sausages were actually created by the Greeks and the Romans, who taught the Germans how to make them. Today, as in the past, preparing sausages is regarded as a good way to use up the least attractive cuts of meat, such as certain kinds of offal (which are rarely put to any other use in North America). This is just one of the reasons that sausages have remained popular for centuries.

There is an almost infinite variety of sausages; over 1,500 different kinds are made in Germany alone. In fact, the names of many sausages are German in origin, especially those that end with the suffix *wurst,* the German word for "sausage." The numerous methods used to make sausages, which vary from one country to another, affect their appearance and composition (and thus their taste and nutritional value).

Although most sausages are still made with the traditional ingredients – lean and fat cuts of pork – they can also be made from beef, veal, lamb, mutton, horse meat, poultry, offal (primarily beef liver, heart, and stomach used to make large cooked sausages), or tofu. Sausages made from mechanically deboned meat may also contain particles of nerves, tendons, blood vessels, or bones. The other ingredients added to sausages include water, fillers (flour, starch, skim-milk powder, etc.), sugars (sucrose, lactose, glucose, etc.), spices, and preservatives (salt, sodium nitrate, sodium erythrobate, etc.). All of the ingredients are chopped coarsely or finely, depending on the desired result, and mixed together to form what is known as the filling or stuffing, which is sometimes smoked. This mixture is inserted into a natural or synthetic casing. Synthetic casings made from collagen (edible) or cellulose (inedible) have almost completely replaced natural casings, which usually consist of a piece of animal (mainly pork or lamb) intestine or the lining of a pig's intestine (a thin, transparent membrane or caul that is veined with fat). Natural casings are now used primarily to make specialty sausages.

There are four main types of sausages: small fresh sausages, small cooked sausages, large dried sausages, and large cooked sausages.

As their name suggests, fresh sausages are either raw (long sausages, Toulouse sausages, merguez, *crépinettes,* chipolatas, breakfast sausages, etc.) or cured *(gendarmes,* frankfurters, Lyon saveloy sausages); the cured varieties are sometimes smoked and dried. Before being eaten, fresh sausages can be grilled, braised, boiled, or fried. Pierce them with a fork before cooking them to allow the fat to escape as it melts. Start cooking them gently, adding a little water if necessary to prevent them from sticking; there is no need to add fat because sausages release more than enough fat when heated. Cured fresh sausages are usually poached, but *gendarmes* can be eaten uncooked because they are thoroughly dried and heavily smoked.

As its name suggests, the frankfurter is a European sausage that originated in Germany. Traditional frankfurters are cold-smoked pork sausages. Today, the best-known frankfurter is the hot dog (or wiener), which was created in the United States at the beginning of the 20th century.

In addition to inferior cuts of meat (beef, pork, chicken, turkey, mutton) and mechanically deboned meat, hot dogs may also contain pork or beef by-products such as skin, fat, liver, stomach, and blood plasma. The other ingredients include water, fillers (often flour, soy proteins, and starch), salt, sweeteners (syrup, sugar, etc.), flavorings, and additives.

Hot dogs are manufactured by means of a highly mechanized process. The meat is mixed, then chopped, cut, or ground. The remaining ingredients are then added, and the entire mixture is reduced to a fine paste, which is subsequently poured into a machine and automatically stuffed into an endless series of linked cellulose casings. The resultant hot dogs are then cooked, usually in a mechanical smoker, where they acquire their characteristic flavor. Once they have been cooked, the hot dogs are chilled and peeled, then vacuum-packed and refrigerated. Although hot dogs have already been cooked, it is best to cook them again before eating them.

Cooked sausages (Strasbourg saveloy sausages, cocktail sausages, Vienna sausages, etc.) are usually steamed before they are sold, but they are sometimes smoked.

Dried sausage is an uncooked product that is salted, fermented (in a heated environment), and dried. It may also be smoked. Fermentation is a natural process during which lactic bacteria transform the sugars added to the sausage into lactic acid; dried sausage is a relatively stable product with a long shelf life because it is acidic, highly salted, and contains very little water. Dried sausages usually contain about 35% water, and semi-dried varieties between 45% and 50%.

The consistency of sausage mixtures ranges from very fine to quite coarse. Sausages stuffed with fine mixtures look relatively homogenous, but those made from coarser mixtures contain visible pieces of meat, fat, and spices. The finer varieties of sausage include some types of salami and pepperoni, while the coarser varieties include the *saucisson de montagne,* the *saucisson de ménage,* and the *rosette.*

Cooked sausage is cooked only once; it is neither dried nor fermented but may be smoked. As in the case of dried sausage, its filling may contain a variety of meats, each of which influences its consistency, taste, and color. Mortadella is often classified as a cooked sausage, as are *saucisson de Paris, saucisson de Lyon,* Cambridge sausage, bologna sausage (baloney), liver sausage, and tongue sausage.

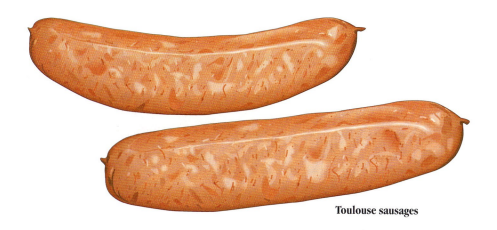

Toulouse sausages

Buying

Buy smooth, evenly colored sausages that do not feel sticky. Dried sausage should be firm, have a pleasant odor, and be covered with a "bloom" (small white spots about the size of the head of a pin). Check the expiration date on vacuum-packed products.

Serving Ideas

Sauces, such as Worcestershire sauce, ketchup, mustard, chutneys, and marinades, go very well with sausages. In fact, the practice of eating sausages with mustard dates back to the Greeks and the Romans. Many larger varieties of sausage are usually served in thin slices, either as hors d'oeuvres or as main-course dishes. They are also served on canapés and in sandwiches.

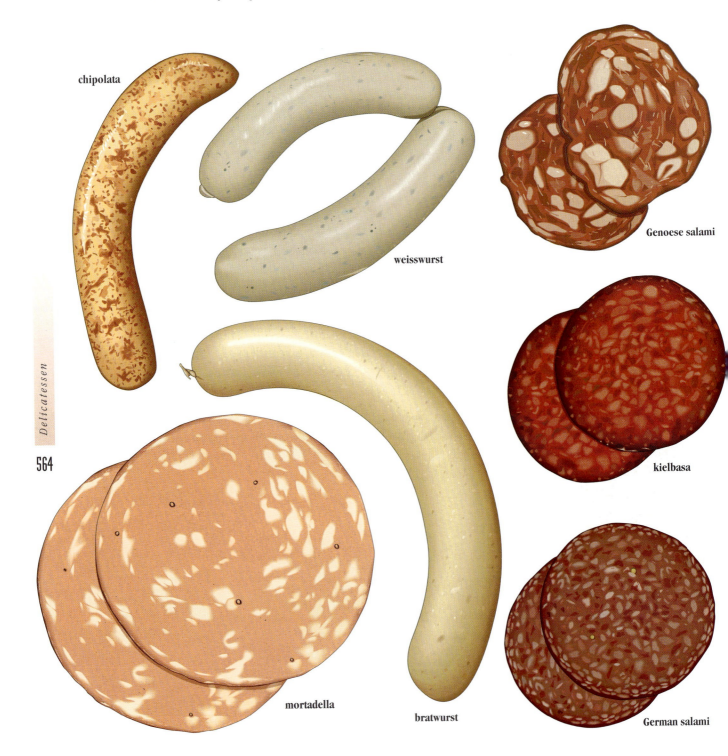

chipolata

weisswurst

Genoese salami

kielbasa

mortadella

bratwurst

German salami

Nutritional Information

	dried pork salami	bologna sausage	smoked sausage (beef and pork)	cooked pork sausage fresh
protein	23 g	15 g	11 g	20 g
fat	34 g	20 g	29 g	31 g
cholesterol	79 mg	59 mg	50 mg	83 mg
calcium	407 mg	247 mg	320 mg	369 mg
sodium	2,260 mg	1,184 mg	1,120 mg	1,294 mg
				per 100 g

The nutritional value of sausages depends on the kind and proportions of ingredients used to make them. Sausage ingredients are generally salty, as as well high in fat and calories; sausages usually contain less protein and more additives than meat. One of the additives commonly found in sausages is sodium nitrate, which prevents the development of bacteria such as *Clostridium botulinum* – a microorganism that can cause botulism, a severe form of food poisoning; sodium nitrate also affects the taste and enhances the characteristic pinkish color of salted foods. However, its use is somewhat controversial, because under certain conditions it can turn into nitrosamine, which may be carcinogenic. As for smoked sausages such as hot dogs, water and fat make up almost three quarters of their total weight.

Storing

Fresh or cooked sausages can be refrigerated for about 3 days and frozen for 2 to 3 months. If they are in sealed packages, they can be frozen "as is"; otherwise, wrap them well before freezing them.

Whole dried sausages can be stored for up to 3 months in a cool, dry place. When they are very ripe, or if they have been partially or completely sliced, store them in the refrigerator and eat them within 3 to 5 days. Cover them and store them well away from foods with strong odors. Sliced cooked sausages can also be refrigerated for 3 to 5 days.

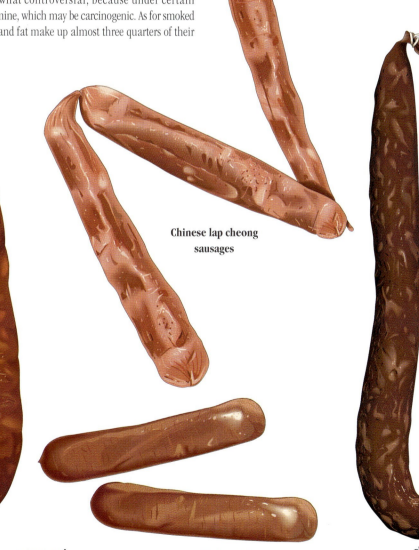

Chinese lap cheong sausages

pepperoni

merguez sausages

chorizo

Andouille

andouillette

A ndouille, a French specialty, is a type of pork or veal sausage made from chitterlings and, in many cases, the animal's head, heart, and breast. The viscera are cut into strips and stuffed into a section of the intestine. The andouille is then tied, dried, cold-smoked, and either steamed or cooked in broth. Each sausage is 10 to 12 inches long. A smaller version, known as "andouillette," is 4 to 6 inches in length. Andouillette is sometimes breaded or coated in meat jelly or lard.

Nutritional Information

protein	10 g
fat	29 g
cholesterol	143 mg
calories	303
	per 100 g

Simmered andouille is high in fat and calories.

Storing

 Andouille and andouillette can be kept for 3 to 4 days in the refrigerator.

Serving Ideas

 Andouille is served cold, normally thinly sliced, as an appetizer. Andouillette should be fried or pan-roasted and is traditionally served with mustard; it goes well with legumes (red kidney beans or lentils), sauerkraut, red cabbage, and French fries.

Rillettes

C ooked gently in lard until they develop a smooth consistency, rillettes, or potted meat, are then potted, chilled, and covered with a layer of fat (lard, goose fat, etc.). Usually made with pork or goose, rillettes can also be made with rabbit, poultry, duck, veal, or fish. Various parts of these animals are used, including the neck, breast, belly, and thighs.

Nutritional Information

	(beef, chicken, turkey)
protein	16 g
fat	19 g
calories	280
	per 100 g

Serving Ideas

Rillettes are always eaten cold, usually on canapés, in sandwiches, or with toast.

Storing

Unopened rillettes can be refrigerated for several weeks. However, they should be eaten within a few days once opened.

Foie gras

goose foie gras

Foie gras is duck or goose liver that has been hypertrophied (enlarged) by force-feeding the birds; prepared and cooked with great care, it is regarded as a delicacy by food connoisseurs. The use of the term "foie gras" is regulated in several countries, including France, in order to avoid confusion and misleading claims. At least 20% of any product labeled "foie gras" should consist of fattened goose or duck liver. If the product contains the livers or flesh of other animals, it should be referred to as foie-gras "pâté," "terrine," or "galantine."

The force-feeding of geese and ducks is an ancient practice that dates back to the time of the Egyptians; they noticed that wild geese would prepare for migrations by eating vast amounts of food and storing the excess energy in the form of fat in their livers. It has also been determined that while the Greeks force-fed geese with a mixture of crushed wheat and water, the Romans used figs. Geese and ducks are now usually force-fed a gruel-like mixture of corn, lard, beans, and salt. Fattened goose livers generally weigh between 28 and 36 ounces, but fattened duck livers rarely weigh more than 12 to 16 ounces. Those opposed to the force-feeding of animals contend that the practice is inhumane. Foie gras is produced in various ways: in France, force-feeding birds by means of tubes is an increasingly popular method; an alternative method is to induce bulimia in geese by destroying their ability to determine whether or not they are hungry, which makes it easier to force-feed and fatten them.

Serving Ideas

Foie gras is sold raw and ready to eat. It should be refrigerated the day before it is eaten; open the container 1 hour before it is to be served, returning it to the refrigerator. Run the blade of a knife under hot water, then cut the foie gras into slices. It can be eaten with a fork or on toasted bread.

Cooking

Slice the uncooked foie gras and sauté it in a small amount of butter for no more than 30 seconds; afterwards, deglaze the pan with cognac or Madeira wine.

Nutritional Information

	foie-gras pâté
protein	11 g
fat	44 g
calories	462
	per 100 g

The nutritional value of foie gras and related products varies according to the other ingredients that are added, which can include the unfattened livers of animals such as pigs, calves and turkeys, as well as other meat, fat, seasonings, truffles, alcohol, sugar, egg whites, and various additives. Since most of these ingredients are high in fat and calories, foie gras should be eaten in moderation.

Storing

Since foie gras is perishable, it can be kept, refrigerated, for no longer than 3 or 4 days once the package has been opened. Reseal the package carefully to prevent the foie gras from drying out or absorbing food odors.

Blood sausage

Blood sausage consists mainly of pig's blood and fat that is cooked and seasoned, then stuffed into a section of intestine. It may also contain ox, calf's, or sheep's blood. Thought to be one of the first prepared meats consumed by humans, it is mentioned in texts dating back over 5,000 years. Blood sausages are made in an infinite variety of ways; it has been suggested that in France there are as many different kinds of blood sausages as there are butchers, because the proportions of blood and fat can be varied and a broad range of optional ingredients can be added (onions, spinach, raisins, apples, prunes, chestnuts, milk, cream, brandy, semolina, crustless bread, oats, spices, herbs). This mixture is inserted into a casing (usually the intestine of the animal), then poached. There is a clear distinction between blood sausage and white-meat sausage, a much more recent variety. During the Middle Ages, a Parisian butcher expanded on the Christmas custom of eating milk-based gruel after midnight Mass by adding eggs, white meat, pork fat, and seasoning to the milk, then stuffing this mixture into a piece of animal intestine; and *voilà* – white-meat sausage! In fact, this kind of sausage is still referred to as Parisian sausage and is most widely available at Christmastime.

Nutritional Information

protein	15 g
fat	35 g
cholesterol	120 mg
calories	378
	per 100 g

Blood sausage is rich in iron and vitamin B_{12}, and contains a relatively large amount of sodium (approximately 700 milligrams per 100 grams). It may also contain additives, which are normally included on the list of ingredients.

Serving Ideas

 Blood sausage is usually cut into slices, then fried, poached, or grilled for about 10 minutes. It is often served with apples or puréed potatoes. White-meat sausage is usually fried over low heat, poached, baked, or cooked in aluminum foil.

Storing

 Blood sausage can be refrigerated for 3 or 4 days. Since it deteriorates quickly, it should be eaten as soon as possible.

Poultry

Introduction

The term "poultry" is derived from the Latin word *pulla,* meaning "young female animal," and refers to all domestic fowl (duck, turkey, hen, chicken, pigeon, cockerel, goose, guinea fowl). In cooking, the term generally refers to the flesh of the chicken or hen; recipes for other kinds of poultry usually specify the particular variety of fowl.

Most of these birds have been raised in captivity for centuries, and they are sometimes bred for very specific purposes: the goose for its liver, which is made into foie grass, the duck for its liver and for cutlets, the hen for its eggs, and other poultry for their flesh. Chicken is the most popular kind of poultry because it can be produced very cheaply, has a pleasant taste, and can be prepared in numerous ways. Since the introduction of industrial poultry farms, all of these birds have been available year-round.

It is important to consider the risk of salmonella food poisoning when preparing poultry. A bacterium, salmonella is one of several microbes that make a significant number of people sick on a yearly basis. In Canada, for example, approximately 8,500 cases of salmonella poisoning (salmonellosis) were reported annually between 1970 and 1991, and this figure does not include cases that went unreported or were not diagnosed.

The symptoms of salmonellosis (abdominal pain, fever, diarrhea, vomiting, shivering, headaches) usually appear between 12 and 24 hours after the ingestion of contaminated food and last for about 2 or 3 days. The illness can be more serious when it affects particularly vulnerable people, such as children or seniors.

Salmonella is frequently found in the intestines of poultry and can spread to the surface of a bird when it is slaughtered. It is also found in meat, fish, eggs, and dairy products. In most cases, salmonella poisoning can be avoided by taking very simple precautions when storing, freezing, handling, and cooking these foods (see *Preparation.*)

Buying

Poultry is divided into various categories in accordance with norms that vary from one country to another. Since poultry is generally graded on the basis of its appearance, these categories have no bearing on the quality of flesh, which is largely dependent on the age of the bird. A substandard bird that is missing a wing or a leg, or has discolored or torn skin, can be just as flavorful as a whole bird, even though it is classified as a less expensive grade of poultry. Such birds can be an excellent buy if used to prepare salads, sandwiches, casseroles, or other dishes where the appearance of the poultry is less important.

Poultry is sold fresh or frozen, either raw or cooked. Turkey and chicken are available whole and in halves, quarters, and pieces; they are also sold in boneless pieces such as fillets, scallops, and roasts. As a rule, whole birds are less expensive, and the larger the bird, the greater the amount of flesh on the bones. When buying fresh poultry, choose plump birds with supple, moist, intact skin without feathers and without dry or discolored patches. Avoid frozen poultry that appears to have dried out or whose packaging has been damaged or is covered with frost; the presence of pinkish ice is a sign that the poultry has been defrosted and refrozen.

Depending on the variety of poultry, the selection of pieces, and the number of bones it contains, 2 pounds of fresh poultry yields between two and eight cooked 3-ounce portions; it is thus very important that you calculate the cost per portion when comparing prices. You should also consider the per-pound yield when determining how much poultry you should buy.

Preparing

Poultry can be cooked and eaten right after it is killed because the flesh does not have to age. It is never eaten raw. Before cooking poultry, check to ensure that all the feathers have been removed. Any remaining feathers or down can be burned off with a gas or alcohol flame, or with a candle or match; they can also be removed with pliers or a brush. Rinse and dry both the inside and the outside of the bird. If you want to ensure that the flesh remains white when the poultry is cooked, rub the skin with lemon. Remove the bitter-tasting uropygial gland, which is situated at the base of the rump (the rear part of the bird's back). This gland produces an oil that birds use to preen their feathers; it is usually removed before drawn poultry is sold. The V-shaped bone known as the wishbone can also be removed; this makes the breast meat easier to slice.

Poultry cooks more quickly when cut into pieces or when prepared *en crapaudine* – that is, flattened but whole.

Since poultry is often contaminated with samonella, it must be handled and cooked with a certain amount of care:

• Always prepare the poultry in a specific area of your kitchen to lower the risk of contamination.

• Before storing poultry, remove and discard its packaging; remove the giblets from inside the bird and store them separately; wipe the bird with a damp cloth.

• Loosely wrap the poultry in waxed paper or aluminum foil, and refrigerate it for a maximum of 2 or 3 days.

• Defrost frozen poultry completely and cook it within 24 to 48 hours.

• Do not cook poultry at low temperatures (less than 300°F/150°C) because the internal temperature should reach 140°F (60°C) – the temperature at which salmonella is destroyed – as quickly as possible. Preheat the oven to 160°C (325°F) and use a meat thermometer. Cook the poultry until the internal temperature of the thickest portion of the thigh reaches 210°F/85°C (196°F/77°C for an unstuffed turkey).

• Wash your hands carefully after handling poultry, and use hot soapy water to thoroughly wash all the utensils and surfaces that came into contact with the poultry. Wash the knife and the cutting board with particular care before using them to cut other food, especially cooked meat or any other food that will not be cooked before being eaten.

• Avoid leaving raw or cooked poultry at room temperature for any longer than 2 hours.

• Do not freeze previously frozen poultry without cooking it first.

Do not stuff poultry until just before it is cooked; never stuff it the day before, because stuffing is the perfect breeding ground for bacteria. Avoid overfilling the bird, because the stuffing tends to expand as it cooks. Immediately after the meal, remove the remaining stuffing from the bird and refrigerate it separately in a sealed container for up to 3 days. It can also be frozen for 3 to 4 weeks.

Poultry (especially a whole turkey) should be defrosted completely before it is cooked to ensure that it is well done in the center.

Poultry can be defrosted in several ways, but defrosting it in the refrigerator is the safest method, and defrosting it at room temperature the riskiest.

When poultry is defrosted in the refrigerator, the flesh retains more moisture and fewer bacteria develop; however, this is the slowest method (allow 5 to 6 hours per pound). Leave the poultry in its packaging, and pierce the underside of the package in several places to allow the juice to escape.

When defrosting poultry in the microwave, leave it whole in its packaging (remove the metal fastener, if there is one), and pierce the packaging to allow the juice to escape. Place the poultry on a microwaveable dish and cook it at 30% (medium-low) power for 10 to 12 minutes per pound, or for as long as the manufacturer of the microwave suggests.

When the poultry is half defrosted, remove the plastic packaging and cover the top of the bird with aluminum foil to prevent it from cooking.

Poultry can also be defrosted in cold water by soaking it in its original packaging. Change the water from time to time to ensure that it remains sufficiently cold.

Defrosting poultry at room temperature is the riskiest method, because the outside of the bird thaws before the inside and reaches room temperature very quickly.

Serving Ideas

 Poultry can be eaten hot or cold, but never raw. It can be prepared in many different ways. Cold poultry is delicious in salads and sandwiches.

Cooking

 The cooking method can influence the fat content of poultry. You can remove the skin and the fat before cooking poultry, or pierce the skin to allow the juice to escape as it cooks.

Roasting

Whole birds as well as pieces of poultry (thighs, breasts, wings, halves, quarters) can be roasted, in a conventional oven. Coat the skin with a thin layer of oil, or melted butter or margarine, to prevent it from drying out as it cooks. Truss the bird if you want it to hold its shape. Insert a meat thermometer into the fleshiest part of the breast or thigh, and preheat the oven to 350°F (180°C). Place the poultry on the rack in a roasting pan, breast-side up (skin-side up for pieces). Cover the poultry with aluminum foil, turning the shiny side toward the skin, and put the bird in the oven. Remove the foil 30 minutes before the poultry is ready, and allow the skin to brown. Baste the skin with the cooking juices from time to time.

Remove the poultry from the oven when the meat thermometer reads 210°F/85°C (196°F/77°C for an unstuffed turkey and 205°F/82°C for a stuffed turkey). The juices should be clear, not pinkish, and the thighs should be easy to move.

The flesh surrounding the bones sometimes becomes reddish when poultry is cooked. This occurs when the pigments in the bones are absorbed by the flesh and has no impact on the flavor or quality of the poultry. It is more likely to happen with young birds because their bones are more porous.

The flesh of older birds (such as stewing hens, for example) is firm and strong-tasting. Young birds are often roasted or grilled, which makes the skin crispy.

Grilling

This method of cooking is particularly appropriate for pieces of poultry. They can be grilled on a medium-hot barbecue or in a conventional oven that has been heated to "broil". Grilling poultry is a little trickier than roasting it because the flesh can dry out or burn quite easily and the skin can catch fire. Place the poultry at least 4 to 5 inches away from the heat source, avoid piercing the skin, and baste and turn the pieces a few times while they are cooking.

• If cooked poultry is allowed to sit for a few minutes before it is served, the juices will spread throughout the flesh, making it more moist and tender.

Microwaving

Poultry can be cooked quite successfully in a microwave oven because its flesh is comprised of short muscular fibers. It cooks faster in a microwave than in a conventional oven, but it will not brown. To improve its appearance, coat it with a browning sauce, barbecue sauce, soy sauce, or Worcestershire sauce, or with melted butter or margarine seasoned with parsley or paprika.

To ensure that it cooks evenly, defrost the bird completely, cover the ends of the wings, the breastbone, and the thigh bones with aluminum foil, and truss the bird by attaching the free ends of the limbs to the body.

Pierce the skin of whole birds and place them on a microwaveable dish deep enough to hold the fat that melts as the poultry cooks. Arrange the pieces of poultry in radiating lines, placing the thicker parts toward the edge of plate and ensuring that the pieces do not touch. Cook the poultry for as long as the microwave manufacturer suggests, removing the juices that accumulate and turning the whole bird or the pieces at least once. Use a meat thermometer to check the internal temperature of the poultry in several places, after allowing it to finish cooking outside of the oven.

Nutritional Information

Poultry contains the same amount of protein as butchered animals. The fat content varies greatly depending on the species (goose and duck are fattier than quail, chicken, pheasant, guinea fowl, and turkey), the part of the animal (breast meat is slightly less fatty than thigh meat and much less fatty than the skin), and the breeding method. The flesh of wild birds is less fatty than that of domesticated poultry.

There is less saturated fat and more polyunsaturated fat in poultry than in meat from butchered animals. Some of the fat is intramuscular, some is contained in the skin, and some is located beneath the skin, where it forms a yellow layer, which can comprise up to 2.5% of the total weight of a chicken. The water absorbed by poultry when it is being prepared for market can also comprise a significant percentage of its weight. After poultry has been scalded, plucked, and drawn, it is chilled with ice water or cold air; poultry that is immersed in ice water becomes slightly waterlogged. Governmental regulations usually stipulate the percentage of water that frozen and fresh chicken can contain. However, chicken is being chilled with cold air more and more frequently.

Breast meat not only has a more delicate flavor than thigh meat, it is also generally more tender and less moist, particularly in the case of large birds. The general preference for white meat has led to a surplus of brown meat, especially since many fast-food restaurants have added products made primarily from white chicken to their menus.

Storing

Fresh poultry is perishable because it is an ideal breeding ground for bacteria (providing food, moisture, and a low level of acidity). Remove it from its packaging, wipe it with a damp cloth, and remove the giblets from inside the bird. Place the poultry on a plate and loosely cover it with waxed paper or aluminum foil, then put it in the refrigerator and cook it within 2 or 3 days.

Defrosted poultry (the label should indicate whether or not the bird has been frozen) should be cooked within 24 hours.

Poultry that is frozen whole can be stored for up to 12 months; poultry pieces that are purchased frozen can be stored for up to 6 months; and cooked poultry that is not covered with a sauce or stock can be stored for 1 or 2 months.

Poultry

573

Turkey

Meleagris gallopavo, Galliformes

T urkeys are large poultry or game birds with a featherless, purplish-red head and neck with warty excrescences. The females are called turkey hens and the males are referred to as toms or gobblers. Native to North America, they were introduced to Europe by the Spanish. In England, the birds were dubbed "turkey-cocks," a name that, until then, had been applied to Guinea fowls native to "Turkish" (i.e., Muslim) lands. In the United States and Canada, stuffed turkey with cranberry sauce or jelly is traditionally served at Christmas and Thanksgiving; the latter practice dates back to November 1620, when the famished *Mayflower* pilgrims dined on turkey upon arriving in today's Massachusetts.

In Europe, turkey was initially served only at royal tables. The taste for the meat gradually spread through a number of countries, and the birds eventually replaced the traditional Christmas goose in places such as England. In France, turkeys were introduced and raised intensively by the Jesuits; indeed, even today, French people sometimes refer to them as "Jesuits."

Unlike wild turkeys, which have little flesh, domesticated strains are considerably heavier (up to 40 pounds), thanks to years of careful cross-breeding. In Canada, depending on consumer needs, turkeys are killed young, at 12 to 16 weeks of age. The eviscerated birds generally weigh 7 to 18 or more pounds.

Turkey meat is coarser and drier than chicken. The larger the turkey, the less tasty its flesh.

Cooking

Make sure your turkey is completely thawed before you put it in the oven, to ensure even cooking and full destruction of all pathogenic bacteria (salmonella) that may be present. Ideally, the bird should be thawed in the refrigerator in its original wrapping; this takes about 5 hours per pound. You can also thaw it in cold water (plan on about 1½ hours per pound) or the microwave (see the manufacturer's instructions for thawing poultry).

Avoid cooking turkey at under 300°F, as not all pathogenic bacteria will be destroyed. The ideal cooking temperature is 325°F.

To ensure optimum cooking, insert a meat thermometer in the fleshiest part of the breast or thigh. The ideal internal temperatures are 162°F (breast) and 171°F (thigh).

	Weight (pounds)	Roasting time (hours)
Whole turkey	4 - 6.5	3 h - 3 h 30
	6.5 - 7.75	3 h 30 - 4 h
	7.75 - 10	4 h - 4 h 30
	10 - 12	4 h 30 - 5 h
	12 - 15.5	5 h 30 - 6
	17.5 - 20	5 h 45 - 6 h 30
	20 - 24	6 h 15 - 7h
Half turkey	4.5	2 h 30 - 3 h
	9	4 h - 4 h 30
	13	4 h 30 - 5 h
Quarter turkey	4.5	3 h - 3 h 30
	6.5	3 h 30 - 4 h
Drumsticks (6)	3.3	1 h 30 - 1 h 45
Thighs (6)	4.5	1 h 30 - 1 h 45
Wings (8)	4.5	1 h 15 - 1 h 30
Half breast	2	1 h 45 - 2 h

Nutritional Information

	raw white and dark meat	with skin	roasted white and dark meat	with skin
protein	22 g	20 g	29 g	28 g
fat	3 g	8 g	5 g	10 g
cholesterol	65 mg	68 mg	76 mg	82 mg
calories	119	160	170	208
				per 100 g

Turkey is high in protein, niacin, vitamin B_6, zinc and potassium. It is also a good source of vitamin B_{12} and phosphorus.

Turkeys have almost twice as much white meat than dark. The white meat is drier, less fatty and generally more popular. About 40% of the bird's weight is edible. Each pound of raw turkey thus provides about ⅖ pound of cooked meat, slightly over half of which can be served sliced.

Lemon turkey cutlets

4 SERVINGS

4 thin turkey cutlets
2 tbsp. of butter
2 tbsp. of olive oil
1 tbsp. of flour
1 can (10 oz.) of beef consommé

8 slices of lemon
2 tbsp. of softened butter
1 tbsp. of lemon juice
Salt and white pepper

1. Salt, pepper and lightly flour the cutlets. In a frying pan, heat the unsoftened butter and olive oil at medium temperature. Brown the cutlets for about 2 minutes to seal them. Remove them from the pan and keep them warm.

2. Drain the grease and pour in ¾ cup of consommé, scraping the bottom of the pan as you add the liquid. Put the cutlets back in the pan and garnish them with the lemon slices. Cover and let simmer for 10 minutes.

3. Place the cutlets on a serving platter and keep them warm.

4. Add the remaining consommé to the juice in the pan and reduce it to a syrupy liquid. Add the lemon juice. Stir. Remove the pan from the heat and add the softened butter. Pour the sauce over the cutlets.

Buying

As turkeys are often too large for the needs of today's consumers, the turkey industry markets a wide range of products. Consumers can choose from boneless turkey, turkey pieces (breasts, thighs, drumsticks, etc.), chopped or cubed turkey, turkey cutlets, turkey rolls and a number of processed products (pastrami, salami, kolbassa sausage, etc.). Boneless turkey is available with or without the skin, can consist in white or dark meat, and may also be precooked, smoked or even ham-flavored. Generally speaking, ready-to-cook and precooked products are sold frozen; to find out what they contain, consult the list of ingredients.

Some turkeys available in stores have been injected with oil products; this increases their weight by 3% and makes them less dry when cooked. In addition to costing more per pound, they contain a high percentage of saturated fat (often margarine or coconut oil). You can obtain equally savory turkey by roasting a bird at medium temperature (325°F) and basting it during cooking.

Serving Ideas

Although turkey is traditionally stuffed and roasted, you can cook it in a number of other ways. Prepare it like chicken, which it can replace in most recipes. It is also delicious cold - in salads, aspics and sandwiches, for example.

Goose

Anser anser, Anatidae

The goose is a webfooted bird with a long neck and a large beak. Wild geese travel in flocks, which have been a favorite target of hunters since ancient times. The goose was probably first domesticated during the Neolithic period, when small wild geese were captured and fattened. The Egyptians were the first to force-feed domestic geese and ducks to produce the fattened livers required to make foie gras (see *Foie gras*).

Geese form couples and remain with the same partner throughout their lives; if one partner dies, the surviving member waits for a long period of time before mating again. In Europe and central Asia, geese are traditionally killed on the day of the winter solstice. During the Middle Ages, goose was the second most popular meat after pork. Turkey only recently replaced goose as the meat most commonly served at the New Year and on other festive occasions. Roast goose, stuffed or unstuffed, is still a traditional dish in Germany, England, central Europe, and Scandinavia.

There are numerous species and various sizes of geese. Certain small varieties are bred for their tender and flavorful flesh; they are generally killed when they weigh between 6 and 11 pounds. Other larger varieties are bred for their fattened livers; they grow to be between 22 and 26 pounds (their livers generally weigh 14 to 19 ounces).

Buying

Buy a goose with pink or light red flesh, a plump breast, and light, smooth feet. The older the goose, the hairier and redder its feet, the harder its beak, and the firmer and drier its flesh. Allow 14 ounces of goose meat per person.

Cooking

To make goose less fatty, pierce the skin in several places and roast the bird on a grill, turning it halfway through the cooking process. Skim the fat from the drippings. When roasting a goose at 325°F (160°C), allow approximately 15 minutes per pound.

Serving Ideas

Goose can be cooked like other poultry. The flesh of wild geese is relatively firm and is most flavorful when braised or when used to make pâté. Recipes for turkey and duck are particularly appropriate for goose. In Europe, goose stuffed with chestnuts and served with apples or sauerkraut is a classic dish. The flesh of old or very large geese is used to make conserves, pâté, or potted meat, or is braised or cooked in stews. Stuffings and fruit preparations go especially well with goose because it is quite fatty.

Goose fat, which is off-white and pasty at room temperature, can be used like butter. Gourmet cooks often use it to brown potatoes.

Nutritional Information

	raw flesh	raw unskinned flesh	roasted flesh	roasted unskinned flesh
protein	23 g	16 g	29 g	25 g
fat	7 g	34 g	13 g	22 g
cholesterol	84 mg	80 mg	96 mg	91 mg
calories	160	370	238	305
				per 100 g

The nutritional value of goose is similar to that of duck, although it is even fattier.

Chicken

Gallus gallus, Gallinaceae

T he word "chicken" refers to male and female offspring of the hen that are least 4 months old. This bird was first domesticated in the Indus river valley in southern Asia over 4,000 years ago and was found in Greece in the 5th century B.C. Chickens are easy to raise and and feed because they can live on table scraps or on food they find on the ground.

Chicken is now eaten in almost every part of world, but its popularity has fluctuated throughout history. During certain periods, chicken was regarded as a luxury food to be eaten on Sundays and other festive occasions, while at other times it fell into disregard. However, chicken has reached unprecedented heights of popularity since the development of industrial poultry farming after the Second World War. New breeding methods and genetic manipulation are some of the advances that have made it possible to breed better-quality chickens (with greater muscle mass, for example) more rapidly and in greater numbers. Chicken became even more popular when researchers identified it as a relatively healthy alternative to red meat.

Chickens are rarely eaten before they reach the age of 6 weeks because their flesh is not mature enough. Chickens marketed as "broilers" are killed when approximately 7 weeks old and weigh between 2½ and 4 pounds, while "roasting chickens" are killed at 10 weeks and weigh over 4 pounds. The Rock Cornish hen is a cross between the White Rock chicken and the Cornish hen; a drawn Rock Cornish hen weighs between 1½ and 2 pounds.

Gourmets seek out "free-range" chickens, which are allowed acess to the outdoors rather than being confined to henhouses and are fed a vegetarian diet. These conditions result in tastier meat but are costly; free-range chickens are generally much more expensive than mass produced birds.

Chicken that is chilled with water contains between 3% and 5% water, while air-chilled chicken contains none. Air-chilled chicken is thus a better buy than it appears to be because it loses less moisture as it cooks. The relatively dark skin of air-chilled chicken also makes it more attractive to consumers. Poultry that is fed a diet rich in carotene is also darker in color.

Buying

The price of chicken should reflect the amount that is lost when it is being prepared (bones, fat, skin) and cooked (water, fat). It is thus better to base comparisons on the price per portion rather than the price per pound. The per-pound price of whole chickens is usually lower than that of chicken pieces. Large chickens are a better buy than small chickens because there is more flesh on the bones.

A whole chicken yields three 3½-ounce cooked portions. Serve 12 ounces of wings, 8 ounces of legs or drumsticks, and 7 ounces of breasts per person.

Nutritional Information

	raw flesh	*with the skin*	*roasted flesh*	*with the skin*
protein	21 g	19 g	29 g	27 g
fat	3 g	15 g	7 g	14 g
cholesterol	70 mg	75 mg	89 mg	88 mg
calories	119	215	190	239
				per 100 g

Raw chicken generally contains less fat than red meat or other white meats, but the same amount of cholesterol.

Chicken is rich in protein, niacin, and vitamin B_6. It is also a good source of vitamin B_{12}, zinc, phosphorus, and potassium.

1 *Insert a sharp chef's knife into the cavity of the chicken and cut it lengthwise along the spine.*

2 *Turn the bird over and open it up; then cut it along the wishbone.*

3 *Cut the spine off the half to which it is attached, and discard it.*

4 *Place one half of the bird on a flat surface, and insert the blade of the knife between the leg and the breast.*

5 *Insert the tip of a knife into the wing joint and cut off the wing.*

6 *You should end up with 6 pieces: 2 wings, 2 legs, and 2 breast halves.*

Serving Ideas

Chicken can be eaten hot or cold but must always be cooked. It can be cooked in any way, and with any number of ingredients and seasonings. Chicken is delicious roasted, grilled, or sautéed. You can enhance the flavor of chicken by stuffing it or by marinating it for a few hours. Since all chickens are killed when very young, the meat is always tender and stands up very well when cooked with dry heat.

Oven-Roasted Chicken

SERVES 4

One 3-pound (1.5 kg) chicken
1 small onion
1 carrot
1 rib celery
Salt and ground pepper

Dried tarragon and thyme, to taste
¼ cup (60 ml) butter
1 tbsp. dry mustard
Hot water, chicken stock, or white wine

1. Preheat the oven to 375°F (190°C).

2. Cut the onion in half. Cut the carrot and celery into small sticks.

3. Salt and pepper the inside of the chicken, then stuff it with the vegetables and herbs. Tie the opening shut or close it with a trussing skewer.

4. Soften the butter with a fork and combine it with the dry mustard; then brush the chicken with this mixture.

5. Put the chicken on the roasting pan and place it in the oven. Cook it for 25 minutes per pound (500 g).

6. Turn off the oven. Remove the chicken from the roasting pan and place it on a platter in the oven. Defat the pan juices, and deglaze the pan with a few tablespoons of hot water, chicken stock, or white wine. Scrape the bottom of the pan with a wooden spatula to dislodge all the browned bits. Carve the chicken and serve with the sauce.

Hen

Gallus gallus, Phasianidae

The word "hen" usually refers to the female domestic fowl, but it can also refer to the female of other gallinaceous species. In such cases it usually combined with another term, as in "hen pheasant," "hazel hen," and "moorhen."

Hens are raised to lay eggs and are killed only when they become infertile, which usually occurs after 12 to 24 months. At this age, they can weigh anywhere from 3 to 7 pounds, but those under 5 pounds are best for eating.

Serving Ideas

The flesh of the hen is always firm and somewhat fatty. It is tenderest when gently simmered for a long period of time. It can be used to make excellent soups and stews. Before roasting a hen, braise it for about 1 hour in a very small amount of water.

Nutritional Information

	boiled skinless hen	*with the skin*
protein	39 g	27 g
fat	12 g	19 g
cholesterol	83 mg	79 mg
calories	237	285
		per 100 g

Rich in protein and niacin, hen is a good source of vitamin B$_6$, phosphorus, zinc, and potassium.

Capon

Gallus gallus, Galliformes

Capons are male chickens that have been castrated and fattened – a technique invented by the Romans and practiced ever since antiquity. Slow and costly, it is still used in Europe but is less common in North America.

Capons grow to twice the size of other young chickens. Their flesh stays tender and succulent, as their muscles are marbled with layers of fat. They have a higher proportion of white meat than other chickens and are more flavorful. They generally weigh about 8 or 9 pounds.

Nutritional Information

	uncooked (flesh and skin)
protein	19 g
fat	17 g
cholesterol	75 mg
calories	234
	per 100 g

Serving Ideas

People generally prefer to cook capons simply, in order to avoid overpowering their delicate-tasting flesh. They are usually roasted (stuffed or unstuffed).

Guinea fowl

Numida meleagris, Numididae

An omnivorous bird with dark plumage and a piercing call, the guinea fowl originated in Africa. It was known to the Egyptians, Greeks, and Romans, who named the bird the Numidian or Carthage hen, after its regions of origin. Some Europeans still refer to the bird as the "Bohemian pheasant," because gypsies revived the practice of eating guinea fowl around the 14th century.

There are over 20 different species of guinea fowl, several of which have been domesticated. The most common is the *Numida meleagris,* which has silver-gray plumage with light spots. The guinea fowl is difficult to breed in captivity because it will not lay eggs if confined to small area. The domestic guinea fowl is about the same size as a small chicken, and its flesh tastes somewhat musky. The flesh of young guinea fowl *(pintadeau),* weighing less than 2 pounds, is particularly flavorful.

Serving Ideas

Usually roasted or braised, guinea fowl can be cooked like pheasant, partridge, and chicken, which it can replace in most recipes.

Cooking

 Since the lean flesh of the guinea fowl tends to dry out, it should be brushed or barded with fat before being cooked, and basted while cooking. Roast a guinea fowl for 1 to 1½ hours at 375°F (190°C), basting it frequently.

Nutritional Information

	raw flesh	*with the skin*
protein	21 g	23 g
fat	3 g	7 g
cholesterol	63 mg	74 mg
calories	110	158
		per 100 g

Guinea fowl is low in fat and calories.

Pigeon

Columba spp., Columbidae

T he pigeon is a seed-eating bird with short broad wings, a small beak and attractive plumage; it mates with the same partner throughout its life and abstains from mating for a long period of time if its partner dies. Wild pigeons are found on every continent, and certain species have been domesticated. Pigeons have been bred in captivity since they were first domesticated by the Greeks in about 1500 B.C.

The flesh of wild pigeons has been eaten since ancient times; it is leaner, darker and stronger-tasting than that of domesticated pigeons. Farm-bred pigeons are usually killed very young, at about 4 weeks old, before they start to fly; pigeons killed at this age weigh about 12 ounces and have very tender flesh. Most pigeons are killed by means of suffocation, and their blood is allowed to spread throughout their bodies, darkening the skin and flesh.

Serving Ideas

Pigeon is traditionally served with peas. It can be cooked and served whole.

Buying

Serve one pigeon per person.

Cooking

Pigeon can be cooked like other poultry. Young pigeons with tender flesh are often roasted, sautéed or grilled; adult pigeons are best when cooked with liquid (braised, poached). Seal pigeons by baking them at 425 to 475°F (220 to 250°C) for the first 10 to 20 minutes, then reduce the temperature to 350°F (175°C). Since the liver of the pigeon does not contain bile, it does have to be removed before the bird is cooked.

Nutritional Information

	raw flesh	*with the skin*
protein	18 g	19 g
fat	8 g	24 g
cholesterol	90 mg	95 mg
calories	142	294
		per 100 g

Quail

Coturnix spp. and *Colinus* spp., **Phasianidae**

A small migrating bird thought to have originated in Asia or Africa, the quail first appeared in Europe over 10,000 years ago. By that time, the Egyptians were already breeding quails. Very easy to maintain in captivity, quails are now bred all over the world.

There are over 200 different species of quails, which are the smallest gallinaceous birds in existence. Some species of quails have a tuft or crest of feathers on top of their heads.

The northern bobwhite *(Colinus virginianus)* is a related American species that is much larger than European quails. This bird was dubbed the quail by the first European settlers because it resembles European quails. Since the quail inhabits flat fields and grasslands, and runs rather than flies to escape danger, it can be captured with ease. The quail is a rather plump little bird; hence the expression "plump as a partridge," partridge being another inexact common name for the bobwhite. The domestic quail usually weighs between 5 and 10 ounces. It has delicate, flavorful flesh, and its eggs, which are often beige with brown spots, are tiny but edible (they usually weigh less than half an ounce).

Buying

 Allow 2 to 3 quails per person.

Nutritional Information

	raw flesh	*with the skin*
protein	22 g	20 g
fat	5 g	12 g
cholesterol	70 mg	76 mg
calories	134	192
		per 100 g

Serving Ideas

Quail can used to make a pâté or terrine. The small, delicate bones can be eaten, especially if the bird is well cooked. Grapes, cherries, prunes, and lemons go particularly well with quail. Quail eggs are usually served hard-boiled, often as a snack or as a garnish. Renowned for their delicate flavor and smooth, creamy texture, they are regarded as a delicacy in China and Japan.

Cooking

Quail can be a very delicate dish, as long as the flesh is not allowed to dry out when cooked. It is usually roasted, braised (with grapes), cooked in casseroles, or grilled. Quail takes about 20 to 25 minutes to cook.

Storing

Fresh quail is extremely perishable. It should be stored in the coldest part of the refrigerator and cooked as soon as possible, preferably within 2 or 3 days.

Pheasant

Phasianus colchicus, Phasianidae

An omnivorous bird with magnificent plumage that is often reddish brown with black spots, the pheasant originated in Asia and was brought to Europe by the Romans. Hunters have always prized this bird, especially the male of the species, which is renowned for the beauty of its brightly colored feathers and for its long tail. During the Middle Ages, pheasant hunting was the preserve of the nobility. Hunting has since led to considerable declines in pheasant populations, but pheasant breeding has begun to replenish their numbers.

An initial attempt was made to introduce the pheasant into the United States in 1790, but it was unsuccessful. The bird did not successfully adapt to North American conditions until 1881, in Oregon. Since wild pheasants have never managed to survive the rigors of the Canadian winter, hunters in Canada have to make do with farm-bred pheasants.

Breeding pheasants can be quite difficult because the bird is sensitive to stress and will perish in less than ideal conditions. Cannibalism is a common problem, which is usually solved by removing the end of the pheasants' beaks or, occasionally, by covering the eyes of the birds. Breeders also have to encourage the birds to mate throughout the year, rather than only during the spring mating season. Domestic pheasants can be raised in an indoor henhouse or in an aviary (a large outdoor cage measuring over 2,500 square feet). Pheasants raised in aviaries have more beautiful plumage than those raised indoors, and a certain number of them are released into the wild and then hunted. Domestic pheasants are fleshier and heavier than wild pheasants; their flesh is also fattier and less musky. Killed when 18 to 25 weeks old, they usually weigh between 2 and 2½ pounds.

Preparing

Pheasant is traditionally hung (for 4 to 12 days, depending on the season) until the proteins begin to decompose, which tenderizes the flesh and enhances its flavor. However, this practice is now less common; if the pheasant is young and farm-bred, it is usually cooked about 48 hours after being killed.

Storing

Pheasant is perishable. Store it in the coldest part of the refrigerator and cook it as soon as possible – within 2 to 3 days.

Cooking

Young pheasant is usually roasted. Since the flesh can be quite dry, pheasant is often filled with a moist stuffing (stuff the bird just before it is cooked to prevent the development of bacteria). It can also be barded (covered with strips of lard) or brushed with melted fat. Older birds tend to be less moist and tender. They can be roasted with lard, cooked in casseroles, or used to make terrines or pâtés. Pheasant is particularly good when cooked with wine or other kinds of alcohol. Roast pheasant for 1 to 1½ hours at 375°F (190°C), basting it frequently.

Buying

Cook one pheasant for every two people, or one stuffed pheasant for three to four people.

Valeur nutritive

	raw flesh	with the skin
protein	24 g	23 g
fat	4 g	9 g
cholesterol	66 mg	71 mg
calories	133	181
		per 100 g

Duck

Anas platyrhynchos, **Anatidae**

The duck is a web-footed bird thought to have been domesticated in China over 4,000 years ago. Affectionate and easy to tame, ducks tend to follow their keepers around – a habit that children find particularly delightful. Ducks live in couples and mourn the loss of their mates, which is why the bird has long been a symbol of marital fidelity in China.

Duck is very popular in Europe, especially in France, which raises more ducks than any other European country, largely to satisfy the demand for *foie gras* (the liver of fattened ducks or geese). It also plays an important role in Asian cuisine, especially in Chinese cooking. The species of ducks raised in captivity include the Barbary duck, which has firm, strong-tasting flesh, and the Nantes duck, whose delicately flavored flesh can be quite fatty. The most common species of wild duck is the mallard; its flesh is much sought after, but usually only the breast and thigh meat is eaten. Several other species of wild ducks are highly prized by those with a taste for fine food.

There are approximately 80 different species of ducks, some of which are fleshier, fattier, more flavorful (muskier), or richer in nutrients than others. The most widely available ducks are usually between 7 and 12 weeks old and have tender flesh; they generally weigh between 4 and 7 pounds. Birds served as "duckling" in restaurants should be no more than 2 months old. Ducks are usually killed by chopping their heads off or bleeding them; but some, such as the Rouen duck, are smothered, and the blood is allowed to spread throughout bird, darkening its flesh. Since this method of killing not only enhances the flavor of the flesh but also promotes the development of bacteria, these ducks are usually killed just before they are cooked. The French call this kind of duck *canard au sang*.

Buying

Ducks contain very little meat. Ensure that there is at least 1 to 1½ pounds of raw duck per person.

Serving Ideas

Duck is often cooked with fruit such as oranges, cherries, and apples, because their acidity complements the fatty flesh. Duck *à l'orange* is a classic French recipe, and duck is also frequently served with chestnuts. Peking duck is a traditional Chinese dish that takes several hours to prepare and involves coating the duck with a sweet-and-sour sauce, then roasting it.

Duck eggs are rarely eaten in Western countries but are very much appreciated in Asia. They are sometimes hard-boiled and are never eaten raw, because they often contain bacteria that cannot be eliminated without cooking the eggs.

Duck is also prized for the foie gras that is produced by fattening the bird; some people prefer it to the foie gras obtained from fattened geese. The breast meat of ducks is cut into "magrets," then grilled, fried, or smoked.

Duck à l'Orange

SERVES 4

2 oranges	1 tbsp. honey
½ tsp. salt	2 tbsp. Cointreau
½ tsp. curry powder	(orange liqueur)
1 duck, weighing 3 lb.	Salt and ground pepper
(1.5 kg)	Parsley or watercress
3 tbsp. butter	
½ cup (250 ml) orange	
juice	

1. Preheat the oven to 425°F (220°C).

2. Prepare the duck for cooking:

Peel 1 orange with a zester, reserving the zest.

Cut the pulp into pieces.

Mix the salt and the curry powder together, then add the orange pieces. Stuff the duck with this mixture, then seal the opening tightly. Tie the free ends of the legs and the wings to the body of the bird.

Melt 2 tablespoons of the butter. Then place the duck in a roasting pan and brush it with the melted butter.

3. Roast the duck in two stages, for a total of 1 hour (or 20 minutes per pound): first roast the duck for 20 minutes; then baste it with a mixture of the orange juice, honey, and Cointreau, reduce the heat to 350°F (180°C), and continue to cook the duck. Baste it every 10 minutes with the pan juices.

4. While the duck is cooking, blanch the orange zest, then strain it and set it aside. Peel the second orange and cut it into slices.

5. When the duck has finished cooking, remove it from the roasting pan, remove the trussing, cover it with aluminum foil, place it on a serving platter, and put it back in the cooling oven.

6. Skim the fat off the pan juices, then bring the liquid to a boil. Reduce the liquid, thoroughly deglazing the bottom of the pan. Add salt and pepper to taste, along with the remaining butter, the orange zest, and the orange slices. Continue to cook the sauce until has a nice consistency. Remove the orange slices and pour the sauce through a fine strainer. Adjust the seasonings and pour the sauce into hot gravy boat.

7. Serve the duck on a hot serving platter, garnishing it with the orange slices and bunches of parsley or watercress.

Nutritional Information

	flesh	flesh and skin roasted
protein	24 g	19 g
fat	11 g	28 g
cholesterol	89 mg	84 mg
calories	201	337
		per 100 g

The nutritional value of duck varies depending on the breeding methods and the species. The raw flesh of wild ducks contains about 30% less fat than that of domesticated species. However, this difference diminishes once the flesh is cooked and some of the fat is eliminated. Duck is rich in iron and B-complex vitamins. It can be difficult to digest, especially if the skin is eaten.

Cooking

Roast duck is particularly good. Roasting eliminates some of the fat from the bird, especially if the skin is pierced in various places with a fork before the duck is cooked and if it is grilled on a rotisserie. Allow the bird to cook for 20 to 25 minutes per pound at 320°F (160°C). As the fat melts, the skin of the bird will turn crispy and golden. Very large ducks, which are less tender, are often cooked with steam heat (in a braising pan containing liquid) or are used to make pâtés, meat loaves, or cassoulets (bean-based stews).

Egg

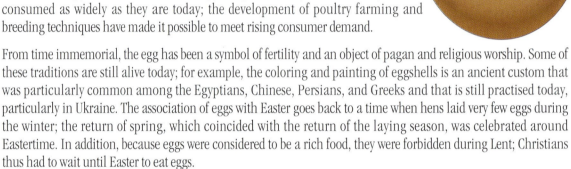

T he egg is an organic reproductive body laid by the female of bird and animal species; it contains the germ of an embryo and nutritional reserves. Eggs come in various sizes, depending on the species; they are most commonly laid by birds and reptiles (quail, duck, turkey, goose, partridge, ostrich, crocodile, turtle, etc.). Unless otherwise specified, the word "egg" is usually taken to refer to hen's eggs. While we tend to take eggs for granted, they have not always been consumed as widely as they are today; the development of poultry farming and breeding techniques have made it possible to meet rising consumer demand.

From time immemorial, the egg has been a symbol of fertility and an object of pagan and religious worship. Some of these traditions are still alive today; for example, the coloring and painting of eggshells is an ancient custom that was particularly common among the Egyptians, Chinese, Persians, and Greeks and that is still practised today, particularly in Ukraine. The association of eggs with Easter goes back to a time when hens laid very few eggs during the winter; the return of spring, which coincided with the return of the laying season, was celebrated around Eastertime. In addition, because eggs were considered to be a rich food, they were forbidden during Lent; Christians thus had to wait until Easter to eat eggs.

The egg is composed of four main parts: the shell, the membranes, the albumen, and the yolk.

The egg **shell** is the porous, fragile covering that protects the egg; its multiple tiny pores make it pervious to air, water, and odors. An effective barrier against germs, the shell also preserves the humidity of the egg. The shell of a medium-size egg has between 6,000 and 8,000 pores and represents 9% to 12% of the total weight of the egg; it is composed mainly of calcium carbonate (94%), magnesium carbonate (1%), calcium phosphate (1%), and organic matter (4%). The color of the shell is a genetic trait that depends on the breed of hen; as such, it is not an indication of the nutritive value or flavor of the egg. The shell's thickness depends both on hereditary factors and on the hen's diet; the more eggs a hen lays, the thinner the shells. Since hens that lay white eggs are more fertile than hens that lay brown eggs, the shells of white eggs tend to be thinner and more fragile. Eggshells are often coated with an odorless mineral oil which partially clogs the pores, thus prolonging freshness, preserving the humidity of the eggs, and preventing the absorption of odors; this is why eggs should not be washed.

The **shell membranes** are made up of two or three thin layers of protein fibers that cling to the shell and provide additional protection against undesirable elements such as mold and bacteria. When it is first laid, the egg's contents fill the shell completely; however, with the subsequent drop in temperature, the contents shrink, causing an air chamber to form at the rounder end. The size of this air chamber varies with the storage conditions, particularly the temperature and the degree of humidity; a loss of humidity or dehydration causes the air chamber to increase in volume. The size of this chamber is thus an indication of freshness: the larger it is, the older the egg.

The **albumen**, or "white," consists of 87% water and 12.5% albumin, a protein substance; it represents two thirds of the total weight of the egg.

The chalazae are two spiral membranous cords of albumin located at either end of the yolk; they hold the yolk in position. The fresher the egg, the denser and firmer the white around the yolk. The albumen coagulates at 144° to 149°F.

The **yolk** is formed of several layers of a substance called "vitellus," alternating between a pale yellow and a dark yellow; it is protected by a transparent membrane (the vitelline membrane). The yolk of unfertilized eggs contains a small, irregularly shaped, pale spot called the embryonic disk. The color of the yolk varies according to the hen's diet; for instance, a diet rich in wheat produces eggs with pale yellow yolks, while a diet of corn produces yolks of a deeper yellow. The yolk is made up of approximately 50% solids, 16% protein, and 30% fat; it coagulates between 150° and 158°F.

After they have been laid, eggs are dispatched to a packing station for assessment of their inner and outer quality. Those that are cracked are set aside, while the rest are examined in front of an intense light for the position of the yolk and the size of the air chamber; following inspection, the eggs are washed, graded, and packaged.

Buying

When buying eggs, make sure that the shells are not cracked, and choose refrigerated eggs, as they will stay fresh much longer. Always check the side of the carton for the expiration date, which indicates how the long eggs' qualities will be preserved without significant deterioration. The "Best Before" date is reliable only if the eggs are stored at an adequate temperature (below 40°F) and degree of humidity (70% to 80%). Eggs that are left at room temperature deteriorate 7 times faster than eggs stored in proper conditions. The expiration date is established by the producer with a standard delay of 4 to 5 weeks after packaging.

The criteria for grading eggs differ from one country to another. In the United States, eggs are graded AA, A, and B, AA being the best quality. Eggs graded C are used in the food processing industry only.

Eggs are also classified according to the weight per dozen: a dozen "small" eggs weighs at least 18 ounces (540 grams), "medium" eggs weigh at least 21 ounces (600 grams), "large" eggs at least 24 ounces (720 grams), and "extra-large" eggs 27 ounces (810 grams). The smallest eggs ("peewee") weigh a minimum of 15 ounces (450 grams), and the largest ("jumbo") weigh in at a minimum of 30 ounces (900 grams) per dozen.

Preparing

When breaking eggs into a mixing bowl, it is possible to contaminate the other foods in the bowl by inadvertently adding a rotten egg. To avoid such unpleasant surprises, break each egg into a separate dish before adding it to the other ingredients.

Certain preparations require that the eggs be at room temperature; this is the case for mayonnaise (all ingredients should be at room temperature), when beating egg whites (cold whites will not peak as well), and when boiling eggs (cold eggs tend to crack when they are plunged into boiling water).

Plain Omelet

SERVES 4

6 eggs   2 tbsp. butter
Salt and ground pepper

1. Break the eggs into a bowl, season with salt and pepper, and beat lightly with a fork.

2. Melt the butter in a frying pan. When it is very hot, add the beaten eggs and cook them on high heat for a few minutes, mixing the omelet with a fork or wooden spoon to ensure that the bottom cooks evenly.

3. The omelet is ready when it begins to dry around the edges but is still soft in the center. Remove the pan from the heat. Fold the omelet in half, and slide it onto a serving dish. Serve immediately.

Chopped *fines herbes* (parsley, chervil, chives, tarragon) may be added to the beaten eggs before cooking.

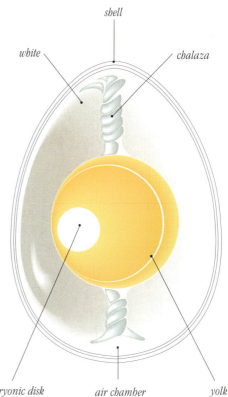

shell

white

chalaza

embryonic disk   air chamber   yolk

Serving Ideas

Eggs are consumed on their own or incorporated into an infinite number of other foods, including crêpes, quiches, cakes, pastries, ice cream, and beverages. They are used both as a thickening and binding agent and to give a smooth and creamy texture to various preparations (sauces, soups, stuffings, flans, cream fillings, puddings, purées, croquettes, pasta). Egg yolk is used in bread crumbs, breads, rolls, pies, and other baked goods to give them an attractive golden color. Eggs can also be emulsified to make mayonnaise and sauces, and the whites can be whisked into a foam for mousses, meringues, and soufflés. Eggs, and particularly egg yolks, should never be added directly to a hot liquid (soup, white sauce, custard, etc.), as the heat will cause them to curdle. Instead, heat the eggs slowly, incorporating a little of the hot liquid into the eggs while stirring constantly; then stir this heated mixture into the rest of the hot liquid and cook as required. Custards should be cooked neither too quickly nor too long, as this will cause them to curdle. For the best results, use a double boiler, which ensures a constant temperature. When heating custard in a saucepan, remove the pan from the heat as soon as the mixture begins to thicken, and cool it immediately by placing the pan in cold water.

Cracked or stained eggs may be contaminated and should never be consumed raw, although cooking will destroy any bacteria. To test the freshness of eggs, place them in cold water; fresh eggs will sink to the bottom, while older eggs will float to the surface because of their enlarged air chamber.

quail egg

Cooking

Because of their high water (75%) and protein (13%) content, it is best to cook eggs for a short time and over low heat. Prolonged cooking at a high temperature will give eggs a rubbery texture.

Soft-boiled eggs, medium-boiled eggs, hard-boiled eggs

Eggs that are boiled in their shells. The cooking method is identical in all three cases; only the cooking time varies, as this determines the firmness of the final product.

Eggs with a slightly set white and a liquid yolk are called soft-boiled eggs, while medium-boiled eggs have a firm white and a runny yolk. In a hard-boiled egg, both the yolk and the white are firm.

Whatever the cooking method used, the eggs should always be at room temperature before they are immersed in boiling water. A small hole can be made at the large end of the egg (using a needle or a specially designed tool) to release the air and prevent the shell from cracking. Cooking may be started with cold or hot water. A pinch of salt or 1 tablespoon of vinegar can be added to the water to prevent the egg from leaking out of a cracked shell (salt and vinegar cause the egg to coagulate immediately, thus sealing the crack).

• Cold-water method: Place the eggs in a saucepan and add enough cold water to cover them completely. Add salt or vinegar. Bring the water to a simmer and then begin timing: allow 3 minutes for soft-boiled eggs, 3 to 4 minutes for medium-boiled eggs, and 7 to 10 minutes for hard-boiled eggs.

Remove the eggs from the hot water immediately, and refresh hard-boiled eggs under cold water to halt the cooking process and to avoid the formation of a grayish or greenish ring around the yolks; rinsing the eggs under cold water also makes them easier to peel. To peel the egg, tap it gently with a spoon to crack the shell, which can then be removed under cold water.

• Hot-water method: Fill a saucepan with a generous amount of water; bring it to a simmer, and add salt or vinegar. Gently lower the eggs into the boiling water and begin timing, allowing 3 to 4 minutes for soft-boiled eggs, 7 to 9 minutes for medium-boiled eggs, and 10 to 15 minutes for hard-boiled eggs (refresh hard-boiled eggs under cold water).

It is important to cook eggs in simmering water; a rolling boil may cause the shells to crack and the whites to become rubbery. Once cooled, the cooking water

goose egg

duck egg

brown egg

white egg

can be used to water plants, as it is rich in nutrients. Freshly laid eggs are more difficult to peel when hard-boiled because the whites tend to cling to the shell; it is easier to peel hard-boiled eggs that are 3 or 4 days old. In addition, freshly laid eggs should be cooked a little longer. On the other hand, eggs that are too old do not taste as good.

Poached eggs

Shelled eggs that are boiled in water and vinegar (2 to 3 tablespoons). It is important for the whites to coagulate quickly enough to prevent them from spreading in the water. Never add salt to the water, as it causes the white and yolk to separate. Break each egg into a small dish and slide it into a frying pan filled with boiling water, leaving the egg as close to the surface as possible. Lower the heat to a simmer, and poach the eggs for 3 to 5 minutes for firm whites and soft, runny yolks. Remove the eggs with a skimmer or spatula, and drain them on paper towels. Serve immediately.

Depending on the size of the pan, two to four eggs can be poached at a time.

Poached eggs may also be served cold.

Scrambled eggs

Eggs that are lightly beaten (just enough to break the yolk) and to which seasoning or other ingredients can be added; milk is often added for a smoother texture. To cook scrambled eggs, use a buttered or greased heavy frying pan and cook the eggs over a low, even heat, stirring constantly with a wooden spoon (6 to 10 minutes, depending on the quantity). It is generally suggested to use two eggs per person. When the eggs begin to set, they can be flavored with vegetables, mushrooms, cheese, ham, poultry, or seafood. Add salt and pepper at the end of cooking.

Fried eggs, sunny-side up

Eggs that are cooked on one side only in a frying pan over low heat. Using an egg ring will limit the spreading of the egg white in the pan. The eggs are ready when the white is firm and the yolk is runny and shiny. (When cooked, the albumen forms a thin translucent layer over the yolk, giving it this shiny appearance; if you want to avoid this, simply cover the eggs with a sheet of aluminum foil while they are cooking.) Shirring is another method of cooking eggs sunny-side up: the eggs are baked or broiled in individual shallow ramekins, requiring very little fat.

Fried eggs, over

Eggs that are fried in hot oil (peanut or corn) or butter, then carefully flipped over and quickly cooked on the other side. (The trick is to avoid breaking the yolk, and then to avoid overcooking it.) The eggs are ready when the white begins to turn golden; they are often served on toast.

Egg threads

Eggs or egg whites that are beaten and dropped through a fine strainer into a boiling liquid. The fine threads of egg set instantly upon contact with the hot liquid. This preparation is often used as a garnish for soups and consommés.

Omelet

Lightly beaten eggs that are seasoned with salt and pepper (and sometimes herbs) and cooked in a frying pan. There are different versions of the omelet, from the thick Italian *frittata* and the Spanish *tortilla* to the classic French omelet, which is soft on the inside, to lighter versions, like the Chinese *foo yung,* in which the eggs serve merely to bind the garnish. The classic French omelet is cooked quickly over high heat and folded in half; it is usually left slightly soft on the inside. Cheese or a precooked filling (vegetables, meat) can be added to the omelet before it is folded. In the flat omelet, or frittata, the filling (often potatoes, ham, onion, and peppers) is folded into the beaten eggs before they are cooked, making for a thicker consistency. The flat omelet is cooked more slowly and must be flipped or briefly run under the broiler in order to brown it on both sides.

pheasant egg

Beaten egg whites

Room-temperature egg whites that are whisked until they become thick and form peaks. When beaten, egg whites can expand to 8 times their original volume, especially if they are whisked in a copper bowl (the reaction between copper and conalbumin, a protein that is particularly abundant in egg whites, increases the volume and firmness of the foam).

When whisking egg whites, the following points should be observed:

• The whites should be at room temperature.

• The equipment should be immaculate; avoid using plastic utensils, as they tend to retain fatty substances which inhibit the frothing power of egg whites.

• Use a copper bowl if possible; avoid aluminum bowls.

• There should be no trace of yolk in the whites. Because yolks contain 35% fat, a single drop is enough to reduce the volume of the beaten whites by more than two thirds. When separating eggs, it is a good idea to collect each white in a small dish, ensuring that it contains no yolk before adding it to the others;

• A pinch of salt or cream of tartar can be added at the start to help obtain firm peaks. Sugar should be incorporated when the whites begin to foam; beat the whites until they form peaks that are stiff but not dry.

• When adding other ingredients to the whites, fold them in gently to avoid deflating the foam.

	large egg
protein	6.3 g
fat	5 g
carbohydrates	0.6 g
calories	75
	(50 g)

Storing

Eggs left out at room temperature will lose as much freshness in 1 day as eggs that are properly stored (at 40°F and 70% to 80% humidity) will lose in a week. The best place to keep eggs is in the refrigerator, where they will stay fresh for over a month; store them in their carton or in a covered container to prevent the loss of humidity and the absorption of odors. While it is common practice to place eggs in the door of the refrigerator, this may not be the best place to store them, since frequent opening of the door causes variations in temperature. Place eggs with the pointed end downward to prevent compression of the air chamber and displacement of the yolk. Avoid washing eggs, as this removes their protective layer and allows germs to penetrate; if they are dirty, wipe them with a dry cloth. Place unused raw whites or yolks in a covered container in the refrigerator, where they will keep for 4 days (cover the yolks with cold water to prevent them from drying out, and simply drain them before using them). Slightly beaten whole eggs or egg whites can be frozen for 4 months; yolks can be frozen on their own or beaten with whites. Never freeze eggs in their shell, as the cold causes them to crack.

Hard-boiled eggs will keep in the refrigerator for a week.

Nutritional Information

Considering that they contain the germ of a new life, it is not surprising that eggs are a highly nutritious food. There is no difference whatsoever between the nutritive value of white eggs and brown eggs, although the quantity of nutrients may vary with the size of the egg and the yolk. Egg protein is said to be «complete» because it provides the eight essential amino acids. These acids are essential to the human body and must be supplied by the food we eat, since the body is unable to produce them itself. Not only does egg protein provide these amino acids, but it does so in ideally balanced proportions; as a result, egg protein is used as a reference in assessing the content and value of proteins found in other foods.

Therefore, eggs are an excellent source of high-quality protein. The fat in eggs is composed of 32% saturated fatty acids, 38% monounsaturated fatty acids, and 14% polyunsaturated fatty acids; a large egg contains 5% cholesterol (213 milligrams). Eggs also contain vitamins and minerals. An egg weighing 50 grams is rich in vitamin B_{12} and is a good source of riboflavin; it also supplies vitamin D, folic acid, pantothenic acid, phosphorus, zinc, iron, and potassium.

The egg's nutrients are not equally distributed between the white and the yolk. The white supplies more than half of the protein and the larger portion of the potassium and riboflavin, while the yolk provides the A and D vitamins as well as most of the other vitamins and minerals; the yolk also contains all of the fat and three fourths of the total calories.

Egg whites can cause an allergic reaction in some people, which is why they are not recommended for children under 1 year of age. Raw egg whites contain avidin, a protein that combines with the vitamin biotin, thus blocking its absorption by the body; however, the risk of biotin deficiency is small, since this vitamin is found in many other foods and raw egg whites are not usually a significant part of a diet. Avidin is neutralized by cooking. Other types of protein present in egg whites inhibit the action of trypsin, a gastric enzyme secreted by the pancreas. Once again, however, this becomes a problem only in the unlikely event that large amounts of egg white are consumed. Like avidin, trypsin is neutralized by cooking.

Milk Products

Milk

Milk is the liquid secreted by the mammary glands of female mammals as food for their newborns. Human beings regard animal milk as a food that can be consumed throughout their lives, not just in infancy.

Cow's milk is the most common variety, but milk from sheep, goats, donkeys, horses, zebus (oxen), buffaloes, and reindeer is also consumed. Only 8.6% of the milk produced worldwide comes from buffaloes, goats, and sheep. At certain times in history, the milk of various animals (ewes, zebus, asses, buffaloes) was considered to be sacred. Unless otherwise specified, the word "milk" in this article refers to cow's milk.

Cow's milk and dairy products are commonly consumed in many parts of the world, including the United States, Canada, western and northern Europe, Australia, and New Zealand. Milk is consumed much less frequently in Asia and Africa.

The ability to digest lactose (a sugar found in milk from mammals) after early childhood is a genetic adaptation among milk-consuming populations. Asians, Africans, African Americans, Native Americans, and Inuit generally have some difficulty digesting lactose, as do people from the Middle East and northern Africa.

Lactose intolerance is caused by a deficiency in lactase, a digestive enzyme that transforms lactose into a substance that can be assimilated in the intestine. Within 2 hours of consuming milk, people who lack this enzyme can experience various symptoms, including abdominal pain, diarrhea, flatulence, bloating, nausea, and cramps. However, some people who are lactose intolerant can consume small amounts of milk (about 1 cup) without experiencing any symptoms.

These symptoms are rarely associated with the consumption of yogurt or aged cheeses, because the lactose in yogurt is decomposed or hydrolyzed and there is little or no lactose in cheese. However, cottage cheese, cream cheese, and cheese spreads do contain a certain amount of lactose and may provoke some of these symptoms.

As for milk, it appears that whole milk is easier to digest than skim milk. Most lactose-intolerant adults can digest milk from which 50% of the lactose has been removed: it is possible to buy dairy products that contain only 10% of the lactose normally found in milk.

Pasteurized milk – named for its inventor, the famous French chemist and microbiologist Louis Pasteur – is heated to a temperature below the boiling point, then rapidly chilled; this destroys most of the pathogenic bacteria and extends the shelf life of the milk.

In the pasteurization process, dairy products containing less than 3.25% milk fat are heated to 145°F (62.8°C) for 30 minutes or, in the case of rapid high-temperature pasteurization, to 163°F (72.8°C) for 16 seconds.

Milk can thus be pasteurized at different temperatures for various lengths of time. Ultra-rapid high-temperature pasteurization involves heating the milk to 192.2°F (89°C) for 1 second, then cooling it rapidly to 39.2°F (4°C). Milk that is pasteurized in this way retains more of its flavor and color, as well as more of its heat-sensitive nutrients such as thiamine, vitamin B_{12}, and lysine. However, pasteurization does involve the loss of a small amount (generally less than 10%) of certain water-soluble vitamins.

Homogenized milk is milk containing fat that has been forced through very small openings, which breaks the fat globules up into tiny particles that remain suspended in the liquid and cannot accumulate on the surface of the milk.

Ultrafiltered milk is milk that is filtered, then subjected to minimal pasteurization – a process that eliminates 99.9% of the bacteria found in milk, as opposed to the 99.4% eliminated by pasteurization alone. Ultrafiltration further prolongs the shelf life of milk without diminishing its nutritional value.

Raw milk is untreated milk. It is illegal to sell raw milk in many states, as well as in Canada and numerous European countries, because its consumption is regarded as a major health risk. An ideal medium for bacterial growth, raw milk can be easily contaminated; drinking it can cause illnesses such as tuberculosis and salmonellosis (food poisoning). (Pasteurization destroys virtually all of the pathogenic bacteria found in milk.) Where it is legal, raw milk is usually found in health-food stores.

Whole milk generally contains 3.5% fat. If it is not homogenized, the fat rises to the surface, forming a layer of cream. This layer does not form in homogenized milk because the fat is suspended in the liquid. Whole milk is fortified with vitamin D.

Lowfat or **partially skimmed milk** contains 1% to 2% fat and tastes slightly less rich than whole milk. It has practically the same nutritional value as whole milk but contains less fat and calories. Extra vitamin A is added to lowfat milk to compensate for the nutrients lost when the fat is removed. It is also fortified with vitamin D.

Nonfat or **skim milk** contains no more than 0.3% fat. Vitamin A is added to compensate for the nutrients lost when the fat is removed. It is also usually fortified with vitamin D.

Buttermilk is nonfat or lowfat milk with added bacteria that give it a tangy flavor; it is also slightly thicker than whole milk.

Acidophilus milk is whole, lowfat, or nonfat milk containing *Lactobacillus acidophilus,* bacteria that benefit the digestive system.

UHT or **ultrapasteurized milk** is subjected to a special kind of pasteurization known as "ultra heat treatment" (UHT). The milk is heated to very high temperatures, between 269.6°F (132°C) and 302°F (150°C), for 2 to 6 seconds, then chilled to room temperature and packaged in aseptic containers. This sterilization process destroys all of the organisms present in the milk, including the pathogenic bacteria and those responsible for coagulation, without substantially altering its nutritional value; the only nutrient that is affected is the vitamin C, but milk is not regarded as an important source of vitamin C. Some consumers do not like the flavor of UHT milk, which can taste slightly "cooked" and overrich.

UHT milk is packaged in sealed aseptic containers; it can be stored at room temperature for up to 3 months. Once the container is opened, the milk should be consumed within a few days, because it is particularly vulnerable to contamination by colon bacilli *(E. coli)*. Since UHT milk that has been contaminated does not curdle or show any other signs of deterioration, open containers should not be stored for any longer than 24 to 36 hours.

Dairy Products

593

Evaporated milk is whole, lowfat, or skim milk from which approximately 60% of the water has been evaporated. The milk is first evaporated, homogenized, and rapidly chilled; next, vitamins and stabilizers are added, and the milk is packaged in cans, tubes, or cartons; then it is sterilized. Evaporated milk contains at least 7.5% fat and 25.5% milk solids. It is slightly darker than regular milk, and it tastes somewhat caramelized as the result of a reaction that occurs between proteins and lactose when they are exposed to extreme heat.

To ensure that evaporated milk remains viscous when stored, stabilizers such as disodium phosphate, sodium citrate, or calcium chloride are added, along with the preservative sodium ascorbate. Since all of the nutrients in evaporated milk are concentrated, it is nourishing and high in calories (182 calories/125 ml for whole milk, 123 calories for lowfat milk, and 106 calories for skim milk). All varieties of evaporated milk are enriched with vitamins D and C; lowfat and skim evaporated milk must also be enriched with vitamin A.

Do not buy evaporated milk if the can appears to be swollen.

Since evaporated milk curdles very little when cooked, it can be used to make thick sauces and puddings. Evaporated whole milk can be whipped, but not until just before it is served, because it collapses very quickly.

Since evaporated milk is slightly sweet, add a little less sugar when using it in recipes.

Condensed milk is very much like evaporated whole milk, but it contains added sugar in the form of sucrose, dextrose, viscous glucose, semisolid glucose, lactose, or a mixture of these sweeteners. As with evaporated milk, 60% of the water is removed. Condensed milk contains 40% to 45% sugar, as well as at least 8% fat and 28% milk solids. It also contains stabilizing agents. The milk is pasteurized during the evaporation process; this exposure to high temperatures and the added sugar make further sterilization unnecessary. With the exception of the iron and the vitamin C, which are almost completely eliminated, all of the nutrients in the milk are concentrated. Condensed milk is particularly high in fat and calories (519 calories/125 ml). Regulations require that it be fortified with vitamin A, but vitamin D is an optional ingredient.

Condensed milk is used to make numerous desserts, candies, and cake decorations. You can reduce the number of calories in recipes that call for condensed milk by cutting down on the sugar.

Condensed milk thickens and caramelizes when it is boiled for 2 to 3 hours. Boil it in its sealed can, and do not open the can until it has cooled to avoid burning yourself. Caramelized condensed milk is delicious in desserts.

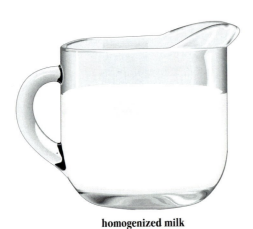

homogenized milk

evaporated milk

Flavored milk is milk to which a flavoring has been added. The most famous kind is of course chocolate milk, but there are several other varieties, including malted milk, fruit- or vanilla-flavored milk, and mixtures of milk and fruit juice. Lowfat flavored milk must contain between 0.3% and 3% fat.

The nutritional value of flavored milk, especially its fat content, depends mainly on the kind of milk that is used and on the amount of sugar that is added. Malted milk, which contains ground barley and wheat, can be sold plain, flavored, or dried.

Most flavored milks are ultra heat treated (UHT). Due to the nature of its ingredients, chocolate milk has to be thoroughly pasteurized – for a minimum of 30 minutes at 165.9°F (74.4°C) or for 25 seconds at 178°F (81.1°C); it may even be sterilized.

Powdered milk is dehydrated whole milk containing no more than 2.5% moisture or dehydrated skim milk containing no more than 4% moisture.

Most powdered milk is made with skim milk because it is less perishable; the fat in powdered whole milk tends to oxidize unless the product is vacuum-packed. Like fresh milk, powdered milk may be enriched with vitamins A and D. An unopened package of powdered milk can be stored for up to 1 year at room temperature, but it should be used within 1 month once opened. It will remain fresh longer if stored in a glass jar in the refrigerator.

Before it is dehydrated, the milk is usually heated until it attains a concentration of 35% milk solids.

Powdered whole milk contains a minimum of 26% fat, while powdered lowfat milk contains 9.5% and powdered skim milk 0.8%.

Prepare the milk as directed on the package; about 1 cup of non-instant powdered milk is usually combined with 1 pint of water, while about 1½ cups of instant powdered milk is required to make 1 quart of milk. Non-instant powdered milk should be diluted in a mixer or in lukewarm water. Two pounds of powdered milk yields approximately 10 quarts of reconstituted milk.

Plain non-instant powdered milk can be used to enhance the nutritional value of foods or to thicken sauces and puddings. Since 3 tablespoons of powdered skim milk is equivalent to a 1-cup serving of milk, it is a convenient way to add calcium and protein to foods. Instant powdered milk cannot be used in this way because rather than dissolving when combined with dry ingredients, it makes them lumpy. However, it dissolves easily in water, cereal, and drinks.

Powdered milk can be used as substitute for whipped cream: beat ¾ cup of powder with ½ cup of ice water and 1 tablespoon of lemon juice (to make the foam more stable) to make approximately 1 quart of whipped milk. Do not beat the milk until just before it is served because the foam collapses quickly.

Like milk solids, powdered skim milk is often added to baked goods, soups, prepared meats, candies, and dairy products. Reconstituted powdered milk can be used like any other kind of milk and should be stored with same amount of care.

Dairy Products

595

Buying

Cow's milk is usually sold pasteurized, homogenized, and in some cases sterilized; it is available whole, lowfat, nonfat, evaporated, flavored, and powdered.

Cooking

Milk has to be cooked in accordance with certain rules in order to preserve its nutritional value, taste, and consistency. It is also important to remember that milk "burns" very easily.

It is best to heat milk over low heat, in a double boiler if possible, because it boils over very quickly once it reaches the boiling point and readily sticks to the bottom of the pan, forming a precipitate that tends to turn brown.

A skin forms on the surface of milk when it is heated uncovered or without being stirred (or after it cools down). Milk proteins coagulate not only when heated but also when they come into contact with an acid ingredient or with enzymes. To prevent milk from coagulating when an acid ingredient is added, mix some cornstarch into the milk or into the acid ingredient, then heat the mixture gently.

Homogenization changes the way milk reacts when it is cooked. Homogenized milk coagulates more quickly; it also takes longer to cook because the heat penetrates the fat particles more slowly. Cooked homogenized milk has a softer texture, a milder taste, and a smoother consistency.

powdered milk

Nutritional Information

The rich taste of milk comes from the milk fat, which is among the most digestible of all edible fats because it is so finely emulsified. Forty-nine percent of the calories in whole milk come from the fat, which consists of 62% saturated fatty acids, 29% monounsaturated fatty acids, and 3.7% polyunsaturated fatty acids. The composition of the fat in skim milk is slightly different: 60% saturated fatty acids, 24% monounsaturated fatty acids, and 4% polyunsaturated fatty acids. Milk also contains an essential fatty acid, linoleic acid.

The proteins found in milk are excellent. They make up 38% of the non-fatty milk solids. Eighty-two percent of this protein is casein; found in no other food, casein gives milk its characteristic white color. Whey (the liquid that remains after the fat and casein are extracted from milk) makes up the remaining 18% of the protein.

Casein curdles when it comes into contact with an acid ingredient. Lactoglobulins and lactalbumins coagulate when heated, forming the skin on boiled milk. All of the essential amino acids in milk are present in sufficient quantities to perform their respective functions. Milk is particularly rich in lysine, which makes it a good complement for foods that lack this acid, such as cereals, nuts, and grains (see *Complementary proteins*).

Lactose makes up virtually all (97%) of the carbohydrates in milk; a disaccharide consisting of the monosaccharides glucose and galactose, lactose is found only in milk. The least sweet of all sugars, it is only about one sixteenth as sweet as sucrose. Depending on the type of milk, lactose makes up 30% to 56% of the calories. It also facilitates the absorption of calcium and enhances the absorption of magnesium, phosphorus, and zinc.

Milk is rich in calcium, phosphorus, and potassium; it also contains a moderate amount of sodium. Few foods provide as much calcium as milk, and the relative proportions of calcium and phosphorus, as well as the lactose, promote the intestinal absorption of calcium.

Rich in vitamin B_{12}, milk is also good source of riboflavin, a B-complex vitamin. However, it contains very little vitamin D. In North America and many European countries, vitamins A and D are added to liquid milk in order to prevent rickets and other health problems. In Canada, all types of milk must be enriched with vitamin D; lowfat and skim milk must also be fortified with vitamin A, while vitamin C must be added to evaporated milk. However, these vitamins do not have to be added to milk used to make dairy products such as cheese and yogurt. Milk is also a good source of magnesium and zinc, but it contains very little iron.

Betacarotene is the pigment that makes milk slightly yellowish; milk becomes yellower when made into butter because the carotene is concentrated.

Opinion is divided on the nutritional value of cow's milk. Its proponents claim that it is an indispensable food because it is plentiful, cheap, and very nourishing; they point to the fact that it is an excellent source of protein, vitamins, and minerals. It is also promoted as an important source of calcium, which is required for the development of healthy teeth and bones; calcium also helps to prevent osteoporosis and high blood pressure, and may play a role in the prevention of colorectal cancer and high cholesterol levels. Furthermore, it is thought that the population as a whole would be less likely to consume sufficient quantities of calcium, riboflavin, vitamin D, and vitamin B_{12} if dairy products were not consumed on a daily basis. It is important to note that even though bones stop growing when we reach our early thirties, bone cells are constantly renewed throughout our lives. Calcium also plays a role in the functioning of heart cells, nerves, and muscles.

Milk's detractors point out that it is meant to be eaten by calves, animals that become very large very quickly (they weigh about 75 pounds at birth and 350 pounds at 6 months), a characteristic not shared by humans. They note that in nature milk is consumed by newborns, not by adult animals.

Another concern of those opposed to the consumption of dairy products is the use of a hormone that increases the amount of milk that cows produce by 10% to 20%. The scientific name of this hormone is sometribove, but it is commonly known as bovine somatotropin. Over 25 countries have approved the use of this controversial hormone. The U.S. Food and Drug Administration approved it in 1993; the Canadian government is still studying the matter. In 1994 the European Economic Community banned the use of BST until at least 1999, when researchers are expected know more about its effects.

According to several researchers, bovine somatotropin hormone (BST) poses no danger to consumers because it is destroyed and rendered biologically inactive by the human digestive system. Produced by genetic recombination, BST is biologically equivalent to a naturally occurring hormone that controls lactation; it is thus present in all cow's milk, and there is no detectable difference between the milk produced by cows treated with the hormone and milk from untreated cows. Furthermore, the hormone does not affect the nutritional value of milk. Although there is no guarantee that the hormone will not have unforeseen effects, this seems quite unlikely in light of the numerous studies that have been done and the results obtained thus far.

As for the contention that the prevalence of inflamed udders among cows treated with this hormone leads to an increase in the use of antibiotics (and thus to possibility that antibiotics will show up in milk), somatotropin is said to be less likely to be the cause of this problem than other factors, such as the age of the animal or the time of year. Furthermore, some countries have adopted guidelines restricting the sale of dairy products containing traces of veterinary medicines. In Canada, for example, milk from cows treated with antibiotics must be discarded for a specific length of time, depending on the antibiotic in question. The use of organochlorinated pesticides for agricultural purposes is also prohibited.

	3.25% m.f.	2.0% m.f.	1.0% m.f.	skim
protein	8.5 g	8.6 g	8.5 g	8.8 g
fat	8.6 g	5.0 g	2.7 g	0.5 g
carbohydrates	12.0 g	12.4 g	12.3 g	12.6 g
cholesterol	35 mg	19 mg	10 mg	5 mg
				per cup (250 ml)

Serving Ideas

Milk is a key ingredient in the cuisines of many countries, especially Western countries. It is consumed as a drink and added to a vast array of foods, including soups, sauces (such as béchamel sauce), pancakes, cakes, pastries, desserts (such as flans, custards, and ice cream), purées, and a variety of cooked dishes. It is the basic ingredient in yogurt and cheese.

High-fat dairy products can be replaced with skim-milk products in most recipes.

Storing

Heat, oxygen, and light alter the nutritional value of milk. Their combined effects destroy many of the vitamins; in fact, over 90% of the vitamins can be eliminated within 2 hours. Since a single hour of exposure to light destroys 20% to 30% of the vitamin A, milk should be refrigerated as soon as possible. Buy milk sold in opaque containers whenever possible, and reseal the container tightly after each use.

Never pour excess milk back into the original container, because it may contaminate all of the remaining milk; store it in a separate sealed container. Milk can be refrigerated for about 10 days, but it will not last as long if left at room temperature for extended periods of time, such as during meals.

Reconstituted powdered milk is just as perishable as fresh milk and should also refrigerated.

Powdered milk can be stored at room temperature for about 6 months if the package is well sealed. Although powdered milk is regarded as a stable product, its taste, appearance, and nutritional value can change if it is stored at temperatures over 68°F (20°C). The same is true of UHT milk.

Open packages of powdered milk should be carefully resealed and stored in a cool, dark place because powdered milk readily absorbs humidity, which makes it lumpy and less flavorful.

Goat's milk

Goat's milk is whiter than cow's milk and has a stronger taste. It has been consumed by humans since prehistoric times. Unlike cow's milk, goat's milk does not have to be homogenized because its fat globules, which are very small in diameter, tend to remain suspended rather than floating to the surface.

Nutritional Information

Goat's milk contains slightly less cholesterol than cow's milk, but more or less the same proportions of fatty acids. However, there is one major difference between the fat in goat's milk and the fat in cow's milk: goat's milk is easier to digest because it contains more short-chain fatty acids. Tiny globules of these acids are dispersed throughout the milk, creating a very fine emulsion.

Goat's milk is rich in potassium, calcium, and phosphorus; a good source of riboflavin, it also contains vitamin A, magnesium, niacin, pantothenic acid, thiamin, zinc, vitamin B_{12}, vitamin B_6, and copper. Goat's milk does not have to be enriched; if it is labeled as "enriched," however, it must contain between 35 and 45 IU of vitamin D and between 140 and 300 IU of vitamin A per 100 ml, depending on the country.

	whole goat's milk
water	87%
protein	9.2 g
fat	10.7 g
carbohydrates	11.5 g
cholesterol	29 mg
sodium	128 mg
calories	177
	per cup (250 ml)

Buying

Goat's milk is usually available in health-food stores.

Serving Ideas

Goat's milk is used like cow's milk, for which it can often serve as a substitute. It can be consumed fresh, used in recipes, or made into cheese, yogurt, or butter.

Buttermilk

Buttermilk is a whitish, slightly sour-tasting liquid that separates from cream during the production of butter. Somewhat creamy, buttermilk separates into two layers when left undisturbed; the relatively light top layer is comprised of lactoserum and the bottom layer consists of fine lumps of coagulated casein. The buttermilk sold today is not a byproduct of the traditional butter-making process; it is made by adding a bacterial culture to skim, or partially skim, milk. This transforms a portion of the sugar naturally found in milk (lactose) into lactic acid, thus creating the sour taste associated with traditional buttermilk.

Buying

 Check the expiration date on the package to ensure that the buttermilk is fresh.

Serving Ideas

Buttermilk is a natural emulsifier that is often used to make baked goods, pastry, and ice cream; it is a very common ingredient in breads and cakes, especially in the form of a powder. Powdered buttermilk is an excellent emulsifier because it is rich in phospholipids, and it also has an appetizingly rich flavor. Buttermilk is added to soups and certain cheeses; it can also be blended with fruit to make delicious refreshing drinks or combined with fragrant herbs and lemon juice to make a cold sauce. Fresh milk to which vinegar has been added (2 teaspoons per cup) can replace buttermilk (and sour milk) in most recipes.

Storing

Unopened containers of buttermilk can be refrigerated for about 2 weeks. Once the container is opened, the buttermilk will remain fresh for about 1 week. Reseal the container tightly.

Nutritional Information

protein	8.6 g
fat	2.3 g
carbohydrates	12.4 g
cholesterol	9 mg
sodium	272 mg
	per cup (250 ml)

The nutritional value of buttermilk is similar to that of the skim, or partially skim, milk from which it is made. It is an excellent source of potassium, vitamin B_{12}, calcium, and riboflavin, and a good source of phosphorus. It also contains zinc, magnesium, pantothenic acid, niacin, thiamin, folic acid, and vitamin B_6. Low in fat, it is rich in lactic acid and nitrogen. It is often recommended for people with digestivem problems.

Sour cream

Sour cream (or soured cream) is an acidic-tasting cream equivalent to unpasteurized cream that has turned. The sour cream sold today is pasteurized cream that has been soured with a bacterial culture. "Cultured" and "acidified" sour cream are slightly different. Cultured sour cream is homogenized pasteurized cream that is soured with *Streptococcus lactis* at 71°F (22°C) until the level of acidity reaches at least 0.5%. Acidified sour cream is pasteurized cream that has been soured with bacteria that produce lactic acid. The cream is left to ferment for 12 to 14 hours, much like yogurt; it is sometimes stabilized with additives (gelatin, sodium alginate, carrageen) and may contain milk solids or whey, buttermilk, and salt. It is thick, uniform, and smooth.

Buying

Be sure to check the expiration date on the outside of the package.

Preparing

Sour cream can be made at home by adding 2 tablespoons of buttermilk to 2 cups of fresh cream and allowing the mixture to sour at room temperature, without disturbing it, for at least 24 hours. This cream will keep for 3 days in the refrigerator.

Cooking

Add sour cream to hot food at the last minute and reheat it gently without allowing it to boil, or the sour cream may separate.

Storing

Sour cream can be refrigerated for 2 to 3 weeks. It should not be frozen because it will separate when defrosted.

Serving Ideas

Sour cream makes food taste slightly acidic. It is a common ingredient in German, British, Russian, and Polish cuisine; it is frequently added to soups, dips, sauces, stuffed cabbage, goulash, breads, and cakes. Two of the most common sour-cream dishes are eastern European borscht and Smetana sauce, which is traditionally served with game in Russia. In the United States, baked potatoes are rarely eaten without a touch of sour cream. Add sour cream to hot food at the last minute and reheat it gently without allowing it to boil, or the sour cream may separate.

Plain yogurt can be substituted for sour cream in most recipes, which can help to reduce the number of calories and the amount of fat. Yogurt that is too runny can be thickened with powdered milk.

Nutritional Information

	14% (m.f.) cultured sour cream	18% (m.f.) cultured sour cream
water	78.1%	74%
protein	0.8 g	1.0 g
fat	4 g	5.2 g
carbohydrates	1.2 g	1.2 g
cholesterol	12 mg	12 mg
		per 30 ml

Saturated fatty acids make up 63.5% of the fat in regular sour cream, and 62.7% of the fat in 18%-milk-fat cultured sour cream.

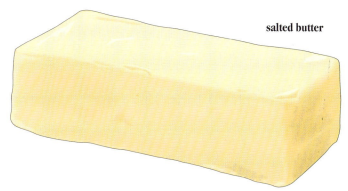

salted butter

Butter is a smooth, fatty substance that is made by churning cream. Churning causes the fat in the cream to separate from the liquid (the remaining watery portion is known as buttermilk). It takes about 10 quarts of milk to make 1 pound of butter. Before it can be churned, the cream has to be separated from the milk because the fat is the only part of the milk that can be made into butter.

Although butter is usually made from cow's milk, it can also be made from the milk of other mammals such as goats, donkeys, horses, buffalos, and camels. Usually produced by local dairies, these rather strong-tasting butters are used mainly in Asia, Africa, and certain parts of South America. The word "butter" also refers to creamy, fatty substances derived from a variety of sources; the names of these butters specify the source (peanut butter, cocoa butter, almond butter, coconut butter). In ancient times, butter was used in religious ceremonies and as a medication; for example, it was applied as a plaster to infected or burned skin. The ancient Greeks and Romans rarely cooked with butter, but they did use it as a medicine, especially as a salve. And no matter what the source, they always referred to butter as *butyrum* (Latin) or *bouturon* (Greek), meaning "cow's cheese." Butter was not used in Italy or France until the 15th century. During the Middle Ages, the butter produced on farms and in dairies was put in stoneware pots and covered with salted water, then sold at markets. North African and Arab cooks rely on clarified butter, or *smeun,* which fares much better than regular butter in hot climates. Butter is now produced in such vast quantities that many countries have enormous stockpiles of surplus butter.

Preparing

Measuring butter is no easy task in countries like the United States and Canada, where recipes specify the volume rather than the weight required. One solution to this problem is to measure the butter in water:

• If you need a quarter cup of butter, put a quarter cup of water in a measuring cup and add butter until the water reaches the half-cup mark; then pour off the water and drain the butter. (It may be useful to know that 500 g of butter is equivalent to 500 ml of butter.) Butter can be "clarified" by removing the whey. Known as *ghee* in Indian cuisine, clarified butter is a clear, oil-like liquid that can be fried.

To clarify butter, melt it over very low heat and allow it to separate into three layers: the layer of foam on the surface, the layer of pure fat in the middle (a thick yellow liquid) and the whey at the bottom of the pan.

• Skim the foam off the surface with a spoon, then slowly pour the butter (through muslin if desired) into a container without disturbing the whey at the bottom of the pan. The butter can also be refrigerated after it has been heated and skimmed; when chilled, the clarified butter forms a crust that can be easily removed from the liquid whey.

Home-made clarified butter can be refrigerated for about 2 months and frozen for up to 3 months. Store-bought clarified butter can be left at room temperature.

Storing

Butter readily absorbs odors and can lose moisture if it is not well packaged; dehydration heightens its color and alters its flavor. Butter can also be discolored by mold or other marks caused by bacteria or fungi. If stored for too long at room temperature, it can taste rancid. Seal it tightly in its original packaging or ensure that it is well covered, and store it in the refrigerator away from foods whose odors it is likely to absorb. Butter is usually packaged in material that protects it from the light and prevents oxidization, the absorption of odors, moisture loss, and discoloration. Unopened unsalted butter should not be refrigerated for any longer than 8 weeks, but salted butter in its original packaging can be refrigerated for up 12 weeks. Once a package of butter is opened, it should be used within 3 weeks.

Butter can be frozen, but it begins to lose some of its flavor after about 6 months. Freezing can also make butter taste more salty.

Serving Ideas

Butter is a key ingredient in the cuisines of many countries, because it gives food an incomparable flavor. It is used primarily in sauces (kneaded butter, roux, Béarnaise sauce, hollandaise sauce), pastry (French butter cream, puff pastry), creams, and soups. A staple food, it is eaten on bread, canapés, toast, and sandwiches.

Various ingredients are added to cold butter to make the flavored butters used to season grilled foods, fish, snails, seafood, canapés, vegetables, and soups. The butter is first creamed with a wooden spoon or spatula. Ingredients such as garlic, shallots, parsley, horseradish, caviar, mustard, Roquefort cheese, sardines, watercress, lemons, and almonds are then finely chopped and puréed; some ingredients are cooked until the water they contain evaporates. Finally, the chosen ingredients are combined with the butter, which is then formed into a roll, wrapped, and refrigerated or frozen. Whipped butter should not be used in recipes that call for ordinary butter; nor should "light" butter, which contains much more water than regular butter. These butters are normally used only as sandwich spreads.

Cooking

Since butter burns more easily than oil, it should not be cooked at high temperatures. However, it can withstand higher temperatures when used in combination with oil (heat the oil before adding the butter).

Solid butter is easier to digest than melted butter that has begun to separate. The fat in butter begins to break down at temperatures as low as 250° to 260°F (120° to 130°C). When heated to higher temperatures, butter becomes dark and releases an indigestible toxic substance called acrolein that can lead to increases in blood-cholesterol levels.

Nutritional Information

	light butter	whipped butter	salted butter	unsalted butter
protein	0.4 g	0.1 g	traces	traces
fat	3.9 g	7.8 g	8.2 g	8.2 g
carbohydrates	0.6 g	traces	traces	traces
cholesterol	12 mg	21 mg	22 mg	22 mg
sodium	69 mg	79 mg	82 mg	2 mg
				per 10 g

Whipped butter, salted butter, and unsalted butter all contain vitamin A.

Regular butter is comprised of 80% to 82% animal fat, 14% to 16% water, and up to 4% salt. Sixty-two percent of the fat is made up of saturated fatty acids containing 22 mg of cholesterol per 10 g. Also high in calories, butter contains 72 calories per 10 g. It contains only minuscule amounts of protein, carbohydrates, vitamins, and minerals, with the exception of vitamin A and added sodium, which makes up 2% of salted butter and 1% of lightly salted butter. Unsalted butter does not contain any sodium.

Whipped butter is slightly lower in calories (69 calories/10 g) and fat (7.8 g/10 g) than regular butter.

"Light" butter contains only half as many calories as regular butter, as well as 50% less fat, 46% less cholesterol, and 25% less salt. Low-fat butter should not contain any more than 39% fat. Softer than regular butter, it may contain emulsifying agents, stabilizers and preservatives, salt, and artificial coloring.

A controversial food, butter is defended by dairy producers as a "natural" product and condemned by those concerned about the high percentages of saturated fatty acids and cholesterol it contains. Oil and margarine manufacturers are among its most vocal critics. It is important to note, however, that the total amount of fat in your diet is much more significant than your consumption of one particular kind of fat. That being said, butter should be eaten in moderation because it does contain high levels of fat, saturated fatty acids, and cholesterol.

C ream is the fat that rises to the surface of nonhomogenized milk during the first stage of the butter-making process. American regulations stipulate that cream must contain at least 18% fat, but in Europe the term "cream" is reserved for products made from cow's milk that contain at least 30% fat. Until the end of the 19th century, cream was produced by allowing milk to separate for 24 hours in a cool place, then skimming the concentrated fat off the surface with a ladle. A smooth, yellowish white substance, cream is now obtained by means of centrifugation. Nine quarts of milk are required to make 1 quart of cream. In order to be whipped, cream must contain at least 30% fat; the tiny air bubbles produced when cream is whipped make it light, doubling its volume and creating firm peaks. Chantilly cream is made by adding sugar and vanilla to whipped cream; it is named for the French château where it was invented by the famous chef Vatel.

Cream is sold under various labels according to its fat content. Regulations stipulating the amount of fat each variety of cream must contain vary from one country to another.

In the United States, a distinction is made between light whipping cream (the more widely available), which must contain at least 30% but no more than 36% fat, and heavy whipping cream, which must contain at least 36% fat. In Europe, this kind of cream is known simply as heavy cream and must contain at least 30% fat; it is sold untreated, pasteurized, or ultra-heat-treated (UHT).

In Canada, whipping cream contains between 32% and 40% fat. A product referred to as heavy cream or country cream is also available; it contains only 15% fat but has the same consistency as 35% cream and can be whipped.

Light cream, which is also known as table cream, contains between 15% and 18% fat. In Europe, this kind of cream is known as single cream and contains between 12% and 30% fat.

Coffee cream contains 10% fat. Half-and-half cream is mixed with milk, then pasteurized and sometimes homogenized; it contains between 10.5% and 18% fat.

Double cream contains approximately 40% fat.

Dried cream contains 40% to 70% fat.

Cream substitutes

There are numerous artificial creams or creamers on the market. They are sold dried or frozen, in the form of a liquid or in pressurized cans. These products, which include coffee cream and whipped cream, are made with hydrogenated vegetable and animal fats such as coconut oil and cabbage-palm oil, or with partially hydrogenated soy oil; they also contain sweeteners (sugar, glucose) and additives. Used mainly to modify the texture, these additives help the products retain the desired consistency. They include emulsifiers, gelling agents, stabilizers, and thickeners. The number and quantity of additives vary, depending on how the product is manufactured.

Cream substitutes and coffee creamers are practical, but their nutritional value is questionable because they contain virtually no vitamins and very few minerals. They are also higher in saturated fat than the products they replace and are made from hydrogenated oils. (Hydrogenation is a process that solidifies oils by transforming polyunsaturated fatty acids into substances that act like saturated fatty acids, which raise blood-cholesterol levels and increase the risk of heart disease.)

Dairy Products

Buying

Cream is pasteurized and homogenized before it is sold; it may also be sterilized, either by normal means or by means of ultra-heat treatment (UHT). Cream has to be heated to higher temperatures than the milk from which it is derived because it contains more bacteria. It is thus heated to a minimum of 150° to 154.9°F (65.6° to 68.3°C) for 30 minutes or to 170° to 174.9°F (76.7° to 79.4°C) for 16 seconds. Light creams and table creams also have to be homogenized to make them thicker, as well as to prevent the whey and the fat from separating. Whipping cream does not have to be homogenized because pasteurization liquefies the fat globules.

Be sure to check the expiration date on the package.

Serving Ideas

Cream is widely used in cooking because its taste and texture are hard to match. It is added to coffee, vinaigrettes, soups, sauces, omelets, terrines, desserts, candies, and liqueurs. Milk and yogurt are being substituted for cream more and more frequently, as people become increasingly concerned about their consumption of fat and calories. However, it is interesting to note that, in terms of volume, creams containing 35% fat or less are lower in calories than butter, margarine, or oil.

Whipped cream decorates and enriches pastries, soufflés, pies, ices, charlottes, Bavarian creams, sauces, and fruit. It is an essential ingredient in *vacherins* (cream-filled meringues) and cream puffs.

Cream can still be used once it turns sour, especially in cooking. However, it is a less versatile ingredient than commercial sour cream, because pasteurization alters its lactic acids, making it taste a little too bitter.

Preparing

Whipped cream should be beaten at the last minute unless it can be refrigerated, because it tends to deteriorate in the heat. Use chilled utensils if possible; refrigerate them for 30 minutes or put them in the freezer if you are short of time. Do not add anything (sugar, vanilla) to the cream until it begins to foam. Whipped cream will hold up for a few hours, but once it starts to turn yellow, it can turn into butter.

Cooking

Cream should not be added to soups or simmered dishes until the last minute to prevent it from going lumpy, nor should it be allowed to boil hard (it can be simmered).

Nutritional Information

	light cream (15% m.f.)	*whipping cream (35% m.f.)*
water	77.5%	59.6%
protein	0.8 g	0.6 g
fat	4.6 g	10.6 g
carbohydrates	1.2 g	0.8 g
cholesterol	16 mg	38 mg
		per 30 ml

Whipping cream (35% milkfat) contains vitamin A. Cream is high in calories because it is a relatively fatty food. Sixty-two percent of the fat is comprised of saturated acids; and like all animal fats, it contains cholesterol. Depending on its fat content, cream contains between 10 and 38 milligrams of cholesterol per 30 milliliters.

Storing

Fresh cream is a very perishable food, unless it is pasteurized and sterilized or ultra-heat-treated (UHT), then packaged in sterile containers. Like milk, it is an ideal medium for the development of bacteria and turns sour when exposed to heat and light. It should be stored in the refrigerator and used before its expiration date. Unopened UHT or long-storage cream can be stored for up to 45 days at room temperature; once opened, however, it is just as perishable as other dairy products and should be refrigerated. Whipped cream will retain its consistency for several hours when refrigerated. Cream should not be frozen, because freezing alters its flavor and tends to give it a granular texture. Furthermore, cream that has been frozen cannot be whipped.

plain yogurt

Yogurt is a fermented dairy product obtained by adding lactic bacteria to milk. The word "yogurt" (or "yoghurt" or "yoghourt") is derived from the Turkish word *yoghurmak,* meaning "to thicken." Yogurt is in fact the modern version of "curds."

Yogurt is thought to have originated in Bulgaria – a country where people eat yogurt on a regular basis and where an unusually high number of people live to be at least 100 years old. At the beginning of the century, Metchnikoff, one of Pasteur's collaborators, identified the two lactic bacteria used to make yogurt – *Streptococcus thermophilus* and *Thermobacterium bulgaricus.*

The fact that milk curdles was almost certainly discovered by accident, but people have probably relied on curdling as a means of preserving milk since the earliest days of the history of agriculture. Yogurt is a traditional food in several parts of the world, including Greece, Turkey, Mongolia, India, the Middle East and certain parts of Asia. It has been a staple food in the Balkans, Turkey and Asia for centuries, but it was not widely consumed in western Europe until the 1920s. Furthermore, attempts to market yogurt in the West during the first half of the 20th century were largely unsuccessful because people found the taste too bitter. In fact, yogurt did not become popular until producers started flavoring it with fruit and fruit juices. In North America, it took even longer for yogurt to gain acceptance, but the consumption of yogurt has increased dramatically in recent years. During the 1970s and 80s, yogurt sales in some parts of North America increased by as much as 500%. However, Europeans still consume 3 to 5 as much yogurt as North Americans.

Yogurt is made with milk (cow's milk, goat's milk, ewe's milk or soy milk) by adding fermenting agents that transform part of the lactose (the main sugar in milk) into lactic acid. These agents, which are different from those used to make cheese, are the two bacteria *Lactobacillus bulgaricus* and *Streptococcus thermophilus,* which work together to produce more lactic acid than either of them could separately. During the first part of the fermentation process, the *streptococcus* bacteria do most of the work, but once the milk starts to become acidic the *lactobacilli* take over, because they remain more active in acidic environments. Ideally, equal amounts of the two bacteria should be used, but store-bought yogurt often contains less *Lactobacillus bulgaricus,* because it makes yogurt more acidic and more bitter-tasting.

The milk coagulates once a sufficient quantity of lactic acid has been produced; biological transformations that make the milk proteins easier to assimilate occur at the same time. The bacteria are most active at temperatures between 104° and 122°F (40° and 50°C). Once the yogurt has fermented for the appropriate length of time, it need only be chilled to stop the bacteria from fermenting it any further. Unlike cheese, yogurt is not drained.

Whether plain, stirred or firm, yogurt is made with the same basic mixture of ingredients: a specific amount of whole or partially skimmed milk enriched with a dry extract – whole or skim-milk powder, or milk that has been concentrated by means of evaporation. Stabilizers (gelatin or pectin) are added to this mixture when it is preheated. The mixture is then homogenized and hyperpasteurized to make it thicker and smoother. At this point, it is cooled to 111°-115°F (44°- 46°C) in preparation for the addition of the *Lactobacillus bulgaricus* and the *Streptococcus thermophilus.* The incubation period lasts anywhere from 2 to 6 hours, depending on the desired degree of acidity. The yogurt is then chilled to 39°F (4°C), which slows down the bacterial action, allowing the yogurt to be stored for about 1 month.

Commercially produced yogurt is firmer and less likely to secrete whey, the yellowish liquid that often accumulates on the surface of natural yogurt. The separation of the whey does not affect the quality of the yogurt, but manufacturers and consumers prefer a more homogeneous product.

There is wide variety of yogurt on the market, including firm yogurt (the oldest kind of yogurt), stirred yogurt (a Swiss innovation) and products such as frozen yogurt, yogurt drinks and dried yogurt.

Firm yogurt looks like compact jelly. It is fermented and chilled in the containers in which it is sold; if it is flavored with natural or artificial products, they are deposited in the bottom of the containers.

Stirred yogurt is mixed after it is fermented and chilled, which makes it more homogeneous and smoother. It often contains solidifying agents such as carrageen or gelatin, as well as natural and artificial flavorings.

Yogurt drinks, which are marketed as an alternative to soft drinks, consist of fermented milk sweetened with fruit-flavored syrups or a mixture of sugar and fruit; **frozen yogurt** is similar to ice cream.

It is important to note that many of these products are pasteurized or subjected to ultra heat treatment (UHT) — processes that destroy the bacterial culture and eliminate many of the benefits of fermentation. Many of them also contain additives. For example, frozen yogurt often contains modified cellulose gum, guar gum, polysorbate 80, carrageen, mono- and diglycerides, potassium sorbate, as well as artificial colorings and flavorings.

Yogurt is just one of the many foods made with fermented milk, which also include curd, kefir and kumiss.

Curd is milk that is fermented naturally at room temperature, without the addition of a bacterial culture. Heat activates the lactic flora in the milk, producing lactic acid that curdles the milk. Curdled milk separates into two distinct substances — curd and whey. It is stirred or drained before it is eaten.

kefir

yogurt with fruit

Although once very popular, curd is now extremely rare because pasteurization and homogenization destroy some of the lactic flora required to curdle milk. Sterilized milk and UHT milk cannot be fermented. Since curd is very perishable, it should be stored in the refrigerator and eaten as soon as possible.

Kefir is whole or partially skimmed milk that has been fermented by the combined action of several species of bacteria and yeasts. Slightly fizzy and alcoholic, it has a piquant, somewhat bitter flavor. Its alcohol content is usually about 1% but can be as high as 2%. Thought to have originated in Caucasia, kefir is a very common drink in eastern Europe, Russia and the Middle East. It is produced industrially in Russia.

The fermenting agents in kefir consist of a mixture of yeasts *(Saccharomyces kefir* and *Candida kefir)* and various bacteria (such as *Lactobacillus caucasicus, L. casei, Streptococcus lactis* and *Streptococcus diacetilactis).* This combination of microorganisms forms a zoogloea — i.e., gelatinous grains that can be easily strained out of the fermented milk. The bacteria produce lactic acid that creates a bitter, yogurt-like taste, and the yeasts transform the lactose into a mixture of carbon dioxide and alcohol. The amount of alcohol in the kefir, as well as the thickness and smoothness of the final product, depend on the length of the fermentation process. When poured, kefir froths and bubbles like beer. It can be also be made with dried fruit or lemons, but this requires a different combination of fermenting agents.

Kefir is easy to make: add kefir grains to milk that has been warmed to between 68° and 72°F (20° to 22°C) and allow the mixture to ferment at room temperature for 1 or 2 days. The closer the temperature is to 72° F, the faster it will ferment. Traditionally, the milk is fermented with tiny yellow kefir grains, which become whiter when combined with milk. Often difficult to find in stores, kefir grains can be saved after each use and stored at 39°F (4°C) for up to 10 days. Freeze-dried kefir cultures are also available; they can be stored almost indefinitely. It is also possible to use a powdered culture or a portion of previously made kefir that is less than a month old. Kefir can be used like yogurt.

Kefir is more perishable than yogurt and should be stored in the refrigerator. It can still be used once it turns sour, especially for cooking. Kefir is delicious when served ice cold with mint leaves, or when served over fruit. It can be served as a drink or eaten like yogurt.

Kumiss (or **koumiss)** resembles kefir, but it can contain as much as 2.5% alcohol. It is made with mare's, ass's or cow's milk, and its flavor sometimes approximates that of white wine. It has been widely consumed on the Russian steppes and in Asia for centuries, and was particularly popular during the time of the Tatars, the Cossacks and the Russians — i.e., from the 13th to the 19th century. It is a traditional drink in central Asia.

Buying

 Check the expiration date when buying yogurt to ensure that it is as fresh as possible. Yogurt can be eaten after its expiration date as long as it still has a pleasant taste and there are no visible molds or bubbles – a sign that it has begun to ferment. The accumulation of liquid on the surface does not mean that the yogurt has begun to deteriorate.

Serving Ideas

Yogurt can be eaten "as is" or combined with other foods. Used in a wide variety of ways, it is added to savory as well as sweet dishes (soups, salads, meat, poultry, fish, rice, pasta, bread, cakes, pies, brioches, desserts, drinks). Yogurt is the basic ingredient in a variety of hot and cold soups, as well as cold sauces served with grilled meats; it is also used as a marinade for meat, poultry and game, which it tenderizes.

Yogurt is a key ingredient in the cuisines of many countries, especially in the Middle East and India. In Indian cuisine, yogurt is served with curries and is the basic ingredient in *raita,* a mixture of flavored yogurt and finely chopped fruit or vegetables that is served as a cool refreshment throughout meals.

Whether liquefied, whipped or sour, plain yogurt can replace cream; it can also be added to mayonnaise or vinaigrettes to reduce their content in fat and calories. When using yogurt as a substitute for cream in hot dishes, add a little cornstarch to prevent it from separating. Leave yogurt at room temperature for 1 or 2 hours before adding it to cooked foods, and whenever possible, add it at the last minute to prevent it from boiling.

Preparing

Making yogurt at home is a cheap and easy way to obtain sugar-free yogurt that contains vitamins A and D.

The first step is to carefully clean the required utensils, then rinse them under very hot water or sterilize them.

Next combine the milk with 3 to 5% skim-milk powder and heat this mixture to 185°F (85°C) for about 30 minutes. The fresh milk can be whole, partially skimmed or even UHT milk.

The amount of fat and milk solids in the milk affects the texture, the flavor and the nutritional value of the yogurt. Yogurt made with whole milk is firmer, more flavorful, and higher in fat and calories than yogurt made with skim milk. Adding powdered milk (3 to 8 tablespoons per quart of milk) thickens the yogurt, making it creamier and enhancing its nutritional value.

Once the milk reaches the boiling point, gelatin or pectin can be added (1 teaspoon per quart of milk). Before adding the gelatin or pectin, allow it to soak in a small amount of milk until it swells completely (there is no need to add pectin when using dried cultures, because they will thicken the yogurt).

A thermometer can help you control the temperature and lets you know precisely when to add the fermenting agent.

Cool the milk to 111°-115°F (44°-46°C), then add the fermenting agent or the dehydrated (freeze-dried) culture; it is also possible to use home-made yogurt (2 to 5 tablespoons per quart of milk) that is less than 5 days old, or plain store-bought yogurt that is as fresh as possible and contains active bacteria but no starch or gelatin. To minimize the risk of contamination, the amount of yogurt required to make the next batch should be set side before the current batch is consumed.

Yogurt made with a dried culture is the creamiest variety, and is thicker and less acidic than yogurt made with commercially produced yogurt; it also remains fresh longer and can be used to make a few additional batches of home-made yogurt. After about 1 month or 3 uses as a fermenting agent, the yogurt begins to deteriorate and should not be used again.

Avoid stirring yogurt once it begins to coagulate, or it will evaporate and become watery. It should be left undisturbed for 4 to 6 hours at a constant temperature of 108°F (42°C).

The temperature at which yogurt is incubated is crucial. The ideal temperature is between 104° and 115 F (40° and 46°C). The bacteria will be destroyed at temperatures over 115°F, and the yogurt will not coagulate; if the temperature is under 104°F, the yogurt will take longer to coagulate and will taste more bitter.

Yogurt-makers are practical but not essential. Any constant source of heat that is protected from drafts will do. Yogurt can be curdled in an oven preheated to 120°F

(50°C) or in an oven with a light bulb that provides sufficient heat. It is also possible to use a preheated thermos, or a dish or frying pan filled with hot water and covered with a thick cloth to retain the heat; another option is to wrap the container and place it inside an unheated oven, on a radiator or near some other source of low, constant heat.

Once the yogurt coagulates – i.e., once it achieves the desired taste and consistency – it should be refrigerated immediately to stop the bacteria from coagulating it any further. Fruit and other ingredients should not be added until the yogurt is served.

If the yogurt fails to thicken, it may be the result of any one of a number of factors: the bacterial culture may be too old, the temperature may be too hot or too cold, or it may need more time or extra milk powder. Add a new fermenting agent or additional milk powder before attempting to thicken the yogurt again.

If the yogurt is sour or the whey separates from the curd, it may have been heated for too long or cooled too slowly. You can beat the whey back into yogurt, but the final product will still be quite runny.

Homemade yogurt can be refrigerated for up to 3 weeks.

1 *Heat the milk to 185°F (85°C) for about 30 minutes.*

2 *Chill the milk to 111°-115°F (44°-46°C), then add the fermenting agent.*

3 *Pour the mixture into a container, then cover it with plastic wrap and keep it warm for 4 to 8 hours.*

Nutritional Information

Yogurt is an excellent source of protein, calcium, phosphorus, potassium and vitamins A and B. The nutritional value of unsweetened plain yogurt is almost identical to that of the milk with which it is made, with the additional benefits associated with fermentation. It is important to note, however, that unlike milk that is marketed as a drink, the milk used to make yogurt does not have to be enriched with vitamins A, D and C.

The nutritional value of commercially produced yogurt varies greatly, especially in terms of its content in fat, carbohydrates and calories. Certain kinds of yogurt contain as much as 10% fat, which is significantly more than the 3.4% found in whole milk. As for the cholesterol content of yogurt, plain and flavored varieties contain between 7.5 and 12.5 milligrams per 125 g. Plain yogurt usually contains about 7% carbohydrates, but yogurt with fruit can contain anywhere from 11 to 18% and is thus higher in calories (usually between 79 and 144 calories/125 g). Yogurt often contains additives (stabilizers, thickeners, flavorings, colorings), which may or may not be essential and are sometimes omitted.

Various medicinal properties are ascribed to yogurt; it is not only said to promote longevity when consumed on a regular basis (this theory has yet to be proven), but is also reputed to benefit the digestive system by, among other things, repairing intestinal flora that have been damaged by antibiotics; it may also help to prevent cancer and may alleviate insomnia when eaten just before bedtime. However, further research is required before it can be said with certainty that dairy products such as yogurt can play a role in the prevention of cancer.

Yogurt is also used to treat vaginitis; the bacteria *L. acidophilus* is thought to be the active and curative ingredient. However, in order to be beneficial, the acidophil bacterial culture must be alive, which is not the case when yogurt made with active cultures is pasteurized.

Yogurt is more digestible than milk because it dissolves in the stomach three times faster – i.e., in about an hour. It also contains bacteria that make lactose easier to digest. It remains to be shown whether the body can absorb and retain the calcium in some dairy products better than the calcium in others. Furthermore, there is as yet very little data with regard to whether the fat in yogurt is more readily absorbed than the fat in unfermented milk.

Storing

Yogurt should not be left at room temperature for any longer than is absolutely necessary. It can be refrigerated for 2 to 3 weeks.

Freezing does not appear to affect the fermenting agents in yogurt, but it should not be frozen for any longer than 1 month. It is best to defrost yogurt slowly in the refrigerator rather than at room temperature.

The dried fermenting agents used to make yogurt can be stored at room temperature for 6 months, refrigerated for 12 months and frozen for 18 months.

Tzatziki

SERVES 4

2 cups (500 ml) plain yogurt
1 medium cucumber
2 cloves garlic
1 tbsp. olive oil

3 tbsp. Italian parsley
1 tbsp. dill
Salt and ground pepper

1. Peel the cucumber and cut it in two lengthwise, then remove the seeds and grate it coarsely. Peel and crush the garlic. Chop the parsley and dill.

2. Combine all the ingredients and season them to taste. Chill the mixture for at least 1 hour to allow the flavors to blend.

Serve with grilled fish or as a dip.

Ice cream

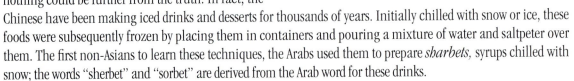

Ice cream is a sweet, flavored substance made from frozen dairy products. Although we tend to assume that ice cream (which is sometimes referred to simply as ice) is a recent invention made possible by modern freezing techniques, nothing could be further from the truth. In fact, the Chinese have been making iced drinks and desserts for thousands of years. Initially chilled with snow or ice, these foods were subsequently frozen by placing them in containers and pouring a mixture of water and saltpeter over them. The first non-Asians to learn these techniques, the Arabs used them to prepare *sharbets,* syrups chilled with snow; the words "sherbet" and "sorbet" are derived from the Arab word for these drinks.

Ices were first produced in Europe during the 13th century, when Marco Polo brought the secret of ice-making back to Italy after a trip to China. Iced products were initially reserved for royalty, but street vendors began to sell ices at the end of the 19th century. Ices and ice creams were an immediate success, and they continue to be just as popular. In the United States, for example, 1.3 billion gallons of ice cream were produced in 1988.

Traditional ice cream contains milk, cream, sugar, natural flavors, and, usually, eggs. To prevent the formation of ice crystals, this mixture is beaten shortly after it starts to freeze, thus ensuring that the final product is light and creamy. Some countries have passed regulations specifying the minimum amount of milk fat that a product must contain in order to be called "ice cream"; any product that does not meet this standard must be labeled "milk dessert."

Industrially produced ice cream is generally made from a mixture of cream, fat-free milk solids, and milk or evaporated milk (or both). It also contains sugar, emulsifiers, stabilizers, essences, and coloring agents, which can be natural but are usually artificial. The milk solids usually come from concentrated or powdered skim milk, but they sometimes come from concentrated or powdered lactoserum; concentrated lactoserum proteins may even be used. Milk solids comprise 16% to 24% of ice cream. The sugar in ice cream can be either sucrose or sugars derived from corn syrup (dextrose, maltose, dextrine).

A specific amount of sugar (14% to 16%) should be used to make ice cream, in order to ensure that it has a rich and delicate flavor. The sugar promotes the formation of small ice crystals, thus preventing the ice cream from becoming sticky and hard. Egg yolk – a natural emulsifier containing lecithin, which plays a key role in the homogenization process – is almost always replaced with less expensive emulsifiers (mono- and diglycerides, polyoxyethylene derivatives, lecithin). Texturing and stabilizing agents (carrageen or Irish moss, guar gum, carboxymethylcellulose) ensure that the ice cream retains the desired consistency, minimize the formation of large ice crystals, and prevent the ice cream from melting too quickly at room temperature. These additives can also act as preservatives.

When using liquid milk, commercial ice-cream manufacturers condense it to remove surplus water before adding the milk solids, the sugar, and the various additives (as well as optional ingredients like fruit, nuts, raisins, candies, etc.). This mixture is then pasteurized at 150° to 175°F (70° to 85°C) for 2 to 20 seconds; the bacteria cannot be eliminated at lower temperatures because the mixture is so thick and sticky. Ice cream can also be sterilized by means of UHT pasteurization – i.e., at 200° to 265°F (100° to 130°C) for 1 to 40 seconds. After it is pasteurized, the mixture is homogenized in order to smooth out and stabilize the emulsion. It is then insufflated with air as it is frozen. It is quickly chilled to a temperature of about 22° or 23°F (-5° or -6°C) to promote the formation of numerous small ice crystals.

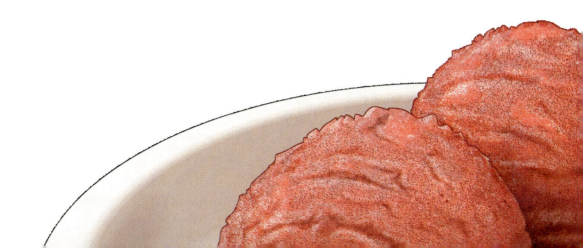

The term "yield" refers to the extent to which the volume of an iced product is increased by the addition of air. The volume can increase by as much as 80%; for example, 250 gallons of ingredients can yield up to 450 gallons of ice cream. In countries where ice cream is sold by volume rather than weight, and where there are no limits on the amount of air that can be added, consumers have no of way of knowing how much ice cream they are really getting for their money. Ice cream that has not been insufflated with air is richer in nutrients. One way of determining how much air has been added is to weigh the ice cream; one quart of non-insufflated ice cream usually weighs about 1 pound. Once the air has been added, the ice cream is poured into containers and chilled until it freezes; it should harden very quickly.

Buying

Choose containers that are free of frost and whose contents are still thoroughly frozen. For maximum freshness and taste, it is best to buy frozen products in stores whose stock turns over on a regular basis. If you want to avoid food additives, read the label; some iced products are "all natural" and others contain relatively few additives.

Storing

Avoid leaving frozen products at room temperature for any longer than necessary, because they lose flavor when refrozen and are more likely to contain ice crystals. It is best to store containers of ice cream in the coldest part of the freezer, where the temperature is most consistent. It is also important to ensure that the container is tightly sealed in order to prevent the formation of ice crystals. Ice cream can be kept in the freezer for about 1 month.

Nutritional Information

An average portion of ice cream contains about 1 tablespoon (15 ml) of sugar. Soft ice cream contains 2% to 3% less sugar. Ice cream contains various mineral salts and vitamins.

Vanilla ice cream (11% milk fat) is a good source of vitamin B_{12}; it also contains potassium, riboflavin, calcium, zinc, vitamin A, phosphorus, and pantothenic acid. Vanilla ice cream that is 16% milk fat contains vitamin B_{12}, vitamin A, potassium, riboflavin, calcium, zinc, and phosphorus.

Soft vanilla ice milk is an excellent source of vitamin B_{12} and a good source of potassium and riblofavin; it also contains calcium, phosphorus, pantothenic acid, and magnesium. Firm vanilla ice milk is a good source of vitamin B_{12} and also contains potassium, riboflavin, calcium, phosphorus, and pantothenic acid. Orange sherbet contains potassium, zinc, and calcium. Ice cream is just one of many iced treats, which also include ice milk, frozen yogurt, sherbet, granita, and tofutti.

Ice milk contains less fat than ice cream; it should contain between 2% and 7% milk fat. Ice milk is made from a mixture of pasteurized cream, milk, and other sweetened dairy products. It contains as much, if not more, sugar than ice cream, because sugar is used to provide some of the texture and flavor that fat adds to ice cream. Since ice milk contains only about half as much fat as ice cream, it can be slightly less creamy and flavorful; it is also denser than ice cream because it contains less air.

Sherbet is traditionally made with fruit juice or puréed fruit, but wine, liqueurs, alcohol, or tea can also be used. It is sweetened with sugar syrup, and beaten either very gently or not all; it does not contain egg yolk or fat, but egg whites may be added in the form of Italian meringue once the sherbet has set. Sherbet can also contain milk or milk solids, which slow down the crystallization process and promote the formation of smaller crystals. Store-bought sherbet is often nothing more than a mixture of water, sugar, milk solids (approximately 5%), and artificial flavors; this kind of sherbet can contain up to twice as much sugar as ice cream, which means that it contains more calories than firm ice milk but less than ice cream.

Granita is an Italian sherbet made from slightly sweetened syrup flavored with fruit, liqueurs, or coffee; it does not contain Italian meringue. Only half-frozen to prevent it from becoming too hard, it has a granular texture (hence its name); it is served between courses or as a refreshment.

Tofutti or **frozen tofu** is a product made from soy milk, vegetable oil, and sugar. It thus contains only vegetable fat and no lactose or cholesterol. However, it does contain just as many calories as ice cream because it is higher in fat. Tofutti was created in the United States in 1981, after several years of research. The goal of its inventor, David Mintz, was to provide Jews with a non-dairy alternative to ice cream (kosher dietary laws proscribe the consumption of dairy products and meat during the same meal). Tofutti was also welcomed by the many people who cannot digest lactose (milk sugar). Unlike ice cream, tofutti contains very few saturated fatty acids and is cholesterol-free. It contains twice as much protein as ice cream but equally as many calories, because sugar is the second most important ingredient (firm tofutti contains more sugar than the soft variety). Tofutti also contains natural or artificial flavorings, isolated soy proteins, soy lecithin, and, like ice cream, several stabilizers.

Serving Ideas

Ice cream and other frozen products are eaten as desserts and as snacks. If they are too frozen to eat when removed from the freezer, let them soften in the refrigerator for a little while.

Ice cream is often covered with caramel or chocolate sauce, or beaten into milk shakes. It is also frequently served with cakes, pies, pancakes, waffles, fruit, and cookies. It can be garnished with fresh or canned fruit, or even with fruit sauces *(coulis)*.

Ice cream can be heated in the oven without melting in dishes like baked Alaska (Norwegian omelet), as long as it is completely covered with meringue; the egg white in the meringue creates a barrier that prevents the heat from penetrating the ice cream.

	vanilla ice cream (11% m.f.)	vanilla ice cream (16% m.f.)	vanilla ice milk (soft)	vanilla ice milk (firm)	orange sherbet
water	61%	57%	69.6%	68%	66%
protein	3.5 g	3.5 g	4.9 g	3.8 g	1.1 g
fat	11 g	16 g	2.6 g	4.3 g	2 g
carbohydrates	23.6 g	22.4 g	21.8 g	22.7 g	30.4 g
cholesterol	44 mg	61 mg	12 mg	14 mg	7.3 mg
					per 100 g

sherbet

ice cream

Cheese

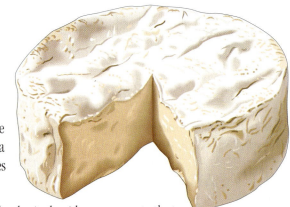

Cheese is a dairy product obtained from the coagulation and draining of milk or cream or a combination of milk and cream. In general, it takes 11 pounds of milk to make 1 pound of cheese.

While the exact origins of cheese are unknown, archeological evidence suggests that cheesemaking dates back to the beginning of animal husbandry, approximately 10,000 years ago. It is thought that the discovery of cheese was an accident. Having observed that milk curdled when left out at room temperature, the first cheesemakers found that the curd could be drained to separate it from the whey (a process accelerated by heat), and thus obtained cheese. According to legend, a shepherd carrying milk in a pouch made from the lining of a sheep's stomach discovered that the milk had coagulated into cheese along the way.

Milk and cheese were the food of gods and heroes in mythology. Cheeses made from goat's and ewe's milk were common fare in ancient Roman times, an era which saw cheesemaking attain an unprecedented level of sophistication. Knowledge of the art of cheesemaking spread throughout the empire and a number of firm cheeses were developed by the Romans, including Parmesan and Pecorino. After the fall of the Roman empire and the barbarian invasions, Benedictine and Cistercian monasteries became the major centers of cheesemaking during the Middle Ages. A number of cheeses still bear the name of their monastic origin (Saint-Paulin, Pont-l'Évèque, Livarot, Limburger, Munster).

There are over 1,000 varieties of cheese in the world, with France alone producing more than 350 of these varieties. The quality, nutritive value, and characteristics of cheese are dependent upon a number of factors, including the type of milk used (cow, goat, ewe, mare, reindeer, yak, water buffalo), the method of production, and local preferences. To the connoisseur, cheeses are too often robbed of their full flavor in order to conform with strict rules of food hygiene whose purpose is to protect the public against the spread of bacteria. This has led to the uniformization of production methods, which include the pasteurization (almost systematic) of milk, a process that destroys the bacteria present in milk; it is known, however, that these organisms cannot survive more than 60 days in cheese if the milk was not previously pasteurized. In a number of countries, including Canada, cheeses that are sold without having been aged for at least 2 months must be made from pasteurized milk.

There are four basic steps in the cheesemaking process: coagulation (or curdling) of the milk, the shaping of the curd, salting and inoculation, and ripening.

Coagulation (curdling) is the curd-formation stage; a ferment or rennet is added to the milk and acts on a group of proteins in milk called casein, causing it to coagulate into curds. Rennet is an enzyme extracted from the fourth stomach of suckling calves; rare and costly today, it has been largely replaced by bovine or porcine pepsin, or, more commonly, by bacterial cultures. The freshness, natural acidity, and temperature of the milk all influence the process of coagulation. For example, a lack of freshness increases the acidity of the milk, causing it to coagulate more quickly. In industrial cheesemaking, the milk is pasteurized in order to destroy harmful bacteria and to neutralize the lactic acid ferments so as to obtain a more predictable product.

Draining consists of separating the water (the whey) from the curd, thus giving it a firmer texture. The quantity of whey remaining in the curd after it has been drained determines the firmness and texture of the cheese. At this stage, all cheeses are still unfermented and unripened soft white cheeses. Depending on the type of cheese, draining may also include cutting (to drain off more whey), kneading, pressing, or cooking. The cheese is also shaped into molds during this stage.

Salting has an antiseptic effect, while also retarding the development of microorganisms, improving the keeping qualities of the cheese, and accelerating drying and the formation of a rind. The salt can be spread over the surface of the cheese (dry salting) or the cheese can be immersed in brine. The salting stage lasts an average of 2 to 4 days. Some cheeses are inoculated with mold spores in order to obtain a bloomy rind (Brie, Camembert) or the veining characteristic of blue cheeses (Roquefort, Gorgonzola). The development of mold can also be induced under certain controlled storage conditions. The cheese is then ripened.

During **ripening** (also called maturing or aging), the cheese is transformed by the biochemical action of the bacteria spores it contains. The lactose is converted into lactic acid and the proteins break down into amino acids. This is a crucial stage in cheesemaking, for it determines such characteristics as the consistency, odor, flavor, and rind of the cheese (soft white cheeses and process cheeses do not undergo ripening). Successful ripening depends on several factors, including temperature and humidity, both of which are carefully controlled. Temperature has a direct effect on the microbial and enzyme activity, and each category of cheese has an optimal ripening temperature; for example, soft cheeses are ripened at between 46° and 50°F, semi-firm cheeses at 50° to 54°F, and firm cheeses at up to 68°F. The duration of ripening also varies: the longer the ripening process, the lower the moisture content of the cheese, the firmer its texture, and the more pronounced its flavor.

The classification of cheeses is complex and may be based on a number of characteristics, although they are normally classified according to firmness, which varies with the degree of moisture. The moisture content of firm cheeses may be as low as 30%, while that of soft or fresh cheeses may be as high as 80%. The most common designations include fresh (or unripened) cheeses, soft ripened cheeses, semi-firm (or semi-hard), firm (or hard), and blue-veined cheeses, processed cheeses, cheese substitutes, and goat's-milk cheeses.

Fresh (or unripened) cheeses are coagulated under the action of lactic acid ferments in the milk instead of by adding rennet. While they are drained after formation of the curd, they are neither ripened nor fermented. This category includes cottage cheese, ricotta, mascarpone, cream cheese, Petit-Suisse, and quark. Made from pasteurized, skim, part-skim, or whole milk, sometimes enriched with cream (or from partly skimmed milk mixed with whey in the case of ricotta), these cheeses have a short storage life and must be consumed soon after purchase. Fresh cheeses contain up to 80% water and are generally low in fat (0.1% to 13%) and calories. However, those that are made with cream naturally have a higher fat and calorie content (for example, cream cheese has a fat content of 30%). Several cheeses in this group contain food additives, including food coloring agents, thickening agents, and food preservatives. Fresh cheeses are soft, creamy, or lumpy in texture, and are usually mild tasting, with some having a slightly acid taste. Mainly used in baking and desserts, they are available plain or flavored with vegetables, fruit, or herbs and spices. The storage life of these cheeses is usually about 1 week, but it can vary according to the moisture content and storage conditions.

cottage cheese

cream cheese

ricotta

Unripened stretched-curd cheeses are produced by kneading and stretching the curd (known as "stringing"), which is stored in water until the desired consistency is obtained. This process gives them a slightly rubbery texture. Cheeses in this category include mozzarella, Scarmoza, Provolone, Bocconcini, and Caciotta. Mozzarella is widely used as a topping on pizzas and pasta dishes baked au gratin.

Soft cheeses are ripened for a relatively short period of time before being drained and turned into molds without being pressed or cooked. They have a moisture content of 50% to 60% and their fat content represents 20% to 26% of the cheese's weight. Cheeses in this category develop a soft rind that can be more or less satiny. Fermentation starts on the surface of the cheese and moves toward the interior. Soft cheeses are rarely used in cooking because they tend to lose a lot of flavor when heated.

Soft cheeses are divided into two categories according to the characteristics of the rind:

• **Surface-ripened soft cheeses** are covered with a thin layer of a white down or mold that is satiny in appearance (Camembert, Brie, Brillat-Savarin, Coulommiers); this rind is edible but should be removed if its flavor is too pronounced.

• **Interior-ripened soft cheeses** are washed in light brine in order to maintain the moisture level and softness of the cheese and the rind and to eliminate certain ferments. These delicately flavored and strong-smelling cheeses include Munster, Pont-l'Évèque, Livarot, Bel Paese, and Époisses. To ensure an appropriate interior degree of humidity and adequate fermentation, these cheeses are stored in a humid atmosphere (close to 90% humidity) at a mild temperature varying between 53° and 59°F. Some of the cheeses in this category are soaked in an alcohol such as wine or beer as part of the ripening process.

Brie

Camembert

mozzarella

Pont-l'Évèque

Munster

Bel Paese

Semi-firm cheeses are uncooked pressed cheeses that are ripened for a relatively long period in a cool (45° to 50°F) and very humid (90%) atmosphere. The curd is cut into small grains, pressed, and turned out of the molds to be soaked in brine. Semi-firm cheeses are dense and are usually pale yellow in color. This family of cheeses includes Cheddar, Cantal, Reblochon, Gouda, Edam, Fontina, Saint-Nectaire, Morbier, Tommes, Tilsit, and Monterey Jack.

Firm (or hard) cheeses are cheeses that have been cooked and pressed. The curd is heated for at least 1 hour in order to make it more concentrated, which, upon pressing, produces a more compact cheese. Firm cheeses, which include Gruyère, Emmenthal, Jarlsberg, Comté, Raclette, Beaufort, Parmesan, and Romano, may or may not have a hard rind; the rind is sometimes rubbed with oil to reduce moisture loss, or washed and scraped, which helps to ripen the cheese. The fermentation process usually lasts for 4 to 12 months. In certain cases, carbon dioxide forms and is trapped in the cheese, producing holes (eyes) that vary in size and quantity from one cheese to another. The texture of the cheese is usually firm, although some hard cheeses, such as Parmesan and Romano, may have a rather granular texture. These cheeses are sometimes produced in wheels that can weigh as much as 85 to 300 pounds.

Emmenthal

Romano

Raclette

Gruyère

Parmesan

Jarlsberg

Edam

Cheddar

Monterey Jack

Gouda

Blue-veined (or blue) cheeses are neither cooked nor pressed; the curd is first cut into pieces, then molded, drained, salted, and inoculated with a species of blue-green mold such as *Penicillium roqueforti* or *P. gorgonzola,* which is injected into the cheese by means of long needles. Fermentation occurs from the inside toward the outside; the action of the bacterial culture causes the development of a network of blue-green veins that becomes denser over time. These cheeses (Roquefort, Gorgonzola, Bleu de Bresse, Danish Blue, Stilton) have a strong and sharp, peppery flavor and are often crumbly in texture.

Process cheeses are made from one or a blend of pressed cheeses (cooked or uncooked) that are remelted and to which milk, cream, or butter is added. They have the advantage of keeping longer than natural cheeses. These cheeses may contain stabilizing agents, emulsifiers, salt, food coloring, sweeteners (sugar, corn syrup), or flavorings (herbs, spices, fruits, nuts, Kirsch). They are more or less soft and rubbery in texture, with a flavor that is usually quite mild. In North America, most process cheeses are made using Cheddar, while Emmenthal and Gruyère are more commonly used in Europe. Process cheeses are labelled differently depending on the amount of cheese they contain (processed cheese, process cheese food, and cheese spread are all available on grocery shelves).

Cheese substitutes are imitation cheeses that are often made using only the casein element in milk, to which emulsifiers (disodium phosphate, sodium citrate) and artificial flavoring and food coloring are added. Natural ingredients like soybean or corn are also sometimes added after being processed.

Roquefort

Gorgonzola

Stilton

Danish Blue

process cheeses

Goat's-milk cheeses are soft cheeses with a natural rind; they may be made from 100% goat's milk (pure goat's-milk cheese) or from a mixture of goat's milk and cow's milk. They are available unripened, soft and surface-ripened, or in some cases hard. Whiter than cheeses made from cow's milk, goat cheeses also tend to have a more pronounced flavor. They are generally moist and smooth-textured. The intensity of the flavor depends on the breed and diet of the animal, the season, and the method of production. These cheeses are often very salty, a factor which has the effect of prolonging their storage life. Most goat cheeses today are made from a blend of goat's and cow's milk, that makes for a mild and creamy cheese. Cheeses in this family include Chabichou, Crottin de Chavignol, Valençay, Chevrotin, and feta (feta is made from goat's or cow's milk or a blend of the two).

Buying

When purchasing cheese, check the expiration date on the package and avoid cheeses that have been stored at room temperature. Each category of cheese has specific characteristics that are important to look for at the moment of purchase. Certain problems are easy to spot, and any cheeses showing signs of these defects should be avoided.

For example, soft cheeses should be soft both inside and out; they are fully ripe when the cheese is creamy, smooth, and uniformly colored, and when it fills out the crust. The crust itself should be soft, not too dry, and uncracked. Avoid cheeses that are overly firm or chalky white in the center, a sign of underripeness. Overripe soft cheeses have a sticky rind that is often darker colored or that smells like ammonia. Soft cheeses that have been improperly stored will have a hard crust and will be dry on the inside.

Semi-firm cheeses should be neither too dry nor too crumbly; if the cheese near the crust is darker than at the center, the cheese has likely been improperly stored. These cheeses should be neither rancid nor sharp tasting.

Firm cheeses should be uniform in color and texture, with a firm rind. Avoid dried-out, bulging, pasty, or overly granular cheeses with a cracked rind, all of which point to improper storage conditions. Firm cheeses should be neither too salty nor too bitter tasting.

Blue cheeses should be more or less generously veined depending on the variety, and the veining should be evenly distributed throughout the cheese. The cheese, which is usually white, should be neither too crumbly nor too dry nor too salty.

Preparing

Only firm cheeses are suitable for grating, and they are easier to grate when cold than when at room temperature. Once grated, hard cheeses will stay fresh for about a week in the refrigerator.

fresh goat's-milk cheese

Crottin de Chavignol

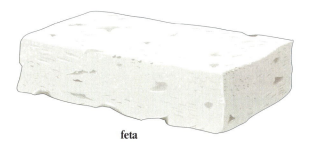

feta

Storing

The duration of the storage life of cheeses is mainly a matter of moisture content. For example, because soft cheeses have a higher moisture content than firm cheeses, they do not keep as long.

• Fresh cheeses and blue-veined cheeses will keep for only a week to 10 days and must be refrigerated in airtight wrapping or container.

• Soft cheeses do not keep for very long once they are fully ripened.

• Semi-firm cheeses can be stored for several weeks in the refrigerator provided that they are well wrapped.

• Firm cheeses will keep for 2 weeks in the refrigerator or in a cool place if they are well wrapped in wax paper or aluminum foil.

All cheeses can be stored in the refrigerator. They should be well wrapped in plastic wrap or aluminum foil and placed in the warmest section of the refrigerator (some cheeses, including soft cheeses, lose flavor when stored at inappropriate temperatures). Cheeses can also be stored at cool temperatures ranging from 50° to 54°F. Surface-ripened cheeses should not be stored in vacuum-sealed or airtight packages.

Cold cheeses are more flavorful if they are taken out of the refrigerator at least 30 minutes before being served. Avoid leaving them out at room temperature for too long, however, or they may dry out and spoil.

If mold has developed on the surface of a firm cheese, cut out ½ to 1 inch of the cheese around the mold just to be safe, and cover the cheese with a fresh piece of wrapping. It is preferable to discard fresh and soft cheeses that contain mold, as they could cause food poisoning.

While it is possible to freeze cheese, this method of preservation is not recommended, as it tends to detract from the flavor of the cheese and to make it more crumbly. Should freezing prove necessary, it is best to cut the cheese into wedges about 1 inch thick and weighing no more than 1 pound. Dry cheeses stand up better to freezing than those with a high moisture content; fresh cheeses cannot be frozen. When well wrapped, cheese will keep for 2½ to 3 months in the freezer. Frozen cheeses are best thawed in the refrigerator to minimize alteration of their texture; it is better to reserve frozen cheeses for cooking.

Warm Chèvre Salad

SERVES 4

8 slices of baguette
1 clove garlic
Salt and ground pepper
2 tbsp. white wine vinegar
¼ cup (60 ml) olive oil
4 small semi-dry goat's-milk cheeses
6 oz. mesclun

Mesclun is a mixture of different kinds of baby lettuce available ready-prepared in gourmet grocery stores; it can also be prepared at home using the greens at hand.

1. Preheat the oven to 400°F (200°C).

2. Rub the bread slices with the peeled garlic clove. Toast them lightly on both sides in the oven.

3. To make the vinaigrette, place the salt and pepper in a bowl, add the vinegar and oil, and mix well.

4. Divide each cheese in half. Place one half on each slice of toast. Place under the broiler and leave until the cheese begins to soften and turn slightly golden.

5. Toss the mesclun with the vinaigrette. Serve the warm cheese-topped toasts on top of the salad.

Serving Ideas

Cheese can be consumed as a snack or as part of a meal, in addition to having a wide array of uses in cooking as a main ingredient, a condiment, a stuffing, a coating for meats and vegetables, and in desserts. Indeed, cheeses blend just as nicely with savory foods (salads, sauces, soups, croquettes, pizzas, pasta, crêpes, soufflés, fondues, raclette, croque-monsieur, omelets) as with sweet dishes (cakes, pies, donuts); fresh cheeses are the type most commonly used in baking. When seasoning dishes that include cheese, it is important to remember that most cheeses are salted and to adjust the seasoning of the dish accordingly; this is particularly true of blue cheeses, whose salty taste is actually accentuated by cooking. Cheeses within the same family can be easily interchanged in recipes; for example, Gruyère and Emmenthal can be replaced by Edam, Brick, or Jarlsberg. Cheeses are often served at the end of a meal, and many consider that they are best accompanied by a good wine.

Cooking

Cheese will melt more quickly during cooking if it is crumbled, grated, or cut into pieces beforehand. When adding it to a sauce, cook it over a gentle heat until it melts; but do not let it boil, as this causes the proteins in the fat to separate. Firm cheeses such as Parmesan, Emmenthal, and Gruyère withstand high temperatures better than other cheeses, and are thus more suitable for gratinéed dishes. Remove the cheese from the heat as soon as it has melted.

Cheese	Type	Appearance	Texture	Flavor	Type of milk	Comments
COTTAGE CHEESE	soft white cheese	white	small curds, creamy	mild, milky	skimmed or unskimmed cow's milk	Low fat content. Easy to make. Creamed cottage cheese contains cream and at least 4% fat.
CREAM CHEESE (United States)	soft white cheese	white	creamy, soft	mild, acidic, unripened	milk and cream or only cream	Fat content over 30% .
RICOTTA (Italy)	soft white cheese	white	soft and moist	mild, unripened, slightly sweet	whey from cow's milk	Used to stuff Italian cannelloni. Contains up to 10% fat.
MOZZARELLA (Italy)	stretched-curd cheese	white	semi-soft to hard	mild, slightly salty	cow's milk or water buffalo's milk	Spongy when fresh but soon becomes rubbery. Quintessential pizza cheese.
CAMEMBERT (France)	surface-ripened cheese	yellowish inside; downy white rind	creamy	mild to sharp	cow's milk	Named after the French village where it has been made for over 2 centuries.
BRIE (France)	surface-ripened cheese	yellowish inside; downy white rind	creamy when ripe	mild to sharp	cow's milk	Comes from the Brie area, near Paris.
BEL PAESE (Italy)	washed-rind cheese	yellow inside; brown or grayish rind	soft	very mild, fruity	cow's milk	Turns sharp if rind is fermented.
MUNSTER (France)	washed-rind cheese	whitish with orange-colored surface	soft; filled with small holes	mild, slightly salty	cow's milk	Strong, penetrating smell. Created in the 17th century.
PONT-L'ÉVÂQUE (France)	washed-rind cheese	yellowish inside; golden or orange-colored rind	soft but not runny	strong	cow's milk	Named after a town in Normandy. Rind should not be sticky.
CHEDDAR (Great Britain)	semi-firm pressed cheese	whitish to dark orange	firm	mild to sharp (depending on aging)	cow's milk	Named after the town of Cheddar. First cheese to be produced on an industrial scale. Wide variety available in English-speaking countries.
EDAM (Netherlands)	semi-firm pressed cheese	yellowish or orange with an orange or red surface	semi-firm, elastic	velvety	partially skimmed cow's milk	Similar to Cheddar and Gouda. Contains less fat than Gouda due to the use of skimmed milk.

Cheese

Cheese	Type	Appearance	Texture	Flavor	Type of milk	Comments
GOUDA (Netherlands)	semi-firm pressed cheese	yellow with a paraffin rind	semi-firm to firm; small holes	neutral when fresh	cow's milk	Comes from Gouda, near Rotterdam, Holland.
HAVARTI (Denmark)	semi-firm cheese	white to yellowish	soft; small irregular holes	mild to sharp	cow's milk	Named after a farm in Denmark.
MONTEREY JACK (United States)	semi-firm pressed cheese	ivory colored with a waxy surface	semi-firm	mild	cow's milk	Originally from Monterey County, California. Resembles Cheddar and Colby.
JARLSBERG (Norway)	firm cheese	ivory colored with a waxy surface	firm; large holes	sweet; nutty flavor	cow's milk	Resembles Swiss cheese, but sweeter and less strong.
EMMENTHAL (Switzerland)	firm cheese	yellow with a hard dry surface	firm; large holes	mild and sweet; taste can be strong depending on aging.	cow's milk	Resembles Swiss cheese, but sweeter and less strong.
GRUYÈRE (Switzerland)	firm cheese	whitish to ivory-yellow	firm; small scattered holes	semi-sweet; mild to strong	cow's milk	Holes caused by bacteria, *Propionibacterium shermanii,* which produce gas bubbles and give the cheese its mild flavor.
ROMANO (Italy)	firm cheese	whitish with a brownish black surface	dry and granular	sharp	cow's, sheep's, or goat's milk or a mixture of the above	Also called Pecorino Romano in Italy, which means it is made from goat's milk.
PARMESAN (Italy)	firm cheese	yellow with a very hard brown or blackish rind	dry and granular	strong	skimmed cow's milk	Sold in wheels or grated. Called Parmigiano-Reggiano in Italy, after the Italian provinces where it was created 1,500 years ago.
ROQUEFORT (France)	blue-veined cheese	creamy white with blue veins and spots	creamy	sharp; slightly peppery	sheep's milk	Comes from the Roquefort region in France.
BLUE (France, Denmark)	blue-veined cheese	creamy white with blue veins	crumbly; semi-soft	sharp; somewhat peppery	cow's milk	Injected with a special mold, *Penicillium roqueforti,* which gives it its distinct color and flavor.
GORGONZOLA (Italy)	blue-veined cheese	creamy white with blue veins and spots	crumbly; semi-soft	sharp	cow's milk	Italian version of blue cheese.
GOAT CHEESE	soft white cheese; pressed or unpressed	white; rind sometimes covered with mold	soft; becomes harder as it ages	acquires a strong taste when aged	goat's milk	Italian version of blue cheese.
FETA (Greece)	soft cheese	white and rindless	crumbly	sharp, salty	cow's, sheep's, or goat's milk	Greece's national cheese. Kept in brine.

Sugar, Cacao, and Carob

Sugar

S ugar is a sweet-tasting, water-soluble sub-
stance that is extracted from sugar cane and sugar beets.
Its scientific name is "sucrose." In ancient Rome, sugar was known as *saccharum*.
The words for sugar in European languages *(zucchero* in Italian, *sucre* in French, *azúcar* in Spanish and
Zucker in German) are all derived from the Sanskrit word *sakara,* meaning "grain."

Sugar cane *(Saccharum officinarum)* grows in tropical regions and is thought to have originated in India or New Guinea. Today, the leading producers of sugar cane are Brazil, India, Cuba, China, Pakistan and Mexico. In 1990, a total of one billion tons of sugar was produced worldwide. Approximately three fifths of the world's output of refined sugar is made with cane sugar. The sugar-cane plant is a fragile grass that requires special care, including a steady supply of water and fertilizer. A large perennial plant, it can grow to be between 6 and 23 feet high, and approximately 2 inches in diameter. Depending on the climate, it is harvested 8 to 16 months after the first shoots appear; the harvest is now usually highly mechanized, but in several countries sugar cane is still cut by hand with a machete. After the cane is cut off at ground level, the plants grow new shoots.

The carbohydrates in sugar cane are found in the pith of the stems; they contain 12 to 15% sucrose. One ton of sugar cane yields approximately 275 pounds of sugar.

The **sugar beet** *(Beta vulgaris spp.)* is related to the beets eaten as vegetables *(Chenopodiaceae).* The sugar beet plant originated in Europe and can grow in northern climates. A large bulbous biannual root, it usually weighs about 2 pounds, and contains between 15 and 20% sugar. It is harvested approximately 20 to 30 weeks after it is planted. About two fifths of the world's output of refined sugar is made with beet sugar. Today, the leading producers of sugar beets are Russia, France, Germany, the United States, Poland and China.

For centuries, the only sweetener available in the West was honey, which was used throughout the ancient world – i.e., in China, India, Egypt, Greece and Rome. Sugar cane was first cultivated in India approximately 2,500 years ago; the Greeks and Romans used it only for medicinal purposes.

From the Middle Ages until modern times, Europeans regarded sugar as a medicine or as an exotic luxury food that was reserved for the rich. The Arabs are thought to have been the first to grow and refine sugar cane on a large scale; they also grew or sold sugar cane in the countries they conquered. The Spanish were the sole distributors of sugar in Europe during the 8th and 9th centuries, but as of about 900 A.D., Venice became a major sugar distribution center.

Most Europeans were first introduced to sugar during the Crusades. The economic power of the major Mediterranean ports resulted from the spice trade in general and the sugar trade in particular. During the 15th century, the discovery of America, as well as the presence of Europeans in the East Indies and on the islands in the Indian Ocean, served as the catalysts for a major boom in sugar-related economic activity; the islands comprising the West Indies became leading producers of sugar at this time, and their economic fortunes have been closely tied to the sugar trade ever since. The production of sugar cane on a large scale in the West Indies required a great deal of manpower, most of which was supplied by African slaves. This expansion of production lowered the price of sugar, which in turn led to a significant increase in sugar consumption.

Beets were not regarded as a major source of sugar until the end of the 18th century, when sugar beets were first grown on a relatively large scale in France, Austria, Hungary and Russia. In response to the English blockade of West Indian sugar, Napoleon ordered that sugar beets be grown in France and its territories; in 1811, a Frenchman named Delessert established the first viable beet-sugar refinery and received an award from the emperor for his efforts. Over the next two years, approximately 300 such refineries were set up, leading to a considerable increase in sugar consumption.

During the 20th century, the uses of sugar as a foodstuff have changed dramatically, and sugar consumption has reached unprecedented levels. Whereas for centuries the average person consumed about 4 ½ pounds of sugar per year, per capita annual consumption of sugar increased to 110 pounds or more in some industrialized countries during the second half of the 20th century. In the United States, it reached 139 pounds in 1990; this amount represents sugar consumed in various forms, but consists mainly of refined sugar. The consumption of refined sugar has decreased somewhat since the beginning of the 1980s; for example, recent studies suggest that Canadians consume an average of 43 pounds of sugar per year.

Sugar is often "invisible," in that we consume it without realizing we are doing so. It is estimated that 75 to 80% of the sugar we consume is "hidden" in other foods; over half of the sugar consumed in France is said to come from indirect sources. Sugar often turns up in the most unexpected places; it is added to prepared meats, pizzas, soy sauce, bouillon cubes, sauces, peanut butter and mayonnaise.

Food chemistry

Food chemists have identified approximately one hundred sweet substances, including glucose, fructose and maltose. Known collectively as "carbohydrates" or "glucides," they are comprised of carbon (C), hydrogen (H) and oxygen (O). Carbohydrates are one of the three food groups that are regarded as the essential building blocks of a healthy diet (the other two being fat and carbohydrates).

Carbohydrates are not found only in sweet foods; in fact, most foods — especially cereal, pasta, vegetables and fruit — contain significant amounts of these organic compounds. Honey, maple syrup, corn syrup, sugar and molasses consist almost entirely of carbohydrates.

The main forms of carbohydrates include simple sugars, complex sugars and fiber, as well as polyhydric sugar alcohols such as sorbitol, mannitol and xylitol.

Each source of carbohydrates is distinguished by the size of the molecules it contains and the manner in which they are assimilated by the body. Carbohydrates provide the body with energy. They are converted into glucose that is used by the brain, the spinal cord, peripheral nerves and red blood cells.

Simple sugars are either monosaccharides or disaccharides.

Monosaccharides are comprised of a single sugar molecule. Since they cannot be broken down into other sugars, they are assimilated directly; they dissolve in water and turn into alcohol in the presence of a fermenting agent. The most common monosaccharides include glucose, fructose, galactose and mannose.

Disaccharides are comprised of two monosaccharides that share one water molecule. Like monosaccharides, they are water-soluble. The most common disaccharides include sucrose, lactose and maltose. Simple sugars can be isolated in the form of crystals. Ordinary table sugar is comprised of crystallized sucrose.

Glucose (or dextrose) is the most common naturally occurring monosaccharide. It is found in such things as fruit, cereals, honey, nuts, flowers and leaves. The body generally converts more complex carbohydrates into glucose in order to assimilate them.

The glucose in the bloodstream provides the energy required to maintain body temperature and sustain vital bodily functions. After a meal, the liver transforms glucose into glycogen, which it stores for future use. Between meals, the liver converts the glycogen back into glucose, so as to maintain a blood-sugar level of approximately 0.1% at all times.

Fructose (or levulose) is a monosaccharide that is found in its natural form in fruit (2 to 7%), honey (40%) and various other foods. The sweetest of all sugars, it is about one and a half times as sweet as table sugar (sucrose) and three times as sweet as glucose. Refined fructose is available in the form of crystals or a syrup. Crystallized fructose is 100% pure. A corn syrup containing a high concentration of fructose is also available; it is produced by treating the syrup with enzymes that transform a portion of the glucose into fructose. As a general rule, any sugar solution that is heated in presence an acid, or to which enzymes are added, will break down into a combination of glucose (dextrose) and fructose (levulose) known as "invert sugar."

Invert sugar, like corn syrup, is resistant to crystallization and is capable of absorbing humidity – properties that make these products ideal for making baked goods and candy. They are also used to make other sweet snacks, preserves and icing. Sweeter than table sugar, invert sugar is available only in the form a liquid.

Sucrose (or saccharose) is a disaccharide composed of glucose and fructose. Present in all plants that produce organic compunds by means of photosynthesis, sucrose is particularly abundant in sugar cane, sugar beets and maple syrup. It is commonly known as white sugar or table sugar.

Lactose is a disaccharide composed of glucose and galactose. It is found only in milk (from 5 to 8% in mother's milk and from 4 to 6% in cow's milk). The intestinal flora convert lactose into lactic acid, which inhibits the growth of pathogenic bacteria. Lactose will not crystallize and is added to various foods for a number of reasons, including to improve the taste.

Maltose is a disaccharide composed of two glucose molecules. It is not a naturally occurring sugar. It is created by hydrolyzing starch with a diastasic enzyme found in malt. Maltose is commonly used in the food industry; it is added to products such as beer, bread, baby food and coffee substitutes.

Complex sugars (polysaccharides or complex carbohydrates) are organic compounds like starch and fiber. They consist of at least three simple sugar molecules linked together in a complex fashion. The resultant molecules are of course larger than the simple sugars of which they are comprised. **Starch** is insoluble in water and cannot be isolated in the form of crystals; powdered starch (or amylum) forms a gel when boiled in water. Starch granules

icing sugar

white sugar

swell to up to 30 times their original size in water. However, starch molecules can be broken down into simple sugar molecules such as maltose by means of hydrolysis (which involves combining the starch with a water molecule). Vegetables – more specifically, cereals, legumes, roots and tubers – are the only foods that contain starch. Starch is stored in plant tissue for the purpose of fueling new growth. Complex carbohydrates moderate the levels of glucose and insulin in the bloodstream. Eating large amounts of complex carbohydrates is also thought to lower blood-cholesterol levels.

Fiber includes polysaccharides such as cellulose, hemicellulose, pectin and lignin. Unlike the digestive secretions of ruminating animals, the substances secreted by the human digestive system do not contain the enzymes required to break down all varieties of fiber, especially cellulose and lignin. However, the human body requires dietary fiber to, among other things, regulate gastrointestinal functions and prevent constipation. A high-fiber diet plays an important role in the reduction of the incidence of heart disease and certain cancers (such as colon cancer). The North American diet is deficient in fiber; in fact, most North Americans consume less than half of the recommended amount of dietary fiber.

Cellulose is found mainly in legumes and vegetables, while pectin is particularly abundant in apples and citrus fruits.

Hemicellulose, the main fiber found in cereals, speeds up the digestive process.

Pectin, which is generally soluble in water, is found in citrus fruits, apples, squash and cabbage. It slows down the digestive process, thus reducing the rate at which glucose is absorbed; it also lowers blood-cholesterol levels.

The human body cannot break pectin down into simple sugars by means of hydrolysis. Unlike other polysaccharides, pectin is water-soluble and becomes gelatinous when combined with liquid. The granules are rich in mucilages, glutinous complex carbohydrates that contain pectic substances and absorb water. Found mainly in legumes, oats and barley, mucilages have the same effects as pectic substances.

Lignin is not a carbohydrate, but it is a basic fibrous component of the cell walls of certain vegetables; it does not dissolve in water and has the same properties as other insoluble fiber.

Harvesting and refining sugar

Sugar is extracted from sugar cane and sugar beets in very similar ways, the only difference being that sugar cane is crushed and sugar beets are sliced.

Sugar cane is harvested when still green; the leaves are usually removed and left in the fields as mulch for the next harvest, but they are sometimes burned off before the cane is harvested. Immediately after the harvest, the sugar cane is cut into kindling-like sections and carted off to the refinery, where it is crushed then placed in cylinders that extract the blackish juice (vesou) from which sugar is made. The remaining portions of the stem (bagasse) – the bark, the pith and the fiber – are used mainly as fuel in the refinery.

The cane juice is then processed in a various ways – i.e., refined, clarified, lightened and crystallized. The steps involved include concentrating the juice in a boiler and purifying it, usually with lime and carbon dioxide (the lime also the prevents the juice from fermenting). The goal of the refining process is to wash the sugar crystals and separate the layers of molasses from the impurities found in raw sugar, without dissolving the crystals themselves.

The sugar is sometimes purified with soluble phosphates or sulfuric anhydride. The goal of the clarification process is to dissolve any remaining impurities and prepare the sugar crystals for decolorization. The yellow syrup, which can be relatively light or dark, is decolorized with bone charcoal in preparation for the production of white sugar crystals. The decolorization process removes all of the remaining impurities, as well as the molasses. Lastly, the decolorized syrup is transformed into pure crystallized sugar. This is done either by evaporating the syrup or by separating the crystals in centrifugal machines. The crystallized syrup or "cooked mass" contains approximately 50% crystals; the remaining 50%, which is known as the "mother liquor," is liquid. After the crystals are removed, the mother liquor is referred to as "poor molasses." A thin layer of liquid remains on the crystals, which are then pulverized with hot water; this process melts them slightly, producing a liquid known as "rich molasses."

Molasses is the sugar syrup obtained during the last stage of the crystallization process, at the point when it becomes impossible, or economically inefficient, to extract any more sugar crystals. Once the crystallization process has been repeated three times, the remaining syrup is referred to as "blackstrap molasses," a cane-sugar byproduct. The clarified and decolorized refined sugar is then dried with hot air, graded and packaged.

Sugar beets are cut into strips or slices (cossettes), then the juice is extracted by means of diffusion – i.e., by submerging the strips in hot water (sugar-cane juice can also be extracted in this way). The water becomes increasingly sweet and takes on a blackish-blue color. After all the sugar has been extracted from the beets, they are used as feed. The sugar-beet juice is refined in much the same way as sugar-cane juice.

Several products result from the refining of sugar-cane juice and sugar-beet juice, including raw sugar, brown sugar, white sugar, powdered sugar, molasses and liquid sugar (sugar syrup).

Raw sugar is produced during the first stage of the crystallization process. It is covered with a thin layer of syrup and may contain impurities (dirt, pieces of plants or insects, molds, bacteria, wax). Raw sugar contains 96 to 99% sucrose. Raw sugar made with sugar beets is a yellowish color, while raw cane sugar is brownish.

A portion of the raw sugar is sold "as is," but most of it is refined until it becomes granulated white sugar. Raw sugar is rarely (or never) available in stores; it cannot be sold in the United States unless all of the impurities have been removed. It is sometimes partially refined and sold in loaves known as "turbinado" or "demerera" sugar, which contain approximately 95% sucrose. The nutritional value of the minute amounts of minerals in this kind of sugar is insignificant.

Traditional brown sugar consists of fine crystals that have been only slightly refined and are still covered with thin layer of molasses. It is made exclusively from cane sugar because the taste of beet-sugar molasses is too strong.

Today, brown sugar is almost always made by adding molasses, and sometimes artificial colorings, to white sugar. One of these colorings, caramel, consists entirely of burnt sugar. The color and taste of brown sugar depend on the amount of molasses it contains; the darker the sugar, the stronger it tastes. For cooking purposes, these sugars are generally interchangeable. Brown sugar contains between 91 and 96% sucrose.

White sugar (table sugar, refined sugar or granulated sugar) is the most commonly available kind of sugar. It is comprised of pure dried sugar crystals that have been completely refined. White sugar contains 99.9% sugar, and is entirely devoid of vitamins and minerals.

Powdered sugar (icing sugar, confectioner's sugar) is finely milled white sugar that is mixed with 3% cornstarch to prevent it from becoming lumpy.

Molasses is a byproduct of the sugar-refining process; only cane-sugar syrup is marketed as molasses because beet-sugar syrup is bitter and has a strong odor. The color and sugar content of molasses vary, depending on the number of times sugar has been extracted from the syrup. Unsulfured molasses, which is produced during the first stage of the sugar-extraction process, is light and very sweet; sulfured molasses, which results from the second extraction, is darker and moderately sweet; and blackstrap molasses, a product of the third and final extraction, is a very dark, strong-tasting substance that is only slightly sweet. Blackstrap molasses contains more nutrients than the other varieties. Molasses contains 35% sucrose, and 20% glucose and fructose.

Molasses can be eaten "as is" or used to produce alcohol, yeast, or rum.

Liquid sugar (or sugar syrup) is a clear solution containing highly refined sugar. It is used to can foods and to make candies, pastries, ice cream, etc.

Invert sugar is sucrose that has been hydrolyzed with acid; it is available only as a liquid and is sweeter than noninverted sucrose. Comprised of glucose (or dextrose) and fructose (or levulose), it absorbs humidity and prevents crystallization. Invert sugar is widely used in the food industry, to make products such as candies, pastries, soft drinks and table syrups.

corn syrup

molasses

Serving Ideas

Refined sugar is used in a wide variety of ways. It is used to adjust the texture and taste of foods, especially those with an acidic or bitter taste, as well as to activate yeast (in bread, for example) and preserve foods.

Sugar is an essential ingredient in many foods, including meringues, syrups, ice cream, sherbet and other sweet snacks. It is also used as a condiment because it enhances the flavor of other foods (glazed vegetables, glazed ham, sweet-and-sour dishes). It is an indispensable ingredient in pastries and candies.

If you want to reduce the amount of sugar in your diet, you can:

• gradually cut down on the optional sugar you add to foods such as coffee, tea, salad dressings, juices, yogurt and grapefruit, until you have eliminated it entirely;

• compensate for the reduction of sugar by adding spices such as cinnamon, ginger and nutmeg, or simply replace all of the sugar with fruit, which can give cereal, muffins and cookies a naturally sweet taste;

• cut the sugar in half in most recipes for cakes, muffins, quick breads, pastries and other desserts that call for more than ⅔ of a cup (175 ml);

• read labels carefully: most ingredients that end with the suffix "ose" are sugars, and products that contain several sugars are generally far too sweet;

• when eaten with whole-grain bread or dairy products, sugar can be part of a well-balanced diet and a good substitute for the empty calories in sweetened tea or coffee and soft drinks;

• significantly reducing the amount of sugar you consume can make you feel irritable and tired, but these symptoms usually last no longer than a week or so.

Nutritional Information

Sugar has very little nutritional value. It contains no protein, fat or fiber, and is lacking in vitamins and minerals; it consists mainly of carbohydrates. Granulated sugar contains 9 calories per gram or 16 calories per teaspoon, and icing sugar contains 9 calories per teaspoon.

Sugar and very sweet foods are often said to contain "empty calories" because they are deficient in nutrients. Since consuming too much sugar, especially sucrose, is thought to cause cavities, dentists suggest that people brush their teeth after eating sweet or chewy foods that tend to stick to tooth enamel.

As for the suspected link between the amount of sugar in your diet and glucose intolerance, current levels of sugar consumption do not appear to constitute a risk factor. Furthermore, there is no conclusive evidence linking sugar consumption to the development of heart disease or obesity, or to behavioral changes in children.

Like salt, sugar tends to absorb liquid, which is why people often feel thirsty after eating sweet foods.

Storing

Most kinds of sugar can be stored indefinitely as long as they are protected from insects and humidity. Sugar should be stored in a tightly sealed container in a dry, cool place.

Since molasses can go moldy if exposed to heat and humidity, it should be stored in a cool, dry place. It can also be refrigerated, but this makes it thick and difficult to pour.

brown sugar

cyclamate

Artificial sweeteners are very sweet synthetic substances that are used as sugar substitutes because they contain few or no calories. The first such substance, saccharin, was discovered by a German researcher in 1879. It dominated the market for 60 years, until the development of cyclamates during the 1950s and '60s, and has more recently given way to aspartame. At the beginning of the century, the search for artificial sweeteners focused on developing relatively cheap substances with the same properties as sugar. Today the principal goal of this research is to create products that contain fewer calories than sugar.

In many countries, the use of certain artificial sweeteners is restricted or prohibited because they have not yet been proven to be safe. The Canadian Food and Drug Act defines artificial sweeteners as food additives because they are synthetic substances not naturally found in foods. In the United States, saccharin and cyclamates are approved food additives; in Canada they can be sold only as substitutes for table sugar.

The main artificial sweeteners are saccharin, cyclamates, aspartame, and sucralose.

Saccharin, derived from coal tar, is 300 to 500 times sweeter than sugar and contains no calories; nor does it promote tooth decay. The use of saccharin has been restricted since 1978, when it was linked to cancer of the bladder in rats. Although it is now illegal to sell foods containing saccharin in Canada, it can still be sold there as an artificial sweetener. In many countries, including the United States, saccharin can still be used as a food additive. Following protests from the soft-drink industry, manufacturers, and consumers, Congress passed a 2-year moratorium preventing the Food and Drug Administration (FDA) from banning the use of saccharin, and this moratorium has been renewed on a regular basis ever since. At any rate, the FDA no longer plans to attempt to ban the use of saccharin because there is now some doubt about the conclusions of the studies that initially identified the substance as a potential carcinogen.

Cyclamates are substances derived from benzene. They were discovered accidentally in 1937, when an American academic noticed that the cigarette he had inadvertently placed on a derivative of cyclohexylsulfamic acid, a crystalline powder, had a pleasantly sweet flavor. Cyclamates are 30 times sweeter than sugar, contain no calories, and do not promote tooth decay.

Cyclamates were once commonly used in combination with saccharin; this not only masked the bitter taste of the saccharin and made both substances taste sweeter, it also made them more stable and prolonged their shelf life. The United States and Canada restricted the use of cyclamates in 1969, then prohibited their use as food additives and artificial sweeteners the following year when several studies suggested that they might be harmful; tests on rats linked cyclamates to cancer of the testicles, while a cyclamate by-product was shown to cause the testicles to atrophy. Health Canada revised its position in 1978. Cyclamates are now sold in approximately 40 countries, including Canada and France, where they are used exclusively as a substitute for table sugar. Cyclamates are sold as artificial sweeteners in the form of tablets, cubes, a powder or a liquid.

Sugar, Cocoa, and Carob

631

In the United States, the manufacturer and the food industry are lobbying to have the restrictions on the use of cyclamates lifted, on the basis that there is no conclusive proof that they are harmful and because various studies suggest that they pose no health risk. But the issue remains unresolved; the U.S. government's position is that although there is no definitive research proving that cyclamates are carcinogenic, nor is there any clear evidence that they do not cause cancer or genetic problems. The ban thus remains in effect, but the FDA is currently reevaluating cyclamates.

Aspartame was discovered in the United States in 1969 as the result of research on ulcer medications. It is a combination of two amino acids, aspartic acid and phenylalanine (glucose or lactose is sometimes added). Equal amounts of aspartame and sugar contain the same number of calories – 4 calories per gram – but since aspartame is about 180 times sweeter than sugar, much less has to be added to achieve the same level of sweetness. Furthermore, aspartame does not promote tooth decay and has no aftertaste. However, it cannot be used for cooking because it loses all of its sweetening power when heated.

Aspartame has been a controversial substance since it was first created. The FDA and Health Canada did not approve its use until 1981; and although it is the only artificial sweetener that both the American and Canadian governments have approved for use as a food additive, the scientific community and the media continue to raise concerns about its possible harmful effects.

The maximum daily allowance of aspartame (for life) has been set at 40 milligrams per kilogram of body weight, which corresponds to 16 ten-ounce cans of diet soft drinks for a person weighing 132 pounds (60 kilograms). The only official contraindication pertaining to aspartame concerns people with phenylketonuria, a relatively rare hereditary metabolic disorder characterized by abnormally high levels of phenylalanine, one of the main components in aspartame; the phenylalanine accumulates in the blood and can cause brain lesions. A complicating factor is that about 2% of the population – that is, 4.5 million people in the United States alone – carry one of the two genes that cause phenylketonuria, although they do not have any symptoms of the disease. These people may be unaware that they have a reduced capacity to metabolize phenylalanine and may be adversely affected by increases in the level of phenylalanine in their blood. However, since these concentrations of phenylalanine are only slightly higher than normal, they are not considered to be neurotoxic.

Since phenylalanine is concentrated in the placenta, pregnant women who are unaware that they carry one of the two genes in question can expose their unborn child to abnormally high levels of phenylalanine. Therefore women should not consume any more than 40 mg of aspartame per kilogram of body weight per day during pregnancy. In any case, all pregnant women should avoid all foods containing high-powered sweeteners because they tend to replace foods that are rich in much more beneficial nutrients.

In the United States, several people have reported experiencing various symptoms after eating foods sweetened with aspartame.

Aspartame was first approved for use in dry foods in 1981, then for use in soft drinks in 1983, despite the fact that it becomes very unstable when added to these drinks (since they are acidic, soft drinks rapidly alter the chemical composition of aspartame, reducing its sweetening power by 80% within 3 months). Aspartame can now be added to cereals, drinks, desserts, and chewing gum. When aspartame breaks down, it not only becomes less sweet, it also produces methanol, a substance that is known to be harmful.

Aspartame is now being used as a food additive more and more frequently. It is added to a vast number of products, including medicines and vitamins. The astonishing array of foods containing aspartame includes cereals, juice, cookies, puddings, cakes, pastries, pies, ice cream, yogurt, salad dressing, chewing gum, and candies. In 1992, 4,200 different products in the United States were sweetened with aspartame. As the number of products containing aspartame rises, it becomes increasingly difficult to avoid the substance or to control the amount you consume. However, the data produced thus far indicate that among all segments of the Canadian population, at least, aspartame consumption is still well below the maximum daily allowance.

Many researchers suggest that pregnant women and children under the age of six should avoid consuming aspartame, but several studies indicate that children can safely consume moderate quantities of drinks containing this sweetener. All members of the population are advised to limit their consumption of aspartame, especially people who may be particularly sensitive to its effects.

Sucralose, the most recently developed synthetic sweetener, was discovered in Great Britain in 1976 after many years of experimentation. Health Canada approved its use in 1991, but as of yet Canada is the only country to have done so. Sucralose has the sweet taste of sugar, but its sweetening power is 600 times as great as sugar. It remains stable when stored and when exposed to heat, and it does not promote tooth decay.

In Canada, sucralose can be added to cereals, drinks, desserts, chewing gum, candies, pastries and baked goods, as well as other products. Since it is extremely sweet, only minute quantities are required; it is thus mixed with powdered starch to make it easier to measure. The calories in sucralose come from the starch, not from the sweetener itself. The maximum daily allowance of sucralose is 9 grams per kilogram of body weight, or the equivalent of four small packages a day. It is sold in granules and small packages.

The studies conducted to date indicate that sucralose and hydrolyzed sucralose have no harmful effects on the human body. However, as of 1995, the long-term effects of sucralose on diabetics had yet to be examined.

The use of synthetic sweeteners raises many questions, including the effect of the consumption of artificially sweetened foods on obesity. It appears that the consumption of these foods has had little impact on the rate of obesity. Although artificial sweeteners allow people who are concerned about their weight to eat sweet foods, they do not necessarily improve eating habits, which is the real solution to obesity. In fact, sugar-free sweet foods tend to maintain the taste for sugar.

Sugar, Cocoa, and Carob

633

Honey

Honey is the sweet substance manufactured from flower nectar by bees (which use it as a source of nourishment) and consumed by humans ever since ancient times. The practice of apiculture, or beekeeping, dates back to 700 B.C.

For thousands of years, honey was the only sweetening agent known in the Western Hemisphere, whereas in Asia, sugar cane was widely cultivated. Across the ages, honey acquired mythological status, coming to be regarded as a symbol of life and of wealth. This can be attributed to its numerous medicinal properties. Indeed, honey is held to have the qualities of a purifier, an antiseptic, a skin toner, a sedative, and a digestive; it is believed to reduce fever and to stimulate the appetite. A rare commodity in early times, honey was reserved for use in religious ceremonies and for medicinal purposes. Among other things, it was used to pay tribute to the gods, in baptismal rites, to feed sacred animals, to treat the sick, to embellish the skin, and to embalm the dead. Only the wealthy could afford honey, and its use in cooking was widely regarded as a mark of refinement. Although honey was long used as a preserving agent for fruits, it was gradually replaced by sugar. From the Middle Ages onward, Europeans began to use it mainly in confectionery and for medicinal purposes.

The fabrication of honey by bees is a fascinating process. The bees first gather the nectar by means of specially adapted mouth parts; the nectar is projected into the honey sac (a pocket located in the bee's esophagus), where it accumulates and mixes with the bee's saliva. The nectar is converted into honey by the action of enzymes in the saliva and in the gastric juices, which convert the sucrose in the nectar into glucose and fructose. This nectar is then deposited by the bees in the cells of the beehive, where it is ventilated by means of wing movements in order to reduce the degree of moisture to between 14% and 20%; this ventilation process can take up to 20 minutes, after which the honey is ready for consumption. Bees use the honey as a source of nourishment.

The proportion of glucose and fructose in the honey determines its consistency and varies according to the source of the nectar. Roughly 5 gallons of nectar are required to produce 1 gallon of honey, and a single quart of nectar represents between 20,000 and 100,000 trips for the bee. A colony of bees (30,000 to 60,000 bees) is able to store about 2 pounds of honey per day.

The quantity and quality of the honey are determined by geographic, seasonal, and botanical factors. Bees have a tendency to gather a single type of nectar, resulting in the production of distinct types of honey, each of which has its own specific flavor. However, it should be noted that the different types of honey are not subject to regulation in all countries.

Among the wide variety of honeys available on the market, some are made from the nectar of one variety of flower, while others are a mixture of different nectars that have either been culled from different flowers by the bees or been combined by producers. The source of the nectar determines the color, flavor, and texture of the honey. Honey ranges in color from white to different shades of brown, red, and blond, with some varieties being almost black. While flavor varies as widely as color, generally speaking, the darker the honey, the stronger its flavor. The most common types of honey include the pale-colored and mild tasting varieties such as clover honey and alfalfa honey, the reddish brown and strongly flavored heather honey, and acacia honey, which is very mild, clear, and runny.

Buying

Honey is sold in liquid or crystallized form and is often pasteurized to destroy any fermenting agents present. Creamy honey has a fine texture and is obtained by adding finely crystallized honey to liquid honey in order to induce crystallization. When purchasing honey, check the label to make sure that it is 100% pure, meaning that it consists solely of honey and has not been adulterated. This does not mean that the honey has not been pasteurized, however.

Preparing

Honey tends to crystallize at room temperature (cold temperatures accelerate this process), but it can be returned to its liquid state by heating the container in hot water for about 15 minutes. It is not advisable to heat honey in a microwave oven, as this increases its hydroxymethylfurfural (HMF) content, altering its taste.

Baklava

6 PORTIONS

2 cups (500 ml) whole blanched almonds	For the syrup:
¼ cup (60 ml) sugar	3 cups (750 ml) sugar
1 tsp. ground cinnamon	2 cups (500 ml) water
1 lb. (500 g) filo pastry	1 cup (250 ml) honey
1½ cups (375 ml) melted butter	1 tsp. ground cinnamon
	½ tsp. ground cloves
	1 tbsp. lemon juice

1. Preheat the oven to 350°F.

2. Finely chop the almonds.

3. In a small bowl, mix the chopped almonds with the sugar and cinnamon.

4. Brush six sheets of filo pastry with melted butter, and place them in the bottom of a greased cake pan. Spread a layer of the almond mixture over the pastry, and cover it with a layer of two buttered pastry sheets. Alternate layers of almond mixture and pastry sheets (two per layer) until there is no almond mixture left. End with a layer of six sheets of filo. Using a sharp knife, cut a diamond-shaped pattern on the top layer. Bake in the oven for about 1 hour, or until the pastry is golden brown. Let cool in the pan.

5. To prepare the syrup, dissolve the sugar in the water in a saucepan; add the honey, cinnamon, and cloves. Bring the syrup to a boil and simmer for 10 minutes. Add the lemon juice.

6. Pour the hot syrup over the cooled baklava, and let stand for 2 hours. When it is completely cooled, cut it into triangles and serve.

Serving Ideas

Honey is used in a rich variety of dishes, both sweet (pastry, cakes, flans, creams, yogurts, cookies, candies, nougats, syrups, gingerbread, Greek baklava) and savory (chicken, ham, lamb, duck, couscous). It is also commonly used as a spread in tea, coffee, and infusions, as well as in sweet-and-sour sauces.

Honey is easier to measure if it is heated slightly before being poured into a measuring cup that has been lightly greased to prevent the honey from sticking. Honey is the basic ingredient in mead, an alcoholic beverage made from fermented honey and water. Mead can also be distilled or processed to make vinegar. Honey is also used outside of the food industry, notably in the manufacture of medicines and beauty products.

It is not recommended to feed honey to children under 1 year of age, as it may contain a toxin known as *Clostridium botulinum,* which can cause botulism in small babies (it is harmless in infants over 1 year old and in adults).

creamy honey

Nutritional Information

water	14% to 20%
protein	0.3% to 0.5%
carbohydrates	76% to 80%

The carbohydrates in honey are composed, on average, of 5% sucrose, 25% to 35% glucose, 35% to 45% fructose, and 5% to 7% maltose. By volume, honey contains more calories than sugar: 1 teaspoon (5 milliliters) of honey contains 64 calories, while 1 tablespoon (15 milliliters) of sugar contains 48 calories; by weight, however, honey contains fewer calories: .75 ounce (21 grams) of honey contains 64 calories, while the same amount of sugar contains 84 calories. This difference can be explained by the higher water content of honey.

Honey contains only small traces of vitamins and minerals. While it does not really have a nutritional advantage over sugar, because its sweetening power is higher, it is used in smaller quantities.

Cooking

Sugar can be replaced with honey in recipes, but the quantity of honey should be reduced to take into account that it is sweeter than sugar; replace 1 cup of sugar with ½ to ¾ cup (4 to 6 ounces) of honey and reduce the amount of liquid by ¼ cup (2 ounces). The baking time should also adjusted slightly and the temperature lowered by 25°F, as honey tends to make foods brown more rapidly when cooked or baked. Honey can be used in place of all or part of the sugar in jams and jellies without any appreciable modification of consistency and color, although it does change the flavor somewhat.

Storing

Honey will keep almost indefinitely if it is stored in a sealed container and placed in a cool, dry place; its acid pH and high sugar content inhibit the growth of microorganisms. Low temperatures cause honey to thicken and crystallize, while high temperatures alter its flavor and may cause it to darken. Honey can be frozen.

Maple syrup

Upon arriving in America, French settlers were surprised to discover that the Indians would cut the bark of maple trees in order to harvest the sap, from which they made a syrup.

Maple syrup is a sweetener that is made by reducing the sap of certain species of maple trees (the sugar maple, *Acer saccharum,* the red maple, *Acer rubrum,* and the black maple, *Acer nigrum).* These trees are found only in North America, mainly in Quebec, New York and Vermont, which are major maple syrup producing regions. Canada – and more specifically, Quebec – produces over 80 million quarts of maple syrup annually, while the United States produces 12 million.

The sap is collected at the end of winter, between January and April, when the days are warm enough to melt snow and the nights are cold enough to prevent the trees from budding. An ancient Native American practice, the collection of sap astonished the French settlers who colonized this part of North America. The natives cut slits in the trees when the sap started to mount, attaching containers to them to collect the sap, then concentrated the sap to make syrup.

The sap was condensed in one of two ways: hot stones were plunged into the sap, which would turn into a dark syrup as the water evaporated, or the sap was frozen on successive nights and the layer of ice that formed on its surface was removed each morning, until the relatively clear syrup achieved the desired consistency. The natives used maple syrup as a medicine as well as a food.

Today, the sap is still gathered by cutting slits in the trees, but the process is gradually becoming more mechanized; the sap is often pumped through tubes directly to the "sap house", where it is boiled. This technique increases the amount of maple sap that is collected, while reducing labor costs. A productive maple tree can yield between 15 and 40 gallons of sap per season.

Several factors, including climatic conditions, appear to influence the amount of sap produced by a tree. A combination of warm days and freezing nights helps increase the flow of sap.

Maple sap is a clear, relatively tasteless liquid that contains 4 to 10% sugar, mainly in the form of sucrose. It usually takes 30 to 40 quarts of sap to produce one quart of syrup. Unlike maple sap, the syrup contains 66.5% sugar.

A considerable amount of heat energy is required to turn the sap into syrup, which is one of the reasons that maple syrup is so expensive. A recently invented process known as inverted osmosis has begun to supplant the traditional method of concentrating sap; since the sap is concentrated before it is boiled, only about 10 quarts of liquid is required to produce a quart of syrup.

Buying

Governments have adopted legislation to prevent maple syrup substitutes from being sold as pure syrup. Norms specify the colors of various grades of syrup; in Quebec, for example, there are five different colors and two grades of syrup, and the name "maple syrup" is reserved for products that are 100% pure.

The quality of maple syrup depends on its color and consistency. Runny syrup is unstable because it tends to ferment and turn sour, while syrup that is too thick tends to crystallize. The flavor of maple syrup varies as much as the color.

Serving Ideas

Maple sap can be made into syrup, toffee, sugar (hard or soft) or butter. Maple syrup is the most versatile of these products and is used in a variety of desserts, either as replacement for sugar or as a flavoring (maple-syrup pies, soufflés, mousses, cakes). It is used to cook ham and eggs, to sweeten tea and coffee, and as a topping for pancakes and waffles. Like maple sugar, it can be eaten alone or used as a sandwich spread.

Maple toffee is usually eaten during maple syrup season and mainly at the sap houses themselves, where hot syrup is hardened instantaneously by pouring it directly onto the snow.

When using maple syrup as a replacement for sugar, reduce the amount of liquid in the recipe by approximately half a cup for every cup of syrup used.

Nutritional Information

	maple syrup
water	34%
carbohydrates	32.5 g
	per 50 g (40 ml)

Maple syrup contains fewer calories than an equivalent amount of honey. It also contains more minerals than honey, and these minerals (calcium, iron, phosphorus and potassium) are present in relatively high concentrations.

Storing

Unopened containers of maple syrup can be stored in a cool, dry place but should be refrigerated once opened. Even if mold appears only on the surface of the syrup it best to throw it all away, because harmful toxins can develop inside the container, and some of them are resistant to heat.

The maple syrup on the bottom and sides of the container can crystallize – i.e., clear crystals of sucrose can separate and harden – if the syrup is not 100% pure or if it is stored for too long, especially if it has been overcooked.

Like maple butter, sugar and toffee, maple syrup can be frozen (the syrup remains liquid but becomes difficult to pour; it becomes runnier again when defrosted).

Sugar, Cocoa, and Carob

637

Carob

Ceratonia siliqua, Leguminosae-Caesalpinioideae

carob powder

Fruit of the carob tree, an evergreen believed to have originated in Syria and cultivated since ancient times, eventually spreading to the Mediterranean region. The word "carob" comes from the Arab *kharrub,* meaning "pod."

The carob tree is a relative of the tamarind tree. It is also known as "locust bean" and as "St. John's bread"; according to legend, John the Baptist lived on its seeds mixed with honey during his crossing of the desert.

The food industry makes wide use of carob as a cacao substitute and as an additive (it has stabilizing, binding, and gelling properties). It also serves as a coffee substitute and as animal feed. A popular food in Europe until the early 1920s, carob subsequently fell into relative obscurity, only to make a massive comeback in the 1980s, particularly in North America, when the food industry began using it to replace cacao, which had become a rare and expensive commodity following a shortage.

The carob tree can live to be 100 years old and grows in warm climates, attaining up to 40 feet in height. This decorative tree has large, tough leaves that are shiny and green. Clusters of small reddish flowers produce the fruits, which are flat brown pods measuring 4 to 12 inches in length. Inside, a sweet and juicy pulp encloses a row of three to ten reddish brown seeds that are shiny, hard, and flat. Cultivation of carob has spread to many parts of the world, including Mexico, the southern United States, the Indies, South Africa, Australia, and the Near East.

Two distinct products are derived from carob. The first, carob powder, is similar to cacao and is obtained from the pods; the second product is carob bean gum, which is derived from the beans encased in the pod. Carob is available in solid form (powder, chips) or liquid form (syrup). Carob powder is obtained by drying, roasting, and grinding the pod after removal of the beans.

Unlike cacao, carob does not contain theobromine, a stimulant similar to caffeine. Moreover, since carob is always very sweet, it is not necessary to add sugar when using it in place of cacao, although it may be a good idea to enhance its flavor with a little cinnamon or mint.

The degree of roasting modifies the color and flavor of carob; the more it is roasted, the darker the carob and the blander its flavor. Solid carob and carob syrup and chips are made from the powder, while carob bean gum comes from the white, translucent endosperm of the beans contained in the pods.

Buying

Carob is generally available in health-food stores.

Serving Ideas

Carob has the same uses as cacao and chocolate; it is a common ingredient in cakes, biscuits, beverages, and confectionery and can be used either on its own or in combination with cacao or chocolate. Most recipes allow the replacement of 1 part cacao by 1½ to 2 parts carob by weight, although carob is best used in the presence of strong-flavored ingredients, as it is not as flavorful as cacao.

Since carob powder contains more sugar than cacao, reduce the quantity of sugar called for in the recipe by half when using it in place of cacao.

Carob also dissolves less easily than cacao, with the result that some of the powder remains suspended in liquids, producing a lumpier consistency and forming a deposit at the bottom of the container. Mixing the carob with a little hot water will help to dissolve it better. In addition, carob melts at a lower temperature than chocolate and liquefies more rapidly, which can be a problem when preparing certain dishes, such as mousse.

Carob Chip Muffins

MAKES 8 TO 12 MUFFINS

1 cup (250 ml) rolled oats
⅓ cup (80 ml) sugar
1 cup (250 ml) milk
¼ cup (60 ml) vegetable oil
1 egg, lightly beaten
1 pinch of salt
1 cup (250 ml) whole wheat flour
3 tsp. baking powder
¾ cup (185 ml) carob chips
1 tsp. grated orange zest

1. Preheat the oven to 400°F (200°C). Grease a muffin tin.

2. In a large bowl, combine the rolled oats, sugar, milk, oil, lightly beaten egg, and salt.

3. In a small bowl, combine the flour and baking powder.

4. Add the flour mixture to the other ingredients and fold it in gently with a wooden spatula. Incorporate the carob chips and the orange zest.

5. Spoon the dough into 8 large muffin cups or 12 medium-size cups.

6. Bake in the oven for 15 minutes. Let the muffins cool in the pan, then remove.

Nutritional Information

	carob powder
water	3.6%
protein	1.4 g
fat	0.2 g
carbohydrates	26.7 g
fiber	3.7 g
calories	114
per 75 ml (30g)	

Carob powder has a much lower protein and fat content than cacao. Its mineral and vitamin content also differs from that of cacao; for example, it contains much less phosphorus, potassium, and iron, but is twice as rich in calcium.

Carob powder is a rich source of fiber. It contains tannins, but no caffeine or theobromine; it does not cause allergies and is easily digested.

The nutritional value of products made using carob depends on the added ingredients; for example, sugar (sometimes more than is added to chocolate) and vegetable oil are frequently added to such products.

Storing

Store carob in a hermetic container away from humidity in order to keep it from becoming lumpy.

carob pod

Cacao

Theobroma cacao, Sterculiaceae

The product extracted from the beans of the cacao tree, a native of tropical America, cacao is the basic ingredient used in the making of chocolate.

The term "cacao" is derived from *cacahuaquchtl,* the word used by the Mayan Indians to designate the cacao tree, and more particularly the tree of the Mayan gods. "Chocolate" comes from *tchocoatl,* meaning "bitter water"; this was the name of a chocolate beverage greatly appreciated by the Aztecs. Made from the dried beans of the cacao tree, this drink also contained peppers, musk, honey, and vanilla, and was thickened with annato juice, which gave it a blood-red color.

Cultivation of the cacao tree dates back some 3,000 years. The beans of this tree played an important role in Mayan society and later in Toltec and Aztec cultures, where they were used both as food and as a form of payment; for example, a slave could be bought for the price of 100 cacao beans. Various properties, including those of an aphrodisiac, were attributed to the cacao bean by these peoples. According to Aztec legend, the god of the forest, Quetzalcoatl, was the creator of the sacred cacao tree, *cacahuaquchtl,* which was believed to bring fortune and strength. When Cortés landed in Mexico, he was greeted with mountains of cacao instead of the gold he was seeking. The Spanish conquistador brought cacao back to Spain with him in 1527, and the flavorings traditionally mixed with it were eventually replaced by vanilla, sugar, and cream. Cortés was responsible for the planting of cacao trees in numerous countries in the Caribbean, in the West African islands, and in Trinidad, thus creating a Spanish monopoly over the cacao trade that lasted for close to a century. In 1737, the renowned botanist Carl von Linné classified the cacao tree in the genus *Theobroma,* which means "divine food."

Cacao made its way to Africa around 1822, and the largest cacao-producing countries today are located on this continent (Ivory Coast, Ghana, Cameroon, and Nigeria), as well as in South America (Brazil and Ecuador).

The first chocolate bar (made from dark chocolate) appeared on the market in 1847, created by the English company Fry and Sons, which came up with the idea to mix cocoa butter, chocolate liquor, and sugar.

Switzerland, which specializes in chocolate production, has earned a reputation for the excellent quality of its chocolate. The development of the cacao and chocolate industry in the United States is largely attributable to Milton Snavely Hershey, who opened a chocolate factory in Pennsylvania in 1888. Switzerland has the highest per capita consumption of chocolate, which stood at about 24 pounds per person in 1994, while the Belgians consume close to 17 pounds of chocolate per year, the English 16.5 pounds, and the Germans 15.5 pounds.

There are about 20 varieties of the cacao tree, which are generally divided into two classes: the first group produces high-quality cacao and is usually found in South America, while the second group, primarily grown in Africa, produces a higher yield but inferior quality of cacao that is grown mainly for industrial use.

At maturity, the cacao tree attains a maximum height of 26 feet and produces leaves, flowers, and pods year-round. Its long leaves average 1 foot in length and between 2½ and 5 inches in width. Initially a pale rose color, they turn dark green at maturity and acquire a shiny, leathery appearance. The cacao tree grows only in humid tropical climates along the equatorial belt. The largest producers are Ivory Coast, Brazil, Malaysia, Ghana, Nigeria, and Indonesia.

The cacao tree flowers continually, but there are two periods in the year when its small flowers are more abundant. The flowers, which vary in color from pink to yellow, white, bright red, or pale orange tinged with pink, grow in small clusters directly on the trunk and lower branches of the tree. An average of 30 to 40 flowers are pollinated in the course of a year.

The oblong fruit, called the pod, grows up to 1 foot long and 2½ to 5 inches wide and can have a smooth or warty surface that hardens as the fruit matures, changing color and becoming yellow, scarlet, red, or various shades of green, depending on the variety. The pods are harvested with a knife. They contain a sticky pinkish-colored pulp enclosing 30 to 40 pink or light purple seeds, or beans, that can measure up to 1 inch in width. The beans consist of a nib, a tegument, or seed coat, and a germ. The nibs are the only part that is eaten, but they must be treated first, as they are very bitter. The various stages of processing include fermentation, sorting, roasting, cooling, cracking, and grinding.

Fermentation, which generally lasts for 3 to 9 days, modifies the composition of the beans. Temperatures as high as 122°F kill any bacteria and activate the enzymes that produce the substances from which chocolate derives its characteristic flavor. The fermented beans are sun-dried until their moisture level is between 6% and 8%.

Once dried, the beans are sorted to remove any foreign matter (pebbles and other debris), after which they are graded. The roasting process is a very important step that transforms part of the tannins present in the beans, reducing their bitterness and developing their flavor. Roasting determines the flavor and color of the final product and varies according to the intended use of the beans and to their variety. Once roasted, the bean are cooled.

The cracking process separates the beans from their shell by grinding them between steel rollers at a high temperature (between 122° and 190°F). The sticky paste obtained at this stage is called chocolate liquor or chocolate mass and consists of 53% cocoa butter, a yellow fat.

Cocoa powder is obtained by pressing the chocolate liquor to extract the cocoa butter; the resulting paste is cooled, ground, and sifted. Cocoa powder can contain 10% to 25% fat.

The Dutch method of making cocoa powder consists of extracting the cocoa butter from the bean and making the paste soluble by adding alkaline compounds such as sodium carbonate, sodium hydroxide, potassium, or magnesium to the chocolate liquor before pressing. Also called solubilization, this process was invented by C.J. Van Houten in 1828 and produces a darker, more bitter cocoa.

Manufacture of Chocolate

Making chocolate is a complex art, mainly because the divergent physical properties of sugar and cacao make it difficult to obtain a homogenous liquor or paste.

Several steps are involved in the chocolate-making process: the chocolate mass, or liquor, is first mixed with sugar and cocoa butter; it is then heated and agitated (conched) in order to obtain a soft-textured paste; then cooling, or tempering, brings the cacao to the temperature of crystallization, at which point chocolate is obtained.

The many different chocolate products available on the market are defined according to their cacao content and to their added ingredients. Each country sets its own norms regulating the various types of chocolate and their composition.

Unsweetened chocolate is the chocolate mass once it has solidified; no sugar or milk solids are added. It is used by chocolate makers and confectioners for baking; although it has a chocolate flavor, it is too bitter to be edible on its own.

The oblong fruit, known as a pod, encloses 30 to 40 beans; the beans contain nibs, which are edible once they have been treated to reduce their bitterness.

Sugar, Cocoa, and Carob

641

Dark chocolate includes both bittersweet and semisweet chocolate; it contains between 35% and 70% chocolate liquor, sugar, and sometimes emulsifiers. These types of chocolate can be eaten on their own or used in baking.

Milk chocolate contains varying amounts of milk powder, sugar, and flavorings (vanilla) that are blended with the cocoa butter and that give the chocolate its sweet flavor and rich texture. However, it is not suitable for use in cooking because the milk solids tend to burn.

White chocolate does not contain any chocolate liquor; it is made from cocoa butter to which evaporated or powdered milk, sugar, and vanilla extract are added. This chocolate has a sweeter flavor and creamier consistency than milk chocolate and is not as widely used in confectionery.

There are also numerous chocolate substitutes on the market, some of which may contain cacao while others contain none at all. Various additives are added to these products to imitate the color, texture, and flavor of real chocolate.

Buying

Good-quality chocolate is pleasant smelling, shiny, and brown or dark brown in color; it should break cleanly and have no white spots or small holes (burst bubbles). It should also melt evenly on the tongue and upon contact with the skin. Soft, tender chocolate contains more cocoa butter than hard, crisp chocolate. Chocolate that is dull, grayish, whitish, or crystallized should be avoided; it likely either lacks freshness, was inadequately stored, or contains a fat other than cocoa butter. Traces of white on the surface are a sign that the chocolate was subjected to temperature variations and do not alter its taste.

Whenever possible, check the ingredients to ensure that you are buying real chocolate and not a substitute.

Preparing

Cocoa powder's high starch content makes it difficult to dissolve it in liquids. It is best to combine it with a cold liquid first (if the liquid is hot, lumps will form) or to add sugar, which separates the starch particles. Cocoa powder can also be sifted beforehand.

Serving Ideas

Cocoa and chocolate are widely popular flavorings in a rich variety of foods, including cakes, tarts, puddings, biscuits, sauces, icings, ice cream, mousses, flans, breads, candies, syrups, milk, beverages, and liqueurs. Chocolate is the essential ingredient in a number of classic desserts, including Black Forest cake and Sacher torte.

Various ingredients can be added to chocolate bars, including peanuts, almonds, hazelnuts, caramel, cherries, wafers, nougat, fruit paste, and alcohol. Chocolate is also used to make truffles and Easter eggs.

Some countries, Spain and Mexico in particular, make use of chocolate in savory dishes as well as in desserts. It is used notably to flavor sauces accompanying seafood, chicken, duck, rabbit, and turkey, as in the well-known *mole poblano*, a turkey stew that also includes bittersweet chocolate, peppers, and sesame.

Chocolate fondue, a Swiss specialty, is prepared by melting chocolate containing almonds, nougat, and honey to which a little cream and a drop of alcohol are added; fresh fruit, pieces of bread, or dry biscuits are dipped in the delicious chocolate sauce.

Chocolate Fondue

Fresh fruits
Sponge cake
8 oz. (250 g) baking
chocolate

½ cup (125 ml)
whipping cream
2 tbsp. kirsch or rum

Each guest spears a piece of fruit or cake with a fork and dips it in the chocolate fondue.

1. Cut a selection of fresh fruits into bite-size pieces: bananas, pears, oranges, grapefruit, pineapple, and apples can all be used. Do the same with the sponge cake (or similar dense type of cake).

2. Break the chocolate into small pieces and melt it in a double boiler over very low heat.

3. Pour this sauce into a fondue pot placed over a table burner. Add the cream and the rum or kirsch, and mix well.

Cooking

During cooking, the starch in cacao is converted, making it more digestible and more flavorful.

When melting chocolate for use in a recipe, it is important to observe the following simple but indispensable rules: First, the temperature of the chocolate should never exceed 120°F (to avoid altering its flavor), and second, no water (not even a drop) must ever come into contact with the chocolate, as this causes lumps to form.

Usually the chocolate is broken into pieces and heated gently in an uncovered double boiler. It is important not to overcook it and to stir it continuously. Remove the chocolate when the temperature reaches 115°F.

white chocolate

cocoa powder

	powdered cacao
protein	5.4 g
fat	7.8 g
carbohydrates	15.6 g
fiber	12 g
	per 90 ml (30 g)

milk chocolate

dark chocolate

Nutritional Information

The cacao bean nib contains various substances, including proteins, fat (cocoa butter), carbohydrates, xanthines (caffeine and theobromine), tannins, fiber, oxalic acid, small quantities of minerals (including phosphorus, potassium, and iron), and negligible quantities of vitamins A and B. Cacao processed using the Dutch method has a higher potassium content.

The protein content of cacao and chocolate is between 10% and 20%.

Chocolate contains about 50% fat and cacao between 10% and 22%, depending on the percentage of cocoa butter that has been extracted. The cocoa butter is frequently removed (for use in cosmetics notably) and replaced by coconut butter or palm oil.

Cocoa powder and low-fat cocoa powder are both excellent sources of copper, potassium, vitamin B_{12}, and iron; they are also good sources of phosphorus and contain riboflavin, pantothenic acid, niacin, and thiamine, as well as traces of calcium and vitamin B_6. They are very rich in fiber. Their calorie content depends on the ingredients in the chocolate.

Cacao and chocolate contain the stimulants theobromine and caffeine in quantities that vary from one type of chocolate to another. For example, 30 grams (1 ounce) of cacao contains 617 milligrams of theobromine and 72 milligrams of caffeine, while 30 grams of milk chocolate supplies 51 milligrams of theobromine and 7.5 milligrams of caffeine. A square of unsweetened chocolate (30 grams) contains 351 milligrams of theobromine and 59 milligrams of caffeine, while 30 grams of semisweet chocolate contains only 138 milligrams of theobromine and 18 milligrams of caffeine. Chocolate contains lower quantities of these stimulants than coffee; although the effect is the same, it is somewhat less intense.

Contrary to popular belief, consuming chocolate before doing physical exercise will not provide the body with more energy, since the muscles use energy that has been stored in the body in the form of glycogen for at least 18 hours. It is actually not recommended to eat sweet foods before engaging in physical activity.

Chocolate contains phenylethylamine, a chemical substance that acts on the brain's neurotransmitters; this substance is a bio-amine, similar to amphetamines, which produces the sensation of euphoria associated with being in love.

Storing

Chocolate should be stored at room temperature (about 65°F) and will keep for several months if it is well wrapped, protected from humidity and heat, and stored at a fairly constant temperature. It can also be stored in the refrigerator or the freezer, but this may result in the appearance of a whitish film, caused by the resurfacing of the cocoa butter; this does not alter the flavor of the chocolate and disappears during melting. It is important to avoid moisture both when cooking with chocolate and when storing it.

Fats
and Oils

Margarine

Margarine was developed in France in 1869 as the result of a contest sponsored by Napoleon III, who was interested in finding an alternative to butter, which was quite rare and expensive during the 19th century. In addition to being relatively inexpensive, the winning product had to be capable of being stored without going rancid and could not have a strong odor. The word "margarine" is derived from the adjective "margaric," which means "of or resembling pearl" and is itself derived from the Greek word for pearl, *margaron*. Margarine is thought to have been named by its inventor, the chemist Hippolyte Mège-Mouriès, who was apparently inspired by its color. Margarine made from beef fat was first sold in 1872. Scientists subsequently began to experiment with margarines made from tropical oils and eventually discovered how to raise the melting point of vegetable oils, as well as to prolong their shelf life, by means of hydrogenation.

Margarine was initially made from refined tallow, but vegetable oils were used after scientists discovered a process that prevented vegetable fat from oxidizing too quickly; the discovery of hydrogenation (a process that solidifies liquid fats) at the beginning of the 20th century also led to the development of new kinds of margarine.

Margarine is usually made of one or more vegetable fats (soy, corn, sunflower, peanut, safflower, palm, cabbage palm, and colza oil are among the most common), but it may also contain animal fats (tallow, lard, and fish oil). Most of the margarines now sold in North America are made from a single vegetable oil or a mixture of various vegetable oils. Since animal fats and tropical oils such as copra, palm, and cabbage palm oil are naturally high in saturated fat, manufacturers can use small quantities of these oils to give their products the consistency usually achieved by means of hydrogenation, thus producing non-hydrogenated margarine. In Europe, the term "margarine" refers to any edible substance that looks like butter and is meant to be used like butter.

Margarine was not an immediate success; it gradually began to replace butter in the home, as well as in institutions, restaurants, and the food industry, but it was quite some time before it had a significant impact on the sales of butter. It eventually succeeded because it was relatively cheap and was marketed as a healthy alternative to butter. The margarine sold today looks so much like butter that some countries have implemented regulations stipulating that it cannot be dyed the same shade of yellow as butter, to ensure that consumers can distinguish between the two products. North Americans now consume almost twice as much margarine as butter.

As part of their effective marketing campaign, margarine manufacturers emphasize the fact that their product contains polyunsaturated fatty acids, which are generally regarded as "healthy" fat. However, most margarines contain at least some hydrogenated oil. Hydrogenation involves combining hydrogen atoms with the fatty-acid molecules, which solidifies the oil, raises its melting point, prevents it from going rancid, and improves the consistency of foods to which it is added. Unfortunately, hydrogenation also alters the nature and structure of fatty acids, turning naturally occurring "cis" fatty acids into "trans" fatty acids, small amounts of which are found in milk and butter. This modification has a dramatic impact on how these polyunsaturated fatty acids behave; in fact, once they become "trans" fatty acids, they act very much like saturated fatty acids – i.e., they raise levels of "bad" cholesterol and reduce levels of "good" cholesterol (see *Fats*). It is impossible to determine the proportion of "trans" fatty acids a margarine actually contains because measuring them requires very expensive and imprecise technology. However, the consistency of the margarine is a good indication: harder margarines are generally more hydrogenated and contain more "trans" fatty acids.

When "trans" fatty acids were introduced into the food chain by means of hydrogenation, very little was known about their metabolic impact or their effects on health in general. Toward the end of the 1960s, it was established that the chemical structure of "trans" fatty acids is very similar to that of saturated fatty acids, and subsequent research has confirmed that they increase levels of "bad" cholesterol in much the same way as saturated fat. It is important to note, however, that some of the soft margarines on the market contain less than 10% "trans" fatty acids and others consist exclusively of non-hydrogenated fats. In terms of their capacity to raise blood cholesterol levels, these soft margarines are less dangerous than either butter or hard margarines.

People who want to restrict the total amount of fat, saturated fat, or cholesterol in their diets should choose a soft margarine that is low in saturated fat and "trans" fatty acids rather than butter.

Buying

Margarine can be hard, soft, liquid, or whipped, and either salted or unsalted. There are regular, spreadable, and diet margarines on the market. For information about the composition of the fatty acids in a margarine, consult the nutritional-information table on the outside of the package. Soft margarines are much less hydrogenated and contain far fewer "trans" fatty acids than hard margarines. Check the list of ingredients on the label to determine whether or not the margarine contains hydrogenated fat; margarines that contain a high proportion of liquid oil tend to be less hydrogenated.

Serving Ideas

Since they contain a high percentage of water, diet margarines are used mainly as sandwich spreads and should not be used for cooking. Regular margarine has a much broader range of uses; it can replace butter in most recipes and can also be used for cooking, although it cannot always match the flavor of butter. Like butter, margarine should not be used for deep-frying. To prevent margarine from turning brown or burning when cooked, choose a product that does not contain any powdered milk or whey.

Storing

Margarine can be stored in the refrigerator or the freezer. To prevent it from absorbing food odors, ensure that the container is tightly sealed or that the margarine is well wrapped.

Nutritional Information

Like butter, margarine is high in fat and calories, and should be eaten in moderation. In fact, most margarines contain just as much fat and as many calories as butter: 11 grams of fat and 100 calories per tablespoon (15 ml). Unlike butter, margarine made exclusively from vegetable oils does not contain any cholesterol.

Regular margarine contains 82% fat and 16% water. Diet margarine contains less fat (approximately 40%) and more water (55% to 59%).

A broad range of other ingredients are added to margarine in various proportions. These include milk solids like buttermilk, vegetable dyes, preservatives, emulsifiers, antioxidants, flavorings, sweeteners, modified starch, and salt. Since it is regarded as a substitute for butter, margarine must be enriched with vitamins A and D.

Salt enhances the flavor of margarine and acts as a natural preservative. It can be replaced with various other substances, including potassium chloride, sodium benzoate, and potassium carbonate, or combined with them, in order to extend the shelf life or to adjust the pH of the product. The antioxidants BHT (butylated hydroxytoluene) and BHA (butylated hydroxyanisole) preserve the freshness and flavor of margarine. Emulsifiers, mono- and diglycerides, sodium alginate, and lecithin are added to prevent the water from separating from the fat and to limit the amount of splattering that occurs when the margarine is heated. Sugar is added to ensure that foods fried in margarine will brown.

Fats and Oils

647

Fats

ghee

In the food industry, the term "fats" generally refers to solid or liquid substances that are used as a cooking medium for other foods, as a flavoring, a binding agent, an emulsifier, or a preserving agent. These fats can be of animal origin (butter, pork fat or lard, beef fat, suet, goose fat), of vegetable origin (vegetable fat, most margarines, corn oil, sunflower oil, nut oil), or in the form of shortening, a fatty substance made from several vegetable oils to which animal fats are sometimes added and which is solidified by a process called hydrogenation.

Serving Ideas

Fats and oils have been known to man since the beginning of time. They have been used as food, to make soap and lubricants, as fuel for lighting and heating, and for cosmetics and medicines. However, patterns of fat consumption have shifted over time, and modern-day diets often include excessive quantities of fat; this in turn has led to a higher incidence of heart disease among certain populations. For this reason, nutritionists recommend lowering the intake of fats by choosing less fatty dairy products and leaner meats, and by minimizing the amount of fat used in cooking.

For a long time, it was believed that foods rich in the more harmful saturated fats (butter, red meat, cheese, etc.) could be replaced by foods high in unsaturated fatty acids (oil and polyunsaturated margarines, white meat, etc.) without regard for the overall fat intake. However, it now appears that it is more important to reduce the overall quantity of fats consumed, while avoiding saturated fats in particular. We also recognize that the health effects of polyunsaturated fatty acids are not as positive as was originally believed and that monoun-saturated fatty acids may be at least as valuable as polyunsaturated fatty acids; thus, products that are rich in monounsaturated fats (such as olive oil) are a healthy part of a daily diet.

In active people who have a well-balanced ratio of calories consumed to calories spent, the daily fat intake should not exceed 35% of the total energy intake (the average fat intake in the U.S. and Canada is about 40%). In the case of sedentary people, fat intake should not exceed 30% of the total energy intake. However, it is not always easy to reduce the quantity of fat consumed, since close to 60% of the fat in our diet comes from invisible sources. For example, most of the calories contained in many commercially prepared and restaurant foods are provided by fat. Nevertheless, by following a few simple guidelines, it is possible to lower one's fat intake:

• Reduce the size of portions of meat, and choose lean meats or meats from which the fat can be easily removed before cooking, such as beef round, flank, or sirloin; pork loin, shoulder, or tenderloin; veal cutlet, chop, or leg; as well as poultry and game.

• Use a nonstick pan when cooking meat, and add little or no fat.

• Switch to low-fat dairy products; check the label for the percentage of milk fat (% MF) present, and choose cheeses containing less than 20% MF.

• Choose foods that can be either baked, broiled, steamed, or microwaved, all methods that require little fat.

• Avoid foods containing hydrogenated fats, including solid margarines, shortenings, fried foods, crackers, cookies, cake mixes, snacks, processed cheeses, and chips. Choose nonhydrogenated margarines that are rich in polyunsaturated and monounsaturated fatty acids.

• Include different types of fat in the diet, using vegetable oil (cold-pressed or not), a little butter, and nonhydrogenated margarine. Whenever possible, avoid foods rich in tropical oils, which include some cookies, certain baked products, and certain cereals.

Above all else, carefully read the list of ingredients and the nutritional table on food product labels, paying special attention to fat content. It is also important to keep in mind that only foods of animal origin contain cholesterol; thus it is somewhat misleading to label a vegetable oil "cholesterol-free." Moreover, foods labeled "light" are not necessarily less fatty; for example, the only thing lighter about "light" olive oil is usually its taste. On the other hand, "light" butters and margarines actually do contain only half the calories of regular products, but their high water content makes them unsuitable for cooking, so they are used mainly as a spread.

In short, the simplest and most effective way to reduce one's overall intake of dietary fat is to eliminate the consumption of "added" fats. Finally, any effort to reduce one's overall intake of dietary fat should include a decrease in the quantity of saturated fats, in order to lower the risk of heart disease.

Fat substitutes

To help consumers maintain a dietary fat intake of around 30%, the food industry has sought to create substitutes that play the same role as fat, but without the calories and cholesterol. A few years ago, Canada and the United States approved the use of a fat substitute made from a blend of egg and milk proteins that are heated in order to convert the proteins into minute round particles. This fat substitute has the same smoothness characteristic of fats, but supplies only 1 or 2 calories per gram, as opposed to the 9 calories provided by normal fats. This substance is digested and absorbed by the body in the same manner as other proteins. So far, this substitute is used only by the food industry, notably in the manufacture of ice cream and as a thickening and texture-modifying agent in frozen desserts. Because it cannot withstand very high temperatures, it is not suitable for frying.

Another replacement for fat was created in the United States by manipulating fat molecules. Comprised of eight fatty acids joined to a sugar molecule, this substitute has the same qualities of taste, texture, and appearance as fat and is also suitable for frying. While it contains neither calories nor cholesterol, it does inhibit the body's absorption of vitamin E.

While these substitutes can help to reduce fat intake, unlike fats, they do not produce a feeling of satiety. Moreover, foods made with these substitutes do not necessarily contain fewer calories, since additives and ingredients that increase their calorie content are often added.

Nutritional Information

In nutrition, the term «fats» is often used as a synonym for lipids, although this can lead to confusion since not all lipids are fats, whereas all fats are lipids. Like carbohydrates, lipids are made up of different proportions of carbon, hydrogen, and oxygen, with hydrogen and oxygen being present in a larger quantity. Fats release over 2 times more energy (9 calories per gram) than do carbohydrates and proteins (4 calories per gram); they are thus an important source of energy and heat, and they contribute to the formation of body fat. Because they supply more calories than any other nutritional element, fats play a very important role in maintaining good health. Fatty acids serve as a direct source of energy for all of the body's cells (with the exception of red blood cells and the central nervous system).

In addition to making foods more palatable, dietary fats transport the fat-soluble vitamins A, D, E, and K, which would not be absorbed by the body in the absence of dietary fat. Dietary fat also supplies two essential fatty acids that cannot be synthesized by the body, namely linoleic acid and alpha-linolenic acid, both of which are more abundant in polyunsaturated fats.

Among other things, essential fatty acids contribute to the harmonious functioning of the circulatory and immune systems, while also contributing to the development of individual cells.

The category of alpha-linolenic acid includes the omega-3 fatty acids. This type of fat, a primary source of which is fish oils, is held to be of value in combatting chronic inflammatory diseases such as rheumatoid arthritis, as well as having a beneficial effect on the immune system and lowering the incidence of atherosclerosis and heart disease. While the health benefits of essential fatty

Fats and Oils

acids have been well established, it should be noted that only small quantities of these acids are required in order to reap their benefits. Indeed, excessive consumption of fats can have a negative effect on health, notably by increasing blood cholesterol levels and by contributing to the problem of obesity.

Fats are metabolized slowly by the system, since they slow down gastric emptying, thus prolonging the process of digestion.

Fatty acids (the simplest form of lipids) are molecules made up of carbon atoms arranged in chains of varying lengths to which are joined a variable number of hydrogen and oxygen atoms. Each fatty acid is characterized by the length of its carbon chain and by the amount of hydrogen it can hold. The structure of this carbon chain may or may not include a double bond between the carbon atoms. The three main types of fatty acids are distinguished by their chemical structure:

• Saturated fatty acids have a single bond between carbon atoms; because there are no double bonds, they cannot receive any additional hydrogen atoms.

• Monounsaturated fatty acids have one double bond between two carbon atoms, and can therefore each receive an additional hydrogen atom; this structure is flexible, as opposed to the rigid structure of saturated fats.

• Polyunsaturated fats have several double bonds, resulting in a large degree of flexibility as well as a greater structural vulnerability; polyunsaturated fats oxidize easily and rapidly, causing the substance to turn rancid.

Hydrogenation

Hydrogenation is a process by which hydrogen is added to the molecules of unsaturated fats. This treatment is applied to oils high in polyunsaturated fatty acids that are liquid at room temperature (some animal fats comprised mainly of saturated fatty acids are solid at room temperature). Hydrogenation converts the unsaturated bonds of fatty acids into saturated bonds, resulting in the solidification of the oil as well as increasing its melting temperature, delaying rancidity, and improving the consistency of foods. All-vegetable shortening is obtained by the complete hydrogenation of the vegetable oil in order to solidify it, while pure shortening may contain animal or vegetable fats. One negative effect of hydrogenation is that it changes the configuration of fatty acids by converting them from their natural "cis" form to a new "trans" form. Trans fatty acids have the same effect in the body as saturated fatty acids; they increase the level of low-density cholesterol (LDL), or so-called bad cholesterol, in the blood and reduce the level of high-density cholesterol (HDL), or "good cholesterol."

Cholesterol

Cholesterol is a fatlike substance present in blood cells and in food of animal origin. Unlike lipids, cholesterol does not supply energy, but it does play a role in the synthesis of bile salts, adrenalin hormones, and sex hormones. It is also an important constituent of myelin, which forms a protective layer around the nerves. Cholesterol is also a precursor of vitamin D. The human body, principally the liver, synthesizes close to 80% of the cholesterol it requires, while the remaining 20% is provided by food of animal origin. Cholesterol is important for the functioning and development of the nervous system.

Since studies have linked saturated fats and cholesterol to heart disease, obesity, and a number of cancers, including colon and breast cancer, consumers have been encouraged to reduce their consumption of these substances. However, there is as yet no evidence that the risk of developing cancer can be reduced merely by limiting fat intake to 30% or by simply modifying the type of fat consumed. Cholesterol and lipids have also been linked to the development of atherosclerosis, the accumulation of fat deposits on the walls of the coronary arteries, causing the thickening and hardening of the tissue (sclerosis), which can seriously reduce the flow of blood. The risk of heart disease increases when the level of cholesterol in the blood is too high. The most important factor in high blood cholesterol is an excessive consumption of fats, particularly saturated fats.

The notion of "good" and "bad" cholesterol is actually a question of transportation means. In order to fulfill its functions, cholesterol is transported in the blood by specialized proteins called lipoproteins, of which there are two types: low-density lipoproteins (LDL's) and high-density lipoproteins (HDL's).

The LDL's transport the cholesterol from the liver to the cells; when the quantity of cholesterol being transported is too high, the surplus adheres to the walls of the arteries, which is how LDL's earned the reputation of being "bad cholesterol."

On the other hand, it is believed that HDL's play the role of a scavenger, picking up the excess cholesterol in the arteries and transporting it to the liver, where it is eliminated by the bile. It is because of their cleansing effect that HDL's are termed "good cholesterol."

Triglycerides are another fatlike substance found in the blood. A high level of triglycerides is caused by the excessive consumption of alcohol, fat, and sugar. The influence of triglycerides as a risk factor for heart disease is, however, lower than that presented by low-density lipoproteins.

Although the notion of "good" and "bad" cholesterol applies only to blood cholesterol, the different types of fat found in foods have a different effect on "good" and "bad" blood cholesterol, since the three types of fatty acids affect the body differently. While foods contain a combination of these fatty acids in varying proportions, one type of fat is always predominant. For example, meat and dairy products are rich in saturated fat, while olive oil and almonds are rich in monounsaturated fat and sunflower oil is high in polyunsaturated fat.

Saturated fats tend to cause an increase in the blood cholesterol level of people whose diet is rich in such fats. Saturated fats are found mainly in foods of animal origin and, exceptionally, in tropical oils such as palm oil and coconut oil. This type of fat is solid at room temperature.

When monounsaturated fatty acids are added to the diet, they protect and even increase the level of "good" cholesterol (HDL) while lowering "bad" cholesterol (LDL). These fats are found in olive and canola oil, almonds, hazelnut oil, and avocados. They are liquid at room temperature and are more resistant to oxidation than polyunsaturated fatty acids.

Polyunsaturated fatty acids in the diet lower the level of both "bad" and "good" cholesterol. They are also very rich in essential fatty acids. The main sources of polyunsaturated fats are vegetable oils such as corn, soybean, wheat germ, safflower, sunflower, and sesame oil. The family of polyunsaturated fats also includes fats from fish, commonly known as omega-3 fatty acids. Because the omega-3 fatty acids reduce the tendency of blood to form clots by making it more fluid, it is recommended to include two to three portions of fish rich in omega-3 (including mackerel, herring, tuna, and salmon) in one's weekly diet. However, it is still too early to recommend the consumption of fish oil supplements.

shortening

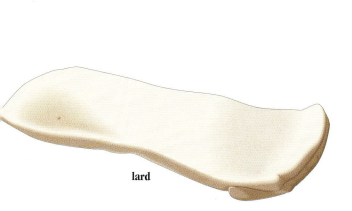

lard

il is an unctuous fatty substance that is insoluble in water and usually liquid at room temperature. The use of oil dates back to primitive times; the first form of oil used by man was melted animal fat. It is known that the olive tree was cultivated in the Mediterranean basin over 6,000 years ago; the first pressed oils were probably sesame oil and olive oil. In addition to its use as a foodstuff, oil was used as fuel, notably to provide lighting. The most commercially important oils in the world today are soybean oil, palm oil, and rapeseed (canola) oil. The production and use of oils vary from one country to the next. For example, in Canada the most important oil is canola oil; in Europe, canola oil, sunflower oil, soybean oil, and peanut oil are particularly important; and the countries along the Pacific rim use mainly palm and soybean oils.

Vegetable oils are particularly important as a foodstuff. The primary sources of vegetable oil are legumes (soybeans, peanuts), seeds (sunflower, rapeseed, pumpkin), cereals (corn), fruits (olives, palm, nuts, hazelnuts, grape seeds, sweet almonds), and cotton. Oil is also extracted from animals (whale, seal, halibut, cod), notably for use as a dietary supplement, and from minerals (hydrocarbons); paraffin oil is the only edible mineral oil, although it must never be heated and it is indigestible.

For a long time, the extraction of vegetable oil was performed according to traditional methods; nowadays, industrial methods are used, allowing for the mass production of oil. Regardless of the raw material, the first step in the oil-manufacturing process always involves the cleaning and shelling (as in the case of peanuts, sunflower seeds, almonds, hazelnuts, etc.) of the oil-bearing material. It is then ground into a pulp that is subjected to mechanical extraction by cold or hot pressing.

Cold pressing is performed mechanically using hydraulic presses at a maximum temperature of 172°F, and was long the only process used. To be profitable, cold extraction requires that the seeds or fruits have a minimum fat content of 30%. Only seeds grown using organic methods of cultivation are suitable for pressing to make oil. After the oil is extracted, it is decanted and filtered before being bottled in opaque bottles. Cold-pressed oils are not subjected to further treatment. It should be noted that since there is no legal definition of "cold-pressed oil," oils marketed as such may not actually be cold-pressed.

"First-extraction cold-pressed oil" is the oil obtained from the first pressing; "extra-virgin oil" is oil obtained from the first pressing with an acid content of less than 1%, while «virgin oil» is a first-extraction oil with a maximum acid content of 3%. "Fine" oil is a blend of extra-virgin and virgin oil. The mention "100% pure" refers to the fact that the oil comes from a single source, as opposed to being a blend of different oils; it is often obtained from a second pressing of the fruits. The process of cold pressing leaves close to one third of the oil in the residual pulp, while expressing by heat limits loss to about 5%, and the addition of a solvent lowers it to 1%. The solvent most commonly used is a solution of hexane (hexane, acetone, and water).

Heat pressing is a mechanical process by which the pulp is passed through heated screw presses at a temperature of between 208° and 280°F. The oil obtained is called crude oil (also known as raw oil or unrefined oil). The residue, called cake oil meal, is subsequently treated with a solvent to extract any remaining oil. Crude oil pressed using the heat method must be subjected to several treatments before it can be used; these treatments include degumming, refining or neutralization, bleaching, hydrogenation (sometimes), deodorization, and antioxidation.

Degumming involves removing the free fatty acids and small quantities of proteins, phospholipids, and other substances that contribute to the instability of the oil and to the production of froth and smoke during deep-frying.

Refining or neutralization consists of adding an alkaline substance (often caustic soda) to the degummed oil in order to transform its free fatty acids into soap, which is then extracted by centrifugation.

Bleaching eliminates the pigments present in the crude oil.

Hydrogenation involves treating the saturated bonds of the oil with hydrogen to prevent oxidation and to convert liquid oils into semisolid or solid shortenings. The higher the degree of hydrogenation, the more solid the fat and the higher its degree of saturation (see *Fats*).

Fractionation is performed to prevent the oils from crystallizing at low temperatures (in the refrigerator, for example). The crystals are removed by filtration after the oil has been cooled.

Deodorization produces oil with a neutral flavor that does not transfer any specific flavor to foods; this process eliminates traces of substances that cause the oil to go rancid, thus prolonging its keeping qualities once it is bottled.

The **antioxidation treatment** usually involves adding synthetic antioxidants that prevent oxidation of the oil as long as the container is sealed. (Oxidation is a chemical reaction occurring between the unsaturated bonds in fatty acids when an unsaturated fat is exposed to oxygen.) Although a natural antioxidant, vitamin E, is present in oil and in vegetable fats (it is more abundant in cold-pressed than in hot-pressed oils), the oil is protected against oxidation only until these natural antioxidants are used up, after which the fatty acids begin to deteriorate. That is why cold-pressed oils must be stored with greater care than refined oils. Under proper storage conditions, oxidation takes place very slowly. However, once it begins, it very quickly imparts an acrid taste to the oil, which must then be discarded.

Unrefined oils are darker and have a more pronounced flavor than refined oils. However, this stronger flavor is not to be confused with rancidity. Refining has an effect on the nature and the quantity of fatty acids in oils, as well as on their vitamin and mineral content, color, flavor, and cooking qualities. Consequently, after refining, an antioxidant (vitamin E or an additive) is added to the oil if its vitamin E content is not adequate to protect the oil against oxidation. Unlike refined oils, cold-pressed oils contain several substances, including free fatty acids and pigments, that may cause oxidation. Moreover, hydrogenation can destroy up to 50% of the polyunsaturated fatty acids in oil, lowering the quantity of linoleic acid, an essential acid that cannot be synthesized by the body.

Buying

A wide variety of oils, both refined and cold-pressed, are available on the market. It is important to read the list of ingredients on the label, as the number of additives in oil varies according to the brand; some brands contain no additives. Also, in the case of cold-pressed oils it is a good idea to verify the expiration date.

Storing

Oil should be stored in a sealed container in a cool, dark place. The container should be airtight, narrow, and deep; in the case of cold-pressed oils, it is best to use a small container that is opaque or dark. Cold-pressed oils should be stored in the refrigerator, where they will keep up to 1 year unopened or for a few months once opened. Linseed oil will keep for only a few months while sealed and for a few weeks once the bottle has been opened. When refrigerated, cold-pressed oil has a tendency to harden, forming whitish masses of flakes; this phenomenon affects neither the quality nor the taste of the oil, which returns to its liquid state at room temperature.

Serving Ideas

Vegetable oil has many culinary uses. It often replaces butter, both as a cooking agent for other foods and as an ingredient in such preparations as sauces, cakes, muffins, and cookies. However, the use of vegetable oil instead of butter can change the flavor and texture of foods.

Oil is one of the main ingredients in salad dressings. Oils extracted from nuts make particularly tasty vinaigrettes. The distinctive flavor of sesame oil is often found in Asian cuisine, which makes wide use of it.

Oil is commonly used in marinades to tenderize meat, poultry, fish, and game. It can also be lightly brushed on foods to be broiled or barbecued; and it serves as a preserving agent, notably with purÇed garlic, dried tomatoes, and fresh herbs.

Oil emulsifies when it is beaten, which is how mayonnaise is obtained. For an effective emulsion, the ingredients in the mayonnaise should all be at room temperature. Choose a bland-tasting oil so as not to mask the flavor of the egg and vinegar (or lemon juice).

To lower the quantity of fat in one's diet, it is best to steam foods instead of browning, frying, or sauteing them. It is also a good idea to use stock, tamari sauce, or tomato juice instead of oil.

olive oil   peanut oil   sesame oil   sunflower oil   corn oil

Oils	Saturated Fat g/100 g	Monounsaturated Fat g/100 g	Polyunsaturated Fat g/100 g	Smoke Point	Oxidation	Uses	Comments
PEANUT	16.9	46.2	32	high 425°F - 220°C	slow	all	withstands high heat
SAFFLOWER	9.1	12.1	74.5	higher than 425°F - 220°C	very quick	especially cold	unrefined: yellow to dark amber; mild nutty flavor refined: very pale yellow neutral flavor
CANOLA	7.2	55.5	33.3	high 425°F - 220°C	slow	all	unpleasant smell at high heat due to high acid content
COCONUT	86.5	5.8	1.8	high	very slow	all	widely used by the food industry
CORN	12.7	24	58.7	unrefined: 340°F - 170°C refined:450°F - 230°C	average slow	all	unrefined: amber to dark golden; often tastes like popcorn refined: pale amber
WALNUT	9.1	22.8	63.3	325-400°F 160-200°C	quick	cold only	strong taste
PALM	49.3	37	9.3	400- 415°F 200- 210°C	slow	cold cooking	unrefined: yellow or green; strong taste; withstands high heat but leaves a lingering smell
OLIVE	13.5	73.7	8.4	435°F - 225°C	slow	all	widely used by the food industry
GRAPE SEED	9.6	16.1	69.9		quick	cold only	strong taste
SESAME	14.2	39.7	41.7	higher than 450°F - 230°C	average	table	unpleasant smell at high heat
SOYBEAN	14.4	23.3	57.9	higher than 450°F - 230°C	average	table cooking	unrefined: pronounced taste and color; high vitamin B content refined: whitish; milder flavor
SUNFLOWER	10.1	45.2	40.1	410 - 425°F 210 - 220°C	very quick	table cooking	unrefined: amber; strong taste refined: whitish; neutral taste

Nutritional Information

Oils contain neither proteins nor carbohydrates, and vegetable oils do not contain cholesterol. Oil does contain fats and vitamins A, D, and E and is a valuable source of energy.

Because they are comprised mainly of fats, which produce more calories than proteins and carbohydrates (9 calories per gram versus 4 calories per gram), all oils are energizing. All oils have the same energy value: 15 millileters of oil provides 122 calories and contains 14 grams of lipids.

Each type of oil is made up of a combination of several fatty acids in proportions that vary according to the oil. The fatty acids can be saturated, monounsaturated, or polyunsaturated. Monounsaturated and polyunsaturated fats are regarded as being healthier than saturated fatty acids (see *Fats*). Thus it is recommended that oils rich in monounsaturated and polyunsaturated fatty acids be consumed in moderation and that consumption of oils with a high saturated fat content be kept to a minimum.

Palm oil and coconut oil are comprised mainly of saturated fatty acids, and like animal fats, they are solid at room temperature. On the other hand, most vegetable oils (peanut, safflower, canola, corn, linseed, nut, sesame, soybean, sunflower) consist mainly of polyunsaturated fats and are liquid at room temperature. Olive oil, canola oil, peanut oil, and hazelnut oil are composed mainly of monounsaturated fatty acids. While it was long believed that polyunsaturated fats were healthier, recent research suggests that monounsaturated fats are actually more beneficial, which is why the consumption of olive oil is increasingly recommended. Oils recommended for consumption (in moderation) include those that are rich in monounsaturated fatty acids, such as canola oil, which also contains omega-3 fatty acids (see *Fats*), olive oil, and peanut oil. Oils that are high in polyunsaturated fatty acids include corn oil, safflower oil, soybean oil, sunflower oil, and sesame oil, which has a very distinctive flavor.

Cooking

Certain oils, including cold-pressed walnut, linseed, safflower, corn, and soybean oils, are not able to withstand high temperatures. Generally speaking, it is best to reserve cold-pressed oils such as these for use in vinaigrettes and to avoid exposing them to direct heat, although most of them withstand indirect heat very well (for example, when used in baked goods).

Avoid heating oil to the point that it begins to smoke and decompose; it will produce toxic substances that are irritating to the lungs and the digestive system. The formation of smoke at the surface of oil is also an indication that the oil could ignite spontaneously. The fatty acids that make up the oil determine its smoke point, and accordingly its possible uses. The higher the oil's smoke point, the higher the temperature it can withstand. Oils used for deep-frying should have a smoke point of over 488°F, a criterion met by sunflower, peanut, and canola oil. Polyunsaturated fatty acids are not very tolerant of high temperatures and are not suitable for repeated frying, which causes them to oxidize and deteriorate, producing toxic substances.

Because the smoke point varies with the oil, it should be indicated on the label, although unfortunately this is rarely the case. Each time a batch of oil is reused for frying, its smoke point decreases and the oil deteriorates, with the result that after a batch has been used for frying a certain number of times (which varies depending on the oil), it becomes unfit for consumption and must be discarded. To ensure the safe reuse of oil for frying, follow these guidelines:

• Do not exceed the smoke point; to be on the safe side, keep the temperature below 450°F.

• Pour the oil through a coffee filter or several layers of cheesecloth after each use in order to filter out any food particles or other debris.

• Keep the oil in an opaque airtight container in a cool place.

• Do not reuse the same batch of oil more than five to seven times.

• Avoid using copper, bronze, or brass utensils, which may cause the oil to oxidize and deteriorate; stainless steel is preferable.

• Discard any oil that has smoked or that is too dark, smells rancid, produces foam, or does not bubble when the food is added.

Adding fresh oil to a batch of old oil does not improve its quality; it is best to replace old oil with a totally new batch. To prevent hot oil from splattering, drain and dry the food as completely as possible before immersing it in the oil.

The cooking thermometer is an indispensable tool for deep-frying; the food can be immersed at exactly the right temperature, and the temperature can be controlled during the cooking process and reduced before the oil reaches the smoke point. Do not fry too much food at once, which can reduce the temperature of the oil, causing the food to absorb too much oil and to lose flavor. By frying small batches at a time, the food will be golden and crispy on the outside and cooked to perfection inside.

Cooking Ingredients

Arrowroot

Maranta arundinacea, **Marantaceae**

The word "arrowroot" originally referred only to a starch extracted from maranta, a tuberous-root plant thought to have originated in South America, but it has gradually come to be associated with starches derived from the rhizomes or roots of various other plants, such as *Zamia, Curcuma,* and *Musa.* There is some disagreement among etymologists with regard to the origin of the word "arrowroot." Some believe that it is derived from *araruta,* a word meaning "root flour" in a dialect spoken by native South Americans; others suggest that the word refers to the aboriginal custom of treating poison-arrow wounds with this starch or to the practice of coating arrows with starch made from roots of poisonous plants.

Arrowroot is produced in various countries, including several in South America, as well as India, Mexico, and the United States. The roots of the maranta plant are 8 to 12 inches long and 1 to 1¼ inches in diameter. These roots (or rhizomes) are ground and mixed with water, then filtered, dried, and reduced to a fine white powder that is used like cornstarch or flour. Arrowroot can be substituted for flour, but only half as much should be used. Unlike cornstarch, arrowroot does not cloud clear liquids or alter the taste of sauces (if cooked only briefly). It is also used to make low-protein foods for people with liver or kidney problems or with certain allergies.

Nutritional Information

protein	0.3 g
fat	0.1 g
carbohydrates	88.1 g
	per 100 g

Arrowroot is easy to digest.

Serving Ideas

 Arrowroot is used to thicken soups, sauces, puddings, creams, and flans. Dilute it in a small amount of cold liquid before adding it to hot dishes. It is a common ingredient in cakes and cookies, especially in biscuits for nursing infants.

Storing

Arrowroot should be protected from insects and stored at room temperature.

Baking powder

Baking powder is a fine white substance that reacts in the presence of liquid and heat, releasing carbon dioxide, which leavens dough. It is made up of a mixture of alkaline and acid salts. The various combinations of ingredients used as baking powder include:

• monocalcium phosphate, sodium bicarbonate, aluminum sulfate, sodium sulfate, and cornstarch;

• aluminum sulfate, sodium sulfate, calcium carbonate, monocalcium phosphate, and sodium bicarbonate;

• anhydrous monocalcium phosphate and sodium bicarbonate;

• sodium bicarbonate, calcium sulfate, monocalcium phosphate, cornstarch, aluminum sulfate, and sodium sulfate.

Baking powder was perfected toward the end of the 19th century, shortly after the invention of baking soda. A crude form of baking powder was used in the United States around 1790, but it had a bitter aftertaste. The first baking powder containing cream of tartar was developed around 1835; it was a mixture of sodium bicarbonate and the residue of cream of tartar from barrels in which wine was made. This kind of baking powder was first sold commercially in 1850. At the end of the 19th century, the cream of tartar was replaced with the acid salts monocalcium phosphate, aluminum sulfate, and sodium sulfate.

A much more effective leavener than baking soda, baking powder reacts with the wet ingredients at lower temperatures and has no aftertaste, unless an excessive amount is used. Fast-acting, slow-acting, double-action, and low-sodium baking powder are among the most widely available varieties.

Fast-acting baking powder contains monohydrous monocalcium phosphate. It begins to produce carbon dioxide as soon as it is combined with liquid. Since over 90% of the carbon dioxide is released within the first few minutes, dough containing fast-acting baking powder has to be prepared quickly and baked immediately to ensure that it retains the gas and rises as desired. The baked goods made with this kind of baking powder include angel food cakes, *craquelins* (small light, crunchy cakes or cookies), donuts, and pizza dough.

Slow-acting baking powder is made by combining anhydrous monocalcium phosphate with sodium phosphate and aluminum phosphate, or with sodium sulfate and aluminum sulfate. The phosphate is in the form of tiny particles coated with an insoluble substance that makes them react more slowly in the presence of liquid. Most of the carbon dioxide is produced after the phosphate is heated in the oven. Since virtually no gas is produced before the dough is baked, dough made with slow-acting baking powder can be stored in the refrigerator overnight.

Double-action baking powder contains two acids that react with liquid ingredients at different speeds: monohydrous monocalcium phosphate, which reacts very quickly, mainly at room temperature, and a mixture of aluminum phosphate and sodium phosphate (or aluminum sulfate and sodium sulfate), which reacts very slowly and not until it is heated in the oven. This kind of baking powder can be used to make angel food cakes or donuts, as well as doughs that have to be refrigerated before they are baked.

Low-sodium baking powder contains potassium salts rather than sodium salts; it is ideal for people on low-sodium diets.

Cooking Ingredients

Preparing

You can make your own baking powder by combining 2 parts cream of tartar, 1 part sodium bicarbonate (baking soda) and 1 part cornstarch or arrowroot. For example, to make 1 teaspoon of baking powder, mix ½ teaspoon of cream of tartar with ¼ teaspoon of sodium bicarbonate; if preparing this mixture in advance, add ¼ teaspoon of cornstarch, which absorbs humidity, thus preventing the alkaline and acid ingredients from reacting prematurely.

Serving Ideas

Baking powder is used to make cakes, puddings, muffins, pancakes, waffles, and cookies. Generally, 1½ teaspoons of baking powder is added for each cup of flour. Sift the baking powder with the flour and the salt. It is important to note that the amount of baking powder used to make cakes has to be adjusted at high altitudes. Approximately 10% less baking powder is required at altitudes of about 3,000 feet, and 20% to 40% less is required at altitudes of 6,000 feet or more.

Storing

Baking powder should be stored at room temperature, away from heat and humidity. It can be less effective if stored for a long period of time. To ensure that it is still active, pour 4 to 5 tablespoons of boiling water over 1½ teaspoons of baking powder; if it is still fresh, it will bubble vigorously; if it is less than fresh, only a few bubbles will form or there will be no reaction whatsoever.

Cream of tartar

A fine white powder used as a stabilizer, cream of tartar is a by-product of the wine fermentation process. Crystals containing potassium bitartrate form on the interior walls of the barrels in which wine is fermented. The tartaric acid, produced when grapes ferment, is first isolated in the form of potassium salt. The crystals are then ground, purified, dehydrated, and reground to the powder known as cream of tartar. Since about 1835, cream of tartar has been combined with baking soda to be used as dry yeast. Cream of tartar reacts rapidly in the presence of baking soda and liquid, which makes dough rise very quickly. However, dough that is leavened in this way begins to lose volume if it is not baked immediately; for this reason, manufacturers have developed dry yeasts containing slower-acting agents like monocalcium phosphate.

Serving Ideas

Cream of tartar is often used to stabilize the egg whites beaten into angel food cakes, sponge cakes, chiffon cakes, meringues and soufflés, and to stop the sugar in candy from crystallizing. It is also added to omelets and cookies.

Storing

Store cream of tartar at room temperature, away from heat and humidity.

Preparing

You can make your own dry yeast by combining 2 tablespoons cream of tartar and 2 teaspoons baking soda or potassium bicarbonate (available in drugstores, this product contains no sodium and is thus recommended for people on salt-restricted diets).

Nutritional Information

Cream of tartar contains an amount of potassium equivalent to 3.8% of its total weight (0.11 g potassium/3 g cream of tartar); however, some of this potassium is lost when heated.

Baking soda

A leavening agent, baking soda is a fine white powder that consists of a mixture of alkaline salts. It has been in common use since the middle of the 19th century, when it revolutionized culinary practices by making it easier to produce leavened baked goods. It was partially responsible for the boom in the production of commercial bakery products like cakes, cookies, and donuts. It also expanded the range of ingredients used in breads and pastries by making it possible to use flours containing less gluten and to incorporate ingredients like nuts, wheat germ, cheese, and raisins.

Baking soda was initially produced by treating sodium ash with carbon dioxide, but most baking soda is now manufactured by adding carbon dioxide to huge vats of water containing sodium chloride and ammonia. Once the resultant insoluble sodium bicarbonate settles on the bottom of the vats, it is filtered, washed in cold water and dried, then ground to a fine powder.

The only mineral contained in baking soda is sodium, the usual concentration being 1,370 mg per 5 ml (5 g). When dissolved in water and heated, sodium bicarbonate decomposes into sodium carbonate, water, and carbon dioxide (which is what makes dough rise). Although the residue of sodium bicarbonate can create a bitter aftertaste, the production of sodium bicarbonate can be entirely avoided by using baking soda in combination with an acid ingredient, which will transform all of the bicarbonate of soda into water or carbon dioxide. It is thus important to ensure that dough made with baking soda is sufficiently acidic.

Molasses, honey, malt, fruit or fruit juice, chocolate, cocoa, lemon juice, yogurt, sour cream, buttermilk, and vinegar are the acidic ingredients most frequently added to dough. Even when used in combination with acidic ingredients, baking soda can still create an aftertaste because it is a rather stable compound that has to be heated to very high temperatures before it will decompose.

If a recipe calls for 1 cup (250 ml) of sour milk or buttermilk and none is available, it can be replaced with 1 cup (250 ml) of milk and 1½ teaspoons (8 ml) cream of tartar, or 1 cup of milk soured with 1 tablespoon (15 ml) vinegar or lemon juice.

Depending on the recipe, 2 teaspoons of dry yeast can be replaced with 2 pinches (2 ml) of baking soda and 1 cup (250 ml) of molasses, or with 2 pinches of baking soda and 1 rounded teaspoon (6 ml) of cream of tartar. It is very important to use the correct amount of baking soda with acid ingredients: 2 pinches of baking soda to 1 cup of buttermilk, sour milk, or yogurt, or to 1 tablespoon of lemon juice or vinegar.

Serving Ideas

Baking soda is often used when fruit is added to pastry, in order to neutralize the acidity. It is usually combined with the dry ingredients, which should be sifted to ensure that the baking soda does not clump together. If the dry ingredients are not well mixed, the baking soda can turn portions of the food yellow, altering the taste.

When baking soda is used in combination with an acid ingredient, it should be mixed with the dry ingredients, and the acid ingredient should not be added until just before the dough is cooked. Otherwise too much of the carbon dioxide, which makes the dough rise, will be lost. Baking soda should never be diluted in buttermilk or any other liquid acid ingredient.

Cooking

Baking soda is sometimes added to the water in which vegetables and legumes are cooked because it helps preserve the color of vegetables and reduces the amount of time required to cook legumes. However, this reduces the nutritional value of these foods and can often result in soggy, overcooked legumes, because baking soda rapidly breaks down fiber, making the legumes soft. Baking soda can be used to remove stuck or burned-on food from the bottom of pans: Put a little water in the bottom of the pan, sprinkle in some baking soda, and boil the water for 1 or 2 minutes; then let it cool. Baking soda can also be used to smother oil fires or other minor kitchen fires.

Storing

Baking soda should be stored at room temperature in a dry place.

Cooking Ingredients

661

Yeast

east is a microscopic fungus, usually a unicellular organism, that is used primarily to make bread. Scientists have identified 39 different yeast genuses, comprising over 350 species. The most commonly used species of yeast is *Saccharomyces cerevisiae,* which is also known as "brewer's yeast" (it is a byproduct of the beer-fermentation process) or "baker's yeast." Yeast should not be confused with baking powder, a mixture of several ingredients that is used as raising agent in cakes, cookies, pancakes, muffins and puddings (see baking powder).

The fungus develops rapidly when it comes into contact with a sweetened solution, or with the starchy sugars in flour, transforming the sugar into alcohol and carbon dioxide. In the presence of oxygen, yeast transforms sugar into water and carbon dioxide; alcohol is produced when no oxygen is present because the yeast cannot be completely oxidized. Although alcohol has been produced by means of fermentation since ancient times, brewer's yeast was not used to make bread until 1665. Louis Pasteur, the famous French chemist and microbiologist, began to study yeast in 1857 and discovered that the agent responsible for the fermentation of alcohol was a living microorganism capable of reproducing itself.

When yeast is added to flour that is rich in gluten, the carbon dioxide becomes trapped in the gluten, which makes the dough rise. The alcohol evaporates when the dough is cooked, and the trapped bubbles of carbon dioxide form air pockets that make the final product relatively light.

Yeast is also eaten as a dietary supplement. Brewer's yeast, a byproduct of the beer-making process, does not ferment and is usually consumed in the form of a dry powder; it is rich in vitamin B and high-quality proteins (35%). Torula yeast *(Torulopsis utilis)* is grown specifically for use as a dietary supplement for humans and animals. It has a more pleasant taste than brewer's yeast, which can be very strong-tasting. These food yeasts cannot be used as fermenting agents because their cells have been destroyed by heat.

Buying

Live yeast is sold fresh and compressed, or dried. Dry yeast can consist of a single yeast or a mixture of several yeasts; often obtained as a byproduct of the fermentation of alcohol, it is also grown specifically for use as a raising agent. Compressed yeast is usually sold by weight and should contain 70% moisture.

Dry yeast is available in regular or fast-acting varieties, either in grains or as a powder. Be sure to check the expiry date on the package.

Yeast that is used as a dietary supplement is sold as a powder or in tablets.

Storing

Fresh compressed yeast should not be refrigerated for any longer than 1 week. When stored for too long, it becomes inactive and starts to turn brown. Prolonged refrigeration can diminish its effectiveness as a raising agent.

Dry yeast can be stored for a longer period of time - up to a year, if is refrigerated or stored in a cool place.

Yeast that is consumed as a dietary supplement can be stored at room temperature.

Serving Ideas

Fresh compressed yeast and dry yeast can be used in same ways. They both become active at temperatures of between 77 and 82°F (25 and 28° C). The colder the temperature, the longer it will take for the dough to rise; the yeast will become inactive at temperatures over 130°F (54°C).

Yeast that is consumed as a dietary supplement cannot be used as a raising agent. If it is in the form of a powder, it can be diluted in juice, water or broth, or added to soups, stews, breads and salads. This kind of yeast, especially brewer's yeast, has a very strong flavor.

Nutritional Information

A very nutritious food, yeast is rich in protein, vitamins (especially B-complex vitamins), minerals, trace elements and enzymes. 30 milliliters of powdered brewer's yeast or torula yeast contains 5 grams of protein, 3 grams of carbohydrates and 23 calories. Brewer's yeast and torula yeast are particularly rich in B-complex vitamins, iron, folic acid, potassium and phosphorus; they are sometimes fortified with vitamin B_{12}. Since these yeasts contain 5 grams of protein per 30 milliliters, they can be consumed as a protein supplement between meals.

Dried torula yeast is an excellent source of high-quality proteins (50 to 62% protein), minerals and vitamin B, including vitamin B_{12}. Relatively bland, it does not have the bitter taste associated with brewer's yeast.

Since yeast is rich in phosphorus, which can affect calcium levels, people who use yeast as a dietary supplement should ensure that they are consuming enough calcium.

Active yeast should not be used as a dietary supplement because it consumes B-complex vitamins.

Coffee
and Tea

Tea

Camellia sinensis, Theaceae

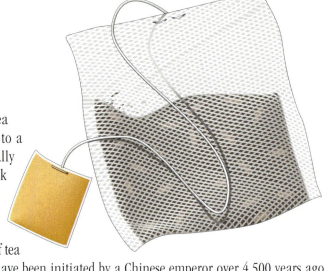

Tea is made from the dried leaves of the tea plant, a bushy evergreen that can grow to a height of 30 feet in the wild. Commercially grown tea plants, however, are pruned back to a more modest height of about 4½ feet to facilitate picking. The shrubs are likely indigenous to a region covering Tibet, western China and northern India. Although the exact origin of tea growing is uncertain, the practice is said to have been initiated by a Chinese emperor over 4,500 years ago. The leaves have been used since ancient times to produce a drink more popular than even coffee. Indeed, next to water, tea is world's leading beverage. There are various legends about the discovery of the drink known as tea, which dates back to the dawn of Chinese civilization. According to the best-known tale, in 2374 B.C., reigning sovereign Chen-nung decided to boil some water to quench his thirst. He placed the pot in the shade of a tea bush, and a breeze blew some leaves into the hot water. Upon tasting it, Chen-nung was pleasantly surprised by its flavor and aroma. Tea nevertheless became a popular drink in China only around the 16th century. Prior to this period, people had chewed the leaves and, around the year 1000, began drying and crushing them and adding boiling water. Tea has long been a ritual drink in Japan. The plants were first grown in Java and other tropical and subtropical regions. The Dutch introduced the beverage to Europe in the 17th century. The drink became popular in France and, above all, England, where, in the 18th century, all classes of society set began to partake twice daily in what has become a veritable institution: the tea break.

In North America, English and Irish colonialists made tea a highly popular beverage – up until the Boston Tea Party in 1773, when settlers opposed to taxation without representation stormed tea ships in the Boston harbor and dumped their cargoes overboard.

Today, England is the world's number-one tea consumer. The beverage is also popular in most other English-speaking countries, including Australia and New Zealand, as well as in Arabic countries, where it is prepared with sugar and mint, and in Russia. The world's leading producers are India, China, Sri Lanka, Kenya, Indonesia, Turkey and Russia.

The tea plant's elliptical, persistent leaves are bright green, slightly hairy, partially serrated and scattered with glands containing an essential oil. The best teas are cultivated at high altitudes where the plants grow slowly in relatively cool climates. Once a year, they bear tiny white flowers similar in appearance to camellias; these lightly scented blossoms fetch a high price. Tea plants continue to produce leaves for close to a century.

There are three broad categories of tea plants, originating respectively from China, Southeast Asia and India. These varieties are divided into a huge range of subcategories.

In tea plantations, the leaves are picked up to 20 to 30 times a year. Increasingly, traditional hand-picking is being replaced by mechanized means. Only the young leaves at the tips of the branches are harvested. Although the best teas are made from the leaf buds and next two leaves, the third, fourth and sometimes fifth leaves are also used to produce a less high-quality beverage. The end bud is known as a "pekoe," a term derived from the Chines *pa ko,* meaning "white down," in reference to the delicate down that covers the lower surface of the emerging leaf.

Depending on the process, the leaves are used to produce black tea (fermented), oolong tea (semifermented) or green tea (unfermented).

There are five steps in the production of **black tea:** withering, rolling, fermentation, drying and grading. During withering, the leaves lose part of their water and become flaccid. Rolling destroys the leave's inner membranes, thus freeing and mixing components required for fermentation. Fermentation, which is carried out in a wet environment, is aimed at developing the aroma and coppery color of black tea; the duration of this step depends on the desired results. The main purpose of drying is to end fermentation and extract the remaining water. During grading, the leaves are sorted according to quality.

The main sources of black teas are Sri Lanka, India and China. India is known for highly aromatic teas such as the fruity Darjeeling.

Oolong tea, which comes from Taiwan, is partially fermented. Its characteristics are half way between those of black tea and green tea. Its greenish-brown leaves have a richer flavor than green tea but a more delicate taste than black tea. The best oolong teas are produced during the summer months.

Green tea is unfermented. The enzymes in the leaves, which cause discoloring and fermentation, are deactivated by several minutes of steam heating. The leaves are then rolled and dried like black tea. They are fired as soon as they are picked. Green tea is more astringent than black tea, as its tannins are less oxidized. Although it formerly dominated the market, black tea now monopolizes 98 percent of world production. Green tea is particularly popular in China, Japan and Muslim countries.

In addition to black, oolong and green teas, consumers can also choose between a variety of flavored, instant and decaffeinated teas.

The leaves of **flavored teas** have been mixed with spices, orange peel, bergamot or flowers (jasmine, gardenia, rose, lotus, cinnamon, mint, etc.). Earl Grey tea, for example, is flavored with bergamot oil.

Instant tea is made from tea that has been steeped and evaporated. The resulting powder, which has been very popular in the United States since the 1950s, has existed for much longer in countries such as Japan.

Decaffeinated tea is tea from which part of the caffeine (an alkaloid also known as "theine") has been removed; this reduces the stimulating effect of the resulting beverage. As the caffeine content of tea varies widely, however, some decaffeinated teas can contain almost as much of the alkaloid as regular teas.

Buying

Buy tea in a store with a high inventory turnover to obtain optimum taste. Bulk tea is almost always cheaper than tea bags; in addition, it is often of higher quality, as the leaves are uncrushed. Tea bags often contain inferior quality leaves mixed with tea powder and dust and bits of branches.

Serving Ideas

Like coffee, tea can be used to flavor various foods, especially sherbets and pastries. Prunes and other dried fruits that are soaked in tea take on a very pleasant taste. Green tea is used to flavor soba noodles.

Tea can also be used for a number of non-culinary purposes, including skin and hair care and to polish glass, mirrors and varnished floors.

Preparing

The preparation of tea has evolved over the ages. Whereas people used to boil the leaves, today's preferred method consists in steeping.

It is easy to make good tea if you follow a few simple rules. Heat the teapot with boiling water, empty it and add the tea. For medium-strength tea, use 1 teaspoon of tea per cup plus an extra spoon for the teapot (or an equivalent number of tea bags). Pour hot water over the tea and let the mixture steep for 3 to 5 minutes. Stir the liquor to distribute the aromatic components and serve the tea (or remove the tea bags or tea ball). Water temperature and steeping time are crucial. Water that has boiled for too long is flat and makes mediocre tea. Ideally, you should pour the water over the leaves just before it reaches a full boil. The length of time you allow the mixture to steep has an impact on the taste, bitterness and caffeine content of the resulting beverage. As mentioned above, 3 to 5 minutes is enough; for stronger tea, add more leaves rather than extending steeping time. A tea ball is a handy solution if you wish to make a single cup.

Hot tea can be drunk plain or with sugar or milk; it can also be flavored with lemon, orange, a drop of vanilla or almond extract, or a clove. Methods of preparation and tea-drinking customs vary from one culture to another. Iced tea, which is particularly popular in North America, can be made from scratch or from instant powder, which is presweetened, flavored and contains various additives. To make iced tea, let the hot beverage steep for twice as long as for hot tea. Remove the bags or leaves, add sugar and garnish with slices or lemon or other fruits. As the tea cools, it may become somewhat cloudy under the effect of the tannins. If you wish, you can also make iced tea from cold water. Use 8 to 10 tea bags per quart of water and let the mixture steep in the refrigerator for at least 6 hours.

green tea

black tea

Nutritional Information

Tea contains a number of substances, including caffeine, essential oils, enzymes, tannins and phenolic compounds. When drunk plain, it has only 2 to 3 calories per 6 ounces. It also contains potassium and magnesium.

Theine, an alkaloid belonging to the methylxanthine family, is identical to caffeine. Tea also contains small amounts of two other methylxanthines, namely theophylline and theobromine. The caffeine content of tea varies depending on the type of leaves used and how long they are allowed to steep (the longer the beverage steeps, the more caffeine it contains).

Tea leaves have more caffeine (2.5 to 4.5 percent) than coffee beans (1 to 2 percent). However, as less leaves are used to make a cup of tea, the beverage's caffeine content is lower. A stimulant, tea eases digestion and has various other effects on the body (see *Coffee*). Its impact seems to be less negative than that of coffee, as the effects of theine are mitigated by the other nutrients contained in tea.

Unlike the consumption of pure caffeine, tea drinking brings about a slight drop in blood pressure. According to research carried out in Japan and epidemiological studies performed in the 1980s, green tea may be a natural protection against cancer, and five cups of green tea per day are thought to help prevent strokes. Further studies will have to be carried out to confirm or invalidate these findings.

The tannins in tea, like those contained in coffee, hinder the absorption of iron found in vegetables, fruits, cereals, nuts, eggs and dairy products. (Some people believe tea to have an even more negative effect than coffee with this respect). Tea that is steeped for over 5 minutes is bitter due to its high concentration of tannins, which can be neutralized by the addition of milk.

Storing

Keep tea in an airtight container in a dark, cool place (under 85°F). Ideally, it should be stored in a sealed metallic container, which will protect it from dampness and odors. Less fragile than coffee, it can be kept for up to 18 months; for optimum flavor, however, you should use it within 6 months. Chinese teas keep for up to 3 years.

tea bag

oolong tea

Earl Grey tea

Herbal tea

chamomile

Herbal tea has been drunk since ancient times. The first known variety was an infusion of barley, but the term "herbal tea" or "tisane" now refers to infusions made from a broad range of medicinal and nonmedicinal plants. Almost every civilization has used plants for medicinal purposes. One of the oldest Chinese texts on the use of plants as medicines dates back approximately 4,700 years. Traditional Chinese prescriptions make use of the roots, stems, bark, leaves, flowers, and fruit of plants. Inscriptions found on Egyptian tombs and in Egyptian temples indicate that plants were commonly used as medicines in 3000 B.C. Numerous medicinal plants are still used today because they do in fact contain chemicals that have beneficial effects; however, others are used despite the fact that their active ingredients have yet to be identified. Herbal teas are hot (and sometimes cold) infusions made from the dried leaves or flowers of edible plants. They can also be made from the seeds of certain plants or aromatic herbs.

Buying

When buying herbal teas, it is advisable to ensure that the mixtures contain only nontoxic plants. To be absolutely safe, buy products whose ingredients are listed on the package. In view of the recent surge in the popularity of herbal teas, the U.S. Food and Drug Administration has published a list of plants that cannot be used in foods, drinks, and medicines. Health Canada requires that manufacturers document any health claims made about their products. It is thus important to read the label when buying herbal teas and other herbal products. It also important to be extremely careful when picking your own plants and herbs or when using herbal remedies. You must be able to identify the variety of herb you are looking for with absolute certainty, and it is essential that you are familiar with its chemical composition and pharmacological properties. Most of the herbal teas on the market are comprised of well-known, harmless products.

Preparing

It is easy to make good herbal tea; all you have to do is pour boiling water over the product in question in order to extract the active ingredients. 1 tablespoon of dried herbs or 2 tablespoons of fresh herbs is usually enough to make 2 cups (400 to 500 ml) of hot tea. It is best to start with cold water. The length of time the herbs are infused depends on their size and the part of the plant that is used; 5 minutes is usually sufficient. The tea should be covered while it is steeping to prevent the active ingredients from escaping.

Serving Ideas

You can dry aromatic plants yourself and then use them to make tea. Tie the stems, leaves, or flowers together and hang them in a well-ventilated dark place for 2 to 3 weeks. Once the plant has dried, remove the leaves from the stems and store them in a tightly sealed container. Most herbal teas are served hot, but fruitier varieties such as rose hip or verbena are delicious cold. Herbal tea can be drunk plain or with a little sugar, honey, or lemon.

The most common varieties of herbal tea include linden, verbena, mint, chamomile, and sage.

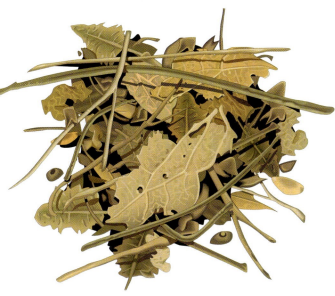

verbena

linden

Nutritional Information

Very little research has been done on the nutritional value of herbal teas, but it is known that they contain very few calories and sometimes contain traces of vitamin C. Unlike tea and coffee, herbal teas do not contain tannin or caffeine and are said to have calming, digestive, tonic, and curative properties. However, it is difficult to be sure if they have any beneficial effects. Although it has been determined that certain plants contain substances that do have effects on the human body, these effects do not provoke the same reactions among all individuals. Chamomile tea is often said to be a relaxant and an effective remedy for neuralgia; lemon-balm tea is reputed to alleviate palpitations, migraines, menstrual cramps, indigestion, and insomnia. Rosemary tisanes are thought to have a beneficial impact on the liver, the circulatory system, and migraines; thyme is said to be an expectorant and an antiseptic; and verbena is reputed to be a digestive; violet is thought to have expectorant, sodorific and diuretic properties, and may alleviate bronchitis and rheumatism. Borage, marjoram, thyme, and sage can be used to make excellent teas that are used as tonics, while bergamot, fennel, dill, lemon balm, and rosemary are said to have calming and relaxing effects.

Storing

Herbal teas can be stored for up to 6 months in a cool place in tightly sealed containers.

Coffee and Tea

669

Coffee

Coffea spp., Rubiaceae

Coffee is brewed from the seeds of the coffee plant, an evergreen shrub indigenous to the high plateaus of Ethiopia and tropical Africa. The origin of the beverage has given rise to various legends. According to one version, coffee was discovered around 850 A.D. in the area now known as Ethiopia. Noting that his goats frolicked about queerly after eating the leaves and berries of a certain bush, a goatherd took a branch of the shrub to a monk, who brewed a drink from the plant's seeds. Surprised by the drink's stimulating effect, the monk and his peers ascribed the creation of the beverage to a divine spirit. Another legend relates that, upon observing the erratic behavior of goats that nibbled the shrub's berries, the monk decided to boil the seeds to make a potion that would help him stay awake for nightly prayers.

The term "coffee" is likely derived from the Arabic *kawbah*. Some linguists, however, trace the origin of the word to Kaffa, the name of the Ethiopian province where the plant was ostensibly discovered.

Arab growers began cultivating coffee plants around 1575. For years they exercised a monopoly over the coffee trade, going so far as to sell only boiled seeds to ensure that no one could grow plants from them. The first breach in the monopoly occurred in 1616, when the Dutch brought a coffee plant back to Europe with them. They subsequently began cultivating coffee in places such as Ceylon, Java, Sumatra, and Bali. The French first planted coffee in Martinique in the early 1700s, and the Spanish introduced the shrub to the Philippines and Latin America in the same century. This marked the start of the phenomenal spread of coffee growing and consumption around the world. Today coffee is second only to oil as a world trade item, and its price is listed in commodity exchanges. The price of coffee is listed on stock exchanges. On occasion, the beans are even used by the World Bank in lieu of currency, and producer countries exchange them for foreign aid from wealthy nations. The International Coffee Organization, which groups together close to 98% of producers, sets export quotas and determines minimum and maximum prices. In order of importance, the world's leading producers are Brazil, Colombia, Indonesia, Mexico, Vietnam, and Côte d'Ivoire (formerly known in English as the Ivory Coast).

Depending on the variety, coffee plants can grow to a height of 20 feet. Commercially grown species are generally pruned back to about 13 feet to facilitate picking. The shrubs begin to bear fruit only between their fifth and sixth years. Their white flowers produce oval "cherries," which turn dark red when ripe. Between ½ and ¾ inch long, they contain two pale-green seeds covered with a tough membrane called the endocarp (also known as the parchment); depending on the species, the caffeine content is 1% to 2%. To this day, coffee cherries are picked by hand, as they ripen at different times and machine picking has yet to be perfected. The plants produce year-round; at any given time, a single branch can bear flowers, green cherries, and red cherries. The harvest lasts an average of 3 months. Coffee plants that are pruned to shrub size remain highly productive for over 30 years.

Once picked, the cherries are cleaned and the seeds are freed from the pulp and parchment. The green beans are then dried in the sun or in dryers, sorted, graded, and packed in bags. The decorticated seeds are roasted only after they arrive in consumer countries.

Although there are about a dozen varieties of coffee plants, the market is dominated by the beans of just two species: *Coffea arabica,* the oldest and best known (approximately 75% of world production), and *Coffea robusta* (about 25% of production). Each type of coffee has its own taste, aroma, caffeine content, and other characteristics. Arabica beans, which are relatively large, are divided in half by a crooked crease. Coffee brewed from these beans, which contain only 1% caffeine, is highly appreciated for its mild, refined taste and fragrance. The species is cultivated mainly in Arabia, Ethiopia, India, Brazil, Mexico, and Colombia, and is also found in certain mountainous regions of Asia and Africa (Kenya, for example). Robusta beans are smaller and rounder with a straight crease. Robusta coffee has a less refined, somewhat bitter taste, and the beans contain about 2% caffeine. The term "robusta" refers to the plants' better resistance to diseases and heat than their Arabica cousins. Grown mainly in Africa, robusta coffee fetches a lower price.

Coffee beans are named after the variety of plant, the place of origin (Brazil, Colombia, Java, Mocha, etc.), or the port from which they are shipped. These appellations are not, however, exclusive, and beans can come from parts of the planet other than those indicated by their names.

Coffee sold on the world market is still "green," i.e., unroasted, as green beans can be stored for several years with no loss in flavor. Indeed, the characteristics of certain coffees are enhanced by aging in warehouses. Before roasting, the beans undergo a final grading aimed at eliminating any remaining impurities as well as unripe or fermented beans, and then are blended with other varieties to improve the quality of individual batches and ensure consumers of a consistent taste.

During **roasting,** a key process that brings out the coffee's flavor and aroma, the beans are subjected to high dry heat in cylindrical ovens. They are then cooled immediately to minimize the loss of aromatic substances, and covered with a thin coating of resin, gum arabic, or sugar to make them shiny and to preserve their flavor. Roasting transforms the beans in various ways:

• Their color changes from greenish gray to brown. This color change is due to the caramelization of sugars. The longer coffee is roasted and the higher the roasting temperature, the darker the beans' hue (brown beans have been roasted more briefly than medium-black or black beans).

• The beans expand by up to 60 percent and, in releasing water, lose 15% to 20% of their initial weight. The characteristic aroma of roasting coffee may be explained by the production of carbon dioxide and caramel. Roasting also causes volatile essential oils and certain fatty acids to rise to the surface of the beans, giving them their gloss, flavor and aroma.

• The beans' caffeine content remains stable.

• The longer they are roasted, the more bitter but less acidic the beans become.

Instant coffee is soluble coffee powder that can be reconstituted into a beverage by the addition of hot water. The beans used to produce the powder (often robusta) are generally of inferior quality. They are ground, roasted, and percolated to produce a coffee solution, which is then dehydrated. The resulting powder contains various components absent from freshly brewed coffee, which have a negative impact on taste. Although the powder can be sold as is, it is generally processed into larger particles by means of steam or water, so that it looks more like freshly ground coffee. In some cases, the instant powder is flavored with concentrated coffee.

Another method consists in quickly freezing the coffee solution and extracting the water in a vacuum, to produce instant coffee with a crystalline structure and better flavor. Known as freeze-drying, this process is more costly and, as a result, less common. It nevertheless preserves all of the coffee solution's aromatic qualities.

Although instant coffee is less flavorful than freshly brewed coffee, its simple, quick preparation makes it highly popular.

Coffee and Tea

671

Decaffeinated coffee is coffee from which most of the caffeine has been removed prior to roasting. One of the earliest decaffeination processes uses solvents such as methylene chloride, ethyl acetate, and carbon dioxide (considered to be food additives) to extract the caffeine; given their high volatility, these substances quickly evaporate. Chemical extraction consists in eliminating caffeine through direct contact with the solvents. The beans are treated with water and steam until their moisture content reaches a predetermined level and they become soft and porous. They are then washed in various solvents and drained, following which the solvent solution is removed by steam. Coffee from which 97% of the caffeine has been removed has been treated up to 24 times. Finally, the beans are dried, roasted, and in some cases, ground. Roasting eliminates any remaining traces of solvent. "Swiss" or "natural" decaffeination is much less widespread due to its higher cost. The beans are soaked in hot water to bring the caffeine to the surface, then dried, roasted, and ground.

Coffee substitutes are caffeine-free substances used to prepare beverages with a similar taste to coffee. The most widespread substitute is chicory, the roots of which are dried, roasted, and ground (and, in many cases, mixed with barley and rye). Coffee to which chicory has been added is more bitter, thicker and blacker than pure coffee.

Be it natural or decaffeinated, roasted coffee must be packaged immediately as it is highly fragile and quickly loses its volatile aromatics. The beans are also prone to oxidization by dampness and oxygen.

Vacuum packing protects ground coffee for about 3 months, and pressurized packing, which involves the removal of air from a metal container, allows consumers to store coffee for up to 3 years.

Roasted beans

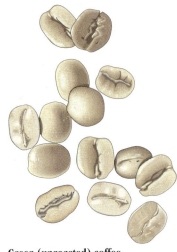

Green (unroasted) coffee

Ground coffee

Buying

Coffee quickly loses its flavor and aroma, particularly if it is ground and kept in an unsealed container. You are therefore best advised to buy a small amount of vacuum-packed coffee (enough to meet your immediate needs) in a store with a high inventory turnover. Be sure to specify the type of coffeemaker you plan to use to ensure you are given the right grind of coffee. Too fine a grind produces bitter coffee, and the drink made from an overly coarse grind tends to be tasteless. For maximum flavor, buy whole coffee beans and grind them just before use.

Preparing

Coffee-making can be extremely simple or more complicated, depending on whether you use instant coffee or create your own blends from different types of beans, grind the beans yourself, etc.

There are various ways of brewing coffee, each of which requires a different grind. The finer the coffee, the stronger and more flavorful the resulting brew. Finer grinds are also more economical, as fewer beans are required per cup of coffee.

Steeped coffee is made by pouring water over the coffee, allowing the brew to infuse and then pouring it off the grounds.

In **percolation,** water is forced through the ground beans by means of pressure or gravity. The amount of beans needed to produce a cup of coffee depends on the grind, type of coffee, and desired taste. According to how strong you like your coffee, use 1 to 3 tablespoons of coffee per 6 ounces of water.

Drip coffee is produced by pouring boiling water over coffee measured into a paper, cloth, or mesh filter placed in a special conical basket, and allowing the water to trickle into a cup or pot positioned underneath. The grind is all important: if it is too fine, the pores in the filter will clog and prevent the water from flowing through the coffee; if it is too coarse, the brew will be bland.

Coffee lovers can choose between a wide range of coffeemakers, which work according to a variety of principles.

Espresso coffeemakers (also known as "Moka" or "Cona" coffeemakers) consist in three parts: a base (equipped with a safety valve), a funnel-shaped filter in the middle and an upper container that screws onto the bottom. Water poured in the base is transformed by heat into steam, which is forced through finely ground coffee placed in the filter. The resulting brew, which is strong and aromatic, collects in the upper container. Once the water comes to a boil, the process takes only 20 to 30 seconds. The coffeemaker must be taken off the burner as soon as the boiling stops.

Percolators use a leaching process to produce a less flavorful brew that can often be bitter. Medium-grind coffee is placed in a container atop a narrow cylinder; when the water in the pot comes to a boil, it is forced upward through the cylinder and drips back through the coffee. As the process is repeated over a period of 7 to 10 minutes, there is a risk of boiling, which decreases the coffee's aroma and greatly increases its tannin content.

Piston coffeemakers (generally sold under the trade name "Bodum" or "Mélior") consist in a glass pot and a piston filter. Heat the pot with boiling water, discard the water and add finely ground coffee. Pour boiling water over the coffee, stir, and let the liquid steep for 5 minutes. Push the piston to the bottom of the pot just before serving. Coffee made in this way is rich and full bodied; its strength depends on the amount of water and coffee used.

Ibrik coffeemakers, which are wide based and conical, are used to make Turkish coffee. This strong brew still contains the coffee grounds, and should thus be sipped (many fans, however, also drink the spent coffee). To make Turkish coffee, add very finely ground coffee to bubbling water with an almost equal amount of sugar. Bring the mixture to a boil three times, adding a bit of cold water after each boiling. At the end of the process, add a few drops of cold water to cause the grounds to settle to the bottom and serve the unfiltered, boiling hot coffee in small cups.

For many people, coffee-making is an art governed by highly specific rules. The basic principle is to extract the maximum amount of caffeine and aromatic substances from the ground beans, while limiting the amount of tannin.

In Finland, people drink an average of over a quart of coffee per day. Americans consume slightly less than half this amount and Canadians drink even less.

To make good coffee:

• Grind the beans just before using them.

• Use fresh, cold water. Bring to a simmer (195 to 205°F); do not boil, as the water will lose its oxygen and become flat. Avoid water that is high in calcium, chlorine, sulfur, or iron, as the taste of these elements will be transferred to the coffee.

• Avoid oversteeping, as this increases tannin content. If the water is at the proper temperature (see next point) and is in constant contact with the grounds, 2 minutes is long enough.

• Do not boil or reheat coffee; to extract the maximum amount of soluble substances (other than those that can make the coffee bitter), steep the brew at a temperature of 185° to 205°F.

• Avoid using metallic coffeemakers or cups that alter the taste of the coffee. Stoneware and earthenware cups retain more heat than glass cups.

• Wash the coffeemaker thoroughly to get rid of the oily residue, which can turn rancid and give an unpleasant taste to your coffee. Rinse off all traces of dishwashing detergent.

Serving Ideas

Many people like their coffee black and unsweetened, while others prefer to add sugar, milk, or cream. Coffee can also be flavored with cardamom seeds, alcohol, chocolate powder, or cinnamon. It is often used in sweets and desserts such as mocha cake, éclairs, and ice cream, as well as in frostings and *café liégeois* (a drink made of cold coffee and ice cream). To obtain optimum taste in desserts, use extra strong coffee brewed with half the usual amount of water.

Coffee is also an ingredient of certain liqueurs.

Nutritional Information

From the nutritional viewpoint, coffee is low in protein, carbohydrates, and fat. The beans contain about a hundred different substances, including caffeine, tannins (chlorogenic acid, etc.), oils, and nitrogeneous constituents. A stimulant, caffeine belongs to the xanthine family (like theobromine, found in tea and cocoa). Its effects on the body are numerous and varied: it is diuretic, stimulates the central nervous and respiratory systems, dilates blood vessels, speeds up the heart rate, boosts striated-muscle effort, and delays mental and muscular fatigue. People who are used to drinking large quantities of coffee can suffer withdrawal symptoms such as headaches, irritability, tense muscles, and nervousness if they stop consuming the beverage; the ingestion of caffeine causes these symptoms to disappear.

The maximum recommended daily coffee intake varies depending on the type of coffee, how the drink is prepared, personal tolerance (people who seldom drink coffee are particularly sensitive to caffeine and react more strongly than those who consume coffee on a regular basis), and consumption of other substances containing caffeine, such as tea (strong tea contains 78 to 108 mg of caffeine per 6 ounces), cocoa, colas (28 to 64 mg of caffeine per 355 ml can), and certain medications such as diuretics, analgesics, and cold remedies. An average cup of drip coffee (6 ounces) contains 108 to 180 mg of caffeine, compared with 72 to 144 mg for percolated coffee, 60 to 90 mg for regular instant coffee, and less than 6 mg for instant decaffeinated coffee. You are best advised to limit your coffee consumption to the equivalent of 4 cups a day.

To date, health studies have failed to show a link between caffeine consumption and high blood pressure, cancer, or congenital defects. Women are nevertheless advised to drink only moderate amounts of coffee while pregnant or breast-feeding, as caffeine filters through the placenta and is found in mother's milk. Caffeine has an undeniable effect on sleep during the 4 hours following coffee consumption.

Storing

Coffee beans start to lose their flavor as soon as they are roasted, and this flavor loss accelerates after grinding. Store coffee away from air and light, ideally in an airtight container made of opaque glass kept in the refrigerator or freezer. Ground coffee keeps well at room temperature for 7 to 10 days and for up to a month in the freezer. Whole coffee beans can be stored for several months in the refrigerator.

Glossary

à blanc
a term used to describe foods that are cooked or partially cooked but not browned; the phrase *cuire à blanc* also means "to bake blind" (see below).

abaisse
a French term referring to a sheet of rolled-out pastry.

additives
substances that are added to foods to prolong their shelf life, and to improve their flavor, texture and appearance.

antiarthritic
a substance that prevents arthritis.

antiseptic
a substance that prevents or alleviates infections.

au gratin
a French term referring to dishes that are topped with bread crumbs or grated cheese then browned in the oven.

bake blind
to bake an empty pie crust by half filling it with dried peas, etc., to ensure that it holds its shape.

baste
to pour a liquid (fat, cooking juices, etc.) over food as it cooks to prevent it from drying out.

Béarnaise
a sauce made from eggs, melted butter, wine, vinegar, tarragon and shallots that is served with fish, meat or eggs.

béchamel
a sauce made by adding milk and a selection of seasonings to a mixture of butter and flour (roux).

blanch
to cook food briefly (1 to 2 minutes) in boiling water. After being blanched, food is usually chilled under running water then drained. The purpose of blanching is to make food taste less bitter, to make it more tender or to improve its flavor.

boil
to immerse food in water that has been heated to 212°F (100°C). The phrase «bring to a boil» means to heat liquid until bubbles break on its surface.

Bordelaise
a brown sauce served with grilled foods that is made by reducing a mixture of red or white wine, marrow, shallots, pepper and herbs.

bouquet garni
herbs (usually thyme, parsley and bay leaves) that are tied together or wrapped in cloth, then added to soups or sauces to enhance their flavor.

braise
to cook food gently and slowly in a covered dish containing a small amount of liquid; meat is sometimes braised in its own juices.

bread
to coat food with pieces of crustless bread or bread crumbs.

bread crumbs
bread that is crumbled and sifted, then used as a coating for foods.

brine
a heavily salted liquid preparation (which may contain various other seasonings) used to preserve foods such as olives and fish.

cheesecloth (muslin)
a fine, light cotton fabric that is used to strain certain ingredients or to enclose ingredients so they can be removed from a preparation.

cholagogue
a substance that promotes the elimination of bile.

chutney
a sweet-and-sour condiment comprised of fruit or vegetables that have been cooked in vinegar, various spices and sugar.

coagulation
the transformation of a substance from a liquid or semi-liquid state to a solid or semi-solid state by means of heat or the addition of an acid ingredient.

coral
a portion of the stomach of certain crustaceans that is removed from the shell and added to sauces.

coulis
a fine hot or cold purée made from fruit, vegetables or shellfish.

court bouillon
a flavored liquid preparation containing vinegar or other acidic ingredients that is used to cook fish and shellfish, as well as certain types of offal and meat; it is sometimes prepared in advance.

deglaze
to dissolve (with wine, alcohol, stock, water, etc.) the caramelized juices at the bottom of a pan in order to make a sauce or gravy.

depurative
a substance that purifies the body by promoting the elimination of toxins and waste products.

desalt
to remove the salt from food, usually by soaking it in water.

digestive
a substance that promotes digestion.

diuretic
a substance that increases the flow of urine.

émincer
a French term meaning to cut fruit, vegetables or meat into thin slices (not «to mince»).

emmenagogue
a substance that promotes or regulates menstrual flow.

emulsify
to beat or whisk an ingredient that cannot generally be combined with fat into a fatty substance so as to create a mixture that is temporarily homogenous and stable (vinaigrette, mayonnaise, etc.).

essence
a concentrated aromatic substance.

675

expectorant
a substance that promotes the oral elimination of respiratory secretions.

fermentation
the transformation of certain food substances by the enzymes produced by microorganisms.

fish steak
a thick cross-section of a large fish that is sliced before the fish is cooked.

fry
to cook food in a hot fatty substance.

garam masala
an Indian mixture of spices available in an infinite number of varieties, most of which contain cinnamon, bay leaves, cumin seeds, coriander seeds, cardamom seeds, black pepper corns, dried chiles, cloves and nutmeg.

gelatin
an odorless, tasteless mixture of proteins extracted from animal tissue that becomes a jelly-like thickening and stabilizing agent when heated.

hollandaise
a sauce made with egg yolks, butter and lemon juice that is served lukewarm with eggs, vegetables and fish.

hollow (or scoop) out
to remove the flesh or the heart from fruits or vegetables.

hull
to remove the outer covering from fruit, nuts or seeds.

infusion
a liquid preparation made by pouring boiling water over herbs so as to release their flavor and active ingredients.

julienne
to cut meat or vegetables into thin stick-shaped pieces.

laxative
a substance that promotes the elimination of feces.

marinade
a mixture of wine, vinegar, oil and other condiments in which meat or fish is soaked before it is cooked to make it more tender and flavorful.

mayonnaise
a sauce made from oil, eggs and various condiments (mustard, salt, vinegar, garlic, etc.) that is beaten at room temperature until the oil and egg yolks form an emulsion.

meringue
a light baked preparation made from stiffly whisked egg whites and sugar; it contains no added fat.

mirepoix
a mixture of diced vegetables (carrots, celery, onions) and herbs (thyme, bay leaves) that is used to flavor foods.

moisten
to add liquid to a preparation.

papillote
greaseproof paper or aluminum foil in which food is cooked to ensure that none of its flavor is lost.

paupiette
a thin slice of fish or meat that is spread with stuffing then rolled.

pectin
a substance found in numerous fruits that is used by the food industry as a thickening and stabilizing agent in products such as jam.

phyllo (pastry)
pastry dough comprised of numerous very thin sheets made from flour and water.

poach
to cook food in simmering liquid, usually court bouillon.

pod
to remove the pods or shells from certain vegetables, especially legumes.

rancid
an adjective used to describe fats whose taste and nutritional value have deteriorated due to prolonged exposure to air, light or heat.

remineralizing
an adjective used to describe foods that replenish the body's supply of minerals.

reserve
to set food or a preparation aside for future use.

roast
to expose food to the direct heat of an oven, wood fire or grill.

roux
a cooked mixture of flour and butter that is used to make sauces and soups.

sashimi
thin slices of raw fish eaten as an appetizer, usually with wasabi or ginger rather than rice.

sauté
to pan-fry tender foods very quickly over high heat in a small amount of fat.

seal (or sear)
to cook food briefly over intense heat, usually in very hot fat.

shell
to remove the husk or shell from nuts or eggs.

smoke point
the temperature at which a fatty substance begins to deteriorate and smoke, and becomes combustible.

smoking
to preserve food by exposing it to smoke.

soufflé
sweet or savory dishes comprised of a light custard containing whipped egg whites that rises as it cooks.

starch
carbohydrates from vegetable sources that increase in volume when exposed to moist heat.

steam
to cook food by placing it above boiling or simmering water in a covered saucepan, in order to preserve all of its nutritional and organoleptic properties; fish is sometimes steamed in its own juices.

stew
a dish consisting of pieces of meat, fish or vegetables cooked in sauce.

strain
to pour a semi-liquid preparation through cheesecloth, a sieve or a cone-shaped strainer.

stuff
to fill foods such as fish, poultry and vegetables with a flavorful mixture.

sushi
a preparation comprised of raw or cooked fish or shellfish that is covered with seasoned rice and is sometimes rolled in a sheet of dried seaweed.

sweat

to sprinkle certain vegetables with salt in order to eliminate some of the water they contain, thus making them less bitter-tasting and easier to digest.

tonic

any food that fortifies or stimulates the body.

tops

the stems and leaves left on certain vegetables when they are harvested.

trim

to remove the fins from a raw fish.

verjuice

juice extracted from unripe grapes that is used to make Dijon mustard.

vermifuge

any food or substance that promotes the elimination of intestinal worms.

vinaigrette

a basic sauce usually containing oil, vinegar, salt, pepper and various other seasonings that is used to dress salads or crudités.

wasabi

a very hot-tasting green condiment made with the root of an Asian plant; it is sometimes referred to as «Japanese horseradish.»

zest

the colorful outer layer of a citrus peel.

Selected Bibliography

GENERAL INTEREST

BENNION, Marion. *The Science of Food*, San Francisco, Harper & Row, 1980, 598 p.

COURTINE, R.J. *Larousse gastronomique*, Paris, Librairie Larousse, 1984, 1142 p.

COYLE, Patrick L. *The World Encyclopedia of Food*, New York, Facts on File, 1982.

ENSMINGER, Audrey H. *et al. Foods and Nutrition Encyclopedia*, 2ᵉ éd., Boca Raton (Floride), CRC Press, 1994, 2 vol., 2415 p.

GRIFFITHS, Mark. *Index of Garden Plants*, The Royal Horticultural Society, Portland, Timber Press, 1994, 1234 p.

Harper's Review of Biochemistry, 20ᵉ éd., États-Unis, Lange Medical Publications,1985, 718 p.

Larousse de la Cuisine, Paris, Larousse, 1990, 800 p.

Larousse des cuisines du monde, Paris, Librairie Larousse, 1993, 544 p.

PENNINGTON, J.A.T. *Bowes & Church's Food Values of Portions Commonly Used*, 6ᵉ éd., Philadelphie, J.B. Lippincott Company, 1994, 483 p.

Present Knowledge in Nutrition, Nutrition Reviews', 5ᵉ éd., États-Unis, The Nutrition Foundation, 1984, 900 p.

ROGERS, J.O. *What food is that ? and How Healthy is it ?*, Toronto, Stewart House, 1990, 480 p.

SOUCI, S.W., W. FACHMANN et H. KRAUT. *La composition des aliments. Tableaux des valeurs nutritives 1989/90*, 4ᵉ éd., Stuttgart, Wissenschaftliche Verlagsgesellschaft mbH, 1989, 1028 p.

SPECIALIZED BOOKS

ABBOTT, R. Tucker. *American Seashells. The Marine Mollusca of the Atlantic and Pacific Coasts of North America*, 2ᵉ éd., Toronto, Van Nostrand Reinhold Company, 1974, 663 p.

BIRCH, J.J. et K.J. PARKER. *Sugar : Science and Technology*, Londres, Applied Science Publishers Ltd, 1979, 475 p.

BRODY, Jane. *The Seafood Handbook*, Rockland (Maine), Seafood Business, 1989, 160 p.

CARPER, Jean. *Les aliments et leurs vertus*, Montréal, Éditions de l'Homme, 1994, 543 p.

CHERNET, Daniel. *Levures, algues et ferments*, Paris, Retz, 1990, 157 p.

CLÉMENT, J. *La santé par les fruits et les légumes*, Montréal, Dezclez, 1981, 184 p.

COAD, B.W. *Guide des poissons marins de pêche sportive de l'Atlantique canadien et de la Nouvelle-Angleterre*, Éditions Broquet, 1993, 400 p.

DAHLSTRÖM, Preben et J. Muus BENT. *Guide des poissons d'eau douce et pêche*, 3ᵉ éd., Neuchâtel (Suisse), Delachaux et Niestlé S.A., 1981, 242 p.

DIEUDONNÉ, Marie-Paule et Pascal. *Les nouveaux aliments — soja-algues*, Colmar, Éditions SAEP, 1991, 95 p.

DLOUHÀ, Jana, Miloslav RICHTER et Pavel VALICEK. *Les fruits*, Paris, Gründ, 1995, 223 p.

DOUCET-LEDUC, Hélène. *Échec à la contamination des aliments*, Modulo Éditeur, 1993, 147 p.

DOUCET-LEDUC, Hélène. *La contamination des aliments*, Modulo Éditeur, 1991, 248 p.

DUMAIS *et al. Science et technologie du lait : principes et applications*, Fondation de technologie laitière du Québec inc., 1984, 532 p.

ELLIOT, Rose. *The Complete Vegeterian Cuisine*, New York, Pantheon Books, 1988, 352 p.

ENSRUD, Barbara. *Le guide des fromages*, Éditions Optimum internationales, 1982, 165 p.

FRASER, Margaret *et al. Cuisine micro-ondes*, Éditions Trécarré, 1990, vol. 2, 184 p.

GAYRAL, P. *Les algues : morphologie, cytologie, reproduction, écologie*, Paris, Doin éditeurs, 1975, 164 p.

GEISTDOERFER, Patrick. *Poissons des mers d'Europe*, Guide Point vert, Hatier, 1983, 125 p.

GENEST, Françoise. *Guide pratique de l'alimentation*, Collection Protégez-vous, 1992, 125 p.

GENEST, Lyse et Monique LE ROUZÈS. *Les fibres de la santé*, Éditions Québécor, 1990, 267 p.

HEINERMAN, John. *The Complete Book of Spices : their Medical, Nutritional and Cooking Uses*, États-Unis, Keats Publishing, 1983, 183 p.

HILLMAN, Howard. *Kitchen Science : A Compendium of Essential Information for Every Cook*, New York, Houghton Mifflin Company, 1981, 263 p.

HODGES, Anne. *Le livre du chocolat*, Paris, M.A. Éditions, 1989, 80 p.

HOFFMANN, G. *The Chemistry and Technology of Edible Oils and Fats and their High Fat Products*, Academic Press Ltd, 1989, 384 p.

HOWARTH, A. Jan. *Délices de la mer et du Canada*, Montréal, Lidec inc., 1983, 286 p.

JACOBSON, Micheal F. *et al.. Safe Food. Eating Wisely in a Risky World*, Los Angeles, Center for Science in the Public Interest et Living Planet Press, 1991, 234 p.

KYBAL, Jan. *Plantes aromatiques et culinaires*, Paris, Gründ, 1981, 223 p.

LABENSKY, Sarah et Alan M. HAUSE. *On Cooking ; techniques from expert chefs*, New Jersey, Prentice-Hall, Inc, 1995, 1080 p.

LA MÈRE MICHEL. *Le Grand livre des fines herbes*, Guy Saint-Jean Éditeur inc., 1987, 230 p.

LAMBERT-LAGACÉ, Louise et Michelle LAFLAMME. *Bons gras mauvais gras*, Montréal, Éditions de l'Homme, 1993, 172 p.

LAMBERT-LAGACÉ, Louise. *Le défi alimentaire de la femme*, Montréal, Éditions de l'Homme, 1988, 248 p.

LAWSON, Harry. *Foods Oils and Fats Technology, Utilization, and Nutrition*, États-Unis, Chapman & Hall, 1995, 339 p.

LINDSAY, Anne. *Au goût du cœur*, Éditions du Trécarré, 1991, 250 p.

MABEY, Richard. *The New Age Herbalist*, New York, Macmillan Publishing Co., 1988, 288 p.

MALLOS, Tess. *Fèves, Haricots et autres légumineuses : comment les apprêter et les cuisiner*, Montréal, Éditions de l'Homme, 1982, 196 p.

MATTEAU, Hélène. *Les mots de la faim et de la soif*, Montréal, Éditions de l'Homme, 1990, 207 p.

MAURO, Frederic. *Histoire du café*, Éditions Desjonquères, 1991, 249 p.

NANTET, Bernard. *Le goût du fromage*, Paris, Flammarion, 1994, 255 p.

OLNEY, Richard et Jacques GANTIÉ. *Saveurs des terroirs de Povence*, Paris, Éditions Robert Laffont, 1993, 256 p.

PERROT, Émile et René PARIS. *Les plantes médicinales*, France, Presses Universitaires de France, 1974, vol. 1 -2, 245 p.

PHILLIPS, Roger et Martyn RIX. *The Random House Book of Vegetables*, New York, Random House, 1993, 270 p.

POMERLEAU, René. *Flore des champignons au Québec*, Montréal, Éditions La Presse, s.d.

RÉDACTEURS DES ÉDITIONS TIME-LIFE. *Les boissons*, Éditions Time-Life, Amsterdam, 1982, 176 p.

REIX, Alain. *Poissons ; techniques et saveurs*, Lucerne, Dormonval, 1991, 251 p.

RICHARDSON, Julia. *Fruits et légumes exotiques du monde entier*, Éditions Héritage , 1990, 256 p.

SABATIER, Patrick Pierre. *La pomme de terre c'est aussi un produit diététique*, Paris, Éditions Robert Laffont, 1993, 275 p.

SMITH, Allan K. « Soybeans : Chemistry & Technology », dans *Proteins*, États-Unis, Avi Publishing Company, 1980, vol. 1, 470 p.

Sophie Grigson's Ingredients book, Londres, Reed Consumer Books Limited, 1993,192p.

SOUTH, G. Robin et Alan WHITTICK. *Introduction to Phycology*, Oxford, Blackwell Scientific Publications, 1987, 341 p.

STADELMAN, William J. et Owen J. COTTERILL. *Egg Science and Technology*, 2ᵉ éd., AVI Publishing Company Inc., 1977, 323 p.

SWAHN, J.O. *Les épices*, Paris, Gründ, 1993, 208 p.

TOUSSAINT-SAMAT, Maguelonne. *Histoire naturelle et morale de la nourriture*, Paris, Bordas, 1987, 590 p.

TRÉMOLLIÈRES *et al. Les bases de l'alimentation*, Paris, Éditions ESF, 1984, tome 1, 57 p.

TYLER, Varro E. *The Honest Herbal : A sensible Guide to the Use of Herbs and Related Remedies*, 3ᵉ éd., États-Unis, Pharmaceutical Product Press, 1993, 375 p.

VALNET, Jean. *Aromathérapie : Traitement des maladies par les essences des plantes*, Paris, Librairie Maloine S.A., 1964, 389 p.

VALNET, Jean. *Phytothérapie : traitement des maladies par les plantes*, 5ᵉ éd., Paris, Maloine S.A. Éditeur, 1983, 942 p.

VALNET, Jean. *Traitement des maladies par les légumes, les fruits et les céréales*, 8ᵉ éd., Paris, Maloine S.A. Éditeur, 1982, 527 p.

WHITEHEAD, P.J.P. *et al. Poissons de l'Atlantique du Nord-Est et de la Méditerranée*, Paris, UNESCO, 1986, 3 vol., 1473 p.

WILLIAM, Anne. *Cuisine Succès : l'école de la cuisine*, Paris, Librairie Larousse, 1991, 528 p.

GOVERNMENTAL ORGANISMS PUBLICATIONS

AGRICULTURE CANADA.

Ce qu'il faut savoir sur les œufs.

Haricots, pois et lentilles, publication 1 555, 1981, 18 p.

La congélation des aliments, 1978, 38 p.

La mise en conserve de fruits et légumes du Canada, 1981, 41 p.

Les légumes frais canadiens, publication 1 476, 1982, 42 p.

Les produits laitiers maison, mai 1983.

Edible and Poisonous Mushrooms of Canada, 1979, publication 1 112, 326 p.

L'irradiation des aliments.

La congélation des aliments, 1986, publication 892, 38 p.

CENTRE D'INFORMATION SUR LE BŒUF. *Bœuf Canada, un choix supérieur — Votre guide pour du bœuf de première qualité.*

Découpe du bœuf, charte.

La structure du bœuf.

COMMITTEE ON SCIENTIFIC AND VERNACULAR NAMES OF MOLLUSKS OF THE COUNCIL OF SYSTEMATIC MALACOLOGISTS. *Common and Scientific Names of Aquatic Invertebrates from the United States and Canada : Mollusks*, Bethesda (Maryland), American Fisheries Society, 1988, Special Publication 16, 277 p.

COMMITTEE ON THE NAMES OF DECAPOD CRUSTACEANS OF THE CRUSTACEAN SOCIETY. *Common and Scientific Names of Aquatic Invertebrates from the United States and Canada : Decapod crustaceans*, Bethesda (Maryland), American Fisheries Society, 1989, Special Publication 17, 77 p.

CONSEIL CANADIEN DU MIEL. *La miellée*, Fédération des apiculteurs du Québec, été 1994.

CONSOMMATION ET AFFAIRES COMMERCIALES CANADA. *Guide sur l'étiquetage nutritionnel*, gouvernement du Canada, 1991.

DIRECTION GÉNÉRALE DE LA PROTECTION DE LA SANTÉ, GOUVERNEMENT DU CANADA,

La manipulation de la volaille... en toute sécurité, Ottawa, 1985, feuillet H49 -15/7.

La salubrité des aliments, c'est votre affaire, Ottawa, gouvernement du Canada, 1983, 18 p.

ENVIRONNEMENT CANADA, *Poisson et Fruits de mer*, n° 2.

FÉDÉRATION DES PRODUCTEURS DE BOVINS DU QUÉBEC et AGRICULTURE, PÊCHERIES ET ALIMENTATION QUÉBEC, *Le renouveau du veau*, 1989, 15 p.

FÉDÉRATION DES PRODUCTEURS DE PORCS DU QUÉBEC, *Les différents modes de cuisson du porc du Québec.*

FÉDÉRATION DES PRODUCTEURS DE VOLAILLES DU QUÉBEC. *La petite encyclopédie du poulet québécois*, 1994. 105 p.

679

LAMOUREAUX, Gisèle *et al.* « Plantes sauvages printanières », dans *La documentation québécoise*, Québec, Éditeur officiel du Québec, 1975, 247 p.

MINISTÈRE DE L'AGRICULTURE, DES PÊCHERIES ET DE L'ALIMENTATION, GOUVERNEMENT DU QUÉBEC,

Caractéristiques à observer lors de l'achat des poissons et fruits de mer, carte de renseignements.

Principales espèces de poissons pêchées commercialement au Québec.

Teneur en gras et en cholestérol des produits de la pêche, carte de renseignements.

MINISTÈRE DES TERRES ET FORÊTS, « Petite flore forestière du Québec », dans *La documentation québécoise*, Québec, Éditeur officiel du Québec, 1974, 216 p.

MONGEAU, Estelle, *Le rôle des produits laitiers dans l'alimentation des Canadiens*, Conseil de recherches agro-alimentaires du Canada, juillet 1995, 104 p.

OFFICE CANADIEN DE COMMERCIALISATION DU DINDON, *La dinde au gril.*

La dinde au menu du jour, 28 p.

Recommandations sur la température interne de cuisson du dindon, Fédération des producteurs de volailles du Québec, 1994.

PÊCHES ET OCÉANS CANADA. Série *Le monde sous-marin.* Ottawa, gouvernement du Canada.

Produits de la pêche du Canada. Région du Pacifique, 1985, 35 p.

Fish and Seafood for the Microwave, Ottawa, 1985, 18 p.

Le Grand Brochet, Plan d'action Saint-Laurent dans la collection « Espèces en difficulté dans le Saint-Laurent ».

Poissons et fruits de mer en une leçon, Ottawa, 1985, 18 p.

Produits de la pêche du Canada. Région de l'Atlantique, Ottawa, 1985, 51 p.

Produits de la pêche du Canada. Région des eaux douces, Ottawa, 1985, 16 p.

Les mollusques du Québec et leur contrôle Ottawa, 1985.

BUREAU LAITIER DU CANADA. *Les fabriquants de mythes attaquent.*

L'ABC des produits laitiers, mai 1983.

Nos fromages par goût et par cœur, 1987, 72 p.

Guide pratique des produits laitiers, mai 1993.

SANTÉ CANADA.

Le Guide alimentaire pour manger sainement, Ottawa, 1992.

Loi et règlements des aliments et drogues, Ottawa, s.d.

À propos des sulfites, publication 1 992.

Botulisme et conserve maison, 1976.

Dictionnaire de poche sur les additifs alimentaires, 1990, 31 p.

Nutrition durant la grossesse, 1986, 139 p.

Questions et réponses sur les additifs alimentaires, 1983, 21 p.

Recommandations sur la nutrition, Rapport du Comité de révision scientifique, 1990, 223 p.

SCOTT, W.B. ET A. H. LEIM. *Poissons de la côte atlantique du Canada*, Office des recherches sur les pêcheries du Canada, 1972, bulletin 155, 530 p.

SCOTT, W.B. et E.J. CROSSMAN. *Poissons d'eau douce du Canada*, Ottawa, Office des recherches sur les pêcheries du Canada, Service des pêches et des sciences de la mer, Environnement Canada, 1974, bulletin 184, 1 026 p.

SCOTT, W.B. et M.G. SCOTT. *Atlantic Fishes of Canada*, University of Toronto Press en collaboration avec le ministère des Pêches et Océans et le Centre d'édition du gouvernement du Canada, 1988, 731 p.

PERIODICALS

Essentiel, Nutrition Action, Québec Science, Protégez-vous, Journal of the American Dietetic Association, Diététique en Action, Le Point INN.

681

The terms in CAPITAL LETTERS refer to a main entry. Those in **bold type** refer to a recipe.

The terms in CAPITAL LETTERS refer to a main entry. Those in **bold type** refer to a recipe.

The terms in CAPITAL LETTERS refer to a main entry. Those in **bold type** refer to a recipe.

684

The terms in CAPITAL LETTERS refer to a main entry. Those in **bold type** refer to a recipe.